History of the Reformation in Germany

HISTORY

OF THE

REFORMATION IN GERMANY.

BY

LEOPOLD RANKE,

AUTHOR OF

THE HISTORY OF THE POPES, &c., &c.

TRANSLATED FROM THE LAST EDITION OF THE GERMAN,

BY

SARAH AUSTIN.

COMPLETE IN ONE VOLUME.

PHILADELPHIA:
LEA AND BLANCHARD.
1844

Printed by T K & P G Collins

PREFACE.

From the first ten years of the fifteenth century, to the beginning of the thirty years' war, the constitution and political condition of Germany were determined by the periodical diets and the measures there resolved on.

The time was long past in which the public affairs of the country were determined by one supreme will; but its political life had not yet (as at a later period) retreated within the circle of the several constituent members of the empire. The imperial assemblies exercised rights and powers which, though not accurately defined, were yet the comprehensive and absolute powers of sovereignty. They made war and peace; levied taxes; exercised a supreme supervision, and were even invested with executive power. Together with the deputies from the cities, and the representatives of the counts and lords, appeared the emperor and the sovereign princes in person It is true they discussed the most important affairs of their respective countries in their several colleges, or in committees chosen from the whole body, and the questions were decided by the majority of voices. The unity of the nation was represented by these assemblies. Within the wide borders of the empire nothing of importance could occur which did not here come under deliberation, nothing new arise, which mu' not await its final decision and execution here

Spite of all these considerations, the history of the diets of the empire has not yet received the attention it deserves. The Recesses* of the diets are sufficiently well known; but who would judge a deliberative assembly by the final results of its deliberations? Projects of a systematic collection of its transactions have occasionally been entertained, and the work has even been taken in hand, but all that has hitherto been done has remained in a fragmentary and incomplete state.

* The Recess (*Abschied*—Recessus), the document wherewith the labours of a deliberative assembly are closed, and in which they are summed up All the resolutions of the assembly, or the decisions of their sovereign on their proposals or petitions, were collected into one whole, and the session, or, according to the German expression, day (*Tag*) was thus closed, with the publication of the Recess. Each separate law, after having passed the two colleges, that of the electors and that of the princes, received the emperor's assent or ratification, and had then the force of law. It was called Resolution of the Empire (*Reichsceluss* of *Reichsconclusum*). The older recesses of the empire (*Reichsabschiede*) are lost. Since the year 1663, as the diet remained constantly sitting down to 1806, no recess, properly so called, could be published. The sum of all the decisions or acts of a diet was called *Reichsabschied* The correspondence of this with the English term Statute will be seen in the following extract "For all the acts of one session of parliament taken together make properly but one statute, and therefore when two sessions have been held in one year we usually mention stat. 1 or 2. Thus the Bill of Rights is cited as 1 W. & M. st. 2, c 2, signifying that it is the second chapter or act of the second statute, or the laws made in the second session of parliament in the first year of King William and Queen Mary."—*Blackstone's Comment.* vol. i. p 85, 15th ed.

The speech with which the emperor opened the diet was called the Proposition

As it is the natural ambition of every man to leave behind him some useful record of his existence, I have long cherished the project of devoting my industry and my powers to this most important work. Not that I flattered myself that I was competent to supply so large a deficiency; to exhaust the mass of materials in its manifold juridical bearings, my idea was only to trace with accuracy the rise and development of the constitution of the empire, through a series (if possible unbroken) of the Acts of the Diets.

Fortune was so propitious to my wishes, that, in the autumn of 1836, I found in the Archives of the city of Frankfurt a collection of the very kind I wanted, and was permitted to use these precious documents with all the facility I could desire.

The collection consists of ninety-six folio volumes, which contain the Acts of the Imperial Diets from 1414 to 1613. In the earlier part it is very imperfect, but step by step, in proportion as the constitution of the empire acquires form and development, the documents rise in interest. At the beginning of the sixteenth century, from which time the practice of reducing public proceedings to writing was introduced, it becomes so rich in new and important documents, that it lays the strongest hold on the attention. There are not only the acts, but the reports of the deputies from the cities—the Rathsfreunde, which generally charm by their frankness and simplicity, and often surprise by their sagacity. I profited by the opportunity to make myself master of the contents of the first sixty-four of these volumes, extending down to the year 1551. A collection of Imperial Rescripts occasionally afforded me valuable contributions.

But I could not stop here. A single town was not in a condition to know all that passed. It is evident that the labours of the electoral and princely colleges were not to be sought for in the records of a city

In the beginning of the year 1837, I received permission to explore the Royal Archives of the kingdom of Prussia at Berlin, and in the April of the same year, the State Archives of the kingdom of Saxony at Dresden, for the affairs of the empire during the times of Maximilian I. and Charles V. The former were of great value to me, as containing the records of an electorate; the latter, down to the end of that epoch, those of a sovereign principality. It is true that I came upon many documents which I had already seen at Frankfurt; but, at the same time, I found a great number of new ones, which gave me an insight into parts of the subject hitherto obscure. None of these collections is, indeed, complete, and many a question which suggests itself remains unanswered, yet they are in a high degree instructive. They throw a completely new light on the character and conduct of such influential princes as Joachim II. of Brandenburg, and still more, Maurice of Saxony.

Let no one pity a man who devotes himself to studies apparently so dry, and neglects for them the delights of many a joyous day. It is true the companions of his solitary hours are but lifeless paper, but they are the remnants of the life of past ages, which gradually assume form and substance to the eye occupied in the study of them. For me (in a preface an author is bound to speak of himself—a subject he elsewhere gladly avoids) they had a peculiar interest.

When I wrote the first part of my History of the Popes, I designedly treated the origin and progress of the Reformation with as much brevity as the subject permitted. I cherished the hope of dedicating more extensive and profound research to this most important event of the history of our country.

This hope was now abundantly satisfied. Of the new matter which I found, the greater part related directly or indirectly to the epoch of the Reformation. At every step I acquired new information as to the circumstances which prepared the politico-religious movement of that time; the phases of our national life, by which it was accelerated; the origin and working of the resistance it encountered.

It is impossible to approach a matter originating in such intense mental energy, and exercising so vast an influence on the destinies of the world, without being profoundly interested and absorbed by it. I was fully sensible that if I executed the work I proposed to myself, the Reformation would be the centre on which all other incidents and circumstances would turn

But to accomplish this, more accurate information as to the progress of opinion in the evangelical* or reforming party, especially in a political point of view, antecedent to the crisis of the Reformation, was necessary than any that could be gathered from printed sources. The Archives common to the whole Ernestine line of Saxony, deposited at Weimar, which I visited in August, 1837, afforded me what I desired. Nor can any spot be more full of information on the marked epochs at which this house played so important a part, than the vault in which its archives are preserved. The walls and the whole interior space are covered with the rolls of documents relating to the actions and events of that period. Every note, every draft of an answer, is here preserved. The correspondence between the Elector John Frederic and the Landgrave Philip of Hessen would alone fill a long series of printed volumes. I endeavoured, above all, to make myself master of the two registers, which include the affairs of the empire and the Schmalkaldic League. As to the former, I found, as was to be expected from the nature of the subject, many valuable details; as to the latter, I hence first drew information which is, I hope, in some degree calculated to satisfy the curiosity of the public.

I feel bound here publicly to express my thanks to the authorities to whom the guardianship of all these Archives is entrusted for the liberal aid—often not unattended with personal trouble—which I received from them all. How much more easy are existence and study become than they formerly were!

At length, I conceived the idea of undertaking a more extensive research into the Archives of Germany. I repaired to the Communal Archives of the house of Anhalt at Dessau, which at the epoch in question shared the opinions and followed the example of that of Saxony; but I soon saw that I should here be in danger of encumbering myself with too much matter of a merely local character. I remembered how many other documents relating to this period had been explored and employed by the industry of German inquirers The work of Bucholz on Ferdinand I. contains a most copious treasure of important matter from those of Austria, of which too little use is made in that state. The instructive writings of Stumpf and Winter are founded on those of Bavaria The Archives of Wurtenberg were formerly explored by Sattler; the Hessian, recently, by Rommel and Neudecker. For the more exclusively ecclesiastical view of the period, the public is in possession of a rich mass of authentic documents in the collections of Walch, and the recent editions of Luther's Letters by De Wette, and still more in those of Melanchthon by Bretschneider. The letters of the deputies from Strasburg and Nurnberg, which have been published, throw light on the history of particular diets It is hardly necessary for me to mention how much has lately been brought together by Forstemann respecting the Diet of Augsburg of 1530, so long the subject of earnest research and labour.

Recent publications, especially in Italy and England, lead us to hope for the possi-

* It is, perhaps, hardly necessary to remark, that I have retained this word throughout the following work in its original acceptation, viz as denoting the party which, at the time of the Reformation, adhered to the Confession of Augsburg In our own age and country it has been adopted by a party which stands in nearly the same relation to the Church of England as the party called pietistical (*pietistisch*) to the Lutheran Church of Germany But this did not seem to me a sufficient reason for removing it from its proper and authorised place in German history —Transl.

bility of a thorough and satisfactory explanation of the foreign relations of the empire.*

I see the time approach in which we shall no longer have to found modern history on the reports even of contemporaneous historians, except in so far as they were in possession of personal and immediate knowledge of facts; still less, on works yet more remote from the source; but on the narratives of eye-witnesses, and the genuine and original documents. For the epoch treated in the following work, this prospect is no distant one. I myself have made use of a number of records which I had found when in the pursuit of another subject, in the Archives of Vienna, Venice, Rome, and especially Florence. Had I gone into further detail, I should have run the risk of losing sight of the subject as a whole; or, in the necessary lapse of time, of breaking the unity of the conception which arose before my mind in the course of my past researches.

And thus I proceeded boldly to the completion of this work; persuaded that when an inquirer has made researches of some extent in the authentic records, with an earnest spirit and a genuine ardour for truth, later discoveries may throw clearer and more certain light on details, but can only strengthen his fundamental conceptions of the subject: — for truth can be but one.

* Researches and publications of this kind have been going on ever since the first edition of the two first volumes of this work were published; I have availed myself of them as far as was possible in the second. Nor have I neglected to introduce the additional matter which presented itself to me in Brussels and in Paris. (*Note to the second edition.*)

TRANSLATOR'S PREFACE.

In the Preface to the first volume of this work, I said that, according to the view of the Author, it might be divided into three epochs: the first comprehended in the first two volumes, the next, in the third; and the last, in the two concluding volumes

The second of these historical divisions I now, after a considerable and unwilling delay, offer to the English reader.

If, in the volumes already translated, he watched the early struggles, the partial and doubtful triumphs of the church founded by Luther, he will here accompany it, through the various stages of growing strength, to maturity. At the close of this volume, we leave it in possession of all the attributes of a regularly constituted Church, we leave it protected by the civil power, and yielding in return cordial obedience and firm support

We leave it also (such is the infirmity, and such the presumption of man) already laying claim to the possession of absolute truth; already forging instruments for restraining the inquiry it had so ardently promoted, and so largely used; and for establishing an authority akin to that which it had risen to overthrow.

In their ardour to overthrow the authority of the ancient church, the Reformers had not measured the aberrations of which undisciplined minds, suddenly freed from habitual restraint, are capable. and now, alarmed at the frightful and apparently boundless extent of the moral disorder, they felt the necessity of fixing certain limits, beyond which the extravagance of man should not pass

But if they had not calculated the amount of evil they had let loose on the world, neither had they understood all the value and potency of the great conservative and corrective principle to which they were the first to give a general and systematic application. It is in the promptitude, the energy, the inflexible perseverance, with which Luther seized and pursued the idea of the connexion between the Church and the School (i. e. the joint and inseparable culture of the religious affections and the intellectual faculties), and of the duty incumbent on a Christian State to provide with equal care for both, that we recognize the pre-eminent genius of the first German Reformer. This idea was adopted by most of his successors; but none of them—nor, indeed, even the great author of it himself—was as yet sufficiently secure of its results, to dare to intrust religion to the guardianship of enlightened reason, or the order of the world to the slow but sure operation of moral discipline.

The experience of three centuries has shown that religion and morality have, at best, a precarious hold on minds too gross to understand their foundations or their value; that all modes of governing men which take no account of their reason are inefficacious or depraving, and, in either case, fraught with danger; and thus the political expediency (as well as the Christian duty) of educating the people, which the dauntless innovator was the first to proclaim, has come to be admitted, even by the selfish and the timorous. Nor is the recognition of this great necessity confined to the countries which adopted his ecclesiastical reforms. In many of those where the Catholic Church retains her authority, the State has provided (more or less amply) for the instruction of all its subjects.

The origin and course of the Reformation in England sufficiently explain the absence of any such presiding thought among its authors and leaders. Exactly three hundred years have passed since Luther's death (1546): are we too sanguine in believing the time to be at hand, when, in a country calling herself the champion of Protestantism, some attempt may be made to act up to that sublime conception of the duties of a Reformed Church and a Protestant State, which he bequeathed to the world?

S. A.

December, 1846.

HISTORY

OF THE

REFORMATION IN GERMANY.

INTRODUCTION.

VIEW OF THE EARLY HISTORY OF GERMANY.

For purposes of discussion or of instruction, it may be possible to sever ecclesiastical from political history; in actual life, they are indissolubly connected, or rather fused into one indivisible whole.

As indeed there is nothing of real importance in the moral and intellectual business of human life, the source of which does not lie in a profound and more or less conscious relation of man and his concerns to God and divine things, it is impossible to conceive a nation worthy of the name, or entitled to be called, in any sense, great, whose political existence is not constantly elevated and guided by religious ideas. To cultivate, purify and exalt these,—to give them an expression intelligible to all and profitable to all,—to embody them in outward forms and public acts, is its necessary as well as its noblest task.

It is not to be denied that this process inevitably brings into action two great principles which seem to place a nation at variance with itself. Nationality (i e the sum of the peculiar qualities, habits, and sentiments of a nation) is necessarily restricted within the bounds marked out by neighbouring nationalities, whereas religion, ever since it was revealed to the world in a form which claims and deserves universality, constantly strives after sole and absolute supremacy.

In the foundation or constitution of a State, some particular moral or intellectual principle predominates, a principle prescribed by an inherent necessity, expressed in determinate forms and giving birth to a peculiar condition of society, or character of civilisation. But no sooner has a Church, with its forms of wider application, embracing different nations, arisen, than it grasps at the project of absorbing the State, and of reducing the principle on which civil society is founded to complete subjection: the original underived authority of that principle is, indeed, rarely acknowledged by the Church.

At length the universal religion appears, and, after it has incorporated itself with the consciousness of mankind, assumes the character of a great and growing tradition, handed down from people to people, and communicated in rigid dogmas. But nations cannot suffer themselves to be debarred from exercising the understanding bestowed on them by nature, or the knowledge acquired by study, on an investigation of its truth In every age, therefore, we see diversities in the views of religion arise in different nations, and these again react in various ways on the character and condition of the State It is evident, from the nature of this struggle, how mighty is the crisis which it involves for the destinies of the human race Religious truth must have an outward and visible representation, in order that the State may be perpetually reminded of the origin and the end of our earthly existence; of the rights of our neighbours, and the kindred of all the nations of the earth, it would otherwise be in danger of degenerating into tyranny, or of hardening into inveterate prejudice,—into intolerant conceit of self, and hatred of all that is foreign. On the other hand, a free development of the national character and culture is necessary to the interests of religion Without this, its doctrines can never be truly understood nor profoundly accepted without incessant alternations of doubt and conviction, of assent and dissent, of seeking and finding, no error could be removed, no deeper understanding of truth attained. Thus, then, independence of thought and political freedom are indispensable to the Church herself, she needs them to remind her of the varying intellectual wants of men, of the changing nature of her own forms; she needs them to preserve her from the lifeless iteration of misunderstood doctrines and rites, which kill the soul.

It has been said, the State is itself the Church, but the Church has thought herself authorised to usurp the place of the State. The truth is, that the spiritual or intellectual life of man—in its intensest depth and energy unquestionably one—yet manifests itself in these two institutions, which come into contact under the most varied forms; which are continually striving to pervade each other, yet never entirely coincide; to exclude each other, yet neither has ever been permanently victor or vanquished. In the nations of the West, at least, such a result has never been obtained. The Califate may unite ecclesiastical and political power in one hand; but the whole life and character of western Christendom consists of the incessant action and counter-action of Church and State; hence arises the freer, more comprehensive, more profound activity of mind, which must, on the whole, be admitted to characterise that portion of the globe. The aspect of the public life of Europe is always determined by the mutual relations of these two great principles.

Hence it happens that ecclesiastical history is not to be understood without political, nor the latter without the former. The combination of both is necessary to present either in its true light; and if ever we are able to fathom the depths of that profounder life where both have their common source and origin, it must be by a complete knowledge of this combination.

But if this is the case with all nations, it is most pre-eminently so with the German, which has bestowed more persevering and original thought on ecclesiastical and religious subjects than any other. The events of ten centuries turn upon the struggles between the Empire and the Papacy, between Catholicism and Protestantism. We, in our days, stand midway between them.

My design is to relate the history of an epoch in which the politico-religious energy of the German nation was most conspicuous for its growth and most prolific in its results. I do not conceal from myself the great difficulty of this undertaking; but, with God's help, I will endeavour to accomplish it. I shall first attempt to trace my way through a retrospect of earlier times.

CAROLINGIAN TIMES.

One of the most important epochs in the history of the world was the commencement of the eighth century; when, on the one side Mahommedanism threatened to overspread Italy and Gaul, and on the other, the ancient idolatry of Saxony and Friesland once more forced its way across the Rhine. In this peril of Christian institutions a youthful prince of Germanic race, Karl Martell, arose as their champion; maintained them with all the energy which the necessity for self-defence calls forth, and finally extended them into new regions. For, as the possessor of the sole power which still remained erect in the nations of Roman origin—the Pope of Rome—allied himself with this prince and his successors; as he received assistance from them, and bestowed in return the favour and protection of the spiritual authority, the compound of military and sacerdotal government which forms the basis of all European civilisation from that moment arose into being. From that time conquest and conversion went hand in hand. "As soon," says the author of the life of St. Boniface, "as the authority of the glorious Prince Charles over the Frisians was confirmed, the trumpet of the sacred word was heard." It would be difficult to say whether the Frankic domination contributed more to the conversion of the Hessians and Thuringians, or Christianity to the incorporation of those races with the Frankic empire. The war of Charlemagne against the Saxons was a war not only of conquest but of religion. Charlemagne opened it with an attack on the old Saxon sanctuary, the Irminsul; the Saxons retorted by the destruction of the church at Fritzlar. Charlemagne marched to battle bearing the relics of saints; missionaries accompanied the divisions of his army; his victories were celebrated by the establishment of bishoprics; baptism was the seal of subjection and allegiance; relapse into heathenism was also a crime against the state. The consummation of all these incidents is to be found in the investiture of the aged conqueror with the imperial crown. A German, in the natural course of events and in the exercise of regular legitimate power, occupied the place of the Cæsars as chief of a great part of the Romanz world; he also assumed a lofty station at the side of the Roman pontiff in spiritual affairs; a Frankic synod saluted him, as "Regent of the true religion." The entire state of which he was the chief now assumed a colour and form wherein the spiritual and temporal elements were completely blended. The union between emperor and pope served as a model for that between count and bishop. The archdeaconries into which the bishoprics were divided, generally, if not universally, coincided with the Gauen, or political divisions of the country. As the counties were divided into hundreds, so were the archdeaconries into deaneries. The seat of them was different; but, in respect of the territory over which their jurisdiction extended, there was a striking correspondence.* According to the view of the lord and ruler, not only was the secular power to lend its arm to the spiritual, but the spiritual to aid the temporal by its excommunications. The great empire reminds us of a vast neutral ground in the midst of a world filled with carnage and devastation; where an iron will imposes peace on forces generally in a state of mutual hostility and destruction, and fosters and shelters the germ of civilisation; so guarded was it on all sides by impregnable marches.

But every age could not produce a man so formed to subdue and to command; and for the development of the world which Charlemagne founded, it remained to be seen what would be the mutual bearing of the different elements of which it was composed; whether they would blend with or repel each other, agree or conflict: for there can be no true and enduring vitality without the free motion of natural and innate powers and propensities.

It was inevitable that the clergy would first feel its own strength. This body formed a corporation independent even of the emperor:

* See Wenck, Hessische Landesgeschichte, ii. 469.

originating and developed in the Romanz nations, whose most remarkable product it had been in the preceding century, it now extended over those of Germanic race; in which, through the medium of a common language, it continually made new proselytes and gained strength and consistency.

Even under Charlemagne the spiritual element was already bestirring itself with activity and vigour. One of the most remarkable of his capitularies is that wherein he expresses his astonishment that his spiritual and temporal officers so often thwart, instead of supporting each other, as it is their duty to do. He does not disguise that it was the clergy more especially who exceeded their powers: to them he addresses the question, fraught with reproach and displeasure, which has been so often repeated by succeeding ages — how far they are justified in interfering in purely secular affairs? He tells them they must explain what is meant by renouncing the world; whether that is consistent with large and costly retinues, with attempts to persuade the ignorant to make donations of their goods and to disinherit their children; whether it were not better to foster good morals than to build churches, and the like.*

But the clergy soon evinced a much stronger propensity to ambitious encroachment.

We need not here inquire whether the pseudo-Isidorian decretals were invented as early as the reign of Charlemagne, or somewhat later; in the Frankic church, or in Italy: at all events, they belong to that period, are connected with a most extensive project, and form a great epoch in our history. The project was to overthrow the existing constitution of the church, which, in every country, still essentially rested on the authority of the metropolitan; to place the whole church in immediate subjection to the pope of Rome, and to establish a unity of the spiritual power, by means of which it must necessarily emancipate itself from the temporal. Such was the plan which the clergy had even then the boldness to avow. A series of names of the earlier popes were pressed into the service, in order to append to them forged documents, to which a colour of legality was thus given.†

And what was it not possible to effect in those times of profound historical ignorance, in which past ages were only beheld through the twilight of falsehood and fantastic error? and under princes like the successors of Charlemagne, whose minds, instead of being elevated or purified were crushed by religious influences, so that they lost the power of distinguishing the spiritual from the temporal province of the clerical office?

It is indisputable that the order of succession to the throne which Louis the Pious, in utter disregard of the warnings of his faithful adherents, and in opposition to all German modes of thinking, established in the year 817,‡ was principally brought about by the influence of the clergy. "The empire," says Agobardus, "must not be divided into three; it must remain one and undivided." The division of the empire seemed to endanger the unity of the church: and, as the emperor was chiefly determined by spiritual motives, the regulations adopted were enforced with all the pomp of religious ceremonies, — by masses, fasts, and distributions of alms; every one swore to them; they were held to be inspired by God himself.

After this, no one, not even the emperor, could venture to depart from them. Great, at least, were the evils which he brought upon himself by his attempt to do so, out of love to a son born at a later period of his life. The irritated clergy made common cause with his elder sons, who were already dissatisfied with the administration of the empire. The supreme pontiff came in person from Rome and declared in their favour; and a universal revolt was the consequence. Nor did this first manifestation of their power satisfy the clergy. In order to make sure of their advantage, they formed the daring scheme of depriving the born and anointed emperor, on whom they could now no longer place reliance, of his consecrated dignity,—a dignity which, at any rate, he owed not to them,—and of bestowing it immediately on the successor to the throne who had been nominated in 817, and who was the natural representative of the unity of the empire. If, on the one hand, it is indisputable that, in the eighth century, the spiritual authority contributed greatly to the establishment of the principle of obedience to the temporal government, it is equally certain that, in the ninth, it made rapid strides towards the acquisition of power into its own hands. In the collection of capitularies of Benedictus Levita, it is treated as one of the leading principles, that no constitution in the world has any force or validity against the decisions of the popes of Rome; in more than one canon, kings who act in opposition to this principle are threatened with divine punishment.§ The monarchy of Charlemagne seemed to be about to be transformed into an ecclesiastical state.

I do not hesitate to affirm that it was mainly the people of Germany who resisted this tendency; indeed, that it was precisely this resistance which first awakened Germany to a consciousness of its own importance as a nation. For it would be impossible to speak of a German nation, in the proper sense of the word, during the preceding ages. In the more remote, the several tribes had not even a common name by which they recognised each

* "Capitulare interrogationis de iis quæ Karolus M. pro communi omnium utilitate interroganda constituit Aquisgrani 811."—*Monum. Germaniæ Histor. ed. Pertz*, iii. p. 106.

† A passage from the spurious Acts of the Synods of Pope Silvester is found in a Capitulary of 806. See Eichhorn, Ueber die spanische Sammlung der Quellen des Kirchenrechts in den Abhandl. der Preuss. Akad. d. W. 1834. Philos. Hist. Klasse, p. 132.

‡ Fauriel, Histoire de la Gaule Mérid. iv. 47, examines this point more in detail.

§ Benedicti Capitularia, lib. ii. p. 322. "Velut prævaricator catholicæ fidei semper a Domino reus existat quicunque regum canonis hujus censuram permiserit violandam." Lib. iii. 346. "Constitutiones contradecreta præsulum Romanorum nullius sunt momenti."

other: during the period of their migration, they fought with as much hostility among themselves as against the stranger, and allied themselves as readily with the latter as with those of common race. Under the Merovingian kings they were further divided by religious enmities, the Saxons, in presence of Frankic Christianity, held the more pertinaciously to their forms of government and to their ancient gods. It was not till Charlemagne had united all the Germanic tribes, with the exception of those in England and Scandinavia, in one and the same temporal and spiritual allegiance, that the nation began to acquire form and consistency; it was not till the beginning of the ninth century, that the German name appeared as contra-distinguished from the Romanz portion of the empire *

It is worthy of eternal remembrance, that the first act in which the Germans appear as one people, is the resistance to the attempt of the clergy to depose their emperor and lord.

The ideas of legitimacy which they had inherited from their past political life and history, as members of tribes, would never have led them to derive it from the pretended grace of God,—that is to say, from the declaration of the spiritual authorities. They were attached to Louis the Pious, who had rendered peculiar services to the Saxon chiefs, their aversion to his deposition was easily fanned into a flame at the call of Louis the Germanic, who kept his court in Bavaria, the other tribes, Saxons, Swabians, and Franks, on this side the Carbonaria, gathered around his banner, for the first time they were united in one great object As they were aided by an analogous, though much feebler, movement in the south of France, the bishops soon found themselves compelled to absolve the emperor from the penance they had imposed, and to acknowledge him again as their lord. The first historical act of the united nation is this rising in favour of their born prince against the spiritual power. Nor were they any longer inclined to consent to such a deviation from their own law of succession, as was involved in the acknowledgment of a single heir to the whole monarchy. When, after the death of Louis the Pious, Lothair, in spite of all that had passed, made an attempt to seize the reins of the whole empire, he found in the Germans a resistance, at first doubtful, but every moment increasing, and finally victorious. From them his troops received their first important defeat on the Riess, which laid the foundation of the severance of Germany from the great monarchy †

Lothair relied on his claims recognised by the clergy; the Germans, combined with the southern French, challenged him to submit them to the judgment of heaven by battle Then it was that the great array of the Frankic empire split into two hostile masses; the one containing a preponderance of Romanz, the other of Germanic elements. The former defended the unity of the Empire; the latter demanded, according to their German ideas, its separation. There is a ballad extant on the battle of Fontenay, in which one of the combatants expresses his grief at this bloody war of fellow-citizens and brethren, "on that bitter night in which the brave fell, the skilful in fight." For the destiny of the West it was decisive.‡ The judgment of heaven was triumphantly pronounced against the claims of the clergy; three kingdoms were now actually established instead of one. The secular Germanic principles which, from the time of the great migration of tribes, had extended widely into the Romanz world, remained in possession of the field they were steadfastly maintained in the subsequent troubles.

On the extinction of one of the three lines in which the unity of the empire should have rested, dissensions broke out between the two others, a main feature of which was the conflict between the spiritual and secular principles.

The king of the French, Charles the Bald, had allied himself with the clergy, his armies were led to the field by bishops, and he abandoned the administration of his kingdom in a great measure to Hinkmar, archbishop of Rheims. Hence, when the throne of Lotharingia became vacant in the year 869, he experienced the warmest support from the bishops of that country. "After," say they, "they had called on God, who bestows kingdoms on whom he will, to point out to them a king after his own heart; after they had then, with God's help, perceived that the crown was of right his to whom they meant to confide it," they elected Charles the Bald to be their lord.§ But the Germans were as far now as before from being convinced by this sort of public law. The elder brother thought his claims at least as valid as those of the younger, by force of arms he compelled Charles to consent to the treaty of Marsna, by which he first united transrhenane Germany with that on the right bank of the Rhine. This same course of events was repeated in the year 875, when the thrones of Italy and the Empire became vacant. At first, Charles the Bald, aided now by the pope, as heretofore by the bishops, took possession of the crown without difficulty.‖ But Carlmann, son of Louis the Germanic, resting his claim on the right of the elder line, and also on his nomination as heir by the last emperor, hastened with his Bavarians and high Germans to Italy; and in spite of the opposition of the pope, took possession of it as his unquestionable inheritance If this were the case in Italy, still less could Charles the Bald succeed in his attempts on the German fron-

* Rühs Erlauterung der zehn ersten Capitel von Tacitus Germania, p 103, Mone Geschichte des Heidenthums im Nördlichen Europa Th ii p 6

† In Retiense (Annales Ruodolfi Fuldensis, Monumenta Germaniæ Hist i p. 352) According to Lang (Baierische Gauen, p 78,) belonging to the Swabian territory

‡ Angilbertus de bella quæ fuit Fontaneto

§ "Caroli Secundi Coronatio in Regno Hlotharii, 869"—*Monum* iii 512

‖ "Papa invitante Romam perrexit Beato Petro multa et pretiosa munera offerens, in imperatorem unctus est" —*Annales Hincmari Remensis*, 875 et 876, *Monum Germ* i 498

tiers. He was defeated in both countries; the superiority of the Germans in arms was so decisive that, at length, they became masters of the whole Lotharingian territory. Even under the Carolingian sovereigns, they marked the boundaries of the mighty empire; the crown of Charlemagne, and two-thirds of his dominions, fell into their hands: they maintained the independence of the secular power with dauntless energy and brilliant success.

SAXON AND FRANKIC EMPERORS.

The question which next presents itself is, what course was to be pursued if the ruling house either became extinct, or proved itself incapable of conducting the government of so vast an empire, attacked on every side from without, and fermenting within.

In the years from 879 to 887, the several nations determined, one after another, to abandon the cause of Charles the Fat. The characteristic differences of the mode in which they accomplished this are well worthy of remark.

In the Romanz part of Europe the clergy had a universal ascendancy. In Cisjurane Burgundy it was "the holy fathers assembled at Mantala, the holy synod, together with the nobles," who "under the inspiration of the Holy Spirit," elected Count Boso king.* We find from the decretal for the election of Guido of Spoleto, that "the humble bishops assembled together from various parts at Pavia chose him to be their lord and king,† principally because he had promised to exalt the holy Roman church, and to maintain the ecclesiastical rights and privileges." The conditions to which Odo of Paris gave his assent at his coronation are chiefly in favour of the clergy; he promises not only to defend the rights of the church, but to extend them to the utmost of his information and ability.‡ Totally different was the state of things in Germany. Here it was more especially the temporal lords, Saxons, Franks and Bavarians, who, under the guidance of a disaffected minister of the emperor, assembled around Arnulf and transferred the crown to him. The bishops (even the bishop of Mainz) were rather opposed to the measure; nor was it till some years afterwards that they entered into a formal negotiation§ with the new ruler: they had not elected him; they submitted to his authority.

The rights and privileges which were on every occasion claimed by the clergy, were as constantly and as resolutely ignored by the Germans. They held as close to the legitimate succession as possible; even after the complete extinction of the Carolingian race, the degree of kindred with it was one of the most important considerations which determined the choice of the people, first to Conrad, and then to Henry I. of Saxony.

Conrad had, indeed, at one time, the idea of attaching himself to the clergy, who, even in Germany, were a very powerful body: Henry, on the contrary, was always opposed to them. They took no share in his election; the consecration by the holy oil, upon which Pepin and Charlemagne had set so high a value, he declined; as matters stood in Germany, it could be of no importance to him. On the contrary, we find that as in his own land of Saxony he kept his clergy within the strict bounds of obedience, so in other parts of his dominions he placed them in subjection to the dukes;‖ so that their dependence on the civil power was more complete than ever. His only solicitude was to stand well with these great feudatories, whose power was almost equal to his own, and to fulfil other duties imperatively demanded by the moment. As he succeeded in these objects,—as he obtained a decisive victory over his most dangerous enemies, re-established the Marches, which had been broken at all points, and suffered nothing on the other side the Rhine that bore the German name to be wrested from him,—the clergy were compelled by necessity to adhere to him: he bequeathed an undisputed sceptre to his house. It was by an agreement of the court and the secular nobles that Otho was selected from among Henry's sons as his successor to the throne. The ceremony of election was attended only by the dukes, princes, great officers of state, and warriors; the elected monarch then received the assembled body of the clergy.** Otho could receive the unction without scruple; the clergy could no longer imagine that they conferred a right upon him by that ceremony. Whether anointed or not, Otho would have been king, as his father had been before him. And so firmly was this sovereignty established, that Otho was now in a position to revive and carry through the claims founded by his Carolingian predecessors. He first completely realised the idea of a Germanic empire, which they had only conceived and prepared. He governed Lotharingia and administered Burgundy; a short campaign sufficed to re-establish the rights of his Carolingian predecessors to the supreme power in Lombardy. Like Charlemagne, he was called to aid by a pope oppressed by the factions of Rome; like him, he received in return for his succour the crown of the western empire (2d February, 962.) The principle of the temporal government, the autocracy, which from the earliest times had held in check the usurpations of ecclesiastical ambition, thus attained its

* "Nutu Dei, per suffragia sanctorum, ob instantem necessitatem."—*Electio Bosonis; Monum.* iii. 547.

† "Nos humiles episcopos ex diversis partibus Papiæ convenientibus pro ecclesiarum nostrarum ereptione et omnis Christianitatis salvatione," &c.—*Electio Widonis Regis, Monum.* iii. 554.

‡ Capitulum Odonis Regis. Ibid.

§ "De collegio sacerdotum gnaros direxerunt mediatores ad præfatum regem," &c.—*Arnulfi Concilium Triburience, Monum.* iii. 560. He says, "Nos, quibus regni cura et solicitudo ecclesiarum commissa est."

‖ "Totius Bajoariæ pontifices tuæ subjaceant potestati," is the promise of Liutprand the king to Duke Arnulf. Buchner, Geschichte der Baiern, iii. 38, shows what use the latter made of it. See Waiz, Henry I., p. 49.

** Widukiveli Annales, lib. ii. "Duces ac præfectorum principes cum cætera principum militumque manu—fecerunt eum regem; dum ea geruntur a ducibus ac cætero magistratu, pontifex maximus cum universo sacerdotali ordine præstolabatur."

culminating point, and was triumphantly asserted and recognised in Europe.

At the first glance it would seem as if the relation in which Otho now stood to the pope was the same as that occupied by Charlemagne; on a closer inspection, however, we find a wide difference.

Charlemagne's connection with the see of Rome was produced by mutual need; it was the result of long epochs of a political combination embracing the development of various nations; their mutual understanding rested on an internal necessity, before which all opposing views and interests gave way. The sovereignty of Otho the Great, on the contrary, rested on a principle fundamentally opposed to the encroachment of spiritual influences. The alliance was momentary; the disruption of it inevitable. But when, soon after, the same pope who had invoked his aid, John XII., placed himself at the head of a rebellious faction, Otho was compelled to cause him to be formally deposed, and to crush the faction that supported him by repeated exertions of force, before he could obtain perfect obedience; he was obliged to raise to the papal chair a pope on whose co-operation he could rely. The popes have often asserted that they transferred the empire to the Germans; and if they confined this assertion to the Carolingian race, they are not entirely wrong. The coronation of Charlemagne was the result of their free determination. But if they allude to the German emperors, properly so called, the contrary of their statement is just as true; not only Carlmann and Otho the Great, but their successors, constantly had to conquer the imperial throne, and to defend it, when conquered, sword in hand.

It has been said that the Germans would have done more wisely if they had not meddled with the empire; or at least, if they had first worked out their own internal political institutions, and then, with matured minds, taken part in the general affairs of Europe. But the things of this world are not wont to develop themselves so methodically. A nation is often compelled by circumstances to increase its territorial extent, before its internal growth is completed. For was it of slight importance to its inward progress, that Germany thus remained in unbroken connexion with Italy?—the depository of all that remained of ancient civilisation, the source whence all the forms of Christianity had been derived. The mind of Germany has always unfolded itself by contact with the spirit of antiquity, and of the nations of Roman origin. It was from the contrasts which so continually presented themselves during this uninterrupted connexion, that Germany learned to distinguish ecclesiastical domination from Christianity.

For however signal had been the ascendancy of the secular power, the German people did not depart a hair's breadth either from the doctrines of Christianity, the ideas upon which a Christian church is founded, or even from the forms in which they had first received those doctrines and ideas. In them the nation had first risen to a consciousness of its existence as a united body; its whole intellectual and moral life was bound up with them. The German imperial government revived the civilising and Christianising tendencies which had distinguished the reigns of Charles Martell and Charlemagne. Otho the Great, in following the course marked out by his illustrious predecessors, gave it a fresh national importance by planting German colonies in Slavonian countries, simultaneously with the diffusion of Christianity. He Germanised as well as converted the population he had subdued. He confirmed his father's conquests on the Saale and the Elbe, by the establishment of the bishoprics of Meissen and Osterland. After having conquered the tribes on the other side the Elbe in those long and perilous campaigns where he commanded in person, he established there, too, three bishoprics, which for a time gave an extraordinary impulse to the progress of conversion.* In the midst of all his difficulties and perplexities in Italy, he never lost sight of this grand object; it was indeed while in that country that he founded the archbishopric of Magdeburg, whose jurisdiction extended over all those other foundations. And even where the project of Germanising the population was out of the question, the supremacy of the German name was firmly and actively maintained. In Bohemia and Poland bishoprics were erected under German metropolitans; from Hamburg Christianity found its way into the north; missionaries from Passau traversed Hungary, nor is it improbable that the influence of these vast and sublime efforts extended even to Russia. The German empire was the centre of the conquering religion; as itself advanced, it extended the ecclesiastico-military State of which the Church was an integral part; it was the chief representative of the unity of western Christendom, and hence arose the necessity under which it lay of acquiring a decided ascendancy over the papacy.

This secular and Germanic principle long retained the predominancy it had triumphantly acquired. Otho the Second offered the papal chair to the abbot of Clugny; and Otho the Third bestowed it first on one of his kinsmen, and then on his instructor Gerbert. All the factions which threatened to deprive the emperor of this right were overthrown; under the patronage of Henry III., a German pope defeated three Roman candidates for the tiara. In the year 1048, when the see of Rome became vacant, ambassadors from the Romans, says a contemporaneous chronicler, proceeded to Saxony, found the emperor there, and entreated him to give them a new pope. He chose the Bishop of Toul, (afterwards Leo IX.), of the house of Egisheim, from which he himself was descended on the maternal side. What took place with regard to the head of the church was of course still more certain to befall the rest of the clergy. Since Otho the Great, in all the troubles of the early years of his reign, succeeded in breaking down the re-

* Adami Brem. Histor. Ecclesiastica, lib. ii. c. 17.

sistance which the duchies were enabled by their clan-like composition to offer him, the ecclesistical appointments remained without dispute in the hand of the emperor.

How magnificent was the position now occupied by the German nation, represented in the persons of the mightiest princes of Europe and united under their sceptre; at the head of an advancing civilisation, and of the whole of western Christendom; in the fulness of youthful, aspiring strength!

We must here however remark and confess, that Germany did not wholly understand her position, nor fulfil her mission. Above all, she did not succeed in giving complete reality to the idea of a western empire, such as appeared about to be established under Otho I. Independent and often hostile, though Christian powers arose through all the borders of Germany; in Hungary, and in Poland, in the northern as well as in the southern possessions of the Normans; England and France were snatched again from German influence. Spain laughed at the German claims to a universal supremacy; her kings thought themselves emperors; even the enterprises nearest home—those across the Elbe—were for a time stationary or retrograde.

If we seek for the causes of these unfavourable results, we need only turn our eyes on the internal condition of the empire, where we find an incessant and tempestuous struggle of all the forces of the nation. Unfortunately the establishment of a fixed rule of succession to the imperial crown was continually prevented by events. The son and grand-son of Otho the Great died in the bloom of youth, and the nation was thus compelled to elect a chief. The very first election threw Germany and Italy into a universal ferment; and this was shortly succeeded by a second still more stormy, since it was necessary to resort to a new line—the Franconian. How was it possible to expect implicit obedience from the powerful and refractory nobles, out of whose ranks, and by whose will, the emperor was raised to the throne? Was it likely that the Saxon race, which had hitherto held the reins of government, would readily and quietly submit to a foreign family? It followed that two factions arose, the one obedient, the other opposed, to the Franconian emperor, and filled the empire with their strife. The severe character of Henry III. excited universal discontent.* A vision, related to us by his own chancellor, affords a lively picture of the state of things. He saw the emperor, seated on his throne, draw his sword, exclaiming aloud, that he trusted he should still avenge himself on all his enemies. How could the emperors, thus occupied during their whole lives with intestine dissensions, place themselves at the head of Europe in the important work of social improvement, or really merit the title of supreme Lords of the West?

It is remarkable that the social element on which they propped their power was again principally the clergy. Even Otho the Great owed his triumph over intestine revolt and discord, in great measure to the support of the bishops; for example, of his brother Bruno, whom he had created Archbishop of Cologne, and who, in return, held Lotharingia in allegiance to him: it was only by the aid of the clergy that Otho conquered the Pope.† The emperors found it expedient to govern by means of the bishops; to make them the instruments of their will. The bishops were at once their chancellors and their counsellors; the monasteries, imperial farms. The uncontrollable tendency, at that time, of all power and office to become hereditary would naturally render the heads of the church desirous of combining secular rights, which they could dispose of at pleasure, with their bishoprics. Hence it happened, that just at the time when the subjection of the clergy to the imperial authority was the most complete, their power acquired the greatest extension and solidity. Otho I. already began to unite the temporal powers of the count with the proper spiritual authority of the bishop. We see from the registers of Henry II. that he bestowed on many churches two and three countships; on that of Gandersheim, the countship in seven Gauen or districts. As early as the eleventh century the bishops of Würzburg succeeded in totally supplanting the secular counts in their diocese, and in uniting the spiritual and temporal power; a state of things which the other bishops now strove to emulate.

It is evident that the station of an emperor of Germany was no less perilous than august The magnates by whom he was surrounded, the possessors of the secular power out of whose ranks he himself had arisen, he could hold in check only by an unceasing struggle, and not without force. He must find a prop in another quarter, and seek support from the very body who were in principle opposed to him. This rendered it impossible for him ever to attain to that predominant influence in the general affairs of Europe which the imperial dignity would naturally have given him. How strongly does this everlasting ebb and flow of contending parties, this continual upstarting of refractory powers, contrast with the tranquillity and self-sufficiency of the empire swayed by Charlemagne! It required matchless vigour and fortitude in an emperor even to hold his seat.

In this posture of affairs, the prince who possessed the requisite vigour and fortitude, Henry III., died young (A. D. 1056), and a child, six years old, in whose name the government was carried on by a tottering regency, filled his place:—one of those incidents which turn the fortunes of a world.

EMANCIPATION OF THE PAPACY.

The ideas which had been repressed in the

* Hermannus Contractus ad an. 1053. "Regni tam primores quam inferiores magis magisque mussitantes, regem se ipso deteriorem fore causabantur"

† Rescriptum patrum in concilio, in Liutprand, lib. vi. contains the remarkable declaration: "Excommunicationem vestram parvipendemus, eam potius in vos retorquebimus."

ninth century now began to revive; and with redoubled strength, since the clergy, from the highest to the lowest, were become so much more powerful.

Generally speaking, this was the age in which the various modifications of spiritual power throughout the world began to assume form and stability; in which mankind found repose and satisfaction in these conditions of existence. In the eleventh century Buddhaism was re-established in Thibet; and the hierarchy which, down to the present day, prevails over so large a portion of Eastern Asia, was founded by the Lama Dschu-Adhischa. The Califate of Bagdad, heretofore a vast empire, then took the character of a spiritual authority, and was greatly indebted to that change for the ready reception it met with. At the same period, in Africa and Syria arose the Fatimite Califate, founded on a doctrine of which its adherents said, that it was to the Koran what the kernel is to the shell.

In the West the idea of the unity of the Christian faith was the pervading one, and had taken strong hold on all minds (for the various conversions which awakened this or that more susceptible nation to fresh enthusiasm belong to a later period). This idea manifested itself in the general efforts to crush Mahommedanism: inadequately represented by the imperial authority, which commanded but a limited obedience, it now came in powerful aid of the projects and efforts of the hierarchy. For to whom could such an idea attach itself but to the bishop of the Roman Church, to which, as to a common source, all other churches traced back their foundation; which all western Europeans regarded with a singular reverence? Hitherto the Bishop of Rome had been thrown into the shade by the rise and development of the imperial power. But favouring circumstances and the main course of events now united to impel the papacy to claim universal and supreme dominion.

The minority of the infant emperor decided the result. At the court of Rome, the man who most loudly proclaimed the necessity of reform—the great champion of the independent existence of the church—the man ordained by destiny to make his opinion the law of ages,—Hildebrand, the son of a carpenter in Tuscany, acquired supreme influence over all affairs. He was the author and instigator of decrees, in virtue of which the papal elections were no longer to depend on the emperor, but on the clergy of the Church of Rome and the cardinals. He delayed not a moment to put them in force; the very next election was conducted in accordance with them.

In Germany, on the contrary, people were at this time entirely occupied with the conflicts of the factions about the court; the opposition which was spread over Italy and Germany (and to which Hildebrand also belonged) at length got a firm footing in the court itself: the adherents of the old Saxon and Salic principles (for example, Chancellor Guibert) were defeated; the court actually sanctioned an election which had taken place against its own most urgent interest; the German rulers, plunged in the dissensions of the moment, abandoned to his fate an anti-pope who maintained himself with considerable success and who was the representative of the ancient maxims.

Affairs, however, changed their aspect when the youthful Salian, with all his spirit and talents, took the reins of government into his own hand. He knew his rights, and was determined to assert them at any price. But things had gone so far that he fell into the most perilous situation at the very outset of his career.

The accession to the throne of a young monarch, by nature despotic and violent, and hurried along by vehement passions, quickly brought the long-fermenting internal discords of Germany to an open breach. The German nobles aspired after the sort of independence which those of France had just acquired. In the year 1073 the Saxon princes revolted; the whole of Saxony, says a contemporary, deserted the king like one man. Meanwhile at Rome the leader of the hostile party had himself gained possession of the tiara, and now advanced without delay to the great work of emancipating not only the papacy but the clergy from the control of the emperor. In the year 1074 he caused a law to be proclaimed by his synod, the purpose and effect of which was to wrest the nomination to spiritual offices from the laity; that is, in the first place, from the emperor.

Scarcely was Henry IV. seated on his throne when he saw its best prerogatives, the crown and consummation of his power, attacked and threatened with annihilation. He seemed doomed to succumb without a contest. The discord between the Saxons and Upper Germans, which for a time had been of advantage to him, was allayed, and their swords, yet wet with each other's blood, were turned in concert against the emperor; he was compelled to propitiate the pope who had excommunicated him, to travel in the depth of winter to do that penance at Canossa by which he so profoundly degraded the imperial name.

Yet from that very moment we may date his most strenuous resistance.

We should fall into a complete error were we to represent him to ourselves as crossing the Alps in remorse and contrition, or as convinced of the rightfulness of the claims advanced by the pope. His only object was to wrest from his adversaries the support of the spiritual authority, the pretext under which they threatened his highest dignity. As he did not succeed in this,—as the absolution he received from Gregory was not so complete as to restrain the German princes from all further hostilities,*—as, on the contrary, they elected another sovereign in spite of it,—he plunged into the most determined struggle against the assumptions of his spiritual as well as of his

* Lambertus Schaffnaburgensis: (*Pistor.* i. p. 420.) "His conditionibus absolutus est ut . . . . accusationibus responderet et ad papæ sententiam vel retineret regnum . . . . vel æquo animo amitteret."

temporal foes. Opposition and injury roused the man within him. Across those Alps which he had traversed in penitential lowliness, he hurried back burning with warlike ardour; in Carinthia an invincible band of devoted followers gathered around him. It is interesting to follow him with our eye, subduing the spiritual power in Bavaria, the hostile aristocratical clans in Swabia; to see him next marching upon Franconia and driving his rival before him; then into Thuringia and the Meissen colonies, and at length forcing him to a battle on the banks of the Elster, in which he fell. Henry gained no great victories; even on the Elster he did not so much as keep the field; but he was continually advancing; his party was continually gaining strength; he held the banner of the empire aloft with a steady and vigorous grasp. After a few years he was able to return to Italy (A. D. 1081). The empire had been so long and so intimately allied with the episcopal power that its chief could not be without adherents among the higher clergy: synods were held in the emperor's behalf, in which it was resolved to maintain the old order of things. The excommunications of the pope were met by counter-excommunications. Chancellor Guibert, who had suffered for his adherence to Salic principles, was nominated pope under the auspices of the emperor; and after various alternations of success in war, was at length conducted in triumph to Rome. Henry, like so many of his predecessors, was crowned by a pope of his own creation. The second rival king whom the Saxons opposed to him could gain no substantial power, and held it expedient voluntarily to withdraw his pretensions.

We see that the emperor had attained to all that is attainable by war and policy, yet his triumph was far from being as complete and conclusive as we might thence infer; for the result of a contest is not always decided on a field of battle. The ideas of which Gregory was the champion were intimately blended with the most powerful impulses of the general development of society; while he was a fugitive from Rome, they gained possession of the world. No later than ten years after his death his second successor was able to take the initiative in the general affairs of the West—a power which was conclusive as to results. One of the greatest social movements recorded in history — the Crusades — was mainly the result of his policy; and from that time he appeared, as the natural head of the Romano-Germanic sacerdotal and military community of the West. To such weapons the emperor had nothing to oppose.

The life of Henry, from this time till its close, has something in it which reminds us of the antique tragedy, in which the hero sinks, in all the glory of manhood and the fulness of his powers, under an inevitable doom. For what can be more like an overwhelming fate than the power of opinion, which extends its invisible grasp on every side, takes complete possession of the minds of men, and suddenly appears in the field with a force beyond all control? Henry saw the world go over, before his eyes, from the empire to the papacy. An army brought together by one of the blind popular impulses which led to the crusades, drove out of Rome the pope he had placed on the throne: nay, even in his own house he was encountered by hostile opinions. His elder son was infected with the zeal of the bigots, by whom he was incited to revolt against his father; the younger was swayed by the influence of the German aristocracy, and, by a union of cunning and violence, compelled his own father to abdicate. The aged warrior went broken-hearted to his grave.

I do not think it necessary to trace all the various alternations of the conflict respecting the rights of the church.

Even in Rome it was sometimes deemed impossible to force the emperor to renounce his claims. Pope Paschal at one time entertained the bold idea of giving back all that the emperors had ever granted to the church, in order to effect the radical separation of the latter from the state.*

As this proved to be impracticable, the affairs of the church were again administered for a time by the imperial court under Henry V., as they had been under Henry IV.†

But this too was soon found to be intolerable; new disputes arose, and after long contention, both parties agreed to the concordat of Worms, according to which the preponderant influence was yielded to the emperor in Germany, and to the pope in Italy; an agreement, however, which was not expressed with precision, and which contained the germ of new disputes.

But though these results were little calculated to determine the rights of the contending powers, the advantages which gradually accrued to the papacy from the course of events were incalculable. From a state of total dependence, it had now attained to a no less complete emancipation; or rather to a preponderance, not indeed as yet absolute, or defined, but unquestionable, and every moment acquiring strength and consistency from favouring circumstances.

RELATION OF THE PAPACY TO THE PRINCES OF THE EMPIRE.

THE most important assistance which the papacy received in this work of self-emancipation and aggrandisement arose from the natural and tacit league subsisting between it and the princes of the Germanic empire.

The secular aristocracy of Germany had, at one time, made the strongest opposition, on

* Heinrici Encyclica de Controversia sua cum Papa. Monum. iv. 70. The emperor asked, most justly, what was to become of the imperial authority, if it were to lose the right of investiture after the emperors had transferred so large a share of their privileges to the bishops.

† Epistola Friderici Coloniensis archiepiscopi: Codex Vdalrici Babenbergensis, n. 277. "Synodales episcoporum conventus, annua consilia, omnes denique ecclesiastici ordinis administrationes in regalem curiam translata sunt."

behalf of their head, to the encroachments of the Church, they had erected the imperial throne, and had invested it with all its power but this power had at length become oppressive to them, the supremacy of the imperial government over the clergy, which was employed to keep themselves in subjection, became their most intolerable grievance. It followed that they at length beheld their own advantage in the emancipation of the papacy

It is to be observed that the power of the German princes and that of the popes rose in parallel steps.

Under Henry III, and during the minority of his successor, both had laid the foundation of their independence they began their active career together Scarcely had Gregory VII established the first principles of his new system, when the princes also proclaimed theirs, —the principle, that the empire should no longer be hereditary Henry IV. maintained his power chiefly by admitting in detail the claims which he denied in the aggregate his victories had as little effect in arresting the progress of the independence of the great nobles as of the hierarchy Even as early as the reign of Henry V these sentiments had gained such force that the unity of the empire was regarded as residing rather in the collective body of the princes than in the person of the emperor For what else are we to understand from the declaration of that prince—that it was less dangerous to insult the head of the empire than to give offence to the princes? * —an opinion which they themselves sometimes expressed In Wurzburg they agreed to adhere to their decrees, even if the king refused his assent to them. They took into their own hands the arrangement of the disputes with the pope which Henry found it impossible to terminate they were the real authors of the concordat of Worms

In the succeeding collisions of the papacy with the empire every thing depended on the degree of support the emperor could, on each occasion, calculate on receiving from the princes

I shall not here attempt to give a complete view of the times of the Welfs and the Hohenstaufen, it would not be possible, without entering into a more elaborate examination of particulars than is consistent with the object of this short survey let us only direct our attention for a moment to the grandest and most imposing figure with which that epoch presents us—Frederic I.

So long as Frederic I. stood well with his princes he might reasonably entertain the project of reviving the prerogatives of the empire, such as they were conceived and laid down by the emperors and jurists of ancient Rome. He held himself entitled, like Justinian and Theodosius, to summon ecclesiastical assemblies, he reminded the popes that their possessions were derived from the favour and bounty of the emperor, and admonished them to attend to their ecclesiastical duties. A disputed election furnished him with a favourable occasion of acquiring fresh influence in the choice of a pope.

His position was, however, very different after the fresh rupture with his powerful vassal, Henry the Lion. The claims of that prince to a little town in the north of Germany, —Gosslar in the Harz,—which the emperor refused to admit, decided the affairs of Italy, and hence of the whole of western Christendom. * In consequence of this, the emperor was first stripped of his wonted support, he was beaten in the field, and, lastly, he was compelled to violate his oath, and to recognise the pope he had rejected

It is true that, having turned his arms against his rebellious vassal, he succeeded in breaking up Henry's collective power but this very success again was advantageous to the princes of the second rank, by whose assistance he obtained it, and whom, in return, he enriched with the spoils of his rival; while the advantage which the papacy thus gained was never afterwards to be counter-balanced

The meeting of Frederic I. and Alexander III at Venice is, in my opinion, far more important than the scene at Canossa. At Canossa, a young and passionate prince sought only to hurry through the penance enjoined upon him at Venice, it was a mature man who renounced the ideas which he had earnestly and strenuously maintained for a quarter of a century; he was compelled to acknowledge that his conduct towards the church had been dictated rather by love of power than of justice † Canossa was the spot on which the combat began, Venice beheld the triumph of the church fully established.

For whatever might be the indirect share which the Germans had in bringing about this result, both the glory and the chief profit of the victory fell entirely to the share of the papacy. From this moment its domination began

This became apparent on the first important incident that occurred, viz, when, at the end of the twelfth century, a contest for the crown arose in Germany

The papacy, represented by one of the most able, ambitious, and daring priests that ever lived, who regarded himself as the natural master of the world,—Innocent III., did not hesitate an instant to claim the right of deciding the question

The German princes were not so blinded as not to understand what this claim meant. They reminded Innocent that the empire, out of reverence for the see of Rome, had waived the right which it incontestably possessed to interfere in the election of the pope; that it would be an unheard-of return for this moderation, for the pope to assume an influence

* "Unius capitis licet summi dejectio reparabile damnum est, principum autem conculcatio ruina regni est" Fragmentum de Hoste facienda —*Monum* iv 63.

† "Dum in facto ecclesiæ potius virtutem potentiæ quam rationem justitiæ volumus exercere, constat nos in errorem merito devenisse" Oratio Imperatoris in Conventu Veneto —*Monum* iv 151

over the election of the emperor, to which he had no right whatever. Unfortunately, however, they were in a position in which they could take no serious steps to prevent the encroachment they deprecated. They must first have placed on the throne an emperor equally strong by nature and by external circumstances, have rallied round him, and have fought the papacy under his banners. For such a course they had neither the inclination, nor, in the actual state of things, was it practicable. They had no love for the papacy, for its own sake; they hated the domination of the clergy; but they had not courage to brave it. Innocent's resolute spirit was again victorious. In the struggle between the two rivals, the one a Welf, the other a Hohenstaufe, he at first supported the Welf, because that family was well inclined to the church; but when, after the accession of this prince to power, and his appearance in Italy, he manifested the usual antipathy of the empire to the papacy, Innocent did not hesitate to set up a Hohenstaufe in opposition to him. He had contended against the Hohenstaufen with the resources of the Welfic party: he now attacked the Welfs with those of the Hohenstaufen. It was a struggle in which the agitations of the rest of Europe were mingled. Events, both near and remote, took a turn so favourable, that Innocent's candidate again remained master of the field.

From that time the papacy exercised a leading influence over all German elections.

When, after the lapse of many years, Frederic II., (the Hohenstaufe whom he had raised to power,) attempted in some particulars to restore the independence of the empire, the pope thought himself justified in again deposing him. Rome now openly avowed her claim to hold the reins of secular as well as spiritual authority.

"We command you," writes Innocent IV. to the German princes in 1246, "since our beloved son, the Landgrave of Thuringia, is ready to take upon himself the office of emperor, that you proceed to elect him unanimously without delay."*

He formally signifies his approbation of those who took part in the election of William of Holland; he admonishes the cities to be faithful to the newly-elected emperor, that so they may merit the apostolical as well as the royal favour.

In a very short time no trace of any other order of things remained in Germany. Even at the ceremony of homage, Richard of Cornwall was compelled to dispense with the allegiance of the cities, until it should be seen whether or not the pope might choose to prefer another aspirant to the throne.

After Richard's death, Gregory X. called upon the German princes to prepare for a new election: he threatened that if they delayed, he and his cardinals would nominate an emperor. The election being terminated, it was again the pope who induced the pretender, Alfonso of Castile, to abandon his claim and to give up the insignia of the empire; and who caused the chosen candidate, Rudolf of Habsburg, to be universally acknowledged.†

What trace of independence can a nation retain after submitting to receive its head from the hands of a foreign power? It is manifest that the same influence which determines the elections, must be resistless in every other department of the state.

The power of the princes of Germany had, it is true, been meanwhile on the increase. In the thirteenth century, during the struggles between the several pretenders to the throne, and between the papacy and the empire, they had got possession of almost all the prerogatives of sovereignty; they likewise took the most provident measures to prevent the imperial power from regaining its vast preponderance. At the end of the thirteenth and the beginning of the fourteenth century, the emperors were chosen almost systematically out of different houses. Consciously or unconsciously, the princes acted on the maxim, that when power began to be consolidated in one quarter, it must be counterbalanced by an increase of authority in another; as, for example, they curbed the already considerable power of Bohemia by means of the house of Habsburg, and this again, by those of Nassau, Luxemburg, or Bavaria. None of these could attain to more than transient superiority, and in consequence of this policy, no princely race rose to independence: the spiritual princes, who conducted the larger portion of the public business, were almost of more weight than the temporal.

This state of things tended greatly to increase the power of the papacy, on which the spiritual princes depended; and to which the temporal became very subordinate and submissive. In the thirteenth century they even made the abject declaration that they were planted in Germany by the church of Rome, and had been fostered and exalted by her favour.‡ The pope was, at least, as much indebted to the German princes as they were to him; but he took good care not to allude to his obligations, and nobody ventured to remind him of them. His successive victories over the empire had been gained by the assistance of many of the temporal powers. He now possessed, uncontested, the supreme sovereignty of Europe. Those plans of papal aggrandisement which were first avowed in the ninth century, and afterwards revived in the eleventh, were, in the thirteenth, crowned with complete success.

During that long period a state of things had been evolved, the outlines of which may, I think, be traced in a few words.

The pretensions of the clergy to govern Europe according to their hierarchical views — pretensions which arose directly out of the

* Ex Actis Innocentii. Monum. iv. 361.

† Gerbert, Introductio ad Cod. Epist. Rudolfi, c. iv. n. 30.

‡ Tractatus cum Nicolao III. Papa, 1279. "Romana ecclesia Germaniam decoravit plantans in ea principes tanquam arbores electas."—*Monum.* iv. 421.

ecclesiastical institutions of Charlemagne—were encountered and resisted by the united body of the German people, still thoroughly imbued with the national ideas of ancient Germania. On this combined resistance the imperial throne was founded. Unfortunately, however, it failed to acquire perfect security and stability; and the divisions which soon broke out between the domineering chief and his refractory vassals, had the effect of making both parties contribute to the aggrandisement of that spiritual power which they had previously sought to depress. At first the emperors beheld in a powerful clergy a means of holding their great vassals in check, and endowed the church with liberal grants of lands and lordships; but afterwards, when ideas of emancipation began to prevail, not only in the papacy but in all spiritual corporations, the temporal aristocracy thought it not expedient that the emperor should be stripped of the resource and assistance such a body afforded him: the enfeebling of the imperial authority was of great advantage, not only to the church, but to them. Thus it came to pass that the ecclesiastical element, strengthened by the divisions of its opponents, at length obtained a decided preponderance.

Unquestionably the result was far different in the twelfth and thirteenth centuries from what it would have been in the ninth. The secular power might be humbled, but could not be annihilated; a purely hierarchical government, such as might have been established at the earlier period, was now no longer within the region of possibility. The national development of Germany had been too deep and extensive to be stifled by the ecclesiastical spirit; while, on the other hand, the influence of ecclesiastical ideas and institutions unquestionably contributed largely to its extension. The period in question displayed a fulness of life and intelligence, an activity in every branch of human industry, a creative vigour, which we can hardly imagine to have arisen under any other course of events. Nevertheless, this was not a state which ought to satisfy a great nation. There could be no true political freedom so long as the most powerful impulse to all public activity emanated from a foreign head. The domain of mind, too, was enclosed within rigid and narrow boundaries. The immediate relation in which every intellectual being stands to the Divine Intelligence was veiled from the people in deep and abiding obscurity.

Those mighty developments of the human mind which extend over all generations, must, of necessity, be accomplished slowly; nor is it always easy to follow them in their progress.

Circumstances at length occurred which awakened in the German nation a consciousness of the position for which nature designed it.

FIRST ATTEMPTS AT RESISTANCE TO THE ENCROACHMENTS OF THE PAPACY.

The first important circumstance was, that the papacy, forgetting its high vocation in the pleasures of Avignon, displayed all the qualities of a prodigal and rapacious court, centralizing its power for the sake of immediate profit.

Pope John XXII. enforced his pecuniary claims with the coarsest avidity, and interfered in an unheard-of manner with the presentation to German benefices: he took care to express himself in very ambiguous terms as to the rights of the electoral princes; while on the contrary, he seriously claimed the privilege of examining into the merits of the emperor they had elected, and of rejecting him if he thought fit; nay, in case of a disputed election, such as then occurred, of administering the government himself till the contest should be decided *: lastly, he actually entered into negotiations, the object of which was to raise a French prince to the imperial throne.

The German princes at length saw what they had to expect from such a course of policy. On this occasion they rallied round their emperor, and rendered him real and energetic assistance. In the year 1338 they unanimously came to the celebrated resolution, that whoever should be elected by the majority of the prince-electors should be regarded as the true and legitimate emperor. When Louis the Bavarian, wearied by the long conflict, wavered for a moment, they kept him firm; they reproached him at the imperial diet in 1334 with having shown a disposition to accede to humiliating conditions. A change easily accounted for; the pope having now encroached, not only on the rights of the emperor, but on the prescriptive rights of their own body—on the rights of the whole nation.

Nor were these sentiments confined to the princes. In the fourteenth century a plebeian power had grown up in Germany, as in the rest of Europe, by the side of the aristocratic families which had hitherto exercised almost despotic power: not only were the cities summoned to the imperial diets, but, in a great proportion of them, the guilds, or trades, had got the municipal government into their own hands. These plebeians embraced the cause of their emperor with even more ardour than most of the princes. The priests who asserted the power of the pope to excommunicate the emperor were frequently driven out of the cities; these were then, in their turn, laid under excommunication; but they never would acknowledge its validity; they refused to accept absolution when it was offered them.†

Thus it happened that in the present instance

* "Attendentes quod imperii Romani regimen, cura et administratio (another time he says, imperii Romani jurisdictio, regimen et administratio), tempore quo illud vacare contingit, ad nos pertineat, sicut dignoscitur pertinere."—*Literæ Johannis in Rainaldus*, 1319; and *Olenschläger*, *Geschichte des Rom.-Kaiserthums, &c., in der ersten Hälfte des 14ten Jahrhunderts*. p. 102. In the year 1323 he declares that he has instituted a suit against Lewis the Bavarian; "super eo quod electione sua *per quosdam qui vocem in electione hujusmodi habere dicuntur*, per sedem apostolicam, ad quam electionis hujusmodi et personæ electæ examinatio, approbatio, admissio ac etiam reprobatio et repulsio noscitur pertinere, non admissa," &c.—*Olenschläger*, *Urk.* n. 36.

† *e.g.* Basel. Albertus Argentinensis in Urstisius, 142.

the pope could not carry the election of his candidate, Charles of Luxemburg; nobles and commons adhered almost unanimously to Louis of Bavaria: nor was it till after his death, and then only after repeated election and coronation, that Charles IV. was gradually recognised.

Whatever he might previously have promised the pope, that sovereign could not make concessions injurious to the interests of his princes; on the contrary, he solemnly and firmly established the rights of the electors, even to the long-disputed vicariate (at least in all German states). A germ of resistance was thus formed.

This was fostered and developed by the disorders of the great schism, and by the dispositions evinced by the general councils.

It was now, for the first time, evident that the actual church no longer corresponded with the ideal that existed in men's minds. Nations assumed the attitude of independent members of it; popes were brought to trial and deposed; the aristocratico-republican spirit, which played so great a part in the temporal states of Europe, extended even to the papacy (the nature of which is so completely monarchical), and threatened to change its form and character.

The ecclesiastical assembly of Basle entertained the project of establishing at once the freedom of nations and the authority of councils; a project hailed with peculiar approbation by Germany. Its decretals of reformation were solemnly adopted by the assembly of the imperial diet*: the Germans determined to remain neutral during its controversies with Eugenius IV.; the immediate consequence of which was, that they were for a time emancipated from the court of Rome.† By threatening to go over to his adversary, they forced the pope, who had ventured to depose two spiritual electors, to revoke the sentence of deposition.

Had this course been persevered in with union and constancy, the German Catholic church, established in so many great principalities, and splendidly provided with the most munificent endowments in the world, would have acquired a perfectly independent position, in which she might have resisted the subsequent polemical storms with as much firmness as that of England.

Various circumstances conspired to prevent so desirable a result.

In the first place, it appears to me that the disputes between France and Burgundy reacted on this matter. France was in favour of the ideas of the council, which, indeed, she embodied in the pragmatic sanction; Burgundy was for the pope. Among the German princes, some were in the most intimate alliance with the king, others with the duke.

The pope employed by far the most dexterous and able negotiator. If we consider the character of the representative and organ of the German opposition, Gregory of Heimburg, who thought himself secure of victory, and, when sent to Rome, burst forth at the very foot of the Vatican into a thousand execrations on the Curia;—if we follow him there as he went about with neglected garb, bare neck, and uncovered head, bidding defiance to the court,—and then compare him with the polished and supple Æneas Sylvius, full of profound quiet ambition, and gifted with the happiest talents for rising in the world; the servant of so many masters, and the dexterous confidant of them all; we shall be at no loss to divine which must be the successful party. Heimburg died a living death in exile, and dependent on foreign bounty; Æneas Sylvius ended his career, wearing the triple crown he had so ably served. At the very time we are treating of, Æneas had found means to gain over some councillors, and through them their sovereigns, and thus to secure their defection from the great scheme of national emancipation. He relates this himself with great satisfaction and self-complacency; nor did he disdain to employ bribery.‡

The main thing, however, was, that the head of the empire, King Frederic III., adhered to the papal cause. The union of the princes, which, while it served as a barrier against the encroachments of the church, might have proved no less perilous to himself, was as hateful to him as to the pope. Æneas Sylvius conducted the negotiation in a manner no less agreeable to the interests and wishes of the emperor than to those of the pope: the imperial coffers furnished him with the means of corruption.

Hence it happened that on this occasion also the nation failed to attain its object.

At the first moment, indeed, the Basle decretals were accepted at Rome, but under the condition that the Holy See should receive compensation for its losses. This compensation, however, was not forthcoming; and Frederic III., who treated on the part of the empire, at length conceded anew to Rome all her old privileges, which the nation had been endeavouring to wrest from her.§ It would have been impossible to carry such a measure at the diet; the expedient of obtaining the separate consent of the princes to this agreement was therefore resorted to.

The old state of things was thus perpetuated.

* Johannes de Segovia; Koch, Sanctio pragmatica, p. 256.

† Declaration in Müller, Reichstagstheater, unter Fred. III. p. 31. "In sola ordinaria jurisdictione citra præfatorum tam papæ quam concilii supremam auctoritatem ecclesiasticæ politiæ gubernacula per dioceses et territoria nostra gubernabimus."

‡ Historia Frederici III. ap. Kollar, Analecta, ii. p. 127.

§ In the second half of the foregoing century attention had been strongly drawn to the assertion, that all the decrees of the council of Basle, which had not been expressly altered by the concordat, acquired legal validity in virtue of the same. Against this, Spittler has made the objection, that the brief runs thus: "donec per legatum concordatum fuerit vel per legatum aliter fuerit ordinatum;" and, assuming that an "aliter" is wanting in the first part of the sentence, has concluded that the whole of the decrees had only been suffered to hold good *till the* conclusion of the concordat. (Werke, viii. p. 473.) But in the relation of Æneas Sylvius in Koch, Sanctio pragmatica, p. 323, the "aliter" missed by Spittler stands expressly next to "concordatum;" "usque quo cum legato aliter fuerit concordatum." (Vide Koch, ii. § 24.) The sense of these words cannot therefore be doubted. For in no case can it be supposed that "aliter" had been left out with any sinister design.

Ordinances which the papal see had published in 1335, and which it had repeated in 1418, once more formed, in the year 1448, the basis of the German concordat. It is hardly necessary to say that the opposition was not crushed. It no longer appeared on the surface of events, but deep below it, it only struck root faster and acquired greater strength. The nation was exasperated by a constant sense of wrong and injustice.

ALTERED CHARACTER OF THE EMPIRE.

The most remarkable fact now was, that the imperial throne was no longer able to afford support and protection. The empire had assumed a position analogous to that of the papacy, but extremely subordinate in power and authority.

It is important to remark, that for more than a century after Charles IV. had fixed his seat in Bohemia, no emperor appeared, endowed with the vigour necessary to uphold and govern the empire. The bare fact that Charles's successor, Wenceslas, was a prisoner in the hands of the Bohemians, remained for a long time unknown in Germany: a simple decree of the electors sufficed to dethrone him. Rupert the Palatine only escaped a similar fate by death. When Sigismund of Luxemburg, (who, after many disputed elections, kept possession of the field,) four years after his election, entered the territory of the empire of which he was to be crowned sovereign, he found so little sympathy that he was for a moment inclined to return to Hungary without accomplishing the object of his journey. The active part he took in the affairs of Bohemia, and of Europe generally, has given him a name, but in and for the empire, he did nothing worthy of note. Between the years 1422 and 1430 he never made his appearance beyond Vienna; from the autumn of 1431 to that of 1433 he was occupied with his coronation journey to Rome, and during the three years from 1434 to his death he never got beyond Bohemia and Moravia;* nor did Albert II., who has been the subject of such lavish eulogy, ever visit the dominions of the empire. Frederick III., however, far outdid all his predecessors. During seven-and-twenty years, from 1444 to 1471, he was never seen within the boundaries of the empire.

Hence it happened that the central action and the visible manifestation of sovereignty, insofar as any such existed in the empire, fell to the share of the princes, and more especially of the prince-electors. In the reign of Sigismund we find them convoking the diets, and leading the armies into the field against the Hussites; the operations against the Bohemians were attributed entirely to them.†

In this manner the empire became, like the papacy, a power which acted from a distance, and rested chiefly upon opinion. The throne, founded on conquest and arms, had now a pacific character and a conservative tendency. Nothing is so transient as the notions which are handed down with a name, or associated with a title, and yet, especially in times when unwritten law has so much force, the whole influence of rank or station depends on the nature of these notions. Let us turn our attention for a moment to the ideas of Empire and Papacy entertained in the fifteenth century.

The emperor was regarded, in the first place, as the supreme feudal lord, who conferred on property its highest and most sacred sanction; as the supreme fountain of justice, from whom, as the expression was, all the compulsory force of law emanated. It is very curious to observe how the choice that had fallen upon him was announced to Frederic III.,—by no means the mightiest prince in the empire,—how immediately therefore the natural relations of things are reversed, and "his royal high mightiness" promises confirmation in their rights and dignities to the very men who had just raised him to the throne.‡ All hastened to obtain his recognition of their privileges and possessions; nor did the cities perform their act of homage till that had taken place. Upon his supreme guarantee rested that feeling of legitimacy, security and permanence, which is necessary to all men, and more especially dear to Germans. "Take away from us the rights of the emperor," says a law-book of that time, "and who can say, this house is mine, this village belongs to me?" A remark of profound truth; but it followed thence that the emperor could not arbitrarily exercise rights of which he was deemed the source. He might give them up; but he himself must enforce them only within the narrow limits prescribed by traditional usage, and by the superior control of his subjects. Although he was regarded as the head and source of all temporal jurisdiction, yet no tribunal found more doubtful obedience than his own.

The fact that royalty existed in Germany had almost been suffered to fall into oblivion; even the title had been lost. Henry VII. thought it an affront to be called King of Germany, and not, as he had a right to be called before any ceremony of coronation, King of the Romans.§ In the fifteenth century the emperor was regarded pre-eminently as the successor of the ancient Roman Cæsars, whose rights and dignities had been transferred, first to the Greeks and then to the Germans in the persons of Charlemagne and Otho the Great; as the true secular head of Christendom. Emperor Sigismund commanded that his corpse should be exposed to view for some days; in order that every one might see that "the Lord of all the world was dead and departed."‖

* The acts of his reign are dated from Ofen, Stuhlweissenburg, from Cronstadt "in Transylvanian Wurzland," from the army before the castle of Taubenburg in Sirfey (Servia). Häberlin, Reichsgeschichte, v. 429, 439.

† Matthias Doring in Mencken, iii. p. 4. "Eodem anno principes electores exercitum grandem habentes contra Bohemos se transtulerunt ad Bohemiam."

‡ Letter of the Frankfort Deputies, July 5, 1440. Frankfurter Arch.

§ Henrici VII. Bannitio Florentiæ, Pertz, iv. 520, "supprimentes (it is there said) ipsius veri nominis (Regis Romanorum) dignitatem in ipsius opprobrium et despectum."

‖ Eberhard Windeck in Mencken, Scriptt. i. 1278.

"We have chosen your royal grace," say the electors to Frederic III. (A. D. 1440), "to be the head, protector, and governor of all Christendom." They go on to express the hope that this choice may be profitable to the Roman church, to the whole of Christendom, to the holy empire, and the community of Christian people.* Even a foreign monarch, Wladislas of Poland, extols the felicity of the newly-elected emperor, in that he was about to receive the diadem of the monarchy of the world.† The opinion was confidently entertained in Germany that the other sovereigns of Christendom, especially those of England, Spain, and France, were legally subject to the crown of the empire: the only controversy was, whether their disobedience was venial, or ought to be regarded as sinful.‡ The English endeavoured to show that from the time of the introduction of Christianity they had never been subject to the empire.§ The Germans, on the contrary, not only did what the other nations of the West were bound to do—they not only acknowledged the holy empire, but they had secured to themselves the faculty of giving it a head; and the strange notion was current that the electoral princes had succeeded to the rights and dignities of the Roman senate and people. They themselves expressed this opinion in the thirteenth century. "We," say they, "who occupy the place of the Roman senate, who are the fathers and the lights of the empire."‖ .... In the fifteenth century they repeated the same opinion.** "The Germans," says the author of a scheme for diminishing the burthens of the empire, "who have possessed themselves of the dignities of the Roman empire, and thence of the sovereignty over all lands."†† .... When the prince-electors proceeded to the vote, they swore that "according to the best of their understanding, they would choose the temporal head of all Christian people, *i. e.* a Roman king and future emperor." Thereupon the elected sovereign was anointed and crowned by the Archbishop of Cologne, who enjoyed that right on this side the Alps. Even when seated on the coronation chair at Rheims, the King of France took an oath of fealty to the Roman empire.‡‡

It is obvious in what a totally different relation the Germans stood to the emperor, who was elevated to his high dignity from amidst themselves, and by their own choice, from that of even the most puissant nobles of other countries to their natural hereditary lord and master. The imperial dignity, stripped of all direct executive power, had indeed no other significancy than that which results from opinion. It gave to law and order their living sanction; to justice its highest authority; to the sovereignties of Germany their position in the world. It had properties which, for that period, were indispensable and sacred. It had a manifest analogy with the papacy, and was bound to it by the most intimate connection.

The main difference between the two powers was, that the papal enjoyed that universal recognition of the Romano-Germanic world which the imperial had not been able to obtain: but the holy Roman church and the holy Roman empire were indissolubly united in idea; and the Germans thought they stood in a peculiarly intimate relation to the church as well as to the empire. There is extant a treaty of alliance of the Rhenish princes, the assigned object of which was to maintain their endowments, dioceses, chapters, and principalities, in dignity and honour with the holy Roman empire and the holy Roman church. The electors lay claim to a peculiar privilege in ecclesiastical affairs. In the year 1424, and again in 1446, they declare that the Almighty has appointed and authorised them, that they should endeavour, together with the Roman king, the princes, lords, knights, and cities of the empire, and with all faithful Christian people, to abate all crimes that arise in the holy church and Christian community, and in the holy empire.§§

Hence we see that the German people thought themselves bound in allegiance to the papal, no less than to the imperial authority; but as the former had, in all the long struggles of successive ages, invariably come off victorious, while the latter had so often succumbed, the pope exercised a far stronger and more wide-spread influence, even in temporal things, than the emperor. An act of arbitrary power, which no emperor could ever have so much as contemplated—the deposition of an electoral prince of the empire—was repeatedly attempted, and occasionally even accomplished, by the popes. They bestowed on Italian prelates bishoprics as remote as that of Camin. By their annates, pallia, and all the manifold dues exacted by the curia, they drew a far larger (Maximilian I. said, a hundred times larger) revenue from the empire, than the emperor: their vendors of indulgences incessantly traversed the several provinces of the empire. Spiritual and temporal principalities and jurisdictions were so closely interwoven as to afford them continual opportunities of interfering in

* Letter of the Prince-Electors, Feb. 2, 1440, in Chmel's Materialien zur Oestreich. Gesch. No. ii. p. 70.

† Literæ Vladislai ap. Kollar Anal. ii. p. 830.

‡ Petrus de Andlo de Romano Imperio: an important book, not indeed with reference to the actual state of Germany, but to the ideas of the time in which it was written. It dates from between 1456, which year is expressly mentioned, and 1459, in which year happened the death of Diedrich of Mainz, of whom it speaks. The author says, ii. c. 8: "Hodie plurimi reges *plus de facto quam de jure* imperatorem in superiorem non recognoscunt et suprema jura imperii usurpant."

§ Cuthbert Tunstall to King Henry VIII., Feb. 12, 1517, in Ellis's Letters, series 1, vol. i. p. 136. "Your Grace is not nor never sithen the Christen faith the kings of England wer subgiet to th' Empire, but the crown of England is an Empire of hitself, mych bettyr than now the Empire of Rome: for which cause your Grace werith a close crown."

‖ Conradi IV. electio 1237: Pertz, iv. 322.

** P. de Andlo ii., iii. "Isti principes electores successerunt, in locum senatus populique Romani."

†† Intelligentia Principum super Gravaminibus Nationis Germanicæ. MS. at Coblenz. See Appendix.

‡‡ Æneas Sylvius (Historia Friderici III. in Kollar's Anal. ii. 288.) tries to make a distinction between the three crowns, and to assign them to the different kingdoms; but in this case we do not ask what is true, but what was commonly thought. The opinions which he disputes are exactly those of importance in our eyes: namely, those generally entertained.

§§ Müller Rtth. Fr. iii. 305.

the civil affairs of Germany The dispute between Cleves and Cologne* about Soest, that between Utrecht and East Friesland about Groningen, and a vast number of others, were evoked by the pope before his tribunal In 1472 he confirmed a toll, levied in the electorate of Treves† like the emperor, he granted *privilegia de non evocando*

Gregory VII's comparison of the papacy to the sun and the empire to the moon was now verified. The Germans regarded the papal power as in every respect the higher When, for example, the town of Basle founded its high school, it was debated whether, after the receipt of the brief containing the pope's approbation, the confirmation of the emperor was still necessary, and at length decided that it was not so, since the inferior power could not confirm the decisions of the superior, and the papal see was the well-head of Christendom ‡ The pretender to the Palatinate, Frederic the Victorious, whose electoral rank the emperor refused to acknowledge, held it sufficient to obtain the pope's sanction, and received no further molestation in the exercise of his privileges as member of the empire. The judge of the king's court having on some occasion pronounced the ban of the empire on the council of Lubeck, the council obtained a cassation of this sentence from the pope §

It was assuredly to be expected that the emperor would feel the humiliation of his position, and would resist the pope as often and as strenuously as possible

However great was the devotion of the princes to the see of Rome, they felt the oppressiveness of its pecuniary exactions, and more than once the spirit of the Basle decrees, or the recollections of the proceedings at Constance, manifested themselves anew. We find draughts of a league to prevent the constitution of Constance, according to which a council should be held every ten years, from falling into utter desuetude ‖ After the death of Nicholas V. the princes urged the emperor to seize the favourable moment for asserting the freedom of the nation, and at least to take measures for the complete execution of the agreement entered into with Eugenius; but Frederic III. was deaf to their entreaties Æneas Sylvius persuaded him that it was necessary for him to keep well with the pope. He brought forward a few common-places concerning the instability of the multitude, and their natural hatred of their chief,—just as if the princes of the empire were a sort of democracy. the emperor, said he, stands in need of the pope, and the pope of the emperor; it would be ridiculous to offend the man from whom we want assistance.** He himself was sent in 1456 to tender unconditional obedience to Pope Calixtus. This immediately revived the old spirit of resistance. An outline was drawn of a pragmatic sanction, in which not only all the charges against the papal see were recapitulated in detail, and redress of grievances proposed, but it was also determined what was to be done in case of a refusal; what appeal was to be made, and how the desired end was to be attained †† But what result could be anticipated while the emperor, far from taking part in this plan, did every thing he could to thwart it? He sincerely regarded himself as the natural ally of the papacy.

The inevitable effect of this conduct on his part was, that the discontent of the electors, already excited by the inactivity and the absence of the emperor, occasionally burst out violently against him As early as the year 1456 they required him to repair on a given day to Nürnberg, for that it was his office and duty to bear the burthen of the empire in an honourable manner if he did not appear, they would, at any rate, meet, and do what was incumbent on them ‡‡ As he neither appeared then nor afterwards, in 1460 they sent him word that it was no longer consistent with their dignity and honour to remain without a head. They repeated their summons that he would appear on the Tuesday after Epiphany, and accompanied it with still more vehement threats They began seriously to take measures for setting up a king of the Romans in opposition to him.

From the fact that George Podiebrad, king of Bohemia, was the man on whom they cast their eyes, it is evident that the opposition was directed against both emperor and pope jointly. What must have been the consequence of placing a Utraquist at the head of the empire? This increased the zeal and activity of Pope Pius II (whom we have hitherto known as Æneas Sylvius), in consolidating the alliance of the see of Rome with the emperor, who, on his side, was scarcely less deeply interested in it The independence of the prince-electors was odious to both. As one of the claims of the emperor had always been, that no electoral diet should be held without his consent, so Pius II, in like manner, now wanted to bind Diether, Elector of Mainz, to summon no such assembly without the approbation of the papal see. Diether's refusal to enter into any such engagement was the main cause of their quarrel. Pius did not conceal from the emperor that he thought his own power endangered by the agitations which prevailed in the empire. It was chiefly owing to his influence, and to the valour of Markgrave Albert Achilles of Brandenburg, that they ended in nothing.

From this time we find the imperial and the papal powers, which had come to a sense of their common interest and reciprocal utility, more closely united than ever.

The diets of the empire were held under their joint authority; they were called royal

* Schuren, Chronik von Cleve, p 288

† Hontheim, Prodromus Historiæ Trevirensis, p 320

‡ Ochs, Geschichte von Basel, iv p 60

§ Sartorius, Gesch des Hanse ii p 222

‖ e g Resolution of the spiritual Electors, &c Properly, a report upon the means of restoring tranquillity to the empire, and upon the necessity of a council, of about the year 1453, in the archives of Coblenz See Appendix

** Gobellini Commentarii de Vita Pii, ii p 44.

†† Æneæ Sylvii Apologia ad Martinum, Mayer, p 710, and the above cited Intelligentia

‡‡ Frankfurt Sep 10, 1456, a hitherto unknown and very remarkable document Frankf Arch

and papal, papal and royal diets. In the reign of Frederic, as formerly in that of Sigismund, we find the papal legates present at the meetings of the empire, which were not opened till they appeared. The spiritual princes took their seats on the right, the temporal on the left, of the legates it was not till a later period that the imperial commissioners were introduced, and proposed measures in concert with the papal functionaries.

It remains for us to inquire how far this very singular form of government was fitted to satisfy the wants of the empire.

STATE OF GERMANY IN THE MIDDLE OF THE FIFTEENTH CENTURY.

We have seen what a mighty influence had, from the remotest times, been exercised by the princes of Germany.

First, the imperial power and dignity had arisen out of their body, and by their aid ; then, they had supported the emancipation of the papacy, which involved their own now, they stood opposed to both Although strongly attached to, and deeply imbued with, the ideas of Empire and Papacy, they were resolved to repel the encroachments of either their power was already so independent, that the emperor and the pope deemed it necessary to combine against them

If we proceed to inquire who were these magnates, and upon what their power rested, we shall find that the temporal hereditary sovereignty, the germ of which had long existed in secret and grown unperceived, shot up in full vigour in the fifteenth century, and (if we may be allowed to continue the metaphor), after it had long struck its roots deep into the earth, it now began to rear its head into the free air, and to tower above all the surrounding plants.

All the puissant houses which have since held sovereign sway date their establishment from this epoch.

In the eastern part of North Germany appeared the race of Hohenzollern, and though the land its princes had to govern and to defend was in the last stage of distraction and ruin, they acted with such sedate vigour and cautious determination, that they soon succeeded in driving back their neighbours within their ancient bounds, pacifying and restoring the marches, and re-establishing the very peculiar bases of sovereign power which already existed in the country.

Near this remarkable family arose that of Wettin, and by the acquisition of the electorate of Saxony, soon attained to the highest rank among the princes of the empire, and to the zenith of its power. It possessed the most extensive and at the same time the most flourishing of German principalities, as long as the brothers, Ernest and Albert, held their united court at Dresden and shared the government; and even when they separated, both lines remained sufficiently considerable to play a part in the affairs of Germany, and indeed of Europe.

In the Palatinate we find Frederic the Victorious. It is necessary to read the long list of castles, jurisdictions, and lands which he won from all his neighbours, partly by conquest, partly by purchase or treaty, but which his superiority in arms rendered emphatically his own, to form a conception what a German prince could in that age achieve, and how widely he could extend his sway

The conquests of Hessen were of a more peaceful nature. By the inheritance of Ziegenhain and Nidda, but more especially of Katzenelnbogen, a fertile, highly cultivated district, from which the old counts had never suffered a village or a farm to be taken, whether by force or purchase, it acquired an addition nearly equal to its original territory

A similar spirit of extension and fusion was also at work in many other places. Juliers and Berg formed a junction. Bavaria-Landshut was strengthened by its union with Ingolstadt; in Bavaria-Munich, Albert the Wise maintained the unity of the land under the most difficult circumstances, not without violence, but, at least in this case, with beneficial results In Wurtemberg, too, a multitude of separate estates were gradually incorporated into one district, and assumed the form of a German principality.

New territorial powers also arose. In East Friesland a chieftain at length appeared, before whom all the rest bowed, Junker* Ulrich Cirksena, who, by his own conquests, extended and consolidated the power founded on those of his brother and his father. He also conciliated the adherents of the old Fokko Uken, who were opposed to him, by a marriage with Theta, the granddaughter of that chief Hereupon he was solemnly proclaimed count at Emden, in the year 1463 But it was to Theta, who was left to rule the country alone during twenty-eight years, that the new sovereignty chiefly owed its strength and stability This illustrious woman, whose pale, beautiful countenance, brilliant eyes and raven hair survive in her portrait, was endowed with a vast understanding and a singular capacity for governing, as all her conduct and actions prove

Already had several German princes raised themselves to foreign thrones In the year 1448, Christian I, Count of Oldenburg, signed the declaration or contract which made him king of Denmark in 1450, he was invested with the crown of St Olaf, at Drontheim, in 1457, the Swedes acknowledged him as their sovereign, in 1460, Holstein did homage to him, and was raised on his account to the rank of a German duchy These acquisitions were not, it is true, of so stable and secure a character as they at first appeared, but, at all events, they conferred upon a German princely house a completely new position both in Germany and in Europe.

The rise of the princely power and sove-

* Junker, literally, the younger son of a noble house, became the title of the lesser aristocracy of Germany It corresponds pretty nearly to squire in its common English acceptation —TRANSL

reignty was, as we see, not the mere result of the steady course of events; the noiseless and progressive development of political institutions, it was brought about mainly by adroit policy, successful war and the might of personal character.

Yet the secular princes by no means possessed absolute sovereignty, they were still involved in an incessant struggle with the other powers of the empire.

These were, in the first place, the spiritual principalities (whose privileges and internal organization were the same as those of the secular, but whose rank in the hierarchy of the empire was higher), in which nobles of the high or even the inferior aristocracy composed the chapter and filled the principal places In the fifteenth century, indeed, the bishoprics began to be commonly conferred on the younger sons of sovereign princes the court of Rome favoured this practice, from the conviction that the chapters could only be kept in order by the strong hand and the authority of sovereign power,* but it was neither universal, nor was the fundamental principle of the spiritual principalities by any means abandoned in consequence of its adoption.

There was also a numerous body of nobles who received their investiture with the banner, like the princes, and had a right to sit in the same tribunal with them, nay, there were even families or clans, which, from all time, claimed exemption from those general feudal relations that formed the bond of the state, and held their lands in fee from God and his blessed sun They were overshadowed by the princely order, but they enjoyed perfect independence notwithstanding

Next to this class came the powerful body of knights of the Empire, whose castles crowned the hills on the Rhine, in Swabia and Franconia, they lived in haughty loneliness amidst the wildest scenes; girt round by an impregnable circle of deep fosses, and within walls four-and-twenty feet thick, where they could set all authority at defiance: the bond of fellowship among them was but the stricter for their isolation Another portion of the nobility, especially in the eastern and colonized principalities in Pomerania and Mecklenburg, Meissen and the Marches, were, however, brought into undisputed subjection, though this, as we see in the example of the Priegnitz, was not brought about without toil and combat.

There was also a third class who constantly refused to acknowledge any feudal lord The Craichgauer and the Mortenauer would not acknowledge the sovereignty of the Palatine nor the Bokler and Löwen-ritter,† that of Bavaria We find that the Electors of Mainz and Treves, on occasion of some decision by arbitration, feared that their nobles would refuse to abide by it, and knew not what measure to resort to in this contingency, except to rid themselves of these refractory vassals and withdraw their protection from them ‡ It seems, in some cases, as if the relation of subject and ruler had become nothing more than a sort of alliance

Still more completely independent was the attitude assumed by the cities Opposed to all these different classes of nobles, which they regarded as but one body, they were founded on a totally different principle, and had struggled into importance in the midst of incessant hostility A curious spectacle is afforded by this old enmity constantly pervading all the provinces of Germany, yet in each one taking a different form In Prussia, the opposition of the cities gave rise to the great national league against the supreme power, which was here in the hands of the Teutonic Order. On the Wendish coasts was then the centre of the Hanse, by which the Scandinavian kings, and still more the surrounding German princes, were overpowered. The Duke of Pomerania himself was struck with terror, when, on coming to succour Henry the Elder of Brunswick, he perceived by what powerful and closely allied cities his friend was encompassed and enchained on every side On the Rhine, we find an unceasing struggle for municipal independence, which the chief cities of the ecclesiastical principalities claimed, and the Electors refused to grant In Franconia, Nurnberg set itself in opposition to the rising power of Brandenburg, which it rivalled in successful schemes of aggrandisement Then followed in Swabia and the Upper Danube (the true arena of the struggles and the leagues of imperial free cities), the same groups of knights, lords, prelates, and princes, who here approached most nearly to each other Among the Alps, the confederacy formed against Austria had already grown into a regular constitutional government, and attained to almost complete independence On every side we find different relations, different claims and disputes, different means of carrying on the conflict, but on all, men felt themselves surrounded by hostile passions which any moment might blow into a flame, and held themselves ready for battle It seemed not impossible that the municipal principle might eventually get the upper hand in all these conflicts, and prove as destructive to the aristocratical, as that had been to the imperial, power.

In this universal shock of efforts and powers,—with a distant and feeble chief, and inevitable divisions even among those naturally connected and allied, a state of things arose which presents a somewhat chaotic aspect; it was the age of universal private warfare. The *Fehde*§ is a middle term between duel and

* "Si episcopum potentem sortiantur, virgam correctionis timent"—*Æneas Sylvius*

† In 1488, Albert IV, of Bavaria, imposed a tax instead of personal service The Order of Knights having vainly protested against this, formed the association called the Lion League (Löwenbund), and entered into alliance with the Swabian League The other associations were probably of a similar kind.—TRANSL

‡ Jan 12, 1438 Document in Hontheim, ii p 432. "So sall der von uns, des underseaiss he ist, siner missig gain und sine queine schirm, zulegunge oder handhabunge widder den anderen von uns doin"—"Then shall that one of us, whose vassal he is, abandon him and yield him no protection, support or defence, against the rest of us"

§ Some resemblance in sound probably led to the use

war. Every affront or injury led, after certain formalities, to the declaration, addressed to the offending party, that the aggrieved party would be his foe, and that of his helpers and helpers'-helpers. The imperial authorities felt themselves so little able to arrest this torrent, that they endeavoured only to direct its course, and while imposing limitations, or forbidding particular acts, they confirmed the general permission of the established practice.*

The right which the supreme, independent power had hitherto reserved to itself, of resorting to arms when no means of conciliation remained, had descended in Germany to the inferior classes, and was claimed by nobles and cities against each other, by subjects against their lords, nay, by private persons, as far as their means and connections permitted, against each other.

In the middle of the fifteenth century this universal tempest of contending powers was arrested by a conflict of a higher and more important nature—the opposition of the princes to the emperor and the pope; and it remained to be decided from whose hands the world could hope for any restoration to order.

Two princes appeared on the stage, each of them the hero of his nation, each at the head of a numerous party; each possessed of personal qualities strikingly characteristic of the epoch—Frederic of the Palatinate, and Albert of Brandenburg. They took opposite courses. Frederic the Victorious, distinguished rather for address and agility of body than for size and strength, owed his fame and his success to the forethought and caution with which he prepared his battles and sieges. In time of peace he busied himself with the study of antiquity, or the mysteries of alchemy; poets and minstrels found ready access to him, as in the spring-time of poetry. he lived under the same roof with his friend and songstress, Clara Dettin, of Augsburg, whose sweetness and sense not only captivated the prince, but were the charm and delight of all around him. He had expressly renounced the comforts of equal marriage and legitimate heirs, all that he accomplished or acquired was for the advantage of his nephew Philip.

The towering and athletic frame of Markgrave Albert of Brandenburg (surnamed Achilles), on the contrary, announced, at the first glance, his gigantic strength. he had been victor in countless tournaments, and stories of his courage and warlike prowess, bordering on the fabulous, were current among the people,—how, for example, at some siege he had mounted the walls alone, and leaped down into the midst of the terrified garrison; how, hurried on by a slight success over an advanced party of the enemy, he had rushed almost unattended into their main body of 800 horsemen, had forced his way up to their standard, snatched it from its bearer, and after a momentary feeling of the desperateness of his position rallied his courage and defended it, till his people could come up and complete the victory. Æneas Sylvius declares that the Markgrave himself assured him of the fact.† His letters breathe a passion for war. Even after a defeat he had experienced, he relates to his friends with evident pleasure, how long he and four others held out on the field of battle, how he then cut his way through with great labour and severe fighting, and how he was determined to re-appear as soon as possible in the field. In time of peace he busied himself with the affairs of the empire, in which he took a more lively and efficient part than the emperor himself. We find him sharing in all the proceedings of the diets, or holding a magnificent and hospitable court in his Franconian territories, or directing his attention to his possessions in the Mark, which were governed by his son with all the vigilance dictated by the awe of a grave and austere father. Albert is the worthy progenitor of the warlike house of Brandenburg. He bequeathed to it not only wise maxims, but, what is of more value, a great example.

About the year 1461 these two princes embraced, as we have said, different parties. Frederic, who as yet possessed no distinctly recognised power, and in all things obeyed his personal impulses, put himself at the head of the opposition. Albert, who always followed the trodden path of existing relations, undertook the defence of the emperor and the pope,‡

of the word *feud* (feodum), as the equivalent of *Fehde* (faida), a confusion which however sanctioned by custom I have thought it better to avoid. Eichhorn (Deutsche Staats und Rechtsgeschichte, vol. i. p. 111.) says:—"In case of robbery, murder, &c., the injured party, or his heirs was not bound to pursue the injurer at law; but private help or self revenge (Privathulfe und Selbstrache)—*Fehde* (faida) was lawful, and the *Befehdete* (faidosus) could only escape this by paying the appointed fine." For the earliest mention of this fine, he refers to Tacitus (Germ. 21). It is remarkable, too, that the authority from which he quotes these terms is the laws of Friesland, a country where, as is well known, feudalism never existed. And indeed the parties by whom diffidations (*Fehdebriefe*) were often sent, were obviously subject to no feudal relations. Although we appear to have lost the English cognate of the Anglo Saxon Fæhthe (*capitalis inimicitia*), it is found in the Scotch *feid, fede, feyde*, (see Gawin Douglas, Jamieson's Dict. &c.), and in most of the Teutonic languages.—TRANSL.

* *e. g.* the "Reformation" of Frederic III. of 1442 orders, "dass nymand dem andern Schaden tun oder zufugen soll, er habe ihn denn zuvor—zu landlaufigen Rechten erfordert."—"that none should do, or cause to be done, injury to another, unless he have previously challenged him, according to the customary laws of the land." The clause of the golden bull, de Diffidationibus, is then repeated.—[This clause is as follows:—"Eos qui de cetero adversus aliquos justam diffidationis causam se habere fingentes, ipsos in locis ubi domicilia non obtinent aut ea communiter non inhabitant, intempestive diffidant, declaramus damna per incendia, spolia, vel rapinas, diffidatis ipsis, cum honore suo inferre non posse." *Bulla Aurea*, cap. XVII.—TRANSL.]

† Historia Frederici III., in the part first published by Kollar, Anal. ii. p. 166.

‡ In the collection of imperial documents in the Frankfurt Archives, vol. v. there is a very remarkable report by Johannes brun, of an audience which he had of Albrecht Achilles, in Oct. 1461. He had to entreat him for a remission of the succours demanded. Markgrave Albrecht would not grant this, "Auch erzalte er, was Furnemen gen unssen gn. Herrn den Keyser gewest ware und wy ein Gedenken nach dem Ryche sy, auch der Kunig von Behemen ganz Meynung habe zu Mittensommer fur Francfort zu sin und das Rych zu erobern, und darnoch wie u. g. H. der Keiser yne, sine Schweher von Baden und Wirtenberg angerufen und yne des Ryches Banyer bevolhen habe, uber Herzog Ludwig, um der Geschicht willen mit dem Bischof von Eystett, den von Werde und Dinkelsbul und umb die Pene, darin er deshalben verfallen sy,—in den Dingen er uf niemant gebeitet oder gesehen, sondern zu Stund mit den sinen und des von Wirten-

fortune wavered for a time between them. But at last the Jorsika, as George Podiebrad was called, abandoned his daring plans. Diether of Isenburg was succeeded by his antagonist, Adolf of Nassau, and Frederic the Palatine consented to give up his prisoners victory leaned, in the main, to the side of Brandenburg The ancient authorities of the Empire and the Church were once more upheld

These authorities, too, now seemed seriously bent on introducing a better order of things By the aid of the victorious party, the emperor found himself, for the first time, in a position to exercise a certain influence in the empire, Pope Paul II wished to fit out an expedition against the Turks. with united strength they proceeded to the work at the diet of Nurnberg (A. D 1466) *

It was an assembly which distinctly betrayed the state of parties under which it had been convoked Frederick the Palatine appeared neither in person nor by deputy, the ambassadors of Podiebrad, who had fallen into fresh disputes with the papal see, were not admitted nevertheless, the resolutions passed there were of great importance It was determined for the next five years to regard every breach of the Public Peace† as a crime against the majesty of the empire, and to punish it with the ban. It was found that the spiritual tribunals must come in aid of the temporal sword, and accordingly the pope denounced the heaviest spiritual penalties against violators of the Public Peace The emperor formally adopted these resolutions at an assembly at Neustadt, in the year 1467, and for the first time revoked the articles of the Golden Bull and the Reformation of 1442, in which private wars were, under certain conditions, permitted ‡ A peace was proclaimed, "enjoined by our most gracious lord the king of the Romans, and confirmed by our holy father the pope," as the electors express themselves.

Sometime afterwards—at Regensburg, in the year 1471—the allied powers ventured on a second yet more important step, for the furtherance of the war against the Turks, which they declared themselves at length about to undertake 'they attempted to impose a sort of property tax on the whole empire, called the Common Penny,§ and actually obtained an edict in its favour They named in concert the officers charged with the collection of it in the archiepiscopal and episcopal sees; and the papal legate threatened the refractory with the sum of all spiritual punishments, exclusion from the community of the church ||

These measures undoubtedly embraced what was most immediately necessary to the internal and external interests of the empire. But how was it possible to imagine that they would be executed? The combined powers were by no means strong enough to carry through such extensive and radical innovations. The diets had not been attended by nearly suf-

berg mit des Rychs Banyer zu Feld gelegen und unsern Herrn den Keyser geledigert und die Last uf sich genommen darin angesehen sine Pflicht, und was er habe das er das vom Ryche habe, und meyne Lip und Gut von-u H dem Keiser nit zu scheiden "—" He also recounted what manner of enterprise there had been against our gracious lord the emperor and how there was a design upon the empire, also how the king of Bohemia had the full intention of being at Frankfort at midsummer, and of getting possession of the empire and how, thereupon, our gracious lord the emperor had summoned him his brothers in law of Baden and Wirtenburg and committed the banner of the empire to him rather than to Duke Ludwig by reason of the affair with the bishop of Eystett, those of Werde and Dinkelshol and of the punishment he had incurred on that account in these things he had tarried or looked for no one but forthwith taken the field with his men and those of him of Wirtenberg with the banner of the empire, and relieved our lord the emperor, and taken the burthen upon himself, and had therein beheld his duty, and that what he had, he had from the empire, and had no thought of separating his life and lands from the cause of the emperor" As to the prayer of the cities, he says —"wywol yme das Geld nutzer ware und er mer schicken wolle mit den die er in den Sold gewonne denn mit den die in von den Stadten zu geschicket werden, ye doch so stehe es ime nit zu und habe nit Macht eynich Geld zu dehmen und des Keisers Gebote abzustellen" "Although money was needful to him, and he should spend more with troops he took into his pay than with those the cities should send him, still it would not become him, and he had not power anyhow to take money and to set aside the emperor's command" Dispositions such as befit a prince of the empire It were much to be wished there were some one capable of giving a more full and accurate account of the life and deeds of this remarkable prince

* Proceedings at the papal and imperial diet held at Nurnberg on account of the Turkish campaign in the 4th vol of the Frankfort Acts of the Diet of the Empire as published by Schilter and Muller, with some small variations

† *Landfriede*—Peace of the land The expression, public peace, which, in deference to numerous and high authorities, I have generally used in the text, is liable to important objections *A breach of the public peace* means, in England, any open disorder or outrage But the *Landfriede* (Pax publica) was a special act or provision directed against the abuse of an ancient and established institution,—the *Fehderecht* (jus diffidationis, or right of private warfare) The attempts to restrain this abuse were, for a long time, local and temporary, as, for example, in the year 1382, Markgrave Sigismund of Brandenburg, and some of the neighbouring princes, concluded a Landfriede for six years. In such cases tribunals called Peace Courts (*Friedensgerichte*), for trying offences against the *Landfriede*, were instituted and expired together with the peace The first energetic measure of the general government to put down private wars was that of the diet of Nurnberg (1466)

Peace of the realm, internal or domestic peace (as distinguished from foreign or international), would come nearer to the meaning of *Landfriede*. It is sufficient, however, if the reader bears in mind that it is opposed not to chance disorder or tumult but to a mode of voiding differences recognised by the law, and limited by certain forms and conditions, as e g that a *Befehdete* (faidosus) could not be attacked and killed in church or in his own house See Eichhorn, Deutsche Staats und Rechtsgeschichte, vol ii p 433 —Transl

‡ The constitution of the 18th of August, 1467, in Muller Rtth ii 293 The provisions for the maintenance of peace contained in those laws were not to be annulled, "dann allain in den Artickel der gülden Bull, der do inhellt von Widersagen, und in den ersten Artickel der Reformation der da inhellt von Angreifen und Beschedigen, dieselben Artickel sollen die obgemeldten funf Jar ruhen —auf dass zu Vehde Krieg und Aufrur Anlass vermitten und der Fride Stracks gehriten werde" "Then alone in the article of the Golden Bull, concerning challenges, and the first article of the Reformation, concerning assaults and damages these articles shall remain unaltered the above mentioned five years —that all occasion of challenge, war, and disorder, be avoided, and peace be thoroughly maintained" Unluckily the worthy Muller read Mulbenstadt for Neuenstadt in this important passage, a mistake which has found its way into a number of histories of the empire

§ *Das gemeine Pfennig* —I have not been able to find in any French or English writer the literal translation of this name given to the first attempt at general taxation in the empire, but I have retained it as characteristic of the age, and of the nature of the tax —Transl

|| The Duke of Cleves was named executor for Bremen, Münster, and Utrecht, Duke Ludwig of Bavaria, for Regensburg and Passau

ficient numbers, and the people did not hold themselves bound by the resolutions of a party The opposition to the emperor and the pope had not attained its object, but it still subsisted. Frederic the Victorious still lived, and had now an influence over the very cities which had formerly opposed him. The collection of the Common Penny was, in a short time, not even talked of, it was treated as a project of Paul II, to whom it was not deemed expedient to grant such extensive powers

The proclamation of the Public Peace had also produced little or no effect. After some time the cities declared that it had occasioned them more annoyance and damage than they had endured before * It was contrary to their wishes that, in the year 1474, it was renewed with all its actual provisions The private wars went on as before Soon afterwards one of the most powerful imperial cities, Regensburg, the very place where the Public Peace was proclaimed, fell into the hands of the Bavarians. The combined powers gradually lost all their consideration. In the year 1479 the propositions of the emperor and the pope were rejected in a mass by the estates of the empire, and were answered with a number of complaints

And yet never could stringent measures be more imperiously demanded

I shall not go into an elaborate description of the evils attendant on the right of diffidation or private warfare (*Fehderecht*) they were probably not so great as is commonly imagined. Even in the century we are treating of, there were Italians to whom the situation of Germany appeared happy and secure in comparison with that of their own country, where, in all parts, one faction drove out another † It was only the level country and the high roads which were exposed to robbery and devastation But even so, the state of things was disgraceful and insupportable to a great nation It exhibited the strongest contrast to the ideas of law and of religion upon which the Empire was so peculiarly founded

One consequence of it was, that as every man was exclusively occupied with the care of his own security and defence, or could at best not extend his view beyond the horizon immediately surrounding him, no one had any attention to bestow on the common weal; not only were no more great enterprises achieved, but even the frontiers were hardly defended In the East, the old conflict between the Germans and the Lettish and Slavonian tribes was decided in favour of the latter As the King of Poland found allies in Prussia itself, he obtained an easy victory over the Order, and compelled the knights to conclude the peace of Thorn (A D 1466), by which the greater part of the territories of the Order were ceded to him, and the rest were held of him in fee. Neither emperor nor empire stirred to avert this incalculable loss In the West, the idea of obtaining the Rhine as a boundary first awoke in the minds of the French, and the attacks of the Dauphin and the Armagnacs were only foiled by local resistance But what the one line of the house of Valois failed in, the other, that of Burgundy, accomplished with brilliant success As the wars between France and England were gradually terminated, and nothing more was to be gained in that field, this house, with all its ambition, and all its good fortune, threw itself on the territory of Lower Germany In direct defiance of the imperial authority, it took possession of Brabant and Holland, then Philip the Good took Luxemburg, placed his natural son in Utrecht, and his nephew on the episcopal throne of Liege; after which an unfortunate quarrel between father and son gave Charles the Bold an opportunity to seize upon Guelders A power was formed such as had not arisen since the time of the great duchies, and the interests and tendencies of which were naturally opposed to those of the empire This state the restless Charles resolved to extend, on the one side, towards Friesland, on the other, along the Upper Rhine. When at length he fell upon the archbishopric of Cologne and besieged Neuss, some opposition was made to him, but not in consequence of any concerted scheme or regular armament, but of a sudden levy in the presence of imminent danger The favourable moment for driving him back within his own frontiers had been neglected. Shortly after, on his attacking Lotharingia, Alsatia, and Switzerland, those countries were left to defend themselves Meanwhile, Italy had in fact completely emancipated herself If the emperor desired to be crowned there, he must go unarmed like a mere traveller, his ideal power could only be manifested in acts of grace and favour. The King of Bohemia, who also possessed the two Lusatias and Silesia, and an extensive feudal dominion within the empire, insisted loudly on his rights, and would hear nothing of the corresponding obligations.

The life of the nation must have been already extinct, had it not, even in the midst of all these calamities, and with the prospect of further imminent peril before it, taken measures to establish its internal order and to restore its external power, — objects, however, not to be attained without a revolution in both its spiritual and temporal affairs

The tendency to development and progress in Europe is sometimes more active and powerful in one direction, sometimes in another. At this moment temporal interests were most prominent; and these, therefore, must first claim our attention.

* "Dass die erbb Stadte und die iren in Zeitten solichs gemainen Friden und wider des Inhalt und Mainung mer Ungemachs Beschadigung verderblicher Rost Schaden und Unfrid an iren Leuten Leiben und Guten gelitten dann sy vorher in vil Jaren und Zeytten je empfangen" "That the hereditary cities and their people, in times of such common peace, and contrary to the intent and meaning, had suffered under more inconvenience, damage, cost, mischief, and disturbance, to the persons and possessions of their inhabitants, than had been undergone before during many years and seasons' — *Proceedings at Regensburg*, 1474 *Frankfurter AA*, vol viii

† Æneas Sylvius, Dialogi de Autoritate Concilii, introduces in the second of these dialogues a Novanese, who calls out to the Germans "Bona vestra vere vestra sunt pace omnes fruimini et libertate in communi, magisque ad naturam quam ad opinionem vivitis Fugi ego illos Italiæ turbines" — *Kollar*, *Anal* ii 704.

BOOK I.

ATTEMPT TO REFORM THE CONSTITUTION OF THE EMPIRE.

1486—1517.

SIMILAR disorders, arising from kindred sources and an analogous train of events, existed in all the other nations of Europe It may be said, that the offspring and products of the middle ages were engaged in a universal conflict which seemed likely to end in their common destruction.

The ideas upon which human society is based are but partially and imperfectly embued with the divine and eternal Essence from which they emanate, for a time they are beneficent and vivifying, and new creations spring up under their breath But on earth nothing attains to a pure and perfect existence, and therefore nothing is immortal When the times are accomplished, higher aspirations and more enlightened schemes spring up out of the tottering remains of former institutions, which they utterly overthrow and efface, for so has God ordered the world

If the disorders in question were universal, the efforts to put an end to them were not less so Powers called into life by the necessity of a change, or growing up spontaneously, arose out of the general confusion, and with vigorous and unbidden hand imposed order on the chaos.

This is the great event of the fifteenth century The names of the energetic princes of that time, whose task it was first to awaken the nations of Europe to a consciousness of their own existence and importance, are known to all In France we find Charles VII. and Louis XI The land was at length delivered from the enemy who had so long held divided sway in it, and was united under the standard of the Lilies, the monarchy was founded on a military and financial basis, crafty, calculating policy came in aid of the practical straightforward sense which attained its ends, because it aimed only at what was necessary, all the daring and insolent powers that had bid defiance to the supreme authority were subdued or overthrown the new order of things had already attained to sufficient strength to endure a long and stormy minority.

Henry VII. of England, without attempting to destroy the ancient liberties of the nation, laid the foundation of the power of the Tudors on the ruins of the two factions of the aristocracy, with a resolution nothing could shake and a vigour nothing could resist The Norman times were over,—modern England began At the same time Isabella of Castile reduced her refractory vassals to submission, by her union with a powerful neighbour, by the share she had acquired in the spiritual power, and by the natural ascendency of her own grand and womanly character, in which austere domestic virtue and a high chivalrous spirit were so singularly blended. She succeeded in completely driving out the Moors and pacifying the Peninsula. Even in Italy, some stronger governments were consolidated five considerable states were formed, united by a free alliance, and for a while capable of counteracting all foreign influence. At the same time Poland, doubly strong through her union with Lithuania, climbed to the highest pinnacle of power she ever possessed, while in Hungary, a native king maintained the honour and the unity of his nation at the head of the powerful army he had assembled under his banner

However various were the resources and the circumstances by which it was surrounded Monarchy—the central power—was every where strong enough to put down the resisting independencies, to exclude foreign influence to rally the people around its standard, by appealing to the national spirit under whose guidance it acted, and thus to give them a feeling of unity.

In Germany, however, this was not possible The two powers which might have effected this most were so far carried along by the general tendency of the age, that they endeavoured to introduce some degree of order, we have seen with what small success. At the very time in which all the monarchies of Europe consolidated themselves, the emperor was driven out of his hereditary states, and wandered about the other parts of the empire as a fugitive.* He was dependent for his daily repast on the bounty of convents, or of the burghers of the imperial cities; his other wants were supplied from the slender revenues of his chancery. he might sometimes be seen travelling along the roads of his own dominions in a carriage drawn by oxen; never—and this he himself felt—was the majesty of the empire dragged about in meaner form · the possessor of a power which, according to the received idea, ruled the world, was become an object of contemptuous pity.

If any thing was to be done in Germany, it must be by other means, upon other principles, with other objects, than any that had hitherto been contemplated or employed

* See Unrest, Chronicon Austriacum, Hahn. 660—688. Kurz, Oestreich unter Friedrich III. vol ii

FOUNDATION OF A NEW CONSTITUTION.

:T is obvious at the first glance, that no ›mpt at reform could be successful which not originate with the States themselves. ıce they had taken up so strong a position linst the two co-ordinate higher powers, they re bound to show how far that position was ely to prove beneficial to the public interests. t was greatly in their favour that the empe- had sunk into so deplorable a situation.

Not that it was their intention to make use this to his entire overthrow or destruction; the contrary, they were determined not to ›w him to fall. What for centuries only › emperor had accomplished, and he, in the ness of his power and by dispensing extra- inary favours (viz. to secure the succession his son), Frederic III. achieved in the mo- nt of the deepest humiliation and weakness. e prince-electors met in the year 1486, to ›ose his son Maximilian king of the Romans. this measure, Albert Achilles, of Branden- rg, took the most prominent and active part. ›twithstanding his advanced age, he came ›e more in person to Frankfurt: he caused nself to be carried into the electoral chapel a litter, whence, at the close of the proceed- gs, he presented the sceptre; he was in the ; of performing his high function as arch- amberlain of the empire, when he expired. ›ould not escape the electors, that the claims the house of Austria to the support of the ıpire were greatly strengthened by this event. ıximilian, the son-in-law of Charles the ld, who had undertaken to uphold the rights the house of Burgundy in the Netherlands, ›ountered there difficulties and misfortunes t much inferior to those which beset his her in Austria, and must, on no account, be andoned. His election could hardly be re- rded as fully accomplished, until the coun- es which had hitherto maintained a hostile itude were subjected to him, and thus re- ›red to the empire. It was precisely by de- mining to send succours in both directions, ıt the states acquired a two-fold right to dis- ss internal affairs according to their own dgment. They had rendered fresh services the reigning house, which could not defend hereditary possessions without their aid, d their voices must now be heard.

At this moment, too, a coolness arose be- een the emperor and the pope. There was arge party in Europe which had always re- rded the rise of the Austrian power with dis- ›e, and was now greatly offended at the elec- ›n of Maximilian to the Roman throne. To is party, in consequence of the turn Italian airs had taken, Pope Innocent VII. belong- . He refused the emperor aid against the ungarians, and even against the Turks. The ıperial ambassador found him, as Frederic mplained to the diet, "very awkward to deal ith" (*gar ungeschickt*,*) and could do nothing ith him. There was also a difference with e pope about the nomination to the see of Passau, as well as about a newly-imposed tithe. In short, the intervention of the Roman see was, for a moment, suspended. For the first time, during a long period, we find nume- rous assemblies of German princes without the presence of a papal legate.

Under these circumstances the deliberations of the States were opened with a better pros- pect of useful results.

It was evidently not necessary to begin from the beginning; all the elements of a great commonwealth were at hand. The diets had long been regarded as the focus of legislation and of the general government: peace (*Land- friede*) had been proclaimed throughout the realm; an imperial court of justice existed; as long ago as the Hussite war a census had been taken with a view to the general defence of the empire. Nothing remained but to give to those institutions that steady and pervading action which they had hitherto entirely wanted.

To this effect deliberations were incessantly held from the year 1486 to 1489. Ideas em- bracing the whole land of the German people, and directed to the restoration of its unity and strength, were in active circulation. In order to obtain a more complete and accurate concep- tion of the several important points, we will consider them, not in their historical connexion either with each other or with contemporane- ous events, but each separately.

The first was the Public Peace, which had again been broken on every side, and now, proclaimed anew in 1486, had been rendered clear by some more precise provisions annexed in 1487; yet it differed little from those which had gone before it. The execution of it was now, as heretofore, left to the tumultuous levy of the neighbourhood within a circle of from six to ten miles (German); nay, the declara- tion of 1487 expressly declares that a party in whose favour sentence had been pronounced might use force to secure its execution.† The only difference was that the co-operation of the pope was no longer invited. There was no further mention of sending papal conservators with peculiar powers of executing justice, in order to the maintenance of the Public Peace. This, however, rendered it doubtful whether the clergy, to whom the pope and the church were much more proximate and formidable than the emperor and the state, would choose to regard themselves as bound by the peace. No other means could be found to obviate this evil than that the emperor should declare, as the bishops had done in regard to their own nobility, that he would put the disobedient out of the favour and protection of the law, and would not defend them from any aggression or injury.

We see what a state of violence, insubordi- nation, and mutual independence still prevail- ed, and even manifested itself in the laws:

* Muller, Rtth. unter Friedrich III., v. 122.

† Muller, Rtth. Fr. VI., 115. "Wo aber der, der gewal- tige Tate furneme und ube, das thete uf behapte Urtheil, so solt daruber nyemant dem Bekricgten das mahl Hilf zuzuschicken schuldig seyn." "When, however, any one, undertaking and exercising acts of violence, does so upon judgment received in his favour, then shall no one be bound to send help thereupon to him who is attacked."

and how necessary it was to establish internal regulations, by the firmness and energy of which arbitrary power might be held in check, and the encroachments of an authority which, at the very first meeting of the estates, was regarded as foreign, might be repelled.

The most essential point was to give to the imperial diets more regular forms and greater dignity; and especially to put an end to the resistance offered to their edicts by the cities.

The cities, which were so often hostilely treated by the other estates, and which had interests of so peculiar a nature to defend, held themselves from the earliest period studiously aloof During the Hussite war they were even permitted to send into the field a separate municipal army under a captain of their own appointment * In the year 1460 they declined going to council with the princes, or uniting in a common answer to the emperor's proposals † In the year 1474 the deputies refused to approve the Public Peace concluded by the emperor and princes, and obstinately persisted that they would say nothing to it till they had consulted their friends ‡ In 1486 the princes having granted some subsidies to the emperor to which the cities were called upon to contribute, they resisted, and the more strenuously, since they had not even been summoned to the meeting at which the grant was made Frederic replied that this had not been done, because they would have done nothing without sending home for instructions

It was evident that this state of things could not be maintained. The imperial cities justly deemed it an intolerable grievance that they should be taxed according to an arbitrary assessment, and a contribution demanded of them as if it were a debt; on the other hand, it was just as little to be endured that they should obstruct every definitive decision, and send home to consult their constituents on every individual grant

So powerful was the influence of the prevailing spirit of the times, that, in the year 1487, the cities came to a resolution to abandon the course they had hitherto pursued

The emperor had summoned only a small number of them to the diet of this year; they determined, however, this time to send the whole body of their deputies, and not to require them to send home for instructions. The Emperor Frederic received them at the castle of Nurnberg, sitting on his bed, "of a feeble countenance," as they express themselves,§ and caused it to be said to them that he was glad to see them, and would graciously acknowledge their coming The princes too were well satisfied therewith, and allowed the cities to take part in their deliberations Committees were formed—a practice that afterwards became the prevailing one—in which the cities too were included. The first which sat to deliberate on the Public Peace consisted of six electors, ten princes, and three burghers. From the second,—to consider the measures to be adopted against the Hungarians,—the cities were at first excluded, but afterwards were summoned at the express desire of the emperor. Our reporter, Dr. Paradeis of Frankfurt, was one of the members of this committee. Nor was the share taken by the burgher delegates barren of substantial results; of the general grant of 100,000 gulden, nearly the entire half, (49,390 gulden) was at first assessed to them they struck off about a fifth from this estimate, and reduced it to 40,000 gulden, which they apportioned to each city at their own discretion.

At the next diet, in 1489, the forms of general deliberation were settled. For the first time, the three colleges, electors, princes, and burghers, separated as soon as a measure was proposed, each party retired to its own room, the answer was drawn up by the electoral college, and then presented for acceptance to the others Thenceforth this continued to be the regular practice. At this juncture there was a possibility of the constitution of the empire assuming a form like that which arose out of similar institutions in other countries, viz that the commons, who regarded themselves (in Germany as elsewhere) as the emperor's lieges (Leute),—as in an especial manner his subjects,—might have made common cause with him against the aristocracy, and have formed a third estate, or Commons' House Sigismund was very fond of joining his complaints of the princely power with theirs: he reminded them that the empire had nothing left but them, since everything else had fallen into the hands of the princes, he liked particularly to treat with them, and invited them to come to him with all their grievances ‖ But the imperial power was far too weak to foster these sympathies to any practical maturity, or to give a precise and consistent form to their union, it was incapable of affording to the cities that protection which would have excited

* In the year 1431 Datt de Pace Publica, 167

† Protocol in Muller, i p 782 with this addition, however "Sie wolten solch freundlich Furbringen ihren Frunden berumen" "They would commend so friendly a proposition to their friends"

‡ The answer given by them in Muller, ii p 625, is vague and obscure In the Frankfurt Archives (vol viii) it runs thus "Als die des Friedens notdurftig und begerlich sind, setzen sy (die Stadte) in kein Zweifel, E K M (werde) gnediglich darob und daran seyn dass der vestiglich gehandhabt und gehalten werde dazu sy aber nicht halb zu reden mit bedacht sind auch kein Befel haben unterteniglich bittend, das S K M das also in Gnaden und Guten von in versten und sy als ir allergnedigster Herr bedenken wolle"—"As they have need, and are desirous of peace, they (the cities) make no doubt, your Imperial Majesty will graciously strive to bring about that it be firmly maintained and kept, but beyond this they have no thought of speaking on their own behalf nor have any command so to do submissively entreating, that his Imperial Majesty will therefore take this in good and gracious understanding from them, and think of them like their most gracious master" It is evident that their acceptance is only very general, and that they would not suffer the more essential resolutions to be pressed upon them, the emperor at last concedes the point relating to the instructions

§ Dr Ludwig zum Paradeis of Frankfurt, Monday after Judica April 2 1487 With this diet of the empire begin the detailed reports of the Frankfurt deputies The earlier ones were more fragmentary —*Rs A*, vol xii

‖ See Sigismund's Speech to the Friends of the Council at Frankfurt Printed by Aschbach, Geschichte Kaiser Sigmunds, i 453 He there says, he will discuss with them "was ir Brest (Gebrechen) sy,"—"what may be their wants"

or justified a voluntary adherence to the head of the empire on their part. The German Estates generally assumed a very different form from all others. Elsewhere the lords spiritual and temporal used to meet separately in Germany, on the contrary, the electors, who united the spiritual and temporal power in their own persons, had so thoroughly defined a position, such distinct common privileges, that it was not possible to divide them Hence it happened that the princes formed a single college of spiritual and temporal members the committees were generally composed of an equal number of each. The cities in Germany were not opposed, but allied to the magnates These two estates together formed a compact corporation, against which no emperor could carry any measure, and which represented the aggregate power of the empire

In the consciousness of their own strength and of the necessity of the case, they now made a proposal to the emperor, which, however moderate in its tone, opened the widest prospect of a radical change in the constitution.

It was obvious that if order and tranquillity were really restored, and all were compelled to acknowledge him as the supreme fountain of justice, the emperor would necessarily acquire an immense accession of power. This the estates were little inclined to concede to him, the less, since justice was so arbitrarily administered in his tribunal, which was therefore extremely discredited throughout the empire. As early as the year 1467, at the moment of the first serious proclamation of the Public Peace, a proposal was made to the emperor to establish a supreme tribunal of a new kind for the enforcement of it, to which the several estates should nominate twenty-four inferior judges * from all parts of Germany, and the emperor only one as president.† To this Frederick paid no attention he appointed his tribunal after, as he had before, alone, caused it to follow his court, and even decided some causes in person, revoked judgments that had been pronounced, and determined the amount of costs and fees at his pleasure He of course excited universal discontent by these proceedings, people saw clearly that if any thing was to be done for the empire, the first step must be to establish a better administration of justice. The subsidies which they granted the emperor in the year 1486 were saddled with a condition to that effect. The estates were not so anxious to appoint the judges of the court, as to secure to it first a certain degree of independence, they were even willing to grant the judge and his assessors a right of co-optation for the offices becoming vacant. The main thing, however, was, that the judge should have the faculty of sentencing the breakers of the Public Peace to the punishment upon which the penal force of the law for the preservation of that peace—the punishment of the ban—mainly rested, as well as the emperor himself, and also that it should rest with him to take the necessary measures for its execution So intolerable was the personal interference of the emperor esteemed, that people thought they should have gained every thing if they could secure themselves from this evil They then intended in some degree to limit the power of the tribunal, by referring it to the statutes of the particular part of the empire in which the particular case arose, and by having a fixed tax for the costs and fees ‡

But the aged emperor had no mind to renounce one jot of his traditional power He replied, that he should reserve to himself the right of proclaiming the ban, "in like manner as that had been done of old" (*immaassen das vor Alters gewesen*). The appointment of assessors also must in future take place only with his knowledge and consent Local statutes and customs should only be recognised by the court in as far as they were consistent with the imperial written law, *i e.* the Roman (a curious proof how much the Idea of the Empire contributed to the introduction of the Roman law) with regard to taxing the costs and fees, he would be unrestrained, as other princes were, in their courts of justice and chanceries § He regarded the supreme tribunal of the realm in the light of a patrimonial court. It was in vain that the electors observed to him that a reform of the supreme court was the condition attached to their grants, in vain they actually stopped their payments, and proposed other and more moderate conditions the aged monarch was inflexible.

Frederic III. had accustomed himself in the course of a long life to regard the affairs of the world with perfect serenity of mind. His cotemporaries have painted him to us,—one while weighing precious stones in a goldsmith's scales, another, with a celestial globe in his hand, discoursing with learned men on the positions of the stars. He loved to mix metals, compound healing drugs, and in important crises, predicted the future himself from the aspects of the constellations he read a man's destiny in his features or in the lines of his hand. He was a believer in the hidden powers that govern nature and fortune. In his youth his Portuguese wife, with the violent temper and the habitual opinions of a native of the South, urged him in terms of bitter scorn to take vengeance for some injury he only answered, that every thing was rewarded, and punished, and avenged in time.‖ Complaints of the abuses in his courts of justice made little impression on him he said "things did not go quite right or smooth anywhere." On one occasion representations were made to him by the princes of the empire, against the influence which he allowed his councillor Pruschenk to

* The passage, as Harpprecht, Archiv i par 109, gives it, is quite unintelligible, for instead of urtailsprecher (utterer of a sentence), urtel sprechen (to pronounce sentence) is printed, just as if the states themselves were to sit in judgment It is more exact and connected in Konig von Königsthal, ii p 13

† The words in the text are *Urtheiler* and *Richter* As *Urtheil* is *judgment* or *decision*, and *Recht law* or *right*, these titles seem to imply some analogy with the offices of the English jury and judge —Transl

‡ Essay on an Ordinance of the Imperial Chamber, Muller, vi 29

§ Moruta Cæsareanorum Muller, vi 69

‖ Grunbeck, Historia Frederici et Maximiliani in Chmel, Oestreichischer Geschichtsforscher, i p 69.

exercise he replied, "every one of them had his own Pruschenk at home" In all the perplexities of affairs he evinced the same calmness and equanimity In 1449, when the cities and princes, on the eve of war, refused to accept him as a mediator, he was content he said he would wait till they had burnt each other's houses and destroyed each other's crops, then they would come to him of their own accord, and beg him to bring about a reconciliation between them; — which shortly after happened.

The violences and cruelties which his hereditary dominions of Austria suffered from King Matthias did not even excite his pity he said they deserved it, they would not obey him, and therefore they must have a stork as king, like the frogs in the fable In his own affairs he was more like an observer than a party interested, in all events he saw the rule by which they are governed, — the universal, inflexible principle which, after short interruptions, invariably recovers its empire. From his youth he had been inured to trouble and adversity. When compelled to yield, he never gave up a point, and always gained the mastery in the end. The maintenance of his prerogatives was the governing principle of all his actions, the more, because they acquired an ideal value from their connection with the imperial dignity. It cost him a long and severe struggle to allow his son to be crowned king of the Romans, he wished to take the supreme authority undivided with him to the grave in no case would he grant Maximilian any independent share in the administration of government, but kept him, even after he was king, still as "son of the house,"* nor would he ever give him anything but the countship of Cilli · "for the rest, he would have time enough." His frugality bordered on avarice, his slowness on inertness, his stubbornness on the most determined selfishness yet all these faults are rescued from vulgarity by high qualities. He had at bottom a sober depth of judgment, a sedate and inflexible honour, the aged prince, even when a fugitive imploring succour, had a personal bearing which never allowed the majesty of the empire to sink. All his pleasures were characteristic Once, when he was in Nürnberg, he had all the children in the city, even the infants who could but just walk, brought to him in the city ditches; he feasted his eyes on the rising generation, the heirs of the future, then he ordered cakes to be brought and distributed, that the children might remember their old master, whom they had seen, as long as they lived. Occasionally he gave the princes his friends a feast in his castle In proportion to his usual extreme frugality was now the magnificence of the entertainment he kept his guests with him till late in the night (always his most vivacious time) when even his wonted taciturnity ceased, and he began to relate the history of his past life, interspersed with strange incidents, decent jests and wise saws. He looked like a patriarch among the princes, who were all much younger than himself

The Estates saw clearly that with this sort of character, with this resolute inflexible being, nothing was to be gained by negotiation or stipulation If they wished to carry their point they must turn to the young king, who had indeed no power as yet, but who must shortly succeed to it. On his way from the Netherlands, whence he was hastening to rescue Austria from the Hungarians, for which end he had the most urgent need of the assistance of the empire, they laid their requests before him and made a compliance with these the conditions of their succours Maximilian, reared in the constant sight of the troubles and calamities into which his father had fallen, had, as often happens, adopted contrary maxims of conduct, he looked only to the consequences of the moment he had all the buoyant confidence of youth, nor did he think the safety of the empire involved in a tenacious adherence to certain privileges. His first appearance in public life was at the diet at Numberg, in 1439, where he requited the support granted him by the empire with ready concessions as to the administration of justice. He could indeed only promise to use every means to induce his father to have the Imperial Chamber (Kammergericht) established as soon as possible on the plan proposed In this, as was to be expected, he did not succeed, but he was at all events morally bound to fulfil the expectations he had raised it was a first step, though the consequences of it lay at a distance. This promise was registered in the recess of the diet †

This was the most important point of the administration of the empire. All internal order depended on the supreme court of justice. It was of the highest moment that it should be shielded from the arbitrary will of the emperor, and that a considerable share in the constitution of it should be given to the States.

Maximilian too now received the succours he required for the restoration of the Austrian power. While one of the bravest of German princes, Albert of Saxony, called the Right Arm of the empire, gradually, to use his own expression, "brought the rebellious Netherlands to peace,"‡ Maximilian himself hastened to his ancestral domains. Shortly before, the aged Archduke Sigismund of Tyrol had allowed himself to be persuaded to give the emperor's daughter, who had been confided to him, in marriage to Duke Albert of Bavaria-Munich, and had held out to that prince the hope that he would leave him Tyrol and the Vorlande as an inheritance But the sight of Maximilian awakened in the kindhearted and childless old man a natural tenderness for the manly and blooming scion of his own race; he now dwelt with joy on the thought that this was the rightful heir to the country, and instantly determined to bequeath it to him. At this moment King Matthias of Hungary, who

* Letter from Maximilian to Albert of Saxony, 1492, in the Dresden Archives

† Muller, vi p 171 A register of this imperial diet in the Frankfurt Archives, vol xiii

‡ From a letter of Albrecht to his son, in Langenn, Duke Albert, p 205.

was still in possession of Austria, died. The land breathed again, when the rightful young prince appeared in the field surrounded by the forces of the empire and by his own mercenaries; drove the Hungarians before him, delivered Vienna from their hands, and pursued them over their own borders. We find this event recorded, even in the journals of private persons, as the happiest of their lives:*—a district that had been mortgaged raised the mortgage money itself, that it might belong once more to its ancient lords.

Such was the vast influence of the good understanding between Maximilian and the States of the empire, on the re-establishment of the power of Austria. It had, at the same time, another great effect in conducing to the conciliation of one of the most eminent of the princes, and to the consolidation of all internal affairs.

The Dukes of Bavaria, spite of the family alliance into which they had been forced with the emperor by the marriage above mentioned, adhered to the opponents of Austria—the Roman see, and King Matthias.† They would hear nothing of furnishing aids to the emperor against the king; they refused to attend the diets, or to accept their edicts: on the contrary, they made encroachments on the domains of their neighbours, enlarged the jurisdiction of their own courts of justice, and threatened neighbouring imperial cities — for example, Memmingen and Bibrach. Regensburg had already fallen into the possession of Duke Albert of Munich.‡

Immediately after the renewal of the Public Peace, in the year 1487, it became evident that there was no chance of its being observed if these partial and turbulent proceedings were not put an end to.

This was the immediate and pressing cause of the Swabian league, concluded in February 1488, by the mediation of the emperor,§ and some of the more powerful princes. The order of knights, who the year before had renewed their old company of St. George's shield, quickly joined the league, as did also the cities. They mutually promised to oppose a common resistance to all strangers who sought to impose foreign (*i. e.* not Swabian) laws upon them, or otherwise to injure or offend them. But in order to secure themselves from disputes or disorders among themselves, and at the same time to observe the Public Peace —for this general object was, from the very first, included among the more particular ones, and gave the whole union a legitimate character, — they determined to settle their mutual differences by the decision of arbitrators, and appointed a council of the league, composed of an equal number of members chosen from each body. In a very short time the league was joined by neighbouring princes, especially Würtenberg and Brandenburg, and formed, as contra-distinguished from the knights and the cities, a third body, taking equal share in its council, submitting to the decisions of the arbitrators, and promising, in case of a war, to send the contingent agreed upon into the field. Here, in the very focus of the old quarrels, a firm and compact union of the several classes arose, affording a noble representation of the Ideas of the constitution of the empire, and of public order and security; though its main and proximate object was resistance to the encroachments of Bavaria. Nevertheless, Duke Albert held himself aloof in haughty defiance, while the emperor, relying on the league, would hear of no reconciliation till the pride of the Duke was humbled. At length resort was had to arms. In the spring of 1492 the troops of the league and of the empire assembled on the Lechfeld. Frederic of Brandenburg, "whose doublet had long been hot against Bavaria," carried the banner of the empire; Maximilian was there in person. At this moment Albert, abandoned by his kinsmen, at strife with his knights, felt that he could not withstand such an overwhelming force; he relinquished the opposition which he had hitherto maintained, consented to give up Regensburg, and to abandon all claims founded on the assignments made by Sigismund. By degrees even the old emperor was appeased, and received his son-in-law and his granddaughters with cordiality. After some time Albert himself found it expedient to join the Swabian league.

We see that the reign of Frederic III. was by no means so insignificant as is commonly believed. His latter years especially, so full of difficulties and reverses, were rich in great results. The house of Habsburg, by the acquisition of Austria and the Netherlands, had acquired a high rank in Europe. A short campaign of Maximilian's sufficed to establish its claims to Hungary.‖ The intestine wars

* Diarium Joannis Tichtelii, in Rauch, Scriptt. Rer. Austriacarum, ii. 559. He writes the name of Maximilian four times, one after the other, as if unable to write it often enough for his own satisfaction.

† In Lent, 1482, Albert and George determined, "with their several states, that, without the countenance of the holy father, help should not be given to King Matthias against the emperor." "Mit ihr beder Landschaft dass man ohne Gunst des h. Vaters dem Kaiser wider König Matthias nit helfen sollte." Anonymous contemporary Chronicle in Freiberg's Collection of Historical Papers and Documents, i. 159. All these circumstances deserved a closer examination. For the modern relations and political system of these states did not begin so late as is believed. From Hagek, Pöhmischer Chronik, p. 828, it appears that the Bohemians would not put up with their exclusion from the election of Maximilian. They entered into a league with Matthias, drawing Poland into it also. (Pelzel. Geschichte von Böhmen, i. 494). The deputies of Matthias tried to set the Italian princes in motion. (Philippus Bergomas, Supplementum Chronicorum.) France likewise belonged to this party. The reason why Bavaria joined it is evident. The eyes of her dukes were always turned either towards Lombardy or the Netherlands. Freiberg: Geschichte der Baierischen Landstände, I. 655.

‡ Pfister, Geschichte von Schwaben, v. p. 272.

§ In his very first address the emperor declares the object of the league to be, that the states, "bei dem heiligen Reiche und ihren Freiheiten bleiben," "should remain in adherence to the holy empire, and in possession of their liberties."—*Datt, de Pace Pub.* 272. Who could believe, that for the history of this most important of all early leagues we have still to refer chiefly to Datt?

‖ The treaty of Oedenburg, 1463, July 29, had already secured the succession to the house of Austria, upon the extinction of the Hunniads. The new treaty, 1491, Nov. 7, the Monday after the feast of St. Leonard, renewed this right in case of failure of male issue from Wladislas.

of Germany were almost entirely suppressed. The Swabian league gave to the house of Austria a legitimate influence over Germany, such as it had not possessed since the time of Albert I. The diets had acquired a regular form, the Public Peace was established and tolerably secured, and important steps were taken towards the formation of a general constitution. What form and character this should assume, mainly depended on the conduct of Maximilian, on whom, at the death of his father (August 19, 1493), the administration of the empire now devolved.

DIET OF WORMS, 1495.

IDEAS had long been universally current, and schemes suggested, pregnant with far more extensive and important consequences than any we have yet contemplated.

Among the most remarkable were those put forth by Nicholas von Kus, whose capacious and prophetic mind was a storehouse of new and just views on the most various subjects. At the time of the council of Basle he devoted himself with earnest zeal and perspicacious judgment to the internal politics of the empire. He began by observing that it was impossible to improve the church without reforming the empire; since it was impossible to sever them, even in thought.* He therefore urgently recommends, though an ecclesiastic, the emancipation of the secular authority. He is entirely opposed to the right claimed by the papacy, of transferring the empire to whom it will: he ascribes to the latter a mystical relation to God and Christ, absolute independence, and even the right and the duty of taking part in the government of the church. He desires that the confusion arising from the jurisdiction of the spiritual and temporal courts be put an end to. He proposes a plan for superior courts of justice, each provided with three assessors, chosen from the nobles, clergy, and citizens respectively,† and empowered not only to hear appeals from the inferior courts, but to decide the differences between the princes in the first instance. It was only by such means, he thought, that the legal practice could be brought into greater harmony with the principles of natural justice. Above all, however, he looked to the establishment of yearly diets for the revival of the authority, unity, and strength of the empire (*Reich*); for he clearly perceived that no such results were to be expected from the power of the emperor (*Kaiserthum*) alone.‡ Either in May or in September he would have a general meeting of the Estates held at Frankfurt, or other convenient city, in order to arrange any existing dissensions, and to pass general laws, to which every prince should affix his signature and seal, and engage his honour to observe them. He strenuously contends that no ecclesiastic shall be exempted from their operation, otherwise he would want to have a share in the secular power, which was to be exercised for the general good. He goes on to remark that, in order seriously to maintain order and law and to chastise the refractory, it is necessary to have a standing army, for to what end is a law without the penal sanction? He thinks that a part of the revenues of the numerous tolls granted to individuals might be kept back by the state, and a fund thus formed, the application of which should be every year determined at the diet. There would then be no more violence, the bishops would devote themselves to their spiritual duties, peace and prosperity and power would return.

It is clear that the reforms suggested by this remarkable man were precisely those which it was the most important to put in practice; indeed the ideas which are destined to agitate the world are always first thrown out by some one original and luminous mind. In the course of time some approach was made, even on the part of the authorities of the empire, to the execution of these projects.

Even during their opposition to Frederic III. in 1450—1460, the Electors were of opinion that the most salutary measure for the empire would be, when they were with the emperor in person—for example, in an imperial city,—to form a sort of consistory around him, like that of the cardinals around the pope, and from this central point to take the government of the empire into their own hands, and to provide for the preservation of public order. It was their notion that a permanent court of justice should be established, like that of the parliament of Paris, whose judgments should be executed by certain temporal princes in the several circles of the empire, the ban should be pronounced by the emperor according to justice and conscience, and should then be duly executed and obeyed.§

Similar suggestions appeared from time to time. In the archives of Dresden there is a report of a consultation of the year 1491, in

* Nicolai Cusani de Concordantia Catholica, lib. iii. Schardius, Sylloge de Jurisdictione Imperiali, f. 467.

† Lib. iii. c. xxxiii. "Pronunciet et citet quisque judicum secundum conditionem disceptantium personarum, nobilis inter nobiles, ecclesiasticus inter ecclesiasticos, popularis inter populares, nulla tamen diffinitiva feratur nisi ex communi deliberatione omnium trium. Si vero unus duobus dissenserit, vincat opinio majoris numeri." It is not to be believed that the customs of German law also had not given rise to many complaints. It is here said: "Sæpe simplices pauperes per cavillationes causidicorum extra causam ducuntur, et a tota causa cadunt, quoniam qui cadit a syllaba, cadit a causa, ut sæpe vidi per Treverensem diocesim accidere. Tollantur consuetudines quæ admittunt juramentum contra quoscunque et cujuscunque numeri testes."—iii. c. 36.

‡ This is one passage among many in which the want of two words corresponding to Reich and Kaiserthum, both Englished by *empire*, is grievously felt. Reich, and its numerous derivatives and compounds, Reichstag, Reichsabschied, &c., always relate to the great Germanic body called the Empire. Kaiserthum, to the office and state of Kaiser, relates to the personal dignity, power, functions, &c., of the individual occupying the imperial throne. As it is impossible every time these words occur to resort to a long paraphrase, the meaning is often lost or obscured. Reich is also applied to a monarchical state, and then stands in a like relation to Konigthum (the kingly office or state), somewhat as *realm* does to *royalty*. The title of a former section presents a difficulty of a somewhat similar nature,—it is, Papsthum and Fursteuthum—Popedom and Princedom; for the former we have Papacy, for the latter abstraction, nothing.—TRANSL.

§ Final Edict of the spiritual Electors. See p. 58. n. 1.

which dissatisfaction is expressed with the plan of a supreme court of justice, and a scheme of a general government and military constitution for the whole empire, not unlike that of Nicholas von Kus, is proposed; an annual diet for the more important business of the general government, and a military force, ready for service at a moment's notice, proportioned to the six circles into which it was proposed to divide the empire, and under twelve captains or chiefs.

With the accession of a young and intelligent prince, a tendency to improvement and a leaning towards innovation took the place of the invincible apathy of the old emperor; and these dispositions, both in the chief of the empire and the Estates, were strengthened by other circumstances attending the new reign.

Maximilian had received some offences of an entirely personal nature from the King of France. According to the terms of a treaty of peace, that prince was to marry Maximilian's daughter, and, till she reached years of maturity, she was confided to French guardianship: Charles now sent her back. On the other hand, Maximilian was betrothed to the princess and heiress of Bretagne, an alliance on which the people of Germany founded various plans reaching far into the future, and hoped to draw that province under the same institutions as they intended to give to the empire. Charles VIII., however, got the young princess into his power by violence, and forced her to accept his hand.* The rights of the empire were immediately affected by these hostile acts. Whilst Maximilian was preparing to go to Rome to be crowned, and cherished the hope of restoring the imperial dignity and consideration in Italy, the French, anticipating him, crossed the Alps, marched unchecked through the Peninsula from north to south, and conquered Naples. We cannot affirm that Charles VIII. had any positive design of seizing the imperial crown; but it is undeniable that a power, such as he acquired throughout Italy by the nature and the success of his enterprise, was calculated to oppose a direct obstacle to the revival of the authority of the German empire.

Irritated by such reiterated wrongs, and deeply impressed with the necessity of making a stand against French aggression; availing himself of his incontestable right to demand succours from the States for his journey to Rome; urged likewise by his Italian allies, Maximilian now appeared at Worms, and on the 26th March opened his diet with a description of the political state of Europe. "If we continue," exclaimed he, "to look on passively at the proceedings of the French, the holy Roman Empire will be wrested from the German nation, and no man will be secure of his honour, his dignity, or his liberties." He wished to invoke the whole might and energy of the empire to take part in this struggle. Independent of a hasty levy to keep alive the resistance of Italy, he likewise demanded a permanent military establishment for the next ten or twelve years, in order that he might be able to defend himself, "whenever an attack was attempted against the Holy Empire." He pressed for it with impetuous earnestness; he was in a position in which the interests of the public were identical with his own.

The Estates also, which had assembled in unusual numbers, were fully impressed with the necessity of resisting the French. But in the first place, they regarded affairs with more coolness than the young emperor; and, secondly, they deemed the accession of a new sovereign who had already pledged himself to them and was now in need of considerable assistance, a moment well adapted for the prosecution of their schemes of reform and the introduction of order into their internal affairs. They met the warlike demands of the king with one of the most comprehensive schemes ever drawn up for the constitution of the empire.

They too assumed the necessity of a strong military organization, but they found the feudal system, now in its decline, no longer available; they deemed it better to impose a general tax, called the Common Penny. This tax was to be levied not according to the territorial extent, but the population of the several parts of the empire. The application of it was not to devolve on the king, but to be entrusted to a council of the empire composed of members of the States, the cities included. This council was to be invested with large general powers. It was to execute the laws, to put down rebellion and tumult; to provide for the reintegration of any domains that had been subtracted from the empire; to conduct the defensive war against the Turks and other enemies of the Holy Empire and of the German nation; in short, it is evident that it was to have the sum of the powers of government in its hands;† and certainly a large share of independence was to be awarded to it for that purpose. The weightiest affairs it was bound to lay before the king and the electors, subject to the revision of the latter; but in all other respects the members were to be freed from the oath whereby they were bound to the king and the Estates, and act only in conformity with the duties of their office.‡

The ideas by which this project was dictated show a very strong public spirit; for it was

* The old emperor says in his proclamation of the 4th of June, 1492, "Rather would we depart in peace and blessedness from this world, than suffer so unchristian-like and foul a deed to remain unpunished, and the Holy Empire and German people to put up with this scandalous and irreparable injury under our rule." "Wir—lieber von dieser Welt seliglich scheiden, dann einen solchen unkristlichen snoden Handel ungestrafft beleiben und das heil Reich und deutsche Nation in diesen lesterlichen und unwiederpringlichen Vall bei unserer Regierung wachsen lassen wolten."

† See the first scheme which the elector of Mainz communicated first to the king, and then to the cities. Protocol in Datt, de Pace Pub. p. 830. The protocol is the same with that found in the Frankfurt Acts, vol. xv.

‡ The latter is a provision of the larger draft, p. 838, nr. 17. "Sollen dieselben President und Personen des vorgemeldten Rathes aller Gelübd und Aide—damit sie uns oder inen (denen von welchen sie gesetzt worden) verbunden oder verstrickt wären, gentzlich ledig seyn." "The same president and persons of the before-mentioned council shall be wholly freed from all promise and oath, having the effect of binding them to, or connecting them with, us or them" (those by whom they had been appointed).

by no means the king alone whose power was limited. The general interests of the country were represented in a manner which would admit of no division or exclusion. How utterly, for example, is the idea of a general tax, to be collected by the parish priest, and delivered under his responsibility to the bishop, at variance with any further augmentation of the influence of the territorial lords! Which among them would have been strong enough to resist a central national power, such as this must have become?

The first result, however, would have been that the power of the monarch—not indeed that which he exercised in the usual troubled state of things, but that which he claimed for better times—would have been limited.

It remained now to be seen what he would say to this project. The fiefs which he granted out, the knightly festivities devised in his honour, or given by him in return, the manifold disputes between German princes which he had to accommodate, occupied him fully. It was not till the 22d of June that he gave his answer, which he published as an amendment of the project. On closer examination, however, its effect was in fact entirely to annul it. He had said at the beginning that he would accept the project with reservation of his sovereign prerogatives; now, he declared that he thought these assailed in every clause. I will give an example of the alterations he made. According to the project, the council of the empire was charged to see that no new tolls were erected without the previous knowledge of the electors; a precaution suggested by the tolls continually granted by Frederic and Maximilian. The clause, in its altered state, set forth that the council of the empire should itself take care to erect no toll without the previous knowledge of the king.

Strange that such a complete reversal of an original scheme should be announced as an amendment! but such were the manners, such the courtesy of that time. The opposition in temper and opinion was not the less violent on that account. A visible irritation and ill-humour prevailed at the diet. The king one day summoned to his presence the princes on whose friendship he could most confidently rely,—Albert of Saxony, Frederic of Brandenburg, and Eberhard of Würtenberg, to consult them on the means of maintaining his sovereign dignity.*

So directly opposed were the views of the monarch and those of the States at the very commencement of this reign. Both parties, however, made the discovery that they could not attain their ends in the way they had proposed to themselves. Maximilian clearly perceived that he should obtain no subsidies without concessions. The States saw that, at present at least, they would not be able to carry through their scheme of a general government.† While trying, however, to hit upon some middle course, they came back to experiments attempted under Frederic III.

In the first place, they settled the basis of that Public Peace which has rendered this diet so celebrated. On a more accurate examination, we find indeed that it is in detail rather less pacific than the former ones; as, for example, it restores a right, lately abrogated, of the injured party to make forcible seizure of a mortgaged estate; the only advantage was, that this peace was proclaimed, not as before for a term of years, but for ever. By this act the law, in fact, ceased to contemplate the possibility of any return to the old fist law (Faustrecht).

The question of the Imperial Chamber (Kammergericht), or supreme court of justice for the empire, was next discussed. Maximilian had hitherto treated this tribunal exactly as his father had done: he made it follow his court; in 1493 it accompanied him to Regensburg, in 1494 to Mechlin and Antwerp, in 1495 to Worms. We have, however, seen that he was bound by the concessions he made in 1489 to reform the administration of justice. When, therefore, the proposals formerly laid before his father were submitted to him, he felt himself compelled to accept them. Under what pretext, indeed, could he have rejected an institution, the establishment of which he had so solemnly undertaken to promote with all his might? This, however, was one of the most important events in the history of the empire. Maximilian gave his assent to the maxim that the statute law should have force in the supreme court, and that no more than the regular fees should be exacted; above all, he ceded to the judge the office of proclaiming the ban of the empire in his name; nay, he bound himself not to remove the ban when pronounced, without the consent of the injured party. When we reflect that the judicial power was the highest attribute of the imperial crown, we feel all the importance of this step. Nor was it only that the supreme court of the empire was secured from the arbitrary interference which had hitherto been so injurious to it—its offices were also appointed by the Estates. The king nominated only the president (Kammerrichter); the assessors were appointed by the Estates; and the cities, to their great joy, were invited to propose certain candidates for that office: a committee was then appointed to examine and decide on the presentations.‡ Later jurists have disputed whether the court derived its penal sanction

* Notice in the Archives of Berlin, which contains, however, only fragmentary remarks upon this imperial diet.

† Later Declaration of the Elector Berthold of Mainz in Datt, p. 871. "Daruf wäre erst fürgenommen ain Ordnung im Reich aufzurichten und Sr. ko. Mt. furgehalten, darab S. M. etwas Beswërung und Missfallens gehabt, hetten die Stende davon gestanden." "Thereupon it was first determined to establish a regular government in the empire and submitted to his Royal Majesty, so that if H. M. had any objection or dislike to it, the States would have desisted from it." Whether Müller, Rtth. unter M. (i. 329), be right in maintaining that a second scheme of a similar kind had also been presented, whereupon Maximilian had offered to appoint, instead of the imperial council, a court council, I must leave undetermined. It would, in fact, have been but another evasive proposition.

‡ Notice from a document of later date in Harpprecht, Staats-archiv. des Reichskammergerichts, ii. p. 249.

solely from the emperor, or from the emperor and the princes but thus much is certain, that it changed its whole character, and from a simply monarchical institution, became dependent on the whole body of the States It followed, of course, that it was no longer an appendage to the court and a companion of the emperor's travels, but held its stated sittings in one fixed spot in the empire

This great concession was met by the States with a grant of the Common Penny, on the produce of which they allowed the king, who seemed intensely desirous of it on account of the state of his affairs in Italy, to raise a loan. The tax itself is a combination of poll-tax and property-tax, not very different from that formerly levied by the kings of Jerusalem, and also occasionally proposed in Germany, for example, in the year 1207, by King Philip In the fifteenth century, frequent mention of such taxes is made as being applied sometimes to the maintenance of the Hussite, sometimes of the Turkish war. The Common Penny was levied on the following plan —Half a gulden was levied on every five hundred, a whole one on every thousand, gulden, among persons of small means, every four-and-twenty above fifteen years of age, without exception, men and women, priests and laymen, were to contribute one gulden, the more wealthy were to pay according to their own estimate of their property The idea of taxation was still in some degree mixed up with that of alms,* the priests were to admonish the people from the pulpit to give something more than what was demanded The whole plan was still extremely imperfect Its importance consisted only in its being (as the whole course of the transaction proved) a serious attempt at a general systematic taxation of the empire, destined for purposes both of peace and war, for the maintenance of the supreme court of justice, the payment of the Italian allies, and the equipment of an army against the Turks.

It was in accordance with this character of a general tax that the choice of the treasurer of the empire, whose office it was to receive the money from the commissioners or collectors stationed in all parts of the country, was also entrusted to the States Maximilian engaged to levy the Common Penny in the Austrian and Burgundian dominions upon the same plan, and to set the example herein to all other sovereigns

But if the collection of the money could not safely be entrusted to the king, still less could its application. After the proposal for a council of the empire had been suffered to drop, the idea of a yearly meeting of the Estates of the empire for the purpose of controlling the public expenditure, first suggested by Nicholas von Kus, and then proposed in the project of 1491, was revived This assembly was to meet every year on the first of February, to deliberate on the most important affairs, internal and external. To this body the treasurer of the empire was to deliver the money he had received from the taxes; and in it was to be vested the exclusive power of deciding on the application of the same neither the king nor his son was to declare war without its consent, every conquest was to accrue to the empire.† To this body was also committed a peremptory authority for the maintenance of the Public Peace. The question was, when this tribunal (thus rendered independent of the crown and emanating from the Estates) should have pronounced the ban, to whom the execution of it was to be entrusted The king of the Romans wished that it should be left to him. The States, true to the principle on which their legislation was founded, committed it to the annual assembly of the empire

It is obvious that the States, though they gave up their original plan, kept constantly in view the idea on which it was founded. In the conflict of the interests of the monarch and those of the States, the balance clearly inclined in favour of the latter Maximilian had cause to complain that he was made to feel this personally; that he had been forced to withdraw, and to wait before the door, till the resolution was passed He was often inclined to dissolve the diet, and it was only the want of a fresh subsidy (which he then obtained) that restrained him ‡ On the 7th of August, he accepted the project in the form last given to it

There is a grand coherency in its provisions All Germans are once more seriously and practically regarded as subjects of the empire, and the public burthens and public exertions were to be common to all If the States thus lost something of their independence, they received in compensation (according to their ancient organization and their respective ranks) a legitimate share in the supreme administration of justice, as well as of the government The king submitted himself to the same ordinances, and to the same community He retained undiminished the supreme dignity, the prerogatives of a sovereign feudal lord, but in the conduct of public business, he was to be regarded only as president of the college of the Estates of the empire The constitution proposed was a mixture of monarchical and federal government, but with an obvious preponderance of the latter element, a political union, preserving the forms of the ancient hierarchy of the empire. The question whether these projects could be carried into execution, was now of the highest importance to the whole future destiny of Germany.

* So the taxes levied by the contemporary King of England, Henry VIII, were called "benevolences"—Transl

† Maintenance of Peace and Law established at Worms Muller Reth Max i p 434

‡ This second grant amounted to 150 000 gulden "Damit S Konigl Grad unserm h Vater Papist und Italien, bis der gemein Pfennig einbracht werde, dester stattlicher Hulfe thun möchte" "In order that his Royal Grace may be so much the more able to give more liberal help to our holy father the pope and Italy, until the common penny be collected" To collect the loan the king despatched emissaries to single states e g Prince Magnus of Anhalt and Dr Heinrich Friese to the following, the Abbot of Fulda, contributing 300 gulden, the two Counts of Hanau, 500, the Count of Eisenberg, 300, the city of Freiberg, 400, and the city of Frankfort, 2,100 Instruction in Comm Archiv at Dessau

Resolutions of so comprehensive a kind can be regarded as views only;—as ideas, to which an assembly has expressed its assent, but to the execution of which there is a long way yet to be traversed. It is the ground-plan of a building which is intended to be built; but the question remains whether the power and the means will correspond with the intention.

DIFFICULTIES.—DIET OF LINDAU, 1496.

A great obstacle to the execution of the resolutions of the diet occurred at once in the defective nature of its composition. A large number of powerful Estates had not been present, and as the obligatory force of the resolutions of an assembly upon those not present was as yet far from being determined, it was necessary to open separate negotiations with the absent. Among others, the Elector of Cologne was commissioned to negotiate with the bishops in his neighbourhood, those of Utrecht, Münster, Osnabrück, Paderborn, and Bremen; the Elector of Saxony with Lüneburg, Grubenhagen, and Denmark; and it was by no means certain what would be their success. Here again we find the possibility that some one might not choose to be included in, or to consent to, the Public Peace, assumed.*

A still more important organic defect was, that the knightly order had taken no part in the diet. It is manifest that the mighty development which a government composed of different estates (*eine ständische Verfassung*) had reached in England, mainly rests on the union of the lower nobility and the cities in the House of Commons. In Germany it was not the ancient usage to summon the nobility to the diet. The consequence of this was, that the nobles refused to conform to the resolutions passed at it, especially when (as in the present case) these related to a tax. The Franconian knights assembled in December at Schweinfurt, and declared that they were free Franconians, nobles of the empire, bound to shed their blood, and in every war to guard the emperor's crown and sceptre at the head of all their youth capable of bearing arms; but not to pay taxes, which was contrary to their liberties, and would be an unheard of innovation. This declaration had the assent of all their compeers. Unions of the same kind were formed in the several circles.†

We observed how much stress was laid at an earlier period on the spiritual authorisation. The consequence of the want of it now was that the abbots of the empire refused to recognise the authority of so purely secular a tribunal as the Imperial Chamber.

There were yet other Estates whose obedience was very doubtful. The Duke of Lorraine declared that, beyond the jurisdiction of his own tribunals, he was amenable to no other authority than that of the king in person. The Swiss confederates did not indeed as yet dispute the sovereignty or the jurisdiction of the empire, but at the first exercise of it they were offended and irritated into resistance. The king of Poland declared that Dantzig and Elbing were Polish cities, and rejected all claims made upon them on the part of the empire. As the first effect of a vigorous medicine is to set the whole frame in agitation, so the attempts to organise the Germanic body had the immediate result of calling into activity the hostile principles hitherto in a state of repose.

But if so strong an element of resistance existed on the side of the States, to whom the resolutions were clearly advantageous, what was to be expected from the king, whose power they controlled, and on whom they had been forced? In contriving the means for their execution, every thing had been calculated on his sympathy and co-operation; whereas he incessantly showed that he set about the task with repugnance.

He certainly organised the Imperial Chamber according to its new forms. It held its first sittings at the Grossbraunfels at Frankfurt-on-Main,‡ on the 3d of November. On the 21st of February it exercised its right of pronouncing the ban for the first time: the judge and his assessors, doctors and nobles, appeared in the open air; the proclamation of the ban, by which the condemned was deprived of the protection of the law,§ and all and every man permitted to attack his body and goods, was publicly read and torn in pieces. Yet the king was far from allowing the court of justice to take its free course. On more than one occasion he commanded it to stop the proceedings in a cause; he would not suffer his fiscal, when judgment was given against him, to pay the usual fine of the defeated party: he sent an assessor from the Netherlands whom his colleague refused to admit, because he had not been regularly appointed; he made no provision for the pay of the assessors as he was bound at first to do: after appointing Count Eitelfriedrick of Zollern, against the will of the States, who preferred another,‖ he very soon removed him, because he wanted him for other business. Nor did he take any measures for collecting the Common Penny in his own dominions, as he had promised. The meeting had been, as we saw, fixed for the 1st of Feb-

* Recess and ordinances in Müller, 459.

† Müller, Rttb. 688, 689.

‡ Excerpta ex Collectaneis Jobi de Rorbach; Harpprecht, ii. 210. In the Frankfurt Imp. Archives, a letter is still extant from Arnold Schwartzenberg to the council of Frankfurt, dated on the Friday after the Feast of the Assumption (Aug. 21): "Item uf Samstag U L F. Abend hat Graf Hug von Wernberg nach mir geschickt, und vorgehalten, das Kammergericht werde gelegt gen Frankfurt, wo man ein Huss dazu bekommen mocht und ein Stuben daneben züm Gesprech." "Also upon the evening of Saturday, the feast of Our Blessed Lady, Count Hugh of Wernberg sent to me and represented, that the Imperial Chamber was transferred to Frankfurt, where it might be possible to get a house, and a room close to it for conferences." The price of meat and fish was to be determined, and the citizens were to be admonished to behave in a seemly and discreet manner ("zimlich glimpflich") towards the members.

§ "Ans dem Frieden in den Unfrieden gesetzt"—literally, put out of the peace into unpeace.—Transl.

‖ To the Prince Magnus of Anhalt, he says in one of his own notes, "Conventus me elegerunt, sed revocavit rex."

ruary, but he did not appear, and consequently it did not take place *

It is a matter of astonishment that the reputation of founder of the constitution of the empire has so long and so universally been given to a sovereign, on whom the measures tending to that object were absolutely forced, and who did far more to obstruct than to promote their execution.

There is no doubt that all attempts at reform would have been utterly defeated, had not the king's designs been counteracted by a prince who had embraced most of the opinions on which it was founded; who had been the chief agent in bringing it thus far, and was not inclined now to let it drop—Berthold, Elector of Mainz, born Count of Henneberg † Even under Frederic III., whose service he entered at an early age, he had taken an active share in all attempts to introduce better order into the affairs of the empire. In 1186, he became Elector of Mainz, and from that time might be regarded as the most eminent member of the States There are men, whose whole existence is merged in their studies or their business there we must seek them if we wish to know them; their purely personal qualities or history attract no attention To this class of men belonged Berthold of Mainz Nobody, so far as I have been able to discover, has thought it worth while to give to posterity a description of his personal appearance or characteristics but we see him distinctly and vividly in the administration of his diocese. At first people feared his severity; for his administration of justice was as inexorable as it was impartial, and his economy was rigorous, but in a short time every body was convinced that his austere demeanour was not the result of temper or of caprice, but of profound necessity it was tempered by genuine benevolence, he lent a ready ear to the complaints of the poorest and the meanest ‡ He was peculiarly active in the affairs of the empire. He was one of the venerable men of that age, who earnestly strove to give to ancient institutions which had lost their original spirit and their connection with higher things, the new form adapted to the necessities of the times. He had already conducted the negociations of 1486; he next procured for the towns the right of sitting in the committees, it was mainly to him that Germany owed the promises made by Maximilian in the year 1489, and the projects of Worms were chiefly his work. In every circumstance he evinced that serene and manly spirit, which, while it keeps its end steadily in view, is not self-willed as to the means or manner of accomplishing it, or pertinacious on merely incidental points; he was wearied or discouraged by no obstacles, and a stranger to any personal views if ever a man bore his country in his inmost heart, it was he.

In the summer of 1496, at the diet of Lindau, this prince acquired a degree of independent power such as he had not enjoyed before

In the midst of the troubles of that summer, Maximilian thought he discerned the favourable moment in which he needed only to show himself in Italy, in order, with the help of his allies there, to re-establish the supremacy of the imperial power He summoned the States to repair to Lindau, whither they were to bring the amount of the Common Penny, together with as many troops as it would suffice to pay, and whence they were immediately to follow him, at the same time declaring that he would not wait for them, but must cross the Alps without delay with what force God had given him

While he put this in execution, and, equipped rather as for some romantic enterprise of knight-errantry than for a serious expedition, rushed on to Italy, the States of the empire gradually assembled in Lindau They brought neither troops, money, nor arms, their attention was directed exclusively to internal affairs How greatly in acting thus, they relied on Elector Berthold, is shown (among other documents) by the instructions to the ambassador of Brandenburg, ordering him implicitly to follow the course pursued by that prince §

On the 31st of August, 1196, the princes, as many as were assembled, embarked in boats and fetched the king's son, Archduke Philip of Bregenz, across the river, on the 7th of September, the first sitting was held The Elector of Mainz took his place in the centre, on his right sat the princes, the archduke, for the first time, amongst them, on his left the ambassadors or delegates of those who did not appear in person, in front of him stood the deputies of the cities In the middle was a bench for the king's councillors, Conrad Sturzel and Walter von Andlo

The Elector conducted the proceedings with unquestioned authority If he absented himself, which was never but for a short time, they were stopped, when he returned, he was the chief speaker, whether in the assembly or the committee, he brought forward the propositions, demanded the grants, and found means to keep the plenipotentiaries steady to them He did not conceal the grief he felt at seeing the empire in such a state of decline. "Even in the time of Charles IV and Sigismund," exclaimed he, "the sovereignty of the empire was acknowledged in Italy, which is now no longer the case The king of Bohemia is an elector of the empire, and what does

* In the Frankfurt Archives, we meet with several letters from Jülich, Cölln, Mainz, &c, bespeaking a lodging, but also a letter dated from Frankfurt itself on the Saturday after Invocavit, to the effect that no one had as yet appeared

† Of the Romhilde line, born in 1442 Diplomatische Geschichte des Hauses Henneberg, p 377

‡ Serarius, Res Moguntinæ, p 799

§ In the Berlin Archives there is a Convolute concerning this Diet of the Empire, which, along with the Instruction, contains 1st, the letters received up to the time of the arrival of the deputies, and the propositions made by the foreign deputies 2d, the protocol of the proceedings on the Friday after the feast of St Dionysius Oct 14 What is especially remarkable in this protocol, is, that the most distinguished of the plenipotentiaries, Erasmus Brandenburg, parish priest of Cotbus was a member of the committee, and is the reporter of its transactions. The greater part is in his handwriting

he do for the empire? has he not even wrested Moravia and Silesia from it? Prussia and Livonia are liable to incessant attacks and oppression, and no one troubles himself about them, nay, even the little which remains to the empire is daily wrested from it, and given to one or the other. The ordinances of Worms were made to preserve the empire from decay, but the union and mutual confidence which alone could sustain it are wanting. Whence comes it that the confederation enjoys such universal respect? that it is feared by Italians and French, by the pope, nay, by every body? The only reason is, that it is united and of one mind. Germany ought to follow the example. The ordinances of Worms should be revived, not to prate about, but to execute them."*

Berthold's was that powerful eloquence which is the expression of convictions founded on actual experience. The committee resolved to look into the matter, and to see that the empire was better ordered. On the motion of the Brandenburg ambassador, the members examined their credentials, and found that they were sufficient for that purpose. Such being the dispositions of the States, affairs now took a decisive turn.

The Imperial Chamber, which had closed its sittings in June, was induced to open them again in November. It was determined to appropriate the tax which was to be levied on the Jews in Regensburg, Nurnberg, Worms, and Frankfurt, to the payment of the assessors. The Elector insisted that the sentences of the court should be executed, that no sovereign should recal his assesser, and that the cities should have justice against the princes. It was resolved to transfer the chamber to Worms: the reason assigned for which was, that it was easier from thence to reach the four universities of Heidelberg, Basle, Mainz, and Cologne, whenever it was necessary "to ask the law."

On the 23d of December, the edict for levying the Common Penny was renewed in the most stringent form. The knights (Ritterschaft) who complained of the demand made upon them by the king, were reminded that it was not the king who imposed this tax, but the empire, that it was the most equal and the least oppressive that could be devised, and would be of advantage to their Order, if they would only get to horse and endeavour to earn the pay for which this fund was in part raised.

Another meeting of the States was appointed to consider of the disbursement of the Common Penny.

Other points were discussed;—the necessity of instant and effective succours for the attack, new regulations of the courts of justice and of the mint, above all, the firmest determination was expressed to maintain unaltered the measures passed at Worms. Should any attempt be made to thwart or oppose them or those of the diet of Lindau, the matter was to be referred to the Archbishop of Mainz, who should be authorised thereupon to convoke other members, in order that an answer from the whole body of the States might be given, and public order and tranquillity be defended by them in concert.†

All these resolutions the Archbishop carried without much difficulty. If there was occasionally some attempt at opposition on the part of the envoys of the princes, those of the electors and of the cities always supported him and compelled the former to give way. They were, therefore, incorporated in the Recess, the usual practice as to which was, that each member should first write out for himself the resolutions which had been passed: these were then compared in the assembly, a fixed formula was determined on, and signed by the whole body.

On the 10th of February 1497, the diet of Lindau was closed. The States thanked the Archbishop for the trouble he had taken, and entreated his pardon for their negligences. The Elector, on the other hand, excused himself for having, perhaps, sometimes addressed them with too great earnestness, and exhorted them faithfully to enforce the resolutions that had been passed, each in his own territory or sphere, that so the empire might be profited.

DIET OF WORMS AND FREIBURG, 1497, 1498.

The matter was, however, but half settled; the difficulties which had arisen among the States had been removed, but as yet no influence had been obtained over the king, whose co-operation and executive power were indispensable.

Maximilian's romantic enterprise had ended as was to be expected: the same excitable fancy which had flattered him with exaggerated hopes, had prevented him from perceiving the true state of affairs. After a short time the allies, whose assistance was all he had to rely on, had quarrelled among themselves; he had returned to Germany filled with shame, disgust and vexation. Here he found the finances of his hereditary domains exhausted and in the utmost disorder, the empire in an attitude of defiance and sullen reserve, and disastrous tidings following each other in quick succession. When Louis XII. ascended the throne in 1498, Maximilian hoped that troubles would arise in France, and that his allies would support him in a fresh attack upon that power. The very contrary took place: Louis, by pacific and prudent measures, won from his subjects a degree of consideration such as no king had ever before possessed, the Italian league endeavoured to bring about an accommodation with him: but the most unexpected thing was, that Maximilian's own son, Archduke Philip, instigated by his Netherland councillors, with-

* These words were spoken by the Elector on the 28th Nov. A similar effusion is cited in Scherer's extract, and in Fels Erster Beitrag zur Reichsgesch. Preface, § 7. In these contributions is to be found the protocol of Lindau, contained in the Frankf. A. A. vol. xvi.

† In order to avoid the appearance of a conspiracy, it had been previously resolved, 'Die Handhabung, zu Worms versigelt vorzunehmen und aus derselben ain Grund und Einung und Verstendniss zu nehmen und, was des zu wenig seyn will zu erweitern." "To take the declaration sealed at Worms, and from it to construct a groundwork, union, and agreement, and in those respects where it may come short, to enlarge it."—*Brandenburg Protocol.*

out consulting his father entered into a treaty with France, in which he promised not to agitate any of his claims on Burgundy so long as Louis XII. lived, and never to attempt to enforce them by arms, or otherwise than by amicable and legal means. The only consideration in return for this vast concession was the surrender of a few strong places. Maximilian learned this when he had already begun his preparations for war; in June 1498, in a state of the most violent irritation, he summoned the assembly of the empire which he could no longer do without.

The assembly had opened its sittings, as had been determined, in Worms,* but had transferred them at the king's request to Freiburg. Although, in consequence of the proceedings at Lindau, affairs were in a much better state than before,—the Common Penny began to be really collected, the Imperial Chamber at Worms held its regular sittings for the administration of justice, and the diet itself exercised an uncontested jurisdiction as between the several Estates, in the more weighty and difficult cases; yet it was daily felt that so long as the king remained in the equivocal and half hostile attitude he had assumed, nothing permanent would be accomplished. Before the very eyes of the assembled States, Elector John of Treves, with the help of his secular neighbours, Baden, the Palatinate, Hessen and Juliers, invaded the town of Boppard, and forced it to submit and to do homage to him. The Swiss resisted a sentence of the Imperial Chamber against St Gall, held the most insolent language, and were very near issuing formal diffidations. The States pointed out to the king, in remonstrances incessantly reiterated, that, without his presence, neither the Public Peace could be maintained, nor the law executed, nor the taxes duly collected.

At length, on the 8th June, 1498, he arrived in Freiburg, but neither with the views, nor in the temper, that his subjects wished. His soul was galled by the failure of all his plans,—deeply wounded by the defection of the Netherlands, and ardently excited by the thought of a war with France, the more, I think, from a feeling of the difficulty, nay, impracticability of it. At the very first audience (28th June) he vented all this storm of passion upon the princes. He said that he did not come to ask their advice, for he was resolved to make war upon France, and he knew that they would dissuade him; he only wished to hear whether they would support him as they were bound to do, and as they had promised at Worms. It was possible that he might accomplish nothing decisive; but, at any rate, he would give the king of France a slap in the face (Backenstreich) such as should be remembered for a hundred years. "I am betrayed by the Lombards," said he, "I am abandoned by the Germans; but I will not allow myself again to be bound hand and foot and hung upon a nail, as I did at Worms. War I must make, and I will make, let people say what they may. Rather than give it up, I would get a dispensation from the oath that I swore behind the altar at Frankfurt, for I have duties not only to the empire, but to the House of Austria. I say this, and I must say it, though I should be forced on that account to lay the crown at my feet and trample on it."

The princes listened to him with amazement. "Your Majesty," replied the Elector of Mainz, "is pleased to speak to us in parables, as Christ did to his disciples!" They begged him to bring his proposals before the assembly, which would then proceed to deliberate upon them.† Strange meeting of this monarch with this assembly! Maximilian lived in the interests of his House, in the contemplation of the great political relations of Europe, in the feeling that he was the bearer of the highest dignity of Christendom, which was now in jeopardy; he was ambitious, warlike, and needy. The States, on the other hand had their attention fixed on internal affairs; what they desired above all things was a government of order and law; they were cautious, pacific, frugal; they wanted to check and control the king; he to excite and hurry on the States.

Nothing less than the singular prudence, moderation, and sense which distinguished the Archbishop of Mainz were necessary to prevent a total breach between them.

He conciliated the king by placing before his eyes the prospect of the revenue likely to accrue from the Common Penny. He prevailed on the assembly to offer the king immediate payment of the sum formerly proposed at Worms, on the understanding that Maximilian should himself contribute to the fuller and more exact collection of the tax by his own example and assistance. This brought on a more distinct explanation. Every individual was called upon to state how much of the Common Penny he had collected. A slight review of these statements will give us an insight into the situation of the German princes of that day.

Elector Berthold of Mainz has collected and paid in the tax, but some persons in his dominions had resisted. To these he has announced that they subjected themselves to the ban of the empire, from which he would not protect them.—Cologne and Treves have received only a part of their share of the tax; they have met with not less refractory subjects, who excused themselves with the delays of the Netherlands.—The Electors of Brandenburg and of Saxony have collected the greater

* Transactions of the States of the Holy Empire at the Royal Diet at Worms, Fr. A. vol. xvii. We see by them, amongst other things, as a matter of complete certainty, that Maximilian did not appear at Worms. As Haberlin (Reichsgeschichte, ix. 84), however, assumes that he did, he must have been deceived by certain documents which were only laid before the Imperial Diet in the King's name. 'At Freiburg, July 3d, the Tuesday after the Visitation of the Holy Virgin, Maximilian made excuses for not having appeared at Worms: "he had been obliged to establish an excellent government (Regiment) in his hereditary states," &c.; "it had been commented on as folly in him," &c., "but now he was present." (Brand. Protocol.)

† The Brandenburg protocol, our chief source of information regarding the Diet of Freiburg, adds, the king spoke "with many marvellous words and gestures, so as to be completely obscure and incomprehensible."

part of the tax, and are ready to pay it in; but there are certain lords in Saxony of whom the Elector says, he can do nothing with them, he does not answer for them.*—The ambassador of the Elector Palatine, on the other hand, has not even instructions to give any distinct explanation, George of Landshut, too, gave only an evasive answer Albert of Bavaria expressed himself better disposed, but he complained of the great number of recalcitrants he met with Nor was this to be regarded as a pretext the Bavarian states had, in fact, made great difficulties,—they had enough to do with the wants of their own country, they thought it strange that the empire, also, should make claims upon them † The resistance in Franconia was not less vehement, the Margraves of Brandenburg were forced in some cases to resort to distraint —The cities, already prepared for contributions of this kind, had a much easier task Only three out of the whole number were still in arrear—Cologne, Muhlhausen, and Nordhausen, the others had paid in their whole contingent

Although the matter was, as we see, far from being perfectly accomplished, it was put into a good train, and Maximilian was highly satisfied with the result. He now condescended to give a report of what his own hereditary dominions had raised. From Austria, Styria, and Tyrol he had collected 27,000 gulden, in the Netherlands, on the contrary, great resistance had been made. "Some," says the king's report, "those of the Welsch (i e foreign, not German) sort, said they were not under the empire Those who hold to the German nation, on the other hand, declared that they would wait and see what their neighbours on the Rhine did."

Unfortunately it is impossible, from the reports before us, to arrive at any statistical results. The payments were too unequal, and the accounts are generally wanting

It was, however, for the moment a great point gained, that the States could either pay the king the money he required immediately, or at least promised it with certainty. He was thus induced, on his side, to devote his attention and interest to the affairs of the empire

The Public Peace was guarded with fresh severe clauses, especially against the abettors of the breakers of it The president of the Imperial Chamber was empowered, in peculiarly weighty and dangerous cases, to call together princes of the empire at his own discretion, and to require their help. A former proposition of the Imperial Chamber, viz to confer the right of representation on the heir, was at length carried, in spite of the objection that a third part of the nation held to the rules of the Sachsenspiegel (Mirror of Saxony), which were at direct variance with that right ‡ A regular criminal procedure was taken into consideration, chiefly on account of the frequent illegal infliction of the punishment of death. In order to put a stop to the confusion in the currency, it was resolved to coin all gulden of the size and form of the gulden of the Rhenish electors. In short, this diet of Frieburg, which opened so stormily, gradually despatched more business of various kinds than any that had yet met.

The question now remained what view the States would take of European affairs. The French had made the proposal that Genoa and Naples should be ceded to them, in which case they would not disturb Milan, and would conclude a permanent peace on all other points;—a proposal which, if sincere, had much to recommend it, and was especially agreeable to the German princes They urged that Genoa was little to be depended upon in any case, and was seeking a new master every day; and what had the empire to do with Naples and Sicily? It would, in fact, be far more advantageous to them to have a powerful prince there, who could hold the Turks in check. The sovereignty of Italy was a matter of indifference to them, they declared themselves generally opposed to all alliances with the Welsch (non-Germans) Such, however, was not the opinion of the electors, and least of all, the ecclesiastical. They reminded their opponents that Genoa had been called by Frederic I. a chamber of the empire; that Naples was a fief of the papal see, and must therefore be held by the King of the Romans, the steward of the church. But above all, that they must not suffer the King of France to become too powerful, lest he should attempt to get possession of the empire They would not abate a single iota of the idea of the Germanic empire, with which indeed their own importance was indissolubly associated These sentiments, which rendered them at once partisans of the king, were at length triumphant the negotiations which Frederic of Saxony had set on foot with Louis XII fell to the ground at the moment when the States had placed the institutions of the empire on something like a firm footing, they were forced into a war.

Two great conflicting tendencies had been at work from the beginning of this reign; that of the king, to hurry the nation into warlike enterprises, and that of the States, to establish its internal tranquillity They now seemed resolved on concession, union, and concert. The king had confirmed and established the proceedings of Worms, which were disagreeable to him, and the States acceded to his desire to defend the majesty of the empire by arms.

EVENTS OF THE WAR.

It remained however to be asked, whether either party had distinctly conceived, or ma-

* In the Instruction of the Elector of Brandenburg it was further said, "Scarcely half of the Common Penny had been got in, on account of the great mortality His electoral Grace would either deliver up what had been hitherto received, separately, or would be responsible for the whole together"

† Freiberg, Gesch der Baier Landst i 568, 603

‡ A very important protocol, which serves to complete the others, in Harpprecht, ii p 341 In the Berlin Archives, we find the document, which Muller, ii 442, gives under the title "An Explanation of the Imperial Chamber," with some additions, however, e g "with respect to the article concerning the succession of daughters and grandchildren, this article has been deferred till the arrival of the king's majesty" The presence of the king himself was needful to bring the affair to a conclusion

turely weighed, with what they were about to undertake.

There may be governments to which war is a source of strength; but it can never be so to those which have a strong federative element, yet in which the danger attendant on failure is not common to the whole body. For Germany, nothing was more necessary than peace, in order that institutions yet in their infancy might be allowed tranquil growth, and identify themselves with the habits of the people, and the scarcely recognised principle of obedience have time to take root. The collection and expenditure of the Common Penny needed above all to become habitual. But the diet at which these measures had been concluded was hardly closed when the nation rushed forth to war.

Nor was this all. The power they were about to attack was the earliest and the most completely consolidated of any in Europe, a new sovereign, who had long enjoyed universal consideration, had assumed the reins of government and commanded the entire and cordial obedience of his subjects. Such was the monarch, and such the kingdom, which Maximilian, in daring reliance on the assistance of the empire, now proceeded in person to attack. After having regained for his troops the advantages they had lost in Upper Burgundy,* he fell upon Champagne with a considerable army. A truce was now offered by the enemy, which he declined.

I do not doubt that the leading princes saw the danger of the course Maximilian was taking; but they could not prevent it. The agreement they had come to at Freiburg was obtained solely by the consent of the States to assist him in his campaign —they must let him try his fortune.

The great superiority of the political position which Louis XII. had contrived to acquire, now manifested itself. He had gained over the old allies of Maximilian in Spain, Italy, and even the Netherlands. Milan and Naples, which he had resolved to attack, had no other allies than the King of the Romans himself.

But even in Germany itself, Louis found means to excite enmities sufficient to furnish Maximilian with occupation. The Palatinate had always maintained a good understanding with France, active negotiations were set on foot with Switzerland and the Grisons. Duke Charles of Gueldres, (of the house of Egmont, deposed by Charles the Bold, but which had never renounced its claims,) was the first to take up arms.

Maximilian was driven out of Champagne by incessant rain and the overflow of the rivers. He turned his arms upon Gueldres, and, with the assistance of Juliers and Cleves, gained some advantages, but they were not decisive: the country adhered faithfully to Duke Charles, who had secured its attachment by granting it new privileges. Hence it happened, that Maximilian could not attend the assembly of the empire fixed to be held on the eve of St. Catherine (November 21st) at Worms, indispensable as that was to the completion and execution of the ordinances agreed on this meeting, where, if he had been present, resolutions of the utmost practical importance would probably have been passed, broke up without doing any thing.† But, besides this, the troubles in Switzerland now broke out in the form of regular war. The empire was as yet far from renouncing its sovereignty over the confederated cantons: it had cited them before the imperial chambers, nor had any objection been taken to the legality of such a proceeding, the Common Penny had been levied in them, so lately as at the diet of Freiburg, the resolution was passed "to keep the powerful cities of the Confederation which bear the imperial eagle in their arms, in their duty and allegiance to the empire, and to invite them again to attend the meetings of the States. But these invitations could have no effect in a country where the want of internal peace was not felt, because they had secured it for themselves and were already in possession of a tolerably well-ordered government. A party which had always been hostile to the King of the Romans, and which found it more expedient to earn French money than to adhere to the empire, gained the upper hand. In this state of things, the Grisons, who were threatened by Tyrol on account of the part they had taken injurious to the peace of the empire, by sheltering persons under the king's ban, found immediate assistance from the confederates. In one moment the whole frontier, Tyrol and Grisons, Swabia and Switzerland, stood in hostile array.

Strange that the measures taken to introduce order into the empire should have had results so directly contrary to the views with which they were undertaken! The demands of the diet and of the imperial chamber set the Swiss Confederation in a ferment, the summoning of the Grisons to deliver up a fugitive under ban occasioned their defection. If, on the other side, the city of Constance, after long hesitation, joined the Swabian league, this act was regarded with the utmost disgust by the Swiss, because the city possessed the jurisdiction over the Thurgau, a district of which it had obtained possession some years before. Independently of this, there existed, ever since the formation of the league, a hatred between Swabia and Switzerland which had long vented itself in mutual insults and now broke out in a wild war of devastation.

The constitution of the empire was far from being strong enough—its unity was far from having sunk deeply enough into the mind and consciousness of the people—to allow it to put forward its full strength in the conflict with France: the States convened, or rather huddled together in the utmost hurry at Mainz, passed partial and infirm resolutions; it was, in fact,

* The Fugger MS relates at length that the Germans had kept the advantage in a skirmish, Sept 22, 1498 and had re conquered castles they had previously lost. It is incredible that Maximilian, as Zurita asserts, should have had 25,000 infantry, and 5000 horse in the field.

† Letter from Maximilian to Bishop Henry of Bamberg. Harpprecht ii 399. The king invited the assembly to meet at Cologne where however, many of the members did not appear, as their instructions only spoke of Worms.

only the members of the Swabian league who supported the king, and even these were not inclined to risk their lives in a battle with sturdy peasants

Under these circumstances the empire was in no condition to make a successful resistance to those designs of King Louis upon Italy which Maximilian had vainly desired to prevent Whilst the Upper Rhine was torn by private wars, the French crossed the Alps and took Milan without difficulty Maximilian was compelled to make a very disadvantageous peace with the Swiss, by which not only the jurisdiction of the Thurgau was lost, but their general independence was fixed on an immovable basis

A successful war would have strengthened the constitution of the empire the inevitable effect of these reverses was to overthrow, or, at the least, to modify it

DIET OF AUGSBURG, AND ITS CONSEQUENCES.

The immediate result of this assembly was that the authority of the king was even more limited than before, the principle of representative government (ständische Princip) gained another victory, by which it appeared to have secured a fresh and lasting ascendancy *

At the diet which was opened at Augsburg on the 10th of April, 1500, it was agreed that the means which had been hitherto adopted for the establishment of a military organisation and a more regular government were insufficient The prospect of collecting the Common Penny was too remote, events succeeded each other too rapidly to allow of the possibility of the States constantly assembling first for the purpose of guiding or controlling them Adhering to the idea which had got possession of their minds, they now resolved to try other means to the same end They proposed to collect the forces they wanted by a sort of levy. Every four hundred inhabitants, assembling according to their parishes, were to furnish and equip one foot soldier,— a method which had been tried some time before in France · the cavalry proportioned to this infantry was to be raised by the princes, counts, and lords, according to a certain scale. A tax was to be laid on those who could not take an active share in the war,— clergy, Jews, and servants, and the amount was to form a fund for the war, propositions which, as it will be seen, are immediately connected with the former ones, and which assume an equally complete and comprehensive unity of the empire Maximilian embraced them with joy; he made his calculations, and gave the Spanish ambassador to understand that he would shortly have 30,000 men in the field On the other hand, he adopted a plan which he had rejected five years before, and which must have been odious to a man of his character, he now acknowledged the necessity of having a permanent imperial council, which might relieve him and the States from incessant recurrence to the diets, and to whose vigilance and energy the execution of the ordinances when issued might be entrusted † A committee was formed for a fresh discussion of this institution, and its suggestions were then submitted to the general assembly of the States Every member had the right of proposing amendments in writing.

The business was treated with all the gravity it deserved. There were two points to be considered, the composition, and the rights and functions, of the proposed council. In the first place, a position suited to their high rank, and to the influence they had hitherto possessed in the country, was assigned to the electors. Each of them was to send a delegate to the council; one of them, according to regular rotation, to be always present The much more numerous college of princes was less favourably treated The intention had at first been to let the spiritual side be represented according to the archbishoprics, the temporal, according to the so-called countries, Swabia, Franconia, Bavaria, and the Netherlands,‡ but these divisions neither corresponded with the idea of a compact and united empire, nor with the existing state of things, and the assembly now preferred to include spiritual and temporal princes together within certain circles or districts. Six of these were marked out, and were at first called provinces of the German nation, Franconia, Bavaria, Swabia, Upper Rhine, Westphalia, and Lower Saxony; they were, however, not as yet called by these names, but were distinguished according to the several states which inhabited them §. The interests whose disseverance would, in any case, have been absurd and purposeless were thus more closely united. Counts and prelates and cities were all included within these circles It was also determined that one temporal prince, one count and one prelate should always have a seat in the council Austria and the Netherlands were to send two delegates Little notice had at first been taken of the cities, nor, indeed, in spite of the original intention, had they at a later period been admitted to a place in the imperial chamber, but they thought this extremely injurious to them, and the more unjust since the

* *Ständsche Princip* is not literally "representative principle," or rather, it is that and something more *Ständisch*, the adjective of Stand, (status, class, order,) as applied to government, signifies representation of the several states or orders of the nation The English and the Swedish constitutions are *ständisch*, the American, though representative, is not *ständisch* at all, since there are no *Stände* to represent I may here point out another difficulty arising out of the double and often equivocal use of the word state, which represents both *Staat* and *Stand*—two words of totally different meaning *Staat*, the state, is the whole civil and political body of the nation, *Stand* (status) is a class or order of the nation The United States of America are *Staaten*, the States of the Empire were *Stände* —Transl

† Protocol of the Imperial Diet of Augsburg in the Frankfurt Archives, vol xix, unfortunately not so circumstantial as might be wished, *e g* the objections which the cities had made, contained in three bills or advertisements, are not inserted, "as every city deputy knew them"

‡ These are Salzburg, Magdeburg, Bremen, and Besançon, the electorates were of course excluded, the Netherlands on the Maass were instead of Saxony Datt, de Pace Publica, p 603

§ Order of the Regency (Regiment) established at Augsburg, in the collections of the Recesses of the Imperial Diets

burthen of raising the funds for the expenses of the States must fall mainly upon them, and at length they succeeded in obtaining the right of sending two members to the imperial council. The cities which were to enjoy this privilege in turn were immediately named Cologne and Strasburg for the circle of the Rhine, Augsburg and Ulm for the Swabian, Nurnberg and Frankfurt for the Franconian; Lubeck and Gosslar for the Saxon the delegates were always to be sent by two of these districts.* A curious illustration of the old and fundamental principle of the Germanic empire,—that every right should be attached as soon as created, in a certain form, to a certain place; so that the general right wears the air of a special privilege.

Thus the three colleges of which the diet consisted were also the component parts of the imperial council, which may, indeed, be regarded as a permanent committee of the States The king had no other right there than to preside in person, or to send a representative (*Statthalter*) The preponderance was doubtless on the side of the States, and especially in the hands of the electors, who were now so firmly united and so strongly represented.

This council, the character of which was so decidedly that of class representation (*standisch*), was immediately invested with the most important powers Every thing that regarded the administration of justice and the maintenance of public tranquillity, every thing relating to the measures of defence to be taken against the infidels and other enemies, foreign as well as internal affairs, lay within its domain; it had power " to originate, to discuss, to determine." It is evident that the essential business of the government was transferred to it, and indeed it assumed the title of the government or regency of the empire† (Reichsregiment) ‡

It seemed now as if not only the judicial but the legislative and administrative parts of the government must assume a thoroughly representative *standisch* character

If Maximilian suffered himself to be persuaded to make such large concessions in Augsburg, it was, doubtless, only because the preparations for war depended on them, because he hoped by this means to obtain from the States a durable, voluntary, cordial and effective support in his foreign enterprises. On the 14th of August, after every thing was concluded, he urged the States to take example from him, and to do something for the empire, as he had done He worked himself up, as it were intentionally, to the expectation that this would take place, he wished to believe it; but his hopes alternated with secret fears that, after all, it would not take place, and that he should have surrendered his rights in vain. He betrayed the greatest agitation of mind, a feeling of impending danger and of present wrong, as he himself expressed it Whilst he reminded the assembly of the oaths and vows by which each of them was bound to the holy empire, he added that unless more and better was done than before, he would not wait till the crown was torn from his head, he would rather himself cast it down at his feet §

Very little time elapsed before he got into various disputes with the States He was obliged to consent to publish an edict against the disobedient, the penalties attached to which were of a less severe nature than he deemed necessary

A Captain-general of the empire, Duke Albert of Bavaria, was appointed, with whom Maximilian speedily felt that he could never agree

The armament of the succours agreed upon did not proceed, in spite of the new council of the empire, which assembled in the year 1500. In April, 1501, the lists of the population of the several parishes, which were the necessary basis of the whole levy, were not yet sent in.

Lastly, the imperial council assumed an attitude utterly disagreeable to the king. Negotiations were set on foot. and a truce concluded, with Louis XII of France, whom Maximilian had thought to crush with the weight of the empire The council was not averse to grant the king of France Milan as a fief of the empire, at his request ‖

At this the whole storm of anger and disgust which Maximilian had so long with difficulty restrained burst forth He saw himself thralled and fettered as to internal affairs, and as to external, not supported His provincial Estates in Tyrol remarked to him how insignificant he was become in the empire.

He appeared for a moment at the Council of Regency in Nurnberg, but only to complain of the indignities offered him,** and of the in-

* Chiefly from the letter of Johann Reysse to the City of Frankfurt, Aug 17 1500 "So die Fursten kai en von Stetten zu Reichsradt verordnet hatten, so haben die Stette bedacht" &c "As the princes had appointed none of the cities to the council of the empire, the cities had therefore bethought themselves," &c He further remarks that the princes immediately caused three candidates to be proposed to them from each city, out of whom they chose one

† That this was regarded as a sort of abdication is shown by the expression of the Venetian ambassador Relatione di S Zaccaria Contarini venuto orator del re di Romani 1502 in Sanuto's Chronicle, Vienna Archives, vol iv "Fo terminato et fo opinion del re rinontiar il suo poter in 16, nominati il senato imperial quali fossero quelli avesse (i quali avessero) a chiamar le diete e tuor le impresse"

‡ The translation commonly in use for Reichsregiment (council of regency) does not convey any definite or correct idea to the mind of the reader nor does any better suggest itself *Das Regiment*, is as nearly as possible, *the government*, according to the common and inaccurate use of the word, but that is far too vague and general What its powers and functions were we see in the text Eichhorn (vol iii p 127) says "This institution was agreeable neither to the emperor nor to the States For the former it was too independent, and for the latter too active and hence it remained only two years assembled" —Transl

§ Letter from Reysse, Aug 17

‖ Muller Reichstagsstaat, p 63

** In this Maximilian was not entirely wrong It is not to be believed to what lengths the French Ambassador went He said without reserve that the reason why Maximilian took the part of Naples so warmly was that he had been paid 10 000 ducats, though the negotiator of the affair had pocketed one half of the sum and the remainder only had come into the hands of the emperor He said the King of France had no thought of injuring the empire But if they made war on him, then the king would find his way into the enemies' quarters as readily as they into his —And yet to this ambassador the council of the empire gave a testimonial, to the effect

creasing disorders of the empire. He remained but a few days.

It had been determined that the Council of Regency should be empowered to summon an assembly of the States in cases of urgency. The state of things now appeared to that body highly urgent, and it did not delay to use the right conferred upon it. The king did every thing he could to thwart it.

Another ordinance bound the king not to grant the great fiefs without consulting the electors. As if to punish the States for their negotiations with Louis XII., he now granted, of his own sole authority, the fief of Milan to this his old enemy.*

But if the king had not power enough to enforce order in the empire, he had enough to trouble that which was as yet but imperfectly established. In the beginning of the year 1502, every thing that had been begun in Augsburg had fallen into a state of utter dissolution. The Council of Regency and the assessors of the imperial chamber, who neither received their salaries nor were allowed to exercise their functions, dispersed and went home. To the king, this was rather agreeable than otherwise. He erected a court of justice exactly similar to that of his father, with assessors arbitrarily appointed, over which he presided himself. It is evident from one of his proclamations that he meditated establishing in like manner a government (Regiment) nominated solely by himself, and, by its means, carrying into execution the plan of a military organisation determined on in Augsburg.

This conduct necessarily excited a universal ferment. A Venetian ambassador, Zaccharia Contarini, who was in Germany in the year 1502, was astonished at the great unpopularity of the king,—how ill people spoke of him, how little they respected or cared for him. Maximilian himself said, "He would he were Duke of Austria, then people would think something of him, as King of the Romans he received nothing but indignities." †

Once more did the electors resolve jointly and resolutely to oppose his will. On the 30th of June, 1502, at a solemn congress at Gelnhausen, they bound themselves to hold together in all important affairs, to act as one man at the imperial diets, and always to defend the wishes of the majority; to allow of no oppressive mandates, no innovations, no diminution of the empire, and, lastly, to meet four times every year, for the purpose of deliberating on the public affairs and interests. It does not distinctly appear whether they really, as was reported, came to the resolution to dethrone the king, but what they did was in fact the same thing. Without consulting him, they announced a meeting of the empire on the 1st of the November following; every member communicated to the one seated next him the topics on which they were to deliberate. They were the same which had formed the subject of all former deliberations of the Germanic body: the Turkish war, the relations with the pope, the public expenditure, but, above all, the establishment of law, tranquillity and order, with a view to the maintenance of which, some new ordinances were presently inserted, to come into force after the Imperial Chamber and Council of Regency should cease to exist.‡

The Elector Palatine, who had rather opposed the former measures of the diet, now that it had come to a breach with the king, distinguished himself by his active and zealous co-operation.

Maximilian was in the greatest perplexity. While he complained that attacks were made on the sovereignty which was his of right as crowned king of the Romans,—while he sought to take credit for having of his own accord established the Council of Regency and the Chamber,§ he did not feel himself strong enough to forbid the proposed assembly of the empire; he therefore took the course of proclaiming it himself, announcing that he would be present at it, and would take counsel with the princes and electors on an expedition against the Turks, the necessity for which daily became more urgent. This was, in truth, not very unlike the conduct of King Rupert, or the manner in which, at a later period, the kings of France put themselves at the head of factions which they could not subdue.

But the electoral princes of Germany would not even make this concession. Some had already arrived at Gelnhausen for the proposed diet, among them a papal legate, and many others had bespoken dwellings, when a proclamation of the Elector Palatine of the 18th October was circulated, putting off the diet.‖

To compensate for this they held an extraordinary meeting in Wurzburg, at which they renewed their opposition, and announced a general assembly of the empire for the next Whitsuntide.

Maximilian, who was about to set out on a journey to the Netherlands, issued a proclamation, in which he invited the States to repair to his court, and to consult with him concerning the Turkish war and Council of Regency.**

that if he had not accomplished the king's object the fault lay not in him but in circumstances. Recreditive, May 23, 1501, Muller, p. 110.

* Contarini alleges the following very peculiar motive—"Lo episcopo di Magonza voleva per il sigillo 80m due onde paise al re di Romani d'accordarsi et aver lui questi danari."

† Relatione l. c. of 1502. "Il re è assa odiato, a poca obedientia in li tre stadi. questi senatori electi è venuti inimici del re, adeo il re dice mal di loro e loro del re. Il re a ditto più volte vorria esser duca d'Austria, perche saria stimato duca, che imperator è vituperato."

‡ I found them in the Archives of Berlin and Dresden; to the Duke of Saxony they had sent the united electors of Brandenburg and Saxony. Muller has but a very unsatisfactory notice of the subject.

§ Letter from Schwabischwerd, Nov. 2. Frankf. R. A., tom. xx.

‖ Hirsburg, near Frankfurt, Oct. 20. (Thursday after Galli.) Gelnhausen sent to Frankfurt the letter of the elector Berthold, which arrived on the 19th, wherein the latter also declared "the diet appointed at Gelnhausen was delayed from special causes, and removed to another place."

** Antorf, April 7. Fr. A. "Des Reichsregiments wegen der Personen so daran geordnet seyen wir dann nit so pald erlangen haben mugen und dadurch wiederum in Anstand kommen ist."—"As to the Council of Regency, on account of the persons fitted for it, we have not been able to create it so quickly, and accordingly it is again delayed."

Of the meeting summoned by the king there exists not a trace, that appointed by the electors, however, certainly took place in June 1503, at Mainz, though we are unable to discover whether it was numerously attended Maximilian's measures were here opposed, on the ground that they were injurious to the empire As there was nothing to be feared from his Council of Regency (since he was obliged to confess that he had been unable to find fitting members), the meeting contented itself with attacking his tribunal. They declared to him that no prince of the empire would consent to submit to its decisions They reminded him of the ordinances passed at Worms and Augsburg, and urged him to adhere to them.

Such was the result of the attempts made in the year 1503 to constitute the Germanic body

The authority of the empire was restored neither in Italy, nor in the Swiss Confederation, nor on the eastern frontier, where the Teutonic knights were incessantly pressed upon by the Poles and Russians At home, the old disorders had broken out anew Not only had the attempt to establish a firm and durable constitution for war and peace utterly failed, but there was no longer any tribunal of universally recognised authority.

The highest powers in the nation, the king and his electors, had fallen into irreconcilable discord In Elector Berthold, especially, Maximilian beheld a dangerous and determined foe. It had already been reported to him from Augsburg that Mainz had spoken contemptuously of him to the other princes, and obsequious people had given him a list of not less than twenty-two charges which the Elector brought against him. Maximilian had stifled his anger, and had said nothing; but the impression now made upon him by every opposition he encountered, by every consequence of the Augsburg constitution that he had not anticipated, was the more profound, he ascribed everything to the crafty schemes of the sagacious old man. A hostile and bitter correspondence took place between the king and the arch-chancellor.* Maximilian retorted upon his adversary a list of charges, twenty-three in number, — one more than those brought against himself by Mainz, which he still kept concealed, but with whose contents he only fed his resentment the more constantly in secret.†

A state of things most perilous to himself.

The other Electors adhered firmly to Berthold, who, in the midst of all these troubles, had formed a fresh and strict alliance with the Palatinate The cities clung to him as closely as ever. There was a general feeling through the nation that the fate of Wenceslas was impending over Maximilian;—that he would be deposed. It is said that the Elector Palatine had formally proposed this measure in the electoral council; that shortly after, the king arrived one day unexpectedly at a castle belonging to that prince where his wife was residing, and that during their morning's repast, he gave her to understand that he was perfectly acquainted with her husband's designs Such, however, was the grace and charm of his manner and the imposing dignity of his person and bearing, that the project was abandoned.‡ However this may be, his affairs were in as bad a situation as possible. The European opposition to Austria once more obtained that influence on the interior of Germany, formerly acquired through Bavaria, and now through the Palatinate, which maintained a close connexion with France and Bohemia

Yet Maximilian had still powers and resources in store; and it was the Palatinate which soon afforded him an opportunity to rally and to apply them

IMPROVED FORTUNES OF MAXIMILIAN DIFT OF COLOGNE AND CONSTANCE, 1505 AND 1507.

In the first place Maximilian had connected himself with one of the most powerful houses of Europe The marriage of his son Philip with the Infanta Johanna of Spain not only directly opened very brilliant prospects to his family, but indirectly afforded it a defence against the aggressions of France, in the claims, the policy, and the arms of Spain. After a momentary good understanding in Naples, a war had just broken out between these two powers, the results of which inclined in favour of Spain, so that the consideration of France began to decline in Germany, and the public confidence in the fortunes of Austria, to revive.

Moreover, Maximilian had (which was much more important) a party at home among the States If the electors and the cities in alliance with Mainz were hostile to him, he had won over devoted friends and adherents among the princes, both spiritual and temporal.

For the name and state of King of the Romans was not an empty sound. In the general affairs of the realm his power might be controlled, but the functions and the sacred dignity of sovereign head of the empire, still gave him considerable influence over individual families, districts and towns He was exactly the man to turn this influence to advantage.

By means of unremitting attention and timely interference he gradually succeeded in getting a certain number of bishoprics filled according to his wishes. We find among them the names of Salzburg, Freisingen, Trent, Eichstadt, Augsburg, Strasburg, Constance, Bamberg all these sees were now, as far as their chapters would permit, partisans of Maximilian, and favourers of his projects § In these ecclesiastical affairs his connexion with the pope was especially useful to him For example,

* Gudenus IV, 517, 551

† "Königl Maj Anzeigen item die Ursach darumb des Reichs Regiment und Wolfart zu Augsburg aufgericht stocken beliben ist" — "Declarations of his Royal Majesty, also the cause why the government and welfare of the empire established at Augsburg have stood stock still." —Frankf A A

‡ Anecdote in Fugger, the truth of which, however, I will not warrant

§ Pasqualigo, Relatione di Germania (MS in the Court Library at Vienna), to whom I am indebted for this remark, says of the bishops "Li quali tutti dependono dal re come sue fatture, e seguono le voglie sue"

when a prebend of the cathedral of Augsburg became vacant in 1500, it was the papal legate who conferred it on the king's chancellor, Mathew Lang (the vacancy having occurred in a papal month) The chapter raised a thousand objections, it would admit no man of the burgher class, and, least of all, a son of a burgher of Augsburg but Maximilian said, one who was good enough to be his councillor and chancellor was good enough to be an Augsburg canon At a solemn mass Matthew Lang was unexpectedly placed among the princes, and afterwards seated within the altar At length the canons were satisfied, upon Lang's promising them that if he delegated to another the business of the provostship, he would appoint no one whom the chapter did not approve

Still more direct was the influence which Maximilian gained over the secular princes. In most cases he attached them to his cause, partly by military service, partly by the favours which he had to dispense as head of the empire Thus the sons of Duke Albert of Saxony were indissolubly bound to the Netherland policy of Austria by the possession of Friesland, which Maximilian granted to their father as a reward of his services. Albert's son-in-law, too, Erich of Calenberg, connected through him with the house of Austria, gained fame in the Austrian wars the whole house of Welf was attached to Austria Henry der Mittlere* of Luneburg, as well as his cousins, won new privileges and reversions of estates in the service of the king In the same position stood Henry IV. of Mecklenburg † Bogislaw X. of Pomerania did not indeed accept the service offered him at his return from the East, nevertheless Maximilian thought it expedient to conciliate him by the grant of the tolls of Wolgast and other favours ‡ The granting of tolls was, indeed, with Maximilian, as with his father, one means of carrying on the government Juliers, Treves, Hessen, Wurtenburg, Luneburg, Mecklenburg, the Palatinate even, and many others, acquired at different times new rights of toll. Other houses transferred to Austria their ancient alliances with Burgundy. Count John XIV. of Oldenburg alleged that a secret treaty had existed between his ancestors and Charles the Bold, in consideration of which the king promised to support him in his claims on Delmenhorst § Count Engilbert of Nassau fought by the side of Charles at Nancy, and of Maximilian at Guinegat, for which he was made Stadtholder-General of the Netherlands in 1501 From this moment we may date the firm establishment of the power of that house (which shortly after gained possession of Orange) in the Low Countries ‖ Hessen and Wurtenberg were won over by Maximilian himself. He at length determined to grant the Landgrave of Hessen the investiture which he had always refused his father. At the diet of 1495 he presented himself in front of the throne with the great red banner, upon which, round the arms of Hessen, were displayed not only the bearings of Waldeck, but of Katzenelnbogen, Diez. Ziegenhain, and Nidda the banner was so splendid that it was not torn up, as was usual on such occasions, but was borne in solemn procession and consecrated to the Virgin Mary ** Such was the investiture of the house of Hessen; and we find that William der Mittlere took an ardent share in Maximilian's campaigns.

Still more intimate was the connexion of Wurtenberg with Austria. Maximilian put the seal to the acquisitions of centuries made by the counts of that house by consolidating them into a duchy, from that time he took a warmer interest in the affairs of that state than in any other in the year 1503, in defiance of the law, he declared the young Duke Ulrich of age when only in his sixteenth year, and thus secured his entire devotion The Markgraves of Brandenburg were still true to the ancient allegiance of their founder Later historians complain bitterly of the costly journeys and the frequent campaigns of Markgrave Frederic, whose succours always far exceeded his contingent We find his sons also, from the year 1500, commanding small bodies of men in the Austrian service.

These princes were, for the most part, young men who delighted in war and feats of arms, and at the same time sought profit and advancement in the king's service The gay and high-spirited Maximilian, eternally in motion and busied with ever-new enterprises, good-natured, bountiful, most popular in his manners and address, a master of arms and all knightly exercises, a good soldier, matchless in talents and inventive genius, was formed to captivate the hearts and to secure the ardent devotion of his youthful followers

How great was the advantage this gave him, was seen in the year 1504, when the Landshut troubles broke out in Bavaria. Duke George the Rich of Landshut, who died on the first of December, 1503, in defiance of the feudal laws of the empire and the domestic treaties of the house of Bavaria, made a will, in virtue of which both his extensive and fertile domains, and the long-hoarded treasures of his house, would fall, not to his next agnates, Albert and Wolfgang of Bavaria-Munich, but to his more distant cousin, nephew, and son-in-law, Rupert of the Palatinate, second son of the elector, to whom, even during his lifetime, he had ceded his most important castles

Had the Council of Regency continued to exist, it would have been empowered to prevent the quarrel between the Palatinate and Bavaria which this incident rekindled with great violence; or had the Imperial Chamber still been constituted according to the decrees of Worms and Augsburg, members of the States of the empire would have had a voice in the decision of the question of law: but the Regency had

* Der Mittlere—the mid brother of three —Transl

† Lutzow, Geschichte von Meklenburg, ii p 458.

‡ Kanzow, Pomerania, ii p 260 Barthold im Berlin Kal 1838, p, 41

§ Hamelmann, Oldenb Chronik p 309.

‖ Arnoldi, Gesch. v. Oranien, ii 202

** The ballad on this subject, which Muller, Rtth unter Max I 538, has inserted, is of later date, the thing itself is correct

fallen to nothing, and the court of justice was constituted by the king alone, according to his own views; he himself was once more regarded as "the living spring of the law,"* and every thing was referred to his decision

His conduct in this case is extremely characteristic He insisted upon the preservation of peace he then appeared in person, and presided at long sittings of the diet, in order to preserve a good temper and understanding he did not shrink from the labour of hearing both parties, even to the fifth statement of each, and, lastly, he summoned the judge and assessors of his chamber to assist him in forming a just and lawful decision † But in all these laudable efforts he had chiefly his own interest (he calls it himself by that name) in view

He now called to mind all the losses he had sustained on account of Bavaria,—for example, how the expedition to the Lechfeld had caused him to neglect the defence of his rights in Brittany and Hungary. He found, on the one side, that Duke George had incurred heavy penalties by his illegal will; on the other that Albert's claims, founded on family contracts, were not incontestably valid, since those contracts had never been confirmed by the emperor or the empire Hereupon he himself set up a claim to one part of the land in dispute, and a not inconsiderable one.

Duke Albert, the king's brother-in-law, was quickly persuaded to acquiesce, and at length published a formal renunciation of the disputed districts This was not surprising, he was not yet in actual possession of them, and he hoped by this compliance to establish a claim to still larger acquisitions. On the other hand, the Count Palatine Rupert was utterly inflexible Whether it were that he reckoned on his father's foreign alliances, or that the hostile spirit of the electoral college towards the king gave him courage,—he rejected all these proposals of partition Maximilian had an interview with him one night, and told him that his father would bring ruin on himself and his house: but it was all in vain, Rupert immediately afterwards had the audacity to take possession in defiance of the king

Upon this Maximilian lost all forbearance. The lands and securities left by Duke George were awarded by a sentence of the Chamber to the Duke of Bavaria-Munich, the crown fiscal demanded the proclamation of the ban, and on the same day (23d April, 1504) the King of the Romans uttered it in person in the open air ‡

The neighbours of the Palatine attached to the king's party only waited for this proclamation to break loose upon him from all sides The recollection of all the injuries they had been compelled to endure from "that wicked Fritz" (so they called Frederic the Victorious), and the desire to avenge themselves and redress their wrongs, was aroused within them Duke Alexander the Black of Veldenz, Duke Ulrich of Wurtenberg; Landgrave William of Hessen, who led the Mecklenburg and Brunswick auxiliaries, fell with devastating bands upon the Rhenish Palatinate § In the territory on the Danube, the troops of Brandenburg, Saxony, and Calenberg joined the magnificent army which Albert of Munich had collected The Swabian league, once so dangerous an enemy, was now his most determined partisan, Nurnberg, which indeed wished to make conquests for itself, sent succours to the field four times as great as had originally been required of it ‖ The King of the Romans first appeared on the Danube It added not a little to his glory, that it was he who had gone in quest of a body of Bohemian troops—the only allies who had remained faithful to the Count Palatine—and had completely defeated them behind his own Wagenburg, near Regensburg He then marched on the Rhine, the bailiwick of Hagenau fell into his hands without resistance. Here, as on the Danube, his first care was to take possession of the places to which he himself had claims The Palatinate, in any case little able to withstand so superior and general an assault, was now totally incapacitated by the death of the young and warlike Count Palatine, the author of the whole disturbance, who fell in battle. The old elector was obliged to employ another son (whom he had sent to be educated at the Court of Burgundy) as his mediator with Maximilian. An assembly of the empire, which had been talked of in the summer of 1504, had at that time been evaded by the king It was not till the superiority of his arms was fully established in February, 1505, that he concluded a general truce, and summoned a diet at Cologne (which assembled in the June of that year), for the settlement of all the important questions arising out of this affair, and now once more referred to his decision.**

How different was his present from his former meeting with the States! He now appeared among them at the close of a war successfully terminated, with added renown of personal valour, surrounded by a band of devoted adherents, who hoped to retain by his favour the conquests they owed to their own prowess, respected even by the conquered,

* Expression of Lamparter in his address to the States at Landshut, Freiberg, ii p 173 Gesch der baier Land stande, ii p 33

† Harpprecht, Archiv des Kammergerichts, ii p 178

‡ Frieberg, *passim*, ii p 52

§ Trithemius Zayner, and others, describe this devastation minutely See Ranke, Gesch der romanisch german Volker, p 231

‖ In the true historical account of the cities usurped by Nurnberg, &c 1791, par 15, this reproach is again brought against that city

** One of the strangest reports of these occurrences is to be found in the Viaggio in Alemagna di Francesco Vettori Paris, 1837, p 95, from the mouth of a goldsmith at Ueberlingen First, the Count Palatine is in league with the Swiss and the French, even the Swiss war is brought about by him hereupon Maximilian concludes a treaty with France at Hagenau, in 1502 (it took place, as we know, in 1505), and forthwith attacks the Count Palatine, who calls upon the Bohemians for help, but then leaves them himself in the lurch, so that they get beaten This is another example how rapidly history turns into myth, every detail is incorrect, while the whole is not entirely devoid of truth Vettori himself finds the statements of the goldsmith wanting in order, and not to be depended on, but he readily admits them into his book which has more the air of the Decameron than of a Diary of a Journey

who surrendered their destiny into his hands. Nor was this all. The affairs of Europe were propitious. Maximilian's son Philip was become King of Castile, upon the death of his mother-in-law. Many a good German cherished the hope that his mighty and glorious chief was destined to chase the Turks from Europe, and to add the crown of the Eastern empire to that of the West. They thought that the united force of the empire was so great, that neither Bohemians, Swiss, nor Turks could withstand it.*

The first matter discussed at Cologne was the decision of the Landshut differences. The king had the power of determining the fate of a large German territory. He recurred to the proposals which he had made before the beginning of the war: for the issue of the Count Palatine Rupert, he founded the new Palatinate on the other side the Danube, which was to yield a rent of 21,000 gulden, the constituent parts of it were calculated to produce that amount. Landshut now, indeed, devolved on the Munich line, but not without considerable diminution: the dukes themselves had been compelled to pay by cessions of lands for the succours they had received; the king kept back what he had advanced to others before the sentence was pronounced: not only did he not sacrifice, he promoted, his own interests. The Palatinate sustained still greater losses; the loans, the claims to ceded lands, and the king's claims, were more considerable in that territory than in any other. It availed little that the old elector could not bring himself to accept the terms offered him; he was only the more entirely excluded from the royal favour: some time later his son was obliged to conform to them. If the possessions of the two houses of Wittelsbach were regarded as a whole, it had suffered such losses by this affair as no house in Germany had for ages sustained; and it left so deep and lasting a resentment as might have proved dangerous to the empire, had not their mutual animosity been enkindled anew by the war, and rendered all concert between them impossible.

The position of Maximilian was, however, necessarily changed, even as to the general policy of the empire, by the course things had taken.

The union of the electors was broken up. The humiliation of the Palatinate was followed by the death of the Elector of Treves in the year 1503, to whose place Maximilian, strengthened by his alliance with the court of Rome, succeeded in promoting one of his nearest kinsmen, the young Markgrave James of Baden,† and, on the 21st December, 1504, by the death of the leader of the electoral opposition, Berthold of Mainz. How rarely does life satisfy even the noblest ambition! It was the lot of this excellent man to live to see the overthrow of the institutions which he had laboured so earnestly to establish, and the absolute supremacy of the monarch on whom he had sought to impose legal and constitutional restraints.

Maximilian had now a clear field for his own enterprises. It seemed to him possible to use the ascendency which he felt he had acquired, for the establishment of organic institutions. Whilst he endeavoured to ascertain why the measures taken at Augsburg had failed (the blame of which he mainly attributed to Berthold of Mainz), he published a plan for carrying them into execution, with certain modifications.‡

His idea was, at all events, to form a government (*Regiment*) composed of a viceroy, chancellor, and twelve counsellors of the empire; and for their assistance, and under their supervision, to appoint four marshals, each with twenty-five knights, for the administration of the executive power in the districts of the Upper and Lower Rhine, the Danube, and the Elbe. The imposition of the Common Penny was again expressly mentioned.

But a glance is sufficient to show the wide difference between this scheme and the former. The king insisted on having the right of summoning this governing body to attend his person and court; it was only to be empowered to decide in the more insignificant cases, in all matters of importance it was to recur to him. He would himself nominate a captain-general of the empire, if he could not come to an understanding with Albert of Bavaria.

In short, it is clear that the obligations and burdens of government would have remained with the states, the power would have fallen to the lot of the king.

His ascendancy was, however, not yet so great as to induce, or compel, the empire to accept such a scheme as this at his hands.

Was it indeed possible to revert to institutions which had already proved so impracticable? Was not the sovereignty of the lords of the soil far too firmly and fully developed to render it probable that they would lend or even submit themselves to such extensive and radical changes? The only condition under which this could have been imagined possible was, that a committee chosen from the body of the princes should be invested with the sovereign power, but that they would voluntarily abandon their high position in favour of the king, it would have been absurd to expect.

The diet of Cologne is remarkable for this — that people began to cease to deceive themselves as to the real state of things. The opinions which prevailed during the last years of Frederic's and the first of Maximilian's reign, the attempts made to establish an all-embracing unity of the nation, — a combined action of all its powers, — a form of government which might satisfy all minds and supply all wants, are to be held in eternal and honourable remembrance, but they were directed towards an unattainable Ideal. The estates

* The sentiment of the admirable song, "die behemsch Schlacht" (the Bohemian Fight), 1504 by Hormayr, from some publication of the day, and repeated by Soltau, p. 193.

† Browerus, p. 320. He saw the Brief by which the Pope recommended the candidate of the king of the Romans.

‡ Protocol of the Imperial Diet in the Frankfort Acts, which adds considerably to the particulars found in Müller's Reichstagsstaat.

were no longer to be reduced to the condition of subjects, properly so called: the king was not contented to be nothing more than a president of the estates. It was therefore necessary to abandon such projects.

The estates assembled at Cologne did not refuse to afford succours to the king, but neither by a general tax (Common Penny) nor by an assessment of all the parishes in the empire, but by a matricula.* The difference is immeasurable. The former plans were founded on the idea of unity, and regarded the whole body of the people as common subjects of the empire; the matricula, in which the States were rated severally, according to their resources, was, in its very origin, based on the idea of the separateness of the territorial power of the several sovereigns.

They declined taking any share in a central or general government (*Reichsregiment*) of the empire. They said his majesty had hitherto ruled wisely and well; they were not disposed to impose restraints upon him.

Public opinion took a direction far less ideal, far less satisfactory to those who had cherished aspirations after a common fatherland, but one more practical and feasible.

Maximilian demanded succours for an expedition against Hungary; not against the king, with whom, on the contrary, he was on a good footing, but against a portion of the Hungarian nobles. The last treaty, by which his hereditary rights were recognised, had been agreed to only by a few of them individually; it was not confirmed at the diet. The Hungarians now began to declare that they would never again raise a foreigner to the throne, alleging that none had consulted the interests of the nation. A resolution to this effect which was as offensive to their monarch as it was injurious to the rights of Austria, was solemnly passed and sent into all the counties.† This Maximilian now resolved to oppose. He observed that the maintenance of his rights was important not only to himself but to the Holy Empire, for which Bohemia had been recovered, and with which Hungary was, through him, connected.

In a proclamation, in which the edicts concerning the Council of Regency (*Regiment*) and the Common Penny were expressly repealed, Maximilian asked for succours of four or five thousand men for one year. He expressed a hope that this might perhaps also suffice for his expedition to Rome. The States assented without difficulty: they granted four thousand men for a year, raised according to a matricula. The levy was to consist of 1058 horse, and 3038 foot. Of these, the secular princes were to furnish the larger proportion of horse, namely, 422; the cities the larger of foot,—1106: on the whole, the electors had to bear about a seventh, the archbishops and bishops a half, the prelates and counts not quite a third; of the remaining seven parts, about one half was borne by the secular princes, the other half by the States.

These more moderate levies had at least one good result—they were really executed. The troops which had been granted, were, if not entirely (which the defective state of the census rendered impossible), yet, in great measure, furnished to the king, and did him good service. His appearance on the frontier at the head of forces armed and equipped by the empire, made no slight impression in Hungary; some magnates and cities were quickly reduced to obedience. As a son was just then born to King Wladislas, whereby the prospect of a change of dynasty became more remote, the Hungarian nobles determined not exactly to revoke their decree, but not to enforce it. A committee of the States received unconditional powers to conclude a peace, which was accordingly concluded in July 1506 at Vienna; Maximilian having again reserved to himself his hereditary right. Although the recognition of the states of Hungary expressed by accepting this treaty is only indirect, Maximilian thought his own rights and those of the German nation sufficiently guaranteed by this treaty.

He now directed his attention and his forces upon Italy. Till he was in possession of the crown and title of emperor he did not think he had attained to his full dignity.‡

It was evident, however, that he would not be able to accomplish his purpose with the small body of men that followed him from Hungary.

Louis XII., with whom he had shortly before concerted the most intimate union of their respective houses, was led into other views by his States. He no longer thought it advisable to permit the ambitious, restless Maximilian, sustained by the power of a warlike nation, to get a footing in Italy. In this the Venetians agreed. At the moment when Maximilian approached their frontiers, they hastened (favoured by a revolt among the Landsknechts, which gave them time) to organise a very strong defence. Maximilian saw that, if he would obtain the crown, he must conquer it by force of arms and in strenuous warfare. He hastened to summon a new diet.

Once more, in the spring of 1507, the States assembled in the plenitude of their loyalty and devotion to the king. They were still under the influence of recent events; strangers were astonished at their unanimity, and at the high consideration the king of the Romans enjoyed among them. A remark made by the Italians is not without foundation—that a calamity which had befallen the king had been of advan-

* The Matricula partook of the nature both of census and rate or assessment. It was the list of the contingents, in men and money, which the several States were bound to furnish to the empire, and was founded on their population and pecuniary resources respectively.—Transl.

† Istuanffy, Historia Regni Hungarici, p. 32.

‡ In his declaration to the states, Maximilian designates the convention of Vienna as a treaty "whereby his Imperial Majesty and the German nation, God willing, might suffer no loss of their rights in the kingdom of Hungary, when the crown becomes vacant:"—"dadurch I. K. Mt. und deutsche Nation, ob Gott will, an ihrer erblichen und andern Gerechtigkeit des Königreichs Ungern, wenn es zu Fällen kommt, nicht Mangel haben werde."

tage to him in the affairs of Germany.* His son Philip had hardly ascended the throne of Castile when he died unexpectedly in September, 1506. The German princes had always regarded the rising greatness of this young monarch with distrust. They had feared that his father would endeavour to make him elector, or vicar of the empire, and, after his own coronation, king of the Romans; and this first idea of a union of the imperial authority with the power of Burgundy and of Castile had filled them with no little alarm. The death of Philip freed them from this fear; the sons he left were too young to inspire anxiety. The princes felt disposed to attach themselves the more cordially to their king; the more youthful hoped to conquer new and large fiefs in his service.

On the 27th of April, 1507,† Maximilian opened the diet at Constance, in the immediate neighbourhood of Italy. Never was he more impressed with the dignity of his station than at this moment. He declared, with a sort of shame, that he would no longer be a little trooper (*kein kleiner Reiter*), he would get rid of all trifling business, and devote his attention only to the great affairs. He gave the assembly to understand that he would not only force his way through Italy, but would engage in a decisive struggle for the sovereignty of Italy. Germany, he said, was so mighty that it ought to receive the law from no one; it had countless foot soldiers, and at least sixty thousand horses fit for service; they must now make an effort to secure the empire for ever. It would all depend on the heavy fire-arms; the true knights would show themselves on the bridge over the Tiber. He uttered all this with animated and confiding eloquence. "I wish," writes Eitelwolf von Stein to the elector of Brandenburg, "that your grace had heard him."

The States replied, that they were determined to aid him, according to their several means, to gain possession of the imperial crown.‡

There remained, indeed, some differences of opinion between them. When the king expressed his determination of driving the French out of Milan, the States dissented. They were only disposed to force a passage through the country in defiance of them, for a regular war with France was not to be engaged in without negotiations. Nor would they grant the whole of the supplies the king at first demanded. Nevertheless, the subsidy which they assented to, in compliance with a second proposal of his, was unusually large. It amounted to three thousand horse, and nine thousand foot.

Maximilian, who doubted not that he should accomplish some decisive stroke with this force, now promised, on his side, to govern any conquests he might make according to the counsels of the States. He hinted that the revenue she might derive from these new acquisitions would perhaps suffice to defray the charges of the empire.§

The States accepted this offer with great satisfaction. Whatever, whether land or people, cities or castles, might be conquered, was to remain for ever incorporated with the empire.

This good understanding as to foreign affairs, was favourable to some progress in those of the nation. The diet of Cologne, while it gave up all the projects of institutions founded upon a complete community of interests and of powers, had continued to regard a restoration of the Imperial Chamber as necessary. This, however, they had never been able to accomplish: the Chamber which Maximilian had established by his own arbitrary act had held no sittings for three years; the salaries of the procurators had even been stopped.‖ Now, however, the diet assembled at Constance resolved to re-establish the Imperial Chamber according to the edicts of Worms. In the nomination of the members of it the electors were to retain their privileges; for the other estates, the division into circles which had been determined on in Augsburg was adopted, so that it was not entirely suffered to drop: no notice was taken of the cities. The question now was, how this tribunal was to be maintained? Maximilian was of opinion that it would be best that each assessor should be at the charge of the government which had appointed him: he would take upon himself that of the judges and the chancery of the court. Unquestionably however the States were right in desiring to avoid the predominancy of private interests which this arrangement would have favoured:** they offered to tax themselves

* Somaria di la Relatione di Vic. Querini, Dottor, ritornato dal Re di Romani, 1507, Nov. Sanuto's Chronicle, Vienna Archives, tom. vii. He is of opinion, that the Elector of Saxony indulged the hope of one day getting possession of the crown. "Il re a gran poder in Alemagna," he also says, "è molto amato, perche quelli non l' ubediva è morti."

† Tuesday after the feast of St. Mark. Letter from Eitelwolf von Stein to the elector of Brandenburg, April 6, 1507, in the Berlin Archives. The previous accounts are incorrect.

‡ Answer of the States, Frankf. A. A., tom. xxiii.: "They had appeared at this Imperial Diet, at his majesty's request, as his lieges fully inclined to advise, and according to their ability to aid in obtaining the imperial crown, and to offer resistance to the design of the King of France, which he is practising against the holy empire."—"Sie syen uf diesen Richstag uf irer Mt. Erfordern als die Gehorsame erschienen, ganz Gemütz zu raten und ires Vermögens die kaiserliche Krone helfen zu erlangen und des Königs von Frankreich Fürnemen, des er wider das h. Reich in Uebung steht, Widerstand zu tun."

§ In the declaration in which he asks for 12,000 men, he adds: "And if the States now show themselves in such measure ready and prompt with help, then is his imperial majesty willing to act after their counsel, with respect to what money, goods, land and people will be requisite, how the same should be managed and applied, how also the conquered domains and people are to be treated and supported by the empire, so that the burdens in all future times may be taken off the Germans, and, according to what is reasonable, laid upon another nation; also, how every king of the Romans may be supported honourably in due state without heavily burdening the German nation" — "Und wo sich die Stend des Reichs jetzo dermaassen dapferlich mit der Hilf erzaigen, so ist k. Mt. willig jetzo nach irem Rat zu handeln, was von Geld Gut Land und Lüten zuston wird, wie dasselb gehandelt und angelegt werden soll, wie auch die eroberte Herrschaften und Lut by dem Rich zu hanndhaben und zu erhalten syn, dadurch die Bürden in ewig Zeiten ab den Deutschen und der Billichait nach uf andre Nation gelegt, auch ein jeder romisch Konig eehrlich und statlich on sunder Beswerung deutscher Nation erhalten werden mög."

‖ Harpprecht, ii. § 240, § 253.

** "Es sy not, das Cammergerichte als ain versampt Wesen von ainem Wesen unterhalten und derselbtige

to a small amount in order to pay the salaries of the law officers. They did not choose that the court should be stripped of the character of a tribunal common to the whole body of the States, which had originally been given to it. With this view they determined that every year two princes, one spiritual, the other temporal, should investigate its proceedings, and report upon them to the States.

If we pause a moment and reflect on what preceded the diet of Constance, and on what followed it, we perceive its great importance. The matricular assessment (or register of the resources of the empire) and the Imperial Chamber were, during three centuries, the most eminent institutions by which the unity of the empire was represented; their definitive establishment and the connexion between them were the work of that diet. The ideas which had given birth to these two institutions were originally founded on opposite principles; but this was exactly what now recommended them to favour; the independence of the several sovereignties was not infringed, while the idea of their community was kept in view.

Another extremely important affair, that of Switzerland, was also decided here.

Elector Berthold had been desirous of incorporating the Swiss in the diet, and giving them a share in all the institutions he projected. But exactly the reverse ensued. The Confederates had been victorious in a great war with the King of the Romans. In the politics of Europe they generally adhered to France, and they continued to draw one city after another into their league; and yet they pretended to remain members and subjects of the empire. This was a state of things which became manifestly intolerable when disputes with France arose. Whenever war broke out with France and Italy, a diversion was to be feared on the side of Switzerland, the more dangerous because it was impossible to be prepared for it.

The diet resolved to come to a clear understanding on this point. An embassy was sent by the States of the empire to Switzerland for that purpose.

The members of it were, however, by no means confident of success. "God send his Holy Spirit upon us," exclaims one of them: "if we accomplish nothing, we shall bring down war upon the Swiss, and be compelled to regard them as our Turks."

But the Confederates had already, in the course of their service, fallen out with the French, so that the ambassadors found them more tractable than they had expected. They recalled all their troops still in Italy at the first admonition. They promised without the slightest hesitation to remain faithful to the empire. A deputation from them appeared at Constance, and was most graciously received by the king, who kept them there at his own expense and dismissed them with presents, after entering into an agreement to take into pay, in the next war, six thousand Swiss under the banners of the empire.

On the other hand, Maximilian made a most important concession to them. He formally emancipated them from the jurisdiction of the imperial courts; declaring that neither in criminal nor in civil causes should the Confederation, or any member of it, be subject to be cited before the imperial chamber or any other royal tribunal.*

This measure decided the fate of Switzerland to all succeeding ages. At the very time when the empire agreed to subject itself to a general assessment and enrolment, and to the jurisdiction of the imperial chamber, it abandoned all claim to impose them on the Swiss: on the contrary, it took their troops into its pay and renounced its jurisdiction over them. They were, as Maximilian expressed himself, "dutiful kinsmen of the empire," who however must be kept in order when they were refractory.

Although it is not to be disputed that the real political grounds of these concessions was the increasing inclination of the Swiss to a separation from the empire, still it was the most fortunate arrangement for that moment. The quarrel was for a time appeased. Maximilian appeared more puissant, more magnificent than ever. Foreigners did not doubt that he would have, as they heard it affirmed, thirty thousand men to lead into the field: the warlike preparations which they encountered in some of the Swabian cities filled them with the idea that the empire was rousing all its energies.

Maximilian indulged the most ambitious and romantic hopes. He declared that with the noble and efficient aid granted to him, he hoped to reduce to obedience all those in Italy who did not acknowledge the sovereignty of the holy empire. But he would not stop there. When he had once reduced that country to order, he would confide it to one of his captains, and would himself march without delay against the infidels; for he had vowed this to Almighty God.

The slow march of the imperial troops, the procrastination of the Swiss, the well-defended Venetian passes, doubly difficult to force in the approaching winter season, were indeed calculated to rouse him from these dreams of conquest, and turn his attention on what was really attainable. But his high spirit did not quail. On the 2d of February he caused a religious ceremony to be performed in Trent, as a consecration of his intended expedition to Rome. Nay, as if the very object for which he was going thither was already accomplished, he assumed, on the very same day, the title of elected emperor of the Romans.† Foreigners always called him so, and he well knew that the pope, at this moment his ally, would not oppose it. He was led to this act by different motives: on the one side, the sight of the formidable opposition he had to encounter, so that

underhaltung nit zerteilt werden."—"It is needful that the imperial chamber, as a collective body, be maintained by one body, and that the maintenance of the same be not divided."—*Protocol of the Imperial Diet in Harpprecht*, ii. 443.

* Fryheitsbull bei Anshelm, iii. 321.

† There is a closer examination of this point in the Excursus upon Fugger.

he already feared he should not succeed in getting to Rome; on the other, the feeling of the might and independence of the empire, for which he was anxious at all events to rescue the prerogative of giving a supreme head to Christendom: the mere ceremony of coronation he did not regard as so essential. To Germany, too, his resolution was of the utmost importance: Maximilian's successors have always assumed the title of Emperor immediately after their coronation at Aix-la-Chapelle; though only one of the whole line was crowned by the pope.* Although Pope Julius appeared well pleased at this assumption, it was, in fact, a symptom of the emancipation of the German crown from the papacy. Intimately connected with it, was the attempt of Maximilian at the same time to revive the title of King of Germany, which had not been heard for centuries. Both were founded on the idea of the unity and independence of the German nation, whose chief was likewise the highest personage in Europe. They were expressions of that supremacy of the nation which Maximilian still asserted: a supremacy, however, which rapidly declined.

VENETIAN WAR. DIET OF WORMS.

It had been debated at Constance whether the imperial forces should first attack the French or the Venetian possessions in Italy. Whatever conquests might be made, it was not the intention of the diet to grant them out as fiefs (Milan had not even been restored to the Sforza), but to retain them in the hands of the empire, as a source of public revenue.

Among the princes some were advocates for the Milanese, others, who like the dukes of Bavaria had claims against Venice, for the Venetian, expedition. Even among the imperial councillors, difference of opinion prevailed. Paul von Lichtenstein, who was on good terms with Venice, was for attacking Milan; Matthew Lang and Eitelfriz of Zollern, on the other hand, deemed it easier to make conquests from the Venetians than from the French.†

The latter opinion at length prevailed. The Venetians were not to be brought to declare that they would not take part against the king of the Romans: on the other hand, France held out hopes that if no attempt was made upon Milan, she would offer no obstacle to the steps taken by the empire for the assertion of its other claims in Italy.‡ Strongly as the Alps were defended, Maximilian was not to be deterred from trying his fortune there. At first he was successful. "The Venetians," he says, in a letter to the Elector of Saxony, dated the 10th of March, "paint their lion with two feet in the sea, one on the plain country, the fourth on the mountains; we have nearly caught the foot on the Alps; there is only one claw missing, which, with God's help, we will have in a week; and then we hope to conquer the foot on the plain."§

But he had engaged in an enterprise which was destined to plunge his affairs in general, and those of Germany in particular, into inextricable difficulties.

In Switzerland, spite of all treaties, the French faction, especially supported by Lucern, soon revived;‖ the confederate troops hung back. This so greatly weakened the German forces (the emperor having intended to draw two-thirds of the infantry from Switzerland), that the Venetians soon had the advantage of the imperialists. They did not rest satisfied with driving the Germans from their territory, they fell on the emperor's own dominions, just where he was least prepared for an attack. Görz, Wippach, Triest, and forty-seven places, more or less strongly fortified, rapidly fell into their hands.

Germany was struck with astonishment and consternation. After subsidies which had appeared so considerable, after the exertions made by every individual for the empire, after such high-raised expectations, the result was shame and ignominy. It was in vain that the emperor alleged that the levies had not been furnished complete; the fault of this was in part ascribed to himself. The Duke of Lüneberg, for example, had never received the estimate of his contingent. But putting that aside:—To set out without having the least assurance of success!—to risk his whole fortunes on the levies of a Swiss diet! The common lot—loss of reputation for one abortive undertaking—now fell with double and triple force on Maximilian, whose capacity and character had always been doubted by many.

Compelled to return immediately to Germany, Maximilian's first act was to call the electors together. The elector palatine he did not include with the rest; Brandenburg was too far; he contented himself with sending a messenger to him. But the others assembled in

* The title of Emperor, though commonly given to Maximilian, belonged, of right, only to those who had been crowned at Rome by the hands of the Pope,—conditions which, as we shall see, Maximilian was never able to fulfil. At the head of the "Holy Roman empire (Reich) of the German nation," stands the King, elected by the German estates of the empire, who, however, by his election and his coronation in Germany (at Aachen) obtains only the rights and title of King of the Romans, (Romischen Konigs.) and acquires the rights and title of Roman Emperor (Romischen Kaisers) only by his coronation at Rome; to which all the vassals of the empire must accompany him, and which the Pope, if he be lawfully and duly elected, cannot refuse him. His successor bears the title of King of the Romans. Eichhorn, Deutsche Staats-und Yechts-geschichte, vol. ii. p. 365.—Transl.

† Relatione di Vicenzo Quirini. He mentioned some of the council by name as nottri "capitali inimici;" for a time, Maximilian said: "I Venetiani non mi a fato dispiacer e Franza si. E su queste pratiche passa il tempo."

‡ Pasqualigo, Relatione. "Non saria molto difficil cosa che la (S. M.) Dirizzasse la sua impresa contra questo stato, massime per il dubbio che li è firmato nell' animo che le Ecce Vostre siano per torre l'arme in mano contra a lei quando la fusse sul bello di cacciar li Francesi d'Italia, et a questo ancora l' inclineria assai li onorati partiti che dal re di Francia li sono continuamente offerti ogni volta che la voglia lassar la impresa di Milano e ricuperar le altre jurisditioni imperiali che ha in Italia."

§ Letter from Sterzing, March 1, accompanied by a letter from Hans Renner of the same date. He also has the best hopes.

‖ In the Relatione della Nazione delli Suizzeri 1508, Informm. politiche, tom. ix., the different persons who brought about this change are mentioned, but their names are difficult to decipher in our copy; "Amestaver at Zug, Nicolo Corator at Solothurn, Manforcsini at Frieburg." Lucerne was the centre of the whole movement.

the beginning of May 1508, at Worms. Maximilian declared to them that he called on them first, on whom the empire rested as on its foundations, for their aid in his great peril: he craved their counsel how he might best obtain valiant, safe, and effective succours; but, he added, without employing the Swabian league; whose help he should stand in need of elsewhere; and without convoking a diet of the empire.*

Among the assembled princes, Frederic of Saxony was the most powerful. By his advice they declined the emperor's invitation to meet him in Frankfurt; principally because they found it impossible to come to any resolution without a previous conference with the other states of the empire.† Maximilian replied that he was in the most perilous situation in the world; if the troops of the empire, whose pay was in arrear, were now to withdraw, his country of Tyrol was inclined to join the French and the Venetians, out of resentment against the empire, by which it was not protected: he could in no case wait for a diet; the loss of time would be too great; the utmost that could be done would be hastily to call together the nearest princes.‡ The electors persisted in demanding a diet. They would not believe that the Swabian league entertained the thought of separating itself from the other states; to grant any thing on their own responsibility and in the absence of the others, said they, would bring hostility upon them, and be useless to the king.§ They were worked upon by the pressing and obvious exigency of the case, only so far as to facilitate a loan of the emperor's, by their intercession and guarantee.

The consequences of war must, in every age and country, have an immense influence on the current of internal affairs. We have seen how all the attempts to give to the empire a constitution agreeable to the wishes and opinions of the States were ultimately connected with the alliance by which Maximilian was elected king of the Romans, Austria and the Netherlands were defended, and Bavaria reduced to subjection. On the other hand, at the first great reverse—the unfortunate combat with Switzerland,—that constitution received a shock from which it never recovered. The position too which the king himself assumed, rested on the success of his arms in the Bavarian war. It was no wonder, therefore, that after the great reverses he had now sustained, the whole fabric of his power tottered, and the opposition which seemed nearly subdued arose in new strength. Success is a bond of union; misfortune decomposes and scatters.

Nor was this state of the public mind changed by the circumstance that Maximilian, favoured by the disgust which the encroachments of the Venetians had excited in other quarters, now concluded the treaty of Cambrai, by which not only the pope and Ferdinand the Catholic, but the King of Bavaria, against whom he had just made war, combined with him against Venice.‖ This hasty renunciation of the antipathy to France which he had so loudly professed, this sudden revolution in his policy, was not calculated to restore the confidence of the States.

Perhaps the present might really have been the moment in which, with the co-operation of such powerful allies, conquests might have been made in Italy; but there was no longer sufficient concert among the powers of Germany for any such undertaking. On the 21st of April, 1509, the emperor made his warlike entry into the city of Worms (where, after long delays, the States had assembled),** armed from head to foot, mounted on a mailed charger, and followed by a retinue of a thousand horsemen, among whom were Stradiotes and Albanians. He was destined to encounter such an opposition as never awaited him before.

He represented to the States the advantages which would accrue to the empire from the treaty just concluded, and exhorted them to come to his aid with a formidable levy of horse and foot as quickly as possible, at least for a year.†† The States answered his appeal with complaints of his internal administration. A secret discontent, of which the fiery impetuous Maximilian seemed to have no suspicion, had taken possession of all minds.

The chief complaints arose from the cities; —and indeed with good reason.

Under Elector Berthold they had risen to a very brilliant station, and had taken a large share in the general administration of affairs. All this was at an end since the dissolution of the

* The instruction for Matthias Lang, Bishop of Gurk; Adolf, Count of Nassau: Erasmus Dopler, prebendary of St. Sebaldus at Nürnberg; and Dr. Ulrich von Schellenberg, is dated the last day of April, the feast of St. Wendel, 1508. (Weimar Archives.)

† The Archives at Weimar contain the advice of Frederic, and the answer. (May 8, Monday after Misericordia.)

‡ Letters of Maximilian from Linz, May 7, and from Siegburg, May 10. (Weimar Archives.)

§ Answer, dated May 13, Saturday after Misericordia. (Weimar Archives.) In return for their guarantee, they desired some security from the emperor. The latter replied, "he could bind himself to nothing further, than to release them from their guarantee within a year's time, upon his good faith."

‖ Matthias von Gurk informs the elector Frederic, Sept. 24, that he was going with certain councillors and the daughter of the emperor to a place on the French frontier, in order to treat concerning the peace with the Cardinal de Rohan, who was also to come thither. "Frau Margareta handelt und tnuet sich mit allem Vleiss und Ernst umb ain Frid." "The Lady Margaret negotiates and exerts herself with all industry and earnestness for a peace."

** By a letter of summons, Cologne, May 31, 1508, after the above-mentioned meeting of the electors, "ein eilender Reichstag," "a speedy diet of the empire" was announced for July 16: deferred at Boppart, June 26, "bis wir des Reichs Nothdurft weiter bedenken,"—"till we have further considered the necessities of the empire," at Cologne, July 16, fixed for All Saints' day; at Brussels, Sept. 12, this term is once more resolved upon; at Mechlin, Dec. 22, the reason of the fresh delay is explained, viz. the negotiations with France; at last, March 15, 1509, the emperor renews his letter of summons, and fixes the term for Judica. Fr. Ar., vols. xxiv. and xxv.

†† Verhandelung der Stennde des h. Reichs uff dem kaiserlichen Tage zu Worms ao dni 1509. Frankft. Ar. vol. xxiv. Address of his majesty, Sunday, April 22, at one o'clock. "Wo S. Heiligkeit nit gewest, hätte Kais. Mt. den Verstand und Practica nit angenommen." Had it not been for his holiness, his imperial majesty would not have accepted the treaty. Yet he remarks, the affair "werde sich liederlich und mit kleinen Kosten ausführen lassen,"—"might be executed easily and at little cost."

Council of Regency (*Regiment.*) Nor were any municipal assessors admitted into the Imperial Chamber. Nevertheless, they were compelled to contribute not only to all the other taxes, as well as to the expenses of the administration of justice, but the rate imposed on them at Constance was disproportionately high Even at Cologne they were not spared, as we saw, they were compelled to furnish nearly two-sevenths of the subsidies; but at Constance a full third of the whole amount of foot soldiers and of money was levied upon them * Nay, as if this was not enough, immediately after the diet the emperor caused the plenipotentiaries of the cities to be cited before the fiscal of the empire, who called them to account for the continuance of the great merchants' company, which had been forbidden by previous imperial edicts, and demanded a fine of 90,000 gulden for carrying on unlawful traffic. The merchants loudly protested against this sentence; they said that they were treated like serfs, it were better for them to quit their native country, and emigrate to Venice or Switzerland, or even France, where honourable trade and dealing was not restricted; but they were forced at last to compound by means of a considerable sum The cities were not so weak, however, as to submit quietly to all this, they had held town-meetings (*Stadtetag*) and had determined to put themselves in an attitude of defence at the next imperial diet,† the members of the Swabian league as well as the others. They had not the slightest inclination to strain their resources against a republic with which they carried on the most advantageous commercial intercourse, and which they were accustomed to regard as the model and the natural head of all municipal communities ‡

Among the princes, too, there was much bad blood The demands of the imperial chamber, the irregularities in the levies of men and money which we shall have occasion to notice again, had disgusted the most powerful among them The Palatinate was still unreconciled The old Count Palatine was dead, his sons appeared at Worms, but they could not succeed in obtaining their fief. The warlike zeal which had recently inflamed many for the emperos, had greatly subsided after the bad results of his first campaign.

But the circumstance which made a stronger impression than all the rest, was the conduct of Maximilian with regard to his last treaties. At the diet of Constance, the States had proposed sending an embassy to France in order to renew negotiations with that power; for they did not choose to commit the whole business of the empire implicitly to its chief. Maximilian had at that time rejected all these proposals, and professed an irreconcilable enmity to the French Now, on the contrary, he had himself concluded a treaty with France, and without consulting the States, nay, he did not even think himself called upon to communicate to them the treaty when ratified § No wonder if these puissant princes, who had so lately entertained the project of uniting all the powers of the empire in a government constituted by themselves, were profoundly disgusted. They reminded the emperor, that they had told him at Constance that the grant he then received was the last, and that he, on his side, had abandoned all claim to further aids He was persuaded, they said, by his councillors, that the empire must help him as often as he chose to require help, but this notion must not be allowed to take root in his mind, or they would have perpetually to suffer from it.

A very strong opposition thus arose on various grounds to the king's proposals. It made no change in public opinion, that the French obtained a brilliant victory over the Venetians, and that the latter for a moment doubted whether they should be able to retain their possessions on the main land On the contrary, the first obstacle to the victorious career of the league of Cambrai was raised in Germany. At the same moment in which the Venetian cities in Apulia, Romagna and Lombardy fell into the hands of the allies after the battle of Aguadello, a committee of the States advised, and the whole body thereupon resolved, that an answer should be sent to the emperor, refusing all succours They declared that they were neither able to support him in the present war, nor were they bound to do so. Unable, because the last subsidies had been announced to their subjects as final, and no fresh ones could be levied without great difficulties and discontents not bound, since the treaty had not even been communicated to them, as was the custom from time immemorial in all cases of the kind ||

* Accounts in the genuine Fugger It appears to me that the sum amounted to 20,000 gulden See Jager, Schwabisches Stadtewesen 677

† The resolutions of these municipal diets deserve much more accurate examination A letter from the Swabian league Oct 21, 1508, calls to mind, " welchermaass auf vergangen gemeinem Frei und Reichsstett Tag zu Speier der Beschwerden halben, so den Stettboten uf dem Reichstag zu Costnitz begegnet sind gerathschlagt und sunderlich verlassen ist, so die Rom Konigl Mt wiederum ein Reichstag furnehmen wird, dass alsdann gemeine Frei und Reichsstette gen Speier beschrieben werden sollten "—" In what manner, at a former common diet of the free and imperial cities held at Spires by reason of complaints with regard to the treatment the deputies of the cities had met with at the imperial diet at Constance, it had been discussed and specially resolved on, in case his majesty, the King of the Romans, should again propose a diet of the empire that then the free and imperial cities should be convened in common at Spires "

‡ Very curious indications of the light in which Venice was regarded by the trading towns of Germany are still to be found at Nurnberg That magnificent city endeavoured in all its institutions to imitate the queen of the Adriatic I have seen, in MS, an application from the council of Nurnberg to the senate of Venice for the rules of an orphan asylum, in which this sentiment is strongly expressed.—Transl.

§ The Weimar Archives contain an opinion upon the necessity of refusing succours, in which persons are especially complained of, "so bei S Kais Mt sein und sich allwege geflissen Ks Mt dahin zu bewegen Hilf bei den Stenden des Reiches zu suchen zu solchem Furnemen das doch ohne Rad und Bewusst der Stennde des h Reichs beschehen ist "—" who are about his imperial majesty, and in all ways strive to move his imperial majesty to seek help from the states of the empire, towards such undertaking, which, however, has been entered upon without the advice and knowledge of the states of the holy empire "

|| Transactions, &c " Dweile die Stende des Reichs davon kein grundliches Wissen tragen, so hab I Ks Mt wohl zu ermessen, dass wo ichts darin begriffen oder verleipt das dem h Reich jetzo oder in Zukunft zu Nachtheil thate reichen, es were mit Herzogthum Mailand

The emperor's commissioners (for he had quitted the diet again himself a few days after his arrival, in order to hasten the armaments on the Italian frontier,)* were in the utmost perplexity. What would the church, what would France, say if the holy empire alone did not fulfil its conditions? The States declined any further explanation on the matter; if the commissioners had any proposition to make concerning law and order, concerning the administration of justice, or the coinage, the States were ready to entertain it. The commissioners asked whether this was the unanimous opinion of all the States; the States replied, that was their unanimous resolution. The commissioners said, that nothing then remained for them but to report the matter to the emperor, and await his answer.

It may easily be imagined what a tempest of rage he fell into. From the frontiers of Italy — from Trent — he dispatched a violent answer, printed, though sealed. He began by justifying his own conduct; especially the conclusion of the last treaty, for which he had power and authority, "as reigning Roman Emperor, according to the ordinance of the Almighty, and after high counsel and deliberation;" he then threw the blame of his reverses back on the States, alleging, as the cause of them, the incompleteness of the subsidies. Their inability he could not admit. They should not try to amass treasure, but think of the oath they had sworn, and the allegiance they owed to him. Nor was that the cause of their refusal; it was the resentment which some had conceived because their advice was not taken.

Before this answer arrived, the States had dispersed. No final Recess was drawn up.

DIET OF AUGSBURG, 1510; OF TREVES AND COLOGNE, 1512.

Before I proceed further, I feel bound to make the confession that the interest with which I had followed the development of the constitution of the empire, began to decline from this point of my researches.

That, at so important a moment, when the most desirable conquest was within their grasp — a conquest which would have more than freed them from the burdens they bore so reluctantly, and would have constituted an interest common to all the States—they came to no agreement, shows that all these efforts were doomed to end in nothing, and that the impossibility of reaching the proposed end lay in the nature of things.

Although the emperor by no means took the active, creative part which has been ascribed to him in the establishment of national institutions, he evinced a strong inclination towards them; he had a lofty conception of the unity and dignity of the empire; and occasionally he submitted to constitutional forms, the effect of which was to limit his power. Nor were there ever States so profoundly convinced of the necessity of founding settled coherent institutions, and so ready to engage in the work, as those over which he presided. Yet these two powers could not find the point of coincidence of their respective tendencies.

The States saw in themselves, and in their own union, the unity of the empire. They had in their minds a government composed of representatives of the several orders in the empire (*ständisches Regiment*)† such as really existed in some of the separate territories of the empire; by which they thought to maintain the dignity of the emperor, or, if occasion demanded, to set fixed bounds to his arbitrary rule; and to introduce regularity and order into the establishments for war, finance, and law, even at the expense of the power of the territorial sovereigns. But the calamities of an ill-timed campaign, and the dissatisfaction of the emperor with the part they took in foreign affairs, had destroyed their work.

Maximilian then undertook to renovate the empire by means of similar institutions, only with a firmer maintenance of the monarchical principle; resolutions to that effect were actually passed, not indeed of such a radical and vital character as those we have just mentioned, but more practicable in their details: but when these details came to be carried into execution, misunderstandings, reluctances without end appeared, and suddenly every thing was at a stand.

The States had been more intent on internal, Maximilian on external, affairs; but neither would the king so far strip himself of his absolute power, nor the States part with so much of their influence, as the other party desired. The States had not power to keep the emperor within the circle they had drawn round him, while the emperor was unable to hurry them along in the path he had entered upon.

For such is the nature of human affairs, that little is to be accomplished by deliberation and a nice balance of things: solid and durable foundations can only be laid by superior strength and a firm will.

Maximilian always maintained, and not without a colour of probability, that the refusal of the empire to stand by him gave the Venetians fresh courage.‡ Padua, which was already

oder anderm, dem Reich zuständig, dass sie darin nit willigen können." — "Seeing that the states of the empire have no thorough knowledge thereof, his imperial majesty has to consider well that if anything be therein contained or embodied which might tend now or hereafter to the injury of the holy empire, be it with regard to the duchy of Milan, or any other belonging to the empire, they cannot give their consent thereunto."

* Not out of anger, as has been commonly believed. He declared as early as the 22d of April, that he could not await the conclusion, and went away two days afterwards, before the diet had fully met: the real proposition of the diet took place only on May 16, Wednesday before the Feast of the Assumption; Casimir of Brandenburg acting as his Lieutenant (*Statthalter*). Adolf von Nassau and Frauenberg as his councillors. Frankf. Ar., vol. xxiv. The letters of the Frankfurt friend of the council (*Rathsfreund*), Johannes Frosch, repeat nearly what is contained in the Archives, with some additions. It appears from both that no final resolution was come to, although Müller and Fels seem to imply the contrary.

† See note, p. 62.

‡ Rovereyt, Nov. 8, 1509. "Als uns der Stend Hilf und Beistand vorzigen und abgeschlagen, und den Venedigern das kund, wurden sy mehr gestärkt, suchten erst all ir Vermogen und bewegten daneben den gemein Popl in Stetten."—"When the help and assistance of the states

invested, was lost again, and Maximilian besieged this powerful city in vain. In order to carry on the war, he was obliged to convoke the States anew. On the 6th of March, 1510, a fresh imperial diet was opened at Augsburg.* Maximilian represented the necessity of once more bringing an army against Venice. Already he had extended the empire over Burgundy and the Netherlands, and established an hereditary right to Hungary, he would now annex to it these rich domains, on which the burdens of the state might fall, instead of resting wholly on Germany.

The prospect thus held out produced a certain impression on the States, yet they still remained very pacific They wished to bring the affair to a conclusion by a negotiation with Venice The Republic had already promised a payment of 100,000 gulden down, and 10,000 gulden yearly tax, and the diet was extremely inclined to treat on this basis This will appear intelligible enough, when it is remembered with how much difficulty a grant of a few hundred thousand gulden was obtained It would at least have relieved them from the small tax raised for the support of the Imperial Chamber, which was collected with great difficulty †

To the emperor, however, these offers appeared almost insulting He calculated that the war had cost him a million; that Venice derived an annual profit of 500,000 gulden from Germany; he declared that he would not suffer himself to be put off so.

The misfortune was now, as before, that he could not inspire the States with his own warlike ardour All projects that recalled the Common Penny or the four-hundredth man, were rejected at the first mention. A grant was indeed at length agreed on, they consented to raise succours according to the census and rate (matricula) fixed at Cologne (for they rejected that of Constance), and to keep them in the field for half a year ‡ but how could they hope to drive the Venetians from the terra firma by so slight an effort? The papal nuncio spoke on the subject in private to some of the most influential princes. They answered him without reserve, that the emperor was, so ill-supported because he had undertaken the war without their advice.

It followed by a natural reaction, that Maximilian felt himself bound by no considerations towards the empire. When he was requested at Augsburg not to give up his conquests at his own pleasure, he replied, that the empire did not support him in a manner that would make it possible to do otherwise; he must be at liberty to conclude treaties, and to make cessions as he found occasion. So little advance was made at this diet towards a good understanding and co-operation between the emperor and the States

The emperor rejected even the most reasonable and necessary proposals. The States required that he should refrain from all interference with the proceedings of the Imperial Chamber. This had been the subject of continual discussion, and was at total variance with the idea upon which the whole instution was founded Maximilian, however, did not scruple to reply, that the Chamber sometimes interfered in matters beyond its competence: that he could not allow his hands to be tied

No wonder if the States refused to assent to a plan which he submitted to them for the execution of the sentences of the Imperial Chamber, notwithstanding its remarkable merits. Maximilian proposed to draw out a scheme of a permanent levy for the whole empire, calculated on the scale of Cologne, of from one to fifty thousand men, so that, in any exigency, nothing would be needed but to determine the amount of the subsidy required. For, he said, a force was necessary to chastise the rebellious who break the Public Peace or disregard the ban of the Chamber, or otherwise refuse to perform the duties of subjects of the empire. The fame of such an organisation would also intimidate foreign enemies. A committee might then sit in the Imperial Chamber, charged with the duty of determining the employment of this force in the interior § This was evidently a consistent mode of carrying out the matricular system. Maximilian, with the acuteness and sagacity peculiar to him, had once more touched and placed in a prominent light the exact thing needed. The States declared that this scheme was the offspring of great wisdom and reflection; but they were not to be moved to assent to it—they would only engage to take it into consideration at the next diet. This was natural enough. The very first employment of the levy would have certainly been in Maximilian's foreign wars. The emperor's councillors, too, with whom the States were

was withdrawn and refused us, and this became known to the Venetians they felt further strengthened and examined into all their resources, and moreover stirred up the common people in the cities"—*Frankf Ar*

* Häberlin is uncertain whether the imperial diet had been summoned for the feast of the three kings, or for the 12th of Jan The summons is addressed to the observers of the feast of the three kings, *i e* Jan 13

† Proceedings at the Imperial Diet held at Augsburg in 1510 (Fr Ar) Answer of the States second Wednesday after Judica They advised the measure, in order neither to let the matter drop entirely for the future, "oder veil nachtheiliger und beschwerlicher Rachtigung annehmen zu mussen, als jetzt dem heil Reich zu Ehr und Lob erlangt werden moge"—"nor to be obliged to accede to a more disadvantageous and oppressive arrangement, than might now be got to the honour and praise of the holy empire"

‡ The emperor desired a free promise of "the grant made at Constance for as long as his majesty should have need of it" He was willing to give a secret promise in return, that he wanted them for one year only The States proposed the levy of Cologne The emperor replied that this shocked him, that many of the States were able to contribute more than that singly They persisted however, and all they resolved on was, to grant the levy of Cologne for half, as they had before done for a whole, year.

§ Commissioners for the maintenance of the law "Also dass Kais Mt Jemand dazu verordnet, desgleichen auch das Reich von jedem Stand etliche, mit voller Gewalt, zu erkennen ob man Jemand der sich beklagt dass ihm Unrecht geschehen, Hulfe schuldig sey und wie gross"—"So that his imperial majesty do appoint some one, in the same manner, also, the empire, certain persons from each state, with full power to discover whether help, and to what extent, be due to any man complaining that wrong has been done him" In each quarter of the empire was to be a president, who would summon help upon such discovery There was also to be a general captain for the empire.

extremely dissatisfied, would have gained a new support in their demands.

It was not to be expected that affairs would turn out otherwise than they did

No new disputes arose at Augsburg to appearance a tolerable harmony prevailed, but in essentials no approach was made to union.

Maximilian carried on the Venetian war for a few years longer, with various success, and involved in ever new complications of European policy. He interwove some threads in the great web of the history of that age, but all his attempts to draw the empire into a fuller participation in his views and actions were vain. neither the cities, nor even the Jews who inhabited them, gave ear to his demands for money; the results of his levies were so inadequate that he was obliged to dismiss them as useless, the utmost he could hope was, that the succours granted him in Augsburg would arrive at last The surrender of one city after another, the loss of the hope of some alleviation of the public burthens, were partly the consequence, partly the cause, of all these misunderstandings.

In April, 1512, a diet again assembled at Treves, whence its sittings were afterwards transferred to Cologne *

The emperor began by renewing his proposal for a permanent rate and census, and by praying for a favourable answer The princes answered, that it was impossible to carry this measure through in their dominions, and with their subjects; they begged him to propose to them other ways and means. Maximilian replied, that he trusted they would then at least revert to the resolutions of the year 1500, and grant him the four-hundredth man that he might gain the victory over the enemy, and a Common Penny wherewith to maintain the victory when gained The States did not venture entirely to reject this proposal, feeling themselves, as they did, bound by the promises made at Augsburg. The scheme of a Common Penny was now resumed, but with modifications which robbed it of all its importance they lowered the rate extremely; before they had determined to levy a tax of one gulden on every thousand, capital; now, it was to be only one on every four thousand † They likewise exempted themselves: before, princes and lords were to contribute according to their property; now they alleged they had other charges for the empire, to defray out of their own exchequer. Even the representations of the knights were immediately yielded to, they were only to be bound to include their vassals and subjects within the assessment Maximilian made less objection to this than to the insufficiency of the tax generally; but the States answered that the common people were already overladen with burthens, and that it would be impossible to extort more from them. He then requested that at least the tax might be granted until so long as it should have produced a million of gulden The States replied that the bare mention of such a sum would fill the people with terror.

The emperor's other proposition, concerning the execution of the sentences of the Imperial Chamber, was received and discussed with greater cordiality Rejecting the division of the empire into four quarters, which Maximilian, like Albert II, had once thought of adopting, the States conceived the idea of employing the division into circles (hitherto used only for the elections for the Council of Regency and the Imperial Chamber) for that purpose, and of rendering it more generally applicable to public ends. The electoral and imperial hereditary domains were also to be included among the circles Saxony and Brandenburg, with their several houses, were to form the seventh, the four Rhenish electorates the eighth, Austria the ninth, Burgundy the tenth circle In each a captain or governor was to be appointed for the execution of the law

But this subject also gave rise to the most important differences The emperor laid claim to the nomination of these captains, and demanded moreover a captain-general, whom he might employ in war, and a council of eight members who should reside at his court, a sort of ministry (*Regiment*), from whose participation in affairs he promised himself peculiar influence in the empire The States, on the contrary, would hear nothing either of these councillers, or of the captain-general, and they insisted on reserving to themselves the nomination of the captains of their circles.

These points gave rise to fresh and violent disputes at Cologne, in August, 1512 On one occasion the emperor refused to receive the answer sent by the States, which, he said, was *no answer*, and should not remain a moment in his hands

It was only through the zealous endeavours of the Elector of Mainz, that the proposal for the eight councillors was at length accepted. Their chief office was to be that of putting an end to quarrels by conciliation. Of the captain-general, no further mention occurs I do not find that there was any intention of limiting the circles in the nomination of the subordinate captains The subsidy was granted in the way determined by the States, and the emperor abandoned his demand for a million

At length therefore, resolutions were passed, and finally embodied in a Recess of the empire.

When, however, we come to examine whether it was executed, we find not a trace of it There was a numerous party which had never, from the first, assented to the resolutions, though they had not been able to prevent their adoption; at the head of which was one of the most experienced and the most respected princes of the empire—Frederic, Elector of Saxony The projected subsidy was never

* The acts of this diet are to be found tolerably complete in vol xxvi of the Frankfurt Collection The letters of the Frankfurt deputy, Jacob Heller, from the 4th of May to the 29th of June, are dated from Treves, one on the 12th of July from Cologne, in vol xxix

† This is the principle —Whoever possessed 50 gulden was to pay one *sixtieth of a Rhenish gulden*, *between* 50 and 100, one fortieth, 100 and 400, one twentieth, 400 and 1000, one tenth, 1000 and 1500, one fifth, 2000 and 4000, one half, 4000 and 10,000, one gulden

even called for, much less raised. The eight councillors were never appointed, nor the captains, whether supreme or subordinate. The division of the empire into ten circles did not assume any positive character till ten years later.

Intestine Disorders.

Had the attempts to give a constitution to the empire succeeded, a considerable internal agitation must necessarily have ensued, until an adaptation and subordination of the several parts to the newly-created central power had taken place. But that attempts had been made, and had not succeeded,—that existing institutions had been rudely shaken and no real or vital unity been produced,—could result in nothing but a universal fermentation.

The reciprocal rights and duties of the head of the empire and the States, were now for the first time thrown into utter uncertainty and confusion. The States had demanded a share in the jurisdiction and the government; the emperor had conceded some points and had held tenaciously to others; no settled boundary of their respective powers had been traced. It was an incessant series of demands and refusals—extorted grants, inadequate supplies—without sincere practical efforts, without material results, and hence, without satisfaction on any side. Formerly the union of the electors had, at least, possessed a certain independence, and had represented the unity of the empire. Since 1501 this also was dissolved. Lastly, Mainz and Saxony had fallen into a bitter strife, which entirely broke up the college. The only institutions which had come to any real maturity, were the Imperial Chamber and the matricula. But how carelessly was this constructed! Princes who no longer existed, except in old registers, were entered in the list; while no notice was taken of the class of mediate proprietors which had gradually arisen. Countless appeals were the consequence. The emperor himself named fifteen secular, and five spiritual lords, whose succours belonged to the contingent of his own dominions, and not to the matricula of the empire; Saxony named fifteen secular lords and three bishops*; Brandenburg, two bishops and two counts; Cologne, four counts and lords; every one of the greater States put forward mediate claims which had not been thought of. A number of cities, too, were challenged. Gelnhausen, by the Palatinate; Göttingen, by the house of Brunswick; Duisburg, Niederwesel, and Soest, by Juliers; Hamburg, by Holstein.† In the acts of the diets we find the memorial of an ambassador of Denmark-Holstein to the States of the empire, wherein he pleads that he has travelled two hundred miles (German) to the emperor, but could obtain no answer either from him or his councillors; and now addressed himself to the States, to inform them that there was a city called Hamburg, lying in the land of Holstein, which had been assessed as an imperial city, but of which his gracious masters were the natural hereditary lords and sovereigns.‡ There was no dispute about the principle. It was always declared in the Recesses, that the States should retain their right over all the succours which belonged to them from remote times; yet in every individual case the question and the conflicting claim were always revived. Even the most powerful princes had to complain that the fiscal of the Imperial Chamber issued penal mandates against their vassals.

In short, the Imperial Chamber excited opposition from every side. The princes felt themselves controlled by it, the inferior States, not protected. Saxony and Brandenburg reminded the diet that they had only subjected their sovereign franchises to the chamber under certain conditions. Joachim I. of Brandenburg complained that this tribunal received appeals from the courts of his dominions; which had never been done in his father's time.§ The knights of the empire, on the other hand, were discontented at the influence exercised by the powerful princes over the chamber; when a prince, they said, saw that he would be defeated, he found means to stop the course of justice. Maximilian, at least, did not think their complaints unfounded: "Either," says he, "the poor man can get no justice against the noble, or if he does, it is 'so sharp and fine pointed' that it avails him nothing." Nor were the cities backward with their complaints. They thought it insufferable that the judge should receive the fiscal dues; they prayed for the punishment of the abandoned men by whose practices many cities were, without any crime or offence, dragged before the court: in the year 1512 they again demanded that two assessors appointed by the cities should have seats in the chamber;‖—of course, all in vain.

The natural consequence of this inability of the supreme power either to enforce obedience

* In the Archives at Dresden there is an instruction from Duke George for Dr. G. von Breyttenbach, according to which the latter was to declare at Worms (in 1509), "das wir uns nicht anders zu erinnern wissen, denn das alles, so wir uf dem Reychstage zu Costnitz zu Underhaltung des Kammergerichtes zu geben bewilligt, mit Protestation beschehen, also das dye Bischoffe und Stifte desgleichen Graven und Herrn die uns mit Lehen verwandt und auch in unsern Fürstenthumen sesshaftig seyn, welche auch an dem Kammergericht nie gestanden, ichtes dabei zu thun nicht schuldig, bei solcher Freiheit bleiben."—"That we have no other remembrance than that all which we consented to give at the diet at Constance for the maintenance of the Imperial Chamber, was accompanied with a protest; that thus the bishops and chapters of such counts and lords as hold of us by feudal tenure and are vassals of our principalities, and who have never appeared before the Imperial Chamber and are under no obligation to do so, continue to be exempt."

† Proceedings concerning the Imperial Chamber, and such as claim exemption from its jurisdiction. Harpprecht, Staats Archiv. iii. p. 405.

‡ We know that he did not succeed. The decision of the imperial diet of 1510 is the main foundation of the freedom of the empire possessed by Hamburg. Lünig, Reichsarch. Pars Spec. Cont. iv. p. 965.

§ Letter from Frederic of Saxony to Renner, on the Wednesday after the feast of the Three Kings, 1509 (Weim. Ar.); Joachim I. die crps. Christi, 1510.

‖ Jacob Heller to the city of Frankfurt, June 11. "Wir Stett sein der Meinung auch auzubringen zween Assessores daran zu setzen auch Gebrechen und Mangel der Versammlung fürzutragen."—"We cities are of the opinion that we should introduce two assessors to sit there (in the court), and to bring forward the abuses and defects of the assembly."

or to conciliate approbation and respect, was an universal striving after separate and independent power — a universal reign of force, which singularly characterizes this period. It is worth while to try to bring before us the several States under this aspect.

I. In the principalities, the power of the territorial lord was much extended and increased. In particular ordinances we clearly trace the idea of a legislation for the whole territory, intended to supersede local unions or associations, traditional rules and customs; and of an equally general supervision, embracing all the branches of administration. A remarkable example of this may be found in the ordinances issued by Elector Berthold for the government of his archbishopric.* In some places, a perfect union and agreement subsisted between the princes and their estates; *e. g.* in the dominions of Brandenburg, both in the Mark and Franconia: the estates contract debts or vote taxes to pay the debts of the sovereign.† In other countries, individual administrators become conspicuous. We distinguish the names of such men as George Gossenbrod in Tyrol, created by Maximilian, Regimentsherr (master or chief of the government), and keeping strict watch over all the hereditary rights of the sovereign. In Styria, we find Wallner, the son of that sacristan of Altötingen in Bavaria who accumulated the treasure of Landshut; in Onolzbach, the general accountant Prucker, who for more than thirty years conducted the whole business of the privy chancery and the chamber of finance. It is remarkable too that these powerful officials seldom came to a good end. We often see them dragged before the tribunals and condemned to punishment: Wallner was hanged at the door of the very house in which he had entertained princes, counts, and doctors as his guests; Gossenbrod was said to have ended his life by poison; Wolfgang of Kolberg,‡ raised to the dignity of count, died in prison; Prucker was forced to retreat to a prebend in Plassenburg.§ In order to put an end to the arbitrary acts of the detested council of their duke, the Würtenbergers extorted the treaty of Tübingen in 1514. Here and there we see the princes proceeding to open war in order to extend their territory. In the year 1511 Brunswich, Lüneburg, Bremen, Minden, and Cleves fell with united forces on the country of Hoya, which could offer them no resistance. In 1514, Brunswick, Lüneburg, Calenberg, Oldenburg, and Duke George of Saxony, turned their arms against the remnant of the free Frieslanders in the marshes. The Butjadinger swore they would rather die than live exposed to the incessant vexations of the Brunswick officials, and flew to arms behind the impassable ramparts of their country; but a traitor showed the invading army a road by which it fell upon their rear: they were beaten, and their country partitioned among the conquerors and the Worsaten and Hadeler compelled to learn the new duty of obedience to a master.‖

In some cases the princes tried to convert the independence of a bishop into complete subjection; as, for example, Duke Magnus of Lauenburg demanded of the bishop of Ratzeburg the same aids** as were granted him by his States, perhaps with twofold violence, because that prelate had formerly served in his chancery; he encountered a stout resistance, and had to resort to open force.†† Or a spiritual prince sought to extort unwonted obedience from the knights of his dominions, who thereupon, with the aid of a secular neighbour, broke out in open revolt; as the dukes of Brunswick took the knights of Hildesheim, and the counts of Henneberg the chapter of Fulda and the nobility connected with it, under their protection.

II. For the increasing power of the princes was peculiarly oppressive to the knights. In Swabia the associations of the knights of the empire (Reichsritterschaft) consolidated themselves under the shelter of the league. In Franconia there were similar struggles for independence; occasionally (as, for instance, in 1511 and 1515), the six districts (Orte) of the Franconian knights assembled, mainly to take measures for subtracting their business under litigation from the tribunals of the sovereign: the results of these efforts, however, were not lasting; here and on the Rhine every thing remained in a very tumultuous state. We still see the warlike knights and their mounted retainers, in helm and breastplate and with bent cross-bow before them — for as yet the horsemen had no fire-arms—riding up and down the well-known boundary line, marking the halting places, and lying in ambush day and night in the woods, till the enemy whom they are watching for appears; or till the train of merchants and their wares, coming from the city they are at war with, is seen winding along the road: their victory is generally an easy one, for their attack is sudden and unexpected: and they return surrounded by prisoners and laden with booty to their narrow stronghold on hill and rock, around which they cannot ride a league without descrying another enemy, or go out to the chase without harness on their back: squires, secret friends, and comrades in arms, incessantly come and go, craving succour or bringing warnings, and keep up an incessant alarm and turmoil. The whole night long are heard the howlings of the wolves in the neighbouring forest. While

* Boddmann, Rheingauische Alterthümer, ii. 535.

† Buchholz, Geschichte der Mark, iii. 363. Lang, i. p. 111.

‡ Report in the manuscript Fugger.

§ Lang, i. p. 147.

‖ Rehtmeier, Braunschweigsche Chronik., ii. p. 861.

** *Bede*—precaria: (*beten*, to pray)—grants of money to the prince on extraordinary occasions, such as attendance on the emperor, the marriage of a daughter, &c.—Transl.

†† Chytræus, Saxonia, p. 222. By Masch, Gesch. von Ratzeburg, p. 421, we perceive that there were many other points of dispute. On the 28th of March, 1507, bishop and chapter were obliged to promise, "that when the sovereign received a land-tax from his knights, it should be paid by the peasants on the church lands just as by the peasants of any other lords."

the States of the empire were consulting at Treves as to the means of ensuring the execution of the laws, Berlichingen and Selbitz seized the train of Nurnberg merchants coming from the Leipzig fair, under the convoy of Bamberg, and thus began the open war against the bishop and the city. The decrees of the diet were of little avail.* Gotz von Berlichingen thought himself entitled to complain of the negotiations that were opened, for otherwise he would have overthrown the Nurnbergers and their Burgermeister "with his gold chain round his neck and his battle-mace in his hand."† At the same time another notorious band had collected under the command of the Friedingers in Hohenkrahn (in the Hegau), originally against Kaufbeuern, to avenge the affront offered to a nobleman who had sued in vain to the fair daughter of a citizen afterwards they became a mere gang of robbers, who made the country unsafe, so that the Swabian league at length stirred itself against them, and the emperor himself sent out his best men, the Weckauf (Wake up) of Austria, and the Burlebaus,—at whose shots, as the historical ballad says, "the mountain tottered, the rocks were rent, and the walls riven, till the knights fled, their people surrendered, and the castle was razed to the ground."‡ But there was also many a castle in Bavaria, Swabia, and Franconia for which a similar fate was reserved. The insecurity of the roads and highways was greater than ever, even poor travelling scholars who begged their way along, were set upon and tortured to make them give up their miserable pittance.§ "Good luck to us, my dear comrades," cried Gotz to a pack of wolves which he saw fall upon a flock of sheep, "good luck to us all and every where." He took it for a good omen.

Sometimes this fierce and lawless chivalry assumed a more imposing aspect, and constituted a sort of tumultuary power in the State. Franz von Sickingen had the audacity to take under his protection the enemies of the council which had just been re-established in Worms by the emperor; he began the war with that city by seizing one of its vessels on the Rhine. He was immediately put under ban. His answer to this was, instantly to appear before the walls of that city, to fire upon it with carronades and culverins, lay waste the fields, tear up the vineyards, and prevent all access to the town. The Whitsuntide fair could not be held either in 1515 or 1516. The States of the circle of the Rhine assembled, but dared not come to any resolution, they thought that could only be done at an imperial diet.|| It is indisputable that some princes, out of opposition either to the emperor or to the Swabian league, favoured, or at least connived at, these acts of violence. The knights were connected with the party among the princes which was inclined neither to the emperor nor to the league.

III. The cities were exposed to annoyance and injury from all sides, from the imperial government, which continually imposed fresh burthens upon them; from these lawless knights, and from the princes, who in 1512 agitated the old question of the Pfahlburger.** But they made a most gallant defence. How many a robber noble did Lubeck drag from his stronghold! Towards the end of the fifteenth century that city concluded a treaty with neighbouring mediate cities, the express object of which was to prevent the landed aristocracy from exceeding the powers they had hitherto exercised. It availed nothing to King John of Denmark that the Emperor Maximilian for a time favoured his attempts. In the year 1509, the Hanse towns or rather a part of them,

* Emperor and States disputed as to the amount of the levy necessary. The emperor thought they wanted to put the affair off, and reminded them that what had happened to-day to Bamberg, might happen to-morrow to another city. If the succours demanded appeared too considerable, he would ask Bamberg to be content with a hundred horses fit for service. This the States agreed to, but only under the condition that the ban must be first proclaimed against outlaws or suspected persons before the troops were employed. (Frankf. A.) The universal state of division extended even to this matter.

† Gotzens von Berlichingen ritterliche Thaten. Ausgabe von Pistorius, p. 127. Mullner's Chronicle (MS.) relates the whole affair after the documents in the Nurnberg Archives, in the following manner:—The attack was made between Forchheim and Neusess, May 18, 1512, by a band of 130 horse, 31 persons were carried off, the damage done amounted to 8800 gulden, the horses were foddered and the booty divided in a wood near Schweinfurt. The prisoners were concealed by the knights of Thungen, Eberstein, Buchenau. The council of Nürnberg hereupon took 300 foot soldiers into their pay, and announced to the Great Council their determination to do every thing to bring the perpetrators to punishment. Meanwhile, 'solten sie ihre Kaufmannschaft so enge es seyn konnte einziehen, bis die Laufte etwas besser wurden.'—"they must draw in their dealings as much as possible till the ways became somewhat better." And he actually produces a proclamation of ban of the 15th of July, accompanied, however, by a proposal for a commission before which the accused might clear themselves. Some did thus clear themselves, others not. Among the last are mentioned Caspar von Rabenstein, Balthasar and Reichart Steinruck, Wilhelm von Schaumburg, Dietrich and Georg Fuchs, Conrad Schott. Among them are many Wurzburg officials, who were jointly declared under ban by the Imperial Chamber. As in the mean time a number of fresh attacks had taken place, at Vilseck, Ochsenfurt, Mergentheim (in which the Commander of the Order at Mergentheim had drawn suspicion upon himself), the Swabian league at last came forward with an armed force, to which the Nurnbergers added 600 men on foot, a squadron of cavalry, and a small body of artillery. Gangolf von Geroldseck led the troops of the league, their first move was against Frauenstein, belonging to Hans von Selbitz, several castles were carried, and lands taken, and at last the way was opened to a treaty. The emperor decreed that the knights should pay 14,000 gulden as compensation. Muller asserts that of this sum the Bishop of Wurzburg paid 7,000 gulden, the Count Palatine Ludwig 2000, the Duke of Wurtenberg as much, the Master of Mergentheim 1000, and Gotz himself 2000. He infers that those princes, 'dieser Fehd heimlich verwandt gewesen.'—"had been privily concerned in this Feud." On the other hand, he speaks with praise of the bishop of Bamberg and Markgrave Frederic of Brandenburg.

‡ Anonymi Carmen de Obsidione et Expugnatione Arcis Hohenkrayen, 1512. Fugger, both MS. and printed. Gassari Annales ad ann. 1512.

§ Plater's Lebensbeschreibung. The period he speaks of is about the year 1515, as he immediately afterwards mentions the battle of Marignano.

|| Zorn's Wormser Chronik in Münch's Sickingen, iii.

** Pfahlburger (from *Pfahl*, pale or stake) were originally persons inhabiting a town, but not enjoying all the rights of citizenship. (See Golden Bull, cap. 16.) They were often free peasants, subject to the sovereign lord's jurisdiction, but not his serfs. It seems that they availed themselves of the protection and security afforded by the cities to the prejudice of the lord's feudal rights, and formed associations to resist him. (See Eichhorn, ii. 162.)

attacked his islands, beat his ships at Helsingör, carried away his bells for their chapels, and remained absolute masters on the open sea. A Lübeck vessel boarded by three Danish ones near Bornholm beat off two of them and captured the third: in the year 1511 the Lübeck fleet returned to the Trave with eighteen Dutch ships as prizes.*

Nor did the inland cities make a less spirited resistance to those aggressions from which they were not protected by the Swabian league. How admirably did Nürnberg defend herself! For every injury she sustained, she carried her vengeance home to the territory of the aggressor, and her mounted bands frequently made rich captures. Woe to the nobles who fell into their hands! No intercession either of kinsmen or of neighbouring princes availed to save them; the council was armed with the ever-ready excuse that the citizens absolutely demanded the punishment of the offender. In vain did he look out from the bars of his prison towards the forest, watching whether his friends and allies were not coming to his rescue: Berlichingen's story sufficiently shows us with how intense a dread even those of her neighbours who delighted the most in wild and daring exploits regarded the towers of Nürnberg. Noble blood was no security either from the horrors of the question or the axe of the executioner.†

Sometimes, indeed, commercial difficulties arose — for example, in the Venetian war — which could not be met with the same vigour by the inland towns as the Hanseats displayed at sea, but the effects of which they found other means to elude. All intercourse with Venice was in fact forbidden, and the Scala which had obtained the proclamation of the ban, often arrested the merchandise travelling along that road; though this was done only in order to extort money from the owners for its redemption. I find that one merchant had to pay the emperor three thousand ducats transit duty, on three hundred horse-load of goods: the Tyrol government had formerly appointed a commissary in Augsburg, whose business it was to collect regular duties on those consignments of goods the safety of which it then guaranteed. The towns accommodated themselves to the times as they could; thankful that their trade was not utterly destroyed. The connexion with the Netherlands, established by the house of Austria, had meanwhile opened a wide and magnificent field for commercial enterprise. Merchants of Nürnberg and Augsburg shared in the profits of the trade to the East and West Indies.‡ Their growing prosperity and indispensable assistance in all pecuniary business gave them influence in all courts, and especially that of the emperor. In defiance of all decrees of diets, they maintained "their friendly companies;" associations to whose hands the smallest affairs as well as the largest were committed. There is sufficient ground for the belief that they gave occasion to many just complaints of the monopoly which was thus vested in few hands; since the importers of wares had it in their power to regulate the price at will.§ But they nevertheless maintained a strong position in the assemblies of the empire. The abortive results of the diets held from 1509 to 1513 were chiefly caused by their opposition. They found means to get the proposed measures concerning the Pfahlbürger, in virtue of which goods were to pay duty, not to the town in which the owner of them lived, but to the sovereign or lord in whose dominions that town was situated, indefinitely adjourned. (A. D. 1512.)||

It is evident that the peaceful security, the undisturbed prosperity, which are often ascribed to those times, had no existence but in imagination. The cities kept their ground only by dint of combination, and of unwearied activity, both in arms and in negotiation.

There was also a vehement and continual ferment in the interior of the towns. The old struggle between the town councils and the commons or people was continually revived by the increasing demands for money made by the former and resisted by the latter; in some places it led to violence and bloodshed. In the year 1510 the Vierherr** Heinrich Kellner was executed in Erfurt for having, in the financial straits of the city, allowed the house of Saxony to redeem Capellendorf for a sum of money; all the following years were marked with violence and disorder. In Regensburg the aged and honest Lykircher, who had frequently held the offices of chamberlain, hansgrave, and judge of the peace, was brought to trial; and, though the treasonable acts of which he was accused were never proved against him, was barbarously tortured in the Holy Week of 1513, and shortly afterwards put to death.†† In Worms, first the old council, and afterwards its successor, was driven out. In Cologne the commons were furiously incensed against the new contributions with which they were vexed; and still more against an association or company called the Garland, to which the most criminal designs were imputed.‡‡ Similar disturbances took place in Aix-la-Chapelle, Andernach, Speier, Hall in Swabia, Lübeck, Schweinfurt,

* Becker, Geschichte von Lübek, vol. i. p. 488.

† Müllner's Chronicle is full of anecdotes of this kind.

‡ Gassarus (Annales in Mencken, i. 1743) names those of the Welser, Gossenbrot, Fugger, Hochstetter, Foëlin: the last are without doubt the Vehlin. He reckons the dividends from the first voyage to Calcutta at 175 per cent.

§ Jäger, Schwäbisches Städtewesen, i. 669. As early as 1495, the plan was entertained of taxing the great companies. Datt. p. 844. nr. 16. Things remained in this state from one diet to another.

|| A counter representation from Wetzlar and Frankfurt: "Es würde dem Reich und ihnen ein merklicher Abbruch seyn und wider ihre Privilegien laufen."—"It would be a signal injury to the empire and to them, and go against their privileges." (Fr. A.)

** Vierherr and Hansgraf are among the numerous titles of magistrates used in different parts of Germany. The former was probably the title of the four chief magistrates, like the four Syndics of Hamburg. The Hansgraf was a sort of president of the board of trade (if I may so apply the words) in the Hanse towns. There are still, I am told, two Hansgrafen in Lübeck.—Transl.

†† Chronicle of Regensburg, vol. iv. part iii.

‡‡ Rhythmi de Seditione Coloniensi in Senkenberg, Selecta Juris et Hist. iv. nr. 6.

and Nürnberg:* in every direction we meet with imprisonments, banishments, executions. Domestic grievances were often aggravated by the suspicion of a criminal understanding with neighbouring states. In Cologne it was Guelders; in Worms and Regensburg, Austria; in Erfurt, Saxony, which was the object of their suspicions. The feeling of public insecurity burst forth in acts of the wildest violence.

IV. Nor was this excitement and agitation confined to the populations of towns; throughout the whole breadth of the empire, the peasantry was in an equal state of ferment. The peasants of the Swiss mountains had completely changed their relation to the empire: from the condition of subjects, they had passed to that of free and independent allies: those of the marches of Friesland on the contrary had succumbed to the neighbouring sovereigns; the Ditmarschers alone stood for a while after a glorious and successful battle, like a noble ruin amidst modern edifices. The antagonist principles which, in distant lands and from the furthest marches of the empire, gave rise to these conflicts, came into contact under a thousand different forms in the heart of the country. The subsidies for the empire and its growing necessities fell ultimately on the peasant; the demands of the sovereign, of the holders of church lands, and of the nobility, were all addressed to him.† On the other hand, in some countries the common people were made to bear arms; they formed the bands of landsknechts which acquired and maintained a name amongst European troops; they once more felt the strength that was in them. The example of the Swiss was very seducing to the south of Germany. In the country round Schletstadt, in Alsatia, a society of discontented citizens and peasants, the existence and proceedings of which were shrouded in the profoundest secrecy, was formed as early as the year 1493. Traversing almost impassable ways, they met at night on solitary mountains, and swore never in future to pay any tax which was not levied with their own free consent; to abolish tolls and duties, to curtail the privileges of the clergy, to put the Jews to death without ceremony, and to divide their possessions. They admitted new members with strange ceremonies, specially intended to appal traitors. Their intention was in the first place to seize on Schletstadt, immediately after to display the banner with the device of the peasant's shoe‡, to take possession of Alsatia, and to call the Swiss to their aid.§ But in spite of the fearful menaces which accompanied the admission to the society, they were betrayed, dispersed, and punished with the utmost severity. Had the Swiss in 1499 understood their own advantage and not excited the hatred of their neighbours by their cruel ravages, the people along their whole frontier would, as contemporaries affirm, have flocked to join their ranks. An incident shows the thoughts that were afloat among the people. During the negotiations preceding the peace of Basle, a peasant appeared in the clothes of the murdered Count of Fürstenberg. "We are the peasants," said he, "who punish the nobles." The discovery and dispersion of the conspiracy above-mentioned by no means put an end to the Bundschuh. In the year 1502 traces of this symbol were found at Bruchsal, from whence the confederates had already gained over the nearer places, and were extending their ramifications into the more remote. They declared that in answer to an inquiry addressed to the Swiss they received an assurance that the Confederation would help the right, and risk life and limb in their cause. There was a tinge of religious enthusiasm in their notions. They were to say five Pater nosters and Ave Marias daily. Their war-cry was to be, "Our Lady!" They were to take Bruchsal, and then march forth and onward, never remaining more than twenty-four hours in a place. The whole peasantry of the empire would join them, of that there was no doubt; all men must be brought into their covenant, that so the righteousness of God might be brought upon earth.‖ But they were quickly overpowered, scattered, and their leaders punished with death.

The imperial authorities had often contemplated the danger of such commotions. Among the articles which the electors projected discussing at their diet of Gelnhausen, one related to the necessity of alleviating the condition of the common people.** It was always the conclusive argument against taxes like the Common Penny, that there was reason to fear they would cause a rebellion among the people. In the year 1513, the authorities hesitated to punish some deserters from the Landsknechts, because they were afraid that they might enter into a combination with the peasants, whose permanent conspiracy against the nobles and clergy had been discovered from the confessions of some who had been arrested in the Breisgau. In the year 1514, they rose in open and complete rebellion in Würtenberg under the name of Poor Kunz (der armer Kunz): the treaty of Tübingen did not satisfy the peasants; it was necessary to put them down by force of arms.†† We hear the sullen mutterings of a fierce un-

* Baselii Auctarium Naucleri, p. 1016. "Ea pestis pessimæ rebellionis adversus senatum in plerisque — civitatibus irrepsit. Trithemius (Chronic. Hirsaug. ii. p. 629) reckons them up, adding the remarks, "et in aliis quarum vocabula memoriæ non occurrunt."

† Rosenblüt complains that the noble draws his maintenance from the peasant, and yet does not insure him any peace; that he is constantly pushing his demands further, whereupon the peasant answers with abuse, and the noble rides down his cattle.

‡ The Bundschuh; the large rude shoe bound on the foot with thongs of leather, commonly worn by the Swabian peasantry, and borne on their banner in the servile war to which they were driven by intolerable oppression. The *Bund* or league of the peasants, was afterwards called the Bundschuh. (See Vol. II.)—Transl.

§ Herzog, Edelsasser Chronik., c. 71, p. 162.

‖ Frankf. Acten, vol. xx. Baselii Auctarium, p. 997.

** "Der mit Fron Diensten Atzung Steure geistlichen Gerichten und andern also merklich beschwert ist, dass es in die Harre nicht zu leiden feyn wird."—"Who is so signally burthened with feudal services, taxes, ecclesiastical courts, and other things, that in the long run it will not be to be borne."

†† Wahraftig Unterrichtung der Ufrur bei Sattler Herzoge, i. App. no. 70.

tamed element, incessantly going on under the very earth on which we stand.

While such was the state of Germany, the emperor was wholly occupied with his Venetian war,—at one time fighting with the French against the Pope and the Venetians, at another with the Pope and the English against the French the Swiss, now in alliance with him, conquer Milan and lose it again, he himself, at the head of Swiss and Landsknechts, makes an attempt to recover it, but in vain We see him repeatedly travelling from Tyrol to the Netherlands, from the sea-coast back to the Italian Alps, like the commander of a beleaguered fortress, hurrying incessantly from bastion to bastion, and watching the propitious moment for a sortie. But this exhausted his whole activity, the interior of Germany was abandoned to its own impulses

A diet was appointed to be held at Worms again, in the year 1513; and on the 1st June we find a certain number of the States actually assembled The emperor alone was wanting At length he appeared, but his business did not allow him to remain under the pretext that he must treat in person with the dilatory electors of Treves and Cologne, he hurried down the Rhine, proposing to the States to follow him to Coblentz. They chose rather to disperse altogether * "Of a truth, writes the Altburgermeister of Cologne to the Frankfurters, "you have done wisely that you stayed at home, you have spared much cost, and earned equal thanks"

It was not till after an interval of five years (A. D 1517), when not only Sickingen's private wars threw the whole of Upper Germany into confusion, but the universal disorder of the country had become intolerable, that a diet was held again,—this time at Mainz, in the chapter house of which city it was opened on the 1st July.

The imperial commissioners demanded vast succours for the suppression of the disturbances — not, as before, every four hundredth, but every fiftieth man, the States, however, did not deem it advisable to resort to arms The poor husbandman, already suffering under the torments of want and famine, might, "in his furious temper," be still further exasperated, the rage which had long gnawed at his heart might burst forth, a universal rebellion was to be feared. They desired rather to put down the prevailing disturbances by lenity and conciliation, they entered into negotiations on all sides — even with Sickingen, above all, they appointed a committee to inquire into the general state of the country, and into the causes of the universal outbreak of disturbances The imperial commissioners wanted to dissolve the assembly on the ground that they could do nothing without ascertaining the opinion of his imperial majesty, but the States would not consent to be put off so the sittings of the committee, two members of which were nominated by the cities, were solemnly opened by a mass for the invocation of the Holy Ghost (Missa Sancti Spiritus) On the 7th August, 1517, they laid their report before the diet.

It is very remarkable that the States discover the main source of the whole evil in the highest and most important institution that had been founded in the empire—in the Imperial Chamber, and in the defects in its constitution and modes of procedure. The eminent members of that tribunal, they said, were gone, and incapable ones put in their places. The procedure was protracted through years; one great cause of which was, that the court received so many appeals on trifling matters that the important business could not be despatched Nor was this all. The court had not free course, it was often ordered to stay all proceedings. If, after long delays and infinite trouble, a suitor succeeded in getting judgment pronounced, he could not get it executed, his antagonist obtained mandates to prevent its execution The consequence was, that the highest penalties of the law, the ban and reban (*Acht und Aberacht*), had no longer terrors for any one The criminal under ban found shelter and protection, and as the other courts of justice were in no better condition—in all, incapable judges, impunity for misdoers, and abuses without end—disquiet and tumult had broken out in all parts. Neither by land nor by water were the ways safe. no safe-conduct, whether of the head or the members of the empire, was the least heeded, there was no protection, whether for subjects or for such foreigners as were entitled to it the husbandman, by whose labours all classes were fed, was ruined, widows and orphans were deserted, not a pilgrim or a messenger or a tradesman could travel along the roads, whether to fulfil his pious duty, or to deliver his message, or to execute his business. To these evils were added the boundless luxury in clothing and food; the wealth of the country all found its way into foreign lands, especially to Rome, where new exactions were daily invented lastly, it was most mischievous to allow the men at arms, who had sometimes been fighting against the emperor and the empire, to return to their homes, where they stirred up the peasantry to rebellion

And while such was the statement of public grievances, the particular petitions and remonstrances were countless. The inhabitants of

* In the Frankfurt Acts vol xxx there is a letter from Worms to Frankfurt, according to which the States present, "prima Sunii nechst verruckt einhelliglich entschlossen und den kais Commissarien fur endlich Antwort geben, dass sie noch zehn Tag alliie bei einander verziehen und bleiben und wo inen in mitler Zeit mit weiter Geschefte oder Befel von Kais Mt zukommen wollen sie alsdann sich alle wieder von dannen anheim thun"—"On the first of June just past, unanimously resolved and give this their final answer to the imperial commissioners that they shall tarry and remain here together ten days longer, and if, meantime, no farther business or command reach them from his imperial majesty, they shall all in that case betake themselves thence home" In an address of the 20th of August Maximilian announces a new diet of the empire, 'Die geringe Anzahl der erschienenen Stande habe ihren Abschied genommen, da sie sich keiner Handlung verfangen mogen"—"The small number of states which had appeared, had taken their leave, as they were unwilling to meddle with any business"

Worms complained of "the inhuman private warfare (*Fehde*) which Franciscus von Sickingen, in despite and disregard of his honour, carried on against them," to which the deputies from Spires added, that Sickingen's troops had the design to burn down the Spital of their city. Muhlhausen complained in its own name, and those of Nordhausen and Gosslar, that they paid tribute for protection and were not protected. Lubeck enumerated all the injuries it sustained from the King of Denmark, from nobles and commons, it could obtain no help from the empire, by which it was so heavily burthened, it must pay its money to the Imperial Chamber, which always gave judgment against it, and never in its favour. Other towns said nothing of their grievances, because they saw it was of no avail. Meantime the knights held meetings at Friedberg, Gelnhausen, Bingen, and Wimpfen, whither the emperor sent delegates to appease them. Anna of Brunswick, the widowed Landgravine of Hessen, appeared in person at the diet, and uttered the bitterest complaints: she said she could obtain no justice in Hessen, that she vainly followed the emperor and the Imperial Chamber from place to place, her dowry of Melsungen was consumed, she was reduced to travel about like a gipsy, with a solitary maid-servant, and to pawn her jewels and even her clothes; she could not pay her debts, and must soon beg her bread.

"Summa Summarum," writes the delegate from Frankfurt, "here is nothing but complaint and wrong, it is greatly to be feared that no remedy will be found.* The States made the most urgent appeals to the emperor: they conjured him for God's sake, for the sake of justice, for his own, for that of the holy empire, of the German nation, nay of all Christendom, to lay these things to heart;—to remember how many mighty states had fallen, through want of inward tranquillity and order; to look carefully into what was passing in the minds of the common people, and to find a remedy for these great evils.

Such were the words addressed to him; but they were but words. A remedy—a measure of the smallest practical utility—was not so much as suggested, the diet was dissolved without having even proceeded to one resolution.

And already the excited mind of the nation was turned towards other evils and other abuses than those which affected its civil and political condition.

In consequence of the intimate union between Rome and Germany, in virtue of which the Pope was always a mighty power in the empire, a grave discussion on spiritual affairs had become inevitable. For a time, they had fallen into the back-ground, or been the subject only of chance and incidental mention: now, however, they attracted universal attention; the vigorous and agitated spirit of the nation, weary and disgusted with the present and the past, and eagerly striving after the future, seized upon them with avidity. As a disposition was immediately manifested to go to the bottom of the subject, and to proceed from a consideration of the external interference of the church, to a general and thorough examination of its rights, this agitation speedily acquired an importance which extended far beyond the limits of the internal policy of Germany.

* Philip Furstenberg, July 26. In the 32d vol. of the Frankf. A., where generally the transactions of this diet are to be found. "Wo Kais. Mt." he says, on the 16th of Aug., of the representations which were made, "dieselbig als billig und wol ware verwilligen wurde, hoff ich alle Dinge sollten noch gut werden, wo nicht so helft uns Gott." "If his imperial majesty would comply with the same as were reasonable and right, I should hope that all things might yet go well, if not, then God help us."

BOOK II.

EARLY HISTORY OF LUTHER AND OF CHARLES V.

1517—1521.

CHAPTER I.

ORIGIN OF THE RELIGIOUS OPPOSITION.

WHATEVER hopes we may entertain of the final accomplishment of the prophecies of an universal faith in one God and Father of all which have come down to us in the Hebrew and Christian Scriptures, it is certain that after the lapse of more than ten centuries that faith had by no means overspread the earth The world was filled with manifold and widely differing modes and objects of worship.

Even in Europe, the attempts to root out paganism had been but partially successful, in Lithuania, for example, the ancient worship of the serpent endured through the whole of the 15th and 16th centuries, and was even invested with a political significancy,* and if this was the case in Europe, how much more so in other portions of the globe! In every clime men continued to symbolise the powers of nature, and to endeavour to subdue them by enchantments or to propitiate them by sacrifices throughout vast regions the memory of the dead was the terror of the living, and the rites of religion were especially designed to avert their destructive interference in human things, to worship only the sun and moon supposed a certain elevation of soul, and a considerable degree of civilisation.

Refined by philosophy, letters, and arts, represented by vast and powerful hierarchies, stood the mightiest antagonists of Christianity —the Indian religion and Islam, and it is remarkable how great an internal agitation prevailed within them at the epoch of which we are treating.

Although the Brahminical faith was, perhaps, originally founded on monotheistic ideas, it had clothed these in a multiform idolatry But at the end of the 15th and beginning of the 16th century, we trace the progress of a reformer in Hindostan. Nanek, a native of Lahore, endeavoured to restore the primitive ideas of religion, and to show the advantages of a pure morality over a merely ceremonial worship. he projected the abolition of castes, nay, even a union of Hindoos and Moslem, he presents one of the most extraordinary examples of peaceful unfanatical piety the world ever beheld † Unfortunately, his efforts were unsuccessful. The notions he combated were much too deeply rooted, even those who called themselves his disciples—the Sikhs—paid idolatrous honours to the man who laboured to destroy idolatry.

A new and very important development of the other branch of the religions of India—Buddhism—also took place in the fifteenth century The first regenerated Lama appeared in the monastery of Brepung, and was universally acknowledged throughout Thibet, the second incarnation of the same (from 1462 to 1542) had similar success in the most remote Buddhist countries,‡ from that time hundreds of millions revere in the Dalailama at L'Hassa the living Buddha of the present,—the unity of the divine trinity,—and throng thither to receive his blessing It cannot be denied that this religion had a beneficial influence on the manners of rude nations, but, on the other hand, what fetters does such a fantastic deification of human nature impose on the mind! Those nations possess the materials for forming a popular literature, a wide diffusion of the knowledge of the elements of science, and the art of printing, but the literature itself—the independent exercise and free utterance of the mind, can never exist, § nor are such controversies as these between the married and unmarried priests, or the yellow and the red professions which attach themselves to different chiefs, at all calculated to give birth to it The rival Lamas make pilgrimages to each other, and reciprocally recognise each other's divine character

The same antagonism which prevailed between Brama and Buddha, subsisted in the bosom of Islam, from its very foundation, between the three elder Chalifs and Ali, in the beginning of the sixteenth century the contest between the two sects, which had been dormant for awhile, broke out with redoubled violence. The sultan of the Osmans regarded himself (in his character of successor to Abubekr and the first Chalifs) as the religious head

---

* Æneas Silvius de Statu Europæ c 20 Alexander Guagninus in Resp Poloniæ Elz. p 276

† Bhai Guru the Bhale in Malcolm's Translation, Sketch of the Sikhs Asiatic Researches xvi 271 That holy man made God the Supreme known to all—he restored to virtue her strength, blended the four castes into one—established one mode of salutation

‡ Fr Georgi Alphabetum Tibetanum p 320, says of it "Pergit inter Tartaros ad amplificandam religionem Xacaicam in regno Kokonor eis murum magnum Sinorum inde in Kang multa erigit asceteria redit in Brepung" He bears the name of So nam kiel Vachiamtzho, and is notwithstanding the old Reval Keuun, who died in 1399

§ Hodgson, Notice sur la Langue, la Littérature, et la Religion des Bouddhistes "L'écriture des Tubetains n'est jamais employée à rien de plus utile que des notes des affaires ou de plus instructif que les rêves d'une mythologie absurde," &c The objections of Klaproth, Nouv Journ Asiatique, p 99, are not in my opinion of much weight, as the question is not concerning a literature, which may be old, or the existence of which may be unknown, but a living one of the present day

of all Sunnites, whether in his own or foreign countries, from Morocco to Bokhara. On the other hand, a race of mystic Sheiks of Erdebil, who traced their origin from Ali, gave birth to a successful warrior, Ismail Sophi, who founded the modern Persian monarchy, and secured once more to the Shiites a powerful representation and an illustrious place in history. Unfortunately, neither of these parties felt the duty or expediency of fostering the germ of civilisation which had lain in the soil since the better times of the early Chalifat. They only developed the tendency to despotic autocracy which Islam so peculiarly favours, and worked up political hostility to an incredible pitch of fury by the stimulants of fanaticism. The Turkish historians relate that the enemy who had fallen into Ismail's hands were roasted and eaten.* The Osman, Sultan Selim, on the other hand, opened the war against his rival by causing all the Shiites in his land, from the age of seven to seventy, to be hunted out and put to death in one day; "forty thousand heads," says Seadeddin, "with base souls." The antagonists were, as we perceive, worthy of each other.

In Christendom, too, a division existed between the Græco-Oriental and the Latin church, which, though it did not lead to acts of such savage violence, could not be healed. Even the near approach of the resistless torrent of Turkish power which threatened instant destruction, could not move the Greeks to accede to the condition under which the assistance of the West was offered them — the adoption of the distinguishing formulæ of confession—except for the moment, and ostensibly. The union which was brought about at Florence, in the year 1439, with so much labour, met with little sympathy from some, and the most violent opposition from others: the patriarchs of Alexandria, Antioch, and Jerusalem, loudly protested against the departure from canonical and synodal tradition, which such a union implied; they threatened the Greek emperor with a schism on their own part, on account of the indulgence he showed to the Latin heterodoxy.†

If we inquire which of these several religions had the greater external and political strength, we are led to the conclusion that Islam had unquestionably the advantage. By the conquests of the Osmans in the 15th century, it had extended to regions where it had been hitherto unknown, almost on the borders of Europe; combined too with political institutions which must inevitably lead to the unceasing progress of conversion. It reconquered that sovereignty over the Mediterranean which it had lost since the eleventh century. Its triumphs in India soon equalled those in the West. Sultan Baber was not content with overthrowing the Islamite princes who had hitherto held that land. Finding, as he expressed it, "that the banners of the heathen waved in two hundred cities of the faithful—that mosques were destroyed and the women and children of the Moslem carried into slavery," he proclaimed a holy war against the Hindoos, as the Osmans had done against the Christians. On the eve of a battle he resolved to abjure the use of wine; he repealed taxes which were inconsistent with the Koran, and enkindled the ardour of his troops by a vow sworn upon this their sacred book; his reports of his victories are conceived in the same spirit of religious enthusiasm, and he thus earned the title of Gazi.‡ The rise of so mighty a power, actuated by such ideas, necessarily gave a vast impulse to the propagation of Islam throughout the East.

But if, on the other hand, we endeavour to ascertain which of these different systems possessed the greatest internal force,—which was pregnant with the most important consequences to the destiny of the human race,—we can as little fail to arrive at the conviction (whatever be our religious faith), that the superiority was on the side of Latin Christendom.

Its most important peculiarity lay in this—that a slow but sure and unbroken progress of intellectual culture had been going on within its bosom for a series of ages. While the East had been convulsed to its very centre by torrents of invasion like that of the Mongols, the West had indeed always been agitated by wars, in which the various powers of society were brought into motion and exercise; but neither had foreign tribes overrun the land, nor had there been any of those intestine convulsions which shake the foundations of a society in an early and progressive stage of civilisation. Hence all the vital and productive elements of human culture were here united and mingled: the development of society had gone on naturally and gradually; the innate passion and genius for science and for art constantly received fresh food and fresh inspiration, and were in their fullest bloom and vigour; civil liberty was established upon firm foundations; solid and symmetrical political structures arose in beneficent rivalry, and the necessities of civil life led to the combination and improvement of physical resources; the laws which eternal Providence has impressed on human affairs were left to their free and tranquil operation; what had decayed crumbled away and disappeared, while the germs of fresh life continually shot up and flourished: in Europe were found united the most intelligent, the bravest, and the most civilised nations, still in the freshness of youth.

Such was the world which now sought, like its eastern rival, to extend its limits and its influence. Four centuries had elapsed since, prompted by religious motives, it had made attempts at conquest in the East; but after a momentary success these had failed—only a few fragments of these acquisitions remained in its possession. But at the end of the fifteenth century, a new theatre for boundless activity was opened to the West. It was the

* Hammer, Osmanische Gesch., ii. 345.

† Passages from their letter of admonition, in Gieseler, Kirchengeschichte, ii. 4, p. 545.

‡ Baber's own Memoirs, translated into English by Leyden and Erskine, into German by Kaiser, 1828, p. 537, and the two firmans thereto annexed.

time of the discovery of both Indies. All elements of European culture—the study of the half-effaced recollections of antiquity, technical improvements, the spirit of commercial and political enterprise, religious zeal—all conspired to render the newly-discovered countries tempting and profitable. All the existing relations of nations, however, necessarily underwent a change, the people of the West acquired a new superiority, or at least became capable of acquiring it.

Above all, the relative situation of religions was altered. Christianity, especially in the forms it had assumed in the Latin Church, gained a fresh and unexpected ascendancy in the remotest regions. It was therefore doubly important to mankind, what might be the present or the future form and character of the Latin Church. The pope instantly put forth a claim, which no one contested, to divide the countries that had been, or that yet might be found, between the two States by which they were discovered.

POSITION OF THE PAPACY WITH REGARD TO RELIGION.

THE question, at what periods and under what circumstances the distinguishing doctrines and practices of the Romish Church were settled, and acquired an ascendancy, merits a minute and elaborate dissertation.

It is sufficient here to recal to the mind of the reader, that this took place at a comparatively late period, and precisely in the century of the great hierarchical struggles.

It is well known that the institutions of the Seven Sacraments, whose circle embraces all the important events of the life of man, and brings them into contact with the church, is ascribed to Peter Lombard, who lived in the twelfth century.* It appears upon inquiry that the notions regarding the most important of them, the Sacrament of the Altar, were by no means very distinct in the church itself, in the time of that great theologian. It is true that one of those synods which, under Gregory VII., had contributed so much to the establishment of the hierarchy, had added great weight to the doctrine of the real presence by the condemnation of Berengar: but Peter Lombard as yet did not venture to decide in its favour: the word transubstantiation first became current in his time, nor was it until the beginning of the thirteenth century, that the idea and the word received the sanction of the church: this, as is well known, was first given by the Lateran confession of faith in the year 1215; and it was not till later that the objections which till then had been constantly suggested by a deeper view of religion, gradually disappeared.

It is obvious, however, of what infinite importance this doctrine became to the service of the church, which has crystallized (if I may use the expression) around the mystery it involves. The ideas of the mystical and sensible presence of Christ in the church were thus embodied in a living image; the adoration of the Host was introduced; festivals in honour of this greatest of all miracles, incessantly repeated, were solemnized. Intimately connected with this is the great importance attached to the worship of the Virgin Mary, the mother of Christ, in the latter part of the middle ages.†

The prerogatives of the priesthood are also essentially connected with this article of faith. The theory and doctrine of the priestly character were developed; that is, of the power communicated to the priest by ordination, "to make the body of Christ" (as they did not scruple to say) "to act in the person of Christ." It is a product of the thirteenth century, and it is to be traced principally to Alexander of Hales and Thomas Aquinas.† This doctrine first gave to the separation of the priesthood from the laity, which had indeed other and deeper causes, its full significancy. People began to see in the priest the mediator between God and man.‡

This separation, regarded as a positive institution, is also, as is well known, an offspring of the same epoch. In the thirteenth century, spite of all opposition, the celibacy of the priesthood became an inviolable law. At the same time the cup began to be withheld from the laity. It was not denied that the efficacy of the Eucharist in both kinds was more complete, but it was said that the more worthy should be reserved for the more worthy—for those by whose instrumentality alone it was produced. "It is not in the participation of the faithful," says St. Thomas, "that the perfection of the sacrament lies, but solely in the consecration of the elements."§ And in fact the church appeared far less designed for instruction or for the preaching of the Gospel, than for the showing forth of the great mystery, and the priesthood is, through the sacrament, the sole depository of the power to do this; it is through the priest that sanctification is imparted to the multitude.

This very separation of the priesthood from the laity gave its members boundless influence over all other classes of the community.

It is a necessary part of the theory of the sacerdotal character above alluded to, that the priest has the exclusive power of removing the obstacles which stand in the way of a participation in the mysterious grace of God: in this not even a saint had power to supersede him.‖ But the absolution which he is authorized to grant is charged with certain conditions, the

* It would amount to little, if what Schrockh (Kirchengeschichte, xxviii. p. 45) assumes were true, viz. that Otto of Bamberg had already preached this doctrine to the Pomeranians; but it has been justly remarked, that the biography of Otto in which this statement appears, was written at a later time.

† See the researches of Thomas Aquinas concerning the Birth of Christ: "Utrum de purissimis sanguinibus virginis formatus fuerit &c." Summæ pars iii. quæstio 31. It is evident what value was set upon the point.

‡ "Sacerdos," says Thomas, "constituitur medius inter Deum et populum. Sacerdos novæ legis in persona Christi operatur." Summæ, pars iii. quæstio 22, art. 4. concl.

§ "Perfectio hujus sacramenti non est in usu fidelium sed in consecratione materiæ."—Pars iii. qu. 80, a. 12, c. 2m.

‖ Summæ Suppl. Qu. 17, a. 2, c. 1m. "Character et potestas conficiendi et potestas clavium est unum et idem." But I refer to the entire question.

most imperative of which is confession. In the beginning of the thirteenth century it was peremptorily enjoined on every believer as a duty, to confess all his sins, at least once in a year, to some particular priest.

It requires no elaborate argument to prove what an all-pervading influence auricular confession, and the official supervision and guidance of consciences, must give to the clergy. With this was connected a complete, organized system of penances.

Above all, a character and position almost divine was thus conferred on the high-priest, the pope of Rome; of whom it was assumed that he occupied the place of Christ in the mystical body of the church, which embraced heaven and earth, the dead and the living. This conception of the functions and attributes of the pope was first filled out and perfected in the beginning of the thirteenth century; then, too, was the doctrine of the treasures of the church, on which the system of indulgences rests, first promulgated. Innocent III. did not scruple to declare, that what he did, God did, through him. Glossators added, that the pope possessed the uncontrolled will of God; that his sentence superseded all reasons: with perverse and extravagant dialectic, they propounded the question, whether it were possible to appeal from the pope to God,* and answered it in the negative; seeing that God had the same tribunal as the pope, and that it was impossible to appeal from any being to himself.

It is clear that the papacy must have already gained the victory over the empire,—that it could no longer have any thing to fear, either from master or rival,—before opinions and doctrines of this kind could be entertained or avowed. In the age of struggles and conquests, the theory of the hierarchy gained ground step by step with the fact of material power. Never were theory and practice more intimately connected.

Nor was it to be believed that any interruption or pause in this course of things took place in the fifteenth century. The denial of the right of the clergy to withhold the cup was first declared to be heresy at the council of Constance: Eugenius IV. first formally accepted the doctrine of the Seven Sacraments; the extraordinary school interpretation of the miraculous conception was first approved by the councils, favoured by the popes, and accepted by the universities, in this age.†

It might appear that the worldly dispositions of the popes of those times, whose main object it was to enjoy life, to promote their dependents and to enlarge their secular dominions, would have prejudiced their spiritual pretensions. But, on the contrary, these were as vast and as arrogant as ever. The only effect of the respect inspired by the councils was, that the popes forbade any one to appeal to a council under pain of damnation.‡ With what ardour do the curialist writers labour to demonstrate the infallibility of the pope! John of Torquemada is unwearied in heaping together analogies from Scripture, maxims of the fathers and passages out of the false decretals, for this end; he goes so far as to maintain that, were there not a head of the church who could decide all controversies and remove all doubts, it might be possible to doubt of the Holy Scriptures themselves, which derived their authority only from the church; which, again, could not be conceived as existing without the pope.§ In the beginning of the sixteenth century, the well-known Dominican, Thomas of Gaeta, did not hesitate to declare the church a born slave, who could have no other remedy against a bad pope, than to pray for him without ceasing.‖

Nor were any of the resources of physical force neglected or abandoned. The Dominicans, who taught the strictest doctrines in the universities and proclaimed them to the people from the pulpit, had the right to enforce them by means of fire and sword. Many victims to orthodoxy were offered up after John Huss and Jerome of Prague. The contrast between the worldly-mindedness and sensuality of Alexander VI. and Leo X., with the additional stringency and rigour they gave to the powers of the Inquisition, is most glaring.** Under the authority of similarly disposed predecessors, this institution had recently acquired in Spain a more fearful character and aspect than it had ever yet presented to the world; and the example of Germany shows that similar tendencies were at work in other countries. The strange distortion of the fancy which gave birth to the notion of a personal intercourse with Satan, served as the pretext for bloody executions; the "Hexenhammer" (Hammer for Witches) was the work of two German Dominicans. The Spanish Inquisition had originated in a persecution of the Jews: in Germany, also, the Jews were universally persecuted in the beginning of the sixteenth century, and the Dominicans of Cologne proposed to the emperor to establish an Inquisition against them. They had even the ingenuity to invent a legal authority for such a measure. They declared that it was necessary to examine how far the Jews had deviated from the Old Testament, which the emperor was fully entitled to do, since their nation had formally acknowledged before the judgment-seat of Pilate the authority of the imperial majesty of Rome.†† If they had succeeded, they would certainly not have stopped at the Jews.

* Augustini Triumphi Summa in Gieseler, Kirchengeschichte, ii. iii. 95.

† Baselii Auctarium Naucleri, p. 993.

‡ Bull of Pius II. of the 18th of Jan. 1460. (XV. Kal. Febr., not X., as Rain. has it.) Bullar. Cocq. tom. iii. pars iii. p. 97.

§ Johannes de Turrecremata de Potestate Papali (Roccaberti, tom. xiii.), c. 112. "Credendum est, quod Romanus pontifex in judicio eorum quæ fidei sunt, spiritu sancto regatur et per consequens in illis non erret: alias possit quis eadem facilitate dicere, quod erratum sit in electione quatuor evangeliorum et epistolarum canonis." He laments, however, over the "multa turba adversariorum et inimicorum Romanæ sedis," who will not believe this.

‖ De Autoritate Papæ et Concilii. Extracts in Rainaldus, 1512, nr. 18.

** Decretals in Rainaldus, 1498, nr. 25, 1516, nr. 34.

†† Report in Reuchlin's Augenspiegel (Mirror), printed by v. d. Hardt, Historia Liter. Reformationis, iii. 61.

Meanwhile the whole intellectual energy of the age flowed in the channels marked out by the church. Germany is a striking example to what an extent the popular mind of a nation of the West received its direction from ecclesiastical principles

The great workshops of literature, the German universities, were all more or less colonies or branches of that of Paris—either directly sprung from it, like the earlier, or indirectly, like the later. Their statutes sometimes begin with a eulogy on the Alma Mater of Paris.* From that most ancient seat of learning, too, had the whole system of the schoolmen, the controversy between Nominalism and Realism, the preponderancy of the theological faculty,—"that brilliant star from which everything received light and life,"—passed over to them. In the theological faculty the Professor of Sentences† had the precedency, and the Baccalaureus who read the Bible was obliged to allow him to determine the hour of his lecture. In some universities, none but a clerk who had received at least inferior ordination, could be chosen Rector. The whole of education, from the first elements to the highest dignities of learning, was conducted in one and the same spirit. Dialectical distinctions intruded themselves into the very rudiments of grammar,‡ and the elementary books of the eleventh and twelfth centuries were constantly retained as the groundwork of learning § here, too, the same road was steadily pursued which had been marked out at the time of the foundation of the hierarchical power

Art was subject to the same influences The minsters and cathedrals, in which the doctrines and ideas of the church are so curiously symbolised, rose on every side. In the year 1482, the towers of the church of St Sebaldus at Nürnberg were raised to their present height, in 1494, a new and exquisitely wrought gate was added to Strasburg minster, in 1500, the king of the Romans laid the first stone of the choir of the Reichsgotteshaus (Church of the Empire) St. Ulrich, in Augsburg, with silver trowel, rule, and hod, he caused a magnificent block of stone to be brought from the mountains, out of which a monument was to be erected "to the well-beloved lord St. Ulrich, our kinsman of the house of Kyburg" upon it was to stand a king of the Romans, sword in hand ‖ In 1513, the choir of the cathedral of Freiburg, in 1517, that of Bern, was finished; the porch on the northern transept of the church of St Lawrence in Nurnberg dates from 1520. The brotherhoods of the masons, and the secrets which arose in the workshops of German builders, spread wider and wider It was not till a later period that the redundancy of foliage, the vegetable character, which so remarkably distinguishes the so-called gothic architecture, became general At the time we are speaking of, the interior of churches was principally adorned with countless figures, either exquisitely carved in wood, or cast in precious metals, or painted and enclosed in gold frames, which covered the altars or adorned the aisles and porches It is not the province of the arts to produce ideas, but to give them a sensible form, all the creative powers of the nation were now devoted to the task of representing the traditional conceptions of the church. Those wondrous representations of the Mother of God, so full of sweet and innocent grace, which have immortalized Baldung, Schaffner, and especially Martin Schon, are not mere visions of an artist's fancy; they are profoundly connected with that worship of the Virgin which was then peculiarly general and fervent I venture to add that they cannot be understood without the rosary, which is designed to recal the several joys of the Holy Mary,—the angelic salutation, the journey across the mountains, the child-bearing without pain, the finding of Jesus in the temple, and the ascension, as the prayer-books of that time more fully set forth.

These prayer-books are altogether singular monuments of a simple and credulous devotion. There are prayers to which an indulgence for 136 days, others to which one for 7000 or 8000 years, are attached one morning benediction of peculiar efficacy was sent by a pope to a king of Cyprus, whosoever repeats the prayer of the venerable Bede the requisite number of times, the Virgin Mary will be at hand to help him for thirty days before his death, and will not suffer him to depart unabsolved. The most extravagant expressions were uttered in praise of the Virgin "The eternal Daughter of the eternal Father, the heart of the indivisible Trinity" it was said, "Glory be to the Virgin, to the Father and to the Son"** Thus, too, were the saints invoked as meritorious servants of God, who, by their merits, could win our salvation, and could extend peculiar protection to those who believed in them, as, for example, St Sebaldus, "the most venerable and holy captain, helper and defender of the imperial city of Nurnberg"

Relics were collected with great zeal. Elector Frederick of Saxony gathered together in

* Principium Statutorum Facultatis Theologicæ Studii Viennensis ap Kollar Analecta, i 137, p 240 n 2 Statute of Cologne in Bianco, Endowments for Students at Cologne p 451 "Divinæ sapientiæ fluvius descendens a patre luminum—ab alveo Parisiens studii tanquam cisterna conductu capto per canalia prorumpit Rheni partes ubertando" The genealogy is as follows —From the university of Paris issued those of Prague, Vienna Heidelberg and Cologne, from Prague,—Leipzig, Rostock, Greifswald, and for the greater part, Erfurt, from Cologne,—Louvain and Treves, from Vienna —Freiburg and, according to the Statutes Ingolstadt At Basle and Tübingen at first, deference was paid to Bologna also, but even in Basle, the first Bursa was called the Parisian and in Tübingen the first teacher of Theology was a magister from Paris

† Professor Sententiarum, the expositor of the "Sententiæ" of Peter Lombard.—TRANSL

‡ Geiler, Navicula "In prima parte de subjecto attributionis et de habitibus intellectualibus, quod scire jam est magistrorum provectorum"

§ Johannes de Garlandia Alexander's Doctrinale. Du fresne, Præfatio ad Glossarium, 42, 43

‖ Account in the Fugger MS. We remember that St. Ulrich was the first saint canonised by a pope (Johannes, xv 973) for the whole church

** Extracts from the prayer-books Hortulus Animæ, Salus Animæ Gilgengart, and others in Riederer, Nachrichten zur Buchergeschichte, ii 137—411

the church he endowed at Wittenberg, 5005 particles, all preserved in entire standing figures, or in exquisitely wrought reliquaries, which were shown to the devout people every year on the Monday after Misericordia.* In the presence of the princes assembled at the diet, the high altar of the cathedral of Treves was opened, and "the seamless coat of our dear Lord Jesus Christ," found in it, the little pamphlets in which this miracle was represented in wood-cuts, and announced to all the world, are to be found in the midst of the acts of the diet.† Miraculous images of Our Lady were discovered,—one, for example, in Eischel in the diocese of Constance, at the Iphof boundary, by the road-side, a sitting figure of the Virgin, whose miracles gave great offence to the monks of Birklingen, who possessed a similar one, and in Regensburg, the beautiful image, for which a magnificent church was built by the contributions of the faithful, out of the ruins of a synagogue belonging to the expelled Jews. Miracles were worked without ceasing at the tomb of Bishop Benno in Meissen, madmen were restored to reason, the deformed became straight, those infected with the plague were healed, nay, a fire at Merseburg was extinguished by Bishop Bose merely uttering the name of Benno, while those who doubted his power and sanctity were assailed by misfortunes.‡ When Trithemius recommended this miracle-worker to the pope for canonization, he did not forget to remark that he had been a rigid and energetic supporter of the church party, and had resisted the tyrant Henry IV.§ So intimately were all these ideas connected. A confraternity formed for the purpose of the frequent repetition of the rosary (which is, in fact, nothing more than the devout and affectionate recollection of the joys of the Holy Virgin), was founded by Jacob Sprenger, the violent and fanatical restorer of the Inquisition in Germany,—the author of the "Hexenhammer."

For it was one single and wondrous structure which had grown up out of the germs planted by former ages, wherein spiritual and temporal power, wild fancy and dry school-learning, the tenderest devotion and the rudest force, religion and superstition, were mingled and confounded, and were bound together by some mysterious quality common to them all;—and, amidst all the attacks it sustained, and all the conquests it achieved—amidst those incessant conflicts, the decisions of which constantly assumed the character of laws,—not only asserted its claim to universal fitness for all ages and nations—for this world and the next—but to the regulation of the minutest particulars of human life.

I know not whether any man of sound understanding—any man, not led astray by some phantasm, can seriously wish that this state of things had remained unshaken and unchanged in Europe, whether any man persuades himself that the will and the power to look the genuine, entire and unveiled truth steadily in the face—the manly piety acquainted with the grounds of its faith—could ever have been matured under such influences. Nor do I understand how any one could really regard the diffusion of this most singular condition of the human mind (which had been produced by circumstances wholly peculiar to the West) over the entire globe, as conducive to the welfare and happiness of the human race. It is well known that one main ground of the disinclination of the Greeks to a union with the Roman church, lay in the multitude of rules which were introduced among the Latins, and in the oppressive autocracy which the See of Rome had arrogated to itself.‖ Nay, was not the Gospel itself kept concealed by the Roman church? In the ages in which the scholastic dogmas were fixed, the Bible was forbidden to the laity altogether, and even to the priesthood, in the mother tongue. It is impossible to deny that, without any serious reference to the source from which the whole system of faith had proceeded, men went on to construct doctrines and to enjoin practices, shaped upon the principle which had become the dominant one. We must not confound the tendencies of the period now before us with those evinced in the doctrines and practices established at the Council of Trent; at that time even the party which adhered to Catholicism had felt the influences of the epoch of the Reformation, and had begun to reform itself: the current was already arrested.** And this was absolutely necessary. It was necessary to clear the germ of religion from the thousand folds of accidental forms under which it lay concealed, and to place it unincumbered in the light of day. Before the Gospel could be preached to all nations, it must appear again in its own lucid, unadulterated purity.

It is one of the greatest coincidences presented by the history of the world, that at the moment in which the prospect of exercising dominion over the other hemisphere opened on the Romano-Germanic nations of the Latin church, a religious movement began, the object of which was to restore the purity of revelation.

Whilst other nations were busied in the conquest of distant lands, Germany, which had little share in those enterprises, undertook this mighty task. Various events concurred to give that direction to the mind of the country, and to incite it to a strenuous opposition to the See of Rome.

* Zaigung des Hochlobwurdigsten Heiligthums, 1509 (The Showing of the most venerable Relics, 1509). Extract in Heller's Lucas Kranach, i. p. 350.

† Chronicle of Limpurg in Hontheim, p. 1122. Browerus is again very solemn on this occasion.

‡ Miracula S. Bennonis ex impresso Romæ 1521, in Mencken, Scriptores Rer. Germ. ii. p. 1857.

§ His letter in Rainaldus, 1506, nr. 42.

‖ Humbertus de Romania (in Petrus de Alliaco de Reform. Eccles. c. 2.) "dicit quod causa dispositiva schismatis Græcorum inter alias una fuit propter gravamina Romanæ ecclesiæ in exactionibus, excommunicationibus, et statutis."

** I hold it to be the fundamental error of Mohler's Symbolik, that he considers the dogma of the Council of Trent as the doctrine from which the Protestants seceded, whilst it is much nearer the truth to say, that itself produced Protestantism by a reaction.

OPPOSITION RAISED BY THE SECULAR POWERS.

The efforts to obtain a regular and well-compacted constitution, which for some years had occupied the German nation, were very much at variance with the interests of the papacy, hitherto exercising so great an influence over the government of the empire. The pope would very soon have been made sensible of the change, if that national government which was the object of such zealous and ardent endeavours had been organised.

The very earliest projects of such a constitution, in the year 1487, were accompanied with a warning to the pope to abolish a tithe which he had arbitrarily imposed on Germany, and which in some places he had actually levied.* In 1495, when it became necessary to form a council of the empire, the intention was expressed to authorize the president to take into consideration the complaints of the nation against the church of Rome † Scarcely had the States met the king in 1498, when they resolved to require the pope to relinquish the Annates which he drew to so large an amount from Germany, in order to provide for a Turkish war In like manner, as soon as the Council of Regency was formed, an embassy was sent to the pope to press this request earnestly upon him, and to make representations concerning various unlawful encroachments on the gift and employment of German benefices ‡ A papal legate, who shortly after arrived for the purpose of causing the jubilee to be preached, was admonished by no means to do anything without the advice and knowledge of the imperial government, § care was taken to prevent him from granting indulgences to breakers of the Public Peace: on the contrary, he was charged expressly to uphold it, imperial commissioners were appointed to accompany him, without whose presence and permission he could not receive the money when collected

We find the Emperor Maximilian occasionally following the same course. In the year 1510 he caused a more detailed and distinct statement of the grievances of the German nation to be drawn up, than had hitherto existed, he even entertained the idea of introducing into Germany ‖ the Pragmatic Sanction, which had proved so beneficial to France. In the year 1511 he took a lively interest in the convocation of a council at Pisa we have an edict of his, dated in the January of that year, wherein he declares that, as the court of Rome delays, he will not delay, as emperor, steward and protector of the Church, he convokes the council of which she is so greatly in need. In a brief dated June, he promises to those assembled his protection and favour till the close of their sittings, "by which they will, as he hopes, secure to themselves the approbation of God and the praise of men."** And, in fact, the long-cherished hope that a reform in the church would be the result of this council, was again ardently indulged The articles were pointed out in which reforms were first anticipated For example, the cumulation of benefices in the hands of the cardinals was to be prevented; a law was demanded, in virtue of which a pope whose life was stained with notorious vice, might be summarily deposed.†† But neither had the council authority enough to act upon ideas of this sort, nor was Maximilian the man to follow them out. He was of too weak a nature; and the same Wimpheling who drew up the statement of grievances, remarked to him how many former emperors had been deposed by an incensed pope leagued with the princes of the empire—certainly no motive to resolute perseverance in the course he had begun Independent of this, every new turn in politics gave a fresh direction to his views on ecclesiastical affairs ‡‡ After his reconciliation with Pope Julius II in 1513, he demanded succours from the empire in order to take measures against the schism which was to be feared. Had there really been reason to fear it, he himself would have been mainly to blame for the encouragement he had given to the Council of Pisa.

It is sufficiently clear that this opposition to Rome had no real practical force The want of a body in the state, armed with independent powers, crippled every attempt, every movement, at its very commencement. But in the public mind, that opposition still remained in full force, loud complaints were incessantly heard

Hemmerlin, whose books were in those times extensively circulated and eagerly read, exhausted the vocabulary for expressions to paint the cheating and plunder of which the court of Rome was guilty.§§

In the beginning of the sixteenth century there were the bitterest complaints of the ruinous nature of the Annates. It was probably in itself the most oppressive tax in the empire occasionally a prelate, in order to save his subjects from it, tried to mortgage some lordship of his see. Diether of Isenburg was deposed chiefly because he was unable to fulfil the engagements he had entered into concerning his Pallium.

* Letter, with the seals of Mainz Saxony, and Brandenburg, June 26, 1487, in Muller, Rtth Fr vi 130

† Datt, de Pace Publ p 840

‡ Instructions of the Imperial Embassy Müller, Reichstaggsstaat, 117

§ Articuli tractati et conclusi inter Revmam Dominationem Dnum Legatum ac senatum et conventum Imperii in Muller, Reichstagsstaat, p 213

‖ Avisamenta Germanicæ Nationis in Freher, ii 678 Yet more remarkable is the Epitome pragmaticæ sanctionis in Goldast s Constitutt Imp ii 123

** Triburgi XVI mensis Januarii and Mildorf V Junii in Goldast, i 421, 429

†† In the Fugger MS the decrees which were expected are noted down

‡‡ Baselius 1110 "Admonitus prudentium virorum consilio—quem incaute pedem cum Gallis contra pontificem firmaverat, citius retraxit "

§§ Felix Malleolus Recapitulatio de Anno Jubileo "Pro nunc de præsentis pontificis summi et aliorum statibus comparationis præparationem fecimus, et nunc facie ad faciem experientia videmus quod nunquam visus est execrabilioris exorbitationis direptionis deceptionis circumventionis derogationis decerptationis deprædationis expoliationis exactionis corrosionis et omnis si audemus dicere simoniacæ pravitatis adinventionis novæ et renovationis usus et exercitatio continua quam nunc est tempore pontificis moderni (Nicolas V) et in dies dilatatur "

The more frequent the vacancies, the more intolerable was the exaction. In Passau, for example, these followed in 1482, 1486, 1490, 1500 the last-appointed bishop repaired to Rome in the hope of obtaining some alleviation of the burthens on his see, but he accomplished nothing, and his long residence at the papal court only increased his pecuniary difficulties.* The cost of a pallium for Mainz amounted to 20,000 gulden, the sum was assessed on the several parts of the see the Rheingau, for example, had to contribute 1000 gulden each time † In the beginning of the sixteenth century vacancies occurred three times in quick succession—1505, 1508, 1513; Jacob von Liebenstein said that his chief sorrow in dying was that his country would so soon again be forced to pay the dues, but all appeal to the papal court was fruitless, before the old tax was gathered in, the order for a new one was issued.

We may imagine what was the impression made by the comparison of the laborious negotiations usually necessary to extract even trifling grants from the diet, and the great difficulty with which they were collected, with the sums which flowed without toil or trouble to Rome They were calculated at 300,000 gulden yearly, exclusive of the costs of law proceedings, or the revenues of benefices which lapsed to the court of Rome ‡ And for what purpose, men asked themselves, was all this? Christendom had, nevertheless, lost two empires, fourteen kingdoms, and three hundred towns within a short space of time it was continually losing to the Turks,' if the German nation were to keep these sums in its own hands and expend them itself, it would meet its hereditary foe on other terms, under the banners of its valiant commanders

The financial relations to Rome, generally, excited the greatest attention It was calculated that the barefooted monks, who were not permitted by their rule to touch money, collected a yearly income of 200,000 gulden, the whole body of mendicant friars, a million

Another evil was the recurrence of collisions between the temporal and spiritual jurisdictions, which gradually became the more frequent and obvious, the more the territorial sovereignties tended towards separation and political independence In this respect Saxony was pre-eminent In the different possessions of the two lines, not only the three Saxon bishops, but the archbishops of Mainz and Prag, the bishops of Wurzburg and Bamberg, Halberstadt, Havelberg, Brandenburg and Lebus, had spiritual jurisdiction. The confusion which must, at all events, have arisen from this, was now enormously increased by the fact that all disputes between laity and clergy could only be decided before spiritual tribunals, so that high and low were continually vexed with excommunication. In the year 1454, we find Duke William complaining that the evil did not arise from his good lords and friends the bishops, but from the judges, officials, and procurators, who sought therein only their own profit In concurrence with the counts, lords, and knights of his land, he issued certain ordinances to prevent this abusé,§ in support of which, privileges granted by the popes were alleged, but in 1490 the old complaints were revived, the administration of justice in the temporal courts was greatly obstructed and thwarted by the spiritual, and the people were impoverished by the consequent delays and expenses ‖ In the year 1518, the princes of both lines, George and Frederic, combined to urge that the spiritual jurisdiction should be restricted to spiritual causes, and the temporal to temporal; the diet to decide what was temporal and what spiritual. Duke George was still more zealous in the matter than his cousin ** But the grievances and complaints which fill the proceedings of the later diets were universal, and confined to no class or portion of the empire.

The cities felt the exemptions enjoyed by the clergy peculiarly burthensome. It was impossible to devise any thing more annoying to a well-ordered civic community, than to have within their walls a corporate body which neither acknowledged the jurisdiction of the city, nor contributed to bear its burthens, nor deemed itself generally subject to its regulations. The churches were asylums for criminals, the monasteries the resort of dissolute youth, we find examples of monks who made use of their exemption from tolls, to import goods for sale, or to open a tavern for the sale of beer. If any attempt was made to' assail their privileges, they defended themselves with excommunication and interdict We find the municipal councils incessantly 'occupied in putting some check to this evil. In urgent cases they arrest offenders even in sanctuary, and then take measures to be delivered from the inevitable interdict by the interposition of some powerful protector, they are well inclined to pass over the bishops and to address themselves directly to the pope, they try to effect reforms in their monasteries. They thought it a very questionable arrangement that the parish priest should take part in the collection of the Common Penny; the utmost

* Schreitwein, Episcopi Pataviensus, in Rauch, Scriptt ii 527

† This is shown by the Articles of the inhabitants of the Rheingau in Schunck's Beitragen, i p 183 Jacob of Treves also reckons in 1500, " Das Geld, so sich an dem papstlichen Hofe fur die papstlichen Bullen und Briefe, daruber Anhaten, Minuten, Servitien und andere dem selben anhangend, zu geben geburet," " the money, which it behoves to give to the papal court for the papal bulls and briefs, moreover annats minutes, services, and the rest belonging to the same," at 20,000 guldens Document in Hontheim, ii ser xv

‡ This is, for instance, the calculation of the little book, Ein klagliche Klag (A mournful Complaint) 1521 which, however, I am not for adopting It might very likely be impossible to reckon the gains of the Romish court The tax of the annates at Treves, for instance, legally amounted to 10,000 gulden, and yet the actual charge was 20,000.

§ Ordinance of Duke William, Gotha, Monday after Exaudi, 1454 in Muller, Rth Fr i 130

‖ Words of an ordinance of Duke George in Langenn's Duke Albrecht, p 319

** Articles of the negotiations of the diet, as my gracious lord has caused them to be given in. 1518. In the Dresden Archives

that they would concede was that he should be present, but without taking any active share.* The cities always vehemently opposed the emperor's intention of appointing a bishop to be judge in the Imperial Chamber.

The general disapprobation excited by the church on such weighty points, naturally led to a discussion of its other abuses. Hemmerlin zealously contends against the incessant augmentation of ecclesiastical property, through which villages disappeared and districts became waste; against the exorbitant number of holidays, which even the council of Basle had endeavoured to reduce; against the celibacy of the clergy, to which the rules of the Eastern Church were much to be preferred; against the reckless manner in which ordination was granted, as, for example, that two hundred priests were yearly ordained in Constance: he asks to what all this is to lead.†

Things had gone so far that the constitution of the clergy was offensive to public morals: a multitude of ceremonies and rules were attributed to the mere desire of making money; the situation of priests living in a state of concubinage and burthened with illegitimate children, and often, spite of all purchased absolutions, tormented in conscience and oppressed with the fear that in performing the sacrifice of the mass they committed a deadly sin, excited mingled pity and contempt: most of those who embraced the monastic profession had no other idea than that of leading a life of self-indulgence without labour. People saw that the clergy took from every class and station only what was agreeable, and avoided what was laborious or painful. From the knightly order, the prelate borrowed his brilliant company, his numerous retinue, the splendidly caparisoned horse, and the hawk upon his fist: with women, he shared the love of gorgeous chambers and trim gardens; but the weight of the mailed coat, the troubles of the household, he had the dexterity to avoid. If a man wishes to enjoy himself for once, says an old proverb, let him kill a fat fowl; if for a year, let him take a wife; but if he would live joyously all the days of his life, then let him turn priest.

Innumerable expressions of the same sentiment were current; the pamphlets of that time are full of them.‡

CHARACTER AND TENDENCIES OF THE POPULAR LITERATURE.

THIS state of the public mind acquired vast importance from its coincidence with the first dawnings of a popular literature, which thus, at its very commencement, became deeply and thoroughly imbued with the prevalent sentiment of disapprobation and disgust towards the clergy.

It will be conceded on all sides that in naming Rosenblüt and Sebastian Brant, the Eulenspiegel (Owleglass) and the edition of Reineke Fuchs (Reynard the Fox) of the year 1498, we cite the most remarkable productions of the literature of that time. And if we inquire what characteristic they have in common, we find it to be that of hostility to the Church of Rome. The Fastnachtspiele (Carnival Sports) of Hans Rosenblüt have fully and distinctly this character and intention; he introduces the Emperor of Turkey, in order through his mouth to say the truth to all classes of the nation.§ The vast success of the Eulenspiegel was not to be attributed so much to its own clownish coarseness and practical jokes, as to the irony which was poured over all classes; the wit of the boor, "who scratches himself with a rogue's nails," put that of all others to shame. It was under this point of view alone that the German writer recast the fable of the fox; he saw in it the symbolic representation of the defects and vices of human society, and he quickly detected its application to the several classes of men, and laboured to develop the lesson which the poet reads to each. The same purpose is obvious to the first glance in Brant's Ship of Fools. The ridicule is not directed against individual follies: on the one side is vice, nay crime, on the other, lofty aspirations and pursuits which rise far above vulgar ends, (as, for example, where the devotion of the whole mind to the task of describing cities and countries, the attempt to discover how broad is the earth, and how wide the sea,) are treated as folly.‖ Glory and beauty are described as transient; "nothing is abiding but learning."

In this general opposition to the prevailing state of things, the defects in the ecclesiastical body are continually adverted to. The Schnepperer declaims violently against the priests, "who ride high horses, but will not do battle with the heathen." The most frequent subject of derision in the Eulenspiegel is the common priests, with their pretty ale-wives, well-groomed nags, and full larders; they are represented as stupid and greedy. In Reineke too the Papemeierschen — priests' households, peopled with little children—play a part. The commentator is evidently quite in earnest; he declares, that the sins of the priests will be rated more highly than those of the laity on account of the evil example they set. Doctor Brant expresses his indignation at the premature admission into the convent, before the age of reason; so that religious duties are performed without the least sentiment of devotion: he leads us into the domestic life of the uncalled priests, who are at last in want of the

* Jäger, Schwäbisches Städtewesen: Müllner's Nürnberger Annalen, in several passages.

† The books De Institutione novorum Officiorum, and De Libertate Ecclesiasticâ, are especially remarkable with reference to this matter.

‡ Wimpheling also mentions, "scandalum odium murmur populi in omnem clerum."

§ In the description also of the battle of Hembach in Reinhart's Beitrage zur Historie Frankenlandes, the nobles are mentioned "as a sharp scourge, which chastises us on account of our sins;" "their hearts are harder than adamant."

‖ Dr. Brant's Farrenschiff. 1506, f. 83.

means of subsistence, while their soul is heavy laden with sins, "for God regardeth not the sacrifice which is offered in sin by sinful hands."*

This, however, is not the exclusive, nor, indeed, the principal matter of these books, their significance is far more extensive and general

While the poets of Italy were employed in moulding the romantic materials furnished by the middle ages into grand and brilliant works, these excited little interest in Germany Titurel and Parcival, for example, were printed, but merely as antiquarian curiosities, and in a language even then unintelligible

While, in Italy, the opposition which the institutions of the middle ages encountered in the advancing development of the public mind, took the form of satire, became an element of composition, and as it were the inseparable but mocking companion of the poetical Ideal; in Germany that opposition took up independent ground, and directed its attacks immediately against the realities of life, not against their reproduction in fiction.

In the German literature of that period the whole existence and conduct of the several classes, ages and sexes were brought to the standard of the sober good sense, the homely morality, the simple rule of ordinary life, which, however, asserted its claim to be that "whereby kings hold their crowns, princes their lands, and all powers and authorities their due value"

The universal confusion and ferment which is visible in the public affairs of that period, proves, by inevitable contrast, that the sound common sense of mankind is awakened and busy in the mass of the nation, and prosaic, homely, vulgar, but thoroughly true, as it is, constitutes itself judge of all the phenomena of the world around it.

We are filled with admiration at the spectacle afforded by Italy, where men of genius, reminded by the remains of antiquity around them of the significancy of beautiful forms, strove to emulate their predecessors, and produced works which are the eternal delight of cultivated minds, but their beauty does not blind us to the fact that the movement of the national mind of Germany was not less great, and that it was still more important to the progress of mankind. After centuries of secret growth it now became aware of its own existence, broke loose from tradition, and examined the affairs and the institutions of the world by the light of its own truth

Nor did Germany entirely disregard the demands of form. In Reinecke Fuchs, it is curious to observe how the author rejects every thing appropriate to the style of romantic poetry; how he seeks lighter transitions, works out scenes of common life to more complete and picturesque reality, and constantly strives to be more plain and vernacular (for example, uses all the familiar German names) his main object evidently is to popularise his matter,—to bring it as much as possible home to the nation, and his work has thus acquired the form in which it has attracted readers for more than three centuries. Sebastian Brant possesses an incomparable talent for turning apophthegms and proverbs, he finds the most appropriate expression for simple thoughts; his rhymes come unsought, and are singularly happy and harmonious. "Here," says Geiler von Keisersperg, "the agreeable and the useful are united; his verses are goblets of the purest wine, here we are presented with royal meats in finely wrought vessels"† But in these, as well as in many other works of that time, the matter is the chief thing,—the expression of the opposition of the ordinary morality and working-day sense of mankind to the abuses in public life and the corruptions of the times.

At the same period another branch of literature,—the learned, took an analogous direction, perhaps with even greater force and decision

CONDITION AND CHARACTER OF LEARNED LITERATURE

Upon this department of letters Italy exercised the strongest influence.

In that country neither the metaphysics of the schools, nor romantic poetry, nor Gothic architecture, had obtained complete dominion recollections of antiquity survived, and at length in the fifteenth century, expanded into that splendid revival which took captive all minds and imparted a new life to literature.

This reflorescence of Italy in time reacted on Germany, though at first only in regard to the mere external form of the Latin tongue

In consequence of the uninterrupted intercourse with Italy occasioned by ecclesiastical relations, the Germans soon discovered the superiority of the Italians; they saw themselves despised by the disciples of the grammarians and rhetoricians of that country, and began to be ashamed of the rudeness of their spoken, and the poverty of their written language. It was not surprising, therefore, that young aspiring spirits at length determined to learn their Latin in Italy At first they were only a few opulent nobles—a Dalberg, a Langen‡, a Spiegelberg, who not only acquired knowledge themselves, but had the merit of bringing back books, such as grammatical treatises and better editions of the classics, which they communicated to their friends A man endowed with the peculiar talent necessary for appropriating to himself the classical learning of the age then arose—Rudolf Huesmann of Groningen, called Agricola. His scholarship excited universal admiration, he was applauded in the schools

* The 72d Fool fol 94.

† Geiler Navicula Fatuorum, even more instructive as to the history of morals, than the original, J. u "Est hic," he continues, "in hoc speculo veritas moralis sub figuris sub vulgari et vernacula lingua nostra teutonica sub verbis similitudinibusque aptis et pulchris sub rhitmis quoque concinnis et instar cimbalorum concinentibus"

‡ Hamelmann published in 1580 an Oratio de Rodolpho Langio, which has some merit, but which has also given rise to many errors

as a Roman, a second Virgil.* He had, indeed, no other object but his own advancement in learning; the weary pedantries of the schools were disgusting to him, nor could he accommodate himself to the contracted sphere assigned to a learned man in Germany. Other careers which he entered upon did not satisfy his aspirations, so that he fell into a rapid decline, and died prematurely. He had, however, friends who found it less difficult to adapt themselves to the necessities of German life, and to whom he was ever ready to afford counsel and help. A noble and intimate friendship was formed in Deventer, between Agricola and Hegius, who attached himself to him with all the humility and thirst for knowledge of a disciple; he applied to him for instruction, and received not only assistance but cordial sympathy.† Another of his friends, Dringenberg, followed him to Schletstadt. The reform which took place in the Low German schools of Munster, Hervord, Dortmund, and Hamm, emanated from Deventer, which also furnished them with competent teachers. In Nurnberg, Ulm, Augsburg, Frankfurt, Memmingen, Hagenau, Pforzheim, &c., we find schools of poetry of more or less note.‡ Schletstadt at one time numbered as many as nine hundred students. It will not be imagined that these literati, who had to rule, and to instruct in the rudiments of learning a rude undisciplined youth compelled to live mainly on alms, possessing no books, and wandering from town to town in strangely organized bands, called Bachantes and Schutzen,§ were very eminent scholars themselves, or made such, nor was that the object: their merit, and a sufficient one, was that they not only kept the public mind steady to the important direction it had taken, but carried it onwards to the best of their ability, and founded the existence of an active literary public. The schoolbooks hitherto in use gradually fell into neglect, and classical authors issued from the German press. As early as the end of the fifteenth century, Geiler of Keisersberg, who was not himself devoted to these pursuits, reproached the learned theologians with their Latin, which, he said, was rude, feeble, and barbarous—neither German nor Latin, but both and neither.‖

For since the school learning of the universities, which had hitherto entirely given the tone to elementary instruction, adhered to its wonted forms of expression, a collision between the new and humanistic method, now rapidly gaining ground, and the old modes was inevitable. Nor could their collision fail to extend from the universal element of language into other regions.

It was this crisis in the history of letters that produced an author whose whole life was devoted to the task of attacking the scholastic forms prevailing in universities and monasteries, the first great author of the modern opposition, the champion of the modern views,—a Low German, Erasmus of Rotterdam.

On a review of the first thirty years of the life of Erasmus, we find that he had grown up in ceaseless contradiction with the spirit and the systems which presided over the conventual life and directed the studies of that time,—indeed that this had made him what he was. We might say that he was begotten and born in this contradiction, for his parents had not been able to marry, because his father was destined to the cloister. He had not been admitted to a university, as he wished, but had been kept at a very imperfect conventual school, from which he soon ceased to derive any profit or satisfaction; and, at a later period, every art was practised to induce him to take the vows, and with success. It was not till he had actually taken them, that he felt all the burthen they imposed: he regarded it as a deliverance when he obtained a situation in a college at Paris: but here, too, he was not happy; he was compelled to attend Scotist lectures and disputations; and he complains that the unwholesome food and bad wine on which he was forced to live, had entirely destroyed his health. But in the meanwhile he had come to a consciousness of his own powers. While yet a boy, he had lighted upon the first trace of a new method of study,** and he now followed it up with slender aid from without, but with the infallible instinct of genuine talent, he had constructed for himself a light, flowing style, formed on the model of the ancients, not by a servile imitation of particular expressions, but in native correctness and elegance far surpassing any thing which Paris had to offer. He now emancipated himself from the fetters which bound him to the convent and the schools, and boldly trusted to the art of which he was master, for the means of subsistence. He taught, and in that way formed connections which not only led to present success, but to security for the future; he published some essays which, as they were not less remarkable for discreet choice of matter than for scholar-like execution, gained him admirers and patrons, he gradually discovered the wants and the tastes of the public, and devoted himself entirely to literature. He composed school-books treating of method and form of instruction; translated from the Greek, which he learned in the process; edited

* Erasmi Adagia. Ad de Cane et Balneo.

† Adami Vitæ Philosophorum, p. 12, mentions this correspondence: "unde tum ardor proficiendi, tum candor in communicando elucet."

‡ They are so called, e. g. in the Chronicle of Regensburg. A list of the schools, very incomplete, however, is given by Erhard, Hist. of the Restoration of the Sciences, i. 427. Eberlin von Gunzburg names in 1521 as pious schoolmasters, "deren trewe Unterweisung fast genutzt," "whose faithful instruction had been profitable," Crato and Sapidus at Schletstadt, Mich. Hilspach at Hagenau, Spiegler and Gerbellius at Pforzheim, Brassicanus and Henrichmann at Tubingin, Egid. Krautwasser at Stuttgart and Horb, Joh. Schmidlin at Memmingen, also Cocleus at Nürnberg, and Nisenus at Frankfurt. See Dr. Karl Hagen, Deutchlands literarische und religiose Verhaltnisse im Reformations Zeitalter, 1841, vol. i. p. 164–237.

§ Platter's Autobiography places this practice in a very lively manner before us. (Thomas Platter, after the autograph manuscript lately edited by Fechner, Basle, 1840.)

‖ Geiler Introductorium, ii. c. "Quale est illud eorum Latinum, quo utuntur, etiam dum sederint in sede majestatis suæ, in doctoralis cathedra lecturæ!"

** He cannot, however, be properly considered as a scholar of Hegius. "Hegium," he says in the Compendium Vitæ, "testis diebus audivi." It was the exception.

the classics of antiquity, and imitated them, especially Lucian and Terence. His works abound with marks of that acute and nice observation which at once instructs and delights; but great as these merits were, the grand secret of his popularity lay in the spirit which pervades all he wrote. The bitter hostility to the forms of the devotion and the theology of that time, which had been rendered his habitual frame of mind by the course and events of his life, found vent in his writings; not that this was the premeditated aim or purpose of them, but it broke forth sometimes in the very middle of a learned disquisition—in indirect and unexpected sallies of the most felicitous and exhaustless humour. In one of his works, he adopts the idea, rendered so popular by the fables of Brant and Geiler, of the element of folly which mingles in all human affairs. He introduces Folly herself as interlocutor. Moria, the daughter of Plutus, born in the Happy Islands, nursed by Drunkenness and Rudeness, is mistress of a powerful kingdom, which she describes, and to which all classes of men belong. She passes them all in review, but dwells longer and more earnestly on none than on the clergy, who, though they refuse to acknowledge her benefits, are under the greatest obligations to her. She turns into ridicule the labyrinth of dialectic in which theologians have lost themselves,—the syllogisms with which they labour to sustain the church as Atlas does the heavens,—the intolerant zeal with which they persecute every difference of opinion. She then comes to the ignorance, the dirt, the strange and ludicrous pursuits of the monks, their barbarous and objurgatory style of preaching; she attacks the bishops, who are more solicitous for gold than for the safety of souls; who think they do enough if they dress themselves in theatrical costume, and under the name of the most reverend, most holy, and most blessed fathers in God, pronounce a blessing or a curse; and lastly, she boldly assails the court of Rome and the pope himself,* who, she says, takes only the pleasures of his station, and leaves its duties to St. Peter and St. Paul. Amongst the curious wood-cuts, after the marginal drawings of Hans Holbein, with which the book was adorned, the pope appears with his triple crown.

This little work brought together, with singular talent and brevity, matter which had for some time been current and popular in the world, gave it a form which satisfied all the demands of taste and criticism, and fell in with the most decided tendency of the age. It produced an indescribable effect: twenty-seven editions appeared even during the lifetime of Erasmus; it was translated into all languages, and greatly contributed to confirm the age in its anticlerical dispositions.

But Erasmus coupled with this popular warfare a more serious attack on the state of learning. The study of Greek had arisen in Italy in the fifteenth century; it had found its way by the side of that of Latin into Germany and France, and now opened a new and splendid vista, beyond the narrow horizon of the ecclesiastical learning of the West. Erasmus adopted the idea of the Italians,—that the sciences were to be learned from the ancients; geography from Strabo, natural history from Pliny, mythology from Ovid, medicine from Hippocrates, philosophy from Plato; and not out of the barbarous and imperfect schoolbooks then in use: but he went a step further—he required that divinity should be learned not out of Scotus and Thomas Aquinas, but out of the Greek fathers, and, above all, the New Testament. Following in the track of Laurentius Valla, whose example had great influence generally on his mind, he showed that it was not safe to adhere to the Vulgate, wherein he pointed out a multitude of errors;† and he then himself set about the great work,—the publication of the Greek text; which was as yet imperfectly and superficially known to the West. Thus he thought, as he expresses it, to bring back that cold word-contender, Theology, to her primal sources; he showed the simplicity of the origin whence that wondrous and complicated pile had sprung, and to which it must return. In all this he had the sympathy and assent of the public for which he wrote. The prudence wherewith he concealed from view an abyss in the distance, from which that public would have shrunk with alarm, doubtless contributed to his success. While pointing out abuses, he spoke only of reforms and improvements, which he represented as easy; and was cautious not to offend against certain opinions or principles to which the faith of the pious clung.‡ But the main thing was his incomparable literary talent. He worked incessantly in various branches, and completed his works with great rapidity; he had not the patience to revise and polish them, and accordingly most of them were printed exactly as he threw them out; but this very circumstance rendered them universally acceptable; their great charm was that they communicated the trains of thought which passed through a rich, acute, witty, intrepid, and cultivated mind, just as they arose, and without any reservations. Who remarked the many errors which escaped him? His manner of narrating, which still rivets the attention, then carried every one away. He gradually became the most celebrated man in Europe; public opinion, whose pioneer he had been, adorned him with her fairest wreaths; presents rained upon his

* Μωρίας ἐγκώμιον. Opp. Erasmi, t. iii. "Quasi sint ulli hostes ecclesiæ perniciosiores quam impii pontifices, qui et silentio Christum sinunt abolescere et quæstuariis legibus alligant et coactis interpretationibus adulterant et pestilente vita jugulant."

† In the edition of Alcala de Henares, on the other hand, the Greek text has been changed according to the Vulgate; e. g. 1 Joh. v. 7. Schröckh, KGsch. xxxiv. 83. As to the rest, this adherence to the Vulgate was regarded at a later period, and especially when his canonisation was talked of, as the chief merit of Ximenes, "ut hoc modo melius intelligeretur nostra vulgata in suo rigore et puritate."—*Acta Toletana in Rainaldus*, 1517, nr. 107.

‡ A few years later he thus describes his situation: "Adnixus sum ut bonæ literæ, quas scis hactenus apud Italos fere paganas fuisse, consuescerent de Christo loqui." Epistola ad Cretium, 9 Sept. 1526. Opp. III. i. p. 953.

house at Basle; visitors flocked thither, and invitations poured in from all parts.* His person was small, with light hair, blue, half-closed eyes, full of acute observation, and humour playing about the delicate mouth his air was so timorous that he looked as if a breath would overthrow him, and he trembled at the very name of death.

If this single example sufficed to show how much the exclusive theology of the universities had to fear from the new tendency letters had acquired, it was evident that the danger would become measureless if the spirit of innovation should attempt to force its way into these fortresses of the established corporations of learning The universities, therefore, defended themselves as well as they could George Zingel, pro-chancellor of Ingolstadt, who had been dean of the theological faculty thirty times in three-and-thirty years, would hear nothing of the introduction of the study of heathen poets. Of the ancients, he would admit only Prudentius, of the moderns, the Carmelite Baptista of Mantua these he thought were enough Cologne, which had from the very beginning opposed the introduction of new elementary books,† would not allow the adherents of the new opinions to settle in their town: Rhagius was banished for ten years by public proclamation, Murmellius, a pupil of Hegius, was compelled to give way and to become teacher in a school, Conrad Celtes of Leipzig, was driven away almost by force; Hermann von dem Busch could not maintain his ground either in Leipzig or Rostock; his new edition of Donatus was regarded almost as a heresy ‡ This was not, however, universal According to the constitution of the universities, every man had, at least after taking his degree as Master of Arts, a right to teach, and it was not every one who afforded a reason or a pretext for getting rid of him § In some places, too, the princes had reserved to themselves the right of appointing teachers. In one way or another, teachers of grammar and of classical literature did, as we find, establish themselves, in Tübingen, Heinrich Bebel, who formed a numerous school, in Ingolstadt, Locher, who, after much molestation, succeeded in keeping his ground, and left a brilliant catalogue of princes, prelates, counts, and barons, who had been his pupils,‖ Conrad Celtes in Vienna, where he actually succeeded in establishing a faculty of poetry in the year 1501; and in Prague, Hieronymo Balbi, an Italian, who gave instructions to the young princes, and took some share in public affairs. In Freiburg the new studies were connected with the Roman law; Ulrich Zasius united the two professorships in his own person with the most brilliant success, Pietro Tommai of Ravenna, and his son Vincenzo, were invited to Greifswald, and afterwards to Wittenberg in the same double capacity ** it was hoped that the combined study of antiquity and law would raise that university. Erfurt felt the influence of Conrad Muth, who enjoyed his canonry at Gotha "in blessed tranquillity" ("*in glückseliger Ruhe*") as the inscription on his house says he was the Gleim of that age — the hospitable patron of young men of poetical temperament and pursuits Thus, from the time the new spirit and method found their way into the lower schools, societies of grammarians and poets were gradually formed in most of the universities, completely opposed to the spirit of those establishments as handed down from their fountain-head, Paris They read the ancients, and perhaps allowed something of the petulance of Martial, or the voluptuousness of Ovid, to find its way into their lives, they made Latin verses, which, stiff and barbarous as they generally were, called forth an interchange of admiration; they corresponded in Latin, and took care to interlard it with a few sentences of Greek, they Latinised and Græcised their names †† Genuine talent or accomplished scholarship were very rare, but the life and power of a generation does not manifest itself in mere tastes and acquirements for a few individuals these may be enough, but, for the many, the tendency is the important thing The character of the universities soon altered. The scholars were no longer to be seen with their books under their arms, walking decorously after their Magister, the scholarships were broken up, degrees were no longer sought after—that of bachelor especially (which was unfrequent in Italy) was despised On some occasions the champions of classical studies appeared as the promoters of the disorders of the students,‡‡ and ridicule of the dialectic theologians, nominalists as well as realists, was hailed with delight by the young men.

The world, and especially the learned world, must be other than it is for such a change to be effected without a violent struggle.

The manner, however, in which this broke out is remarkable It was not the necessity of warding off a dangerous attack or a declared enemy that furnished the occasion this was reserved for the most peaceful of the converts

* He afterwards complains of the want of contradiction "Longe plus attulissent utilitatis duo tresve fidi moni tores quam multa laudantium millia" Epp III i 921

† According to Chytræus (Saxonia, p 90) Conrad Rithberg, the bishop of Münster, was warned by the university of Cologne against the establishment of a school upon the new method, but he who had himself been in Italy, was far more strongly worked on by the recommendations which Langen had brought with him thence, e g even from Pope Sixtus

‡ Hamelmann, Oratio de Buschio, nr 49

§ Erasmi Epistolæ, i p 689 In the Epp Obsc Vir ed Münch, p 102 a Socius from Moravia is complained of who wanted to lecture at Vienna without having taken a degree

‖ "Qui nostri portarunt signa theatri"—*Catalogus Illustrium Auditorum Philomusi* "Doctorum insignium magistrorum nobilium ac canonicorum infinitum pene numerum memorare nequeo qui ore magnifico laudi,o naque voce me præceptorem salutare gestiunt Hæc citra omnem jactantiam apposuimus"—*Extract in Zapf Jacob Locher, called Philomusus*, p 27

** Tiraboschi also mentions them vi p 410 Their catastrophe at Cologne is not yet, however, thoroughly cleared up

†† Chraebenberger entreats Reuchlin to find some Greek name, "quo honestius in Latinis literis quam hoc barbaro uti possim" Lynz, Febr 19, 1491

‡‡ Acta Facultatis Artium Friburgensis in Riegger, Vita Zasii i 42 "Conclusum, ut dicatur doctori Zasio quod scholaribus adhæreat faciendo eos rebelles in universitatis præjudicium"

to the new system, who had already fulfilled the active task of life, and at that moment devoted himself to more abstruse studies,—John Reuchlin.

Reuchlin, probably the son of a messenger at Pforzheim, was indebted to his personal gifts for the success which attended him in his career. A fine voice procured him admittance to the court of Baden; his beautiful handwriting maintained him during his residence in France, the pure pronunciation of Latin which he had acquired by intercourse with foreigners, caused him to be appointed member of an embassy to Rome, and this led to an important post and considerable influence at the court of Wurtemberg, and the Swabian league generally.* His qualities, both external and internal, were very unlike those of Erasmus. He was tall and well made, and dignified in all his deportment and actions, while the mildness and serenity of his appearance and manner won instant confidence towards his intellectual superiority.† As an author, he could never have gained the applause of the large public of Latin scholars, his style is not above mediocrity, nor does he evince any nice sense of elegance and form. On the other hand, he was inspired by a thirst for learning, and a zeal for communicating, which were without a parallel. He describes how he picked up his knowledge bit by bit,—crumbs that fell from the lord's table—at Paris and in the Vatican, at Florence, Milan, Basle, and at the Imperial Court, how, like the bird of Apollonius, he left the corn for the other birds to eat.‡ He facilitated the study of Latin by a dictionary, which in great measure supplanted the old scholastic ones, and of Greek, by a small grammar, he spared neither labour nor money to get copies of the classics brought across the Alps, either in manuscript, or as they issued from the Italian press. What no prince, no wealthy city or community thought of doing, was done by the son of a poor errand man, it was under his roof that the most wondrous production of distant ages—the Homeric poems—first came in contact with the mind of Germany, which was destined in later times to render them more intelligible to the world. His Hebrew learning was still more highly esteemed by his contemporaries than all his other acquirements, and he himself regarded his labours in that field as his most peculiar claim to distinction. "There has been none before me," exclaims he with well-grounded self-gratulation, to one of his adversaries, "who has been able to collect the rules of the Hebrew language into a book; though his heart should burst with envy, still I am the first. Exegi monumentum ære perennius."§ In this work he was chiefly indebted to the Jewish Rabbis whom he sought out in all directions, not suffering one to pass by without learning something from him: by them he was led to study not only the Old Testament, but other Hebrew books, and especially the Cabbala. Reuchlin's mind was not one of those to which the labours of a mere grammarian or lexicographer are sufficient for their own sake. After the fashion of his Jewish teachers, he applied himself to the study of the mystical value of words. In the name of the Deity as written in the Holy Scriptures, in its elementary composition, he discovers the deepest mystery of his being. For, he says, "God, who delights in intercourse with a holy soul, will transform it into himself, and will dwell in it. God is Spirit, the Word is a breath; Man breathes; God is the Word. The names which He has given to Himself are an echo of Eternity; in them is the deep abyss of his mysterious working expressed; the God-Man called himself the Word."‖ Thus, at its very outset, the study of language in Germany was directed towards its final end and aim—the knowledge of the mysterious connection of language with the Divine—of its identity with the spirit. Reuchlin is like his cotemporaries, the discoverers of the New World, who sailed some north, some south, some right on to the west, found portions of coast which they described, and while at the beginning, often thought they had reached the end. Reuchlin was persuaded that he should find in the road he had taken, not only the Aristotelic and Platonic philosophers, which had already been brought to light, but that he should add to them, the Pythagorean,—an offspring of Hebraism. He believed that by treading in the footsteps of the Cabbala, he should ascend from symbol to symbol, from form to form, till he should reach that last and purest form which rules the empire of mind, and in which human mutability approaches to the Immutable and Divine.**

But while living in this world of ideas and abstractions, it was his lot to be singled out by the enmity of the scholastic party: he unexpectedly found himself involved in the heat of a violent controversy.

We have already alluded to the inquisitorial attempts of the Dominicans of Cologne, and their hostility to the Jews. In the year 1508, a book was published by an old Rabbi, who at the age of fifty had abandoned his wife and child, and become a Christian priest. In this he accused his former co-religionists of the grossest errors, for example, adoration of the sun and moon, but, above all, of the most horrible blasphemies against the Christian faith, which he endeavoured to prove from the Talmud.†† It was mainly on this ground that

* Schnurrer, Nachrichten von den Lehrern der Hebraischen Literatur, p. 11. A small essay of Michael Coccinius De Imperii a Græcis ad Germanos Translatione, 1506, is dedicated to Reuchlin, together with his two colleagues in the court of the Swabian league, Streber and Winkelhofer (confœderatorum Suevorum judicibus consistorialibus et triumviris.)

† Joannis Hiltebrandi Præfatio in Illustrium Virorum Epistolas ad Reuchlinum.

‡ Præfatio ad Rudimenta Linguæ Hebraicæ, lib. iii. Cf. Burkhard, de Fatis Linguæ Latinæ, p. 152.

§ Reuchlini Consilium pro Libris Judæorum non abolendis in v. d. Hardt, Historia Ref. p. 49. This is moreover a fine specimen of German prose.

‖ Reuchlin de Verbo Mirifico, ii. 6, 15; iii. 3, 19.

** Reuchlin de Arte Cabbalistica, p. 614, 620, 696.

†† Notices of this little Jewish book in Riederer's Nach-

the theologians of Cologne urged the emperor to order the publication of the Talmud, and gave him, at his request, the opinion in which they affirmed his right to proceed against the Jews as heretics. The Imperial Council, however, deemed it expedient to consult another master of Hebrew literature They referred the matter to the reviver of the cabbalistic philosophy—Reuchlin.

Reuchlin gave his opinion, as might be expected, in favour of the Judaical books His report is a beautiful monument of pure dispassionate judgment and consummate sagacity But these qualities were just those fitted to draw down the whole storm of fanatical rage upon himself

The Cologne theologians, irritated to fury by the rejection of their proposition, which they ascribed, not without reason, to the adverse opinion of Reuchlin, incited one of their satellites to attack him, he answered they condemned his answer, he rejoined, upon which they appointed a court of inquisition to try him

This was the first serious encounter of the two parties. The Dominicans hoped to establish their tottering credit by a great stroke of authority, and to intimidate the adversaries who threatened to become dangerous to them, by the terrors which were at their disposal. The innovators—the teachers and disciples of the schools of poetry whom we have mentioned—were fully sensible that Reuchlin's peril was their own; but their efforts and aspirations were checked by the consciousness of opposition to existing authority, and of the dubious position which they occupied.

In October, 1513, a court of inquisition was formed at Mainz, composed of the doctors of the university and the officers of the archbishopric, under the presidency of the inquisitor of heretical wickedness—Jacob Hogstraten, and it remained to be seen whether such a sentence as that pronounced some years before against John of Wesalia, would now be given

But times were totally altered. That intensely Catholic spirit which had rendered it so easy for the Inquisition to take root in Spain, was very far from reigning in Germany The Imperial Council must have been, from the outset, indisposed towards the demands of the Cologne divines, or they would not have appealed to such a man as Reuchlin for advice The infection of the prevalent spirit of literature had already spread too widely, and had created a sort of public opinion We have a whole list of members of the higher clergy who are cited as friends of the literary innovation—Gross and Wrisberg, canons of Augsburg, Nuenar of Cologne, Adelmann of Eichstadt, Andreas Fuchs, dean of Bamberg, Lorenzo Truchsess, of Mainz, Wolfgang Tanberg, of Passau, Jacob de Bannissis, of Trent. Cardinal Lang, the most influential of the emperor's councillors, shared these opinions. The superior clergy were not more disposed than the people to allow the Inquisition to regain its power

Elector Diether had consented to the trial of Wesalia, against his will, and only because he feared the puissant Dominicans might a second time effect his deposition,* now, however, the heads of the church were no longer so timorous, and after the tribunal had already taken its seat to pronounce judgment, Dean Lorenz Truchsess persuaded the Elector to command it to suspend its proceedings, and to forbid his own officers to take part in them †

Nay, another tribunal, favourable to Reuchlin, was appointed to hold its sittings under the Bishop of Spires, in virtue of a commission obtained from Rome, the sentence pronounced by this court on the 24th April, 1514, was, that the accusers of Reuchlin, having falsely calumniated him, were condemned to eternal silence and to the payment of the costs ‡

So widely diffused and so powerful was the antipathy which the Dominicans had excited. So lively was the sympathy which the higher and educated classes testified in the efforts of the new school of literature. So powerful already was the opinion of men of learning. It was their first victory.

Persecuting orthodoxy found no favour either with the emperor or with the higher clergy of Germany But its advocates did not give up the contest. At Cologne, Reuchlin's books were condemned to be burnt unanimous sentences to the same effect were obtained from the faculties of Erfurt, Mainz, Louvaine, and Paris, thus fortified, they applied to the supreme tribunal at Rome, the representatives of orthodox theology presented themselves before the pope, and urged him to give his infallible decision in aid of the ancient champions of the Holy See against innovators

But even Rome was perplexed Should she offend public opinion represented by men so influential from their talents and learning? Should she act in opposition to her own opinions? On the other hand, would it be safe to set at nought the judgment of powerful universities? to break with the order which had so zealously contended for the prerogatives of the Roman see, and had preached the doctrine and furthered the sale of indulgences all over the world?§

In the commission appointed by the pope at Rome, the majority was for Reuchlin, but a considerable minority was against him, and the pope held it expedient to defer his decision He issued a *mandatum de supersedendum* ‖

Reuchlin, conscious of a just cause, was

richten, I i p 34 It appeared in Latin in 1509, as an "opus aureum ac novum"

* Cogentibus Thomistis quibusdam, veritus ne denuo ab episcopatu ejiceretur jussu Romano pontificis"—*Examen Wesaliæ*, fasc i 327

† Hutten's Preface to Livy, opp iii p 334 ed Munch proves the share of Lorenz Truchsess "quodam suo divino consilio"

‡ Acta judiciorum in v d Hardt, Hist Lit Reformationis, 111 The chief source of information respecting these events

§ Erasmus ad Vergaram, Opp III, 1015 "Quis enim magis timet monachos quam Romani pontifices?"

‖ Reuchlin de Arte Cabbalistica, p 730. Acta Judiciorum, p 130.

not perfectly satisfied with this result, especially after all that had gone before: he expected a formal and complete acquittal; nevertheless, even this was to be regarded as little less than a victory. The fact that the party which assumed to represent religion and to have exclusive possession of the true doctrines, had failed to carry through their inquisitorial designs, and even, as secret reports said, had only escaped a sentence of condemnation by means of gold and favour,* was enough to encourage all their adversaries. Hitherto the latter had only stood on the defensive; they now assumed an attitude of open, direct offence. Reuchlin's correspondence, which was published expressly to show the respect and admiration he enjoyed, shows how numerously and zealously they rallied round him. We find the spiritual lords we have mentioned; patricians of the most important cities, such as Pirkheimer of Nürnberg, who delighted in being considered as the leader of a numerous band of Reuchlinists; Peutinger of Augsburg, Stuss of Cologne; preachers like Capito and Œcolampadius; the Austrian historians, Lazius and Cuspinian; doctors of medicine—all, in short, who had any tincture of letters; but chiefly those poets and orators in the schools and universities who beheld their own cause in that of Reuchlin, and now rushed in throngs to the newly-opened arena; at their head Busch, Jäger, Hess, Hutten, and a long list of eminent names.†

The remarkable production in which the whole character and drift of their labours is summed up, is, the Epistolæ Obscurorum Virorum. That popular satire, already so rife in Germany, but hitherto confined to generals, here found a particular subject exactly suited to it. We must not look for the delicate apprehension and tact which can only be formed in a highly polished state of society, nor for the indignation of insulted morality expressed by the ancients: it is altogether caricature,—not of finished individual portraits, but of a single type;—a clownish, sensual German priest, his intellect narrowed by stupid wonder and fanatical hatred, who relates with silly *naïveté* and gossiping confidence the various absurd and scandalous situations into which he falls. These letters are not the work of a high poetical genius, but they have truth, coarse strong features of resemblance, and vivid colouring. As they originated in a widely-diffused and powerful tendency of the public mind, they produced an immense effect: the See of Rome deemed it necessary to prohibit them.

It may be affirmed generally that the genius of the literary opposition was triumphant. In the year 1518, Erasmus looked joyfully around him; his disciples and adherents had risen to eminence in every university—even in Leipsig, which had so long resisted: they were all teachers of ancient literature.‡

Was it indeed possible that the great men of antiquity should have lived in vain? That their works, produced in the youth-time of the human race,—works with whose beauty and profound wisdom nothing that has since arisen is to be compared, should not be restored to later ages in their primitive form and perfection? It is an event of the greatest historical importance, that after so many convulsions by which nations were overthrown and others constituted out of their ruins,—by which the old world had been obliterated and all its elements replaced by other matter,—the relics of its spirit, which could now exercise no other influence than that of form, were sought with an avidity hitherto unknown, and widely diffused, studied, and imitated.

The study of antiquity was implanted in Germany as early as the first introduction of Christianity; in the 10th and 11th centuries it had risen to a considerable height, but at a later period it was stifled by the despotism of the hierarchy and the schools. The latter now returned to their original vocation. It was not to be expected, that great works of literary art could as yet be produced; for that, circumstances were not ripe. The first effect of the new studies showed itself in the nature and modes of instruction — the more natural and rational training of the youthful mind which has continued to be the basis of German erudition. The hierarchical system of opinions which, though it had been wrought up to a high point of brilliancy and refinement, could not possibly endure, was thus completely broken up. A new life stirred in every department of human intelligence. "What an age!" exclaims Hutten, "learning flourishes, the minds of men awake; it is a joy to be alive." This was peculiarly conspicuous in the domain of theology. The highest ecclesiastic of the nation, Archbishop Albert of Mainz, saluted Erasmus as the restorer of theology.

But an intellectual movement of a totally different kind was now about to take place.

EARLY CAREER OF LUTHER.

The authorities, or the opinions which rule the world, rarely encounter their most dangerous enemies from without; the hostilities by which they are overthrown are usually generated and nurtured within their own sphere.

In the bosom of theological philosophy itself, discords arose from which a new era in the history of life and thought may be dated.

We must not omit to notice the fact, that the doctrines of Wickliffe, which had spread from Oxford over the whole of Latin Chris-

* In Hogstratus Ovans, 336, it is said, through the intercession of Nicolaus von Schomberg.

† Even before the letters to Reuchlin, we find set down the Exercitus Reuchlinistarum. Pirkheimer, Epistola Apologetica, in Hardt, p. 136, has another list. Later lists, *e. g.* in Mayerhoff, must, in several cases, be taken with restrictions.

‡ In the Essay De Ratione conscribendi Epistolas, the dedication of which belongs to the year 1522, he exclaims (ed. of 1534, p. 71), "Videmus quantum profectum sit paucis annis. Ubi nunc est Michael Modista, ubi glossema Jacobi, ubi citatur Catholicon brachylogus aut Mammætrectus, quos olim ceu rarum thesaurum aureis literis descriptos habebant monachorum bibliothecæ." It is evident how much the method had changed.

tendom, and broke out with such menacing demonstrations in Bohemia, had not, in spite of all the barbarities of the Hussite wars, been extirpated in Germany. At a much later period we find traces of them in Bavaria, where the Boklerbund drew upon itself the suspicions of Hussite opinions; in Swabia and Franconia, where the council of Bamberg at one time thought it necessary to compel all the men in that city to abjure the Hussites, and even in Prussia, where the adherents of Wickliffite and Hussite doctrines at length submitted, though only in appearance.* It was the more remarkable that after such measures, the society of the Bohemian brethren arose out of the fierce tempest of Hussite opinions and parties, and once more exhibited to the world a Christian community in all the purity and simplicity of the primitive church. Their religion derived a new and singular character from the fundamental principle of their secession—that Christ himself was the rock on which the church was founded, and not Peter and his successors.† Their settlements were in those districts where the German and Slavonic elements are intermingled, and their emissaries went forth and traversed unnoticed the wide domain of either language, seeking those already allied to them in opinion, or endeavouring to gain over new proselytes. Nicholas Kuss of Rostock, whom they visited several times, began at this period to preach openly against the pope (A. D. 1511.)‡

The opposition to the despotism of the Dominican system still subsisted in the universities themselves. Nominalism, connected at the very moment of its revival with the adversaries of the papacy, had found great acceptance in Germany, and was still by no means suppressed. The most celebrated nominalist of that time, Gabriel Biel, the collector, is mainly an epitomizer of Occam. This party was in the minority, and often exposed to the persecutions of its enemies who wielded the powers of the Inquisition,§ but it only struck deeper and firmer root. Luther and Melanchthon are the offspring of nominalism.

And perhaps a still more important circumstance was, that in the 15th century the stricter Augustinian doctrines were revived in the persons of some theologians.

Johann de Wesalia taught election by grace; he speaks of the Book in which the names of the elect are written from the beginning. The tendency of his opinions is shown by the definition of the Sacrament which he opposes to that given by Peter Lombard: the former is that of St. Augustine in its original purity, while the latter is an extension of it, the general aim of his works is, the removal of the additions made in later times to the primitive doctrines of the church.‖ He denies the binding force of priestly rules, and the efficacy of indulgences; he is filled with the idea of the invisible church. He was a man of great intellectual powers, capable of playing a distinguished part at a university like that of Erfurt; he arrived at these convictions by degrees, and when convinced did not conceal them even in the pulpit; nor did he shrink from a connexion with Bohemian emissaries. At length, however, when advanced in age, he was dragged, leaning on his staff, before the Inquisition, and thrown into prison, where he died.

Johann Pupper of Goch, who founded a convent of nuns of the rule of St. Augustine at Mechlin about the year 1460–70, made himself remarkable by accusing the dominant party in the church of a leaning to Pelagianism.** He calls Thomas Aquinas the prince of error. He attacked the devotion to ceremonies, and the Pharisaism of vows, upon Augustinian principles.

How often have the antagonists of the church of Rome made this the ground of their opposition!—from Claudius of Turin in the beginning of the ninth, to Bishop Janse in the 17th century, and his followers in the 18th and 19th. The deeper minds within her pale have always felt compelled to point back to those fundamental doctrines on which she was originally based.

The principles of the opposition now assumed the form of a scientific structure. In the works of Johann Wessel, of Groningen, we see a manly mind devoted to truth, working itself free from the bonds of the mighty tradition which could no longer satisfy a religious conscience. Wessel lays down the maxim that prelates and doctors are to be believed only so far as their doctrines are in conformity with the Scriptures, the sole rule of faith, which is far above pope or church,†† he writes almost in the spirit of a theologian of later times. It was perfectly intelligible that he was not permitted to set foot in the university of Heidelberg.

Nor were these efforts completely isolated.

At the time of the council of Basle, the German provincial society of the Augustin Eremites had formed themselves into a separate congregation, and had from that moment made it their chief endeavour to uphold the more rigorous doctrines of the patron of their order. This was peculiarly the aim of the resolute and undaunted Andreas Proles, who for nearly a half century administered the Vicariate of that province.‡‡ Another and a

* Zschokke, Baier. Gesch. ii. 429. Pfister, Gesch. von Schwaben, v. 378. Baczko, Gesch. von Preussen, i. 256.

† What it was which appeared dangerous in their doctrines is shown particularly in the Refutations of the Dominican Heinrich Institoris, from which Rinaldus (1498, nr. 25.) gives copious extracts.

‡ Wolfii Lectiones memorabiles, ii. 27.

§ In the Examen Magistrale Dni Joh. de Wesalia the Concipient describes these disputes at the conclusion: "adeo ut si universalia quisquam realia negaverit, existimetur in spiritum sanctum peccavisse, immo—contra deum, contra Christianam religionem,—deliquisse."

‖ Joh. de Wesalia, Disputatio adversus indulgentias in Walch Monumenta Medii Ævi. tom. i. fasc. p. 131.

** Dialogus de Quatuor Erroribus circa Legem Evangelicam in Walch, Monum. I. iv. p. 151. "Hæc fuit insania Pelagii hæretici, a qua error Thomistarum non solum in hoc loco sed etiam in multis aliis non multum degenerare videtur." What impression this made we perceive from Pantaleon's description.

†† Ullmann, Johann Wessel, p. 337.

‡‡ Joh. Pelz, Supplementum Aurifodinæ, 1501, in Kapp, Nachlese, iv. p. 400.

congenial tendency came in aid of this in the beginning of the 16th century The despotism of the schools had been constantly opposed by all those who were inclined to mystical contemplation the sermons of Tauler, which had several times issued from the press, became extremely popular from their mild earnestness, their depth of thought and reason, and the tone of sincerity so satisfactory to the German mind and heart The Book of German Theology, which appeared at that time, may be regarded as an offspring of Tauler's teaching It chiefly insisted on the inability of the creature, of himself, to comprehend the Infinite and the Perfect, to attain to inward peace, or to give himself up to that Eternal Good, which descends upon him of its own free motion Johann Staupitz, the successor of Proles, adopted these ideas, and laboured to develope and to diffuse them * If we examine his views of the subject,—as for example, the manner in which he treats of the love "which a man can neither learn of himself nor from others, nor even from the Holy Scriptures,—which he can only possess through the indwelling of the Holy Spirit,"—we are struck with their perfect connexion and accordance with the stricter ideas of grace, faith, and free-will, a connexion, indeed, without which these doctrines would not have been intelligible to the age. We must not assume that all Augustine convents, or even all the members of the one in question, were converted to these opinions; but it is certain that they first struck root among this order, whence they spread abroad and tended to foster the resistance to the prevailing doctrines of the schools

It is manifest that all these agitations of opinion, from whatever source they proceeded, were allies of the literary opposition to the tyranny of the Dominican system. The fact that these various but converging tendencies at length found representatives within the circle of one university, must be regarded as in itself an important event for the whole nation

In the year 1502, Elector Frederic of Saxony founded a new university at Wittenberg He accomplished this object chiefly by obtaining the pope's consent to incorporate a number of parishes with the richly endowed church attached to the palace, and transforming the whole into a foundation, the revenues of which he then allotted to the new professors. The same course had been pursued in Treves and in Tubingen, the clerical dignities of the institution were connected with the offices in the university The provost, dean, scholaster, and syndic formed the faculty of law, the archdeacon, cantor, and warden, that of theology, the lectures on philosophy and the exercises of the candidates for the degree of master of arts were attached to five canonries The eminent Augustine convent in the town was to take part in the work †

We must recollect that the universities were then regarded not only as establishments for education, but as supreme tribunals for the decision of scientific questions. In the charter of Wittenberg, Frederic declares‡ that he, as well as all the neighbouring states, would repair thither as to an oracle, "so that," says he, "when we have come full of doubt, we may, after receiving the sentence, depart in certainty."

Two men, both unquestionably belonging to the party hostile to the reigning theologico-philosophical system, had the greatest influence on the foundation and first organization of this university The one was Dr Martin Pollich of Melrichstadt, physician to the elector, whose name stands at the head of the list of the rectors of the Leipzig university, where he was previously established We know that he had contended against the fantastic exaggerations of scholastic learning, and the strange assertions to which they gave birth; such as that the light created on the first day was theology, that discursive theology was inherent in the angels We know that he had already perceived the necessity of grounding that science on a study of letters generally §

The other was Johann Staupitz, the mystical cast of whose opinions, borrowed from St. Augustine, we have just mentioned; he was the first dean of the theological faculty, the first act of which was, the promotion of Martin Pollich to the doctor of theology ‖ as director of the Augustine convent, he likewise enjoyed peculiar influence It was not an insignificant circumstance that the university had just then declared St. Augustine its patron Notwithstanding his strong tendency to speculation, Staupitz was obviously an excellent man of business, he conducted himself with address at court, and a homely vein of wit which he possessed, enabled him to make his part good with the prince; he undertook an embassy, and conducted the negotiation with success; but the deeper spring of all his conduct and actions is clearly a genuine feeling of true and heartfelt religion, and an expansive benevolence.

It is easy to imagine in what spirit these men laboured at the university But a new star soon arose upon it. In the year 1508, Staupitz conducted thither the young Luther.

We must pause a moment to consider the early years of this remarkable man.

"I am a peasant's son," says he; "my father, grandfather, and ancestors were genuine peasants; afterwards, my father removed to Mansfeld, and became a miner; that is my native place "** Luther's family was from Mohra, a village on the very summit of the Thuringian forest, not far from the spot celebrated for the

* Grimm de Joanne Staupitzio ejusque in sacrorum Christianorum restaurationem meritis, in Illgen Zeitschrift fur die Hist Theologie. N F i ii 78

† The papal privilege in Grohmann, Geschichte der Universitat Wittenberg, comp p 110

‡ Confirmatio ducis Frederici, ib p 19

§ Loscher, in the unoffending accounts of 1716, and in the Acts of the Reformation i 88 has given extracts from his writings In his epitaph in the parish church at Wittenberg, he is rightly called hujus gymnasii primus rector *et parens*

‖ Liber decanorum facultatis theologorum Vitebergensis, ed Foerstemann, p 2

** Tischreden, p 581

first preaching of Christianity by Boniface; it is probable that Luther's forefathers had for centuries been settled on their hide of land (Hufe) as was the custom with those Thuringian peasants, one brother among whom always inherited the estate, while the others sought a subsistence in other ways Condemned by such a destiny to seek a home and hearth for himself, Hans Luther was led to the mines at Mansfeld, where he earned his bread by the sweat of his brow, while his wife, Margaret, often fetched wood from the forest on her back Such were the parents of Martin Luther He was born at Eisleben, whither his sturdy mother had walked to the yearly fair; he grew up in the mountain air of Mansfeld

The habits and manners of that time were generally harsh and rude, and so was his education. Luther relates that his mother once scourged him till the blood came, on account of one miserable nut, that his father had punished him so severely that it was with great difficulty that he could get over the child's terror and alienation, at school he was flogged fifteen times in one forenoon. He had to earn his bread by singing hymns before the doors of houses, and new year's carols in the villages Strange—that people should continually exalt and envy the happiness of childhood, in which the only certain foretaste of coming years is the feeling of the stern necessities of life; in which existence is dependent on foreign help, and the will of another disposes of every day and hour with iron sway In Luther's case, this period of life was full of terrors

From his fifteenth year his condition was somewhat better In Eisenach, where he was sent to the high school, he found a home in the house of some relations of his mother; thence he went to the university of Erfurt, where his father, whose industry, frugality and success had placed him in easier circumstances, made him a liberal allowance* · his hope was, that his son would be a lawyer, marry well and do him honour.

But in this weary life the restraints of childhood are soon succeeded by troubles and perplexities The spirit feels itself freed from the bonds of the school, and is not yet distracted by the wants and cares of daily life; it boldly turns to the highest problems, such as the relation of man to God, and of God to the world, and while eagerly rushing on to the solution of them, it falls into the most distressing state of doubt We might be almost tempted to think that the Eternal Source of all life appeared to the youthful Luther only in the light of the inexorable judge and avenger, who punishes sin (of which Luther had from nature an awful and vivid feeling) with the torments of hell, and can only be propitiated by penance, mortification and painful service As he was returning from his father's house in Mansfeld to Erfurt, in the month of July, 1505, he was overtaken in a field near Stotternheim by one of those fearful tempests which slowly gather on the mountains and at length suddenly burst over the whole horizon. Luther was already depressed by the unexpected death of an intimate friend There are moments in which the agitated desponding heart is completely crushed by one overwhelming incident, even of the natural world Luther, traversing his solitary path, saw in the tempest the God of wrath and vengeance, the lightning struck some object near him, in his terror he made a vow to St Anne, that if he escaped, he would enter a convent He passed one more evening with his friends, enjoying the pleasures of wine, music, and song, it was the last in which he indulged himself, he hastened to fulfil his vow, and entered the Augustine Convent at Erfurt

But he was little likely to find serenity there, imprisoned, in all the buoyant energy of youth, within the narrow gates and in the low and gloomy cell, with no prospect but a few feet of garden within the cloisters, and condemned to perform the lowest offices. At first he devoted himself to the duties of a novice with all the ardour of a determined will. 'If ever a monk got to heaven by monkish life and practices (*durch Moncherei*), I resolved that I would enter there," were his words † But though he conformed to the hard duty of obedience, he was soon a prey to the most painful disquiet Sometimes he studied day and night, to the neglect of his canonical hours, which he then passed his nights in retrieving with penitent zeal. Sometimes he went out into some neighbouring village, carrying with him his midday repast, preached to the shepherds and ploughmen, and then refreshed himself with their rustic music, after which he went home, and shutting himself up for days in his cell, would see no one. All his former doubts and secret perplexities returned from time to time with redoubled force

In the course of his study of the Scriptures, he fell upon texts which struck terror into his soul, one of these was, "Save me in thy righteousness and thy truth" "I thought," said he, "that righteousness was the fierce wrath of God, wherewith he punishes sinners" Certain passages in the Epistles of St Paul haunted him for days The doctrine of grace was not indeed unknown to him, but the dogma that sin was at once taken away by it, produced upon him, who was but too conscious of his sins, rather a sense of rejection—a feeling of deep depression, than of hope He says it made his heart bleed—it made him despair of God.‡ "Oh, my sins, my sins, my sins'" he writes to Staupitz, who was not a little astonished when he received the confession of so sorrowful a penitent, and found that he had no sinful acts to acknowledge. His anguish was the longing of the creature after the purity of the Creator, to whom it feels itself profoundly and intimately allied, yet from whom it is severed by an immeasurable gulph a feeling which Luther nourished by incessant solitary

* Luther's Erklarung der Genesis, c 49, v 15, Attenb tom. ix p 1525

† Short answer to Duke George Altenburg t vi p 22 Exposition of the eighth chapter of John, v 770

‡ He relates this in the Sermo die S Joh 1516, in Löscher, Reformations Acta, i. p 258

brooding, and which had taken the more painful and complete possession of him because no penance had power to appease it, no doctrine truly touched it, no confessor would hear of it. There were moments when this anxious melancholy arose with fearful might from the mysterious abysses of his soul, waved its dusky pinions over its head, and felled him to the earth. On one occasion when he had been invisible for several days, some friends broke into his cell and found him lying senseless on the ground. They knew their friend, with tender precaution they struck some chords on a stringed instrument they had brought with them, the inward strife of the perplexed spirit was allayed by the well-known remedy, it was restored to harmony and awakened to healthful consciousness.

But the eternal laws of the universe seem to require that so deep and earnest a longing of the soul after God should at length be appeased with the fulness of conviction.

The first who, if he could not administer comfort to Luther in his desperate condition, at least let fall a ray of light upon his thick darkness, was an old Augustine friar who with fatherly admonitions pointed his attention to the first and simplest truth of Christianity,—the forgiveness of sins through faith in the Redeemer, and to the assertion of St Paul (Rom iii.), that man is justified without works, by faith alone * doctrines which he might indeed have heard before, but obscured as they were by school subtleties, and a ceremonial worship, he had never rightly understood. They now first made a full and profound impression on him. He meditated especially on the saying, "The just shall live by faith." He read St Augustine's commentary on this passage. "Then was I glad," says he, "for I learned and saw that God's righteousness is his mercy, by which he accounts and holds us justified, thus I reconciled justice with justification, and felt assured that I was in the true faith." This was exactly the conviction of which his mind stood in need. it was manifest to him that the same eternal grace whence the whole race of man is sprung, mercifully brings back erring souls to itself and enlightens them with the fulness of its own light; that an example and irrefragable assurance of this is given us in the person of Christ. he gradually emerged from the gloomy idea of a divine justice only to be propitiated by the rigours of penance. He was like a man who after long wanderings has at length found the right path, and feeling more certain of it at every step, walks boldly and hopefully onward.

Such was Luther's state when he was removed to Wittenberg by his provincial (A. D 1508). The philosophical lectures which he was obliged to deliver, sharpened his desire to penetrate the mysteries of theology, "the kernel of the nut," as he calls it, "the heart of the wheat." The books which he studied were, St Paul's Epistles, St. Augustine against the Pelagians, and, lastly, Tauler's sermons: he troubled himself little with literature foreign to this subject, he cared only to strengthen and work out the convictions he had gained.†

A few years later we find him in the most extraordinary frame of mind, during a journey which he took for the affairs of his order to Rome. As soon as he descried the towers of the city from a distance, he threw himself on the ground, raised his hands and exclaimed, "Hail to thee, O holy Rome!" On his arrival, there was no exercise in use among the most pious pilgrims which he did not perform with earnest and deliberate devotion, undeterred by the levity of other priests, he said he was almost tempted to wish that his parents were dead, that so he might have been able certainly to deliver them from the fire of purgatory by these privileged observances.‡ Yet, at the same time, he felt how little such practices were in accordance with the consolatory doctrine which he had found in the Epistle to the Romans and in St Augustine. While climbing the Scala Santa on his knees in order to obtain the plenary indulgence attached to that painful and laborious work of piety, he heard a reproving voice continually crying within him, 'The just shall live by faith.'"§

After his return in 1512, he became Doctor of the Holy Scripture, and from year to year enlarged his sphere of activity. He lectured at the university on both the Old and New Testament; he preached at the Augustine church, and performed the duties of the priest of the parochial church of the town during his

* Short notice by Melancthon on the Life of Luther Works Altenb viii 876. See Matthesius Historien Dr Luthers First Sermon, p 12. Bavarus in Seckendorf, Hist Lutheranismi, p 21.

† In the "Histori, so zwen Augustinerordens gemartert seyn zu Brussel in Probandt,"—"History, how two monks of the order of St Augustine underwent martyrdom at Brussels in Brabandt,"—there is in sheet B the following excellent and authentic passage upon Luther's studies "In welchen Verstand (dass er die Schrift so klar und gnadenreich erklärt) er kummen ist erst durch manche Staupen dye er erlitten hat von Got, und mit vleissigen Bitten zu Got steten Lesen, und nemlich Augustinus wider die Pelagianer hat ym grosse hilff gethan tzur erkenntnuss Pauli yn seyn Episteln. Sunderlich ein Predigbuchlin der Tawler genanndt yhm deutschen das hat er uns oft zu erkauffen ermant unter seym lesen yn der Schul welches yn gefurt hat yn geist als er offt uns bekannt auch ist eyn Buchlyn genandt die deutsch Theologen hat Er allzeyt hochgebrufft als er den schreibtt yn der Vorrede gedachten Buchlyns — Hat auch oft gesagt, das seyn Kunst mer yhm geben sey auserfarendenn lesen, und das vyll Bucher nit gelert machen. Darumb findt man (Spater 1523) yhn seiner Wonung nit vyll Bucher, den eyn Bibel und Concordanz der Bybel."—"To what understanding (enabling him to explain the Scriptures with such clearness and grace) he has arrived, first by manifold chastisements which he has suffered from God, and through diligent prayer to God, and constant reading, and for instance, Augustine against the Pelagians has been of great help to him towards the comprehension of Paul in his Epistles. Especially a little book of sermons by Tawler he has often admonished us to buy in the middle of his teaching in the school, as what has guided him in spirit, as he as often acknowleged to us, there is also a little book called the German Theology, which he has at all times highly praised, as he writes in the preface to the said little book. He has also often said, that his skill was given him more by experience than reading, and that many books do not make a man learned. Therefore many books are not to be found (this is later in 1523) in his dwelling, but one Bible and a Concordance of the Bible."

‡ Exposition of the 117th Psalm to Hans von Sternberg Luthers Werke, Altenb v 251.

§ Story told by Luther in the Table Talk, p 609.

illness; in 1516, Staupitz appointed him administrator of the order during his absence on a journey, and we trace him visiting all the monasteries in the province, appointing or displacing priors, receiving or removing monks. While labouring to introduce a profounder spirit of piety, he did not overlook the smallest economical details; and besides all this, he had to manage his own crowded and extremely poor convent. Some things, written in the years 1515 and 1516, enable us better to understand the state and workings of his mind during that period. Mystical and scholastic ideas had still great influence over him. In the first words of his on religious subjects in the German language which we possess,—a sketch of a sermon dated November, 1515,—he applies, in somewhat coarse terms, the symbolical language of the Song of Songs to the operations of the Holy Ghost, which acts on the spirit through the flesh; and also to the inward harmony of the Holy Scriptures. In another, dated December of the same year, he endeavours to explain the mystery of the Trinity by the Aristotelic theory of being, motion, and rest.* Meanwhile his thoughts were already turned to a grand and general reform of the church. In a speech which appears to have been intended to be uttered by the provost of Lietzkau at the Lateran council, he sets forth that the corruption of the world was to be ascribed to the priests, who delivered to the people too many maxims and fables of human invention, and not the pure word of God. For, he said, the word of life alone is able to work out the regeneration of man. It is well worthy of remark, that, even then, Luther looked for the salvation of the world far less to an amendment of life, which was only secondary in his eyes, than to a revival of the true doctrines: and there was none with the importance of which he was so penetrated and filled as with that of justification by faith. He continually insists on the absolute necessity of a man denying himself, and fleeing for refuge under the wings of Christ; he seizes every opportunity of repeating the saying of St. Augustine, that faith obtains what the law enjoins.† We see that Luther was not yet completely at one with himself; that he still cherished opinions fundamentally at variance with each other; but all his writings breathe a powerful mind, a youthful courage, still restrained within the bounds of modesty and reverence for authority, though ready to overleap them; a genius intent on essentials, tearing asunder the bonds of system, and pressing forward in the new path which it has discovered. In the year 1516, we find that Luther was busily occupied in defending and establishing his doctrine of justification.‡ He was greatly encouraged by the discovery of the spuriousness of a book attributed to Augustine, on which the schoolmen had founded many doctrines extremely offensive to him, and which was quoted almost entire in Lombard's book, "De verâ et falsâ Penitentiâ;" and he now took heart to attack the doctrine of the Scotists on love, and that of the Magister Sententiarum on hope; he was already convinced that there was no such thing as a work in and for itself pleasing to God—such as prayer, fasts and vigils; for, as their whole efficacy depended on their being done in the fear of God, it followed that every other act or occupation was just as good in itself.

In opposition to some expressions of German theologians which appeared to him of a Pelagian tendency, he embraced with uncompromising firmness even the severer views of Augustine: one of his disciples held a solemn disputation in defence of the doctrine of the subjection of the will, and of the inability of man to fit himself for grace, much more to obtain it, by his own powers.§

If it be asked wherein he discovered the mediating power between divine perfection and human sinfulness, we find that it was solely in the mystery of the redemption, and the revealed word; mercy on the one side, and faith on the other. These opinions led him to doubt of many of the main dogmas of the church. He did not yet deny the efficacy of absolution; but no later than the year 1516, he was perplexed by the doubt how man could obtain grace by such means: the desire of the soul was not appeased by it, nor was love infused; those effects could only be produced by the enlightenment of the mind, and the kindling of the will by the immediate operation of the Eternal Spirit; for, he added, he could conceive of religion only as residing in the inmost depth of the heart.‖ He doubted whether all those outward succours for which it was usual to invoke the saints, ought to be ascribed to them.

Such were the doctrines, such the great general direction of mind immediately connected with the opinions implanted by Pollich and Staupitz, which Luther disseminated among the Augustine friars of his convent and his province, and, above all, among the members of the university. For a time Jodocus Trutvetter of Eisenach sustained the established opinions; but after his death in the year 1513, Luther was the master spirit that ruled the schools. His colleagues, Peter Lupinus and Andreas Carlstadt, who for a time withstood his influence, at length declared themselves overcome and convinced by the arguments of Augustine and the doctrines of the Holy Scripture which had made so deep an impression on him; they were almost more zealous than Luther himself. A totally different direction was thus given to the university of Wittenberg from that in which the other seats of learning continued to move. Theology itself, mainly in-

* Sermo Lutheri in Nativitate Christi, 1515.

† Fides impetrat quæ lex imperat.

‡ From the Sermo de propria Sapientia, it appears that he had already been attacked on this point. "Efficitur mihi et errans et falsum dictum."

§ Quæstio de viribus et voluntate hominis sine gratia, in Löscher, i. 328.

‖ Sermo Xma post Trinitatis. He still says himself occasionally, "Ego non satis intelligo hanc rem; manet dubium," &c.—*Löscher*, p. 761.

deed in consequence of its own internal development, made similar claims to those asserted by general literature. In Wittenberg arose the opposition to the theologians of the old and the new way, the nominalists and the realists, and more especially to the reigning thomistical doctrines of the Dominicans; men now turned to the scriptures and the fathers of the church, as Erasmus (though rather as a conscientious critic than an enthusiastic religionist) had recommended. In a short time there were no hearers for the lectures given in the old spirit.

Such was the state of things in Wittenberg when the preachers of papal indulgences appeared in the country about the Elbe, armed with powers such as had never been heard of before, but which Pope Leo X. did not scruple, under the circumstances in which he found himself, to grant.

For no fear whatever was now entertained at Rome of any important division in the church.

In the place of the council at Pisa, one had been convoked at the Lateran, in which devotion to the see of Rome, and the doctrine of its omnipotence, reigned unalloyed and undisputed.

At an earlier period, the college of Cardinals had often made an attempt to limit the powers of the papacy, and to adopt measures with regard to it like those employed by the German chapters towards their bishoprics; they had elected Leo because they thought he would submit to these restraints. But the event proved how utterly they had miscalculated. The men who had chiefly promoted Leo's election were precisely those who now most severely felt his power. Their rage knew no bounds. Cardinal Alfonso Petrucci several times went to the college with a dagger concealed beneath the purple; he would have assassinated the pope had he not been withheld by the consideration of the effect which the murder of a pope by a cardinal would produce on the world. He therefore held it to be more expedient to take another and less violent way to the same end—to get rid of the pope by poison. But this course required friends and allies among the cardinals and assistants in the palace, and thus it happened that he was betrayed.*

What stormy consistories followed this discovery! The persons standing without, says the Master of the Ceremonies, heard loud clamours,—the pope against some of the cardinals, the cardinals against each other, and against the pope. Whatever passed there, Leo did not allow such an opportunity of establishing his power for ever, to escape him. Not only did he get rid of his formidable adversary, but he proceeded to create at one stroke thirty-one cardinals, thus insuring to himself a majority in all contingencies, and a complete supremacy.†

The state, too, was convulsed by a violent storm. Francesco Maria, Duke of Urbino, who had been driven out of his territory, had returned, and had set on foot a war, the result of which long kept the pope in a state of mingled exasperation and shame: gradually, however, he mastered this opposition also; the war swallowed up streams of gold, but means were found to raise it.

The position which the pope, now absolute lord of Florence and master of Siena, occupied, the powerful alliances he had contracted with the other powers of Europe, and the views which his family entertained on the rest of Italy, rendered it absolutely indispensable for him, spite of the prodigality of a government that knew no restraint, to be well supplied with money. He seized every occasion of extracting extraordinary revenues from the church.

The Lateran council was induced, immediately before its dissolution (15th of March, 1517), to grant the pope a tenth of all church property throughout Christendom. Three different commissions for the sale of indulgences traversed Germany and the northern states at the same moment.‡

These expedients were, it is true, resorted to under various pretexts. The tenths were, it was said, to be expended in a Turkish war, which was soon to be declared; the produce of indulgences was for the building of St. Peter's Church, where the bones of the martyrs lay exposed to the inclemency of the elements. But people had ceased to believe in these pretences.

Devoted as the Lateran council was to the pope, the proposition was only carried by two or three votes: an extremely large minority objected to the tenths, that it was impossible to think of a Turkish war at present.§ Who could be a more zealous catholic than Cardinal Ximenes, who then governed Spain? Yet even in the year 1513, he had opposed the attempt to introduce the sale of indulgences into that country; ‖ he made vehement professions of devotion to the pope, but he added, as to the tenths, it must first be seen how they were to be applied.**

For there was not a doubt on the mind of any reasonable man, that all these demands were mere financial speculations. There is no positive proof that the assertion then so generally made—that the proceeds of the sale of indulgences in Germany was destined in part for the pope's sister Maddelena — was true. But the main fact is indisputable, that the ecclesiastical aids were applied to the uses of the pope's family. We have a receipt now lying before us, given by the pope's nephew

* All doubts whatsoever in the reality of this conspiracy cease, upon reading the discourse held by Bandinelli upon receiving his pardon, in which he acknowledges, "qualiter ipse conspirarat cum Francisco Maria, . . . et cum Alfonso Petrutio machinatus erat in mortem sanctitatis vestræ præparando venena," &c. &c.

† Paris de Grassis, in Rainaldus, 1517, 95. Comp. Jovius, Vita Leonis, iv. 67.

‡ Leoni, Vita di Francesco Maria d'Urbino, p. 205.

§ Paris de Grassis, in Rainaldus, 1517, un. 16.

‖ Gomez, Vita Ximenis, in Schott, Hispania illustrata, i. p. 1065.

** Argensola, Anales de Aragon, p. 354.

Lorenzo to the king of France, for 100,000 livres which that monarch paid him for his services. Herein it is expressly said that the king was to receive this sum from the tenths which the council had granted to the pope for the Turkish war.* This was, therefore, precisely the same thing as if the pope had given the money to his nephew; or, perhaps even worse, for he gave it him before it was raised.

The only means of resistance to these impositions were therefore to be sought in the powers of the state, which were just now gradually acquiring stability, as we see by the example of Ximenes in Spain; or in England, where the decision of the Lateran council could not have reached the government, at the time when it forced the papal collectors to take an oath that they would send neither money nor bills of exchange to Rome.† But who was there capable of protecting the interests of Germany? The Council of Regency no longer existed; the emperor was compelled by his uncertain political relations (especially to France) to keep up a good understanding with the pope. One of the most considerable princes of the empire, the Archchancellor of Germany, Elector Albert of Mainz, born Markgrave of Brandenburg, had the same interests as the pope,—a part of the proceeds were to go into his own exchequer.

Of the three commissions into which Germany was divided, the one which was administered by Arimbold, a member of the Roman prelature, embraced the greater part of the dioceses of Upper and Lower Germany; another, which included only Switzerland and Austria, fell to the charge of Cristofero Numai of Forli,‡ general of the Franciscans; and the Elector of Mainz himself had undertaken the third in his own vast archiepiscopal provinces, Mainz and Magdeburg; and for the following reasons.

We remember what heavy charges had been brought upon the archbishopric of Mainz by the frequent recurrence of vacancies. In the year 1514 the chapter elected Markgrave Albert for no other reason than that he promised not to press heavily on the diocese for the expenses of the Pallium. But neither was he able to defray them from his own resources. The expedient devised was, that he should borrow 30,000 gulden of the house of Fugger of Augsburg, and detain one half of the money raised by indulgences to repay it.§ This financial operation was perfectly open and undisguised. Agents of the house of Fugger travelled about with the preachers of indulgences. Albert had authorized them to take half of all the money received on the spot, "in payment of the sum due to them."‖ The tax for the plenary indulgence reminds us of the measures taken for the collection of the Common Penny. We possess diaries in which the disbursements for spiritual benefits are entered and calculated together with secular purchases.**

And it is important to examine what were the advantages which were thus obtained.

The plenary indulgence for all, the alleged object of which was to contribute to the completion of the Vatican Basilica, restored the possessor to the grace of God, and completely exempted him from the punishment of purgatory. But there were three other favours to be obtained by further contributions: the right of choosing a father confessor who could grant absolution in reserved cases, and commute vows which had been taken into other good works; participation in all prayers, fasts, pilgrimages, and whatever good works were performed in the church militant; lastly, the release of the souls of the departed out of purgatory. In order to obtain plenary indulgence, it was necessary not only to confess, but to feel contrition; the three others could be obtained without contrition or confession, by money alone.†† It is in this point of view that Columbus extols the worth of money: "he who possesses it," says he seriously, "has the power of transporting souls into Paradise."

Never indeed were the union of secular objects with spiritual omnipotence more strikingly displayed than in the epoch we are now considering. There is a fantastic sublimity and grandeur in this conception of the church, as a community comprehending heaven and earth, the living and the dead; in which all the penalties incurred by individuals were removed by the merit and the grace of the collective body. What a conception of the power and dignity of a human being is implied in the belief that the pope could employ this accumulated treasure of merits in behalf of one or another at his pleasure!‡‡ The doctrine that the power of the pope extended to that intermediate state between heaven and earth, called purgatory, was the growth of modern times.

* Molini, Documenti storici, t. i. p. 71.

† Oath of Silvester Darius, the papal collector (in curia cancellaria in aula palatii Westmonasteriensis) April 22, 1517, in Rymer's Fœdera, vi. i. p. 133.

‡ His deputy plenipotentiary was Samson, of whom it was said in a pamphlet of 1521: er habe den Bauern "Bassporten geben in den Hymel durch ein Tollmetschen, von welchem Kaufmannschatz hatt er gut silberin Platten gefiret gen Mailand."—He had given the peasants "passports into Heaven through an interpreter, by means of which stock in trade he had taken good silver coin back to Milan."

§ Notices from a manuscript essay, from which Rathmann Gesch. von Magdeburg, iii. p. 302, has made extracts. In Erhard's Überlieferungen zur vaterländ. Gesch. part iii. p. 12, is to be found a calculation addressed to Leo X., and a motuproprio by him referring to this point. The money advanced by the Fuggers to the archiepiscopal oratores in Rome towards the payment for the pallium amounted to 21,000 ducats (100 ducats are equal to 140 gold gulden): the Fuggers received 500 Rhenish gulden over, as commission.

‖ Gudenus, Diplom. Moguntiac, iv. 587.

** *e. g.* Johannis Tichtelii Diarium. in Rauch, ii. 558. "Uxor imposuit pro se duas libras denariorum, pro parentibus dimidiam 1 d., pro domino Bartholomæo dimidiam 1 d."

†† Instructio summaria ad subcommissarios, in Gerdes, Historia Evangelii, i. App. n. ix. p. 83. For the most part agreeing word for word with the Avvisamenti of Arcimbold in Kapp's Nachlese.

‡‡ Summa divi Thomæ Suppl. Qu. 25 art. 1 concl. "Prædicta merita sunt communia totius ecclesiæ: ea autem quæ sunt alicujus multitudinis communia, distribuuntur singulis de multitudine secundum arbitrium ejus qui multitudini præest." Further: art. 2, "Nec divinæ justitiæ derogatur, quia nihil de pœna dimittitur, sed unius pœna alteri computatur."

The pope appears in the character of the great dispenser of all punishment and all mercy And this most poetical, sublime idea he now dragged in the dust for a miserable sum of money, which he applied to the political or domestic wants of the moment Mountebank itinerant commissioners, who were very fond of reckoning how much they had already raised for the papal court, while they retained a considerable portion of it for themselves, and lived a life of ease and luxury, outstripped their powers with blasphemous eloquence They thought themselves armed against every attack, so long as they could menace their opponents with the tremendous punishments of the church.

But a man was now found who dared to confront them

While Luther's whole soul was more and more profoundly embued with the doctrine of salvation by faith, which he zealously diffused not only in the cloister and the university, but in his character of parish priest of Wittenberg, there appeared in his neighbourhood an announcement of a totally opposite character, grounded on the merest external compromise with conscience, and resting on those ecclesiastical theories which he, with his colleagues, disciples and friends, so strenuously combated. In the neighbouring town of Juterbock, the multitude flocked together around the Dominican friar, John Tetzel, a man distinguished above all the other pope's commissioners for shamelessness of tongue. Memorials of the trafic in which he was engaged are preserved (as was fitting) in the ancient church of the town Among the buyers of indulgences were also some people from Wittenberg; Luther saw himself directly attacked in his cure of souls

It was impossible that contradictions so absolute should approach so near without coming into open conflict.

On the vigil of All Saints, on which the parochial church was accustomed to distribute the treasure of indulgences attached to its relics,—on the 31st October, 1517,—Luther nailed on its gates ninety-five propositions,—"a disputation for the purpose of explaining the power of indulgences"

We must recollect that the doctrine of the treasure of the church, on which that of indulgences rested, was from the very first regarded as at complete variance with the sacrament of the power of the keys. The dispensation of indulgences rested on the overflowing merits of the church all that was required on the one side was sufficient authority: on the other, a mark or token of connexion with the church,—any act done for her honour or advantage. The sacrament of the keys, on the contrary, was exclusively derived from the merits of Christ, for that, sacerdotal ordination was necessary on the one side, and, on the other, contrition and penance. In the former case the measure of grace was at the pleasure of the dispenser; in the latter, it must be determined by the relation between the sin and the penitence. In this controversy, Thomas Aquinas had declared himself for the doctrine of the treasure of the church and the validity of the indulgences which she dispensed: he expressly teaches that no priest is necessary, a mere legate can dispense them; even in return for temporal services, so far as these were subservient to a spiritual purpose In this opinion he was followed by his school *

The same controversy was revived, after the lapse of ages, by Luther, but he espoused the contrary side. Not that he altogether denied the treasures of the church; but he declared that this doctrine was not sufficiently clear, and, above all, he contested the right of the pope to dispense them For he ascribed only an inward efficacy to this mysterious community of the church He maintained that all her members had a share in her good works, even without a pope's brief; that his power extended over purgatory only in so far as the intercessions of the church were in his hand; but the question must first be determined whether God would hear these intercessions: he held that the granting indulgences of any kind whatsoever without repentance, was directly contrary to the Christian doctrine. He denied, article by article, the authority given to the dealers in indulgences in their instructions On the other hand, he traced the doctrine of absolution to that of the authority of the keys † In this authority, which Christ delegated to St Peter, lay the power of the pope to remit sin. It also extended to all penances and cases of conscience; but of course to no punishments but those imposed for the purpose of satisfaction; and even then, their whole efficacy depended on whether the sinner felt contrition, which he himself was not able to determine, much less another for him If he had true contrition, complete forgiveness was granted him, if he had it not, no brief of indulgence could avail him for the pope's absolution had no value in and for itself, but only in so far as it was a mark of Divine favour.

It is evident that this attack did not originate in a scheme of faith new to the church, but in the very centre of the scholastic notions; according to which the fundamental idea of the papacy — viz. that the priesthood, and more especially the successors of St. Peter, were representatives and vicegerents of Christ,— was still firmly adhered to, though the doctrine of the union of all the powers of the church in the person of the pope was just as decidedly controverted. It is impossible to read these propositions without seeing by what a daring, magnanimous, and constant spirit Luther was actuated. The thoughts fly out from his mind like sparks from the iron under the stroke of the hammer.

* Scti Thomæ Summæ, Supplementum tertiæ partis Quæstio xxv art ii, expounds this doctrine very clearly Its main ground however, always remains the same, that the church says thus for, "si in prædicatione ecclesiæ aliqua falsitas deprehenderetur, non essent documenta ecclesiæ alicujus autoritatis ad roborandam fidem"

† Just as the adversaries, whom Thomas Aquinas refutes, maintained "indulgentiæ non habent effectum nisi ex vi clavium."

Let us not forget to remark, however, that as the abuse complained of had a double character, religious and political, or financial, so also political events came in aid of the opposition emanating from religious ideas.

Frederick of Saxony had been present when the Council of Regency prescribed to Cardinal Raimund very strict conditions for the indulgence then proclaimed (A. D. 1501) he had kept the money accruing from it in his own dominions in his possession, with the determination not to part with it, till an expedition against the infidels, which was then contemplated, should be actually undertaken, the pope and, on the pope's concession, the emperor had demanded it of him in vain * he held it for what it really was—a tax levied on his subjects; and after all the projects of a war against the Turks had come to nothing, he had at length applied the money to his university. Nor was he now inclined to consent to a similar scheme of taxation His neighbour, Elector Joachim of Brandenburg, readily submitted to it: he commanded his States to throw no obstacles in the way of Tetzel or his sub-commissioners;† but his compliance was clearly only the result of the consideration that one half of the amount would go to his brother For this very reason, however, Elector Frederick made the stronger resistance he was already irritated against the Elector of Mainz in consequence of the affairs of Erfurt, and he declared that Albert should not pay for his pallium out of the pockets of the Saxons The sale of indulgences at Juterbock and the resort of his subjects thither, was not less offensive to him on financial grounds than to Luther on spiritual.

Not that the latter were in any degree excited by the former, this it would be impossible to maintain after a careful examination of the facts; on the contrary, the spiritual motives were more original, powerful, and independent than the temporal, though these were important, as having their proper source in the general condition of Germany The point whence the great events arose which were soon to agitate the world, was the coincidence of the two.

There was, as we have already observed, no one who represented the interests of Germany in the matter. There were innumerable persons who saw through the abuse of religion, but no one who dared to call it by its right name and openly to denounce and resist it. But the alliance between the monk of Wittenberg and the sovereign of Saxony was formed; no treaty was negotiated; they had never seen each other, yet they were bound together by an instinctive mutual understanding. The intrepid monk attacked the enemy; the prince did not promise him his aid—he did not even encourage him, he let things take their course.

Yet he must have felt very distinctly what was the tendency and the importance of these events, if we are to believe the story of the dream which he dreamt at his castle of Schweinitz, where he was then staying, on the night of All Saints, just after the theses were stuck up on the church door at Wittenberg He thought he saw the monk writing certain propositions on the chapel of the castle at Wittenberg, in so large a hand that it could be read in Schweinitz; the pen grew longer and longer, till at last it reached to Rome, touched the pope's triple crown, and made it totter, he was stretching out his arm to catch it, when he woke ‡

Luther's daring assault was the shock which awakened Germany from her slumber. That a man should arise who had the courage to undertake the perilous struggle, was a source of universal satisfaction, and as it were tranquillised the public conscience § The most powerful interests were involved in it,—that of sincere and profound piety, against the most purely external means of obtaining pardon of sins, that of literature, against fanatical persecutors, of whom Tetzel was one, the renovated theology against the dogmatic learning of the schools, which lent itself to all these abuses, the temporal power against the spiritual, whose usurpations it sought to curb, lastly, the nation against the rapacity of Rome.

But since each of these interests had its antagonist, the resistance could not be much less vehement than the support. A numerous body of natural adversaries arose.

The university of Frankfurt on the Oder, like that of Wittenberg, was an off-shoot of Leipzig, only founded at a later date, and belonging to the opposite party Determined opponents to all innovation had found appointments there Conrad Koch, surnamed Wimpina, an old enemy of Pollich, who had often had a literary skirmish with him, had acquired a similar influence there to that possessed by Pollich at Wittenberg Johann Tetzel now addressed himself to Wimpina, and with his assistance (for he was ambitious of being a doctor as well as his Augustine adversary) published two theses, on one of which he intended to hold a disputation for the degree of licentiate, on the

* At the Diet of Augsburg, 1510, the Saxon deputies declared to the papal nuncio as appeared in one of their letters to Frederic the Wise "es habe Pp Heiligkeit leiden mogen, das E Gn das Geld so in iren Landen gefallen zu sich genommen mit einer Verpflichtung wann es zum Streit wider die Unglaubigen komme es wiederum darzulegen aus der Ursach hab E Gn wyewol mehrmal darum angesucht von Keys Mt wegen, die auch gerne E Gn gemelte Summe um ihre Schuld geben hatt dy Summa noch wy sy gefallen ist " "His Papal Holiness has been obliged to allow that your Grace should take into your keeping the money collected in your States under an obligation to produce it again whenever a war with the infidels should come about, from this cause, your Grace, although many times applied to for it on behalf of his Imperial Majesty, who would gladly have given the before mentioned sum to your Grace in payment of debts, still has the entire sum, as it was collected "

† Mandate of Joachim in Walch, Werke Luthers, xv 415

‡ A divine and scriptural dream from Caspar Rothen, Gloria Lutheri, in Tentzel's Histor Bericht, p 239

§ Erasmus to Duke George of Saxony, Dec 12 1524 "Cum Lutherus aggrederetur hanc fabulum, totus mundus illi magno consensu applausit,—susceperat enim optimam causam adversus corruptissimos scholarum et ecclesiæ mores, qui eo progressi fuerant ut res jam nulli bono viro tolerabilis videretur "

other, for that of doctor both were directed against Luther. In the first he attempted to defend the doctrine of indulgences by means of a new distinction between expiatory and saving punishment The pope, he said, could remit the former, though not the latter * In the second thesis he extols most highly the power of the pope, who had the exclusive right of settling the interpretation of Scripture, and deciding on articles of faith, he denounces Luther, not indeed by name, but with sufficient distinctness, as a heretic, nay a stiff-necked heretic This now resounded from pulpit and chair Hogstraten thundered out invectives, and clearly intimated that such a heretic was worthy of death; while a manuscript confutation by an apparent friend, Johann Eck of Ingolstadt, was circulated, containing insinuations concerning the Bohemian poison † Luther left none of these attacks unanswered and in every one of his polemical writings he gained ground. Other questions soon found their way into the controversy; *e. g.* that concerning the legend of St. Anne, the authenticity of which was disputed by a friend of Luther's at Zwickau, but obstinately maintained by the Leipzig theologians ‡ The Wittenberg views concerning the Aristotelian philosophy and the merit of works spread abroad Luther himself defended them at a meeting of his order at Heidelberg, and if he experienced opposition from the elder doctors, a number of the younger members of the university became his adherents The whole theological world of Germany was thrown into the most violent agitation

But already a voice from Rome was heard through the loud disputes of excited Germany Silvester Mazolini of Prierio, master of the sacred palace, a Dominican, who had given out a very equivocal and cautious opinion concerning the necessity of repentance and the sinfulness of lying, but had defended the system of teaching practised by his order with inflexible zeal,—who, in Reuchlin's controversy, had been the only member of the commission that had prevented it from coming to a decision favourable to that eminent scholar, now deemed himself called upon to take up arms against this new and far more formidable assailant He rose, as he said, from the commentary in "Primam Secundæ" of St. Thomas, in the composition of which he was absorbed, and devoted a few days to throw himself like a buckler between the Augustine monk and the Roman See, against which he had dared to rear his head §; he thought Luther sufficiently confuted by the mere citation of the opinions of his master, St. Thomas An attack emanating from Rome made some impression even upon Luther feeble and easy to confute as Silvester's writing appeared to him, he now paused; he did not wish to have the Curia his open and direct foe On the 30th May he sent an explanation of his propositions to the pope himself, and seized this occasion of endeavouring to render his opinions and conduct generally intelligible to the Holy Father. He did not as yet go so far as to appeal purely and exclusively to the Scriptures, on the contrary, he declared that he submitted to the authority of the fathers who were recognized by the church, and even to that of the papal decrees But he could not consider himself bound to accept the opinions of Thomas Aquinas as articles of faith, since his works were not yet sanctioned by the church "I may err," he exclaims, "but a heretic I will not be, let my enemies rage and rail as they will."

Affairs, however, already began to wear the most threatening aspect at Rome

The papal fiscal, Mario Perusco,‖ the same who had rendered himself celebrated by the investigation of the conspiracy of cardinals, commenced criminal proceedings against Luther, in the tribunal which was appointed, the same Silvester who had thrown down the gauntlet to the accused on the literary ground was the only theologian. There was not much mercy to be expected.

There is no question that German influences were also at work here. Elector Albert, who instantly felt that the attack from Wittenberg was directed in part against himself, had referred Tetzel to Wimpina; the consequence of this was, that Frederic was attacked in Tetzel's Theses (indirectly indeed, but with the utmost bitterness), as a prince who had the power to check the heretical wickedness, and did not—who shielded heretics from their rightful judge ** Tetzel at least affirms, that the Elector had had an influence in the trial. Personal differences, and the jealousies of neighbouring states, had influenced, from the very beginning, the course of these events ††

Such was the state of the spiritual power in Germany. As yet, a secession or revolt from the pope was not thought of, as yet, his power was universally acknowledged, but indignation and resistance rose up against him from all the depths of the national feeling and the national will. Already had his sworn defenders sustained a defeat,—already some of the foundations of the edifice of dogma, on which his power rested, tottered; the intense desire of the nation to consolidate itself into a certain unity, took a direction hostile to the authority of the Court of Rome An opposition had arisen which still appeared insignificant, but which found vigorous support in the temper of the nation and in the favour of a powerful prince of the empire

* Disputatio prima J Tetzelii Thesis, 14 To this refers the passage in Luther's second sermon on Indulgences, in which he calls such a distinction mere talk

† Obelisci Ockii, nr 18 et 22

‡ Job Sylvii Apologia contra Calumniatores suos, in qua Annam nupsisse Cleophæ et Salomæ evangelicis testimoniis refellitur Reprinted in Rittershusii Commentarius de Gradibus Cognationum, 1674

§ Dialogus revdi patris fratris Sylvestri Prieriatis—in præsumptuosas Martini Lutheri conclusiones, in Loscher, ii 12.

‖ Guicciardini (xiii p 384) and Jovius mention him

** Disputatio secunda, J Tetzelii Thesis, 47, 48

†† Tetzel to Miltitz in Loscher, ii 568 "so doch hochbenannter Erzbischof inen bestellt hat zu citiren und nicht ich"—"Thus then the above-named archbishop has summoned him (Luther) and not I"

CHAPTER II.

DESCENT OF THE IMPERIAL CROWN FROM MAXIMILIAN TO CHARLES V

DIET OF AUGSBURG, 1518.

Had there been at this moment a powerful emperor, he might have turned these agitations to vast account. Supported by the nation, he would have been able to revive the ancient opposition to the papacy, and to inspire his people with a new life founded upon religious ideas.

Maximilian was by nature far from being inaccessible to such a project. Indeed, the expression he once let fall to Elector Frederic, that he wished "to take good care of the monk," for that it might be possible some time or other to make use of him, betrays what was passing in his mind; but for the moment he was not in a condition to follow it out.

In the first place, he was old, and wished to secure to his grandson Charles the succession to the empire. He regarded this as the closing business of his life. He had laboured all his days, as he said, to aggrandize his house: all his trouble would, however, be lost, if he did not attain this his final aim.* But, for this, he especially required the support of the spiritual power; for the minds of men were not yet so far emancipated from the ideas of the middle ages, as that they could be brought to recognize in him the full dignity of emperor, without the ceremony of coronation. While meditating the project of raising his grandson to the rank of king of the Romans, the first difficulty that occurred to Maximilian was, that he himself had not been crowned. He conceived the idea of causing himself to be crowned, if not in Rome, at least with the genuine crown of a Roman emperor, which he hoped to induce the papal court to send across the Alps, and opened negotiations with that view. It is evident how necessary it became for him, not only not to irritate, but to conciliate the pope.

On another point also, advances were made towards a good understanding between the emperor and the pope. We have mentioned the grant of a tenth for a Turkish war, which the Lateran council was induced to consent to, just before its close. It is a very significant fact, that while this excited amazement and resistance throughout Europe, Maximilian acquiesced in it. He, too, wished nothing more earnestly than once more to levy a large tax on the whole empire, we know, however, what a mighty opposition he encountered, and that even the grants which he wrung from the States had been fruitless: he now hoped to obtain his end in conjunction with the pope. He therefore assented without a question to the plan of the Court of Rome. It seems as if not only his self-interest was moved, but his imagination captivated. He exhorts the pope, in letters of the greatest ardour and vivacity, to undertake the campaign in person, surrounded by his cardinals, under the banner of the cross, then, he says, every one would hasten to his aid. He, at least, had from his youth had no higher ambition than to do battle against the Turks.† The victories of Selim I. over the Mamelukes revived his sense of the general danger. He convoked the States of the empire, in order at length to conclude on means of raising efficacious succour against the Turks, to whom already all Asia, as far as the domains of Prester John, belonged; by whom Africa was occupied, and whom it would soon become utterly impossible to resist.‡ He hoped that the moment was come for realising his long-cherished project of establishing a permanent military constitution. Thus, after long interruption, the ancient union of the spiritual and temporal powers was once more beheld at the diet. Instead of opposing the pope, the emperor united with him; while the pope sent a legate to assist the emperor in his negotiations with the States.

His choice fell on the Dominican, Thomas de Vio, the same who had so zealously defended the papal prerogatives; this had opened to him the way to higher dignities, which had terminated in that of cardinal. The brilliant appointment of legate, now superadded, placed him at the summit of his ambition. He determined to appear with the greatest magnificence, and almost acted in earnest upon the pretension of the Curia, that a legate was greater than a king.§ At his nomination he made special conditions as to the state and splendour of his equipments, for example, that a white palfrey with bridle of crimson velvet, and hangings for his room of crimson satin, were to be provided for him: even his old master of the ceremonies could not refrain from laughing at the multiplicity of demands which he had to make. When at Augsburg he delighted beyond all things in magnificent ceremonies; such as the high mass which he celebrated before all the princes, spiritual and temporal, in the cathedral, on the 1st of August, when he placed the cardinal's hat on the head of the Archbishop of Mainz, kneeling at the altar, and delivered to the emperor himself the consecrated hat and sword—the marks of papal grace and favour. He indulged also in the most extravagant ideas. While exhorting the emperor to march forth against the hereditary enemy who thirsted for the blood of Christendom, he reminded him that this was not only the day on which Augustus had become master of the world at the battle of Actium, but also that it was sacred to St. Peter: the emperor might accept it as an augury of the conquest of Constantinople and Jerusalem, and the extension of the empire and

* Letter of the 24th of May, 1518.

† Letter of Maximilian, Feb 23, in Rainaldus, 1617, 2–5.

‡ Address of the 9th February in the Frankf. A., vol xxxiii. By a letter from Furstenberg (July 3 1518) it appears that the States had met by the beginning of July.

§ "Legati debent esse supra reges quoscunque."—*Paris de Grassis in Hofmanns Scriptores nove, p. 408.*

the church to the farthest ends of the earth.* Such was the style of a discourse, framed according to all the rules of rhetoric, which he delivered to the assembly of the States

It may easily be imagined, that it cost him no labour to persuade the emperor, after a short deliberation they now made the joint proposal, that in order to bring an army against the Turks into the field, every fifty householders should furnish one man, and the clergy should pay a tenth, the laity a twentieth, of their income for its maintenance.

It was extremely difficult, however, to carry this measure through the States Whatever were the real designs of the emperor, people refused, whether in Germany or abroad, to believe that he was in earnest Publications appeared, in which the intention of the See of Rome to make war on the infidels was flatly denied; these were all Florentine arts, it was affirmed, to cajole the Germans out of their money, the proceeds of indulgences were not even applied to the building which was represented as so urgently wanted, the materials destined for the building of St Peter's wandered by night to the palace of Lorenzo de Medici;—the Turks whom they ought to make war upon were to be found in Italy † As to the emperor, it was suggested that his object was to impose a tax on the empire under these pretexts

The answer which the States returned on the 27th of August, therefore, was a decided negative. They observed, that it would be impossible to raise so considerable a tax, in the state to which the country had been reduced during the last years by war, scarcity, and intestine disorder. But that, independently of this, the common people complained of all the money that was sent out of Germany to no purpose, the nation had already frequently contributed funds for a Turkish war by means of indulgences and *cruciata*, but it had never yet heard that any expedition against the Turks had been attempted The refusal thus assumed the character of an accusation The States seized the opportunity afforded by the demand on the part of the See of Rome to retort upon it a multitude of grievances e g the annates which were now exacted from abbeys, prebends, and parishes, the constantly increasing costs of the confirmation in spiritual offices caused by the creation of new officia, the apparently eternal burthens imposed by the rules of the Roman chancery; all the various encroachments on the right of patronage, the appointment of foreigners to spiritual posts in Upper and Lower Germany, and, generally, an incessant violation of the concordat with the German nation ‡ A memorial presented by the Bishop of Liege to the head and princes of the empire, served to give additional force to these complaints It contained a complete catalogue of acts of injustice which the German church had to suffer from the courtiers of Rome; those mighty huntsmen, sons of Nimrod, as it said, sallied forth daily in chase of benefices, day and night they meditated on nothing but how to thwart the canonical electors, the German gold, formerly too heavy for an Atlas, had fled across the Alps.§ Such a writing, "so full of boldness," said the Frankfurt envoy, had never been seen.

How greatly had the emperor deceived himself in imagining that he should more readily attain his end by the aid of the spiritual power!

Charges against the pope were now also advanced at the discussions on the grievances which had been brought forward a year before at Mainz, *e. g.* his encroachment on the right of collation, the conduct of the clergy generally; above all, the use of excommunication, to which the people had no mind to concede a validity equal to that of the sentence of the civil tribunals. But in urging these complaints, they did not lose sight of those against the emperor. They again demanded a better composition of the courts of justice, and a more perfect execution of the judgments of the Imperial Chamber; a commission was appointed in order to deliberate on the code of criminal procedure

Nor was this all; the opposition to the imperial authority took a perfectly new direction in the important discussions on the Turkish war.

The States did, indeed, after much debate, at length seem to come to some agreement as to the nature and mode of a new tax; it was actually decreed in the Recess, that for three years every one who communicated at the Lord's Supper should pay at least a tenth of a gulden, and that the sum resulting from this collection should be kept by the government till the commencement of a Turkish war; but even a grant of so strange and equivocal a kind was rendered nearly illusory by a condition attached to it. The princes declared that they must first consult with their subjects upon it The emperor's answer shows how astonished he was at this innovation He said, that was not the usage in the Holy Empire; the princes were not bound by the consent of their subjects, it was the duty of the latter to execute the decisions of their lords and rulers ||

* Jacobi Manlii Historiola duorum Actuum, Freher, ii p 700

† Oratio Dissuasoria, Freher, ii 701 The "conclusion of this discourse makes against the opinion that it is by Hutten But how is the fact to be explained, that the dialogue, unquestionably Hutten's, 'Pasquillus Exul, has so extraordinary a resemblance in many passages to this discourse, that it cannot possibly be accidental? It might, however, very well have had an influence upon the consultations, as it reached Wittenberg on the 2d of September"—*Luther's Letters*, i nr 79

‡ Answer of the States Friday after the Feast of St Bartholomew Frankft A

§ Erardus de Marca Sacratæ Cæsæ Majestati Kapps Nachlese, ii nr 1

|| Declaration of the emperor on the 3th of Sept "Item, dass in dem allen Churfursten Fursten und Stande kein Ausred noch Entschuldigung furnemen, noch solch Zusage thun mit eynicher Weigerung oder Condicion auf ihre Unterthanen, denn solichs in bisher bewilligten Hulfen nie bedacht worden und darauf gestellt ist, sondern Churff FF und Stend haben allezeit frei gehandelt und bewilligt, nachdem sy Kais Mt und des Reichs Churf belehnt seyen, auch die Unterthanen schuldig seyn den Willen der Fursten und Obern und mit die Fursten und Obern der Unterthanen Willen zu verfolgen und Gehorsam zu beweisen" "Also that in all these things the electors, princes, and States, take upon themselves no

The princes replied, that they had often made promises without consulting their subjects, and the consequence had been, that it had generally been found impossible to execute them continuance in such a course could end in nothing but disgrace and contempt. The Recess, accordingly, contained nothing more than that the princes promised to treat with their subjects, and to report the result at the next diet.

It is evident that the disposition which this betrays must have rendered it impossible to come to any agreement on the other affairs of the empire.

A great deal was done about the Imperial Chamber, but without any results * The Electors protested in a body that in virtue of their franchises they were not subject to the Imperial Chamber: they could not agree on the suggestions for a reform, the old objections to the matricula for the contributions were urged again, its operation was no longer felt, and in a short time it was entirely at a stand †

Disorder once more prevailed on all sides. The same torrent of complaints poured in upon the diet at Augsburg, as the year before at Mainz.

The Count von Helfenstein invoked assistance against Wurtemberg, Ludwig von Boyneburg against Hessen, the Archbishop of Bremen against the Worsats all in vain. The disputes between the city of Worms and their bishop, between the Elector Palatine and a company of merchants who were robbed when under his escort, were brought to no conclusion. The behaviour of the Elector Palatine in this affair, and the support which he appeared to find, raised the indignation of the city to the highest pitch ‡ There was hardly a part of the country which was not either distracted by private warfare, or troubled by internal divisions, or terrified by the danger of an attack from some neighbouring power. Those who wished for peace must take their own measures to secure it it was in vain to reckon upon the government.

Such a state of anarchy necessarily led to a general conviction that things could not go on thus. For a long time the emperor could come to no agreement with the Estates on any measure whatever, whether for tranquillity at home, or against the enemy abroad · what he had been unable to accomplish single-handed, he had tried to effect in conjunction with the pope — an attempt which had ended in more signal failure than before. The highest authorities could no longer fulfil the prime duties of a government.

In so far it was of great importance that the States of the Empire made the innovation we have just mentioned; viz to render the grants dependent on the will of their subjects. The life of the nation showed a tendency to fall off from what had hitherto been its centre, and to form itself into independent self-sufficing powers in the several territories. This tendency was now greatly increased by the interests connected with the election of an emperor, which were already very active in Augsburg, and shortly afterwards began to occupy all minds

In fact, we cannot advance a step further without some preliminary inquiry into the relations of the German principalities.

MUTUAL RELATIONS OF THE GERMAN PRINCES.

It was impossible as yet to speak of German states, properly so called. The unity of even the larger principalities was not yet sufficiently cemented — attempts were here and there made at a common government, which, however, seldom succeeded, so that people constantly returned to the principle of division, — nor was there any settled system of representation. A vast number of independent powers and privileges still existed, incompatible with any form of government whatever. But, in the larger territories, there were efforts towards the establishment of unity and order; in the smaller, local associations took the place of the princely power in all directions the force of the local spirit struggled for ascendancy with the imperial authorities, and with the greater success, the more vain were the attempts of the latter at concentration and general efficient control.

It was unquestionably an important circumstance, that the head of the empire was less intent on the tranquil exercise of his legal sovereignty, than on acquiring influence by personal and irregular interference. It was only in moments of enthusiasm and excitement that Emperor Maximilian beheld his high station in its national point of view; in ordinary moments he regarded it rather as a fraction of his personal power. The nature of his administration was exactly calculated to excite agitations of every kind in the somewhat formless world around him.

evasion or excuse, nor make such promise with any hesitation or condition having reference to their subjects, for none such had ever been made, nor grounded thereon, on occasion of succours granted heretofore, but electors, princes, and estates, have in all times freely acted and made grants, as lieges of his Imperial Majesty and electors of the empire, also the vassals are bound to follow the wills of, and to show obedience to princes and superiors, and not princes and superiors to follow the will of, and to show obedience to, subjects '—*Frankft Acten*.

* The reason of the bad appointments lies in the bad pay Furstenberg (Letter of the 8th of Sept) remarks that no better pay could be obtained "Daraus folgt dass es auch nit mit dem Inkommen, so jetzunder geben wird, mit gelehrt fromm und verstandig Leuten besetzt mag werden " "Thence follows, that it (the Imperial Chamber) cannot, with the income which is now given, be provided with learned, pious and sensible men "

† Furstenberg, Sep 14 "Somma Sommarum aller Handelung die uf diesem Reichstag gehandelt ist, dass von Friede und Recht nichts beschlossen wird dass die Schatzung des Turkenzugs, wie K Mt dawider, bei den Unterthanen anbracht (wird) "The sum total of all the affairs which have been transacted at this Imperial Diet is, that nothing is determined as to the peace and the laws, and that the taxation for the Turkish war, although his Imperial Majesty is opposed to it, is laid on the vassals "

‡ Furstenberg, in transmitting the correspondence, expresses his dissatisfaction "Hie ist nit anders ein jeder sehe sich fur Die Churf Fürsten und Andre haben nit alle ob der Handlung Gefallens es will aber diess Mal aus Ursachen nit anders seyn Gott erbarms" "Here things are not otherwise let each man look to himself The electors, princes, and others, are not all content with the transaction, but this time there are causes why it cannot be otherwise God have mercy on us."

In Upper Germany the emperor had naturally, after all that had passed, to encounter much opposition. The Elector Palatine could not yet forget the injuries he had sustained in the last war; he was still unappeased, nor had he received his investiture. Although the emperor had then espoused the party of Bavaria, the people of that country were not the less sensible to what the two branches of the sovereign house, viewed collectively, had lost. The young princes, William and Louis, had such a profound sense of this, that they arranged the disputes which had broken out between them as to their respective shares in the government, as quickly as possible, when they thought they detected, on the part of the emperor, a design of turning their disagreements to advantage in order to promote another interest, as in the year 1504.* They remembered what Bavaria had been stripped of, and the first act of their combined government was to pledge themselves mutually to reconquer all that had been lost, as soon as the emperor, their uncle, was dead.†

It appeared that Maximilian might reckon more securely on Duke Ulrich of Wurtenberg, whom he had declared of age before the legal term, who had accompanied him in his wars, had made conquests under his banner, and to whom he had given a consort. Ulrich seemed bound to him by every tie of gratitude. But this prince soon began to display a determined spirit of resistance to the emperor's designs, inspired by the most arrogant self-conceit. He was displeased that he was of so little importance in the Swabian league. He considered it an insufferable abridgement of his power, that of the one-and-twenty votes in the council of that body, fourteen belonged to the lower states,—prelates, counts, knights, and above all, cities, and had the right of deciding on peace and war, so that "his will and possession were in the hands of strangers."‡ In the year 1512, when the league was renewed, he obstinately refused to join it. He thus offended the league, began consequently to fear its hostility, and allied himself with its enemies, especially the Elector Palatine and the Bishop of Wurzburg. He thus got into innumerable difficulties and quarrels with the emperor, with all his neighbours, and even with his own states and councils, which would rather have adhered to the emperor and the league. In all these affairs his behaviour became more and more violent, harsh, and overbearing. The peasants revolted against his taxes, the estates of his dominions compelled him to sign a contract limiting his authority, which he showed an inclination to break; his councillors meditated setting a regency over him, which filled him with rage. At length the consummation of all these evils burst upon him in his own house.

Unhappily he had suffered himself to be carried away by an inclination for the wife of one of his courtiers, Hans von Hutten, his comrade in the field and the chase. Hutten at length seized an occasion to speak to his lord on this subject; the duke threw himself at his feet, extended his arms imploringly to him, and conjured him to permit him to see and to love her; he had tried in vain, he said, to conquer his passion—he could not.§ It is reported, that in a short time they exchanged characters; Hutten became the lover of the duchess Sabina. One day Ulrich thought he saw the betrothing ring which he had given his wife, on Hutten's finger, and fell into the most violent transports of jealousy. It is impossible, in the dearth of authentic accounts,‖ to say how much of the story is true. According to the legal documents, what peculiarly incensed the duke was, that Hutten had not kept the secret of his master's passion, and had given currency to reports by which he appeared at once vicious and ridiculous. It seemed that the servant was little alarmed at the anger which his lord gave vent to on this occasion; he thought he should have to encounter some sharp words, to which he could return others as sharp and as proud. But Ulrich was now worked up to deeds of vengeance. They were riding together, and as they came into the Boblinger wood, the duke took the knight aside, upbraided him with his falsehood, called out to him to defend his life; and, as Hutten was not armed, overpowered and killed him.** He then stuck his sword into the ground, and tied the lifeless body fast to it with a girdle twisted round the neck. He said that as Freischoffe, as initiated member of the Fehme, he had the right and authority to do so. He carried home the bloody sword, and laid it by his wife's bedside. Alarmed for her freedom, and even for her life, she fled, first to her uncle the emperor, who was taking the diversion of hunting in the neighbourhood, and then to her brothers in Bavaria, between whom and Ulrich there was already much bad blood. Sabina accused her husband to the emperor, and demanded that her enemies should be delivered up. Ulrich, on the other hand, persecuted with vindictive fury her friends and all those whom he regarded as adherents of the emperor and the league. Attempts at reconciliation only served to bring the secret hostilities fully to light: a treaty was concluded, but imme-

* From a letter of Duke Ludwig, Freiberg Landstande, ii 149.

† The first document in the Urkundenbuch to Stumpf, Baierns Politische Gesch. i.

‡ "Beswerung so wir Herzog Ulrich zu Wirtemperg haben, des Pundts Schwaben Erstreckung anzunemen." "Difficulty which we, Duke Ulrich of Würtenberg, have to consent to the extension of the Swabian League." Sattler, Herzoge, i. Appendix, nr. 56, p. 120.

§ The printed address of the family of von Hutten in Sattler, a. a. O. p. 213.

‖ See Heyd, Duke Ulrich, i. p. 394. It is not to be forgotten that a certain respect was observed in the statement in spite of all its violence. The Huttens would not have brought forward the connection with the wife of the murdered man, had not the Duke first mentioned it.

** Address of Duke Ulrich, a. a. O. p. 305. The relations maintained, that Hutten had been positively invited to join in the ride; the Duke, that he had been warned and yet had obstinately accompanied them. The account of the Duke seems to me to have greater moral probability.

diately broken; letters injurious to the honour of both parties were interchanged. never, in short, did a prince rend asunder all the ties that bound him to a party, as whose ally and associate he had risen to power, with greater violence than Duke Ulrich At the diet of 1518 it was reported that he had arrested followers of the emperor, put them to horrible tortures, and threatened them with death. On the other hand, Maximilian intimated that he would appoint a criminal tribunal to try the duke, and would execute whatever sentence it might pronounce * he immediately issued a special writ to the States, not only authorising, but summoning them to set at liberty their lord's prisoners † This furnished an additional motive to the emperor for desiring a reconciliation with the Elector Palatine This he accomplished so far that that prince appeared at the diet and received his investiture It is clear that the emperor's policy acquired by this event, and by his influence over the league and Bavaria, the ascendency in Upper Germany, nevertheless, affairs wore a very perilous aspect, and it was easy to foresee that, be the event what it might, differences could not be adjusted in an amicable manner Their ramifications extended over the whole empire.

Another and far more formidable opposition to the emperor arose out of the affairs of Lower Germany connected with the house of Burgundy.

One of the earliest acts of Maximilian's government, in 1486, the year of his election, had been to grant the reversion of Juliers and Berg to the house of Saxony, in case that those provinces should, "by reason of failure of lineal heirs male," become vacant ‡ In the year 1495 he confirmed this for himself and all his successors in the empire, 'now as then, and then as now." The event in question seemed not far distant, since Duke William VII. had only a daughter, this opened to the house of Saxony a prospect of a more commanding, indeed of what might be called an European position, since Friesland had then been transferred to the younger line

But difficulties soon arose This assignment to so distant a master was by no means popular in the country itself, which would have thought itself better provided for by an union with the neighbouring province of Cleves. Princes and states were unanimous in this opinion. In the year 1496 they already determined to marry the daughter of the Duke of Juliers with the heir of Cleves, and to unite the two countries. A solemn treaty, which may be regarded as effecting a union of all these provinces, was entered into and signed by nobles and cities.§ They prayed the emperor to confirm it, and to acknowledge the Princess of Juliers as heiress of her father's possessions

The emperor, however, would have paid little attention to this petition, and would have adhered to the grant of reversion, had not certain political events occurred to change his designs.

From the time that Duke Charles, son of the Duke of Gueldres, formerly deposed by Charles the Bold, had returned to his hereditary dominions, and, in defiance of the unfavourable decrees of the empire, had found means, with the aid of his estates, to maintain himself, there had not been one moment's peace in those parts He was closely allied with France, all the enemies of Austria found in him an ever-ready protector It was, therefore, a serious thing to make another powerful enemy in that neighborhood The Duke of Cleves threatened, in case his petition was refused, to enter into a matrimonial connexion and an indissoluble alliance with the Duke of Gueldres—a threat which filled the Netherlands with alarm ** The Governess Margaret, Maximilian's daughter, thought it would be impossible to wrest Juliers and Berg from the Duke of Cleves, the only effect would be to cause him to unite with Gueldres, Arenberg, and Liege, all foes of the house of Burgundy. this would furnish a power strong enough even to drive the emperor's posterity out of the Netherlands

In Saxony it was believed that the emperor connected schemes of another kind with this design. Elector Frederic enjoyed singular consideration in the empire He steadily adhered to the principles and sentiments of the old electors, and his power was constantly on the increase His intellectual superiority checked the inclination which his cousin George now and then betrayed to oppose him,

* Fürstenberg, Sept 9, calls it, "eine scharfe und ubermessliche Antwort" "a sharp and immoderate answer" "Wo er sich nicht fuge, wolle ihn S M ein Halsgericht setzen, dass er daselbst in Schranken komme, und wess von anderen und Sr Maj Interessen wegen an ihn erlangt wird, dass dem auch Vollzug geschehe"—"In case he do not yield, his Majesty will sit in judgment on him that he may be thereby brought within bounds and whatever, by reason of his Majesty's and other interests may be decreed against him, that the same may also be executed"

† July 17, 1518 Sattler, i App 263

‡ Document in Muller, Imp Rth Fr vi 48

§ Treaty of Marriage and Agreement in Teschenmacher, Annales Cliviæ, Cod dipl nr 98, 99, wherein the two princes promised one another—the Duke of Juliers that his daughter should bring the son of his brother of Cleves his principalities of Juliers, Berg his countship of Ravensburg, with all his other lordships—the Duke of Cleves, that his son should bring the daughter of his brother of Juliers his principality of Cleves, his countship of the Mark and all his other lordships, now actually possessed, or still to be acquired

** The emperor says to Cesar Pflug "Die klevisch Tochter hindre I M Frau Tochter Margr" "The daughter of the Duke of Cleves stands in the way of the Lady Margaret, his Imperial Majesty's daughter" Reuber states 'Clef lasst sich vernehmen, wolt man die Lehen nit thun, so musste sich Clef mit den Herrn verbinden, von denen es Trost und Hulf haben mecht das Sine zu erhalten" "Cleves says thus—if they will not bestow the fief then Cleves must join the lords from whom she may have comfort and help to hold her own"—*Weimar Acts* Comp Correspondance de l Empereur Maximilien I et de Marguerite d'Autriche I p 390 Margaret further wrote in 1511 to the emperor, as is said in his answer "Que se povons tant faire que nostre cousin le duc de Zaxssen voulsist quicter ou du moins mectre en delay la querelle qu il pretend à la duche de Juillers, le jeusne duc de Cleves et son pere se condescendroient facilement à eulx declairer a la guerre et aydier a la reduction de nostre pays de Gheldres' The emperor hoped to conciliate the elector at the approaching imperial diet, but in this he did not succeed

so that the house of Saxony might still be regarded as one power. His brother Ernest had been Archbishop of Magdeburg up to the year 1513, and certainly one of the best that see had ever possessed; his cousin Frederic was Grand Master in Prussia; his sister Margaret, Duchess of Lüneburg, ancestress of that house. It is evident how extensive was the influence of this family; an influence further augmented by the act of the States of Hessen, which, on the death of Landgrave William, in 1510, excluded his widow Anne from the guardianship of the minor, claimed by her, and committed it to the elector and house of Saxony, to which the regency thereupon appointed was subject. Boyneburg, the governor of the province, who was at the head of affairs, was entirely devoted to Frederic.* It appeared to the emperor highly inexpedient to throw Juliers, and Berg also, which must soon be without a sovereign, into the hands of this powerful prince, who might thus become too mighty a vassal.

Under the influence of these considerations, Maximilian retracted the promise he had made at the time of his election (and doubtless with a view to that), and in various documents of the years 1508–9 revoked the contingent rights on Juliers and Berg which had been conferred: he declared that the duke's daughter, Maria, was the worthy and competent successor of her father.† In the year 1511 William VII. died; his son-in-law, John of Cleves, took possession of the country without opposition. All attempts to recall the past, all persuasions and negotiations on the part of the house of Saxony, were vain.

The effect of this certainly was to induce Cleves to refuse the alliance with Gueldres, and to adhere faithfully to Austria. Saxony, on the contrary, declined in importance. The spiritual principalities which were occupied by members of that house passed into other hands on the death of their possessors. Boyneburg, by his somewhat tyrannical mode of governing, provoked the discontent of the States of Hessen, and especially of the cities (A. D. 1514). By a sort of revolution, the Princess Anne was restored to the guardianship of which she had been deprived; Elector Frederic retaining nothing more than the name. Another proof of this anti-Saxon spirit was, that the emperor, at the suggestion of the order of knights, declared the young Landgrave Philip of age when only fourteen years old (March 1518); alleging that he would be better off so, than under any guardianship or tutelage whatsoever. In these Hessian transactions, Duke George took part against the elector: so far from raising any cordial opposition to the designs of Anne, he betrothed his son with her daughter. Meanwhile he had already restored Friesland to Austria.

In this case, too, the policy of Austria was triumphant; the dreaded coalition of the Netherland adversaries was prevented, and Saxony kept at a distance and depressed.‡ On the other hand, however, the hostility of the most able and prudent of all the princes of the empire was provoked. What the weight of that hostility was, soon appeared at the diet of Cologne (A. D. 1512). Frederic's resistance sufficed to defeat all the emperor's plans; at least his biographer imputes to his opposition the rejection of the project of a new tax. This enmity affected even the Netherlands through another channel. The niece of the elector, a Lüneburg princess, married Charles of Gueldres (of whom we have already spoken), who thus secured in two of the most powerful princely houses, such a support as he had never before been able to obtain.

While the house of Saxony was thus weakened by a contest with Austria, Brandenburg rose upon her favour. It was with the emperor's assistance that Brandenburg princes succeeded to those of Saxony both in the grand mastership of the Teutonic Order and the see of Magdeburg: he then further favoured the elevation of the young archbishop, who was also bishop of Halberstadt, to the Electorate of Mainz, which had formerly been enjoyed by a brother of Elector Frederic: we have already seen what was the nature of the relations which subsisted between these two princes. Maximilian also renewed his alliance with the Franconian line of this house. He confirmed the removal of the old Margrave, who had been declared idiotic, from the government; and marrying the Margrave's eldest son Casimir to his own niece, Susanna of Bavaria, he gave that prince the whole support of his authority and an important advantage over his brothers. For this very reason, however, he did not win them over completely; with one of them, indeed, the Grand Master, he had a serious difference. The emperor had at first induced him to assume a hostile attitude towards King Sigismund of Poland,§ who was

* See Rommel, Philipp der Grossmüthige, vol. i. p. 26.

† The document in Teschenmacher, nr. 100, is inconclusive; nr. 101, leaves no room for doubt.

‡ The Saxon councillors, as early as 1512, dreaded further disfavour: "Darum er (der Kaiser, nach jener Erklärung für Cleve) fort und fort auf Wege trachten mocht, Ewer Aller Fürstl. Gnaden zuzuschieben so viel ihm möglich, damit Ew. Aller Fürstl. Gn. in Dempfung und Abfall kämen."—"Lest he (the emperor, after that declaration in behalf of Cleves) should more and more strive after means of embarrassing your most Princely Grace as much as possible, so that your most Princely Grace may fall into weakness and decline."—*Letter from Cologne written Thursday after Jacobi*, 1512. *Weimar Records.*

§ The Fugger MS. "Deswegen die Kais. Maj. nach solchem Wege getrachtet, dieweil S. M. erachtet, dass König Sigmund seinem Schwager Graf Hansen von Trentschin Grossgrafen in Ungarn Rath und Hülfe erzeiget und denselben nach Absterben des Königs Lasslew zu dem Reich Ungarn . . . befördern mocht, dass er demselben etliche Könige und Fürsten zu Feinden machen wollt, und ward durch S. Mt. so vil gehandelt, dass Markg. Albrecht von Brandenburg Hochmeister in Preussen den Hochernannten König Sigmundt von Polen anfeindet." "His Imperial Majesty on this account, because his Majesty considered that King Sigismund had yielded counsel and aid to his brother-in-law, Count Hans von Trentschin Grossgraf in Hungary, and after the decease of King Ladislas might advance the same to the kingdom of Hungary, that he wished to render sundry kings and princes enemies to the same; and so much was done by his Majesty, that Margrave Albert of Brandenburg, Great Master in Prussia, opposes the above-named King Sigismund of Poland." The alliance with Russia was concluded expressly for the

rendered extremely formidable to the Austrian claims on the kingdom of Hungary, by his connexion with the House of Zapolya. Maximilian wished to hold him in check, on the one side by the Grand Duke of Moscow, on the other by the Teutonic Order. But the situation of things was now much altered. In the year 1515, Sigismund of Poland had formed very amicable relations with the emperor; he now recognised the hereditary right of Austria to Hungary, and took a wife out of the Italian branch of that house. Maximilian, on his side, waived the claims of the empire: he granted Danzig and Thorn an exemption from the jurisdiction of the Imperial Chamber in 1515, as he had to Switzerland in 1507; a measure the more important in this case, since it substituted a Polish for a German jurisdiction; it was, in fact, a sort of cession. It may readily be imagined how much less inclined he must now be to interpose earnestly on behalf of the Order; and accordingly we find it stated in the preamble to the agreement, that the emperor recognised the peace of Thorn,—the very thing against which the Grand Master protested, and by which he had been made a vassal of the crown of Poland. Prussia was thus again alienated from the emperor, and this re-acted on the other members of the house of Brandenburg. Elector Joachim, at least, was not disinclined to give the same support to the Grand Master as he did to his brothers in Franconia.

It may easily be imagined that the position of the other sovereign houses was affected in various ways by all these friendships and enmities.

Pomerania, forced to give way before the claims of Brandenburg to the supreme feudal lordship, was alienated from Austria by the support its rival received from that power. The Pomeranian historians ascribe it to the influence of Joachim I. that the projected marriage of a Pomeranian princess with King Christian II. of Denmark did not take place; and on the contrary, that that monarch married a grand-daughter of Maximilian.* The result of this again was, that the uncle and rival of Christian Frederic of Holstein, who thought himself unjustly dealt with in the partition of the ducal inheritance, and, as king's son, believed himself to have claims even on Norway,† now sought to ally himself with the house of Pomerania; whilst the third member of this house, the Count of Oldenburg, adhered firmly to the Austro-burgundian alliance, and once more received a stipend from the Netherlands. Every event that occurred in the northern states immediately affected the dynastic houses of Germany through these various combinations.

It must not be imagined that open hostility broke out amongst them. There was a greater or lesser influence of the house of Austria; a more or less visible favour shown by or inclination towards it; but they remained on the footing of good neighbours, met at diets, interchanged visits at family festivals, endured what they could not alter, and kept their eye steadily on the point in view.

The discord was most fierce and undisguised in the house of the turbulent Welfs. Calenberg and Wolfenbüttel held to the friendship of Austria; indeed it was in her service that the duke of the former state had revived the ancient warlike renown of his house. Lüneburg sided with the opposition. There were a multitude of old disputes between them, mainly caused by an attempt of the Bishop of Minden, a Wolfenbüttler by birth, to appropriate to himself the countship of Diepholz, to which Lüneburg had ancient contingent claims.‡ Lauenburg was now drawn into these quarrels. During the absence of the Archbishop of Bremen — another Wolfenbüttel — the Worsats, who had recently been conquered, killed his officers; Magnus of Lauenburg, to whom they appealed as the true Duke of Lower Saxony, lent them aid, and destroyed the fortress erected by the archbishop.§ On his return, open war among all these princes appeared imminent, and was only prevented from breaking out by Mecklenburg, which stood in a tolerably impartial situation in the midst of all these disputes; or rather, in that of an ally of both parties.

This example suffices to prove that there was but little distinction between temporal and spiritual princes.

For the highest posts in the church had long been distributed, not in consequence of spiritual merits, but in compliance with the wishes of some powerful prince, especially the emperor; or of the interests of the neighbouring nobles, who had seats in the chapters: indeed it was, as we have seen, a maxim of the court of Rome, ever since the last century, to use its influence in promoting the younger sons of sovereign houses.‖ In the beginning of the sixteenth century this policy had been pursued with success in many sees. In Lower Germany, Brunswick, and Lauenburg in particular, rivalled each other in this respect. The house of Brunswick-Wolfenbüttel and Grubenhagen had got possession of the archbishopric of Bremen, the bishoprics of Minden, Verden, Osnabrück and Paderborn; the house of Lauenburg, of Münster and Hildesheim. We have seen how richly Brandenburg was provided for. We find princes of Lorraine as bishops of Metz, Toul and Verdun. The palatinate possessed Freisingen, Regensburg, Speier, Naumburg, and afterwards Utrecht. Bavaria obtained

re-conquest of the lands of the Order seized on by Poland. This is the famous document in which Zar was translated into Kaiser (emperor). — *Karamsin, Hist. of Russia*, vii. 45, 450.

* Kanzow, Pomerania, ii. 313.

† Chief points of complaint, as set forth in the different publications on the dispute; Christiani, Neuere Gesch. von Schleswig-Holstein, i. p. 318. These complaints sufficiently refute the supposition of a good understanding, to which Christiani previously adheres.

‡ Delius, Hildesheimische Stiftsfehde, p. 96.

§ Chytræus, Saxoniæ Chronicon, lib. vii. p. 227.

‖ See p. 16. Æneas Sylvius, Epistola ad Martinum Maier, p. 679.

Passau. In the year 1516, the chapter of Schwerin chose Prince Magnus of Mecklenburg, although not yet seven years old, its bishop.* It were impossible to enumerate all the prebends which came into the hands either of members of the less powerful houses, or favourites of the emperor. Melchior Pfinzing, his chaplain and secretary, was dean of St. Sebald, in Nürnberg, of St. Alban and St. Victor in Mainz; and prebendary both in Trent and Bamberg. Hence it followed that the interests of the house to which a dignitary of the church belonged, or to which he owed his elevation, influenced the exercise of his functions: we find the spiritual principalities implicated in all the intrigues or dissensions of the temporal rulers.

These circumstances re-acted on the other states of the empire, though perhaps less obviously. The cities of the Oberland, for example, whose strength was the main support of the Swabian league, belonged to the one party; while the Franconian knights, who were at open war with the league, sided more with the other.

For imperfect and undefined as all relations were, the powers of Germany may be ranged under two great political parties. On the side of Austria were Bavaria, the League, Brandenburg (for the most part), Hessen, Cleves, the Count of East Friesland (which had lately joined this party), Oldenburg, Denmark, Calenberg, Wolfenbüttel, and Albertine Saxony. On that of the opposition, were Ernestine Saxony, Pomerania, Lauenburg, Lüneburg, the Franconian knights, Würtemberg, and Gueldres. The Duke of Gueldres was indeed in a state of open warfare. In the year 1517, his troops devastated the whole of Holland; he gave up Alkmaar to pillage for eight days: in the year 1518, the Frisian corsair, Groote Pier, appeared in the Zuyder Zee, and made himself complete master of it for a considerable time. The duke employed all his influence to keep the Frieslanders in a continual state of revolt. The palatinate and Mecklenburg occupied a sort of neutral or middle ground between these two parties. The Elector palatine inclined to the house of Austria for a singular reason. His brother Frederic, who had served for many years at the court of Burgundy, had formed an attachment to the Princess Leonora. One of his letters was found in her possession, and excited such displeasure, that the unhappy prince was obliged to quit the court, with the persuasion that he had thus thrown away all his well-earned claims on the emperor's favour, unless he could re-establish them by still more important services. But his brother was not disposed to forget what he had suffered in the war of inheritance. On the contrary, the brave knight who had risen to fame and honour in his service, Franz von Sickingen, now took revenge on Hessen for those very injuries.† While the diet was sitting at Augsburg, he marched an army of 500 horse and 8000 foot upon the fortified town of Darmstadt, and extorted from the inhabitants contributions to the amount of 45,000 gulden, on the hardest and most oppressive terms. A deputation of the empire made representations to the emperor against this breach of the Public Peace; but he did not venture to do anything; he had formerly taken Sickingen into his own service, and he had no mind to alienate the palatinate again.

Such is the situation in which we find Maximilian towards the close of his career.

The received opinion which recognises in him the creative founder of the later constitution of the empire, must be abandoned. We saw above that the ideas of organisation which first became currrent in the early years of his reign experienced far more opposition than encouragement from him; and that he was incapable of carrying even his own projects into execution. We now see that he had not the power of keeping the princes of the empire together; that, on the contrary, everything about him split into parties. It followed of necessity that abroad he rather lost than gained ground. In Italy nothing was achieved: Switzerland acquired greater independence than she possessed before; Prussia was rather endangered than secured. The policy of France had obtained new influence in the heart of Germany; first Gueldres and then Würtemberg openly declared for that power.

The glory which surrounds the memory of Maximilian, the high renown which he enjoyed even among his contemporaries, were therefore not won by the success of his enterprises, but by his personal qualities.

Every good gift of nature had been lavished upon him in profusion; health up to an advanced age, so robust that when it was deranged strong exercise and copious draughts of water were his sole and sufficient remedy;‡ not beauty, indeed, but so fine a person, so framed for strength and agility, that he outdid all his followers in knightly exercises, outwearied them in exertions and toils; a memory to which everything that he had learnt or witnessed was ever present; so singular a natural acuteness and justness of apprehension, that he was never deceived in his servants; he employed them exactly in the services for which they were best fitted; an imagination of unequalled richness and brilliancy; everything that he touched came new out of his hands; a mind, as we have already remarked, which always seized with unerring instinct on the necessary, though unfortunately the execution of it was so often embarrassed by other conditions of his situation! He was a man, in short, formed to excite admiration, and to inspire enthusiastic attachment; formed to be

* Born July 4, 1509, elected June 21, 1516. Rudloff, Mecklenburgische Gesch. iii. 1, 37.

† That this was the motive, is asserted in the Chronicle of Flersheim, by Münch, iii. 210.

‡ Pasquaglio, Relatione di 1507: "Non molto bello di volto ma bene proportionato, robustissimo, di complessione sanguinea e collerica, e per l'età sua molto sano, nè altro il molesto che un poco di catarro che continuamente li discende, per rispetto del quale ha usato e usa sempre far nelle caccie gran esercitio."

the romantic hero, the exhaustless theme of the people.

What wondrous stories did they tell of his adventures in the chase! How, in the land beyond the Ens, he had stood his ground alone against an enormous bear in the open coppice: how in a sunken way in Brabant he had killed a stag at the moment it rushed upon him: how, when surprised by a wild boar in the forest of Brussels, he had laid it dead at his feet with his boar-spear, without alighting from his horse. But above all, what perilous adventures did they recount of his chamois hunts in the high Alps, where it was he who sometimes saved the practised hunter that accompanied him, from danger or death. In all these scenes he showed the same prompt and gallant spirit, the same elastic presence of mind. Thus, too, he appeared in face of the enemy. Within range of the enemy's fire, we see him alight from his horse, form his order of battle, and win the victory: in the skirmish, attacking four or five enemies single handed: on the field, defending himself in a sort of single combat against an enemy who selected him as his peculiar object; for he was always to be found in the front of the battle, always in the hottest of the fight and the danger.* Proofs of valour which served not merely to amuse an idle hour, or to be celebrated in the romance of Theuerdank: the Venetian ambassador cannot find words to express the confidence which the German soldiers of every class felt for the chief who never deserted them in the moment of peril. He cannot be regarded as a great general; but he had a singular gift for the organization of a particular body of troops, the improvement of the several arms, and the constitution of an army generally: the militia of the Landsknechts, by which the fame of the German foot soldiers was restored, was founded and organised by him. He also put the use of fire-arms on an entirely new footing, and his inventive genius displayed itself pre-eminently in this department, he surpassed even the masters of the art, and his biographers ascribe to him a number of very successful improvements:† they add, that he brought even the Spaniards who served under him to the use of fire-arms. Wherever he was present he found means to allay the mutinous disorders which often arose in these bands of mercenaries, in consequence of the irregular state of his finances. We are told that once in extremity he appeased the discontent of his men by the jests and antics of a court fool, whom he sent among them. He had a matchless talent for managing men. The princes who were offended and injured by his policy could not withstand the charm of his personal intercourse. "Never," says the sagacious Frederic of Saxony, "did I behold a more courteous man." The wild turbulent knights against whom he raised the empire and the league, yet heard such expressions from his lips, that it was, as Gotz von Berlichingen said, "a joy to their hearts, and they could never bear to do any thing against his Imperial Majesty or the house of Austria." He took part in the festivals and amusements of the citizens in their towns—their dances and their shooting matches, in which he was not unfrequently the best shot, and offered prizes—damask for the arquebusiers, or a few ells of red velvet for the cross-bowmen: he delighted to be among them, and found in their company and diversions a relief from the arduous and weary business of the diet. At the camp before Padua he rode up to a suttler and asked for something to eat. John of Landau, who was with him, offered to taste the food; the emperor inquired where the woman came from. From Augsburg, was the reply. "Ah!" exclaimed he, "then there is no need of a taster, for they of Augsburg are God-fearing people." In his hereditary dominions he often administered justice in person, and if he saw a bashful man who kept in the back-ground, he called him forward to a more honourable place. He was little dazzled by the splendour of the supreme dignity. "My good fellow," said he to an admiring poet, "thou knowest not me nor other princes aright."‡ All that we read of him shows freshness and clearness of apprehension, an open and ingenuous spirit. He was a brave soldier and a kind-hearted man, people loved and feared him.

And in his public life, we should do him injustice if we dwelt exclusively on his abortive attempts to re-constitute the empire. It is an almost inevitable defect of that form of government which excites a competition between the highest person in the state and a representative body or bodies, that the sovereign separates his personal interests from those of the community. Maximilian, at least, was far less intent on the prosperity of the empire than on the future fortunes of his house. When a youth of eighteen, he went to the Netherlands, and, by the union of Burgundy and Austria, founded a new European power. In states, as in the world of science, there are certain minds whose vocation it is to act as the pioneers of those gifted with the genius of construction. Incapable of bringing any thing new into existence, they are actively employed in preparing the materials and the instruments with which their more creative successors are

* See the Geschichtbibel of Seb. Frank, and particularly the Key to Theuerdank, reprinted in the edition of Theuerdank by Haltaus, p. 111.

† Grünbeck in Chmel, p. 96. "Bellicas machinas in minutas partes resolvere, parvis viribus bigis aptari et quocunque fert voluntas faciliter deduci primus invenit." The Fugger MS. "Durch S. Mt. Erfindung sind die Poller und Mörser zu dem werfen, auch die langen Ror zu dem weitraichen, desgleichen die weited kurzen Ror zu dem Haglschiessen in die Streichwehre darin auch etwa eisern Ketten und Schrot geladen werden, alsdann auch die grossen Karthaunen von neuen erfunden und zu gebrauchen aufbracht worden." "By his majesty's invention, mortars for throwing, also long tubes for distant range, likewise broad short tubes for firing canister shot from fortifications, and which may also be loaded with iron chains and balls, moreover large carronades have been afresh discovered and brought into use."

‡ The Fugger MS. Cuspinian. Querini paints him, Nov. 1507, as "homo virtuoso religioso, forte, liberal, quasi prodego. Adeo tutti l' ama ... nia mancha di prudentia."—*Sanuto*, vol. vii.

to work. The force that was in embryo did not assume its complete form under Maximilian. But by maintaining the sovereign prerogatives in the Netherlands, as well as in Austria; by defending the former against the French, the latter against the Hungarians; by securing for his house the great Spanish inheritance; by definitively founding that of Hungary and Bohemia, he exerted a vast and permanent influence on succeeding ages. How different was the position of his grandson from that of his father, an exile from his paternal land, or from his own, a prisoner in Bruges! Never did a family enjoy more magnificent or more extensive prospects than those which now lay before that of Austria. This was the point of view from which Maximilian regarded the affairs of Germany. Until the latter half of the fifteenth century, Austria was almost shut out from Germany: she now interfered with a high hand in the affairs of every state and province, temporal or spiritual—territories of cities or of knights; nothing could stir, whether in an amicable or a hostile direction, by which she was not immediately affected. If it be undeniable that the empire, regarded as a whole, had sustained losses, it is not less true that it was the union of the house of Austria with Burgundy which restored the province of the Low Countries again to a conscious connection with Germany; and that the remote prospects which were involved in the Hungarian, and still more in the Spanish family alliance, opened a new theatre of activity to the nation. The shadows of coming events continually flitted before the mind of Maximilian: it was this presentiment which influenced his whole conduct and actions, and produced all that was apparently unsteady, mysterious, and one-sided in his policy. It was not given to him to perfect or to found; his mission was solely to prepare, to maintain, and to extend the views and the claims of his house, amidst the conflicting powers of the world.

The last decisive moment still remained; and although he would never hear any thing on the subject at an earlier period of his reign, it is clear how earnestly he must have desired to secure his grandson's succession.

From the situation of things in Germany which we have just contemplated, it is easy to infer what was the support he might reckon upon, and what the obstacles he was likely to encounter. He had already made great progress in his negotiations at the diet of Augsburg. The renewal and confirmation of his good understanding with the Hohenzollern, and the large promises he made to that family, secured to him two electoral votes, those of Brandenburg and of Mainz, both of which had very recently been extremely dubious.* Hermann of Cologne, of the family of Wied, who was intimately connected with Cleves, and hence well inclined to the emperor, was completely won by presents made to himself, and by pensions promised to his brothers and kinsmen:† lastly, the old misunderstandings with the palatinate were arranged by the mediation of the Count Palatine Frederic; the elector received his investiture, entered into an agreement with Austria as to the inheritance, and gave his sanction to the order of succession. After certain preliminary arrangements had taken place, these four electors had a meeting with the emperor, who was surrounded by his own council and that of his nephew, on the 27th August, 1518, and ratified their consent by a formal treaty. The ambassadors of Bohemia, who was now restored to her place in the Germanic body (as since the league of 1515, Austria was sure of her vote), gave their assent.

On the other hand, Frederic of Saxony, as may readily be believed, did not forget his numerous wrongs and affronts, and was not to be propitiated. With him was Elector Richard of Treves, a Greifenklau by birth, who had already been opposed to the Prince of Baden, and had, at a more recent vacancy, obtained the electorate. Their chief objections were, that it was an unheard-of thing to place a king of the Romans by the side of an uncrowned emperor, and that a papal constitution forbade the union of the kingdom of Naples, which Charles possessed, with the crown of Germany.

Maximilian laboured incessantly to remove these objections, as well as the deeper reasons for which they were only a cover. Active negotiations were carried on with the court of Rome, both as to the sending of the crown across the Alps,‡ and the repeal of the above-mentioned constitution. The strangest plans were suggested. Maximilian once thought of abdicating and passing the rest of his life at Naples; not, indeed, without receiving the crown of that country as compensation for the one which he renounced, so as to remove both of those obstacles at once. Besides this, the physicians had told him he might recover his health in Naples. The German negotiations he thought he should conclude at a meeting which was to take place in the following

* Albert and Joachim had made preliminary promises in 1517 to the king of France, which they now retracted. The state of things appears from a memorandum which the emperor had drawn up for his grandson in Oct. 1518, wherein it is said: "Le mariage de dame Catherine avec le fils du Marquis Joachim n'importe pas moins; le marquis pour-donner sa voix, Charles à dû renoncer à son mariage avec dame Renée de France et à une grande somme d'argent que le roi de France luy avoit promis."

† Argent Comptant et Pensions pour l'Archevesque de Coulongne: Mone, Anzeiger für Kunde der teutschen Vorzeit, 1836, p. 409. The records therein inserted from the Archives of Lille have all been of great use to me. M. Mone had, however, left a great many untouched, from which M. Gachard of Brussels has lately given an extract in a "Rapport à Monsieur le Ministre de l'Intérieur sur les Archives de Lille," Annexè C. p. 146. In addition to printed sources, I made use of a correspondence of the Venetian ambassador at Rome, who transmits home the news which reaches him, and paints admirably the varying dispositions of the court.

‡ Maximilian even demanded that the pope himself should come to Trent and crown him. He alleged that the pontiff had gone to meet Francis I. at Bologna. But the master of the ceremonies held a coronation out of Rome to be thoroughly inadmissible. Even were pope and emperor in one province, the pope might not, he said, then and there crown the emperor: he must rather suffer him to proceed alone to Rome and be there crowned by a cardinal.—*Paris de Grassis, in Hoffmann*, p. 425. Another idea was, that the cardinals, Giulio de' Medici and Albert of Mainz, should perform the ceremony at Trent.

March at Frankfurt. He begged Elector Frederic in the most urgent manner not to fail to be present, and added that he himself intended to set out soon after the new year.

But this was not permitted him. He fell sick on the journey, at Wels, within his own dominions. His illness did not prevent him from carrying on the negotiations concerning the succession: in his sleepless nights he had the genealogical history of his early progenitors read to him; he was occupied with the past and the future fortunes of his race, when he expired, on the 12th January, 1519.

His death suddenly plunged the issue of the pending negotiations into fresh uncertainty. The engagements already entered into related only to the election of a king, as next in dignity and succession to the emperor; the affair altered its aspect now that the subject of them was an immediate, reigning king and emperor. But so much more weighty was now the decision, both as it regarded the distant future, and the present, pressing, tempestuous moment.

Possibilities of every kind still presented themselves.

ELECTION OF EMPEROR IN 1519.

HAD the powers and functions of the head of the empire been defined by a regular constitution, such as was once contemplated, the most illustrious princes of the empire might have chosen one out of their own body to fill that station. But as the project had failed, who among them all would have been powerful enough to allay the storm of hostilities that raged on all sides, and to uphold the dignity of the empire among the powers of Europe? It was a great question whether any one of them would venture upon such a task.

Maximilian had entertained and declared various singular projects before he would suffer it to be known that he had designs for his grandson. He had offered the succession to the king of England: in one of the most extraordinary documents existing, he at another time nominated the young king Louis of Hungary and Bohemia, administrator of the empire during his lifetime, and after his death, his successor; and these two princes now actually cherished some hopes of the imperial crown: but the one was at too great a distance, the other not sufficiently powerful at home; it was impossible to entertain serious thoughts of either.

In declaring himself openly in favour of his grandson, Archduke Charles, King of Spain and Naples, Maximilian now proposed a scheme which had much to recommend it. Charles was of German blood, heir to Austria, and to many provinces of the German Netherlands, and sprung of the house which had already acquired a sort of title to the imperial dignity. There was, however, no want of objections to this young prince. It was observed that he did not even understand German, and had given no proofs of personal valour or ability; the multitude of his dominions would leave him no time to devote to the empire; lastly, he was expressly excluded by the papal constitution. His prospects, indeed, began to be overclouded. The electors, as we have observed, did not think themselves bound by their promises; nor did Maximilian's daughter Margaret, who now conducted the negotiations, deem it expedient to lay before them the sealed copies of their several compacts, as she had been advised to do; she contented herself with reminding them in general terms of their expressions of goodwill. Added to this, disturbances of a very serious nature had broken out in Austria after Maximilian's death, in which the States established a government of their own* without troubling themselves about the young and absent princes; "poor boys, of whom nobody could tell whether they would ever be seen in Germany." In Tyrol similar troubles broke out.† Louis, King of Hungary, thought it expedient to recall his sister Anna from Austria, where she had already arrived in order to conclude her marriage with one of the brothers.

Under these circumstances, a foreign monarch, already the natural rival of the Austro-Burgundian power,—Francis I. of France,—determined to grasp at the supreme dignity of Christendom.‡

The fortune and fame of Francis were still in the ascendant. The battle of Marignano, by which he had reconquered Milan, and the personal valour which he had displayed there, had secured him a high station in Europe, and a great name. He was on an intimate footing with Leo X. We find that this pope communicated the briefs which he intended to address to the German princes, first to the court of France. King Henry of England, after a short hesitation, promised him his co-operation "by word and deed." A still more essential thing was, that he had gained an influence over at least a portion of the German opposition. We have spoken of the Dukes of Gueldres and Würtemberg; the existence of the one, and all the hopes of the other, depended on France: old relations, never entirely broken, united the palatinate to that country, and Duke Henry der Mittlere of Lüneburg now also took part with the king. "I rejoice in his good fortune," says he in a letter, "I grieve at his bad fortune; whether he be up or down I am his." The king affirmed that he was solicited by Germany to try to acquire the crown. His adherents insisted particularly on his bravery; they urged that no other prince was so well fitted to conduct the war against the Turks, which, sooner or later, must be undertaken.

* Narratio de Dissensionibus Provincialium Austriæ. Pez. Scriptt. ii. 990.

† Zevenberghen to Margaret, March 23, Mone, p. 292.

‡ Il Cl. di Bibbiena al Cl. de' Medici, 13 Ott. 1518. He gives an account of an audience he had of the king relating to the elettion del Catholico (the grants which had been made at Augsburg for Charles): "sopra che in sustanza mi disse, in grandissimo secreto, sua opinione et volontà essere, che per Nostro Signore (the pope) e per sua Mtà si faccia ogni opera possibile, accioche ella non vada innanzi et che si corrompano con danari et con promesse et con ogni possibil mezzo gli elettori."—*Lettere di Principi*, i. p. 47. The whole correspondence, which is printed in this collection, ought to be read: it perfectly shows the relations between Leo X. and Francis I

Kings of France, both before and after Francis, have entertained similar projects—for example, Philip of Valois and Louis XIV.; but none ever had so much encouragement from the posture of affairs, none such favourable prospects, as Francis I.

Two things were necessary to the success of his undertaking; the electors must be won over, and the anti-Austrian party must be supported and strengthened. Francis was resolved to do everything in his power to accomplish both these ends, especially to spare no money; he gave out that he would spend three millions of kronthalers to become emperor. In February 1519, Germany was again filled with his emissaries. Somewhat later, his confidential minister, Admiral Bonnivet, in whose talents the public had great confidence from his late successful conclusion of the peace with England and Spain, set out for the Rhine, largely provided with money; whence he ventured, but in profound secrecy, further into the interior of Germany.*

At one time it really appeared as if the king would attain his object with the electors.†

He had long had the most perfect understanding with Richard Greifenklau, Elector of Treves. Whatever were the cause,—whether ancient dissensions between Treves and the house of Burgundy concerning their claims on Luxemburg, or perhaps the hope which the Elector (who was already "Archchancellor through Gallia and the kingdom of Arles") might entertain of an accession to his power and importance in case France were once more so closely united to the empire,—it is certain that Elector Richard had been equally deaf to the seductions of Maximilian and to the prayers of delegates from the Spanish Netherlands. On the other hand, the terms of the credentials given him by Francis show the most implicit confidence in him. "Convinced of his fidelity, his zeal, his honour, and his prudence," the king nominated him his lawful and unquestioned procurator, envoy and commissary, with full powers to grant to the remaining electors and their confidential servants, or to any other princes of the empire, as much money as he thought fit, either in one sum, or in the form of yearly pension; and to that intent, to mortgage the crown lands in the name of the king, and even in that of his successors: whatever he agreed to was to have the same force and validity as if concluded by the king in person. While he declared himself ready to protect the rights and privileges of the princes, the nobles and the cities; and, generally, to do everything appertaining to an emperor,—especially to undertake the war against the Turks for the defence and extension of the faith,—he empowered the Elector of Treves, should the occasion present itself, to take the required oath on the salvation of his soul.

Nor were the king's negotiations fruitless in other quarters. A complete outline of a treaty with the Elector Palatine was drawn up by his envoys,‡ and in the beginning of April that prince raised his pecuniary demands on Austria threefold, and revived his claim to the Stewardship (*Landvogtei*) of Hagenau. Cologne received a warning from Austria not to allow herself to be seduced into the wrong way, while the French sometimes thought themselves nearly sure of her support.

All these Rhenish electors feared the violence and vengeance of Francis I. in case they resisted him; they were alarmed at perceiving no refuge or defence on the other side. But the support of the See of Rome was still more advantageous to the king's cause, than the fears or the sense of weakness of these princes. Pope Leo X. indeed sometimes expressed himself doubtfully, and it appeared as if he would not take part against Austria; but he was far too deeply versed in the policy of Italy, not to see the dangers that would impend over himself if Naples were united to the empire. The Venetian ambassador, who enjoyed his confidence, affirms that Leo would on no account consent to that.§ Nor was the court of Spain deceived; King Charles once ordered the pope's messengers to be arrested in Tyrol, in order to obtain proof of the illicit practices of the court of Rome in that country.‖ He knew that the legate spoke ill of him; one of his councillors was astonished when the Elector of Mainz showed him all the letters he had received from the papal court in the interest of the French. Of all the electors he was the one whom it was the most important to gain; and who had such ample means of gaining him as the pope? One of the favourite objects of the elector of Mainz was to get himself nominated legate of Germany, like Amboise in France and Wolsey in England. It is well known how difficult it was to induce the See of Rome to grant that dignity to a native; but at the present moment, and in favour of Francis I., it was disposed to do so. In a letter dated from St. Peter's, March 14, 1519, and bearing the seal of the fisherman's ring, Leo X. authorized the king, in the event of his obtaining the imperial crown by the vote and influence of the Elector of Mainz, to promise the same the dignity of legate in Germany: he, Leo X., binding himself, on the word of a true pope of Rome, to fulfil the engagement. There seemed little reason to doubt that the elector would yield to such a temptation.**

* In Rome it was asserted, "che l'era in Augusta el dito Amirante," according to letters of the 1st of April; but I find no further proof of it.

† The statements of Flassans, Histoire de la Diplom. Fr. i. 322, are not of importance. But he there mentions a "liasse contenant des mémoires, lettres et instructions données par François I. à ses envoyés auprès des électeurs," in the Trésor des Chartes. (I looked them over myself in the year 1839, and have extracted from them some remarkable notices.) The accounts of the jeune aventureux (Mémoires de Fleuranges, Coll. univ. xvi. 227,) though well worth reading, do not go deep enough.

‡ In the extract in Stumpf, Baierns polit. Gesch. i. p. 24.

§ "Il papa dice vol far ogni cosa in favor del re christianissimo, et non vol sia il re cattolico per niuno partido per esserli troppo vicino, e poi S. Stà è in liga col re christianissimo dicendo, aver mandato al re cattolico il juramento ha fatto per il reame di Napoli accio si aricordi; poi pregò l'orator tenesse silentio." Roma, 12. April.

‖ "Pour dévoiler ses illicites poursuites." From the letter of the 31st of March in Gachard.

** I give in the Appendix the letter from the Archives of Paris.

The bait which he held out to Joachim I., Elector of Brandenburg, brother of the Cardinal, was at least equally alluring. Joachim, to whom Maximilian had promised his granddaughter Catherine, the sister of Charles, in marriage to the hereditary prince, with a very large dowry, had conceived some suspicions that there was a design to disappoint him The contract was indeed ratified, but only by Charles, not by the princess, without whose consent it could not be considered binding The Fuggers declared themselves not authorized to fulfil the pecuniary obligations contracted with the Elector Joachim, whether at home or in his foreign relations, was fiery, resolute, and suspicious, in money matters, above all, he was not to be trifled with. He was already mortified that the affair had not been terminated a year sooner, as he wished He therefore fixed a term within which the promises made him were to be fulfilled, and meanwhile gave audience to the French ambassador, de la Motte. The French now in their turn promised him a princess of the blood for his son, — Madame Rénée, daughter of Louis XII. and Queen Anne, — with a still larger dowry, for the payment of which they offered greater security than their rival But they did not fail to accompany these promises with others of a far more extensive character. In case Francis I was really chosen, they declared themselves empowered to acknowledge the elector his lieutenant or viceroy, but if that was found to be impracticable, they would use all their influence to raise Joachim himself to the throne. Joachim was not so free from ambition as not to be captivated by proposals of such a kind The moment of Brandenburg's greatness seemed to him arrived It was something that he should be lieutenant of the future emperor, his brother, legate of the pope, the highest secular and spiritual honours would thus be united in his house Behind these, floated the far more splendid vision of the imperial crown.

While however the French became thus deeply implicated with the house of Brandenburg, they did not desist from attempts to gain over the elector of Saxony * We have no accurate knowledge of the negotiations carried on with him, but we have evidence that the French were perfectly well informed of the disgusts the elector had latterly had to endure respecting the Netherlands, and presumed that he would not be very willing to recognize the sovereign of that province as his emperor

During these negotiations, which awakened such lively hope, the opposition in the interests of France, so long kept down by the late emperor, broke out in acts of open violence Ulrich of Würtemberg, even on his way home from the obsequies of Maximilian, made an attack on Reutlingen, where one of his stewards was killed, took the town, and, with the aid of French money,† collected a numerous army, with which he thought to revenge himself on all his enemies, especially the Duke of Bavaria He negotiated with the Swiss, and hoped to excite them to take up arms against the Swabian league Somewhat later, the Bishop of Hildesheim also put himself at the head of his troops, and, during Passion week, under the invocation of the Blessed Virgin, inflicted the most fearful devastations on the territory of his Brunswick enemies The Duke of Luneburg, who had also received money from France, acted in concert with him, gained friends on all sides, and made magnificent preparations for war The Duke of Gueldres had promised to send him succours, and took troops into his service.

The French endeavoured to gain over other military chiefs, as for example, in Upper Germany, Sickingen; in Lower, Henry of Mecklenburg The latter was to bind himself to appear with his troops at Coblentz in the territory of Treves, immediately after the election, in order to earn the pension premised him by the king ‡ French money was offered to the Counts of the Harz, and to the nobles of Westphalia, through the mediation of Guel-dres §

The idea of the French doubtless was, that they should best attain their end by a union of negotiation and warlike demonstrations, — of persuasion and terror. The court already regarded the event as nearly certain It is said that the king's mother had ordered the jewels in which she meant to appear at the coronation ‖ The ambition of her son took a higher flight When the English ambassador asked him whether it was his serious intention, if he became emperor, to take any active measures as to the long-talked of Turkish war, he solemnly assured him, laying his hand on his heart, that in three years he would either not be alive, or be in Constantinople **

But he was far from being so near the goal of his wishes as he and his courtiers imagined. The attachment to Austria was not so weak in Germany as to have lost all its force on the death of the emperor The electors might indeed vacillate, but they were not yet won by France. Enemies of the House of Austria might arise, but it found friends who adhered to it with constancy. Above all, too, that house possessed a head resolved to defend his claims, prepared to accept the challenge of his French rival, and to sustain the combat to the last.

Some former councillors of Maximilian, Matthew Lang, Villinger, Renner, and certain delegates from the court of the Netherlands, among whom the most conspicuous was Maximilian of Zevenberghen, formed a commission in Augsburg, which,

* Letter from the Venetian ambassador, dated Poisy, March 28 " Del duca di Saxonia si confida, non vorrà il re catolico "

† Francis complained afterwards that Ulrich had declared the sum which he had received. See Sattler, ii 92 A letter in Sanuto, dated April 27, 1519 " S M Xma era quello che dava danari al duca de Virtemberg, accio tenesse la guerra in Germania "

‡ Rudloff, Neuere Gesch von Mecklenberg i p 50

§ The Count of Schwarzburg declared, according to a letter of Nassau, of the 20th of March, in Mone (p 136), that a pension of 600 livres for his life had been offered him, and that he had not accepted it

‖ Le Ferron, v 118

** Sir Thomas Boleyn to King Henry Ellis Letters, i 147

under the presidency of Margaret, watched over the interests of Austria. Able and devoted as these men were, they sometimes took a very gloomy view of affairs, and feared for the event. At one time the thought passed through their minds, that it would be better to put forward the Archduke Ferdinand, Charles's brother, who was just arrived in the Netherlands from Spain: they were at all events very desirous that he should come to Germany without loss of time. But they little knew their master, King Charles, if they thought this could be agreeable to him. He was not only displeased, but incensed at it. He declared to the Archduchess Margaret, that he was absolutely determined to have the crown himself, by whatever means it was to be obtained, and at whatever cost; he forbade his brother's journey.* He who united in his person so many monarchies, felt that his ambition would be unsatisfied till he had achieved the supreme dignity of Christendom. He had long reflected not only on the advantages likely to result from it, but on the disadvantages he had to expect if he failed, and that dignity was bestowed on another. He resorted without delay to every form of canvass. To the electors he represented that his great-grandfather, and his grandfather, the late Maximilian, when invested with the imperial majesty, had governed the German nation long and well; he was resolved to tread in their footsteps, and to protect all franchises, spiritual and temporal, particular and general; and to abate everything which could be prejudicial to the liberties of Germany. He declared that his sole object was to maintain peace throughout Christendom; and, after the pattern of his other grandfather, the King of Arragon, to make war upon the unbelievers, and to reserve his whole force for the defence and diffusion of the Catholic faith.† From this time Ferdinand was no more thought of: the councillors reverted to their original project — to raise their elder lord, the King of Spain, to the station of "Prince of princes," at whatever risk or sacrifice.

We must here examine a little in detail what were the means to which they resorted, what the circumstances which favoured them, and what the obstacles they encountered.

Their greatest advantage was precisely that from which their antagonist had hoped the most—the connection between Francis and the Pope.

At a meeting of the Rhenish electors at Wesel, in the beginning of April, the papal legate formally admonished them, in virtue of a prohibitory bull of Clement IV., not to elect the King of Naples, which country, he said, was the property of the Church of Rome. Though the negotiations between the French and the electors were at that moment peculiarly active, such a demand as this roused their spirit of independence. They replied that they were astonished that the Pope should endeavour to throw a prohibition in the way of the election—a thing which the See of Rome had never done; and expressed their hope that his holiness would desist from such an attempt. The legate answered with some bitterness; he reminded them of their not altogether lawful transactions with Maximilian. A correspondence arose which betrayed great irritation, and was not much fitted to advance the cause the pope had espoused.‡

The warlike movements of Francis and his allies were, if possible, yet more advantageous to his rival; above all, the rising of the restless Würtemburger. Some few of the imperial council thought to settle the affair in good German fashion, by peaceful means; but the more sagacious prevented this: they foresaw with certainty on whose side the superior strength lay, who would be victorious, and what an advantage would result to the interests of the election; they wished for war.§ The Swabian league, irritated by former and by recent affronts, and now strengthened by considerable subsidies, was ready to take the field. Franz von Sickingen at length accepted a yearly pension from the house of Burgundy, broke off all negotiations with France, and promised to come to the aid of the league with his cavalry. It was, however, at the same time, necessary to restrict the struggle within these limits, to prevent a general conflagration, and especially to keep the Swiss from siding with Würtemberg.

Duke Ulrich had already taken 16,000 Swiss into his pay; and it was to be feared that the old hostility between the Confederation and the Swabian league might break out anew, as it had done twenty years before. This would have been as welcome a sight to Francis as it was to his predecessor Louis XII. It was all-important not only that it should be avoided, but that contrary dispositions should be excited.

The election of emperor had already been discussed in the Swiss diet. French ambassadors had presented themselves to seek the support of the Confederation: the Swiss in Paris, among them Albert von Stein, advised their countrymen to declare for the king, were it only in order to enjoy the credit and the favour resulting from an event which was no longer to be averted.‖ The Confederation was not, however, so decidedly French as to follow this course. The Cardinal von Sitten, the old enemy of the French, well skilled in all the secret ways of diplomacy, was then in Zürich, and in the enjoyment of great consideration. In the middle of March, Zevenberghen came from Augsburg to his aid. They had, indeed, no easy task. Zevenberghen makes loud complaints of the bad words and threats he was obliged to endure from the pensionaries and speakers; what it

* Margaret to Zevenberghen, May 15. "Absolument le roi est délibéré de lui-mesme parvenir à l'empire, comment que ce soit et quoi que il luy doibve couster."

† Papiers d'Etat du Cl. Granvelle, t. i. p. 112.

‡ Correspondence in Bucholtz, iii. 670. Acta Legationis in Goldast, Political Imper., p. 102. This coincides with the fact of the electors demanding back so seriously and pressingly their circular letters from Augsburg.

§ Letter from Zevenberghen, March 28. Mone. Matth. Schiner, Feb. 12. "Que ce Duc de Wirtemberg estoit le plus grand ami du roi (Charles)—car à cause de sa folie la grande lighe feront de si grosses armées qui feront crainte aux François et autres qui veuillent empescher son election."

‖ Anshelm, Chronicle of Berne, v. 375.

cost him to acknowledge "this low rabble as gentlemen, and to pay them respect; he would rather carry stones;" but he bore it all: he did among them, he said, as if at a fair—paid much and promised more; at length he succeeded. The main cause of his success was, indeed, the interests of Switzerland herself; not only the recollection of the Swiss blood shed in the late wars, or of the numerous claims which still remained unsatisfied; but above all, the consideration that France would, by the acquisition of the imperial dignity, become too mighty, would no longer need the assistance of the Swiss, and would consequently trouble herself no more about them—still less, pay their pensions. On the 18th of March, the Swiss diet came to a formal resolution to oppose the election of the French king to the imperial crown, with body and soul (as they expressed it); and on the contrary to promote the election of a German prince, whether an elector or another. In pursuance of this they wrote to the electors, and to Francis himself; they took the liberty to admonish the latter to content himself with his own kingdom. The Austrian ambassadors wished the Confederation to declare openly for King Charles, but this they could not accomplish. "Wherever they fall," says Zevenberghen, "there they abide."* Nevertheless, much was effected. The ancient union with Austria was renewed. The diet determined to recall from the field those of their people who had joined the duke, and with such unanimous earnestness that they should not dare to resist.

This decided Duke Ulrich's ruin. Zevenberghen justly gloried in having persuaded the diet to pass such a resolution.

At the moment when letters of challenge (*Fehdebriefe*) poured in upon the duke from all sides—when even some of his own vassals renounced their allegiance, and the powerful troops of the league were preparing to fall upon his country—at that moment he was abandoned by those who alone could have defended him. His Würtemberg militia did not understand regular warfare; his cavalry was no match whatever for that of the league. The league encountered no resistance. On the 21st of April they took Tubingen, where the duke's children were residing: and he himself was compelled to abandon his country.

So complete a victory—deciding the conquest of a considerable principality—turned the scale in favour of the Austrian interest through the whole of Upper Germany.

A similar change soon followed in Lower Germany. Towards the end of May the dukes of Calenberg and Wolfenbuttel had completed their preparations, and appeared in the field, with their auxiliaries from Hessen and Meissen, in undisputed superiority. They destroyed Waldenstein, stormed Peine, and plundered the Luneburg territory. Fifty villages were seen in flames at once on their path, nor did they spare a single church; they defaced the arms of their own house, the house of Welf, on their cousin's castle, and carried off rich booty. "They were of a proud spirit," says a song of that day; "they had silver and the red gold; they went in velvet with golden chains; they had two thousand chariots with them." They challenged the Duke of Luneburg in mockery to do battle, while he was still waiting for the succour promised him from Gueldres.

But if the French thought to attain their end by the aid of the intestine wars of Germany, they soon found how completely they had deceived themselves. Exactly at the decisive moment, these private wars took a turn in favour of Austria.

Under the impressions produced by these events, the plenipotentiaries of King Charles renewed their negotiations with the electors with the greatest diligence.

Towards the end of April, a Spanish chargé-d'affaires arrived, bringing the archbishop of Mainz the assent to all his demands. Very remarkable concessions and promises were made to him; full power over the chancery of the empire; the protection of the emperor in the dispute of the archbishopric with Saxony about Erfurt, and in that with Hessen about a newly-erected toll; the emperor's intercession with the pope that he would allow the archbishop to hold a fourth bishopric in Germany; and, lastly, (for the example of France was to be followed in this) his appointment as legate of the Apostolical See in the empire. Moreover, the pensions promised him were secured to him by special legal instruments from Mechlin and Antwerp.† From this time we find the archbishop, who had vacillated for a moment, unshaken in his attachment to Austria and doubly zealous in her cause. He threw the whole weight which the dignity of archchancellor gave him in Germany, into the scale of King Charles.

The elector palatine's support was secured by similar means. He had wavered, only because the publication of his new agreement with Austria as to the succession, and the promised compensation for the stewardship of Hagenau were delayed; while, on the other hand, the Swabian league threatened to espouse the pecuniary claims urged against him by the Rhenish merchants. The Austrian plenipotentiaries hastened to allay these troubles; they satisfied the demands of the merchants at their own cost. Count Palatine Frederic, moreover, exerted all his influence with his brother in favour of Austria, and considerable sums of money were granted to both.‡ Though the elector had said at first, that whatever wind blew, he would always be for Austria, he had not entirely kept his word; but he gradually returned to his first intention, and remained constant to it.

The difficulties with Cologne were not so great. The Count of Nassau, who conducted the negotiations in this part of the country, un-

* Mars 22. "Là où ils tombent, ils demeurent comme tels gens qu'ils sont." Gachard, 178. See Maroton to Margaret, April 10, Mone, 397.

† Carolus ad Albertum 12 Martii, in Gudenus, iv. 607. Jean de le Sauche à Marguer. 29th April; Mone, p. 403.

‡ Correspondence in Mone, p. 34. See Hubert Thomas Leodius, Vita Friderici Palatini, iv. p. 100. sq.

derstood the means of conciliating the Rhenish counts generally, and the archbishop—who was by birth one of that body—in particular The concessions made to that prelate at Augsburg were now extended We have a letter of his, dated the 6th of June, in which he treats the affair of the election as settled, as soon as Bohemia shall be secured *

The King of Bohemia had indeed at first contemplated availing himself of the engagements entered into with him by Maximilian, and had in consequence sent his ambassadors to Italy, but he soon saw how little he had to expect The pope treated his documents with the greatest contempt, as some of the many *privilegia* which Maximilian had created in order to put money into the pockets of his clerks Upon this the government of Bohemia resolved to support the house of Austria, with which it was about to enter into so near a family alliance Perhaps the circumstance that John, brother of the Margrave George of Brandenburg, who had great influence at that court, was just married to the widow of Ferdinand the Catholic, and nominated Viceroy of Valencia,† contributed greatly to this result

There remained, therefore, only Treves, Brandenburg, and Saxony, and the Austrian plenipotentiaries showed no lack of zeal in their endeavours to secure these important votes

With Treves there was nothing to be done Although the dependents of the elector gave some hope, he himself declared he would keep his vote free, and from this resolution no representations could induce him to depart If, notwithstanding this, he had entered into the close connexion with France which we have already noticed, it must have been under some reservation which secured to him his freedom of voting at the decisive moment Such, at least, was the case with Brandenburg

On the 20th of April, the plenipotentiaries of King Charles, the Count of Nassau, M de la Roche, and Nicholas Ziegler, who enjoyed the especial confidence of the archbishop of Mainz, arrived at Berlin They were commissioned to renew to Elector Joachim all the promises which had formerly been made to him, especially in relation to the marriage of his son with the archduchess and infanta Catherine They brought with them the infanta's ratification, and placed it in the hands of a kinsman of the elector, Markgrave Casimir But they found Joachim little disposed to listen to them The utmost that he would promise was, that he would vote for Charles, if the four electors who preceded him had done so, and even for this very unsatisfactory engagement, he made greater demands than they were empowered to grant Nor had he given any promise to the King of France, but with the condition that two electors should have voted on that side before it came to his turn, yet that sovereign had, in addition to various other concessions, agreed to these exorbitant demands. According to the first proposal made by Margaret, her ambassadors certainly gave the elector reason to hope that he would have the lieutenancy of the empire, but I do not find whether this was confirmed by Charles or not. The ambassadors did not accede to a suggestion of Joachim's as to the vicariate of the empire for the Saxon provinces, still less would they permit him to hope for the crown, in any case or under any condition As this was the prospect that first allured the elector, we need not wonder that they had no success with him

It was the more important to obtain the vote of him whom Austria had lately so deeply offended, and whom the councillors regarded as their most formidable opponent—Frederic of Saxony ‡ As the Bohemian vote did not carry great weight (and indeed the last election was concluded without Bohemia), the vote of Saxony was necessary to the formation of a majority that would be universally recognised The refusal of the elector to take part in the measures agreed on at Augsburg, which excited great discontent in the nation when they were known, had increased the already high consideration he enjoyed Moral authority and the consent of public opinion were attached to this vote, every effort must be made to secure it

The elector himself remained inaccessible. He would hear of no promises, he forbade his servants to receive presents, and referred all inquiries to the day of election, when it would be seen to whom he gave his vote, till then he would keep it free

But there is no position on earth so lofty or so impregnable, that it cannot be reached by some means or other The deputies determined to take a step which, if successful, would certainly put an end to all the animosities that had been accumulating between Saxony and Austria They now offered the Archduchess Catherine, sister of King Charles, who had just been the subject of their fruitless negotiations with Joachim I, to Duke John, brother of the elector, for his son, John Frederic, the future heir to the electorate.

To this proposal Duke John replied, that the king would be able to place his sister in a more exalted position The ambassadors answered, that the king only wished to renew the ancient alliance of the two houses They overruled the objections raised by his modesty in the most dexterous and flattering manner, by reminding him that the sister of Emperor Frederic was the grandmother of the dukes of Saxony §

The elector took no part in these negotiations, but he allowed them to go on The ambassadors thought they discovered that the whole business of the election depended on the success of them They wrote first from Lochau, and again on the 16th of May from Rudolstadt, to the king, in Spain, urging him to send them full powers to conclude this treaty

* Bucholtz, iii 671

† Letter from Charles to Casimir on this subject, March 6, 1519 Spiess, Brandenburgische Munzbelustigungen, i p 320

‡ Marnix to Margaret, March 16, traces the unfavourable disposition of Bohemia, amongst other sources, to Saxony Mone, p 131

§ Muller Geschichte der Protestation, p 689

of marriage as quickly as possible, if he would not have their endeavours prove fruitless, this was the only means of arriving at the desired end * This was so obvious to the king that he did not hesitate an instant. On the 30th of May he signed the act empowering his envoys to negotiate this marriage and everything relating to it, in his name, and to arrange the terms with an authority equal to his own † Hereupon Duke John granted his council full powers to treat, in the preamble to which he said that, "bearing in mind the dignity of the crown of Spain, and the name and race of the honourable house of Austria, he wished most especially to see his son, who was also well inclined thereto, advised to a friendly marriage with the most illustrious princess, the Lady Catherine" The Austrian ambassadors had now only to ascertain what effect this good understanding with the duke was likely to have on the elector, and to act accordingly

At all events, it is evident that they had successfully employed the interest of the house they served

But the affair was not decided thus

Austria had now unquestionably a majority of declared friends in the electoral college, but the French, too, could reckon on more than one partisan, and did not relinquish the hope of gaining over one or two of the others They had just made a vehement, and, as they believed, successful attempt on the elector of Cologne they thought that even if they had only three votes, the pope would declare the election valid, and his legate, at least, adhered firmly to their side up to the middle of June

Austria was indeed victorious, and remained with arms in her hands; but the partisans of France in Lower Germany were by no means crushed We find traces of very extensive and unexpected plans, *e g* an original document, in which Francis promises to pay whatever troops the electors of Treves and Brandenburg should levy in Germany, under the extraordinary pretext that they were to maintain the peace of the country and the freedom of the roads for the meeting in Frankfurt The Duke of Gueldres was already up in arms again The French troops did not yet advance upon the German frontier, but they were prepared to do so ‡

The two powers vied with each other in prodigal expenditure of money It was a peculiar advantage on the side of Austria that the great mercantile house of Fugger, which conducted nearly the whole monetary business of Germany, refused its services to the French § Admiral Bonnivet had, however, brought large sums in hard money to Germany, which many might think better than any bills of exchange whatsoever

Had the event depended exclusively on pecuniary interests, its decision would have remained very doubtful

But considerations of a totally different nature evidently had weight

We must do the princes of Germany in old times the justice to admit, that, spite of the many scandalous transactions they engaged in, the interests of the nation always prevailed at last

To uphold the ancient privileges of the empire against all attacks or encroachments of the See of Rome, was the motive which led the Rhenish electors to reject the proposals and arguments of the legate

But was not Francis also a foreigner? Could the electoral college venture so lightly to alienate from the nation that imperial crown which, at every diet, they solemnly promised to maintain? There were those who did not fail to remark that Francis was an absolute monarch, accustomed to implicit obedience and possessed of great power, under whose sceptre the maintenance of German liberties could hardly be expected The violent acts of his partisans were not calculated to make quiet patriots his friends

On the other hand, the young King of Spain was without question a German He reminded the German princes that the tree stem and the first blossom of his nobility were from Austria, were he not a German, had he not land and lordships in Germany, he would withdraw from the contest

How profound an effect was produced by this difference in the pretensions of the rivals, is distinctly shown by a remark of the papal delegates They say, every one will, in the end, deem it infamous to receive money from France, but to take it from King Charles, is thought nothing of

Public opinion had also already declared itself on the matter The electors had it in their power to choose one of their own body—a German prince Had they chosen the King of France, taking money too for their votes, the result might have been dangerous to themselves

All these things were gradually so distinctly felt, that, by the middle of June, Charles's superiority was decided, and no further doubt was entertained of the event

Henry VIII of England for a moment cherished the hope of placing the crown on his own head, during the contest of the other two sovereigns, but his ambassador acted with great discretion and reserve He looked at the affair like a man of business, and, on calculation, he found his crown too dear a purchase for its value and utility ‖ A letter of his, of the 12th of June, shows that he had then given up all hope

At this conjuncture Carracciolo, one of the pope's chargés-d'affaires, caused himself to be carried, ill as he was, to the archbishop of Mainz, in order that he might once more recommend to that prelate the interests of the

* Nassou et Peine, May 16 Mone, p 40.

† Document in Arnoldi's Denkwurdigkeiten, p 8

‡ Letter from France, May 26 "In Franza non è alcun motivo di arme, ma ben la zente preparata"

§ Letter from Zevenberghen, Mone p 30 In the Netherlands Margaret forbade business relating to French bills of exchange to be transacted Ibid p 293 But we find the imperial agents not always on a good understanding with the Fuggers The Welsers seem to have done business on lower terms

‖ Richard Pace, Ellis, i. 156 See Herbert, Life of Henry VIII, p 74.

church and of the King of France. The archbishop answered, that he took upon his own head the affairs of the church, but that he would have nothing to do with the King of France. The envoy asked upon whom the choice of the electors would fall? The cardinal said, on the King of Spain; and, if not upon him, then upon the Elector of Saxony. The envoy was perfectly astonished that the cardinal, notwithstanding such repeated misunderstandings, still preferred the Elector of Saxony to the King of France.* These words perhaps decided the conduct of the Roman see. When Pope Leo found what the dispositions of Germany were, he was heard to exclaim that it would not do to run one's head against the wall; an expression characteristic of his policy, which was always that of giving way before an obstinate resistance. After having so long held out, he at length yielded (June 24th), and announced to the electors his assent to the election of the King of Spain and Naples.

When the electors assembled in Frankfurt there was not the smallest hope left for Francis: the only remaining obstacle to Charles's success was the wish which had existed among them, of having a native of the soil of Germany for their emperor.† The elector Joachim, who now put forward urgent claims,‡ was thought of; but his own relations, above all his brother of Mainz, were against him; they found that the maintenance of the imperial dignity would necessitate exertions and expenses which would consume the resources of the Mark, and those of their whole family; they knew, too, that the princes of the empire would not choose a head of so harsh, severe and self-willed a character. Joachim would never have conciliated a sufficient number of voices. A far more formidable rival existed in the person of Frederic of Saxony, on whom the eyes of the assembly were now turned. Richard of Treves went to him once by night, and offered to take a part of the labour of the canvass on himself. His own hopes being utterly at an end, the King of France determined to use his influence in favour of Frederic. Considering the conduct of that prince in the Lutheran affairs, and the national tendencies with which these affairs were connected, this certainly opened one of the grandest prospects for the destiny of Germany. The electors were, on the whole, well disposed towards the measure; indeed it was afterwards said, in the way of reproach, that if there had been one among them "capable of sustaining the empire," he would have been chosen. Had Frederic only been inspired by a more daring ambition! Had he not been of so cautious a nature, rendered still less enterprising by age! But he had too long and too profound an acquaintance with the history of the empire, not to know that a vast preponderance of power was necessary to hold together in union and subordination these haughty, energetic princes and states, all striving for independence.

Although his resolution was taken, he once asked his follower, Philip of Solms, his opinion. Philip replied, that he feared his lord would not be able to use his power of punishing with due severity. Frederic answered, that he was of the same opinion; and declined the proffered support.§ The time was come, too, when no more reserves could be maintained: he declared himself openly for King Charles. This declaration decided those who had till then been wavering.

On the 28th of June, the tocsin was sounded, according to ancient custom, and the electors assembled, clad in their scarlet robes of state, in the small dark chapel in the choir of the church of St. Bartholomew, which served them as conclave. They were already unanimous. Mainz addressed himself first, according to ancient precedent, to Treves, who replied that he voted for the Archduke Charles of Austria, Prince of Burgundy, King of Spain. So said they all; the King of France had not a vote.‖

The electors were however mindful, in choosing so puissant a prince, immediately to take measures for securing the rights of the empire. They laid before the elected King of the Romans a rigorous capitulation, constructed on the principles which had been established during the last negotiations with Maximilian.¶ In this it was decided that the public offices should be filled exclusively by Germans, the public proceedings carried on exclusively in the German language, and the assemblies of the empire invariably held within the frontiers of the German nation. Nor did the electors forget their own privileges. They stipulated that they were to have seats in the Council of Regency; that no war was to be declared, no alliance concluded, no diet convoked—it is hardly necessary to add, no tax imposed—without their consent; whatever was acquired by the counsel and aid of the States in war, should remain for ever the property of the empire.**

And here another reflection suggests itself. The princes, it is true, elected a puissant monarch as their chief. But it may be asked, was not his position, which rendered inevitable his frequent absence, favourable to the development of their own power?

* "La esso Moguntino habbi gran inimicitia con Saxonia, lo vel avanti che il re christianissimo."

† The Italians, for instance, could not at all comprehend why such an one was not chosen. "Li electori," says Lippomano, the Venetian ambassador at Rome, "saranno pazzi a non si far uno di loro." On this ground they willingly believed that the Elector of Brandenburg would be chosen. "Scrive il Cl. Sedunese, sarà il Brandenburg, 5 Giugno." Hereon rests also Vettori's opinion, that Leo had never wished to give his support to the king, in whose behalf, however, he had expressed himself far too decisively.

‡ According to a letter from the admiral, of the 17th or 18th of June, "Il Treverese havea rimosso il Marchese di Brandenburg qual volea esser electo lui;" but he concluded thence, that the king had fresh hope.

§ Extract from Lucas Geierberg, Leben Philipsen, Grafen von Solms, after the preface to Göbel's Beiträgen zur Staatsgeschichte von Europa, p. 19.

‖ Protocollum Electionis in Goldast's Polit. Reichshändeln, p. 41. The speeches said to have been delivered on this occasion are fictitious. See Ranke, Zur Kritik neuerer Geschichtschreiber, p. 62.

¶ Revers in Bucholtz, iii. 663.

** Capitulation, amongst others, in Dumont, iv. 1. Unfortunately I have not been able to examine the documents.

Under a prince like this, who had to govern so many countries, to provide against so many wars, they could most easily obtain that representative constitution, that share in the government of the empire, which it had been the constant object of their endeavours to acquire under Maximilian.

How strange a mixture of the most heterogeneous motives combined to bring about the election of Charles V! Pecuniary bribes (it is not to be denied) to a large amount, both to the princes, among whom were even Treves and Duke John of Saxony, and to their dependents and councillors, the concession of new privileges, family alliances, near or remote, which either already existed, or were now concluded, or contracted for the future: on the other hand, some degree of dread of the army of the Swabian league, which was still in the field and in the pay of Austria,* and, lastly, antipathy to the stranger, in spite of his still more profuse offers of money, attachment to the house which had already given several emperors to Germany, and which enjoyed traditional respect; the dangers attending every other course; the expectation of good results from that pursued, — in short, a mixture of purely personal considerations and of sincere regard for the public weal! Among the various influences which determined the event, we must not omit to add that of luck. On the very day, nay the very hour, of election, an event took place in Lower Saxony, which, had it occurred earlier, might easily have rendered the issue once more doubtful, and have revived the hopes of the French party.

The cavalry of Gueldres had at length joined Duke Henry of Luneburg, who had set out without delay to seek in the field the plunder-laden army of his cousins. He came up with this near Soltau on the Haide, and began the attack without waiting for his infantry. His strength lay in his cavalry, which rushed up to the enemy's artillery and took it, then broke the lines of the infantry, partly mercenaries, who took to flight and threw their arms into the sand: animated by this success, the conquering troop then made a violent attack on the squadron of Calenberg horse. Here they met with a gallant resistance. Duke Eric of Calenberg, distinguishable by his white plume, forced his way into their ranks, but, in spite of his bravery, the Luneburgers overpowered him by their numbers, and gained a complete victory. Eric himself, his brother William, and a hundred and twenty knights, were made prisoners by the partisans of the King of France.†

But since, as we have observed, the election of the emperor was concluded on the same day, this victory was utterly fruitless. The victors were now compelled to avoid all connexion with France, while the vanquished found favour and assistance from the commissioners of Charles V at Augsburg. In October, Henry the Younger of Wolfenbuttel took up arms anew, aided, as it was believed, by money from Augsburg, and committed devastations in Hildesheim, estimated at a hundred and fifty thousand gulden, and it was with difficulty that he could be induced by the neighbouring princes to grant a truce. He would agree to no definitive terms proposed by the mediators. He quitted Zerbst, where they were assembled, by night, without bidding them farewell, and only leaving word that he must reserve the matter for the decision of his imperial majesty (May 1520). If France had defended the Luneburgers, Austria and her fortunes now lent more powerful support to their adversaries.

The affairs of Upper Germany at the same moment took a still more decisive turn in the same direction. Wurtemberg passed entirely into Austrian hands.

The cause of this was that Duke Ulrich, in this unexpected attack in August, had driven out the government of the league, taken the country again into his own possession, and was only expelled from it by renewed efforts of that body.‡ This conquest was now burdensome to the conquerors: the expenses of the former war, for which they earnestly desired some compensation, were now, on the contrary, increased by new ones. The members of the league, therefore, joyfully accepted the emperor's proposition to take into his charge and custody the country, together with the duke's children, and in consideration of this concession, he promised to accede to the demands of the States.§ In February 1520, the imperial commissioners took the administration into their own hands, and by confirming the treaty of Tubingen, which Ulrich at his return had been imprudent enough to revoke, they secured a considerable party in the country.

This first act of Charles's government wore a very arbitrary aspect. For it was utterly unheard of that, as the Swiss expressed it, "a prince of the Holy Empire should be driven from his illustrious house, contrary to all law and forcibly despoiled of the principality which was his by paternal inheritance and right." But the commissioners regarded the election as a triumph of the Austrian party, and were only anxious to turn it to their own advantage.

This had not been the intention of the electors—least of all that of Frederic of Saxony; on the contrary, they had immediately considered how to introduce an uniform representative government, to convoke an imperial diet, and to appoint a Council of Regency. The court of Spain appeared to approve cordially of these measures, a proclamation arrived, in which Elector Frederic was nominated lieutenant (Statthalter) of the Regency, and was also entreated to give his good counsel in public affairs. But the commissioners did not think fit to convoke a diet, still less to nominate a Council of Regency. They carefully avoided

* Richard Pace to Cardinal Wolsey, i 157. "Suerly they wold nott have electidde hym yff fere of these persons hadde not dryven them thereunto."

† Chytræus, Saxonia, lib viii p 207. Carmen prolixius, in Leibnitz, Scriptores Rer Brunsv iii 257.

‡ Stumphart, Chronica gwaltiger Verjagung Herzog Ulrichs (Chronicle of the forcible Expulsion of Duke Ulrich) Sattler, Herzoge, ii Appendixes, p 43.

§ Gwalt K Karls V auf seine Commissarien, ibid p 73.

consulting the elector and kept the diploma of his nomination to themselves They were as fully determined now, as under Maximilian, to resist all interference on the part of the States, they chose to retain the whole of the public business in their own hands

This ought to excite no wonder These imperial functionaries remained firmly attached to those views which had become current under Maximilian, and regarded the new government as a mere continuation of the old

It therefore became a matter of double solicitude to ascertain in what light the young prince, on his arrival in Germany, and those around him, would regard affairs, or in what spirit he would undertake their management His commanding station and wide sovereignty naturally led people to expect views proportionally grand and elevated, and such indeed were displayed in all his letters He wrote to Elector Frederic that he should find that he had given his vote to the most grateful of princes, that he would shortly appear in person, hold a diet, and order the affairs of the empire with the counsel and approbation of his well-beloved, the Elector, "for," said he, "we esteem marvellously the designs, the counsel, and the wisdom of thy rule"*

Before, however, Charles could arrive, the religious affairs of Germany had assumed a character which rendered the question, what course he would embrace, no less important to the church than to the empire

CHAPTER III.

FIRST DEFECTION FROM THE PAPACY, 1519–20

CAJETAN AND MILTITZ

During the interval we have been treating of, it had more than once appeared probable that the Lutheran controversy would be brought to a peaceful termination, to this both sides were inclined

During the diet at Augsburg, Elector Frederic prevailed on himself to pay a visit to the papal legate, and to invite his mediation I do not find that the latter had any special commission from Rome to this effect, but his general powers gave him full liberty to accept such an office. He promised the elector to listen to the monk whenever he should appear before him, and to dismiss him with paternal kindness †

The business of the meeting was already ended, when Luther, well pleased at not being obliged to go to Rome, set out to present himself before the cardinal. He travelled indeed in a most lowly guise, the cowl he wore was borrowed, and he wandered on, craving hospitality from convent to convent, ill, and sometimes exhausted even to fainting ‡ He often said afterwards, that if the cardinal had treated him kindly, he might easily have induced him to keep silence. When he came into his presence, he fell down at his feet

Unhappily, however, this legate, Thomas de Vio of Gaeta (Cajetan), was not only a representative of the Curia, but a most zealous Thomist His mother, it is said, dreamt when she was with child of him, that she saw St. Thomas in person teaching him, and afterwards bearing him to heaven § In his sixteenth year, in spite of the great reluctance of his family, he was not to be withheld from entering a Dominican convent, where laying aside his original name of James, he took that of his saint, and exerted all his powers thoroughly to imbue his mind with the doctrines of St. Thomas, whom he esteemed the most perfect theologian that ever existed He undertook to defend his great work, the Summa, step by step, against the objections of the Scotists ‖

Luther, therefore, was already extremely odious to him as a nominalist, as an impugner of the theological despotism of St Thomas, and as leader of an active opposition party in a newly-created university At first he replied to Luther's humility with the official fatherly condescension of a spiritual superior But the natural antagonism between them soon broke out. The cardinal was not disposed to be satisfied with mere silence, nor would he permit the matter to come to a disputation, as Luther proposed, he thought he had demonstrated the monk's error to him in a few words, and demanded a recantation. This awakened in Luther a feeling of that complete contrariety of opinions and systems, which acknowledges no subordination, whether spiritual or temporal. It appeared to him that the cardinal did not even understand his idea of faith, far less confute it a conversation arose in which Luther displayed more reading, more distinctness and depth of views, than the legate had given him credit for, speculations of so extraordinary a kind had never come before him; the deep-set glittering eyes, fixed upon his, inspired him with a sort of horror, at length he exclaimed that Luther must either recant or never venture into his sight again ¶

It was the dominican system which here, clad in purple, repulsed its antagonist. Luther, though furnished with a safe-conduct from the emperor, thought himself no longer secure from violence, he drew up an appeal to the pope, praying him to inquire into the matter,

* Instruction to Hieronymus Brunner, Barselona, Sept 25, 1519 in a register in the Weimar archives, which lays open the whole of the circumstances

† Frederic's letter to Cajetan (Loscher, ii 543) "Persuaseramus nobis, vestram pietatem audito Martino secundum vestram multiplicem promissionem eum paterne et benevole dimissuram esse" See Luther, wider Hans Worst Altenb vii 402 Letter to Lang in de Wette, i 141

‡ Luther to Spalatin, Oct 10, 1518, in de W. 142.

§ So says the Biography in Roccaberti, Bibl Max t xix p 443

‖ "Divi Thomæ Summa cum commentariis Thomæ de Vio, Lugduni, 1587 Præfatio Inter theologos quem divo Thomæ Aquinati præferre ausis, invenies neminem"

¶ Luther's report in the Acta Augustana, his letters, the addresses of the legate, finally a letter from Staupitz, in Grimm (passim, p 123) give sufficient information about this interview It is to be regretted that the account sent by the legate to Rome has never come to light

and took to flight His going corresponded with his coming Escaping through a secret gate which his Augsburg friends opened for him by night, mounted on a horse procured for him by his provincial, Staupitz, habited in his cowl, and without any proper riding garments, he rode, accompanied by a mounted guide, eight long German miles the first day, on alighting, he fell half dead from fatigue by the side of his horse on the straw But he was happily out of the immediate jurisdiction of the legate

Cajetan's accusations soon followed him to Saxony. He conjured the elector not to stain the glory of his house for the sake of an heretical friar, if he did not choose to send him to Rome, at least to get rid of him out of his country, he declared that Rome would never suffer this affair to drop But he could no longer produce any impression, his indiscreet and violent conduct had robbed him of all credit with Frederic. The university wrote to their prince that they knew no otherwise than that Luther showed all due reverence for the church, and even for the pope, were there wickedness in the man, they would be the first to notice it. This corporation was irritated that the legate should treat one of its members as a heretic, before any sentence had been pronounced.* Thus seconded, Frederic replied to the legate, that it had not yet been shown by any of the numerous learned men in his own states, or those contiguous, that Luther was a heretic; and refused to banish him †

Luther however did not conceal from himself that the sentence pronounced by Rome might very probably be unfavourable to him He hastened to secure himself against this as far as possible by a fresh appeal to the general council which was just about to be called

But the conduct of the cardinal did not obtain the approbation of Rome That court was not disposed to alienate so considerable and respected a sovereign as Frederic, who had just acquired twofold weight by his conduct at the election, and with whom it had probably rested to raise the King of France to the imperial throne, as the pope had desired Leo therefore now made an attempt to bring the discussion concerning Luther to an amicable conclusion. He determined to send the elector the golden rose, a mark of the apostolical favour, for which that prince had always been very anxious In order to draw the loosened ties closer between them, he likewise despatched a native of Saxony, and agent of the elector at Rome, to him as nuncio

Karl von Miltitz unquestionably showed great address in the manner in which he set about the affair

On his arrival in Germany he abstained from visiting the legate, who indeed had lost all influence, and now showed a sullen resentment against the elector, even on the journey, Miltitz contracted an intimacy with one of Frederic's privy councillors, Degenhard Pfeffinger He did not scruple among friends, over the convivial table, or even in inns and taverns, to join in the complaints which were made in Germany of the Curia, and of the abuses of the church, nay, to confirm them by anecdotes of what he had himself witnessed But he assured his hearers that he knew the pope, and had influence with him, and that Leo did not approve these things He pronounced the most entire and distinct disapprobation of the scandalous proceedings of the vendors of indulgences, and in short the reputation which preceded him was such that Tetzel did not dare to present himself before him ‡

On the other hand, the prince, towards whom he maintained the demeanour of a subject and servant, and Luther himself, whom he treated very indulgently, conceived great confidence in him Without much trouble, he succeeded in bringing about that degree of approximation between himself and the anti-dominican party, which was absolutely necessary to the success of his negotiation

On the 3d January, 1519, he had an interview with Luther at Altenburg The nuncio represented to the monk the evils which arose from his vehemence, and the great breach which he would thus make in the church he implored him with tears to lay these things to heart Luther promised to remedy, by a public explanation of his doctrine, whatever mischief he might have done On the other hand, the nuncio gave up the idea of bringing Luther to a recantation They came to an agreement that the matter should be referred to a German bishop, and that, meanwhile, both parties should be bound to observe silence § So, thought Luther, the controversy would die away They embraced and parted

The explanation which Luther soon after published, in consequence of this conversation, is very remarkable He touches on all the controverted points of the moment Without abandoning the free attitude he had assumed, he shows that he considers himself as still within the pale of the Roman church, for example, he maintains that the saints ought to be invoked for spiritual, rather than for temporal gifts, but he does not deny that God works miracles at their graves, he still admits the doctrine of purgatory, and of indulgences in a certain sense, he wishes for some relaxation of the commandments of the church, but is of opinion that this could only be granted by an ecclesiastical council, although he ascribes salvation to the fear of God and the state of the thoughts and intentions, he does not entirely reject good works It is evident that on every point he insists on inward, rather than outward influences and merits, but he does so with great moderation, and endeavours to maintain external observances In the same spirit he speaks of the church He sees her essence in

* With regard to the brief in which mention is made of a sentence already passed (in Loscher, ii 438) I think I have shown in an Excursus, that it is not genuine

† Correspondence in Loscher, 537-542.

‡ His letter of apology, subscribed "Brother Tetzel, on the last day of Dec 1519," (i e 1518,) in Walch xv p 860 The rest of Miltitz's Correspondence, first published by Cyprian, is also to be found in Walch

§ 'In ir selbs vorgehn" — *Luther to the Electors*, in *De Wette*, i 213

"inward unity and love," but he does not reject her constitution, he acknowledges the supremacy of the church of Rome, "where St Peter and St Paul, forty-six popes, and hundreds of thousands of martyrs, poured out their blood, and overcame hell and the world" no sin that can be committed in her can justify us in separating ourselves from her, or in resisting the commands of the pope *

With this explanation the ecclesiastical authority might for the moment be content—and indeed was forced to be content For, if Elector Frederic chose to accept it, there was no other power that could be turned against Luther so great was the interest which the nation already took in his cause, so strong the aversion which repelled all interference of the court of Rome

In the early months of the year 1519, when the demands of the last diet in behoof of the Turkish war were made to the several States in all parts of Germany, the doubts expressed in that assembly as to the reality of the intention which served as pretext were now repeated in various circles, and were more and more widely diffused, all the well-founded complaints which had there been more distinctly stated than ever, were now the topic of discourse through the whole nation

Moreover, the interest which the papal legate had evinced in the views of Francis I on the imperial crown, excited great disgust It is a fact well worth notice, that the whole Austrian party thus naturally fell into a state of hostility to the Roman see At the court of its leader, the Elector of Mainz, there appeared satires in which the pompous inanity of the legate, his personal peculiarities and the oppressive nature of his office, were ridiculed in the bitterest manner In the spring of 1519,† it was with difficulty that he could find a boatman in Mainz who would consent to take him down the river to Niederwesel, where the Rhenish electors held a meeting he was once told that he must renounce all his French schemes if he wished to get home in a whole skin ‡

This universal unpopularity compelled the court of Rome to observe a discreet reserve, to which its interest in the election contributed; and thus it happened that Rome once more tried by every means in its power to be upon a footing of amity with Elector Frederic Another plenipotentiary of the Curia besides Miltitz appeared in Saxony The legate, although with obvious ill will, was at length prevailed upon to deliver to the elector the golden rose which had been entrusted to him, and which he had till now withheld The prospect of putting an end to the controversy in Germany was desirable and commodious even to him The Archbishop of Treves was selected as judge §

ARRIVAL OF MELANCHTHON

The state of suspended controversy and preliminary calm that now arose was peculiarly advantageous to the university of Wittenberg. There was a general sentiment of an undertaking successfully begun, increasing in force of opposition, but yet not obnoxious to the condemnation of the church. The members of the university had time to carry forward the proper studies of the place in the spirit that had from the first presided over them The most eminent teachers still held the same opinions on the main question Besides this, in the summer of 1518, they had acquired a youthful assistant, whose labours from the first moment gave new life to their whole proceedings

Philip Schwarzerd, surnamed Melanchthon, was, in the truest and most perfect sense, a disciple of Reuchlin Reuchlin was one of his nearest relations, and had directed his education the young man followed the precepts and example of his master with intelligent docility; the native powers which well-conducted studies never fail to develop, the sympathy he received from his fellow-students, and, above all, a matchless capacity, certain, from the first, of its vocation, led him rapidly forwards. In his 17th or 18th year he had already begun to teach in Tubingen, and had published two or three little books on grammatical subjects ‖

But the mind of the pupil, like that of the master, was not satisfied with philological studies He attended lectures in all faculties; for the sciences were not as yet cultivated in such detail, or in so special a manner, as to render that impossible; they could still furnish nutriment to a large and liberal curiosity. Melanchthon felt peculiarly attracted towards the study of philosophy, in comparison with which all his other pursuits appeared to him mere waste of time But the rigid, stationary spirit of the old universities still reigned in Tübingen; and while his whole intellectual powers were stretching forward to unknown regions, his instructors sought to bind him down to a lifeless routine

A circumstance, however, occurred which decided both his outward destiny and the direction of his mind In the spring of 1518, Elector Frederic applied to Reuchlin to send him a teacher of the Greek language for his university Without a moment's hesitation, Reuchlin recommended "his kinsman and friend," whom he himself had instructed ¶ This might be regarded as involving Melanchthon's decision: for between master and disciple there was that noble relation which exists between a youth who beholds the world in the imperfect light shed over distant objects, and the admitted superiority of a matured judgment. "Whither thou wilt send me," writes Melanchthon to Reuchlin, "there will I go, what thou wilt

* D M L Unterricht auf etliche Artikel so ihm von seinen Abgönnern aufgelegt worden Walch, xv 822

† Hutten's Febris Prima (op iii 109,) belongs to this period

‡ Letter to Zurich in Anselm, Berne Chronik, v 373

§ Miltitz to the Electors Walch, xv 879 he had seen the legate at Coblentz The instruction to Miltitz, I 1, must likewise be assigned to the month of May, as it refers to his journey into Saxony, which he mentions in his letter, dated Wednesday after Misericordia, May 11

‖ Schnurrer de Phil Melanchthonis rebus Tubingensibus Orationes Academ ed Paulus, p 52. Præfatio in primam editionem operum Bretschneiders Corpus Reformatorum, iv 715.

¶ Correspondence in the Corp Ref i 28.

make of me, that I will become." "Get thee out," answered Reuchlin, "from thy country and from thy kindred." With the words once addressed to Abraham, he blessed him and bade him depart.

In August 1518, Melanchthon came to Wittenberg. His first determination was, as he says, to devote himself entirely to the university, and to raise its fame in the classical studies, which had as yet been cultivated with little success. With the high spirits of youth he reckoned up the labours he had before him, and hastened to enter upon them.* Before September was over, he dedicated to the elector the translation of one of Lucian's works; in October he printed the Epistle to Titus and a little dictionary; in November he wrote the preface to a Hebrew Grammar. He immediately undertook a more elaborate work—his Rhetoric, which appeared in three books, in January 1519. In February followed another discourse; in March and April, editions of several of Plutarch's writings, with a preface—all during an equally varied and laborious course of teaching; for the youthful stranger undertook to give instructions in Hebrew as well as Greek.†

Yet these immediate occupations led neither to the scope, nor to the results, of his laborious studies.

It was an important circumstance that a perfect master of Greek arose at this moment at a university, where the development of the Latin theology already led to a return to the first genuine documents of primitive Christianity. Luther now began to pursue this study with earnestness. His mind was relieved, and his confidence strengthened, when the sense of a Greek phrase threw a sudden light on his theological ideas; when, for example, he learned that the idea of repentance (pœnitentia), which, according to the language of the Latin church, signified expiation or satisfaction, in the original conception of the Founder and the apostles of Christianity signified nothing but a change in the state of mind;‡ it seemed as if a mist was suddenly withdrawn from before his eyes.

It was also of inestimable value to Melanchthon that he could here devote himself to subjects which filled his whole soul, and that he now found the substance of those forms to which his attention had hitherto been principally directed. He embraced with enthusiasm the theological views of Luther, and, above all, his profound exposition of the doctrine of justification. But he was not formed to receive these opinions passively. He was one of those extraordinary spirits, appearing at rare intervals, who attain to the full possession and use of their powers at an early period of life. He was now but just twenty-one. With the precision which solid philological studies seldom fail to impart, with the nice instinct natural to the frame of his mind, he seized the theological element which was offered to his grasp.

The somewhat unfavourable impression which the youthful and unpretending appearance of the new-comer had at first made, was quickly effaced. The scholars caught the infection of their teacher's zeal. "They are as industrious as ants at the university," says Luther. Reforms in the method of instruction were proposed. With the approbation of the court, lectures were discontinued which had no value but for the scholastic system, and others were instituted, founded on classical studies; the conditions upon which academical degrees were granted were rendered less severe. These measures unquestionably tended to place Wittenberg in stronger contrast to the other universities; new views and ideas were introduced. Luther's letters show the ferment that was going on within him, but they equally show that neither he nor those associated with him were conscious of being involved in a general struggle with the church of Rome. We saw how carefully Luther kept within the bounds prescribed by the church; and Melanchthon, in one of his prefaces, extols the services rendered by his sovereign to monasteries.§ This, as well as the conduct pursued by Miltitz, and finally also by the legate, shows that every thing wore a peaceful aspect.

But at this very moment, when external peace at least was restored, and when, though vehement struggles were to be anticipated from differences of opinion and of education, it was possible they might be confined within the region of school learning, there arose a contest touching those important doctrines whereon the Church and the State are founded, and lighting up that war which has never since been extinguished. It must be admitted that Luther was not the person who caused its outbreak.

DISPUTATION AT LEIPZIG.

DURING the diet of 1518, Eck had appeared in Augsburg, dissatisfied that his polemical writings had as yet procured him neither emolument nor honour:‖ he had called on Luther, and had agreed with him, in a perfectly amicable manner, publicly to fight out an old controversy which he had with Dr. Carlstadt in Wittenberg, concerning grace and free will. Luther had readily offered his mediation, in order, as he says, to give the lie to the opinion that theologians cannot differ without hostility. Carlstadt consented to dispute with Eck in Erfurt or Leipzig; upon which Eck immediately published a prospectus of the disputation, and made it known as widely as possible.

Luther's astonishment was extreme when he saw in this prospectus certain opinions announced as the subject of the debate, of which he was far more the champion than Carlstadt. He held this for an act of faithlessness and duplicity which he was called upon openly to resist; the agreement he had just concluded

* To Spalatin, Sept. 1518. Corp. Ref. i. 43.

† Luther to Spalatin, Jan. 25, in de Wette, i. 214. Upon these two correspondences, as may be imagined, my whole narrative is founded.

‡ μετάνοια.

§ Dedication of Lucian in Calumniam. C. R. i. 47.

‖ Bartholini Commentarius de comitiis Augustanis. p. 645.

with Miltitz seemed to him broken; he was determined to take up the gauntlet.*

It was of vast importance that Eck had annexed to the dogmatic controversy, a proposition as to the origin of the prerogatives of the papacy. At a moment when anti-papal opinions were so decidedly triumphant throughout the nation, he had the clumsy servility to stir a question, always of very difficult and dubious solution, yet from which the whole system of the Church and State depended, and, when once agitated, certain to occupy universal attention: he ventured to irritate an adversary who knew no reservations, who was accustomed to defend his opinions to the utmost, and who had already the voice of the nation on his side. In reference to a former assertion of Luther's, which had attracted little attention, Eck propounded the maxim, that the primacy of the Pope of Rome was derived from Christ himself, and from the times of St. Peter; not, as his opponent had hinted, from those of Constantine and Sylvester. The consequences of this gross imprudence were soon apparent. Luther, who now began to study the original documents of the papal law—the decretals, and had often in the course of this study felt his Christian convictions wounded, answered with a much bolder assertion, namely, that the primacy of Rome had been first established by the decretals of the later popes in the last four centuries (he meant, perhaps, since Gregory VII.), and that the primitive church knew nothing of it.†

It is not surprising that the ecclesiastical authorities in Saxony, (for example, the bishop of Merseburg) and even the theologians of the university, were not much pleased that a disputation of the kind at last agreed upon between the parties, should be held in Leipzig. Even the elector hesitated for a moment whether he should allow Luther to go. But as he had the firmest conviction that hidden truth would best be brought to light in this manner, he at length determined that it should take place, and endeavoured to obviate every objection that stood in its way. It was settled that, together with various other important points of doctrine on the mysteries of faith, the question, whether the papacy was established by God, or whether it was instituted by man, and consequently might be abolished by man (for that is in fact the point at issue in the two doctrines), was to be argued in a public disputation, at a great university, in the face of all Germany; that this question, the very one in which all political and ecclesiastical interests met as in a point, was to be thus discussed in a period of ferment and of ardent innovation.

At the very moment when the electors assembled at Frankfurt to choose an emperor, (June, 1519,) the theologians met to perform an act of no less importance.

Eck arrived first from Ingolstadt. Johann Mayr von Eck was unquestionably one of the most eminent scholars of his time—a reputation which he had spared no pains to acquire. He had visited the most celebrated professors in various universities: the Thomist Süstern at Cologne, the Scotists Sumenhard and Scriptoris at Tübingen; he had attended the law lectures of Zasius in Freiburg, those on Greek of Reuchlin, on Latin of Bebel, on cosmography of Reusch. In his twentieth year he began to write and to lecture at Ingolstadt upon Occam and Biel's canon law, on Aristotle's dialectics and physics, the most difficult doctrines of dogmatic theology, and the subtleties of nominalistic morality; he then proceeded to the study of the mystics, whose most curious works had just fallen into his hands: he set himself, as he says, to establish the connexion between their doctrines and the Orphicoplatonic philosophy, the sources of which are to be sought in Egypt and Arabia, and to discuss the whole in five parts.‡ He was one of those learned men who held that the great questions which had occupied men's minds were essentially settled; who worked exclusively with the analytical faculty and the memory; who were always on the watch to appropriate to themselves a new subject with which to excite attention, to get advancement, and to secure a life of ease and enjoyment. His strongest taste was for disputation, in which he had made a brilliant figure in all the universities we have mentioned, as well as in Heidelberg, Mainz, and Basle: at Freiburg he had early presided over a class (the Bursa zum Pfauen) where the chief business was practice in disputation; he then took long journeys,—for example, to Vienna and Bologna,—expressly to dispute there. It is most amusing to see in his letters the satisfaction with which he speaks of his Italian journey: how he was encouraged to undertake it by a papal nuncio; how, before his departure, he was visited by the young Markgrave of Brandenburg; the very honourable reception he experienced on his way, in Italy as well as in Germany, from both spiritual and temporal lords, who invited him to their tables; how, when certain young men had ventured to contradict him at one of these dinners, he had confuted them with the utmost ease, and left them filled with astonishment and admiration; and lastly, how, in spite of manifold opposition, he had at last brought the most learned of the learned in Bologna to subscribe to his maxims.§ He regarded a disputation with the eye of a practised fencer, as the arena of unfailing victory; his only wish was to find new adversaries on whom to try his weapons. He therefore seized with avidity on an opportunity of extending his fame in North Germany. He was now seen in the midst of the Leipzig professors (who welcomed him as an ally against their neighbouring rival and enemy), taking part in the procession of the Corpus Christi, dressed in his priestly garments and with an air of great devotion. In his letters we find that he did not neglect to institute a nice comparison between the Saxon

* Luther's letters to Sylvius, Feb. 3; Spalatin, Feb. 7; Lang, April 13.

† Contra novos et veteres errores defendet D. Martinus Lutherus has sequentes positiones in studio Lipsensi. It is the thirteenth proposition. Opp. lat. Jen. i. 221.

‡ Eckii Epistola de ratione, studiorum suorum, in Strobel's Miscellaneen, iii. p. 97.

§ Riederer, Nachrichten, &c., iii. 47.

beer and that of Bavaria, and also that the fair sinners of Leipzig did not escape his notice.*

On the 24th of June the Wittenbergers arrived, the professors in low open waggons on rollers or solid wooden wheels (Rollwagen), Carlstadt first, then Luther and Melanchthon, and some young licentiates and bachelors, with them was Duke Barnim of Pomerania, who was then studying in Wittenberg and held the dignity of rector, around them, on foot, some hundreds of zealous students armed with halberds, battle-axes, and spears. It was observed that the Leipzigers did not come out to meet them, as was the custom and the courtesy of those times.†

With the mediation of Duke George, the terms of the combat were next settled. Eck reluctantly acquiesced in the condition that the speeches and rejoinders should be written down by notaries, while Luther was forced to concede that the decision was to be left to certain universities, he himself proposed Paris and Erfurt. The duke insisted, with peculiar earnestness, on these things, he treated the affair like a trial at law, and wanted to send the documents, as it were to a court of appeal for its decision. Meanwhile he ordered a spacious hall in the castle to be got ready for the literary duel, two pulpits were placed opposite to each other, covered with tapestry, on which were the figures of the warrior saints, St George and St. Martin, there was ample provision of tables for the notaries, and of benches for the audience. At length, on the 27th of June, the action was commenced with a mass and invocation of the Holy Ghost.

Carlstadt had insisted on his right of opening the debate, but he acquired little glory from it. He brought books, out of which he read passages, then hunted for others, then read again, the objections which his opponent advanced one day, he answered the next.‡ How different a *disputator* was Johann Eck! His knowledge was all at his command, ready for use at the moment, he required so little time for preparation, that immediately after his return from a ride he mounted the chair. He was tall, with large muscular limbs, and loud penetrating voice, and walked backwards and forwards while speaking, he had an exception ready to take against every argument; his memory and address dazzled his hearers. In the matter itself—the explanation of the doctrine of grace and free-will—no progress was, of course, made. Sometimes the combatants approximated so nearly in opinion, that each boasted he had brought over the other to his side, but they soon diverged again. With the exception of a distinction made by Eck, nothing new was produced,§ the most important points were scarcely touched upon, and the whole affair was sometimes so tedious that the hall was emptied.

The interest was therefore the more intense, when at length, on Monday the 4th of July, at seven in the morning, Luther arose, the antagonist whom Eck most ardently desired to meet, and whose rising fame he hoped to crush by a brilliant victory. Luther was of the middle size, at that time so thin as to be mere skin and bone, he possessed neither the thundering organ, nor the ready memory stored with various knowledge, nor the skill and dexterity acquired in the gladiatorial exercises of the schools, that distinguished his opponent. But he, too, stood in the prime of manhood, and in the fulness of his strength. he was in his thirty-sixth year, his voice was melodious and clear, he was perfectly versed in the Bible, and its aptest sentences presented themselves unbidden to his mind, above all, he inspired an irresistible conviction that he sought the truth. He was always cheerful at home, and a joyous, jocose companion at table, he even, on this grave occasion, ascended the platform with a nosegay in his hand, but, when there, he displayed the intrepid and self-forgetting earnestness arising from the depths of a conviction till now unfathomed, even by himself. He drew forth new thoughts, and placed them in the fire of the battle, with a determination that knew no fear and no personal regards. His features bore the traces of the storms that had passed over his soul, and of the courage with which he was prepared to encounter those that yet awaited him, his whole aspect breathed profound thought, joyousness of temper, and confidence in the future. The battle immediately commenced on the question of the authority of the papacy, which, at once intelligible and important, riveted universal attention. Two sons of German peasants (for Eck, too, was the son of a peasant—Michael Mayr, who was for many years Ammann‖ of Eck, as Luther's father was Rathsherr‖ of Mansfeld) represented the two great tendencies of opinion which divided the world then, and divide it now; the future condition of the Church and the State mainly hung on the issue of their conflict—on the success of the one in attack, and of the other in defence.

It was immediately obvious that Luther could not maintain his assertion that the pope's primacy dated only from the last four centuries. he soon found himself forced from this position by ancient documents, and the rather, that no criticism had as yet shaken the authenticity of the false decretals. But his attack on the doctrine that the primacy of the pope (whom he still persisted in regarding as the ecumenical bishop) was founded on Scripture and by divine right, was far more formidable. Christ's words, "Thou art Peter, feed my sheep," which have always been cited in this controversy, were brought forward.¶ Luther laboured to support the already well-known explanation of them,

* Eck to Haven and Burkard July 1, in Walch xv p 1456. In this respect he had the very worst reputation.

† Pfeiter's Beschreibung, ibid p 1175.

‡ Rubeus, in Walch, xv 1491.

§ Rogatus largireturne totum opus bonum esse a deo respondit totum quidem, non autem totaliter.—*Melanchthon*.

‖ Titles of local magistrates.—Transl.

¶ In the exposition by Nicolaus von Lire (Lyranus) also, of which Luther made the most use, there occurs this explanation, differing from that of the curia, of the passage in Matthew, chap xvi. "Quia tu es Petrus, i e confessor veræ petræ qui est Christus factus,—et super hanc petram, quam confessus es, i e super Christum, ædificabo ecclesiam meam."

at variance with that of the curia, by other passages which record similar commissions given to the apostles. Eck quoted passages from the Fathers in support of his opinions, to which Luther opposed others from the same source. As soon as they got into these more recondite regions, Luther's superiority became incontestable. One of his main arguments was that the Greeks had never acknowledged the pope, and yet had not been pronounced heretics; the Greek church had stood, was standing, and would stand, without the pope; it belonged to Christ as much as the Roman. Eck did not hesitate at once to declare that the Christian and the Roman church were one; that the churches of Greece and Asia had fallen away, not only from the pope, but from the Christian faith — they were unquestionably heretics: in the whole circuit of the Turkish empire, for instance, there was not one soul that could be saved, with the exception of the few who adhered to the pope of Rome. "How?" said Luther, "would you pronounce damnation on the whole Greek church, which has produced the most eminent fathers, and so many thousand saints, of whom not one had even heard of a Roman primate? Would Gregory of Nazianzen, would the great Basil, not be saved? or would the pope and his satellites drive them out of heaven?" These expressions prove how greatly the omnipotence and exclusive validity of the forms of the Latin church, and the identity with Christianity which she claimed, were shaken by the fact that, beyond her pale, the ancient Greek church, which she had herself acknowledged, stood in all the venerable authority of her great teachers. It was now Eck's turn to be hard pressed: he repeated that there had been many heretics in the Greek church, and that he alluded to them, not to the Fathers—a miserable evasion, which did not in the least touch the assertion of his adversary. Eck felt this, and hastened back to the domain of the Latin church. He particularly insisted that Luther's opinion — that the primacy of Rome was of human institution, and not of divine right—was an error of the poor brethren of Lyons, of Wickliffe and Huss; but had been condemned by the popes, and especially by the general councils wherein dwelt the spirit of God, and recently at that of Constance. This new fact was as indisputable as the former. Eck was not satisfied with Luther's declaration that he had nothing to do with the Bohemians, nay, that he condemned their schism; and that he would not be answered out of the Collectanea of inquisitors, but out of the Scriptures. The question had now arrived at its most critical and important moment. Did Luther acknowledge the direct influence of the Divine Spirit over the Latin church, and the binding force of the decrees of her councils, or did he not? Did he inwardly adhere to her, or did he not? We must recollect that we are here not far from the frontier of Bohemia; in a land which, in consequence of the anathema pronounced in Constance, had experienced all the horrors of a long and desolating war, and had placed its glory in the resistance it had offered to the Hussites: at a university founded in opposition to the spirit and doctrine of John Huss: in the face of princes, lords and commoners, whose fathers had fallen in this struggle; it was said that delegates from the Bohemians, who had anticipated the turn which this conflict must take, were also present: Luther saw the danger of his position. Should he really reject the prevailing notion of the exclusive power of the Roman church to secure salvation? oppose a council by which John Huss had been condemned to the flames, and perhaps draw down a like fate upon himself? Or should he deny that higher and more comprehensive idea of a Christian church which he had conceived, and in which his whole soul lived and moved? Luther did not waver for a moment. He had the boldness to affirm, that among the articles on which the council of Constance grounded its condemnation of John Huss, some were fundamentally Christian and evangelical. The assertion was received with universal astonishment. Duke George, who was present, put his hands to his sides, and, shaking his head, uttered aloud his wonted curse, "A plague upon it!"* Eck now gathered fresh courage. It was hardly possible, he said, that Luther could censure a council, since his Grace the Elector had expressly forbidden any attack upon councils. Luther reminded him that the council of Constance had not condemned all the articles of Huss as heretical, and specified some which were likewise to be found in St. Augustine. Eck replied that all were rejected; the sense in which these particular articles were understood was to be deemed heretical; for a council could not err. Luther answered that no council could create a new article of faith; how then could it be maintained that no council whatever was subject to error? "Reverend father," replied Eck, "if you believe that a council regularly convoked can err, you are to me as a heathen and a publican."

Such were the results of this disputation.† It was continued for a time, and opinions more or less conflicting on purgatory, indulgences, and penance were uttered. Eck renewed the interrupted contest with Carlstadt; the reports were sent, after the solemn conclusion, to both universities; but all these measures could lead to nothing further. The main result of the meeting was, that Luther no longer acknowledged the authority of the Roman church in matters of faith. At first, he had only attacked the instructions given to the preachers of indulgences, and the rules of the later schoolmen, but had expressly retained the decretals of the popes: then he had rejected these, but with appeal to the decision of a council; he now emancipated himself from this last remaining human authority also; he recognised none but that of the Scriptures.

* "This I myself heard and saw."—*Fröschel's Report in Walch*, xv. 1400.

† "Disputatio Excellentissimorum Theologorum Johannis Eccii et D. Martini Lutheri Augustiniani quæ Lipsiæ cœpta fuit iv die Julii aō 1519. Opera Lutheri, Jen. i. 231.

PROGRESS OF THE THEOLOGICAL OPPOSITION

AT this period Luther conceived an idea of the Church different from any he had before entertained—deeper and more comprehensive He recognised in the Oriental and Greek Christians true members of the universal church he no longer admitted the necessity of a visible head; he acknowledged none but the Invisible, the ever-living Founder, whom he regarded as standing in a mystical relation to his faithful disciples of every nation and clime This was not only a dogmatical innovation, but at the same time the recognition of an incontestable fact—the validity of Christianity without the pale of the Latin church In asserting this opinion, Luther now took up a position which enabled him to appropriate all the various elements of opposition to the papacy that were afloat in the world He made himself better acquainted with the doctrines of the Greek church, and finding, for example, that it did not admit the doctrine of purgatory, of which he also found no mention in Scripture, he ceased to maintain it, as he had done even in Leipzig * A far stronger impression was made on him by the works of John Huss, which now reached him from Bohemia; he was perfectly astonished at finding therein the doctrines expounded by St Augustine, and derived from St Paul, which he had adopted after such violent mental struggles "I taught Huss's opinions," says he, in February, 1520, "without knowing them, and so did Staupitz we are all Hussites, without knowing it Paul and Augustine are Hussites I do not know what to think for amazement" He denounces woe to the earth, and predicts the fearful judgments of God, because evangelical truth had been known for a century, and had been condemned and burnt.† It is evident that he not only receded in opinion from the church of Rome, but at the same time conceived a religious disgust, nay hatred, of her In the same month, the treatise of Laurentius Valla, on the donation of Constantine, first fell into his hands. It was a discovery to him that this donation was a fiction his German honesty was shocked and exasperated at finding that, as he says, "such shameless lies had been incorporated into the decretals, and almost made articles of faith" "What darkness!" exclaims he, "what wickedness!" All spirits and powers that had ever waged war against the papacy now gathered around him, those which had never submitted from the beginning; those which had emancipated themselves and never been reclaimed, and all the tendencies of the opposition that existed in the bosom of Latin Christendom, whether theological or literary He had no sooner begun to study the papal laws, than he thought he perceived that they were in contradiction to the Scriptures he was now persuaded that the Scriptures and the papacy stood irreconcilably opposed It is quite in accordance with Luther's character that, while seeking a solution of the problem, how this could be permitted by Divine providence, while struggling to recover the broken unity of his religious convictions, he fell, after violent contention and torture of mind, on the hypothesis that the pope was the antichrist whom the world was taught to expect ‡ This mythical notion tended, no doubt, to obscure the historical view which might perhaps have been obtained of the subject, but it had, in fact, no other meaning than that the doctrine of the church was corrupted, and must be restored to its original purity

Melanchthon, meanwhile, who had taken the part of an ally and adviser in the Leipzig disputation, was occupied with a parallel, but peculiar train of speculation, and now devoted himself to theological studies with the quiet ardour natural to him, with the enthusiasm which a successful and steady progress in a new path always excites

The principles on which protestant theology rest are to be traced, at least as much to him as to Luther One of the first that he enounced, referred immediately to the controversy in Leipzig

Maxims of the Fathers of the church were appealed to by each side, and with equal justice To extricate the matter from this contradiction, Melanchthon laid it down in a little treatise, published August, 1519, that the Scripture was not to be expounded according to the Fathers, but that these were to be understood to the sense of Scripture § He maintained that the expositions of the great pillars of the Latin church, Ambrose, Jerome and even Augustine, were often erroneous This principle—that a Christian (or, as he expresses it, a Catholic) is not bound to receive any thing but what is contained in Scripture—he treated more at large in September, 1519 What he had said of the Fathers, he now repeated of councils—that their authority was of no account when compared to that of Scripture Having reached this point, doubt on doubt inevitably presented itself to his mind, as to the entire system of authoritative dogmas If Luther was resolute in action, Melanchthon was no less so in speculation Even in September, 1519, he stated the polemical maxims in which he attached the two most important funda-

* Letter to Spalatin, Nov 7

† To Spalatin, in De Wette, nr 208

‡ To Spalatin, Feb 23, (not 24) 1520 nr 201 "Ego sic angor ut prope non dubitem papam esse proprie antichristum" This notion sprang from the old chiliastic notions still maintained in the West (see the passage of Commodian "venturi sunt sub antichristo qui vincunt," in Giesler, Kirchengeschichte i 281) and was especially cherished in Germany One of the oldest German works in print, the first mentioned by Panzer in the Annalender älteren deutschen Literatur, is, Das Buch vom Entkrist (The Book of Antichrist), or also, "Buchlin von des Endte Christs Leben und Regierung durch verhengniss Gottes, wie er die Welt tuth verkeren mit seiner falschen Lere und Rat des Teufels, auch wie darnach die zween Propheten Enoch und Helyas die Christenheit wieder bekeren mit predigen den Christen Glauben" "Little Book concerning Antichrist's Life and Rule through God's Providence, how he doth pervert the World with his false Doctrine and Counsel of the Devil, also how, thereafter, the two Prophets, Enoch and Elias, again convert Christendom with preaching of Christ's faith" In 1516, this book was reprinted at Erfurt We see how it came about that Luther was occasionally called Elias by his followers

§ Defensio contra J Eckium C R i p 1813 "Patres judice Scriptura recipiantur"

mental doctrines of the whole system, that of transubstantiation, and that of the sacerdotal character, whereon the mystery of the visible church, as well as the sacramental ritual which governs the whole course of human life, rest.* The boldness of the attack, and the ingenuity with which it was carried on, filled every one with surprise. "He has now appeared to all," says Luther, "as wonderful as he really is. He is the most powerful enemy of Satan and of the schoolmen, he knows their folly and the rock of Christ, he has the power and the will to do the deed. *Amen*." Melanchthon now applied himself with fresh fervour to the study of the New Testament. He was enchanted by its simplicity, and found in it true and pure philosophy: he refers the studious to it as the only refreshment to the soul, and the afflicted, as pouring peace and joy into the heart. In his course of study, too, he thought he perceived that much was contained in the doctrines of former theologians, which not only could not be deduced from Scripture, but was at variance with it, and could never be brought into accordance with its spirit. In a discourse on the doctrines of Paul, pronounced on the 18th of January, 1520, he first declared this without reserve. In the following month he remarked that his objections to transubstantiation and the sacerdotal character, were applicable to many other doctrines, he finds traces of Jewish ceremonies in the seven sacraments, and esteems the doctrine of the pope's infallibility an arrogant pretension, repugnant to Holy Scripture and to common sense:—most pernicious opinions, he says, which we ought to combat with all our might, more than one Hercules is needed for the work.†

Thus we perceive that Melanchthon arrives at the same point which Luther had already reached, though by a calmer and more philosophical path. It is remarkable how each expresses himself concerning the Scripture, in which both live. "It fills the soul," says Melanchthon, "it is heavenly ambrosia."‡ "The word of God," exclaims Luther, "is a sword, and war, and destruction: it meets the children of Ephraim like a lioness in the forest." The one views it in reference to the inward thoughts of man, with which it has so strong an affinity, the other, in its relation to the corruptions of the world, against which it wars, but they come to the same conclusion. They quitted each other no more. "That little Greek (*Griechlein*)," says Luther, "outdoes me even in theology." "He will make up to you," exclaims he, "for many Martins." All his solicitude is that any of those misfortunes should befall him which are incident to great minds. On the other hand, Melanchthon was deeply impressed and penetrated with the thorough comprehension of St Paul, peculiar to Luther, he prefers the latter to the fathers of the church, he finds him more admirable every time he sees him, even in ordinary intercourse, he will not admit the justice of the censures which his joyous and jocose humour brought upon him. It was truly a divine dispensation that these two men lived together and united at this crisis. They regarded each other as two of God's creatures endowed with different gifts, each worthy of the other, joined in one object, and holding the same convictions, a perfect picture of true friendship. Melanchthon is careful not to trouble Luther's mind;§ Luther confesses that he abandons an opinion when Melanchthon does not approve it.

So immeasurable was the influence which the literary spirit had obtained over the new and growing theology; an influence which we shall now see it exercising in another manner.

HUTTEN.

The minds which took part in the poetical and philological movement of Germany of which we have treated, may be arranged under two distinct classes. Those of the one class, eager to acquire and apt to give instruction, sought by tranquil and laborious study to master the erudition they were afterwards to diffuse. The whole character of their labours, which from the first were directed to the Holy Scriptures, was represented by Melanchthon, and had formed in his person the most intimate union with the deeper theological tendencies which were exhibited in that of Luther, and had gained an ascendency at the university of Wittenberg. We have seen what were the results of this union. The peaceful study of letters acquired solidity, depth, and intensity of purpose, theology, scientific form and an erudite basis. But literature exhibited another phase: by the side of the tranquil students were to be seen the combative poets,—well content with the ground they had gained, self-satisfied and arrogant, incensed at the opposition they had experienced, they filled the world with the noise of their war. At the beginning of the Lutheran controversy, which they regarded as a mere dispute between two monastic orders, they had remained neutral. But now that this revealed a character of such vastness, and opened a vista so remote—now that it appealed to all their sympathies, they too took part in it. Luther appeared to them in the light of a successor of Reuchlin, John Eck as another Ortwin Gratius, a hired adherent of the Dominicans, and in that character they attacked him. In March 1520, a satire appeared with the title of "The Planed-off Angle," (*Der abgehobelte Eck*), which for fantastic invention, striking and crushing truth, and Aristophanic wit, far exceeded the "Literæ Obscurorum Virorum," which it somewhat resembled. And

* Unluckily these propositions, which play a chief part in the construction of the protestant system of belief, are no longer to be met with. From a letter of Melanchthon to John Hess, Feb 1520 (C. R. i. 138.) we get a knowledge of three of them, which are moreover the most important. According to Luther's letter to Staupitz in de Wette, i. nr. 162 they must date from the month of September. The propositions which appear in the C. R. p. 126. are, as Forstemann there remarks, of later origin, seemingly of the date of July, 1520.

† Dedication to Bronner, C. R. p. 138. Letter to Hess.

‡ To Schwebel, Dec. 1519, 128.

§ To John Lange, Aug. 1520. "Spiritum Martini nolim temere in hac causa, ad quam destinatus ὑπὸ προνοίας videtur, interpellare." (C. R. i. 221.)

at this moment a leader of the band entered the lists, not nameless like the others, but with his visor up. It was Ulrich von Hutten, the temper of whose weapons and his skill in wielding them had long been well known.

The whole course of Hutten's life had, like that of Erasmus, been determined by his being very early condemned to the cloister, but to him this constraint was far more intolerable: he was the first-born of one of the most distinguished equestrian families of the Buchen, which still laid claim to the freedom of the empire. On his friends earnestly pressing him to take the vows, he ran away, and sought his fortune, as Erasmus had done, in the newly opened career of literature.* He encountered every variety of suffering: plague and shipwreck, the banishment of a teacher whom he followed; robbery, and disease, the scorn with which indigence and a mean garb are commonly regarded, especially in a strange land, the utter neglect of his family, who acted as if he did not belong to them, nay, his father even treated him with a sort of irony. But his courage remained buoyant, his mind free and unshackled, he bid defiance to all his enemies, and a state of literary warfare became a second nature to him. Sometimes it was his own personal quarrels which he fought out on the field of literature, for example, the ill-treatment he sustained from his hosts at Greifswald, who robbed him, he called upon all his companions of the school of poets to take part against this act of injustice, which was, as it were, committed against them all.† Another time he replied to the reproach which even in that age he had to encounter, that a man must *be* something, *i. e.* must fill some office, or hold some title, or some deed of violence, like the unjustifiable conduct of the Duke of Wurtemberg to one of his cousins, moved him to vehement accusation. But his warlike muse was still more excited by the affairs of his country.

The study of Roman literature, in which the Germans have taken so eminent a part, has not unfrequently had the effect of awakening the patriotism of their descendants. The ill-success of the emperor in the Venetian war did not deter Hutten from eulogizing him, or from treating the Venetians, in their contest with him, as upstart fishermen, he contrasts the treachery of the pope and the insolence of the French, with the achievements of the Landsknechts and the fame of Jacob von Ems. He writes long poems to prove that the Germans have not degenerated, that they are still the ancient race. Just as he returned from Italy, the contest between the Reuchlinists and the Dominicans had broken out, and he rushed to the side of his natural ally, armed with all the weapons of indignation and of ridicule; he celebrated the triumph of his master in his best hexameters, which were embellished with an ingenious wood-cut. Hutten is not a great scholar, nor is he a very profound thinker; his excellence lies more in the exhaustlessness of his vein, which gushes forth with equal impetuosity, equal freshness, in the most various forms—in Latin and in German, in prose and in verse, in eloquent invective and in brilliant satirical dialogue. Nor is he without the spirit of acute observation, here and there (for example in the Nemo) he soars to the bright and clear regions of genuine poetry. His hostilities have not that cold malignant character which disgusts the reader, they are always connected with a cordial devotion to the side he advocates: he leaves on the mind an impression of perfect veracity, of uncompromising frankness and honesty, above all, he has always great and single purposes which command universal sympathy, he has earnestness of mind, and a passion (to use his own words) 'for godlike truth, for common liberty.' The victory of the Reuchlinists had turned to his advantage also. He had found an asylum at the court of the Elector Albert of Mainz, and formed an intimacy with the formidable Sickingen, he was cured of his illness, and now thought of marrying and entering upon his paternal inheritance, he thus hoped to enjoy the tranquillity of domestic life, while the brilliancy of the reputation he had already acquired secured to him an eminent station. Under these circumstances, the spirit which Luther had awakened in the nation breathed upon him; a prospect opened, compared to which all previous results had been mere child's-play, it took possession of his whole convictions, of every impulse and energy of his mind. For a moment Hutten deliberated. The enemy to be attacked was the mightiest in existence, who had never been subdued, and who wielded power with a thousand hands, whoever engaged in a conflict with him must be aware that he would never more find peace so long as he lived. Hutten did not disguise this from himself, it was discussed in the family, who dreaded the losses and evils to which it would expose them. "My pious mother wept," said he. But he tore himself away, renounced his paternal inheritance, and once more took up arms.‡

In the beginning of the year 1520 he wrote some dialogues, for which he could never hope to obtain pardon. In the one, called the Spectators (*Anschauenden*), the jests on the papal legate are no longer, as before, confined to certain externals, all his spiritual faculties, his anathema and excommunication which he hurls against the sun, are treated with the bitterest scorn and derision. In another—Vadiscus, or the Roman Trinity—the abuses and pretensions of the Curia are described in striking triplets. In confirmation of the Wittenberg opinion that the papacy was inconsistent with the Scriptures, Hutten drew a picture of the actual state of the court of Rome, in which he represented it as an abyss of moral and religious corruption, which the duty of Germans to God and their country equally called upon them to shun.§ His

* Mohnike, Ulrich Huttens Jugendleben, p 43. Hutten was born in 1488, in 1499 he entered the convent, and in 1504 deserted it.

† Querelarum, lib. ii eleg. x "nostros, communia vulnera casus."

‡ Apology for Ulrich von Hutten in Meiner's Lebensbeschreibungen beruhmter Manner, &c iii 749.

§ Vadiscus, Dialogus qui et Trias Romana inscribitur. Inspicientes Dialogus Hutteni. Opera ed Munch iii 427, 511.

ideas were profoundly national. An old apology for Henry IV having accidentally fallen into his hands, he published it in March, 1520, with a view of reviving the recollections of the great struggle with Gregory VII, and the extinct sympathy of the nation with the empire, and of the empire with the nation * He sent it to the young Archduke Ferdinand, who had just arrived in the Netherlands from Spain, with a dedication, in which he calls upon him to lend his aid to the restoration of the ancient independence of Germany, which had withstood the warlike and victorious Romans of old, and was now become tributary to the effeminate Romans of modern times † It appeared as if the nation might reasonably look with hope to the two brothers of the house of Austria, whose elevation to the throne had been so earnestly opposed by the papal court Most of their friends were indeed at this moment enemies of the papacy We have already alluded to the disposition of the court of Mainz In Switzerland, all who had approved Luther's first book were adherents of Cardinal von Sitten, who had so successfully conducted the affairs of the house of Austria at the diet, partly by their assistance. Sickingen, who had contributed so much to the decision taken by Wurtemberg, was likewise a partisan of Reuchlin, and found means to compel the Cologne Dominicans, although the process was still pending in Rome, to obey the sentence of the Bishop of Spires, and to pay the costs to which they had there been condemned No one had contributed more to the election of Charles V than Frederic of Saxony by the protection which he had afforded to Luther and his university, he had rendered possible the national movement in that prince's favour He now absolutely refused to allow Luther to be tried at Rome On the day of the emperor's election the Archbishop of Treves had actually undertaken the office of umpire, and Elector Frederic declared that no steps should be taken against Luther till that prelate had pronounced his decision, by which he would abide ‡ There was a secret connection between all these incidents, these various manifestations of opinion—people were resolved to get rid of the interference of Rome Hutten preached in all parts, that Germany must abandon Rome and return to her own bishops and primates "To your tents, O Israel!" exclaimed he, and we perceive that sovereigns and cities responded to his appeal § He deemed himself destined to accomplish this change, and hastened to the court of the archduke, in order, if possible, to gain him over by personal intercourse, and to inspire him with his own ardour He felt the most confident assurance of success In an essay written on the road, he predicted that the tyranny of Rome would not long endure, already the axe was laid to the root of the tree He exhorted the Germans only to have confidence in their brave leaders, and not to faint in the midst of the fight; for they must go on—on, in this propitious state of things, with this good cause, with these noble energies "Liberty for ever—Jacta est alea," was his motto The die is cast, I have ventured all upon the throw ||

Such was the turn which Luther's cause now took—not without great faults on the side of the defenders of the See of Rome The attack, which, though only levelled at one side of the great system, would unquestionably have been very troublesome to the head of the Church, was now directed against his entire position and functions,—against that idea of his authority and prerogative which he had so successfully laboured to establish It was no longer confined to the domain of theology; for the first time, the literary and political elements of opposition existing in the nation came into contact and mutual intelligence, if not into close union, with the theological; thus allied, they turned their united strength against the prerogatives of the Pope of Rome.

This led to a similar combination on the other side, and the See of Rome, which had hitherto always maintained reserve, was now induced to pronounce a definitive sentence.

BULL OF LEO X

We must bear in mind that the advocates of the old opinions were not satisfied with opposing Luther with all the authority they possessed (for example, the Dominican universities of Louvain and Cologne pronounced a solemn condemnation of his works), but sought to prove themselves the strictest and most faithful allies of the Roman See The attacks of the Germans furnished them with an opportunity to exalt the omnipotency of the papacy more extravagantly than ever Silvestro Mazzolini, the Master of the Sacred Palace, of whom we have spoken, published a pamphlet,¶ in which, indignant that Luther had dared to appeal from his judgment to the pope, and in the last resort to a council, he tries to demonstrate that there can be no judge superior to the pope; that the Roman pontiff is the infallible arbiter of all controversies and of all doubts; and further sets forth that the papal sovereignty is the only true monarchy, the fifth monarchy mentioned by Daniel, that the pope is the prince of all spiritual, and the father of all temporal princes, the head of the whole world, nay, that he is, virtually, the whole world ** In his former work, he had only said

* Waltramus de Unitate Ecclesiæ conservanda, etc., in Schardius, Sylloge, Part I

† Præfatio ad Ferdinandum Opp iii 531

‡ Transactions, Walch, xv 916, 919 The chief reason why this did not come to pass was, that Frederic wanted to bring Luther with him to the Imperial Diet, which was to be held in Nov 1519, but which the Imperial Commissioners prevented

§ Agrippa a Nettesheim Johanni Rogerio Brennonio ex Colonia, 16 Junii, 1520 (Epp. Agrippæ, lib ii p 99) "Relinquat Romanos Germania et revertatur ad primates et episcopos suos"

|| Ad libros in Germania omnes Opp iii 563.

¶ De Juridica et Irrefragabili Veritate Romanæ Ecclesiæ Romanique Pontificis Roccaberti, Bibl Max tom xix p 264

** C iv "Etsi ex jam dictis constat Romanum præsulem esse caput orbis universi, quippe qui primus hierarcha et princeps sit omnium spiritualium ac pater omnium temporalium principum, tamen quia adversarius negat eum esse ecclesiam catholicam virtualiter aut etiam esse ecclesiæ caput, eapropter ostendendum est quod sit caput orbis et consequenter orbis totus in virtute"

that the whole collective church was in the pope, now he affected to prove that the pope was the world. In another place, too, he did not hesitate to declare that all the power of temporal sovereigns was a sub-delegation of the papal.* The pope, he says, is more superior to the emperor than gold to lead: a pope can appoint or depose an emperor, appoint or depose electors, make or abolish positive laws: the emperor, he exclaims, together with all laws and all Christian peoples, could effect nothing contrary to his will.† The proofs that he adduces in support of his opinion are, indeed, strange enough, but it was not necessary to substantiate them; it was enough that they were adduced by a man of so eminent a station, and that they emanated from the papal palace. German obsequiousness hastened to furnish Roman arrogance with a somewhat better groundwork for its pretensions. In February, 1520, Eck also completed a treatise on the primacy, in which he promises triumphantly and clearly to confute Luther's assertion, "that it is not of divine right," and also to set forth various other rare and notable things, collected with great labour, partly from manuscripts which he had most diligently collated. "Observe, reader," says he, "and thou shalt see that I keep my word."‡ Nor is his work by any means devoid of learning and talent; it is an armoury of very various weapons, but it affords the most distinct evidence of the importance of this controversy to science, independent of all theological considerations, and of the profound darkness in which all true and critical history still lay buried. Eck assumes, without the slightest hesitation, that Peter resided twenty-five years at Rome, and was a perfect prototype of all succeeding popes, whereas, historical criticism has shown that it is a matter of doubt whether the apostle ever was at Rome at all: he finds cardinals, and even under that title, as early as the year 770, and assigns the rank and functions of cardinal to St. Jerome. In the second book, he adduces the testimony of the Fathers of the Church in support of the divine right of the pope, and places at their head Dionysius Areopagita, whose works are, unfortunately, spurious.—Among his favourite documents are the decretals of the elder popes, from which much certainly is derived that we should not otherwise be inclined to believe; the only misfortune is, that they are altogether forgeries. He reproaches Luther with understanding nothing whatever of the old councils; the sixth canon of the council of Nice, from which Luther deduced the equality of the ancient patriarchate, he interprets in a totally different manner, but here again he had the ill luck to rest his arguments on the spurious canon, which belongs not to the Nicene, but the Sardicene, synod. And so on.

It is important to have a distinct idea of the actual state of things. With these claims of an absolute power, including all other earthly powers, were connected, not only dogmatic theology as elaborated in the schools, but this gigantic fiction, this falsification of history, resting on innumerable forged documents, which, if not overthrown, as it subsequently was (and we must add chiefly by truly learned men of the Catholic church itself), would have made all authentic and well-founded history impossible: the human mind would never have arrived at the true knowledge of ancient times, or at the consciousness of the stages itself had passed through. The newly-awakened spirit of the German nation seized at once upon this entire system, and laboured energetically to open new paths in every direction of human thought and action—politics, religion, science and letters. Equal zeal was displayed on the other side in maintaining the old system entire. As soon as Eck had finished his book, he hastened to Rome to present it himself to the pope, and to invoke the severest exercise of the ecclesiastical authority against his opponents.

It was asserted at the time that Eck was in fact sent to Rome by the house of Fugger, which was alarmed at the prospect of losing the profit arising from the money exchanges between Rome and Germany. It is at least certain that the doctor had some intimate connection with those eminent merchants. It was in their behalf that he defended usury in his disputation at Bologna.§

But his chief aid was derived from the judgment pronounced against the new opinions by Cologne and Louvain. Cardinals Campeggi and Vio, who were well acquainted with Germany, gave him all the support in their power. His book was fully calculated to place the imminence of the danger before their eyes. A commission of seven or eight zealous theologians was appointed, of which Giovan Pietro Caraffa, Alcander, and probably also Silvestro Mazzolini and Eck himself, were members; their judgment could not be for one moment doubtful; already, in the beginning of May, the draft of the bull by which Luther was condemned was prepared.

In the trial of Reuchlin, it was matter of doubt how far the See of Rome made common cause with the Dominicans, now, however, that order had completely succeeded in restoring the ancient alliance. In the present case the trial was hardly begun, when we hear that the monks at Cologne triumphed in a sentence

* De Papa et ejus Potestate, ibid. p. 369. "Tertia potestas (the first is that of the Pope, the second that of the prelates) est in ministerium data, ut ea quæ est imperatoris et etiam principum terrenorum, quæ respectu Papæ est subdelegata subordinata."

† "Papa est imperatore major dignitate, plus quam aurum plumbo (371).—Potest eligere imperatorem per se ipsum immediate—ex quo sequitur quod etiam possit eligere electores imperatoris et mutare ex causa: ejus etiam est electum confirmare,—et dignum depositione deponere (372).—Nec imperator cum omnibus legibus et omnibus Christianis possent contra ejus voluntatem quicquam statuere."

‡ De Primatu Petri. In Eckii Opp. contra Lutherum, tom. i. f. iii.

§ Literæ cujusdam e Roma. From the Pirkheimer papers in Riederer, Nachrichten zur Kirchen Gelehrten und Büchergeschichte, i. p. 178. As a letter, this document certainly inspires me with some suspicion; at all events however it is of the same date, and expresses the opinion of a well informed contemporary. Welser also says, (Augspurgische Chroniken, ander theil, p. 275) that that disputation had been held "at the cost of Jacob Fugger and his partners."

which had been pronounced in their favour, and caused it to be affixed on their church-doors.*

The Elector of Mainz was called to account for the protection he had afforded to Ulrich von Hutten, and exhorted to show severity against the author of so many libels. The main object, however, was the condemnation of Luther. The jurists of the Curia were of opinion that a citation and fresh hearing of the accused were necessary, adding that "God had summoned even Cain once and again before him;" but the theologians would accede to no further postponement. They at length came to a compromise, and determined that the propositions extracted from Luther's writings were to be judged without delay, but that an interval of sixty days was to be granted to him for recantation. The draft of the bull, framed by Cardinal Accolti, underwent many alterations. A consistory was held four times, to consider of each separate proposition; Cardinal Vio, though suffering under a severe attack of illness, would on no account stay away; he was carried to the meeting every time. A smaller conference met in the presence of the pope himself, at his country-house at Malliano, and in this Eck took part. At length, on the 16th of June, the bull was completed. Forty-one propositions from Luther's writings were declared false, dangerous, scandalous, or absolutely heretical; and the damnatory decrees of the universities of Louvain and Cologne as learned, true, and even holy. Christ was invoked to protect his vineyard, the management of which he had, at his ascension, entrusted to St. Peter. St. Peter was besought to take the cause of the Church of Rome, the mistress of the faith, under his care. Luther, if he did not recant within the sixty days allowed him, was to be considered a stubborn heretic, and to be hewn off, as a sere and withered branch, from Christendom. All Christian authorities were exhorted to seize his person and to deliver him into the hands of the pope.†

It appears that no doubt of the complete success of this measure was entertained in Rome. Two vigorous champions who had a personal interest in the matter, Aleander and John Eck himself, were entrusted with its execution. In Germany there was no need of a royal *placet;* the commissioners had their hands completely free.

How proud and elated was Eck on reappearing in Germany with the new title of papal prothonotary and nuncio! He instantly hastened to the scene of the conflict, and in the month of September caused the bull to be fixed up in public places in Meissen, Merseburg and Brandenburg. Meanwhile Aleander descended the Rhine for the same purpose.

It is said, and with perfect truth, that they did not every where meet with the best reception; but the arms they wielded were still extremely terrible. Eck had received the unheard of permission to denounce any of the adherents of Luther at his pleasure, when he published the bull; a permission which, it will readily be believed, he did not allow to pass unused. Amongst others, he had named Adelmann of Adelmannsfeld, his brother canon at Eichstädt, with whom he had once nearly gone to blows at dinner concerning the questions of the day. In pursuance of the bull, the bishop of Augsburg now set on foot proceedings against Adelmann, who was compelled to purge himself of the Lutheran heresy by oath and vow. Eck had not scrupled also to denounce two eminent and respected members of the council or senate of Nürnberg—Spengler and Pirkheimer: the intercessions of the city, of the Bishop of Bamberg, even of the Dukes of Bavaria, were of no avail; they were forced to bow before Eck, who made them feel the whole weight of the authority of one commissioned by the See of Rome.‡ In October 1520, Luther's books were seized in all the bookseller's shops of Ingolstadt, and sealed.§ Moderate as was the Elector of Mainz, he was obliged to exclude from his court Ulrich von Hutten, who had been ill received in the Netherlands, and to throw the printer of his writings into prison. Luther's works were first burnt in Mainz. Aleander's exultation at this was raised to a pitch of insane insolence. He let fall expressions like those of Mazzolini—that the pope could depose king and emperor; that he could say to the emperor, "Thou art a tanner" (*Du bist ein Gerber*); he would soon, he said, settle the business of a few miserable grammarians; and even that Duke Frederic would be come at by some means or other.‖

But though this storm raged far and wide, it passed harmless over the spot which it was destined to destroy. Wittenberg was unscathed; Eck had indeed instructions, if Luther did not submit, to execute on him the menaces of the bull, with the aid of the surrounding princes and bishops.¶ He had been authorized to punish as a heretic the literary adversary whom he was unable to overcome; a commission against which the natural instinct of morality so strongly revolted, that it more than

* Letter from Hedios to Zwinglius in Meiners, *passim*, p. 236. This matter deserved closer examination. That it had been really agitated again in Rome at that very time, is clear from the letters of the Elector Palatine and the Dominicans, assembled at Frankfort, (Friedlander, Beitrage zur Reformations-geschichte, pp. 113, 116), May 10 and 20, 1520. But might not the letter of the Dominicans have been merely a consequence of the extorted agreement with Sickingen? If so, no weight could be attached to it by the court of Rome. Even at Leipzig, Eck had drawn attention to the necessity of that reunion; he blamed the pope for his leaning to the grammarians (grammaticelli), adding that he was not proceeding in the via regia: July 24, 1519 (not 1520); in Luther's Opp. Lat. ii. p. 469.

† Frequently printed in Luther's and Hutten's works. The authentic copy is in Bull. Cocq. III. iii. p. 487. It surprises me that Rainaldus, who gives it, should have taken it from Cochlaus. On all these subjects he is very scanty. Pallavicini is somewhat better. A few notices are to be found in the Parnassus Boicus, iii. p. 205.

‡ Riederer's little work, Beiträge, &c., is specially devoted to these events. The privilege possessed by Eck appears from a paragraph of his Instructions, quoted by him word for word, p. 79.

§ Letter of Baumgartner to the Council of Nürnberg, Oct. 17.

‖ Erasmi Responsio ad Albertum Pium, in Hardt, Hist. Lit. Ref. i. 169. For the διπλωματοφόρος is no other than Aleander.

¶ Extract from the Breve Apostol. 15 Kal. Aug. Winter, Geschichte der Evangel. Lehre, in Baiern, i. p. 53.

once endangered Eck's personal safety, and which, moreover, it was found impossible to execute The Bishop of Brandenburg had not the power, even had he had the will, to exercise the rights of an ordinary in Wittenberg, the university was protected by its exemptions, and, on receiving the bull from Eck, he resolved not to publish it The authorities assigned as a reason that his Holiness either knew nothing about it, or had been misled by the violent instigations of Eck That Eck had, on his own authority, specified by name two other members of the university, Carlstadt and Johann Feldkirchen, as partisans of Luther, created universal indignation Luther and Carlstadt were allowed to be present at the sittings in which the resolutions as to the bull were passed * Already the university had greater authority in this part of Germany than the pope Its decision served as a rule to the electoral government, and even to the official of the bishopric of Naumburg-Zeiz

The only question now was, what the Elector of Saxony, who was just gone to meet the emperor on his arrival at the Rhine, would say Aleander met him in Cologne and instantly delivered the bull to him But he received a very ungracious answer. The elector was indignant that the pope, notwithstanding his request that the affair might be tried in Germany, notwithstanding the commission sent to the Archbishop of Treves, had pronounced sentence in Rome, at the instigation of a declared and personally irritated enemy, who had then come himself to publish, in the sovereign's absence, a bull, which, if executed, would ruin the university, and must inevitably cause the greatest disorder in the excited country But, besides this, he was convinced that injustice was done to Luther. Erasmus had already said to him at Cologne, that Luther's sole crime was that he attacked the pope's crown and the monks' bellies † This was likewise the prince's opinion, it was easy to read in his face how much these words pleased him His personal dignity was insulted, his sense of justice outraged, he determined not to yield to the pope He reiterated his old demand, that Luther should be heard by his equals, learned and pious judges, in a place of safety, he would hear nothing of the bull ‡ This, too, was the opinion of his court, his brother, and his nephew,—the future successor to the throne—nay, of the whole country §

For it was in the nature of things that the partial and ill-considered proceedings of the See of Rome should awaken all antipathies We may safely affirm, that it was the bull which first occasioned the whole mass of public indignation to burst forth

CRISIS OF SECESSION

During the early months of the year 1520, Luther had remained comparatively passive, and had only declared himself against auricular confession and against the administration of the Lord's Supper in one kind, or defended the propositions he had advanced at Leipzig, but when the tidings of Eck's success at Rome and of the impending excommunication, reached him, at first as a vague rumour, but daily acquiring consistency and strength, his ardour for spiritual combat awoke the convictions which had meanwhile been ripening in him burst forth, "at length," exclaimed he, "the mysteries of Antichrist must be unveiled " In the course of June, just as the bull of excommunication had been issued at Rome, he wrote his Book to the Christian Nobility of the German Nation, which was, as his friends justly observed, the signal for a decisive attack The two nuncios with their bulls and instructions, were met by this book, which was published in August at Wittenberg ‖ It consists of a few sheets, the matter of which however was destined to affect the history of the world, and the development of the human mind — at once preparative and prophetic How loud had been the complaints uttered in all countries at this time of the abuses of the Curia, and the misconduct of the clergy ! Had Luther done nothing more, it would have signified little, but he brought into application a great principle which had taken firm hold on his mind Since Melancthon's disputation, he denied the *character indelebilis* conferred by ordination, and thus shook the whole groundwork of the separation and privileges of the clergy He came to the decision that in regard to spiritual capacity all Christians are equal, this is the meaning of his somewhat abrupt expression that "all Christians are priests" Hence followed two consequences, first, that the priesthood can be nothing but a function, "no otherwise separate or superior in dignity," says he, "than that the clergy must handle the Word of God and the Sacraments, that is their work and office," but also that they must be subject to the sovereign power, which has another office to perform, "which holds the sword and the rod in its hand wherewith to punish the wicked and to protect the good "¶ These few words run counter to the whole idea of the papacy as conceived in the middle ages, on the other hand they furnish a new basis to the secular power, for which they vindicate the scriptural idea of sovereignty; and they include in themselves the sum of a new and grand social movement which was destined by its character to be prolonged

* Peter Burcard (Rector) to Spengler Riederer, p 69

† Spalatin, Life of Frederic, p 132 The "Axiomata Erasmi Roterodami pro causa Lutheri Spalatino tradita, 5 Nov 1520 in Lutheri Opp Lat ii p 314" are very remarkable, as throwing light upon the notions of Erasmus

‡ Narrative of the proceedings at Cologne (W xv 1919), the idea that this is by Heinrich von Zutphen is an error caused by the signature in the earlier edition, which, however, only refers to an annexed correspondence

§ Veit Warbeck, Walch, xv 1876.

‖ Probably, however, in the beginning of August On the third of August, Luther writes to his brother Augustine, Voigt, " *jam edo* librum vulgarum contra Papam de statu ecclesiæ emendando " (De W i 475)

¶ An den christlichen Adel deutschen Nation, von des christlichen Standes Besserung Altenb Ausg Werke, i 483

through centuries. Yet Luther was not of opinion that the pope should be overthrown. He would have him remain, neither, of course, as lord paramount of the emperor, nor as possessor of all spiritual power; but with well-defined limited functions, the most important of which would be to settle the differences between primates and archbishops and to urge them to the fulfilment of their duties. He would retain cardinals also, but only as many as should be necessary—about twelve—and they should not monopolise the best livings throughout the world. The national churches should be as independent as possible; in Germany, especially, there should be a primate with his own jurisdiction and his chanceries of grace and justice, before which the appeals of the German bishops should be brought; for the bishops, too, should enjoy greater independence. Luther strongly censured the interference which the See of Rome had recently been guilty of in the diocese of Strasburg. The bishops should be freed from the oppressive oaths with which they were bound to the pope: convents might still be suffered to exist, but in smaller number, and under certain strict limitations: the inferior clergy should be free to marry. It is not necessary to enumerate all the changes which were connected with these in his mind; his meaning and purpose are clear. It could not be said that he wished to break up the unity of Latin Christendom, or completely destroy the constitution of the church. Within the bounds of their vocation, he acknowledges the independence, nay, even the authority of the clergy;* but to this vocation he wishes to recall them, and at the same time to nationalise them and render them less dependent upon the daily interference of Rome. This wish, indeed, he shared with every class of the community.

This was, however, only one point of his attack—the mere signal for the battle, which soon after followed in all its violence. In October, 1520, appeared the treatise on the Babylonish captivity of the church;† for Luther regarded the gradual establishment of the Latin dogmas and usages, which had been effected by the co-operation of the schools and the hierarchy, in the light of a power conferred on the church. He attacked them in the very centre of their existence—in the doctrine of the sacraments—and, in the first place, in the most important of these, the Eucharist. We should do him injustice were we to look for a thoroughly elaborated theory on this subject; he only points out the contradictions which subsisted between the original institution and the prevailing doctrine. He opposes the refusal of the cup, not because he did not believe that the bread contained the whole sacrament, but because nobody ought to attempt to make the smallest change in the original institutions of Christ. He does not, however, counsel the resumption of the cup by force;‡ he only combats the arguments with which it had been attempted to justify the refusal of it from Scripture, and zealously traces out the vestiges of the pure and primitive practice. He then treats of the doctrine of transubstantiation. The reader will recollect that Peter Lombard had not ventured to maintain the transformation of the substance of the bread. Later theologians did not hesitate to do this; they taught that the accidens alone remained; a theory which they supported by a pretended Aristotelic definition of subject and accident.§ This was the point taken up by Luther. The objections raised by Peter of Ailly to this hypothesis had, at a former period, made a great impression upon him; but he now also thought it dishonest to introduce into Scripture any thing which was not found in it, and that its words were to be taken in their plainest and most precise meaning; he no longer acknowledged the force of the argument, that the Church of Rome had sanctioned this hypothesis; since she was that same Thomist Aristotelic church, with which he was engaged in a mortal struggle. Moreover, he believed himself able to prove that Aristotle had not even been understood on this point by St. Thomas.‖ But a yet more important doctrine, as affecting the practical views of Luther, was, that the celebration of the sacrament was a meritorious work—a sacrifice. This dogma was connected with the mysterious notion of the identity of Christ with the Church of Rome, which Luther now entirely rejected. He found nothing of it in the Scripture; here he read only of the promise of redemption connected with the visible sign or token, and with the faith; nor could he forgive the schoolmen for treating only of the sign, and passing over in silence the promise and the faith.¶ How could any man maintain that it was a good work—a sacrifice—to remember a promise? That the performance of this act of remembrance could be profitable to another, and that other absent, was one of the most false and dangerous doctrines. In combating these dogmas, he does not conceal from himself the consequences:—that the authority of countless writings must be overthrown; the whole system of ceremonies and external practices altered: but he looks this necessity boldly in the face; he regards himself as the advocate of the Scripture, which was of higher significance and deserved more careful reverence than all the thoughts of men or angels. He said he only proclaimed the Word in order to save his own soul; the world might then look

* "It does not beseem the pope to exalt himself above the temporal power, save only in spiritual offices, such as preaching and absolving." (p. 494.)

† De Captivitate Babylonica Ecclesiæ Præludium M. L., ubi præcipue de natura, numero et usu sacramentorum agitur. Opp. ed. Jen. ii. 259.

‡ "Contra tam patentes potentes scripturas; contra evidentes Dei scripturas," p. 262.

§ One principal passage is in the Summa Divi Thomæ, pars iii. qu. 75, art. iv. c. 1m. v. 4.

‖ Opiniones in rebus fidei non modo ex Aristotele, tradere, sed et super eum, quem non intellexit, conatus est stabilire: infelicissimi fundamenti infelicissima structura. (p. 263.)

¶ If at a later period, Bellarmin, as Möhler, p. 255, relates, requires before all things "exparte suscipientis voluntatem fidem et pœnitentiam," still it was exactly conclusions of this kind which Luther missed in the then prevailing thomistic writings; and before we blame him, it must be shown that these doctrines had been really taught and inculcated in his time. Their readmission into the Roman church is, as has been said, only the reaction of the spirit of reform.

to it whether it would follow that Word or not. He would no longer adhere to the doctrine of the seven sacraments Thomas Aquinas delights to show how their order corresponds with the incidents of the natural and social life of man — baptism with his birth; confirmation with his growth, the eucharist with the nutriment of his body, penance with the medicine of his diseases; extreme unction with his entire cure —how ordination sanctified public business; marriage, natural procreation * But these images were not calculated to make any impression on Luther, he only inquired what was to be clearly read in the Scriptures, what was the immediate relation between a rite, and faith and redemption he rejected, almost with the same arguments as those to be found in the confession of the Moravian brethren, four of the sacraments, and adhered only to baptism, the Lord's Supper, and penance The others could not even be derived from the See of Rome, they were the product of the schools, to which, indeed, Rome was indebted for all she possessed,† and hence there was a great difference between the papacy of a thousand years ago and that of the present day

The hostile systems of opinion on the destiny and duties of man, and on the plan of the universe, now stood confronted in all their might Whilst the papal see proclaimed anew in every bull all the privileges which it had acquired during the gradual construction of its spirituo-temporal state in the middle ages, and the principles of faith connected with them, the idea of a new ecclesiastical constitution according to which the priesthood should be brought back to a merely spiritual office, and of a system of faith emancipated from all the doctrines of the schools, and deduced from the original principles of its first apostles—an idea conceived by one or two teachers in a university, and emanating from a little town in Germany—arose and took up its station as antagonist of the time-hallowed authority This the pope hoped to stifle in its birth What if he could have looked down that long vista of ages through which the conflict between them was destined to endure!

We have already observed that the pope's bull did not touch Wittenberg Luther had even the audacity to denounce the pope as a suppresser of the divine word, for which he substituted his own opinions—nay, even as a stubborn heretic. Carlstadt also raised his voice against the fierce Florentine lion, who had never wished any good to Germany, and who now condemned the truest doctrines, contrary to laws divine and human, without even having granted the defenders of them a hearing The whole university rallied more and more firmly round its hero, who had in fact given it existence and importance When the intelligence arrived that in some places the authorities had begun to execute the bull, and to burn Luther's books, the monk felt himself sufficiently strong to revenge this arbitrary act on the pope's writings. On the 10th of December, 1520, the academic youth,‡ summoned by a formal proclamation posted on a black board, assembled in unwonted numbers before the Elster Gate of Wittenberg, a pile of wood was collected, to which a Master of Arts of the university set fire in the full feeling of the orthodoxy of his secession, the mighty Augustine, clad in his cowl, advanced to the fire, holding in his hand the pope's bull and decretals "Because thou hast vexed the Lord's saints," exclaimed he, "mayst thou be consumed in eternal fire!" and threw it into the flames Never was rebellion more resolutely proclaimed "Highly needful were it," said Luther another day, "that the pope (that is, the papacy) with all his doctrines and abominations should be burnt"

The attention of the whole nation was now necessarily drawn to this open resistance. What had first procured for Luther the general sympathy of the thinking and serious-minded among his contemporaries, was his theological writings By the union of profound thought and sound common sense which distinguishes them, the lofty earnestness which they breathe, their consolatory and elevating spirit, they had produced an universal effect "That know I," says Lazarus Spengler in the letter which was imputed to him as a crime, "that all my life long no doctrine or sermon has taken so strong hold on my reason Divers excellent and right learned persons of spiritual and temporal estate are thankful to God that they have lived to this hour, that they might hear Dr Luther and his doctrine"§ The celebrated jurist Ulrich Zasius in the most explicit and animated terms proclaims his adoption of Luther's opinions as to absolution, confession and penance; his writings on the ten commandments, and on the Epistle to the Galatians || The collections of letters of that time afford abundant proof of the interest which the religious publications—for example, the exposition of the Lord's Prayer, or the new edition of the German Theology—excited, societies of friends were formed for the purpose of communicating them to each other, of getting them reprinted and then distributed by messengers sent about with these books and no others, in order that the attention of the buyers might not be diverted, preachers recommended them from the pulpit ¶

The boldness of this attack, so formidable and so immediately connected with the deepest feelings of religion, was another cause of popular interest. Some, and among them Zasius whom we have just quoted, disapproved the turn it had taken, but its temerity only served

* Tertia pars, qu lxv conclusio

† "Neque enim staret tyrannis papistica tanta, nisi tantum accepisset ab universitatibus, cum vix fuerit inter celebres episcopatus alius quispiam qui minus habuerit eruditionem pontificum"

‡ According to Sennert, Athenæ et Inscriptiones Vitebergenses, pp 58 and 59, the names in the university books amounted in the year 1512 to 208, in 1513 to 151, in 1514 to 213, in 1515 to 218, in 1516 to 162, in 1517 to 232, in the year 1518 the number of the students entered already rose to 273, in 1519 to 458, in 1520 to 578.

§ Speech in defence, Riederer, p 202

|| Zasii Epp p 394 I cannot possibly believe this letter to be spurious, as the same opinion reappears in so many others

¶ Beatus Rhenanus to Zwinglius Huldrici Zwinglii Opera, tom vii pp 77, 81

to heighten the admiration and the sympathy of the majority; all the elements of opposition naturally congregated around a doctrine which afforded them that of which they stood most in need—justification in their resistance on religious grounds. Even Aleander remarked that a great proportion of jurists declared themselves against the ecclesiastical law; but how great was his error if he really thought what he asserted—that they only wished to be rid of their canonical studies: he little knew the scholars of Germany, who were actuated by a far different motive,—the vexatious collisions between the spiritual and temporal courts, complaints of which had been laid before so many diets and assemblies of the empire. The very latest proceedings of the court of Rome had drawn down severe criticism from the lawyers of Germany. Jerome of Endorf, an imperial councillor, declared that the mode taken by the pope of enforcing his bull by the threat of "attainder for high treason, loss of inheritance and fief," was an encroachment of the spiritual power on the temporal, which he exhorted the emperor not to endure.* It was not, however, the jurists alone, but even the clergy, whom Aleander found wavering, especially the inferior clergy, who severely felt the pressure of the hierarchical power; he was of opinion that throughout Germany they approved Luther's doctrines.† Nor did it escape him that the religious orders too were infected: among the Augustines this arose from the influence of the later vicars, and partiality for a brother of their own order; with others, from hatred of the tyranny of the Dominicans. It was also inevitable that in the heart of many a reluctant inmate of a cloister, the events now passing would awaken the wish and the hope of shaking off his fetters. The schools of the humanists belonged of course to this party; no dissension had as yet broken out among them, and the literary public regarded Luther's cause as their own. Already two attempts had been made to interest the unlearned in the movement. Hutten perfectly understood the advantage he possessed in writing German: "I wrote Latin," he says, "formerly, which not every one understands; now I call upon my fatherland." The whole catalogue of the sins of the Roman Curia, which he had often insisted upon, he now exhibited to the nation in the new light thrown upon it by Luther, in German verses.‡ He indulged the hope that deliverance was at hand, nor did he conceal that if things came to the worst, it was to the swords and spears of brave men that he trusted; by them would the vengeance of God be executed. The most remarkable projects began to be broached; some particularly regarding the relation of the German church to Rome; as that no man should for the future possess an ecclesiastical dignity, who could not preach to the people in the German tongue; that the prerogatives of the papal months, accesses, regresses, reservations, and, of course, annates, should be abolished; that no sentence of excommunication issued by Rome should have any validity in Germany; that no brief should have any force till a German council had pronounced whether it were to be obeyed or not; the bishops of the country were always to hold in check the papal power.§ Others added proposals for a radical reform in details; that the number of holydays should be diminished, the curates regularly paid, fit and decorous preachers appointed, fasts observed only on a few days in the year, and the peculiar habits of the several orders laid aside; a yearly assembly of bishops should watch over the general affairs of the German church. The idea even arose that a christian spirit and life would, by God's especial ordinance, spread from the German nation over the whole world, as once from out Judæa. Thereunto, it was said, the seeds of all good had sprung up unobserved—"a subtle sense, acute thought, masterly skill in all handicrafts, knowledge of all writings and tongues, the useful art of printing, desire for evangelical doctrine, delight in truth and honesty." To this end, too, had Germany remained obedient to the Roman emperor.‖

All hopes now rested on Charles V., who was at this moment ascending the Rhine. Those who opposed the new opinions wished him the wisdom of Solomon and of Daniel, "who at as early an age were enlightened by God;" they even thought the state of things so desperate, that if not changed by a serious and thorough reformation, the last day must quickly come."¶ The partisans of innovation approached him with the boldest suggestions. He was asked to dismiss the grey friar his confessor, who boasted that he ruled him and the empire; to govern with the counsels of temporal electors and princes; to entrust public business, not to clerks and financiers, but to the nobles, who now sent their sons to study; to appoint Hutten and Erasmus members of his council, and to put an end to the abuses of Rome and to the mendicant orders in Germany. Then would he have the voice of the nation for him; he

* To the Landeshauptmann of Styria, Siegm. v. Dietrichstein. Walch, xv. 1902.

† Extracts from the Report of Aleander in Pallavicini.

‡ Klage und Vermanung gegen die ungeistlichen Geistlichen.

§ "Etliche Artickel Gottes Lob und des heyligen Römischen Reichs und der ganzen Deutschen Nation ere und gemeinen nutz belangend." "Divers articles touching God's praise, and the honour and the common profit of the holy Roman empire and of the whole German nation." At the end, printed at Hagenau, by Thomas Anshelm, in Feb. 1521.

‖ "Ein Klagliche Klag an den Christlichen Röm. Kayser Carolum von wegen Doctor Luthers und Ulrich von Hutten," &c.—"A Doleful Complaint to the Christian Roman Emperor Charles, relating to Dr. Luther and Ulrich von Hutten," &c.; the work known by the title of "The Fifteen Confederates." Panzer, Annals of the earlier German Literature, ii. p. 39, has shown that it is by Eberlin von Günzburg. In the Epistola Vdelonis Cymbri Cusani de Exustione Librorum Lutheri, 1520, the contrast between the Romans and the Germans is described in the following manner: "Nos Christum, vos chrysum, nos publicum commodum, vos privatum luxum colitis, vos vestram avaritiam—et extremam libidinem, nostram nos innocentiam et libertatem tuentes pro suis quisque bonis animose pugnabimus."

¶ Verbatim, from Hieronymus Emser against the unchristian book of Martin Luther the Augustine, sheet iv He adds, all ranks are sinful, and "foremost the clergy, from the highest to the lowest." He also applies to them the saying, "from the heel to the crown of the head there is no soundness."

would no longer stand in need of pope or cardinal, but, on the contrary, they would receive confirmation from him, "then," said one, "will the strong Germans arise with body and goods, and go with thee to Rome, and make all Italy subject to thee; then wilt thou be a mighty king. If thou wilt settle God's quarrel, he will settle thine "*

"Day and night," exclaims Hutten to him, "will I serve thee without fee or reward, many a proud hero will I stir to help thee, thou shalt be the captain, the beginner, and the finisher, thy command alone is wanting "

* Ein Klagliche Klag, sheet ††III

CHAPTER IV.

DIET OF WORMS A D 1521.

THE most important question for the intellectual and moral progress of the nation now unquestionably was, in what light Charles V would regard exhortations of this kind, what disposition he would evince towards the great movements of the national mind

We have seen that as yet every thing was wavering and unsettled no form had been found for the government; no system of finance, no military organisation perfected, there was no supreme court of justice, the public peace was not maintained All classes in the empire were at strife—princes and nobles, knights and citizens, priests and laymen, above all, the higher classes and the peasants In addition to all these sources of confusion, arose the religious movement, embracing every region of mind, originating in the depths of the national consciousness, and now bursting forth in open revolt against the head of the hierarchy The existing generation was powerful, intelligent, inventive, earnest, thoughtful It had a presentiment that it contained the germ of a great moral and social revolution

The want of a sovereign and chief, felt by all mankind, is in fact but the conscious necessity that their manifold purposes and endeavours should be collected and balanced in an individual mind, that one will should be the universal will, that the many-voiced debate should ripen into one resolve, admitting of no contradiction. This, too, is the secret of power, when all the energies of a nation give voluntary obedience to its commands, then, and then only, can it wield all its resources

This was the important result which now hung upon the question, whether Charles would understand the sentiments and the wants of his nation, and thence be able to secure its full obedience.

In October, 1520, he proceeded from the Netherlands to Aix-la-Chapelle, where he was to be crowned The newly elected emperor was a young man of twenty, still imperfectly developed, who had just learned to sit his horse well and to break a lance, but of feeble health, a pale and melancholy countenance, with a grave, though benevolent expression He had as yet given few proofs of talent, and left the conduct of business to others, it was principally in the hands of the high chamberlain, William of Croi, Lord of Chievres, who possessed, as it was said, absolute authority over finances, court and government The minister was as moderate as his master, who had formed himself upon his model, his manner of listening and answering satisfied every body, nothing was heard to fall from his lips but sentiments of peace and justice †

On the 23d October Charles was crowned, he took the title of Roman Emperor Elect,‡ which his predecessor had borne in the latter years of his life No later than December we find him in Worms, where he had convoked his first diet, and whither the sovereigns and states of Germany now flocked together His whole soul was filled with the high significance of the imperial dignity He opened the diet on the 28th January, 1521, the day sacred to Charlemagne The reigning idea of his opening speech was, that no monarchy on earth was to be compared with the Roman empire, which the whole world had once obeyed, to which "God himself had paid honour and allegiance, and had left behind him " Unhappily it was now but the shade of what it had been, but he hoped, with the help of the monarchies, the powerful countries and the alliances which God had granted him, to raise it again to its ancient glory §

This seemed the echo of the common wish of Germany, it remained to be seen how he would understand his work—how he would endeavour to perform it

SECULAR AND INTERNAL AFFAIRS OF THE EMPIRE

Charles's first care at the diet was to strengthen the advantageous relation in which, from the circumstances attending his election, he stood to the several German sovereigns The Elector of Mainz received an extension of his powers as arch-chancellor Whenever he was present in person at court, the despatch of all the internal business of the empire was to rest with him; but in his absence, to be in

† "Relatione di Francesco Corner venuto orator di la Cesa e catolica Mta 6 Zugno 1521 Chievres zentilhuomo per esser il secondo genito non di molta facolta, ma adesso più non potria essere, per haver al governo suo non solum la persona del re, ma la caxa li stati li danari e tutto quello è sotto la S Mta E homo di bon ingegno parla pocho, perho molto humanamente ascolta e benignamente risponde non dimostra esser colerico, ma più presto pacifico e quieto che desideroso di guerra et e molto sobrio nel suo viver, il che si ritrova in pochi Fiaminghi "

‡ A description of the place (in which the journey of Charlemagne to Jerusalem is still treated as an historical fact) and of the ceremonies, by an eye witness, in Passero, Giornale Napol p 284.

§ The Proposition, which is the first document in the Frankfurt and Berlin Archives relating to this Imperial Diet, was followed on the 14th of March, Monday after Oculi, by a special statement, which explains it, this is given also by Olenschlager, Explanation of the Golden Bull Records, nr vii p 15. One of the best printed works of that time, but not, however, quite exact As to the rest, Charles's statement recalls strongly some passages in Peter von Andlo

the charge of a secretary appointed by himself, to act with the grand chancellor.* The Elector of Saxony obtained the sanction of his nephew's marriage with the infanta Catharine. As the Saxon government wished, on account of the expense, to avoid a marriage by proxy, the emperor pledged himself to see that the infanta should arrive in Germany six months after his own return to Spain. Markgrave Casimir of Brandenburg had the reversion of the next considerable fief of the empire which might fall vacant in Italy The Count Palatine Frederic, who had been promised the dignity of Viceroy of Naples, received as compensation the post of imperial lieutenant in the Council of Regency; Calenberg, and Wolfenbüttel, the old and devoted friends of Austria, were readily favoured in the matter of Hildesheim, upon which the Lüneburgers quitted the diet in disgust; they saw that they should have to pay severely for their inclination towards the French. Shortly after, a very ungracious decree was issued against them.† The proceedings of the Swabian league, on the other hand, met with a no less cordial approbation. The exiled Duke of Würtemberg, who had neglected to repair to the Netherlands, as he had promised, now declared himself ready to appear at the diet. He received for answer, that it was no longer convenient to his imperial majesty to give audience to the duke; nor would any intercession induce Charles to change this determination. Proceedings were instituted against him, which terminated as unfavourably as those of Lüneburg: both were shortly after placed under ban.‡ The affair of Würtemberg was the more important, since that country belonged to the territory which it was proposed to incorporate into the newly constituted state of Austria. Archduke Ferdinand, the emperor's brother, who was educated in Spain, but had been fortunately removed from that country,§ where he might have become dangerous, received the five Austrian duchies, which Maximilian had once entertained the project of raising into a kingdom in his favour, as his portion of the inheritance of the German domains. The day on which this contract was ratified (28th April, 1521),‖ is one of the most memorable in German history. It witnessed the foundation of the German line of the house of Burgundian Austria, which was destined to occupy so great and conspicuous a station not only in Germany but in the whole of western Europe. Emperor Maximilian's former plans were adopted; and those reciprocal engagements with the royal houses of Bohemia and Hungary which were pregnant with such vast and immediate results, were contracted. The emperor at first intended to keep Würtemberg and the upper hereditary domains for himself, and to appoint a government for the joint administration of them; but he did not carry this into execution; with great magnanimity he left first the government and then the possession of them to his brother, as his *alter ego*.¶ Many thought Ferdinand a man of greater talents than Charles; at all events he was evidently more animated, daring and warlike, and kept a vigilant eye on what occurred in every direction.

It cannot be said that in these transactions Charles showed a constant regard to the national feelings or interests. He suffered himself to be persuaded to strip the Bishop of Lübeck of the inferior feudal dominion of Holstein, to which he had a right, and to transfer it to the King of Denmark and his heirs: he forbade the duke, "under pain of his grievous displeasure and that of the empire," to oppose any obstacle. He had certainly no other motive for this measure than that the king was his brother-in-law, and forgot that that monarch would never be regarded in any other light than as a foreign prince.** Nor was his conduct towards Prussia untainted by similar considerations: the emperor negotiated a truce between the Grand Master and the King of Poland for four years, within which time he promised, with the aid of his brother and the King of Hungary, to endeavour to adjust the difference. The Grand Master would acknowledge no other allegiance than that he owed to the emperor and empire, and rejected every other demand. The emperor took this occasion to institute an inquiry whether his vassal could, or could not, render feudal service to a foreign king. He appointed the King of Hungary one of the umpires; that prince being now related to the house of Austria through the Jagellon alliance, which, as we have observed, was the main cause of the change in the late emperor's policy with regard to Prussia.

It is evident that it was Charles's earnest purpose to maintain the position prepared by Maximilian, and occupied, even before his arrival, by his own commissioners. Kinsmen and old partisans were favoured, and, as far as possible, promoted; recently acquired friends, more closely attached; the decision of difficult disputes, for example, those between Cleves and Saxony, Brandenburg and Pomerania, Hessen and Nassau, were, if possible, postponed, and rendered dependent on future favour: the old opposition was, for the moment, broken up and reduced to inactivity.

Such were the auspices under which the deliberations on the institutions of the empire now commenced.

We shall not examine what would have happened, or what course Charles's councillors would have entered on, if their hands had been perfectly free. It is enough to say that this was not the case.

In the third article of the election capitulations, the emperor had promised to establish a government, or Council of Regency, "such as

* Haberlin, Reichsgeschichte, x. p. 375.

† In Delius Stiftsfehde, p. 175.

‡ Sattler, Herzöge, ii. p. 75.

§ Corner: "Credo non si hanno fidato di lassarlo in Spagna nè al governo di Spagnoli dubitando di qualche novità."

‖ Bucholtz, Ferdinand, i. p. 155.

¶ Extracts from the Records, ib. 158.

** Copies of the Records, printed in Christiani, i. p. 541.

had formerly been devised and had been in course of formation, of pious, acceptable, brave, wise and honest persons of the German nation, together with certain electors and princes." The purpose of this stipulation was not doubtful. The nation wished now to establish, on a permanent basis, the representative form of government which had been under discussion in 1487, planned and proposed in 1495, and brought into operation in 1500, but abolished again by Maximilian. The opinions and designs of Archbishop Berthold were now revived.

At Worms the electors renewed their ancient union, and interchanged their word to press for the performance of the promises contained in the capitulations. In March a scheme of the Council of Regency was submitted to the emperor. This scheme was no other than a repetition of the ordinance for the establishment of the Regency of the year 1500. It was to be composed exactly in the same manner — a lieutenant of the emperor as president, delegates from the electors and the six circles (for the division of the empire into ten circles was not yet carried into effect), and representatives of the different states in rotation: to remain in existence and in force when the emperor was present within the empire, as well as in his absence; to have power to carry on negotiations, in urgent cases to contract alliances and to decide feudal questions. In short, now, as at the former period, the greater part of the powers and functions of emperor were to be transferred to this representative body.

It was not in the nature of things that the emperor should assent to such a project. He was surrounded by the same school of German councillors who had been about his predecessor: the ideas of Elector Berthold were once more encountered by the views of Maximilian. The emperor declared, that his predecessor on the throne had found that the Council of Regency tended to the diminution of his own power and to the prejudice of the empire, and therefore had not established it, that it could not be expected of him to attempt to repeat the experiment of an institution which could only lower his dignity in the eyes of foreign nations. He sent the States a scheme of a totally different nature for their consideration, according to which the most important element of the Regency was six permanent imperial councillors; the fourteen councillors named by the Estates, who were to be assessors to the former, were to be constantly changed. Although the interests of the emperor would thus be far more powerfully represented than before, yet the Council of Regency thus constituted was neither to make alliances, nor to decide important feudal questions, nor to remain in existence, except during the emperor's residence out of the limits of the empire. The oath was to be pronounced, not to the emperor and the empire, but to the emperor alone. The imperial hereditary dominions, which it was one of the main objects of the States to render subject to the common duties and burdens of the empire, Charles insisted on keeping under a perfectly independent administration, even Wurtemberg was not included within the boundary he had assigned to the circles.

This led to a very animated encounter. The States considered the expressions about Maximilian as "more than highly vexatious." Had not that prince, they said, suffered himself to be persuaded by false friends to recede from the original plan, it would have been honourable, useful, and glorious for himself and the holy empire, and terrible to all adversaries. And this time they were unmovably steadfast to their project. The emperor could obtain nothing but some mitigation of subordinate points.

The most vexatious thing to him was the mention of an administration of the empire which should continue its functions during his presence. He regarded this as a sort of tutelage—a stain upon his honour. On this point they yielded to him, and acceded to the title he proposed, "His Imperial Majesty's Regency in the Empire," also that it should at first be established only for the period of his absence. This was subject to the less difficulty, because its duration could not be fixed, and the emperor on his part promised to decide whether the existence of the institution should be prolonged or not, according to the situation of affairs at the time of his return.

Concessions were made to the emperor on some other matters of detail. The composition of the Council of Regency, which was the most important matter, was indeed to be precisely on the model of the former, but the number of assessors was increased from twenty to twenty-two, the two additional members to be nominated by the emperor. On the more important feudal questions, and in alliances with foreign powers, the approbation of the emperor was justly made a necessary condition, but the initiative in affairs, and the negotiation of them, were to be left to the Regency.—Wurtemberg was restored to the Swabian circle. Austria and the Netherlands were to send deputies as before. The oath was unquestionably to be taken in the first place to the emperor, but a distinct pledge was given that the honour and welfare of the Holy Empire were to be mentioned immediately after in the formula of the oath.*

In a word, the emperor succeeded in maintaining his honour and authority—a point on which he showed great susceptibility, but, at the same time, the States carried through their long-cherished idea, and obtained a share in the government of the empire, which Maximilian, after the first experiment, would never again grant them. The Electors of Saxony and of Treves were peculiarly satisfied with the result.

The Imperial Chamber, which had fallen into utter decay, was reconstituted upon the same principles. The original scheme was a

* The documents exchanged in this contest are tolerably complete in Harpprecht. In the Frankfort Archives there is, besides, an essay "ungeverlich Anzeyg, was in Keys. Mt. übergebenem Regiment zugesetzt und umbgangen ist"—"a tolerably exact Account of what has been determined and done in the Regency appointed for his Imperial Majesty."

very extensive one. As there were about three thousand causes undecided, it was proposed to name so many assessors that they might be divided into two senates; the one of which should be entirely occupied in disposing of old causes. There was a project for reforming the procedure on the model of the Rota Romana and the parliament of France. But it was soon evident how little could be done. "I have as yet seen no doctor," writes the Frankfurt delegate home, "who has proposed any good scheme of reform. People say the judges' hearings should be increased, the holydays curtailed, and proceedings the only purpose of which is delay, abolished: any peasant might have advised that." "They are deliberating," says he, another time, "on the reform of the Imperial Chamber; but that is like a wild beast, every body knows his strength, but nobody where to attack him; one advises here, the other there." At last the States, with whom this proposal likewise originated, came to the conviction that nothing could be invented more expedient than the old ordinance of the year 1495, with the improvements it had afterwards undergone, and some new additions.* The chief alteration was, that the emperor should be allowed to appoint two new assessors to the court of justice as well as to the Regency. The constitution of the court was in other respects the same as that agreed to at Constance; here, too the division of the six circles was retained. The three spiritual electors and the three first circles, Franconia, Swabia and Bavaria, were to send assessors learned in the law; the three temporal electors and the three last circles, Upper Rhine, Westphalia and Saxony, assessors of the knightly class. Charles V. promised to send from his hereditary dominions two of the former and two of the latter description. He had also the joint nomination, with the States, of the judge or president of the court, and of the two assessors out of the class of counts and lords. The character of the tribunal, as we perceive, remained essentially that of class representation (*ständisch*); and this was the more unequivocal, since it was to hold its sittings in the same place as the Council of Regency, which was so decidedly representative, and was to be subject to the supervision of that body.

What likewise contributed to impress this character on it was, that the States took upon themselves (as indeed they had from the first offered to do) the maintenance of all these authorities. Many extensive plans were devised for that end: *e. g.*, the keeping back the annates and the revenues of spiritual fiefs, which now went to Rome; or a tax on the Jews; or the imposition of an import duty throughout the empire, which had the most numerous and the warmest advocates; at last, however, they came back to a matricula on the pattern of that proposed at Constance, only that the rate was much higher. The cost of the courts of justice was estimated at 13,410 gulden; that of the Council of Regency, the assessors of which must receive much higher salaries, at 28,508.† But as it was foreseen that there would be many deficits, it was determined to make the estimates at 50,000 gulden. The assessment of Constance was altered as follows: the principle was, to multiply the contributions then required by five; and this rule was generally adhered to, though not without many exceptions. Many of the counts and lords, who were always very intractable, were left at the old assessment; others were raised, but only threefold at the highest. On the other hand, some cities which had the reputation of being very flourishing and wealthy, were compelled to submit to a contribution above fivefold higher than the last. Nürnberg and Ulm were raised from 100 to 600 gulden; Danzig, from 70 to 400. In this manner was the only permanent impost on the States of the empire, which, together with the supreme tribunal, had begun to fall into oblivion, revived.

Larger demands, with a view to a military organisation, and also more immediately to the emperor's coronation journey to Rome, necessarily came under discussion.

It might have been thought that the projects of a general tax, and of a military training of the people in parishes, would have been revived in conjunction with that of the Council of Regency; representative government and popular armament had always hitherto been kindred notions. On this occasion, however, the latter was not suggested; either because it had always been found to be impracticable, or because, since it was last entertained, the power of the princes had so greatly increased. On the 21st of March, Charles V. appeared in person in the assembly of the States, and, with much circumlocution, demanded, through the mouth of Dr. Lamparter, succours for his ex-

* The ordinance of the Imperial Chamber of 1521 is almost word for word the same as this project of the states. The beginning only is different. "Dienstag nach Lätare," lautet er, "ist auf Römisch. Ks. Mt. unsres Allergnädigsten Herrn Beger von Churfürsten Fürsten Stennden des heil. Röm. Reychs beratschlogt, da hievor auf erstgehalltenem Reychstag allhie zu Wormbs im xcv. I. ain Ordnung desselben Kaiserl. Cammergerichts aufgericht, welche nachmals zu vorgehalten Reychstagen zum Thail weiter declarirt und gebessert worden, das dieselbe als notturfdeglich und hochlich ermessen und bedacht, im h. R. zu hallten und zu vollziehen auch nachmals nit wol stattlicher zu machen oder zu ordnen seyn mocht dann wie hernach folgt; darum Ir der Stennde getreur Rate, das die kais. Mt. jetzo solich (Ordnung?) wider, allhie gegen und mit den Stennden des heyl. Reychs und herwiderumb sambt hernachgemeldten Enderungen Ratschlag und Zusatz genädigklich annem, approbir und wie bei S. K. Mt. Anherrn geschehen verpflicht und dieselben also zu halten und zu vollziehen als Römischer Keiser handhabe."—"On Thursday after Lætare," it proceeds, "at the desire of the Roman emperor, our most gracious lord, the electors, princes, and states of the Roman empire have debated on a new constitution of the Kammergericht having been, on a former diet here at Worms, in 1495, decreed, which constitution afterwards, at other diets, has been farther interpreted and amended; that the same, as requisite and highly fitting and well-considered, should be kept and executed in the empire, since the same could not well be made or constituted more excellent than here follows. Therefore it is the loyal advice of the said states, that his imperial majesty do now, in a common accord with the states of the empire, with the alterations, suggestions, and additions hereafter mentioned, graciously accept and approve of the said constitution, and, like his imperial majesty's predecessors, engage to keep and execute the same and uphold it as Roman emperor."

† Harpprecht IV., iii. 35, has, it is true, only 27,508 gulden, but this is an error. In the Frankfurt copy the sums are given more correctly than in Harpprecht.

pedition to Rome, which he himself estimated at 4000 horse and 20,000 foot, for a year He then promised to contribute 16,000 foot soldiers, 2000 heavy horse, and a considerable body of light horse, at his own cost Elector Joachim of Brandenburg answered in the name of the States, "his brothers, lords and good friends,"* and prayed time for consideration To the demand itself, which was founded on the ancient customs of the empire, or to the number of troops specified, which was not unreasonable, there was no objection to be urged But again the States would promise nothing, till they were certain of the establishment of the supreme court and of the Council of Regency, which latter institution they more than ever felt bound in duty to insist on At length they granted the required number of troops, but only for half a year; it was also agreed that they should furnish the men, and not money for raising them, they would not give occasion a second time to all the disorders that had prevailed in this matter under Maximilian † Lastly, care was taken that the German troops should not be left to the command of foreigners they were all to march under their own officers; the emperor was only to have the appointment of the commander-in-chief, who also must be a German For every leader wished to see his own men in the field under his own banner A matricula was drawn out on the principles of that of Constance of 1507 As to the cavalry, it was almost exactly the same, in addition to the 3791 men then registered, there were now 240 from Austria and Burgundy, so that all the electors, and many other of the states, had only to furnish their old contingent. For the infantry (to which Austria and Burgundy now contributed 600 men each), the former demand of 4722 was generally quadrupled, though with many exceptions ‡ Thus arose the matricula of 1521, which was the last, and formed the model for the military organisation of the German empire for ages.

Such were the most important measures proposed by the new emperor at this first diet It could not be said that they were fully adequate to the wants of the nation The resolutions adopted were chiefly to the advantage of the sovereign princes; the preliminary ordinances concerning the execution of the judgments of the Imperial Chamber—which was chiefly intrusted to them—were, for example, manifestly in their favour: even in his capitulation, the emperor had proposed to forbid alliances or leagues between the nobles and vassals, and this might have the effect of forming more compact local powers. On the other hand, nothing was done for the mass of the people, among whom such a ferment prevailed, though it had been so much and so often talked of The nobility remained excluded from all share in the business of the empire, counts, lords and nobles were in a constant state of excitement concerning the legal decision of their disputes with princes and electors, which they wanted to have more expeditious and equitable, and some rather acrimonious correspondences on this subject passed at the diet The cities had vainly demanded a seat in the Imperial Chamber for their deputies, the great subsidies of the empire were discussed and voted without consulting them, many of them were recently aggrieved by the new rate of contributions imposed on them; and, besides this, they were threatened with an import duty for the whole empire, from which they feared a universal disturbance to commerce They made incessant complaints, and at last only agreed to the project because they would not, as they said, be the only members of the empire who resisted; they would not have to bear the blame if peace and justice were not established §

Notwithstanding these defects, it was a great point gained that the disorders of the last years of Maximilian's reign were checked; and that the ideas of a representative government, which had never been realised under him, were revived with such considerable success The constitution of 1521, like that of 1507, was founded on a combination of matricular with representative forms, but the latter were now far more comprehensive, since they did not, as on the former occasion, regard the administration of justice only, but, according to the propositions of 1495 and 1500, formed the basis of a Council of Regency, enjoying considerable independence of the emperor The attempt to revive an administration adapted to the momentary interests of the policy of the house of Austria, such as that constantly carried on by Maximilian, was met by a national institution, which, if it could but acquire consistency and development, promised the most important future results

FOREIGN RELATIONS — LUTHER

While these political arrangements were concluded, the spiritual interests of the empire were also frequently discussed they opened another field to the emperor's policy

On all the other questions which came before him, he had been able to keep in view Germany, his relation to the interior of the empire, and the interests of his family, but

* Letter from Fuerstenburg to Frankfurt, March 24 "S Maj sey auch willens gen Rom zu ziehen und dasjenige so dem Reich entwandt wieder zu erlangen"—"His majesty purposes to go to Rome, and to regain possession of that which has been wrested from the empire"

† Fürstenberg, May 13 "Damit kein Finantz in den gesucht werde"—"In order that it might not be turned into a matter of financial speculation"

‡ Neueste Sammlung der Reichsabschiede, ii p 211

§ Hans Bock and Dr Peutinger, who had sat in the committee, got little credit "Etlich geben" schreibt Furstenberg, am 20 sten Mai, "Hr Hansen Bock etwa spitz Wort, als ob er sich und die rheinischen Stadte erhalten und sie im Pfeffer habe stecken lassen Dazu verdriesst sie und uns alle, dass sie die Grafen fast gelachert (erleichtert) und die Beschwerung auf uns getrieben haben. Dr Peutinger der ist der aller onlustigst, er wolt gern dass man es beim alten Anschlag liess will nit ansehn dass Eine Stadt aufgeht die andre in Abfall kommt"—"Some give" writes Furstenberg on the 20th of May, "Herr Hans Bock hard words, as if he had taken care of himself and the Rhenish cities, and left them (the others) in the lurch Moreover, it vexes them and all of us that they have greatly relieved the counts, and forced the burden upon us Dr Peutinger is the most discontented of all he would gladly have abided by the old assessment: he does not like to see that whilst one city rises, another falls into decline"

the Lutheran agitation extended so widely that it affected even the most important foreign relations.

Charles V. was the child and nursling of that Burgundian court which had been mainly composed of French elements under Philip the Good and Charles the Bold, and had followed the peculiar line of policy dictated by the position of those princes. Even as opposed to Ferdinand the Catholic and the Emperor Maximilian, this court had maintained and acted on its own independent views, often in direct hostility to the former. The prospects which had been contemplated under Charles the Bold, and opened under Philip I., appeared to find a necessary fulfilment in the position and the rights of Charles V. The court of Brussels, which was not properly a sovereign court and wielded no extraordinary powers, was suddenly called, by the hereditary rights of its prince, to play the greatest part in Europe. To take possession of this pre-eminent station was of course its first care.

For the attainment of this end, the policy of the Netherlands was conducted with singular prudence and success by the Archduchess Margaret and the Lord of Chièvres. Friesland had been annexed to the Netherlands, which had also been strengthened by the appointment of a kinsman to the bishopric of Utrecht, and by the closest alliance with Liége and Cleves. The crowns of Castile and Aragon, with all their dependencies, had been taken possession of. Rebellious commotions had indeed been universal, even in Naples and Sicily, but they had all been put down: the national pride of the Castilians, offended by the dominion of a court composed of foreigners, burst forth in an insurrection of the communes, but the monarch possessed natural allies there in the clergy and the grandees, and needed not to fear the people.

The inheritance of Maximilian was now added to these vast territories. The Austrian hereditary dominions, with all their rights or expectancies in the east of Europe, which had been acquired by the late emperor, were now left to the younger scion of the house, who, however, was kept in constant dependence by his need of assistance: the empire Charles took into his own hands, and founded the ascendency of his house in Germany—with what care, we have just seen.

All this was carried into effect in the midst of continual irritations and collisions with France, originating in the disputes between former dukes and kings, but matters were so skilfully conducted in Brussels, that peace was maintained under the most difficult circumstances. The successors of Louis XI. were compelled, however reluctantly, to allow the posterity of Charles the Bold to consolidate a power which infinitely exceeded all that could have been anticipated in his time.

Nothing now remained but for the Burgundian monarch to take possession of the imperial rights in Italy, which appeared the more practicable, since he already ruled Naples and Sicily, and since his expedition to Rome would be supported by the whole might of the Spanish monarchy,—a combination which had never existed before. The Proposition* with which he opened the diet sufficiently showed that the young emperor was determined to avail himself of it. During the proceedings, frequent allusion was made to the recovery of the imperial dominions that had been lost, and grants for that purpose were made by the diet: negotiations were entered into with the Swiss, even at Worms.

The maintenance of peace with France, the country the most nearly interested, was no longer possible. Francis I. held the duchy of Milan without having received or even sought the investiture; the emperor's first efforts must be directed to this point. Other plans, which gradually attained to maturity, lay in the back ground; for example, that of recovering the duchy of Burgundy, taken by Louis XI., the loss of which the Netherlands had never learned to brook. The consolidation of two great European powers completely opposed to each other, which had long been silently preparing, became at this moment fully manifest. France,—by her internal unity and her wide-spread connexions, both early in the 14th and (after the expulsion of the English) at the close of the 15th and beginning of the 16th centuries, unquestionably the most powerful country in Europe,—saw herself surrounded and overshadowed on all her frontiers by a vassal who had gradually arisen to power, whom she thought she had crushed, but who, by a few easy and fortunate matrimonial alliances, had come into possession of a combination of crowns and dominions such as the world had never beheld. Here we first perceive the hidden motives which rendered Francis so eager to obtain the imperial crown; he could not endure that his ancient vassal should rise to a dignity superior to his own. That this nevertheless had come to pass,—that his rival could now set up legitimate claims to the very country the possession of which was peculiarly dear to the king as the conquest of his own sword,—inflamed him with bitter and restless irritation. Growing ill will was observable in all the negotiations, and it became evident that a breach was inevitable between these two powers.†

This was the grand conjuncture destined to develope the political life of Europe; the several states of which necessarily inclined to the one side or the other, according to their peculiar interests. Its more immediate consequence was, to determine the position of the empire and the application of its forces.

For however highly Charles V. estimated the imperial dignity, it was natural that he should not look upon Germany as the central point of his policy. The sum of all his opinions and feelings was, of necessity, the result of the aggregate of his various dominions and relations.

* The Proposition was the speech with which the emperor opened the diet. It contained the topics proposed for discussion.—Transl.

† What were the mutual reproaches appears in the French Apologiæ Madritæ Conventionis Dissuasoria, and the Imperial Refutatio Apologiæ in Goldast, Politica Imperialia, pp. 863, 864.

He ever felt himself the Burgundian prince who united the highest dignity of Christendom with the numerous crowns he had inherited from his ancestors; and he thus, like his grandfather, necessarily regarded the rights he enjoyed as emperor as only a part of his power, indeed the extent and variety of the countries subject to his sway rendered it even more impossible for him to devote himself completely to the internal affairs of Germany, than it had been for Maximilian

Of the workings of the German mind, he had not the faintest idea, he understood neither the language nor the thoughts of Germany.

It was a singular destiny that the nation, in the moment of an internal agitation so mighty, so peculiar to itself, had called to its head a stranger to its character and spirit, in whose policy, which embraced a much wider sphere, the wants and wishes of the German people could appear but as a subordinate incident

Not that religious questions were indifferent to the emperor—they were very interesting to him; but only in as far as they affected or threatened the pope, and afforded a new view of his own connexion with the court of Rome, or new weapons with which to encounter it

Amidst all the various political relations of the emperor, this, however, was unquestionably now the most important

For as a conflict with France was obviously inevitable—a conflict of which Italy must be the principal scene—the main question for the emperor was, whether he should have the pope with him or not The two monarchs already rivalled each other in their efforts to gain Leo's favour. Both were lavish in their promises, the king, in case he should conquer Naples, which he was resolved to attack, the emperor, in the event of an attempt upon Milan, which he was about to make in favour of the pretender and the house of Sforza, and for the purpose of restoring the rights of the empire over that province

This, however, was not the only close relation of the emperor to the see of Rome, others of an ecclesiastical nature, but involving not less important results, existed in his other dominions, and especially in Spain

It is matter of notoriety that the main prop of the government of that country, as constituted under Ferdinand the Catholic, was the inquisition. But this institution was now the object of a simultaneous attack in Castile, Aragon and Catalonia. That powerful body, the Cortes of Aragon, had applied to the pope, and had actually obtained from him some briefs, according to which the whole constitution of the inquisition was to be altered and approximated to the forms of the common law* In the spring of 1520, Charles sent an ambassador to Rome to effect a revocation of these briefs, which he foresaw must have important consequences in his other dominions, and endanger his whole government.

The negotiations were pending when Charles arrived in the Netherlands, and a loud and almost universal voice, expressing both a political and a religious opposition, called upon him to assume a bold attitude of resistance to the pope

Charles's acute and able envoy, who arrived in Rome while Eck was there, and Luther's controversy gave rise to so many deliberations of the theologians and sittings of the consistory, immediately perceived all the advantage which might accrue from it to his master "Your Majesty," he writes to the emperor on the 12th of May, 1520, "must go to Germany, and there confer some favour upon a certain Martin Luther, who is at the court of Saxony, and excites great anxiety in the court of Rome by the things he preaches"† This view of the case was actually adopted at the imperial court When the papal nuncio arrived there with the bull against Luther, the prime minister let fall the expression, that the emperor would do what was agreeable to the pope, if his holiness would oblige him, and not support his enemies ‡ On another occasion, Chievres said that if the pope embarrassed the affairs of the emperor (with France), other people would stir up embarrassments for him, out of which he would not easily extricate himself

This, therefore, was the real point on which the affair, from the first moment, turned, not the objective truth of the opinions, nor the great interests of the nation connected with them—of which the newly arrived sovereign was not conscious, and with which he could have no sympathy, but the general situation of politics, the support which the pope was willing to grant the emperor, and the footing upon which the former intended to place himself with regard to him

This was well known at Rome Great pains were taken to gain over the emperor's confessor, Glapio, a Franciscan, who was not well disposed towards Rome, "by civilities" It was determined, after long hesitation, to nominate the Bishop of Liége, Eberhard of the Mark, who had gone over from the side of France to that of Austria, cardinal, offensive as this must be to the former power § The same motives had dictated the mission of Aleander, who had been in the bishop's service before he came to Rome, and from the influence which that prelate enjoyed over the government of the Netherlands, appeared there as the natural mediator between Rome and the empire This bishop, Aleander thought, too, would be an active instrument in securing a favourable result to the negotiations with the empire, though his language was generally frank and audacious All the measures which the nuncio suggested or employed were conceived in this spirit The Bishop of Tuy, who had followed the emperor from Spain, and enjoyed great consideration with the prime minister, was to

* Llorente, Hist de l'Inquisition, i. p 395, or x

† Extract from Manuel's Despatches Llorente, i p 398.

‡ From Aleander's letters Pallavicini, i c 24, p 136 To what does the emperor refer, when he afterwards reproaches the court of Rome with having tried to delay the coronation at Aix? Caroli Rescr Goldast, Const p 992

§ Molini, Documenti di Storia Italiani, i p 84.

be conciliated by the gift of a benefice which had been already promised to one who had every possible claim to it. Aleander paid one of the imperial secretaries fifty gulden, for which sum the latter engaged to render him "secret and good service," and promised the same man a pension for some years, in consideration of his pledging himself to report to him all the deliberations of the Council of Regency hostile to the court of Rome. He expresses himself persuaded that most of these councillors and secretaries, although they hate the papacy, will "dance to Rome's piping," if they do but see her gold.* His bribes extended even to the door-keepers and beadles who were to seize Luther's works; his sole and continual complaint is, that his employers send him too little money. By a similar course of "cunning and promptitude," as he boasts, he had carried into effect the mandate for the burning of Luther's books in Flanders. "the emperor and his councillors saw the books burning, before they were fully aware that they had assented to the mandate." Aleander's letters present an odious and disgusting spectacle, a most immoral mixture of cunning, cowardice, arrogance, affected devotion and mean ambition, the vilest means employed in so great a cause. It is not probable that these were without influence, though of course others were needed to produce a decisive effect. But what had not been put in practice? In the matter of the inquisition, especially, the pope agreed to make the most important concessions. On the 21st of October, 1520, he declared to the grand inquisitor of Spain, that he would give no further encouragement to the demands of the cortes of Aragon, that he would not confirm the briefs he had issued, and that he would introduce no innovation in the affairs of the inquisition without the approbation of the emperor. Even this did not satisfy Charles, he demanded the entire revocation of the briefs. On the 12th of December, the pope offered to declare all steps that had been taken against the inquisition null and void. On the 16th of January, 1521, he at length actually permitted the emperor to suppress the briefs, and expressed the wish that they might be sent back to Rome in order that he might annul them.†

It is obvious that this state of things was little calculated to meet the wishes of the people of Germany. Charles's position and connexions required of him an alliance with the pope, instead of that opposition which the spirit of the nation would have dictated. How grievously were the hopes which such men as Hutten and Sickingen had placed on the young emperor disappointed! The papal bull was executed without hesitation in the Low German hereditary dominions, where the higher clergy and confessors seemed to engross all the consideration of the court. In January, 1521, there was a general belief that the emperor was determined to destroy Luther, and if possible to exterminate his followers.‡ A brief arrived, probably together with the last concessions, wherein the pope exhorted the emperor to give the force of law to his bull by an imperial edict. "He had now an opportunity of showing that the unity of the church was as dear to him as to the emperors of old. Vainly would he be girded with the sword, if he did not use it, not only against the infidels, but against heretics, who were far worse than infidels."§

One day in the month of February on which a tournament was to be held, the emperor's banner was already displayed, when the princes were summoned, not to the lists, but to the imperial quarters, where this brief was read to them, and at the same time an edict commanding the rigorous execution of the bull was laid before them.

Strange and unlooked for entanglement of events! The Lutheran controversy led the pope to revoke that mitigation of the severities of the inquisition in Spain which he had already determined on at the request of the cortes, while in Germany, on the other hand, the emperor prepared to crush the monk who so audaciously incited the people to rebel against the authority of Rome. The resistance to the power of Dominican inquisitors was in both countries a national one. This fully explains the fact that, among the Spaniards who accompanied the court, those at least of the middle classes took the liveliest interest in Luther and his writings.

In Germany however the emperor could accomplish nothing without the approbation of the empire, and in submitting the draft of the mandate before alluded to to the States, he had added, "that if they knew of any thing better, he was ready to hear it." This gave rise to a very warm discussion in the imperial council. "The monk," says the Frankfurt deputy, "makes plenty of work. Some would gladly crucify him, and I fear he will hardly escape them, only they must take care that he does not rise again on the third day." The same doubt and fear, that condemnation by a party would produce no permanent effect, prevailed in the States. The emperor had intended to publish the edict without further trial,‖

* He asks on one occasion for "denari si per uno vivere come per donar a segretarii et a sbirri, li quali ancorche siano infensissimi alla corte di Roma, tutta volta qualche danaro li farebbe saltar a nostro modo. quia aliter nihil fit et vix faciemus aliquid."—*Extracts from Aleander's Letters in Munster, Beitrage zur Kirchengeschichte*, p. 78.

† Extracts in Llorente, i. pp. 396 and 405.

‡ Spengler to Pirkheimer, Dec. 29. Jan. 10, in Riederer, pp. 113, 131.

§ "Deus accinxit te terrenæ potestatis supremo gladio, quem frustra profecto gereres juxta Pauli apostoli sententiam, nisi eo uterere cum contra infideles tum contra infidelibus multo deteriores hæreticos."—*Fr. Arch.*

‖ In the draft it is said: "Und (weil) dann der gedacht Martin Luther alles das so muglichen gewesen ist offentlichen gebredigt, geschrieben und ausgebraitet, und yetzt am jungsten etlich Articul, so inn viel Orten in Behem gehalten werden und die von den hailigen Concilien fur katzerisch erkannt und erklart seyn, angenommen, und ine darum die papstlich Heylikeit fur einen offenbaren Ketzer wie obstet erklart und verdammt hat und deshalben inen weiter zu horen nit rat noch geburlich ist."— "And (since) then the said Martin Luther has openly preached, written, and spread all this as much as possible, and has now lately accepted certain articles which are maintained in many places in Bohemia, and which are recognised and declared by the holy councils to be heretical, and his papal holiness has, therefore, as beforesaid, declared and condemned him as an avowed heretic, and therefore it is neither advisable nor fitting to hear him further."

according to the advice of Alcander, who declared that the sentence of condemnation already pronounced was sufficient; Doctor Eck, too, sent in a little memorial, full of flatteries and admonitions, to the same effect.* It was the same question which had been discussed in the curia, but the Estates of Germany were not so obsequious as the jurists of Rome. They begged the emperor to reflect what an impression would be made on the common people, in whose minds Luther's preaching had awakened various thoughts, fantasies, and wishes, if he were sentenced by so severe a mandate, without being even called to take his trial. They urged the necessity of granting him a safe-conduct, and summoning him to appear and defend himself. But a new question arose. On what basis was this trial to be conducted? The states distinguished between two branches of Luther's opinions, the one relating to church government and discipline, which they were for handling indulgently, even if he refused to recant (and they seized this occasion of once more strongly impressing on the emperor the complaints of the nation against the See of Rome), the other, against the doctrine and the faith "which they, their fathers, and fathers' fathers, had always held." Should he also persist in these, and refuse to recant, they declared themselves ready to assent to the imperial mandate, and to maintain the established faith without further disputation.†

Such were the views with which Luther was summoned to Worms. "We have determined," says the imperial citation, "we and the States of the Holy Roman empire, to receive information from thee concerning the doctrine and the books that have been uttered by thee." An imperial herald was sent to conduct him.

With regard to the opposition to the temporal interference of Rome, the States were essentially of the same opinion with Luther. As the emperor was bound even by his capitulation to restore and maintain the Concordat and the ecclesiastical liberties of the nation, which had been continually violated to an insufferable extent, the lesser committee was now employed in drawing up a complete statement of the grievances of the nation against the See of Rome. Their manner of proceeding was this, each prince delivered in a list of the grievances of which he had more particularly to complain, and every charge alleged by more than one was received and recorded. Already it was feared that the spiritual princes would draw back, but the councillors of the temporal were determined in that case to carry the matter on to the end alone. A statement of grievances was produced which reminds us of the writings of Hutten and the Book to the German Nobles; so strong was the censure of the papal See generally, and above all, of the government of Pope Leo X.‡ It is filled with the cunning and malignant devices, the roguery and cheating, which prevailed at the court of Rome. The curia was also directly accused, in practice, of simony. If Luther had done nothing more than attack the abuses of the curia, he could never have been deserted by the States, the opinion he had expressed on this subject was the general one, and was indeed their own. Probably the emperor himself would not have been able to withstand it, his father confessor had threatened him with the chastisements of Heaven if he did not reform the church.

We feel almost tempted to wish that Luther had remained for the present satisfied with this. The nation, engaged under his conduct in a common struggle against the temporal sway of the church of Rome, would have become for the first time strongly united and completely conscious of its own unity. But the answer to this is, that the strength of a mind like his would have been broken, had it been fettered by any consideration not purely religious. Luther had been incited not by the wants of the nation, but by his own religious convictions, without which he would never have done any thing, and which had indeed led him further than would have been either necessary or expedient in a political struggle.

Some still hoped, however, that he would recall one step, that he would at least not persist in his last most offensive expressions which occurred in the Book of the Babylonish Captivity. This was in particular the opinion of the emperor's confessor. He did not regard the papal anathema as an insuperable obstacle to an amicable adjustment. Luther had not yet had a hearing, a door remained open to the pope for restoring him to the bosom of the church, if he would but consent to retract this last book, which was full of the most untenable assertions and not comparable to his other writings. But by maintaining these passages he laid a stumbling block in his own path; he would cause that the precious wares which he might otherwise bring safely to port would be shipwrecked.§ At first he proposed to the Elector of Saxony to nominate two or three councillors with whom he could consult as to the means of arranging the affair. The elector replied that he had not learned councillors suf-

* "Ad Carolum V. de Ludderi causa. Ingoldstadt, 18 Feb. Saxones sub Carolo magno colla fidei et imperio dedere: absit ut sub Carolo maximo Ludder Saxo alios fidem veram et unicam deponere faciat."

† "Der Stennd Antwurt aufkeyserlicher Mt. Beger des Mandats."—"The answer of the States to the desire of his imperial majesty to the mandate." Without a date. Unfortunately, also Furstenberg has not dated his letters precisely. The one, for instance, which refers to this resolution, he has inscribed Saturday after Matthiæ. Saturday after Matthiæ, March 2, is certainly meant. In which case this resolution of the States is of that date. For that their answer should have referred to a command of the emperor of the 7th of March, is impossible, since the letter of summons to Luther is dated the 6th of March.

‡ This document is republished from the old printed edition, in Walch xv. 2058. The copy in the Frankfort Archives, which agrees with the printed one, shows more plainly that the work consists of three parts, the first reaching to E iii, upon which follows an episode, the second, with a fresh superscription, touching especially the usurpations of the spiritual courts of justice, reaching to G iii, finally, a third, containing chiefly the complaints of the clergy themselves, and of the ordinaries, against the court of Rome, which was presented on the Monday after Jubilate, April 22, Luther himself being by.

§ Seckendorf, Comm. de Lutheranismo, i. 142.

ficient. Glapio hereupon asked whether the parties would submit the matter to chosen arbitrators, by whose decision the pope himself would abide. The elector did not believe it possible to induce the pope to consent to this, especially since the emperor intended so soon to leave Germany. On hearing this, Glapio sighed. The silent, reserved prince, who repelled all attempts at intimacy or sympathy from others, and who was in fact the only human being that had any influence over Luther, was absolutely unapproachable; it was impossible to obtain from him even a private audience. The confessor, therefore, addressed himself to other friends of Luther. He went to the Ebernburg to visit Sickingen, who had just then re-entered the emperor's service and was esteemed one of Luther's most distinguished patrons, in the hope of obtaining his mediation. Here, too, Glapio expressed himself in such a manner on some points, that he might have been supposed to be an adherent of Luther. I am not of opinion that this was a stratagem, as so many have assumed; Aleander, at least, was very uneasy about it, and neglected no means of interrupting the course of the negotiations. It is obvious that Luther's opposition to the pope promised to be a doubly powerful instrument of the imperial policy, if the government did not find itself compelled absolutely to condemn him on account of his open schism, and could keep the matter pending before a court of arbitration. Sickingen sent an invitation to Luther to visit him in passing by.*

For Luther was already on his way from Wittenberg to Worms. He preached once on the road, and in the evening when he arrived at his inn, amused himself with playing the lute; he took no interest whatever in politics, and his mind was elevated far above all subjects of mere personal interest, whether regarding himself or others. At various places on the road he had to pass through, might be seen posted up the decretal condemning his books, so that when they arrived at Weimar the herald asked him whether he would go on. He replied that he would rely on the emperor's safe-conduct. Then came Sickingen's invitation. He replied, if the emperor's confessor had any thing to say to him, he could say it in Worms. Even at the last station, a councillor of his sovereign sent him word that he had better not come, for that he might share the fate of Huss. "Huss," replied Luther, "was burnt, but not the truth with him. I will go, though as many devils took aim at me as there are tiles on the roofs of the houses."† Thus he reached Worms, on the 18th of April, 1521, one Tuesday, about noon, just as people sat at dinner. When the watchman on the church tower blew his trumpet, every body crowded into the streets to see the monk. He sat in the open waggon (*Roll-wagen*) which the council of Wittenberg had lent him for the journey, in the cowl of his order; before him rode the herald, with his tabard, embroidered with the imperial eagle, hung over his arm. Thus they passed through the wondering, gaping crowd, regarded by some with sympathy, by all with various and unquiet emotions. Luther looked down upon the assembled multitude, and his daring courage rose to the height of firm confidence; he said, "God will be with me." In this state of mind he alighted.

The very next day towards evening he was conducted into the assembly of the empire. The young emperor, the six electors (among whom was his own master), a body of spiritual and temporal princes before whom their subjects bowed the knee, numerous chiefs celebrated for deeds in war and peace, worshipful delegates of cities, friends and foes, were there, awaiting the entrance of the monk. The sight of this majestic and splendid assemblage seemed for a moment to dazzle him. He spoke in a feeble and almost inaudible voice. Many thought he was frightened. Being asked whether he would defend his books (the titles of which were read aloud) collectively, or consent to recant, he replied that he begged for time to consider; he claimed, as we have seen, the benefit of the forms and customs of the empire.

The following day he appeared again before the diet. It was late before he was admitted; torches were already lighted; the assembly was perhaps more numerous than the day before; the press of people so great, that the princes hardly found seats, the interest in the decisive moment, more intense. Luther now exhibited not a trace of embarrassment. The same question as before being repeated to him, he answered with a firm, distinct voice, and with an air of joyful serenity. He divided his works into books of Christian doctrine, writings against the abuses of the See of Rome, and controversial writings. To be compelled to retract the first, he said, would be unheard of, since even the papal bull acknowledged that they contained much that was good; the second, would afford the Romanists a pretext for the entire subjugation of Germany, the third, would only give his adversaries new courage to resist the truth;—an answer which was more directed against the erroneous form in which the questions had been arranged, than against the views with which the States had entered on the trial. The official of Treves put the matter in a more tangible shape, by advising Luther not to give a total and unqualified refusal to the proposal to retract. Had Arius, he said, retracted some points, his good books would not have been destroyed together with the bad. In his (Luther's) case, too, means would be found to rescue some of his books from the flames, if he would recant what had been condemned by the Council of Constance, and what he had repeated in defiance of that condemnation. The official insisted more on the infallibility of councils than on that of the pope.

* See Luther's Narrative. Works, Altenb. Ed. t. i. p. 733.

† Muller, Staatscabinet, viii. 296. I retain the expression, which he himself makes use of in a subsequent letter. "Wenn ich hatte gewusst, dass so viel Teufel auf mich gehalten hatten, als Ziegel auf den Dachern sind, ware ich dennoch mitten unter sie gesprungen mit Freuden."—"If I had known that as many devils would have set upon me as there are tiles on the roofs, I should still have sprung into the midst of them with joy."—*Letters*, ii. 139.

But Luther now believed as little in the one as in the other; he replied, that even a council might err This the official denied Luther repeated that he would prove that this might happen, and that it had happened The official could not of course go into the inquiry in that assembly He asked again definitively whether Luther meant to defend all his works as orthodox, or to retract any part He announced to him that, if he utterly refused to recant, the empire would know how to deal with a heretic Luther had expected that a disputation or confutation, or some attempt at demonstrating his errors, awaited him in Worms, when, therefore, he found himself at once treated as a false teacher, there arose in his mind during the conversation the full consciousness of a conviction dependent on no act of the will, founded on God's word, regardless of and untroubled by pope or council threats alarmed him not, the universal sympathy, the warm breathings of which he felt around him, had first given him strength and courage his feeling was, as he said at going out, that had he a thousand heads he would let them all be struck off sooner than recant. He repeated now, as he had done before, that, unless it were demonstrated to him by texts from the Holy Scripture that he was in error, he could not and would not recant, since his conscience was captive to God's word "Here I stand," exclaimed he "I can do no otherwise; God help me! Amen"*

It is remarkable how different was the impression which Luther made upon those present The Spaniards of high rank, who had always spoken of him with aversion and contempt, who had been seen to take a book of Luther's or Hutten's from a book-stall, tear it in pieces and trample it in the mire,† thought the monk imbecile A Venetian, who was otherwise perfectly impartial, remarks, that Luther showed himself neither very learned nor remarkably wise, nor even irreproachable in his life, and that he had not answered to the expectations conceived of him ‡ It is easy to imagine what was Aleander's judgment of him But even the emperor had received a similar impression. "That man," said he, "will never make a heretic of me" The next day (19th of April) he announced to the states of the empire, in a declaration written in French and with his own hand, his determination to maintain the faith which had been held by his predecessors, orthodox emperors and catholic kings In that word he included all that had been established by councils, and especially that of Constance To this he would devote his whole power, body and soul After the expressions of obstinacy which they had yesterday heard from Luther, he felt remorse that he had spared him so long, and would now proceed against him as against an avowed heretic He called upon the princes to act in the same spirit, according to their duty and their promises

Luther had, on the contrary, completely satisfied his own countrymen § The hardy warriors were delighted with his undaunted courage, the veteran George of Frundsperg clapped him on the shoulder encouragingly, as he went in; the brave Erich of Brunswick sent him a silver tankard of Eimbeck beer through all the press of the assembly At going out a voice was heard to exclaim, "Blessed is the mother of such a man!" Even the cautious and thoughtful Frederic was satisfied with his professor "Oh," said he to Spalatin in the evening, in his own chamber, "how well did Doctor Martinus speak before the emperor and states!" He was particularly delighted at the ease and ability with which Luther had repeated his German declaration in Latin From this time, the princes rivalled each other in the frequency of their visits to him. "If you be right, Sir Doctor," said Landgrave Philip of Hessen, after a few jocose words, which Luther gently rebuked with a smile, "may God help you" Luther had already been told, that if his enemies burned him, they must burn all the German princes with him Their latent sympathy was aroused and set in motion by the emperor's peremptory manifesto, so foreign to all the forms of the empire A paper was found in his apartments on which were written the words, "Wo to the land whose king is a child!" A declaration of open hostility was fixed on the town-hall, on the part of four hundred allied knights against the Romanists, and especially against the Archbishop of Mainz, for trampling under foot honour and divine justice They had sworn not to abandon the upright Luther "I am ill at writing," said the author of this proclamation, "but I mean a great mischief, with 8000 foot soldiers at my back Bundschuh, Bundschuh, Bundschuh!"‖ This seemed to announce a combination between the knights and the peasants to protect Luther against his enemies In fact, the courtiers did not feel perfectly at ease, when they saw themselves thus unarmed and defenceless, in the midst of a warlike nation in a state of violent excitement and agitated by conflicting passions

For the moment however, there was nothing to fear, since Sickingen and many other knights and captains had entered Charles's service, in the hope of soon reaping an ample harvest of glory and gain under his banners.

Before the States entered on the discussion of the emperor's proclamation, they proposed that an attempt should be made to induce Luther to renounce his most offensive opinions, they intimated that there was danger of a rebellion, if the proceedings against him were of

* Acta, Revdi Patris Martini Lutheri coram Cæsa Majestate, etc Opp Lutheri, lat ii p 411 The account which Pallavicini drew from the letters of Aleander contains somewhat more a good deal of the detail which he gives, as well as different pieces of news, I found in the letters of the Frankfurt delegates, Fürstenberg and Holzhausen

† Buschius ad Huttenum Opp Hutt iv p 237

‡ Contarenus ad Matthæum Dandulum Vormatiæ, 26mo d April, 1521, in the Chronicle of Sanuto, tom xxx

§ "Contarenus ad Tiepolum 23mo d Apr Habet in fentissimos inimicos et maximos fautores res agitur tanta contentione quantam nemo crederet"—*Letter of Tonstall from the Diet of Worms, in Fidde's Life of Wolsey*, p 242 The Germans everywhere are so addicted to Luther, that rather than he shall be oppressed by the pope's authority a hundred thousand of the people will sacrifice their lives

‖ The war cry of the league of the peasants of the Upper Rhine in 1501-2 (See note, p 82).—TRANSL.

so hasty and violent a kind: for this purpose the emperor granted a delay of some days.

But it was easy to foresee that little could be accomplished by such means. Representations were made to Luther concerning his opinions on the councils;—he persisted in affirming that Huss was unjustly condemned at Constance. He was again asked to acknowledge the emperor and states as judges of his doctrines;—he declared that he would not allow men to be the judges of God's word.

Aleander maintains that Luther had really, at one moment, been advised to abandon some of the opinions he had last proclaimed, and to defend only those immediately directed against Rome. No trace of this is to be found in German authorities. It does not even appear that the question contained in the memorial of the States was very precisely put; but all his declarations were so clear and explicit, so profoundly religious, that no personal considerations were to be expected from him: he had emancipated himself for ever from the forms of the church of Rome; in rejecting the decision of one council, he rejected the whole idea on which it rested: a compromise was now impossible.

But as he quitted Worms without having consented to the smallest limitation of his opinions, the former resolution of the States, which had given occasion to his being summoned before them, was now put in force as an instrument of his condemnation. The emperor, at least, could not have contemplated a revision of this decree or a fresh debate upon it, since he had just formed the most intimate relations with the See of Rome.

The ill-concealed hostile disposition in which Don Juan Manuel had found the court of Rome in the spring of 1520, had been converted into the strictest union by his efforts, within the space of a year. On the 8th of May, 1521, an alliance was concluded between Charles and Leo, in which they mutually promised "to have the same friends and the same enemies, without exception; the same will in consent and denial, in attack and defence." They began by making common cause against France; the pope having at length determined completely to take the side of the emperor, and to exert all his powers to drive the French out of Milan and Genoa. The immediate object, however, was the spiritual affairs of Germany.

In the 16th article of the treaty, the emperor promised that, "inasmuch as certain men had arisen, who fall off from the Catholic faith and wickedly slander the apostolic see, he would employ all his powers in punishing them and avenging the wrong they had committed against the apostolic see, in like manner as if it had been done against himself."*

It cannot be affirmed that the conduct of Charles V. in the affair of Luther was dictated exclusively by political motives; it is very probable that a denial of the infallibility of councils and an attack on the sacraments, was as offensive as it was unintelligible to him; but it is perfectly clear that he was mainly determined by politics. To what purposes might not Luther have been turned, if he had moderated his tone so as to render it unnecessary to condemn him? But as this was not to be avoided, it was made a condition of the great war which was about to be declared.

There was, however, still a certain difficulty in adopting decisive measures, arising from the universal sympathy which Luther had excited during his presence. The resolution passed by the States was now repugnant to a considerable number of them. The question was, whether they would acquiesce without contest in an edict founded upon this resolution.

In order to obtain this result, the following course was adopted.

Nothing was said for some time; meanwhile many quitted Worms, as all the other business was ended.

On the 25th of May, when the emperor appeared at the town-hall to go through the formalities of receiving the resolutions concerning the Council of Regency, the courts of justice, and the matricula, in person, he requested the States to adjourn their departure for three days, in order to terminate some matters which were still undecided.† According to ancient usage, the members of the diet escorted him back to the bishop's palace, where he resided; the electors of Saxony and the Palatinate had left Worms, but the four others were present. On their arrival at the palace, they found the papal nuncios awaiting them. In consequence of Aleander's urgent representations of the necessity of sending this mark of honour, briefs had arrived from the pope to the electors, and were presented to the nuncios. A brief had also arrived addressed to the emperor, the publication of which had been designedly delayed till this moment. Under the impressions made by these flattering communications, the emperor now declared that he had caused an edict on the Lutheran affair to be drawn up, on the basis of the former resolution of the States. This document had even been composed—such was the confidence now prevailing between emperor and pope—by one of the nuncios; the present was esteemed the favourable moment for communicating it to these members of the diet. There was now no legitimate or efficient line of opposition open to them, even had they been disposed to pursue it; and the Elector of Brandenburg, Joachim I., replied that the opinion of the States was certainly conformable to the measure in question. Aleander hastened to place this instantly on official record.‡

We perceive that the edict was not laid before the States in Assembly; it was not submitted to any new deliberation; it was an-

* Tabulæ Fœderis, &c. in Dumont, t. iv. part iii. p. 98. "Quoniam sanctissimo domino nostro cura est aliquanto etiam major rerum spiritualium et pastoralis officii quam temporalium——"

† Letter of Fürstenberg, May 23. Frankf. Arch.

‡ Pallavicini, lib. i. c. 28, from Aleander's Letters. It is evident what pleasure the narrator takes in the success of so dexterous a proceeding: "Era ignoto il misterio all' istesso Grancancelliere—crucciava forte i ministri di papa, veggendo nel discioglimento della dieta rimanerse con le mani vacue; ma i principi se vogliono adoperare prudentemente, conviene," &c. &c.

nounced to them unexpectedly, in the emperor's apartments, and after every artifice had been employed to incline them to listen favourably to any proposal. their assent, which cannot even be called a formal one, was extorted by a sort of surprise *

It was, however, as severe and peremptory as possible Sentence of ban and re-ban was declared against Luther as a member lopped off from the church of God, together with all his adherents, patrons and friends His writings and those of his followers were prohibited and sentenced to be burnt And that no similar works might appear in future, a censorship was appointed to control the press ‡

Aleander had thus attained the long-desired object of all his negotiations In the course of the day he had two fair copies made, the one in German, the other in Latin the next morning—Sunday—he hastened with them to the emperor, he found him with the States and the court in the church, but even this did not prevent him from laying the paper before Charles on the spot, in the church it received the imperial signature This was on the 26th of May, but Aleander had thought it expedient to date it the 8th, at which time the assembly was still tolerably full

By this act the temporal power, as well as the spiritual, declared open resistance to the spirit of religious innovation which was awakened in the nation The opposition had not succeeded, as they had hoped, in inspiring the emperor with their own hostility to the papacy; on the contrary, he had drawn closer all the ties which bound him to the pope The two representatives of the secular and ecclesiastical powers had united, in order to uphold the established constitution of the church

Whether they would succeed was, indeed, another question

BOOK III.

ENDEAVOURS TO RENDER THE REFORMATION NATIONAL AND COMPLETE.

1521—1525,

INTRODUCTION.

THE peculiar character and form which the Latin church had gradually assumed gave rise, as we have already seen, to the necessity for its reform,—a reform demanded by the state of the world, and prepared by the national tendencies of the German mind, the advancement of learning, and the divergencies of theological opinion. We have likewise remarked how the abuse of the traffic in indulgences, and the disputes to which it gave birth, led, without design or premeditation on the part of any concerned, to a violent outbreak of opposition.

While we regard this as inevitable, we cannot proceed further without pausing to make some observations on its extreme danger.

For every member and every interest of society is enlinked with the whole established order of things which forms at once its base and its shelter, if once the vital powers which animate this mass are thrown into conflict, who can say where the victorious assailants will find a check, or whether every thing will not be overwhelmed in common ruin?

No institution could be more exposed to this danger than the papacy, which had for centuries exercised so mighty an influence over the whole existence of the European nations.

The established order of things in Europe was, in fact, the same military-sacerdotal state which had arisen in the eighth and ninth centuries, and, notwithstanding all the changes that had been introduced, had always remained essentially the same—compounded of the same fundamental elements. Nay, even those very changes had generally been favourable to the sacerdotal element, whose commanding position had enabled it to pervade every form of public and private life, every vein of intellectual culture. How then would it have been possible to assail it without producing an universal shock, to question it, without endangering the whole fabric of civilisation?

It must not be supposed that so resistless a power of persuasion resided in a merely dogmatic faith, wrought out by the hierarchy and the schools. The establishment of this would, on the contrary, have excited incessant controversy, which, though generally confined within

† Dr Caspar Riffel, in his Christl Kirchengesch der Neuesten Zeit, vol i p 214, cannot, in fact, avoid admitting this But he rejoices that "the emperor, by means of this 'surprise,' removed all opportunity for even one of them (the princes) to break his word at the decisive moment" It could not well be said more plainly that a serious difference prevailed between the emperor and the princes

‡ Edict of Worms in Walch, xv 2204 It is remarkable that in all other departments the censorship is conferred on the bishop alone, but in that of theology only in conjunction with "the faculty of the Holy Scriptures of the nearest situated university"—§ 30

the region of received ideas, would sometimes have been carried beyond that limit But the intimate connexion which the papacy maintained with all established authorities had defeated every attempt at opposition. How, for example, could an emperor have ventured to take under his protection religious opinions opposed to the dominant system of faith, not on particular and unimportant points, but profoundly and essentially? Even as against a pope on whom he was making war, he could not have dared to do it, he must have feared to undermine the spiritual basis on which his own rank and power were founded, to be the first to break through the circle of ideas and associations by which the minds of men were bounded The civil authorities felt, at every moment, the indissoluble nature of their connexion with the hierarchy, and generally made themselves the instruments of the persecution of all who dissented from the faith prescribed by the church

It was now also to be considered that projects and attempts of the most dangerous kind had been connected with the more recent attacks on the doctrine and discipline of the church of Rome

A century and a half had elapsed since John Wicliffe had engaged in a similar contest with the papacy in England (with nearly the same weapons, and supported by the same national impulses) to that which Luther now entered upon in Germany, this was instantly accompanied by a tumultuous rising of the lowest classes of the people, who, not content with reforms in the creed, or an emancipation from the see of Rome, aimed at the abolition of the whole beneficed clergy,* and even at the equalisation of the nobleman and the peasant, *i. e* at a complete overthrow of Church and State It is uncertain whether Wicliffe had any share in these proceedings or not. At all events, the resentment they excited fell upon him, and he was removed from Oxford, the scene of his labours, whence he might have exercised a singular influence over England and the world, to the narrow and obscure sphere of a country parish.

The disorders in Bohemia, which broke out in consequence of the teaching and the condemnation of Huss, at first related exclusively to the spiritual matters whence they arose,† but the severity with which they were repressed soon excited an extremely dangerous fanaticism. The Taborites not alone rejected the doctrines of the Fathers of the church equally with those of later times, but they demanded the destruction of all the books in which those doctrines were contained. They declared it vain and unevangelical, nay, sinful, to prosecute studies and to take degrees at the universities‡, they preached that God would destroy the world, and would only save the righteous men of five cities§, their preachers deemed themselves the avenging angels of the Lord, sent to execute his sentence of annihilation. Had their power corresponded with their will, they would have transformed the earth into a desert in the name of the Lord.

For a thirst for destruction is inevitably excited by successful opposition, and is the more violent, the more powerful the enemy with whom it has to contend.

Was not then, we must now inquire, a similar storm to be feared in Germany, where the pope had hitherto wielded a portion of the imperial power?

The nation was in a state of universal ferment, a menacing revolt against the constituted authorities was already stirring in the depths of society, would not this be called into action by an attack on the highest of all acknowledged earthly authorities? Would not the destructive forces which every society harbours in its bosom, and which this sacerdotal-military state had certainly not been able to neutralise or destroy, now rear their heads?

The whole future destiny of the German nation was involved in the question whether it could withstand this danger or not; whether it would succeed in severing itself from the papacy, without imperilling the state and the slowly won treasures of civilisation in the process; and what form of constitution—for without political changes the separation was impossible—the nation would then assume On the answer to these questions rested, at the same time, the possible influence of Germany on the rest of the world.

The immediate course of events assumed a most menacing and dangerous character.

CHAPTER I.

DISTURBANCES AT WITTENBERG—OCTOBER, 1521, TO MARCH, 1522.

Once more had the supreme temporal power in Germany allied itself with the papacy, and this at first could not fail to make a deep impression The edict of Worms was published in all parts of the empire, and in some places the confessors were instructed by the bishops to refuse absolution to every one who should be guilty of avowing Lutheran tenets Luther's own sovereign could only save him by seizing him on his way through the Thuringian forest, and carrying him, in feigned captivity, to the safe asylum of the Wartburg. A report was

* See Prioris et Capituli Cantuarensis Mandatum, Sept 16, 1381, in Wilkins's Concilia Magnæ Britanniæ, iii p 152

† One chief cause of this movement which is commonly overlooked, is mentioned by the well informed Hemmerlin in his tract De Libertate Ecclesiastica I will give this in his own words "In regno Bohemiæ quasi omnes possessiones et terrarum portiones et portiones portionum quasi per singulos passus fuerunt occupatæ, intricatæ, et aggravatæ per census, reditus et proventus clero debitos Unde populeres nimis exasperati—insultarunt in clerum et religiosos—et terram prius occupatam penitus liberarunt."

‡ Formula fidei Taboritarum apud Laur Byzynium (Brzezina) Ludewig Reliquiæ MSS, tom vi p 191.

§ Byzynii Diarium belli Hussitici, ib p 155 sq

spread that an enemy of the elector had imprisoned and perhaps killed him.

It soon however, became manifest how little had been effected by these severities.

In the towns of the Netherlands in which Charles happened to be residing, Luther's writings were collected and publicly burned, but the emperor might be seen to smile ironically as he passed these bonfires in the market-place, nor do we find any trace of such executions in the interior of Germany. On the contrary, the events of the diet and the new edict only gained fresh partisans for Luther's cause. It appeared a powerful argument for the truth of his doctrines, that when he publicly avowed his books at Worms, and declared that he was ready to retract them if any one could confute him, no one had ventured to accept the challenge.* "The more Luther's doctrine is pent up," says Zasius, "the more it spreads."† If this was the experience of the university of Freiburg, where the orthodox party was so strong, what must it have been elsewhere? The Elector of Mainz did not think it expedient to grant the Minorites the permission begged by their provincial, to preach against Luther in his diocese, fearing that it would but increase the agitation of the public mind.‡ In despite of the new regulations for the censorship contained in the edict, pamphlet after pamphlet appeared in favour of the new doctrines. These were mostly anonymous, but Hutten ventured to put his name to a direct attack on the pope's nuncio, Alcander, the author of the edict. In this he asks him whether he imagines that he can crush religion and freedom by means of a single little edict, artfully wrung from a youthful prince, or that an imperial command had any power against the immutable word of God. Were not rather the opinions of a prince subject to change? The emperor, he believed, "would learn to think very differently in time."§ The agents of Rome themselves were astonished to find of how little avail was the edict they had obtained with so much difficulty. The ink, they said, was scarcely dry with which the emperor had signed it, when already it was violated on every side. They are said, however, to have consoled themselves with the reflection, that if it had no other results, it must lay the foundation for inevitable dissension among the Germans themselves.

It was a most significant circumstance that the university of Wittenberg was as little affected by the imperial edict as it had been by the papal bull. There the new doctrines had already taken root and flourished independently of Luther's personal influence, and thither the flower of the German youth flocked to receive and adopt them. It made indeed but little difference whether Luther was present or not, the lecture rooms were always crowded, and his doctrines‖ were defended with the same enthusiasm, both orally and in writing. In short, this infant university now took the boldest ground. When the Sorbonne at last broke silence, and declared itself against Luther, Melanchthon thought himself not only bound to undertake the defence of his absent friend, but he even dared to fling back the accusation upon the university of Paris, the source of all theological learning, the parent stem of which the German universities were branches, the Alma Mater to whose decision the whole world had ever bowed, and to charge her herself with falling off from true Christianity. He did not hesitate to declare the whole of the doctrines current at the universities, especially the theology of the schools, false and heretical when tried by the standard of Scripture.¶ The highest powers in Christendom had spoken, the pope had issued an anathema, and his sentence had been confirmed by that of the great mother university, and, finally, the emperor had ordered it to be executed, and yet, in the small town of Wittenberg, which a few years before was hardly known, a professor little more than twenty years of age, in whose slight figure and modest bearing no one could have detected any promise of heroism or boldness, dared to oppose all these mighty powers, to defend the condemned doctrines, nay, to claim for them the exclusive glory of Christianity.

One cause of this singular phenomenon was, that it was well known that the appearance was more formidable than the reality —the motives which had determined the course taken by the court of Rome (chiefly dominican influence), and the means by which the edict had been extorted from the emperor, and the manner of its publication, were no secret. The three men from whom the condemnation in Paris originated were pointed out and called by the most opprobrious names.** The reformers, on the other hand, were conscious of pure motives, and a firm and impregnable foundation for their opinions. The influence of their prince, who afforded them undoubted though unacknowledged protection, was a safeguard against actual violence.

But those who ventured to take up so independent and imposing a position, at variance

* "Ein schoner dialogus und gesprech zwischen eim Pfarrer und eim Schulthayss, betreffend allen ubelstand der Geystlichen," &c. "A fine dialogue and conversation between a parish priest and a sheriff touching the ill condition of the clergy," &c., doubtless written immediately after the meeting of the diet, in which are these words "Warum hand ir dan nit Doctor Luther mit disputiren yez zu *Worms* uberwunden?" "Why did you not then overcome Doctor Luther in the disputation now held at Worms?" This is the argument with which the sheriff brings over the parish priest to his views.

† Epp i 50

‡ Capito ad Zwinglium Hallis, iv Aug 1521 (Epp Zw, i 78) He required sermons, "citra perturbationem vulgi, absque tam atrocibus affectibus."

§ Invectiva in Alcandrum. Opera, iv p 240

‖ Spalatini Annales, 1521 October "Scholastici, quorum supra millia ibi tum fuerunt." Nevertheless in the course of the winter, the electors of Brunswick and Brandenburg forbade their subjects to attend this University Mencken, Script ii 611 The number of matriculations fell off considerably during the winter term Sennert, p 59

¶ Adversus furiosum Parisiensium theologastrorum decretum Phil Melanchthonis pro Luthero Apologia Corp Reformatorum i 398

** Glareanus ad Zwinglium Lutetiæ 4 non Julii, 1521. Beda, Quercus, Christophorus Bellua, Stercus, Christotomus Epp Zw p 176 The work of Glareanus, p 156, in which the death of Leo X is mentioned, does not belong to the year 1520, but to the following year

with all established authorities, and supported only by opinions which had not yet attained their full development nor acquired a precise form, obviously incurred an enormous weight of responsibility. In carrying out the principles professed, it was necessary to be the pioneers of a numerous, susceptible and expecting crowd of sympathising spirits Here, where all the elements of a state at once military and sacerdotal were to be found as abundantly as elsewhere, the experiment was to be tried, how far the authority of the priesthood might be destroyed without endangering the safety of the state

It was, however, become impossible to remain stationary. Men's minds were too much excited to be content with doctrines alone On the faith which was now so profoundly shaken, were founded practices that influenced every day and hour of common life, and it was not to be expected that an energetic generation, conscious of its own power, and impelled by new and mighty ideas, should do violence to its own convictions and submit to ordinances it had begun to condemn

The first remarkable incident that occurred was of a purely personal nature. Two priests in the neighbourhood, Jacob Seidler and Bartholomew Bernhardi, both professing the doctrines of Wittenberg, solemnly renounced their vows of celibacy. Of all the institutions of the hierarchy, this, indeed, was the one which, from the strong taste for domestic life inherent in the nation, had always been most repugnant to the German clergy, and, in its consequences, most profoundly offensive to the moral sense of the people. The two priests declared their conviction that neither pope nor synod were entitled to burden the church with an ordinance which endangered both the body and the soul * Hereupon they were both claimed for trial by the spiritual authorities; Seidler alone, who resided in the territory of Duke George of Saxony, was given up to them, and perished in prison, the Elector Frederic refused to lend his authority to the Bishop of Magdeburg against Bernhardi; he refused, as Spalatin expresses it, to let himself be employed as a constable. Carlstadt now took courage to attack the institution of celibacy in a work of considerable length.

As the vow of celibacy was originally confined to the monastic orders, and had subsequently been extended to the whole priesthood, its dissolution necessarily affected the whole idea of the monastic system. In the little Augustine church which had been the scene of Luther's first appearance, Gabriel Zwilling, one of his most able fellow-labourers, preached a series of fervent discourses, in which he attacked the very essence of monachism, declaring that it was not only lawful but necessary to renounce it; for that ' under the cowl there was no salvation " Thirteen Augustine monks left the convent at once, and took up their abode, part among the students and part among the townspeople One of them who understood the trade of a cabinet-maker, applied for the right of citizenship and proclaimed his intention of marrying † This was followed by a general disturbance the Augustines who had stayed in the convent thought themselves no longer safe, and the Carmelite convent in Wittenberg had to be protected every night by a strong guard.

Meanwhile Brother Gabriel made another still more formidable attack upon the Catholic church. He carried Luther's doctrines about the sacrament so far as to declare the adoration of it, and even the celebration of the mass without communicants, simply as a sacrifice (the so-called private mass), an abuse and a sin.‡ In a short time the prior of the convent was compelled by the general agitation to discontinue the celebration of private masses in his church, in order, as he said, to avoid still greater scandal. This of course produced a great sensation both in the town and university. On the 3d of December, 1521, when mass was going to be sung in the parish church, several of the students and younger burghers came with knives under their coats, snatched away the mass books and drove the priests from the altar The town council summoned the offenders subject to its jurisdiction, and showed an intention of punishing them; upon which the townspeople rose tumultuously and proposed terms to the council, in which they demanded the liberation of the prisoners in a tone almost amounting to open rebellion.§

All these were attempts made without plan or deliberation to overthrow the existing form of divine worship. The Elector, to whose decision such affairs were always referred, wished, as was usual with him, to take the opinion of some constituted authority

His first step was to summon to Wittenberg a council of Augustines from the provinces of Meissen and Thuringia. These monks all more or less shared Luther's opinions and regarded his cause as their own. Their judgment, as he afterwards declared, coincided with his own, even during his absence; they did not go so far as brother Gabriel, who denounced the monastic vows as sinful, but they no longer acknowledged them to be binding. Their decision was as follows. " Every creature is subject to the word of God, and needs not allow

* "Quid statuerint Pontificii canones, nihil refert Christianorum "—*Epistle from the Theologians of Wittenberg to the Bishop of Meissen, Corp Ref* i 418.

† Report of Gregorius Bruck to the Elector, Oct 11 Corp Ref i 459

‡ Report from Helt the prior of the Augustines to the Elector, Nov 12 Corp Ref p 483

§ The Council of Wittenberg to the Elector Dec 3. and 5 Corp Ref, p 487 The impression made by these innovations in distant countries is remarkably displayed by a passage in vol xxxii of the Venetian Chronicle of Sanuto, in the Archives of Vienna " Novita di uno ordine over uso de la fede christiana comenzada in Vintibergia La frati heremitani di S Augustino hanno trovato e provato per le St Scripture che le messe secondo che se usano adesso si è gran peccato a dirle o a odirle (thus it appears that the whole innovation was looked upon as an invention of the Augustine order) e dapoi el zorno di S Michiel, 1521 in qua ogni zorno questo hanno predichado e ditto, e stanno saldi in questa soa oppinione, e questo etiam con le opre observano e da poi la domenega di S Michiel non hanno ditto piu messe nella chiesia del suo monasterio, e per questo è seguito gran scandalo tra el popolo li cantori e acnonici spirituali e temporali ——"

himself to be oppressed by burdensome human institutions; every man is at liberty to leave the convent or to remain in it,* but he who leaves it must not abuse his freedom according to the lusts of the flesh; he who prefers to stay, will do well to wear the cowl and render obedience to his superiors from choice and affection" They determined at the same time to desist from the practice of begging, and to abolish votive masses.

Meanwhile the prince had called upon the university to pronounce an opinion on the mass in general. A commission was accordingly chosen, of which Melanchthon was a member, and which decided for the entire abolition of the mass, not only in Wittenberg but throughout the country, be the consequences what they might.† When, however, the moment arrived for the whole corporation to confirm this sentence, they absolutely refused to do so, several of the most influential members stayed away from the meeting, declaring that they were too insignificant to undertake to reform the church ‡

Thus as neither the Augustine order nor the university declared themselves distinctly in favour of the innovators, the Elector refused to move any further in the matter, saying that if even in Wittenberg they could not agree, it was not probable that the rest of the world would think alike on the proposed change they might go on reading, disputing and preaching about it, but in the mean while they must adhere to established usages §

The excitement was, however, already too great to be restrained by the command of a prince whose leniency was so well known, and accordingly Dr Carlstadt announced, in spite of it, that on the feast of the circumcision he should celebrate the mass according to a new rite, and administered the Lord's Supper in the words of the Founder. He had already attempted something of the kind in the month of October, but with only twelve communicants, in exact imitation of the example of Christ As it seemed probable that difficulties would be thrown in his way, he determined not to wait till the day appointed, and on Christmas Day, 1521, he preached in the parish church on the necessity of abandoning the ancient rite and receiving the sacrament in both kinds. After the sermon he went up to the altar and said the mass, omitting the words which convey the idea of a sacrifice, and the ceremony of the elevation of the host, and then distributed first the bread and next the wine, with the words, "This is the cup of my blood of the new and everlasting covenant" This act was so entirely in harmony with the feelings of the congregation that no one ventured to oppose it On New Year's Day he repeated this ritual, and continued to do so every succeeding Sunday, he also preached every Friday ‖

Carlstadt belonged to a class of men not uncommon in Germany, who combine with a natural turn for deep speculation the boldness to reject all that has been established, or to maintain all that has been condemned, yet without feeling the necessity of first arriving at any clear and precise ideas, or of resting those ideas upon arguments fitted to carry general conviction Carlstadt had at first adopted the doctrines of the schoolmen, he was afterwards urged by Luther to the study of the sacred writings, though he had not, like him, patience to acquire their original languages, nor did he hesitate at the strangest and most arbitrary interpretations, in which he followed only the impulse of his own mind. This led him into strange aberrations; even at the time he was preparing for the disputation of Leipzig, he used the most singular expressions with regard to the Holy Scriptures, applying to them as a whole that which has generally been understood of the law only; viz. that they lead to transgression, sin, and death, and do not afford the true consolation the soul requires In the year 1520 he entertained doubts whether Moses was really the author of the books which bear his name, and whether the Gospels have come down to us in their genuine form; speculations which have since given so much occupation to learning and criticism, presented themselves at this early period to his mind.¶ At that time he was overawed by the presence and authority of Luther, now, however, he was restrained by no one; a wide arena for the display of his ambition lay before him, and he was surrounded by an enthusiastic public. Under these circumstances he was himself no longer the same, the little swarthy sun-burnt man, who formerly expressed himself in indistinct and ambiguous language, now poured forth with the most vehement eloquence a torrent of mystical extravagant ideas, relating to a totally new order of things, which carried away all imaginations.

Towards the end of the year 1521 he was joined by allies who had entered on a similar career from another direction, and who pursued it with still greater audacity

It is well known that at the beginning of the Hussite troubles, two strangers, Nicolas and Peter of Dresden, who had been banished by the Bishop of Meissen and found an asylum in Prague, were the persons who, during the absence of Huss and Jerome, instigated the populace to demand a change of the ritual, especially in the administration of the sacrament; and that various other fanatical opinions were quickly combined with these **

* Decreta Augustinianorum Corp Ref i 456 This meeting is not to be placed in the month of October, but rather in December or in the beginning of January, as is remarked by Seckendorf (Historia Luther i s 54 § 120) on the authority of a contemporary letter See Spalatini Ann 610

† Ernstlich Handlung der Universitat, &c Corp Ref i 465

‡ Report of Christian Beiers, Dec 13 ib 500

§ Instruction of the Elector, Lochau, Dec 19 ib. 507

‖ Zeitung aus Wittenberg account of what took place in 1521, &c, in Strobel's Miscellanien, v 121

¶ See extracts from his works in Löscher's Historia Motuum, i 15.

** The notice of this is very remarkable in Pelzel's Wenceslas, ii (Urkunden, nr 238. ex MS coævo capituli) They declared at the very beginning "quod papa sit antichristus cum clero sibi subjecto"

Whether it was that these opinions re-acted on the country in which they originated—or whether they had from the first taken deeper and more lasting root there,—the same spirit which had formerly directed the movement at Prague, now revived at Zwickau (a town in the Erzgebirge, where Peter of Dresden had for some time resided), and appeared likely to guide the agitation now prevailing at Wittenberg.

This spirit was remarkably displayed in a sect which congregated round a fanatical weaver of the name of Claus Storch, of Zwickau, and professed the most extravagant doctrines. Luther did not go nearly far enough for these people. Very different men, they said, of a much more elevated spirit, were required; for what could such servile observance of the Bible avail? That book was insufficient for man's instruction, he could only be taught by the immediate inspiration of the Holy Ghost.* Their fanaticism soon rose to such a pitch as to convince them that this was actually granted to them, that God spoke to them in person, and dictated to them how to act and what to preach.† On the strength of this immediate inspiration from Heaven, they pressed for various alterations in the services of the church. Above all, they maintained that a sacrament had no meaning without faith, and therefore entirely rejected the baptism of infants, who are incapable of faith. But their imaginations took a much wilder flight. They asserted that the world was threatened with a general devastation, of which the Turks were perhaps to be the instruments, no priest was to remain alive, not even those who were now contracting marriage, nor any ungodly man; but after this bloody purification the kingdom of God would commence, and there would be one faith and one baptism.‡ They seemed well inclined to begin this work of violent convulsion themselves. Finding resistance from the moderate portion of the citizens and town council of Zwickau, they collected arms in the house of one of their party, with the design of falling suddenly on their opponents and putting them all to death. Fortunately they were anticipated by Wolf of Weissenbach, the chief magistrate of the place, he arrested a number of the misguided men, kept the peace and compelled the ring-leaders to quit the town.§ The fanatics hoped to accomplish abroad what they had failed in at home. Some of them went to Prague with a view to reviving the old Taborite sect there,—an attempt which proved abortive. The others, of whom it is more especially our business to speak, came to Wittenberg, where they found the ground admirably prepared for the seed they had to sow, by the universal restlessness of minds craving for some unknown novelty, not only among the excitable class of students, but even among the townspeople. We accordingly find that after their arrival in Wittenberg the agitation assumed a bolder character.

Carlstadt, with whom they immediately allied themselves, introduced more striking innovations every day. The priestly garments were abolished and auricular confession disused. People went to receive the sacrament without preparation, and imagined that they had gained an important point, when they took the host with their own hands instead of receiving it from those of the priest. It was held to be the mark of a purer Christianity to eat eggs and meat on fast days especially. The pictures in the churches were now esteemed an abomination in the holy place. Carlstadt disregarded the distinction which had always been made between reverence and adoration, and applied all the texts in the Bible directed against idolatry to the worship of images. He insisted upon the fact that people bowed and knelt before them, and lighted tapers, and brought offerings, that, for example, they contemplated the image of St. Christopher, in order that they might be preserved against sudden death; he therefore exhorted his followers to attack and destroy "these painted gods, these idol logs." He would not even tolerate the crucifix, because he said men called it their God, whereas it could only remind them of the bodily sufferings of Christ. It had been determined that the images should be removed from the churches, but as this was not immediately executed, his zeal became more fiery‖; at his instigation an iconoclast riot now commenced, similar to those which half a century afterwards broke out in so many other countries. The images were torn from the altars, chopped in pieces and burnt. It is obvious that these acts of violence gave a most

* A report sent from Zwickau to the elector of which he informs the university, gives this account of their opinions. Acta Einsiedeln cum Melanthonio, C. R. p. 536. The statements in Enoch Widemann Chronicon Curiæ, in Mencken, Scriptt. R. G., iii. 744., show a somewhat later development of the fantasies of Storch. Tobias Schmidt's Cronica Cygnea, 1656, is not without its value for the events of the thirty years' war, but is insufficient for the times of the Reformation.

† Official Report of Melanchthon, Jan. 1. 1522. C. R., i. 533, from which it is evident that half a year before, these people had not begun to boast of this communion with God.

‡ *Zeitung aus Wittenberg*, p. 127.

§ According to G. Fabricius, Vita Richii, in Melchior Adam, Vitæ Philosophorum, p. 72.

‖ Von Abtuhung der Bylder. Und das keyn Betdler unther den Christen seyn Soll. Carolstatt in der christlichen Statt Wittenberg. Bog. D. (Concerning the Abolition of Images. And that there should be no worshipper among Christians. Carlstadt in the Christian Town of Wittenberg. Sheet D.) The decree was made on Friday after St. Sebastian, Jan. 24. 1522. The dedication to the paper on the first sheet, which also was first printed, is dated Monday after the conversion of St. Paul, 27th Jan. Carlstadt then had the greatest hopes. The date shows how zealous he was. When he came to the fourth sheet, he plainly saw that matters would not proceed so rapidly. "Ich hette auch gehofft, der lebendig got solt seine eingegeben werk das ist guten willen tzu abtuhung der bilder volzogen und yns eusserlich werk gefurt haben. Aber ess ist noch kein execution geschehen, vileicht der halben, das got seinen tzorn vber vns lest treuffen yn meynung seynen gantzen tzorn ausszuschutten, wu wir alsso blind bleiben vnd furchten vns vor dem dass vns nicht kan thun. Das weiss ich das die Obirsten deshalb gestrafft werden. Dan die schrifft leugt ye nit."—"I had also hoped that the living God would have carried into execution and openly brought to bear his appointed work, that is, good will towards the abolition of images. But no execution has yet taken place, perhaps because God lets his anger drip upon us, intending to pour out all his wrath if we remain thus blind, and fear not that which he is able to do. Thus much I know, that they in high places will be punished therefor. For the Scripture lieth not."

dangerous and menacing character to the whole controversy. Carlstadt not only quoted the Old Testament to show that the secular authorities had power to remove from the churches whatever could give scandal to the faithful, but added, that if the magistrates neglected this duty, the community was justified in carrying out the necessary changes Accordingly the citizens of Wittenberg laid a petition before the council, in which they demanded the formal abolition of all unbiblical ceremonies, masses, vigils, and processions, and unlimited liberty for their preachers. The council was forced to concede these points one after the other;* nor did even these concessions satisfy the innovators Their project was to realise without delay their own conception of a strictly Christian community The council was called upon to close all places of public amusement, not only those which the law prohibited, but those which it had sanctioned; to abolish the mendicant orders who, they said, ought not to exist in Christendom, and to divide the funds of the religious communities, which were pronounced to be altogether mischievous and corrupt, among the poor. To these suggestions of a bigoted fanaticism, blind to the real nature and interests of society, were added the most pernicious doctrines of the Taborites. An old professor like Carlstadt suffered himself to be carried away by the contagion to such a degree as to maintain that there was no need of learned men, or of a course of academic study, and still less of academic honours. In his lectures he advised his hearers to return home and till the ground, for that man ought to eat his bread by the sweat of his brow. One of his most zealous adherents was George Mohr, the rector of the grammar school, who addressed the assembled citizens from the window of the schoolhouse, exhorting them to take away their children Of what use, said he would learning be henceforth? They had now among them the divine prophets of Zwickau, Storch, Thoma, and Stubner, who conversed with God, and were filled with grace and knowledge without any study whatsoever. The common people were of course easily convinced that a layman or an artisan was perfectly qualified for the office of a priest and teacher.

Carlstadt himself went into the houses of the citizens and asked them for an explanation of obscure passages in Scripture, acting on the text that God reveals to babes what he hides from wise men. Students left the university and went home to learn a handicraft, saying that there was no longer any need of study †

The conservative ideas to which Luther had still clung were thus abandoned, the idea of temporal sovereignty, on which he had taken his stand to oppose the encroachments of the priesthood, was now rejected with no less hostility than the spiritual domination. Luther had combated the reigning faith with the weapons of profound learning, one of the rudest theories of inspiration that has ever been broached now threatened to take its place. It is evident, however, that its success was impossible. All the powers of the civilized world would have arisen against such a wild, destructive attempt, and would either have utterly crushed it, or at all events have driven it back within the narrowest limits Had such anarchical dreams ever become predominant, they must have destroyed every hope of improvement which the world could attach to the reforming party.

In Wittenberg there was no one capable of resisting the general frenzy. Melanchthon was then too young and inexperienced, even had he possessed sufficient firmness of character. He held some conferences with the prophets of Zwickau, and finding not only that they were men of talent, but well grounded in the main articles of a faith which was likewise his own; being also unable to refute their arguments concerning infant baptism, he did not feel himself competent to enter the lists against them We find disciples and friends of Melanchthon among their adherents ‡

The elector was equally incapable of offering any efficient resistance. We are already acquainted with the character of this prince,—his temporising policy, his reluctance to interfere in person, his habit of letting things take their own course. His was the most peaceful nature produced by this troubled and warlike age, he never had recourse to arms, when advised to seize Erfurt, on the plea that he might accomplish it with the loss of only five men, he replied, "One were too many"§ Yet his quiet, observant, prudent and enlightened policy had ever been crowned with ultimate success His pleasure was to adorn his own territories, which he thought as beautiful as any on earth, with castles, like those of Lochau, Altenburg, Weimer and Coburg; to decorate his churches with pictures from the admirable pencil of Lucas Kranach, whom he invited to his court; to keep up the high renown of his chapel and quire, which was one of the best in the empire, and to improve the university he had founded

Although not remarkable for popular and accessible manners, he had a sincere affection for the people. He once paid back the poll-tax which had been levied, when the purpose to which it was to be applied was abandoned. 'Truly," said he of somebody, "he is a bad man, for he is unkind to the poor folk" Once, when on a journey, he gave money to the children who were playing by the road-side· "one day, "said he," they will tell how a duke of Saxony rode by and gave each of them something" We read of his sending rare fruits to a sick professor.‖ The elector was now in years, most of the older German princes with whom he had lived in habits of intimacy,

* Strobel, v 128

† Fröschel Tractat vom Priesterthum (Appendix,) 1565 Reprinted in the Unschuldigen Nachrichten, 1731, p 698

‡ e g Martin Borrhaus (Cellarius) of Stuttgard had set on foot a private school for Melanchthon Adam, Vitæ Theolog p 191

§ Luther to John Frederic and Moritz, 1542

‖ Epistola Carlstadii ad Spalatinum in Gerdes Scrinium, vii ii 345.

"his good comrades and friends," as he called them, were dead, and he had many annoyances and vexations to bear. He was in doubt and perplexity as to the real inclinations of the young emperor. "Happy is the man," he exclaimed, "who has nothing to do with courts!" The disagreement between himself and his nearest neighbour and cousin, the turbulent Duke George, became more and more serious and evident. "Ah, my cousin George!" said he,—"truly I have no friend left but my brother,"—and to him he gradually confided the greater share of the government. The protection he afforded to Luther had arisen naturally out of the course of events; at first, partly from political motives, then from a feeling of duty and justice.* Nor was this all; he conscientiously shared the profound, unquestioning veneration for the Scriptures inculcated by Luther. He thought that every thing else, however ingenious and plausible, might be confuted; the word of God alone was holy, majestic, and truth itself. He said that this word should be "pure as an eye." He had a deep reverential fear of opposing or disobeying it. The basis of all religion is this sense of what is sacred—of the moral mystery of the universe; this awe of offending against it under the momentary influence of impurer motives. Such was eminently the religion of Frederic the Wise, and it had withheld him from interfering decidedly and arbitrarily in Luther's behalf, but it also hindered him from exerting his power to put down these new sectarians in Wittenberg, displeasing as they were to him. He did not venture, any more than Melanchthon, to pronounce an absolute condemnation of them. After listening to the doubts and scruples of his counsellors and learned men at Prettin on this subject, he appeared perplexed and overpowered at the idea that these people might possibly be in the right. He said that as a layman he could not understand the question; but that, rather than resist the will of God, he would take his staff in his hand and leave his country.†

It certainly might have come to this. The movement that had begun could lead to nothing short of open rebellion,—to the overthrow of civil government in order to make room for a new Christian republic; violence would then certainly have called forth violence, and good and evil would have perished together.

How much now depended on Luther! Even these disturbances were the offspring or the consequence of ideas that he had set afloat, or were closely connected with them: if he sanctioned them, who would be able to stem the torrent? if he opposed them, it seemed doubtful whether his opposition would have any effect, or whether he himself would not be overwhelmed in the common ruin.

During the whole of this time he was in the Wartburg, at first keeping closely within the walls, then venturing out timidly to gather strawberries on the castle hill, and afterwards, grown bolder, riding about as Junker George, accompanied by a groom. He once even ventured into Wittenberg, trusting to the disguise of his long hair and beard, and completely cased in armour. But though his mode of life and his accoutrements were those of a Reiter, his soul was ever in the heat of ecclesiastical warfare. "When hunting," says he, "I theologized:" the dogs and nets of the hunters represented to him the bishops and stewards of antichrist seeking to entrap and devour unhappy souls.‡ In the solitude of the castle he was again visited by some of the struggles and temptations which had assailed him in the convent. His chief occupation was a translation of the New Testament, and he likewise formed the project of giving to the German nation a more correct translation of the Bible than the Latin church possesses in the Vulgate.§ Whilst endeavouring to fortify his resolution for the accomplishment of this work, and only wishing to be in Wittenberg that he might have the assistance of his friends, he heard of the excitement and disorder prevailing there. He was not for a moment in doubt as to their nature. He said that nothing in the whole course of his life had given him greater pain; all that had been done to injure himself was nothing in the comparison. The pretensions of these men to the character of divinely inspired prophets and to immediate communion with God, did not impose on him; for he too had fathomed the mysterious depths of the spiritual world, and had gained a far deeper insight into it, and a far too exalted conception of the divine nature, to allow himself to be persuaded that God would appear visibly to his creatures, converse with them, or throw them into ecstacies. "If you want to know the time and place and nature of the divine communications," writes he to Melanchthon,‖ "hear; 'Like as a lion he hath crushed my bones,' and 'I am cast out from before thy countenance, my soul is filled with heaviness, and the fear of hell is upon me.' God spake by the mouths of his prophets, because if he spoke himself we could not endure it." He wishes his prince joy of the cross which God has laid upon him, and says that the Gospel was not only persecuted by Annas and Caiaphas, but that there must be a Judas even among the apostles; he also announces his intention of going to Wittenberg himself. The elector entreated him not to leave his retreat so soon, saying that as yet he could do no good, that he had better prepare his defence for the next diet, at which it was to be hoped he would obtain a regular hearing.¶ But Luther was no longer to be restrained by

* His counsellors in Wittenberg declared, on the 2d Jan 1522, "S Ch G hatt sich Doctor Martinus Sachen bisher nicht anders—angenommen, denn allein weil er sich zu Recht erboten, dass er nicht bewaltigt wurde"—"His Christian grace, the elector, had as yet taken up Dr Martinus's cause in no other way beyond offering to see that he had justice, and was not overpowered by force."—*Corp Ref* p 537

† Spalatin, Leben Friedrichs des Weisen. Vermischte Abhandlungen zur sachsischen Gesch. B. v

‡ To Spalatin, 15th Aug. D. W., ii 43

§ To Amsdorf, 13th Jan. p. 123

‖ 13 Jan. 1522, to Amsdorf, p. 125

¶ Instructions to Oswald, Corp. Ref. i. 561

these arguments. never had he been more firmly convinced that he was the interpreter of the divine word and that his faith would be a sufficient protection; the occurrences in Wittenberg seemed to him a disgrace to himself and to the Gospel.* He accordingly set out on his way, regardless of the pope's excommunication or the emperor's ban, bidding his prince have no care about him. He was in a truly heroic state of mind.

A party of young Swiss who were on their way to the University of Wittenberg stopped to dine at the sign of the Black Bear at Jena On entering they saw a horseman who sat at the table resting his right hand on the hilt of his sword, with a Hebrew psalter before him, this horseman, as they afterwards discovered, was Luther, and we read in the notes of one of them, how he invited them to dine with him, and how gentle and dignified was his deportment.† On Friday 7th of March he arrived at Wittenberg; on the Saturday the same Swiss found him surrounded by his friends, inquiring minutely into all that had occurred during his absence On Sunday he began to preach, in order immediately to ascertain whether his popularity and influence were still sufficient to enable him to allay the disturbance Small and obscure as was the scene to which he returned, his success or failure was an event pregnant with important results to the whole world, for it involved the question, whether the doctrine which had forced itself on his conviction from its own inherent weight, and which was destined to give such an impulse to the progress of mankind, had also power to subdue the elements of destruction fermenting in the public mind, that had already undermined the foundations of society and now threatened it with total ruin It had now to be tried whether it were possible to reform without destroying, to open a fresh career to mental activity, without annihilating the results of the labours of former generations Luther's view of the question was that of a preacher and pastor of souls, he did not denounce the changes that had been made as utterly pernicious, nor the doctrines from which they had sprung as fundamentally bad, and he carefully refrained from any personal attacks on the leaders of the new sect. He merely said that they had acted with precipitation, and had thus laid a stumbling-block in the way of the weak and transgressed the commandment of charity. He allowed that there were practices which undoubtedly ought to be abolished, such, for instance, as private masses; but that these reforms ought to be effected without violence or scandal. As to a number of other usages, he thought it indifferent whether a Christian observed them or not That it was a matter of very small importance whether a man received the Lord's Supper in one kind or in both, or whether he preferred a private confession to the general one, or chose rather to remain in his convent or to leave it, to have pictures in the churches, and to keep fasts or not; but that to lay down strict rules concerning these things, to raise violent disputes, and to give offence to weaker brethren, did more harm than good, and was a transgression of the commandment of charity

The danger of the anarchical doctrines now broached, lay in the assumption that they were an indispensable part of true Christianity, an assumption maintained with the same vehemence and confidence on the side of the anabaptists, as the divine and thence infallible origin of every decree of the church was on that of the papists

These doctrines, therefore, like those of the papacy, were intimately bound up with the whole system of morals, and the whole fabric of civil life It was therefore most important to show that religion recognised a neutral and independent province, over which she was not required to exercise a direct sway, and where she needed not to interfere in the guidance of every individual thought This Luther did with the mildness and forbearance of a father and a guide, and with the authority of a profound and comprehensive mind. These sermons are certainly among the most remarkable that he ever preached, they are, like those of Savonarola popular harangues, not spoken to excite and carry away his hearers, but to arrest them in a destructive course, and to assuage and calm their passions ‡ How could his flock resist the well-known voice, the eloquence which carried the conviction it expressed, and which had first led them into the way of inquiry? The construction commonly put upon moderate counsels, namely, that they arise from fear of consequences, could have no place here. Never had Luther appeared in a more heroic light, he bid defiance to the excommunication of the pope and the ban of the emperor, in order to return to his flock, not only had his sovereign warned him that he was unable to protect him, but he had himself expressly renounced his claim to that protection, he exposed himself to the greatest personal danger, and that not (as many others have done) to place himself at the head of a movement, but to check it; not to destroy, but to preserve At his presence the tumult was hushed, the revolt quelled, and order restored; a few even of the most violent party leaders were converted to his opinions and joined him. Carlstadt, who could not be brought to confess his error, was condemned to silence He was reproached with having intruded himself uncalled into the ministry, and was forbidden to enter the pulpit again Some approximation took place between the moderated opinions now maintained by Luther, and those of the civil authorities, who were delivered from the danger that had threatened the state. A treatise of Carlstadt's, written in the same spirit as heretofore, part of which was already printed, was suppressed by the university, and a

* To the elector, 5th March, ii 137.

† From the Chronicle of Kessler, in Bernet, Leben Kesslers, p. 27

‡ "Sieben Predigten D M L so er von dem Sontage Invocavit bis auf den andern Sontag gethan, als er aus seinem Pathmos zu Wittenberg weider ankommen" ("Seven sermons of Doctor Martin Luther delivered by him during the week between the Sunday Invocavit and the following Sunday, when he returned from his Patmos to Wittenberg"—Alt 99

report of it sent to the elector. The Zwickauers once more sought an interview with Luther; he exhorted them not to suffer themselves to be deceived by the illusions of the devil, they answered, that as a proof of their divine mission, they would tell him what were his thoughts at that instant, to this he agreed, upon which they said that he felt a secret inclination towards themselves "God rebuke thee, Satan!" exclaimed Luther He afterwards acknowledged that he had, indeed, been conscious of such a leaning, but their guessing it, he held to be a sign of powers derived from Satan rather than from God,* he accordingly dismissed them with a sort of challenge to their demon to resist his God. If we soften the coarseness of his language, this struggle between two antagonist spirits, the one destructive, the other tutelary, is the expression of a mighty and profound truth.

Wittenberg was now once more quiet, the mass was as far as possible restored, preceded by confession, and the host was received as before with the lips It was celebrated in hallowed garments, with music and all the customary ceremonies, and even in Latin, nothing was omitted but the words of the canon which expressly denote the idea of a sacrifice † In every other respect there was perfect freedom of opinion on these points, and latitude as to forms Luther himself remained in the convent and wore the Augustine dress, but he offered no opposition to others who chose to return to the world. The Lord's Supper was administered in one kind or in both, those who were not satisfied with the general absolution, were at full liberty to require a special one. Questions were continually raised as to the precise limits of what was absolutely forbidden, and what might still be permitted The maxim of Luther and Melanchthon was, to condemn nothing that had not some authentic passage in the Bible,—"clear and undoubted Scripture," as the phrase was,—against it This was not the result of indifference; religion withdrew within the bounds of her own proper province, and the sanctuary of her pure and genuine influences It thus became possible to develope and extend the new system of faith, without waging open warfare with that already established, or, by the sudden subversion of existing authorities, rousing those destructive tendencies, the slightest agitation of which had just threatened such danger to society Even in the theological exposition of these doctrines, it was necessary to keep in view the perils arising from opinions subversive of all sound morality. Luther already began to perceive the danger of insisting on the saving power of faith alone; already he taught that faith should show itself in good conduct, brotherly love, soberness and quiet.‡

The new religious opinions, in assuming the character of a distinct creed, threw off from themselves all that was incongruous, and assumed a more individual, and at the same time a more universal character,—the character inseparable from its origin and tendency. As early as December 1521, in the heat of the disturbances, appeared the first elementary work on theology, founded on the new principles of faith—Melanchthon's 'Loci Communes' This was far from being a complete work, indeed it was originally a mere collection of the opinions of the apostle Paul concerning sin, the law, and grace, made strictly in accordance with those severe views to which Luther had owed his conversion, but remarkable on account of its entire deviation from all existing scholastic theology, and from being the first book which had appeared for several centuries in the Latin church containing a system constructed out of the Bible only Sanctioned by Luther's approbation, it had great success, and in the course of repeated editions it was recast and perfected § The translation of the New Testament by Luther, which he corrected with Melánchthon's assistance on his return to Wittenberg, and published in September 1522, had a still more extensive effect, and acted immediately on the people. Whilst with one hand he emancipated them from the forms imposed on religion by the schools and the hierarchy, with the other he gave to the nation a faithful, intelligent and intelligible translation of the earliest records of Christianity. The national mind had just acquired sufficient ripeness to enable it to apprehend the meaning and value of the gift: in the most momentous stage of its development it was touched and penetrated to its very depths by the genuine expression of unveiled and unadulterated religion. From such influences everything was to be expected. Luther cherished the noble and confident hope that the doctrine alone would accomplish the desired end; that wherever it made its way, a change in the outward condition of society must necessarily follow.

The course pursued by the authorities of the empire, in the altered form they had mean-

* Camerarius, vita Melanchthonis, cap xv

† 'Luther von beider Gestalt des Sacraments zu nehmen "—*Altenb* ii p 126

‡ Eberlin of Gunzberg quotes a remarkable passage from one of his sermons "Vermanung an alle frumen Christen zu Augsburg am Lech "—"Ich hab gehort," says he, "von D Martin Luther in ainer Predig ain gross war wort, das er sagt wie man die sach anfacht, so felt unrat darauf predigt man den glauben allein, als man thon sol so unterlesst man alle zucht und ordnung, prediet man zucht und ordnung so fелt man so gantz darauff das man alle selickait darein setzt und vergisst des glauben, das mittel aber were gut, das man also den glauben lehre das er ausbreche in zucht und ordnung, und also ubte sich in guten siten und in brüederlicher liebe das man doch selickait allein durch den glauben gewertig were"—' An Exhortation to all pious Christians at Augsburg on the Lech "—"I have heard in one of Luther's sermons a great and true saying that as you stir up the matter, some mischief arises, if a man preach faith alone, as he should do, he omits all soberness and order, he insists upon them alone, and places all salvation therein, forgetting faith, the middle course, however, would be the best, that man should so use faith that it should break out in soberness and order, and that they should so exercise themselves in good habits and in brotherly love, as to look for salvation only through faith"

§ The original composition of this book is to be seen by a comparison of the first sketch of it in 1520 (which appears written by many different hands, in Strobel's Neuen Beitragen, v 323) with the first edition of 1521, printed in V D Hardt's Hist Lit Ref, iv

while acquired, not only justified this hope, but led to results calculated to give it still greater assurance.

CHAPTER II

TEMPORAL AND SPIRITUAL TENDENCIES OF THE COUNCIL OF REGENCY.

1521—1523

It is a remarkable and striking coincidence, that the mighty national movement we have just been considering was exactly coeval with the institution of that representative (*ständisch*) form of government which had been the object of such various and persevering exertions.

The emperor, powerful as he was, had been forced to grant it as the condition of his election; the plan was agreed upon at Worms, and was carried into execution in the autumn of 1521. The electors and the circles severally elected deputies, who, as we find, were freed from their feudal obligations, and exhorted to attend only to the general welfare of the empire. The old acts of the Imperial Chamber, weighing many hundred weight, and containing the pleadings in about 3500 long pending and yet undecided suits, and a vast number of fresh plaints on which no proceedings had yet been taken, were transported to Nurnberg.* One by one the deputies arrived; those from the emperor, the last of all. During the course of the month of November they got so far as to open first the Council of Regency, and then the Imperial Chamber.

At first they had to endure a great deal from the interference of the imperial councillors,† the same, for the most part, with whom the States had had such frequent disputes under Maximilian, and who were still unwilling to give up any of their lucrative privileges, and still, as formerly, accused of taking bribes. Very strange things occurred; among others, the Bishop of Würzburg had seized the person of a certain Raminger, who was furnished with a safe conduct from the emperor, and kept him prisoner. The Council of Regency very properly took the injured man under their protection. Their surprise may be conceived when a declaration arrived from the emperor, that he had given the safe conduct without reflection, and that it could not be supposed that the Bishop of Wurzburg had violated a real imperial safe conduct. It made no difference whether the States supported the Regency or not. The States met in March 1522, and both bodies jointly interceded for the Bishop of Hildesheim, who complained of the ban which had been pronounced against him and his friends, without any previous summons and trial. But the emperor would not endure any interference with "his affairs," and rejected the intercession with some short unmeaning answer.

Towards the end of May the emperor quitted the Netherlands. His presence was required in Spain to quiet the disturbances of the Comunidades, and his mind fully occupied with the perplexities of the war he had begun in Italy, and with the extraordinary conquests and discoveries made on a distant continent by a handful of fortunate and intelligent Castilian adventurers serving under his banner. Even the German councillors who accompanied him could not possibly influence the details of the administration of Germany from so distant a country as Spain. At this time, therefore, the Council of Regency first acquired complete independence. The young emperor's presence had been needed to confer upon it the authority which his absence now left it at liberty to exercise.

Let us first consider the temporal part of its administration.

Several very important matters had come under consideration, above all, the executive ordinance, on the plan proposed in the year 1512, and then so violently resisted by Maximilian, was determined upon, namely, that the circles should elect their own captains or governors. The affairs of Turkey and Hungary also urgently demanded attention. Whilst the two principal rulers of Christendom inflamed their natural jealousy into bitterer antipathy in the Italian wars, the potentate of the Osman empire led out his armies, fired by hatred of the Christians and love of conquest, and took possession of Belgrade, the ancient bulwark of Christendom, which was but feebly defended on that frontier. Germany was not insensible to the danger. The States met expressly on this account in the spring of 1522.‡

* Hans v. d. Planitz to Friederich v. Sachsen, 18 Oct 1521, according to communication made by Adam v. Beichlingen. The correspondence of Planitz, in two volumes, and a smaller pamphlet in the Archives of Weimar, are the authorities for the following. Harpprecht and Müller (Statts Cabinett, i.) give very superficial information.

† Planitz says, as early as the 18th October, "Churfursten Fursten und Andre so itzund allhie vorhanden haben Beisorge es werde bei etzlichen Kaiserischen gefleissigt, ob sülch Vornemen des Regiments in Verhinderung oder Aenderung gestellt werden mocht."—"The electors, princes and others, at this present here assembled, have a fear that some of the imperial court are busied in endeavours to hinder, or at least to alter, this project of the Council of Regency." On the 14th of May he mentions a certain Rem, who after long imprisonment succeeded in obtaining an imperial absolution. "Ist vermuthlich weil das Regiment die Sach zu sich forderet und die Sach den Hofretten nicht gestatten wollte, hierin zu handeln, das sie die Absolution gefürdert, damit das Regiment auch nichts daran haben solt."—"It is probable, since the Regency brought the matter within its own jurisdiction, and did not allow the imperial councillors to act in it at all, that the latter furthered the absolution in order to take it out of the hands of the Regency." The letters are full of similar expressions.

‡ The summons is dated Feb. 12. for the Sunday Oculi (March 23, 1522) so as to allow time to arm. On March 28, a number of the States were present, and processions and prayers were ordered. "Damit S. gottlich Barmherzigkeit den Zorn, ob und wie wir den durch unsre Schuld und Missethat verschuldet hatten, von uns wende."—"In order that the Almighty mercy may turn from us the wrath which we have brought upon ourselves by our guilt and misdeeds." The Proposition was made on the 7th of April: the emperor therein declared that he gave up the supplies voted for his expedition to Rome to be applied to the war against the Turks. The States determined to vote three-eighths thereof to the war,—not, how-

and again in the autumn, a part of the supplies which had been granted to the emperor for his expedition to Rome were, with his permission, appropriated to the succour of the Hungarians. Schemes for the complete equipment of an army, to be kept always in readiness for the same purpose, were proposed and discussed. The main point, however, on which every thing else depended, was the secure establishment of the form of government itself. Every day showed the inconveniencies of allowing the salaries of the members of the Imperial Chamber and the Regency to be dependent on the matricular taxes, which were granted from year to year, and were always difficult to collect, neither would it do to leave these salaries to be paid by the emperor, as it was justly feared he would then raise a claim to appoint the members himself. Many other expedients were proposed, such as the application of the annates to this purpose, a tax upon the Jews; or finally, the re-imposition of the Common Penny, in connection with a permanent war establishment. But all were alike impracticable. For the annates, a previous agreement with the see of Rome was necessary, and that was not so easily made. The towns which had obtained from earlier emperors the right of taxing their own Jews (a right which they had lately maintained in opposition to the imperial fiscal) absolutely refused to surrender it. As to a return to the Common Penny, it did not get beyond a mere project, and was not even seriously debated. Under these circumstances, the Council of Regency adopted a plan which had formerly been entertained, and which, in itself, must have been productive of very important national consequences, besides being connected with other views of the administration of the empire well worthy of our attention.

Among the charges and complaints which the several classes of the community made against each other in those times, one which was urged with the greatest frequency and vehemence was directed against the merchants.

Commerce still travelled along its accustomed roads, the Hanse Towns still enjoyed most of their privileges in foreign countries, peace had restored the markets of Venice; but the splendour and importance of this traffic was eclipsed by the brilliant and adventurous commerce across the seas, to which the discovery of both the Indies had given rise. Some of the great commercial houses of Upper Germany placed themselves in immediate communication with Lisbon, or shared in the West Indian enterprises of the Spaniards. Antwerp owed its prosperity chiefly to being the emporium of German maritime trade.

In Germany, however, no one was satisfied; the stricter part of the community disapproved the importation of new luxuries and wants; others complained of the quantity of money sent out of the country, and almost all were discontented at the high prices of the wares. During the years 1516 to 1522, especially, a general rise in prices was observed. Cinnamon cost upwards of a gulden the pound, sugar from twelve to twenty gulden the cwt., and some of the East Indian spices had risen to four times their former price.* Several causes might conduce to this effect, such as increased luxury and consequent demand, the Venetian war, which had interrupted the course of trade, and a diminution of the value of money, arising from the importation of precious metals from America, which began to be felt, though far from what it afterwards became. At that period, however, the cause was chiefly sought, and perhaps not without justice, in the system of monopoly arising from the combination of the great commercial houses, a practice which had continued to increase, in spite of the repeated enactments of the diets. They were already, it was alleged, possessed of such an amount of capital and such numerous and extensive factories; that no one could possibly compete with them. They were willing to give the King of Portugal higher prices even than he had previously asked, only on condition that he would demand still higher from those who came after them. It was calculated that every year 30,000 cwt. of pepper and 2000 cwt. of ginger were imported into Germany, and that within a few years, the first had risen in price from 18 to 32 kreutzers per lb., and the second from 21 kreutzers to one gulden, 3 kreutzers; this must, of course, have afforded an enormous profit.

As Rome was constantly assailed for her sale of indulgences, and the knights for their robberies, so the merchants and commercial towns were now incessantly inveighed against for their extortions. At all events, the Frankfurters attributed the disfavour shown them for some time past in their transactions with the Estates of the empire, almost exclusively to the unpopularity of monopolists.

At the diet of 1522–23, the resolution was taken to interdict all companies possessing a capital of more than 50,000 gulden. they were to be allowed a year and a half to dissolve their

ever in men, but in money everything was done in haste, as a better method of equipment was to be arranged in a conference with the Hungarian commissioners. The Frankfort deputy thought that little would be effected, but "aufs fürderlichste wieder zum Thor hinaus"—"That they would be out of the gate again as fast as possible." The chief delay was caused by the disputes in the sessions of the colleges. "Der Sachen halber bleiben andre Handel unausgerichtet und wir verzehren das Unsre ohne Nutzen."—"For the sake of these, other affairs remained undetermined, and we eat up our substance without profit." The order is dated May 7 (Frank A.) At the following diet, in Dec. 1522 two fourths more of the money intended for the expedition to Rome were voted for this service.

* I have extracted the following tables from a decree of the select Committee on Monopolies in 1523 (Frank A.) —

The best saffron from Catalonia, which in	1516	cost 3 g. 6 kr	cost, in	1522,	4 g 15 kr
Second rate do	1519	2 g 21 to 27 kr		—	4 g
Cloves	1512	19 schill	—	—	2 g
Stick cinnamon	1516	1 g 18 kr.	—	1518	2 g 3 ort
Short do	1513	3 ort	—	1519	1 g 21 kr
Nutmeg	1519	27 kr	—	1522	3 g 28 kr
Mace	1518	1 g 6 kr	—	—	4 g 6 kr.
Best pepper in the husk	1518	18 kr	—	—	32 kr
Ginger, formerly from 21 to 24 kr			—	1516	1 g 3 kr
Galingal — 1 g 36 kr			—	—	1 g 39 kr
Sugar, the hundred weight	1516	11 to 12 g	—	1518	20 g
Sugar candy	1516	16 to 17 g	—	1522	20 to 21 g.
Venetian almonds, the cwt	1518	8 g	—	—	— 12 g.
Do raisins	1518	5 g	—	—	— 9 g
Do. figs	1518	3 g 2 sch.	—	—	4 g 1 ort

partnership. It was hoped that this would enable the smaller commercial houses to enter into competition with the great ones, and would also have the effect of preventing the accumulation of money and merchandise in few hands

Overlooking the enormous advantages afforded by foreign commerce, however carried on, the diet conceived the idea of covering the general deficiencies of the state by a tax upon trade. It was notorious that each individual prince drew the greater part of his revenues from the tolls, the right of levying which had been granted to him by former emperors, and as it was evident that no direct tax could be collected, a plan was adopted for an indirect one, in the form of a general system of import duties to be levied for the use of the empire.*

This project is worthy of a moment's attention; if carried into execution it must have produced incalculable results, but it is remarkable that it could even be entertained. So early as the year 1521 it was discussed, the Elector Joachim I. of Brandenburg adopted it with great eagerness and continually recommended it.

In the spring of 1522 the States were really resolved to accede to it, principally because it did not appear burdensome to the common people, but in order to make sure of carrying it into effect, they determined to ask the previous consent of the emperor, before taking any further step.

This consent having been received from Spain, accompanied, however, with the condition that the further provisions should be again submitted to him for approbation, a commission was appointed at the diet of 1522–23, by the general vote of the States, to work out the plan in detail.*

The commission went on the principle of leaving all the necessaries of life duty-free. Under this head were classed corn, wine, beer, cattle for draught and slaughter, and leather All other articles were to pay both an import and export duty, not to be regulated either by weight or by a tariff, which would have occasioned a great deal of troublesome investigation, but by the price at which the article was bought, to be stated by the purchaser, upon this the duty was to be four per cent.

The whole extent of the Roman empire inhabited by the German race was to be surrounded by a line of custom-houses, which was to begin at Nikolsburg in Moravia, and thence pass towards Hungary through Vienna and Gratz to Villach or Tarvis, thence to extend along the Alps towards Venice and Milan. Custom-house stations were to be erected in Trent, Brunegg, Insbruck, and Feldkirchen. The frontier of Switzerland, which refused to submit to the imposition of the duty, was to be guarded by custom-houses, the line was then to cross the Rhine and run through Strasburg, Metz, Luxemburg, and Treves, to Aix-la-chapelle, which would bring it near the coast and within the region of maritime commerce. The Netherlands were without hesitation considered as part of the empire, Utrecht and Dordrecht, as well as Cologne and Wesel, were proposed as custom-house stations for inland trade, Antwerp, Bruges and Bergen-op-zoom, for maritime trade, especially that with England and Portugal The line was thence to follow the coast northward and eastward. Towards Denmark, which according to public law was still regarded as a permanent confederate of the empire, the Hanse towns, from Hamburg to Danzig inclusive, were to be the custom-house ports, towards Poland, Konigsberg in the Newmark and Frankfurt on the Oder, besides a few other towns in Silesia and Lusatia.

Much was still left undetermined in this project; for instance, it was immediately proposed that the frontiers should be surveyed, in order to ascertain whether better places could not be found for the prevention of smuggling, than those already named it was still a matter of doubt whether Bohemia could be included, and neither Prussia nor Livonia had yet been taken into consideration, but all these were mere details which could easily be determined when the project was carried into execution,—the main point was seriously resolved upon

As might have been expected, the whole commercial body thought it would be injured by this measure, which it attributed merely to the hostility generally shown towards itself, and accordingly raised numerous objections to it, more or less well founded. An attempt was made to answer all these objections at length. The example of neighbouring kingdoms was cited, where much heavier restrictions existed, and where, nevertheless, trade was most flourishing. It was argued that the duty by no means fell on the merchant, but on the consumer, and that it would be a prodigious advantage to commerce if, by means of this tax, the disturbances in the empire could be put down, and general security restored

At all events, it cannot be denied that this project might have been the means of producing the most important results for the future fate of Germany The establishment of accurately defined and well guarded frontiers, the entire circumference of which were closely bound to a common active centre, would in itself have been a great advantage, this alone would have at once awakened a universal feeling of the unity of the empire Besides, the whole administration would have assumed a different character. The most important national institution, the Council of Regency, the formation of which had cost so much labour, would by this means have acquired a natural and firm basis, and sufficient power for the maintenance of order As yet there was no peace throughout the country, all the roads were unsafe, it was impossible to reckon on the execution of any sentence or decree. But had this ordinance been vigorously carried into effect, the Regency would have had the means of paying the governors and councillors in the circles, so often discussed, and of maintaining a certain number of troops under their own orders and those of the subordinate authorities.

* "Ordnung ains gemainen Reichs Zolls in Ratschlag verfast"—*Fr Ar* vol xxxviii "Ordinance for customs' duties for the whole empire,"—a document which I intend to give in the Appendix

In the spring of 1523 it seemed as if this point would certainly be achieved: the plan was again sent for final confirmation to the emperor, who was already bound by his former consent.

It is evident that the Council of Regency entertained the project of constituting itself a powerful central government, and, in conjunction with the States, resorted to every possible expedient to accomplish this end, in spite of all opposition.

Hence the question, what course this rising power would take with respect to the religious movement, acquired additional importance.

At the beginning of the year 1522 the feelings of the Council of Regency were much opposed to the innovation. Duke George of Saxony was present, in whom a natural attachment to traditionary opinions,* the various old quarrels with his cousins of the Ernestine line, and a personal dislike to the bold and reckless monk, combined to raise a violent and active hostility to the new doctrines. The disturbances in Wittenberg happened opportunely to give more weight to his accusations; and he actually obtained an edict in which the Regency exhorted the neighbouring bishoprics of Naumburg, Meissen, and Merseburg not to allow the innovations to be forced upon them, but to maintain the customary rites and practices of the church.†

But in the course of the next three months, when news arrived that the disturbances had ceased, the feelings of the Council of Regency underwent a total change. One subject of discussion, of course, was Luther's return to Wittenberg, by which he had openly bidden defiance to the imperial ban, and Duke George even proposed an appeal to the immediate intervention of the emperor; this, however, merely wounded the self-love of the Council of Regency. John of Planitz, the envoy of Elector Frederic, would not hear his master blamed for permitting Luther to remain in Wittenberg; nor would he allow it to be said that the monk's doctrine was heresy. "The receiving the sacraments in both kinds, the marriage of a few priests, and the desertion of the convent by a few monks, could not, he said, be called heresies; these acts were merely opposed to regulations established not long since by popes and councils, and which would perhaps be eventually abolished. If, on the other hand, Luther were banished, imitators of him would arise, but animated with a different spirit; who, instead of preaching only against the dogmas of the church, might declaim against Christianity and God himself; and not only a rebellion, but complete unbelief might be the result." This envoy was a man of talent, equally resolute and dexterous: he was strongly in favour of Luther, less indeed from religious belief—although in the main their opinions were the same—than from the conviction that Luther's cause was equally the cause of his prince, of the Council of Regency, and of the empire.

In the summer of 1522 it was the turn of the Elector Frederic to attend the Council of Regency in person. He was one of the few who remained of the old school of princes, to whom that body owed its establishment, and he had lately taken the most active part in the firm settlement of its constitution. He had already been frequently consulted concerning questions of form. His calm judgment, his well-known experience, and the universal respect paid to his acknowledged integrity and talents for business, invested him with singular authority.‡ He might indeed at this time be said to govern the empire, in as far as it could be governed at all.

Under these circumstances, it is evident that Luther, who enjoyed so fully the favour of this prince, had nothing to fear from the Council of Regency. Duke George continued to attack him before that assembly: he repeatedly complained of the monk's violence, and of the abuse which he poured forth against the princes of the empire, the emperor, and the pope. Never perhaps was a more evasive answer given than that which he received from the Council of Regency, to one of these accusations. "We perceive," they write on the 16th of August, "that your grace feels displeasure at insults to the pope's holiness and the emperor's majesty, and we thereupon make known to your grace, that we would not patiently endure insult or injury to the emperor's majesty, wherever we should see or hear of it."§ No wonder that, when the duke afterwards complained of this answer to the lieutenant of the empire, Count Palatine Frederic, he replied that at that time there was nothing to be done in matters of this kind.

An independent party favourable to Luther was now forming in the Council of Regency. It was, it is true, subject to fluctuations from the entrance of new members every quarter of a year; but from the permanent operation of

* Duke George said to our informant Planitz: "Wenn S. F. Gn. nicht micht der Tatt und Gewalt dazu thät, würd S. Gn. Land schyr gar ketzerisch: wollten alle die behemische Weis an sich nemen, und sub utraque communiciren: *er gedächt es aber mit Gewalt zu weren.*"—"If his princely grace did not interfere with might and deed, his grace's subjects would soon become sheer heretics, for they all wanted to follow the Bohemian fashion, and to communicate sub utraque; *but that he intended to prevent it by force.*"—*Letter of the 2d Jan.* 1522.

† Resolution und Decisum, &c., 20th Jan. 1522. Walch xv. 2616. The Appendix No. 10 is remarkable; "Bis so lang durch Versehung der gemeinen Reichsstände, christliche Versammlung oder Concilia solcher Sachen halben, eine bedächtliche wohlerwogene gegründete gewisse Erklärung—vorgenommen werde."—"Until such time as, by the care of the general Estates of the empire, a christian assembly, or council for such matters, shall have made a prudent, deliberate, well grounded, and certain declaration of faith." From this passage we may perceive the existence of another tendency, although as yet vague.

‡ The Elector of Treves hearing that Frederic was ill, sent him word through his minister, "E. Ch. Gn. solten vest halten, nicht krank werden noch abgehen, denn man hett im Reich E. Ch. Gn. nye als wol bedurft als itzund, nachdem E. Ch. Gn. wusste, wye es allenthalben im Reiche stünde."—"Your Electoral Grace must stand firm, and not fall sick nor die, for your Electoral Grace was never so greatly needed by the empire as now, for your Electoral Grace knows how matters stand in the empire." —*Planitz*, 1st Nov. 1521.

§ Instruction to the Regency at Nürnberg. Answer to the same; letter from Duke George, dated the Tuesday after the Nativity of the Virgin (9th Sept.), and from Otto Pack to the duke, the Monday before the XImille Virginum (20th Oct.)—*Dresden Archives*

principles once imbibed, it always regained the upper hand, and, in fact, constituted a majority. Here was, indeed, a wonderful change in the aspect of affairs!—In 1521 the emperor published sentence of ban against Luther, and in 1522–23, the body which represented the imperial power, took him, though still under ban, under its protection, and even approximated to his opinions. That body was, of course, not affected by the political combinations which had influenced the emperor.

The bias it had received was all the more important, since the States had assembled during the last months of the one year and the first of the ensuing; and at the instigation of the new pope, Adrian VI., were to come to a decision concerning the Lutheran affairs.

Adrian VI. was undoubtedly an extremely well-intentioned man. He had formerly been professor at Louvain, and had even then zealously reproved the arrogance of the priesthood, and the waste and misapplication of church property.* He subsequently became tutor to Charles V., and took part in the administration of affairs in Spain, where he imbibed a thorough disgust of the worldly tendencies of the papacy. He was therefore strongly disposed to attempt some reform. He declared that he had only bent his neck under the yoke of the papal dignity, in order to restore the defiled bride of Christ to her original purity. At the same time he was a decided opponent of Luther, and belonged to those 'Magistri nostri' of Louvain, who had so long waged war against the innovating literature and theology; he had expressed unqualified approbation of the opinions professed by that university. The orthodox dominican tendency, which, as early as 1520, had once more formed a close alliance with the court of Rome, had now obtained a temporary sovereignty in his person.

In conformity with these sentiments were the instructions which Adrian gave to his nuncio Chieregati, whom he sent to the German diet. He looked upon the spread of Lutheran doctrines as a punishment for the sins of the prelates. "We are aware," said he, "that, some years ago, many abominations took place in this chair: every thing was turned to evil, and the corruption spread from the head to the members, from the pope to the prelates." Whilst he now declared himself willing to reform the existing abuses, he at the same time exhorted the States of Germany to offer a determined resistance to the diffusion of Luther's opinions;† and brought forward eight arguments in favour of that course, which he thought of irresistible cogency.

An answer to these propositions of the pope had now to be given, and a resolution to be formed upon them. This duty devolved on the Council of Regency.

At the first appearance of the nuncio, a trial of strength ensued between the two parties in that body. The orthodox minority brought forward a complaint from the nuncio, concerning two or three preachers who proclaimed the Lutheran tenets under the very eyes of the Regency, to their and his serious offence. Archduke Ferdinand, who then filled the office of lieutenant of the empire, and the Elector of Brandenburg, who was the next in succession for the ensuing quarter, declared themselves in favour of the nuncio. The majority, however, led by Planitz, resolutely opposed them. This gave rise to several violent discussions. Ferdinand exclaimed, "I am here in the place of the emperor."—"Yes, certainly," rejoined Planitz, "but in conjunction with the Council of Regency, and subject to the laws of the empire;"—and, in accordance with his suggestion, the affair was referred to the States;‡ i. e. indefinitely adjourned. It is easy to imagine that this increased the boldness and vehemence of the Lutheran preachers. "Even if the pope," exclaimed one of them in the church of St. Lawrence, "had a fourth crown added to the three he already wears, he should not make me forsake the word of God." Thus was defiance hurled from the pulpit against the pope, before the very eyes of his nuncio.

Under these circumstances the Council of Regency appointed a committee to draw up the answer which the States should give to the nuncio. This committee, like the Regency itself, contained representatives of both parties; some of its members belonging to the clergy, and others to the laity, and for a time it was doubtful which side had the majority. This was however very soon decided.

The most influential member was undoubtedly Johann von Schwarzenberg, the Hofmeister of Bamberg, who was now advanced in life. In his early youth he had quitted the dissipation of a court which had threatened to hurry him along in its vortex, and, in consequence of his father's admonition, had formed earnest and effectual resolutions of a virtuous life; from that time he had devoted himself with untiring perseverance to study and to the service of the state. We have translations of some of Cicero's works, bearing his name, in which he has carefully adopted the purest and most intelligible forms of the language of his age.§ The first criminal code for Bamberg, if not

* Extracts from his "Commentary in Quartum Sententiarum," in the letter of Joh. Lanoy to Henr. Barillon; Burman's Vita Adriani, p. 300.

† "Expergiscantur, excitentur—et ad executionem sententiæ apostolicæ ac imperialis edicti præfati omnino procedant. Detur venia iis qui errores suos abjurare voluerint."—*Instructio pro Cheregato.*

‡ Planitz relates this himself, on the 4th Jan. 1523. The States answered, that it was a grave matter which required much consideration: they asked for copies of the brief and of the instruction, and wished "etzliche darüber verordnen, die die Sach mit Fleiss bewegen." "In der Stadt ist gross Murmeln, will nicht rathen, das man einen gefangen annehme."—"To appoint certain people who should manage the matter with diligence." "In the town is much murmuring. I cannot advise that any person should be imprisoned."

§ *e. g.* De Senectute. Neuber's was revised and collated with the text by Hutten, and put into Hoffränkisch Deutsch by Schwarzenberg. Neuber's translation of the De Officiis was put into "zierlicher Hochteutsch,"—"elegant High German,"—by Schwarzenberg, and then revised by a third person to see "obs dem Lateyn gemess sey,"—"whether it were according to the Latin." Christ praises it for the "emergens e stilo nativa et vere Germanica simplicitas." De Amicitia was translated "von Synnen zu Synnen, nicht von Worten zu Worten,"—"from sense to sense, not from words to words."—*See Degen, Literatur der Ubersetzungen*, i. 55.

entirely his work, was at least in great measure constructed by him. In this he evinces as much capacity for appreciating the value of traditional and local usages (for he adheres in the main to the old customary law of the city of Bamberg) as the scientific merits of the Roman law. Wherever he applies the principles of the latter to supply some deficiency, he does it in a manner corresponding with existing maxims.* He was, as we see, a man of original and productive talent, both in literature and in politics: he expressed his wonder how any one could find the time too long. He eagerly embraced the Lutheran cause at its very first appearance, finding in it the scientific and practical tendencies of his own mind exalted by an alliance with religious sentiments and aims. He accordingly exchanged several very serious letters on the subject with one of his sons, and removed one of his daughters from her convent; indeed his mind was entirely engrossed by the new opinions.† With all the force of a full and well-grounded conviction, armed against every objection, he adopted them, and, partly perhaps owing to the high and important station he filled, he carried with him the minds of his colleagues; some because they already inclined to those opinions—like Sebastian von Rotenhan and Dr. Zoch, and others, like the Bishop of Augsburg, because they knew not, just then at least, what resistance to offer. Those who did not share these opinions, such as Dr. v. Werthern, the envoy from Duke George, and the Archbishop of Salzburg, found it better to stay away from the assembly. Thus, with very slight opposition, this committee, which now represented the central government of the empire, agreed upon a report in a spirit of decided opposition to the papacy, and of the greatest importance to the whole future progress of the new doctrines.

This report was based on the admissions and promises of reform made by the pope, which the committee accepted, but without giving in return the promise which the pope demanded,—to unite with him in the endeavour to crush the Lutheran doctrines. On the contrary, it declared that these admitted abuses rendered it impossible to carry into execution the bull of Leo X. and the edict of Worms, for that Luther had been the first to expose these abuses, and any display of rigour towards him would make every one believe that it was the object of the government "to suppress the truth of the Gospel by tyranny, and to maintain unchristian abuses, wherefrom nothing could arise but resistance to authority, sedition and heresy." The pope was exhorted to adhere to the concordats, to redress the grievances of the German nation, and above all, to abolish annates; it was not indeed pretended that these reforms would now suffice to put an end to the schism; that, it was said, could only be effected by a council. The convocation of a council, which would occupy men's minds for half a century, had already been the subject of a serious conversation between the nuncio and Planitz, and was now officially agitated by the committee of the Council of Regency. Some of the conditions were at once stated by it; they were as follows:—The council to be convoked by the pope's holiness, with the assent of the emperor's majesty, as befitted the respective privileges of the two sovereigns; to be held at a convenient neutral town without delay; to begin within a year, and under a form materially differing from any previous council. One important innovation was, that the laity were to be allowed a seat and a voice in it, and all present were to be absolved from every obligation which might restrain them from bringing forward whatever might be of service in "godly, evangelical, and other generally profitable affairs." An assembly thus constituted would have answered to the Lutheran ideas respecting the Church, and would have been totally different from what the Council of Trent afterwards was. In answer to the inquiry, what course would be pursued till the council had given its decision, the committee answered, that they should hope, in case the pope agreed to their proposals, to prevail on the Elector Frederic and on Luther, that neither the latter nor his followers should write or preach any thing which might occasion irritation and disorder; they should only teach the Holy Gospel and the authentic Scriptures according to the true Christian sense. These last conditions were of course the most important; all the rest was vague and remote, but these would serve as a rule of conduct for the present moment. They were, as may be easily perceived, entirely in accordance with the opinions which prevailed at Wittenberg and at the court of Saxony, and were evidently proposed with the intention of promoting the free development of the doctrine embraced there. The 13th January, 1523, was the day on which this ever-memorable decision of the States was announced for further discussion. Hans von Planitz joyfully sent it to his master on the very same day.‡

A great fermentation, and sharp collisions between the clerical and lay members began moreover to be observable in the States. It had indeed at first appeared as if both intended to make common cause against Rome, and at Worms the bishops had stated their own peculiar grievances in addition to those of the German nation; yet it was there that the division began; the clergy found that their interests were touched by the complaints of the laity, and resolved to defend their prescriptive rights. Several outbreaks of this animosity had already taken place in that assembly. A memorial from the cities, full of the most violent invective, was read, and the head of the German clergy, the Elector of Mainz, warmly expressed his

* Zöpfl das alte Bamberger Recht als Quelle der Carolina, pp. 166, 170.

† There is a notice of him in Strobel Vermischte Beiträge, 1775, No. 1. Heller, Reformationsgeschichte von Bamberg, p. 45.

‡ "Wess der Ausschuss zu pepstlicher Heiligkeit Antwurdt den lutherischen Handell betreffen verordnet derhalb gerathschlagt hat."—"What the committee argued and decided with respect to his papal holiness's answer concerning the Lutheran affairs."—*Frankf. R. A. A.*, tom. xxxviii. f. 99.

displeasure at it It appeared, he said, as if the clergy were to be treated like criminals, and not to be secure from personal violence. But even the most zealously catholic lay princes demanded reforms, and if a prince had given no instructions on the subject himself, his councillors of their own accord inclined to that side The grievances of the nation were again recapitulated,—this time indeed without the participation of the clergy, but with much more vehemence, and with many additions, chiefly directed against the clergy themselves, for the thousandfold abuses enumerated, no reform was more strongly urged than the separation of the spiritual from the temporal jurisdiction

Nothing could be more calculated to drive these two hostile parties into open warfare than the report which the committee of the Council of Regency had sent in to the States

The clergy did, however, succeed in introducing some modifications into it.

First of all, the admissions quoted from the papal brief were only allowed to stand as far as they regarded the pope himself the words relating to priests and prelates were struck out * Then no mention was made of the claims of the laity to a seat and voice in the council A single phrase was frequently the cause of violent disputes, for instance, the clergy would not admit the word "evangelical" into the article concerning obligations, whereupon such offensive expressions were used by the lay party, that the Elector of Mainz left the assembly and rode home to his lodging. In the end however the majority decided in his favour, and the word was omitted.

Whatever were the changes made in particular expressions, the main point was left unaltered, the States declined to carry into execution the edict of Worms, † a council was demanded, which was to begin, if possible, within a year, in a German town, and with the co-operation of the emperor a suggestion was even made to alter the form of such an assembly, and the participation of the temporal states in it was tacitly assumed; both clergy and laity were to be relieved from all obligations restrictive of the free utterance of opinion. In short, the party which strove to alter the entire constitution of the Church had now decidedly the upper hand in both estates of the empire The clergy were aware of the necessity of a change, and the laity eagerly pressed for it,—it is said that even Duke Louis of Bavaria insisted upon it, in spite of the opposition of the adherents of Rome ‡

The only points that now remained to be discussed—and for the present the most important —were, the conduct of affairs in the interval before the convocation of the council, and the degree of liberty of speech and action which was to be allowed to writers and preachers.

On this question the clergy succeeded in introducing still further restrictions They insisted that the elector should be requested not alone to prohibit whatever might lead to disorder, but to allow nothing whatever to be written, printed or done by Luther or his followers; and also that the request should be made immediately, without waiting for the pope's consent to the council The Saxon envoy to the diet, Philip von Feilitzsch, endeavoured to maintain the terms proposed by the Council of Regency, and failing in this, protested that "his prince could not consider himself bound by this resolution, and would always know how to act in a christian, praiseworthy and irreproachable manner."

Thus we see that in this contest the victory inclined first to one side and then to the other. The two parties collected all their forces for the last point at issue, which was, perhaps, still more important than the preceding one, as it was to decide the latitude to be allowed to preaching, a matter which immediately concerned the mass of the people The clergy were not satisfied with merely directing the preachers to confine themselves to the Gospel and to writers approved by the Church, but required a more accurate specification of what was meant by the latter, and wished to include the four great Latin fathers, Jerome, Augustin, Ambrose and Gregory, to whom they ascribed canonical authority. This is the more remarkable, since a century earlier the more explicit of the Hussite doctrines had been regarded mainly as a departure from these four founders of the Latin church But the nation was now so deeply imbued with the spirit of Luther's teaching, that it would no longer be bound by the particular form and character assumed by the Latin church; the common sense of the people revolted against the imputing to St Paul less authority than to Ambrose. The time was past in which the clergy could carry their point. After a great deal of debating, a resolution was passed, which was in reality only a more complete expression of the meaning of the original proposition. It was decreed, that nothing should be taught but the pure, true and holy Gospel, mildly, piously and in a Christian spirit, according to the doctrine and interpretation of writings approved and accepted by the

* In the rough draft it is stated "Ist von Ppl Heilig keit woll angezeigt dass solches von wegen der Sund beschee und dass die Sund des Volks von den Sunden der Priester und Pralaten herfliessen, und dass darum dieselben zuforderst und am ersten als die endlich Ursach solcher Krankheit von der Wurzel geheilt gestraft und abgewendet werden soll"—"It is well shown by his holiness the pope that such things happen on account of sin, and that the sinfulness of the people flows from the sins of the priests and prelates, that these therefore should, first and fore most as the ultimate cause of such evil, be cured from the root upwards, and should be cured, punished and turned from their evil ways" This passage is wanting in the answer which was really sent to the papal nuncio —*See the reprint in Walch*, xv p 2551 No 8.

† This was expressed in the following manner in the answer given to the nuncio "Majori namque populi parti jam pridem persuasum est nationi Germanicæ a curia Romana per certos abusus multa et magna gravamina et incommoda illata esse ob id si pro executione apostolicæ sedis sententiæ vel imperatoriæ majestatis edicti quippiam acerbius attemptatum esset, mox popularis multitudo sibi hanc opinionem animo concepisset ac si talia facerent pro evertenda evangelica veritate et sustinendis manutenendisque malis abusibus, unde nihil aliud quam gravissimi tumultus populares intestinaque bella speranda essent"—*Fr A*

‡ Planitz names him as early as on the 18th Jan with Schwarzenburg and Feilitzsch

Christian church.* Perhaps the adherents of the established faith were satisfied by the decision, because it recognised the authority of the expositions of the Latin fathers; but this recommendation was couched in vague, general and uncertain language, whereas that of the evangelical doctrine was precise, decided and emphatic, and therefore was alone likely to make an impression.

Thus, after all, the answer went back to the Council of Regency, having undergone a few partial changes, but agreeing in the main with the spirit of the original plan. Contrary to all expectation, it caused another very stormy debate in that assembly. Some of the members (among whom was the Bishop of Augsburg) who had repented of the part they had taken in the original scheme, made another attempt to retain the express mention of the four fathers of the Church. Planitz reports that he had to endure many proud and wicked words, and to resist a violent storm on this question. He expresses the greatest indignation at the apostacy of the bishop, whom, he says, God had raised out of the dust and made a ruler over his people, and who in return persecuted the Gospel.† However, with resolution and patience, and the assistance of Schwarzenberg, he succeeded in maintaining the form which had at last been decided upon, and the answer was delivered to the nuncio as it had been returned from the assembly of the States.‡

The nuncio did not attempt to conceal his astonishment and vexation. Neither the pope nor the emperor, nor any other sovereign, he said, had expected such a decision from them. He renewed his request for the execution of the edict of Worms and the establishment of an episcopal censorship, but it was impossible to persuade a body which moved so slowly and with so much difficulty, to think of retracting a resolution once formed, and all his endeavours were fruitless.

The substance of the answer was published in an imperial edict. The Elector of Saxony and Luther himself were highly pleased with it, Luther, indeed, thought that the ban and excommunication which had been proclaimed against him were virtually revoked by it.

It is indisputably true that these decisions of the diet of Nurnberg were exactly the contrary of those passed at Worms. The important step which had been expected of Charles V., namely, that he would place himself at the head of the national movement, was now actually taken by the Council of Regency. The political opposition which had so long been gathering its forces, offered a more vigorous resistance than ever to the pope; allied with it, and protected by the representatives of the imperial power, religious discussion was now left to its free and unfettered course.

CHAPTER III.

DIFFUSION OF THE NEW DOCTRINES.

1522—1524.

No new arrangement needed to be made, no plan to be concerted, no mission to be sent; like the seed which shoots up on the ploughed field at the first genial rays of the sun in spring, the new opinions, the way for which had been prepared by all the events and discussions we have endeavoured to trace, now spread abroad through the whole land where the German language was spoken.

A religious order was destined to afford the first common centre to the various elements of opposition.

The Augustines of Meissen, and of Thuringia generally, had made the first step towards emancipation, by a formal resolution. Among them were old friends of Luther, who had followed the same career of studies and of opinions as he had; even among the more distant Augustine convents, there were few in which similar questions had not been agitated, and similar changes of opinion manifested; indeed, a list is still extant, of those who took part in the movement at Magdeburg, Osnabrück, Lippe, Antwerp, Regensburg, Dillingen, Nurnberg and Strasburg,§ and in the territories of Hessen and Wurtemberg. Many of these reformers were men advanced in life, who had held these doctrines ever since the time of Johann Proles, and who now exulted to see them attain a fuller development and greater power; others again were youthful and fiery spirits, inspired with admiration for their victorious brother of Wittenberg. Johann Stiefel of Esslingen beheld in him the angel of the Apocalypse flying through the heavens, and holding in his hand the everlasting Gospel; he composed a mystical and heroic poem in his

* "Quod nihil preter verum purum sincerum et sanctum evangelium et approbatam scripturam pie mansuete christiane juxta doctrinam et expositionem approbatæ et ab ecclesia christiana receptæ scripturæ doceant." This is the passage in the answer given to the papal nuncio.

† Planitz, 4th Feb. "Ich will aber Patienz und Geduld tragen. Es haben die Stände obangezeigte wort (he has inserted them in his letter) haben wollen und nit die vier Doctores zu benennen und sulchs dem Regiment anzeigen lassen, dabei es bliehen."—"I will however, have patience and temper. The States would have the words I have before mentioned, and would not allow the four doctors to be named or specified to the Council of Regency, so it remained as it was."

‡ Planitz, 9th Feb. "Die Schrift ist dem papstl. Nuntius auf die Mass ubergeben wie ich E. Chf. G. zugeschickt. Der ist der nicht zu frieden und hat darauf replicirt. Er will den Kayser dabei nit haben, so gefallt ihm auch nit dass es so gar frei seyn soll wie begehrt."—"The paper is handed over to the papal nuncio, on the whole much as I have sent it to your electoral grace. The nuncio is not satisfied with it, and has replied, he will not allow the emperor to be mentioned in it, nor does he like that there should be so much freedom as is demanded."

§ According to Eberlin's "Syben frumme aber trostlose Pfaffen," "Seven devout but comfortless Priests," Dr. Casper Amon, "ain erwirdig Man," "a reverend man," taught at Dillengen. This is doubtless the same person who in 1523 published a Psalter done into German from the genuine text in the Hebrew tongue,—"geteutscht nach warhaftigem text der hebreischen zungen." The dedication of this book is dated Lauingen. Panzer, ii. p. 131.

praise.* This body, moreover, had the glory of being the first to draw down persecution on itself. Two or three Augustine friars at Antwerp were the first martyrs of the new faith. Jean Chatelain of Mêtz was soon afterwards condemned to the flames for the attacks he had made on the prerogatives of the clergy in the Advent of 1523, and the Lent of 1524.†

A number of Franciscans, not, like the Augustines,† supported by their order, but separating themselves entirely from it, and, as we may infer from that act, men of more energetic temper, were the next to join the new sect. Some of these were learned men, like Johann Brismann of Cottbus, who had been for many years devoted to the study of the schoolmen and had become doctor of theology, but who now, like Luther, drew from their works entirely opposite opinions.‡ Others were spirits full of deep religious yearnings, which the conventual rule and discipline failed to satisfy; such was Friedrich Myconius. It is related that on the night following his investiture, he dreamed that whilst wandering in steep and tortuous paths, he was met by a holy man, baldheaded, and clothed in an antique dress, as St Paul is painted, who led him first to a fountain whose waters flowed from a crucified body, whereat he slaked his thirst, and then through endless fields of thick standing corn, in which the reapers were making ready for the harvest.§ This vision is sufficient to show the turn of his mind; and we may easily infer from it the impression which must have been produced on him by the revival of the apostolical doctrine, and the prospect of an active co-operation in its diffusion. Others again were men who in the various intercourse with the lower classes, to which the duties of a Franciscan convent leads, had perceived the pernicious effects of the doctrine of justification by works, and now attacked it with all their might; among these were Eberlin of Gunzburg, and Heinrich of Kettenbach, who came out of the same convent at Ulm, and who possessed, in an extraordinary degree, the gift of popular oratory. Eberlin's opponents said of him, that he alone had power to mislead a whole province; so great was the effect of his eloquence on the common people. Among them were found the most steadfast champions, like Stephen Kempen, whose brave and warlike bearing was worthy of his name. The Franciscans were almost everywhere among the first reformers: Kempen was the founder of the new doctrines in Hamburg, where he defended them nearly single-handed for three years against all opponents.

But there was not, perhaps, a single religious order which did not furnish partisans to the new opinions, many of whom were among its most celebrated champions. Martin Butzer had been appointed professor of the Thomist doctrines by the Dominicans, but he dissolved his connexion with that order by a kind of lawsuit, and from that time forward took a most active and successful part in the establishment of the new system of faith. Otto Brunnfels came out of the Carthusian convent at Mainz and became the follower of Hutten, whose labours he shared with rival ardour. The young reading-master of the Benedictine abbey of Alperspach, P. Ambrosius Blaurer, was incited by the general ferment to the study of the sacred writings, and formed opinions which soon rendered a longer residence in the convent impossible to him. Œcolampadius, who had but lately taken the vows in the convent of St Bridget at Altomunster, raised his voice in favour of the new views: he had hoped to find in the convent undisturbed leisure for the learned works he purposed to write, but the conviction which soon forced itself on his mind hurried him into an eager participation in all the mental conflicts of the times. The brothers of Our Lady of Mount Carmel at Augsburg declared themselves for Luther from the very first, with the prior at their head, and to them belonged, for a time at least, Urban Regius,‖ one of the most devoted and favourite disciples of Johann Eck, whom he now, however, deserted for the new cause.¶ he supported it with great effect, first in Upper, and afterwards still more successfully in Lower Germany. Here he was, after a while, assisted by Johann Bugenhagen, who had also for a long time followed a very different course of studies and opinions, in a convent of Præmonstratenses at Belbuck in Pomerania. Bugenhagen, as his history of Pomerania, written in 1518, and vigorously attacking the abuses prevailing in the Church, shows, was even then convinced of the necessity of a complete change in the body of the clergy;** but he was no less

* Von der christförmigen rechtgegründeten Lehre Doctoris Martini Luthers

"Er thut sich worlich fyegen zu Got in rechten mut,
Gwalt mag ihn auch nit biegen er geb er drum sein blut
Zu Worms er sich erzeyget er trat keck auf den plan
Sein feynd hat er geschweyget keiner dorft ihn wenden an"

"Concerning the Christian like well grounded doctrine of Doctor Martin Luther

"He trusted truly in God with a good courage
Force could not bend him for it (the cause) he would have spilled his blood
He proved himself at Worms, stepping boldly into the field
He silenced his enemies, none could answer him"

See Strobel's *Neue Beitrage*, i p 10

† The Reimchronik of Metz speaks very favourably of this Augustine monk

"A Metz prescha ung caresme,
devant grand peuple homme et femme,
qui en sa predication
avoient grande devotion"

His persecutor says to him,—

"Tu as presche de nostre estat,
je te hai plus qu'un apostat
as tousché sur le gens d'eglise,
maintenant te tiens a ma guise

Calmet, Histoire de Lorraine, ii, Preuves cxix

‡ Extract from his sermons in Seckendorf, Historia Lutheranismi, i p. 272

§ Adami Vitæ Theologorum, edition of 1705, p 83.

‖ Braun, Geschichte der Bischöfe von Augsburg, iii 230 He is also called a Carmelite in Welser's Augsburger Chronik

¶ There are a few letters which passed between them in Adami, p 35 Eck is violent and bitter Regius (König), in spite of the firmness of his opposition, never forgets the accustomed reverence towards his master

** J H Balthasar, Præfatio in Bugenhagii Pomeraniam, p 5

strongly opposed to Luther; and when Luther's book on the Babylonish captivity was brought to him one day as he sat at dinner, he exclaimed, that since the Passion of Christ a more pernicious heretic had never existed. But this very book wrought a complete revolution in his mind he took it home with him, read it, studied it, and became convinced that the whole world was in error and that Luther alone saw the truth Of this change of sentiments he informed his colleagues at the conventual school over which he presided, his abbot, and all his friends.* Similar conversions took place in all the religious orders The superiors were often the most strongly impressed, like the priors of the Augustine and Carmelite convents, of whom we have spoken among others were Eberhard Widensee, provost of the convent of St John at Halberstadt, and by his influence, Gottes-Gnaden and St. Moritz, provosts of Nuenwerk and Halle, and Paul Lemberg, abbot of Sagan, who openly declared that if any one of his monks felt his conscience burdened by remaining in the convent, so far from attempting to keep him there, he would rather carry him out of it on his own shoulders †

On a careful examination, I do not find, however, that love of the world, or any licentious desire to be freed from the restraints of the convent, had much effect in producing these resolutions, at all events, in the most conspicuous cases, where motives have been recorded by contemporaries, they were always the result of a profound conviction, in some, gradually developed, in others, suddenly forced on the mind, sometimes by a striking passage in the Bible many did not leave the convent of their own accord, but were driven out of it; others, though of a most peaceful nature themselves, found their abode between the narrow walls embittered by the frequent disputes which arose out of the state of men's minds The mendicant friars felt disgust at their own trade one of them, a Franciscan, entered a smithy at Nurnberg with his alms-box in his hand, and was asked by the master why he did not rather earn his bread by the work of his hands the robust monk immediately threw off his habit and became a journeyman smith, sending back his cowl and box to the convent

There is no doubt that the monastic institutions of the West were originally founded in imitation of the Hindu penitents, who live in lonely forests, clothed in the bark of trees, eating only herbs and drinking only water, free from desires, masters of their passions, beatified even in this life, and a sure refuge to the afflicted ‡ But how widely had the recluses of Europe departed from their model! They took part in all the pursuits, dissensions and troubles of the world, and their main object was the maintenance of a dominion at once temporal and spiritual, aided by masses actuated by the same sentiments and working to the same ends; they were held together by servile vows, frequently taken from interested motives, and as much as possible disregarded. No sooner, therefore, had the validity of these vows, and their religious efficacy to the soul, become doubtful, than the whole structure fell in pieces nay more, the institution on which the Western Church mainly rested, sent forth the most sturdy antagonists to its further hierarchical development.

This general movement among the regular clergy was now seconded by all ranks of the secular priesthood.

There was one even among the bishops, Polenz of Samland, who openly declared himself for Luther, occasionally preached his doctrines from the pulpit at Konigsberg, and took care to appoint preachers of his own way of thinking to a number of places in his diocese. Luther was overjoyed at this; such a peaceable and lawful change was exactly what he desired §

A few other bishops were also supposed to be favourably inclined to the new doctrine. Johann Eberlin of Gunzburg mentions the Bishop of Augsburg, who did not conceal that "the life and conversation of the Lutherans were less sinful than those of their adversaries," the Bishop of Basle, who was pleased when Lutheran books were brought to him, and always read them diligently, the Bishop of Bamberg, who no longer opposed the preaching of Lutheran doctrines in his city, and the Bishop of Merseburg, who sent for the writer to consult him concerning the reforms which were wanted. He assures us that several others sent their canons to study at Wittenberg. Most of the names which we find in the list of Reuchlin's patrons appear among those who took part in the religious innovation.

They were also joined by the patrician provosts of the great towns, such as a Wattenwyl in Berne, and a Besler and Bömer in Nurnberg, under whose protection the evangelical preachers were established in the churches of their respective cities.

Even without this encouragement, a great number of the officiating priests and preachers in Lower, and still more in Upper, Germany, declared themselves converts to Luther's opinions The name of Hermann Tast, one of the twenty-four papal vicars in Schleswig, is well known. In the churchyard at Husum stood two lime-trees, which were called the Mother and the Daughter, under the largest of the two, the Mother, Tast used to preach, escorted to and from the place of meeting by his hearers, who went armed to fetch him and conduct him home. At Emden, in East Friesland, Georg von der Dare was driven out of the great church when he began to preach Luther's doctrines, but the people, after flocking to hear him for some time in the open air, at length obtained re-admittance for him into the church Johann Schwanhauser,

* Chytræi Saxonia, p 287 Lange, Leben Bugenhagens, 1731, contains nothing of importance

† Catalogus Abbatum Saganensium, in Stenzel's Scriptt Rer Siles, i. p 457

‡ Nalas, twelfth song.

§ "Lutheri Dedicatio in Deuteronomium, Reverendo Georgio de Polentis vere episcopo Tibi gratia donata est, ut non modo verbum susciperes et crederes, sed pro episcopali autoritate etiam palam et publice confessus doceres docerique per tuam diocesim curares, liberaliter his qui in verbo laborant provisis"—*Opp* iii p. 75 *Hartknock's Preussische Kirchengeschichte*, i p 273

custos of St. Gangolph in Bamberg, declaimed, in the language of a Carlstadt, against the adoration of the saints * The parish priest of Cronach was one of the first who married. At Mainz, it was the preacher in the cathedral, Wolfgang Kopfl (for a long time the confidential adviser of the elector), at Frankfort, the preacher in the church of St. Catharine, Hartmann Ibach, at Strasburg, the parish priest of St Laurence, Matthew Zell, at Memmingen, the preacher of St Martin's, Schappeler, who were the first to propagate the new doctrines. In the imperial city of Hall, Johann Brenz, a mere youth, but deeply impressed with the doctrines of St Paul, and an imitator of the apostle's style of speaking, pronounced his sermon of trial in September, 1522, and drove his antagonists, the guardian and the reader of the Minorite convent, out of the field without further contest, by the doctrine of the sole merit of Christ.† In the Kreichgau, a band of village priests, united by similarity of opinion, collected around Erhard Schnepf, under the protection of the Gemmingen In Basle, at the procession of the Corpus Christi, Roubli, the priest of St. Alban's, carried a splendidly-bound Bible instead of the host, declaring that he alone bore the true Holy of holies Next followed, at the minister of Zurich, the great secular priest, Ulrich Zwingli, equally courageous and influential in politics and in religion, and in whom the vicar of Constance soon thought he beheld a second Luther. We may follow these movements even into the lofty regions of the Alps. The leading men of Schwytz often timed their rides so as to arrive at Freienbach, where a friend of Zwingli's preached, at the time of divine service, after which they stayed and dined with him.‡ It made no difference that they were Swiss, for in those days the feeling of nationality had not yet separated them from Germany, indeed the people of the Valais called the territory of the confederate cities, Germany. The new doctrines then followed the course of the mountains as far as the valley of the Inn, where Jacob Strauss first expounded them to many thousand converts; then to Salzburg, where Paul von Spretten made the cathedral resound with them and finally into Austria and Bavaria At Altenottingen, where there was one of the most popular miraculous pictures, the regular priest, Wolfgang Russ, had the courage to declaim against pilgrimages.

It may be concluded that all these changes were not brought about without stout resistance and a hard struggle. Many were compelled to yield, but some persevered, and at all events the persecution did no harm to the cause. When that zealous Catholic, Bogislas X of Pomerania, destroyed the Protestant society at Belbuck, and confiscated the property—for the seizure of church lands began on that side—the only result was, that one of their teachers accompanied some young Livonians, who had been studying there, to Riga, and thus scattered the seed of the Word over the most remote parts of Germany.§

Paul von Spretten was expelled from Salzburg, after which we find him preaching in St Stephen's church at Vienna, and when driven thence, at Iglau in Moravia there also he was in imminent danger, and at last found a safe asylum in Prussia With this scene of action, the ardent Amandus was not content, he soon left it and went to Stolpe, where he challenged the monks to a disputation on the truth of the old or the new system he told them they might prepare a stake and faggots, and burn him if he was overcome in argument; and that if he obtained the victory, the sole punishment of his opponents should be conversion

As yet no attention was paid to the place where the Gospel was preached It is almost symbolic of the ecclesiastical opposition, that at Bremen it was a church standing under an interdict, in which two or three Augustine friars who had escaped the stake in Antwerp, first assembled a congregation At Goslar, the new doctrine was first preached in a church in the suburbs, and when that was closed, a native of the town, who had studied at Wittenberg, proclaimed it on a plain covered with lime-trees (the Lindenplan), whence its adherents were there called Lindenbruder (brothers of the lime-tree) ‖ In Worms a movable pulpit was put up against the outer walls of the church. The Augustine Monk, Caspar Guttel of Eisleben, at the request of the inhabitants of Arnstadt, preached seven sermons in the market-place there, according to ancient custom. At Danzig the people assembled on a height outside the town, to hear a preacher who had been driven from within its walls

But even if none of the clergy had embraced the new faith, it would have found many proclaimers and defenders among the laity. At Ingolstadt, under the very eyes of Dr Eck, an enthusiastic journeyman weaver read aloud Luther's writings to assembled crowds, and when, in the same town, a young Master of Arts, called Seehofer, who had begun to teach from Melanchthon's pamphlets, was forced to recant, his defence was undertaken by a lady, Argula von Staufen, whose attention having been directed by her father to Luther's books, she had, in conformity with their precepts, devoted herself exclusively to the study of the Scriptures. Believing herself fully able to compete with them in knowledge of the Bible, she now challenged all the members of the university to a disputation, and hoped to maintain the superiority of her own faith in the presence of the prince and the whole community ¶ It was in this intimate acquaintance

* Extracts from his sermons in Heller, p 62

† Hartmann and Jager, Johann Brenz, i 43. 59

‡ Hottinger, Geschichte der Eidgenossen

§ Andreas Cnoph von Custrin "Er hat viel herrlicher und geistreicher Lieder, darin die Summa von der Lehre von der Gerechtigkeit, dem Glauben und desselbigen Fruchten verfasset" — "He has composed many most beautiful and ingenious songs, wherein is contained the essence of the doctrine of righteousness—faith and its fruits"—*Hiarn Liefländische Gesch*, book v p 193

‖ Hamelmann, Historia renati Evangelii Opp Hist Gen, p 869

¶ Winter, Gesch der evang Lehre in Baiern, i 120. f

with Scripture that the leaders of the religious movement trusted. Heinrich von Kettenbach exultingly enumerates countries and cities—Nürnberg, Augsburg, Ulm, the Rhenish provinces, Switzerland and Saxony—where women and maidens, serving-men and artisans, knights and nobles, were more learned in the Bible than the high schools.*

There was indeed something very extraordinary in this simultaneous and universal conviction, unquestionably religious in its origin, rising up in opposition to forms of ecclesiastical and political life which had been revered for centuries, though now men could see in them only their wide departure from true primitive Christianity, and their subservience to an oppressive and odious power.

As every effort on the one side was followed by a re-action, and every attack by persecution, it was of great importance that there should be one spot in Germany where such was not the case: this spot was the electorate of Saxony.

In the year 1522 the neighbouring bishops made another attempt to re-establish their power here also, in consequence of the favourable tone of the first proclamation of the imperial government; and the Elector Frederic offered no opposition to them so long as they promised to send preachers who should combat the Word with the Word.† When, however, not content with this, they demanded that the priests who had married or dared to administer the Lord's Supper in both kinds, and the monks who had quitted their convents, should be given up to them, he declared, after brief consideration, that the imperial edict did not oblige him to this.‡ By withdrawing his countenance from them, he of course annihilated their influence.

This naturally induced all those who were forced to fly from other places, to take refuge in his dominions, where no spiritual authorities could reach them. Eberlin, Stiefel, Strauss, Seehofer, Ibach from Frankfurt, Bugenhagen from Pomerania, Kauxdorf from Magdeburg, Mustæus from Halberstadt, where he had been barbarously mutilated,§ and numbers more, flocked together from all parts of Germany; they found a safe asylum, and in many cases temporary employment, and then went forth again, confirmed in their faith by intercourse with Luther and Melanchthon. Wittenberg was the centre of the whole movement; without the existence of such a centre, the unity of direction, the common progress, which we observe, would have been impossible; we may add, that the admixture of foreign elements was of great importance to the development of the public mind of Saxony. The university especially thus acquired the character of a national body,—incontestably the true character of a great German high school. Both teachers and hearers resorted from all parts of Germany, and went forth again in all directions.

Wittenberg became equally important as a metropolis of literature.

It was the agitation of these important questions which first obtained for the German popular literature general circulation and influence. Up to the year 1518 its productions were far from numerous, and the range of its subjects very narrow. During the last twenty years of the fifteenth century there appeared about 40 German works; in 1513 about 35; in 1514, 47, in 1515, 46; in 1516, 55; in 1517, 37: these were chiefly mirrors for the laity, little works on medicine, books on herbs, religious tracts, newspapers, official announcements, and travels,—in short, the books fitted to the comprehension of the many. The most original productions were always those of the poetical opposition—the satires which we have already noticed. The increase in the number of German publications which followed Luther's appearance before the public was prodigious. In the year 1518 we find 71 enumerated; in 1519, 111; in 1520, 208; in 1521, 211; in 1522, 347; in 1523, 498. If we inquire whence this wonderful increase emanated, we shall find it was from Wittenberg, and the chief author, Luther himself. In the year 1518 we find 20 books published with his name; in 1519, 50; in 1520, 133; in 1521, when he was interrupted by his journey to Worms, and hindered by a forced seclusion, about 40; in 1522, again 130; and in 1523, 183.‖ In no nation or age has a more autocratic and powerful writer appeared; and it would be difficult to find any other who has united so perfectly popular and intelligible a style, and such downright homely good sense, to so much originality, power and genius; he gave to German literature the character by which it has been ever since distinguished, of investigation, depth of thought, and strenuous conflict of opinions. He began the great discussion which has been carried on in Germany through all the subsequent centuries; though often grievously interrupted by acts of violence and by the influences of foreign policy. In the beginning he stood quite alone, but by degrees, especially after the year 1521, disciples, friends, and rivals began to appear in the field. In the

* "Ein new Apologia vnnd Verantwortung Martini Luthers wyder der Papisten Mortgeschrey, die zehen klagen wyder jn ussblasiniren so wyt die Christenheyt ist, 1523."—"A new Apology and Answer of Martin Luther against the Papist's Cry of Murder, who trumpet forth Ten Complaints against him throughout Christendom."

† Frederic instructs his officers, "An Verkündigung des Wortes Gottes nicht zu hindern."—"Not to hinder the preaching of the Word of God." He takes for granted, "sie würden die Ehre Gottes und die Liebe des Nächsten suchen"—"that they would seek the honour of God and the love of their neighbour."

‡ Geuterbock, St. Lucastag. The very remarkable correspondence in the Sammlung vermischter Nachrichten zur sächsischen Geschichte, iv. 282.

§ What cruelties then took place! "Aliquot ministri canonicorum capiunt D. Valentinum Mustæum,"—"with the sanction of the burgher-master he had preached the Gospel in Neustadt," "et vinctum manibus pedibusque, injecto in ejus os freno, deferunt per trabes in inferiores cœnobii partes ibique in cella cerevisiaria eum castrant."—*Hamelmann*, l. c. p. 880.

‖ I rely upon Panzer's Annalen der ältern Deutschen Literatur, 1788—1802. That his information, useful as it is, is not quite complete, is a defect this has in common with most statistical works. We can, however, gather from them the general facts, which is all we here have to do with. According to Adam, Vitæ Jurisconsult., p. 62., it was Schneidewin's father-in-law—ex honorata familia, quæ nomen gentilitium Turingorum habuit, agnomen vero Aurifabrorum—who established the first printing-press at Wittenberg, socio Luca pictore seniore. This is another of Lucas Cranach's merits.

year 1523, besides his own works, there were published 215 by others, in favour of the new opinions; that is, more than four-fifths of all that appeared, while we do not find above 20 decidedly catholic publications. It was the first time that the national mind, uninfluenced by foreign models, and manifesting itself purely in the form impressed on it by the great events of the times, and the high destinies to which Germany was called, found a general expression; moreover, this expression regarded the most important interests that can occupy the attention of man, and its very first utterance was prompted by ideas of religious freedom.

It was a singular felicity, that at the very instant of full intellectual awakening, the Holy Scriptures, both of the New and Old Testament, were laid open to the nation. It is true that the Bible had long been known in translations; but it is impossible to conceive, without reading them, how full of errors, how rude in style, and how unintelligible these versions are. Luther, on the contrary, spared no labour to obtain an accurate knowledge of the meaning of the original, and gave it utterance in German, with all the clearness and energy of which that language is capable. The imperishable records of the earliest ages of the world, characterised by the freshness of the youth of mankind, and the sacred writings of later date, in which true religion appears in all its child-like candour, were now put into the hands of the German people in their own vernacular tongue, piece by piece, like a periodical work which relates to the immediate interests of the day, and were devoured with equal avidity.

There is one production of the German mind which owes its origin directly to this concurrence of circumstances. In translating the Psalms, Luther conceived the project of making a paraphrase of them for the purpose of congregational singing;* for the idea of a Church, such as he had described and begun to call into existence, supposed that the congregation should take a far more considerable part in the service than it had ever done before. In this case, however, as in some others, a mere paraphrase did not suffice. The devout spirit, tranquil in the conviction of possessing the revealed Word of God; elevated by the strife and danger in which it was placed, and inspired by the poetical genius of the Old Testament, poured forth lyrical compositions, at once poetry and music; words alone would have been insufficient to express the emotions of the soul in all their fulness, or to excite and sustain the feelings of a congregation. This could only be done by the melody which breathed in the solemn old church music, and the touching airs of popular songs. Such was the origin of the evangelical hymns, which we may date from the year 1523.† Detached hymns by Luther and Spretten acquired immediate popularity, and lent their aid to the earliest struggles of the reforming spirit; but it was many years later that the German mind displayed its whole wealth of poetical, and still more of musical, productions of this kind.

The popular poetry also devoted itself in other ways to the new ideas with that spirit of teachableness, and at the same time resistance to arbitrary power, which characterised it. Hutten published his bitterest invectives in verse; Murner depicted the corruption of the clergy in long and vivid descriptions: to this feeling of censure and reprobation was now added, if not in Murner himself, at any rate in most others, a positive conviction of the truth of the new doctrine, and a profound admiration of its champion; the man who maintained the righteous cause among crimson barrets and velvet caps was celebrated in verse. The pope was brought on the stage in carnival farces; he congratulates himself that, in spite of his knavery, men continue to ascribe to him the power of admitting them into heaven or binding them in hell, which brings many birds to his net to be plucked; that he reaps the fruits of the sweat of the poor man's brow, and can ride with a retinue of a thousand horses—his name is Entchristelo; there also appear, uttering like sentiments, Cardinal Highmind (*Hochmuth*), Bishop Goldmouth Wolfsmaw (*Goldmund Wolfsmagen*), Vicar Fabler (*Fabeler*), and a long list of personages held up to ridicule and contempt under such names: the last who enters is the Doctor, who expounds the true doctrine very much in the tone of a sermon.‡ Under the influence of these impressions was educated Burckhardt Waldis, who afterwards made such a happy application of the old fable of the beasts to religious controversies. The greatest German poet of that day warmly embraced Luther's cause. Hans Sachs's poem, the Nightingale of Wittenberg, appeared in 1523; he compares the faith which had prevailed for four hundred years, to the moonlight which had led men astray in the wilderness; now, however, the nightingale announces the rising sun and the light of day, while she herself soars above the dark clouds. Thoughts emanating from a sound understanding, instructed by the infallible Word, and confident of its own cause, form the basis of the many ingenious, gay, and graceful poems—not the less attractive for a slight smack of the work-

* Luther's preface to Johann Walter's Hymns recalls "das Exempel der Propheten und Könige im alten Testament, die mit singen und klingen, mit dichten und allerlei Seitenspiel Gott gelobet haben."—"the example of the prophets and kings in the Old Testament, who, with songs and music, with verses and all manner of stringed instruments, praised God."—*Altenb. A.*, ii. p. 751.

† Riederer, "von Einführung des deutschen Gesanges," p. 95. The remarkable letter to Spalatin concerning the translation of the Psalms into German verse, in De Wette, ii. p. 490., is doubtless earlier than that dated 14th Jan. 1524, ibid. p. 461. In it we see what the Musæ Germanicæ, about which De Wette seems to be in doubt, really meant. It appears from the letters to Hausmann, that Luther was employed in November and December, 1523, in the composition of the liturgy.

* "Ein Fassnachtspyl, so zu Bern uf der Hern Fassnacht in dem MDXXII. Jare von Burgerssonen offentlich gemacht ist, darinn die warheit in Schimpffswyss vom Pabst und siner Priesterschaft gemeldet würt."—"A Carnival Play, the which was publicly enacted in the Lord's carnival of the year 1522, at Bern, by the sons of burghers, wherein the truth is satirically told of the pope and of his priesthood." Newly printed by Grüneisen.—*Nicl. Manuel*, p. 339.

shop—with which the honest master delighted all classes of the nation

In Germany, the proper aim of art—to teach by giving a sensible form to ideas—had never been lost sight of Hence, there is no less fancy displayed in her symbols, than earnestness in her character It so happened that one of the great masters of the time, Lucas Kranach, went to live at Wittenberg, and, in a constant familiar intercourse with Luther, became thoroughly imbued with the modes of thinking of the reformers, and consecrated his talents to embodying them He sometimes entered the ranks as a combatant Some of his smaller pictures, such as the Passion of Christ and Antichrist, in which the lowliness and humility of the Founder, and the pride and pomp of his vicegerent, are contrasted, are protests against Catholicism, and accordingly woodcuts of them were inserted into Luther's writings It may be imagined that his chaste pencil was employed in no works but such as harmonised with the evangelical faith. The grace and loveliness with which he had formerly adorned groups of beatified female saints, he now shed over the little children receiving the blessing of our Saviour. The mysteries shadowed forth in early art, were now expressed in representations of the sacraments retained by Luther, which were sometimes painted on one canvass, and of the sublime work of Redemption. The eminent statesmen and divines by whom he was surrounded, presented forms and features so remarkable and characteristic, that he had no temptation, except in the cause of religion, to strive after the ideal. Albert Durer, though his genius had already reached maturity, was powerfully affected by the prevailing spirit the most perfect, perhaps, of all his works—the evangelists Mark and John, and the apostles Peter and Paul—were produced under the impressions of these times There exist studies for these pictures with the date 1523: they reflect the image suggested by Scripture (now rendered accessible to new views), of the wisdom, devotedness and energy of these first witnesses of the Christian church. Vigour and grandeur of conception manifest themselves in every feature *

The general development of the German mind was closely connected with the new ideas, the same spirit was stirring in the learned, as in the popular branches of mental activity.

Wittenberg was far from being the only university in which the course of studies was changed. At Freiburg, where Luther was detested, the Aristotelian philosophy ceased to be studied and inculcated as hitherto "Petrus Hispanus," says Ulrich Zasius, "has had his day, the books of Sentences are laid aside, our theologians are some of them reading Matthew and others Paul; nay, even the very beginners, those who are but just arrived, crowd to these lectures "† Even Zasius himself, one of the most distinguished German jurists of that time, gives a remarkable testimony to the universal diffusion of the reforming spirit. He complains that his lecture-room is deserted; that he has barely half a dozen hearers, and they, all Frenchmen, and at the same time he can find no better mode of recommending his own exertions in the cause of learning, than by comparing them to the labours of Luther. The glossators of the genuine texts whom he was engaging in combating, appeared to him in the same light as the schoolmen on whom Luther was waging war, he laboured to restore the Roman law to its original purity, just as Luther strove to revive the theology of the Bible

Of all departments of learning, none, however, stood more in need of a similar reform than history. There existed an immense accumulation of materials; but the earlier periods were obscured by the learned fables which were continually receiving fresh and more circumstantial additions; while the later were known only in fragments dressed up to suit the interests of the dominant party the most important parts had been intentionally falsified, in consequence of their necessary connection with the great ecclesiastical fiction. It was impossible to arrive at a true, lively and connected view of history; even minds thirsting for real information shrank from such insuperable masses of reading An attempt to penetrate them was, however, made just about this time by Johann Aventin, who, at an earlier period, had sympathised in the literary tendencies of the new school of thinkers, and now followed its religious direction with the liveliest zeal. In writing his Bavarian chronicle, the contents of which are interesting to Germany generally, and even to the world, he spared no pains in searching libraries and archives in order to substitute genuine records for the shallow and improbable traditions hitherto current. He puts the reader on his guard against the representations of the ignorant; especially "people who have seen nothing of mankind, who know nothing of cities and countries, have no experience of earthly or heavenly matters, and yet pretend to judge of every thing" His endeavour is to understand history in its true and necessary aspect, "such as it should be" The spirit of the national opposition to the papacy is powerfully at work within him whenever he strives to depict the simplicity of the Christian doctrine, or alludes to its origin, he never fails to contrast with it the spiritual power in its rise, progress and operation. His history of Gregory VII. is even now the best extant. he takes a very comprehensive view of the results arising from the dominion of the hierarchical principle, though he had not the peculiar talent requisite to place them distinctly before the reader. His works are indeed generally unfinished; but he was the first labourer in that field of profound and penetrating research into universal history, which in our day occupies so many minds.

For a time, it seemed as if the interest in theological questions would absorb all others.

* How Pirkheimer and Durer disputed about the question of the Lord's Supper in Melanchthon's presence related by Peucer in Strobel's "Nachricht von Melanchthons Aufenthalt in Nurnberg," p 27

† Zasii Epistolæ, i 63.

Erasmus complains that nothing was read or bought but publications for or against Luther, he fears that the study of the humanities, which was but just established, would be stifled under a new system of school learning The chronicles of the time describe how the contempt into which the clergy had fallen reacted on learning. the proverb, "Die Gelehrten, die Verkehrten," (the more learned, the more wrongheaded,) was in every body's mouth, and parents hesitated to devote their children to studies which offered so doubtful a prospect. This, however, was only a momentary aberration, the mind, roused to a desire for authentic knowledge, could not reject the very instrument which had awakened it In the year 1524 Luther published a letter to the "burghermasters and councillors, of all the towns on German ground," exhorting them "to establish Christian schools."* He means by this, especially for the training of priests; for, he says, it is only by the study of languages that the Gospel can be preserved in its purity, to which end it was delivered down to us in writing, otherwise there would be nothing but wild and perilous disorder, and an utter confusion of opinions Yet he does not by any means confine his recommendation to ecclesiastical schools, far from it he deplores that schools have been so exclusively calculated for the education of the clergy, and his chief object is to free them from this narrow destination, and to found a learned class among the laity. He holds out the education of the ancient Romans as an example to Germany, and says that instructed men well versed in history are absolutely necessary for the government of the state; he also insists upon the establishment of public libraries, not only to contain editions and expositions of the sacred writings, but also orators and poets, whether heathen or not, besides books on the fine arts, law and medicine, chronicles and histories, "for they be profitable for the learning of the wonders and works of God." This letter had as great an effect on secular learning, as his book addressed to the German nobility had on the general condition of the laity. Luther first conceived the idea of that learned body of official laymen which has exercised such an incalculable influence over the social and political condition of Germany, he advocated the popular cultivation of knowledge for her own sake, apart from the church, it was he who laid the first stone of that edifice of learning in northern Germany, which succeeding labourers have reared to such a height In this he was vigorously seconded by the indefatigable Melanchthon, who was the author of the Latin grammar used in the schools throughout the North of Germany, till the beginning of the eighteenth century † He completed it in the year 1521, beginning from some notes made for the private instruction of a young Nurnberger, at the same time, the Greek grammar, of which he had previously drawn up the plan, received the form in which it was taught for centuries afterwards. Teachers were formed under Melanchthon's discipline, who adopted all his ideas, and became the founders of the German school-training The most remarkable of these was Valentine Trotzendorf, who was called from Wittenberg to Goldberg in Silesia, in the year 1523, and who was said to be born a schoolmaster as much as Cæsar was born a general, or Cicero an orator Innumerable German schoolmasters were formed by him

A large and coherent survey of all these facts suffices to convince us that the Reformation was by no means confined to theological dogmas; a whole circle of aspirations and thoughts of a peculiar character, and pregnant with a new order of things, had arisen, closely connected, it is true, with the theological opposition, and partly developed under that form, but the existence of which is neither to be ascribed to, nor confounded with that phenomenon. The opposition was itself merely one manifestation of this spirit, the future workings of which were entirely independent of it

The first object of the awakened mind undoubtedly was, deliverance from that mighty power which claimed the right of retaining it captive.

In examining more closely the course of this struggle, as it displayed itself in all parts of Germany, we shall fall into error if we expect to find the same points of variance which exist between the later Protestant and the revived Catholic systems The ideas and intellectual powers which were then arrayed against each other, stood in a far more distinct, broad, and intelligible opposition

One of the most violent conflicts was that concerning faith and good works. We must not understand by this the more deep and abstruse controversy which has since arisen out of the subtilty or the obstinacy of the schools At that time the question was very simple on the one side, by good works were meant those ritual observances through which men then really hoped to merit reward, both in this world and the next—such as pilgrimages, fasting, the foundation of masses for the souls of the dead, the recital of particular prayers, the reverence paid to certain saints, and the gifts to the churches and the clergy which formed so important a part of the piety of the middle ages. To this perversion of the idea of moral obligation, which had been so culpably allowed to gain currency and strength, the other party opposed the doctrine of the efficacy of faith without works But—especially after the troubles in Wittenberg—no one now ventured to inculcate an ideal, abstract, inactive faith. We still possess many of the sermons of that period, and it would be difficult to find one in which faith and charity are not spoken of as indissolubly united Caspar Guttel earnestly inculcates the doctrine, that the conduct which a man pursues towards his neighbour for the love of God is the one

* Altenb edition ii p 804 Eobin Hess caused the letters which he had received on this subject from Luther, Melanchthon, Jonas, Draco and others, to be printed collectively in 1523, in the pamphlet, "De non contemnendis Studiis humanioribus"

† The editions most worthy of note till 1737 are enumerated in Strobel, Von den Verdiensten Melanchthons, um die Grammatik neue Beitruge, ii iii p 43

essential thing.* The preacher blamed those who spent their substance in enriching the clergy, decorating the image of a saint, or going on distant pilgrimages, and at the same time forgot the poor.

The same thing took place with respect to the opinions concerning the church. The reformers entirely refused to recognise the holy church of Christ, out of whose pale there is no salvation, in the persons of the pope, his prelates and priests; they considered it profane to say that the Church commands or possesses any thing; they distinguished that ecclesiastical institution, which, by its scandalous government, gave the lie to the principles on which it was founded, from the mysterious existence of that holy fellowship which appears not outwardly, which, according to the words of the Symbol, is a pure object of faith, and which unites heaven and earth indeed, but without the intervention of the pope.† "Far be it from us to suppose," said Pastor Schmidt, in a sermon he preached with great effect at Küssnacht, "that the Christian church can acknowledge a head so spotted with sin as the pope; and thus forsake Christ, whom St. Paul so often calls 'the head of the church.'"‡

In like manner the institution of the Lord's Supper, freed from all priestly intervention, was contrasted with the compulsory obligation of *confessing* every individual sin,—an obligation which led and still leads to all the odious abuses of the confessional, and to the despotism of a stern and tyrannical orthodoxy. The discretionary power of the priest to grant absolution was denied, together with the doctrine of the actual presence; and people were even dissuaded from too nice a pondering over particular sins, as tending to stimulate the desires anew, or to produce despair: nothing was required but an undoubting, cheerful, steadfast reliance on the mercy of God, and faith in his present favour.§

But perhaps the most strongly and totally opposed were the opinions as to creeds of human origin and the pure word of God. Here again the dispute was not concerning tradition, as it has been defined by the more ingenious and enlightened controversialists of modern times; that is to say, little more than the Christian spirit propagating itself from generation to generation,—the Word living in the hearts of the faithful.‖ What the reformers combated, was the entire system of the Latin church, developed in the course of centuries by hierarchical power and school learning, and claiming absolute authority. They remarked that the fathers of the church had erred, Jerome often, and even Augustin occasionally; that those holy men had themselves been well aware of it; and that nevertheless a system from which no deviation was allowed, had been based on their decisions, and spun out with the aid of heathen philosophy. Thus it came to pass that they had given themselves up to human devices, and that there was not a teacher among them who led his hearers to the true understanding of the Gospel. And to this human doctrine, which neither satisfied the reason nor consoled the heart—which was connected with all sorts of abuses—they now opposed the eternal word of God, "which is noble, pure, cordial, steadfast and comfortable, and should therefore be kept unadulterated and undefiled."¶ They exhorted the laity to work out their own salvation; to gain possession of the word of God, which had now come forth in full splendour from its long concealment, to take it as a sword in their hands, and to defend themselves with it against the preachers of the contrary faith.**

Such were the questions concerning which the warfare of popular literature—preaching, was mainly carried on. On the one side, certain external ecclesiastical observances were deemed meritorious; the idea of a Church was identified with the existing hierarchy; the mystery of the individual relation to God, which is expressed in absolution, was made dependent on absolute obedience to the clergy. These opinions belonged to the system of faith

* Schutzrede wider etzlich ungezemte Clamanten. The very sermons preached at Arnstadt: printed in Olearii Syntagma Rerum Thuringicarum, ii. 274; an edition which Panzer does not mention in his Annals, ii. p. 93.

† Ain Sermon oder Predig von der christlichen Kirchen welches doch sey die hailig christlich Kirche, davon unser Glaub sagt, geprediget zu Ulm von Bruder Heinrich von Kettenbach, 1522.—"A Sermon or Preaching touching the Christian Church—which is the holy Christian Church of which our belief speaketh? Preached at Ulm by Brother Henry of Kettenbach." Johann Brenz took up this doctrine very vehemently. He will not allow that the church is to be believed because it received Christ. "Juden und Heiden die haben Christum angenommen—und sind nachfolgends die äusserliche christliche Kirche geworden, and hat die Kirche ihren Ursprung von dan frommen Christenmenschen und ist nachfolgends die äusserliche christliche Kirche worden, doch nit dass die Menschen ihre Seligkeit haben von der äusserlichen Kirche. . . . Dieweil die Kirche ein geistlicher verborgener Leib ist und nit von dieser Welt, so folgt, dass in diesem Leib kein weltlich äusserlich noch sichtbar haupt ist."—"Jews and Pagans received Christ, and thereupon became the outward Christian church, and the church has its origin from pious Christians, and is thereafter become the outward Christian church, not that men receive salvation from the outward church. . . . For since the church is a spiritual hidden body, and not of this world, it follows that this body cannot have a worldly, outward, and visible head."

‡ Myconius ad Zwinglium. Epp. Zw. p. 195.

§ "Eyn verstendig trostlich Leer über das Wort St. Paulus: Der Mensch sol sich selbst probieren und alsso von dem Brott essen und von dem Kelch trinken: zu Hall in Inthall von D. Jacob Strauss geprediget, MDXXII."—"A reasonable and comfortable Doctrine concerning the Word of St. Paul: 'But let a man examine himself, and so let him eat of that bread, and drink of that cup.' Preached by D. Jacob Strauss, 1522, at Hall, in the valley of the Inn." The body and blood of Christ are taken as the surest sign of his merciful promises to forgive us our sins, if we have faith. This contradiction appears in some later writings of this author.

‖ Möhler Symbolik, p. 361.

¶ Das hailig ewig Wort Gots was das in im kraft, sterke frid, fred, erleuchtung und leben in aym rechten Christen zu erwecken vermag—zugestelt dem elden Ritter—Hern Jörgen von Fronsperg; von Haug Marschalk der genennt wirt Zoller zu Augsburg, 1523.—"The holy eternal word of God, what strength, power, peace and joy, light and life it is able to awaken in a true Christian. Addressed to the noble Knight George von Fronsperg, by Haug Marshalk, who was named tax-master at Augsburg in 1523." In his preface he praises the knight, "dass Eur Gestreng yetzumal so hoch benennt und gepreist wird, dass das edel rain lauter und unvermischt Wort Gottes, das heilig evangelium bey eur gestreng statt hat, und in eur ritterlich gemüt und herz eingemaurt und befestiget," &c.—"that your worship is now so highly famed and praised, for that the noble, clear, plain, and pure word of God, the holy Gospel, has an asylum with your worship, and is enclosed and made fast in your knightly spirit and heart," &c.

** Cunrad Distelmar von Arberg; ain trewe Ermannung, &c. 1523.

which defended its authority with fire and sword. On the other side, was the obligation of faith and love; the idea of the unity of an invisible Church consisting in a community of souls; the forgiveness of sins through faith in the redemption, and reception of the sacrament without the necessity of confession, and, finally, belief in the Bible alone as a rule of faith and doctrine. We are not now treating of the modifications given to their opinions by individual theologians, but simply of the prevalent trains of ideas which were at war in every part of Germany.

So early as the year 1521, a little work was published containing the allegory of this contest, under the name of "The old and the new Gods." On the title-page we see, as representatives of the new God, the pope, some of the fathers of the church, Aristotle, and, at the bottom of the leaf, Cajetan, Silvester, Eck and Faber; on the opposite page, the true and ancient God in his triune form, the four evangelists, St Paul grasping a sword, and lastly, Luther. The contents of the book were quite in character with the frontispiece.* With the ceremonies, rites, and articles of faith which had grown up under the protection of the rising hierarchy and its bloody sword, and turned Christianity into a kind of Judaism, is contrasted the old God, with his authentic word, and the simple doctrine of the redemption, of hope, faith, and love.†

These coarse and naked expressions suffice to show that the nation felt what were the real points in debate. The German mind became conscious that the hour of its maturity was come; boldly resisted the tyranny of those accidental forms which had governed the world, and returned to the only true source of religious instruction.‡

Considering the vast agitation, the strong feeling of conflict, which prevailed, it is doubly remarkable how much control men had over themselves, and with how much caution they often acted.

Heinrich of Kettenbach continued to assume that the Church—by which, however, he understands an invisible community—possessed the treasure of the merits of Christ, of the Virgin Mary, and of all the elect.

Eberlin of Gunzburg, whilst writing from Wittenberg to exhort his friends in Augsburg to procure for themselves each a copy of the New Testament, even if they had to save the price of it out of their food or raiment, admonishes them at the same time not to be too hasty in condemning the opinions of their fathers. There were many things, he said, which God in his wisdom had kept secret, and which they needed not to inquire about, such as purgatory, and the intercession of saints. He adds, that even Luther condemned nothing that had not some distinct passage of Scripture against it.

A young Bohemian critic brought forward a whole train of arguments to prove that it was very doubtful whether St. Peter had ever been in Rome, and the Catholic party clearly perceived that if this question was decided in the negative, the whole doctrine of the primacy would be overthrown. But the theologians of Wittenberg did not allow themselves to be dazzled by the brilliant results to which this line of argument would lead, they pronounced it to be of no avail§ towards furthering faith and piety, and, indeed, in a work wherein this question is treated at length, and the ill effects of the abuse of the doctrine of primacy set forth with great earnestness, a hope is expressed that the new Pope, Adrian VI, would renounce all existing errors, and confine himself entirely to the precepts of the Bible—which some passages in his writings seemed to promise, and that then not only the present differences would be healed, but also the old schism ended, and that even Greeks and Bohemians would return to the bosom of the Church.‖

Others who were less sanguine, were yet of opinion that all violent measures were to be avoided, and that the abolition of abuses should be left to the government. Some, indeed, exhorted their followers to free themselves from the dominion of the priesthood, as the Israelites did from that of Pharaoh. But even such men as the vehement Otho of Brunfels opposed them, saying, that "the Word had power to improve the state of the world without trouble or the sword; and that things rashly and inconsiderately begun never ended well."¶

This was Luther's opinion also, and for a

* Panzer, ii p 20

† See the preface by Hartmann Dulich, printed in Veesenmeier's Sammlung von Aufsatzen, p 135 The following passage in Eberlin of Gunzburg's Fraindlicher Vermanung, p iii, shows how much the purpose of the whole movement was recognised in these its most prominent tendencies "Ich halt, Luther sey von Gott gesandt zu scubern die Biblia von der lerer auslegung vnd zwang, die gewissen zu erlosen von banden der menschlichen gebot od' bapstgesetzen, und den gaistlichen abziehen den titel Christi uñ seiner kirchen, dz furohyn nit irer sollich gross buberey—straffios sey und' dem heyligen namen Gottes auch ist der Luther gesant dz er lere das creutz vnd glauben, welche schier durch alle doctores vergessen seindt, darzu ist Luther beruft von Got vnd Got gibt im weyshait kunst, vernunft, sterke, vnd herz dazu"—"I hold that Luther was sent by God to free the Bible from the empty expositions and restrictions of the teachers to release the conscience from the bondage of human commands or popish laws, and to strip ecclesiastics of the title of Christ and of his church so that in future such great knavery should no longer remain unpunished in the holy name of God Luther is likewise sent to teach the cross and the faith, which are clean forgotten by all the doctors Hereunto was Luther called by God, and to this end has God given him wisdom, knowledge, prudence, strength and courage"

‡ Sermon von der Kirche, at the very beginning

§ Luther to Spalatin, 17th Feb 1520, in De W, i 539

‖ Apologia Simonis Hessi adv dominum Roffensem Episc Anglicanum super concertatione ejus cum Vlrico Veleno Julio mense 1523 The author maintains chiefly, "quod gentiliter et ambitiose pro Petri primatu a multis pugnetur cum hinc nihil lucri accedat pietati quod impie abusi sint potestate sua Romani pontifices in statuendis quibusdam articulis seditiosis magis quam piis" The passage of Adrian in titulo de Sacram baptismi, is "Noverit ecclesia se non esse dominam sacramentorum sed ministram, nec posse magis formam sacramentalem destituere aut novam instituere quam legem aliquam divinam abolere vel novum aliquem fidei articulum instituere Spero fore," he then proceeds, "si ille perstat in sua sententia, ut tota catholica ecclesia, quæ nunc in sectas videtur divisa, in unam fidei unitatem aggregetur adeo ut et Bohemos et Græcos dexteras daturos confidam bene præsidenti Romano pontifici"

¶ Vom evangelischen Anstoss, Neuenberg in Breisgau Simonis und Juda, 1523.

long time it was acted on throughout the whole empire.

Every thing might yet be hoped from the guidance of the Council of Regency; for in directing that the pure word of God should be preached, and in avoiding all reference by name to the fathers of the Church, who were looked upon as the corner-stones of modern Romanism, the Council of Regency had adopted the most important ideas of the reformers.

In the year 1523 it took the cause of reform more expressly under its protection.

When Faber, the vicar of Constance, received a commission from Rome to preach against Luther, and applied to the Council of Regency for protection and safe conduct, they gave him a letter purporting, indeed, to have that effect, but conceived in such terms that, as Planitz says, he would gladly have had a better.

Duke George made fresh complaints to the Regency of Luther's violent attacks, and several members of that body were of opinion that the elector should be admonished to punish him. This, however, was opposed by the majority. Count Palatine Frederic, the emperor's lieutenant, proposed that the duke's letters should, at any rate, be sent to the elector. "Sir," said Planitz, "the voice of the majority decides that my gracious master shall not be written to;" and the duke was told that he might make the application to the elector himself.

In the convocation of a fresh diet, care was taken to make no allusion to the religious troubles.*

The main point, however, was that no step whatever was taken towards the execution of the edict of Worms; but the new doctrines were allowed freely to take their course, in expectation of the ecclesiastical council which had been demanded.

It is evident of what importance to the State as well as to the Church was the question,—whether a government in which sentiments of this kind predominated, would be able to maintain itself or not.

CHAPTER IV.

OPPOSITION TO THE COUNCIL OF REGENCY.—DIET OF 1523–24.

Two great ideas occupied the mind of the whole German nation; that of a national, representative, and at the same time, powerful government, and that of a complete renovation of the religious condition of the country: both these ideas were now, to a considerable extent, represented; each received support from the other; and, united, they seemed to promise a future equally important in a political and intellectual point of view.

All endeavours, however, which are directed towards ends so vast and comprehensive, inevitably provoke strong and various opposition from many quarters.

Not that the connexion between these two important objects was so close as to be evident to all minds, or that the antagonists of the opposition were fully aware of both its bearings; but each of them roused the peculiar antipathies of a class. It by no means followed that those who opposed the Council of Regency were hostile to the reformation of the Church.

We are generally inclined, in our views of the past, to fall into the error of ascribing too soon an exaggerated influence to a new element of social and political life. However powerful it may be, there are other influences at work which it cannot immediately overcome, and which continue to exercise their own independent action.

The hostility to the Council of Regency arose from two causes fundamentally opposed. In the first place, that body seemed destined to become a powerful and efficient government,—a prospect which was far from welcome to every one. In the second, it was at present very feeble; it possessed no executive power. Hence the first obstacle it encountered was disobedience.

SICKINGEN AND HIS ADVERSARIES.

It was not to be expected that the Public Peace proclaimed by Charles V. would be better observed than those of former reigns. Two imperial councillors, Gregory Lamparter and Johann Lucas, the master of the treasury, were attacked and taken prisoners on their way to Augsburg from Worms, where they had assisted at the closing of the diet. Nürnberg, the seat of government and of the courts of law, and at this time in a certain sense the capital city of the empire, was surrounded on all sides by the wildest private wars. Hans Thomas of Absberg, doubly irritated by the resolutions taken against him by the Swabian League, assembled again, in 1522, the most daring and reckless reiters from all the surrounding districts: fresh letters of challenge were brought to Nürnberg every day, or were found stuck on the whipping-post in the neighbouring villages; the roads east and west became unsafe. There was a lonely chapel at Krügelstein, in the territory of Bamberg, where mass was said three times a week. Here, under colour of hearing it, all the bands of robbers and their scouts met together. Woe to the company of merchants that fell in their way, for they not only plundered them of all their wares, but had now adopted the barbarous practice of cutting off the right hands of their prisoners: it was in vain that the wretched sufferers implored them at least to cut off the left and leave the right. Hans Thomas of Absberg thrust the right hand of a shopkeeper, which he had chopped off, into the bosom of the unfortunate man, and told him that when he got to Nürnberg he might give it to the bürgermeister in his name.†

* Letter from Planitz, dated 28th Feb., 3d March, and 18th August, 1523.

† Müllner's Nürnberger Annalen for the years 1522 and 1523 contain this and many other details; for example,

The Frankfurt Acts of 1522 present a very striking example of the general insecurity Philip Furstenberg, who was sent by the town of Frankfurt to the Council of Regency to take part in the government of the empire, found the road he had to travel from Miltenberg to Wertheim so unsafe, that he quitted his carriage, and joining a party of some 'prentice tailors whom he met, assumed their garb, and took a by-road on foot. The carriage was attacked by several horseman with bent cross-bows. In order to reach Wertheim he was forced to take an escort of five or six men armed with firelocks or cross-bows.* "The Reiters are angry," says he: "what they are about I know not."

In this state of things, when the Council of Regency could not even protect its own members, there broke out a private war, more violent than any that had disturbed the peace of the empire during Maximilian's reign. In August, 1522, Franz von Sickingen, with a well-armed force of infantry, cavalry and artillery, ventured to attack an elector of the empire, the Archbishop of Treves, in his own country and strongly fortified capital

In the main this was merely a private war (*Fehde*) like many others, originating in a personal quarrel (this same elector having once earnestly entreated the assistance of the empire against Sickingen's outrages in Hessen), the pretext for which was some doubtful legal claims,—especially concerning a fine which had been transferred from the archbishop to Sickingen; and the real object, the plunder, and, if possible, the conquest of the fortified towns. There exists a most interesting letter from an old confidential friend of Sickingen's, in which the writer dissuades him from the enterprise, and lays before him all the chances of success or failure †

Other motives were also at work, which gave public importance to this undertaking success in a hostile enterprise was no longer Sickingen's ultimate aim; he had an eye to interests of far greater moment.

First of all, to those of the whole body of the Knights of the Empire. We have seen how great was their discontent at the state of public affairs at that time· at the Swabian League, which took upon itself to be at once accuser, judge and executor of its own sentences, at the Imperial Chamber, whose proceedings were only directed against the weak, and left the strong to their own guidance, at the encroachments of the princes, their courts of law, taxes and feudal privileges. In the spring of 1522 the nobility of the Upper Rhine met at Landau, and resolved that they would only allow their feudal affairs to be judged before feudal judges and vassals, according to old custom, and their differences with those of other classes, before tribunals composed of impartial judges, of knightly rank, ‡ and that they would come to the assistance of every man to whom this was refused. They elected Franz von Sickingen their leader in this matter. An address to the imperial towns, written by Hutten and dated 1522,§ is the manifesto of the opinions entertained by Sickingen and his followers Never were the sovereign princes more vehemently accused of violence and injustice, the towns were invited to accept the friendship and alliance of the nobility, and above all, to destroy the Council of Regency, which Hutten looked upon as the representative of the princely power

The religious dissensions gave, of course, a strong additional impulse to hostilities undertaken against one of the most powerful of the spiritual princes. The Ebernburg was, in fact, the first place in which the evangelical service was regularly celebrated in its new form. Sickingen's followers went further than the school of Wittenberg. They considered the administration of the Lord's Supper in both kinds not alone lawful, but absolutely necessary. John Œcolampadius was the first who condemned as pernicious the spiritual satisfaction which the people felt at listening every day to the unintelligible muttering of the mass, being present at the ceremony of benediction, and commending themselves to God without much expenditure of time or attention; and he accordingly read the mass only on Sundays, omitting the elevation of the host, and using none but the German language.‖ There is a letter extant written by Sickingen himself, in which he inveighs against the use of pictures in churches, and pronounces them better fitted for the decoration of stately halls, he also declaims against the invocation of saints The

Rüdigkheim und Reuschlein "haben im Junio 2 Wägen mit Kupfer beladen zwo Meil von Frankfurt angenommen und die Fuhrleut ungescheut benothiget, dass sie das Kupfer in das Schloss Rücking, dem von Rudigkheim zugehörig, führen mussen "—" Rüdigkheim and Reuschlin did in June take, two miles from Frankfurt, two wagons loaded with copper, and in the most shameless manner constrained the drivers to convey the copper to the castle Rücking, which belonged to Rudigkheim" Rudigkheim wrote to the burgher of Nurnberg, to whom the copper belonged, that if he wished to have it back, he might come and buy it of him They were exasperated because the citizens of Nurnberg had complained to the emperor

* Furstenberg writes from Wertheim on St Peter's and Paul's day, 1522 "also hab ich meyn gnedigen Herrn gebeten, uns gen Wirtzburg zu verhelfen ist er willig, Gott helf uns furter"—"I have then besought my gracious Lord to assist us in our journey to Wurzburg, if he be willing, God help us further"

† Balthazar Schlor's letter to Sickingen without date, but immediately before the outbreak of hostilities, in Günther's Codex Diplomaticus Rheno Mosellanus, v. p 202

‡ " wo der Kleger den Antwurter erfordert vor sein des Antwurters Genoss, oder ungefehrlich dem etwas gemess oder daruber, unpartheilichs Rechten oder Austrags, vor die, so inlendisch der Sachen gesessen oder gelegen seyn "—" where the plaintiff cites the defendant before a tribunal composed of his own and the defendant's peers (or nearly so), and having jurisdiction over affairs occurring in the country "

§ "Beklagunge der Freistette deutscher nation"—"Complaints of the free cities of the German nation"—The date is ascertained by these words —

"Der (Kaiser) zeucht nun von uns wider Mher,
Sie wollen nit, dass er widerkheer"

"The emperor now leaves us again,
They wish he may not come back"

These ideas prevailed in the following year also, as we learn from a writing by Kettenbach "Practica practicirt," &c (*Panzer*, ii 190.) wherein the cities are exhorted not to involve themselves in the disputes between the nobles and the princes

‖ Œcolampadii Epistola ad Hedionem in Gerdesius Historia Evangelii, tom i Monumenta, p 166

marriage of Johann Schwebel, one of his preachers, was arranged by him. One of his friends was Hartmuth von Kronenberg, who may be considered as the earliest specimen of a pious and earnest Lutheran in the style of more modern times.*

The connexion with these mighty elements gave unwonted importance to Sickingen's enterprises. The majority of the whole knighthood of the empire was on his side, and exerted itself in his favour; he also called on Luther, to whom he had formerly offered protection, for his support. And assuredly it would have been no mean alliance, had the monk, whom the nation honoured as a prophet, taken up his abode with the brave and puissant knight, and lent to the formidable bands of the Ebernburg the powerful aid of his word. But Luther had the great good sense to avoid all political connexions, to attempt no violence, and to trust solely and entirely to the might of his doctrines. Sickingen received nothing from Saxony but dissuasions. Nevertheless, his manifesto to the inhabitants of Treves shows how much he reckoned on the prevailing national inclinations; for he promises that "he will deliver them from the heavy antichristian yoke of the priesthood and lead them to evangelical freedom."† The ideas and sentiments of a warlike noble, who feels himself a match even for a powerful prince; of the head of the whole order of knighthood, and of a champion of the new religious opinions, were all blended in his mind. It is a significant fact that Hutten, in one of his dialogues, puts into the mouth of Sickingen an ardent panegyric on Ziska, the invincible hero who cleared his country of monks and idle priests, employed their property for the general good, and put a stop to the depredations of Rome.‡

On the 27th of August, 1522, Sickingen declared war against the archbishop, chiefly for those things "wherein he had acted against God and the emperor's majesty." Secretly assisted, rather than hindered, by the Elector of Mainz, he arrived before Treves on the 7th of September, having taken St. Wendel. He crossed the Marsberg with 1500 horse, 5000 foot, and a considerable body of artillery,§ and we have reason to believe that he expected to be joined at this point by his friends, Rennenberg, who was recruiting for him in Cleves and Juliers, the bastard of Sombreff, who was doing the same in the archbishopric of Cologne; and Hanz Voss, who was arming in the territory of Limburg; Nickel Minkwitz, too, was to join him with 1500 men out of Brunswick. In Sickingen's camp, it was rumoured that he would soon be elector, nay, perhaps something even greater still. The eyes of the whole empire were turned upon his movements, the delegate of Duke George of Saxony wrote to his master that nothing so dangerous to the princes of the empire had been attempted for centuries.‖ Others affirmed that affairs were in such a state, that before long it would be impossible to know who was king or emperor, prince or lord.

The turbulent and anarchical power of the knights thus once more threatened the peace and security of the whole empire. It is not easy to imagine what would have been the result had they been successful.

It is scarcely credible that a tolerably well-organised government could have been formed out of the several knightships which were now become absolute and independent sovereignties; or that the wild and arbitrary courses of men who were accustomed to look to their swords for right and security, could easily have been restrained by the sermons of the reformers: it is at least certain that Œcolampadius found a hard and ungrateful soil on Sickingen's mountain fortress. Moreover, the elements of which this body was composed were of the most heterogeneous natures. the knighthood—one of the most peculiar products of the middle ages—arose out of, and existed in, the disorganization of the powers of the state: whereas the declared tendency of the new religious system was to renovate and confirm those powers. The position of Sickingen himself was anomalous. the forces which he led were by no means of a chivalrous kind; he was at the head of a hired army which could only be held together by money, and furnished with the apparatus for a kind of warfare essentially opposed to all knightly modes of combat. Strange spectacle!—the forces which decided the fate of the world in two different ages were here in contact, and it was imagined that they could be brought to unite and co-operate! We, in our days, can see how impossible was such a union, for it is only by keeping pace, sincerely and energetically, with the progress of society, that any thing permanent can be effected. Even at that time, however, it was perceived, that if the power of the princes were overthrown, and the constitution of the empire (which was as yet by no means firmly established) broken up, nothing was to be expected but an exclusive, violent, and at the same time self-conflicting rule of the nobles.

The question then was, who should undertake the defence of public order, thus fearfully menaced.

The Council of Regency did all that was in its power. Remonstrances were sent to Sickingen, and mandates to all the neighbouring princes, enjoining them to resist his attempts. On Sickingen, the warnings from the Regency made little impression: he replied, that he himself intended to introduce a new order of things into the empire.¶ He utterly refused

* Letters from Kronenberg to the four mendicant orders, 25th June, 1522 and to the inhabitants of Kronenberg, Munch's Sickingen, ii pp 145 and 153

† Extracts from the manifestoes in Meiner's Leben Huttens, p 317

‡ Monitor Secundus Opp, iv p 144

§ This number, smaller than that which is usually given, is taken from the Flersheimer Chronik, in Munch's Sickingen, iii p 215

‖ Letter in the Royal Saxon Archives

¶ Planitz to the Elector Frederic, 13th Sept "Sickingen habe gesagt, er wolle sich eines Thuns unterstehn, dessen sich kein romischer Kaiser unterstanden 28th Sept er habe den Boten des Regiments gesagt er wisst vorwar, sein Herr der Kaiser werde nicht zurnen, ob er den Pfaffen ein wenig strafet und ihm die Kronen eintrankt, die er

to submit to a decision of the Imperial Chamber, and said that he had a court of justice of his own, composed of soldiers who argued with muskets and carronades. It is very probable that his whole army did not think as he did; at any rate, the Council of Regency asserted that Franz's following and power were greatly diminished in consequence of their efforts. But a far weightier authority was required to force him to submission, and every thing depended on the resistance he would find from the elector and his allies.

Richard von Greiffenklau, Archbishop of Treves, had made the best possible preparations. He had burned down the convent of St. Maximin, on which the enemy reckoned for stores, bringing in his own hand the first torch that fired it: in the town, his presence kept down the disturbances which certainly had begun. The clergy mounted guard round the cathedral, the citizens in the market-place, the mercenaries on the walls and in the towers, and the conduct of the war was entrusted to the native nobles who had not deserted the cause of the see.

While Sickingen, who had calculated on making a *coup-de-main*, now met with an unexpected and determined resistance, it so happened that all his friends and allies, whose arrival was necessary to the completion of his force, were either detained or beaten. The Duke of Cleves and the Elector of Cologne ordered all the horsemen who had been recruited in their territories, to stay at home, under pain of forfeiture of their fiefs, and even of their lives. The young Landgrave of Hessen succeeded in defeating Minkwitz's troops as they were marching from Brunswick; taking their leader, with all his papers, prisoner, and finally inducing the soldiers to enter his own service.* All these reverses deterred the Luneburg and Westphalian troops from taking the field at all.

On the other side, the Elector Palatine, Sickingen's former patron, as well as his old and bitter enemy the Landgrave of Hessen, took arms and hastened to the assistance of their neighbour and ally, the Elector of Treves.

Sickingen, deprived of the support he had expected, and encamped before a bravely defended town, in an open country, among a people exasperated by his devastations, did not dare to await the conjunction of forces so superior to his own; besides this, he himself did not evince that energy and those resources of talent and bravery, without which no one can venture with impunity on such hazardous enterprises. On the 14th of September he was compelled to abandon Treves.†

That one week sufficed to give a turn to the whole destiny of Germany.

The three sovereigns who represented the threatened princely power, were thus triumphant over the rebellious knights and their leaders. They were not content with clearing the archbishopric of its enemies, and though, strange to say, they did not pursue Sickingen, they immediately attacked his allies.

The Elector of Mainz, who was accused of allowing a detachment of Sickingen's horse to pass the Rhine unmolested, was forced to buy his peace at the cost of 25,000 gulden.‡

Hartmuth von Kronenberg, whom the landgrave wanted above all to punish for the share he had taken in Sickingen's foray on Darmstadt, was beleaguered in his castle near Frankfurt. The landgrave would not hear of pardon or conditions; he helped to point the cannon with his own hand. The knight escaped but just in time for his fortress was forced to surrender on the 16th of October. The three princes received in person the oaths of allegiance from the inhabitants, and the town was for a long time treated as Hessian.§

They next marched against Frowen von Hutten, "because he had taken part in the rebellion, and received proclaimed outlaws in his house:" his castle of Saalmünster was taken.

The same fate was shared by Philip Waiss of Haussen in the Mark of Fulda, and by Rudeken in Rukingen; others endeavoured to save themselves by negotiation.

A similar storm threatened Sickingen's allies in distant parts of the country. The Franconian nobles had not, it is true, directly assisted him, but they had encouraged him in his project, and had generally adhered to his faction. The Swabian League, on the contrary, had made common cause with the princes, especially with the Elector Palatine, and now summoned the Franconian knights before its tribunal, to stand their trial for certain breaches of the Public Peace. The knights did not consider themselves bound to obey this citation, and, accordingly, met at Schweinfurt to protest against it: they were still determined to defend themselves. The vassals of the Bishop of Wurzburg, who had been the last to join the League, were so exasperated at his tardiness, that, in the beginning of the year 1523, they deprived him of all his offices. This threw all Swabia and Franconia into confusion. From the very superior strength of the League, the result of the struggle was easily foreseen, unless the Council of Regency had power to prevent it.

Events indeed now acquired a totally different character and importance, from their

genommen hatte." "Sickingen had said he would dare to do a deed which no Roman emperor had yet dared. 28th Sept. he said to the messenger of the Regency, he knew for certain that his lord the emperor would not be angry because he punished the priest a little, and paid him off for the crowns he had taken." People really began to believe that the emperor might have some understanding with him. The emperor afterwards said, Franz had not served him well enough to induce him to connive at matters of this sort.

* Letter from Landgrave Philip to the Elector of Treves, 5th Sept. 1522, in Rommel's Geschichte von Hessen, vol. v. p. 858.

† These events at Treves are described by Latomus and Browerus, Annal. Trev. ii. 340. who has also quoted Latomus Gesta Trevirorum in Hontheim's Prodromus, p. 858, Chronicon S. Maximini, ibid. p. 1035.

‡ The delegate of Duke George says that this is one of the reasons. "Die andern stecken in der Feder."—"The others stick in the pen."

§ Tendel. "Beschreibung der Belagerung von Kronenberg."—Munch, iii. p. 28.

effect on this supreme administrative body of the empire.

Its authority was formerly resisted and contemned by Sickingen and his friends, for which, on the accusation of the procurator of Treves, Sickingen had been outlawed on the 8th of October, contrary to the laws of the empire, without summons or trial. Now, however, his enemies placed themselves in an attitude of equal defiance, and of equal peril to the Council of Regency: instead of pursuing the outlaw himself, they attacked his supposed allies, frequently without proof of their guilt, and took their fortified dwellings. The Swabian League, which already declared that it had only acquiesced in the creation of the Council of Regency on the supposition of its union, now openly usurped part of the functions of the Imperial Chamber by the citations before its own tribunal to which we have alluded; and it did not deign even to return an answer to an admonition not to molest people about the Public Peace.

Men's pretensions naturally rise with their power. As the attempts of Sickingen, and the insubordinate spirit of the Franconian nobility had not been put down by the Council of Regency, but by the superior force and the arms of their neighbours, it was natural that the latter should now continue the struggle with a view to their own interests, without much regard to the supreme authority of the empire.*

Hence it happened that the Council of Regency soon took under its protection the very men it had but just before treated as its enemies. Frowen von Hutten, after the opinions of the most considerable members of the Imperial Chamber had been heard, obtained without much trouble a mandate wherein the princes were required to restore all his castles to him; and shortly after a formal judgment was given in his favour. At the same time, the Council of Regency pressed the princes to release the Elector of Mainz from the conditions so arbitrarily imposed on him.† These princes had wished for the aid of the empire to put down the outlawed Sickingen; but this they found it impossible to obtain, either from the Regency or from the Estates assembled in the beginning of the year 1523; if the sentence of outlawry had not already been pronounced, we may safely assume that it would not have been pronounced at all.‡ Some members of the Swabian League proposed that all meetings and associations among the order of knights should be forbidden, but to this the Regency could not now be brought to consent; on the contrary, it proclaimed its intention of protecting all the knights, except those who had committed any offence against the Public Peace.

It appears to me that the knights as a body now first became of real importance to the organization and progress of the empire. Their wild project of founding an independent power was at an end. The Council of Regency was their sole support, and they found themselves under the necessity of making common cause with it. The union of these two bodies, essentially distinct, was rendered more strict by the circumstance that the knights and the Regency had both embraced the evangelical doctrines. For the same reason, the Elector of Saxony, who was the main prop of the Regency, entered into a kind of alliance with the knights. In the second quarter of the year 1523, when the duty of personal attendance at the Council of Regency fell upon the Elector of Mainz, his place was filled by his cousin, the grand master, Albert of Prussia, whose sole purpose was to maintain the dominion of his order, *i. e.* the Teutonic knights, and especially those of Swabia and Franconia, in their own country, and to set the whole powers of the empire in motion to that effect.

Little as it had been to be desired a year ago, that Sickingen should conquer Treves, it was of great importance that he should be able to defend himself against the attacks which were preparing against him in the spring of 1523.

Thus, by a strange turn of fate, the safety of the knight who had so often disturbed the Public Peace, and committed so many deeds of violence, became now, after he was outlawed, inextricably bound up with the interests of order in the empire.

Nor did he by any means give up his cause: he expected to receive assistance from Lower Germany, and from the Upper Rhine; to be joined by the Bohemian and Franconian knights, and to be supported by the Lutherans. From his fortress of Landstuhl, where he was then living, he one day descried horsemen among the distant underwood; he flattered himself that they were Lutherans who were coming to see what he was about, but they came no nearer, and tied their horses to the bushes.§ What he saw was the advanced guard of the enemy who were approaching to besiege him.

Meanwhile he had no apprehension. He had just repaired his fortress; and had no doubt that he would be able to stand a siege of three months at least, in which time his allies would come up and relieve him.

But the event proved that he had not rightly calculated the improvement that had taken place in the engines of war during the preceding century. He had no other means of defence than those used by the knights of old: it remained to be seen whether the lofty situation, the vaulted towers—solid as the rocks they stood on—and the massive walls, could afford protection against artillery. It was soon evident that the old defences were far too weak for the modern arts of war. On the 30th of April 1523, the princes began to bombard the castle with carronades and culverins, well supplied

* See the letter from the Elector of Treves, 2d Nov. 1522, in Münch, iii. 33.

† Planitz, 4th Feb. 1523, says, they should release him from his obligations, and give Sickingen an amicable hearing.

‡ Planitz thought on the 24th Nov. that sentence of outlawry would not be pronounced against Sickingen, "man hätte ihn denn citiert; aber geschehn ist geschehn" —"without citing him to appear; but what is done is done."

§ Hubert Th. Leodius, Acta et Gesta Francisci de Sickingen in Freher Script. Rer. Germ. iii. p. 305.

with ammunition and well served. The young landgrave, who appeared in the dress of a landsknecht, showed courage and skill * the great tower, which commanded and threatened their camp, fell the same day. the newness of its walls made them less able to withstand the shock of the cannon-balls. Sickingen seeing this unexpected misfortune, went to a loophole, and leaning on a battering engine, sought to get a view of the state of things, and of what was to be done. A culverin happened at the moment to be pointed in that direction with but too sure an aim; the implements of defence were scattered in all directions, and Sickingen himself was hurled against a sharp beam and mortally wounded in the side

The whole fortress was a ruin. in the only vault which remained standing, lay the lord of the castle, bereft of all hope No help appeared in sight. "Where now," said Sickingen. "are those gentlemen, my friends, who promised me so much? Where is Furstenberg? where are the Swiss and the Strasburgers?" He was at last forced to capitulate †

The princes having refused to allow him liberty to evacuate the castle, as, according to custom, he proposed, he said, "I will not be their prisoner long" He had scarcely strength enough left to sign the conditions, and lay dying when the princes entered the donjon

The Elector of Treves said, "What charge had you to bring against me, Franz, that you attacked me and my poor subjects in my see?" "And what against me," said the landgrave, "that you invaded my land in my nonage?" Sickingen replied, "I have now to render an account to a greater sovereign."

His chaplain Nicolas asked him whether he wished to confess, but he answered, "I have already confessed to God in my heart."

The chaplain addressed to him some last words of consolation, and held up the host, the princes bared their heads and knelt down at that moment Sickingen expired, and the princes said a paternoster for his soul ‡

Sickingen's memory will live for ever, not on account of any great achievements productive of lasting results, nor even on account of his extraordinary bravery, or of any eminent moral qualities he evinced, but for the novelty and importance of the position to which he gradually attained. The first step in his rise was his connexion with the Elector Palatine, who employed him against his enemies, opened a career to him, and afforded him support and assistance both publicly and in secret. Thus in a short time, from an inconsiderable knight, possessor only of two or three mountain castles, he became a powerful Condottiere, who could bring a small army into the field at his own charges. The more considerable he became, the more he felt tempted to pursue his own line of policy, and justified in doing so The Wurtemberg war was the first occasion on which he separated himself from the elector, who did not cordially approve that enterprise. He did not, however, on that account join the Swabian League, on the contrary, he soon entered into the closest alliance with the Franconian knights, with whom that body was at enmity This it was that rendered his position so imposing We have seen how, a few years before, Wurtemberg, the Palatinate, and Wurzburg opposed the Swabian League with the aid of the knights Now, however, the princes had been forced to join the league, and Wurtemberg had been subdued, so that Sickingen and the knights maintained the opposition single-handed Visions of reviving the ancient independence of the nobility, of freeing themselves from the territorial jurisdiction of the temporal and spiritual princes, and of opening the way for the spread of the new religious convictions, floated before their minds Never was there a more singular combination in the midst of the deeds of violence that were committed, there was a lively and ready apprehension of great ideas it is this strange union which characterizes the nobility of that time. Meanwhile they had neither the intellectual power nor the political influence necessary to carry out projects of such a nature When Sickingen at last decidedly attacked the princely authority, mightier powers took the field against him, the Palatinate not only abandoned him, but combined with his enemies for his destruction.§ He then discovered that he was not so strong as he believed himself to be, that he did not owe his elevation to his own powers alone, and that those which had helped to raise, were now turned against him. In this conflict he perished.

The taking of Landstuhl was a victory of the order of princes (*Furstenthum*) over that of knights (*Ritterthum*); of the cannon over the stronghold, and in so far, of the new order of things over the old, it fortified the newly arisen independent powers of the empire.

All the castles belonging to Sickingen and his friends now fell into the hands of the princes They were twenty-seven in all, including those taken in the course of the autumn. Those on the right bank of the Rhine fell to the share of the landgrave, those on the left were divided between the elector palatine and the archbishop In the Ebernberg, the only castle that defended itself for any length of time, rich booty was taken,—splendid jewels and plate, both for worldly and religious purposes, but above all, thirty-six pieces of artillery, the finest of which—the Nightingale, cast by Master Stephen of Frankfurt—measured thirteen feet and a half, weighed seventy hun-

* Lettera da Ispruch a di 12 Mazo, 1523, al Sr Mcb di Mantua "Il Landgraho si è portato magnanimamente, essendo sempre stato de li primi, in zuppone con le calze tagliate et in corsaletto da Lanzichenech, et è giovane di 18 anni"—*Sanuto's Cron Ven* vol xxxiv

† Account of what occurred in the wars of Franz Sickingen, Spalatin, Sammlung zu Sachs Gesch, v p 148.

‡ The Flersheimer Chronik contains the most authentic account Munch, iii 222.

§ Contemporaries saw it in this light, as is shown by the dialogue between the Fox and the Wolf "Wolf Wie mainstu hat der Pfalzgraff gethon, wir wolten gut feiste Bolz erlangt han? Fuchs es ist bei Got war, derselb hat uns allein den Schaden thon des wir uns nit versehen"—"The Wolf How thinkest thou, has the elector palatine done—should we have received good large crossbow bolts? The Fox It is true, by God, he alone has done us the mischief against which we had not guarded."

dred weight, and was decorated with the figures of the knight and his lady, their respective ancestors, and the saint for whom they had formerly had a peculiar devotion — St Francis.* This was part of the landgrave's share. The princes bound themselves to aid each other to keep what they had won in common, after which, on the 6th of June, they separated

At the same moment the Swabian League held a meeting at Nordlingen, to which all the Franconian knights accused of a breach of the Public Peace were summoned for trial Some of them succeeded in clearing themselves from suspicion others appeared, but failing to prove their innocence, they were not admitted to their oath. Many altogether disdained to present themselves before the councillors of the league † Against the two last classes, an army of 1500 horse and 15,000 foot assembled on the 15th June, at Dunkelspiel, under the command of George Truchsess the cities of Augsburg, Ulm, and Nurnberg provided the artillery ‡ Such an army as this was far too powerful to be resisted by the Franconian nobles. Bocksberg, near Mergentheim, was considered the strongest castle in Franconia, and upon it, on the advice of the Nurnbergers, the march was first directed The Rosenbergs, to whom it belonged, had originally meant to defend themselves, and had hired a troop of landsknechts and musketeers to serve their guns; but when they saw such an overpowering force, they gave up all idea of defence, and surrendered their castle with its stores This example put an end to all resistance The castle of Absberg was burnt, and nothing left standing but the bare walls. In the Krugelstein there stood a tower, the walls of which were eight feet thick, even at the top; this was blown up with gunpowder. Waldstein, in the midst of its wilderness, whither many a prisoner had been dragged, was blown up and destroyed by Wolf von Freiberg, the captain of the city of Augsburg twenty-six castles are enumerated, all of which were seized, and most destroyed. Some of these were Bohemian fiefs, and at first the Bohemians had made a show of resistance in the neighbourhood of the mountains, but the League ordered its commander to act up to his instructions, without regard to the Bohemians, who accordingly retreated, leaving him to fulfil his terrible commission.

The independent knights were utterly crushed. Just as they had caught the inspiration of religion, and had hoped by its influence to open a new career for themselves, their power was broken for ever We must not fail to observe a fact intimately connected with this event The man who first brought the warlike spirit of knighthood into contact with the religious agitations of the times, Ulrich von Hutten, was involved in the common catastrophe. He had given to Sickingen's enterprises the incalculable aid of a zealous counsellor and encouraging friend: he was, therefore, naturally struck with consternation at his fall. He dared not endanger the safety of his relations by his presence; and in Upper Germany he was equally obnoxious to the vengeance of the spiritual, and of the victorious temporal authorities; he took refuge in Switzerland, as others had done in Saxony. There he fell again into the same bitter and desponding state of mind which he had once laboured under in his youth. Nor, even here, did he always find a welcome; he wandered from place to place, under the unhappy necessity of asking money and assistance of his literary friends, many of whom shunned him as dangerous Erasmus, who carefully kept up his connexions among the great, was frightened at the idea of receiving a visit from him, and avoided and repulsed him. In addition to this, his old disease broke out again in a dreadful manner Yet the veteran combatant did not lose his courage, once more he poured forth all the vehemence of his rhetoric against Erasmus, whom he looked upon as an apostate But he had now no longer strength to bear such violent emotions and exertions, and before he could receive the answer of Erasmus, disease put an end to his life — he died at Ufnau, on the lake of Zurich, where he had gone at Zwingli's advice to consult a priest skilled in the healing art §

It was fortunate for Luther that he had made no closer alliance with the knights; as both he and the doctrine he preached would have been involved in their evil destiny.

If we now return to the point whence we started, we shall clearly perceive, that the whole turn of affairs was unpropitious, and even dangerous, to the Council of Regency. It would indeed have been unable to do any thing for Sickingen, having tied its own hands by declaring him an outlaw, it would however gladly have afforded protection to the knightly order, but what resistance could it possibly make to two such powerful armies as those of the League and of the princes? Moreover these two powers, emboldened by conquests, assumed an attitude of still greater defiance, and even hostility. The princes declared the judgment in favour of Frowen von Hutten invalid and illegal,|| and rejected the proceedings of the Regency in that and all other cases.

To this dangerous hostility another no less formidable was soon added.

THE CITIES AND THE IMPERIAL COURT.

Under the circumstances we have been describing, the establishment of the proposed import duties, by which the power of the

* Report in Spalatin, p 151

† Letter from Nordlingen in the Dresden Archives, beginning of June, 1523, "der Bund geht teglich zwir in Rath" — "The league meets in council every day" Chiefly from Mullner's Annalen, which contains a journal of the whole expedition

‡ Nurnberg gave 2 cannon, 2 carronades, 2 nightingales, 2 culverins, 6 rabinets, 6 mortars, 60 pole axes.

§ Zwinglius to Wolfhardt, 11th Oct, "libros nullos habuit, supellectilem nullam præter calamum" — *Epp*, p. 313

|| Planitz, 23d July He thinks that, under such circumstances, the Council of Regency could not last long "Denn der dreier Furstent und des Bunds Vornehmen will sicht mit unsern gethanen Pflichten gar nicht leiden" — "The intentions of the three princes and of the league will not square with our duties"

Council of Regency must have been materially increased, could not have failed to produce important results. There ought to have been no hesitation on the subject, the States had resolved on it; the emperor had given his consent beforehand. A messenger from the lieutenant of the Empire had already carried the acts and the Recess of the diet to Spain

But we have already remarked how much the cities thought themselves injured and endangered by such an interference with commerce: they were determined not to submit to it without resistance

They had also many other grievances to allege

In the year 1521, the decree concerning the levies for the expedition to Rome had been passed without summoning the cities, according to ancient usage, to the deliberation The cities immediately complained, whereupon an explanation was given which satisfied them for the moment.

Since then, however, the attempts made to meet the exigencies of the empire by taxes which would have fallen most heavily on the cities; their determined resistance, the attacks on the monopolies on the one side, and the obstinate maintenance of them on the other, had been continually augmenting the ill-will between the cities and the higher classes, and at the diet of 1522–3 it openly burst forth.

A general meeting of the States was announced for the 11th of December, 1522, in order to hear and discuss proposals to be made by the Council of Regency and the committee, for succours to be granted to the Hungarians It had formerly been customary for the Council of Regency, after submitting a proposition, to retire and leave the three colleges to deliberate thereupon. On this occasion, however, the Regency did not retire: the electors and princes assented to its proposal without separating, and it was then laid before the cities The cities, which were peculiarly interested in questions of this kind, and always rather hard to satisfy, asked time for consideration—only till the afternoon. Hereupon they received an answer which they little expected. they were told, that "the usage in the empire was, that when a thing was determined on by the electors, princes and other Estates, the cities should be content to abide by it." The citizens, on their side, contended, that if they were to share weal and woe with the other States, they ought also to have a voice in the deliberations; in short, that those who took their purses must be fain to take their counsel The subsidies in money were what they particularly objected to, like the other States, they would only furnish men. But no attention was paid by the assembly to a resolution they drew up to this effect. A mandate was issued, requiring them to furnish contributions which they had never voted they asked fresh time for deliberation, but were again told that it was not the practice they were preparing to reply when it struck eleven, and the sitting was dissolved.*

The cities were the more confounded at this proceeding, on being told that it was by special favour that two of their deputies were received into the committee, whereas the counts had only one. they thought this betrayed an intention of excluding them from the committees altogether. In the year 1487, they had given up the opposition which, as a body, they had long maintained, because the Elector Berthold of Mainz had, as we saw, obtained for them a practical share in the deliberations, and we know how powerfully this was sometimes exercised they now supposed that the intention was to strip them of all their rights, at the same time that the fulfilment of their obligations was strictly enforced

As measures which threatened to be extremely injurious to their trade and manufactures were now resolved on with reference to monopolies and import duties, and as a fresh petition, in which all their grievances past and present were set forth, had proved as ineffectual as the preceding ones, they determined to resist with all their might.

They steadily withheld their assent to the decisions of the diet, and obstinately refused to grant a loan which they were called upon to advance, and which was to be repaid out of the proceeds of the tax for the Turkish war. Hereupon the princes took care to let them feel their displeasure. "The imperial towns," writes the deputy from Frankfurt,† "are departing under heavy disgrace. time alone can show what will be the result, but my journey home is a sad one."

It was fortunate for the cities that the decisions of the States did not immediately acquire the force of law, but had first to be sent to Spain to receive the emperor's ratification. Their only hope lay in this. In March, 1523, the cities assembled in Spire, and resolved to send an embassy of their own to Spain, to represent to the emperor the injury they apprehended from the proposed duties, as well as their other grievances.

The report of this mission is fortunately still extant, and we will pause over it for a moment, as it affords us a curious specimen of the manner in which the affairs of Germany were conducted at the Imperial court in Spain.

The journey was extremely long and fatiguing On the 15th of June, the delegates met at Lyons, and it was not till the 6th of August that they reached Valladolid. the chief cause of delay was the oppressive heat, which even caused some of the party to fall sick.

They began by visiting Markgrave Johann of Brandenburg, the high chancellor, and above all the councillors to whom the affairs of Germany were referred; Herr von Rosch, Hannart, Provost Marklin of Waldkirchen, and Maximilian von Zevenberghen

Hereupon, on the 9th of August, the emperor gave them a formal audience in the pre-

* Letter from Holzhausen to Frankfort, Dec 1522

Frankf Arch, vol xxxvi, particularly f 110 Die Supplik der Stadte

† Holzhausen, 25th, 26th, 29th Jan 1523 Vol xxxvii. of the Frankf A is here my chief authority

sence of a brilliant assembly of grandees, bishops and ambassadors they addressed him in Latin, and were answered in the same language by the chancellor, in the emperor's name

A commission was then appointed to discuss affairs with them, consisting only of the four German councillors we have named above the proceedings commenced on the 11th of August

The delegates had drawn up a statement of their grievances under six heads,—administration of justice, tolls, subsidies, Public Peace, monopolies, and other things of less importance These they laid before the commissioners in German and Latin, and then went through them together, which gave them an opportunity of expressing their wishes orally.

The councillors at first appeared unfavourably inclined They thought it unjust that the question of the jurisdictions should not have been brought forward till now, when a young emperor had just ascended the throne they complained that no class in the empire would do its part, although neither the Council of Regency nor the courts of justice could be maintained without supplies from the several Estates· they exhorted the cities to submit for a short time longer, and not to refuse their share of the contributions voted by the diet on the part of the whole empire, in aid of the Hungarians. A draught of a ratification of the decree of the diet had actually been prepared at the instigation of another imperial councillor, Doctor Lamparter. But the delegates were not so easily put off they declared that the cities were ready to contribute their share, for example, to pay two members of the Imperial Chamber, and even to pay the contributions, at the rate determined at the diet of Constance, but that they had no intention of submitting to the unjust demands attempted to be enforced against them. They supported their declarations with a very few acute and stringent remarks "Who can foretell," said they, "what will become of the revenues raised from these import duties? It is reported that a scheme has already been proposed by the princes for sharing the proceeds amongst themselves; and even if this be not true, there is a project of electing a king of the Romans, who would be able to maintain his power out of the revenue thus raised" In short, they made it appear that the duty would be dangerous to the emperor himself; remarking, at the same time, that the Council of Regency was not composed in the manner most favourable to the interests of the emperor They also promised the councillors, personally, "to make a grateful return to them for their trouble."

The cities had thus hit upon the means by which any thing was to be accomplished at the imperial court.

At the next meeting the Provost of Waldkirchen gave them to understand, that the emperor, finding how unpopular it was, was not inclined to impose the duty in question; neither was it his intention to continue the Council of Regency, but he must then ask, what the cities were prepared to do for his imperial majesty, if he took the government into his own hands? The delegates replied, that if the emperor granted their petition, and then made any reasonable suggestion to them, they would show themselves grateful and obedient subjects. Waldkirchen reminded them that it appeared from the old registers, that the last emperors on their accession had received a gift of honour from the cities, and asked, why this had been omitted for the first time with the young emperor, who, he said, placed his whole confidence in the cities, and, were it not for the wars, would take a straightforward and royal course with regard to them.

Another matter next fell under discussion. The pope's nuncio had complained that in Augsburg, Strasburg, and Nurnberg, Luther's doctrines were received, and his works printed. The delegates, on being called to account for this, denied the fact. They declared that not a syllable of Luther's writings had been printed in their towns for several years; nay more, that foreign itinerant venders of his books had been punished, and that, however much the common people might thirst after the Gospel and reject human doctrines, it was not from the towns that Luther found protection it was well known who his defenders were, the cities, for their part, were resolved, hereafter as heretofore, to remain Christian members of the Christian church.

Hereupon the two parties came to an agreement on the most important points Another conference between the whole commission and the delegates was held on the 19th of August, and attended also by the Count of Nassau. The doors having been carefully closed, the delegates were informed, that the emperor intended to take the government into his own hands, to appoint a valiant lieutenant, and a noble and dignified Imperial Chamber, and not to allow the imposition of the import duties. The amount of the sum to be offered to him was left to the discretion of the delegates; but they promised to come to an agreement on the subject with Hannart, who was to go to Germany as the imperial commissioner

The delegates were also to treat concerning the monopolies, not exactly on the part of the cities as a body, but in the name of the great mercantile companies. The omnipotence of money and its possessors soon helped them to the attainment of their object It was settled that the Council of Regency was to be directed to pass no resolution with regard to the monopolies, without again asking the consent of his imperial majesty.*

Their commission being thus satisfactorily executed, the delegates quitted Spain. At Lyons they had an audience of Francis I., who vented upon them his anger against the emperor. In December they reached Nürnberg, where a fresh diet had just assembled.

* "Der gemeynen Frey und Reichs Stadt Potschafften Handlung bei Romisch Kayserl Majestadt zu Valedolid in Castilia"—"The Negotiation of the Embassy of the united, free, and imperial Cities, with his Roman Imperial Majesty at Valladolid in Castile" In the month of August, anno 1523 In the Frankf Arch, tom xxxix. fol. 39—56

The final result then was, that the imperial court had entered into a combination with the cities, against the existing form of government in the empire, and especially against the Council of Regency.

And, indeed, it was only natural that the imperial councillors, who had always been in competition with this administrative body, should take advantage of any international dispute to rid themselves of it.

Another and a still stronger motive existed. The idea had really arisen in Germany, as the towns had hinted, of electing a king of the Romans. Ferdinand of Austria, the emperor's own brother, was the man pointed out by the public voice. It was believed, as far as I can discover,* that he would govern in concert with the Council of Regency, according to the forms of the constitution which had just been established; and it is manifest that this could only have attained its completion, had Germany possessed a sovereign of limited power, and dependent on constitutional forms. No wonder that the mere suggestion should be very ill received in Spain; in fact, it almost implied an abdication on the part of the emperor.

Moreover, Ferdinand was very unpopular there. He was constantly making fresh demands, while frequent complaints were preferred against him; besides, the Spaniards believed his most confidential adviser, Salamanca, to be equally ambitious and selfish. When Hannart went to Germany, he was commissioned, if possible, to effect Salamanca's dismissal, and to counteract all his ambitious views.

DIET OF 1524.

If in a former chapter we have endeavoured to show what weighty interests of church and state were involved in the existence of the Council of Regency, we must now turn our attention to the mighty and determined opposition arrayed against it.

Three warlike and victorious princes; the Swabian League, which wielded such formidable forces; wealthy cities; and finally, though as yet in secret, the Emperor, whose whole hope of regaining unlimited authority rested on the overthrow of this representative body.

The Council of Regency was not, however, destitute of support. Archduke Ferdinand promised not to consent to its overthrow, and some of his councillors were its decided adherents, as might be expected, from the prospects it held out to him and to them. The Elector of Saxony, to whom it chiefly owed its existence, attended the diet in person in order to defend it. The Elector of Mainz, who had suffered from the oppression of the three princes alluded to, together with the whole house of Brandenburg, were among its champions. The Regency also enjoyed the whole sympathy of the knightly order (whose only hopes were founded upon it), and of the partisans of the religious innovations.

Thus it still stood on firm ground: in spite of all the changes of individual members, the majority once established, remained: those who did not belong to it, like the Chancellor of Treves, Otto Hundt of Hessen, stayed away.† The imperial fiscal commenced the proceedings against the great mercantile companies, and a judgment against the three princes was prepared. Several most important questions were laid before the diet, which opened on the 14th of January, 1524, concerning the means of maintaining the government and the administration of justice; the execution of decrees of the diet, the code of criminal procedure,‡ &c.

It is a calamity for any power to have produced no great results; and under this disadvantage the Council of Regency laboured. It had been unable to maintain the Public Peace, or to control either Sickingen or his adversaries. The great scheme of customs' duties, on which all the resources for carrying on the government depended, had come to nothing. It was now assailed by blow upon blow.

On the 1st of February the attorney of the three princes, Dr. Venningen, appeared before the general assembly of the States, and made a long, bitter, and insulting speech against the proceedings of the Council of Regency.

A mandate from the emperor was produced, by which the proceedings already commenced against the commercial companies were stayed. The court of Spain demanded to have the documents relating to the case laid before it.

Hannart next arrived, and from the first took part with the opponents of the Regency—the Elector of Treves, in whose company he came, and the cities, from whom he had received a present of 500 gulden.§ At his first interview with the archduke he did not pay him the respect which that prince expected, nor did he attempt to conceal that the emperor wished for the dissolution of the existing form of government.

Such were the circumstances under which the assembly of the States began their deliberations: the debate on the grant necessary to the maintenance of the Council of Regency must, of course, bring the matter to a decision.

The Regency was, after all, the expression of the power of the several States of the empire; was it then credible that the States would themselves assist in its dissolution?

We have seen that the Regency obtained a majority in the former diets of the empire; though after laborious efforts and with precarious results. A host of new antipathies were now added, arising out of the interests of the sovereign princes and the free cities; of

* I extract from a roll of the Weimar Archives, which contains a number of scattered papers written by the chief councillors of the archduke to Elector Frederic, of which I intend to give some further account in the Appendix.

† Otto von Pack to Duke George of Saxony, the Friday after St. Lucia (Dresden Arch.), thinks that they were driven out. "Darnach wissen E. F. Gn. wer die andern seint, welche alle E. F. Gn. Abwesen wol erdulden können."—"Your princely grace will by this know who the others are, that can all well bear your grace's absence."

‡ Frankfurter Acten, vol. xxxix., in which are these documents, and vol. xl., containing the letters of Holzhausen concerning this diet.

§ Letter of Ferdinand's in Bucholtz, ii. p. 46.

money and of religion. The influence of the great capitalists was enormous even in those times. The Fuggers were instrumental in the election of Charles V., and, in all probability, in the publication of the bull of Leo X against Luther. They brought about the alliance between the court and the discontented towns, and it was mainly by their influence that the projected system of duties was abandoned; and now they had the audacity to turn the affair of the monopolies, which had called forth so many decrees of the diet against themselves, into a subject of accusation against the Council of Regency, alleging that that body had assumed judicial powers which properly belonged to the Imperial Chamber alone.* The Bishop of Wurzburg accused the Council of Regency of openly favouring the new creed he said that it had set at liberty two members of his chapter whom he had brought before the ecclesiastical court on the charge of contracting marriage, and that it had given a safe-conduct to a canon whom he had banished for Lutheran opinions. The imperial commissioner was informed that most of the members of the Council of Regency were zealous Lutherans.† The majority which had hitherto been in favour of that body was not compact enough to resist such a multitude of hostile influences, and after some debate and vacillation, turned against it The States did not, indeed, go so far as to propose its total abolition, but resolved not to meet on the 20th of February to consider the means for its maintenance, unless its members were previously changed; and declared they could by no means consent to its continuance, composed as it then was

This was, however, decisive The important point was, the establishment of a vigorous government, chosen out of the body of the States, but what could be expected for the future, if the present members, who had been really earnest in the performance of their duties, and had actually begun to govern, were to be deprived of office, without any charge worthy of a moment's discussion being brought against them? Was it likely that their successors would show any courage or independence?

It was once more rendered evident, that the powerful separate elements, of which the empire was compounded, could never be controlled by one central government.

Frederic the Wise of Saxony felt the whole significance of this decision He now, at the close of his life, saw the idea of a representative government, which had been the object of his whole existence, completely wrecked. He said, that he had never witnessed such a diet ‡ he left it on the 24th of February, and never appeared at one again

Archduke Ferdinand, it is true, still refused his assent to the decision; he even used his personal influence to win over the cities to the side of the Council of Regency; but in the course of a short time, observes the Saxon ambassador, his councillors were no longer of the same opinion it seemed as if Hannart, instead of destroying Salamanca's power, had gained him over; at all events, he never delivered the letter in which the emperor desired the Elector of Saxony to assist in getting rid of Salamanca. These causes at length produced their effect on Ferdinand "after holding out resolutely for nine weeks," writes the Saxon ambassador, on the 1st of March, "he has suddenly fallen away." He consented that not a single member of the old Council of Regency should be admitted into the new.§

The Imperial Chamber underwent the same sort of purification No inquiry was made as to whether the members had been attentive or negligent, capable or incapable; but merely whether they had supported the nobles against the princes, or aided the fiscal in the prosecution of monopolists. Their conduct as to religious matters was also taken into consideration. Dr. Kreutner, the assessor for the circle of Franconia, was dismissed for having eaten meat on a fast-day, without considering that he had a claim for upwards of 1000 gulden, arrears.

This brings us to the main question,—how far these great changes re-acted on the conduct of spiritual affairs. The cause of the Council of Regency and that of the religious reformation were, as we see at every step, connected, though not indissolubly the question now was, whether the States, which had abandoned the Regency to its fate, would be equally unfavourable to the new faith.

After the early and unexpected death of Adrian VI, the purer and severer spirit which he had introduced and exemplified, disappeared. Clement VII, who next ascended the papal chair, was, like his predecessors, exclusively bent on maintaining the papal privileges; and on applying the temporal forces of the States of the church to personal or political ends, without troubling himself seriously about the necessity of reform. He sent to the German diet a man of his own way of thinking,—Lorenzo Campeggi

Campeggi found Germany, which a few years before he had traversed, surrounded with the halo of an unshaken and sacred authority, in a state of complete apostasy In Augsburg he was assailed with derision and mockery when, at his entrance into the town, he raised

* Holzhausen, 12th Feb 1524 It appears from this that only Augsburg offered any resistance to the imperial edicts in the matter of the monopolies All the other towns were in favour of their abolition Dr Rohinger had inserted the article touching monopolies of his own accord in the instruction given to the delegates sent to Spain

† Hannart to the emperor, 14th March —"Et certes je me suis pour vray averty, la pluspart du regiment sont grands Lutheriens car en beaucoup de choses et provisions qu'ils ont fait, ils eussent bien peu user de plus grande discretion et moderation qu'ils n'ont (usé)

‡ At all events the provost of the cathedral of Vienna excused him with these words, to Campeggi, who asked the cause of his absence Letter from Wolfstal, 14th March, Weimar Arch The Italians thought he had gone away because the legate had come "Assai sdegnato," as the Venetian Ziani expresses himself, Disp 29 Martio The same person remarks that Nurnberg had already entirely fallen away from Catholicism "Di qui e totalmente scancellata la sincera fede"

§ According to a letter of Wolf von Wolfstals, Ferdinand, even on the 17th of April, said, "Dass Hannart ihn sampt ihm selbst verführt, wie wenn ein Blinder den andern fuhrt"—"That Hannart had deceived him, as well as himself, like as when the blind lead the blind"

his hand to give the customary benediction After this he was advised by others, and thought it most prudent himself, to enter Nurnberg without any ceremony whatever. He did not wear his cardinal's hat, and made no sign of benediction, or of the cross, and instead of riding to the church of St. Sebaldus, where the clergy were assembled to receive him, he rode straight to his lodging *

His presence, instead of damping the zeal of the reforming preachers, seemed to inflame it to the utmost. The pope was characterised as antichrist, before the face of his legate. On Palm-Sunday no palms were strewed; and in Passion-Week the ceremony of laying down the cross and raising it again, was omitted thousands received the sacrament in both kinds,† and not only among the common people, several members of the Council of Regency were among the communicants, and even the sister of the archduke, Queen Isabella of Sweden, partook of the cup at the castle of Nurnberg.

It is very possible that these public demonstrations produced in the mind of Ferdinand, on whom the new doctrines had made no impression, and who had been brought up in all the rigour of Spanish catholicism, the determination to abandon the Council of Regency; and it is also likely enough that the pope's legate had some influence in the same direction. At all events, the fall of the Council of Regency, which had taken the new doctrines under its protection, would necessarily be very favourable to the maintenance of catholicism

Perhaps the legate founded on this a hope of obtaining from the States a decision agreeable to his wishes on religious affairs generally. He complained of the innovations which were made before his eyes He reminded the States of the edict published at Worms, and expressed his astonishment that ordinances of this kind were so imperfectly enforced in the empire Hannart also demanded the execution of the edict in the emperor's name.

On this occasion, however, it became manifest that religion had by no means decided the course of affairs, however it might have influenced the conduct of some individuals Had no political motives existed, the councillors of the Regency would never have been dismissed on account of their religious inclinations The complaints of the legate made no impression "Some," writes Planitz, "are indignant, but most only laugh." The cities, which had contributed so greatly to the overthrow of the Council of Regency, were furious at the mention of the edict. They declared that the common people were so eager for the word of God, that to deprive them of it would cause rebellion, bloodshed and general ruin, and that the resolutions of the preceding year must be absolutely adhered to. In short, with regard to religious affairs, those who were hostile to Rome still constituted the majority in the States The legate was reminded soon after his arrival of the hundred grievances of the nation which had been sent to Rome by his predecessor. This had been foreseen in Rome; and the legate had been instructed to feign that the memorial containing these complaints had not been delivered in the names of the princes ‡ Accordingly Campeggi answered with a perfectly untroubled countenance, "that no official announcement of those grievances had reached Rome; that three printed copies had been sent thither, it was true, one of which he had seen himself, but that he could not bring himself to believe that any thing so beyond measure ill-written could be produced by the diet" This was certainly not at all calculated to satisfy the temporal Estates, who had been extremely in earnest with regard to the grievances, the statement of which had cost so much trouble and deliberation.

Moreover, the personal behaviour of the legate, who was accused of sordid avarice, and of revolting oppression towards the poorer sort of German priests, was far from favourable to the success of his negotiations §

When the decisive discussion on religious affairs arrived, the order necessary to the transaction of public business and the presence of the imperial commissioner so far influenced the States, that they did not deny the obligation they lay under to carry the edict of Worms into execution; but to this admission they added a clause to a directly contrary effect, namely, that they would execute it "as far as was possible,"—a modification of so vague a nature that it was left to the discretion of each individual to do what he pleased The cities had already represented at length that it was not possible At the same time the demand was renewed, that the pope should convene a council in the German dominions, with the emperor's consent This the legate undertook to advocate faithfully to his holiness

It was, however, questionable whether this was sufficient to tranquillise men's minds, or whether, in such a state of fermentation, they would wait patiently for so remote an event as the convocation and decision of an ecclesiastical assembly lastly, whether the German nation would so far renounce the unity of its anti-Romish tendencies, which had taken so deep a root, as to consent to abide by the results of a council composed of all nations

No sooner were the representatives of the reforming principles dismissed from the Coun-

* The Regency recommended him "dass er seinen Segen und Kreuz zu thun vermeyd, angesehen wie es deshalb jetzund stee "—"To avoid making the sign of the cross or the benediction, seeing how matters then stood" —*Feilitzsch to Frederic of Saxony, 11th March.*

† Planitz (28th March) reckons 4000 "Ist deshalb Muhe und Erbett und sunderlich, dass es des Regiments Personen eines Theyls also genommen"—"On this account is trouble and labour and especially as the persons of the Regency have in part received it thus" He remarks that Ferdinand was very angry at such a manifestation of his sister's opinions "Nicht weiss ich wie es gehn will"—"I know not how it will end."

‡ Pallavicini, i p 222 "che dissimulasse che la scrittura si fosse ricevuta per nome dei principi"

§ A detailed contemporary account of the manner in which the legate induced the learned but poor Schoner to present to him his mathematical instruments on the promise of a benefice, and then neither procured him the benefice nor paid him for his instruments Strobel, Nachricht vom Aufenthalt Melanchthons, in Nurnberg, p 18

cil of Regency, than the necessity of supplying the place of their labours in some other manner was doubly felt. This aroused the champions of the new doctrines to unite in forming a most remarkable determination.

The question which had once before been so important was still unanswered, namely, what was to be done in Germany in the interval till the council met. Spite of all opposition, a resolution still more extraordinary, and of which the results were still more incalculable than that of the former year, was adopted on this point. It was determined that, in the month of November of the current year, a meeting of the States should be convened at Spire, and should there hold a definitive deliberation. To this end the sovereign princes were to direct their councillors and learned clerks to draw up a list of all the disputed points which were to be discussed and decided. Besides this, the grievances of the nation and means for their redress were to be considered anew. Meanwhile it was resolved, as the year before, that the holy Gospel and God's word should be preached.*

It is indeed true that the party favourable to Rome, emboldened by the overthrow of the Council of Regency, had regained somewhat of its influence at this diet, but still it was kept in check by a large majority. The German nation asserted its claim more strenuously than ever to complete independence in ecclesiastical affairs, as against the pope and the unity of the Latin church.

CHAPTER V.

ORIGIN OF THE DIVISION IN THE NATION

There are probably few reflecting men, however well-disposed on other grounds to the cause of ecclesiastical reform, who have not occasionally felt inclined to join in the usual condemnation of it, as the cause of the separation of Germany into two parts,—often at open war and never thoroughly reconciled,—to impute to the adherents of the new opinions all the blame of having broken up the unity, not only of the church, but of the empire.

So long as we regard the facts from a distance, they doubtless wear this aspect; but if we approach nearer to them and contemplate the events which brought about this division, the result we shall arrive at will, if I mistake not, be far different.

No man, to whatever confession he may belong, can deny, what was admitted even by the most zealous Catholics of that day; viz. that the Latin church stood in need of reform. Its thorough worldliness, and the ever-increasing rigidity and unintelligible formalism of its dogmas and observances, rendered this necessary in a religious view; while the interference of the papal court, which was not only oppressive in a pecuniary sense, by consuming all the surplus revenue, but destructive of the unity and independence of the nation, made it not less essential to the national interests.

Nor can it be alleged, either on religious or national grounds, that any unjustifiable measures were resorted to to effect this change.

Independently of all the more precise articles of the protestant creed, which were gradually constructed and accepted, the essence of the religious movement lay in this,—that the spirit of Christianity, so deeply implanted in the German mind, had been, by degrees, ripened to a consciousness of its own independence of all accidental forms, had gone back to its original source,—to those records which directly proclaim the eternal covenant of the Godhead with the human race,—and had there become confident in its own truth, and resolute to reject all untenable theories and subjugating claims.

No one could shut his eyes to the peril impending over the whole existing order of things in the nation, from a departure from those established ecclesiastical forms which had such mighty influence over domestic as well as public life. We have, however, seen with what care all destructive elements were rejected, with how much self-control every violent change was avoided, and how patiently every question was still left to the decision of the empire.

Let it not be objected that discord had already arisen, and that, as we have remarked, action was encountered by re-action; no momentous crisis in the life of a great nation was ever unaccompanied by this stormy shock of conflicting opinions. The important point is, that the divisions should not have sufficient power to overthrow the paramount and acknowledged supremacy of the principle of unity.

Such was the tendency of affairs in Germany in the year 1524.

The adherents of the new faith had hitherto always submitted to the constitutional government of the empire; in the hope of obtaining from its proceedings and favour a reconstruction of the ecclesiastical institutions, in accordance both with the wants of the nation and the commands of the Gospel.

The majority in the Council of Regency, as we have seen, influenced the States in this spirit. In spite of all the efforts of opponents,

* Decree of the Diet of Nurnberg, 18th April, 1524. When after this decree, we read Luther's paper,—"Zwei kaiserliche uneinige und widerwartige Gebote" (Altenb. ii. 762). "Two imperial contradictory and incompatible Orders,"—we are astonished that he was so ill satisfied. The cause of this, however, is, that in the mandate founded on the Recess, the article prescribing the teaching of the holy Gospel was omitted, while, on the other hand, great stress was laid on the observance of the edict of Worms. The clause "so viel moglich" indeed, is there, but almost disappears under the constant reiterations of the edict of Worms; hence we perceive the influence which the imperial chancery obtained after the abolition of the old Council of Regency. Luther does not appear to have been aware of the Recess, and still less of the preceding negotiations. The imperial delegate, Hannart, and the papal legate, took a far more complete view of the matter. They thought it a great gain that at any rate the name of national council had been avoided. Nevertheless, Hannart concludes his letter of the 16th April with the words, "que cependant se fera ung concil national d'Allemagne."

and of the various external difficulties, a majority was formed in the diet, favourable to the reformation. Two Recesses were drawn up and agreed to in its favour. Even after the fall of the Regency, this majority maintained itself, and resolved that a national assembly should be convened at an early date, and should occupy itself exclusively with the endeavour to bring the religious affairs of the empire to a definitive conclusion.

A nobler prospect for the unity of the nation, and for the further progress of the German people in the career they had already entered upon, certainly never presented itself.

To form some notion of the degree to which it occupied the minds of men, we have only to examine the state of Franconia, where, during the summer of 1521, six opinions or reports, destined to be laid before this assembly, appeared, all conceived in the spirit of the evangelical party. Luther felt contented and happy when he saw the judgment of the learned men of Brandenburg, he said that this was coin of the right stamp, such as he and his friends at Wittenberg had long dealt withal. That of Henneberg was not so completely in accordance with his opinions. Luther's doctrine concerning free will was combated in it; but in all other respects it was soundly evangelical, and condemned the invocation of saints, the seven sacraments and the abuses of the mass. The reports of Windsheim and Wertheim were particularly violent against the saints; that of Nurnberg, against the pope. One of the two parties which divided Rothenburg sent in an opinion favourable to the evangelical side.* The other party, however, which was more faithful to the ancient doctrine, was no less active Ferdinand required his universities of Vienna and Freiburg to send in full and minute explanations of the disputed points. At the former university, the faculties immediately prepared to draw up their report, and that of theology exhorted the others to abstain from all mutual offence † It is evident that the most various modifications of opinion must have been in agitation and in conflict at Spire. What results might not have been anticipated, had it been possible to execute the project of holding a peaceful and moderate discussion,—of endeavouring to sever the good from the bad!

It is true that another evangelical majority, like that with which the proposal originated, was fully to be expected, but this was the inevitable consequence of the present state of things, the nation had no alternative, it must resist the encroachments of Rome, or fall, the religious movement could no longer be suppressed, it could only be guided This was the part assigned to the national assembly, nor can it be said that the unity of the nation was thus endangered, on the contrary, had it attained its object, it would have given to that unity a much more solid foundation

In order to discover who it was that, at this decisive juncture, broke the bond of the national unity, we must examine how it happened that an assembly for which such solemn preparation had been made, never took place.

The See of Rome naturally opposed it, for in proportion as the prospect it afforded was full of hope and promise to the German nation, it was threatening and disastrous to the court of Rome.

We have the report of a congregation held at this crisis by Pope Clement VII, at which means were discussed for carrying into effect the bull against Luther, and the edict of Worms, in spite of the Recesses by which they were counteracted A vast variety of schemes were suggested, such as, that Frederic of Saxony should be deprived of his electorate,—a measure proposed by Aleander, or that the kings of England and Spain should be prevailed on to threaten to put a stop to all commerce with the German towns, from which the pope anticipated great results The only conclusion they came to, however, was to oppose the meeting at Spire, both to the emperor and the States, whom the legate was instructed to use every means to prejudice against that assembly.‡

The question for immediate decision—a question which we must here examine—was, whether there could be found estates in Germany who would prefer joining with the pope to awaiting the decisions of a general assembly

The papal court had already found means to secure to itself allies in Germany it had won over one of the most powerful of the sovereign houses—that of the dukes of Bavaria

The government as well as the people of Bavaria had formerly shared the common aversion of the German nation to the ascendency of Rome; neither the bull of Leo X. had been carried into effect, nor the edict of Worms observed § The dukes had been as much displeased at the encroachments made by the spiritual on the temporal jurisdiction, as any other princes; and Luther's doctrines spread among the learned, the clergy, and the commons, as rapidly and as widely as in other parts of the empire.

But as early as the end of the year 1521 the dukes began to incline towards Rome, and had ever since been becoming more and more decided partisans of the old faith

Contemporary writers ascribed this to the great power and extensive possessions of the regular clergy in Bavaria,‖ and certainly this

* Extracts from v d Lith Erlauterung der Frank Reformationshist, p 41

† Raupach Evangel Oestreich, ii p 29 Struve mentions a similar exhortation from the elector palatine to the University of Heidelberg in his Pfälzische Kirchen historie, p 19

‡ Pallavicini, lib ii c x p 227

§ Winter, Geschichte der Schicksale der evangelischen Lehre in und durch Baiern, i pp 62, 76

‖ Pamphlet of Reckenhofer touching the affairs of Seehofer "Denn sobald du fur Munchen herauskompst auf drey Meyl gegen Burg, und fragst wes ist der Grund, Antwort ist meines gnedigen Herrn von Degernsee, Chiemsee, Saunersee also dass mer denn der halb Teil des Bayrlandes der Geistlichen ist"—"For as soon as you leave Munich, about three miles towards Burg and ask whose is the land? the answer is, It belongs to my Lord of Degernsee, Chiemsee, Saunersee, so that more than half of Bavaria belongs to the clergy"—*Panzer* No 2402

had an influence, though rather of a different kind from that supposed

The first symptom of an intimate connexion between Rome and Bavaria was a draft of a bull which Leo X. caused to be prepared on the 14th Nov. 1521, wherein he authorises a commission of prelates, before proposed by the dukes, to visit the convents and restore order and discipline in them * He died before this bull was finished; but not before he had thus pointed out to the Bavarian government what might be done in this direction. A standing commission, independent of the bishopric, and under the influence of the sovereign, was charged with the superintendence of spiritual affairs.

About this time the university of Ingolstadt was almost broken up by a pestilential disease When the contagion had ceased, and the professors re-assembled, they found that it would be impossible to maintain their strict catholic discipline without other support than that of the spiritual jurisdiction; and that a ducal mandate would be necessary to help them to withstand the innovations which threatened to invade even their own body. The three most resolute champions of the old system, Franz Burckhard, George Hauer, and Johann Eck, who had again been at Rome in the autumn, joined in urgent representations of the necessity of such a measure,† of which Duke William's chancellor, Leonhard von Eck, one of the most active and influential statesmen of that time, was fully convinced.‡

The dukes were soon won over to the same opinion, probably the report of the riots which had just then broken out at Wittenberg (but which Luther so quickly tranquillised) made them anxious to prevent similar disturbances in their own territories.

On Ash Wednesday, 5th of March, 1522, the dukes issued a mandate,§ wherein they commanded their subjects, under heavy penalties, to adhere to the faith of their forefathers That which had been considered necessary for the university, was thus extended to the whole nation The duke's officers were directed to arrest all refractory persons, ecclesiastics as well as laymen, and to report upon their offences

In spite of the rigour which was used, these measures had not, at first, the anticipated effect In Saxony the temporal power refused to lend its arm to support the episcopal authority, in Bavaria, on the contrary, the bishops, who had a vague perception of the danger which must accrue to their independent authority from such an alliance, did not second the efforts of the temporal power with much zeal The followers of Luther, arrested by the civil officers, often escaped free and unpunished, from the ecclesiastical court which had jurisdiction over them.

When Dr. Johann Eck returned to Rome in the summer of 1523, at the invitation of Pope Adrian,‖ he was commissioned by the dukes to make a formal complaint against the bishops on this head, and to request an extension of the ducal authority in the proceedings against heretics ¶ It was impossible to refuse the demand of the orthodox doctor, who took part in the most secret consultations on religious affairs. Pope Adrian therefore published a bull empowering a spiritual commission to degrade ecclesiastics who should be convicted of heresy, and to deliver them over to the temporal criminal tribunals, even without the concurrence of the bishops. Adrian added only the limitation, that the bishops were to be once more admonished to perform their duties within a given term; but this was subsequently disregarded

Thus we see that it was not the independent authority of the great institutions of the church, that the dukes took under their protection they raised up a collateral authority, standing under their own immediate influence, and empowered to intervene in the most peculiar sphere of ecclesiastical rights and duties.

Dr Eck is not to be regarded only as one of Luther's theological opponents. He exercised an extraordinary influence on the state, as well as the church in Bavaria, and to him principally is to be attributed that alliance between the ducal power, the university of Ingolstadt, and the papal authority, which checked the progress of the national movement in that country.

Nor was it the authority alone of the church that was assailed, claims were soon advanced to her possessions.

Pope Adrian granted to the dukes one-fifth of all the revenues of the church throughout their territories, "for," said he, "the dukes have declared their readiness to take arms against the enemies of the true faith "** When Pope Clement VII came to the tiara, he revoked all grants of this nature, nevertheless he saw reason to confirm this one for the three following years since then, it has been renewed from time to time, and has always remained one of the chief foundations of the Bavarian financial system.††

On this occasion the university was not forgotten. Adrian consented that in every chapter in Bavaria, at least one prebend might be conferred on a professor of theology, "for the improvement of that faculty, and for the better

* Winter, ii p 325

† He could not have gone thither before October, as he was still at Polling during the months of August and September Leben des berühmten Joh Eckii in the Parnassus Boicus, i ii p 521

‡ Winter, passim, p 81

§ "Erstes baierisches Religionsmandat, Munchen am Eschermittiche angeender Vassten "—*Ibid.* p 310

‖ "Er entbot denselben durch zwei Brevia nach Rom." —"He summoned him by two briefs to Rome."—*Parnassus Boicus*, ii i p 206

¶ "Fragmentum libelli supplicis, quem Bavariæ Ducis oratores, quorum caput celebris ille Eckius, Adriano VI Romæ obtulerunt anno 1521," ap Œfele, ii 274 The date is wrong, as Adrian was not pope in 1521 The bull, which was prepared according to the words of the petition, is dated June, 1523. The Bavarian bishops first appealed against it in December, 1523, so that there can be no doubt that that is the proper date

** Bull of the 1st of June It is there said of the dukes, "Ad arma contra perfidos orthodoxæ fidei hostes sumenda sese obtulerunt "—*Ibid* 279 The Turks were also included in this

†† See Winter, ii p 321

extirpation of the heresies that had arisen in that, as well as in other German countries."*

Thus, before any form of government constituted according to evangelical views, could be thought of, we find an opposing body organised expressly for the purpose of supporting catholic principles, which gradually became of immense importance to the destinies of Germany.

We have already shown that the disturbances of those times mainly arose out of the struggle between the spiritual and temporal power. The rising temporal sovereignties naturally sought to defend themselves against the encroachments of their ecclesiastical neighbours. With this tendency, Luther's views of government exactly coincided; he advocated a total separation of the two powers. The dukes of Bavaria, however, found that such a separation was not the only way to attain the desired end; they took a directly opposite course, which was both shorter and more secure. What others were striving to wrest from the pope by hostile measures, they contrived to obtain with his concurrence. By this means they at once gained possession of a large share of the ecclesiastical revenues, and an authority, sanctioned by the papal see, over the surrounding bishops, even in the most important branch of the spiritual jurisdiction: an authority which was very soon manifested in the proceedings of the Bavarian council for religious affairs. These were advantages which the adherents of the new faith could not yet so much as contemplate.

There was still, however, this immense distinction;—that, while the latter were the representatives of the tendency of the nation to emancipate itself from Rome, Bavaria fell into much more absolute subjection to that power, from whom she held all the privileges she now enjoyed.

Under any circumstances, however, so decisive a step, taken by one of the most powerful houses of Germany, and the example, of the advantages resulting from a renewed connexion with Rome, could not fail to have a great effect on all its neighbours.

We find from a very authentic source, the transactions of the Archbishop of Salzburg with his states, that a compact had already been entered into between Bavaria and Austria, "against the Lutheran sect."†

It is certain that Archduke Ferdinand had likewise formed a closer connexion with the see of Rome, and had obtained thence, in behalf of his defence against the Turks, the enormous grant of a full third of all the ecclesiastical revenues.

Rome did not neglect to conciliate the more influential spiritual, as well as temporal princes. The long-contested appointments to the bishoprics of Gurk, Chiemsee, Seckau, and Lavant, were granted to the Archbishop of Salzburg, even during the disputed months.

By these means the papal see succeeded in regaining a party in the States: no doubt it is to be attributed to these and similar causes, that catholic opinions were more strongly represented at the diet of 1524 than they had been the year before.

Still, as we have already seen, they were not triumphant at that diet. A number of bishops even, offended by the support given by the pope to the claims of the temporal sovereigns, offered a determined resistance to every suggestion emanating from Rome.

The legate Campeggi plainly saw that nothing could be gained from a general assembly in which Lutheran sympathies so greatly predominated. He complained that he could not here venture to speak freely.‡

On the other hand, as he saw around him a number of friends holding the same opinions, he hoped that he should be able to effect more completely all he wanted at a provincial meeting, where only these partisans would be present.

Accordingly, even at Nurnberg, where the national assembly at Spire was resolved on, he proposed another which, in spirit, was directly at variance with it. He made no secret that his object was to obviate the danger which must ensue from an assembly convoked with the avowed intention of listening to the voice of the people.§

This proposal was first agreed to by Archduke Ferdinand and a few bishops, and then by the dukes of Bavaria. At the end of June, 1524, the meeting was held at Regensburg. The dukes, the archduke, the legate, the Archbishop of Salzburg, the Bishop of Trent, who came in the retinue of the archduke, and the administrator of Regensburg, were present. Delegates appeared for the bishops of Bamberg, Augsburg, Spire, Strasburg, Constance, Basle, Freising, Passau, and Brixen: thus not only Bavaria and Austria, but the Upper Rhine, and a considerable portion of Swabia and Franconia, took part in it.

The legate opened the meeting with a discourse on the perils with which the religious troubles threatened both estates: he exhorted them to abandon their disputes, and to unite in measures "for extirpating the heretical doctrines, and making men live after the ordinances of the Christian church." Archduke Ferdinand supported the proposal, and strongly insisted to the assembly on the pecuniary grants he had obtained.

The prelates then divided into three com-

* 30th of August, Œfele, p. 277. In Mederer, Annales, Acad. Ingolstadt, iv. 234, is to be found the bull of Clement VII. concerning this matter; by this bull the dukes of Bavaria are entitled always to promote one of their professors of theology at Ingolstadt to a prebendal stall in the chapters of Augsburg, Freisingen, Passau, Regensburg, or Salzburg. They gave out "quod ecclesie predicte a Ducibus Bavarie fundate vel donationibus aucte fuerunt." The reason assigned was, that they wished to have theologians "hoc tempore periculoso, quo Lutheriana et alie plurime hereses contra sedem apostolicam propagantur, qui se murum pro Israel exponant et contra hereses predictas legendo predicando docendo et scribendo eas confutent dejiciant et extermiment." This is the more important, because in the years immediately after the plague, the university, as is mentioned by the statutes of the faculty of jurists, was almost entirely reconstituted.

† Zauner, Salzburgher Chronik, iv. 359.

‡ From a letter of Ferdinand's, dated Stuttgard, 19th May, in Gemeiners Regensburger Chronik, iv. vi. p. 514.

§ From the letter of the legate, dated 8th May. Winter, i. p. 156.

missions the first of which was to consider the disputes between the clergy and laity; the second, the reforms to be immediately undertaken, and the third, the measures to be taken with respect to doctrine.*

The conference lasted for sixteen days in the town hall at Regensburg, and sittings were held before and after noon The grave course of affairs was on one occasion interrupted by a festive dance.

The affair of the pecuniary grant was the first settled.

The bishops plainly perceived that the popular ferment, which, from its first origin, had been constantly increasing in strength and impetuosity, must be far more dangerous to them, than any supremacy of the temporal sovereign There were few among those we have named who had not had to struggle with a growing opposition in their own capitals. A year before, Cardinal Lang had found it necessary to bring six troops of veteran soldiers into Salzburg He himself rode at their head habited in a red slashed surcoat, under which glittered a polished cuirass, and grasping his marshal's baton; and thus compelled the corporation to sign fresh declarations of submission Perhaps, too, a few such prelates may have been favoured with fresh concessions from the pope; we find many decided partisans of Rome among their delegates, for example, Andreas Hanlin of Bamberg, who was once himself vicerector at Ingolstadt,† Eck and Faber also were present The spiritual lords ended by making a virtue of necessity, those of Bavaria consented to pay to the temporal power (as near as I can discover) a fifth part of their revenues, and those of Austria a fourth.‡

They next proceeded to consider the points of doctrine and life

The most important result of this consultation was a decision which it had been found impossible to carry at the meeting of the States of 1523. The preachers were directed to refer principally to the Latin fathers of the church for the interpretation of difficult passages in Scripture; and (which could not be accomplished on a former occasion) Ambrose, Jerome, Gregory and Augustin were specified as the patterns of faith. In former days, this might have been looked upon as a concession to the literary tendencies of the time, since it relaxed the fetters of the scholastic system; but now, it mainly betokened opposition to Luther and to the majority of the States of the empire, by sanctioning, at any rate, the authorities on which rested the later systems of the Latin church. It was resolved that divine service should be preserved unaltered according to the usages of former generations, and an attempt was made to put an end to Luther's influence. His books were once more forbidden, and all subjects of the allied princes were interdicted, under pain of forfeiture of their patrimonies, from studying at the university of Wittenberg.

At the same time, steps were taken towards the removal of those abuses which had occasioned such a general ferment All the extortions of the inferior clergy which raised so much discontent among the common people, the enforcement of expensive ceremonies, the burdensome fees, the refusal of absolution on account of debts, were abolished The relation of the clergy to their flocks was to be put on a fresh footing, by a commission composed of clerical and lay members The reserved presentations were diminished, the number of holydays materially lessened, the practice of stations abolished. The assembly pledged itself for the future to a more careful consideration of personal merit in the appointment of ecclesiastics The preachers were admonished to show greater earnestness, and to avoid all fables and untenable assertions; and the priests, to follow a chaste and irreproachable course of life §

We are, I believe, warranted in looking on these resolutions as the first effects of the principles of the reformation in reviving the profounder spirit of catholicism. As the alliance of the sovereign princes with the papal see fulfilled the political demands, so this attempt supplied (at first indeed very inadequately) the religious wants, which had given birth to the reforming spirit These attempts at regeneration were unquestionably more important and effective than has been supposed, even by the catholic party itself, and, indeed, modern catholicism is in great measure based upon them, but neither in depth of religious intuition, in the genius which produces a permanent impression on remote nations and ages, or in force and intensity of enthusiasm, could they be compared to those movements which took their name from Luther, and of which he was the centre His opponents offered nothing original, the means they adopted, and by which they thought to keep their ground, were mere analogical imitations of what he had already done. Thus, at Campeggi's suggestion, Dr Eck published, as a corrective to Melanch-

* Letter from Ebner and Nutzel to the Elector Frederic, wherein they inform him, "was eine Schrift enthalt, die ihnen vom Hofe furstlicher Durchleuchtigkeit (Ferdinands) zugekommen ist,"—"of the contents of a letter which had reached them from the court of his Royal Highness (Ferdinand)," 8th July, 1524.—*Weimar A*

† Haller, Reformationsgesch von Bamberg, p 70

‡ Planitz, who had been at Esslingen, writes to the Elector Frederic, Nurnberg, 26th July "Die Geistlichen in des Erzherzogs Landen haben bewilligt, ihm den vierten Pfennig zu geben, 5 Jahr lang, und die Geistlichen unter den Herrn von Baiern geben ihren Fursten den 5ten Pfennig 5 Jahr, allein dass sie in ihren Furstenthumen die lutherische Lehr nicht zulassen und vest uber ihnen halten wollen"—"The ecclesiastics in the archduke's dominions have agreed to give him the fourth penny for 5 years, and the ecclesiastics under the lords of Bavaria will give to their princes the fifth penny for 5 years, but on condition that they shall not suffer the Lutheran doctrines in their dominions, and that they will keep them down with a strong hand" I have not been able to discover whether Planitz was rightly informed as to the duration of this impost According to Winter, ii p 322, it was continued for several years longer

§ "Constitutio ad removendos abusus et ordinatio ad vitam Cleri reformandam per Revdum Dm Laurentium," &c—*Ratisponæ Nonis Julii*, in *Goldast Constitutt. Impp*, iii p 487 What is given by Strobel (Miscel ii p. 109, &c), from an old printed book, which is also before me, by no means embraces the whole contents of the Constitution The abolition of a great number of holydays in the 21st article, which differs but little from the later protestant regulations, is very remarkable

thon's "Loci communes," a handbook of the same kind,* and Emser made a translation of the Bible, as a rival to that of Luther. The works of the Wittenberg teachers had issued forth in the natural course of their own internal development: they were the product of minds goaded by a resistless impulse, pressing forward in their own peculiar path, and were filled with the vigour and originality that forces conviction; the Catholic books, on the contrary, owed their existence to external motives;—to the calculations of a system which looked about for any means of defence against the danger pressing upon it from every side.

But those who adopted such a line of conduct, thus cut themselves off from the great and vigorous expansion which the mind of the German nation was now undergoing. The questions which ought to have been discussed and determined at Spire, with a view to the unity and the wants of the nation, were disposed of by the allied powers in a narrow and one-sided manner. It was said that a single nation had no right to decide on the affairs of religion, and of Christendom generally: this was easily asserted; but what was the nation to do if, from the peculiarities of its constitution and character, it was the only one that had fallen into this state of ferment? At first it had petitioned for the immediate convocation of a council; but as the hope of this grew fainter and more remote, it felt the necessity of taking the matter into its own hands. This is sufficiently proved by the ordinances issued at Regensburg. The difference was this—at Spire, in all probability, resolutions would have been taken in opposition to the Pope of Rome; whereas at Regensburg it was thought expedient, from a thousand considerations, to form a fresh alliance with him. This was the origin of the divisions in the nation. The national duty of awaiting the decisions of a general assembly which was already fixed; of taking part in its deliberations; and, let us add, of influencing them to wise ends, was sacrificed to the narrow and partial expediency of an alliance with Rome.

One part of the projects of the congregation at Rome being thus executed with unhoped-for success, Campeggi next pointed out the necessity of endeavouring to accomplish the other; which was, to induce the emperor to give the cause his cordial support.†

Not a moment was lost at Rome in gaining over Charles V. Whilst the official proclamations from Regensburg dwelt only upon such points in the Recesses as were favourable to the papacy, and affected to consider them as mere confirmations of the edict of Worms, it was at the same time represented to the emperor in Spain how greatly his authority must suffer by his edict being limited by two following Recesses; nay, by an attempt having actually been made to revoke it,—a measure which he himself could not have ventured upon: it was evident, they said, that the people of Germany were preparing to throw off all obedience, both to temporal and spiritual authority. And what insupportable insolence was there in fixing a meeting in that country, to decide on matters of faith, and the affairs of Christianity at large; as if the Germans had a right to prescribe laws to his imperial majesty and to the whole world!‡

Similar arguments were vehemently pressed upon Charles's ally, Henry VIII., who had entered into a literary warfare with Luther, to induce him to use all his credit with Charles V. in support of the pope's exhortations.

The state of political affairs generally was highly favourable for promoting the influence of the papal power over the emperor. War had been formally declared against Francis I., in May, 1524, and was now raging with the utmost violence. The emperor attacked the king in his own territory, from the side of Italy. It would therefore have been extremely dangerous to offend the pope, who was in his rear, and who did not quite approve the invasion; or to refuse him a request which, moreover, was consonant to the Catholic education he had himself received in his youth.

Charles V. did not hesitate a single moment. On the 27th of July, he despatched a proclamation to the empire, entirely in favour of the pope, and expressed with unwonted vehemence. He complained that his mandate from Worms was disregarded, and that a general council had been demanded, without even the due decorum of consulting him. He declared, that he neither could nor would allow the intended assembly to take place; that the German nation assumed to do what would be permitted to no other, even in conjunction with the pope,—to alter ordinances which had been so long held sacred. He pronounced Luther's doctrines to be inhuman, and, like his master, Adrian, he compared him to Mahomet. In short, he forbade the assembly, on pain of being found guilty of high treason, and incurring sentence of ban and reban.§

Thus did the court of Rome succeed in

* "Enchiridion, seu Loci Communes contra Hæreticos:" printed in 1525, and, according to Eck, composed, "Hortatu Cardinalis de Campegiis, ut simpliciores, quibus cortice natare opus est, summarium haberent credendorum, ne a pseudoprophetis subverterentur."

† He complained: "non haver quella causa (Luterana) di costà (della Spagna) il caldo che bisogneria, fa che d'ogni provisione che si faccia si trahe poco frutto."—Giberto Datari agli Oratori Fiorentini in Spagna, *Lettere di Principi*, i. f. 133.

‡ We have not indeed the very letter from the pope to the emperor, but there is a sufficient account of it in the despatch from the papal datarius to the nuncio in England, Marchionne Lango, Lettere di Principi, i. 124. "N. Sre ha di ciò scritto efficacemente alla Mta Ces, accioche la consideri, che facendo quei popoli poco conto di dio tanto meno ne faranno alla giornata della Mta S. e degli altri Signori temporali:...l'absenza della Mta Cesarea ha accresciuta l'audacia loro tanto che ardiscono di ritrattar quell' editto, cosa che Cesare proprio non faria." On the other hand, in the edict given at Regensburg, it is stated, "Darumb so haben wir auf des hochwürdigsten Herrn Lorenzen, etc. Ersuchen uns vergleycht, dass wir und unser Principal obgemelt Kaiserlich Edict zu Worms, auch die Abschied auf beyden Reichstägen zu Nürnberg deshalb beschlossen..vollziehen."—"Wherefore we have, at the request of the most worshipful master Lorenzo, &c., agreed, that we and our principal should execute the above-named imperial edict of Worms, and the recesses of both diets at Nürnberg confirming the same."

§ Frankf. A. It appears from a letter from the Elector of Saxony to Ebner, dated Oct. 1524, Walch, xv. 2711 that in the letter which had been sent to him, the expression, "bei Vermeidung criminis lese majestatis, unser

gaining over to its cause not only several powerful members of the empire in Germany, but even its supreme head in Spain, and by their means, in putting a stop to the dangerous resolutions of the diet. this was its first energetic interference with the ecclesiastical affairs of Germany

The main cause of this was, that the emperor, residing in Spain, followed a line of policy, on which the character and the opinions of Germany had not the slightest effect, and suggested solely by his relations with other countries His government during the first years of his reign exercised merely a negative, decomposing influence Without taking any serious steps for the redress of the grievances charged upon Rome, he allowed himself to be induced by his political position to issue the edict of Worms, which, after all, could not be carried into effect, while on the one hand, it inflamed the antipathy of the nation to the utmost, and, on the other, put fresh arms into the hands of the adherents of the curia. He first checked the growing consolidation of the Council of Regency, by rejecting the system of import duties to which he had at first consented, and then thought it advisable to overthrow that body entirely. Another Council of Regency was, it is true, formed at Esslingen, but it took warning from the fate of the former, and neither enjoyed authority, nor even made the least attempt to acquire any,—it was the mere shadow of a government We have already shown what prospects in favour of religion and of national unity were connected with the projected assembly at Spire. This assembly was forbidden by the court of Spain, as if it were criminal.

The unity of Germany has ever depended, not so much on forms of government, or decisions of the diet, as on an intimate understanding among the more powerful sovereigns Maximilian had found, during the latter half of his reign, what it was to have offended and alienated the Elector of Saxony, and it was only by healing this breach, and entering into a close alliance with the Ernestine line of Saxony, that the election of Charles V could be secured; from that time the Elector Frederic had always been treated, in externals at least, with the confidence and consideration due to a powerful and undoubted ally. This intimate connexion the emperor now broke off. He thought it more advantageous, and more suitable to his own station amongst the powers of Europe, to marry his sister Catharine to John III. of Portugal, than to the nephew of the Elector of Saxony, to whom he had betrothed her. Hannart was commissioned to communicate this resolution to the court of Saxony * We may remember how flattering the proposal had been to Duke John, Frederic's brother, the objections which he raised from mere modesty, and his ultimate joyful acquiescence. Hannart's communication was proportionally mortifying to him. The Saxon court was deeply offended. Such of the elector's friends as were about the archduke, wanted him to use his influence to prevent so offensive a proceeding,† but as he had at first taken no personal share in the negotiation, neither did he now say one word, but suppressed his vexation. Duke John was less reserved. With wounded pride he rejected every communication, every offer, tendered to him on the subject; he expressed to those about him that nothing during the whole course of his life had ever hurt his feelings so deeply.

With the other sovereign princes, too, Austria stood but ill. The house of Brandenburg, which had supported the first Council of Regency for the sake of the interests both of Prussia and Mainz, was much disgusted by its overthrow, and concealed that feeling so little, that overtures were made to the Grand Master, Albert, by France, though, indeed, he did not accept them. In the month of August, the Rhenish electors held a congress, from which Archduke Ferdinand said he expected no good either to himself or his brother.‡ The electoral councillors did not attempt to disguise from the imperial commissioner that people were extremely discontented with the emperor; that his capitulation would be laid before the meeting; and as he had not fulfilled the conditions contained in it, they would proceed to the establishment of a new form of government, either under a lieutenant, the vicars of the empire, or a king of Rome, whom it was intended to elect § This project was discussed at a great cross-bow match at Heidelberg, where several princes were met together, and the palatine house of Bavaria was particularly busied with negotiations to that effect The bond of catholicism between Bavaria and Austria was not strong enough to prevent Duke William of Bavaria from conceiving the idea of obtaining the crown for himself.

Thus the unity of the government of the empire was again dissolved, almost before it had felt its own purposes or destinies. At a crisis so immeasurably eventful, in which all the energies of the nation were rushing with boundless activity into untried regions, and eager for a new state of things, all directing power was wanting

Hence it happened that the local powers

und des Reichs Acht," &c.—"on pain of being found guilty of high treason, and of our ban and that of the empire," &c , had been omitted

* Muller, Geschichte der Protestation, gives the particulars of this event Hannart's letter to the emperor, dated 14th March, shows that the affair was to have come before the diet, which Ferdinand now purposely avoided "Il a semble a mon dit S^r par plusieurs raisons que ne debvai parler à Mr de Saxen de la matière secrète, que savez, que jusque après la fin de cette journée impériale" These letters altogether show a better understanding between Hannart and the archduke than the Saxon documents would lead one to imagine

† Among the secret correspondence between Frederic's and Ferdinand's councillors, there is a note in which one of them says, "S Furstl Durchlaucht begeren sonderlich, das der Heirath vollzogen werd, damit S F Gn desto mer Fug und Statt hab, S Chf Gn als irn angenommenen Vattern um Rath teglich anzusuchen"—"His princely highness greatly desires the consummation of the marriage, so that his princely highness may have more excuse and reason for daily asking counsel of his electoral grace as his adopted father,"—a wish which could scarcely have been shared by the whole court

‡ Letter from Ferdinand, Bucholtz, ii. p 68.

§ Letter from Hannart, ib p 70

proceeded to act upon the principles which severally predominated in them.

Persecution began in those countries which had combined to pass the resolutions of Regensburg.

In Bavaria we find priests ejected or banished, and nobles driven from their estates, till they consented to recant. The tempestuous, oppressive atmosphere of the times is most strikingly exemplified in the fate of an officer of the duke, Bernhard Tichtel von Tutzing. He was travelling towards Nürnberg on the duke's business, when he was joined on the road by Franz Burkhard, one of the orthodox professors of Ingolstadt: they put up together at Pfaffenhofen, and after supper, the conversation turned on religious matters. Tichtel perhaps knew who his companion was; he reminded him that conversations of this kind were forbidden by the new edict, to which Burkhard answered that that did not signify between them. Hereupon Tichtel did not conceal his opinion that the edict could not be carried into effect, and would merely be a disgrace to the dukes; he even went so far as to speak somewhat equivocally of purgatory and of the obligation to fast; sanguinary punishments for differences of opinion he condemned altogether. On hearing these sentiments, Burkhard, who had advised the dukes to all the most odious measures, was seized with the savage fury of a persecutor: he said, in so many words, that decapitation was the proper punishment for Lutheran villains, and at the same time called Tichtel himself a Lutheran. At parting he affected to be reconciled to him, but he hurried to denounce the crime he had detected. Tichtel was arrested and confined in the Falkenthurm, subjected to an inquisition, and compelled to recant: it was only by dint of great exertions and powerful intercession, that he escaped a most degrading punishment which had been suggested to the duke.*

In the territory of Salzburg a priest arrested for Lutheranism was on his way under guard to Mittersill, where he was to remain imprisoned for life, and while the constables were carousing, was set free by two peasants' sons. For this offence the poor youths were, by order of the archbishop, secretly beheaded without public trial, early in the morning, in a meadow in the Nonnthal outside the town—a place never used for execution. Even the executioner had scruples, because the condemned prisoners had not had lawful trial; but the bishop's officer said, "Do what I command you, and let the princes answer for it."†

A citizen of Vienna, one Caspar Tauber, who had expressed anti-catholic opinions respecting the intercession of saints, purgatory, confession and the mystery of the communion, was condemned to make a recantation. On a great holyday — the nativity of the Virgin Mary—two pulpits were erected for this purpose in the churchyard of St. Stephen's; one of these was for the precentor, the other for Tauber, to whom the form of recantation which he was to read was given. But whether it was that he had never promised this, or that an opposite conviction suddenly forced itself more strongly than ever on his mind, he declared from the pulpit whence the assembled multitude was expecting to hear his recantation, that he did not consider himself to have been refuted, and that he appealed to the Holy Roman Empire. He must have been well aware that this would not save him: he was beheaded shortly after, and his body burnt; but his courage and firmness left a lasting impression on the people.‡

There were some other people arrested with Tauber, who, terrified by his fate, made the recantation demanded of them, and escaped with banishment.§

The same severity was practised throughout the Austrian dominions. The three governments of Insbruck, Stuttgart, and Ensisheim appointed a commission at Engen, whose especial business it was to suppress the movement in their provinces. The people of Waldshut gained nothing by dismissing their preacher, Balthasar Hubmaier: the Engen commission declared that they should be punished, or, as it was coarsely expressed, "that the Gospel should be banged about their ears till they were fain to hold their hands over their heads." The weeds were to be pulled up by the roots; and already the other towns had been summoned to furnish subsidies of artillery and infantry for the attack on Waldshut, when a body of Swiss volunteers, principally from Zürich, came to the assistance of the town, and caused the commission to pause awhile.‖

Kenzingen did not escape so well; the little town was actually taken and invested.

Similar disturbances were going on in all parts of the country, though sometimes the measures taken stopped short of bloodshed; Luther's books were forbidden, and his adherents were not endured in the pulpit or the councils of the princes, but were exiled from their country. The government of Würtemberg wanted to break off all communication with Reutlingen, because it tolerated evangelical preachers. Neither were the most barbarous executions wanting. We read of preachers nailed to the pillory by the tongue, so that in order to get free they were forced to tear them-

* Another of the same party, the Chancellor Leonhard v. Eck, had proposed that the duke should follow the merciful course ("den barmherzigen Weg"), viz. that Tichtel should only be placed in the pillory, his crimes be there read aloud, and then by him be orally confessed and renounced: he should then, as a mark of his heretical backsliding, be branded on both cheeks; after this he was to be conveyed back again to the Falkenthurm, and kept there until further orders from the duke. See the Extracts from the Acts, Winter, i. pp. 182–199.

† Zauner, iv. p. 381.

‡ Ein warhafftig Geschicht, wie Caspar Tawber, Burger zu Wien in Osterreich fürein Ketzer und zu dem Todt verurtaylt und aussgefürt worden ist." 1524.—"The true History how Caspar Tawber, a burgher of Vienna in Austria, was condemned and executed as a heretic." The execution took place on 17th Sept.

§ Sententia contra Joannem Væsel—one of the condemned — ult. Septembr, 1524. Raupach Evangel. Oestreich. Erste Fortsetzung; Beilage, No. V.

‖ Letter from Balthasar Hubmaier in the Taschenbuch für Süddeutschland, 1839, p. 67, from the Archives of Switzerland and the Upper Rhine.

selves away, and were thus mutilated for life. The fanaticism of monkish bigotry was awakened, and sought its victims in Lower as well as Upper Germany. The most awful example was made of the wretched Heinrich of Zutphen, at Meldorf in Ditmarsch. A small congregation had formed itself there, which had invited this Augustine monk from Bremen to join them for a time they had obtained permission from the governors of the country, the Forty-eight, that until the meeting of the expected ecclesiastical assembly, the Gospel should be preached pure and unchanged. But their opponents, the prior of the Dominicans of Meldorf and the Minorites of Lunden, were far more powerful, and in combination with the vicar of the bishop's official, they obtained a contrary sentence, which delivered the poor man into their hands, alleging that he had preached against the Mother of God.* A drunken mob, headed by monks bearing torches, went one night in January to the parsonage and dragged forth the preacher, whom they put to death by the most atrocious tortures, executed with equal cruelty and unskilfulness

Meanwhile the other party was aroused to a sense of the necessity of taking more decisive measures.

Immediately after the congress at Regensburg, the cities, seeing the danger that threatened them from the support which their bishops appeared to receive from the princes, held a great town meeting at Spire, and resolved in direct opposition to that adherence to the Latin fathers of the church which had been enjoined, that their preachers should confine themselves wholly to the Gospel and the prophetic and apostolic Scriptures † At that time they still expected that the assembly would be held at Spire, and their intention was to propose some common resolution When, however, this meeting was forbidden by the emperor, and it seemed as if another serious attempt would be made to carry into effect the edict of Worms, they assembled towards the end of the year at Ulm, in order to aid each other in resisting all measures proposed with that view. Weissenburg, Landau, and Kaufbeuren, which had already received some rebukes, were admonished as to their future conduct

The towns were joined by a part of the nobility. Count Bernhard of Solms appeared at the meeting in the name of the counts on the Rhine and the Eifel, of the Wetterau, the Westerwald, and the Neiderland, and asked the towns their opinion concerning a proposed levy and tax of the empire for an expedition against the Turks, and also concerning the Lutheran matter. The towns judged rightly that this combination with the nobles would be very advantageous to them; and after interchanging a few letters, the affair was concluded, and a resolution was taken on the spot at Ulm, "not to act separately in affairs of such weight, and during such perilous times."‡

The most important event of all was, that a considerable number of the princes declared their complete dissent from the compact of Regensburg

Markgrave Casimir of Brandenburg, who had certainly never shown any great religious enthusiasm, could no longer withstand the aroused and declared convictions of his whole country: he rejected the proposal of becoming a party to that compact, alleging the general expectation of the assembly at Spire. When this meeting was forbidden by the emperor, he passed a decree in concert with his estates, that, in his own territories at least, nothing should be preached but the Gospel and the word of God of the Old and New Testament, pure and undefiled, and according to the right and true interpretation Such was the tenour of the recess of the Brandenburg diet of the 1st of October, 1524. His brother George, who lived at the Hungarian court at Ofen, was not satisfied even with this. He thought that the word of God ought not only to be preached, but to be implicitly obeyed, in defiance of all human ordinances §

A most unlooked-for change now took place in Hessen. It was expected that the three warlike princes who had conquered Sickingen and overthrown the Council of Regency, would also combat the reforming ideas which their enemies had supported. The most energetic of the three, however, very soon followed an exactly contrary course.

In May, 1524, one day as Landgrave Philip of Hessen was riding to a cross-bow match at Heidelberg, he met, near Frankfurt, Melanchthon, whose fame was well-known to him, and who was then returning from a visit to his home in the Palatinate, accompanied by a couple of intimate friends who had been there with him. The landgrave stopped him, made him ride some distance by his side, and asked him several questions which betrayed the deep interest he felt in the religious dissensions; and, at last, he only dismissed the surprised and embarrassed professor, on condition that he should send him, in writing, his opinion on the most important points under discussion.‖ Melanchthon executed this task with his usual mastery of his subject; his letter was short, logical, and convincing, and produced a strong impression. Not long after his return from the festivities, on the 18th of July, the landgrave issued a mandate (also in manifest contradiction to the resolutions of Regensburg), wherein, among other things, he commanded that the Gospel should be preached pure and unadulterated. From day to day he became more deeply imbued with the peculiar opinions of the new creed: at the beginning of the following

* Neocorus, edited by Dahlmann, ii p. 21 The judgment of the magistrate runs thus 'Desse Bosewicht hefft gepredigt wedder de Moder Gadess und wedder den Christen Gloven, uth welkerer Orsake ick ehn verordele van wegen mines genedigen Herrn Bischops van Bremen thom Vuere"—"This miscreant hath preached against the mother of God and the Christian faith, for which reason I condemn him to the fire, in the name of my gracious Lord Bishop of Bremen

† Town meeting at Spire, St Margaret's day, 1524 Summary extract in Fels Zweiter-Beitrag, p. 204

‡ Fels Zweiter Beitrag, p 206 Nicolai, 1524

§ Von der Lith, pp 61—65.

‖ Camerarius Vita Melanchthonis, cap 26 Strobel's Neue Beitrage, iv 2, p. 88.

year, he declared that he would sooner give up his body and life, his land and his people, than forsake the word of God

It appears as if some general understanding had been come to at Heidelberg on the subject of religion; for, at first, Philip of Hessen fully expected that the Elector Palatine would follow his example, and although it was not in the nature of that prince to take so decided a part as the landgrave, at least he did not allow himself to be hurried into any acts of persecution.

The banished Duke of Würtemberg, too, might already be regarded as a convert to the cause. Lutheran preachers resided with him at Mümpelgard, and in October, 1524, Zwingli expressed his wonder and joy that this Saul was become a Paul.*

Duke Ernest of Luneburg, the nephew of Frederic of Saxony, who had studied at Wittenberg, showed a similar leaning to the doctrines of the reformers and was strengthened in his opposition to Austria by the affair of Hildesheim. The first beginnings of the reformation at Celle under his protection, date from the year 1524.†

He was joined by Frederic I. of Denmark, who, a year before, had become sole master of Silesia and Holstein His son Christian had attended the Diet at Worms, with his tutor Johann Ranzau. they both returned home filled with admiration of Luther, and deeply imbued with his doctrines. They invited Peter Suave—the very man who had accompanied Luther on that journey—to Denmark, by degrees the duke himself was won over to the same cause While bloody persecutions were set on foot in so many places, Frederic I. published an edict, dated the 7th August, 1524, wherein he made it a capital offence to molest or injure any one on account of his religion every one, he declared, ought so to order his conduct in that behalf, as he could best answer it to Almighty God.‡

A still more important circumstance for the prospects of Lutheranism was, the secession of a powerful spiritual prince, the Grand Master Albert of Prussia, from the doctrines of the papacy. At the diet of Nürnberg he had been much impressed by Osiander's preaching, and having examined the Scriptures himself, he felt convinced that the order to which he belonged was not in accordance with the word of God §. Another motive probably was, that the fall of the Council of Regency, and the depressed state of the nobility in general, deprived him of the last hope of obtaining assistance from the empire against Poland. What then must have been his feelings when no hope was left of successfully resisting his old enemies, while at the same time his mind was agitated by doubts of his own condition and calling He returned to Saxony in the company of Planitz, the Saxon assessor to the Regency, with whose sentiments we are well acquainted Here he saw Luther This intrepid and resolute man, who considered all things with relation to the intrinsic necessity rather than the outward pressure which enforced them, advised him to forsake the rules of his order, to marry, and to convert Prussia into an hereditary principality. The Grand Master had too much of the discretion and reserve befitting a prince, to express his assent to this suggestion but it was easy to read in his countenance how strongly he inclined towards it ‖ We shall see how, impelled by the situation of his country, and by the course which his negotiations took, he soon proceeded to the execution of this project

Such were the results of the prohibition of the national council, the announcement of which had excited such ardent hopes

It cannot be affirmed that violence was met by violence, or that the tenacity with which the old doctrines were maintained was opposed by an equally resolute adoption of the new

How little such was the case, is shown by the example of the Elector of Saxony, who in spite of Luther's continual and violent expostulations, caused the mass to be celebrated throughout the whole of the year 1524. in his chapel of All-Saints, and continually reminded the chapter of their clerical duties.

The state of things may rather be summed up as follows The empire had determined to hold a general deliberation on the important affair which occupied the whole mind of the nation The pope succeeded in preventing the execution of this project, and in drawing a certain number of the German sovereigns into a partial combination in his own favour, but the others still pursued the path they had entered upon conformably with the laws of the empire. They were indeed forced to renounce the general assembly, since the emperor so peremptorily forbade it; but they were not so easily persuaded to relinquish the old decrees of the empire They determined to abide by the provisions of the Recess of 1523, which, in spite of a few additions and amendments, had in the main been confirmed in 1524 Indeed all the various mandates of that year have fundamentally the same character and purport

Such was the origin of a division which has never since been healed, which has constantly been kept open by the same foreign influences that originally caused it. It is very remarkable that all the different party leanings which have lasted through successive centuries, manifested themselves thus early We have still to observe their establishment and further progress; but the first moment of their existence revealed the incalculable amount of the danger with which they were pregnant.

* Zwinglius Œcolampadio, Tiguri, 9th Oct Epp Zwinglii, i p 163

† Hune, Geschichte von Hannover, i p 747

‡ Munter, Kirchengeschichte von Danemark, ii p 565

§ Memorandum of a conversation between Markgrave Albrecht and Achatius v Zemen Beitrage zur Kunde Preussens, vol. iv

‖ Letter from Luther to Brismann in de W, ii 526

CHAPTER VI.

THE PEASANTS' WAR.

Public order rests on two foundations—first, the stability of the governing body; secondly, the consent and accordance of public opinion with the established government, not, indeed, in every particular, which is neither possible nor even desirable, but with its general tenour.

In every age and country there must be disputes concerning the administration of the government, but so long as the foundations of public confidence remain unshaken, the danger is not great. Opinions are in perpetual flux and perpetual progress, so long as a strong government is actuated by the same general spirit, and feels the necessity of moving in the same direction, no violent convulsion need be feared.

But when the constituted powers doubt, vacillate, and conflict with one another, whilst at the same moment opinions essentially hostile to the existing order of things become predominant, then, indeed, is the peril imminent.

The first glance will suffice to show us that such was now the state of Germany.

The government of the empire, which it had cost so much labour to constitute, and which certainly enjoyed the general confidence of the nation, was now broken up, and its place filled by the mere shadow of a name. The emperor was at a distance, and recently the authority he had exercised was merely negative, he had only prevented the execution of whatever was resolved on. The two hierarchies, the spiritual and the temporal, which had been the work of past centuries, were now separated by a deep and wide chasm. The good understanding of the more powerful sovereigns, on which the unity of the empire had always depended, was destroyed. On the most important affair that had ever presented itself, all hope of framing measures in concert was at an end.

This, of course, reacted very powerfully on the state of opinion. A sort of understanding, with regard to which it was unnecessary to fix any precise terms, had hitherto been evinced in the tendencies of the imperial government, and the moderated tone adopted by Luther; and this it was that had enabled them to crush the destructive opinions which arose in 1522. But now that all hope of further change being effected by a decree of the empire was over, Luther could no longer maintain the authoritative position he had assumed, and the anarchical theories he had helped to stifle broke out afresh; they had found an asylum in the territory of his own sovereign—in electoral Saxony.

In Orlamunde, one of the cures which had been incorporated with the endowments of Wittenberg for the benefit of that University, Carlstadt now preached. He had entered into possession of the cure in an irregular manner, in opposition to the proper patrons of it, partly by means of a certain claim which he raised as belonging to the chapter, but mainly, by the election of the parishioners. He now removed the pictures, performed divine service after his own fashion, and promulgated the most extraordinary opinions concerning the doctrines of the church, and especially the obligations of the Mosaic law. We find mention of a man who, by Carlstadt's advice, wanted to marry two wives.* His rash and confused mind led him entirely to confound the national with the religious element of the Old Testament. Luther expected that before long circumcision would be introduced at Orlamunde, and thought it necessary seriously to warn the elector against attempts of this nature.

At Eisenach, Johann Strauss had already struck into a like crooked path. He was particularly violent against the practice of receiving interest on a loan. He declared that the heathenish laws of the jurists were not binding, and that the Mosaic institution of the year of jubilee, "wherein every man shall return unto the inheritance he had sold," still continued to be a valid commandment from God, thus calling all vested rights of property in question.†

Not far from thence, Thomas Munzer had founded a church on the doctrines which had been suppressed at Zwickau and Wittenberg. Like the former propagators of those doctrines, he assumed as its sole basis, those inward revelations to which alone he attached any importance; and he far surpassed them in the vehemence with which he preached the Taborite doctrine, that unbelievers were to be exterminated with the sword, and that a kingdom should be established, composed of the faithful only.

These doctrines could not fail to find a welcome and an echo in all parts of Germany. In Wurtemberg, too, the Israelitish year of jubilee was preached to the peasants. "Oh, beloved brethren!" said Dr. Mantel, "oh, ye poor christian men, were these years of jubilee to arrive, they would indeed be blessed years!"‡ Otto Brunfels, who had previously been very moderate in his language, in 1524 published at Strasburg a series of essays on tithes, wherein he declared them to be an institution of the Old Testament, which was abrogated by the New, and entirely denied the right of the clergy to them.§

While new champions of these opinions started in various parts of Germany, Nicolas Storch re-appeared at Hof, where he found believers in his revelations, and gathered round

---

* Letter of Luther to Bruck, 13th Jan. 1524. (De W., ii. No. 572.)

† "Dass wucher zu nemen und geben unserm christlichen Glauben entgegen ist, 1524."—"To give and take usurious interest is against our Christian faith." C. iii. it is said: "So dann in der Ordnung des Jubel Jars im Text offenbarlich aussgedruckt wirt das Gebot das die notürfftig bruderlich Lieb fordert, muss alle Einrede still halten und allen Christen desgleychen zu thun gebotten ungezweffelt seyn."—"Seeing, then, in the text ordaining the year of jubilee, the command requiring brotherly love is clearly expressed, so all disputes must cease, and there can be no doubt that all Christians are commanded to do likewise."

‡ Sattler, Würtenbergische Geschichte, Herz. ii. p. 105.

§ "De Ratione Decimarum Ottonis Brunfelsii Propositiones." Among others, prop. 115. "Proditores Christi sunt Juda pejores et sacerdotibus Baal, qui pro missis Papisticis et Canonicis preculis decimas recipiunt."

him twelve apostles who were to disseminate his doctrine throughout the nation.*

The exile of Münzer and Carlstadt from Saxony, which was partly effected by Luther's influence,† greatly contributed to the spread and the force of the agitation They both went to the Upper Rhine, where Carlstadt began by unreservedly proclaiming his doctrine of the Lord's Supper; and, however untenable was his own exposition of it, the excitement he thus occasioned was most violent, and productive of incalculable results. Munzer proceeded through Nurnberg to Basle and the frontier of Switzerland, where he was soon surrounded by fanatics who called themselves "the young Munzers," as Carlstadt was by men of learning. He confirmed them in the rejection of infant baptism, which by degrees was become the watchword of the party that meditated a universal revolution.

Thus, to the disorganisation of the supreme authorities, was added the general revolt of opinion against all existing institutions, a state of the public mind, which opened a boundless vista of possible changes in the order of things.

The result was inevitable.

We have already seen in what a state of ferment the peasantry of all parts of the empire had been for more than thirty years; how many attempts they had made to rise, how violent was their hatred to all constituted authorities. Long, however, before the Reformation had been even thought of, their political schemes were tinged with a religious character, this was shown in the case of the Capuchins at Eichstadt, in that of Hans Behaim in the Würzburg dominions, and of the peasantry in Untergrumbach Joss Fritz, who in 1513 renewed the Bundschuh at Lehen, in the Brisgau, was encouraged in his purpose by the parish priest, "because justice would be furthered by it: God approved the Bundschuh, as might be shown from the Scriptures, it was, therefore, a godly thing."‡ Poor Kunz of Wurtemberg declared, in 1514, "that he would stand up for righteousness and divine justice" It was immediately after a sermon of a former very orthodox professor of catholic theology, Dr. Gaislin, that the tumult first broke out on the banks of the Glems §

It was the manifest and inevitable tendency of the reforming movement, which shook the authority of the clergy from its very foundations, to foster ideas of this kind, but it is not less clear that the evangelical preaching, which was undertaken with far different views and aims, was likely to be affected by an excitement already so powerful. The political excitement was not produced by the preaching, but the religious enthusiasts caught the political fever For all had not the sound sense and the penetration of Luther. It was now taught that as all were the children of one father, and all equally redeemed by the blood of Christ, there should no longer be any inequality of wealth or station ‖ To the complaints of the misconduct of the clergy, were added the old accusations against lords and rulers their wars; the harsh, and often unjust administration of their ministers and subordinates, and the oppressions under which the poor groaned; in short, it was asserted that if the spiritual power was antichristian, the temporal was no less so. Both were accused of heathenism and tyranny "Things cannot go on as they have done," concludes one of these writings, "the game has been carried on long enough, and both citizens and peasants are tired of it, every thing will alter—omnium rerum vicissitudo.' ¶

The first disturbances broke out in the same district in which most of the former commotions had begun,—in that part of the Schwarzwald which divides the sources of the Danube from the upper valley of the Rhine. Several causes concurred to render this the scene of peculiar discontent —the vicinity of Switzerland, with which that part of Germany stood in various and close relation, the peculiar severity with which the Austrian government at Ensisheim and the commission at Engen pursued even the most blameless preachers of the new doctrine, the personal share taken in these measures by the Count of Sulz, governor of Insbruck, and hereditary judge at Rothweil, who, as well as the Counts of Lupfen and Fürstenberg, was distinguished for his hatred of Lutherans and peasants, the presence of Duke Ulrich of Wurtenberg at Hohentweil, who beheld his most formidable enemies in these noble partisans of Austria, and used every means to irritate the people against them, lastly, perhaps, the consequences of a hail-storm which, in the summer of 1524, destroyed all hopes of the harvest in the Kletgau The insurrection broke out in the Stuhlinger district, the domain of Count Sigismund of Lupfen. If it be true, as the contemporary chronicles affirm, that the immediate cause of the revolt was a strange whim of the Countess of Lupfen, for winding yarn upon snail-shells which her subjects were forced to collect, it is certain that never did a

* Widemann, Chron Curiense Mencken, iii p 744.

† Who has not read the scenes in Jena, where Luther is said to have given Carlstadt a gulden to write against him, and to be his enemy? Acta Jenensia, Walch, xv 2422. Luther always complained of the malignity of these stories That they are received in Luther's works does not prove their truth, as Fuessli says in his Life of Carlstadt, p 65 Luther was placed in a false position by hinting that Carlstadt's opinions were seditious, like those of Munzer, which could not be clearly proved

‡ Confession of Hans Hummel, Schneider, Bundschuh zu Lehen, p 99.

§ Heyd Herzog Ulrich von Würtenberg, i p 243

‖ "Kurz das e zugang auff Erden, wie mir Theutschen von Schlauraffenland, die Poeten de Insulis fortunatis und die Juden von ihres Messias Zeytten dichten, also auch zum Tayl die Junger Christi gedachten vom Reych Christi"—"In short that it should be on earth, as we Germans romance of the Schlauraffenland (a sort of pays de Cocagne) poets, de Insulis fortunatis, and the Jews of the times of their Messiah, so some of the disciples of Christ thought about the kingdom of Christ"—*Eberlin von Günzberg, Ein Getrewe Warnung an die Christen in der Burgau*

¶ Ein ungewonlicher und der ander Sendtbrieff dess Bauernfeyndts zu Karsthannsen"—"An uncommon and another missive of the peasants' enemy to Karsthannsen" towards the end printed by Johann Locher of Munich Panzer (ii No 2777) mentions a previous letter of Karsthannsen dated 1523 In the second, I find no mention of the peasants' war, and it must have been written, at latest, during the latter half of the year 1524.

more trifling and fantastic cause produce more serious and violent effects.*

On the 24th of August, 1524, Hans Müller of Bülgenbach, a Stuhlinger peasant and soldier, went to the anniversary of the consecration of the church at Waldshut, followed by a considerable troop of insurgent peasants, bearing a black, red, and white flag but resistance to a single count was far too mean and trifling an object for him, he announced his intention of founding an evangelical brotherhood for the purpose of emancipating the peasantry throughout the German empire.† A small contribution paid by the members was destined to pay emissaries who were to extend the confederation over all parts of Germany. This project did not originate with himself. It was suggested by Thomas Munzer, who had long kept up a correspondence with this district, and now arrived there in person. He stayed a few weeks in Griesheim, and then traversed the Hegau and the Kletgau,—for he could find no permanent resting-place,—‡ preaching wherever he went the deliverance of Israel, and the establishment of a heavenly kingdom upon earth. The subjects of the Counts of Werdenberg, Montfort, Lupfen, and Sulz, of the Abbot of Reichenau and the Bishop of Constance, gradually joined the Stuhlingers. Those of Sulz previously consulted the inhabitants of Zurich, in which town their lord possessed the rights of citizenship, and although the latter did not, as they assured the count, approve the insurrection, they did not hesitate to make the toleration of evangelical preachers one of the conditions of their obedience.§ It would be well worth while to examine the course of these movements more narrowly than has yet been done. The various motives which concurred to produce the peasants' war were more distinguishable at this, than at any other period; for this was the moment at which they assumed the form of those general ideas, which from that time to this have possessed such a singular power of inflaming and attaching the minds of men.

The lords vainly called upon the Swabian League for aid in their peril. Here and there a band of insurgents was induced by its persuasions and promises to return home; but wherever a serious engagement took place, the peasants maintained their ground.

Hearing that a body of the infantry and cavalry of the League was advancing against them under Jacob von Landau, they took up a strong position, from which it was impossible to dislodge them.‖ Nor could the most zealous efforts of well-intentioned mediators bring about any reconciliation. The peasants drew up a statement of their grievances in twelve articles, which they did not hesitate to lay before the Council of Regency at Esslingen. If, however, the lords refused to enter on the discussion of the whole of these collectively, the peasants were equally determined not to concede any point. they had indeed far more extensive schemes in reserve. At the end of the year 1524, and the beginning of 1525, the peasants were masters of the whole land.¶ The lords and their ministers were at length compelled to seek safety behind the massive walls of Ratolphzell, defended by its devoted townsmen.

Meanwhile, however, similar disturbances had broken out in larger districts.

Nowhere were the complaints of the people better grounded than in the dominions of the Abbots of Kempten. These ecclesiastical rulers continually vexed their subjects with fresh taxes, which they spent in building or travelling. As long ago as the year 1492, riots had broken out in consequence, but had led to no redress of the people's wrongs. The free peasants, who were very numerous in the Abbacy, were continually ground down to the station of Zinsers,** and those again to that of villeins,†† while the latter were compelled to perform services that rendered their condition more intolerable. Free lands were taken possession of, tithe-free estates subjected to tithes, the money paid by the peasants for protection and defence was raised twenty-fold; the popular courts of justice held at markets or fairs were suppressed; the revenues of the communes or villages were seized; occasionally, even, the spiritual power was applied to carry through these oppressions. It was not surprising, therefore, that, in the year 1523, when a new Abbot, Sebastian von Breitenstein, entered on the government, the peasants refused to do homage, except on condition that he would redress their grievances. At first he held out the hope that he would comply with their demands, thirteen sittings were held to consider of them, but all in vain; the Abbot at length exclaimed that he would leave things as he found them, if his subjects would not obey

* Extract from the Villinger Chronik, Walchner, Ratolphzell, p. 89. According to Anshelm vi. p. 298 the subjects of the Counts von Lupfen and Furstenberg complained, "Dass sie am Fyrtag mussten Schneggenhussli suchen garn winden, Erdbeer, Kriesen, Schlehen gewinnen, und ander dergleichen thun, den Herren und Frouwen werken bei gutem Wetter, ihnen selbs im Ungewetter das gejagd und d hund luffent ohne Achtung einigs Schadens."—"That on holydays they were obliged to hunt for snails wind yarn, gather strawberries cherries, and sloes, and do other such like things, they had to work for their lords and ladies in fine weather, and for themselves in the rain. Their huntsmen and hounds ran about without regarding the damage they did." The matter was laid before the Kammergericht, but the people did not wait for the decision.

† Schreiber, Taschenbuch für Süddeutschland, i. p. 72.

‡ "Certis de causis." Bullinger adversus Anabaptistas, and his Reformations geschichte, p. 224.

§ Fuesslins Beitrage zur Historie der Kirchenreformation vol ii p. 68.

‖ Walchner, Geschichte von Ratolphzell, p. 92.

¶ The instruction given by Archduke Ferdinand to Veit Suter (Walchner and Bensen, p. 538,) shows the state of lawless violence produced under these circumstances.

** The Zinser, or Zinsmann, occupied, as the context shows, an intermediate station between the free peasant and the villein. As the idea is a very complex one, and involves a number of conditions to which we have nothing analogous, any attempt to translate the word could only mislead. Grimm (D. R. A. p. 358) says, "*Zins* is the Latin *census*." The word which seems most nearly to express its meaning, in the cases he cites, is *dues*.—Transl.

†† Haggenmuller, Geschichte der Stadt und Grafschaft Kempten, p. 505, says that four hundred cases of this kind are recorded in the Rotula of the Provincial Acts.

him, George von Frundsberg should come and teach them. This was assuredly a most ill-timed stretch of the spiritual rights of supremacy, just when all men were refusing their belief in the basis on which those rights were founded — the divine authority of the clergy. As the Abbot made this appeal to force, his subjects thought it time to prepare for defence. On the 23d of January, 1525, the seceders, (*Gotteshausleute*—God's house people) held a meeting at their old place on the Luibas. They determined to pursue the matter legally before the judges and councillors of the League, and if they could get no redress, to sound the tocsin, and repel force by force.

Already they beheld allies rising around them on every side. Similar, if not equal wrongs; the force of example, and the hope of success, set the peasantry all over Swabia in motion.

In February, the people of the Allgau, led by Dietrich Hurlewagen of Lindau, rose against the Bishop of Augsburg, and formed a strict alliance with the villages of Kempten. On the 27th of February, the two districts held a meeting on the Luibas. If any inhabitant of them refused to join the association, a stake was driven into the ground before his door, as a token that he was a public enemy. At their call, the peasants all along the Lake of Constance, and across the Alps to Pfullendorf, joined them, led by Eitelhans of Theuringen, whom his followers celebrate as "a good captain of the Lord, who kept a faithful hand over them." No bells could be tolled for divine service; the sound of them instantly gave the alarm, and all the people rushed to the place of meeting at Bermatingen.* A third party, consisting of the subjects of the Abbot of Ochsenhausen, the Baron of Waldburg, and many other lords and cities, rose on the Ried. The villages that refused to join them were threatened with fire and sword;† the people on the Iller hastened to unite with them. Their centre of operations was at Baldringen.

Thus united, and grown to a formidable force, the peasantry now again laid their grievances before the Swabian League. In the course of March, negotiations were again set on foot in Ulm with the three insurgent bands. But it may be doubted whether it was not the character of the League itself which caused these discontents; — the incessant wars, the expenses of which were either thrown directly on the subjects, or raised by an increase of all the established burthens; the support it gave to the several lords individually; being itself composed of the very sovereigns against whom the complaints were made. It now clearly appeared how great a calamity it was for the country that the Council of Regency had recently lost so immensely in power and consideration. It sent, indeed, two of its members to command peace, and to try to bring about a reconciliation; and they proposed to erect a court of arbitration, — each party to nominate one prince and three cities, who should hear the complaints and adjudge the remedy. But the Council of Regency was far too weak to obtain a hearing for even these moderate proposals. For a moment (in February and March) the invasion of his own land by the Duke of Würtenberg had occupied the attention of the League. It is difficult to say what would have happened if the Confederation, on whom this prince again relied, had adhered firmly to his cause, as it appeared its interest to do. For it seemed consistent enough that the Swiss, in opposition to whom the Swabian League was originally formed, should support the duke who attacked, and the peasants who revolted against it; and it was this danger which had induced the councillors of the League to enter into negotiations. But on this occasion, as on former ones, other considerations preponderated with the Swiss diet; and when the duke had already forced his way into the outskirts of Stuttgart, they recalled their troops from him with the greatest urgency,‡ and he was compelled to retreat without gaining any solid advantage.

The League was thus at liberty to act against the peasantry. Without further hesitation, it required them first to lay down their arms, after which it would treat with them.§ As the peasants had gone much too far to agree to these conditions, the League, well prepared for war, determined on an immediate resort to force. But it was destined again to find a wholly unexpected resistance. Detached bands were easily routed and dispersed, and a few small places quickly reduced; but this had no effect on the main body. The duke's enterprise had so far been of use to the peasants, that it had given them time to assemble in masses which kept even such a commander as George Truchsess in check. Many of these men had borne arms in the field. While the League had excited the insurrection by grinding

* Salmansweiler's description in Oechsle, Beiträge zur Geschichte des Bauernkriegs, p. 485.

† See the account of the treaty of Hegöwisch, Walchner, p. 298: "Wie wol es den Frommen und Erbaren nit lieb, sonder ein gros beschwärd was. Nütt dester minder so was der Jungen und auch deren die niemen nutz; so vil das die Allten und auch die Frommen mit innen müsten züchen, oder sy im der nit ziechen wöllt ein Pfal für sin hus schlugent, unnd im darby tröwtend." — "Although, indeed, to the honest and godly it was not welcome, but rather a grievous burthen; nevertheless, not only the young, and those who were of no use to any man, but also the old and godly men even were forced to go along with them. And if any man would not, they thrust a stake into the earth before his door, and threatened him thereat."

‡ Hans Stockar's Heimfahrt und Tagebuch, p. 131: "und dye Botten, die miantend uns ab, das wier hiam zugend mit Mund und mit Brieffen, by Lib und by Leben, ain Eren und Gutt, by Verlürn unser Vatters-land, und ckemend wier, so wettind sy uns aller Straff ledyg lon, und erzalttend uns von dem Schaden, den wier zu Mialand und der Frantzoss Küng hatt aimpfangen. Und also warend wir unseren Heren und Oberen gehorsam, und brachen in der Nacht uff." — "And the messengers warned us to depart to our homes by word of mouth and by letter, as we loved our lives and limbs, our honour and goods, and feared to lose our country; and if we went there they would forgive us all punishment. And they told us of the losses we had suffered in Milan, and those of the French king. And accordingly we obeyed our lords and masters, and set out that same night."

§ Haggenmüller, Kempten, p. 522. A book which I have constantly found very useful. I am surprised to find the movement at Kempten so falsely represented, even in contemporary works, and hence, of course, in all subsequent ones. Cochläus seems to be the originator of the errors.

taxes and religious persecutions, it had also made the insurgents capable of self-defence, by its continual wars. The feeling of their own power of defending themselves was, indeed, one chief motive to the revolt. The foot-soldiers of the League, who had not unfrequently served under the same banners with these peasants, had a natural fellow-feeling with them. And now, from the time that the last negotiations had proved abortive, the disorder began to assume a really serious character

The twelve articles had appeared, and every one knew what he had to expect, and why he had taken arms. These articles contained three different kinds of demands first of all, the liberty of the chase, of fishing, and of hewing wood, and the prevention of or compensation for the damage done by the game.—demands and complaints reiterated by the peasantry of all countries ever since the rise of feudal societies: as early as the year 997, we find them urged in Normandy.* Secondly, the peasants pressed for relief from some newly-imposed burthens, new laws and penalties, and for restoration of the property of the parishes which had been abstracted, as we remarked in speaking of the usurpations of the lords. Lastly, the desire for religious reform was mingled with these secular motives. The peasants were determined no longer to be serfs, for Christ had redeemed them also with his precious blood, they would no longer pay the small tithe, but only the great one,† for God had ordained that alone in the Old Testament Above all, they demanded the right to choose their own preachers, in order to be instructed by them in the true faith, "without which they were mere flesh and blood, and good for nothing" The characteristic feature of these articles is a mixture of spiritual and temporal demands, a derivation of the latter from the former, which is certainly at variance with the sentiments of Luther, and with the pure and unmingled tendencies of the reformation, but which is also far removed from all schemes of general convulsion, and not at variance with common sense and humanity. As to the political demands, the local and particular interests are far less prominent than those of a general or a universal character,—as was indispensable where various bands of men were to combine the author of them, be he who he may, gave evidence of sagacity and address. For thus alone could the articles obtain general approbation, and be regarded as the manifesto of the whole body of the peasantry.‡ But further demands were by no means withdrawn in consequence

All the people of the Black Forest, from Wutachthal to Dreisamthal, now flocked together under Hans Müller of Bulgenbach. This leader journeyed from place to place, brilliantly attired in a red cloak and cap, at the head of his adherents, the great standard and the battle-flag followed him in a cart decorated with leaves and ribbons—a sort of carroccio.§ A herald, or messenger, summoned all the parishes, and read the twelve articles aloud. Nor did their commander stop here; he declared them the symbol of the evangelical brotherhood, which he intended to found; whoever refused to accept them should be put under temporal ban by the union. Already had this been declared against the lords of castles, the monks and priests in convents and chapters: though even these men might be admitted into the association, if they chose to enter it, and to live for the future in common houses like other people; every thing should then be granted them which was their due according to the laws of God Muller's first vague idea of an evangelical brotherhood thus assumed a very distinct form. A radical change in political and even in social relations was the object now clearly aimed at.

In the course of April, 1525, it really appeared likely to come to this

It is a very remarkable circumstance that while Munzer was fomenting the disorders in Upper Swabia, Dr. Carlstadt, a Franconian by birth, was equally active in Franconia. Compelled to quit Strasburg and to return home, but there subject to incessant persecution, and regarded with double horror in consequence of the notoriety of his doubts as to the sacrament, he at length found an asylum at Rothenburg on the Tauber, where his opinions were regarded with sympathy. The citizens of the guilds demanded that the church reform which had just been begun should be carried through, which the patrician families (*die Geschlechter*,) whose domination was, moreover, not wholly

* Gulielmus Gemeticensis, Hist Norm, lib v 2 "Iuxta suos libitus vivere decernebant, quatenus tam in sylvarum compendiis quam in aquarum commerciis nullo obsistente ante statuti juris obice legibus uterentur suis"

† This is shown in the following passage from Mullner's Annals The council at Nurnberg caused it to be proclaimed from all pulpits, "dass aller lebendige Zehent, als Fullen Kalber Lammer, &c, desgleichen der kleine Zehent, den man nennt dan todten Zehent, als Heidel Erbeiss Heu Hopfen, &c, ganz todt und abseyn solle, aber den grossen harten Zehenten von hernach benanntem Getreide, so man die funf Brand nennt, nemlich von Korn Dünkel Waitzen Gerste habern, sollte man zu geben schuldig seyn"—"That all tithes on living things, such as foals, calves, lambs, &c, likewise the small tithes called the dead tithes, such as buck wheat, pasture, hay, hops &c., should be entirely abolished, but the people should be bound to pay the great hard tithes on the following sorts of grain, viz rye, spelt, wheat, barley and oats." (According to custom, the fifteenth, twentieth, or thirtieth sheaf)

‡ "Die grundlichen und rechten Hauptartikel aller Bauerschafft und Hyndersessen" printed among others in Strobel's Beitrage, ii p. 9 Among the editions, one in Panzer, No 2703, has this addition "des monadts Martii" According to Haggenmuller, p 513, their first appearance in the form of a document was during the negotiation between the three united bodies of peasants and the Swabian League, in February and March, 1525, in which case they must have been drawn up by a preacher who had joined the peasants According to the unanimous opinion of contemporaries, among whom was Melanchthon, Christopher Schappeler was the author. Even in the Florentine History of Nardi (viii p 187,) he is called "uno scellerato rinnovatore della setta degli anabattisti chiamato Scifere" Schappeler however, always denied this (Bullinger, p 245), and, indeed, it seems to have been an error It was afterwards supposed and from his own confession (see Strobel ib p 76) that Joh Heughlin of Lindau was the real author, yet his confession relates only to the articles which were granted to the peasants of Sernatingen, to prevent their joining the other peasants the famous twelve articles would have been mentioned in another manner

§ Schreiber der Breisgau im Bauernkriege, Taschenb. für Suddeutschland, i p 235.

legal, opposed. The guilds had a most powerful ally on their side, in the sturdy warlike peasants of the Landwehr, who were also vexed with exorbitant and illegal charges, and who claimed the liberty of the Gospel. We are too well acquainted with the character of Carlstadt, not to know that he would approve all the objects of the people. Already banished by the council, but secretly protected by certain powerful members of it, he suddenly appeared near the crucifix in the great burial-ground, in his peasant's coat and hat of rough white felt, and exhorted the country people not to desist from their endeavours.* It may easily be imagined, however, that the movement was not confined to religious innovations. In the last week of March, disturbances broke out, first in the country, and then in the town, in which a committee of the guilds seized on all the power, while the rural communes formed themselves into a great association, set forth their grievances — which had indeed spiritual grounds, but were by no means of an exclusively spiritual nature—and took up arms to compel redress.

In Franconia the slumbering fires of discontent burst forth with still greater rapidity than in Swabia, either in consequence of the combinations formed by the emissaries sent by Hans Muller, or by the excitement produced in the minds of the disaffected ringleaders by the example of their neighbours. A few thousand peasants, excited by the twelve articles, which had fallen into their hands, assembled in a valley of the Odenwald, called the Schupfergrund, and chose for their leader George Metzler, the inn-keeper at Ballenburg, in whose house the first arrangements had been made, — a bold man, whose life had been passed in the noisy revels of a frequented tavern.† Similar meetings were held at Bockingen, Mergentheim, and many other places The first thing usually was to break the fasts, a banquet was held, at which the most eloquent and the most disaffected spoke; the twelve articles were brought out, read, and approved, a leader was chosen, and the alarm bell sounded. Such was the beginning of the riot, the first act of which, in almost every case, was to seize upon a flour-store or a wine-cellar, or to drag a seigneurial fish-pond The newly chosen commanders might be seen riding about with an air of authority, mounted upon the priest's pony But though these tumults seemed contemptible enough in their beginnings, they became more and more formidable as they advanced. On an appointed day the several bands repaired together from every side, not exactly at the customary meeting-place, but at some convent they had doomed to destruction, as, for example, at Schefersheim, where they swore to pay neither tax, rent, nor tithe, to any lord, temporal or spiritual, till they would come to some terms; and in future, as they had only one God, to acknowledge only one master It was as if the insurgents were led by some secret guidance to one predetermined end. Their object was in the first place to emancipate themselves from their lords, but then to unite with them and take measures in concert against the clergy, and, above all, against the spiritual princes.

To accomplish this work by forcible means, two troops marched into the field, one called the Black, from Rothenburg, under Hans Kolbenschlag, the other, the White, from the Odenwald, under George Metzler The lords were compelled to accept the twelve articles, of which the Odenwald band published a distinct declaration, wherein the abolition of the punishment of death, of the lesser tithes, and of villeinage were especially insisted on, without omitting such local modifications as should seem necessary, and holding out the prospect of further reforms ‡ This band had not, like the Swabian, the forces of the League to deal with, there was nobody capable of resisting them The Counts of Hohenlohe and Lowenstein, the commander of the Teutonic Order at Mergentheim, and the Junker of Rosenberg, were forced in succession to subscribe to the conditions laid before them by the peasants, and to submit beforehand to the reforms they purposed to introduce. The Counts George and Albert, of Hohenlohe, consented to appear before the peasants' army at Grunbuhl "Brother George and brother Albert," said a tinker of Ohringen to them, "come hither and swear to the peasants to be as brothers to them, for ye are now no longer lords, but peasants."§ Terrible, indeed, was the fate of those who ventured to resist, like Count Helferstein at Weinsberg. The natural rudeness of peasants was inflamed by the first opposition into the wildest and most wanton blood-thirstiness they swore that they would kill every man that wore spurs; and when Helfenstein had fallen into their power, it was in vain that his wife, a natural daughter of Emperor Maximilian, threw herself at the feet of the leaders with her little son in her arms a lane was formed, and the victim brought out, preceded by a peasant playing on a pipe, Helfenstein was then driven on the spears of his peasants, amidst the sound of trumpets and horns. Hereupon, every one gave way all the nobility, from the Odenwald to the Swabian frontier, submitted to the laws of the peasants, —those of Winterstetten, Stettenfels, Zobel, Gemmingen, Frauenberg, and the Counts of Wertheim and Rheineck, those of Hohenlohe now even gave up their artillery to the peasants ‖ In order to bring the matter to a conclusion, both bodies now marched against the most powerful lord in Franconia, who bore the title of Duke there, — the Bishop of Wurz-

* Bensen der Bauernkrieg in Ostfranken, p 79 According to the sentence passed on Stephan von Menzingen, this leader of the town movements, an adherent of Duke Ulrich of Wurtenberg associated frequently with Carlstadt See Aufang und Ende des Bauernkriegs zu Rothenburg, Walch, L. W xvi 150

† According to Hubert Thomas Leodius, this occurred about the middle of Lent, at Lätare, 26th March

‡ Explanation of the 12 articles Oechsle, p 572, and Bensen, p 526

§ Letter from Count George to the city of Hall Tuesday after Palm Sunday Oechsle, p 271

‖ Chronik der Truchsessen, ii p 195

burg. On their way, they had not alone enriched and strengthened themselves, but had also secured distinguished commanders of the knightly class. Gotz von Berlichingen had undertaken the command of the Odenwald troop; partly because it would have been dangerous to refuse, partly attracted by the prospect of active war, which was the sole object and passion of his life, and in which he was the more ready to engage, as it was directed against his old enemies of the Swabian League * Florian Geier led the Rothenburgers On the 6th and 7th of May these bands approached Wurzburg in opposite directions, and were joyfully received by the inhabitants of the town, who hoped to gain the privileges of a free imperial city,† the citizens and the peasants swore not to forsake each other till they had conquered the Frauenberg, in which the last remaining forces of the princes and knights of Franconia, who were now united, had assembled.

At the same moment (the end of April and beginning of May, 1525) a similar state of things began throughout Upper Germany Disturbances broke out in all directions, and everywhere they were in effect successful.

The Bishop of Spire had been forced to submit to the conditions imposed by the peasants,‡ the Elector Palatine had met them in an open field near the village of Horst, and promised to redress their grievances on the conditions laid down in the twelve articles § In Alsatia, Zabern, the residence of the bishop himself, had fallen into the hands of the insurgents; the inhabitants of the small towns declared that they had no spears wherewith to pierce the peasants, for a time their leaders, Schlemmerhans and Deckerhans,‖ were all-powerful On Markgrave Ernest of Baden refusing to accept the terms offered by the peasants, his castle was taken and he was forced to fly. The knights of the Hegau were surrounded and besieged by them in the town of Zell on the Untersee. Even the powerful Truchsess, at the head of the forces of the Swabian League, was compelled to come to terms with the peasants of the Allgau, See and Ried, and, with the mediation of the cities, to promise them relief from their oppressions, before they would submit. It was unusual good fortune when they would thus consent to wait for future arrangements In Wurtemberg they would not hear of any more diets of the duchy (*Landtage*), but insisted on instantly placing everything in the hands of their Christian brotherhood, which had already spread over the chief part of the country. Each place sent a certain number of people into the field.

The Bishop of Bamberg, the Abbot of Hersfeld, and the coadjutor of Fulda, had already made concessions of a spiritual, as well as temporal kind. The last-named of the three agreed to these changes with peculiar readiness, and immediately allowed himself to be saluted Prince von der Buchen; his brother, the old Count William of Henneberg, also entered into the peasants' league, and promised to leave in freedom "all whom God Almighty had made free in Christ his Son"¶ The boldest attempt at a complete change in all the relations of life was perhaps that made by the inhabitants of the Rheingau They once more assembled on the old traditional meeting-place, the Lützelau, at Bartholomewtide,** and agreed to demand, above all, the restoration of their ancient constitution, the Haingericht (Bush Court)†† subsisting under their old law, and the Gebick, which converted the country into a sort of fortress besides this they insisted on the participation of the lords, both spiritual and temporal, in the burthens borne by the community at large, and the application of conventual property to the use of the country. They encamped on the Wachholder at Erbach, and actually in open rebellion, compelled the governor, dean and chapter to grant their demands ‡‡ At Aschaffenburg too, the governor for the Archbishop of Mainz was forced to submit to the conditions of the peasants

The whole Swabian and Franconian branch of the German nation was thus in a state of agitation which seemed likely to end in a complete overthrow of all the existing relations of society, a great number of towns were already infected with the prevailing spirit.

The small towns were the first to join the cause of the peasantry,—Kempten, Leipheim, and Gunzburg on the Danube (which, indeed, soon received severe chastisement); the nine Odenwald towns in the see of Mainz, and the towns in the Breisgau, in some of which the town clerk himself opened the gates to the

* Lebensbeschreibung des Gotz, p 201 See his Apology in the Materialien, p 150

† Johann Reinhards Wurzburgische Chronik in Ludwig, Wurzb Geschichtschr, p 886

‡ Gnodalius, ii p 142

§ Letter from the Elector to Melanchthon "Haben uns mit ihnen den 12 Artikel wegen eines Landtags vereinigt, dergestalt wes wir uns derselben mit ihnen vergleichen mochten das hat seine wege, wes wir uns aber nicht vertragen konnen, das solt stehen zu Thurfursten Fursten und Standen des Reichs"—"We have agreed with them about a diet to consider the 12 articles, in such wise that whatever we could arrange with them was to stand, but what we cannot settle was to be referred to the electors, princes, and states of the empire" This was the principle of most of the arrangements that were made (Mel Epp i p 743)

‖ Two names, equivalent to Jack the Guttler and Jack the Tiler —Transl

¶ The formula of the League Ludwig, p 879

** According to Bodmann's Rheingauischen Alterthumern, p 461, Vogt's assertion, that the juniper tree was the ancient place of meeting, is erroneous

†† Grimm, in his Deutsche Rechtsalthumer, p 793, says, "The ancient *Gericht*, was invariably held in the open air, in a wood, under shady trees, on a hillock or near a spring, the assembled multitude could not have been contained in any moderate building, and pagan ideas required that the Gericht should be holden in a holy spot, on which sacrifices were offered, and the judgment of heaven appealed to Christianity abolished the sacrifices but left the old *Gerichtstatten* undisturbed" I have sought in vain for any explanation of the word *Gebick* It has been suggested to me that it is something like a Mark (district), or rather the lines by which each Mark was enclosed These were chiefly formed by forest, and also by rivers, ditches, and other natural boundaries See Grimm's account of the primitive territorial divisions of Germany (book iii p 491).—Transl

‡‡ Artikel gemeiner Landschaft, Schunk, Beitrage zur Mainze Gesch i p 191

peasants, none of these, indeed, were in a condition to resist, and most of them groaned under the same oppressions as the peasantry. The people of Bamberg conceived the bold project of compelling the surrounding nobles to come and live within the walls of their town and become burghers, nearly fifty castles were stormed in this neighbourhood* The Abbot of Kempten being forced to surrender his castle of Liebenthann to the peasants, and to seek refuge in the town, the burghers took advantage of the favourable moment to bring him to an agreement they had long desired, for the release of all his rights of sovereignty. Some of the free imperial towns of the second and third classes were next drawn into the league by persuasion or by force these were Heilbronn, Memmingen, Dunkelspiel, and Wimpfen; Rothenburg entered into an alliance with the peasantry for a hundred and one years, which was ratified at a solemn assembly held in the parish church Windsheim was only restrained from the same course by the dissuasions of Nurnberg Even in the great cities a similar spirit manifested itself Mainz claimed the restitution of its rights as an imperial city, of which it had been deprived since the last disturbances The council of Treves not only demanded that the clergy should be called upon to bear their share in the burthens of the citizens, but even laid claim to a part of the spiritual revenues accruing from the relics in the cathedral.† The council of Frankfurt was forced to agree to the articles laid before it by the commonalty, word by word,‡ alleging as an excuse that the same thing had happened in several other imperial cities. It was remarked that Strasburg received the insurgents as citizens, and that Ulm supplied them with arms, and Nurnberg with provisions A learned writer of this period states it as his opinion, that the movement had originated even more with the towns than with the peasantry, and that the former had been originally stirred up by Jewish emissaries: he believes that the intention of the towns was to shake off the authority of the princes altogether, and to live like Venice, or the republics of antiquity §

Unfounded as was this opinion—for we know how zealously many of the imperial towns, Nurnberg for example, strove to suppress the rising disorders in their own dominions, and we have seen that the disturbances in the towns which corresponded to those of the peasants were only called forth by circumstances.—yet we cannot but perceive what force and extension must have been given to the rebellion by the addition of this second element, and how wide and threatening the danger was become

The ideas to which this crisis gave birth were most remarkable.

The Franconian peasants formed projects for the reform of the whole empire.

So deeply rooted was this purpose in the very heart of the nation. That which the princes had vainly endeavoured to accomplish at so many diets,—which Sickingen and his knights had attempted three years before to execute after their fashion,—the peasants now believed they could effect,—of course in the manner most calculated to raise their own condition.

The first object was to give a general direction and guidance to the present tumultuous movement A common office for the business of all the separate bands, in fact a sort of central government, was to be established at Heilbronn. The masses were to be ordered to return home to their daily work, leaving only a certain levy in the field, whose duty it would be to compel all who still remained unsubdued to accept the twelve articles.

In the further attempts to create some positive institutions, the predominant idea was that of freeing the peasantry from the burthen of all the oppressive privileges of the lords, both spiritual and temporal To accomplish this, it was determined to proceed at once to a general secularisation of the ecclesiastical property As this would involve the abolition of the spiritual principalities, means would thus be obtained for giving compensation to the temporal sovereigns for the loss of their rights, for which some indemnity was thought due. The amount of church property was so enormous, that the people hoped still to have enough left to satisfy all the public exigencies of the empire. All duties and tolls were to be taken off, and all charges for safe conduct, and only every tenth year a tax was to be levied for the Roman emperor,‖ who was in future to be the sole protector and ruler of the country, and to whom alone the people were to owe duty and allegiance. The courts of law were to be remodelled and popularised on one comprehensive principle. There were to be sixty-four free courts (*Freigerichte*¶) in the empire, with assessors of all classes, even the lowest; besides these, sixteen district courts (*Landgerichte*), four courts of appeal (*Hofgerichte*), and one supreme court (*Kammergericht*), all organised in the same manner The members of the Kammergericht were to be as follows —

* Lang's Geschichte von Baireuth, i p 187 Heller, p 88

† Scheckmann Additamentum ad Gesta Trevirorum in Wyttenbach's edition of the Gesta, ii Animadv p 51

‡ Lersner's Frankfurter Chronik

§ Conradi Mutiani Literæ ad Fridericum Electorem, 27th April 1525, in Kohler's Beitrage, i 270

‖ They refused to acknowledge Margrave Ernest of Baden as their sovereign, and were determined to be governed in future by the Emperor and his deputy alone They also meant something similar by the divine right which they conceded to the Duke of Wurtenberg The chief ground of their recognition of the Emperor (*Kaiser*—*Cæsar*) was that he was named in the New Testament

¶ Grimm says, in his Deutsche Rechts Alterthümer (p 829), "Originally almost every *Gau* or *Merkgericht* might be called a *Freigericht* Later, however, when the sovereignty of the princes gained force and consistency, this term acquired a peculiar meaning Particular districts which maintained their independence, and remained immediately subject to the empire, bore the name of *Freigerichte* just as immediate cities were called *Freistadte*" (see further, note at p 225) Courts called *Freigerichte*, of which the lord of the soil appoints the president, and the peasants the assessors, exist, I am told, in the German provinces of Russia —TRANSL

two princes, two reigning counts, two knights, three burghers of the imperial towns, three from the princely residencies, and four from all the communes of the empire These were plans which had often been suggested, and are, for instance, to be found in a work which appeared as early as 1523, called "Need of the German nation" ("*Nothdurft deutscher Nation*")—they were now adopted and developed by two clever and daring peasant leaders, Friedrich Weigant of Miltenberg, and Wendel Hipler, formerly chancellor of Hohenlohe * The doctors of the Roman law were especially hated by the peasantry, they were not to be admitted into any court of law, and only to be tolerated at the universities, in order that their advice might be taken in urgent cases. All classes, too, were to be made to return to their original vocation; the clergy were to be only the shepherds of their flocks, the princes and knights were to occupy themselves in defending the weak, and to live in brotherly love one with another. All the commons were to undergo a reformation consonant to the laws of God and of nature; only one sort of coin was to be current, and uniform weights and measures were to be introduced.

Ideas more radically subversive than were ever again proclaimed till the time of the French Revolution.

But bold and anarchical as they were, they were not without a considerable prospect of being realised. The contagion spread every instant it had already seized on Hessen, whence it threatened to extend its conquests over the Saxon race, as from upper Swabia over the Bavarian, and from Alsatia over that of Lorraine Corresponding disturbances took place in Westphalia; for example, at Munster, where the town demanded the same concessions from its chapter as at Treves, and the bishop already feared that he should see the whole country hurried away by the storm † It also broke out on the Austrian frontiers, where all that offered resistance were put under ban by the peasantry; all the Alpine districts were in the same state: in Tyrol, Archduke Ferdinand found himself compelled, in manifest contravention of the decrees of Regensburg, to concede to the committees of the states of Inn and Wippthal that the Gospel should in future be preached "pure and plain, according to the sense borne by the text,"‡ in the see of Brixen, the bishop's secretary, Michael Geissmayr, headed the insurgents, at Salzburg, the miners flocked to the churches at the sound of the alarm-bell, even between Vienna and Neustadt the labourers in the vineyards talked of a combination which would enable them to send abont ten thousand men into the field within a few hours §

Meanwhile, the rebellion had broken out in Thuringia, and had there assumed another character

It appears probable that in Thuringia and the Harz, traditions of the fanaticism of the flagellants, the effects of which may be traced down even to the end of the 15th century,‖ had prepared the ground for the insurrection of the peasantry. At all events, motives arising out of religious enthusiasm were much more powerful there than political causes. The opinions which Luther had overcome at Wittenberg, and which he had warned his prince not to suffer to take root in Thuringia, were now eagerly listened to by a numerous and excited population Münzer had returned to Thuringia, he had been received at Mühlhausen, where, as at Rothenburg, a change of the constitution and of the council had been brought about by the co-operation of the lower class of burghers with the country people; and from hence he soon spread the ferment far and wide around him He scorned, as we are already aware, the "fabulous gospel" preached by Luther, his "honey-sweet Christ," and his doctrine that antichrist must be destroyed by the Word alone, without violence: he maintained that the tares must be rooted out at the time of harvest, that the example of Joshua, who smote the people of the promised land with the edge of the sword, must

* See the plans of the peasants in Oechsle, p 163 and in the Appendix It has already been remarked by Eichhorn (Deutsche Staats und Rechtsgesch iii p 119, 4th ed) that these designs throw a new light on the so called Reformation of Frederick III Goldast does not indeed deserve the blame which Eichhorn attributes to him he has not given this little work as a reformation of the Emperor's. The old work he quotes bears the title 'Teutscher Nation Notturft die Ordnung und Reformation aller Stend im Rom Reych, durch Kayser Friedrich III Gott zu Lob, der ganzen Christenheit zu Nutz und Seligkait furgenommen" (*Panzer* ii p 226)—'The Needs of the German Nation the ordering and reformation of all the classes of the Roman empire by the Emperor Frederick III, undertaken for the glory of God, and for the benefit and salvation of all Christendom" But this, no doubt, is a mere author's fiction The paper breathes throughout the spirit of the first years of the reformation The calamity at Erfurt, which is there mentioned among those communes which owed their ruin to self interest, refers, no doubt, to the destructive riots of 1510, and not to any previous and less remarkable events

† "Alle und semptliche Artikel durch die van Munster by sick solvest upgericht"—"All and every article drawn up for themselves by those of Munster," and especially the letter of the Bishop Frederic, dated 8th of May, in Niesert, Beitrage zu einem Munsterschen Urkundenbuch, i p 113. 'So juw vorgekommen was grotes uprores jtzont im hylligen Ryke und duitscher nation weder alle Christliche Ordenunge Oberichcit geistlich und weltlich vorhanden is—werden wy berichtet—das sulchs allhier in unserm Gestichte unser Oberichcit und insonderheit dem geistlichen Stande zu gyner geringen Verhonynge Inbrock und Besweringe im Deile och vorgenommen und betenget"—"And it has come to our knowledge what great uproar there now is throughout the holy empire and German nation, against all Christian order and all rulers, both spiritual and temporal, and we are informed that, in our diocese, this has been the cause of no little contempt, resistance, and complaining against our magistrates and especially against those of the ecclesiastical order"

‡ Excerpts in Bucholtz, viii p 330 Bucholtz shows a want of knowledge of the language of this period in assuming that by these concessions the difficulties were avoided

§ Schreiben von Hofrath und Renntkammer, Bucholtz, viii p 89

‖ According to Johann Lindner's Onomasticon (Mencken, ii p 1521) this sect prevailed chiefly in Aschersleben and Sangerhausen In a document which is quoted by Forstemann in his Provincialblattern fur Sachsen (1838, No. 232), we find an inquisition at Castle Hoym against one of these flagellants, in the year 1481 It was perhaps a point of union that they too looked upon their preacher as a prophet and thought that in him they beheld the judge at the day of judgment But, indeed the whole is dressed up with metaphor,

be followed * He was moreover dissatisfied with the compacts made by the peasants of Swabia and Franconia. His views went much farther; he deemed it impossible to speak the truth to the people so long as they were governed by princes. He declared it intolerable that all creatures had been converted into property,—the fish in the water, the birds in the air, and the plants on the earth; these creatures must be free to all before the pure Word of God could be revealed. He utterly rejected all the principles on which the idea of the State rests, and acknowledged nothing but revelation, "but this," he said, "must be expounded by a second Daniel, who will lead the people like Moses." At Muhlhausen he was regarded as a master and a prophet, he had a seat in the council, and gave judgment in the court of law according to revelation; under his direction convents were suppressed, and their property confiscated, cannon of prodigious calibre founded, and warlike enterprises executed. The priests' houses in the territory of Duke George were first attacked, and then the convents stormed, with the assistance of the enraged populace, in the Harz and throughout the great plain of Thuringia, up to the edge of the forest. The monuments of the old Landgraves at Reinhardsbrunn were defaced, and the library destroyed † The next step was to attack the castles and farms of the lords, both in Eichsfeld and in Thuringia. We no longer find any mention of conditions and treaties, or of a future reformation, the object of these fanatics was a general and pitiless destruction. "Beloved brethren," writes Munzer to the miners at Mansfeld, "do not relent if Esau gives you fair words; give no heed to the wailings of the ungodly Let not the blood cool on your swords, lay Nimrod on the anvil, and let it ring lustily with your blows; cast his strong tower to the earth while it is yet day." "Know then," he writes to Count Ernest of Heldrungen, "that God has commanded us to cast thee from thy seat with the might that is given to us "‡ When the country people of Schwarzburg, also in league with the small towns, rose against the count, and assembled in considerable force at Frankenhausen, Munzer feared nothing but the conclusion of a treaty, "a fraud," he calls it, "under colour of justice " he left his stronghold of Muhlhausen in order to prevent this and to attack "the eagle's nest" in person. He proved from the Apocalypse that the power was to be given to the common people. "Come and join in our measure," he writes to his friends at Erfurt, "it shall be right fairly trod; we will pay the blasphemers back all that they have done to poor Christendom ' He signed himself "Thomas Münzer, with the sword of Gideon "

Fanatic as he was, Munzer still occupied a most formidable position In him the mystical notions of former ages were blended with the tendencies toward ecclesiastical and temporal reform which had just arisen. Out of this combination he formed a set of opinions which addressed themselves immediately to the common people, incited them to rise and annihilate the whole existing order of things, and prepared the way to the absolute sway of a prophet. The people assembled in troops all around on the hills of Meissen and Thuringia,§ awaiting the first decisive result of his enterprize, in order to join him immediately after it The popular current would then have flowed in this direction from all parts of Germany.

At length, therefore, the results which might long have been anticipated, appeared. No sooner were the authorities which constituted the State in Germany at variance with themselves and each other, than the elementary forces on which it rested arose The lightnings flashed from the ground, and the streams of public life left their accustomed channels the storm which had so long been muttering underground now poured out all its fury on the upper regions, and everything seemed to threaten a complete convulsion

If we examine more closely this great elemental strife of the German State in all its bearings, we shall be able to distinguish several different steps in its progress

Its origin was, no doubt, to be found in the oppression of the peasantry, which had been gradually increasing during the preceding years, in the imposition of fresh taxes, and, at the same time, the persecution of the evangelical doctrines which had seized on the minds of the common people more strongly than any intellectual influence before or since, and had more effectually stimulated them to individual exertion. Had the peasants been content with resisting all arbitrary claims, and securing the liberty of hearing their own doctrine preached, they would have avoided calling up against them the whole strength of the existing order of things, and might have secured to them-

* Auslegung des andern unterschyds Danielis dess propheten gepredigt aufm Schloss zu Alstedt vor den tetigen thewren Herzogen und Vorstehern zu Sachsen durch Thomas Munzer, 1524."—"Explanation of the other distinction of the Prophet Daniel, preached at the Castle of Alsted, before the active and beloved dukes and governors of Saxony, by Thomas Muntzer " Certainly one of his most remarkable productions He takes great pains to prove the difference between genuine revelations and false visions, e g that the former descends on a man in a joyful amazement ("in eyner frohen Verwunderung") A man must be free from all temporal comforts of the flesh ("abgeschieden sein von allem zeitlichen Trost seines Fleisches") The work of visions should flow not from human endeavours, but simply from the unchangeable will of God ("nit rausser quellen durch menschliche anschlege, sondern einfaltig herfliessen nach Gottes unvorrucklichen Willen"). It is clear that he does not go nearly so far as Ignatius Loyola, at the same time he combats Luther's more moderate theory, which he ascribes to "imaginary goodness" ("einer getichten Gute") He says quite openly, that the ungodly should not be suffered to live "I say with Christ that ungodly rulers, more especially priests and monks, should be put to death" ("Ich sage mit Christo, &c das man die gotlosen regenten, sunderlich pfaffen und monche todten sol") Princes are to exterminate the ungodly, or God will take the sword from them "Oh, my dear masters, how finely will the Lord smite the old pots with an iron rod!' ("Ah, lieben Herren, wie hubsch wirt der Herr unter die alten Topf schmeissen mit einer eysern stangen ")

† Thuringia Sacra, i p. 173

† Letter in Strobel Leben, Schriften und Lehren Thomæ Münzer, p 95

§ Pauli Langii Chronica Nurnburgensia, in Mencken, ii p 67

selves a long course of peaceful and lawful improvement.

Nay, even more might have been obtained; in many places, treaties were concluded by which the lords gave up the most oppressive of the rights they had formerly acquired; it was probable that these would be observed on both sides, and that a lawful and well-defined relation would thus be established between the classes.

But it is not in human nature to rest content with moderate success; it is vain to expect reason or forbearance from a conquering multitude. Here and there a confused tradition of some ancient rights of the commons was revived, or the people found themselves a match for the knights in the field,—indeed the rebellion must be considered partly as a symptom of the revived importance of infantry;—but for the most part, they were goaded by long-cherished hatred and lust of revenge, which now found vent. While some of their chiefs boasted that they would introduce a better order of government into the empire, the wildest destruction was carried from castle to castle, from convent to convent, and even threatened the towns which had refused to join the rebellion. The peasants thought they ought not to rest while a dwelling was left standing in Germany superior to a peasant's cottage.* Their fury was inflamed by the ravings of fanatical preachers, who justified the work of destruction, and thought it a duty to shed blood; and, following the inspiration of the moment, which they called divine, to erect a new kingdom of heaven. Had this movement been successful, there must of course have been an end of all peaceful progress, according to the laws which have ever governed the human race. Happily, it could not succeed; Munzer was far indeed from being the prophet and hero required to execute so gigantic an enterprise; besides which, the existing order of things was too firm to be so completely overthrown. Moreover, the strongest and most genuine element of the reforming party was opposed to it.

Luther had not allowed himself to be hurried into any political enterprise by Sickingen and the knights; nor had the insurrection of the peasantry any attractions for him. At the beginning, ere it assumed its more frightful form, he exhorted them to peace. While he rebuked the lords and princes for their acts of violence and oppression, he condemned the rebellion as contrary to divine and evangelical law, and as threatening destruction to both spiritual and temporal authorities, and hence to the German nation.† But when the danger so rapidly increased, when his old enemies, the "murder prophets and mob spirits," took so prominent a part in the tumult, and when he really began to fear lest the peasants should prove victorious (a state of things which he thought could only be the precursor of the day of judgment), the whole storm of his indignation burst forth. With the boundless influence which he possessed, what must have been the consequences had he taken part with the insurgents! But he remained a staunch advocate for the separation between the spiritual and the temporal, which was one of the fundamental principles of his whole system; and to the doctrine that the gospel gives freedom to the soul, but does not emancipate the body from restraint, or property from the control of the laws. The origin of the rebellion has been often ascribed to preaching, but this is not confirmed by the facts. Luther now, as three years before, did not for one instant hesitate to brave the storm, and to do every thing in his power to prevent the general destruction which he clearly foresaw. A pious Christian, said he, should rather die a hundred deaths than give way one hair's breadth to the peasants' demands. The government should have no mercy; the day of wrath and of the sword was come, and their duty to God obliged them to strike hard as long as they could move a limb; whosoever perished in this service was a martyr of Christ. Thus he supported the temporal order of things with the same intrepidity that he had displayed in attacking the spiritual.‡

The secular authorities, too, aroused themselves, and took courage in this, the greatest peril that had ever threatened them.

The first who rose was the same man who had done the best service against Sickingen,—the young Philip of Hessen. Towards the end of April he assembled his knights and his most trusty subjects of the towns in Alsfeld; he promised them that no new burthens should be laid on the peasants;§ while on their part, in

* According to Mullner's Annalen, the peasants, in anger at receiving some refusal, declared to the council of Nurnberg, that the council might stand in greater need of the peasants than the peasants of the council. "darauf sind sie mit einem solchen Trutz und Hochmuth abgeschieden, als wann die Welt ihr eigen wäre, haben sich auch ingeheim gegen etliche vernehmen lassen, sie gedenken kein Hauss in ganzen land zu gedulden, das besser sey denn ein Bauernhaus."—"thereupon they departed with such insolence and pride, as though the world were their own; they also in private gave many to understand that they were resolved to suffer no house to stand which was better than a peasant's hut." In the ordinance made by Michel Geismair in 1526 ("Lanndsordnung, so Michel Geismair gemacht hat, im 1526 Jar," Bucholz, ix. 651) the fifth article is, "alle Rinkmauern an den Stetten dergl. alle Geschlosser und Bevestigung im Lannd niedergeprochen werden und hinfur nimmer Stätt sonnder Dorfer sein, damit Unterschied der Menschen (aufhöre), und ain gaunze gleichait im Lannd sei."—"That all walls round towns, likewise all castles and fortified houses in the country, should be thrown down, and thenceforth there were to be villages but no towns, so that all distinction among men should cease, and a complete equality should prevail in the land."

† "Ermanung zum Friede auf die 12 Artikel der Baurschaft in Schwaben."—*Altenb.* iii. p. 114.

‡ Wider die rauhischen und mordischen Bauern.—Against the robbing and murderous peasants.—*Ibid.* p. 124. See the letter to Rühel, ii. p. 886. Melanchthon came to his aid on this occasion with his convincing dogmatical, and clear conclusions, *e. g.* to Spalatin, 10th April, 1525, chiefly to be understood as directed against the introduction of the Mosaic laws, but also to be understood generally. "Rationi humanæ commisit Christus ordinationes politicas ... debemus uti presentibus legibus." (*Corp. Ref.* i. 733.) It is necessary to have a front of brass to persist in affirming, as Surius and Cochlæus have done, that Luther abandoned the peasants when he saw that they were beaten. I don't know whether the partial successes of George Truchsess, gained at a great distance were really known to Luther; it is however, certain that they decided nothing: the revolt of the peasants had just taken full possession of Thuringia and Saxony, when Luther, at his own personal risk, opposed it.

§ This information is afforded by a declaration of Land-

answer to his inquiry, they swore with outstretched hands to live and die with him. His first care was to defend his own frontiers; he tranquillised Hersfeld and Fulda, not, indeed, without violence, though his cruelties have been fabulously exaggerated, and then crossed the mountains and marched into Thuringia to the assistance of his Saxon cousins, with whom he stood in hereditary alliance.*

Just at the moment that these disorders reached their height in that district, the Elector Frederic died. How striking was the contrast between the fierce intestine discord which raged throughout Germany, and the quiet chamber at Lochau in which Frederic, calm and collected in the midst of agonizing pain, was awaiting the approach of death! "You do well," said he to his preacher and secretary Spalatin, who after long hesitation had taken courage to demand an audience of him, "you do well to come to me, for it is right to visit the sick." he then caused the low chair in which he reclined to be rolled to the table, and laying his hand in that of the intimate friend and adviser of his latter years, he once more talked of the things of this world, of the peasant's rebellion, of Dr. Luther, and of his own approaching death. He had ever been a gentle master to his poor people, and he now exhorted his brother to act prudently and leniently;† he was not frightened at the danger of the peasants becoming masters, serious as he believed it to be, for if it were not the will of God, it could not happen. This conviction, which had guided and supported him through the whole course of the Lutheran movement, was doubly strong in his last moments. None of his relations were with him; he was surrounded only by servants. The spirit of opposition which every where else divided rulers and their subjects, had not yet reached them. "Dear children," said the prince, "if I have ever offended any of you, I pray you to forgive me for the love of God, we princes do many things to the poor people that we ought not to do." He then spoke only of the merciful God who comforts the dying. For the last time Frederic strained his failing eyes to read one of his friend Spalatin's consolations; he then received the sacrament in both kinds from the hands of a clergyman to whom he was attached. The new doctrine, which had flourished under his prudent and sheltering care, now no longer appeared to him in the light of a power of this world which had to fight for its existence, and the herald of a new order of things,—he only saw in it the true Gospel, the true christian faith, piety, and comfort to the soul. The dying man leaves the world to itself, and withdraws entirely within the circle of his own relations to the Infinite,—to God, and eternity. Thus he died on the 5th of May, 1525. "He was a child of peace," said his physician, "and in peace he hath departed."‡

His successor, now the Elector John, ascended the throne in the midst of the wildest and most formidable confusion. Concessions were no longer to be thought of, there existed the same difference between Frederic and John as between Luther's first and second book, between doubt and cautious counsel and downright hostility. Philip of Hessen came to his assistance at the right moment, Duke George and Duke Henry took the field about the same time, and four princes thus marched with their forces to meet the peasants.

Munzer had taken up a position upon the rising ground above Frankenhausen, which commands the whole length of the valley, the spot was well chosen for preaching to assembled multitudes, but offered no advantages whatever for defence. He showed utter incapacity. he had not even provided powder for his laboriously cast guns, his followers were miserably armed, and had only entrenched themselves behind a feeble barricade of waggons. The prophet who had said so much about the force of arms, and who had threatened to destroy all the ungodly with the edge of the sword, was now reduced to reckon on a miracle, which he saw announced in the portent of a coloured circle round the sun at noon. At the first discharge of the enemy's artillery, the peasants sang a hymn; they were totally routed, and the greater number killed. Hereupon the panic which accompanies a half-accomplished crime seized the whole country. All the troops of peasants dispersed, and all the towns surrendered, even Muhlhausen attempted hardly any resistance.§ Munzer was executed in the camp before Mühlhausen, where for a time he had reigned. He seemed possessed by a savage demon up to his last hour. When, under the pangs of torture, he was reminded of the countless number he had led into destruction, he burst into a loud laugh, and said it was their own desire. When he was led out to death, he could not remember the articles of faith.

At this conjuncture, movements were made in all directions for attacking the forces of the peasants.

Duke Antony of Lorraine came with the various garrisons from Champagne and Burgundy, and a few companies of German landsknechts and reiters, to the assistance of the Landvogt of Morsperg in Alsatia. He cut off some scattered troops in the open field, after which, those who had assembled in Zabern capitulated, they were, however, accused of having made a subsequent attempt to gain over the landsknechts, and were attacked and slaughtered to the number of seventeen thousand, as they were leaving the fortress on the morning of the 17th of May.‖

---

grave William at the Diet of 1576. Rommel, Neuere Geschichte von Hessen. p. 255, 848.

* Haarer, Warhafftige Beschreibung des Bawernkriegs, c. 49, in Gobel's Beitragen, p. 139. Rommel, i. 108.

† His letters of the 14th of April, and 4th of May, in Walch, L. W. xvi. p. 140.

‡ Spalatin, Leben Friedrichs des Weisen, p. 60.

§ Die Histori Thoma Muntzers des Aufengers der Döringischen Urfur." Hagenaw.—This book contains the well known narrative of Melanchthon, also to be found in Luther's works. (Altenb. iii. 126.)

‖ Bellay, No. III. Account by Rappolstein in Vogt's Rheinisch Gesch. vol. iv. p. 49.

Thus Wurtemberg once more fell into the hands of the Swabian League, whose general, Truchsess, having in a great degree secured his rear by a treaty with the peasantry around the lakes, marched upon the Würtemberg insurgents, whom he encountered at Sindelfingen, and having first thrown them into disorder with his field artillery, he charged and cut them down with his numerous and well-armed cavalry Having then taken and garrisoned a succession of towns and cities, he marched on Franconia There he was joined by the other two princes who had fought against Sickengen, —the Electors of Treves and the Palatinate, who marched to meet him from Bruchsal, which had just fallen into their hands The two armies united on the 29th of May, in the open field between Helspach and Neckarsulm They made up together a force of two thousand five hundred horse, and eight thousand foot, and marched on into Franconia.*

It was a most important advantage to them that the castle of Wurzburg still held out against two powerful bodies of Franconian peasants. At first, indeed, the garrison would have consented to accept the twelve articles, and had already received authority from the bishop to do so, a part of the peasants were anxious to come to terms, which would enable them to go to the assistance of their allies, hard pressed on all sides. But the citizens of Wurzburg, determined to get rid of the castle, which had always been a bridle in their jaws, contrived that the conditions offered to the garrison should be such as it was impossible it should accept. Hereupon the latter resolved to resist to the utmost. Sebastian von Rotenhan, who had so greatly promoted the interests of the Lutheran doctrines in the Council of Regency, had supplied the fortress with every requisite, even with powder-mills; erected chevaux-de-frise within the ditches, and palisades all round the castle, and had induced the garrison to swear with uplifted hands that they would stand the storming bravely and faithfully. On the 15th of May, the day of the battle of Frankenhausen, the peasants began the storm at nine o'clock at night, to the sound of trumpets and fifes, with loud shouts and flying colours Pitch, brimstone, and other combustibles were thrown down on them from the castle; and incessant firing kept up from every loop-hole in the walls and tower The lonely castle reared its head in haughty grandeur amid the many-coloured glare of the fire with which it kept off the wild hordes that had overrun Franconia, and now threatened all Germany The artillery decided the victory here, as at Sindelfingen and Frankenhausen, at two in the morning the peasants retreated †

A second assault was entirely out of the question, they received news of the defeat of their friends on all sides, and the storm impending over themselves became every moment more near and threatening.

They made one more effort to save themselves by negotiating; they again offered the twelve articles to the acceptance of the garrison of Wurzburg, and invited Truchsess, the general of the League, who was marching upon them, to appoint time and place for an interview for the purpose of negotiation. In a general address to the States of the empire, they endeavoured to set their views and objects in a favourable light, and called upon the Franconian states especially, to send delegates to Schweinfort, that they might take counsel together with them, "for the establishment of the word of God, of peace and of justice"‡ But all this was now too late They had never had confidence in their own strength, and now fortune had deserted them they must either remain masters of the field or perish.

The united army advanced against them without delay, all the places it passed in its march surrendered unconditionally On the 2d of June it fell in with the first troop of peasants at Konigshofen it was the band from the Odenwald which had had the courage to advance against the victorious enemy. But it consisted of not more than four thousand men,§ and all their measures were thoroughly ill-concerted The peasants had neglected to guard the fords of the Tauber, and had encamped round their baggage, within a barricade of waggons, on the Muhlberg, and it would have been well for them if they had awaited the attack of the enemy even there; but, terrified by the superior force which gradually presented itself, they endeavoured to reach a neighbouring forest, and thus invited an immediate assault The cavalry fell upon their exposed flank, the princes themselves helping to cut them down, in the twinkling of an eye, before even the landsknechts could come up, the whole body of peasants was entirely broken and routed || A false rumour of victory induced the Rothenberg troop to quit its position near Würzburg, and on the 4th of June that also fell into the hands of the cavalry in an open field, between Sulzdorf and Ingolstadt, and was completely dispersed Both victories were accompanied by the most barbarous massacres. Of six hundred peasants who attempted to defend themselves in a fortified house near Ingolstadt, all but seventeen were put to the sword.

A third band which was connected with the Thuringian insurgents was overthrown and routed, after a short conflict, on the Bildberg near Meinengen, where they had entrenched themselves behind waggons, by Elector John of Saxony ¶ The mild and placable prince promised safety to all who would surrender themselves to his protection.

Thus the great Franconian bands, which had

* The autograph diary of the Count Palatine Otto Heinrich, in Freiberg's Urkunden und Schriften, iv p 367, gives these numbers

† Johann Reinhard, in Ludwig, 889

‡ Proclamation in Ochsle, of the 27th of May, p 302 The meeting was fixed for the 31st day of May

§ I hold these to be the true number, as the report of Secretary Spiess, who accompanied the army (Ochsle, p 197), and the Journal of the Elector, p 368, agree on this point Others mention far greater numbers

|| Brower Annales Trevirenses, lib xx p 353.

¶ Spalatin, see Menken, ii 1114 The peasants had one carronade, sixteen cannons and mortars, four arquebusses, and matchlocks Their waggons were buried in the earth.

thought to reform the whole of Germany, were destroyed like those of Alsatia, Thuringia, and Würtemburg; and, like those provinces, Franconia was now garrisoned and chastised by its former masters.

On the 7th of June, Würzburg was forced to surrender at discretion. The aged members of the town council assembled in the market-place, and bared their grey heads to salute the leaders of the army of the League; but they found no mercy from Truchsess, who declared that they were all perjured and dishonoured, and had forfeited their lives. In Würzburg alone, sixty rebels from the town and country were hanged: the executions were equally frequent and terrible throughout the whole bishopric; two hundred and eleven were put to death in different ways; all arms delivered up, new services imposed, and heavy contributions extorted: the ancient ceremonies of the church were restored. Meanwhile Markgrave Casimir of Brandenburg, having taken possession of all the rest of Franconia, of Bamberg, Schweinfurt, and Rothenburg, without encountering any serious resistance, proceeded to take vengeance on the insurgents in his own territories.

All that now remained was, to subdue the remnant of the insurgents who still kept their ground on the Upper and Middle Rhine.

The army of Treves and the Palatinate, on their homeward march, fell in with the insurgents of the Middle Rhine at Pfeddersheim,* and, as on all former occasions, the peasants were dispersed and cut down; the warlike archbishop is said to have slain several with his own hand. These districts hereupon submitted; and even the people of the Rheingau had to give up their arms, and to pay contributions. Mainz was forced to resign the liberties it had but just regained; while the people of Treves, happy that they had not made any serious demonstration, readily dropped all the projects they had entertained.

The great army of the League on the Upper Rhine found a far more arduous task; it was there that the rebellion had originated and taken the deepest root, and nothing decisive had yet been accomplished toward its suppression. The men of the Allgau reappeared in the field; they had occupied a very strong post on a steep hill, at the foot of which is the river Luidas, and on either side, large ponds: a considerable number of experienced landsknechts fought in their ranks. They were able to keep their ground against even the artillery of Truchsess, and indeed had some intention of beginning the attack. Fortunately for Truchsess, the veteran and successful leader, George Frundsberg, came to his assistance in time. It is highly probable† that he exercised a personal influence on many of the peasant chiefs, his old comrades and followers. Contemporary writers positively affirm that he bought over Walter Bach, who treacherously persuaded the peasants to abandon their strong position. Perhaps, however, their stores failed; at all events they separated, and retreated towards the mountains. Truchsess hastened in pursuit of them, and began to burn their farms and villages. This was in direct violation of the orders of the League, at which he only laughed; he, he said, a peasant himself, understood his business better; he knew that this was the way to make every man think of his own home. He kept his troops together, and thus easily beat the separate bands of peasants whenever he met with them. He was not, however, so absolutely master as at Würzburg. George Truchsess was at last obliged to enter into a compact with the large body of rebels who held together on the Kolenberg, by which redress of the local grievances of their several villages was promised them. Not till then did they lay down their arms and give up their ringleaders.‡

At the same moment, Count Felix of Werdenberg put to the rout the peasants of the Hegau, Kletgau, and all that remained in the Schwarzwald—for many were gone home to their harvest—and compelled them to lay down their arms.§

Thus was arrested the great movement which threatened the total subversion of the whole existing order of things in Germany: all the schemes for reconstituting the empire from the groundwork of society upwards, or still more, for visionary changes in the order of the world under the guidance of a fanatical prophet, were now for ever at an end.

Wherever the matter had been decided by arms, the laws of war were enforced. The most barbarous executions took place; the severest contributions were exacted; and in some places, laws more oppressive than ever were imposed.

It was only in districts where the peasants had not sustained a total defeat, that, after all their former vague and ambitious projects had spontaneously died away, some alleviation of their burthens and sufferings was granted them.

The Count of Sulz and his subjects agreed to refer their differences to arbitrators chosen in common, and Archduke Ferdinand consented to appoint a chief umpire.‖

To the people of the Breisgau, Ferdinand promised in his own name that due regard should be paid by magistrates and government officers to the complaints of the subjects.¶ The states of Upper Austria would not allow contributions to be levied upon the people.**

In Tyrol, steps were taken under the influence of the disturbances, towards drawing up a code of laws, whereby the subjects were relieved from all taxes that could not be proved by authentic documents, to have existed for more than fifty years; likewise from the lesser

* Haarer, c. 84–89. I intend to give in the Appendix whatever is necessary to illustrate the relation in which the Latin stands to the German text, as well as that subsisting between Gnodalius and Leontius and Haarer.

† Reisner, Kriegsthaten der Frundsberge.

‡ Haggenmüller Kempten, p. 540.

§ Walchner Ratolphzell, p. 109.

‖ The treaty which the people of Zurich helped to negotiate is to be found in Bullinger's Reformations-geschichte, i. p. 249.

¶ The treaty of Offenburg: extract in Schreiber's Taschenbuch, p. 302.

** Declaration of the Stände, Bucholtz, viii. p. 104.

tithes in kind, and a variety of other dues and services; and the right of fishing, and even of shooting and hunting, granted them. Archduke Ferdinand also made concessions as to religion. Towns and councils were empowered to appoint their own clergy, and the Gospel was to be preached according to the letter.*

Salzburg was the only country in which the peasants kept the field against the advance of a regular army; and even when they were forced to bend before the might of the Swabian League, they began by making singularly advantageous terms.†

These events belong, however, to another state of things, which immediately followed the disturbances, and to which we will now turn our attention.

CHAPTER VII.

FORMATION OF THE ADVERSE RELIGIOUS LEAGUES. DIET OF AUGSBURG, DECEMBER, 1525.

The conflict between the elements of German society was now at an end; the rebellious peasantry, and that portion of the population of the towns which took part with them, were subdued, as the knights had been before them. The local powers which had arisen during the course of ages had again withstood all the storms by which they were assailed: aided by the emperor or the Council of Regency, they had stood fast amidst the ruin of all central authority.

Nevertheless, peace was by no means restored, nor was one of those great questions which had so long occupied public attention decided.

The rebellion had been put down without any reference to religious creed; friends and foes of the new doctrines had taken up arms with equal eagerness against the common enemy; but as soon as that enemy was subdued, the old antipathies broke out with fresh violence.

The Regensburg members of the Swabian League, who at this time exercised the chief influence in that body, seized upon this opportunity of carrying into execution by main force the measures which had been concerted at that city. The victories of the League were everywhere followed by religious persecutions. Among those who were beheaded at Würzburg, many were condemned, not for the rebellion, in which they had taken no part, but for the crime of professing the evangelical faith. Nine of the most wealthy burghers were executed at Bamberg, and it is asserted that some of them were remarkable for their peaceable conduct, and had rather tried to prevent than to encourage the attack of the country people on the bishop's palace; they were punished, as was openly proclaimed, for their adherence to the evangelical party.‡ Their possessions were, by an unexampled exercise of arbitrary power, given to certain individuals, among whom was a secretary of Truchsess. All who professed the evangelical doctrines immediately fled out of both bishoprics. But even in all other territories, spiritual as well as temporal obedience was enforced on the peasantry; the Lutherans stood—under that title—first on the list of those excluded from pardon. The bitterest persecution was directed against the preachers. A provost-martial of the name of Aichili traversed Swabia and Franconia in all directions at the head of a band of reiters, in order to carry into effect the executions that had been decreed; it is calculated that within a small district, he hung forty evangelical preachers on trees by the roadside.§ This was the first restoration of Catholicism by violence in Upper Germany.

Similar attempts were now made also in the north.

After the taking of Mühlhausen, the allied princes had agreed on common measures against the peasants. Duke George relates, that one morning, as his son-in-law Philip was just setting off on a journey, he (Duke George) went to him once more, and entreated him not to attach himself to Luther's cause, "in consideration of the evil which had flowed therefrom;" that he repeated this warning to the Elector of Saxony within the same hour, and that it was kindly received by both of them. Duke George hoped to exercise great authority over his cousin John after Frederic's death, as well as over Landgrave Philip, to whom he stood in the relation of an affectionate father-in-law.

These three princes had agreed at Mühlhausen to communicate their resolutions to their neighbours; and Duke George had an interview as early as in July with the electors of Mainz and Brandenburg and the Duke of Brunswick, at Dessau. These princes still adhered to the Catholic faith, and they allowed their belief, that the insurrection owed its existence to the new doctrines that had been preached, to influence their resolutions. Though we have no authentic document as to the nature of these resolutions, there is sufficient evidence that they were in the highest degree unfavourable to the religious changes. Duke George communicated them to his cousin and his son-in-law, expressing at the same time his persuasion that they had ceased to entertain any Lutheran ideas.‖ At all events, he did not

* Excerpts from the proceedings of the diet, Bucholtz, viii. p. 337.

† Zauner, Chronik von Salzburg, iv. p. 429.

‡ Detailed account in Müllner's Annalen.

§ Bullinger's 140th cap. treats of Provost Aichili ("von Profossen Aichili.") Anshelm also mentions him (vi. p. 291,) as being peculiarly active against the Lutheran parsons; he seized, plundered, mulcted, and hanged them. "Er war sunderlich gflissen, uf die lutherischen Pfaffen, fiengs' beroupts' schatzts' und henkts'."

‖ The only authentic notice of these meetings is to be found in a letter from Duke George in the Dresden Archives. According to that, the determination was "to stand by each other in case the Lutherans attacked any one of them, in order to remain at peace from such rebellion."—"Sich bei einander finden zu lassen, wenn die Lutherischen einen von ihnen angreifen würden, um solches Aufruhrs vertragen zu bleiben." It is not, however, easy to perceive from whom they expected an attack,

suffer himself to be deterred by any consideration for them, from condemning his own subjects to the severest punishments. At Leipzig two citizens were beheaded for no other reason than that some Lutheran books had been found in their possession.*

It appeared probable that the Lutheran movement, from the time it was associated with an insurrection of the peasantry, would, like that of Wicklyffe, be encountered by a reaction which would end in its entire suppression.

But the reform set on foot by Luther stood on a far wider and firmer basis than that of Wicklyffe, and had already found resolute and powerful supporters both in North and South Germany.

Landgrave Philip even brought an evangelical preacher with him to Mühlhausen; and Duke George, while in the act of expressing his conviction of his son-in-law's altered sentiments, was struck with surprise at the appearance of this man. From that time Philip had become more and more deeply imbued with Lutheran opinions. We have only to read the letters he wrote to Duke George during this year,—in which he controverts the doctrine of the canon and the mass, the received idea of the church, and the obligation of vows,—in order to see with what lively and yet earnest zeal he adopted the new doctrines, and what accurate and extensive knowledge he had acquired of the Scriptural grounds on which they rested.†

The same state of things existed in Saxony. Far from forsaking the path trodden by his predecessor, the new elector advanced in it with far more decided steps than Frederic had done. On leaving Weimar in August, 1525, he once more assembled the priesthood of that district—on the 16th of that month—and, after causing their minds to be prepared by two sermons, he announced to them that in future they were to preach the pure word of God, without any human additions.‡ Some old priests who were present having expressed the opinion that this would not be inconsistent with their saying masses for the dead and consecrating salt and water, they were told that the same rule applied to ceremonies as to doctrines.

In consequence of the recess of Mühlhausen, the elector had an interview with Markgrave Casimir of Brandenburg at Saalfeld, at which the evangelical tendencies predominated as much as the catholic had done at Dessau. These princes did not indeed form a regular alliance, but Markgrave Casimir declared that he would hold fast by the word of God.§

At the very time when the military force of the Swabian League was employed in checking the progress of the reformation, some of its most powerful members, the very towns in which it had originated,—Augsburg, and above all, Nürnberg,—organized their churches according to evangelical principles. We shall return to this subject in another place.

The territory of Würtemberg, which had been conquered by the League, and could hardly have been imagined capable of taking any resolutions of its own, now declared itself on the same side; the Estates expressed their conviction that the tranquillity of the country could only be maintained by preaching to the people the pure word of God, unalloyed by the selfishness and vain conceits of men.

Already the evangelical preachers began formally to emancipate themselves from the authority of the bishops. At Wittenberg, in May, 1525, they determined to give ordination themselves. Melanchthon justifies this, on the ground that the bishops neglected their duties.‖ The preachers now asserted their underived vocation as against the bishops, in the same manner as those had done against the pope. Melanchthon says that the princes could not be called upon to support a jurisdiction of whose abusive and corrupt nature they were convinced. In Hessen and Brandenburg, too, even in the towns, the clergy began to emancipate themselves from the episcopal jurisdiction.

We perceive that the two opposite tendencies came out of the conflict with the peasants, exactly in the same state in which they entered it; only with increased activity on either side.

The papal party had the advantage, in so far as in a great part of the empire, the penal power, of which it made such fearful use, was in its hands; but on the whole, the evangelical party had gained still more in the struggle.

Never had the aversion to the spiritual part of the constitution of Germany been so general and so avowed. The clergy were accused of those acts of grinding oppression which had mainly caused the revolt. The hostility of the people was specially directed against them; the peasants of the Allgau, for example, who were besieging Füssen, raised the siege as soon as that town threw off its allegiance to its lord, the Bishop of Augsburg, and hoisted the banner of Austria. On the other hand, though the ecclesiastical princes had contributed very little to extinguish the flame of rebellion, they now made the most tyrannical and merciless use of the victory won by others.

---

if they really believed Philip and the Elector John to have been re-converted; and, indeed, Duke George says, "otherwise he would not have made them a party to the treaty, for he well knew that one could not beat Swiss with Swiss."—"denn sonst würde er ihnen den Vertrag nicht mitgetheilt haben, er wisse wohl, dass man Schweizer mit Schweizern nich schlage." The explanation is, that in those times a defensive form was given to all alliances, even when there was no intention of abiding by mere defence. Duke Henry said to the emperor, that he had signed a treaty with his friends, "against the Lutherans, in case they should attempt by force or cunning to gain them over to their unbelief,"—"wider die Lutherischen, ob sie sich unterstünden, sie mit List oder Gewalt in ihren Unglauben zu bringen."

* Gretschel: Leipzigs kirchliche Zustände, p. 218.

† Rommel's Urkundenbuch, p. 2.

‡ "Das man das lauter rayn evangelion on menschliche Zusatzung predigen soll, fürstlicher Befelch zu Weymar beschehen."—"That the pure Gospel should be preached without any human additions. Sovereign command issued at Weimar."—*Circular from the minister Kisswetter at Erfurt to Master Hainrich at Elxleben*, a. d. Gera, 1525.

§ According to a description by Casimir himself in a letter from Schrauttenbach to the Landgrave Philip, dated 27th Dec. 1525, in Neudeckers Urkunden, p. 16.

‖ De Jure Reformandi. Corp. Reform. i. p. 765.

Hence it happened that the evangelical party found it so easy to shake off the episcopal authority; it is, however, more remarkable that an analogous effect was produced in the catholic party. If the one side questioned the spiritual, the other no less vigorously attacked the temporal jurisdiction

We must here again recur to the events of Tyrol and Salzburg. Archduke Ferdinand had taken up the most remarkable position in the world.

At the diet of Tyrol, which we have already mentioned, there were assembled only the nobles, the cities, and rural districts (*Gerichte**), the ecclesiastical body did not appear. The anti-ecclesiastical temper which this produced was very strongly expressed in the resolutions that were passed In the recess of this diet it was proclaimed, that the appointment to the inferior situations in the church should be rendered totally independent of the bishops, in future, cities and rural districts (*Gerichte*) should have the right of presentation, which the sovereign of the country should confirm, and all complaints of the clergy should be addressed by the former to the latter † The petition of the bishop of Trent for leave to call in foreign troops to punish the insurgents within his see, was refused, for the common people were of opinion, says Ferdinand, that the clergy ought to have no jurisdiction whatever in temporal affairs, were such a permission granted to the bishop, the nobles would complain that he was goading the people to a fresh revolt, which would bring trouble and ruin upon them also ‡ This was even carried much further. The Bishop of Brixen proving himself incapable of restoring order in his see, where one of his secretaries and toll collectors was the leader of the revolt, the Tyrolese determined not to afford him the least assistance, but at once to secularize the see. Archduke Ferdinand took possession of it, and committed the government to one of his council, "till some future council, or the reformation of the empire;" he received the homage from all the vassals and the official persons of the see § The captain of Ehrenberg, which was garrisoned by Tyrolese, would not go to the succour of the town of Fussen till it surrendered itself as an hereditary fief to the house of Austria, and did homage to the Archduke ‖ The Zillerthalers were thus enabled to throw off their allegiance to Salzburg, to attach themselves to Tyrol, and to accept the Archduke, who had already high authority over them, as their lord and sovereign ¶ Nay, even in Bavaria, similar notions prevailed When Matthew, Archbishop of Salzburg, was besieged in his citadel by the peasants, and reduced to the greatest extremity, Doctor Lesch, a Bavarian chancellor, presented himself before the archduke, and proposed to him to sequester the archbishopric in common; so that the part lying on the confines of Bavaria should be taken possession of by the dukes, and that bordering on Austria by the archduke. Ferdinand joyfully acceded to the proposal; he authorized the commissioners he had sent to the peasants to use all their endeavours (but with the knowledge of the archbishop) that the see might be given up to Austria and Bavaria ** In Bavaria, however, this was only a transient thought; the plan here pursued was that of an unconditional restoration, from the accomplishment of which the dukes might justly expect a still greater degree of authority than they had already acquired, over the neighbouring bishoprics They therefore furnished aid in every direction In Tyrol, on the other hand, the province had agreed with the prince on the concessions to be made to the rebels; by a resolute postponement of spiritual interests, they thought they should at once allay the tumults and enhance their own liberty and power The Bavarians, consequently, soon abandoned the plans above-mentioned, and resolved to come to the assistance of the archbishop in this exigency with the forces of the Swabian League. The motives which determined the dukes were not, however, of a very disinterested nature; they calculated on this opportunity of securing the succession to the archbishopric for their brother, Ernest of Passau, which they preferred to contributing to place the greater part of it in the hands of Austria, and thence in a hostile relation to themselves. In vain the states of Tyrol made an attempt to restrain the Swabian League from its intended campaign, by representations of the ancient privileges and alliances of Salzburg †† At Inshruck a strong desire prevailed

* *Gericht* here means a certain community Grimm (Deutsche Rechts Alterthumer, p 755) says, "By *Gericht* we now understand a tribunal for the decision of litigated matters or the punishment of offences Originally, however, the predominant idea was that of a popular assembly (concilium), in which all the public business of the Mark the commune, or the district was discussed, disputes settled and fines adjudged. The main element of the *Gericht* is now the judges, but then, it was the congregated free men All judicial power was exercised by the community of free men under the presidency of an elected or hereditary head"—Transl

† Bucholtz, viii p 338.

‡ Ferdinand to Bishop Bernhard of Trent, Inspruck, 9th July, 1525, Bucholtz, ix p 640

§ Patent of occupation 21st July "Auf Bxger und mit Rat ainer ersamen Landschaft dieser unsrer f G Tirol,—zu furkumung nachtail schadens und geferlichait, so dieselben unsuç Grafschaft und dem Stift zu Brichsen, des Vogt Schirm und Schutzherr wir dann sein, enstehen mechten"—"At the request and with the advice of the honourable province of this our free county of Tyrol—for the prevention of loss, damage, and danger, which might accrue to our country and the see of Brichsen, whereof we are bailiff, lord, and protector"

‖ Martin Furtenbach, the town notary at Füssen report on the insurrection of the peasants, in Occhsle s Beitrage, p 478 'Das Volk schrie Hei Oestreich damit wir nicht gar verderbt werden, der Hauptmann nahm die Erbhuldigung auf ein Hintersichbringen an"—"The people cried, 'Hey Austria,' so that we might not be entirely ruined the governor received our hereditary homage on a hint given him" The delegates of the town went to Inspruck, and were there well greeted (wohl be grusst) Ferdinand declared that he would soon go there himself and receive the homage in person

¶ Instruction to Liechtenstein and Stockel, "was sy mit dem Pfleger zu Kropfsberg mit der Nachparschaft im Zillerthal reden sollen"—'what they should say to the parish priest at Kropfsberg, and to the neighbourhood in Zillerthal"—*Bucholtz*, ix p 630

** Instruction of Ferdinand to the mediating commissioners, Bucholtz, p 621

†† "Die vom Ausschuss der dreier Stande—an Hauptleute und Rathedes Pundts zu Schwaben, 31 Juli."—*Ib* ix. p 624—"The committee of the three estates to the governors and councillors of the Swabian League"

to secure the succession to Don George of Austria, natural son of Emperor Maximilian, and a disposition to afford protection to the peasantry.* But the dukes had already the advantage. Duke Louis of Bavaria, the general-in-chief of the Swabian League, led its armies against Salzburg at the end of August. He, too, deemed it expedient, and strongly urged George Frundsberg, who was general of the county of Tyrol, at first to grant the peasants a favourable treaty—afterwards, indeed, they were as severely dealt with here as elsewhere—as a means of attaining all their other objects. The chapter of the cathedral promised the succession to the bishopric of Salzburg to the Bavarian prince Ernest, to whom the archbishop also made some concessions, the lordships of Laufen, Geisfelden, Titmanning, and Mattsee were mortgaged to the dukes for the expenses of the war. In short, they obtained a general ascendency in Salzburg, nor was it till some time afterwards that the archbishop took courage timidly to admonish them to demand nothing of him at variance with the rights and dignities of his see.†

Thus, as we see, the plans of the League triumphed over the inclinations of the people of Tyrol. The archduke was also forced to cede Füssen again to Augsburg, and the Zillerthal to Salzburg.

Notwithstanding this, Ferdinand did not relinquish the ideas he had once conceived. When the Wurtemberg territory made the demands we have mentioned, and pointed very unequivocally to a secularization of the church lands, as a means of meeting the exigencies of the country, Ferdinand showed not the smallest displeasure: he permitted that country to send deputies to the approaching diet at Augsburg, and promised that whatever should there be determined in regard to a reformation of the clergy, should be carried into effect, as well in Wurtemburg as in his other dominions.‡ The views entertained on these points by Archduke Ferdinand entirely coincided with those of the evangelical party, who, with perfect justice, regarded the revocation of the summons for the meeting at Spire as the immediate cause of the recent tumults. In the autumn of 1525 the project of settling the religious differences at an assembly of the empire, and of there proceeding to a thorough reformation, was once more universally stirred.

In addition to the meetings at Dessau and Saalfeld, there was a third and corresponding one between the Landgrave Philip and the Elector Palatine, at Alzey. They agreed "that things must be put on an equitable footing:" every means must be employed to bring about union among the States.§

Markgrave Casimir proceeded from Saalfeld to Auerbach, to a conference with the Count Palatine Frederic, who governed the Upper Palatinate in the name of his nephew. They determined, in the first place, to lighten the burthens of the common people as much as possible, and in the next, again to petition the emperor to hold an ecclesiastical council in the German nation, 'in order to come to some common understanding as to the exposition of the divine word."

In September the cities held a meeting, and Ferdinand thought he had reason to fear very hostile and objectionable resolutions on their part, but their decision only amounted to this: to urge anew upon himself and the emperor the necessity of introducing a clear and uniform order into the whole empire, with respect to the ceremonies of the church.

In the universal discussion of these subjects, every possible change was suggested, and thus ideas and plans of the most extraordinary nature became current.

In a project drawn up towards the end of the year 1525, and discussed at one or two meetings of the empire, it is assumed in the outset, that the property of the church is no longer of any use or benefit either to religion or to the empire: that some change in the disposition of it is therefore indispensable, that this must not, however, be left to the common people, but must be undertaken by the supreme authorities, i. e. by the emperor and the temporal Estates.

People no longer scrupled to propose the secularization of all ecclesiastical property.

So much might, they said, be assigned to the spiritual princes and prelates as was necessary for the maintenance of a suitable mode of living, nor should any thing, for the present, be taken from the canons, but both they and their superiors should be allowed gradually to die out. Of the convents, a few might be retained for young women of noble birth, but with full right and liberty to quit them.

With the funds thus obtained, the first care must be to supply the new spiritual wants; to appoint pastors and preachers, to nominate in every circle a pious and learned man as bishop, with a fixed salary, but wholly without temporal functions, and solely a superintendent of the other ministers of the church, and, lastly, to establish a high school in every circle, in which the languages and the exposition of the Holy Scriptures according to their true sense, should be taught.

But the party which suggested these reforms also entertained the hope that they should thus acquire strength to give a new form to the whole secular constitution of the country.

The proposal to that effect contained in this project is, to establish a particular Council of Regency, or administrative body, in each circle, consisting of twelve councillors, three from each of the four estates, sovereigns, princes,—counts and lords (nobles),—and imperial cities; and a chief or president, chosen from the states

* Excerpts from a receipt of Ferdinand, ib viii p 109

† Zauner, Salzburger Chronik v p 225, 133

‡ Extractus landschaftlicher Schlusserklarung bei Sattler, Herzoge, Beilagen zum zweiten Theil nr 124, and Landtagsabschied, 30th Oct 1525 nr 125 (iii i 4)

§ Letter from the Elector Louis of the Palatinate, in Neudeckers Actenstucken, i p 16. From the words, "von E. L. und unserm Freund, von ir und uns,"—"from E L and our friend, from him and from us," we may conclude that the Elector of Treves was also there present.

of the circle, but approved by the emperor, with nearly the same powers as the governors and the councillors of the Swabian League. This body was to put in execution all the plans determined on by the States; to form a supreme court of judicature, and, above all, to maintain the public peace, and for that purpose to keep a standing force of horse and foot always in the field. The young nobility were to serve in the army, instead of occupying the posts in the chapters. With these troops any succours granted by the emperor and the empire could then be rendered effective, without imposing burdens on any body. They would constitute so great a permanent force as no emperor had had at his command since the birth of Christ.*

The particular provisions of this project are far less important and interesting than the general ideas upon which it is founded:—the secularization of ecclesiastical property; the empire represented exclusively by temporal estates (the constitution of which was mainly based upon the extension of the functions of the circles); a standing army specially for the advantage of the young nobles:—all things which, in their mature and finished form, gave their character to the succeeding centuries, and constituted modern Germany. The most distant results were boldly contemplated, but the way that led to them was long and arduous.

The ecclesiastical princes were yet far too strong; and it may easily be imagined that plans of the kind above mentioned, which could not remain concealed from them, would make them feel the necessity of collecting all their strength. The clergy already complained that they were kept out of possession of many things of which they had been robbed during the late commotions; and even that their enemies proceeded in depriving them of their accustomed jurisdiction; they showed a determination not to await the attack at the next diet, but to press for a complete restitution of their rights and possessions. To this course they were emboldened by a rescript of the emperor, in which mention was made of the suppression of all things that threatened the destruction of our holy faith, and in such severe terms as seemed to imply that an entire restoration of the old order of things was contemplated.† The Council of Regency which was sitting in Esslingen, and of which we now hear once more, prepared to propose measures in the same spirit.‡ The course taken by the Swabian League was nearly the same. At a meeting held by that body in November, it received a letter from Pope Clement, exhorting it to show the same zeal in the completion of the work, that had inspired the first undertaking of it, and to finish the most glorious deed that had been done for centuries.§ The sovereigns of eastern Germany felt in the same manner; the instruction given by Duke George to his delegate at the diet is still extant. After vehement complaints of the enormous mischief done by the Lutheran Gospel, he demands that no change shall be made in the traditional ordinances without the sanction of a general council; adding, that even if an angel should come down from heaven, he was not to be obeyed, unless in a full Christian assembly.‖ Moreover a papal nuncio was sent to attend the diet.

The idea of a change was, it is true, as widely diffused as it was comprehensive; but the opposite tendency, towards the maintenance of the existing ecclesiastical institutions, or rather towards their restoration in their complete integrity, was still exceedingly powerful. Even while the partisans of the new faith cherished the most sweeping schemes, they could not disguise from themselves that the diet might very possibly take a turn highly unfavourable to their wishes. Some believed that the good and the bad would be destroyed together; that truth would be suppressed together with falsehood; that a rule of faith and life would be established in accordance with the old law, and that those who did not receive it willingly would be compelled by violence to conform to it.

As Elector John and Landgrave Philip had declared themselves most openly for the new doctrines, they had the greatest reason for fear. The landgrave, because his territory was surrounded on all sides by puissant ecclesiastical princes; the elector, because already there was an idea of depriving him of his electorate as a seceder from the Church of Rome; he was advised to place himself on a better footing with his neighbours,—doubtless especially with Duke George,—for that many intrigues were on foot against him in that direction.

It was less the view of effecting any change, than the dread of danger to themselves, and the necessity of maintaining the position which they had taken up, that determined these two princes to enter into a closer alliance with each other.

Landgrave Philip made the first advances in this matter, by sending his chamberlain, Rudolf of Waiblingen, to Torgau, where Elector John was holding his court, charged with the proposal to combine with him in making a common resistance, at the next diet, to any measures that might be attempted in support of abuses, or for the suppression of truth; to accede to no ordinance at variance with the word of God, and to unite steadfastly to that

* "Rathschlag was man mit geistlichen Gütern zu gemeinem und des Reichs Nutz furnemen und handeln soll." "Opinion as to what should be done with ecclesiastical property for the common good and that of the empire." In the Weimar Records. It is indeed true that this is among the acts of 1526, but as the diet of Augsburg is mentioned in it, it was doubtless originally intended for that.

† Tolleten in Castilien, 24th May, 1525. (W. A.)

‡ Feilitsch, Esslingen, Monday after St. Martin's day: "Er hält genzlichen dafür, dass von denen die sich der Aufruhr theilhaftig gemacht, auch denen die Kirchen und Klöster gewaltig zerstört, denselbigen Güter eingenommen und davon wieder geben was ihnen gefällig, dass wider diese auf dem Reichstag gehandelt werden soll."—"He was entirely of opinion that the property should be taken from those who had been parties to the seditious movements, and who had violently destroyed churches and convents, and that such of it should be restored as they thought fit. Proceedings against these persons should be taken at the diet."

§ Papal Brief, delivered in November. Ochsle, p. 305.

‖ Instruction to Otto v. Pack in the Dresden Archives. It also contains some censure of Luther's marriage:—"that he and his Kate wanted as much for themselves alone as the whole Augustine convent had formerly required.

end with all who held the same opinions. This commission was received with great joy by the elector, with whose sentiments and convictions it so fully harmonised. At the beginning of November, his son John-Frederic set out to hold a conference with the landgrave, and to concert the course they were to pursue.*

The interview took place at the strongly defended hunting-seat of Friedewalt, in the Sullinger forest. The two young princes perfectly understood each other. There is in the Weimar archives a note of an opinion "of our dear cousin and brother the landgrave," in the hand-writing of John-Frederic himself, which is, without doubt, the result of this conversation. Its contents do not show that any actual treaty as yet existed; the resolutions were such as the circumstances of the moment called forth: such as, that the contracting parties should come to a fuller understanding as to the evangelical cause, and should induce as many princes, counts, and cities of similar views as possible to join them (they had even the hope of gaining over the Elector of Treves), and should then enter a common protest against the expressions contained in the rescript, which were favourable to old usages, but pernicious to the word of God, and that they should stand as one man for the evangelical cause. The electoral court did not only approve these conditions, but thought it good to extend the agreement to other things, "in which one might be worse treated than the other."†

In the beginning of December the hostile parties thus met at Augsburg, furnished with directly contrary instructions.

The same disagreement which prevailed among the deputies, manifested itself in the imperial commission. This consisted (independently of Archduke Ferdinand, whose behaviour was necessarily ambiguous) of Duke William of Bavaria, the leader and champion of the papists, and Markgrave Casimir of Brandenburg, who had so long been attached to the evangelical party. Casimir declined indeed to enter into the compact proposed to him by the envoys of Hessen and Saxony, but he declared that he would advocate his own convictions in the commission, and thus, he urged, do more service to the cause than he could by joining a formal alliance.

Had the princes been present in person, the struggle must now have become vehement, earnest, and decisive, it would soon have been clearly seen to which side the majority inclined.

But neither party was at bottom sincerely resolved on bringing matters to an issue. Each saw too clearly what might be the consequences of such a decision: they wished to assemble all their forces, and to secure to themselves every kind of support. The princes at Friedewalt thought it expedient to remove the diet of the empire immediately to Spire or to Worms. On the other side, the arrival of the Mainz deputy, without whom no step could be taken, inasmuch as he brought with him the imperial chancery, was unduly delayed. No prince as yet appeared in person, even the commission was not complete, and a great number of the deputies were still missing.

The first preliminary meeting was held on the eleventh of December. Archduke Ferdinand besought those who were assembled to have patience awhile, till a larger number arrived, and promised to report to the emperor the good dispositions of those present.‡

But some weeks elapsed, and their numbers were little augmented: on the renewed application of the States, the commissioners at length held a definitive meeting on the 30th December.§

It was evident to every body that, considering the incompleteness of the assembly of the States, and the importance of the questions at issue, no permanent result could be obtained. Duke William suggested whether it would not be better to adjourn the diet. The three colleges separated, and were unanimously of that opinion. They adjourned the diet to Spire, on the first of May, there, however, they said, every prince must appear in person, "there they would with greater dignity treat of the holy faith, of peace and justice."

In order, however, to have done at least something, and in consideration of the continued ferment among the people, a committee was appointed to draw up a Recess.

The only remarkable circumstance as to this is, that the ordinances of the foregoing diets of 1523 and 1524—that the Gospel should be preached pure and intelligible, according to the interpretations of the received expositors—was repeated, without any mention of the Fathers of the Latin Church, or of the edict of Worms. The States mutually agreed to hold themselves prepared to put down instantly every attempt at insurrection, and so far restored to their rights and station those who had been declared infamous on account of their participation in the disturbances, that the latter were allowed to take part in the sittings of the courts of justice.‖ They were so numerous

* Instruction in Rommel's Urkundenbuch, p 10. Credentials of the same date (5th Oct) in the Weimar Records. There is also a note of the answer that Waiblingen was to deliver to Torgau, 13th Oct.

† "Verzaichniss des Bedenkens unsres lieben Vetters und Bruders auf die vertreuliche Unterrede so wir mit S. L. jetzo allhie gehabt, so viel das h. gottl Wort belangen thut. Friedewalt Mitw. nach Bernardi (8th Nov.)"—"Note of the opinion of our dear cousin and brother, expressed at our confidential meeting held here, so far as they concern the holy word of God. Friedewalt, Wednesday after St Bernard's day, i. e. 8th Nov." The copy which was made in Torgau differs from the paper written in the prince's own hand in this respect:—the prince had only written that they would make an alliance together for the sake of the Gospel; but in the copy the words above quoted are added:—"Auch sunsten in andern Sachen do eyner vor dem andern Recht leyden kunt, ausgeschlossen gegen den, so in der Erbeynung sind." I intend to make ample extracts in the Appendix.

‡ Letter from Feilitsch to the Elector John, 24th December. Weimar Records.

§ Feilitsch und Minkwitz to the Elector John, 2d Jan. 1526.

‖ Recess (Neue Samml.), ii. 271, §§ 1, 4. This was then looked upon as a victory obtained by the Protestants. Letters from the Nurnbergers, quoted by Hortleder, i. viii. 1. Spalatin Annales in Mencken, ii. 652: "Concidit spes sperantium, eo conventu totum Baalem restitutum iri."

that the village tribunals would otherwise have been entirely at a stand.

The whole attention of the public, as well as its active measures of preparation, were now directed towards the approaching meeting, which, indeed, proved to be decisive.

Saxony and Hessen had not as yet found the sympathy they expected in their scheme of an evangelical league, in fact, the Nurnberg deputies alone had really shown an earnest inclination towards it but this discouragement did not induce those princes to abandon the idea: the two ambassadors were of opinion that the affair must be undertaken with redoubled vigour, in a personal interview between their respective masters

Meanwhile, the other party also concentrated its forces The chapter of the cathedral of Mainz brought forward its long-forgotten metropolitan powers, and summoned the chapters of its suffragans to an assembly at the mother-church. The attention of this meeting was called to the danger which threatened the clergy generally; and the resolution was passed, to send a deputation who should lay before the emperor and the pope a complaint that the spiritual jurisdiction was invaded by the temporal authorities, to remind them of the services which the spiritual princes had, from the earliest times, rendered to the empire and the church, and to declare that they were ready to perform similar and yet greater services in future, but that, in return, they should expect their ancient privileges to be protected. They thought it most expedient to entrust this protection to certain princes who had not fallen off from the faith, whom they specified.*

The wishes of these princes seemed to tend to the same point. Duke George of Saxony and Duke Henry of Brunswick met at the residence of the Elector of Mainz at Halle. A few days after, we find them again at Leipzig, together with the Bishop of Strasburg; they, too, determined to address themselves to the emperor. They represented to him that, seeing the uninterrupted progress of the "damnable Lutheran doctrine," nothing could be expected but a repetition of the rebellion; nay, even an open war, between the princes and lords themselves, that attempts were daily made to draw them, too, over to the Lutheran party, and, since these were not likely to succeed by amicable means, it seemed as if it were the design of the Lutherans to force them into it, by instigating their subjects to revolt Against these attempts they now called upon the emperor for support.† Immediately after the meeting, Duke Henry of Brunswick went to Spain, thus throwing the weight of his personal solicitations into the balance

Everything was thus prepared for the decisive battle. If the adherents of innovation found their strongest support in the sympathy of the nation, and in the mighty movement of the public mind generally, on the other hand, the champions of the papacy were sustained by the natural strength of established institutions, and the resolute aversion of some powerful princes to all change.

But they now likewise sought to engage in their behalf the active interference of the two supreme authorities whose dignity was so intimately bound up with the spiritual constitution of the empire They did not doubt that these potentates would bring all their influence to their aid

But they thus came into contact with two great political powers which stood in very different relations to each other, from that which subsisted between them in Germany,—a relation subject at every moment to be changed by the great events of Italy, and the course of European policy.

We shall be unable to understand the affairs of Germany, if we do not first devote our attention to these events -they are also important, as exhibiting another phase of the character and condition of the German people.

* Letter from Count Albert of Mansfeld, sent with a copy of the treaty to the Elector of Saxony, in the Weimar Records Letter from Waldenfels to Vogler in v d Lith, p. 100

† Excerpt from a judgment given at Leipzig, quoted by Schmidt in his Deutsche Geschichte, viii p 202. Yet I know not whether this meeting took place at Leipzig or at Halle

BOOK IV.

FOREIGN RELATIONS.—FOUNDATION OF THE NATIONAL CHURCHES OF GERMANY.

1521—1528.

CHAPTER I.

FRENCH AND ITALIAN WARS, DOWN TO THE LIGUE OF COGNAC, 1521—1526.

In the tenth century, when the peoples of the West, just struggling into intellectual life and culture, were exposed on every side to attacks from mighty and hostile forces, the first great victory was won by the Germans. In defending themselves, they rendered inestimable service to all others. They restored security and independence to the West; their successes in arms revived the idea of a western empire, two-thirds of the great Carolingian heritage devolved upon them.

In the eleventh and twelfth centuries the majesty and supremacy of the empire were recognised by all the surrounding nations, north and south, east and west.

Arles and Lyons, Milan and Pisa, were included within its dominions. At the end of the twelfth, and the former half of the thirteenth century, we find the emperors of Germany founding a strong domestic power in Italy; more than once the idea of annexing the eastern empire to that of the west suggested itself to them. Meanwhile, wide tracts of country in the north and east were covered with settlements; and as outposts in the far distance, those great colonies of military orders were established, which were unquestionably the best constituted and strongest power in the north.

For a while the conquests of the empire continued to advance, although the imperial government no longer retained its pristine energy, but at length the dissolution of internal order, and the annihilation of the real independence of the imperial throne, was felt on its frontiers the empire was no longer able to maintain its lofty station.

The spoliation began with the pope, who wrested Rome, the States of the Church, and Avignon from the empire. In alliance with him, the French crown got possession, noiselessly and bit by bit, of the kingdom of Arles, shortly after, the rising power of Poland and Lithuania gained a decisive victory over the Teutonic order, no longer adequately supported. In the fifteenth century, Bohemia made herself independent; the states of Italy scarcely preserved their allegiance to the empire even in name, and, lastly, the principle of separation reacted even on the races of German blood and language who inhabited the Alps and the Netherlands. The contemplation of so many disasters awoke that sorrowful indignation in the hearts of true patriots to which we have already alluded

As yet, however, no definitive act of cession had been made on the side of the empire; excepting on some points, in favour of the pope, with whom, however, the boundary line of their respective powers had not yet been very firmly settled it was still open to every kind of suggestion or discussion

Never, above all, had the project of giving up the north of Italy been entertained As early as the beginning of the fifteenth century, Rupert, King of the Romans, made a resolute attack on Milan in the middle of it, after the Visconti became extinct, a party arose in Milan disposed to place the city under the power of the emperor, and we have traced the life-long attempts of Maximilian to conquer Lombardy. He did not, it is true, succeed after many fluctuations in the fortunes of war, the French at length kept possession of Milan and Genoa, but the ancient claims were held in the liveliest remembrance, and Francis I, who, moreover, had never received investiture of the fief, was by no means regarded in the empire in the light of a legitimate possessor

On Charles V.'s accession to the throne the magnificent prospect of a recovery of all its rights once more opened on the empire.

We must remember, that this was the point of view which immediately presented itself to men's minds, on the first approximation of Burgundy and Austria. When Charles the Bold sent to offer his alliance to Frederic III, he told him that he would make him more formidable than any emperor had been for three hundred years he represented to him what an irresistible power must result from the union of their possessions and privileges * The youthful prince who now ascended the throne was the great-grandson and heir of both those sovereigns, and his principalities and kingdoms extended beyond the farthest limit that any imagination could at that time have reached How, then, was it possible that ideas of this kind should fail to arise within him!

* The only account which may, however, be considered authentic, is given by Schmidt from the Imperial Archives, book vii cap 24

Of all the nations of Western Europe, the German was, without doubt, the best prepared for war. The nobles of that country were the first to throw off the use of the lance—that chivalrous weapon which the new art of war had rendered nearly useless: lords and vassals fought in the same ranks.* The foot-soldiers, or landsknechts, who were peasants, had no equals except among the Swiss,—also of German race. The citizens were masters in the use of fire-arms; nor could any other nation in the world have measured its naval forces against those of the Hanse towns and the Netherlands combined.

All these elements of strength had been paralysed by the want of an emperor endued with energy enough to put them in motion. Such an one had never yet arisen; but a new era now appeared at hand. The landsknechts hailed its advent in a song, the burden of which is, that they had now a prince who would be able to pay them, and to keep them in the field. At the diet of Worms, the reconquest of the lost or ceded dominions of the empire was discussed with great earnestness. But here again we must not for a moment lose sight of the fact, that the augmentation of the imperial power was not the offspring of any essential change in the sentiments of the nation. The nation was not disposed to grant to Charles V. greater rights than it had granted to his predecessors; nor to rally round him with greater unanimity. The difference consisted in the union of power, such as had never before centred in one house, with the rights and powers of the empire. But the former included elements so heterogeneous that it could never be amalgamated with the power conferred by the imperial throne. The position of Charles V. was twofold; hence it must of necessity in time give birth to difficulties as peculiar as its own nature, and might become perilous to the rights of the German empire in so far as they were distinct from those of the individual then wearing the imperial crown.†

Even the origin of his wars is to be traced far more to the aggregate of his various relations than to the peculiar interests of the empire.

We have already alluded to the revival of the old hostility between France and Burgundy.

In the beginning of the year 1521, the declared enemies of the emperor were favourably received and advanced at the French court. Francis I. formed a connection with the revolted communes in Castile; in Germany, also, the emperor thought he continually detected traces of his enemy's machinations: letters and schemes of the most hostile nature reached him from Italy:‡ in May, Francis I. made an attempt to restore Navarre by force to Albert. When the English expressed their pacific views and wishes, he replied that he could not allow himself to be stopped in his victorious career.§ He openly took under his protection Robert de la Mark, who, in order to avenge a violation of his jurisdiction on the part of the Chancellor of Brabant, was proceeding to acts of violence against Luxemburg.

On the other hand, the emperor now concluded his treaty with Pope Leo X., to whom the ascendency of the French in Italy was extremely oppressive, and any augmentation of it, intolerable.‖ The alliance was destined to revive and restore the rights of the papacy and the empire conjointly, and even remote contingencies were not forgotten. The emperor promised to assist in establishing the pope's claims on Ferrara; the pope, those of the empire on Venice.¶ But they first determined jointly to conquer Lombardy. Parma and Piacenza were to fall to the share of the pope; Milan and Genoa, to be governed by native rulers, who were to acknowledge the emperor as their sovereign lord. There is frequent reference in the treaty to the legitimate subjection of all princes to the pope and the emperor, from whom God would hereafter demand an account of the state of the Christian republic.

In Germany, well-meaning people were anxious to bring about a reconciliation between the king and the emperor. The electors drew up a sort of memorial, exhorting the King of France to a peaceful demeanour, and a recognition of the rights of the empire. But the emperor was not pleased at their interference; he forbade the Elector of Mainz to send this paper; his chancellor declared to the Elector of Treves that no negotiation would have any effect with the king, who would keep the peace only when restrained by force.**

The purposes, moreover, which had dictated the treaty with the pope were wholly irreconcilable with an accommodation of the differences with the King of France.

In August, 1521, it is true, delegates from the emperor and the king, together with plenipotentiaries from Rome and England, met again in Calais; but from the first, little was to be anticipated from this conference. Of the mediators, one was already in alliance with the emperor, while the other had long been negotiating with him, with a view to a stricter alliance. They went over the old treaties, article by article; each party maintaining that it was the other who was chargeable with the breach of it. The greatest impression was

* A passage from Pasqualigo's narrative will explain this further.

† See translator's note, p. 52.

‡ Tractat de subtrahendis omnibus Cæsaris amicis,—solicitat licet frustra sacri imperii electores,—concitat et literis et nunciis turbatos Hispaniæ populos. From these and similar complaints in the Refutatio Apologiæ Dissuasoriæ in Goldest Polit. Imp. p. 870, is seen what especially irritated the emperor, in addition to the direct attacks.

§ Extracts from the despatches of Fitzwilliam, the English minister in Paris, dated 18th Feb. and 29th of May: Raumer, Letters from Paris, vol. i. p. 237.

‖ This motive, which the Italians seemed afterwards to have forgotten, is very apparent in a conference held by Henry VIII. with the French minister: "fere off extreme subjection."—*State Papers, Henry VIII.*, i. p. 13.

¶ "Omnibus viribus suis spiritualibus et temporalibus." Art. 19.—*Dumont*, iv. iii. p. 99.

** "Wurde keine Handlung leiden, er sey denn dermaassen zugericht, dass er das Friedens begere."—"He would hear of no negotiations unless he were in a condition to ask for peace." From the mouth of the Elector of Treves: Planitz to Frederic of Saxony. Nov. 1, 1521.

produced by a letter of Francis to the Count of Carpi, which had fallen into the hands of the imperialists, and in which the king spoke very plainly of the assistance he gave to Robert de la Mark, and of his views on Naples and Sicily. When at length a renewal of these treaties was proposed, the emperor's grand chancellor, without the slightest hesitation, refused, alleging that the basis upon which they were constructed was unsound, the emperor having ancient claims on France, of which they contained no mention He not only denied, as might be expected, the suzerainty of France over Flanders and Artois, which he pronounced a mere momentary concession, but demanded that the inheritance of Charles the Bold should be given back entire and undiminished, he reminded the mediators what the throne of Aragon, and what the empire was entitled to claim in the south of France *—pretensions which, in fact, expressed nothing less than a resolute determination to try the fortune of war, and which it was impossible for Francis to admit unless he had suffered a defeat

From this congress at Calais, Charles V reaped one advantage—he won over the King of England. Henry VIII had before solemnly engaged to declare himself against the one of his neighbours who should first break the peace The intercepted letter in question convinced him that the blame rested with Francis I.† He had, therefore, no hesitation in espousing the side of the emperor, from whom he carefully obtained security for compensation for whatever pecuniary injury might arise to him from his rupture with France His plenipotentiary, Cardinal Wolsey, proceeded from Calais to Bruges, where the stricter alliance, which had formerly been discussed, was concluded

The emperor really wished not to engage in the war without full justification. As, in consequence of the ambiguously worded article in the treaty of peace, there was a doubt which party was in the right in the affair of Navarre, he was rather glad than otherwise when he heard the news of the serious demonstrations of the French in favour of Robert de la Mark "God be praised!" exclaimed he, "it is not I who begin the war, God affords me an occasion for defending myself" He was the more determined to pursue the enterprise to the end. 'I must be a miserable emperor," said he, "or he shall become a pitiable king of France "‡

Such was the beginning of the war between Charles V and Francis I.

It was, in fact, a direct continuation of the ancient hostilities between Burgundy and France At the same time, it was immensely important to the Germanic empire, to which, for the first time, a well-grounded prospect of re-establishing its rights and authority was reopened The war, with the political changes consequent upon it, would then incessantly react on its internal condition, as we have already remarked, and shall soon more distinctly perceive.

CAMPAIGN OF 1521, 1522.

It seemed at first as if the struggle would be decided on the ancient theatre of the Burgundian wars—the border country of France and the Netherlands.

From the territory of Robert de la Mark, which had been subdued without much difficulty, a stately imperial army, under the command of the Count of Nassau, Sickingen, and Frundsberg, marched upon the French frontiers, conquered Mouzon, besieged Mézières, and threatened the whole of Champagne In the mean time, however, Francis assembled his best forces, and had soon so confident a feeling of his own superiority, that he declared that God himself was evidently on the side of France The imperialists were compelled to raise the siege of Mézières, and when they met the French near Valenciennes, esteemed themselves happy to escape without a beating George Frundsberg regarded this retreat as one of his most glorious achievements, and it did, in fact, in some degree restore the balance of affairs the French took some strong places in Artois; the imperialists, Tournay; but these momentary successes led to no great efforts or important results.§

In Italy, on the other hand, events unexpectedly advanced to a crisis.

This was mainly brought about by the Swiss Confederation, which, though still retaining the form of subjection to the empire, and receiving its pay, enjoyed, in fact, political independence, and had for many years been principally instrumental in deciding all the great struggles in the north of Italy. Recently (A D 1512) the Swiss had reconquered Milan for the Sforzas, and its loss, determined in a most bloody battle, was entirely the result of their divisions In the year 1516, Maximilian had undertaken, with their aid, a second expedition into Lombardy, the failure of which was attributed solely to his defective conduct of it Now, too, both the pope and the emperor, in all their plans, reckoned on the assistance of these neighbouring, brave and warlike troops, as indispensable to the success of their arms

* Garnier, Histoire de France, xxiii p 359, from the MSS. of Bethune, which, however he does not mention, gives a very unsatisfactory account of the matter At the time of the first edition I remarked that in time something material should be done (which would be easy enough) in France for the authentic elucidations of this history Since then a beginning has been made by the publication of the papers of Cardinal Gravella In the first volume, p. 125-241 we find a Précis des Conferences de Calais a report written by the Grand Chancellor of the empire in Latin and put into the ' langue Valonne ou Françoise" (so he calls it) by Claude de Chassey

† "Letters sent unto Rome by the Frenshe King to the Counte de Carpye signed with his hande and subscribed by Robt Tett (Robertet), which I have seen, conteyning the hoole discourse of his intended enterprise, as well by Robt de la Marche in those parties as the commotion of Italie and disturbance of Naples wherby the invasion of his partie evidently appeirithe " Wolsey to King Henry —*State Papers*, i 27 From the answer of Pace, p 35 it appears that the king thought this testimony decisive

‡ Aluigi Aleandro de' Galeazzi, Brusselles 3 Luglio, 1521 Lettere di principi, i 93 That is doubtless the meaning of this speech

§ The Memoirs of Bellay and of Fleuranges on one side and of Pontus Heuterus and Sandoval on the other, describe this war I shall insert a very unpoetical, but instructive historical song, in the Appendix

Their intention was to march 16,000 Swiss across the Alps, and to advance upon Milan, at the same time that an imperial fleet appeared before Genoa, and a combined papal and Neapolitan force on the Po.*

It seemed hardly possible to entertain a doubt of the success of their efforts. The Confederation had espoused the part of the House of Austria at the election, and was closely allied with the See of Rome. In the beginning of the year, some thousand Swiss had entered Leo's service, and their captains had been decorated by that pontiff with chains of gold.

But there was another party in Switzerland attached to France. This party had been the cause of the division in the army in 1515, had afterwards concluded the permanent peace with France; and though it did not actually support the pretensions of the king to the imperial crown (which would have given him legitimate claims to their services), being now free from any anxiety on that score, manifested the liveliest desire to enter into a strict alliance with him. The French left nothing undone that could secure or strengthen the attachment of this party. Their means were simple and infallible. They openly promised pensions, and secretly administered bribes. Anshelm declares that not only the members of councils and the burgesses were bribed, but all the loudest village orators, that many were bought with ten gulden, while not less than three thousand found their way, by different channels, into some houses.† Opposition was, indeed, not wanting. It was remarked that the contracting parties bound themselves to a most unequal obligation in engaging mutually to defend each other's territory, the Confederation, the extensive dominions of the king on either side the Alps, the king, the narrow territory of Switzerland. It was said that Francis, by means of pensions, bribes, and promises, would become almost absolute master of the Confederation,‡ but as majorities are generally swayed rather by interests than by arguments, these representations had no effect.

The reply was, that the Confederation wanted something to fall back upon in unexpected emergencies; and where could a better connection be found? that while the only sacrifice demanded of them was to let their hot-blooded youth, whom they could not keep in order, flock to the king's standard, they would derive great advantages from him in return. In Zurich alone a firm resistance was offered—the result in part of more profound religious convictions; but all other parts—even at last Schwyz and Glarus, which held out the longest—gave way. On the 5th of May, 1521, just as these plans were maturing, the alliance was ratified at Lucern, according to the terms of which, the king raised the pensions already granted to the Confederation by one half;§ while the Swiss, on their side, promised to come to his aid whenever any part of his dominions was attacked, with a force of from six to sixteen thousand men. This is the basis of every subsequent treaty between France and Switzerland. How great a weight in Europe would the renewal of that relation to Milan which had subsisted from 1512 to 1515 have given to Switzerland! But this she disregarded; she sold her arm and her strength—the whole of that warlike power by which she had won herself a name among the nations—to the crown of France, and became the hired instrument of its designs. She advanced another step in the career of separation from the empire, to which she was bound by the ties of nationality and of history, and sustained by which, she might have assumed a lofty station among the powers of Europe. In July, 1521, a solemn deputation repaired to Dijon, to deliver to Francis I. the sealed copy of the treaty; and the king's mother was delighted at the marks of reverential homage addressed to her son at this ceremony; immediately after which, bands of Swiss joined the king's troops both in Picardy and in Italy.

It is evident how completely this must have thwarted all the plans of the pope and the emperor.

In Italy, the breaking out of hostilities was hastened by a very ill-concerted attack of the French on the town of Reggio, where they intended to carry off some Milanese emigrants. In July, 1521, Prospero Colonna, to whom the supreme command over the combined papal and imperial forces was given, left Bologna to attack Parma; a fleet was sent to sea against Genoa, in Trent, German foot-soldiers flocked to the standard of Francesco Sforza, son of Luigi il Moro, while the exiled Ghibellines appeared with a few boats on the Lake of Como, where they had always carried on a sort of banditti warfare.‖

But to what could all these detached efforts lead, when the force from which the grand attack on the Milanese was expected had now made common cause with the enemy, whose confidence was thus raised at all points? The enterprises against Genoa and Como completely failed. It was fortunate, that at least the Germans from Trent found means to effect a junction with the army before Parma, where the troops which had been destined for the attack upon Genoa now likewise collected; but, even with this addition, they did not feel themselves strong enough for a serious and decisive attack. On the 12th of September the siege was raised.¶

* This plan is adopted in the treaty of alliance. Art. 9.

† Anshelm, Berner Chronik, vi. p. 25.

‡ Arguments on the other side are to be found, especially in the address of the city of Zurich to the canton, quoted by Bullinger, i. p. 42.

§ "Ut cognoscant intimum amorem, liberalitatem, benevolentiam, et affectionem dicti Christianissimi regis in eos."—*Dumont*, iv. i. p. 334.

‖ Benedictus Jovius Historia Novocomensis in Grævii Thes. Ital. iv. p. 71, names, as leader, Johannes a Brinzia, cognomento stultus, that is, Matto da Brinzi, as he is otherwise called.

¶ The somewhat contradictory details of the raising of this siege are to be found in Guicciardini, Capella, Jovius (Vita Pesc. ii. 300. Leonis Xmi, iii. 100.) See also Nardi, Storie fiorentine, vi. p. 170.

The French at this time possessed an unquestioned superiority over their enemies. The Venetians had sent into the field five hundred men-at-arms, and six thousand foot-soldiers; the Duke of Ferrara, who was not blind to the danger impending over him, fell upon the papal territory; the Swiss came down from their mountains in detachments, at their head the Bernese, led by the most ardent partisans of the French. The historian Guicciardini, who was with the allied armies as papal commissioner, declares, that if the French had attacked them at that moment, when also discords and disorders had broken out among them, they would have obtained an easy victory.*

But just at this moment, hope of succour and of safety dawned in the very point whence the danger had arisen.

Imperial and papal envoys had arrived in Switzerland, richly provided with money and all the means of corruption, and had again found a soil very favourable to the fulfilment of their commission. By pressing on the Swiss their old obligations towards the emperor and Austria, and especially towards the pope, they brought into full and distinct light the extent of the danger into which the Confederation had rushed. They were bound by ancient treaties to defend part of the territories of Austria (*i. e.* Franche Comté), and all those of the Church; yet, in the teeth of these, they had entered into a new treaty, a special clause of which declared that they were to take the field against all parties specified, and especially against Austria and the pope, if they should attack the king's dominions. There were still some Swiss in the papal armies, who had taken part in the attack on Parma, while others of their countrymen co-operated, under Lautrec, in the relief of that place; and it was not easy to see what would be the result of their coming in contact. The French alliance was the work of a party, and nothing was more natural than that another party should be formed in every place to oppose it. The disorderly and ill-timed departure was also a ground of complaint and reproach; in some places the whole labour of getting in the harvest had been left to women. Zürich, which had rejected the French alliance by an unanimous resolution of the council in the city and the communes in the country, was determined at all events to maintain that with the pope. All these various inclinations and passions were now laid hold of, and turned to account by the old master of Swiss intrigues, Cardinal von Sitten. In Zürich he was allowed to levy 2700 men, though under the condition that they were to be employed solely for the defence of the papal possessions, and on no account for the attack on Milan: these troops, however, formed a mere rallying point around which partisans of the pope and emperor gathered from all parts; the cardinal granted still higher pay than the French plenipotentiaries: we find that a banner or company, which had been recruited for the service of France, went over in a body, with the single exception of its captain, to that of the pope: above 6000 men mustered in Coire, towards the end of September, and were quickly joined by troops from the Grisons and the Pays de Vaud.†

The pope was already in great dismay and perplexity at the ill results of his undertakings, when he received these tidings. His nuncio Ennio assured him that the clause in the agreement with Zürich would not restrain the troops of that canton from attacking Parma, Piacenza, and even Ferrara, though they belonged to the Church; nay, that he was confident that if he did but distribute money among some of the leaders, he could induce them to undertake any thing he wished.‡

This revived the almost extinguished hopes of the allies. It was evident that the mere appearance of so strong a Swiss force in the combined army must cripple the strength of the enemy, which mainly consisted of the Swiss in his service. The only question was, how to effect a junction, and to accomplish this the army set itself in motion. Cardinal Giulio de' Medici had just arrived from Florence, and had appeased all the quarrels of the leaders and secured the good will of the troops by the Florentine gold of which he was the bearer; he had thirteen sumpter mules in his train, all said to be laden with money. On the first of October, Prospero Colonna crossed the Po at Casal Maggiore, and marched up the river Oglio. Meanwhile the Swiss who had come down from the Alps across the Morbegno arrived from Chiavenna. Neither mountain nor flood, neither the warnings of their countrymen nor the hostilities of the French, had power to deter them. At the end of October they too appeared on the other side of the Oglio.

It was evident that the safety of the French depended on preventing the junction of these two bodies of troops. Prospero Colonna had taken up a position near Rebecca, so little advantageous, that even the cautious Venetians were tempted to attack him; the Swiss were urgent to do so: they wanted to fight before their countrymen reached the scene of warfare; and in a council of war which was held, the voices were nearly unanimous for the attack. The commander-in-chief, Lautrec, alone was not to be induced to comply with their wishes.§

* Guicciardini, xiv. p. 408. Se fosse sopravenuto Lautrech, gli metteva facilissimamente in fuga.

† The offers made by the imperial and papal party are to be seen in Anshelm. Bullinger is more explicit as to the affairs of Zürich, cap. 24-26. See Hottinger, Geschichte der Eidgenossen (Müller's continuation), i. p. 55, 63.

‡ Galeacius Capella gives, p. 180, an extract from the letter: "Demum pecunia facile esse duces corrumpere, qui milites quo res postularet technis suasionibusque impellerent.

§ The version which Leferron (v. p. 130,) quotes from the mouth of an eye-witness — that Lautrec had really intended to make the attack on the following day, but was prevented by the Venetians—is a mere pretext. Bellay says, "La tardivité de nos chefs fut causè de les nous faire perdre."—*Coll. Univ.*, tom. xvii. p. 180. The particulars are mentioned by the most trustworthy Italians, such as Galeazzo. We may judge of the effect of this event from the Chronicles of Rabbi Josef; he says of the French, "They are a nation voyd of counsel."

Many motives for his refusal were assigned; the most generally received was his want of resolution: he was not a general fitted for enterprising warfare. He chose rather to strengthen the garrisons in the nearest fortified towns, and to take up a strong position behind the Adda. Prospero Colonna soon after joined the Swiss at Gambara without any impediment. A part of them, as the nuncio had predicted, were not reluctant to advance with him upon Milan. The more conscientious, who could not be induced by any promises to do so, marched upon Reggio, whence they were to make an attack on the papal cities of Parma and Piacenza.

The allied army thus acquired an incontestable superiority. The Swiss in the French service, discontented at not having earned the bounty distributed after a battle, dissatisfied with Lautrec, who preferred his German guard to them, and exhorted by messengers from Switzerland, for God's sake not to fight their brother confederates, deserted the ranks, and returned home in troops. If, therefore, in 1515, the dissensions of the Swiss had essentially facilitated the conquest of Milan to the French, the consequences of those dissensions now mainly occasioned their disasters. The allies, at this moment, reinforced by fresh troops from the Grisons, effected their passage across the Adda with equal skill and success. Lautrec found himself entirely confined to the fortified towns.

But these had long been the scene of hostile ferment. The Ghibellines hated the French government; nor were the Guelphs treated by it with all the consideration they expected, their most eminent leader, the aged Trivulzi, whose authority had for a time been superior to that of the French governor, had, on that account, fallen into the disfavour of the king, which had terminated only with his life. To these causes of discontent were added the acts of extortion and violence which generally render the domination of the French hateful to every country subject to their sway. On Lautrec's arrival in Milan, he found so great an agitation, that he thought it necessary to put it down by severe military executions; he caused the aged Christofero Pallavicini, a near relation of the House of Medici, and one of the chiefs of the Ghibelline faction, to be beheaded in the castle.* It is easy to imagine what was the impression produced by this cruelty, combined with the spectacle of a defeated army and the report of the approach of an enemy of overwhelming force. Upon the state of the public mind resulting from such causes, Prospero and Cardinal Giulio had all along placed their hopes.† Francesco Sforza had fostered this by proclamations, breathing nothing but clemency and mildness, and promising the paternal rule of a native prince, which were read with avidity. As the allies approached Milan, they were urged to advance without delay, and to venture on an attack; the whole city, it was said, would rise in their favour. It was in November, the weather and the roads as bad as possible; but under these adverse circumstances they marched forwards. On the evening of the 19th they reached Milan, and immediately pitched their camp before it. Meanwhile, a small party of light-horsemen having reported the bad state of the entrenchments which Lautrec had hastily thrown up round the city, the Marquess Pescara, commander of the Spanish infantry, said, "We must find quarters in the suburbs;" and instantly placing himself at the head of sixty Spanish riflemen, advanced on the Porta Romana, followed by an irregular troop of Landsknechts. The event which was to decide the fate of Italy for centuries, began like an adventure undertaken in wantonness and sport. Prospero Colonna, unwilling to be outdone, collected another party of Germans and Spaniards, and marched on the Porta Ticinese. The entrenchments were easily forced, but, as nearly the whole of the enemy's army lay in the city, and rallied in haste to make resistance, the affair was still doubtful, and a part at least of the assailants held it expedient to retire. At this crisis the population rose; the streets resounded with the cry "the Duke! the Empire for ever! down with the French!" a universal insurrection appeared imminent, and as the main body of the allied army at this moment approached, and the Landsknechts, wading up to their belts in water through the ditches, mounted the entrenchments, Lautrec thought the defence of the city desperate, and retreated through the Porta Comasina on the opposite side. The Venetians were easily disarmed. The Swiss officers would not abandon the French, and hurried after them. In less than two hours the city was taken.‡ On entering it, the imperialists found all the streets brilliantly illuminated. The same evening it was publicly proclaimed that the emperor and pope had determined to restore to the Milanese their hereditary sovereign, Duke Francesco Sforza. Geronimo Morone, the confidential councillor of that prince, who had kept alive the connection with the Ghibelline families, and had contributed more than any other individual to the success of the enterprise, took the reins of government.

Pavia and Lodi, on the one side the Po, Parma and Piacenza on the other, followed the example of Milan. The latter cities received very welcome assistance from the Swiss of Zug and Zurich, who had not accompanied the army to Milan.

The matter was, however, by no means at an end. The French army had not dispersed, as was expected, it took up a strong position

* Cronaca Grumello, in Verri, iii p 221

† Sepulveda, Præfatio in Aristotelem de parvis Naturalibus (Cf Sepulvedæ Vita et Scripta. p cvii), says of Giulio "Non ignarus, in uno Mediolano cetera oppida expugnari" Vettori admirably describes the change of circumstances "In Milano in facto la parte Ghibellina è superiore assai, i popoli sono sempre desiderosi di mutazioni chi lascia la campagna e si retira dentro alle mura, perde di riputazione"

‡ A letter of the Marquis of Mantua to his mother, dated 21st Nov, 1521, and printed in the thirty second volume of Sanuto's Chronicle, contains the best and the most trustworthy account of this event. I shall give it in the Appendix as well as a letter of the Legate Giulio Medici, written between the evening of the 19th and the morning of the 20th

in Cremona, whence it menaced Milan on the one side and Parma and Piacenza on the other, it was still in possession of a number of castles; Novarra, Trezzo, Pizzighetone, in the Milanese, the strongholds in the passes of the Alps; Domo d'Ossola and Arona, with all the others on the Lago Maggiore. The sudden death of Leo X., whom fate summoned away just as he received the first favourable tidings, compelled the allied commanders to be frugal, and to discharge as many of their troops as they could possibly spare For the moment, at least, they could not reckon on any further support from the Tuscan or Papal dominions, which were distracted by troubles of their own, while the French had at their disposal the resources of Venice and Genoa The most important thing, however, was that, after this disaster, of which they were themselves the sole cause, the Swiss acted with greater concert. The emperor invited them to enter into alliance with him; the Council of Regency reminded them of their duties as members of the empire, an embassy from Milan offered them a subsidy, but all was in vain the French party, reinforced by the powerful captains who were returned from Italy, asserted its superiority,* its adversaries themselves were struck by the danger which threatened the Confederation from opposition to the will of the majority Zürich now recalled her citizens from Italy, and the twelve cantons granted the king a levy of 16,000 men they gave leave to the French plenipotentiary to inspect them himself, which had never been granted before, and at the end of January, 1522, whilst falling snow still covered the roads with fresh drifts, they marched across the Alps.

By this event, the whole political face of things assumed a new and most complicated aspect.

The Swiss being thus opposed to the claims of the emperor and the empire, they were only to be maintained (if indeed it was possible to maintain them at all) by purely German resources. no union of hereditary possessions, no negotiation, availed the emperor further, he had nothing to look to but the strong arm and the tried faith of his Landsknechts

A considerable body of these troops were already collected in the Milanese They had been levied the preceding year in Tyrol and Swabia, chiefly with the pope's money it appears from extant documents, that the Wurtenberg government ordered its servants to let every man go who would be better out of the country than in it † Francis of Castelalt had raised five companies ‡ The most renowned of German captains, George of Frundsberg, now set himself in motion. He was personally acquainted with Francesco Sforza, who had once paid him a visit at his castle of Mindelheim. another Italian pretender, Geronimo Adorno, who aspired at regaining his power in Genoa, and had rendered important service at the conclusion of the treaty, appeared in Germany well provided with money, the drum was beat in the streets of Augsburg, and in a very short time twelve companies of Landsknechts flocked to the standard of George Frundsberg, and marched under his orders from Glurns on the 12th of February He had to contend with all the difficulties of the season, and under their severest form, the Grisoners would not allow him to pass over the Valtelline, so that he was obliged to take a much worse road, which the labour of two hundred peasants was required to clear and level, over the Wormser Joch to Lovere and the Lago d'Iseo, notwithstanding which he arrived at the right moment, just as the Swiss and French were about to attack Milan from Monza §

A third German army, 6000 strong, had also assembled at Trent, under the command of Francesco Sforza, Adorno, whose personal hopes and interests all hung on the issue of this campaign, hurried back to lead on these troops to the scene of action

The French made an attempt on Milan; but Prospero had put himself in an excellent state of defence, both against the castle within, and the enemy without He belonged to the classical school of Italy of that time, and it was affirmed that Cæsar's defence of Alesia had served as a model for his operations ‖

The French and Swiss took Novara, Vigevene, and some other places, but—what was much more important—they were unable to prevent the junction of Francesco Sforza with Prospero on the 4th of April, after an absence of twenty-two years, the new duke entered Milan, amidst the ringing of bells, the incessant firing of guns, and the joyous shouts of the whole population a foreign yoke had now taught them the value of a prince of their own race and country, and they deemed that such an one would be more solicitous for their welfare, and more attached to their persons and interests than a stranger. Francesco Sforza lay under the unfortunate necessity of beginning his reign with demands, nevertheless, his people vied with each other in the zeal with which they complied with them. High and low brought money and money's worth, every body strove to show him affection, and to obtain his favour.¶ An Augustine friar, Andrea da Ferrara, fostered this spirit in the people, by the fervid eloquence of discourses in which he represented the French as enemies of God.

The imperialists were thus once more in a condition to appear in the field After relieving Pavia, they took up a strong position at Bicocca, before Milan, in the hope that their impetuous enemy would attack them here

* On the 29th November, we find the French agent, Galeazzo Visconti, in Lucern "Queste lige," he says, "sono in grosso dixordine,—ma a tuto spero troverase bono recapito, etiam che cum faticha et spexa"—*Molini, Doc* i. p 132

† Avvisi di Trento, dated 9th July, 1521, Molini, i p 99 On the 15th the order was published in Würtenberg —*Sattler*, p 77

‡ Jovius, Vita Alfonsi, p 185, names him

§ Reissner, Historia Hern Georgen und Hern Casparen von Frundsberg

‖ Jovius Pescara, p 316 If he must have an example, that of the Thebans when they besieged the Cadmeia, and endeavoured at the same time to defend themselves against Alexander (Arrian, i 7), would be more appropriate

¶ Grumello, quoted by Verri, p 223.

Nor did they long expect in vain. As usual, the error last committed was that most anxiously avoided It was the unanimous opinion in the French army, that nothing had been wanting the preceding autumn at Rebecca but a resolute attack, to have ensured the victory the Swiss, in particular, were convinced of this, they determined not to let the opportunity slip by again, and loudly urged their leaders to lead them on to the enemy Lautrec had lost his judgment and presence of mind Though he did not entirely approve of the proposition of the Swiss, he did not dare resolutely to oppose them, he suffered himself to be overruled On the morning of the 27th of April, the Swiss and the French moved upon Bicocca.

The imperialists had encamped in a spot enclosed by morass, hollow ways, hedges, and ditches; had entrenched themselves here according to the rules of art, as in a fortification, and placed their guns on lofty breastworks The army consisted of the German companies, which occupied the front under George Frundsberg and Rudolf Hal, of Spanish infantry, especially arquebusiers, who had remained in Italy ever since the former wars, and had fought, under Gonsalvo di Cordova, by the side of the Germans; and, lastly, of Italian Ghibellines, who wished to see the power of the empire restored, in order that they might avail themselves of its protection to obtain the mastery over their adversaries. It was an army which fully represented the substantial powers of Spain and Germany, as united under the wearer of the imperial crown Francesco Sforza, whose interests were most immediately at stake, the very next morning occupied a bridge which would have afforded access to the camp, with Milanese troops, horse and foot. He was accompanied by a monk of San Marco, who proclaimed that heaven had decreed the victory to the new duke This patriotic excitement was another ally of the imperial cause

On the other hand, the troops of the Confederation stood now undivided on the side of the French As often as this had been the case before, they had turned the scale of victory, and they were inflamed with confidence in their present success

Their tactic had hitherto always consisted in a headlong, furious, straightforward onset on the camp or the artillery of the enemy, and this was the mode of attack they now adopted They formed into two large bodies; the one out of the country parts, under Arnold von Winkelried of Unterwalden, the other from the cities, under Albrecht von Stein. They would submit to no intermixture with the foreigner, and responded to the exhortations of their leaders, who sought to moderate their impetuosity, with shouts and curses, according to the plan of attack, the body from the villages was to have made the first onset, and that from the cities the second, but they advanced nearly in line, so as to form a right and left wing; the Junkers, pensioners and camp followers were forced by the cries of the multitude to advance into the foremost ranks. Inspired by the ferocity of savages, rather than by the noble enthusiasm of heroes, they trusted only to themselves and despised all discipline and guidance. They knew that they were mercenaries, but every one of them was bent on doing his duty their only thought was to fight out the matter hand to hand, to earn the storming money (*Sturmgeld*), and to conquer their old foes, the Swabians—the Landsknechts.

But the camp upon which they were now advancing was in a better state of defence than any they had before attacked. As they moved forward, their left flank experienced a fearful reception from the enemy's well-posted infantry, and the order of battle was disturbed from that moment, the country troops pressed upon those of the towns. As these, however, did not give way, the former recovered their ranks, and, in spite of the incessant fire of the arquebusiers, both bodies at once charged the lines of the imperial entrenchments

Seeing the enemy approach, George Frundsberg alighted from his horse, took a halberd, and placed himself in the ranks of the landsknechts They fell on their knees and prayed. Meanwhile, the Swiss came on "Be it so," cried Frundsberg, "in a good hour, and in God's name." The landsknechts sprang to their feet; the Swiss advanced in deep columns through the ditches and hollow ways against the landsknechts, and began the fight. "Ha! do I meet thee there, old comrade?" exclaimed Arnold of Winkelried, as he caught sight of George of Frundsberg, with whom he had formerly served, "then by my hand must thou die" "God willing," replied Frundsberg, "thou by mine." Frundsberg received a stab in the thigh; Winkelried was struck to the earth by a shot. The combatants rushed forward into each other's lines, and were mingled in one common struggle The valour of Rudolf Häl and of Castelalt, of the standard-bearer Brandesser and of Stralin's troop, were celebrated in song and story. But the Swiss, too, kept their ground, which was the more remarkable, as they were not yet out of the range of the artillery; they still hoped to overcome the enemy, spite of his present advantages.

Meanwhile, the French cavalry had made an attack on the bridge, and had been repulsed; their retreat had borne along the troops in the rear The cry arose, "The rear is running!" To the effect of the artillery, the impossibility of carrying the entrenchments, and the obstinate resistance of the enemy, was now added the danger of being abandoned. The retreat of the Swiss was characterized by the same impetuosity as their onslaught. They left two or three thousand men dead on the field, but they retreated in tolerably good order.

The Italian cavalry and the Spanish infantry now rushed out upon them from behind the entrenchments, but without doing them much injury.

Frundsberg, too, was urged to pursue them; but he was satisfied with the repulse of so powerful an enemy he said that he had earned honour enough for one day. he felt too sensibly the importance of the victory, to endanger it by a tumultuous pursuit.*

As the military chest of the French was exhausted, the Swiss were no longer to be kept in the field; they betook themselves to their homes. The French, too, now gave up the campaign as lost. At different points, they found their way back across the Alps The whole Milanese territory fell once more into the hands of the Sforzas, and acknowledged the emperor as its feudal lord.

This rendered it impossible for the French party to retain its footing in Genoa Unfortunately, however, though powerless for any effectual resistance, it was powerful enough to prevent the conclusion of a treaty, while it was yet time. The city was taken and given over to pillage. The Adorni now attained the end which they had aimed at from the first, and got possession of the government.

In the Italian historians the share taken in this event by the Germans appears less prominent than it really was The historical ballad,† however, circumstantially relates, "how the eagle was once more let loose, and many a one who had borne his head high must now cower before it; how George Frundsberg led an army at the emperor's command towards the sea-coast to attack Genoa. willingly do the landsknechts follow him; the Genoese feel that they cannot withstand the imperial crown, but the arrival of French succours under Peter Navarra leads them to attempt it: then the cannons are brought into the field, and are cheerily served by the landsknechts, there is a skirmish under the walls, the storming party and the battle are a sport to the Germans; it is they who conquer the city" There is no allusion whatever to any foreign co-operation, to any foreign leader. It is certain that they had the largest share both in the victory and the plunder. "They measured the broad cloth with their spears; they clothed themselves in silk and in velvet" A number of the wealthier families of Genoa bought an exemption from pillage Frundsberg was much displeased that treasure which would have sufficed to maintain the army in the field for months, fell into their hands in so disorderly a manner He selected out of the booty a beautiful mariner's compass for himself, as a memorial of the day. Great as was the loss of the Genoese, it did not seem to affect them much; they had feared the far more serious evil of a shock to their credit ‡

Thus were these dependencies of the Imperial Chamber, Genoa and Milan, after long separation, reannexed: a victorious imperial army, more powerful than any that had existed since the time of Henry VI., placed over them rulers recommended by their hereditary claims, and by their attachment to the empire. The result was in fact greater than the emperor expected—greater than he would even have ventured to aim at At the beginning of the year, he had aspired only to gain over the Swiss, or even to buy their services with a yearly pension; now, they were defeated and repulsed. The forces of Central Germany, which were far more at the emperor's command, had fought the battle and completed the conquest.

And at this moment the prospect and the inducement to enterprises of far wider reach presented themselves to his view.

CAMPAIGN OF 1523, 1521. ATTACK ON FRANCE.

The claims of the empire extended not alone to Italy; they also embraced a large part of the south of France, nor had this portion of them by any means fallen into oblivion. The Elector of Treves still bore the title of arch-chancellor of Arles; in the year 1401, Rupert had destined his son to fill the post of vicar of that kingdom; in 1444, Frederic had summoned the dauphin to his assistance "as the kinsman and vicar of the Holy Roman Empire" At a later period, it had often been remarked that France had neglected to renew its fief as feudatory of the empire.

It was likewise to be considered that Charles V was not merely emperor; as prince of Burgundy, he possessed other rights which he had never renounced; he never ceased to demand the restitution of the French possessions which had been wrested from his house; the blood and the spirit of one of the ancient vassals of France still lived in him.

For his schemes on this side the Alps, Charles now found as powerful an ally in Henry VIII. of England as, for those on the other, in the pope. Henry, too, had not forgotten the ancient claims of his predecessors on France, he still retained the title which expressed them, and Calais was still in the hands of the English. Immediately after the conclusion of the treaty at Bruges, in which the emperor and the king mutually promised to maintain their claims by force of arms, with combined efforts by sea and land, Wolsey laid before his master a long list of provinces, towns, and castles which he meditated wresting from the French § In the correspondence of the king with the cardinal, it is seriously proposed that he should invade France in person,‖ and this project is given as a reason for

* In the account of this battle, I have adhered to the oldest and simplest sources Anshelm among the Swiss, Galeazzo Capra among the Italians, the historical song which I shall publish in the Appendix, and Reissner's Historia der Frundsberge, among the Germans I am not ignorant of the objections made, especially by Bullinger against certain passages of the latter The Swiss would not allow that they had been beaten by the landsknechts but replied to the songs in which the Germans celebrated their deeds, others in which they defended their own One song (reprinted by Gruneisen, p 400,) by Nicholas Manuel, which is grossly false, is very well known But even there it is not positively denied, as Bullinger will have it, that the combatants fought hand to hand According to the information brought the next day by a Venetian spy, about 1000 men fell on the side of the imperialists The statement of Ugo Foscolo, in Sanuto's Chronicle, vol xxxiii, is by no means clear "Non si sa," he finishes by saying "chel causasse, nostri si misseno a ritrare in gran disordine" His description certainly leaves the matter in complete obscurity.

† "Ein Hupsch neü lied von der Stat Genna und wie sy die Lantzknecht erobert haben"—"A pretty new song of the city of Genoa, and how it was conquered by the Landsknechts"—See *Varese, Storia di Genova*, iv p 315

‡ Polydorus Virgilius, Hist Angl 27, 64

§ Pace to Wolsey, 10th Sept 1521 See State Papers, p 52.

‖ Wolsey to Henry, Sept. 1522 Ibid p 107

endeavouring to keep the Scottish border at peace. At one time, the English were inclined to confine themselves within the part of France nearest to them, from Calais to the Somme, as being easier to maintain than the more distant Guyenne; but occasionally the idea of placing the crown of France on his own head floated before Henry's imagination. On hearing a report of the bad state of things in that country, he exclaimed that "they were making a way for him there, as King Richard III. had done for his father in England;* he trusted he should govern France himself." These thoughts were sedulously fostered by Leo, who caused a draft of a bull to be prepared, in which he formally released the subjects of Francis I. from their oath of fidelity.† On the other hand, the king, as well as the emperor, promised him aid against the heretics.‡ It forms a link in this chain of circumstances, that Henry VIII.—like his cardinal, a zealous adherent of Thomas Aquinas—broke a lance with Luther, in behalf of that great teacher of the church: he was delighted with the favourable reception his book experienced in Rome,§ and with the title of Defender of the Faith which it procured him.

In March, 1522, Henry VIII. caused war to be proclaimed against the King of France, by his herald. Already the English merchants had left the ports, and the English students the universities, of France; very little English property fell into Francis's hands. In June, Lord Surrey, admiral of both the imperial and the English fleets, made an attack on the coast near Cherbourg; in September, an army from England and the Netherlands joined and invaded Picardy; but no considerable results ensued either there or elsewhere: a few towns were plundered, and some small districts laid waste; then came the unfavourable time of year, and the troops retreated.

Much more brilliant were the prospects which opened on the campaign of the following year (1523). As in the earlier times of the monarchy, a powerful vassal of the French crown took part with its foes. The constable Bourbon, the second man in the realm, proffered his assistance to the emperor and the king. This fact is of so general an interest, that we may be excused for dwelling upon it somewhat at length, even in a German history.

Louis XI., who had already found means to reduce to subjection so many of the territories of the great vassals, had also meditated a scheme for bringing about the escheat of the possessions of the house of Bourbon to the crown. On the marriage of his daughter with Pierre de Bourbon-Beaujeu, he extorted from that prince a promise that, in default of male issue, he would leave to the crown all the possessions of his house which were alienable.‖ A younger branch of the house still flourished in the person of the Count de Montpensier, whom it was the king's intention to exclude from the succession.

After some time, the event which had been foreseen actually occurred; Duke Peter died and left only one daughter, Countess Susanna.

Meanwhile, however, Louis XII. had ascended the throne, and was not inclined rigidly to enforce the claims of the crown, acquired by such questionable means. He recognised the feudal rights of the house of Montpensier, nor did he contest certain of the hereditary claims of the surviving princess; in order to prevent all dispute, he brought about a marriage between the young Count Charles de Montpensier and the Countess Susanna, and their rights were completely blended by a mutual donation founded on a prudent and equitable basis.

Such was the origin of the vast power of Charles, Duke of Bourbon. He united in his person two principalities, two duchies, four counties, two vis-counties, and seven considerable lordships; his income was reckoned at 120,000 crowns; far more than the richest of German princes then possessed. He had strong places garrisoned by his troops; he convoked his states, and levied taxes; to crown all, King Francis revived the dignity of constable in his person. He was brave, bountiful, and affable, and since he had succeeded in repulsing Maximilian's attack on Milan in the year 1516, he enjoyed the universal respect both of the army and the nation. Even then his thoughts took the highest flights; the lineal succession to the throne was by no means secure, he hoped in time to ascend it himself. The family of Alençon, indeed, possessed nearer claims; but he flattered himself that these had been forfeited by the former rebellion of that line. He even went so far as to solicit the support of the republic of Venice, in case of the king's death.¶

Events however took a totally different course. The succession to the throne became more secure; the government was entirely in the hands of the confidential servants of the king and his mother. Bourbon was recalled from Milan, and excluded from any share in affairs of state at home; in the very next campaign, that of the Netherlands, the privileges of constable were no longer granted him. He might already be regarded as leader of the numerous malcontents created by the disorders in

* More to Wolsey, p. 111. "The kinges grace saied that he trusted in God to be there governour hym selfe, and that they sholl by thys meanys make a way for hym, as King Richard did for his father." 21st Sept. 1522. No one will believe that this was the first time such an idea crossed his mind.

† "Excommunicatio lata per Leonem Papam X. contra Franciscum I. ... qua etiam subditos ejus plenissime absolvit ab omni fide, status nexu et juramento. 4th Sept. 1521."—*Du Mont*, Supplement, iii. p. 70.

‡ Herbert, Life of Henry VIII., p. 118.

§ Pace to Wolsey, 27th Oct. 1521. "Itt is to Hys Graces grete contentacion and comforte."

‖ "En tant qu'il le touchoit ou pourroit toucher, que tous les duchez, contez et vicomtez de la Maison de Bourbon, advenant qu'il n'eust enfans masles de son mariage, appartinssent au Roi."—Extract from the original document in *Pasquier, Recherches de la France*, vi. c. xi.

¶ Notes taken especially from Badoer, Relatione di Milano, in Sanuto's Chronicle. Bourbon explained these claims to the envoy, adding,—"perho in quel caso la ser^ma^ Signoria volesse ajutarlo." Badoer describes him thus: "Prosperoso, traze un pallo di ferro molto gagardamente, teme dio, è devoto, piatoso, humano e liberalissimo."

the government of Francis I, when, in the year 1522, his proud and splendid station was threatened by overwhelming danger.

His wife, Susanna, died without issue; and although she had confirmed by fresh acts the donations made to him at her marriage, the most formidable pretensions to her inheritance were immediately put forward.

The king's mother, Louisa of Savoy, niece of Duke Peter, and hence a member of the elder line, made a general demand to enter upon all the rights enjoyed by Susanna, but scarcely was her suit commenced, when the Crown itself came forward with still more sweeping claims, alleging not only the promise made by Count Peter, but a multitude of other very plausible titles. The more clear and incontestable of these were soon declared valid, and even with regard to the others, the parliament could give no other advice to the duke than that he should endeavour to come to some arrangement with the adverse party.* The constable saw himself in imminent danger of sinking to the rank of an insignificant Count of Montpensier. But to this he was determined not tamely to submit. He addressed himself to that house which was then preparing to avenge on the crown of France the violated and oppressed rights of the great vassals. It was not the emperor who sought him; the first advances were made by Bourbon, and at the same moment in which his suit began, in the month of August, 1522, he sent Adrian de Beaurain to the court of the Netherlands, where the only surprise expressed by Margaret was, that he had so much confidence in so young a man.† The more perilous and uncertain the aspect of his legal affairs, the more earnestly did he prosecute this negotiation. To the emperor and king nothing could be more welcome. Beaurain went backwards and forwards several times, and, at a later period, Sir John Russell visited the constable in disguise, on the part of Henry VIII.‡ It was agreed that a German army should invade Burgundy, a Spanish, Languedoc, and an English, Picardy, at the same moment, and that Bourbon should declare himself independent. He flattered himself that he should be able to bring into the field 500 men at arms and 10,000 foot soldiers. The emperor promised to give him his sister in marriage, and to raise him to the kingly rank, while he, on his side, promised to acknowledge the king of England as his suzerain, if the emperor should desire it.

Francis I had just formed the determination, since his general had been so unfortunate, to make another attempt in person on Milan. A magnificent army was assembled, and Admiral Bonnivet, who commanded the vanguard, had already advanced to occupy the passes of the Alps. the king set out to follow him. The allies intended to put their plan in execution as soon as he should have left France.

But the affair was already known to too many not to transpire. The court of the Netherlands feared it might get wind from England, the English court, from the Netherlands; even in France itself, the conspirators had been compelled to communicate it to some not perfectly trustworthy persons. In short, the king's suspicions were excited, and Bourbon had to esteem himself fortunate that he was able to escape. The king was induced by these circumstances to commit the army of Italy to the sole command of the admiral, and to remain at his post, to take measures of defence against the various dangers with which his kingdom was threatened, from within as well as from without.

Bourbon fled through Besançon to the country of Pfirt, whence he projected making an immediate descent upon France. A few thousand landsknechts under the Count of Furstenberg entered Champagne, and occupied some fortified towns in the neighbourhood of Chaumont and Langres.§ Bourbon's idea had always been that the English should, at the same time, advance as far as possible into the heart of the kingdom carefully abstaining from plunder, and appearing only in the character of liberators from the tyranny of Francis I. Then he thought, every town would open its gates to them.‖ But the landsknechts were soon compelled to retreat, by want of money and provisions, the combined army of English and Netherlanders continued its march through Picardy, and, for a moment, struck terror into Paris. but its leaders followed the traditional mode of warfare, and it could no where obtain a firm footing. The warlike ardour of the Spaniards expended itself before Fuenterrabia, which the French had taken. Bourbon perceived that he could accomplish nothing for the present on this side the Alps, and repaired to Italy.

Italy was destined to be again the field where the fortune of war was to be decided.

When Bonnivet appeared in Lombardy with the fine army which the king had raised to revive his fame and regain his conquests (it was estimated at 30,000 foot and 4000 horse), the imperialists were unable to contest the pas-

* Gaillard (Histoire de Francois I) has given a fuller description of the passion said to be entertained by Louisa for the Constable Bourbon. His remarks on the suit itself in the Appendix have somewhat more value, yet even on this subject he is far surpassed by Garnier vol xxiv. p 17. Neither does Sismondi make the real motives sufficiently clear.

† Notices from the Austrian Archives in Hormayr's Archiv for the year 1810. No 6.

‡ Herbert Records, p 119. According to the extracts in Hormayr (p. 27) the matter was not officially announced to the English court before the 1st June 1523, and, if I am not mistaken, it was to this that Wolsey's undated letter among the State Papers refers (No 73 p. 149). For what else can the "mervailous fordell" mean, the like of which was not to be expected "for the atteyning of Fraunce?" The league was signed the beginning of August (letter of De Praet dated 9th August. Ibid.) It were much to be wished that the authentic instrument itself could be produced. The letters of Wolsey to the English envoys in Spain, Sampson and Jerningham in Fiddes' Collection, appended to his Life of Wolsey, No 69 and 70, give in greater detail, the plans of that period. The precise terms of the treaty I have, however, sought there in vain.

§ Bellay Memoires i p 294. Petri Martyris Epp No 790, who thinks that attempts were made to bribe the German commanders.

‖ More to Wolsey 20th Sept. St P p. 139. "The duke adviseth that the Kinges army shall in the marching proclayme libertie, sparing the cuntre fro burning and spoile. The king thought that they would soon exclaim, 'Home! home!' if they should also forbere the profite of the spoile."

sage of the Tessino, or to meet it in the open country. Prospero Colonna was compelled to confine himself to the defence of the four most important fortified towns—Como, Cremona, Milan and Pavia.

Fortunately he had now nothing to fear from the Italian states usually in alliance with France. Immediately before the arrival of the French army, the emperor had concluded an anti-French alliance with the Italian powers. It was of great advantage to him that his old preceptor, Adrian, now filled the papal chair; and as he entirely disclaimed all the plans of conquest of his predecessors—for example, the designs upon Ferrara—the emperor on his side renounced all views on Venice: the Venetians entered into alliance with the emperor, the pope and the king of England,* and promised to protect Sforza in his duchy.

Every thing now depended on the Milanese, and it was deemed expedient, as the French were advancing, to learn their dispositions. They again declared their entire devotion to the duke and the empire. At the first sound of the bells on the 22d of September, they flocked in as great numbers as ever to the appointed place of meeting, most of them in full armour, many who had come in haste, unarmed.† The duke rode among the assembled crowd. He told them he would govern them with the mildness and magnanimity of his forefathers, and they, on their side, declared their willingness to defend his cause. The aged Prospero Colonna was a man exactly formed to keep alive these sentiments. He enjoyed the reputation of being equally zealous for the happiness of his country, and for the power and glory of the empire. Amidst the horrors and calamities of war, he had ever appeared in the character of protector of the citizen and the peasant. Now, too, he was intent upon the common good. There had been time to lay in abundant stores for the winter, handmills and windmills had been erected within the walls, and there was wine in profusion. The fortifications, spite of the great circumference of the city, were in admirable order. Sorties were daily made, and rarely without the capture of prisoners; the people were grown so daring that they often begged for leave to go out in a mass to attack the French.‡

Even independently of these adverse circumstances, Bonnivet saw himself compelled by frost and snow to raise the siege, and already other and far more formidable forces were gathering around him.

By degrees the newly recruited Italian infantry arrived, Lannoy, the Viceroy of Naples, brought up light and heavy cavalry, the Venetians appeared in the field. but the most important reinforcement consisted of 7000 landsknechts, whom the Archduke Ferdinand§ had taken infinite pains to get together under Ludwig von Lodron and Eitelfritz von Zollern. George Frundsberg had remained at home, but had sent his son Caspar in his place. Some enterprising chiefs like Schartlin von Burtenbach, came at their own charges. The Marquis of Pescara, too, who commanded the Spanish infantry with the same singular and instinctive talent as Frundsberg the German, came again. Fortunately, he arrived just at the moment of Prospero's death, in consequence of which the conduct of things devolved mainly upon him.

If, however, the imperial army was once more in a condition to meet the enemy in the field, it had not a moment to lose; since he too expected reinforcements which would restore to him his former superiority. The king had concluded a new treaty with the Grisons; the Bernese aided him with money, and considerable bodies of men were on their way from both countries.

Nevertheless, the imperialists and their allies did not yet deem it expedient to venture on a battle, the Venetian Provveditore was especially opposed to it. "I do not believe, however," said the general-in-chief of the Venetians, the Duke of Urbino, to the Provveditore, Pier de cha Pesaro, "I do not believe that the republic maintains so many caparisoned horses, so large a body of infantry, and all these arms which glitter around us, for any other reason than to do battle when it is needful." "My lord," replied the Provveditore, "what advantage would it be to the republic if we fought? A defeat would endanger all her possessions; victory cannot escape us if we do not fight. Were the emperor here in person, he would not give battle." This opinion, which convinced the general, prevailed in every council of war from that time. It was agreed not to attempt to overcome the enemy by open attack, but by strategy.

While one division of the army posted itself in the territory of Como and Bergamo to keep off the Grison troops, the main force, accompanied by Bourbon, who was now invested with the rank of Lieutenant of the empire, crossed the Tessino near Pavia, and, by an unexpected attack, took the fortress of Garlasco which commanded all the surrounding country. This compelled Bonnivet to retreat across the Tessino, and to abandon his strong encampment of Abbiate-Grasso, that he might at least defend Vigevene, and the fertile plains of the Lomellino, whence he drew his provisions.‖

* We see in Paruta, p 217, that regard to England on commercial grounds had considerable effect here. Wolsey said plainly to his master that the treaty had come to pass, "by your mediacion and moost for your sake."—State Papers, No 66.

† Lettera di Milano, narra quelli successi de dì 16 Stt a dì 22. Sanuto's Chronicle, vol xxxv.

‡ Lettera di Grotiani, 21 Ott in Sanuto. "Tanto stimano Francesi e Sguizari come se fussero tante puttane." As to the mention of scarcity in Milan alluded to, this could only refer to the first days, before every thing was fully arranged. See Gal Capella and Carpesanus, p 1356.

§ For this the emperor afterwards thanked him. Letter in Bucholtz, ii p 264.

‖ Galeazzo Capella, lib. iii p 191, from whom most other writers have drawn their information. Even Du Bellay's is only a version of Capella's text, with some French additions. Anshelm introduces some particulars about the Swiss, and Sandoval some, but very few, about the Spaniards. In other respects they both merely translate him. It is a great pity that no one who knew the deeds of the Landsknechts took the trouble of supplying the deficiencies in his narrative. Hence we know no-

The imperialists immediately crossed the Gogna and took Sartirana. Whilst Bonnivet, menaced in his new position, as he had been in his former one, prepared to drive them thence, they got possession of Vercelli, by the favour of the Ghibelline faction of the town, and by that means obtained a footing on the other side the Sesia, so as to cut off the admiral from the base of his operations He had now nothing left but to retreat to the Upper Sesia, towards Gattinara, where a new body of Swiss were just arrived from Ivrea. He still did not relinquish the hope, with this reinforcement, of turning round upon the enemy and once more offering him battle But even on his road he found the smaller places occupied by the imperialists When he reached the banks of the Sesia, the Swiss refused to cross to him, and he was obliged to take measures for transporting his troops over the river While thus engaged, he was attacked by Pescara; universal confusion ensued; the bridge broke down; Gattinara was in flames, and, insignificant as was the number of the imperialists on the other side the river (about a thousand light horse and the same number of foot), the loss of the French was immense, nothing remained for them but once more to abandon Italy. It was evident that the mode of warfare by which they had, within the last thirty years, obtained such brilliant triumphs in Italy, was no longer available. Single deeds of arms, momentary advantages, chivalrous bravery, no longer decided the fortune of a war. The awakened national antipathy rendered a more obstinate and regular system of defence possible in the field, the calculations of strategy and the skilful use of the arquebuss carried all before them. In this retreat fell, among other distinguished men, the good knight—the knight without fear and without reproach—Bayard, who united in his own person all the fair and glorious qualities of knighthood, and presented them, for the last time, to the admiration of friend and foe. He had always hated the arquebusiers with all his heart, and reluctantly granted quarter to one who fell into his hands he was doomed to receive his death from a bullet.* There is something at once symbolical, and ominous of universal change in this death, which has been dwelt on emphatically by so many historians, and, indeed, in the defeat of this chivalrous army altogether. Like the fall of Sickingen, they were expressions of a great revolution in human affairs. The coat of mail was conquered by the musket, and the massive wall of the castle fell prostrate before the cannon.

The landsknechts took a very active part in the pursuit Sebastian Schartlin relates that for three days and three nights they followed the enemy to the foot of St Bernard; they dragged the cannon they had taken, crowned with garlands, from the valley of Aosta to the camp. All the places which the French still possessed in Italy immediately surrendered; their defeat was as complete as it was possible to imagine

As a sort of necessary consequence, the thought immediately arose in the minds of the conquerors, that the attack on France, which had failed a year ago, might now be attempted with greater prudence and success Bourbon found the imperial army in admirable order, while his bravery excited their respect and confidence

The state of Italy, too, seemed to render aggressive measures necessary Either peace must be obtained (of which there seemed little prospect),† or employment must be found for the King of France. Lannoy wrote to the emperor, that the Duke of Milan would be a costly bargain to him, if he could not succeed in clipping the wings of his restless neighbour. The emperor reflected that it would be better to seek the enemy in his own country than to await him in Italy, where the army must be kept together at great expense, and gave his consent

On this occasion, as formerly, the idea of attacking France at various points was entertained, but after the experience of the former year, was quickly abandoned. None of the parties concerned had money enough They esteemed themselves fortunate if they could raise sufficient funds to keep the army of Italy quiet for a few months Bourbon hoped to accomplish the most brilliant achievements with this alone.

"Your affairs, sire," says he, in a letter to the emperor, "will prosper If we are able to give battle to the King of France, and win it, as I hope, you will be the greatest man that ever lived, and will give laws to the world"‡

In July, 1524, Bourbon therefore led the imperial army, 5000 Germans under Zollern and Lodron, 3000 Spaniards under Pescara, and a number of Italians, from Italy into France. Francis had no inclination to meet these warlike and victorious bands in the open field. Bourbon met with no resistance, invested Antibes, Frejus, Hières, and Toulon, and caused them to do homage to him He bore the title of Count of Provence, but had taken the oath of vassalage to the King of England.§ On

thing more of them in this campaign than what we gather from the life of Sebastian Schartlin

* I will not dwell long on the circumstances attending his death, the rather because they appear to me doubtful The French (Bellay, 342) relate that Bourbon spoke to him during his last moments, and that Bayard reproached him with his treason It is remarkable that we find nothing of this in the life of Bayard, Coll Univ xv p. 412 But in Italy exactly the reverse was related,—that he died lamenting the injustice of the king and the disorders prevailing in the French government Carpesanus, p 1375 "Questus de injusta in Borbonium ira, de fortuna et male animatorum hominum factione cuncta in Gallia permiscente" His feelings may have vibrated between the two sentiments here expressed, and both may be true Lastly, the Spaniards make him praise God that he died, "en servicio de su rey y a manos de la mejor nacion del mundo."—*Batalla de Pabia MS Alb.*

† The Instruction secrète &c., in Bucholtz, ii p 503 cannot deceive us on this point The multitude of suggestions—and there are no less than nine—shows how impracticable each was Peter Martyr observes this very justly in his Epp 798, p 472, July, 1524, 'Temperate hujus tam incompositi psalterii chordas Dira ferri acies et humano cruore fluentes rivi has diriment querelas"

‡ Extract in Bucholtz, ii p 263

§ Guicciardini says indeed (xiv p 448) "Borbone constantemente ricusò di riconoscere il re d'Inghilterra" It

the 9th of August, he took Aix, the chief town of the province, and on the 19th arrived before Marseilles, well knowing that all his other successes were useless if he did not obtain possession of that fortified city. He felt of what incalculable value it would be to the emperor to command a harbour of such importance between Barcelona and Genoa. Marseilles would form the true defence of Italy, and an incomparable basis for all future operations against France. Beaurain had entertained the design of putting Toulon in a state of defence for the emperor, but he was utterly without the means* These things increased the ardour with which the army engaged in the siege of Marseilles.

Now, however, it became evident how greatly times had altered in France. Italians who knew the country, such as Ludovico Canossa, Bishop of Bayeux, had always predicted this change † Spite of the many causes of discontent afforded by the king, it yet appeared that he was the object of general adoration. On the other hand, Bourbon had lost all credit by his treason. It must be considered that Bourbon's influence, powerful as he was, had not been of sufficient duration to acquire much strength in most of his possessions he was a new master, nor was there any man of importance so independent of the crown as to venture to embrace his cause. This conjuncture suffices to prove to what an extent the consolidation of France had been silently advancing to its completion. Not alone did no one rise in Bourbon's favour, but the attack secured to the king more implicit obedience and more cordial loyalty than had been yielded him before He was able to levy three extremely heavy taxes, amounting in all to five millions, one after the other. The clergy consented to raise contributions, the good cities granted voluntary aids, even the nobility was fain to submit to forced loans What could the tardy and doubtful payments, laboriously obtained from Spain or from England, effect against such abundant pecuniary resources?‡ Francis brought an army into the field which might vie with any former one in magnificence; two thousand men-at-arms, seven thousand French infantry, principally composed of the warlike peasantry of Dauphiné, and six thousand Swiss In the present low state of the German government, he had even found no difficulty in tempting a body of landsknechts to enter his service, by the offer of high pay.

While these troops assembled in the country round Avignon, the imperialists carried on the siege of Marseilles with great pertinacity, they brought up the cannon fit for service, which they had found in the places they had taken from the French, they excavated mines with immense difficulty, and erected a battery from which they made breaches in the walls Pescara was conspicuous above all in the skirmishes, in his singular dress. He wore a red vest and hose, over which was a short black coat without sleeves, and a hat like those of the landsknechts, but with large waving plumes. The eyes of the men followed him like a banner. His nephew Guasto vied with him in enterprising valour The army was in the highest spirits up to the middle of September, on the 21st they intended to storm the city. Pescara drank to his Spaniards, and put them in good humour; Bourbon promised royal gratitude, the soldiers prepared themselves for the last extremities by confession. On the other hand, the garrison, commanded by Renzo da Ceri, an Italian of the Orsini faction, was undaunted, and had put the city in an excellent state of defence. At the first preliminary attempts, the imperialists saw with whom they had to deal. They learned from their prisoners that mines filled with powder were dug behind the breaches, cannon planted at the corners of streets, and the troops posted at all the most exposed points, armed and ready for action § Suddenly Pescara changed his mind "He who has a mind to eat his supper in hell," said he, "may storm the city" A council of war was called, in which not only the probability of a defeat before Marseilles, but even the danger to Italy of a longer delay, were weighed and discussed. The suspicion began to be entertained that the king might, without troubling himself about Marseilles, march directly upon Italy. "Sirs," exclaimed Pescara, "let him who would preserve Italy to the emperor follow me." Bourbon reluctantly abandoned the hope of once more gaining a footing in his own country, but the German leaders, Zollern and Lodron, sided with Pescara. On the 28th of September the siege was raised.

We shall not attempt to decide whether the king really entertained the design attributed to him: thus much at least is certain, — that as soon as he heard of Bourbon's retreat, he seized on this idea with the greatest eagerness, and, in defiance of any representations, determined to lead the noble army he again beheld around him, across the Alps without delay He was determined to strain every nerve for the reconquest of Milan. On the sleeves of

is nevertheless not the less certain that he did take the oaths, as is stated by Herbert (p 133) and as we learn beyond a doubt from a letter of De Praet in Hormayr (p 27) The King of England was besides fully in the secret of the undertaking Richard Pace told the Venetian Suriano, that his monarch had empowered him, by a letter of the 28th June to strengthen Bourbon in his intentions, indeed, that Cardinal Wolsey had offered on the 28th Sept to cause a landing to be attempted if that might be of any assistance. Pace excuses himself for not accurately stating the amount of the succours, on the ground that the emperor had not always done so In the mean while we know that John Russell brought 20,000*l* into the camp before Marseilles That Pace went very honestly to work, is evident from this, that, spite of all appearances he expressed a certain suspicion of the good intentions of the Cardinal, who, he said, was a bad man — "attenta la pessima natura del ditto Cardenal" Whatever may be the case, it is certain that the result of the expedition was anxiously expected in England Bourbon acknowledged no other king than Henry VIII

* The letter in Hormayr He imagines that he could accomplish this with 10,000 ducats

† *E g.* Lettere di Principi, i 132 "E siate certo che Francesi adorano il loro re, e non vi fondate nelle ribellioni altre volte seguite in Francia, perche non vi sono più di quei tali principii che le causavano"

‡ Garnier, p 102. Sismondi, xvi

§ Sandoval, lib xi p i p 598. In this place a mere literal repetition of an old narrative entitled La Batalla de Pabia, by which Sandoval must be here and there corrected, as, for example, for Pisarmo, read *Pisaño*

his body-guard were embroidered the words, "Once more, and no more"*

The two armies rivalled each other in the rapidity with which they crossed the Alps. The imperialists marched as light as possible. They took only a part of their cannon, which they dismounted and placed on mules, the rest were buried or sent to Toulon. They advanced in two columns, but along the same road, so that the first always left their quarters before the other arrived. One day a few of the Germans got drunk and could not march. Pescara set fire to the house in which they lay, without pity, and burned them in it, he would not leave one man in the hands of the peasants, whose vengeance he feared to irritate. Thus they passed Nice, Ventimiglia, and the Maritime Alps, considerably reduced in external appearance, but not dispirited: they had suffered no defeat. they were followed by a long baggage-train, consisting of all the spoils of the wars of preceding years.

Meanwhile, Francis I. marched at the head of his fresh and brilliant army across the Upper Alps, Briançon, Pignerol, &c, and so, without halting, to the plains of Lombardy. He hoped still to be beforehand with the imperial army.

A Milanese chronicle affirms that the two armies crossed the Tessino on the same day, the French at Abbiate Grasso, the imperialists in the neighbourhood of Pavia.†

Be that as it may, the imperialists were at a great disadvantage. They could not take possession of Milan, where the plague had broken out. Francesco Sforza said he was not a bird to let himself be shut up in that cage. They left a garrison in the castle only, the other troops were divided between Pavia, Lodi, and Cremona. The powerful body of troops which a few months before appeared about to make the emperor lord of the world, had suddenly vanished from the field. Maestro Pasquino published an advertisement at Rome, setting forth that an imperial army was lost in the Alps; the honest finder was requested to bring it to the owner, and a handsome reward offered. The French were undisputed masters of the country. They prepared to conquer the fortified towns, and in the first place, Pavia. The attack on France, which was to banish Francis to the other side of the Alps, had only served to knit together all the energies of his kingdom, and to secure to him the ascendancy in Upper Italy.

BATTLE OF PAVIA.

The affairs of the emperor were not, however, in so desperate a condition as they appeared to be. He had now, as before, Germans in his service, and could without difficulty procure more.

In forming the design of laying immediate siege to Pavia, Francis I. was actuated by the hope that he should be able to seduce the Germans who formed the garrison to desert to his side. But he was destined to become better acquainted with their character. The two colonels, Zollern and Lodron, were under manifold obligations to the House of Austria, and even the captains had passed a considerable time under the imperial banner. I shall not attempt to say what course they would have pursued had they now had to take service for the first time, but it is certain that not one of them was disposed to abandon the cause which he had espoused.‡ Nor was the Ghibelline city of Pavia at all the place to suggest thoughts of such a kind. There, women of high rank might be seen taking a part in the labours on the fortifications; the wealthiest citizen, Matteo Beccaria, had raised a company at his own cost, and of his own retainers; when scarcity began already to be felt elsewhere, he gave the officers a splendid feast, and even the common soldiers never wanted "white bread and cool wine." Antonio Leiva, the imperial commander, in praising the young Caspar Frundsberg, who had now risen to the rank of captain, says that he had kept him himself in good spirits. Antonia Leiva, too, was exactly fitted for emergencies of this kind; equally prudent and resolute, devoted to the emperor's cause, and capable of any sacrifice; he took the gold chain from his own neck and gave it to be coined into ducats. The Germans derived great advantage from their skill as miners,§ while the river opposed an insuperable obstacle to the king, the attempt to turn the course of the Tessino having totally failed, as might indeed have been expected. In short, in January, 1525, he found that he could do no more than surround the town, with a view to starve it into submission.‖ He despatched some thousand men under the Duke of Albania with orders to attempt a diversion in central or lower Italy.

Meanwhile fresh troops descended the Alps from Germany. Bourbon had sold the jewels which he had saved in his flight, and had then gone to Insbruck and to Augsburg. Supported by Archduke Ferdinand, he now brought eighteen companies of landsknechts under Marx Sittich of Ems over the mountains. Count Nicholas of Salm accompanied them with two hundred horses of the retainers of the court. At the same time the viceroy of Naples sold every thing for which he could find a purchaser,

* Carpesanus, lib x in Martene, v p 1379

† Martino Verri, in P. Verri, iii p 241

‡ Sandoval, indeed, mentions that Zollern had meditated treason and had been therefore poisoned at a feast. This is also alluded to by G Capella, yet with the addition, "multi existimavere" which has also been repeated by others, with more or less qualification. According to the account of Tægius, physician and knight, who remained in Pavia during the siege (De Obsidione Urbis Ticinensis ed Pez, p 9) Zollern died "post longas vigilias et assiduos labores ex tabida febre xvi Cal Febr" It was said in Pavia that he was related to the imperial family ... aliquali affinitate cum Cæsare conjunctus" He is celebrated in the songs of the time as the person who took the most active part in the defence of the town

§ Carpesanus ascribes the destruction of a bridge, "Germanis ingeniosis viris" Tægius gives high praise on this account to Glurns, who "instrumentis ferreis mirabili arte in medio rescindit" this same bridge

‖ Lettera di Pavia, 10 Genn Chr Ven MS It was understood, 'che il re Xmo avea deliberato di non voler più dar battaglia a Pavia per non far morir gente, ma volea tener quella assediata et in simil modo averla."

and sent a messenger with the money directly to George Frundsberg, who regarded the emperor's Italian power (which he himself had helped to establish) with the most intense interest, and who had a yet stronger motive in the thought that it was his own son whom he was going to relieve The day after Christmas he mustered eleven companies at Meran he was surrounded by twenty-five distinguished captains and brother-soldiers of good family,—younger sons, or gentlemen without inheritance, followed by a retinue of peasants' sons, who, like themselves, could find no employment at home On the 21st of January, the two divisions joined the Italian army at Lodi.*

They saw the necessity of taking the field immediately. In spite of all the exertions that had been made, there was not money enough forthcoming to keep the troops quiet for any considerable time. Most of them had received nothing but their marching money, and had only engaged to serve for a certain fixed period without pay. Pavia, too, must be relieved On the 4th of February, the army arrived in the neighbourhood of that city, threw into it a few troops with munitions of war, and did every thing they could to provoke the king to quit his strong encampment.

These efforts were, however, vain The king would not abandon the strong position he had taken up in the park near Pavia. it was well fortified,† the army was in comfortable quarters, and abundantly supplied with provisions. He thought it more advantageous to wait for an attack, as at Marignano, than to make it, which had proved so disastrous to his army at Bicocca.

On the other hand the imperialists were forced by want, both of money and provisions, to resolve on attacking ‡ They thought it as disgraceful to disperse in sight of the enemy, as to suffer a defeat. "God grant me a hundred years' war, and not one battle," said Pescara; "but now there is no escape" He went into the midst of his Spaniards, and represented to them that they had not a foot of land they could call their own, nor a bit of bread for the morrow, "but there, before you," added he, "is the camp, where there is bread in plenty, and meat and wine and carp from the Lago di Garda. We must have it, we must drive out the enemy; we will make St Matthew's day memorable." Already had George Frunsdberg addressed his Germans in a similar strain With uplifted hands they had promised him to do their best against their splendid foe, and to succour their brethren in Pavia

This was not likely to be one of those brilliant battles in which two chivalrous armies were wont to contend for the prize of honour, a needy band of mercenaries, urged by hunger and privation, and counting the days of the service they had contracted for, must be led on to the assault, or they would disperse. Their objects were, to plunder the rich camp of the enemy, to relieve their brothers in arms, and once for all to secure the possession of the often conquered land. Circumstances were most unfavourable to them "Either," writes Pescara to the emperor, "your majesty must gain the desired victory, or we shall fulfil by our death the duty of serving you"

Pescara's plan was to surprise the enemy by night. In the middle of the park was the farm of Mirabella, where the market of the camp was commonly held; and a part of the cavalry was posted at this point. He wished, if possible, to effect a junction with the garrison of Pavia About midnight they began to pull down the walls of the park. Two thousand Germans of the regiments of Frundsberg and of Ems, and a thousand Spaniards, with linen shirts over their coats of mail, were to fall on the camp But the walls were stronger than they thought, it was daylight before they had made breaches sufficiently large to pass through When, at length—on the morning of the 24th of February—the troops pressed through, the French were fully prepared, and in motion.§ One point was gained,—namely, that they left their strong position and came out into the open ground on the heath; but the imperial army itself incurred the greatest danger. The division of the landsknechts, as they were marching up, were within range of the very superior artillery of the French, and suffered great loss; the light cavalry, too, were in disorder King Francis, who rushed into the thick of the fight at this point and killed a brave knight with his own hand, was delighted when he saw some companies broken and fleeing before him. "To-day," said he to his companion, reining up his horse to let him recover breath, "I call myself Lord of Milan."‖ His army advanced in the best order, the artillery keeping up an uninterrupted fire.

But the moment which seemed that of victory, was, in fact, but the beginning of the battle Pescara had rallied round him the three thousand men, who were now unable to effect any thing, in consequence of the non-appearance of their friends from Pavia; and they were gradually joined by the two large bodies under the command of George Frundsberg, and Marx Sittich of Ems. Frundsberg, with his companions, the Counts of Ortenburg, Hag, Virneburg, and the Lords of Losenstein and Fleckenstein, and by his side Marx Sittich, now formed the left wing,¶ Pescara, with his

* Reissner, Historia Herrn Georgen und Herrn Casparn von Frundsberg, p 18. See G Barthold's Frundsberg

† Extrait des lettres écrites en Allemand a Monseigneur l'Archiduc Ferdinand par Messire George de Fronsberg Urkundenbuch zu Buckholtz, Ferdinand, i p 1

‡ In an anonymous account of that time, Lettere di Principi, i p 153 and from thence transferred by Sismondi to his Hist de France, xvi p 232, it is said indeed, that, two days before the battle, 150 000 scudi reached the camp from Spain this, however, must be a false statement In Pescara's despatch it is expressly said, "De ningumo canto nostra necessidad tenia rimedio" He had foreseen "que deshazer el exercito a lavio del enemigo era tan mal como perdillo con batalia"

§ "Epitre du Roy traitant de son partement de France et de sa prise devant Pavie," in Lenglet and Gobel, p 30

"Au matin ils feirent leur entrée
Et nous aussi estions ja en bataille"

‖ Lettera di Paulo Luzasco al Sr Marchese di Mantua, according to a statement of the king himself, in the Appendix

¶ "This appears from the despatch of Frundsberg,—

Spaniards and two thousand Germans, the right. The cavalry near him had also recovered its order. As it was manifestly no match for the French, Pescara and Frundsberg ordered fifteen hundred arquebusiers to support it. The viceroy, who had always been of opinion that they might entrench themselves opposite to the enemy in the park, now clearly perceived that this was impossible. "There is no help but in God's mercy," said he: "Sirs, do as I do;" so saying, and crossing himself, he put spurs to his horse and charged the enemy.

The mélée thus began on the right wing, where a part of the French men-at-arms, the king at their head, fought with the Spanish-Italian horse, and Salm's reiters; in the centre, but somewhat further off, other French horsemen under Alençon advanced with twenty-eight companies of Swiss: against Pescara and Guasto with their Spaniards and Germans, the black companies (as the Germans from Gueldres and Lorraine in the king's service were called), admirably supported by artillery, moved upon the left wing of the imperialists, consisting of the two great bodies of landsknechts.

On this point the first decisive stroke was struck. The Germans in the service of France, and the imperialists, were those between whom the bitterest and most determined hatred prevailed. An Augsburger, named Hans Langenmantel, stepped from the ranks of the former, and challenged the two German colonels to single combat. But he was held unworthy to do battle with them, in consequence of his having taken service under the French, and was instantly felled to the ground and killed. A landsknecht held up his hand, severed from the body and covered with rings of gold, as a trophy. Upon this the combat became furious. Marx Sittich, by a rapid evolution, threw himself on the flank of the black companies.* They made a most gallant defence, and were killed almost to a man. Their cannon fell into the hands of the imperialists.

Meanwhile the centre had advanced. Already the arquebusiers had made a fearful impression on the men-at-arms, for no armour was stout enough to resist the fire of their matchlocks, when Pescara, at the head of his Spanish veterans, attacked the Swiss.† The fight now became general; the fury of the attack, the effect of the fire-arms on the cavalry, the sight of the defeat of the black companies, and the rush of the victorious squadron of the imperial Germans, threw the French centre into confusion. Alençon was the first of the men-at-arms who took to flight; a part of the Swiss were hurried along with him; a part had their ranks broken: at this moment the garrison of Pavia appeared in the rear of the disordered French troops, and a universal flight followed.

The gallant king was spurring his charger along the right wing, under a heavy fire from the arquebusiers, when he looked round and saw his people in full retreat. "My God, what is this?" exclaimed he. He thought, at least, to rally the Swiss, and hastened after them. But the decided superiority of the enemy rendered this impossible. Even he himself was borne along with the retreating torrent. He wore on his arm an embroidered scarf, given to him in happier days in France by the lady of his love, to whom, in return, he had vowed never, under any circumstances, to give way before the enemy.‡ True knight as he was, he retreated as slowly as possible, and not without continually facing round in an attitude of defence; he was now overtaken by the pursuing Germans. Nicholas von Salm stabbed his horse under him; the king fell, and was compelled to surrender. At this moment the viceroy came up, reached out his hand to him respectfully, and took him prisoner.

Within an hour and a half, the most magnificent army that the world could then behold was annihilated. It was calculated that ten thousand men were left dead on the field, or drowned in the waters of the Tessino: among them many Swiss, the ancient fame of whose arms, established in the Burgundian wars, was now obscured for ever. The leaders of the French, with few exceptions, were killed or taken prisoners: above all, their puissant monarch had fallen into the hands of the enemy. Never was a victory more complete and triumphant.§

The victors seized on the plunder of the camp, to satisfy their most pressing wants. They were at length lords and masters in the

"Moy et ma bande tirasmes à la main senestre vers le dite Marchsith contre les dits François." There is also to be found the number of arquebusiers, who were generally supposed to amount to 500. Tægius mentions as many, but it may have been only the Spaniards. That the landsknechts were armed with arquebusses is proved, among other things, by the line of the song—"Fire into them, you good landsknechts" ("Schiesst Drein, schiesst Drein, ihr frumme Landsknecht.")—*Soltau*, p. 250.

* "Ein schöns neüwes Lied von der Schlacht newlich vor Pavia geschechen."—"A beautiful new song of the battle lately fought before Pavia," by no means poetical, but very accurate, which is proved by its accordance with Frundsberg's despatch: "Da das ersachen die Lanntzknecht, bey dem Frantzosen, mer kendt rechtt, zugendt vnns vnnder augen, Herr Jörgen Hauff gryffen sie an, vnnd thätten in nitt fragenn. Da dz ersach Herr Marxen hauff an disem orth, gryffen sie drauff gar tapfferlich durchtrungen."—"When the landsknechts perceived this among the French, taking good note and marching past us, the Lord George's troop attacked them without asking their leave. When the Lord Marx's troop saw this at this place, they attacked right bravely, and forced their way through."

† His own despatch, agreeing with the statement of the king in Luzazio. When he says that he sent Guasto with the Germans against the king's landsknechts, it is only to be understood that Guasto had a share in Sittich's onslaught. The German accounts prove that he and Frundsberg contributed greatly to the success of this attack.

‡ "L'heureux présent, par lequel te promys
point ne fuir devant mes ennemys.—
Epitre du Roi."

§ In this account of the battle, I have not thought myself bound to adhere exclusively to the earlier historians, such as Capella, Guicciardini, Jovius, and Bellay. I have also avoided all that Reissner has borrowed from Jovius, as we are now enabled to draw more authentic information from the despatches of the commanders themselves: 1. those of Frundsberg in Bucholtz, identical with an old German edition. "Wahrlicher Bericht, &c. ("True Account," &c.) which, however, I never saw: 2. those of Pescara in the Appendix: 3. those of Francis I. in the letters of Luzasco in the Appendix and in the Epitre. Besides these, there exists a detailed Spanish account, which has been used by Sandoval, and which contains some remarkable passages. The song before quoted, which I intend to print in the Appendix, is a bulletin in verse, and therefore worthy of credit.

state of Milan, and had no fresh attack to fear. The Italian powers who, so long as things were in suspense, maintained a very doubtful attitude, now called to mind their old engagements, and consented to pay up the arrears of subsidies they had promised, so that the army at last gradually received its well-earned pay.

But the fears of some, the hopes of others, and the attention of all, were now turned upon the young emperor, for whom this victory had been won; while he, in tranquil retirement in Castile, had been slowly recovering from the quartan ague which had long tormented him.

Charles V was standing in a room of the palace in Madrid, talking of the state of things in Italy, and of the situation of his army, which he still felt to be very dangerous, when a courier from that army arrived. Without announcing to any one the tidings with which he was charged, he walked in he chose to deliver them first to the emperor in person "Sire," said he, "there has been a battle before Pavia. Your Majesty's troops have gained the victory the French army is destroyed, the king himself is a prisoner, and in your majesty's power." Great and unexpected good fortune has at the moment the same effect as a sudden calamity. While Charles listened to these words, the blood seemed congealed in his veins, and for a few moments he did not speak. When at length he found utterance, he only repeated, "The King of France is in my power—the victory is mine!" Hereupon he retired into the adjoining chamber, where his bed stood, and kneeling down before an image of the Holy Virgin, tried to raise his thoughts to God and to the greatness of his vocation. He caused processions to be made and prayers to be offered up, that God would be pleased to grant him still higher favour in the war he meditated with the infidels He spoke of an expedition against Constantinople and Jerusalem *

Projects of this kind, however, were yet at a vast distance. The immediate concern was to improve the present moment.

The first idea which presented itself was, that the great victory could in no way be turned to so much advantage as by a renewal of the so-often-attempted invasion of France.

The Duke of Bourbon began immediately to make preparations for carrying this into execution

The King of England was urgent in his persuasions to the same effect. The instructions drawn up by Henry VIII, for an embassy which he sent to the emperor in consequence of the battle of Pavia, are extremely curious, and show how far that monarch's views extended He expresses his opinion that the King of France should, under no conditions, be reinstated on the throne,—there are none, he says, that Francis will observe he requires that he should be absolutely deprived of the crown. With regard to a successor, there can, he says, be no question as to Bourbon, who could neither plead any defensible claim, nor afford the emperor any satisfactory guarantee, on the other hand, the King of England had the best and most incontestable right to the French crown,—a right, indeed, already recognised by the emperor. In the course of the next summer, Charles might attack France in person from the side of Spain, while he would do the same from that of England he would assist him with large subsidies, no formidable resistance was now to be feared, and he hoped to meet his imperial majesty in Paris. If he were once crowned in that city, he would accompany the emperor to Rome to be present at his coronation. All that had been wrested from the House of Burgundy or the empire should be restored to him, nay, even eventually France and England itself, if, in conformity with the existing treaties, he married the youthful Princess Mary At first he had affected to raise difficulties on this head, but in the end he consented to give his daughter, who was yet a child, into the guardianship of the emperor till she should be of age to marry.†

From time to time, projects like this are revived in Europe,—either of the universal dominion of a single nation, or of a partition of power between two preponderant states, but though at a distance they seem to threaten universal convulsion, they are invariably wrecked against the massive strength of existing institutions

Young as the emperor was, he was of far too sedate a character to be carried away by such extravagant propositions. Nor had England by any means afforded him such a degree of assistance in the war, as would have warranted her claiming so large a share of the fruits of victory. The secret negotiations which the cardinal had carried on with France were well known in Spain.

Chancellor Gattinara advised the emperor to answer, that it would be unseemly to make war upon an enemy who could not defend himself; and that neither did the interests of peace require any such proceeding. He thought that if the King of England resolved to try his fortune, the best way to thwart his schemes was to send him no assistance. He esteemed a union of France and England in the highest degree dangerous to the empire and to Europe· his idea was to maintain the independence of the throne of France, but at the same time to establish for ever the supremacy of Austria A project drawn up by his hand, which is to be found in the Austrian Archives,‡ goes directly

* Letter of the Mantuan envoy Suardin to the Margrave of Mantua, 15th March, 1526 Sanuto, vol xxxviii.

† Fiddes in his Life of Wolsey, 346—352, quotes at length the instruction to Tunstall and Wingfield. Herbert, p 168, gives a very imperfect notice of it Robertson vol iv, who had only read Herbert and not Fiddes, treats it all as a sort of pretext But it is only necessary to read Wolsey's letter to the king, dated 12th Feb, 1525 (State Papers, p 158,) where he already reckons on victory, to be convinced that people promised themselves honour and advantage from this course "The matters succeeding to the advantage of the imperiallis, the thanke, laude, and praise shal comme unto Your Grace" It is impossible, however, to agree with Fiddes, who denies that any arrangement with France had been already entered into The same letter throws light upon this If France were victorious, Wolsey says he had provided against that event "by such communications as be set furth with France aparte"

‡ In Bucholtz, ii p 260 To the same intent are the demands which occur in a letter of the emperor to the king's mother Papiers d'état de Granvelle, i p. 264

to the same decisive object which he already contemplated in the year 1521. The king was to renounce all his claims on Italy, both on Milan and Naples, further, to restore Burgundy to the house to which it appertained; and, lastly, to acknowledge the rights of the empire over the south of France To Provence he made a direct claim, as "an appurtenance of the empire" the emperor's intention was to grant this in fee to the Duke of Bourbon Dauphiné, too, might be demanded back, because the renewal of the investiture had so long been neglected; but the emperor was disposed to leave this to the successor to the throne of France, provided always that he married a princess of the house of Austria. If Francis I. accepted these conditions, he would certainly be too much sunk and enfeebled to be an object of dread. The emperor's supremacy would then be established on an immutable basis he would have no rival remaining who could attempt to measure himself against him A feeling pervaded the whole West, that the emperor was the predestined ruler of Europe A Neapolitan description of the battle of Pavia concludes with the words, "Thou hast placed the world under his feet" "Now," said Wolsey, to one of Charles's ambassadors, "your master will be emperor no longer in title, but in fact also" "The counsels of God," exclaims a minister of the pope, "are a deep abyss."

Such a prospect was not, however, welcome to all. No man had ever yet assumed a station of this kind in Europe without exciting the animosity and the resistance of all that had a feeling of independence The King of England was, of course, offended by the emperor's refusal to accede to his proposals, and every moment increased the coolness between them But this was not all. In another of the emperor's allies—the Papal States—opposition to his schemes arose Indeed, the exclamation of a papal minister which we have just quoted savours more of the terror of one who feels himself menaced, than of the sympathy of an ally For some time past misunderstandings of a very serious nature had arisen between the pope and the emperor They originated, indeed, merely in a question of territory, but soon assumed the character of one of the most important features in the affairs of the times.

MISUNDERSTANDINGS BETWEEN THE POPE AND THE EMPEROR.

When Leo X. concluded his alliance with the emperor, it was, as we have seen, with a view of getting possession of all the countries which were still claimed by the see of Rome, especially Ferrara in this the emperor promised him his assistance.

On the sudden death of Leo, the Duke of Ferrara caused a medal to be struck, with the inscription, "The lamb rescued from the jaws of the lion" But he was not only rescued, he found occasion, during the vacancy of the Holy See, to get possession of Reggio and Rubiera. Over Adrian VI. he gained such an influence, that that pontiff renewed his fief, in spite of these encroachments.

Adrian's successor, however, Clement VII, was of a totally different way of thinking no sooner were the French driven out of Italy in 1524, than he asked the imperialists to assist him against the duke, and, in the first place, to expel the latter from Reggio

This, however, they did not consider themselves bound to do Their thoughts were exclusively bent on the invasion of France, and they wished to excite no troubles in their rear. The viceroy answered, that if the pope loved the emperor, he ought rather to complete his satisfaction by giving him back Modena.*

This suggestion was deeply offensive to the pope If he had not latterly contributed much to the success of the common cause, the share which he had personally taken in the conquest of Milan was still fresh in his memory. Was this now to turn exclusively to the profit of the empire? was the papacy not only not to obtain the extension of territory it desired, but to give up cities it had formerly possessed?

So long as the imperial arms were successful in Provence, Clement was silent, but scarcely could he have received the news of the retreat of Bourbon from Marseilles, than he sent an envoy (the same Geronimo Aleander who is already well known to us) to the King of France,† and as soon as Francis touched the soil of Italy, Giberti, the pope's most confidential minister, who had always been regarded as in the French interest, went to meet him, in order, as his credentials set forth, "to negotiate concerning things and plans which touch the honour and advantage both of the pope and the king"‡ The course and the result of their negotiations are not accurately known, but thus much is certain, that a treaty was agreed on, the basis of which was, that the king should retain possession of Milan In this case the king promised not to demand the restitution of Parma or Piacenza, to import the salt for the consumption of Milan from the papal salt-works (a source of considerable revenue to the apostolic chamber), and to support the pope against his rebellious vassals;—meaning, no doubt, Ferrara § On Giberti's return, people remarked that he never went to the pope without the head-dress which then distinguished the French; the pages of the palace were dressed in the French fashion, and French officers were allowed to recruit in Rome in aid of the Duke of Albania, who had under-

* Giberti agli oratori in Spagna 22 Ott 1524 The duke's retreat, after having made a short advance, was ascribed entirely to the imperialists "Che tal mutatione del duca e determinatione di non rendere è processa del vicere"—*Sanga, 21 Nov Lettere di principi 21 Nov*

† His credentials dated 14th Oct 1524, are to be found in Molini, i 177 "Magnis de rebus christianæque rei publicæ hoc tempore non solum salutaribus sed etiam necessariis"

‡ For Montmorency, dated 30th Oct Ibid p 178 "Mittentes Gibertum ad regem pro rebus ac consiliis utriusque nostrum honorem et commodum spectantibus"

§ The articles of this treaty have never been published in an authentic form, nevertheless the pope communicated them to the Archduke Ferdinand, and in this form Spalatin has preserved them Annales in Mencken Script, ii p 641

taken an expedition against Naples: the Germans at the papal court were persuaded that the pope had even made a grant of Sicily and Naples to the king.*

This was an error it was impossible that the sovereignty of the French in Naples could be agreeable to the pope His view, doubtless, was only to favour a diversion which promised to restore the balance of power in Italy,† but even this design, his whole demeanour, his undeniable defection in the moment of danger, awakened the hostility of the imperial commanders They rejected his offers of mediation with disdain. "He who is not for me," writes the viceroy to him, "is against me." Frundsberg drove a papal agent out of his presence at the point of the sword, and anxiety as to the effect of the papal intrigues certainly hastened on the battle the imperialists threw on the pope the whole blame of the dilatoriness of the Venitians in fulfilling their engagements ‡

This state of things sufficiently explains the painful impression made at Rome by the news of the king's defeat; and indeed Frundsberg actually recommended making an immediate attack on the pope in person. Letters were received in the ecclesiastical States from the other generals, full of threats, and imperial troops instantly invested the territory of Piacenza. Clement VII. avowed that he had been influenced solely by this sort of coercion to pay the imperialists 100,000 ducats, and to conclude a fresh treaty with them §

Unfortunately, too, we have no authentic copy of this treaty, but from the state papers which were afterwards exchanged, it appears that in some articles the pope stipulated for the same conditions as had been granted to him by the king. He demanded the monopoly of salt in the Milanese, the recognition of his claims on Reggio, and assistance in the prosecution of them. He did not doubt that the emperor would accede to these demands

But one of them was no longer possible. Archduke Ferdinand, who had conducted himself so meritoriously in the last expedition, had taken advantage of the favourable moment to conclude a treaty with Francesco Sforza, in virtue of which Milan was to purchase its salt from Austria ‖ This was the first solid advantage Austria derived from her sovereignty in Lombardy.

Nor would the emperor accede to the other condition He had no mind to make a forcible attack on the Duke of Ferrara. Moreover, the feudal rights of the empire came into collision, on this ground, with those of the See of Rome. These the emperor would on no account surrender He accepted the treaty in the main, but these particular articles he refused to ratify.

"As our sovereign lord now saw," says a subsequent papal instruction, "that he was betrayed, that, contrary to all expectation, his footing with the emperor was worse and worse, he lent an ear to the old assertion, that the emperor's design was entirely to subjugate Italy; he therefore, determined to ally himself with those who had a common cause with him, in order to avert the danger which threatened him "¶

It is evident, therefore, that the real questions at issue related to the north of Italy. The pope put forward financial claims on Milan, and territorial ones on Ferrara; and these the emperor refused to admit

Let us examine the conduct of Charles V. By his treaties of 1521, he was bound to make an attack both on France and on Ferrara. His allies, on their side, thought themselves warranted in claiming a share of the advantages of the victory. But their co-operation had been trifling, their behaviour, latterly, equivocal, and hence the emperor thought himself exonerated from all these obligations. The victory was due to his arms alone, and alone he would reap the fruits of it. what inducement could he have to expose himself to new dangers in order to aggrandize allies of so doubtful a kind ?

The situation of the pope was in effect the same as that of England, it marks the spirit of the age, that the pope was the first who had the courage to oppose the rising powers which threatened to become universal, He was afraid the empire might once more become too powerful for the church; and the idea of the independence of Italy haunted him as it had done Julius II The popes had hitherto always given the impulse which led to great political changes, and their views had generally been carried out Clement VII ventured to present himself as the centre of the opposition to Charles V.

His first object necessarily was to bring about a reconciliation between England and France. As early as the 8th of March, Ludovico Canossa, in concert with Giberti,** began to move in this affair in France On the 16th of March, the latter exhorted the papal nuncios in England to use all their influence with Henry VIII. and Wolsey, to effect an amicable arrangement with France †† In April, the negotiations were already known in the Netherlands. They were attended with little difficulty; especially since the emperor's reluctance to fulfil his engagement to marry the king's daughter, became more and more obvious, whereas Francis I. declared that he would enter into no agreement without the good counsel of the king of Eng-

* Ziegler Historia Clementis VII in Schellhorn Amoenitates, ii p 372 Ziegler was then present at the court

† Fr Vettori says that the treaty made by the mediator of Alb Carpi had reference only to the free passage of the troops "Solo a questo che il papa la (gente) lasciasse passare, pagando quello aveva bisogno, et il papa stimò certo, che chome questa gente del re si metteva in camino, che gli imperiali si povessino ritirare verso Napoli, onde seguirebbe che Francesco diventerebbe Signore di Milano et ciascuno di loro avrebbe cura che l'oltro non diventassi maggiore in Italia

‡ Contarini Relatione di Spagna, 1525 Al papa davano principalmente la colpa, che V Celsitudine fosse andata così ritenuta con S M*

§ Instruttione al C Farnese Fursten ond Volker, iv App 15 (Ranke's History of the Popes, vol iii App p 32)

‖ Rescriptum ad criminationes

¶ The fore mentioned Instruttione, (Ranke's History of the Popes, App p 32)

** See a later letter of Giberti, Lett di pr i. 171.

†† Lettere di Principi, 157.

land.* On the 14th of July, Wolsey, according to Giberti's report, appeared not only inclined to a reconciliation with France, but inflamed with ardour for it † On the 30th of June, the nuncios declared that all hesitation was at an end

Another important circumstance was, that the Italian powers once more assumed an attitude calculated to inspire respect To this end, the pope had sought to renew the ancient alliance with Switzerland, that he might be able to command the prompt succour of eight or ten thousand men, in case of need He had already established a good understanding with the Duke of Milan and the Venetians The fortified places belonging to the former, the fine army maintained by the latter, (1000 lances, 500 light horse, and 16,000 foot,) formed an admirable basis for the schemes in agitation ‡ An alliance with France was necessary, and was desired; but the first condition of the treaty was to be, a renunciation on the part of that power of all its Italian claims, of those on Milan in favour of Sforza, and of those on Naples in favour of the pope. Then would Italy—for that name appears once more—bring a magnificent army into the field for the deliverance of Francis I

The persons by whom the pope was surrounded really indulged the hope that it would be possible to keep the French for ever at a distance, to drive out the Spaniards, and to raise Italy to the state in which she was before the year 1491. The feeling of nationality, which had often given signs of its existence, and especially in the unrivalled culture of letters and art, which was the pride and the distinction of Italy, now took possession of all minds The pope was strongly inclined to place himself at the head of the enterprise

Meanwhile, a prospect of reaching the goal of their wishes with unhoped-for rapidity now opened upon the papal party.

Immediately after the battle of Pavia, misunderstandings had broken out between the imperial commanders. Lannoy, who, on that eventful day, had done the least, received the greatest proofs of personal favour, and at length presumed, in direct opposition to the decision of all the others, to take the royal captive on his own authority to Spain § This gave general disgust Pescara, who felt that his services were not duly acknowledged or requited, begged for his dismissal, in order, as he said, to close his life in some obscure corner of the earth, "far from suspicion and from war."||

This was known to the Italians, and it was, indeed, no very far-fetched idea to ground a scheme upon the discontent of such a leader. Had not the first knight and captain of France lately set an example of defection? Was it impossible to lead Pescara to a similar course? He, too, was born in Italy, and was, in the exactest sense of the word, an Italian.

The consequences which would result from gaining over such a man were incalculable. He was the most experienced and the ablest of all the emperor's generals, in every campaign the most signal and successful actions had been his, the Spanish infantry were absolutely devoted to him. If they could succeed in gaining over the general, the best part of the army was sure to follow him, and the rest would easily be destroyed .

And magnificent was the prize they had to offer him The Spaniards were to be driven out of Naples and Sicily Now it was impossible for the pope to administer and to defend these countries himself, and the thought suggested itself, to reward the defection of Pescara with this crown The very act would have bound him closely to the Italian powers. The unity and the freedom of Italy would have been obtained at one stroke

Geromino Morone, the confidential minister of Sforza, who had evinced so much prudence in preparing, and so much energy in effecting, the restoration of his master—who also held all the threads of the intrigues now going on in his hand, one day took courage to open the matter to the marquis, first extorting from him a solemn promise, not to disclose to any human being what he was about to say to him Having fully discussed the political state of Europe, he touched on the possibility of freeing themselves from a foreign yoke which now offered itself to the Italians (among whom he included Pescara) he spoke of the confidence he inspired, of the great deed expected from him, and, lastly, he mentioned the prize by which that deed was to be rewarded ¶

Such a proposal was calculated to excite a storm of contending emotions in the breast of Pescara The prospect opened to him was brilliant and boundless, and he had just causes of displeasure with the court on the other hand, he was incensed at the treachery of the Italians, and his old Spanish blood rose in his veins He instantly saw the necessity, and felt the desire, to come to the bottom of the affair The crafty warrior who had so often surprised the enemy at the right moment, and had never in his life laid himself open to attack, showed all his wonted caution and self-command on this occasion "It is a great thing which you say to me," replied he to Morone; "and it is not less great that you say it *to me*." He admitted that he had cause to

* Instructions to Tonstall and Wyngfield Herbert, 168

† In Wolsey's own handwriting to the king (St P No 88) the demands of the emperor in reference to France as well as to Milan are declared to be exorbitant, his offers to England, to be "lytel or nothing to your commoditie, proufit, or benefit"

‡ Paruta Storia Venetiana, v p 213

§ Letter of Bourbon, 10th June, in Raumer's Briefen, i p 244 It is, however, officially asserted in the Relut Apologia, that the journey was undertaken by the king's own proposal, "inscio atque inconsulto Cæsare"

|| Sepulveda Hist. vi 1 According to Jovius, he wished to retain Carpi or Sora, but was put off with empty words. According to Sandoval, i p 671, the right which he claimed of exacting ransom from the King of Navarre whom he had taken prisoner, was contested

¶ How far matters went is shown by the often quoted answer of the emperor "Cum audivisset marchio nuncium ad id per Vestram Sanctitatem transmissum, eudem sui parte ut ait offerentem sub cujusdam apostolici brevis credentia regni nostri Neapolitani investituram et possessionem ut inde Sanctitas Vestra nos etiam ab omni imperiali dignitate deponeret" — *Goldast Pol. Imp.* 997

be dissatisfied; "but no dissatisfaction in the world," continued he, "could induce me to act contrary to the laws of honour. If I quit the emperor's service, it must be done in such a manner that the best knight in the world could not have behaved otherwise. I should do it only to show the emperor that I am of more importance than certain people whom he prefers before me."* Expressions in which Morone thought he perceived a leaning but slightly veiled, and by no means dubious. This opinion, coinciding with the favourable intelligence from France and England, gave wings to all these projects. "I see the world utterly changed," exclaimed Giberti; "Italy will arise out of the deepest misery to the highest felicity."† Writers were employed completely to remove Pescara's scruples, couriers were despatched to make communications to the allied courts — the commencement of the work was impatiently expected.

But, we may ask, were the means contemplated really of a nature to lead to the desired end? The independence of a people is so vast a good, that, when once lost, it can only be regained by straining every physical power and every moral faculty. In the present case, the need of it was first felt by the literary class alone, the mass of the nation were unconscious of it: they had no military point of honour to wound, nor had they to complain of violated legal or political rights, the right of the emperor was of the highest antiquity, and was incontestable. Hence, therefore, the leaders did not rely on the nation, in the proper sense of the word. They thought chiefly of the favourable conjuncture of circumstances, of foreign aid, and of this unlooked-for defection of Pescara: a lucky political combination was to effect the whole.

But this soon appeared doubtful. As early as the September of 1525, Giberti remarked‡ that the intention of the French was only to take advantage of the connexion with Italy, in order to obtain favourable terms from the emperor.

Whilst the French party continued to reckon on the defection of the imperial general, they learned that the fortified towns in the Milanese were repairing. A courier who had been despatched to France had disappeared in that territory, nay, declarations reached them from the Spanish court, which seemed to contain some allusions to the matter. People knew not what to think. Was Morone a traitor? But what advantage could he propose to himself, that would outweigh the detestation he had to expect from Italy? Or was Pescara playing a double game? "I cannot believe it," says Giberti. "What he had done for the emperor, a kingdom could not requite, can he mean to use this occasion to crouch before him again, and beg for his favour anew? It were a sin to imagine that so base a thought could find place in so noble a soul."§

And yet this was the fact. Pescara was born in Italy, but he had the soul of a Spaniard. All his forefathers had devoted their lives to the one object of establishing the Aragonese sovereignty in Italy. His great-grandfather, Ruy Lopez di Avalos, had attached himself to the person and fortunes of Alfonzo V; his son, Inigo, had been that king's confidential adviser, and his son, Alonzo, had perished by the hand of a Moor, in the attack of the French,|| the existence of our hero was bound up with the prosperity of the same cause. His whole soul was devoted to the command of the Spanish infantry, which was entrusted to him: he knew every one of his men by name; was indulgent to all their offences, even their forbidden pillage, and spared them whenever it was possible. It was enough for him if they fought bravely at the critical moment, and in this they never failed him. When he marched at their head, with his broad shoes of German make, his waving plumes on his hat, and holding his drawn sword straight before him in both hands, he was at the height of his felicity and glory. The Italians, on the contrary, he hated, he held them for cowardly and untrustworthy, there had even been examples at the conquest of a city, of his ordering all the Italian soldiers to be massacred. People asked him, "Why,—since they are your countrymen?" "For that very reason," replied he, "they are my countrymen, and yet serve the enemy." As, in his capacity of general, he curbed his natural intrepidity by prudence and caution, so was he ambitious, high-spirited and arrogant, but always within the bounds of loyalty and honour. The character of the soul is determined, more than is commonly imagined, by the contemplation of some Ideal. To ideas like those which were prevalent in Italy from the study of classical antiquity, Pescara was an utter stranger, but the notions and feelings of personal devotedness and fidelity which form the basis of a feudal state, and from which Italy was the first to emancipate herself, governed all his thoughts and feelings. He had grown up in intercourse with the heroes of Spanish romance; perhaps he compared himself to the Cid, who, though offended and repulsed by his king, remained inflexibly true to him, without bating, for a single moment, one jot of his haughty bearing. Chivalrous feeling and feudal honour were thus opposed to the spirit of Italy, whose national feeling was the offspring of classical culture, and who had thrown off the political morality of the middle ages. That morality did indeed make one more struggle for existence; but in doing so, it betrayed how much it had already been affected by contact with the world of which Machiavelli was the organ and the representative. Pescara had not the refined moral culture which would have led him to reject the proposals made to

* Personal narrative of Pescara in a document dated 30th of July, 1525, in Hormayr's Archiv for 1810, pp 29, 30.

† Lettera a Ghinucci. Lettere di Principi, i 170. How then could Giovio (Vita Pescar., p 403), maintain that Giberti warned the pope against these things?

‡ Al vescovo di Bajusa 4 Sett. Ibid.

§ To Domenico Sauli. Ibid., p 174.

|| Zurita Anales de Aragon, v 58 b.

him with the disgust and scorn they merited. He thought, indeed, while listening to them, that Morone deserved to be thrown out of the window; but he reflected that it was necessary to learn the whole plan in order to counteract it effectually. While, therefore, he kept up a good understanding with Morone, he communicated the affair, from the very first day, to the imperial commissioners, and to his brother commanders, Bourbon and Leiva: he wrote instantly to Insbruck for succours, and sent a courier with the intelligence to Spain. While Giberti was amused with dreams of the dawn of a new freedom for Italy, he was already betrayed.

In September the emperor gave the marquis full powers to act in the matter before him as he should think necessary.*

Nothing was, however, more necessary than to get a firm footing in Milan, and to annul all the claims of the Sforzas. The imperial generals thought that without the concurrence of the marquis they should all have been lost.†

The first step was to secure the person of Morone. On the 14th Oct. 1525, when he paid a confidential visit to Pescara, Leiva was concealed behind the tapestry, for the purpose of overhearing the conversation; and on Morone rising to take his leave, he was arrested. Pescara, however, requested the emperor to grant him the liberty of this man, who might still be of great use if an occasion offered for employing him.

Pescara now required the duke to deliver up the strong places of the duchy to the imperial troops—a measure demanded, as he said, by the interests of the emperor's service. The duke, robbed of his minister, and conscious of his own treacherous conduct, did not venture to refuse; especially since the two strongest, Milan and Cremona, were left him.

But these were passed over in silence only so long as the others were not taken possession of: as soon as that was the case, Pescara demanded the surrender of the citadels of Cremona and Milan. The duke made representations. Pescara replied, that he knew from the letters of Domenico Sauli, the duke's plenipotentiary in Rome, that his excellency had offered the aid of his person and his state in the liberation of Italy from the imperial troops; and insisted that at least the commanders of the castles should take an oath of fidelity to the emperor.‡ As Sforza refused to yield to these demands, Pescara had no hesitation in employing force. He took possession of Cremona, and advanced to besiege the citadel of Milan, which employed three thousand Germans.§ He immediately impeached the duke of felony. He announced to the emperor, that God and the world, and the dictates of common sense, required him to keep Milan in his own hands. The emperor declared his resolution of letting the prosecution take its course, and abiding by the sentence of the judges; though indeed of the nature of this there could be no doubt.‖

Such was the result of this first attempt of the Italians to shake off the yoke of foreign armies. As the principal element of their calculation was the treason of Pescara, their enterprise was rendered abortive by the fidelity with which he adhered to the emperor. Charles could now reasonably entertain the project of keeping Milan in his own hands.

But the matter was not yet decided. The universal hatred entertained for the imperial troops (who lived at the charge of the inhabitants) all over Lombardy, and the obstinacy with which the citadel of Milan defended itself, afforded a hope that what had not been accomplished by cunning might still be effected by force. Another favourable circumstance was, that at this juncture the general, who had always inspired the most fear, and now with good reason the bitterest hate—Pescara—died. Above all, the great questions at issue between the emperor and the King of France were treated in a manner that justified the most confident anticipations of fresh commotions throughout Europe.

It was clear that the emperor, though he did not enter into the English plans, overrated the advantages which might accrue to him from the king's captivity. I shall not enlarge on his want of magnanimity;—though I hold it to be perfectly true, that the power of freely and cordially forgiving his enemies was not in his nature; but it may also be said that his conduct arose from a defect of judgment. He had conquered Milan and Genoa, and he, probably, thought that he might take advantage of the king's captivity to induce him to renounce his Italian claims. He had gained nothing whatever from France itself; his attack on that kingdom having been completely repulsed. He nevertheless demanded, obstinately and peremptorily, the cession of Burgundy. Neither the illness into which Francis fell from vexation and anxiety, nor the negotiations of his sister, who had travelled to Spain on purpose to obtain her brother's liberation, nor the arguments of his own councillors, made the slightest impression on Charles.¶ He would hear of no indemnity; he would have back the heritage of his fathers, whence he derived the name and the arms he bore. But his victory was far from being complete enough for this. The principle of unity and nationality, which daily became more and more powerful in France, had remained unshaken and unharmed, even by the defection of the constable; it was but slightly affected by the disasters in Italy. Ardently as the king's mother desired her son's return, she declared that it were better that he

* Pescara to Archduke Ferdinand, 4th Oct. Bucholtz, iii. ii.

† Letter of Leiva in Hormayr, 29, 30.

‡ Pescara to Ferdinand, 4th Nov. Bucholtz, iii. 14.

§ Custode. Continuation of Varri from the national chroniclers, p. 29.

‖ Sandoval, i. 668, asserts that he saw the instruments of infeudation which were already drawn up for Bourbon; nay, that he had actually been invested with the fief with all due forms.

¶ We see from the Refutatio Apologiæ, p. 877, that the emperor was angry because the Duchess of Alençon, with a view to the machinations going on in Italy, would not agree to all that the king had before pledged himself to; chiefly because she wished to assist him in making his escape.

should remain in prison for ever, than that the kingdom should be dismembered.

On the other hand, purer conceptions of morality and dignity would have taught the king rather to endure his imprisonment than to assent to conditions which he was predetermined not to adhere to. But this would have been asking too much of him he felt his situation insupportable, and was ready to purchase freedom at any price

At length, on the 14th of January, he signed the conditions submitted to him by the emperor He promised to renounce all his claims on Italy, on the suzerainty of Flanders and Artois, and his alliances with the enemies of the emperor in Germany, Wurtemberg, and Gueldres, he consented to give up Burgundy. He did not reject the supposition that these concessions were to put an end for ever to all disputes, and contracted himself in marriage with the emperor's sister, the widowed Queen of Portugal but in the same day—the same hour—nay, one moment before—he had secretly signed a protest, in which he declared that he accepted the treaty only under the pressure of compulsion; that all the stipulations contained in it were, and would remain, null and void, and that he intended nevertheless to maintain all the rights appertaining to his crown *

His ideas of religion did not prevent him from taking an oath at the solemn celebration of the mass, and with his hand on the Gospels, never to break the treaty all the days of his life

He now let the papal legate know that he did not mean to observe the treaty † while he himself made overtures towards an alliance with the Italian powers · at the same time, he went to Illescas to celebrate his betrothal with the emperor's sister, which rested on the presumption that the treaty would be executed

The emperor and the king now saw each other more frequently, rode out together, were carried in the same litter, and called each other brother. They took leave near Illescas, beneath a crucifix which stands at the point where the roads to Madrid and Toledo divide. "Brother," said the emperor, "think on what we have promised each other" The king replied, "I could repeat the articles, without missing a word" "Tell me the truth," said Charles, "are you minded to keep them?" "Nothing in my kingdom shall hinder me from doing so," replied Francis. The emperor then said, "One thing, I pray you, if you mean to deceive me in any thing, let it not concern my sister, your bride, for she," added he, "would not be able to revenge herself"‡

We see the lowering tempest which slumbered behind this appearance of confidence

Immediately after, in a bark on the Bidassoa, Francis was exchanged for his two sons, the dauphin and the future king Henry II, who were to be left as hostages for the performance of his engagements ' "Sire," said Lannoy, "your highness is now free, fulfil now what you have promised." "All will be fulfilled," said the king, and sprang into the French boat. He was now once more among his own people, and saw himself received with all the marks of respect of which he had so long been deprived he felt completely himself again. Mounting, as soon as he touched land, a Turkish horse that stood ready caparisoned, he exclaimed, "I am the king, the king!" and galloped off §

This was the moment for which the Italians had been waiting

When the terms of the peace of Madrid were reported to the pope, he declared that he approved them, provided the king did not observe them the only difference would then be, that the emperor would have the king's sons in his custody, instead of the king, which would avail him little.‖ He now absolved the king from his oath,¶ he caused it to be represented to him in common with the Venetians, what an excellent army was already in the field, that it would not be very difficult to extort better terms, that if he was but resolute, and would take up arms for the relief of his sons and the deliverance of Italy, the Italians too would show themselves men, and would not yield themselves up to the will of the emperor.

For a moment the king paused: he hesitated to enter into this alliance. He convoked the notables of Burgundy, and resting on their declaration, that the King of France, in virtue of the ancient compacts of the province with the crown, had no right whatever to cede it,** he repeated to the emperor his former proposal of giving an indemnity for it in money. He probably thought the ferment in Italy would induce Charles to accept this offer.††

Let us pause to examine the situation of the emperor. At his court and among his most faithful servants the treaty had experienced great opposition, not on account of the exorbitance of its demands, but of the slender security afforded for its observance; they said the conditions were very good as child's play, but nothing more nevertheless, suppressing a secret anxiety which he too felt, he had concluded it —he had already appointed a governor of Burgundy who was on the way thither; his sister waited in Vittoria for the execution of the treaty in order to enter France as queen,—and now he received this proposal,—the same he had before rejected. He saw that Francis

* Treaty and protest in Du Mont, iv 1 399 412

† Giberti to the Bishop of Bajusa, Lettere di Principi, ii p 31, b

‡ Narrative in Sandoval, i 717

§ Report in Sandoval, i 738.

‖ The Bishop of Worcester to Wolsey, 12th Jan 7th Feb Raumer, i 217

¶ Sandoval, i 746 "Embió el papa al rey de Francia relaxacion del juramento que avia hecho"—There is in Rainaldus a similar release from an oath, dated 3d July, 1526 xx 460

** The emperor did not much regard this declaration Apologiæ dissuasoriæ Refutatio, p 884. "Satis plane constat, eos duntaxat vocatos quos rex ipse antea stipendiarios et juratos habebat"

†† Official information in the Oratio ad Proceres Germaniæ in conventu Ratisbon 1527, in Goldast Polit i. p 902 "Conditionem ultro sibi delatam tantisper accipere sustinuit, dum legatis rursus missis ultimum experiretur

thought he should compel him by the fear of hostilities in Italy the consciousness that he had not conducted the affair well, the vexation at being deceived, the wounded feeling of knightly honour, the pride of power—all arose at once within him. He answered the king, that if he was prevented from fulfilling the conditions of his freedom, he had better return to his captivity, where a fresh agreement might then be made.*

In earlier ages this would have been done, those times were past. The king did not hesitate to conclude his treaty with the Italian states on the 22d May, 1526, at Cognac. The terms proposed were, that the emperor should be required to give up the French princes for a ransom, cede Milan to Francesco Sforza, and restore the States of Italy in general to the condition in which they were before the breaking out of hostilities, further, on his progress to his coronation he was to be escorted by no more troops than the pope and Venice thought fit to permit. they thought to treat him as they had formerly treated Maximilian They determined to lay these conditions before him as soon as they had equipped a powerful army, and if he refused to accept them, which did not admit of a doubt, to drive him out of Naples, the subsequent disposal of which the pope reserved to himself †

It was a combination of the whole of Western Europe to counteract the consequences of the battle of Pavia; to check the preponderance, the views and the fortune of the house of Burgundy These objects had the concurrence of England The king and the cardinal exhorted Francis not to fulfil engagements which would make him the servant of Spain.‡ They did every thing in their power to promote the Ligue,§ though Henry VIII did not deem it expedient to become a member of it

At the court of Rome, the ideas which had been cherished a year before, now revived with redoubled strength. There was no longer a question of a struggle for the sovereignty of Italy between the two princes. Francis demanded no more than Asti and the feudal superiority of Genoa, and hopes were really entertained that Italy would be restored to the state in which she was in 1494. The Venetians showed an enthusiasm not inferior to that displayed at Rome their ambassador, Francesco Foscari, boasts that it was he who had held the pope fast to his resolutions; the Republic promised to do wonders. The Florentines were completely at the pope's disposal, and it was reported from Piedmont that the duke wished to emancipate himself from the imperial domination The papal party thought themselves secure of the assistance of the French, as the king had so strong a personal interest in the war; and they reckoned with greater certainty than ever on the Swiss, whose diets would be subject to the combined influence of the courts of France and of Rome, the King of England, it was hoped, would accept the protectorate of the alliance, which was offered him, or at least consent to advance money. Could the imperial army possibly withstand so many united forces? Francesco Sforza still held out in the castle of Milan, the people were ripe for insurrection, they thought they could destroy the flower of the imperial troops on the spot ‖ The letters of the Datarius Giberti, who at length saw himself in the position he had always desired, breathe all the determination which a grand and noble enterprise inspires In June, 1526, the emperor proposed the mildest and most moderate conditions to the pope Clement VII, having already joined the Ligue, rejected them without hesitation ¶

Open war once more broke out between the two greatest powers of Europe But, in the situation of things and the stage of civilization which now prevailed, it became evident that the emperor had other weapons within his grasp than had ever been wielded by his predecessors These he determined to employ

CHAPTER II.

DIET OF SPIRE, A. D. 1526.

The events of Italy necessarily reacted with no inconsiderable force on Germany.

The attack on the emperor was an attack on the rights of the empire, and Charles, with great dexterity and tact, pointed the public attention to the fact that no mention was made of the empire in the treaty of Cognac, it seemed to be regarded indeed as already dispossessed of all its rights. In all former years, it was its German forces which had decided its conquests in Italy. In the present war, more perilous than any preceding, it was to them it must look for efficient support It could not be a matter of indifference to the nation whether the empire should have any significance in Italy, or none.

Weighty, however, as this consideration was, it was in truth the less important side of the matter.

The mind and heart of the nation was in-

* Charles relates this himself in the before quoted Refutation

† Traité de confédération, appellé la Sainte Ligue, in Dumont, iv i 451

‡ Extract from Cheney's Instructions, in Fiddes, 320

§ "That the leegge shold be, by all meanys possibyll, sett forwardys" Clerk to Wolsey, 31st May, St P, p 154 In a paper of the 9th Oct (p 180) Wolsey ascribes the league especially to the king "Your Highness, by whois counsaile this liege had been begon"

‖ Giberti to Don Michele de Silva, 1st July Lett di Princ, i 230 See Provisioni per la guerra che disegnò Pp Clemente VII contra l'imperatore Inform Politt tom xii no 46 It appears from this that there was an intention of acting at the same time against Milan, Genoa, Naples and Sienna, where the imperialist party prevailed,—in Sienna with the aid of the exiled party in Naples with the aid of the Orsini, they were determined to suffer no assemblage of Spaniards in the towns, and no correspondence with Spain They were to accept the offer of the Duke of Savoy, so that the cause might appear to be that of the whole of Italy

¶ Sanga to Sambara, 19th June. Ibid, 210.

comparably more actively engaged in the spiritual interests,—in the great questions which embraced the whole moral and intellectual futurity of the world. We know how mighty an influence political affairs had from the first exercised on the emperor's conduct with regard to these questions the edict of Worms, the revocation of the summons for the assembly at Spire, had been the fruits of his alliance with the pope. to please him, he had assumed an air of strict adherence to the ancient church; it remained to be seen whether he would maintain it.

In the spring of 1526, there was still every appearance that he would not depart from it a hair's breadth Henry of Brunswick, who had just then arrived in Spain, obtained from the emperor declarations which sounded as decided as ever.

In fact he had arrived in a moment the most favourable that could be conceived for the proposal he had to make in his own name and the names of his friends.

The peace of Madrid was concluded, and the court was persuaded that the great dispute with France was thus settled for ever.* Hence the views of the government were rather directed towards Germany. If we examine this peace more nearly, we shall find that it involved not only the adjustment of personal and political disputes, but also an agreement upon a common enterprise against the Turks, and "against heretics who have severed themselves from the bosom of the holy church," the two contracting princes already entreat the pope to co-operate with them by ecclesiastical concessions † It was left to the good pleasure of the emperor with which of these undertakings to begin, and when to set about them It was Francis's own voluntary offer, that if the emperor would make war either upon the infidels or the Lutherans, he would bear half the cost and accompany the army in person ‡

In the days in which people still believed in the execution of this treaty,—when the king returned to his kingdom, Leonora prepared to follow him, and Orange to take possession of Burgundy,—that, in the midst of all the magnificent solemnities of the church with which the marriage of the emperor with a princess of Portugal was celebrated at Seville, the proposals of Duke Henry were brought under discussion in that splendid and stately court. They were extremely welcome, and he received the most encouraging answer. On the 23d of March, 1526,§ the emperor issued an admonition to certain princes and lords of the empire, to remain steadfast in the old faith, and to use their influence with their neighbours, that the heretical doctrines which were the cause of all the disturbances might be wholly eradicated. In this document he commends the anti-Lutheran alliance which had been concluded between Duke Henry, Duke George, Elector Albert, and some other princes. He announces his intention of shortly going to Rome; after which he would resort to every measure for the radical extirpation of heresy Admonitions of this sort were addressed to the Counts of Nassau and Konigstein, to the Bishop of Strasburg, and Duke Erich of Calenberg. The two former were to communicate with the counts on the Rhine, in the Westerwald, and the Netherlands; the bishop with the princes of Upper, and the duke with those of Lower Germany ‖ The emperor, as we perceive, entirely shared the ideas of the orthodox party in Germany, which indeed was observed to display unwonted spirit and boldness from the time of Duke Henry's arrival. Duke George was reported to say that if he liked he could be elector of Saxony ¶ His chancellor one day in Torgau expressed himself to the effect, that the Lutheran affair would not last long; people had better take care what they were about

This, however, necessarily obliged the opposite party to rally all their forces, towards which, indeed, they had already taken some steps The alliance which had been talked of at the end of the former year was now really brought to bear

It is commonly called the league of Torgau, but it was only ratified on the side of Saxony in Torgau, it was concluded about the end of February, 1526, at Gotha.

Here, in pursuance of the arrangement made by their several envoys at Augsburg, the Elector of Saxony and the Landgrave of Hessen met, and agreed to stand by each other with all their might, in case they were attacked on account of the word of God, or the removal of abuses According to the first draft, the union was to subsist only "until a christian and equitable adjustment should be effected at the next diet of the empire." It seems, however, that this clause was afterwards thought too restrictive, and it was omitted. It was also specified that they would afford each other the needful help "at their own cost and damage" As the reigning princes treated in person, no

* "Nach dem langen Trübsal und Krieg," writes Heinrich von Nassau from the Spanish court to his brother in Dillenburg, "hat uns Gott den heiligen Frieden wieder gegeben"—"After the long misery and war, God has again given us blessed peace' Toledo, 22d Jan Arnoldi, p 203

† Pour dresser tous les moyens convenables pour les dites emprises et expeditions tant contre les dits Turcs et infidèles que contre les dits herétiques aliénés du greme de la sainte église Art. 26

‡ Apologiæ Dissuasoriæ Refutatio, in Goldast Pol Imp 884 "Quod inquit (autor apologiæ), quocumque proficisceretur Cæsar, illuc etiam maxima cum militum manu regi eundum erat,"—"on the part of the French this was one motive for refusing to carry out the treaty,"—"hic profecto se proprio gladio percutit, quum potissime rex ipse id obtulerit, ut si Cæsari adversus hostes fidei eundum esset aut in Lutheranos moxendum, is dimidium impensæ custineret, et si Cæsari gratum esset, cum eo personaliter adesset, quam oblationem Cæsar pro Christianæ religionis augmento respuendam non censuit."

§ The exchange of Francis I took place on the 16th March The first letters must have arrived about the 23d in these Francis still promised to hold to the treaty Even in Cognac, Francis I said to the viceroy, Lannoy, that the protest of the Burgundians was of no importance —Refutatio Apologiæ

‖ In the Weim Arch See Rommell, Urkundenbuch, p 13

¶ See Rommel, Ind p 22. From Duke George's answer, it appears that he had only said that the councillors could be electors of Saxony if they willed it, i e they could administer the affairs of the electorate It appears as if he merely sought to explain away what he had said.

protocol was taken of their conferences; but thus much is clear,—that in the course of their deliberations the ties between them were gradually drawn closer.*

But the alliance of two princes, although among the most powerful in the empire, could effect little: they immediately determined, according to their former intentions, to try to induce other states of the empire to join them. Each of them accordingly began with his near friends and old allies, Philip, with those of the Oberland, Elector John, with the Low Germans.

Their success was very unequal. In the Oberland, public opinion was not yet favourable to a positive league. The Nürnbergers had shown themselves well disposed at the last diet, but in Gotha they declared, "they would respectfully await the time of his Imperial Majesty and the next diet." They feared the emperor might conceive displeasure against them and abandon them to their enemies. The Landgrave then applied to Frankfurt, but the council declined the proposal, and an alliance with the people, who, the Landgrave was assured, would find means to force the council to do as they would have it, would have been a dangerous precedent. The Elector of Treves was out of the question; he abandoned, at this very moment, the place in the opposition which he had hitherto held, and accepted a pension of 6000 gulden from the emperor and his brother.† It was impossible to bring the Elector Palatine to a resolution: at a fresh interview with the Landgrave, he declared, indeed, that he would venture person and property in the cause, but he did not accept the proffered alliance; he only held out the hope that he would join it at the diet; he also raised some objections to the draft of the treaty.‡

On the other hand, the negotiations of the Elector of Saxony in Lower Germany were eminently successful. There were a number of princes who had always been attached to the house of Saxony, some of whom were nearly akin to it. After some preliminary negotiations, Duke Ernest of Lüneburg, Philip of Grubenhagen, Henry of Mecklenburg, Prince Wolf of Anhalt, and Count Albert of Mansfeld, repaired, on the invitation of the elector, to Magdeburg.§ On the appointed day, 9th June, Elector John with his son and his cousin also arrived at Lüneburg. All were alarmed at the admonition issued by the emperor from Seville, which had only now come to their knowledge. On the 10th of June, the proceedings were opened, Electoral Saxony spoke first: he reminded the assembled princes of the danger which threatened them from the alliance formed at Mainz, and from the document in question, and of the necessity of giving in an unanimous declaration at the next diet. The compact entered into by Saxony and Hessen was then laid before them, together with the proposal to join it. They were all willing: on the 12th of June they signed the treaty, as it had been drawn up at Gotha and ratified at Torgau, and appended their several seals to it.‖

It is especially remarkable that the princes did not disdain to receive into their alliance a city, which, it is true, enjoyed great franchises, but had by no means the rank or character of an immediate imperial city—Magdeburg, where their meeting was held.¶ It was important to them as a central point for all the States of Lower Germany, and moreover it was desirable for them that it should be able to maintain itself against the archbishop without their aid.

Such was the first formation of a compact evangelical party, in presence of the imminent danger which threatened them from the union of the emperor with their antagonists, they united to defend the truth they acknowledged, and above all, to prevent the passing of any hostile resolution at the ensuing diet. It was an extension of the old Saxon alliance from religious motives.

Such were the preparations made on either side for a decisive struggle, when, in the summer of 1526, the diet was convoked at Spire. The Proposition was laid before the diet on the 25th of June, and brought the affairs of the church immediately under discussion.** It was couched in terms which might be satisfactory to both parties. The States were herein exhorted to consult as to ways and means, "whereby Christian faith and well-established good Christian practice and order might be maintained until the meeting of a free council." Measures were proposed for insuring obedience to the imperial edicts and the decrees which were now about to be passed. It is remarkable how gently the edict of Worms is alluded to in this last passage.††

* The documents in the Weim. Arch. The ratification at Torgau took place on the 4th March. See Hortleder, i. viii. 1.

† Excerpt of the treaty in Bucholtz, ix. 5.

‡ "Da wolle man, sagte er, die Notel weiter stellen."—"It was intended, he said, to extend the terms." Letter of the Landgrave to the Elector, Wednesday after Palm Sunday, 28th March. W. A.

§ It runs thus: "In Meinung und in Sachen des göttlichen Wortes, damit, so der Reichstag Fortgang gewonne, die Sache in christlichen Bedenken zuvor berathschlagt wäre." "In the opinion and cause of the Word of God, so that as the diet proceeded, the affair should first be subjected to Christian deliberation." Instruction for Caspar v. Minkwitz, which was sent to George of Brandenburg, who, however, did not appear. W. A.

‖ Handlung uf den Tag zu Magdeburg. The Proceedings at the Diet at Magdeburg.—properly, instructions for the proceedings at this meeting: "Ferner ist bedacht das Bundniss so uns. gn. Herr mit dem Landgrafen zu Gotha aufgericht, den Fursten freundlich und vertraulich zu zeigen, und wo I. F. Gn. auch darein willigen und schleissen wollten, als u. gn. Hr sich genzlichen versehen auch freundlich bitten thäte, sollt alsdann solch Bundniss durch eine Beschreibung immassen mit u. gnsten Herrn vorgemeldt (dem Landgrafen) auch aufgericht und vollzogen werden." "Further it is intended to show in friendship and confidence to the princes, the treaty which our gracious lord has made with the landgrave at Gotha; and should the princes agree and be willing to enter into it, as our gracious lord fully expected and cordially requested, then should this treaty be concluded and ratified, by a written contract to that intent with our gracious lord aforementioned (the landgrave)."

¶ "At your humble seeking, prayer, and request," says the elector, "we have included the burghermaster, councillors, and guildmasters of the old city of Magdeburg in this Christian agreement, because we know that by God's grace they are well inclined to the godly word."

** According to the report of Esslingen of the 1st of April, signed, "Ferdinandus Archi. Aust. C. in Imp. Locüt." F. A. vol. xli.

†† Extract in Neudecker's Actenstücken, p. 21.

The deliberations began in the Colleges of the Princes, and in them, too, the first resolutions were indifferent. It was laid down as a principle that, in affairs of faith, no decision should be come to, and that the old established good customs should be observed,—a principle which each party might interpret in its own sense. But it was different when they came to speak of the abuses which must be reformed. The clergy required that this matter should be referred to a council; it could not, they said, be within the competence of a diet to separate the good from the evil. On the other hand, the laity did not choose to be again put off: they declared that the common people were so far instructed that they would no longer suffer themselves to be led with the same simple credulity as heretofore. They had on their side the cogency of circumstances, the reasonableness of their purpose, and even the words of the Proposition—that good customs should be maintained and evil ones severed from them and rejected. In spite of the vehement resistance made by the clergy, who appeared in great numbers, it was at length resolved to discuss the reformation of abuses, and to enforce universal obedience to whatever might be agreed on. The clergy had the consolation of thinking that they would have their share of influence in determining what the abuses were which it was desirable to remove.*

But it instantly became evident that they were at a great disadvantage even here.

The cities to which the resolution of the princes was communicated on the 30th of June, received it with joy; but the interpretation which they instantly affixed to it was quite unequivocal. In their answer they declared that, by good customs no other could be understood but such as were not contrary to faith in Christ. But it was notorious to all how many directly opposed to this, had, to the universal corruption, crept into the church. It was a great joy to them to learn that these were to be abolished.†

On the 4th of July, when the bishops took their seats in the council of princes, they opposed the reception of this declaration. They maintained that the disturbed state of the people arose not from the alleged abuses, but from seditious writings and discourses, in the heat of debate, one of them let fall the expression, that it would be better if all the books that were printed were burned every eighth year. Such exaggeration and violence could of course injure only themselves, they were reproached with wishing to stifle all science, art, and reason. The answer of the cities was accepted as it stood.

Upon this the whole diet of the empire was now broken up into various commissions, for the reform of spiritual abuses;—one of electors, one of princes, and one of cities—in the same manner as had been formerly adopted at Worms, for the discussion of the charges against the papal see.

The sentiment of dislike and distrust of the clergy which reigned in the nation became also the prevailing one in the diet. "The clergy," says the Frankfurt envoy, "seek nothing but their own advantage, and neglect the public good."‡ We find the same complaints in the letters of the envoy of Ducal Saxony, notwithstanding the strict catholicism of his master. "The greater part of the clergy," he says, "have only their own aggrandizement in their eye; they cannot deny the mischief created by the abuses that have crept into the church, yet they will eradicate none. There is more solicitude for the true interests of Christianity to be discerned among the laity than among the clergy."§

It may be easily imagined how greatly this disposition of the public mind was heightened by the arrival of the allied princes of the evangelical party.

The Elector of Saxony appeared with the state befitting the most puissant prince of the empire. He rode in at the head of a numerous retinue of horsemen: seven hundred persons lived daily at his charge, and his followers boast how well they fared in his service. He was good-humoured and magnificent. One day he gave a banquet, at which twenty-six princes dined with him, they were seated at four tables, their nobles and councillors at separate ones; some went away early, others stayed till ten o'clock, and played high. The Landgrave, on the other hand, with his earnest and learned zeal, made a great impression. he showed himself more deeply versed in the Scriptures than any of the bishops.‖ Both these princes had admonished their people, that since they had taken a name after the Gospel, they should abstain from all levities. They had preaching in their houses every other day, which, on Sundays and holydays, thousands resorted to hear. The armorial bearings over their doors were encircled with the words, "Verdum Dei manet in æternum."

* The judgment in the Frankf. Acten, vol xlii. Otto von Pack gives to Duke George of Saxony an account of the proceedings, Vis Mar 21 July (Dresden Arch) "Ist daruf gestanden dass der einig Artikel den Reichstag solt zutrennt haben, wenn dy Geystlichen nicht bewilligt das sy von den Missbrauchen wollten handeln lassen." "It is agreed, that the only circumstance which should have power to dissolve the diet should be, the clergy not consenting to any arrangement concerning the abuses of the church."

† The answer of the cities, printed by Kapp and Walch, xvi 240.

‡ Hamman von Holzhusen, 1st ed. "Die Geistlichen bearbeiten sich heftiglich um iren eignen und vergessen den gemeinen Nutzen." — "The clergy exert themselves vehemently for their own, and forget the common interests."

§ Otto von Pack. "Ist am Tage wenn die Geystlichen gemeyne Christenheit also meinten wy dy Laien, so blib Gottes Ehr alle gute christliche Ordnung und bliben darzu sye selbst mit aller irer Hab Ehr und Gut, denn ich hab bisher keyn Leyen vermerkt der da wolt ein Buchstaben von den guten Kirchenordnungen abthun adder der Geystlichen Guter um einen Pfennig schmalern. Nicht weiss ich was der Churfurst von Sachsen und Hessen bringen werden." "It is evident that if the clergy meant the same common Christianity as the laity, the honour of God and good Christian order, as well as they themselves with all their wealth, honour, and property, would remain unhurt, for I have as yet seen no layman who wished to take away an iota from the good discipline of the Church, or to diminish its possessions by one penny. I know not what the Elector of Saxony and Hessen will bring about."

‖ Annales Spalatini in Mencken, 659.

Such were the influences under which the reports of the committees of the diet were made. All the old complaints and charges against the encroachments of Rome were revived; among others, that it exacted far too much subservience from the bishops, since they were also councillors of the empire, against commendams and annates, the monstrosity of the mendicant orders, &c. It was thought that never had language so free been directed against the pope and the bishops. The cities pressed especially for a better provision for the parishes out of the funds of the church, and the right of every civil government to appoint priests to officiate in them; they demanded that the clergy should be subject to the civil burdens and tribunals.*

But by far the most remarkable thing was the report which issued from the committee of the princes, consisting of the bishops of Wurzburg, Strasburg, Freisingen, and of George Truchsess for the spiritual, and of Hessen, the Palatinate, Baden, and the Count of Solms for the temporal bench.† I have not been able to discover which of them had the predominant influence, whether the well-known moderation of the Bishop of Freisingen, or the ardent earnestness of the young landgrave, turned the scale: be that as it may, in the discussions of this committee, the original idea of erecting one norm or standard equally binding on both parties was kept steadily in view; and was, in fact, realised in a resolution passed to that effect. There was as yet, spite of all the struggles between the ruling powers, no actual division in the nation itself. The different races of Germany stood on nearly the same stage of civilisation: all without exception—as we had lately occasion to observe of Tyrol—whether in the north or the south, had the same tendency to reform, though their ideas respecting the means by which it was to be effected might differ. But since these were not yet fixed, they might still be moulded into more than one form. It might be imagined that a well-conceived endeavour to establish a good understanding throughout the nation might yet perhaps destroy those elements of discord, and reconcile those wide divergencies of opinions, which lay in the league of Regensberg and its consequences. In such a spirit of conciliation were these propositions conceived. They particularly insisted on the expediency of permitting the marriage of the clergy, and granting the cup to the laity. It was proposed to leave every man free to receive the Holy Sacrament in one kind or in both, and it was represented to the emperor that it were better for the priesthood to contract matrimony than to live with women of ill fame.‡ The committee proposed that the severity of fasts and confession should be mitigated, private masses abolished, and at the ceremonies of baptism and the Lord's Supper, the Latin and German languages be used jointly; that the other sacraments should not, indeed, be discontinued, but be administered gratuitously. In regard to preaching, the formula of 1523 was repeated,—that God's word should be preached according to right and sound understanding, and according to the interpretation of the expositors acknowledged by the Christian church, but with an addition which evinced a still stronger inclination to reform and to the sentiments of Luther, viz. that Scripture must always be explained by Scripture.§

Such were the propositions which issued from a commission composed of an equal number of spiritual and temporal members. We clearly perceive that if the Council of Regency formerly showed itself favourably inclined to reform, this was not the effect of caprice, nor even of choice: the necessity of this step arose out of the situation of things, and the strength of that universal conviction from whose influence no man can withdraw himself.

After so many abortive attempts and dangerous agitations, the nation once more showed the possibility of preserving its unity on the most important concern that can occupy the mind of man.

On the 1st of August, a committee chosen from all the States was appointed to submit this project to final discussion—a discussion that promised to be of the greatest interest. There is no doubt that the project would have experienced much opposition, since the evangelical party protested against retaining the four sacraments, about which nothing is to be found in Scripture,‖ nor were the catholics satisfied. Duke George remarked that the worst abuses were yet untouched; the origin of all the evil lay in the bad manner in which the prelates found entrance to the church—by the right door or the wrong—by the help of powerful kindred; in short, the most vehement debates would have taken place,¶ but there is no ground for doubting that there would have been a decided majority, and that it would have passed definitive resolutions, binding on the whole empire.

It was a crisis like that which had occurred two years before, when universal preparation was made for a national assembly. The difficulties were now greater, because on both sides independent forms of thought and culture had begun to take root, but it was the more important to oppose some check to their growth, and it was yet possible to do so.

* Memorial of the free and imperial cities against the clergy, in Holzhausen's handwriting in the Frank. A., vol. xlii.

† Report of the Hessian delegate, Schrauttenbach, Thursday after St. Udalric (5th July), in the acts of the diet, Weimar Archives. They are in other respects very confused, and afford but little information for this year.

‡ "Zuzulassen, dass die Empfahung des hochwürdigen Sacraments unter einer oder beiderlei Gestalten eines Jeden Gewissen und Freiem Willen heimgesetzt wurde,—dass mitlerzeit gegen den ehelichen Priestern von keyner Uberkeit geistlichs oder weltlichs Standes etwas strefliches werd furgenomen."—"To concede that the reception of the most venerable Sacrament under one or both kinds should be allowed to every one according to his conscience and free will,—that meanwhile no punishment should be inflicted on married priests, either by the ecclesiastical or temporal authorities."

§ Judgment of the eight commissioners in the Dresden Archives.

‖ Treatise in Walch, xvi. 258. A reply to the principles laid down by the eight commissioners, partly agreeing with, and partly combating them.

¶ Letter of Duke George in the acts of the imperial diet, Dresden Archives.

Again, however, did that power intervene which had forbidden the national assembly, and had so often thwarted the resolutions of the collective empire The emperor seemed determined to adhere inflexibly to his old policy

At the same time that he published the catholic admonition, which we have already mentioned, at Seville, he issued instructions to his commissioners, commanding them to assent to no resolution of the diet that might run counter to the established doctrine or practice of the church, and again urged the execution of the edict of Worms * This affair is involved in some obscurity The instructions must have arrived long before, for a considerable time had elapsed since Duke Henry's return, and it is not easy to see how the commissioners could, nevertheless, feel themselves authorised at first to produce others,—unless we suppose that they did so in pursuance of a hint subsequently given to the archduke Be this as it may, it was not till this advanced stage of the business that the instructions in question were produced, at the instigation, as it was asserted in Spire, of certain powerful ecclesiastics, and not without corruption and intrigue ("*Finanz und Hinterlist*") they created an extraordinary sensation. The great committee preserved its firmness and composure it declared that it would adopt such a course as it could answer to the world, but it seemed impossible to effect any thing, since every new ordinance they might frame would be met by the clear, express words of the emperor.

There was a general persuasion that nothing more whatever was to be accomplished. Many declared they would not stay a moment longer the evangelical party feared that recourse would be had to force For this cause mainly, the cities now inclined to the union with Saxony and Hessen, in order to have a support and defence in case violence should be resorted to against them † Nurnberg, Strasburg, Augsburg, and Ulm, now gave their assent to the proposal of the princes

The complication was most singular Whilst in Italy the pope was employing every means of attack on the emperor, and stirring up an European war against him, the imperial power was once more rendered subservient to the maintenance of the authority of the papal see in Germany.

But such a relation was too wide a departure from the ordinary nature and course of human affairs to endure long.

In Germany people had already ceased to believe in the sincerity of the opinions expressed in the instructions. Though their attention was chiefly engrossed by internal affairs, they knew of the treaty of Cognac, and of the misunderstandings between the pope and the emperor. The cities first remarked how very remote was the date of the instructions At that time, indeed, the emperor and pope were on a good understanding, but now the pope's troops were in the field against the emperor They were told that every improvement must be reserved for the decision of a general council, but how, under the present circumstances, was it possible to expect one? Were the emperor present, he would see that they could not observe his edict, if they would

It was rumoured that a caution had been sent to the Lady Margaret in the Netherlands, to handle all matters connected with the evangelical religion gently. In the persuasion that they were acting in accordance with the emperor's real sentiments, the cities therefore proposed to send a deputation which should represent to him the state of affairs, and pray him either to grant a national council, or at least to recall the order that the edict of Worms should be executed This proposal found a ready hearing in the great committee, in which an anti-ecclesiastical majority had instantly declared itself During the discussion of the grievances of the common people, the abuses of the clergy had, in spite of their opposition, been expressly designated as the chief cause of the late insurrection People now called to mind that the imperial edict had been accepted, only in so far as it should be found possible to execute it,—but it was found utterly impossible Nobody was forthcoming who had executed it, nay, whose conscience would allow him to execute it, according to the letter ‡ And how were they to furnish succours against the Turks, if they saw danger impending over them at home? The great committee assented to the proposition of sending a deputation to Spain, and immediately drew up instructions for it, wherein it ascribed the religious divisions of the country more especially to the prohibition of the national assembly, and prayed the emperor as soon as possible to call a council of the nation at least; and, until then, graciously to suspend the execution of the edict, which,

* Commission of the 23d March, in the Fr A vol xlu p 32

† Then would "solch Ansuchen und Fulgung zu gross em Nutz gereichen"—"such applications and following be of great use" Letter of Holzhusen, 21st August The other cities had their answer by the 25th August They waited to see what the deputies would accomplish before they came to a final decision

‡ A rough draft of the instruction in the Dresden Archives proves that these were the motives alleged, the petition runs thus "Der Kaiser wolle die Execution der Peen und Straf desselbigen Edictes bis uf ein künftig Concilium in Ruw stehn lassen Ursach es haben die Stennd das Edict nicht anders angenommen dan so vil In muglich wie die kaisserliche Instruction selbs mit ir bringt, und nachdem Etlichen unmüglich gewesen das Edict zu halten, so seyen sie auch nicht in die Peen gefallen, zum andern so man die Buchstaben besiebt, so ist kain Furst oder Bischof der das Edict gehallten oder der nicht ein Entsetzen hat dasselbige *ad literam* zu halten." —The emperor wished to let the execution of the pains and penalties imposed by this edict rest until a future council, therefore the estates did accept the edict only so far as it was possible to carry it out, as was set forth in the imperial instruction, and as some had found it impossible to enforce the edict, they were not subjected to the penalties —on the other hand, if the letter of the edict be looked to, it were impossible that any prince or bishop could enforce it or not have a horror of enforcing it *ad literam*" Then follows the instruction itself The Frankfurt deputies say, in a letter written from this diet, "So wollen wir auch E F W nicht bergen, dass auch das kais Edict so aō 21 zu Worms ausgangen, allhie auf diesem Reichstag von Fursten Grafen Herrn und Stedten hochlich und fast als unmuglich in allen Puncter zu halten angefochten wird" "We will not conceal from your princely worships that the imperial edict published at Worms anno 21, will be opposed at this diet by princes, counts, lords, and cities, as being almost impossible to be enforced in all points."

to some, was impossible on conscientious grounds, to others, because they had reason to fear it would cause a rebellion among their subjects; and to a third party, for these reasons combined.

It is very remarkable that while such were the resolutions come to in Germany, they were met by corresponding ideas from Spain.

We know the point of view from which the imperial court from the first regarded the Lutheran opinions. It had opposed them so long as it was in alliance with the papacy, but its devotion to the church did not go the length of requiting the war which Clement VII made upon it in Italy, with friendly offices in Germany. Immediately after the battle of Pavia, when it first became apparent how little reliance could be placed on the pope's good intentions, the Grand Chancellor, Gattinara, proposed to demand a council; not, as he said, really to convoke it, but only to force the pope to show a more compliant spirit in his negotiations.* England at the same time, begged Clement to consider how easily any partiality shown to France might cost him the obedience of that portion of the States of the empire which yet adhered to the church.† But the hostility to him had now become far more decided. From Germany itself he had been apprised that the diet would be more unfavourable than ever to his cause: he himself indeed expected nothing else.‡ Long—almost too long—did the emperor hesitate to declare himself. At length, however, after the latest negotiations had failed, he assumed a more resolute bearing. After many consultations in the council of state which he had just then constituted for affairs of Spain and Germany, he wrote to his brother on the 27th July, that a proposal which he now subjoined had been submitted to that body, for abolishing the penal clauses of the edict of Worms, and for submitting the truth of the evangelical doctrines to the decision of a council. The pope would not have cause to complain, since it was only the secular, and not the spiritual punishments that it was proposed to abolish. It was to be hoped that the emperor might then obtain efficient succours, in horse and foot, against the Turks or against Italy, for the good of Christendom.§

Under these circumstances — the emperor himself having made the concession which Germany urgently demanded—who would not have expected that it would be definitely granted and proclaimed? It appears from the original documents that Markgrave Casimir of Brandenburg, one of the imperial commissioners, zealousy advocated this abolition of penalties.|| It unquestionably depended on Ferdinand alone; but he was not favourable to it.

His chief ground of opposition was doubtless the fear of displeasing those states of Germany which were inclined to the ancient faith. Charles, indeed, had remarked in the letter above mentioned, that a part of his council thought it expedient to put off the repeal of the edict, which might otherwise convert the adversaries of Lutheranism into enemies of his government.¶ Ferdinand doubtless knew even better than his brother how necessary it was to conciliate them. The idea had at this moment been suggested at Rome of offering the Roman crown to some antagonist of the emperor,** and Duke William of Bavaria had already begun to canvass the most influential electors with a view to obtaining that dignity. To wrest from the catholic princes the edict upon which they principally based their persecution of the Lutherans, might have converted them into the most resolute and dangerous enemies. He too thought it prudent to suspend the repeal of the edict of Worms. He thought that when the emperor was once more within the limits of the empire, and had established his power there on a solid basis, this measure might be carried into effect with advantage, and without any shock to the established religion: then too he might obtain a good sum of money from the Lutherans in return for this act of grace and lenity.†† But if he was not disposed to hasten the revocation of the edict of Worms, he had just as little inclination or power to urge its general execution. A complete triumph of the pope's adherents would have been extremely injurious to the house of Austria.

As, therefore, it seemed neither expedient to execute the edict nor to repeal it, as no proposals of a middle course had any chance of acceptance, a principle came into action which had already influenced the course of events, though rather beneath the surface, and without as yet exciting general attention. The principle of the development of the several territorial powers now prevailed even in the affairs of religion. I find that the cities were the first to bring this into public notice and discussion. They alleged that it was no longer possible to re-establish entire the ceremonies of the church: that in many places these had been altered, in others, had been left wholly untouched; that each party thought that his way was the right,

* The decree in Bucholtz, ii p 281

† Extract of a letter from Wolsey to the Bishop of Bath immediately before the battle of Pavia (before Parma, is doubtless a clerical error) Fiddes, Life of Wolsey, 32 Wolsey thought that the course adopted by Campeggi promised to lead to the desired end but "that Germany being now so much infected with the Lutheran heresy, such members of it as still continue in the communion of the church, may be provoked to withdraw their obedience, should his holiness appear to act in favour of the French king against the emperor"

‡ Albert da Carpi au Roi de France, 24th June, 1526 in Molini Docum stor i p 202 "que a cette heure se feroit le tout le pis que se pourroit contre luy et la ste siege" From a declaration of the Elector of Treves of the 9th June

§ Extract in Bucholtz, iii 371 "In his council a draft of a well constructed and well grounded edict was made, the fruit of which was to be, that those who adhered to the errors of Luther were to be drawn away from them by mildness and leniency, and a way be afforded them by which *the truth of the evangelical doctrine might be decided by a good council, which the pope now feared*, at the same time they would support Ferdinand against the Turks or against Italy, for the common good of Christendom"

|| See the Lith Erläuterung, p 172

¶ Cause, "d'estre mauvais avec les autres" Bucholtz, 372 Pity the whole letter is not printed

** In the Provvisioni per la guerra di Clemente VII Inform polit) this is described as a desirable measure

†† Excerpt of a letter from Ferdinand, 22d Sept There is no question that the letter of 27th July arrived in the middle of August Letters from Spain were generally a fortnight on the road

that it was impossible in this case to resort to force, and that nothing remained but to leave every man to the form of religion he had adopted, till such time as a free council should be able, by the help of the divine word, to decide the matter * — A proposal fundamentally at variance with the nature of a diet of the empire, which represented unity, and with the former decrees of the empire, which had always been of universal application and validity, but which was imperiously commanded by the state of things. It was equally impracticable to withdraw the edict of Worms from the catholic states, or to impose it on the evangelical the thought of granting to every district and every state the independence in regard to religion which it had, in fact, begun to enjoy, speedily gained ground It was the most easy and natural solution of the difficulty nobody had any thing better to advise. The impulse towards religious separation which had grown up since 1521, triumphed over all attempts to preserve and to cement unity by means of reform The committee decreed that "each state should act in such wise as it could answer it to God and the emperor,—that is to say, it should do as it thought expedient. The committee immediately inserted this resolution in the instructions for the deputation to the emperor

There is a moment at which all the interests of Europe at large, and Germany in particular, converge and become implicated with each other, a moment which, though it appears unimportant, was in fact the point at which the early history of Germany ends and the modern begins —the moment when the Archduke Ferdinand accepted the report of the committee, sanctioned the sending of the deputation, and approved the instructions drawn up for it It was ordered in the Recess, that until the general or national assembly of the church, which was prayed for, should be convoked, each state should, in all matters appertaining to the edict of Worms, "so live, rule, and bear itself as it thought it could answer it to God and the emperor."†

The reader must pardon the repetition of these words, in consideration of the infinite importance they afterwards acquired. They contain the legal foundation of the constitution of the national churches of Germany, and at the same time they involve (although leaving open the possibility of a future reunion) the separation of the nation into two great religious parties. They are the words which decided the fate of Germany. Catholicism would not have been able to maintain itself if the edict of Worms had been formally repealed. The evangelical party would not have been able to constitute itself legally, if the emperor and the States had insisted on the execution of that edict The future existence and development of both hung on this point.

Generally considered, it was the immediate and necessary consequence of the division between the emperor and the pope. Their alliance had produced the edict of Worms: that alliance being broken, the emperor and his brother revoked the edict in so far as its revocation was consistent with their own interests.

CHAPTER III.

CONQUEST OF ROME, A D. 1527.

While these deliberations were going on in Germany, in Italy war had already broken out

The allies had taken the field in June; unquestionably not with the necessary promptitude and decision, since the imperialists had gained time sufficient to put down the insurrection of the Milanese, and had at length succeeded in taking the citadel. On the other hand, however, the allies took Lodi and Cremona; the Swiss, so long expected in vain, at length arrived in considerable numbers, and a brilliant corps of French men-at-arms joined the army. In September the Ligue were evidently masters of the country, while the imperialists, cooped up in a city inclined to rebellion, ill paid, and almost cut off from the surrounding country, found themselves in a very critical situation ‡

But the emperor had means of resistance and of retaliation at his command, even in Italy itself.

In June he once more made overtures of peace to the pope; at the same time charging his plenipotentiary, Ugo Moncado, in case he received a refusal, to find means of diverting the forces of the enemy from Milan § This was not difficult to accomplish, the state, the city, nay, the Vatican itself, was filled with partisans of the empire When the imperial envoy, the Duke of Sessa, rode home from the last fruitless audience, he took a fool behind him on his horse, who by a thousand antic tricks and buffooneries gave the people to understand that there was nothing to be done ‖

* Memorial of the cities Frankf A A vol xlii

† "Demnach haben wir (die Commissarien) auch Churfursten Fursten und Stande des Reichs und derselben Bottschafter uns jetzo allhie auf diesem Reichstag einmüthiglich verglichen und vereiniget, mittler Zeit des Concilii oder aber Nationalversammlung nichts desto minder (d i ohne die Ruckkunft der Gesandtschaft zu erwarten) mit unsern Unterthanen ein jeglicher in Sachen, so das Edict, durch Kais Mt auf dem Reichstag zu Worms gehalten ausgangen, belangen mochten, fur sich also zu leben, zu regieren und zu halten, wie ein jeder solches gegen Gott und Kais Mt hoffet und vertrauet zu verantworten " "Thereupon have we (the commissioners) also the electors, princes, and estates of the empire, and the ambassadors of the same now here at this present diet, unanimously agreed and resolved, in the midst of the sitting of the council or national assembly (i e without waiting for the return of the deputation) with our subjects, on the matters which the edict published by his imperial majesty at the diet holden at Worms may concern, each one so to live, govern, and carry himself as he hopes and trusts to answer it to God and his imperial majesty "—*New Collection of Recesses*, ii 274

‡ From a letter of Guicciardini to the Datarius, 24th Sept. 1526, it appears that there was an idea of making a new attempt to drive the imperialists out of Milan

§ Letter from Charles Bucholtz, iii 52

‖ Albert da Carpi to Francis I Molini, Documente i 205

The pope's open enemies held meetings under his own eyes in the houses of the Colonnas. In order to fulfil the intention of the emperor, they resorted to what we may be permitted to call the lowest cunning. They began to make warlike preparations on the frontiers of Naples, in the dominions of the Colonnas; upon which the pope too took up arms. They then offered to enter into a treaty with him. Clement consented, and was now so devoid of all solicitude, that he discharged a great number of his troops in Rome. This was exactly the moment they waited for. Having lulled him into security, they determined to attack him.—Pompeo Colonna—the warlike cardinal who had once rent his stole and gone forth to decide a quarrel by single combat—who had always displayed a bitter personal hatred to Clement, now made common cause with Don Ugo, as Sciarra Colonna had done with Nogaret. On the 19th of September, the troops of Colonna appeared before the walls of Rome, and entered without resistance. The city was utterly defenceless: the people did not stir; they were curious to see whether Colonna would really do what he said—take possession of the Vatican in the name of the Roman emperor.* There was no one to prevent his fulfilling this threat; and the pope, who had fled to the castle of St. Angelo, was compelled, in order to have his palace restored to him, to consent to a truce, not only with Naples and the Colonnas, but with Milan and Genoa; in short, in respect of all his own troops by land or sea.† It was only on these terms that Colonna's army left the city, from which it carried off a booty of 300,000 ducats.

Clement must surely now have perceived the feebleness of his resources and the magnitude of the danger; he must have heard the voice that foretells the fall of the avalanche, but again he was under the dominion of exasperation and vengeance. The obligations which he had so solemnly and publicly taken upon himself were, as his plenipotentiary, Guicciardini, wrote to him, far more sacred than these conditions, extorted from him by force;‡ nor was he disposed to observe the truce an hour longer than expediency required,§ no sooner was he in some degree prepared, than he attacked the Colonnas and the Neapolitan territory; in a short time he received French and English subsidies in money, and the celebrated defender of Marseilles, Renzo da Ceri, undertook to lead the papal army into the Abruzzi. Meanwhile, his other troops served against Milan and Genoa, just as they had done before the truce.

At this moment, however, a new and far greater danger arose in another quarter: the emperor had forces at his disposal of a very different character from any that Italy could produce.

In that letter of the 27th July, 1526, which was so decisive for the issue of the diet, Charles had invited his brother either to go to Italy in person, (in which case he meant to give him no instructions, but merely full powers, as his *alter ego*,) or at least to fit out and send a strong army.‖

Ferdinand was prevented from going in person by the affairs of Hungary, which urgently demanded his presence, but he addressed himself to the man who had always led the Landsknechts in Italy to victory—George Frundsberg of Mindelsheim, who was ready once more to devote all the vigour that age had left him to the service of the emperor. The great difficulty was to raise money.¶ Ferdinand gave his plenipotentiaries full powers to mortgage land and people, castles and cities, he declared himself ready to send his jewels to pawn in Augsburg. Frundsberg, too, pawned his wife's jewels, and offered his own lands to mortgage.** The Italian commanders, who declared that they could only hold out for a short time unless they received succours, sent some ready money; at length enough was got together to give the men at least their marching money and half a month's pay. Hereupon the drum was beat in all the imperial cities of the Oberland, and troops flocked to the standard from all quarters.

We run no risk of error in affirming that it was not mere martial ardour that now drew them together, they knew that they were to march against the pope.

This had been foreseen in Rome. Giberti remarked, in the preceding July, that numerous bodies of men might easily be collected in Germany, "on account of the natural hatred which they cherish against us, and of the hope of plunder."

The emperor's exhortations were conceived in the most insidious terms. His brother, he said, had only to give out that the army he was levying was to march against the Turks: every body would know what Turks were meant. In a manifesto published by the emperor in September, 1526, he expressed himself in a

* Contemporary account, in Buder, Sammlung, ungedruckter Schriften, p 563. Negri to Micheli, 24th Sept. Lettere di Principi, i 234. (The date in the printed copy is wrong.)

† Conventione di Clemente VII con Ugo di Moncada in Molini, i 229.

‡ Guicciardini to Datarius, 27th Sept. Lett. di Prin. ii 14. He expressed himself very characteristically: "Nell osservare la triegua veggo vergogna, non si fugge spesa et si augumenta il pericolo perche quanto all' honore più è obligato N S^{re} ad una lega fatta volontariamente et con tante solennita per salute publica, che ad un' accordo fatto per forza et con ruina del mondo."

§ Excerpt of a letter wherein Clement declares that the treaty is not binding on him.

‖ Excerpt in Bucholtz, iii 42.

¶ From the report of Otto von Pack who was sent to Inshruck to collect money for Duke George we see what difficulties he encountered: the Weisers were not in funds, the Fuggers wanted the cash that was in their hands in order to dissolve their partnership after the death of Jacob Fugger (Dr. A.). According to a letter of Ferdinand's to Charles, 28th October, 1526 (Gevay), Documents and Acts, part i p 22,) it appears as if nothing whatever was to be obtained from the money changers.

** "Voire que luy mesmes a voulsu engaiger et mectre ez mains des fouckres les terres et biens quil a a lentour daugspurg, ne luy a este possible sauoir deulx ny autrement recouurer argent ... Neantmoins affin que le tout ne se perde ... non obstant mes grans affaires iay enuoye audict messire george ce dargent quay peu finer, tellement que de ceste heure il passe audict ytalie auec X^m bons pietons et vne bonne bande dartillerie."

manner which no follower of Luther would have needed to disown. he testified his surprise that the pope should be willing to cause bloodshed for any possession whatsoever; a thing wholly at variance with the doctrine of the Gospel.* In October, he begged the cardinals to remind the pope that he was not raised to the pontifical throne "in order to bear arms, nor for the injury of the people of Christendom" he again proposed a council, and urged the cardinals, if the pope continued to refuse it, to call one in his stead he declared that he at least would be guiltless, "if injury should accrue to the Christian republic from its denial."† As to Frundsberg, there is no doubt that he had for some time cherished evangelical opinions, and had, moreover, conceived the bitterest hatred against the pope during the late war.‡ Immediately after the battle of Pavia, he had proposed to march into the States of the Church, and attack him on his own ground. He was encouraged in this way of thinking by his secretary and companion, Jacob Ziegler, who had long been resident at the court of Rome, and whose biography of Clement VII is still extant. From this we learn what the Germans there thought and said among themselves of the pope; — of his illegitimate birth, which ought from the first to have excluded him from the priesthood, his cunning and craftiness, and his insatiable and scandalous rapacity. They accused him of a connection with poisoners, and of the most shameful vices. They caught up and repeated all the rumours of the court, true or false, to feed the national antipathy of which they were themselves full. These stories, combined with the hostility shown by Rome to the emperor, which was esteemed most unjust, awakened in the Germans, both leaders and common men, the same politico-religious zeal against the pope, which had been fatal to so many bishops in the Peasants' War. George of Frundsberg was thoroughly imbued with it,§ added to which, he was sorry, he said, for "the good honest fellows" who were besieged in Milan and Cremona.|| He declared that he was resolved "to make an end of the affair, and to do the pope a mischief, if he could get him into his hands."

If the emperor's policy seconded the religious efforts of the Germans, the religious spirit by which those efforts were prompted was favourable, on the other hand, to the policy of the emperor. No sooner did he show the smallest leaning to the inclinations of the people, than they tendered their whole powers to his assistance.

In November, nearly 11,000 men assembled on the mustering ground at Meran and Botzen ¶ they were joined in Trent by the garrison which had just evacuated Cremona, under Conradin of Glurns they were all willing, spite of the poor pay they received. about 4000 more joined them on their march without any pay whatever, "a choice army, such as had not been beheld in Italy in the memory of man."

The great and immediate difficulty was to get there; to cross the Alps, and then to effect a junction with the troops in Milan.

Frundsberg had no mind to waste his time and strength on the well-garrisoned fortress of Verona he took the far more difficult road over the Sarka mountain, towards the domains of his brother-in-law, the Count of Lodron. Here, again, two roads lay before him: the one on the right practicable for an army, but commanded by the fortress of Anfo, the other on the left, a mere footpath between precipices and chasms, which a single peasant could have rendered completely impassable, but which the enemy had not observed. Along this path Frundsberg began his march on the 17th of November. His brother-in-law, who knew every pass and defile of the neighbourhood of his hereditary castle, gave him escort for three miles, up to the summit of the mountain. They could take but few horses, and even of these some fell over the precipices. of the men, some perished in the same manner, and the boldest did not venture to cast his eyes into the abyss below. A few sure-footed landsknechts, forming a sort of railing with their long spears, guarded the steps of their veteran leader, and thus, holding on one before him and pushed on by another, he traversed the terrific pass. They reached Aa in the evening, and on the 18th arrived at Sabbio, without encountering any resistance. On the 19th they appeared at the foot of the Alps, at the village of Gavardo, in the territory of Brescia. Their provisions were just exhausted, but here they found good Farnazio wine, and having driven together 8000 head of cattle, they made merry after their long privations.**

* Rescriptum ad Papæ Criminationes. "Quod tamen Sti Vtæ non placuit, it is said (Goldast, Constit i 489, nr 19), licet credere non possumus, eum qui Christi vices in terris gerit, vel unius guttæ humani sanguinis jactura quamcunque secularem ditionem sibi vendicare velle, cum *id ab avangelica doctrina prorsus alienum* videretur."

† Epistola Caroli ad Collegium Cardinalium VIto Octobris. Goldast, Pol Imp, p 1013

‡ See the passage quoted at p 96.

§ Schelhorn, de Vita et Scriptis Jacobi Ziegleri, § 21 He refers to an unprinted work of Ziegler's "magnanimo heroi G. F. in expeditione Italica versanti eum fuisse vel a consiliis vel ab epistolis."

|| Letter from Frundsberg to Margaret, 19th Sept, 1526. " where the want of money was such a hinderance to such help and succour, that it was to be feared the good honest fellows would be abandoned, and not only the duchy of Milan lost, but Naples, Calabria, and Sicily also, and likewise that the hereditary and other dominions of his imperial Majesty must be reduced to great extremity."

¶ From the diary in Hormayr's Archiv, 1812, p 424, we see that the army consisted of 10,650 men, and required for its maintenance, and that of the various officers and followers attached to it, 25,900 gulden (with the exchange, 34,842 gulden). The commissaries lent Frundsberg 2000 gulden, "that he might have something in hand." He accepted it "with overflowing eyes."

** Reissner Frundsberge 86. Thun, in Hormayr, 428. Very minute details of this whole enterprise are to be found in Jacob Ziegler's unprinted work, Acta Paparum Urbis Romæ, of which I intend to give a fuller account in the Appendix. I shall only remark here, that it is the main source whence Reissner has taken his book, which it surpasses in brevity and distinctness. It says of the march upon Mantua, "Vnd dieweil gfarlich vnd schwar fur die grosse stett press vnd Bergom vber die grossen wasser, die allenthalb verlegt durch die gwaltigen hauffen der feind, den nechsten auf Mailand zuziehen, hat er sich auf Mantua gewendt."—"And then with danger and difficulty, past the great cities Brescia and Bergamo,

Their intention had been to effect an immediate junction with the army at Milan But the enemy was far too strong in the field to allow this. The Duke of Urbino, commander-in-chief of the Ligue, appeared on their right flank, and kept them off from Oglio They saw the impossibility of attacking any of the neighbouring cities, which were all in a good state of defence, while they themselves were without artillery: nothing remained but to endeavour to cross the Po, where the enemy was not so strong, and where Bourbon might in time be able to join them * Thither Frundsberg took his way, in three close columns The allies had not yet courage to make a serious attack on him, they merely annoyed him with their light cavalry, or with their musketeers, who lay in ambush behind hedges or in ditches. † Once only he was in serious danger. As he entered the fortifications round Mantua, over a long and narrow dam, the enemy attacked him in the rear, and at the same time moved forward to occupy the bridge over the Mincio, which he had to pass at Governolo He would have been lost if he had suffered himself to be hemmed in in this most unfavourable place Frundsberg, however, though chiefly conspicuous for his rough soldier-like bravery, was by no means without a simple and efficient system of tactics. He had secured this bridge exactly at the right moment: the attack in his rear was repulsed by the musketeers, and, just as a considerable body of the enemy's troops appeared on the other side of the river and seemed about to contest the passage with him, fortune favoured him so far that one of his first shots inflicted a mortal wound on their captain, Giovanni de Medici,‡ in whom the Italian soldiery put implicit trust. He was a man completely after the tastes and opinions of Italy at that period—accomplished, prudent, addicted to all the vices and debaucheries of the south, but at the same time energetic and daring, and gifted with every other quality of a good leader Hereupon Frundsberg crossed the Po at Ostiglia, and marched up the right bank as far as the Trebbia. On the 28th of December, he arrived in the neighbourhood of Piacenza "Here we are," he writes to Bourbon, "over the high mountains, and the deep waters, through the midst of the enemy, in hunger and want and misery, we have arrived safe and sound What shall we do?"

Bourbon required the whole of January to reduce Milan to such a state of tranquillity as that he could entrust it to a part of his troops, and march with the remainder to join the German forces On the 12th January the junction was effected near Firenzuola § There could be no doubt as to the course which it was expedient for them to pursue We are already acquainted with the dispositions of Frundsberg, nor can it be matter of wonder that Bourbon now hated the pope more than any man living; since the emperor's demand that he should be created Duke of Milan, to which Clement would never accede, was the condition which had hitherto rendered all negotiations abortive. Their sole ally in Italy was the Duke of Ferrara, who cherished a bitter hatred to the pope, having been incessantly menaced, even in his hereditary domains, both by Leo and by Clement he supplied the troops with provisions on their march, and urged their leaders not to lose a moment, and to seek their common enemy in Rome itself ‖ On the 22d February, the combined army, 20,000 strong, in six divisions, with some cannon and a small body of light horse, broke up their camp at Firenzuola and took the high road to Rome. Leaders and men were equally persuaded of the fact that the pope had begun the war afresh they knew very well that if the emperor allowed them to be without pay it was only from want of means, and they determined to go and seek it for themselves in Rome. Religious antipathy, and the desire to avenge the emperor—perhaps to re-establish the ancient power of the empire in Italy,¶—the just notion that a war is only to be concluded in the enemy's capital, the eagerness to get possession of their well-earned pay, and the rumour of treasures brought from all parts of the globe and accumulated in Rome for centuries,—all these various feelings and motives were blended into one mass of passionate determination to conquer and to plunder Rome

At the very first obstacle that placed itself in their way, this temper—now become independent and untameable—burst out with the most violent explosion

At the end of February and the beginning of

across the great water, which was obstructed on all sides by the strong bands of the enemy, in order to take the nearest way to Milan, he turned upon Mantua"

* Bourbon wrote to Frundsberg that he could not fix a route for him Frundsberg was determined if necessary, to fight, but otherwise "to put himself in no peril"—*Letter in H* p 424.

† Leoni, Vita di Francesco Maria d'Urbino, p 364

‡ The incident that this was exactly the first shot out of the falconet just arrived from Ferrara is first found in Ziegler Reissner also used Jovius (Vita Alfonsi, p 189) and Guicciardini (b 27, p 34), who expresses more clearly what Ziegler tells somewhat obscurely "he (Giov de Medici) had one leg shot off at the knee by a shot from a falconet" "Roppe una gamba alquanto sopra al ginocchio" According to the diary in Hormayr, two falconets and two culverins arrived from the duke, together with 1000 gulden "Had I" says Frundsberg, "had 400 or 500 horse, I would with God's help, have won no slight honour for his imperial majesty and his princely highness You may, in short, believe that I never in my life saw a more hurried retreat" The enemy lost five hundred horse

§ Frundsberg was very discontented at the long delay He began to suspect treachery what is told him, he believes "like St Thomas" Letter passim, 430

‖ As early as November, the Duke of Ferrara had advised him to establish the Bentivogli in Bologna, if that was impossible, "to undertake the campaign against the pope, if Bourbon could raise no money, then to levy contributions on the towns and villages for the support of the landsknechts"

¶ Ziegler "Desshalben aus manigfaltiger getrungner not alle einhellig beschlossen, das sie eilends den papa, den anfaher dess kriegs vnd dieser bundtnus, vberfallen, daselbs bezalung suchen welten wann das haubt bezwungen, so wurden sich die stett vnd das land selbs ergeben, wo es ihnen dann gluckhen vnd dem kaiser geliebt sein wurd, so wolten sie gantz Italia wieder zum reich bringen"—"Therefore from manifold urgent need, all unanimously determined, that they would suddenly fall upon the pope, the beginner of the war, and upon this league and would there seek pay when the head was subdued, the city and the country would surrender of themselves if they had luck, and the emperor pleased, they would bring back the whole of Italy to the empire"

March the papal troops had gained some advantages in the Neapolitan territory, and the viceroy had actually determined to conclude a truce with the pope; in which, however, the sum of money that was to be contributed to the support of the army was either not mentioned at all, or very vaguely; though its retreat into Lombardy was distinctly stipulated.* It was not very likely that this treaty would be ratified by the emperor, or accepted by the leaders of the army; nor, indeed, that it would be executed by the papal general; since the army of the Ligue threatened in that case to separate itself entirely from the papal troops.† But the mere rumour of such a thing, the sight of an envoy coming from Rome and returning thither directly, threw the whole army into agitation.‡ The Spaniards murmured first. They threatened that they would go over to another master who would satisfy their claims better;—an empty threat—for whom could they find? Since the emperor owed them eight months' pay, nothing remained but to stand by their leader. It was fortunate for Bourbon that he was able to make his escape; his tent was plundered, and his best garment found the following day in a ditch. The Spaniards instantly communicated their own mutinous spirit to the Germans: their incessant cry was, Lanz! Lanz! Geld! Geld! (Lance! Lance! Money! Money!) this was all the German they knew; it was like the inarticulate cry of passion. Frundsberg, however, did not as yet see any ground for fear; he still trusted to his well-tried personal influence over the landsknechts. He ordered the drums to beat, a ring to be formed, and had the courage to go into the middle of it, accompanied by the Prince of Orange (who had followed the army from Germany) and the chief commanders: he thought he should still be able to effect something by means of a few words of reason. He called upon them to remember how he had always been their friend,§ and had never left them in good times or in evil: he promised that he would always be true to his good landsknechts; he reminded them that they had sworn to stand by one another in life and in death, till they should all be paid and satisfied; then he meant to stop: the emperor's foe, the beginner of the war, he would carry off with them.‖ But reason has little power over congregated masses of men, nor is their violence to be controlled by any arguments. The rational address of their leader, whom every man of them individually loved and honoured, they answered with the cry, Money! Money! which ran like the muttering of a storm through their ranks: they levelled their lances against the commanders in their centre as if they meant to transfix them. Never could such a moment have presented itself to the imagination or the fears of Frundsberg. It was with him that the organization and tactics of the landsknechts had mainly originated; they called him, and with justice, their teacher and father. He had fought at their head in almost all the wars of the house of Austria during that century; he had conquered the most powerful enemies, spite of every inferiority of numbers or disadvantage of position. His reputation did not rest on the mere animal courage of a soldier; he commanded respect by his coolness and presence of mind in the midst of danger; by the promptitude with which he took a salutary resolution, and the dauntless valour with which he executed it. His homely sayings are very characteristic: "Kriegsrath mit der That" (Counsel in war, with action); "Viel Feinde, viel Ehre" (Many enemies, much honour); they inspired both the officers and men who served under him with boundless confidence. His command fully justified their obedience. He still hoped by their aid to effect every thing; he did not even despair of beating the Turks, and of driving them to the frontiers of Europe. Like a true partisan and servant of the empire, he embraced with a glance Rome and Constantinople. His loyalty never wavered, although, spite of all his services, he was sometimes ill at court; he gave vent to his dissatisfaction in a few rhymes, and at the next trouble or disaster that befel his master, he took down his armour from the wall: he held to the great Idea of the empire with unshaken constancy. He had now to encounter this unlooked-for resistance. He was a man of extraordinary personal strength; on one occasion he had pushed aside a very powerful adversary with one finger, as if in sport; fear he knew not, nor had any sudden mishap ever had power to throw him off his guard;—but that those should rebel against him whom he had made what they were,—that they should turn against him the spears which he had taught them to wield—this was too much for him. Its effect was such as no one could have anticipated; in the same moment—at one stroke—he lost utterance and consciousness; and sank down upon a drum; he had reached the goal of his heroic career. Singular catastrophe! He died on the field, but not by the hands of the enemy; not in the heat of the battle which he had come forth to wage: his simple heroic spirit, which had striven, with all its honour and all its earnestness, to stem

* Treaty in Bucholtz, iii. 605. The contents of this treaty as given by Guicciardini (xviii. 5), do not exactly correspond with this; *e. g.* there is no mention in Bucholz of the 60,000 ducats which, according to Guicciardini, were to be paid. Ziegler says, too, "Er welt sechtzig tausent ducaten, iedem knecht, das sie aus dem land ziehen, ainen monatsold geben;"—"he would give sixty thousand ducats—the amount of a month's pay for all the landsknecht whom they brought out of the country," which is adopted word for word by Reissner, p. 103. I am inclined to think, however, that there were some secret articles, as in the Ligue of Cognac. Vettori speaks of 65,000 ducats.

† These uncertainties reduced the papal agents to despair. "Si è sempre consigliato lo accordo, ma s'intendeva un accordo che fusse fermo e non dubio e intrigato, come questo che si è fatto in Roma e non osservato in Lombardia."

‡ Sepulvedo, vi. 1.

§ In a former letter from the army it is said, "Die Knecht sind vast wohl mit im zufrieden: er ritt auch unter ihnen um wie ein Held, und ist allweg der fördriste beim Haufen." Wittenbach, 4th Feb. 27, in Hormayr's Oestreichischer Plutarch, xiii. 112.

‖ Reissner Frundsberge, 104. (Barthold's Frundsberg, I presume.) True and short account in Buder, p. 526.; and in Goldast, Polit. Reichshändel, p. 443.: there are some small differences which can hardly be reconciled.

the rising torrent of rebellion in the troops by whom he had so long been implicitly obeyed, sank when he saw that the tempest was ungovernable—the passion of revolt triumphant,—it was a sight that struck him with instant death. It has been affirmed, that the crafty enemy who was now advancing against him had stirred up the fire of mutiny by secret practices and emissaries And as against himself, no other weapon was needed. If, however, the pope thought to gain any thing by these means, he was greatly in error. The re-action produced in the army by this sudden calamity was violent as had been the conduct that caused it It effected what no persuasion, no reason could have done. The lances were taken up again, the wild tumult was stilled; the words of the chiefs once more found a hearing, the whole disorderly mass dispersed. Four days after, Frundsberg recovered his speech, but he could no longer lead the army. He could only beg the Duke of Bourbon not to draw back, hitherto, he said, God had guided them, he would not abandon their cause to the end Some money arrived from Ferrara for the Spaniards; the landsknechts had ceased to clamour for it, they themselves entreated Bourbon to lose no more time —all they asked was to be allowed to march

Had Bourbon intended to retreat, he could no longer have induced the army to do so.*

The violence of the hatred entertained against the pope by his enemies, was equalled by the cool indifference manifested by his friends The army of the Ligue followed the imperialists at a distance, and seemed rather intended to obstruct their retreat than their progress All the great towns of the Ecclesiastical States were in as good a state of defence as those of Lombardy, while the army possessed nothing but the road along which it marched, yet it found no obstacles save those presented by inclement weather and alpine passes · it encountered no enemy. Bourbon advanced slowly on the 5th of April we find him at Imola, after taking and plundering smaller towns. He then turned to the right towards the Alps, and took the road of Val di Bagno.† The larger guns he sent to the Duke of Ferrara, the smaller were dragged up the mountains, there was sometimes a scarcity of bread, but never of meat and wine; the heights were ascended without much toil in the neighbourhood where the Sapio, Folia, Metora, and several other tributaries of the Arno rise, and where numerous springs meet and form the sources of the Tiber ‡ On the 18th of April the imperialists appeared at Pieve di San Stefano, whence they threatened at the same time the valleys of the Arno and the Tiber,—Florence and Rome, and left it impossible for the enemy to decide on which side they would first direct their attacks. The whole of this region was panic-stricken.

The pope now perceived that the treaty he had concluded with Lannoy was too favourable to be executed. He could no longer refuse what the imperialists had always demanded of him—money to satisfy the troops He saw that his own safety depended on their dispositions. He commissioned Lannoy to repair to Florence to see what could be raised there. Lannoy obtained the assurance of 150,000 scudi, to be paid at stated terms, and hastened towards the Alps, in order if possible to induce the army by this promise to retrace its steps.§

On the 21st of April he arrived at the camp, where he staid three days He was seen to eat and drink with Bourbon, all their misunderstandings were at an end; but it was clear that the offer of the Florentines was not sufficient for their wants, they declared that they must have at least 240,000 scudi to induce the army to return.

Whether even then they would have found this possible—whether they would have seriously attempted it,—is, I think, extremely questionable. The tumults of that camp were too fresh in men's minds Nor do I find that they received any encouragement from the emperor.

The situation of the emperor, we must remark, is once more extremely singular.

The expressions of paternal kindness and filial obedience which are traditional in the Catholic world, had been frequently and ostentatiously exchanged between him and the pope; the emperor still occasionally spoke of the extirpation of the Lutherans, in respect of Italy, he gave assurances of which the pope said, he would have given the whole world and his own soul into the hands of the emperor upon the faith of them ‖ But Charles's directions to his generals have a totally different tendency. Lannoy was admonished in February, by no means to allow himself to be the dupe of any treaty whatever, if he supported Colonna's party on the one side, and if, on the other, Bourbon came up with his German troops, many great and good things might be accomplisned. "We see clearly," says he in a letter, "that they (in Rome) will do no good unless they are well thrashed. It will be necessary to cut thongs out of foreign leather (i e. to raise money to pay our troops) wherever we can lay our hands on it, and we must not forget Florence, which has also deserved a good castigation "¶ These are nearly the opinions which prevailed in the army The letters to Bourbon are in the same tone The emperor tells him to do every thing he can to make up

* According to Macchiavelli, Speditione a Francesco Guicciardini lettera XIV 29 Marzo Bourbon expressed to the legate, " quanto egli ha desiderato la pace, e la fatica ch' egli ha durata per far contenti quelli soldati a questa tregua, e che in effetto non ha potuto fargli contenti, mostrando che bisogna più danari, nè dice il numero "

† Foscari, Relatione di Fiorenza, 1527, says that Bourbon could pass either the Val di Limone, or the Via della Maria, from Rimini or the Val di Bagno Only the middle and easiest road was fortified The others might also have been fortified with very little trouble, " si fata deum, si mens non læva fuisset " From Macchiavelli's letters it appears that when the army broke up its quarters at San Giovanni it was thought that it might still return, and take the road to Lucca, or attack Ravenna

‡ Plinius, Hist Nat, iii 175, ed Lugd Flavius Blondus, Italia illustr, p 344.

§ Instruction of Lannoy in Hormayr's Archiv 1812, p 377 The Excerpts in Bucholtz, p 71, are taken from the same papers

‖ Instruttione a Farnese, Ranke's History of the Popes, vol iii Appendix, p 19

¶ Excerpts in Bucholtz, iii 57

the accounts of the war "You see, the game lasts long; you will neglect no means of bringing it to a close."* He did not, it is true, break off the negotiations, he even caused a ratification of the truce, and full powers for concluding a peace, to be drawn up, but he at the same time commanded the viceroy to deliver up the ratification only in case no change in the state of affairs had been brought about in the mean time by the army, which might render it possible to make better terms. At the distance at which he was, his instructions could only arrive very late and produce a general effect. But it is most remarkable that on the very same day when Lannoy and Bourbon were together — on the 23d of April — after Charles must have known of the truce — he did not say a single word to his commander-in-chief about observing it "I see, cousin, that you are advancing on Rome," said he, carefully avoiding any expression of disapprobation, on the contrary, he insinuated that a truce or a peace might best be negotiated there; that he would not send him the full powers, although his was the first name that occurred in them, in order that it might not appear as if he came to sue for peace, so that people might know he would compel it by force.† In one word, the emperor was well content that his army marched on Rome to extort its pay there as it could, and to dictate a peace to the enemy.

Let us observe, too, that at this moment, the pope was no longer inclined to observe the truce which separated him from his allies At the very same time—25th April—whether it be that he had already learned the new demands of the army, and had thought them such as it was impossible to comply with, or that he was determined by the general aspect of politics—he concluded a new alliance with the Ligue, the terms of which were kept secret, but which, we learn from his own declaration, contained much that was unfavourable to the emperor ‡

In short, both the emperor and the pope were determined to try their fortune in war

The imperialists, who had felt their hands tied by the former truce, were now set at liberty. Bourbon delayed not a moment to take advantage of this change After some demonstrations against Florence and Arezzo, in which he was supported by Siena, on the 28th of April he took that high road to Rome which for centuries had been trodden alternately by hostile armies and pious troops of pilgrims from the north. The cavalry of the Ligue was close at his heels, but before him he found no obstacle On the 2d of May he was in Viterbo, where he was welcomed by the German leaders, on the 4th he drove the first papal troops that encountered him, under Ranuccio Farnese, out of Romiglione, on the 5th he traversed the Campagna, and appeared towards evening, from the side of Monte Mario, before the walls of the Vatican.§

The German army thus reached Rome in the same state as it had quitted Tyrol and Swabia, without having encountered the slightest resistance, and having seen all its enemies disperse before it, its hatred exasperated by the Spaniards and Italians who had joined it, and who sought in Rome pay and vengeance, led by a general who had already quitted the usual path of the morality and policy of his age and country, and who hated in the pope the most formidable opponent of all his claims and projects

It would be utterly inexplicable how it happened that the prudent Clement did not seek by every possible means to avert this storm, were it not clear that he always believed himself to be the stronger. In Naples he had gained ground, in Lombardy he had lost none; the enemy's unresisted advance he imputed to his own imprudence in concluding a truce which had perplexed his allies: now, as he had recalled this measure and renewed the Ligue. he did not doubt that its army, which was already in Tuscany, would still come to his assistance in time till then, he thought, Rome would be in no danger, the walls were well furnished with cannon, and five thousand arquebusiers were taken into pay · the defence of the city was entrusted to the very captain who had so successfully repulsed the same leader with a similar army from Marseille.

It remained to be seen how the event would justify his security. Bourbon summoned the pope to open the city, over which, he said, the bishop had no right, to the emperor, to whom, as head of the Roman empire, it had of all time belonged The pope sent for answer to the trumpet, that if he did not instantly be-gone, he should be shot.

Hereupon a council of war was called, the issue of which could not be doubtful. The leaders saw very clearly, that they must not allow themselves to be overtaken before these walls by the well-commanded enemy who was marching on their rear They resolved to commend themselves to God, and at once without delay to storm Rome, even though the victory should be dearly bought.

During the night they did not neglect to keep the enemy in breath by incessant alarms. Meanwhile, every thing was prepared for storming

Bourbon gave his confessor a commission which affords a tolerable insight into the sphere of ideas in which his mind moved. He desired him to tell the emperor, in the first place, for the future to keep his troops in good humour —especially the Germans, without whom he could not hold Italy in check in the second, to cause himself to be crowned in Rome, which would be very advantageous to him for securing peace with the pope, and obedience from the

* 14th Feb and 31st March Bucholtz, p 67

† Extract in Bucholtz, p 67

‡ Instruttione al Cl Farnese, App p 31 "consentendo a molte conditioni che erano in pregiudicio della Mta Cesarea"

§ In the 21st hour (between 4 and 5 o'clock) The Commentarius captæ urbis says, that the army arrived before Rome on the 4th A part of it must indeed have appeared there at that time, if it is true that it was exposed for a day and two nights to the fire of the Roman artillery

princes of the empire. As to himself, he declared that his intention was only to force the pope to grant him a loan for the payment of his troops, and to prepare the coronation of the emperor. It is evident that he felt himself entirely a soldier of the emperor; he thought to hold Rome garrisoned by his victorious and contented army, and to procure for his master the rank and dignity of an emperor of antiquity.

It is a remarkable fact, that the sentiments of a portion of the population within the walls were of the same kind. Rome possessed no compact body of citizens, held together by hereditary rights, such as was at that time to be found in almost every other city in Europe, the mass of the inhabitants were recent settlers from other parts, who lived upon the business of the court. As there had been a great and continual falling off in its consideration and revenues, they would not have been sorry to see the government of the priests superseded by the court of a puissant emperor, which would have afforded them the same or greater advantages.*

On the morning of the 6th of May—on a Monday—the imperialists advanced to the assault of the walls surrounding the Vatican. They had got a quantity of trellises from the gardens, which they had converted into scaling-ladders, by binding them together with willow rods. The right side, towards the Porta Santo Spirito, was to be stormed by the Germans, the left, towards the Porta Pertusa, immediately behind St. Peter's church, by the Spaniards. A thick fog rendered it impossible for the enemy to direct his fire from the distant castle of St Angelo against them, or even to see their approach. At the point of their attack, the walls were low and the entrenchments thrown up in haste Meanwhile the fire of the carronades, culverines, and falconets, which were planted on the fortifications, was so effective, that the first assault of both troops was repulsed. They, however, instantly prepared for a second The Germans were animated by the exhortations of Philip Stumpf, who led them to a more favourable spot. Bourbon himself was seen to lead on the Spaniards, upon whom the first repulse had made some impression, and to seize a ladder with his own hand. The forlorn hope of the Germans, though under a heavy fire of musketry, now succeeded in carrying the mound and the entrenchments From this time they encountered no resistance. Claus Seidensticker, a veteran captain, was one of the first to mount the walls with his huge battle sword in his hand; Michael Hartmann, with a few comrades, leaped down; at last they found so little steady resistance that they themselves hardly knew how they had got over, in their fanatical ardour, they thought that God had gone before them in the mist.

The task of the Spaniards was not so easy. Their leader, Bourbon, was struck at the moment in which he was mounting the ladder, by a bullet, whether from the hand of an enemy, or an accidental shot of one of his own troops, is uncertain † He was destined only to conduct events to the point at which they might be left to their own spontaneous movement; they now passed over him, following their own unaided and ungoverned courses But the fury of the Spaniards was roused, by the loss of their leader, to a pitch which nothing could withstand, shouting España, they too scaled the walls. The papal guns were easily taken, and the gates and sally-ports opened to the crowd that pressed on behind, a few hundred Swiss, who here too were opposed to the landsknechts, were routed without difficulty; the Borgo was conquered before the pope actually knew that the attack had begun he had only just time enough left to seek refuge in the Castle of St. Angelo ‡ The original text of one of the oldest accounts states that Bourbon was carried, still living, in front of St Peter's Church, here he must have felt the full sense of victory—and here he breathed his last The body was carried into the Sixtine Chapel

The army was sufficiently well disciplined to preserve its order after his death, to abstain at first from plunder, and to propose further terms to the pope § A few months before, Lannoy had demanded 200,000 scudi, and Bourbon, a few days before, 240,000. The generals now, under the eyes of the pope, demanded 300,000; and, as security for payment, the Trarstevérine city. The pope, who lived in the hope that every moment would bring the army of the Ligue—some pretended that they already descried its advanced guard—and that the city, properly so called, would be able to hold out till its arrival, even at this moment rejected all proposals.

After four hours' delay, the troops once more set themselves in motion to bring their work to a conclusion They took the Trastevere without drawing a sword, the fire of the matchlocks sufficed to clear the battlements, and some blocks that served as battering-rams, to force the gates off their hinges; the bridges that led to the interior of the city were feebly defended. the conquerors advanced unopposed through the deserted streets, the inhabitants had all taken refuge in their houses. At an hour after sunset the whole city was in their hands Until

* Vettori -Sacco di Roma, scritto in dialogo "Gli Romani si persuadevano che l'imperatore avessi a pigliare Roma e farvi la sua residenza, e dovere avere quelle medesime comodita e utile che avevano dal domino de' preti."

† According to the Ferrarese account in Hormayr, 437, Bourbon fell either the first or the third, a musket-ball broke his ribs and penetrated the intestines, in half an hour he was dead

‡ Vettori, Storia d' Italia, relates what he witnessed as follows "La mattina delli sei appresentò (Borbone) la battaglia tra il portone del borgo, che è drieto alla casa del Cᵈ Cesis, e quello di S Spirito, dove ne' più di luoghi non è muro, ma bene vi era facto qualche poco di riparo Era la mattina nebbia grande, che causava che l artigliria non si poteva in modo indirizzare che necesse alli inimici i quali dettono la battaglia, e quelli di drento si difendevano gagliardamente, ma furono tanti quelli di fuori che con le mani guastavano i ripari, che erano di terra e deboli, e si ridussono a combattere a piano" See Sepulveda, who was also present, and fled into the castle with Alberto Carpi, vii 7

§ The Ferrarese account relates that only the camp followers plundered at this moment The attack had cost 200 men

midnight they remained in the order in which they had been posted, the mass of the Spaniards remained on the Piazza Navona, that of the Germans, on the Campofiore,—at that time the most frequented part. at length, as no enemy appeared either in the city or near it, they rushed forth to plunder the houses.

For the last seventy or eighty years, uncounted treasures had flowed in a continual stream into Rome ecclesiastical revenues from every country on earth, gifts of pilgrims, proceeds of jubilees, incomes of benefices held by the prelates the money for which every spiritual favour had been bartered * and all these riches now fell into the hands of naked, hungry, rapacious soldiers, who had so long been only kept in heart by the hope of this hour

Within the first day or two, twenty thousand persons paid contributions those of the imperial party, Ghibellines, were as little spared as the Guelfs; the churches as little respected as private houses. The great basilics before the gates of San Lorenzo and San Paolo were plundered, the tomb of Saint Peter was ransacked, the ring torn from the body of Julius II.. it was calculated that the value of ten millions of gold had fallen into the hands of the army.†

The Spaniards made the richest booty; they might be said to scent gold, they showed equal skill in discovering the most hidden treasures, and in extorting them by torture.

The Neapolitans were personally yet more ferocious and malignant ‡ Fortunately, after some days Pompeo Colonna arrived; he strove to protect the Roman nobles, at least from the most revolting outrages, and opened a sort of asylum in his house

The Germans were satisfied with having once more enough to eat and drink; where they found no resistance, they were rather good-natured than otherwise § They allowed the Jews to make their profit without grudging. There was much gambling in Campofiore, men had grown so suddenly rich, that they staked hundreds of gulden on a throw. Many came laden with vases of gold, which they lost to more successful players. Or they feasted Simon Battista, who had been imprisoned by the papal government for prophesying the pillage of the city. But though they had set him at liberty, he predicted no good to them; he told them that soldiers' riches and priests' lands went the same way. "Take all you can, plunder and spoil," exclaimed he, "you will soon lose it all again'" Their anti-catholic feelings vented themselves in unseemly jests Soldiers dressed as cardinals, with one in the midst bearing the triple crown on his head and personating the pope, rode in solemn procession through the city, surrounded by guards and heralds they halted before the Castle of St. Angelo, where the mock pope, flourishing a huge drinking glass, gave the cardinals his benediction, they then held a consistory, and promised in future to be more faithful servants of the Roman empire the papal throne they meant to bestow on Luther.‖

Occasionally discords broke out between the several nations A committee was then chosen, consisting of three Spanish and three German officers, who patroled the streets all night on horseback, to keep order ¶

The leaders lay in the Vatican; the Prince of Orange occupied the pope's chamber. Every man kept his horse as near him as possible, that it might not be stolen.

Meanwhile, the viceroy had arrived in Rome and renewed the former negotiations. For a time, the pope hoped for succour; the Duke of Urbino appeared in the neighbourhood, and three times every night signals were made from the castle that the garrison still held out. But he appeared to fear that the Germans would defend themselves with more vigour than would be shown in attacking them.**

Nor was it likely that he would be inclined to incur any great danger for the sake of the pope, since, but a few years before, he had been involved in a struggle for life and death with the house of Medici, and driven by them out of his own dominions. He retreated again, without making the slightest attempt at a rescue. The pope was at length compelled to accept, in a greatly aggravated form, the terms he had so often rejected He now promised to pay 400,000 scudi by instalments· as a pledge, he allowed the allies to garrison some of the strongest places which still held out; in Lombardy, Modena, Parma, and Piacenza; and in his own states, Ostia and Civita Vecchia On the 15th June this treaty was concluded, and the following day Spanish and German soldiers mounted guard in the Castle of St. Angelo. Two hundred of the handsomest and stoutest

* Francesco Vettori, Storia d' Italia, MS, adds "Romani vendevano tutte le loro entrate cari et affittavano le loro case a gran pregi ne pagavano alcuna tassa o gabella" He also mentions the profit of each calling "li artigiani il popolo minuto, le meretrici" Never was a richer city plundered

† Nova quomodo Roma capta sit relatio in Schardius, ii 611 "Per decem integros dies ecclesias gyneria monachos moniales et cardinales episcopos prælatos bancarios spoliarunt, deditos ceperunt, libros et registra lacerarunt," &c Vettori "La uccisione fu poca, perche rari si uccidono quelli che non si vogliono defendere, ma la preda fu inestimabile di danari contanti, di gioie, d'oro e d' argento lavorato, di vestiti, d' arazzi, paramenti di case, mercantie d' ogni sorte e di taglie"

‡ An Italian, Jovius, Vita Pompeji Columnæ, pp 191, 192, draws this distinction

§ In the Sacco di Roma, ascribed to Francesco Guicciardini, or to one Jacopo Buonaparte, these details are given at length At first I did not venture to make use of them, as I was not quite sure as to the origin of the work, but after further investigation I think the facts may be as related I shall give, in the Appendix, my views as to the author of this writing, as well as of the book called "Memorie storiche dei principali avvenimenti politici d' Italia seguiti durante il pontificato di Clemente VII opera di Patrizio de' Rossi, Roma, 1837."

‖ Reissner Wahrhaftiger Bericht Much more violent effusions of Grunewald's against the pope, "who acts contrary to the word of God," are related by Cochlæus, and repeated by Rainaldus

¶ "Ἁλωσις Romæ, in Hofmann, Nova Collectio, p 535 The Germans would not allow the Spaniards to commit their abominable outrages,—for example, on the persons of female children, the Spaniards, on the other hand, forbade the Germans to mock at the priests, which they declared one of the most ungodly of sins.

** The Germans, at least, were much inclined to march against him Schwegler writes (Hormayr, passim, p 416), in the camp of the enemy there is hunger and discontent, if they come nearer, we will seek them in the field.

landsknechts were picked out to do duty about the person of the pope.

The emperor now thought his designs on Italy accomplished. He doubted not that his army would be able to make an advantageous convention with the Florentines, who, in the general confusion, had driven out the house of Medici, and deserted the cause of the pope. It was then to march against Venice and encamp in the territory of the republic, in order to compel that state also to make peace. In this enterprise, the assistance of Ferrara would be valuable.*

The title of apostolic, was already exchanged in Rome for that of imperial, chamber.

The Germans had here an opportunity of seeing distinctly how the empire had been the prey and the dupe of the popes, people showed them the ruins of the emperor's palace, and explained to them all the stratagems by which he had been stripped of the country and the city, and even of his own imperial residence within its walls. But they consoled themselves with the thought, that the man who had exalted himself to the station of a god on earth would now be brought low by the might of the jealous and offended God of heaven They were persuaded that He had opened to them a way across the Alps, over the steep rocks which they had climbed like the wild goat, He had preserved them unhurt at Mantua, where their enemies had thought to catch them as in a net; He had commissioned the first shot to lay prostrate the pope's ablest captain; and, lastly, having led them by all the large cities, in face of the enemy, and once more over the trackless mountains, safe and sound, to Rome, He had gone before them in the mist across the strong walls Thus did the mighty God strike Antichrist with the lightnings of his judgment †. They indulged the hope that now times were changed, and the beloved young emperor Charles would rule by his mild virtues according to the word of our Redeemer alone ‡

CHAPTER IV.

OCCUPATION OF BOHEMIA AND HUNGARY.

At the moment of this signal success, the warlike power of Germany, taking another channel, poured itself over Hungary; and here also, for the aggrandizement of the house of Austria.

If we would form a clear conception of the origin and import of this event, we must bear in mind, above all, that the three eastern monarchies of western Christendom,—Hungary, Bohemia, and Poland, had only attained to a somewhat stable government, and to a share in the benefits of Christianity and civilisation, by German influence under various forms At the end of the fourteenth century, it once more seemed as if this connexion were indissolubly restored. The most powerful house of Germany, that of Luxemburg, possessed Bohemia and Hungary, while the heiress of Poland was educated as the affianced bride of an Austrian prince.

But in all these countries there also existed tendencies opposed to German interference. The most formidable enemy of the Germans, the Grand Prince Jagjel of Lithuania, succeeded in driving the Duke of Austria from the throne of Poland, he afterwards sent his nephew, Koribut, to Bohemia, and his son obtained the crown of Hungary. The race of Jagellon thus consolidated its power throughout the east of Europe, on the one side it presented a bulwark against the incursions of the Ottomans, and on the other, excluded all German influence in spite of many turns of fortune, it still maintained itself in the beginning of the 16th century Sigismund I. ruled over Poland and Lithuania, Wladislas II over Bohemia and Hungary

But it no longer possessed any internal strength. Wladislas II was by no means the man to curb the stormy nobles of Hungary § He was fitted only for the simplest private life Those about him remarked that he spoke of the affairs of daily life with a certain degree of good sense, but that this deserted him as soon as the discourse fell on matters of state He would not believe any thing bad that was told him of any man, and could with difficulty be brought to sign a sentence of death,‖ every body, therefore, did what he liked. Under King Matthias, the public revenues had exceeded 800,000 ducats, under Wladislas, they gradually fell off to 200,000; soon after his death, there was not money enough to pay the expenses of the royal kitchen Every thing fell into ruin and decay. "Two things," it is said in the Maxims of Tolna of the year 1518, "are required for the maintenance of every kingdom —arms and laws, in our kingdom of Hungary we have neither the one nor the other."¶

Under these circumstances, the Jagellons gradually saw the expediency of attaching themselves again to the nearest and most powerful German family—to the house of Austria

* Letter of Charles's of the 30th of June, in Hormayr, 1812, 381 His intention was to appoint the Duke of Ferrara captain general Milan, Charles could not promise to any body, but must wait till Sforza's process was decided In a letter of Angerer's of the 1st of July, it is said, if 6000 men were but now sent to the assistance of Leiva, "all Italy would be won and conquered"

† Ziegler's Acta Pp contain these reflections

‡ Words of the Wahrhaftiger Bericht (True Report) It concludes, "In order that our souls, over which God is Lord, at our temporal departure may be taken to eternal joy, therefore did the Lord Jesus come down into this world, and died on the cross for the love of all men This may the Lord God grant us!"

§ They would fain have driven away Matthias too The Relatio Nuncii apostolici of 1840, in Engel, ii 14, says expressly, "Li Baroni cercano di cacciarlo del reame"

‖ Relatione di Sebastian Zustignan venuto orator di Hongaria in Sanuto iv, 1503. "Il re è homo grande d. persona e di degnissima genealogia devoto e religioso, e si d ce, nunquam habuit concubitum cum muliere, e mai si adira mai dice mal di niun, e se niun dice mal di qualcuno, dicit rex, forsan non est verum Dice assa oration, aldi tre messe al zorno, ma in reliquis è come una statua Est più presto homo rectus quam rex"

¶ Ex Ludovici II decretis Tolnensis conventus in Katona Hist crit Ungariæ, xix p. 89

The Emperor Maximilian, who, as he said, had never for a moment lost sight of "his own rights and those of the German nation" on Hungary and Bohemia, had at length, in the year 1515, the singular satisfaction of receiving both kings—Sigismund and Wladislas—at his court, and of concluding the strictest alliance with them. Wladislas betrothed his son and daughter to a grand-daughter and grandson of the emperor, Sigismund promised to marry Bona Sforza, who was also related to the house of Austria. The year after, Wladislas died, and Louis II. ascended the throne, under the joint guardianship of Maximilian and Sigismund. By degrees, a German party took firm root at the court, especially after the marriage between Louis and the grand-daughter of Maximilian, Mary of Austria, had actually been concluded (A. D. 1521). All was, however, still in the greatest confusion. Heberstein cannot find words to describe how the great nobles, spiritual as well as temporal, vied with each other in insolence,"[*] how the frontiers were without defence, while their armed bands obstructed the streets of the capital, how the loud trumpets called the magnates to dinner, while the king sat almost alone,—all places were distributed by favour, and the currency was deteriorated. At length the intelligent queen, at least, formed plans for reviving the authority of the state, but already had a power arisen capable of opposing a formidable resistance to the court.

Under King Matthias the house of Zapolya, so called from a Slavonic village near Poschega, whence it originated, rose to peculiar eminence. To this house, in particular, King Wladislas had owed his accession to the throne, whence, however, it thought itself entitled to claim a share in the sovereign power, and even a sort of prospective right to the throne. Its members were the wealthiest of all the magnates, they possessed seventy-two castles,[†] the chief seat of the family being Trentsin, a fortress perched on a steep rock overhanging the Waag, adorned with the most beautiful gardens, watered from wells dug a hundred fathoms deep by Turkish prisoners, and defended by strong fortifications. It is said that a prophecy early promised the crown to the young John Zapolya. Possessed of all the power conferred by his rich inheritance, Count of Zips, and Woiwode of Transylvania, he soon collected a strong party around him. It was he who mainly persuaded the Hungarians, in the year 1505, to exclude all foreigners from the throne by a formal decree; which, though they were not always able to maintain in force, they could never be induced absolutely to revoke. In the year 1514, the Woiwode succeeded in putting down an exceedingly formidable insurrection of the peasants with his own forces, a service which the lesser nobility prized the more highly, because it enabled them to reduce the peasantry to a still harder state of servitude.[‡] His wish was, on the death of Wladislas, to become Gubernator of the kingdom, to marry the deceased king's daughter Anne, and then to await the course of events. But he was here encountered by the policy of Maximilian. Anne was married to the Archduke Ferdinand; Zapolya was excluded from the administration of the kingdom; even the vacant Palatinate was refused him and given to his old rival Stephen Bathory. He was highly incensed: indeed, at the meeting of the Rakosch, in 1518, the emperor kept a few thousand men ready to come to the aid of the Hungarian government in case of any violence on the part of Zapolya.[§] But it was not till the year 1525 that Zapolya got the upper hand at the Rakosch. The king having nevertheless rejected his proposals, his followers summoned an extraordinary diet at Hatwan, at which they made an attempt to exclude all strangers, to alter the whole government, and take it into their own hands. They deposed the palatine, Bathory, and elected in his stead the Woiwode's most intimate friend, Stephen Verboez. As to Zapolya, no one entertained a doubt that he aimed at the throne. "The Woiwode," says a Venetian report of 1523, "has a good head, he is very clever, and universally beloved: he would be glad if the kingdom suffered some disaster; he would then reconquer it with his own forces and make himself king."[‖] "He strives," says another, of the year 1525, "with all the powers of his mind after the crown, and prepares every thing so that he may be able to seize it."

In order to arrest these hasty and undisguised strides of a vassal towards the final goal of his ambition, his opponents, who had every thing to fear from his success, rallied more closely round the court; declared, at a national assembly, the decrees of Hatwan null and void, reinstated Bathory, and requested the king at length to exert his authority. This the queen was fully prepared to do. She demanded complete liberty in the administration of the finances, and the direct dependence of the frontier troops on the government. She warned the papal nuncio not to put too much fuel on the fire.

But before any thing was accomplished—on the contrary, just as these party conflicts had thrown the country into the utmost confusion, the mighty enemy, Soliman, appeared on the frontiers of Hungary, determined to put an end to the anarchy. Ottomans and Jagellons had long stood opposed to each other on the eastern verge of Europe: the propitious moment had at length arrived, in which the Sultan might hope, at least as far as Hungary was concerned, to fight out this long pending duel. Five years

* Rerum Moscoviticarum Commentarii, Basil, 1571, p. 116.

† According to Turnschwamb (Engel, i. p. 193), many of them were confided only to trusty hands, such as Father John and Stephen Zapolya.

‡ The revolt was directed precisely against the nobility. Zeckel called himself, in one of his proclamations, "Regis Hungariæ tantummodo subditus et non dominorum."—*Katona*, xviii. 720.

§ Maximilian's Instructions to Heberstein in Senkenberg's Sammlung ungedructer Schriften, iv. p. 26.

‖ Relatione del Sr d'Orio, 12th Dec. 1523. "Saria contento che quel regno si perdesse e poi lui con il favor de Transilvani ricuperarlo e farsi re."

before, he had conquered Belgrade, which, it was said, had fallen, partly because the Hungarian government could not raise the fifty gulden necessary for the transport of the ammunition lying ready at Ofen Since then, the strong places on the frontier of Croatia had fallen into the hands of the pachas, and the plain country was laid open to a great blow Such an one the sultan now felt himself encouraged to strike, both by the internal state of Hungary and the general distraction of Europe. In his prison at Madrid, Francis I had found means to entreat the assistance of Soliman, urging that it well beseemed a great emperor to succour the oppressed Plans were laid at Constantinople, according to which the two sovereigns were to attack Spain with a combined fleet, and to send armies to invade Hungary and the north of Italy * Soliman, without any formal treaty, was by his position an ally of the Ligue, as the king of Hungary was, of the emperor On the 23d of April, 1526, Soliman, after visiting the graves of his forefathers and of the old Moslem martyrs, marched out of Constantinople with a mighty host, consisting of about a hundred thousand men, and incessantly strengthened by fresh recruits on its road. He understood the art of keeping his troops under the severest discipline. His diary shows that he ordered men to be beheaded for having driven the horses of the peasantry, or destroyed the standing corn in a village.† Still in the bloom of youth, he displayed those brilliant qualities of energy and love of conquest which had raised his ancestors to greatness

What power had Hungary, in the condition we have just described, of resisting such an attack?

Ibrahim Pacha had already laid siege to Peterwardein before the Hungarians had taken any measures for defence The troops had not long before been called out, but none had appeared, contributions had been demanded, but scarcely any-thing had been raised With great difficulty, Anton Fugger had been induced to advance fifty thousand gulden on the Neusohler mines. The young king took the field with a following of not more than three thousand men ‡

Ibrahim had conquered Peterwardein, and had welcomed his sovereign on the Hungarian soil with an offering of five hundred heads The Ottoman army was now nearly three hundred thousand strong, and had begun to ascend the Danube · Soliman caused it to be proclaimed through his camp that his object was Ofen Meanwhile the troops of some Gespannschafts (counties) and a few magnates collected around the king; a few companies hired by the pope, and a few by Poland, also joined him., On his arrival in Tolna, he might have from ten to twelve thousand men §

The most pressing necessity was to defend the passage of the Drave, whither the palatine, who was certainly not deficient in zeal, now hastened But a number of magnates refused to advance without the king Soliman thus gained time to build a convenient bridge, over which his army marched without interruption for five days. King Louis said, "I see my head must be stuck up instead of yours, well then, I will carry it thither myself!" He proceeded to the fatal plain of Mohacz, fully resolved with his small band to await in the open field the overwhelming force of the enemy

The troops of the kingdom were as yet far from being assembled, the two mightiest vassals, the Ban of Croatia and the Woiwode of Transylvania, were still missing, the Bohemian and Moravian allies had not yet arrived, —with all its recent additions, the army in Mohacz amounted to from twenty to twenty-four thousand men Few of them had ever seen a pitched battle The command was intrusted to a Muscovite friar, Paul Tomory, Archbishop of Colocza, who had formerly distinguished himself in a few marauding expeditions Spite of all these disadvantages, the Hungarians still indulged the most extravagant self-confidence. It would have been impossible to induce them to retreat,‖ they would not even form a barricade of their waggons. As soon as the enemy descended the hills in front of them, into the plain where they lay encamped, without a moment's pause they rushed upon him But Soliman was as prudent as he was daring. The Hungarians thought to decide the battle by an impetuous charge, "they trusted in their harness of the blue steel" Ill provided with infantry or artillery, they made war in the spirit and manner of the past century On the other hand, Soliman, barbarian as he might otherwise be, knew how to avail himself of the most recent improvements in the advancing art of war, he had planted three hundred cannon behind the heights we have mentioned, and his janizaries were as well skilled in the use of the matchlock as any soldiery in the world The Hungarians found no difficulty in dispersing the advanced Turkish squadrons and occupying the hill Already they thought they had conquered, but here they first beheld the boundless camp of the Osmans. They rushed forward headlong, as if the impossible were possible to their valour, and were received by a tremendous fire; the right wing, from the artillery, the centre from the musketry of the janizaries, while the Sipahi horse attacked them on both flanks. Here personal valour could avail nothing. The Hungarians were immediately thrown into disorder,¶ their best men fell, the others took to

* Narrative of Ibraim (the Imbert Wascha) in the Report by Lamberg and Jurischits in Gevay's Urkunden und Actenstucken zur Geschichte der Verhaltnisse zwischen Oesterreich Ungern und der Pforte. 1530, p 42

† Hammer's Geschichte der Osmanen, v iii p 639

‡ Broderithus Descriptio cladis Mohaczianæ in appendice Bonfinii ed Sambucus, p 558. See Thurnschwand, p 204

§ Among them 4000 foot. Brod 559 He does not state the exact number of the cavalry

‖ Ongari si havea potuti ritrar salvo verso Buda Copia di un aviso avuto da Constantinopoli in Hammar's Wiens erste aufgehobene turkische Belagerung App, No viii a simple but good statement

¶ Extract from the Heiduck Nagy's History of the

flight The young king was compelled to flee It was not even granted him to die in the field of battle, a far more miserable end awaited him. Mounted behind a Silesian soldier, who served him as a guide, he had already been carried across the dark waters that divide the plain, his horse was already climbing the bank, when he slipped, fell back, and buried himself and his rider in the morass * This rendered the defeat decisive. The leader of the nation—the king—and a great part of the magnates had fallen † For the present, no further resistance could be thought of The land was ravaged far and wide; the keys of Ofen were carried to the sultan, who celebrated the Beiram there.

Soliman had gained one of those victories which decide the fate of nations during long epochs The great power at the head of which he stood, the power which had carried the principles of Islam, such as they had been established in Asia, under Tartar influence, into the other quarters of the globe, had been raised by him to complete ascendency in eastern Europe. Who was strong enough to overturn it? Troubling himself little about the defence of the places he had taken, he turned back and placed the trophies of Ofen on the Hippodrome and the mosque of Aja Sofia.

That two thrones, the succession to which was not entirely free from doubt, had thus been left vacant, was an event that necessarily caused a great agitation throughout Christendom. It was still a question whether such a European power as Austria would continue to exist,—a question which it is only necessary to state, in order to be aware of its vast importance to the fate of mankind at large, and of Germany in particular Before the nature of the relations which might subsist between Europe and the Ottoman empire could even be discussed, this great question had to be decided

The claims of Ferdinand to both crowns, unquestionable as they might be in reference to the treaties with the reigning houses, were opposed in the nations themselves, by the right of election and the authority of considerable rivals

In Hungary, as soon as the Turks had retired, John Zapolya appeared with the fine army which he had kept back from the conflict the fall of the king was at the same time the fall of his adversaries. The faction which had framed the resolutions of Hatwan was now omnipotent, and, at an assembly at Tokay, they determined that, as nothing could be undertaken without a king and ruler, they would immediately proceed to elect one, and to that end convoke a diet at Stuhlweissenburg ‡ Even in Tokay, however, John Zapolya was saluted as king.

Meanwhile, the Dukes of Bavaria conceived the design of getting possession of the throne of Bohemia · in this they were encouraged by several obsequious nobles of that country, and in September they despatched their councillor Weissenfelder to Prague, who found their prospects so promising that they determined to send a solemn embassy to Bohemia.

Nor was it in the two kingdoms alone that these pretenders had a considerable party. The state of politics in Europe was such as to insure them powerful supporters abroad

In the first place, Francis I. was intimately connected with Zapolya in a short time a delegate from the pope was at his side, and the Germans in Rome maintained that Clement assisted the faction of the Woiwode with money § Zapolya sent an agent to Venice with a direct request to be admitted a member of the Ligue of Cognac.

In Bohemia, too, the French had long had devoted partisans We find that, in the year 1523, they had the project of attacking Austria from the side of Bohemia, and had carried on a correspondence with an ancestor of Wallenstein, with that object ‖ As the King of Poland, who had for some time withdrawn himself from the Austrian alliance, and likewise set up pretensions to the throne of Bohemia, found he had no chance of success, the Polish as well as the French envoys promised their support to the agents of Bavaria.

By this political combination, Duke William of Bavaria was encouraged to form still more ambitious plans

We have already observed, that Rome felt the necessity of placing a king of the Romans by the side of, or rather in opposition to, the emperor Charles. Meanwhile, Duke William, one of the most devoted adherents of the Curia, had already conceived the thought of raising himself to this high station, and had actually taken steps in consequence

At the same diet of 1524, in which the Council of Regency was overthrown, the houses of Bavaria and the Palatinate, engaged in a common struggle against the nobles, laid aside their old hostilities and concluded a new hereditary alliance Leonhard Eck addressed amicable reproaches to the elector, that at the last vacancy of the imperial crown he had forgotten his own pretensions, and had subsequently

Campaign of Mohacz, preserved in Petschewi's Ottoman History (the singular example of a really useful Oriental narrative from an Oriental work) communicated by Hammer, in Hormayr's Archiv for 1827 No 15

* This account (in Nagy and others) is confirmed by the letter in Katona, xix p 697, concerning the discovery of the body

† Katona, p 703 "Magna debinc rerum conversio secuta fuit, pluribus et præsulibus et proceribus una hac dimicatione exstinctis"

‡ Among the contradictory accounts of the chroniclers, the only trustworthy document is the answer of the King of Poland to the invitation sent to him from Tokay Dogiel and Katona, xix p 748

§ Ziegler, Vita Clem VII, in Schelhorn's Amœnitatcs, ii 308 "Ea pecunia (he is speaking of exactions) Trentschinii factionem contra Ferdinandum regem aliquamdiu juvit"

‖ Lettera di Franc Massario in Sanuto, tom xxxv, calls him "Waldestein, barone e gran capitano di Bohemia, volentier veniria a servir la Sta n^ra cum 10, 20, 30^m persone Questo è quel capitano che 'l re X^mo voleva condurre"

ceded his right to the Vicariate to the Council of Regency.*

Shortly afterwards, when the princes met at the cross-bow match at Heidelberg, which we have already mentioned, Duke William no longer concealed that he aspired to the Roman crown for himself.

At an interview at Ellwangen, soon after, they again discussed the matter. Duke William appeared willing to give the precedency to the elector; but as that prince had taken no measures towards the accomplishment of such an object, he commenced negotiations without scruple on his own account In the autumn of 1526, overtures were also made to the Elector of Saxony, though without success. since that prince belonged to a party professing opinions radically different †

The consequences that must have resulted, had this scheme succeeded, are so incalculable, that it is not too much to say they would have completely changed the political history of Europe. The power of Bavaria would have outweighed that of Austria in both German and Slavonian countries, and Zapolya, thus supported, would have been able to maintain his station; the Ligue, and with it high ultramontane opinions, would have held the ascendency in eastern Europe. Never was there a project more pregnant with danger to the growing power of the house of Austria.

Ferdinand behaved with all the prudence and energy which that house has so often displayed in difficult emergencies.

For the present, the all-important object was the crown of Bohemia.

His situation as husband of a Princess of Hungary and Bohemia, and as brother of the widowed queen, brought him into frequent personal contact with the most puissant nobles He perfectly understood the art of turning to his own advantage every favourable disposition arising out of these circumstances, and of extinguishing every germ of antipathy by favours. The influential High Burggrave, Low von Rozmital, received the assurance that the account which he was bound to render of his administration would either be altogether dispensed with, or very slightly inspected. Important concessions were also made to Schwanberg, Schlich, Pflug, and the Duke of Munsterberg The Chancellor Adam von Neuhaus had hastened in the retinue of the Austrian envoy, to use his influence in favour of Ferdinand. While a certain number of Bohemian nobles were quickly induced by these measures to declare that they would acknowledge no other master than the archduke,‡ no means were neglected of conciliating the mass of the population. Though thoroughly convinced that his wife (and therefore he himself) had an unquestionable hereditary right to the throne, he carefully avoided offending the pride which the nation felt in the belief that, in a case like the present, it had absolute freedom of election. He let it appear that his claim was by no means the chief motive for his offering himself to their choice

At first he thought of at once assuming the title of king, but this project he dropped at the advice of his envoys He acceded to the demand of the Bohemians, that he would take upon himself a part of the public debt, inconvenient as that was in the straitened state of his finances Nor did he disdain to give the most careful answers to all the objections which his envoys said were urged against him.§

In a word, all his measures were taken with such skill and prudence, that on the day of election, though the Bavarian agent had, up to the last moment, not the slightest doubt of the success of his negotiations, an overwhelming majority in the three estates elected Ferdinand to the throne of Bohemia.

This took place on the 23d October, 1526. A solemn embassy proceeded to Vienna to invite him to take possession of his new kingdom, one of the fairest in the world, including, as it did, Silesia and Lusatia.

A very important question, deserving a more accurate inquiry, here suggests itself,—what influence religious considerations had in this election

All the countries subject to the Bohemian crown were filled with anti-papal elements In Silesia and the Lusatias, the evangelical doctrines were widely diffused, in Bohemia and Moravia, the Utraquists formed a most powerful community. It is hardly probable that, in the choice of a king, the interests of these different confessions were disregarded.

In this point of view, Ferdinand was infinitely to be preferred to a duke of Bavaria. The dukes were unqualified adherents of the papacy, and fierce persecutors. The archduke, on the contrary, however strict a catholic himself, however careful to appear so (for in all the countries in question there was still a very considerable catholic party), had for some time showed great moderation in his hereditary dominions We have seen how little he was inclined to favour the secular claims of the clergy, and what equivocal decrees the German diet had passed under his influence Moreover, he was at this moment at open war with the pope, the Bohemian election took place while the recruiting for Frundsberg's army was going on

We find no traces of the negotiations which were probably carried on with relation to religious affairs; but from the Recesses it appears that Ferdinand acceded to very remarkable concessions.

It is well known that the court of Rome never fully recognised the Compactata of the Council of Basle (a line of policy it afterwards pursued with many treaties unfavourable to itself), and, since the time of Pius II, had expressly refused to confirm them.

* Mémoires de la Vie et des Faicts de Frederic I (Comte Palatin), in Hoffman's Sammlung ungedructer Nachrichten, ch xlii

† "There are traces" says the Bavarian Staatsarchivar Stumpf, "that Pope Clement VII and the King of France tried to forward the duke's designs"

‡ Extract from a letter of Weissenfelder in Stumpf, Baierns Polit Gesch i p 30

§ Extract from the Instructions and the Ambassador's Correspondence, Bucholtz, ii p 407

Ferdinand now promised to give their full efficacy to the Compactata,* and to assume, in treating with the pope, that they were confirmed.†

One of the greatest grievances of the Utraquists was, that they had long been without bishops to ordain their priests, and that they had been reduced to many strange and even hurtful expedients to supply this want. Ferdinand promised to procure for them an archbishop who should put in force the Compactata in relation to both spiritual and temporal affairs. In short, he solemnly undertook not only to protect the Utraquists, but to obtain for them a fresh recognition of their privileges.

This was, perhaps, rendered less difficult by the fact, that a party hostile to Luther was now formed among the Utraquists themselves; notwithstanding which, however, they were still treated as heretics.

Nor were the general abuses and errors of the church entirely forgotten. Ferdinand promised the Bohemians to take measures to promote a Christian union and reformation—a promise which, indeed, either side might interpret in its own favour,—but which, as it related only to the conduct of the emperor, not to that of the pope,—to some assembly, of whatever nature, not to a general council in which all the nations of Christendom were to take part,‡—could, in fact, hardly be understood in any other sense than that intended by the German diets.

The Silesians expressed themselves still more plainly and unequivocally.

At a meeting of the States at Leobschütz, on the 4th December, 1526, after they had recognised Ferdinand's hereditary right—though not without keeping up the appearance of a certain freedom—they commissioned the delegates who were to be the bearers of this recognition to Vienna, (among whom were princes greatly inclined to evangelical opinions,—for example, Frederic of Liegnitz and George of Brandenburg,) to call the attention of the new king and archduke to the putting an end to religious dissension, "according to the gospel and word of God."§ In conformity with these instructions, the delegates entreated the king to take into consideration the establishment of a Christian ordinance according to the standard of the gospel; that so all might live together in peace and unity. Ferdinand replied, he would do all that could conduce to christian unity and the praise of Almighty God.‖

As opposed to the traditional opinion, it may sound like a paradox to affirm—what however the general combination of events warrants us in concluding,—that the bearing which the house of Austria had at this crisis assumed,—opposed to Rome in its political, and moderate in its religious views, contributed to secure to it the obedience of these countries, which were filled with such various elements of opposition to Rome.

By a singular concatenation of circumstances, the high Romanist opinions, of which Bavaria was the champion, contributed, from the very first, to the defeat of their plans.

On his brother's birth-day, the 24th of February, 1527, Ferdinand was crowned at Prague; on the 11th of May he received the act of homage and allegiance in the market-place in Breslau, and the German princes hastened to accept from the new suzerain a renewal of the fiefs which they held of the Bohemian crown. A Muscovite ambassador, who happened to be then at the court, expressed his surprise that so magnificent a kingdom should have passed into the hands of a new lord without a sword being drawn.¶

The affairs of Hungary were not so easily or so peacefully settled.

That country offered a certain analogy to Bohemia in a religious point of view. Queen Mary, around whom the Austrian party gathered, was esteemed a friend of the new opinions: she did not keep the fasts, read Lutheran writings, and had followers of Luther at her court. In November, 1526, Luther dedicated a psalm to her, for consolation under her misfortune. On the other hand, Zapolya's partisans affected strict orthodoxy: their chief organ, Verböcz, passed among the Lutherans for a great hypocrite; he had caused a covered way to be constructed from his own house to the neighbouring Capuchin convent, that he might enjoy uninterrupted communication with it.**

---

* "Quod rursum ad suum vigorem pervenirent." Ferdinandi Literæ, 15th Dec. 1526, ap. Dumont, iv. pp. 1. 469.

† "Promisimus, cum summo Pontifice illud tractare, ac si Bohemis ac Moravis illa (compactata) cum effectu essent confirmata."

‡ Excerpt of the article inserted in the Landtafel, Bucholtz, ii. p. 420.

§ The words of the instruction in Buckisch, Religionsacten, MS., tom. i. p. 206, are as follows:—"Und nachdem der allm. Gott aus seiner göttlichen Verordnung geschickt und verliehen, dass wir S. Kön. Mt. zu unserm Erbkönige einträchtiglich angenommen, welcher einmütigen und tröstlichen Meinung wir s. Allmächtigkeit billig Lob und Dank sagen, so befinden wir nun in Notturft unser Seel and Leibs glückseliger Wolfahrt, die jetzige vorfallende Irrung und Rweispalt, so sich in dem h. christl. Glauben zugetragen, bei S. K. M. anzuregen, damit dieselb aus solchem Irrthum und Zertrennung erhaben, und nach Verordnung der h. christl. Kirchen dem Evangelio und Worte Gottes gemäss nach S. K. Mt. Aussatz und durch unser aller einmüthig und freundliches Vergleichen in recht christl. Bestand und gleichförmigen Gebrauch gebracht würde, welches E. L. ihn und E. F. Gn. bei S. K. Mt. alles in Unterthänigkeit bitten werden, auf dass S. K. Mt. dasselbe als ein christl. König zu Trost und Heil unrer Seelen Seligkeit, auch zu Dempfung erfolgenden Unraths nach dem h. Evangelio gnädiglich zu verordnen und zu verschaffen geruhe."—"And since Almighty God, in his divine providence, has ordained and granted that we have unanimously accepted H. R. My. to be our hereditary king, for which unanimous and comfortable opinion we give due praise and thanks to the Almighty, we now find it needful for the welfare of our souls and bodies to bring the errors and divisions which now prevail in the holy Christian faith before H. R. My., whereby the same may be raised out of such error and division, and according to the ordinances of the holy Christian church, and agreeably to the gospel and the word of God may, conformably with H. R. My.'s pleasure, and by our unanimous and amicable agreement, be brought to a true Christian understanding, and a uniform practice. Your princely graces will, in all submission, pray H. R. My., in order that H. R. My., as a Christian king, may be pleased graciously to order and procure the same to be done according to the Holy Gospel, for the comfort and benefit of our souls, and for the prevention of future troubles."

‖ Petition and Resolution, in Schickfuss, Schlesische Chronik, iii. 171. Also in the Appendix to Bucholtz, ii 523.

¶ Herberstein R. M. C., p. 154.

** Turnschwamb, in Engel, i. 197. "Stephen Verböcz amicus Stis." Relatio Actorum; Engel, ii. p. 55.

The political consequences of these conflicting opinions were, however, not very obvious in Hungary. The inclinations in favour of a church differing in form from that established, were as yet too scattered, too insignificant, to produce any sensible effect. Ferdinand, who had been reproached with surrounding his wife with Germans, who, it was said, were all Lutherans,* carefully endeavoured to maintain his reputation as a good catholic. On the Good Friday of 1527, he took occasion to admonish his sister concerning her religious leanings.† On Corpus Christi day of the same year, he was seen following the procession through the streets of Vienna, in regal ornaments, with a sword girt at his side and a missal in his hand, looking around to see that every body paid due reverence to the holy elements. From time to time he issued mandates for the maintenance of the ancient practices of the church.

But in Hungary, superiority of force was at that time more important than questions of religion.

It could not be said that the whole nation was split into two hostile parties; rather, that two political tendencies existed in its bosom; the one inclining to the court and the palatine, the other, to the opposition and Zapolya. After the disaster of Mohacz, they stood in the same relation to each other as before; the preponderancy of either was dependent on the momentary assent of the majority, who had attached themselves decidedly neither to the one party nor the other.

At first, when Zapolya came forward, full armed and powerful out of the general desolation, he had the uncontested superiority. The capital of the kingdom sought his protection, after which he marched to Stuhlweissenburg, where his partisans bore down all attempts at opposition:‡ he was elected and crowned (11th of November, 1526); in Croatia, too, he was acknowledged king at a diet; he filled all the numerous places, temporal and spiritual, left vacant by the disaster of Mohacz, with his friends. We have mentioned the negotiations he set on foot in all directions. In Venice and Rome, in Munich and Constantinople, we find his agents. When some one showed him an address of Ferdinand's, exhorting the Hungarians to abandon him, he smiled, and said, "kingdoms were not conquered in that manner."

But Ferdinand soon had recourse to other expedients.

The party of the former court had still sufficient strength and importance to convoke a diet on behalf of Ferdinand, the husband of a Jagellon, who had so many ancient treaties in his favour. It was held at Presburg—also in November, 1526—and elected him king. Stephen Bathory and Alexis Thurzo, the Bishop of Wesprim, were extremely active in his service. There is a diploma of Ferdinand's, in which he names his adherents, expresses his gratitude to them, and promises his supporters the best posts and offices hereafter.§ Nor did he neglect to try the efficacy of gold; mindful of the hint of his sister Mary, that he could accomplish more with a gulden now, than in future perhaps with a large sum. Heavily as they pressed upon him, his gifts were still insufficient to put an end to the waverings of the magnates. Ferdinand saw indeed—for he had too much good sense to indulge in any illusions—that the grand thing was superiority in arms. The acquisition of the crown of Bohemia gradually enabled him to obtain the necessary force, and he received some pecuniary aid from his brother. If he hesitated to reject the negotiations which the King of Poland set on foot at Olmütz, it was, as he expressly says in an extant letter, merely in order to gain time for his preparations. At length he had proceeded far enough.‖

On the 31st July, 1527, Ferdinand reached the half-ruined tower on the high road between Vienna and Ofen, which marks the boundary between Austria and Hungary: he was received by the palatine and a few Hungarian horsemen. As soon as he touched the soil of Hungary, he alighted from his horse and swore to maintain the privileges of the kingdom. He had brought a noble army into the field. The grants of his new kingdom had enabled him to raise an excellent body of infantry: he was preceded by Katzianer; and he now distinguished himself by the most rigorous discipline, which he enforced even on the Bohemians. Rogendorf, who had just returned from Spain, and the veteran captains, Marx Sittich and Eck von Reischach, had brought up the most experienced landsknechts. Besides these, the king's new vassals, Casimir of Brandenburg, George of Saxony, and the aged warrior, Erich of Brunswick, had been induced to send some squadrons of German reiters to his aid. Casimir, notwithstanding that he had adopted decided, though moderate, evangelical opinions, was invested with the chief command. Nicholas von Salm, whose name we met with at the battle of Pavia, and Johann Hilchen, the companion of Sickingen, were with this army. It amounted to 8000 foot and 3000 horse. The king was advised not to expose his person to danger, lest he should share the fate of his predecessor; but as at this moment he received

* Diarium in Comitiis Pesthanis, in Engel, ii. 51. "Dedit ei Germanos qui omnes fuerunt Lutherani." In Katona, xix. 515, Art. v. "Fukkarii ablegentur: oratores Cæsareus et Venetus (the latter only for the sake of the former, as the Venetian Relation expresses) exmittantur; Lutherani etiam omnes de regno extirpentur,—ubicumque reperti fuerint, libere combdrantur."

† Correspondence in Bucholtz, ix.

‡ So at least the Bishop of Nitra, Hodmanizky, excused himself for placing the crown on Zapolya's head. He says he should have been in danger of his life if he had refused.—Diploma Ferdinandi; Katona, xix. p. 752.

§ Katona, xx. 19. "Prælaturas et dignitates et beneficia ecclesiastica ac bona et jura hereditaria et officia quæ ad collationem nostram regiam—devolventur, præfatis, consiliariis et his qui nostras partes sequentur, pro suis cuique meritis ante alios donabimus."—Ferdinand describes the circumstances of both elections in a letter to his brother of 31st Dec. 1526. (Gevay, p. 30.) He asserts that he was elected by a vast majority.

‖ Ferdinand to Mary, 7th April. "Combein que nay nullement en volente—riens traicter ny conclure, neantmoings—pour entretenir les affaires jusques a ce que soie de tout prest pour me mectre aux champs, . . . ie luy (au Roi de Pologne) ay bien voulu accorder icelle journée."—*Gevay*, p. 60.

the intelligence that a son was born to him, and the succession thus secured, he insisted on accompanying the expedition.*

Nor did this assume a very formidable aspect. The first fortified places, Comorn, Tata, and Gran, fell without much resistance: the excellent artillery, the red-hot cannon-balls, quickly reduced the garrison to despair. The Germans advanced without interruption; and as soon as it appeared possible that Ferdinand might be successful, Zapolya's followers began to desert him. The fleet in the Danube went over first, — the military importance of which was equal to its moral effect; next the Ban Bathyany, who had already changed sides more than once, returned to that of Ferdinand. Peter Pereny, who is regarded as the first evangelical magnate in Hungary, and Valentine Török, suspected of being actuated by the desire to retain possession of some sequestrated church lands, appeared with splendid retinues.† The example of these great men was followed by innumerable obscurer ones. Zapolya saw that his antagonist was the stronger, and neither ventured to meet him in the field, nor even to hold the capital against him, but retreated to his own dominions. On the 20th August, St. Stephen's day, Ferdinand made his entry into Ofen.

Whilst the States of the kingdom assembled about him in that city, the German reiters under Nicholas von Salm—Markgrave Casimir having died at Ofen — pursued the Woiwode across the Theis. Never did the German troops display more bravery and constancy.‡ They had often neither meat nor bread, and were obliged to live on such fruits as they found in the gardens: the inhabitants were wavering and uncertain — they submitted, and then revolted again to the enemy; Zapolya's troops, aided by their knowledge of the ground, made several very formidable attacks by night; but the Germans evinced, in the moment of danger, the skill and determination of a Roman legion: they showed, too, a noble constancy under difficulties and privations. At Tokay, they defeated Zapolya and compelled him to quit Hungary; after which they had the honour to escort their royal leader and countryman to Stuhlweissenburg, in silken and embroidered surcoats over their glittering armour. On the 3d November, 1527, Ferdinand was crowned in Stuhlweissenburg: only five of the magnates of the kingdom adhered to Zapolya. The victory appeared complete.

Ferdinand, however, distinctly felt that this appearance was delusive. "Monseigneur," he writes in the same November to his brother, "I do not doubt that the nature of the Hungarians, — the fickleness of their will, is known to you.§ They must be held in with a short rein if you would be sure of them." It was not without great hesitation that he could resolve to leave Hungary again at this moment.

In Bohemia, too, his power was far from secure. His Bavarian neighbours had not relinquished the hope of driving him from the throne at the first general turn of affairs.

The Ottomans, meanwhile, acting upon the persuasion that every land in which the head of their chief had rested belonged of right to them, were preparing to return to Hungary; either to take possession of it themselves, or, at first, as was their custom, to bestow it on a native ruler — Zapolya, who now eagerly sought an alliance with them—as their vassal.

This was a state of things in which the most important events often hang on the fate of a battle. The house of Austria had no other means of maintaining the position it had reached, than the assistance of the empire, to which it was compelled incessantly to appeal.

On the Germans now devolved the defence of Christendom against the Ottoman power.

CHAPTER V.

FOUNDATION OF EVANGELICAL STATES.

So important, in respect of the foreign relations of Germany, were the consequences of the events which coincided with the meeting of the diet at Spire.

But that assembly at the same time gave rise to other consequences, affecting the internal affairs of the empire and the church, which, comparatively insignificant as they at first appeared, were intrinsically, and with relation to the whole future condition of Germany, of far higher and more unequivocal importance than any external acquisitions. Those of the States inclined to evangelical opinions undertook to form new ecclesiastical establishments in their territories, on the basis laid down by the Recess of the empire: they proceeded to sever themselves definitively from the world-embracing hierarchy of the Latin church.

But as it usually happens that, at the beginning of radical changes, the principles most strongly opposed to the existing order of things are the most prominent and influential, so, in the present case, the extremest objects were those most anxiously aimed at; and the ideas most in favour were those most at variance with the absolute dominion of the papacy.

Luther, at an earlier period, had contributed

* Ursinus Velius de Bello Pannonico, ed. Kollar. From the collations in Katona, who has inserted this work entire, it is evident how inferior is Isthuansi and even Zermegh to these contemporaneous and circumstantial accounts.

† Gebhardi Gesch. v. Ungarn, ii. 287. In Bucholtz, ix. 323, there is a document concerning the submission of Pereny, which probably relates to this matter, and is extremely remarkable. Pereny represents the following as his first demand:—"Inprimis cupit D. Petrus der S. M[tem] assecurari, ne a religione sua unquam prohibeatur, quandoquidem verum et bonum Christianum se profiteatur et scientem fidem Ch[anam] *per Christum juxta evangelium.*" Ferdinand answers: "Concedit M. S. uti se gerat verum et bonum Ch[anum] ut cujusque erga deum pietas fidesque nostra vera et catolica dictare et postulare videtur." A concession which, though very equivocal, seems to have satisfied Pereny. Without doubt, he thought himself also in possession of the fides vera et catholica.

‡ Velius; "Haud unquam alias Germani militis virtus et patientia in bello magis enituit."

§ "Leur muable et fragille vouloir." Gevay, p. 120. Bucholtz, iii. 114.

to this result. In the year 1523, the Bohemians, having fallen into intolerable confusion and perplexity, in consequence of their adherence to the necessity of episcopal ordination, he advised them to choose their pastors and bishops themselves without scruple. "First prepare yourselves by prayer," said he, "and then assemble together in God's name and proceed to the election. Let the most eminent and respected among you lay their hands with good courage on the chosen candidate, and, when this has taken place in several parishes, let the pastors have a right to elect a head or superintendent to visit them, as Peter visited the first Christian communities."* Ideas of this kind were at that time very popular and widely diffused, both in Switzerland and Germany. We find even an obscure congregation declaring to its new pastor, that he is not their master but their servant and minister; peremptorily forbidding him to apply to the bishop concerning any one of his congregation, and threatening him with dismissal, if he does not adhere to the single and eternal word of God.† The congregations began to regard themselves as the sources of spiritual power. Had these principles become universal, the edifice of a new church must have been raised on a purely democratical basis.

And, in fact, the experiment was tried in one large principality of Germany.

There is nothing in the history of these times more remarkable than the decree of the synod which Landgrave Philip of Hessen held with the spiritual and temporal estates of his dominions at Homberg. The objection raised by the guardian of the Franciscans of Marburg—that at so small an assembly no decision could be taken on affairs which properly belonged to a general council—was easily overruled; since even at the diet the impossibility of waiting for such a council had been admitted. On the other hand, Francis Lambert succeeded in establishing the contrary principle—that every Christian is participant in the priesthood; that the true church consists only in their fellowship, and that it is for this church to decide, according to God's word, upon articles of faith.‡ The idea was formed of constituting a church consisting solely of true believers. The following was the scheme drawn up to that effect.§

It was proposed that, after a sermon, a meeting should be held, and every one should be asked whether he was determined to submit himself to the laws, or not. Those who refused should be put out and regarded as heathens. But the names of those who chose to be in the number of the saints, should be written down; they must not be troubled if, at first, they should be few, for God would soon increase their number: these would constitute the congregation. The most important business of their meetings would be the choice of their spiritual leaders (here simply called bishops). For this station any citizen of irreproachable life and competent instruction should be eligible, whatever were his profession; but he should be allowed to retain it only so long as he preached the genuine word of God. Each parish or congregation should have some members who should perform military service, and a common chest or treasury, to which all should contribute, and out of which the poor, and those who had been driven from their homes for the Gospel's sake, should receive assistance. The right of excommunicating, it was affirmed, is inherent in every man: the crimes which draw down this punishment are specified: absolution can only be granted after sin has been confessed and repented of. [We see that the most rigid church discipline is united with the fullest independence of the several religious communities. The pretensions set up are sanctified by the profound earnestness of spirit which dictates them.] Every year the churches, represented by bishops and deputies, should assemble in general synod, where all complaints should be heard and doubts resolved. A committee of thirteen should be appointed to prepare the business and lay it before the meeting, to be decided according to God's word. At the general synod, the meeting of which was permanently fixed for the third Sunday after Easter, three visitors were to be chosen, who were to examine the state of each individual church.

It is very remarkable that the man who worked out these ideas into so complete a scheme of church government, was a foreigner—a Frenchman of Avignon—who, converted by Zwingli, had become deeply imbued with evangelical doctrines in the school of Luther. The ideas are the same on which the French, Scotch, and American churches were afterwards founded, and indeed on which the existence and the development of North America may truly be said to rest. Their historical importance is beyond all calculation. We trace them in the very first attempt at the constitu-

* L. de instituendis Ministris Ecclesiæ ad clarissimum Senatum Pragensem. Opp. Jen. ii. p. 554. "Convocatis et convenientibus libere quorum corda Deus tetigerit, ut vobiscum unum sentiant et sapiant, procedatis in nomine Domini et eligite quem et quos volueritis, qui digni et idonei visi fuerint, tum impositis super eos manibus illorum qui potiores inter vos fuerint, confirmetis et commendetis eos populo et ecclesiæ seu universitati sintque hoc ipso vestri episcopi ministri seu pastores. Amen."

† Dorfmaister und Gemaind zu Wendelstains Fürhalten den Amptleuten zu Schwobach iren newangeenden Pfarrherrn gethan Mittw. nach Galli, 1524. Abgedruckt in Riederer's Nachrichten zur Büchergeschichte, &c. ii. 334. "Nachdem ainer christlichen Gemain gebürt, einhellig in sich in die Gemaind zu greifen nach einem erbarn unverleumpten Mann,.. welchen auch dieselbe Gemaind Macht hat wieder abzuschaffen. Der Widerchrist, der sie in der babylonischen Gefangenschaft halte, habe ihnen auch diese Freiheit entzogen," &c. — The master (magistrate) and parish of Wendelstain's charge to the functionaries at Schwobach, as to their new priest, Wednesday after Galli, 1524. Printed in Riederer's Nachrichten, &c., 334. "Afterwards it is incumbent on a Christian congregation to look out unanimously for an honest and blameless man, ... whom the same congregation has power to dismiss again. The antichrist who holds you in Babylonish captivity has robbed you of this liberty among others," &c.

‡ Paradoxa Francisci Lamberti in Scultetus, Annales Evang. p. 68. Tit. vi. § 6. Tit. iii. § 1.

§ Reformatio ecclesiarum Hassiæ juxta certissiman sermonum Dei regulam ordinata in venerabili synodo per clem^mum Hassorum principem Philippum aō 1526, d. 20th Oct. Hombergi celebrata cui ipse princeps interfuit. Schmincke Monumenta Hassorum, ii. p. 588. Bickell Zeitschrift des Vereins für hessische Geschichte i. 63—69.

tion of a church, they were adopted by a small German synod.

It was another question, however, whether they could be carried into execution in Germany generally.

Luther at least had already renounced them In the first place, he found them attended with almost insurmountable difficulties.—Throughout the whole of his labours, he had found a powerful ally in the desire of the higher secular ranks to emancipate themselves from the immediate supervision of the clergy People would not now consent to have an equally galling yoke laid upon them in another form. Moreover, Luther found that he had no men fitted for an institution of this kind. He was often highly incensed at the stubborn indocility of the peasants, who could not even be prevailed on to maintain their clergy. He said "the ordinances of the church fared as they might do if they had to be practised in the market-place, among Turks and heathen. the greater part stood and gaped, as if they were only looking at something new"* In short, the whole state of things was not adapted to such institutions. If these ideas, which we may describe as ecclesiastically democratic, afterwards triumphed in other countries, it was because the new church rose in opposition to the civil power, its real root and strength were in the lower classes of the people. But it was far otherwise in Germany. The new churches were founded under the protection, the immediate influence, of the reigning authorities, and its form was naturally determined by that circumstance.

For the ideas which find their way into the world are modified by external circumstances The moment of their production has an inevitable and permanent effect on their whole existence; they live on under the same conditions which attended their birth.

It is worth while, at the point at which we are arrived, where we have to examine into the foundation of the evangelical church, to endeavour to acquire a precise and comprehensive notion of the circumstances under which it took place. We shall thus be able to form a more exact estimate of the lawfulness of the measures adopted. The principle of the ecclesiastical law of the evangelical church, on which the whole structure is founded, may, if I mistake not, be arrived at by an historical deduction

The first and most important consideration which presents itself is, that the real origin of the movement is to be found in the internal divisions of the church, that the secession took place within her own proper domain. A university, with those nurtured in its bosom, set the example; the lower clergy through a great part of Germany followed; they were the men who changed the opinions of all classes, the lowest as well as the highest—who carried all along with them. In innumerable places the established form of worship fell of itself.

It was the immediate business of the spiritual power to repress this movement,—but it was unable to do so The pope's bulls were not executed. In one portion of the empire the secular power no longer lent its arm to enforce the ordinances of the bishops. The new opinions were become so strong in a number of the princes of the empire, that they no longer regarded this as their duty.

Hence the ecclesiastical power had addressed itself to the emperor, and an edict had been published in its favour, but as this did not spring from any intrinsic necessity, but from partial political considerations, it had been found impossible to carry it into execution. After all the ebbs and flows of the religious agitation, the diet had at length determined not to revoke it, but to leave to the discretion of every member of the empire, whether he would execute it or not.

What under these circumstances could be the result in the territories infected with the ideas of the reformation? Should their princes seek to restore an authority with which they had incessantly been at bitter strife, which had drawn upon itself the hatred of the whole nation, and whose ministry they deemed unchristian? The Recess of the diet did not enjoin this upon them It said, that no man must be robbed of his goods or his revenues; the re-establishment of the spiritual jurisdiction was purposely passed over in silence. Or were they to wait till a council should be convened, and should restore order? It was impossible to foresee when that might take place;—the diet itself had found it impossible. Nor could things be left to their own undirected course, or to chance If the nation were not to be given up to a wild anarchy, the existing lawful authorities must take measures for the restoration of order.

If it be asked, how the princes of Germany were empowered to act thus, their warrant must not be traced to a sort of episcopal authority, at least not at the beginning. It was on this occasion that Luther expressly declared, "that the temporal power was not commanded to govern spiritually." Another opinion then put forward is more plausible, namely, that the church actually existing committed to the sovereign of the country the office of supervision Luther, however, who maturely weighed all these things, and would do nothing without full certainty, only said, "that people prayed the princes, out of love and for God's sake, to take upon themselves this affair." The new church was not yet itself constituted, it is quite certain that it did not esteem itself competent to confer a right on others.

The right, properly so called, is derived, if I mistake not, from another source.

It were hardly possible to question the competency of the empire, in the prevailing state of confusion, to frame ordinances respecting ecclesiastical, as well as civil affairs, at a regular assembly like that intended to be held at Spire. It is true that scruples were urged from more than one quarter, but these scruples were at a subsequent period removed. Other-

* Preface to the Book on the German Mass Altemb iii 468

wise we must call in question the legality of the Religious Peace, as well as of the peace of Westphalia, neither of which was ever acknowledged by the papal power.

Nor was the validity of the Recesses of 1523 and 1524, which were so important to the cause of religion, ever doubted in Germany.

Had the assembly of the empire, proceeding in this course, used its unquestioned right, and organized a reform for all classes, a total revolution must have been the result.

The meeting of the empire could not, it is true, come to any such unanimous decision, but it did not on that account relinquish its powers, as is proved by the way in which it subsequently used them. At the time we are speaking of, the diet deemed it expedient—for that is the point on which the whole depends—to entrust the exercise of its rights to the territorial rulers.

For what other interpretation can be put upon the liberty granted by the diet to the princes, to agree with their respective subjects whether or not they would obey the edict of Worms?—a matter necessitating the most decisive and sweeping measures.* What the assembly of the empire was not unanimous or determined enough to execute, it left to be executed by the several States.

Thus the matter was understood by Landgrave Philip, when he invited his "subjects of spiritual and temporal estate" to repair to Homberg, "in order to come to an agreement with them in affairs relating to the holy faith." Markgrave Casimir of Brandenberg takes the same ground, when, as a god-loving prince (as he calls himself) and a dutiful subject of his imperial majesty, he makes an arrangement with the deputies of his dominions, the spirit of which, notwithstanding a certain discreet reserve, is unquestionably evangelical. We possess a little treatise of that time, in which not only the competency, but the duty of princes to make regulations conformable with the standard of the Divine Word, concerning the whole Christian life and conversation (since the edict was intended to extend to them also), is deduced from the words of the Recess.† To this Luther alludes when he mentions that the Emperor Constantine found himself constrained, during the prevalence of the Arian troubles, to interfere, at least so far as to summon a council in order to put a stop to further disorders

In a word, it was the incontestable right of the highest power in the state, on the breaking out of these dissensions in the church, to take measures for putting an end to them—the right of the whole collective body of the empire, transferred to the several States,—in virtue of which the evangelical princes proceeded to carry through the reform in their own dominions

Hence the democratical ideas we have mentioned could not gain ascendency; the existing facts did not tend that way, the church did not constitute itself from below Nor had that community of true believers, answering to the idea of the invisible Church, to which the right of giving laws to itself might have been committed, any actual existence Luther continued to regard the Church as a divine institution to be supported by all temporal authorities (as heretofore), instituted not for the purpose of representing the great Mystery, but above all, for the instruction of the people; "as a public incitement," as he expresses it, "to faith and Christianity" Whilst he denounced the bishops who had suffered the people to remain in such a state of barbarous ignorance, that they had not even learned the Lord's Prayer or the Ten Commandments, and knew nothing of the Christian faith, he, at the same time, combated the notions of some reformers, who thought that education being rendered more accessible and general, the priesthood might be entirely dispensed with In his view, the Church is a living, divine institution, for the maintenance and the diffusion of the Gospel by the ministering of the sacraments, and by preaching his idea is, as he says, "to drive the doctrine of the Scriptures into the hearts of men; that so present and future generations may be replenished with it"

These were the ideas which presided over the ecclesiastical institutions of the Saxon dominions

The elector had nominated certain Visitors who should examine the state of each parish as to doctrine and life Instructions drawn up by Melanchthon, and approved, nay edited, by Luther, were sent in their name to the respective clergymen.

These are well worthy of attention.

The opposition to the papacy, vehement as was the struggle still pending, had already fallen very much into the back-ground; it was admitted that this was not a fit topic to be debated in the pulpit and before the people. The preachers were admonished not to use reproachful language concerning the pope or the bish-

* "Das ist je die Wahrheit dass das kais Edict anders nichts innen halt, denn die Sachen unsern h Glauben und Religion, auch die Irsallehren und Missbrauch so daraus entsprungen seyn, belangend So denn an denselben, nemlich wie und was man glauben, was man lehren predigen und halten, was man auch in solchem fliehen und vermeiden soll, ein ganz christlich Leben und unser einige Seligkeit ohne Mittel gelegen ist, so folget gewisslich, dass der angezeigte Artikel auf ein ordentlich christlich Leben Regiment und Wesen muss gezogen werden Die hineingebrachten Wort des Edicts machen auch den Artikel viel lauterer" (Worte der gleich anzufuhrenden Schrift)—"That is the truth, that the imperial edict contains nothing but what concerns the affairs of our holy faith and religion, and the false doctrines and abuses that have sprung out of it So then, as upon this,—namely, how and what we must believe what should be taught and preached and held, also what should be eschewed and avoided,—a wholly Christian life and our own salvation immediately depend, so it of a certainty follows that the above mentioned article must extend to the rule and nature of a proper Christian life The words of the edict make the article much clearer" (Words of the writing in which the above edict is quoted)

† "Ein christlicher Rathschlag welcher gestalt sich alle christliche Personum von Obern und Unterthanen halten sollen, dass sie das nach Anzeigung eines sondern Artikels im Abschied des jungstgehaltenen Reichstags zu Speier mogen verantworten"—"A Christian counsel what conduct all Christian persons, rulers, or subjects should observe that they may answer it according to the admonition of a particular article in the recess of the last held diet at Spire"—*Hortleder*, b i c 2.

ops, but to keep solely in view the wants of the many—the implanting of the evangelical doctrine in the minds of the common people. The greatest respect for all that was traditional and established was shown. It was not thought necessary positively to forbid the use of Latin for the mass: the administration of the sacrament in one kind was even deemed allowable, where any one from scruples of conscience was unwilling entirely to throw off the ancient ritual; though the compulsion to auricular confession was rejected as unauthorised by the Holy Scriptures, it was declared salutary for every one to confess the sins by which he felt his conscience burdened, and about which he needed counsel: nor were even all the festivals of the saints abolished; it was enough if they were not invoked or their intercession prayed for.

The idea which we have already frequently expressed—that the reformers rejected only the pretensions to infallibility and to exclusive saving power, which were the growth of later centuries, but by no means abandoned the ground on which the Latin church stands,—here presents itself again in great distinctness. They sought only to get rid of the load of perplexing traditions, to free themselves from hierarchical usurpations, and to recover the pure meaning of the Holy Scripture—the revealed Word.* Whatever could be retained consistently with this, they retained. They took care not to perplex the minds of the common people with difficult controversial doctrines, especially those concerning good works and free will. Not that they had in the least degree fallen off from the convictions they had come to;—from the fundamental doctrine of justification by faith; from the conflict with the error of seeking salvation in the observance of human ordinances: on the contrary, they repeatedly proclaimed these principles with all possible clearness, but they required at the same time penitence, contrition and sorrow, shunning of sin and piety of life. For it is unquestionably in the power of man to flee from evil and to do that which is right; the impotence of the will means only that it cannot purify the heart or bring forth divine gifts; these must be sought from God alone.† The end they proposed to themselves was, to lead men to inward religion, to faith and love, to blameless conversation, honesty and good order. Far from departing on any point whatsoever from genuine Christianity, they made it their chief merit to imbue the minds of their hearers more and more deeply with its principles. Luther deems it his highest praise that he applies the maxims of the gospel to common life. He made it his especial business to instruct the several classes of society in their duties, on religious grounds: the secular authorities and their subjects, the heads of families and their several members. He displayed a matchless talent for popular teaching. He tells the clergy how to preach with benefit to the common people; schoolmasters how to instruct the young in the several stages of learning,—how to connect science with religion, and to avoid exaggeration; masters of families how to keep their servants in the fear of God: he prescribes to each and all texts for the good ordering of their lives; the pastor and his flock, men and women, aged people and children, men-servants and maid-servants, young and old; he gives them the formula of the Benedicite and the Gratias at table; of the morning and evening benediction. He is the patriarch of the austere and devout discipline and manners which characterise the domestic life of Northern Germany. What countless millions of times has his "Das walt Gott,"‡ reminded the tradesman and the peasant, immersed in the dull routine of the working day, of his relation to the Eternal! The Catechism, which he published in the year 1529,—of which he said, that he repeated it himself with devotion, old doctor as he was,—is as childlike as it is profound, as intelligible as simple and sublime. Happy the man whose soul has been nourished with it, and who holds fast to it! It contains enduring comfort in every affliction, and under a slight husk, the kernel of truths able to satisfy the wisest of the wise.

But, in order to insure stability to this tendency towards popular instruction,—this substitution of preachers for priests,—a new external establishment of the churches was immediately necessary.

We must here bear in mind that the property of the church was menaced from every side. We have already remarked how the first dissolution of convents originated in the high catholic party, and what claims were made by the Austrian government on the secular administration of the episcopal domains: these arbitrary acts daily acquired a more open and violent character. Luther said, the papist Junkers were in this respect more Lutheran than the Lutherans themselves; he thought it his duty to complain of the measures of the Elector of Mainz against his convent in Halle.§ Landgrave Philip, too, remarked that people began to scramble among themselves for the conventual lands: every man stretched out his hand after them, though in other respects they would not

* See Luther's Vorrede auf das Büchlin des Herrn Licentiaten Klingenbeil, 1528, Altenb. iv. 456. "Wir haben die Schrift für uns, dazu der alten Väter Sprüche und der vorigen Kirchen Gesetze, dazu des Papsts selbst eigenen Brauch da bleiben wir bei: sie aber haben etlicher Väter Gegensprüche, newe Canones und ihren eignen Muthwillen ohn alle Schrifft und Wort Gottes."—"We have the Scripture for us, and also the maxims of the old fathers and the laws of the early church, and likewise the usage of the pope himself—by that we abide: but they have the contrary maxims of some fathers, new canons, and their own wantonness, without any Scripture and word of God."

† Instructions of the Visitatores to the parish priests of the Elector of Saxony. Altenb. iv. 389.

‡ Literally, that God rules or disposes;—or, as we should say, As it please God.—Transl.

§ Bericht an einen guten Freund aufs Bischofs von Meissen Mandat. Altenb. iii. 895. "Man nehme den Klöstern und Stiftern ihre Barschaft und Kleinodien, greife den Geistlichen in ihre Freiheit, beschwere sie mit Schatzungen, laure auf ihre liegenden Gründe."—Report to a good Friend on the Mandate of the Bishop of Meissen. (Alt. iii. 895. "They strip the convents and abbeys of their money and jewels, assail the freedom of the clergy, oppress them with contributions, and lie in watch for their lands."

be called evangelical * This disposition, however, was not confined to Germany, it showed itself all over Europe. In the two years 1524 and 1525, Cardinal Wolsey dissolved more than twenty convents and abbeys in England, in order to endow with their funds the New College in Oxford, by which he hoped to immortalize his name † We must fully understand the general temper of the times, which was connected with the attempts at reform, before we can be competent to judge the steps taken in the evangelical territories. In Saxony a great number of convents had dissolved of themselves; the monks had dispersed, and the neighbouring nobles already stretched out their hands towards the vacant lands and houses.

Luther's opinion was, that this ought not to be permitted. He said that as the lands were originally designed for the support of God's service, they ought in future to be applied to that destination. He required, above all, that the rural parishes, which were very poorly endowed, and, in consequence of the great falling off in the fees, could not maintain a priest, should be enriched from the funds of the vacant benefices. Whatever remained might be given to the poor, or used for the exigencies of the state. It was only to the highest power, "the supreme head," as he expresses it, that he ascribed "the right, and at the same time the duty, of ordering these things after the papal yoke had been removed from the land" He once forced himself into the apartments of his elector, to impress upon him the duty of protecting the church property from the rapacity of the nobles.‡

The Visitors were now commissioned to order the new establishments conformably with these views It must be acknowledged that they proceeded with great moderation The abbeys and chapters which had become evangelical, as for example, those of Eisenach and Gotha, remained untouched In Hensdorf and Weimar, nuns were tolerated and allowed to adhere strictly to the old ceremonies. The Franciscan convents in Altenburg and Saalfeld, which had made a violent resistance to the new doctrines, were yet suffered to remain, they were only admonished, and, as the original report expresses it, "commended to God" (*Gott befohlen*) § I have not found any trace of the actual abolition of subsisting institutions. The commission only disposed of the estates of benefices already fallen vacant; these were applied to increasing the endowments of parish churches and schools, the existing chapters were compelled to contribute to the same objects Some of the prelates, for example, the Abbot of Bosan, were very well inclined to this; with others, it was necessary to use severe compulsion. Instead of censuring this employment of power, we have only to wish it had been from the first more decisive—more large and sweeping in its plans and operations. In the first freshness and vigour of the religious impulse, much more extensive and beneficial changes might have been effected than could be attempted at a later period What, then, might not have been achieved for the cause of religion and of civilisation, had the empire itself undertaken the guidance of this mighty revolution! As things now stood, the reformers were forced to content themselves with bringing matters to a tolerable condition, not inconsistent with the simple existence of the new church

Nevertheless, even these institutions contained the germ of a vast development

In the centre of Latin Christendom—so essentially hierarchical—a new form of Church and State, emancipated from every kind of hierarchy, arose If, on the one hand, an alliance had been formed in Bavaria between the civil sovereignty, the university and the papacy, which exercised supervision and control over the regular hierarchical authorities, on the other, a union was here effected between the prince, the university and the inferior clergy, which completely excluded the episcopal jurisdiction. The lower clergy acquired great independence. They might be said to govern themselves, by means of the superintendents whom the sovereign chose out of their ranks, and to whom some of the functions of bishops were committed By rejecting celibacy, they secured a new influence over the mind of the nation. The body of married clergy became a nursery for the learned professions and civil offices; the centre of a cultivated middle class It is to the greater care which the tranquillity of a country life enables parents to bestow on the education of their children, and which the dignity of their calling in some measure imposed upon the country clergy, that Germany owes some of its most distinguished men The suppression of monasteries and the restoration of their inhabitants to social life, gradually led to a very sensible increase of the population In the year 1750, Justus Möser reckoned that from ten to fifteen millions of human beings, in all countries and regions of the globe, owed their existence to Luther and to his example, and adds, "A statue ought to be erected to him as the preserver of the species"‖

Institutions of the kind we have been describing were far more consonant with the situation of Germany and the natural course of events, than the rash and subversive ideas, ill suited to the state of things, which had been put forth at Homberg As the instructions to the Saxon Visitatores were adopted in Hessen, as early as the year 1528, the Saxon ordinances very soon followed; in 1531, Landgrave Philip nominated six superintendents,¶ It was only in relation to church property, that the measures employed in Hessen were more sweeping and

* Letter from Philip to Luther, 1526 Rommel Hess Gesch v p 801, es sey "viel Rappens um die geistlichen Guter"—there was "much snatching at the church property"

† Catalogue in Fiddes's Collection, No 76 There are especially many Augustin convents

‡ Letter of Luther to the Elector, 22d Nov 1526, in De Wette, iii p 137, and Spalatin, 1st Jan 1527, ibid 147 See p 153

§ Extracts from the Visitation Acts, Seckendorf, ii p 102.

‖ Lettre a Mr de Voltaire Osn 6th Sept 1750, in Abeken's Reliquien von Justus Moser, p 88.

¶ Rommel Land Philipp, ii pp 123, 124.

uniform than in Saxony. Landgrave Philip was still inflamed by the first ardour of religious and patriotic ideas. "I will help Hessen," exclaimed he once with enthusiasm, yet he did not disguise from himself the danger that "he might be overcome by the flesh, and led away from the right path." He conceived the design of placing the monasteries under an administration dependent on the prince and states conjointly,—providing both for those inmates who chose to remain, and for those who quitted them, and of applying the surplus to the public wants, especially of a spiritual nature he himself would not have the right to touch this fund, without the consent of the states * The interests of the country were here peculiarly powerful.

As a motive for the confiscation of conventual property, it was alleged, that perhaps only a fourth part of the monks and nuns were natives, the rest were foreigners, and therefore such property was of no advantage to the country. Some monasteries which had embraced the evangelical faith were suffered to remain, but by far the greater number were suppressed; some, because they drew their funds from alms, which nobody would now contribute; others, because the members dispersed, either from Christian motives, as they express it,—from conscientious scruples,—or because some favourable opportunity presented itself They accepted compensation in money or in kind; the surplus was, according to the regulations of a diet held in October, 1527, to be given in part to the nobility,† in part to an university which it was determined to found at Marburg, and the remainder to form a fund for the use of the prince, the nobles, and the cities, but only to be resorted to with their joint consent. Many of these dispositions were altered in the course of the slow and gradual execution of them Yet some great institutions were really founded two endowments for young ladies of noble birth, four large public hospitals, and, above all, the university of Marburg, with its Seminarium theologicum For this newly founded evangelical university was more especially a theological school, the other faculties were only slight and incomplete beginnings. The synod of Homberg had decreed that nothing should be studied there which might be "contrary to the kingdom of God," and every member was obliged to take an oath on his admission, that he would attempt no innovation contrary to God's word. It was of great importance that another centre of evangelical theology thus arose by the side of the school of Wittenberg, at first, indeed, without the imperial privilege, but this was afterwards granted.

The influence of these events was felt in the Franconian principalities of Brandenburg, though affairs were here more complicated. Of the two princes who governed conjointly, the one, Markgrave Casimir, married to a Bavarian princess and allied to the house of Austria, adhered as closely as he could to the established party; while the other. Markgrave George, who resided in Silesia, cherished and avowed decidedly evangelical opinions. In October, 1526, Markgrave Casimir held a diet of his estates at Anspach, on occasion of the Recess of Spire, in which resolutions of a still more ambiguous nature were passed than those embodied in the Recess itself It is impossible to doubt of their evangelical tendency: in the very first article it is ordained, that the preachers throughout the country shall preach the pure Gospel and word of God, and nothing contrary to it, nor are the concessions as to the ritual to be judged with rigour, when it is remembered how tolerant even Luther was on that point. To many, doubtless, it must have appeared shocking, that Markgrave Casimir ordered the mass to be said in Latin, that he prayed, though he did not command, his subjects to keep the fasts, and even thought it expedient to maintain the endowed masses for the dead, and the vigils ‡ Markgrave George was extremely dissatisfied the letter which he sent his brother, together with the copy of these resolutions, is full of bitter remarks. The whole country remained in a state of doubt. And as the neighbouring bishops refused their approbation—refused to consent to the loss of their jurisdiction, and still made attempts to present to livings, which were not repressed with sufficient energy,—every thing fell into confusion Under these circumstances it was an event of great importance that Casimir died in the Hungarian campaign, and Markgrave George took upon himself the sole government of the principalities With his accession, the zealous evangelical councillors, Hans von

* "Das eine Oberkeit zu dem Kasten nit kommen kont one Verwilligung der Landschaft, sonst so verkompt das Gut, und der Okerkeit oder Landt wurd es nit gepessert"—"That no one of the authorities should be able to touch the fund without the consent of the country, otherwise the property would be spent and the government or the country not be the better for it"—*Letter to Luther in Rommel*, v p 802

† "S F Gn wollen 30 Mannspersonnen (vom Adel), 15 im odern 15 im nidern Fürstenthumben mit etlicher Steuwer an Frucht Korn und Habern Fürsehung thun, damit sie sich in Rustung erhalten und auf Erforderung desto stattlicher dienen mogen"—"His princely grace will provide 30 men (nobles) 15 in the upper, and 15 in the lower principality, with certain dues in wheat, rye and oats that so they may hold themselves in readiness and serve in more noble wise when called out"—"Was der durchleuchtige Furst Hr Philips mit den Closterpersonen Pfarrkern und abgottischen Bildnussen vorgenommen hat"—"What the most illustrious prince—the Lord Philip—has done and provided as to monks, parish priests, and idolatrous figures" Hortleder, i v 11 § 11—It recalls the ideas which dictated the Augsburg scheme of secularisation, 1525"

‡ Recess and Opinion, Onolzbach, Wednesday after St. Francis (in 1526, St Francis's day fell on a Wednesday, 4th Oct), Hortleder, i i 3. The extract in Lang entirely effaces the evangelical character e g According to Lang, it was said that the holy sacrament should in no case be given in both kinds, and that nothing should be taught contrary to the doctrine of transubstantiation In fact, however, we find there (No 5, Hortleder, p 39) "Wollen uns versehen, dass sich ein jeder mit Empfahung des Sacraments also halte, wie er das gegen Gott und Kais Mt verhoff zu verantworten"—"We will take care that every one carry himself so as to the receiving of the Sacrament, as he may hope to answer it to God and his imperial majesty" which however, involves complete freedom "Es soll auch wider das hochw Sacrament,—als ob in dem h Sacrament der Leib und das Blut nicht gegenwertig ware nit geprediget werden"—"There shall also be nothing preached against the holy Sacrament,—as if the body and the blood were not present in the holy Sacrament" Between the presence and transubstantiation, however, what a difference!

Schwarzenberg and George Vogler, acquired unobstructed influence. At another diet at Anspach, 1st of March, 1528, an explanation of the former Recess, dictated by purely evangelical opinions, was given; and now, too, nothing contrary to God's word was to be tolerated in the ceremonial of the church. A visitation, on the model of that of Saxony, was immediately appointed in connexion with the city of Nürnberg, and by its agency an evangelical church constitution was established in both territories.

For the reform had meanwhile been carried through in Nurnberg. We have already mentioned the great leaning which the burghers of that city had shown from the first to the new doctrines, and the support they experienced from their two provosts—patricians of Nurnberg—in the appointment of evangelical preachers. Here, too, no changes were at first made, except those strictly necessary. In the year 1524, for example, the baptismal service was first read in the German tongue. Although an admonition to that effect had been published a year before by Luther, the Nurnbergers chose rather merely to translate the entire formula of the Bamberg Agenda into German the custom of putting salt into the mouth of the child, of breathing thrice on its eyes, and anointing its breast with oil, was still adhered to; nor was one of the traditionary formulæ of exorcism discontinued.* It deserves to be noticed, as an illustration of the transition going on, that the rector of St Sebaldus altered the ancient form, "Ave Regina, mater misericordiæ'" into, "Ave Jesu Christe, rex misericordiæ'"† The most important changes were, the administration of the Lord's Supper in both kinds, and the omission of the canon; the abolition of vigils, masses and anniversaries for the dead, and particular hours of the day for prayer. But it will be readily concluded that this was far too much for their ordinary, the Bishop of Bamberg. He at length excluded the two provosts from the community of the church, declared their offices vacant, and required those with whom it rested, to proceed to a new election. But things were totally altered since the year 1520. Then, it was still necessary to come to a compromise with the papal commissioners, distant as they were; now, the excommunication of a neighbouring and powerful bishop made no impression. The provosts appealed from him to "a free, sure, Christian, and godly council"‡ The most active members of the council gradually adopted their way of thinking Jerome Ebner, a man distinguished alike for the rigour of his conscience and the mildness of his temper, Caspar Nutzel, Christopher Scheurl, Jerome Baumgartner, and Lazarus Spengler, secretary to the council, who united the highest interest in questions of religion and church government generally, with extraordinary talents for business. At all the meetings of the cities, from the August of 1524, the council of Nurnberg boldly asserted its evangelical opinions, whether against members of the Swabian League, the States of the empire, or the emperor and his representatives. Nurnberg was one of those cities which caused Charles to declare, that he could not act otherwise than he did, on account of the temper of the citizens. But let us not forget that it also gained great political advantages by this conduct. Church reform was the only means of putting an end to the disorders and insubordination of the clergy, with which the civil power had so long had to contend. The Nurnbergers turned the insurrection of the peasants to account for this purpose They urged the clergy to remember their own critical position, the danger that threatened them from the mob, and their pressing need of protection, and at length actually succeeded in persuading the whole body to yield duty and obedience to the civil authorities. Even the Commander and Spital-master of the Teutonic Order submitted, with the consent of the Franconian House-commander, to the obligation of paying taxes § The council was thus, for the first time, master within its own walls. The monasteries were compelled to appoint evangelical preachers, and to promise to admit no new members they soon dissolved, or were closed The jurisdiction of the bishop had no longer an object. To all his complaints the council answered, that it only performed the duties of a Christian government and executed the orders of the Recess of the empire. It did not scruple to unite with the markgrave in the visitation of the churches, "since the bishop had never been in the habit of visiting the churches"

It is obvious how vastly this course of affairs must have tended to increase the independence of the secular power, as well of the cities as of the princes.

Let us here call to mind the primitive organization of the church of Germany under Charlemagne, founded on the combined power and agency of the bishops and counts

While, in those remote ages, the bishops had succeeded in getting into their own hands the secular authority, at least in a part of the ter-

* History of Exorcism in the Church of Nürnberg, Strobel Miscell, iv p 173

† Instead of ' advocata nostra," it is, "mediator noster " instead of "Jesum benedictum fructum ventris tui nobis post hoc exilium ostende," it is, 'O Jesu bene dicte faciem patris tui nobis post hoc exilium ostende."

‡ Appeal and Petition of the Provosts and the Prior of the Augustines at Nurnberg Strobel Miscell., iii p 62

§ Extract from an apologetic Address of the Council of Nürnberg in Müllner's MS Annals "Es sind aber," adds the author, "die Hausscommenthurn mit nachfolgenden Conditionen zu Burgern aufgenommen worden, 1,) dass sie Burgerpflicht thun und hinter die Viertelsmeister schworen sollten, 2) dass sie den deutschen Hof mit seinen zugehorigen Gutern diesseit des Wassers gelegen verlosungen sollten, 3) sollen sie von allem Getrank so im Hof und Spital eingleght wird, das Ungeld zahlen, 4) sollen sie mit dem Holze auf des Reichs Boden sich beschiedentlich halten "—"The House Commanders were, however, admitted citizens under the following conditions 1st that they should perform all civic services and duties and swear behind the Viertel meister (literally, quarter master, i e magistrate of a quarter of the city), 2d, that they should sell the Deutscher Hof (German House) with the lands appertaining on this side of the water, 3d, that they should pay the duty on all drink brought into the Hof or the Spital, 4th, that they should bear themselves modestly as to the wood on the imperial lands."

ritories subject to their spiritual sway, and in constituting themselves sovereign lords, at the time we are treating of, on the other hand, the temporal authorities who exercised, though under another form, the rights and privileges formerly held by the counts, excluded the bishops from all participation in the temporal government of their sees.

We should be misled by appearances, were we to regard this simply as an extinction of the ecclesiastical principle For it cannot be denied that the episcopal authority had been chiefly exerted for the maintenance of all sorts of exemptions, dues, and claims, which had little in common with religion. It was, for example, one of the chief causes of quarrel between Bamberg and Nurnberg, that the city, during the revolt of the peasants, had omitted to pay the small tithes, which the bishop absolutely refused to give up. The temporal power could never have accomplished its purpose, had it not taken upon itself to represent the truly ecclesiastical, *i. e.* the religious principle, for example, to make better provision for the religious instruction of the parishes A deputy of the congregation was summoned out of each parish in Brandenburg and Nurnberg, to give true information as to the life and teaching of the clergyman. The governments were determined to put an end to the disgraceful state of the inferior clergy, to whom no bishop seriously paid any attention. It was impossible to deny that the higher clergy had left the formation and interpretation of doctrine to the universities, and the office of preaching the Word to ill-paid and ill-governed hirelings. It can excite no wonder that, after the high schools had so long acted the part of champions of the clerical claims, one of them at length adopted doctrines of a contrary tendency; or that, in those who had devoted themselves to the proper service of the church, there arose a disgust at so contemptible and already contemned a state of things, a feeling of the peculiar importance of their calling, and a fervent zeal for reform, springing from a conviction of the exclusive authority of the Gospel The temporal power did nothing more than avail itself of the authority given to it by the Recess, to secure freedom for the development of these endeavours which were manifestly of a spiritual nature It is absurd to say that the church was thus become the slave of the state. If by the church is understood the influence of religious principles, it would be more just to say that it only now arose into power, for never were those principles more powerful and efficacious, than in the times which immediately followed those of which we are speaking. What was begun by the evangelical governments, was carried on in an analogous manner by the catholic But it is at the same time clear, that the efficacy of the evangelical church did not rest on wealthy endowments, high rank, or the pomp of hierarchical ordinances; but on inward energy, pious zeal, and the free culture and growth of the intellect On no other foundation can the church ever be established in Germany; and this is the source of her strength.

The same events which had taken place in Nurnberg, occurred also in many of the cities of the Oberland, first in Augsburg and in Ulm,—indeed, meetings of these three cities were frequently held and measures agreed on: in the year 1528, there was again a talk of a new alliance between all the imperial cities; then followed Strasburg, and above all, the towns of Switzerland; in the year 1528, Berne adopted the religious changes. But we must leave the events in these countries for a subsequent part of our work, where we have devoted closer attention to the modifications which the doctrine underwent in Switzerland.

The whole of Lower Germany, on the other hand, adhered to the forms established under Luther's influence in Saxony. The slight variations which they underwent, depended only on the difference of the civil constitution or the form of sovereignty in each country.

In Luneburg, the change took place in consequence of a union of the prince and the nobles at the diet at Scharnebeck in the year 1527 The prelates had refused to appear at previous meetings, and at their instigation the aged prince, who had abdicated and gone to France, where he remained true to the catholic faith, came back to oppose the innovations But it was now too late. At that diet the reigning duke and his subjects promised each other to cause the Gospel to be preached, pure, clear, and plain; they resolved that the prelates should be compelled to do the like in their churches and convents, although they were permitted, in regard to ceremonies, to act as they thought they could answer it to God * From this time the reform gradually spread over the whole country. The Chancellor Klammer rendered the same services here as Bruck had done in Saxony, Feige in Hessen, Vogler in Anspach, and Spengler in Nurnberg.

In East Friesland, the power of the count was still too new to enable him to decide in affairs so delicate and so dependent on the most intimate convictions. When Count Etzard, who at first had been much impressed by the Lutheran opinions, had afterwards come to the determination to hold fast to the existing form of the church, a chieftain, Junker Ulrich of Dornum, took upon himself the conduct of the cause. At his suggestion, a solemn disputation was held at Oldersum It began in a very characteristic manner. "Say the Lord's Prayer," exclaimed Henry Arnoldi, the champion of the Lutherans, "and an Ave Maria," added Prior Laurence, the Dominican who defended the catholic side; and the controversy turned chiefly on the worship of the Virgin Mary. But as the Lutherans persisted in carrying on the argument solely with passages from Scripture, the Dominicans were left without an answer Nor was this all; desertion soon crept into their own ranks On the New Year's day of 1527, Resius, a Dominican, ascended the pulpit in the church at Norden, to defend certain Lutheran propositions which he

* Extract from the ducal edict in Pfeffinger, Historie des Braunschweig Luneburgischen Hauses, ii 347 See Schlegel's Kirchengeschichte, ii 50.

had already advanced; a single antagonist arose, who, however, was soon reduced to silence; whereupon the Dominican, in sign of his conversion, laid aside his cowl in the very pulpit.* In the year 1527, Lutheranism was the prevailing religion in almost all the parishes. In the year 1528, the East Friesland churches published a full confession of faith.

Fortunately for Schleswig and Holstein, the bishops of the dioceses of Schleswig and Lübek offered no strenuous opposition to the Reformation, while on the other hand the government afforded it protection, and left the revenues of its clerical adherents untouched. The transition from the one confession to the other was here peculiarly easy. As one of the four-and-twenty papal vicars, Hermann Tast had been the first to preach evangelical doctrines: his colleagues easily accommodated themselves to the change;—premising always that their incomes were to be secured to them for their lives. Many of the country priests adopted the reformed faith without a struggle; they readily accepted the articles laid before them. In the towns there was almost as much resistance opposed by the anabaptists as by the adherents of the papacy. The immediate disciples of Luther, for example, Marquard Schuldorf of Kiel, lent efficient help against both antagonists.† Here, too, the ecclesiastical institutions were gradually placed on the footing of those of Saxony.

In Silesia, too, as we have already mentioned, the evangelical doctrine had made early and mighty progress. This country, indeed, differed from other parts of Germany, inasmuch as it was not an immediate dependency of the empire, and could therefore ground no pretensions on the Recess of Spire. But the circumstances were nearly akin; its chief city and its princes assumed a scarcely less independent posture with regard to the crown of Bohemia, to which they belonged, than the States of the empire had done towards the emperor: every fluctuation of opinion in central Germany was here immediately answered by an analogous movement. Breslau, which no long time before, in the affairs of Podiebrad, had held with unshaken firmness to the side of the pope, now took the lead in the struggle against him. Here, too, the inclinations of the council and citizens had received an anti-clerical bias from a great number of circumstances. They would no longer have a Bernardine convent, because they thought themselves injured by its connection with the king's court. They were discontented at the disgraceful scenes carried on in the parish of St. Mary Magdalen, where one pretender to the benefice was continually driven out by another.‡ There were a thousand causes of bickering with the canons in the city. The Lutheran tendencies, therefore, found the ground well prepared. In the year 1523, the citizens of Breslau ventured to appoint to the parish in question, of their own authority, Dr. Johann Hess, one of the most intimate friends of Luther and Melanchthon, who had just come from Wittenberg; upon which matters took the same course here as elsewhere. The new principles were triumphantly maintained in a solemn disputation; the people were gained over; the reformers began by altering the ceremonies, keeping as close as possible on various incidental points to the traditionary ritual of the see of Breslau. The Bernardines had quitted the city rather than submit to be united with the Jacobites, as was proposed to them: the monasteries now dissolved themselves; the council offered no impediment to the monks and nuns who quitted them and married. But it must not be imagined that the Lutheran clergy, who unquestionably owed their ascendency to the council, were absolutely at its disposal. In April, 1525, Dr. Hess suddenly left off preaching, upon which the council sent to ask him the cause. He answered, that he saw the blessed Lord Christ lying before the church doors, and that he could not walk over him. What he meant was this;—he had often exhorted the council to provide for the beggars who filled the city, and lay during the time of service before the church doors; but always in vain. This earnest demonstration, however, made an impression. The really indigent were separated from the idle, and placed in six different hospitals. In the year 1526 the first stone of the great spital was laid by Hess himself; the opulent citizens gave the materials, and the various artisans their labour; so that the building was finished in a year—a genuine work of the new-born evangelical zeal. Hess was strongly and actively supported by the town clerk, John Corvinus, who had taken part in the earlier literary movement, and had taught in some of the first schools of poetry. There was a general consent and co-operation: the councillor declared to the court that he had never seen a more obedient community.§ If this was the case with regard to those who had opposed Podiebrad, what was to be expected from his adherents? The son of his son, Duke Charles, ruled over Münsterberg, Ols and Frankenstein; the son of his daughter, Duke Frederic II. of Liegnitz, had united Brieg and Wolau with that domain. It may easily be imagined what opinions they held. Duke Charles wished to see the memory of his grandfather restored to honour by Luther. Duke Frederic not only gave a ready ear to the prayers of his nobles and cities, that he would grant them a freer exercise of their religion, but gradually became inspired by the most ardent zeal in the same cause;‖ he conceived the design of founding another evangelical university, and had not the doctrines and followers of Sewenk-

* Ubbo Emmius Rerum Frisciarum Hist., lib. liv. p. 839.

† Münter's Kirchengeschichte von Dänemark, iii. p. 584, contains a laborious collection of these very scattered notices.

‡ Schutzred des erbarn Raths und ganzen Gemeind der K. Stadt Breslau bei Schickfuss, Neuvermehrte Schlesische Chron., iii. p. 58.

§ Die Jahrbücher der Stadt Breslau von Nicolaus Pol. Bd. iii. die Jahre, 1521—1527. Compared to the veracious account of this simple chronicler, the stories of Bukisch, who borrowed from him, are often like bad caricatures.

‖ Des Erlauchten, &c. Herzog Friedrichs II. Grundersach und Entschuldigung auf etlicher Verunglimpfen in Schickfuss S. 65.

feld caused troubles in his dominions, would have organised one on a noble and comprehensive plan.* Just then Markgrave George of Brandenburg had acquired Jagerndorf, and of course allowed the Lutheran doctrines free course there. The young duke Wenceslas Adam of Teschen, was soon deeply impressed with the new opinions. All these things passed without any serious opposition, either from the spiritual or the temporal authorities. Jacob of Salza, bishop of Breslau, saw very clearly that Christianity did not consist in the presence or absence of a few ceremonies more or less. The evangelical doctrine found powerful protectors at the court of King Louis. King Ferdinand, as we have seen, at least did not venture to reject the demands regarding religion which were laid before him at his election, and if he occasionally published mandates which sounded zealously orthodox, he was not in a condition to give them effect. The Breslauers once represented to him in so lively a manner the impossibility of returning to the ancient practices, that he no longer ventured to press it. "Well, then," said he, at length, "only keep the peace, and believe as you think you can answer it to God and the emperor."† He at the same time extended to his own province the concessions made to the empire. Thus was formed in Silesia the constitution which for a century prevailed there, as well in the Austrian, as in all other dominions: evangelical states strenuously maintained their political and religious privileges, and the government was compelled to use leniency and toleration.

By far the most remarkable and sweeping change took place, however, in Prussia.

Various causes had contributed to prepare this event.

The political importance, nay in effect also the position of the Teutonic Order relatively to the Prussian government, had been annihilated for more than half a century. At the peace of Thorn, in the year 1466, the Order had been compelled to cede the larger half of its territory, with all its richest and most powerful cities, to Poland, and for the smaller, which was left in its possession, to recognise the king of that country as its feudal lord.

If we inquire how this came to pass, we shall find that it was not so much the consequence of the military superiority of Poland, which, though indisputable, would never have sufficed to produce such results, but of the internal situation of the country,—the misunderstandings between the order and the territory over which it ruled.

Prussia was a colony which had gradually risen to independence. The order, which was no longer inspired by the ancient impulses of religion, honour, or love of war, and came into the country only to govern and to enjoy, was most oppressive to the inhabitants. They complained that they were allowed no share in the administration; that they were treated like serfs, subjected to acts of violence, and denied all right and justice. The relation which arose between them was like that between the Creoles and Chapetons in South America, between the Pullains and the Fils Arnaud in Jerusalem, in short, such as must arise in every colony as its civilisation advances. At first the country sought to protect itself by its great union of 1440, but as this was opposed by the emperor, it turned to Poland. It was the native population of Prussia that put those arms into the hands of the King of Poland against the grand master, by means of which the former gained the victory, and extorted so advantageous a peace as that of Thorn. The city of Danzig had expended 700,000 marks in this cause. In return, the King of Poland granted to the allies, for the first time, the blessing of self-government, which the knights had steadily refused them.‡

In the smaller division of the country which had remained in the possession of the order, but which had also taken part in the league and in the war, similar tendencies continued, as may easily be imagined, to show themselves. We find that the states, whose business it was to grant the taxes, more than once refused them. They demanded the right of appointing, jointly with the grand master, a lieutenant to act for him during his absence, a post we sometimes find occupied by a burghermaster. In a scheme for the defence of the country drawn up in the year 1507, fifteen governors, or chiefs of districts, were nominated; and of these fourteen belonged to the order.§

Not only was the order thus checked and controlled in its functions, but its peculiar republican character was gradually superseded by one more monarchical. It was found expedient to choose native princes as grand masters; for example, in 1498, Frederic of Saxony, and in 1511, Albert of Brandenburg, and in order to secure to them a state and maintenance suited to their rank, whole commanderies were confiscated. These princes entrusted the public affairs to chancellors who did not even belong to the order, and to their own particular councillors, after the manner of the German courts. Their position became more and more like that of hereditary rulers, in consequence of the necessity they lay under of granting a great degree of independence to their subordinates out of the country—both the Master in Livonia, and the Teutonic Master (*Deutschmeister*); in fact, of emancipating the former from all important obligations and services.‖ In the place of the wide general relations of the order, arose narrow territorial interests.

* Thebesii Liegnitzische Jahrbücher, iii p 29

† Nic Pol iii. p 52

‡ His very first promise is, "ut in mutatione principum commutatam etiam aut sublatam deprehenderent oppressionem." Litteræ Casimiri Regis, in Dlugoss Historia Pol, ii p 138. See Voigt Preuss Gesch, viii p 378.

§ Baczko Preussische Gesch iv p 142

‖ Albert mentions (Schütz Hist Rer. Pruss, p 331), "was er sich gegen den beiden Meistern verschreiben und obligiren mussen damit sie sich denn ganz und gar aus dem Gehorsam gezogen,"—"to what he must subscribe and bind himself towards both Masters, wherewith they then withdrew themselves entirely from their obedience."

The only question now was, — one which involved a remote and permanent change — whether they should submit to the peace of Thorn, or not. The last grand masters refused to do homage as their immediate predecessors had done; they demanded a revision of the terms of the peace, "according to natural and Christian laws," they made incessant claims on the assistance of the empire (especially of the knightly body), which was afforded to this possession of Prussia. At length, in the year 1519, the grand master (Markgrave Albert of Brandenburg) had once more recourse to arms. But what had been injurious to his predecessors, proved disadvantageous to him. The cities and districts which had fallen off from the order, no longer lent their aid to the support of its power; it was indeed to the cities of Danzig and Elbingen, and to the families of the lords of the league, that the public opinion of that time attributed the breach of the peace; their intention was to strip the order altogether of its territory and subjects;* it was they who urged on the war with the greatest energy and success. From Germany, on the other hand, the order received no efficient help. The grand master was again compelled to cede eleven towns with their territories, and to consent to a truce for four years, during which affairs were to be definitely arranged, under the mediation of the Emperor and the King of Hungary.

Albert went to Germany, in order once more to try in person what he could obtain from the states and nobles of the empire. Had victory declared on the side of Sickingen, with whom he had long been connected, Prussia might have reckoned on assistance. But Sickingen fell; the knights of the empire suffered great losses, they were unable to maintain their independence at home, much less to attempt enterprises abroad. The Council of Regency, too, on which some of its hopes were placed, was overthrown. The emperor was so far from holding out any expectation of assistance, that he rather favoured the claims of the Jagellons. The promised mediation was not even attempted. The grand master had nothing left but either to do homage agreeably to the treaty of Thorn, or to abdicate. And indeed the abdication was seriously discussed. It might either take place according to the views of the order, in which case Duke Erich of Brunswick was suggested as successor, or to those of the country and of Poland, in which case it would have been in favour of Sigismund: the king sent an ambassador to Nurnberg in 1521, in the hope of inducing the grand master to consent to this latter scheme.†

The Order and its government in Prussia, were doubtless the most singular product of the hierarchical and chivalrous spirit of the preceding centuries in the German nation; but to what had it sunk! The greater part of its territory gone; in what remained, powerful and growing states, the internal unity in which its strength lay, broken, its tie to the mother country relaxed and feeble, — submission was become inevitable — its time was over. It was however not easy at present to see what could or ought to be done; there existed no clue by which to escape from the labyrinth of such difficult contingencies. Such were the circumstances under which the new religious doctrine appeared in the country. In no part of the world was it more wanted — in none more welcome. People saw that the institution, so long revered as intrinsically religious, by no means stood in that profound and inward relation to the idea, or the original spirit of Christianity, which had been presumed. The states seized with joy a doctrine which justified their old opposition, on higher grounds. The bishops, who were elsewhere almost universally its opponents, lent a glad ear to it. Under the direction of the bishop of Samland, fasts were abolished, mass said in German, the ceremonies altered, and the monasteries cleared.‡ Even the members of the Order could not withstand the universal current of opinion. They were seen attending the sermons of the Lutheran preachers; many laid aside their cross; some determined to marry. Their number was indeed no longer great, and at last only five remained faithful to the institution. At length the sermons of Osiander, the society of men like Planitz, and the private conversation he held with Luther, imbued the mind of the grand master himself with the evangelical opinions prevalent in Saxony and in Nurnberg. On the one hand, he was convinced that his profession had not the merit which had been imputed to it, nor even conformity with the word of God. On the other, people represented to him that he could not abdicate, since he had duties to perform to the country from which he could not so lightly withdraw himself. The country required him to lay to heart its desolation and its weakness, and to procure for it a lasting peace, to grant it preachers of the pure word of God, and to abolish whatever was repugnant to that; most probably including, in that expression, the vow of the Order.§ Albert, though he still adhered to it, had doubtless in his heart determined on the course he meant to pursue, when he set on foot new negotiations with Poland.

In Poland the diet of Petricau had just then come to the resolution that the grand master should either do homage or be driven out of Prussia, together with his order.‖

* "Eyn newes Geticht von dem negstvorgangenen Krieg zu Preussen." Beitrage zur Kunde Preussens Bd. ii p. 287.

† Memorial of the Grand Master Albert, given by Faber, Beitr. zur Kund. Preussens, iv. 83.

‡ How Rome stirred against and thought to overthrow it. Voigt Preussische Geschichte, ix. pp. 732, 737. That he subscribed himself only by the grace of God, without mentioning the apostolic see, was there regarded as apostasy. This had too, an influence on the safety of the grand master, who was moreover attacked by the Teutonic master.

§ "Sind darum aus geistlichem Suchen und Begern derselben Landschaft zw dieter Verenderung und Vertrag mit der Kron Polen kommen."—"Are thereupon come to this alteration and agreement with the crown of Poland, in consequence of the spiritual request and desire of that country." Albert's answer to the proposals of Grafendorf, the Saxon ambassador. W. A.

‖ Literæ regiæ ad sedem apostolicam. "alioquin hæc tragœdia nullum unquam finem habere potuisset, præser-

It was therefore very fortunate for Markgrave Albert that in Silesia, which in all the previous troubles had adhered to the king, he had two of his nearest relations; his brother, Markgrave George, and his brother-in-law, Frederic of Liegnitz—both like himself, nephews of the king—who undertook once more to conciliate Sigismund, and to procure for Albert favourable conditions.

The king had gone to Cracow with a committee of the diet Here the two princes, both, as we are aware, zealous partisans of the evangelical faith, went to meet him. they adopted the principles laid down by the diet, but at the same time remarked that no arrangement with the Order would be of any avail, since the government was in the hands of so many that no reliance could be placed on its actions They proposed to the king that the grand master should be declared hereditary duke of Prussia *

The king said, he would take into consideration what was to be done, and what Albert's kinsmen required of him † He acquiesced with joy.

When the affair was brought before the royal council of Poland, some voices indeed were raised against it on religious grounds, but to these, others replied, that no injury was inflicted on Catholicism, since the Order had already gone over to Lutheranism, and held nothing in greater abhorrence than the name of the pope,‡ they ought rather to thank God that it had fallen of itself The diet decided in favour of the king's project.

Meanwhile, negotiations were carried on in Beuthen, whither plenipotentiaries of the Order and of the States had repaired to meet the Markgrave. The envoys of the Order, who were unquestionably the most important, spoke first. They entirely approved the proposition, and only urged their claim to certain advantages due to them from Poland The delegates of the States were chiefly solicitous lest they should be attacked by the remnant of the order in Germany, and by the empire, and not sufficiently defended by Poland. They demanded of their new sovereign a promise that he would rather increase than diminish their privileges, and appoint no foreigner to a public office though he did not accede to the latter stipulation, they were on the whole satisfied with his declarations.§ The envoys of the Order, too, were content, on the king consenting to restore the fortified places taken from it in the last war, and granting a small revenue for the new princes.

All parties thus easily and gladly combined to bring about this great change. The King of Poland saw his suzerainty at length willingly acknowledged, and the descendants of his sister established within his extended frontiers. The country acquired the independence of foreign influence it had so long aspired after. The order, which had secularised itself, thus secured protection, it associated itself with the natives of the country whom it had hitherto opposed Markgrave Albert's aim, in short, was not alone to found a hereditary sovereignty, he thought he served his country by securing for it peace, and the free diffusion of evangelical opinions.

On the 10th of April, 1525, the solemn infeudation took place at the Ring at Cracow. The king, in his sacerdotal ornaments, surrounded by his bishops, delivered to the new duke, by the symbol of the banner (which Markgrave George also grasped, in sign that the investiture extended to the whole line of Brandenburg), "the whole land in Prussia which had been held by the Order" Albert took the oath of homage and allegiance in a formula in which no mention was made of the saints.

At his entrance into Königsberg, he was greeted by an evangelical preacher with a religious discourse. He was received with all the festivities and honours which could be offered to an hereditary prince, the bells were rung, the houses hung with tapestry, and the roads strewed with flowers

The States, of course, did not hesitate to approve the negotiations of their delegates, they confirmed the treaty of Cracow, and took the oath of allegiance. The original document, by which Albert had confirmed "the privileges, franchises, and praiseworthy customs' of the country, was delivered into the keeping of the magistrate of the Altstadt of Konigsberg. In the place of the great officers of the Order now appeared Marshal, Landhofmeister, Oberburggraf,‖ and Chancellor, all which officers were in future to be filled by natives. The courts of justice were newly constituted with the advice and assistance of the nobles.

Only one of the knights of the order offered any persevering resistance, Erich of Brunswick, in whose favour Albert had thought of resigning, held out in Memel, he was afterwards provided for by means of a small pension.

The religious establishments were formed

tim cum subditi mei omnes a me exigerent modis omnibus neque ab hoc instituto dimoveri potuerint in conventu generali regni mei novissimo vel cogendum tandem magistrum Prussiæ ad præstandam obedientiam et omagium mihi et regno meo debitum vel illum ac ordinem ex terris illis exturbandum"

* "Literæ Andreæ Critii Episcopi Premisliensis ad Joannem Antonium Puleonem (he should be called Burgonem, for J A v Burgo was then nuncio in Hungary), lib Par et nuncium apostolicum Principes ingenue e vestigio et citra ullas ambages id quod attulerant pronunciarant' —*Samuelis Nakielski Miechovia sive Promtuarium*, &c, p 609

† Literæ regis "conductis conditionibus quæ pro tempore fieri potuerant, et qualis mutua nostra necessitudo postulavit"

‡ "Luteranismum apud ordinem ipsum sacrosanctum, Romanam vero ecclesiam et ejus ritus execrabiles esse (nihil apud eum nomine pontificis contemptibilius esse), plerosque commendatores et sacrificos nubere," &c &c

§ The negotiations are to be found in the last pages of Schutz The duke declared to the deputies of the states, who were in fact not specially commissioned for that purpose, "er werde ihnen dermaassen beweisliche Urkunden mitgeben, dass sie den Ihren entschuldigt seyn sollten,"—"that he would give them such authentic documents that they should stand excused to their constituents" This was shown immediately on the duke's return

‖ Titles of offices to which we have none corresponding —Transl.

without difficulty: the bishops themselves, as we have said, were in their favour. At the very first assembly, Bishop Polenz of Samland abdicated the temporal part of his authority, alleging that the service of the Gospel alone belonged to a bishop, not the enjoyment of worldly honours; he gave his power into the hands of the duke, who took the states to witness this voluntary tradition. This example was soon followed by Bishop Erhard Queis of Pomesania. Their spiritual authority was left entire—the more so, since now, as before, they administered it by officials.* They introduced a liturgy in which they still kept as close as possible to traditional forms: the convents were turned into hospitals: the efforts to spread Christianity in the lowest regions of society and those hitherto the least touched by its influence, here found a wide sphere of action among the Slavonian population, which still occupied a great portion of the land; functionaries called Tolken, i. e. interpreters, were attached to the parish priests, and repeated every sentence of the sermon in the ancient language of Prussia.† In order to keep the clergy themselves in the right way, the Markgrave caused the Postilles‡ to be brought twice a year from Wittenberg, two hundred of each at a time. Lucas Cranach had a general commission to send him all the good and valuable books that appeared.§

Duke Albert's marriage with Dorothea, Princess of Denmark, which took place in the year 1526, appears like the consummation and bond of all these things. Alliances cemented by this kind of uniformity of opinion are now almost universal among the crowned heads of Europe. The duchess gradually gave evidence of as strong evangelical convictions, "as firm a faith and trust in our Saviour," as her husband. Nor was she less fitted to render domestic life happy. He dwells with untired delight on her noble and amiable qualities, and adds that, had she been a poor serving girl, she could not have borne herself with more lowliness and truth, with more unchanging love, to him unworthy.‖ Her brother Christian, afterwards King of Denmark, having married a princess of Lauenburg, out of which house Gustavus Vasa of Sweden afterwards took his wife, all these new evangelical powers of the North were united by the closest bonds.

Let us observe the general direction of the policy of the North, of which these events formed the consummation. In the year 1515, Maximilian had thought to connect all the northern territories of Slavonic and Germanic tongue, in one great alliance, of which he was to be the head. Poland severed itself first, then Christiern II. was driven out of Denmark and Sweden; and now Albert, who had hitherto remained attached to Christiern, formed an alliance of amity and marriage with the new king. Erich of Brunswick was removed from Memel, because he persisted in keeping up an intercourse with Severin Norby, the admiral of Christiern.¶ The position which Albert acquired at his first reception among the northern powers, was extremely strong and advantageous.

The evangelical princes of Germany also afforded him support from another side.

Even at the time when Elector John of Saxony, and his neighbouring co-religionists were negotiating about the meeting at Magdeburg, he sent to Prussia to propose to the new duke, that if he were aggrieved in any thing relating to the evangelical faith, he would stand by him steadfastly. This message was most welcome to the duke. He sent the Bishop of Pomesania, who had the general conduct of his foreign affairs, and had arranged the relations with Poland and Denmark, to Breslau, in 1526, where he was met by Hans von Minkwitz on the part of Saxony. Here a formal agreement was concluded.** The duke had observed that Prussia was so exhausted in the last war, that he could not engage to furnish more than a hundred armed horsemen. Elector John was satisfied and promised the duke an equal number in case he was attacked. The party sending assistance was to pay the troops and bear the losses; the party receiving it, to provide them with necessaries. In December, 1526, the ratification arrived at Weimar. The duke and his bishop had a design of extending this alliance to the states of Silesia, the Markgrave George of Jagerndorf, the Duke of Liegnitz, and the city of Breslau:†† some deliberations had already taken place about a common and more intimate concert with Denmark, for which the elector evinced perfect readiness.

It has often been said, and with perfect truth, that the empire sustained a great loss by the act of homage to Poland. But this was inevitable. The Polish diet had taken the determination to proceed no further on a middle course, and, if necessary, to decide the matter by force; the country was wholly incapable of resistance, and no help was to be expected from the empire. Had the Order not yielded, it would have been driven out of Konigsberg, as it had been out of Danzig; the territory would have become a Polish province, like the kingdom of Prussia. Under these circumstances, it is unquestionably to be regarded as one of the most fortunate events for the maintenance of the Germanic principle in those countries, that a duchy—an hereditary German sovereignty—was erected. If we compare this province with Livonia, we see that though there, too, the Reformation had penetrated, though the powerful Grand Master Pletten-

* Bock Leben Albrechts, i. p. 167.

† Hartknoch Preussische Kirchengeschichte, p. 277.

‡ A book containing expository sermons on the Gospels and Epistles.—Transl.

§ Letter to Cranach, and his account, inserted by Voigt in the Beitragen zur Kunde Preussens, iii. p. 246.

‖ Faber Einiges uder die Herzogin Dorothea. Beitr. z. K. Preussens, iii. p. 126.

¶ See Albert's Instruction, 18th April 1525. Beitr. z. K. Pr., iv. p. 395, and an essay by Faber, vi. p. 539.

** Recess of Konigsberg, 5th July 1526. W. A.

†† Letter from Minkwitz, Leipzig, Sunday after St. Francis's day. "Trost, es soll kein Mangel haben."—"Take comfort, there shall be no want." I do not find, however, that any resolution was come to. The Landgrave of Hessen, too, thought the mutual obligations too insignificant.

berg, who was now absolutely independent, protected it, and found means still to keep the Order in existence for a time,—it was but for a time, the country was afterwards secularised like the rest, but fell under a foreign yoke, and soon lost its sympathy with the German nation Nor did royal Prussia reap any advantage from having no prince at its head, the influence of Poland became overwhelming, and the country had to endure indescribable oppressions, both of a political and religious kind. The progress of German civilisation was not only arrested, but forced back. On the other hand, ducal Prussia gradually became completely German; by its family alliances with a powerful German house, it remained in strict and indissoluble political connection with the great fatherland Amidst all the distraction of the theological and literary controversies which followed in the train of the Reformation, here was an independent centre of German culture, from which the grandest developments of German nationality have sprung

We cannot contemplate Germany at this moment, without a deep sense of the grandeur of her character and position.

Belgium and the Netherlands, Bohemia and the neighbouring countries, might once more be reckoned as parts of the German empire German arms had wrested Italy from the influence of France, as well as from that of Switzerland, which had now severed itself from the empire. they had restored the name of the empire in Italy, and in its ancient metropolis more than once they had made threatening advances from the south and east into France, and in the west, they had aided the Spaniards to reconquer the lost border fortresses, and to vanquish the Moors of Valencia. They had just gained possession of Hungary With the assistance of the German maritime cities, they had put the two northern monarchs in possession of their crowns If Poland had reaped the advantage, she was indebted for it solely to the instigation and the assistance of the German provinces, which sufficiently showed that this was a state of things that could not last. In Livonia, the attacks of the Russians were repulsed in successive engagements, and in the year 1522, peace was obtained on very advantageous terms.

And all this had been accomplished in the absence of any vigorous central government,—amid the storms of the most violent internal dissension. But these very storms were the symptoms of a far wider tendency—one which was destined to embrace the world It was reserved for the mind of Germany to sever the intrinsic truth of Christianity from the accidental forms which, in later ages, had grown around it under the influences of papacy, and with equal moderation and firmness to secure to it a legal adoption in its extensive territories In one electorate, two or three duchies, the largest landgravate, the largest county of the empire, one or two margravates, and a great number of cities, the new doctrine had become predominant, and had pervaded the populations with whose character and turn of mind it had a natural affinity. In order to bring vividly before our minds the original views of a positive and negative kind, we should compare the written confessions of faith which had now been published at so many places, the articles of the Visitation of Saxony and Hessen, and still more those of Brandenburg and Nurnberg; the Confession of East Friesland, the Instructions to the preachers of Schleswig-Holstein; the Apologies of the States of Silesia; the Synodal Constitutions of Prussia In all these documents we perceive the same feeling of an obligatory return from the accidental to the essential., a resistless conviction, not yet indeed defined in articles of faith. but assured of its truth It is manifest that since the development of these opinions took place in narrow territories, the infant church could not enter into the most distant rivalry as to external grandeur and splendour with the established hierarchy, in which was expressed the unity of an aggregate of great kingdoms. its essence and its worth consisted in its intellectual depth and strength. The office it had taken on itself was that of bringing the principles of Christianity home to the minds of the common people; of expounding its meaning and spirit, freed from all disguises of foreign forms and rites; that so it might at length be brought home to the consciousness of all the nations of the earth Already was the new doctrine proclaimed in almost every tongue. We mentioned the interpreters of the Prussian clergy in Breslau Doctor Hess caused the Gospel to be read in Slavonic, Luther's disciples preached it in Denmark and Sweden, one of the first names inscribed at the university of Marburg, was the founder of the Scottish church, in 1527, a society of men inclined to Lutheran opinions was founded in Corpus Christi College, Oxford, which may be regarded as the seminary of the new opinions * Meanwhile, from the year 1528, an immediate effect had been produced on Geneva and the Roman world In Italy, the doctrine pervaded the old literary associations; in Spain, it soon laid hold of the Franciscans, in France, it found a powerful patroness in the Queen of Navarre Luther, who was a stranger to ambition—who had not even a genuine zeal for proselyting,† and expected every thing from the silent inborn force of conviction—yet remarked that his efforts to restore the preaching of the Gospel would some time or other form the subject of a church history. But at present he was occupied with higher hopes "It will draw the cedars of Lebanon to itself," said he. He applied to it the words of Isaiah,‡ "I will say to the North give up, and to the South keep not back, bring my sons from far, and my daughters from the end of the earth."

* Fiddes, Wolsey, p 416

† See his letter to the people of Erfurt, in de W, iii p. 227 'Wer uns nicht horen will, von dem sind wir leicht und bald geschieden "—'He who will not hear us, from him are we easily and quickly departed"

‡ "Eine schone herrliche und tröstliche Vorrede D M L auf das Buchlin der gottseligen Furstin F Ursulen Herzogin zu Munsterberg "—'A fair, noble, and comfortable preface of Dr Martin Luther to the little book of the godly princess the Lady Ursula, Duchess of Munsterberg" Altenb, iv p 416

BOOK V.

FORMATION OF A CATHOLIC MAJORITY.

1527—1530.

RETROSPECT

In the introduction to this history, we endeavoured to lay before our readers a view of the earlier fortunes of the German nation, especially in reference to the struggle between the spiritual and temporal powers We observed how the papacy not only was victorious in this struggle, but raised itself to the condition of a substantial power in the Germanic empire,—a power indeed of the first order We saw, however, that, just as it had placed itself on a footing of amity, and concluded an alliance with the vanquished imperial power, the empire became ungovernable, fell into confusion and anarchy at home, and from year to year lost its consideration abroad, till at length the spirit of the nation, condemned to inactivity, expressed itself only in a general conviction that such a state of things was untenable and fatal

In our first book we traced the earnest efforts made by the nation in the latter part of the 15th and the beginning of the 16th century, to remedy the evils under which it suffered Its first endeavours were directed towards temporal abuses The project was conceived of creating a power in the empire, resting at once on the privileges of the emperor and those of the States, but more especially founded on the co-operation of the latter in the government, not with a view of effecting a centralisation in the sense of modern times, but only as a means of satisfying the most pressing wants,—the establishment of peace and law, and the defence of the country against its neighbours But the end was not attained Certain constitutional forms, which were of more value and importance to later times than to those which gave them birth, were indeed established, but we have seen how small was their practical efficacy The consequence rather was, that the abortive attempt to introduce such radical changes threw the nation into universal confusion As men felt only the restraints which pressed upon themselves, but were ignorant of the benefits of public order, the old spirit of insubordination and private vengeance revived, with the difference, however, that it was now mingled with a lively feeling for the common weal and animated by a disgust at the reigning abuses, bordering on rage.

Such was the temper of the nation, when (as we observed in our second book), after the failure of its attempts to reform its secular affairs, it seized on the affairs of the Church, and on the functions of the papacy, which possessed so large a portion of political power in the empire Here, however, this disposition of the national mind became blended with still more extensive movements of public opinion Though the papacy was still intent upon a more rigorous and minute development of its dogmas and its rites, and a more strenuous assertion of them, tendencies of a scientific kind which were opposed to the reigning system of the schools and longings of the religious spirit which found no satisfaction in the ritual observance of the prescribed ordinances, were at work within its own bosom The wonderful coincidence was, that just as abuses had risen to the most intolerable height, the study of the sacred books in their original tongues once more revealed to the world, in all its radiance, that pure idea of Christianity which had so long been darkened or disguised A man appeared who, in that secret travail and contention of mind to which the remedies usually applied by the Church afforded no relief, seized with his whole soul on an aspect of Christianity hitherto the most profoundly obscured, and such was his own experience of its truth, fulness, and saving power that he would never more suffer it to be wrested from him, but maintained it unshaken through life and death In the contest to which it gave rise, he drew around him all the other elements of innovation, with a consistency and sagacity which at length gained over the whole nation, and secured to himself a degree of sympathy such as no other man ever enjoyed At the same time that he gave a new direction to religious thoughts and feelings, he opened a new prospect of national regeneration Men already felt that the papacy was not to be held in check by constitutional forms, and that if they would free themselves from its usurpations, they must contest the spiritual grounds on which those usurpations rested

The young emperor, who was elected in the midst of these troubles, remained faithful to the old system, but as he left Germany after a short residence, and the representative government which had formerly been projected, was now in actual operation, his conduct was of far less importance than that of the States In the third book we saw how the Council of Regency, after brief hesitation, declared itself decidedly for Luther Even the proposal made in the assembly of the

States, to compel the preachers at least to adhere to the four oldest canonical teachers of the Latin Church, was overruled by the regency; so far were people from considering a strict adherence to doctrines which had been added in later ages as indispensable. The views of this government were indeed on all points of the most enlarged kind. Its plan for the imposition of a general tax of the empire, instead of those taxes on the several states which it was often impossible to collect, would doubtless have given it a firmness and vigour hitherto unknown. Had this succeeded, it would have taken the administration of all the affairs of the country, ecclesiastical as well as temporal, vigorously in hand. It is hardly possible to estimate the consequences which must have resulted from a national council (such as was already appointed) acting under its guidance. But Germany had been too long a stranger to order. Neither the knights, nor the princes, nor even the States, would suffer a regularly constituted power, which they would have been forced to obey, to rise into existence. In defiance of the decrees of the diets of the empire, some princes formed the strictest alliance with the pope; the emperor sent from Spain to forbid the assembling of the national council; the whole government was broken up. The peasants' war was a symptom of the universal dissolution which followed. Nor was this subdued by the constituted authorities of the empire, but by the several associations of princes and states exposed to the attack. Measures for the constitution of a national church, such as had been contemplated by the council of regency, were no longer to be thought of. The several states were compelled to provide for their own wants.

This the emperor was in no present condition to oppose; on the contrary, he himself needed the support of the new tendencies of the public mind.

The attempt to re-establish the rights of the empire in Italy, which he had at first undertaken in concurrence with the papacy, gradually entangled him, as we have shown in our fourth book, in the most violent disputes with that power. With the insignificant means at his disposal, he would never have been able to make any successful resistance to Rome, had not the popular exasperation against the papacy, which increased from year to year, come to his aid. But in order to turn this feeling to account, he was obliged to make concessions to it. A solemn decree of the diet was passed, whereby an almost absolute religious independence was granted to the princes and states within their several dominions. This insured perfect concord and union throughout the empire. While a German army marched into Italy, conquered Rome, and made the Pope himself a prisoner, a great number of the territories of princes and cities on this side the Alps adopted and put in practice the principles of Luther; they emancipated themselves for ever from the yoke of Rome, and established an ecclesiastical organisation of their own.

The fence of those hierarchies which had surrounded the world being thus broken down, the more vigorous and highly civilised among them sought to reconstitute themselves on a new system; the leading principle of which was, to draw religious convictions from the purest and most primitive sources, and to free civil life from the contracting, oppressive influence of a spiritual institution, which assumed the monopoly of piety—an undertaking of the greatest importance and the highest promise to the progress of the human race.

The empire, which from the earliest ages had developed itself under the influence of the See of Rome, was thus invaded by a new element, hostile to the ancient hierarchical order of things: this, if sufficiently powerful to sustain itself, promised to change the whole face and destinies of the German nation.

Changes so radical and extensive are not, however, to be carried into effect without the most violent struggles; nor is this the result of human will or caprice, but inherent in the nature of human affairs.

If, in the case before us, we consider the characters of the men who attached themselves to the great religious innovation, we shall see how impossible it was for them to avoid varieties of opinion, and divergencies of views. Nor was it to be expected that the energetic princes who carried that innovation into effect, should remain perfectly exempt from the excesses and acts of violence which, in their age, had become a second nature.

But far greater dangers presented themselves on the side from which they had seceded.

It would have been absurd to expect that the spirit of absolute domination which had inspired the Church of Rome from her very infancy, and had gradually led her to claim a supreme authority over the world, would allow her to submit to losses so dangerous to her power and interests, without straining every nerve to bring back the seceders.

The German people would doubtless have desired that the emperor should retain the power he had acquired in Italy, and, in return, should allow them to carry into effect those ideas of a Church which they confidently believed to be in conformity with the will and the commands of God. But to this end it would have been necessary that the emperor should himself feel a lively sympathy in those ideas—a sympathy elevated far above the calculations of policy. Were this not the case (and at that time there seemed no trace of any probability of it), his own power stood in far too close and manifold relations to the papacy, for him long to continue at war with Rome.

As, moreover, the attempt to establish a government which might carry through the opposition to Rome and then afford protection to the spiritual Estates, had not succeeded, it followed that the latter, who had reaped nothing from the reformation but loss of revenue and consideration, and who had reason to dread still greater, — if not total ruin, — put themselves in an attitude of defence.

Thus therefore it inevitably followed, that the emperor and the empire once more embraced the cause of the hierarchy; and that the commencement of the fiercest and most perilous struggles dated from this moment.

As yet there was no question of a wider dissemination of the new opinions; it was first to be seen whether the newly organised evangelical church would not share the fate of all the other religious institutions which had attempted to sustain themselves apart from Rome, but had either utterly disappeared, or sunk into insignificance.

We have watched the founding of the edifice; it now remains for us to see whether it will have sufficient strength and solidity to stand erect and unsupported.

We shall begin with a view of the foreign relations of the empire, by which the general position of the emperor was determined, and which consequently exercised a powerful reaction on the affairs of Germany.

CHAPTER I.

CHANGES IN THE GENERAL POLITICAL RELATIONS IN EUROPE.

1527, 1528.

THE Hispano-German army had conquered Rome; and whatever might be the external deportment of the emperor, there is no doubt that he at first founded the most extensive political projects upon this event.

The instructions with which he sent one of his courtiers, Pierre de Verey, to the Viceroy of Naples, have only lately come to light. In these he confesses that his wish was, either to go himself without delay to Italy, or to cause the Pope to come to Spain, in order that they might settle all differences in person and orally: and that he should prefer the latter plan, if the viceroy could find means to bring the pope safely to Spain; but that he was alarmed by the danger of the pontiff falling into the hands of hostile troops by the way. Under these circumstances he thought it best to reinstate the pope in the papal chair in full freedom. But the conditions are worthy of note. This freedom, said the emperor expressly, was only to be understood as relating to the pope's spiritual functions; and even with regard to these, it would be necessary, before setting him at liberty, to obtain full security against treachery and deceit on his part.* The emperor stated what were the securities which he should deem satisfactory; viz., the cession of the cities of Ostia and Civita Vecchia, Parma and Piacenza, Bologna and Ravenna; and lastly, of Civita Castellana. He demands, as we see, all the important places of the ecclesiastical states, as then constituted. The principle upon which he proceeded was, that even if the pope should ever again entertain the wish to injure him, he must not have the power to do so. These strong places he proposed to keep in his own hands, till the pope should call a council for the reformation of the Church.

These views were to a certain degree in accordance with the ideas of the German nation. The church reform which the emperor required was certainly not that proposed by Luther and his followers; nor indeed was it at all of a doctrinal nature: his only object was, to have the administrative abuses removed, as preceding kings and emperors had so often demanded, and Glapio had lately recommended in Worms. It is however obvious that the two projects reciprocally support each other. How vast, moreover, was the prospect of increased temporal power which opened to the emperor, if he could succeed in keeping possession of the States of the Church till the accomplishment of so remote and uncertain an event. Thus Ferdinand had recently seized on the bishopric of Brixen till some accommodation should be come to, and had excited the suspicion that he intended to keep it. Thus too, in this very year, the Bishop of Utrecht, driven out by his warlike neighbour of Guelders, had ceded to the government of the Netherlands all his rights over the temporal administration of his bishopric for an annual sum of money.† The same fate seemed to await the greatest of all spiritual benefices — the States of the Church. It was thought that the emperor would establish his seat of government in Rome, take the temporalities of the ecclesiastical states into his own hands, and depose, or carry off, the pope. What indeed could men think, when Charles was known to have instigated the Duke of Ferrara to undertake without delay the restoration of the exiled dynasts of the ecclesiastical states—the Sassatelli in Imola, the Bentivogli in Bologna, &c.? The Viceroy of Naples actually proposed to the Spanish colonel Alarcon, to whom the safe keeping of the pope in the Castel St. Angelo was entrusted, to bring his captive to Gaeta. Alarcon however refused; "not out of ill will," observes the reporter, "but because he had scruples of conscience." "God forbid," said

* Instructions to Pierre de Verey, Baron de St. Vincent. Excerpts in Bucholtz, Ferdinand, iii. 97—104; especially p. 101. "We have considered that in case there be no means for his Holiness to come hither in safety, notwithstanding what has passed, to use so great liberality towards H. H. as to give him back his freedom, and that by the hand of my viceroy, as representative of our person, he be reinstated in his chair at Rome. But *before* he can be restored to this freedom, which is to be understood of spiritual functions, our viceroy must be so well assured by him as to all things which can happen by human means and by secular power, that we be not deceived therein, and that if H. H. should have the will, he may not have the power to do us ill; that thereby we may not, in return for the kindness we have shown him, continually receive injury and damage, as the experience of the past has shown." Bucholtz places these instructions three weeks after the 30th June, i. e. 21st July, 1527.

† The negotiations of Schoonhoven (Oct. 1527) appear from the speech in the assembly of the Dutch States. Wagenaar, ii. 349.

the brave soldier, "that I should lead the body of the Lord captive"*

It is not always necessary that the schemes of a power should be accurately known in order to excite resistance, the same possibility which, on the one side, suggests the thought of an enterprise, awakens, on the other, the dread of it and the endeavour to counteract it

Charles V had, as we may recollect, still most powerful enemies to contend with The Ligue lay still encamped against him in unbroken force, and just at this moment the King of England, who had for some time shown an inclination that way, made marked advances towards its chiefs Charles's refusal to allow him any share in the advantages resulting from the victory of Pavia, or to conclude the promised marriage between himself and the Princess Mary (a refusal which touched Henry in a very sensible part, inasmuch as it involved a pecuniary damage—an old debt of the emperor's being reckoned as part of the dowry), seemed to the king a sufficient ground for separating himself from his ancient ally As early as the 30th April, a treaty was concluded between Henry VIII and Francis I, the motive for which they declare to be the mutual inclination which nature, who had fashioned them alike in mind and body, had implanted in their hearts, and which had been only heightened by the late interruption of the good understanding between them They agree therein to demand of the emperor, through their common ambassadors, the liberation of the French princes on fair and honourable terms, and the satisfaction of the pecuniary claims of England, and, in case of his refusal to listen to these demands, to declare war against him without delay † It may easily be imagined that their eagerness for war was greatly inflamed by the conquest of Rome Henry VIII says, in the full powers for concluding fresh treaties which he gave to Cardinal Wolsey, that the cause of the Holy See was the common cause of all princes, that never had a greater insult been offered to it than now, and that, as this had been caused by no offence or provocation, but solely by unbridled lust of power, such ungovernable ambition must be opposed betimes by combined forces ‡ His first idea was, that the cardinals still at liberty should assemble in Avignon, where Wolsey should also be present, and that a new central point for the church should thus be created But as the cardinals did not agree to this, the two monarchs mutually promised on no account to consent to any proclamation of a council, so long as the pope was not free, and jointly to oppose every attempt on the part of the emperor to administer the powers of the church § Lastly, they settled the old differences between the two kingdoms Wolsey, who had repaired to Amiens, renounced, in the king's name, all claim to the throne of France A sum of money was agreed on, as compensation, which was to be paid to King Henry and all his successors, "without ceasing, till all the years which divine Providence has appointed to the human race shall have passed away" At first they intended to direct their principal attack against the Netherlands, they now agreed to turn their arms against Italy Henry showed a readiness to advance subsidies, he hoped to obtain ample compensation by means of a perpetual tribute which he intended to exact from the duchy of Milan The proposals made by the emperor at this moment, reasonable as they appeared, were rejected In August 1527, a new French army appeared in Italy under Lautrec, took Bosco, Alexandria and the strong city of Pavia, on which cruel vengeance was taken for the resistance it had made two years and a half before In October 1527, Lautrec crossed the Po, intending to wait only for reinforcements, and then immediately to enter the States of the Church ||

It would have been extremely disagreeable to the emperor, if the pope, still unreconciled to him, had been liberated from the castle by this army, an event which appeared by no means impossible, since the German troops, in consequence of their disorder, and of the diseases caused by an Italian summer, had sustained great losses, and were constantly discontented But this would have been rendered peculiarly vexatious and inconvenient to him by a project which King Henry had conceived, and now followed up with the most impetuous ardour

King Henry VIII was married to Catharine of Aragon, the widow of his brother Arthur, and aunt of the emperor This marriage could not have been contracted without a dispensation from the pope, which Julius II had granted, "in virtue of his apostolical authority; that supreme delegated power which he used as time and circumstances might require."¶ But in the nation, nay, even in the persons immediately surrounding the king, the scruples on this head had never entirely disappeared The death of every son that Catharine brought him, one after another, produced a deep impression on people's minds, and seemed a fulfilment of the words in the 3d Book of Moses,** denouncing childlessness against the man who shall take his brother's wife Even Thomas Aquinas had doubted whether the pope could re-

* Letter of Verey Bucholtz, pp. 110, 118

† Traite de Westminster, 30 Avril, 1527 Du Mont, iv i 476

‡ Ad tractandum super quocumque fœdere pro resarcienda Romanæ sedis dignitate commissio regis Rymer, vi ii p 80

§ "—— præsertim cum juris naturalis æquitate pensata non proprie a summo pontifice factum dici possit, quod ad aliorum arbitrium facit captivus, etiamsi verbis diversissimum profiteatur" Traité d Amiens, 18 Août, Dumont, iv i 494

|| Letter from Angerer (5th Nov), in Hormayr's Archiv 1812, p 436 "We allow ourselves to be restrained by words, and the Ligue follows up its victory I have really no hope or heart left" A letter of Leiva's of the 23d Oct shows, however, that he had not lost heart

¶ Brief in Burnet's Collection p 9 It is said there, "Cum matrimonium contraxissetis illudque carnali copula forsan consummavissetis" It is clear that the dispensation assumed this to be the case

** Leviticus, xx 21, quoted by John the Baptist to Herod St Mark, vi 18

lease men from the obligatory force of a law of the holy Scripture; and we may imagine how greatly the ideas of the reformers, originating in similar questions as to the authority of Scripture, and now become current even in England, must have tended to strengthen this doubt. The king's confessor had for a long time declared to his friends that his highness's marriage would not last.*

In this state of things it happened that Cardinal Wolsey, the king's confidant, quarrelled with the emperor. The emperor, when at Windsor, had promised to raise him to the papal dignity; but when the occasion offered, he did little or nothing in his behalf. It was constantly affirmed in Spain that Wolsey swore eternal vengeance against the emperor for this breach of faith; that he boasted he would bring about such a revolution in affairs as had not taken place for a century;—even though the kingdom of England should perish in the convulsion.† Various other causes now contributed, as we have seen, to create enmity between his royal master and the emperor. In order, however, to render this permanent, it was absolutely necessary that the marriage by which Ferdinand the Catholic and Henry VII. had thought to render the union of their families eternal, should be dissolved. We may believe Wolsey's assertion on his trial,—that it was not he who first suggested the divorce; but it is no less certain that he first seriously proposed it, and with the view above mentioned: he himself affirmed this most distinctly to the French ambassador, Jean du Bellay.‡

Meanwhile, the passion which the king conceived for Anna Boleyn, one of the ladies of the queen's court, though it subserved Wolsey's views, did not form part of his plans. He wished to substitute the French alliance for the Spanish. When he was in Amiens he said to the queen-mother, that if she lived only another year, she would witness the eternal union of England with the one side (the French), and a no less complete separation from the other. He let fall other mysterious expressions, begging her to remember his words, and adding that he would remind her of them at the proper time.

Such being the state of his mind, the differences of the pope with the emperor were entirely in accordance with his wishes; and he therefore urged on the new alliance, and the enterprise against Italy.

We may imagine, however, the effect that schemes and proceedings of this kind naturally produced on the emperor. And here an observation suggests itself, which sounds paradoxical, but, if we mistake not, contains a striking truth.

It is a well-known fact, and one to which we shall often have occasion to recur, that this divorce proved fatal to the influence of the papacy in England. But if we ascend to that higher point of view which commands the general relations of Europe, we shall see that the schemes of Henry VIII. were, at this critical moment, productive of advantage to the papal power. The emperor, whose conduct had been not only imperious but violent towards the pope, now perceived that the head of the church, even in a prison, was a person of importance, and was still able to make him painfully sensible of his power.

The emperor first heard of the project of divorce at the end of July, 1527. In the instructions of the 21st of that month, drawn up for Veroy, no trace of it is (if we may trust our extracts) to be found; but on the 31st of the same month we have a letter of the emperor's in which it is expressly mentioned. In this he commissions the viceroy to speak of the matter to the pope, but with discretion, lest he should avail himself of it "as means to a mischievous understanding with the king." Charles wished that the pope had instantly crushed the scheme by two or three briefs to the king and the cardinal, containing a peremptory refusal.§

It is obvious that a vast weight was thrown into the pope's scale by the need the emperor had of his aid in a domestic affair of such importance.

To this was added the unfavourable impression produced in Spain by the captivity of the sovereign pontiff. The grandees of that kingdom, both temporal and spiritual, who were at the court, took an occasion to speak to the emperor about it, and to remind him of the devoted attachment of the Spanish nation to the see of Rome. The nuncio was even emboldened to entertain the project of suspending the ecclesiastical functions throughout Spain; the prelates were to appear before the emperor in mourning garments, and to demand from him the liberty of Christ's vicegerent on earth. Nothing less than the direct interference of the court was required to prevent his issuing a proclamation of this violent character.‖

Under these circumstances the imperial council of state found it impossible to adhere absolutely to its first instructions. Gattinara declared that they could not keep the pope a prisoner, so long as they continued to recognise him as the true pope. De Praet remarked, that the troops now quartered in Rome were

* Polydorus Virgilius, Historia Anglica, Henricus VIII., p. 82. Jam pridem conjugium regium velut infirmum labefactatum iri censebat idque clam suis sæpe intimis amicis insusurrabat.

† Respuesta del emperador al cartel presentado por Clarençao. Sandoval, lib. xvi. tom. i. p. 358.

‡ Depêche de l'evêque de Bayonne, J. du Bellay, 28th October, 1528. Wolsey complains of certain measures of the French, from which had ensued "totale alienation de Nre dit St. Père avec rompture dudit mariage (the negotiations concerning the affair of the marriage). La quelle rompture, encore que la perte de Nre dit St. Père ne soit pour rien comptée, est de telle importance, ce dit mon dit Seigneur Legat (Wolsey), que tout homme en pourra juger qui *saura que les premiers termes du divorce ont été* mis par luy en avant, afin de mettre perpetuelle separation entre les maisons d'Angleterre et de Bourgogne." Already printed in Le Grand's Histoire du Divorce, iii. p. 185. I have recently looked through the manuscript (Depesches de Messire J. du Bellay. Colbert, v. 468, King's Library, at Paris), which Le Grand used, and have found many new and important circumstances in it.

§ Excerpt from this letter. Bucholtz, iii. 94, note.

‖ Castiglione, 10th Dec. 1527; Pallavicini, lib. ii. c. 14.

wanted for the defence of the kingdom of Naples, and that they could not march till the pope was set at liberty; he advised that the orders issued for the execution of the instructions should be qualified by the very pregnant words, "as far as practicable." The council of state hereupon came to the decision that the pope must, at all events, be set at liberty.*

Negotiations were then set on foot with Clement VII., through Degli Angeli, general of the Franciscans. We unfortunately possess no details of their progress. On the twenty-sixth of November, 1527, a treaty was concluded, in virtue of which the pope was restored, not only to his spiritual functions but to his temporal power. The emperor contented himself with the cession of a few strong places, such as Ostia, Civita Vecchia and Civita Castellana. The pope promised to convoke a council for the union and reformation of the church, and to contribute, as far as lay in his power, to satisfy the soldiery.† Their pay was to be raised chiefly by a large sale of church lands in the Neapolitan territory.

Another point, which is not mentioned in the treaty, was, as it appears, also a subject of negotiation. The pope is said to have promised the emperor that he would not consent to the divorce of the king of England.

Clement VII. was once more free. He garrisoned the castle of St. Angelo with his own troops, caused all the bells in the city to be rung, and nominated anew all the officers of the camera and of the city. The vast schemes of limiting the pope to his spiritual functions, of carrying him off to a distant fortress, and the like, were so far from being realised, that the emperor's own power in Italy was now once more in danger.

At first the pope was far from trusting the emperor or his ministers, or from believing that the peace between them would be of long endurance. It was agreed that he should go to Orvieto. But he was still fearful that Hugo Moncada, who had succeeded Lautrec as viceroy of Naples, would seize upon his person on the way, and carry him off to some fortress in the imperial territory.‡ He determined to escape in disguise through the gates of the garden of the Vatican, on the night before the day appointed for his journey. In this way he reached Orvieto, on the 10th of December, 1527.

For a moment he felt as if he were once more master of his own destiny; but he no sooner raised his eyes, than he found himself surrounded by dangers on every hand.

On the one side, he saw his country in great measure in the hands of the conqueror by whom he had been so injuriously treated. In the course of the winter his capital had been reduced to utter ruin by the imperial troops, to which arrears of pay were still due.

On the other side, the friends who had affected to protect him inspired him only with hatred, distrust and alarm. Florence, which had again expelled the house of Medici, and attempted to found a republic on the plan of Savonarola, found support from France. The Venetians had taken possession of the cities of Ravenna and Cervia, which Julius II. deemed it so great a glory to have reconquered.

Clement feared both parties. That the emperor should possess at once Milan and Naples, seemed to him extremely dangerous;§ in that case Charles would indeed be "lord of all things;" the favour which he himself had shown to the emperor's foes would bring his head upon the block. But the measures of the Ligue caused him, if possible, more anxiety and distress. When the French invited him to sanction and to join the Ligue, as it was then constituted, he replied, that it was a strange proposal to make to him, to sanction and concur in the measures taken against himself:—in Florence his family had been ruined; Ferrara was constantly engaged in hostilities against him; yet with these powers he was asked to ally himself.

The French told him they were determined to wrest not only Milan but Naples also from the emperor; and they wished to know whether the pope would at least openly declare himself for them, when they had made their way to Naples, and driven out the Spaniard. Clement evaded giving a positive answer; he found it difficult to believe that they would, as they asserted, allow him to dispose of Naples at his pleasure; judging from his countenance, people concluded that his intention was to gain time to consider, and then to make such terms as circumstances would allow.‖

Every thing, however, depended on the issue of the enterprise of France, and on the fortune of arms.

In January 1528, Lautrec entered the kingdom of Naples. The German army, which had at length with infinite difficulty been led out of Rome by the Prince of Orange, threw itself in his way at Troja, and offered to give him battle. But Lautrec expected succours from Venice, and was satisfied to let the imperialists feel the superiority of his artillery. This conduct had such an effect, that an inclination in favour of France manifested itself throughout the empire. When the expected reinforcements arrived, the imperial troops,

* Notice in Bucholtz, iii. p. 119.

† Contract between Pope Clement and Charles V.; Reissner, p. 155. The words of the preamble are, however, rather a form of expression than an historical truth.

‡ Jovius, Vita Pompeji Columnæ, 197, f. Guicciardini, lib. xxiii. p. 469.

§ Literæ Gregorii de Cassellis, in Fiddes's Life of Wolsey, p. 467. "Et cum ei persuasissem, ut nihil dubitaret, et quod totum se rejiceret in manus regiæ majestatis et rev. D. Legati, dixit se ita velle facere et quod in eorum brachia se et omnia sua remittat. Et caput jam ponit sub supplicio, nisi a regia Majestate adjuvetur. Si Cæsar permittatur aliquid possidere in Italia præterquam in regno Neapolitano, omnium rerum semper erit dominus, nisi mature confundatur." It is evident he was still of opinion that it was necessary to the security of the see of Rome that Milan should be wrested from the emperor.

‖ Nic. Raince au Gr. Maitre, 28th Jan. 1528. MS. Bethune, 8534.

which had no artillery, found it necessary to abandon the field and retreat upon Naples, the defence of which was of the highest importance;* the head, they said, did not follow the members, but the members the head. Lautrec hastened to pursue them: towards the end of April he encamped on either side of the high road from Capua, and opened the siege of Naples. It appeared almost impossible that this populous city, less able than any other to endure scarcity of food, could long hold out against a conquering army. In England the fall of Naples was already reckoned upon as the termination of the whole affair; for the provinces of the kingdom were already in great measure in the hands of the allies. The Venetians took possession of the ports of Apulia, while Filippino Doria defeated the imperialists in the harbour of Amalfi. Some people began to conceive a hope of a universal overthrow of the imperial power. Wolsey was heard to declare that the pope must be enabled at once to depose the emperor, on account of the grievous outrages he had experienced from him; he had only to proclaim that the electoral princes possessed the right of proceeding to a new election, and to admonish them to choose one of their own body. This would not only have the effect of conciliating them, but would create such a breach between the emperor and the pope that any future reconciliation would be impossible.† A communication to this effect was in fact made to the pope. He deemed it necessary that both kings should agree upon the candidate for the imperial crown, lest a similar confusion to that at the last election (of Charles V.) should occur. He thought he could reckon upon four electoral princes.‡

But here, too, the emperor's lucky star did not forsake him.

In the first place, he succeeded in gaining over one of the most powerful chiefs of Italy, Andrea Doria, of Genoa. He had long been negotiating with him; first before Doria entered into the service of the Ligue, and afterwards during the visit of the arch-chancellor Gattinara to Upper Italy, in May 1527: an Augustinian hermit, in concert with a servant of Doria's named Erasmo, were, on both occasions, the secret mediators.§ It is not surprising if, under these circumstances, the king of France missed in Doria the cordiality and zeal which he expected from him. Doria, on his side, made many complaints of personal offences, as well as of the treatment experienced by his native city, whose ancient rights over Savona were now disputed. In England, where many Genoese then lived, and all these circumstances were known with the greatest accuracy, they created the most violent irritation. Wolsey said the French ought to give Doria all the money and all the honours he might choose to demand; and rather cede Savona seven times over than estrange this man at the moment when they most needed him. But France did not keep one line of policy so rigorously and steadily in view, as to weigh all the consequences of his loss. On the other hand, the emperor subscribed to all the terms proposed by Doria; he rendered the destiny of Genoa, as well as the person and fortunes of Doria, perfectly secure, and he voluntarily added certain marks of favour; for example, a considerable grant of land in the Neapolitan territory. He knew well what he was doing. In a very short time Andrea Doria hoisted on the emperor's ships the very flags which Filippino had taken from the imperialists in the battle of Amalfi.‖ His desertion alone sufficed to establish the emperor's superiority in the Mediterranean. But besides this, it was an important advantage, that a city which formed the link of direct communication between Spain and Milan, once more declared for the emperor.

At this moment, too, the fate of Naples was decided.

Contagious diseases, such as always follow in the train of devastating war, broke out in the French armies before Naples, and spread with dreadful rapidity. "God sent amongst them," says a German report, "such a pestilence that out of 25,000 not above 4000 survived."¶ Lautrec himself was one of its victims; Vaudemont, to whom the crown had been destined, died before the gates which he had hoped to enter in triumph as king. To these disasters were added the fortunate turn of things among the besieged. The German imperialists, as at Pavia, directed their attacks in the first place against their countrymen in the service of France, under the Count of Lupfen, and brought back their colours as a trophy into the city: at length the rest of the French army found itself compelled to prepare for a retreat, when at that moment it was attacked

* Ziegler, Acta Paparum, book xii. "As the imperialists had neither ammunition nor provisions, and nothing could be conveyed to them in safety,—for all places were better inclined to the French than to the imperialists. . . ."

† Bellay au Grandmaitre, 2d Jan. 1528. (MS. Colbert, Ve.)

‡ Gardiner and Cassalis to C. Wolsey. April 28. Strype, Eccles. Mem. v. 427. "It were," says the pope, "to be foreseen before sentence of privation, who were most meet to be chosen."

§ The details which we find concerning this in Hormayr's Archiv. 1810, p. 61, and in Bucholtz, are doubtless taken from the same documents in the Vienna archives. Doria's engagements to Francis were to cease 1st July, 1528, and then those to the emperor to begin. See also Folieta, Historia Genuensis, p. 309. Sigonius de rebus gestis Andreæ Aureæ. Opp. Sigonii, i. 241.

‖ Letter to Salviati, L. d. Principi, ii. 129. In a MSS. biography of Guasto, in the Chigi library at Rome, there is a chapter on the Cambiamento di A. Doria, which certainly sounds rather romantic. Doria's prisoners hear him complaining of king Francis in his sleep: "non basta al rè Franceseo, avermi tolti i ricatti guadagnati col rischio del mio sangue, ma vuol Genova sottoporre a Savona—ma io cambiarò la bandiera, sarò signore del mare, farò libera non che soggetta la patria mia." The motives, however, are clear enough. According to this story, Guasto urged them in his conversation with Doria, adducing the examples of La Palice and Giangiacopo Trivulzio, who had also been very ungratefully treated by Francis. These arguments brought him over.

¶ Ziegler: "es starb ser under ihnen. Gott schiket under des Frantzosen hauffen ain solche pestilenz, das si innerhalb 30 Tagen schir all starben und von 25,000 uber 4,000 nit beliben." "There died many among them. God sent among the troops such a pestilence that within thirty days they sheer all died, and out of 25,000 not 4,000 remained;" a statement which Reissner has altered, after his manner. p. 173.

and totally cut off. This occurred on the 29th August 1528.*

The imperialists, whose condition had so lately appeared hopeless, remained completely victors, and once more took possession of the kingdom.

Fortunate was it for the pope that he had remained neutral. "But for this," writes his secretary of state, Sanga, now his prime minister,† "we should now be in the lowest abyss of ruin." It was in a conference between Clement and Sanga on the 6th of September, that some advances to the emperor were seriously resolved on.

The imperial party had already frequently requested the pope to return to Rome, where they promised to defend him from every danger.‡ He now determined upon this step. On the 6th of October we find him again in Rome.

He was not, however, on that account to be regarded as in any degree an ally of the emperor. Even in November 1528, he encouraged Francis I. to keep alive the agitation in Germany, by which Charles's dignity as emperor was endangered, and to support the Woiwode of Transylvania.§ In December 1528, the French ambassador declares that, "whatever may appear to the contrary, the pope is as much inclined to the French as ever; that at the bottom of his heart he was much displeased that their attack on Naples had succeeded so ill; had they followed his advice, he said, matters would not have ended so. "I venture to affirm," adds the ambassador, "that here is no feint."‖ It is at least certain that one of his intimates, Cardinal Campeggi, who was gone to England to conduct the proceedings on the king's divorce, said publicly, in the plainest terms, that the emperor was full of ill-will, and would do them as much mischief as he possibly could; that to attack him in good earnest was the true way to bring him to his senses; the desirable thing would be to do him some damage in Spain, but as that was not practicable, an expedition against him in Germany was by all means to be undertaken, let it be conducted as it might.¶

No one, therefore, could have ventured to predict a speedy peace. In the year 1528 a formal challenge was sent by the emperor to the king, and it was from no backwardness on the part of the former that a single combat did not take place.**

In Upper Italy the fortune of war was still vacillating, inclining rather to the side of the king than to that of the emperor. The same diseases which had destroyed the French army before Naples, attacked the German troops which, in the summer of 1528, had crossed the Alps under Henry of Brunswick and Marx Sittich of Ems, in aid of the emperor, and were now encamped in Lombardy. Independently of this, Duke Henry was not the man to carry through an undertaking in which he had to contend at once with the jealousy of his allies, the aversion of the country people, the fatal effects of the climate, and the attacks of the enemy. He soon retreated in disgust across the Alps; his troops dispersed, and part of them entered the service of Venice.

Thereupon a fresh French army made its appearance in Ivrea under St. Pol; the Venetians sent money and troops to meet it, and the allies not only reconquered Pavia, which they had a second time lost, but immediately began to indulge the highest hopes. St. Pol was of opinion that they ought instantly to press on to the Neapolitan territory, where a number of strong places were still in possession of the French; he doubted not that the whole kingdom would then fall into his hands. The French government, on the other hand, thought it more urgent first to make an attack on Genoa and Andrea Doria. Although this did not succeed, the army became master of the greater part of Lombardy, and in England hopes were still entertained that it would soon take Milan, and even, by investing Parma and Piacenza, regain its influence over the pope.

Nor was eastern Europe in a state of less confusion. So long as Ferdinand himself was present in Hungary, order was in some measure maintained, but as soon as he absented himself, the old divisions broke out again. Even his own adherents could not agree. The Bishop of Erlau complained of Andrew Bathory, who had insulted and wounded him; "no Socrates," he declared, "had had need of more patience than he." Francis Batthyany could not make his way to the castles of which Louis Pekry had taken possession in his name. A universal cry was raised against the violences of the German army under Katzianer, which levied its supplies directly upon the country, and advanced at a very slow rate against the Joannists. Katzianer sent an energetic and rough answer.†† The assertion, even if untrue, that bread

* Sepulveda, who was then in Gaeta, viii. 34, f.

† Al Cl. Campeggio, Lettere di principi, ii. 127. "Se sua Santità non faceva così, hora si sarebbe nel profondo della total ruina."

‡ Lettera di Roma a B. Castiglione. L. d. pr. ii. 10.

§ Gio Joachim a Montmorency Roma, 7th Nov. 1528. Molini, ii. 122. "Mi disse S. Santità, che l'imperatore fosse quasi costretto, in persona trovarsi ben tosto in Alamagna, per dar ordine a molte cose,—le quali non ordinate—producevano gran pregiudizio e non minor movimento, minacciavano a l'imperatore sua stato, titulo e dignità (he points, no doubt, at the designs of the House of Bavaria, to obtain the dignity of king of Rome). Se mo le cose in Germania fussero nel stato che si dice, a S. Sà parrebbe chel chr^mo re per ben degli suoi affari *le mantenesse, augumentasse e fomentasse.*"

‖ Raince, 14th Dec. 1528, "qu'il n y a fiction aucune."

¶ Bellay, 1 Jan. 1529, "louant fort l'enterprise d'Allemagne, par quel moyen qu'elle se puisse conduire."

** Relacion da Borgoña, Sandoval, 888. He had a solemn audience of the king, who said to him, "Dost thou bring me the place of battle?" The herald answered, "Sire, the Emperor's sacred majesty——" The king broke in upon him, "I bid thee that thou speak to me of nothing, till thou hast brought me assurance of the place of battle." The herald could not fully deliver his message; but at last it came to pass as Wolsey thought. "I trust to God these young courageous passions shall be finally converted into fume." 21st July, St. P. p. 320.

†† Correspondence in Bucholtz, iii. 269—279. In Ursinus Velius de Bello Pannonico, p. 91, we see that the grandees of Hungary quarrelled, "de bonis hostis Joannis jam olim inter se partitis."

mixed with chalk was given to the Germans to poison them, proves the strong national antipathy that had arisen. This rendered it doubly difficult to keep in check the adherents of Zapolya. At the diet of Ofen, in January 1528, they formed three distinct classes; those who, spite of the oath they had sworn to King Ferdinand, endeavoured to seduce his subjects to revolt; the vacillating, who had demanded safe conduct in order that they might go and do homage to the king, and then had never appeared; and lastly, Zapolya's open followers, who carried on a system of plunder, and rendered the country insecure. It does not appear that any effectual measures were taken against any of them. On the other hand, Zapolya neglected no means by which he could, from his exile at Tarnow, keep Hungary in a state of agitation. George Martinuzzi, a monk of the Pauline order, who had formerly been in the service of Zapolya's mother, was so devoted to him that he three times ventured into Hungary on foot. He boasts of the good reception he had experienced from Jacob von Thornaly, Stephen Bathory of Somlyo, and Paul Arthandy. He wandered from castle to castle, revived old connexions, and prepared every thing for his lord's reception.* The main thing was, that he was the bearer of promises of Turkish succours. In the beginning of the year 1528 a treaty had been concluded between Zapolya and Suleiman. This was not the result of presents, for the ambassador, Jerome Lasko, had brought none; nor of any promise of tribute, but solely of political motives. Zapolya had declared that he would, now and always, serve the mighty sultan with all the powers of his kingdom, of his hereditary possessions, and even of his own person. "I, on the other hand," said Suleiman, in the solemn audience of leave, "will be a true friend and ally to your master, and support him against his enemies with all my power. I swear it by the prophet, by the great prophet beloved of God, Mohammed, and by my sword."† Unquestionably nothing could be more conducive to the progress of the Turkish power than a strict alliance with so influential a chief. Suleiman considered himself as the most formidable rival of the House of Austria,—the natural head of the opposition to it, in which he included France, Venice, Poland, and the pope himself; "that poor priest from whom the faith of the Christians emanates, and whom they nevertheless so remorselessly maltreat." He was convinced that he ought immediately to oppose resistance to the power of the emperor Charles V.; "for," said he, "it is like a stream formed of small brooks and melting snows, which at length undermines the strong castle in the mountain gorge."‡ The Austrian ambassadors assert that the King of Poland sent a special messenger in October 1528, inviting the sultan to declare war upon the emperor in the following year; in which case he would come to his assistance. Suleiman was, however, already resolved upon it. When Habordancz, the envoy sent by Ferdinand to Constantinople, to demand the restitution of twenty-four fortresses formerly belonging to Hungary, offered only a pecuniary compensation in return, the sultan replied, that he would come in person, with all his troops, to defend these fortresses. It may easily be imagined what a ferment this prospect of war excited in Hungary. As early as September 1528, Andrew Bathory wrote to King Ferdinand that he lived surrounded by rebels, and with death before his eyes. The same year, Peter Raresch, Hospodar of Moldavia, who had long been a fisherman, but was now recognised as a true Dragoschide of the house of the great Stephen, invaded and laid waste the diocese of Szekler.§ Every thing seemed to tend to a great catastrophe.

While such an universal ferment prevailed in the East and in the West, it was hardly possible that stormy Germany should escape the contagion.

CHAPTER II.

GERMANY DURING THE AFFAIR AND TIMES OF PACK.

We invariably find the Dukes of Bavaria in more or less intimate connexion with the foreign princes hostile to the empire—the King of France,‖ the woiwode, and above all, the pope.

They had still not relinquished their hopes of the imperial crown. They carried on incessant intrigues with the leading electoral princes, and made them magnificent promises. They also tried to set the King of France again in motion.

We are in possession of a project which they communicated to the French court with a view to the attainment of their end.¶ It was proposed that French ambassadors, supported by those of Lorraine and of England, should appear at the next diet of the empire, and should remind the States what numerous and severe losses the church and the empire had sustained, since the House of Austria had occupied the imperial throne. Constantinople, Rhodes, and now Hungary, were lost to christendom; Basle and Constance to the empire; the sole object of the princes of Austria was

* His letter to Verantius in Pray, and thence in Katona, xx. 1. 409. See Isthuansi, p. 126.

† Lasky's Statement in Katona, xx. 1. Lasky declared in Zapolya's name, "non solum Ungariæ regnum, non solum dominia patrimonii sui, sed et personam suam propriam non suam esse vult sed vestram," p. 319.

‡ Habordancz, Report, in Bucholtz, iii. 596.

§ Engel, Geschichte der Wallachei, p. 170.

‖ Lettre de Breton au Gr. Maitre, 17th May, 1528 (MS. Bethune). "Le secretaire du duc de Bavière, que vous savez, est depuis deux (jours ?) ici et a eu fort bonne audience du roi."

¶ Forme et manière de conduire et mener l'affaire d'élection au nom du roi de France. MS. Bethune, 6593, f. 93. See the agreement with Mainz; Stumpf, p. 50.

to make the empire hereditary, and to aggrandise themselves in every possible way; (as an example of which, Don Ferdinand's recent attempt to get possession of Salzburg was to be cited:) hereupon they should call upon the States to proceed to the election of another emperor; to elevate to the throne a man who would rule uprightly, and restore Germany to its former prosperity; who should be a true and good catholic, able to eradicate all heresies. With such an emperor, the King of France should engage to form the strictest alliance.*

It is very probable that these negotiations were carried further. It is at least certain that the Bavarians hoped to gain over the Palatinate and Treves; the Elector of Brandenburg, through the influence of France, and the Elector of Saxony by corrupting his councillors.† This we gather from the expressions of the pope and his legate, as well as from those of Cardinal Wolsey.

It is, however, remarkable enough that the opposite (i. e. the evangelical) party had also made advances to the powers hostile to Austria.

We find an emissary of the Landgrave of Hessen, Dr. Walter, at the court of France. Another we see setting out on his way to John Zapolya, and trace his progress through the whole of his journey. This was the celebrated Dr. Pack. In the Passion-week of 1528, we find him in Senftenberg, where he gave himself out to be a canon of Meissen; at Easter, in Breslau, where he hired a servant who could speak Polish; on the 18th of April, at Cracow. Here, in the church of St. Barbara, he had his first interview with a follower of the woiwode, at which they determined that he should visit that prince in person. When Pack reached the neighbourhood of Tarnow, where the woiwode then resided, he alighted from his carriage and proceeded on foot into the city, in order not to attract attention. On the 26th and 27th April we find him negotiating with the woiwode; a formal treaty was drawn up, and nothing was wanting but the ratification of the landgrave.‡ The landgrave had demanded money to enable him to attack Ferdinand in Germany. The woiwode promised to procure 100,000 gulden from his brother-in-law, the king of Poland. The report that Poland had promised the sultan to attack Ferdinand with German troops, may very probably be traced to this treaty.

It is impossible to calculate the consequences that must have resulted from a prosecution of these schemes, which were aimed by the one party at Charles's imperial dignity, while the other intended to attack Ferdinand in his hereditary domains;§ especially at a time when all other social and political relations were shaken.

But such projects were not destined to be realised. The Dukes of Bavaria and the Landgrave of Hessen were wholly ignorant that they were allies. Indeed, such violent antipathies, chiefly from religious causes, arose among the sovereigns of Germany, that they gave birth to one of the most singular complications that ever occurred in history.

In consequence of so many evangelical princes having thrown off the jurisdiction of the ecclesiastical courts, numerous complaints were laid before the imperial court; and, in the existing state and spirit of the imperial chanceries, these complaints could not fail to meet with a hearing: it is perfectly true that the expediency of resorting to punishments, and even to the ban, was there suggested. Nassau, which had old territorial dissensions with the Landgrave of Hessen, sought to secure itself against this contingency by mandates.‖

A vague rumour of these designs found its way to Germany. The landgrave was warned by a man of great consideration, as he says, "whom he would not name, but who knew from good authority that there was something in hand—extraordinary practices (*merkliche practica*)—against the Lutherans."

The landgrave, however, did not look so far for the origin of the danger. He saw only the hostilities of which the adherents of the new doctrine were the objects, in Bavaria and the whole of Upper Germany; the violent menaces uttered by Duke George of Saxony against his cousin the elector; his declarations that nothing should induce him to be reconciled to that prince so long as he adhered to the Lutheran sect, and that he only waited for the emperor's commands to proceed against him. It appeared to the landgrave a suspicious circumstance that zealous catholic princes had visited King Ferdinand at Breslau, in May 1527, and had afterwards afforded him assistance in Hungary; in short, he was fully persuaded that a plot against him was in agitation among his neighbours.

Just at this time it happened that the steward of the chancery of Duke George—Otto von Pack—the same who undertook the journey to Tarnow—in the course of the year

* The conclusion runs thus: "Au surplus nos princes sont deliberés de n'obmettre rien de leur labeur et vigilance, et d'essayer tous les moyens qu'ils verront être nécessaires pour la fin de cette affaire, et qu'ils ont espérance, Dieu aidant et la bonté du roi tres chrétien, achever l'affaire ainsi qu'ils le désirent."

† "Möchten etliche seiner Räthe durch Geld abzurichten seyn:" "some of his councillors might be to be brought round with money." Extracts from a memoir, probably of Duke William, in Sugenheim, Baierns Zustände, &c., p. 9.

‡ We have taken all the details from the confession of Hans Schuoch of Breslau, the same whom Pack hired as his servant.

§ It was the general opinion that the troubles in the Mark, and the attacks made by Minkwitz upon Lebus, were connected with this. Duke George writes to Hoyer von Mansfeld (March, 1529), "It is credibly reported to us that a very great business was in hand, and although it is set on foot in the name of some of the nobles, we cannot give much heed to it, since a great deal of money is given to the persons employed. It is said that this business is undertaken for the advantage of the Wayda, and against the country of Laussnitz and the elector of Brandenburg." The duke was just then intending to have an interview with the elector. It was he who arrested Minkwitz.

‖ Heinrich v. Nassau to Joh. v. Nassau; Arnoldi, Memoirs, p. 200. The letter is of the 13th April, before Pack's affair, of which nothing was then known, especially in Spain.

1527 came to the landgrave, who was then at Cassel, to give him information and legal advice as to the affair with Nassau. The landgrave disclosed to him his apprehensions, and pressed him to say whether he knew any thing about the matter. Pack sighed, and was silent. This only increased the landgrave's urgency. Pack at length declared, that a league against the Lutherans was indeed not only in hand, but actually concluded. He engaged to procure the original documents for the landgrave, who, in return, promised him his protection and a reward of 10,000 gulden. Landgrave Philip was now inflamed with indignation. In February 1528, we find him in Dresden, whither Pack brought, not, indeed, the original of the treaty, which, he said, the chancellor had laid aside, but a copy of it, bearing all the outward marks of authenticity. The seal of the Saxon chancery was affixed on both sides to the black silk cord which tied the sheets of paper together, and beneath it hung the seal of the signet ring which Duke George wore (and which the landgrave knew perfectly well), with his three escutcheons, in the upper one the rue garland, in the lowest, two lions. Pack allowed the landgrave's secretary to take a copy of it, and received four thousand gulden.*

This document contained the most alarming and hostile matter that it was possible to conceive. It appeared therein that the Electors of Mainz and Brandenburg, the Dukes of Saxony and Bavaria, the Bishops of Saltzburg, Wurzburg, and Bamberg, in conjunction with King Ferdinand, had bound themselves in the first place to fall upon the Elector of Saxony, if he refused to deliver up Luther and his followers, and to partition his territory, and next to attack the landgrave, and if he would not recant, to drive him out of his country, which was then to be given to Duke George. The city of Magdeburg was also to be reduced to subjection to its bishop. The mode, as well as the means of attack were accurately determined.

The landgrave, long filled with suspicions of this kind, did not for a moment doubt the authenticity of the document laid before him: he hurried, with his habitual vehemence, to Weimar, in order to communicate it to the elector. Even he was stunned and hurried away by the amazing, yet precise and urgent nature of the danger, and on the 9th of March a treaty between the two princes was concluded, in which they promised to raise six thousand foot and two thousand horse for their mutual defence. They concluded that it would be better not long to await the attack, but to anticipate it. The landgrave himself went to Nurnberg, and thence to Ansbach. It was under these circumstances that he sent Otto Pack, whom he had now attached more closely to his service, to the woiwode. Warlike preparations began without delay. The Hessian troops assembled near Herrenbreitungen, the Saxon, in the Thuringian forest. The whole of Germany was in motion.

The situation of things in the evangelical part of Germany was not, however, such as to depend solely on the hasty spirit of this or that prince. The theologians too, especially Luther, had a voice to give, and the first question was, what opinion this voice would pronounce.

Luther had as little doubt as the two princes of the genuineness of the treaty laid before him, but he thought it did not justify an immediate resort to arms. Such violent measures were opposed to all his ideas of law and morality. He therefore thought it his duty to remonstrate with the princes on their designs, and beg them to desist from them: an accusation, he said, must first be laid against their enemies, and the answer heard, otherwise, violence and confusion would break out among the princes of Germany, which, to the joy of Satan, would lay waste the country. Of all the men who ever placed themselves at the head of a great movement, Luther was perhaps the most averse to violence and war. He held that self-defence was lawful, especially against princes like those above named, who, as the equals of his master, had no sovereignty over him; but to be the first to take up arms and proceed to acts of offence, — that was beyond his comprehension.† He applied the words, "Blessed are the meek and the peacemakers," to political affairs. "He that taketh the sword shall perish by the sword." "War," said he, "ventures all, wins little and is certain to lose, but meekness loses nothing, risks little, and wins all."

It was easy to persuade Elector John, who understood the gospel as Luther did, and loved it with all his heart; he had merely been hurried away by the vehemence of his impetuous ally. He now represented to Philip that an attack might bring dishonour on the gospel, and that they must therefore refrain from it. The landgrave replied, that the treaty of their enemies, sealed and sworn to by them, was equivalent to an attack; he represented the advantage of taking immediate and active measures for their defence; it would awaken many who now slumbered, and would enable them to obtain safer terms. But the elector could no longer be prevailed on to advance a step. He sent his son, accompanied by a trusty councillor, named Wildenfels, to Cassel, with so decided a refusal, that the landgrave was forced at length to follow Luther's advice, and in the first place to make the treaty known, and demand an explanation from the princes therein named. He instantly sent it to his father-in-law.‡

* Statement of the Landgrave, in a letter to Duke George, of the 28th June, which Rommel (iii 21) speaks of as lost, but which is in the Dresden archives. I shall give it in the Appendix.

† Remarks in De Wette, iii 316. Nos 986, 987 but doubtless to be dated March, and not May. For they are mentioned already in a copy of instructions in Neudecker's Documents, p. 33, which though undated, certainly falls in March, since the elector says therein that he has summoned some of his friends on the Friday after Judica (3d April), "right presently" (schirstkünftig).

‡ Letter in the Weimar archives, undated, but of the earlier half of April, in answer to the above-named instructions. "I will certainly see that I shortly obtain the

It is impossible to describe the astonishment that seized the German courts at the appearance of the accusation founded on this document.

Duke George answered immediately, and denounced the man who affirmed that he had seen the original of such a treaty, as a false and perjured villain. Elector Joachim demanded, as did Duke George, that the name of the liar who had forged this treaty should be published, lest people should think the landgrave himself had invented it. All the others answered in the same manner. The landgrave saw himself compelled to arrest his informer, and to allow him to be brought to trial.*

We too must here discuss the question, which does not seem even yet to be at rest,—what was the real truth concerning this alleged treaty?

In the first place, it is full of the grossest improbabilities. Elector Joachim, for example, was to abandon Hessen to the Duke of Saxony (to which, in virtue of the hereditary union of the houses, he had quite an equal claim), stipulating to receive Beeskow and Storkow as a compensation; though these had for some years become the property of the bishopric of Lebus.† The Dukes of Bavaria were represented as uniting with Ferdinand to give him possession of Hungary—the very country which they were striving to wrest from him. The plan of the campaign, too, was most strange; and there is a certain ironical truth in what Pack afterwards said, when, in order to excuse himself, he described the whole scheme as "foolishly laid" (*närrish gestellt*).‡

We have also to consider the character of Pack. In the Dresden archives there are documents concerning him, from which it is evident that he was untrustworthy, treacherous,—in short, a thoroughly bad man. He made use of his position at court to extort money. For example, he borrowed from the council of Tennstädt some hundreds of gulden, under specious pretexts, and postponed payment from term to term. In the list of his creditors are also four other Saxon towns, Pirna, Meissen, Oschatz and Chemnitz.§

But the following story is still more discreditable to him. On one occasion, when he went to Nürnberg on his lord's business (we find him more than once in the character of envoy to the diet), the Bishop of Merseburg entrusted him with his contingent for the Council of Regency and the imperial chamber, amounting to 103½ gulden. The diet was over, and Pack long returned, when the bishop received a citation to pay his contingent. Pack, being questioned about it, declared, without any embarrassment, that he had given the money to a Nürnberg citizen of the name of Friedemann, who had delivered it to the Council of Regency, but had got no receipt, because some former arrears were still due. As a proof, he subjoined Friedemann's letter and seal. Friedemann was of course immediately called to account. What was the surprise of the council, when the honest citizen declared he hardly knew Dr. Pack,—never had any dealings with him, nor received money from him; he likewise observed that the Council of Regency would certainly have given him a receipt for the sum which he had actually paid in, though not for the whole debt; that the handwriting and seal which the doctor had produced could not possibly be his. Both these documents are in the archives; and, in fact, the handwriting which Pack had sent in, is totally different from that of Friedemann. In fact, Pack was already practised in forgery, when this opportunity of making money, on a larger scale than heretofore, presented itself. He used his skill to such a purpose, that, as we have seen, Germany was very nearly involved in civil war. He himself afterwards did not persist in asserting the genuineness of the forged documents. He abandoned the assertion that he had had in his hands the original, authenticated by the seals of all the princes, and only affirmed that a Bohemian secretary, named Wurisyn, had brought him a copy out of Silesia. But even this turned out to be false. The secretary proved that, at the time mentioned by Pack, he was not in Dresden: he was then a fugitive from his creditors.‖

A document so filled with contradictions, and proceeding from so fraudulent and mendacious a man, must be entirely rejected. I find, too, that the opinion that Pack had practised a cheat, was, even at the time, very generally diffused. Melancthon was persuaded of it the instant he read the first examinations.¶ Chancellor Brück instituted a more searching inquiry, and came to the same conclusion.** Landgrave Philip more than once frankly acknowledged it. He was afterwards reproached with having, on that occasion, undertaken much and accomplished little. "That happened," said he, "because we felt that we

---

same (the original). But had F. L. followed my advice, and that of others, at Weimar, and not grudged a little cost, I should have it already at this time." It is clear that Pack from the very first demanded money. Philip declared in a letter to Duke George (Rommel, iii. 17), that it was only within the last three or four weeks that he had allowed money to be offered to Pack.

* The answers, as well as the pretended treaty itself, are to be found in Hortleder and Walch. In the Dresden archives there is also a copy of instructions of Ferdinand's, in which he requests Duke George to come to the bottom of the affair, and to make out how and where it arose.

† Wohlbrück, Geschichte von Lebus, ii. 414.

‡ Printed in the Acta concerning Doctor Otto v. Pack's examination in Cassel, in Hoffman's collection of unprinted Reports, p. 98.

§ Missives found in Dr. Pack's house when he was arrested. Dresden Archives, No. 7398.

‖ Examination of Wurisyn, in a convolute in the Dresden Archives, entitled, Proceedings concerning the Affair between Dr. Otto Pack and Caspar Wurisyn. I must expressly remark that, in the whole account of this affair, I do not use any thing that Pack confessed on the rack, as evidence.

¶ To Camerarius, Corp. Repert. i. 988. Alter sane odiose extorsit pecuniam nobis valde dissuadentibus: *αἰδὼς δ' οὐκ ἀγαθὴ κεχρημένῳ ἀνδρί.* Camerarius had very much moderated these expressions. Dr. Bretschneider has restored them.

** Oratio de Gregorio Pontano habita a Vito Winshemio. Declam. Melanchthonis, tom. V. p. 205. "Principes *commenticio* fœdere moti, arma ceperunt.—Re inquisita Pontani diligentia exercitus dimissi sunt."

were deceived We found that we had been falsely informed "*

Fortunate would it have been, had he yielded to this conviction sooner than he actually did

But before the falsehood of the supposed project was become perfectly obvious, he had already fallen upon the Wurzburg territory, and threatened Bamberg on the one side and Mainz on the other He now demanded that those who had caused his armament should pay the cost of it As no one was prepared to resist him, the bishops were compelled, in spite of the mediation of the Palatinate and Treves, actually to pay him an indemnity, and to accede to unfavourable terms

Happy as the Elector of Saxony was that an unjust war would be avoided, he was fully sensible of the unpardonable nature of such violence, and of the precipitancy which had characterised the whole affair "It almost consumes me," said Melancthon, "when I reflect with what stains our good cause is covered by it I can only sustain myself by prayer" †

Even the landgrave was afterwards ashamed "If it had not happened," said he, "it would not happen now We know no act of our life that is more displeasing to us "‡

But this did not remedy the evil, which, indeed, was followed by the gravest and the most dangerous consequences

The Protestant chiefs had laid bold plans for availing themselves of the complication of events in Europe, or had endeavoured to bring the religious dissensions of Germany to an open conflict The only result, however, had been an outrageous breach of the public peace, which threw an ill light on all the proceedings and designs of the religious party

For the common sense of what was due to justice and to the empire, now naturally revolted against them

The members of the Swabian league, to which both the landgrave and the bishops belonged, were particularly discontented The landgrave sent apologetic letters, and offered to abide the legal decision of Elector Louis The League answered (November 1528) that no appeal to law was necessary they would adhere to the letter of their act of union "I would that the day of judgment burst upon us," exclaims an envoy in his zeal, "that so we might be delivered out of this and other dangers"

Though there existed in the leaders of both parties a certain inclination to oppose the House of Austria, and to join the European confederation against it, we find that affairs took a totally different direction, and that it was in fact a mistake, a fraud, and an act of rashness which brought all the conflicting passions into play

This could not, indeed, have been the case, had not the internal dissonances become every hour stronger and deeper

As, on the evangelical side, institutions in harmony with the new opinions began to be organised, so on the other, measures were proposed to strengthen the tottering edifice of Catholicism

In some places, similar means to those used by the Lutherans were resorted to In the years 1527, 1528, we find visitations of the churches in Austria, by commissions composed of ecclesiastical and lay members, like those in Saxony, only in a contrary sense These were appointed in the hope of bringing about the observance of the edict of Regensburg, and the archducal mandates founded thereupon, by gentle means,§ but it was soon perceived that the new opinions were already widely diffused Recourse was then had to punishments On the 20th of July 1528, it was ordered that heretics should be punished, not as ordinary criminals, but as malefactors of the highest order ‖ On the 24th of July not only all printers, but all venders of sectarian books, were threatened with death by drowning, as poisoners of the country Edicts were published to restore the spiritual authority which had so greatly declined.¶

In Tyrol the decree of the empire of 1526 was interpreted in favour of Catholicism, and the government declared it would no longer be bound by the concessions made the preceding year

In Bavaria the main point was already gained, and the only solicitude of the government was, not to permit the abhorred doctrines to creep in anew The streets were watched, and those who attended the preachings in the neighbourhood, were immediately seized and punished At first they were fined, but as this was ascribed to the duke's avarice, he would receive no more fines He next caused nine men to be put to death by fire in Landsberg, and twenty-nine by water in Munich The name of the unfortunate Leonhard Kasar is well known He had come from Wittenberg to his birth-place at Schärding, to visit his dying father, here he was betrayed, seized, and carried to Passau, where he was condemned, and soon after burned **

The Swabian league also proceeded with its executions In 1528 the captains of the League received orders to remove all who were suspected of holding anabaptist opinions from the jurisdiction of the ordinary tribunals, and to put them to death without the forms of trial The council of Nurnberg protested against this, not indeed out of any inclination for the anabaptists, but because they thought

* Third reply in Hortleder, iv 19, No 26, p 567

† 13th September, passim p 998

‡ Acts of the proceedings, legation and writings which took place under the most serene Lord Philip in the affairs of Munster, Cassel, May, 1535 "As to the bishops, a plot came before us which we and many others held to be true, and accordingly willed to save our subjects from it, but as we saw that we had been too lightly informed, we paused in our designs The money that we have given, the electors have settled with us with a good will, nor are you to regard this our proceeding as an example, for we know no matter that more displeases us, that we have done in all our life, than even this, had it not happened, it would now never happen"

§ Bucholtz viii 139

‖ Raupach ii 49

¶ E g in Raupach, ii Appendix, N viii

** Schelhorn, in Winter, i 258

that, under the pretext of hunting the wolf, the League meant to seize the sheep;—that this was in fact but a cover for the persecution of the followers and preachers of the Word.

The Bishop of Constance obtained an imperial mandate, in virtue of which all who were settled within the boundaries of his diocese were warned to submit themselves to "his spiritual jurisdictions, bannalia, presentations, first-fruits, and other ancient usages and good customs." The bishop proceeded with great severity against heretics. John Hüglin, of Lindau, was delivered over to the secular tribunal in Mörsburg, "as an enemy of the holy mother church," and committed to the flames.

The same thing took place on the Rhine. A preacher of Halle who was cited to appear at Aschaffenburg, was murdered on the way back; a crime which was openly attributed to the chapter of Mainz.

In Cologne, Adolf Clarenbach was condemned to death; because he would not believe that the pope was the head of the holy church; because he seemed to doubt whether some things had not occasionally been established by councils, or might be established therein, contrary to the divine word;* and the like. The superiority of mind, the knowledge, and the calm courage which the accused displayed at his trial, were truly admirable; and the town council of Cologne accordingly hesitated a long time to consent to his execution. It is affirmed that they were only induced to do so at length, by the declaration of the priests that the havoc made by the sweating sickness in Cologne was a vengeance of God upon the city for not punishing heretics. "Oh Cologne, Cologne!" exclaimed Clarenbach, as he was led to the stake, "why persecutest thou God's word? There is a mist yet in the heavens, but by and by it will disperse."†

North Germany was no longer, indeed, the scene of these barbarous excesses of priestly tyranny; but Duke George still caused the poor people who would not take the Lord's supper because they were not allowed to receive in both kinds, to be whipped out of the country by the beadle and the hangman, in the most ignominious processions. In Brandenburg, at a diet held on the day of the Visitation of the blessed Virgin, in the year 1527, the elector and estates once more agreed to uphold the observance of the ancient ceremonies with all their might; to admit no parish priest without the permission of his ordinary; to protect the clergy in their possessions; and to proceed against offenders according to the mandates of his holiness the pope and his imperial majesty.‡ The country at large, however, was not of the same way of thinking as the sovereign and the states. The first memorable opposition which Joachim I. experienced, was from his own wife, Elizabeth. She sided rather with the Ernestine house of Saxony, from which she sprang, and with her uncle John, than with her husband, against whom she had many other causes of complaint; and her physician, Ratzenberger of Brandenburg, one of the most zealous adherents of the new doctrine, brought her acquainted with Dr. Luther, whose books she had long admired and revered. At last she ventured to take the Lord's Supper in both kinds, in the secrecy of her own apartments in the palace; but the affair did not remain concealed; the whole violence of her husband's temper was excited, and he seemed disposed to execute the just-published mandate on his wife; he locked her up in her chamber, and, it is said, threatened to have her walled up within it. She succeeded, however, in making her escape. Disguised as a peasant, and attended by one male and one female servant, she arrived at Torgau, where the Elector of Saxony then was, in the night of the 20th March, 1528.§ She declared to him that if she was burthensome to him, or likely to bring him into any danger, she would rather go on as far as her eyes could guide her. Elector John, however, invited her to stay with him, and gave her Lichtenburg, where she was free to live in entire accordance with her own pious inclinations.

Such was the state of things in Germany. What was regarded in one part as the most perfect piety, was punished in the other as the most horrible crime. What the one party sought to establish, the other endeavoured, under every condition and by every means, to extirpate.

The troubles caused by Pack are extremely characteristic of the political reactions arising from the spiritual struggle.

Nor were these by any means the only hostilities existing in Germany.

In consequence of the rise of the Swiss church, discords which gradually acquired political importance, had broken out among the Protestants themselves. We cannot advance a step further, without some examination of the religious movement of Switzerland: one of the most important incidents in the general progress of the reformation.

* The first question asked him on the Monday after Palm Sunday, 1528.

† Rabi Martyrerbuch, Part ii. pp. 243, 249. Here, as usual, we find in Rabus an old, contemporaneous, and very circumstantial statement, bearing every mark of authenticity.

‡ Mandate Thursday after Annunciation, 4th July, recently given in Müller, Gesch. der Reform. in der Mark, p. 138.

§ Spalatin's Report in Mencken, ii. 1116. The extracts from Seckendorff are not quite accurate. I also take leave to doubt the truth of the story which is found in this book, and has been disseminated in so many histories of the Mark, and its reformation; namely, that it was a daughter of the electress, named Elizabeth, who betrayed her. It is at least certain, that this princess was not a girl of fourteen, as is said. She was born in 1510, and was married to Erich, Duke of Calenberg, in July, 1527. (Bünting, Braunschw. Chronik. ii. 68.) Is it likely she was in Berlin in March, 1528? In the August of that year she gave birth to her first-born son at Münden. Her husband, who was forty years older than herself, delighted that she had brought him a son, promised to grant her a request. She begged for the liberation of a parish priest who had been imprisoned for administering the Lord's Supper in both kinds. (See Havemann, Duchess Elizabeth, p. 13.) And this was the princess who a few months later accused her own mother! The whole story is equally improbable.

CHAPTER III

REFORMATION IN SWITZERLAND

ALTHOUGH Switzerland formed a distinct community, and pursued a policy independent of the empire, it was imbued with the same moral and intellectual spirit which prevailed in Germany, and more especially in the North

The efforts to throw off the domination of the priesthood which characterized the century, had also, at an early period, shown themselves here The exemption of the clergy from the secular tribunals, and from extraordinary taxes,—the former claimed by the Bishop of Coire, the latter by the prelates and chapter of Thurgau, were disputed

The literary tendencies of the German schools of poetry had also found acceptance here In Lucerne, St Gall, Freiburg, Bern, Coire and Zurich, we find similar institutions for the promotion of learning Here, too, arose an extensive literary public, of which Erasmus formed the active centre from the time he settled in Basle

Hence it happened that Luther's earliest writings excited so much interest in Switzerland. They were first printed in a collected form in Basle As early as 1520, we find "A short Poem in Praise of Luther and in Derision of his Gainsayers," by a peasant of Thurgau This spirit was fostered by the students who returned from Wittenberg The names of those who were present when Luther burned the pope's bull are still preserved The doctrine spread from the plain country and the cities into the mountains, to the Grisons, Appenzell and Schwytz The Administrator of Einsiedeln, one Geroldseck, was described by Zwingli as the father of all them that love God * That, notwithstanding these sympathies, the movement which arose in Switzerland assumed a different character—even as to religious questions—from that of Germany, was mainly the result of the intellectual character and training of the man who commenced and carried through the conflict—Ulrich Zwingli

EARLY LIFE OF ZWINGLI.

Zwingli was born in the parish of Wildenhaus in Toggenburg, within whose boundary the Thur rises, at a height where neither corn-fields nor fruit-trees are to be seen, amidst green alpine meadows, crowned by bare and sturdy pines

He was born on New Year's Day, 1484, a few weeks after Luther His childhood fell about the time when the communes began gradually to emancipate themselves from the most oppressive of the feudal services due from them to the Abbot of St Gall This was effected chiefly under the conduct of his father, who was the most considerable man in those parts, Amman of his village, and proprietor of a large tract of meadows and upland pastures Surrounded by numerous children, eight of whom were sons, he lived in patriarchal dignity It was at that time the constant practice for one of a large family to devote himself to the priesthood —this was the destination of Ulrich,† his uncle who was the first priest chosen by the people of Wildenhaus themselves, and who still held that office, undertook to qualify him for holy orders

The most remarkable trait recorded of Zwingli's youth is, his natural, quick and clear sense of truth He once mentioned that when he first began to reflect on public affairs, the doubt occurred to him whether a lie ought not to be more severely punished than stealing "For veracity," added he, "is the mother and source of every virtue"

With this unperverted sense of right, which he seemed to have imbibed from the pure air of his native mountains, he now entered the field of Literature, public life and ecclesiastical affairs

He studied at the schools of Basle and Bern, thence he went to the university of Vienna, and back again to Basle ‡ It was just the dawn of the revival of classical literature and its substitution for the scholastic learning of the middle ages Zwingli, like his teachers and friends, espoused this cause, to which he steadily adhered when he became, at a very early age, priest in Glarus (1506) He devoted all the leisure his duties left him to study He made some attempts at composition in the style of the Latinists of that time, but he never succeeded in throwing his thoughts with full freedom into antique forms § He rather contented himself with reading and studying the ancients He was more captivated by their matter, by their lofty feeling for the simple and the true, than excited to imitation by their beauty of form He thought that the influences of the divine Spirit had not been confined to Palestine, that Plato, too, had drunk from the sacred fount, he calls Seneca a holy man above all, he reveres Pindar, who speaks of his gods in language so divine, that some sense of the presence and power of the Deity must have inspired him ‖ He is grateful to them all, for he has learned from all and has been led by them to the truth While occupied with such pursuits he took up Erasmus's edition of the New Testament in Greek, and applied himself to it with the greatest industry In order to make himself thoroughly acquainted with St Paul's epistles, he did not shrink

* Letter to Myconius. Aug 25, 1522 Zwinglii Opera, curantibus Melch. Schulero et Jo Schulthessio, tom vii. Epp vol i p 218

† Properly, Huldreich—full of grace —TRANS

‡ His principal teacher in Basle was Thomas Wittenbach, himself a disciple of Paul Scriptor of Tubingen Gualtherus Praefatio ad priorem partem homiliarum in Ev Matthæi ad Josuam Wittenbachium Misc Tigur iii p 103

§ De gestis inter Helvetios et Gallos ad Ravennam Papiam aliisque locis relatio By Freher Struve, iii 171

‖ Nihil est in omni opere, quod non sit doctum, amœnum, sanctum —Quum aliquando Dei munere oculos recipimus eosque ad vetustissimos scriptores attollimus, jam videntur mox et virtus in conspectum venisse See the preface and the conclusion which Zwingli under the name Huldrychus Geminius, wrote for Ceporin's edition of Pindar, 1526 Misc Tig iii 207

from the labour of transcribing them in a fair hand,* and writing on the margin the expositions of the fathers of the Church. Occasionally, he was bewildered by the theological notions he had brought with him from the university; but he soon formed the determination to throw aside all other considerations, and to learn God's will from his pure and simple word. From the time he thus devoted himself exclusively to the text of Scripture, his intellectual sight became clearer. But, at the same time, convictions extremely at variance with the established order of things in the Church, took possession of his mind. At Einsiedeln, whither he had removed in 1516, he said plainly to Cardinal Schinor, that popery had no foundation in Scripture.

But it was another circumstance which gave to his labours their characteristic direction. Zwingli was a republican; reared in the perpetual stir of a small commonwealth, a lively interest in the political business of his country was become a second nature to him. At that time the war with Italy set all the energies of the Confederation in motion, and raised it to the rank of a great power in Europe. Zwingli more than once took the field with his warlike flock. He was present at the battle of Marignano. But war had brought in the evils of foreign enlistment and of pensions. Public opinion was against them, as the disturbances which broke out at short intervals in Lucerne, Solothurn, Bern, and Zürich prove; the common people would hear nothing of treaties, according to which their sons and brothers were led to slaughter in strange lands; they demanded the punishment of the "German-French," the "crown-eaters;" in some cases the Grand Councils were actually forced to forswear "wages and gifts," and not unfrequently the diets published edicts against them; but the interests of those in power were too strongly connected with these abuses for them to be given up; a warlike youth was always ready to enlist in foreign service, and the evil increased from day to day. Zwingli, together with his admiration for the Latin writers, combined that for the German popular literature, (which, as we may recollect, was full of attacks upon prevailing abuses,) and as early as 1510 he wrote a somewhat diffuse fable, in which he set before the Confederation the corrupt practices of which they were the victims: he told them how they were vainly warned by faithful dogs against the seductions of cunning cats; how they must inevitably lose their freedom — freedom, that blessing which, after the example of their ancestors, they were bound to defend with spear and battle-axe, and never to endanger by a connection with foreigners; those, he said, who took pensions and gifts would bring about the destruction of their bond of brotherhood.† In spite of this we find that Zwingli himself lay, for a time, under the obligation of a pension from the pope. It doubtless appeared to him a totally different thing to accept a small salary from the pope, the spiritual head of the Confederation, and to take money from a sovereign with whom they had no connection, like the King of France; and accordingly it was against the partisans of that monarch that his zeal was first directed. In the year 1516, we find him engaged in a warm conflict with the French faction in Glarus, where, as in most parts of Switzerland, it was then in the ascendant. He failed indeed, for the king had gained over the most powerful of the inhabitants; and he makes the bitterest complaints of all he had to endure in consequence. At length he found himself compelled to quit his parish, and to take the subordinate place of vicar at Einsiedeln.‡ This, however, led him to a more complete and consistent development of his opinions. As the French party gradually became the dominant one, so his resistance to it gradually grew into a struggle against the system of pensions in general. The rise, throughout the Confederation, of alliances between families and leaders, founded chiefly upon personal interests, he justly regarded as an event dangerous to the general liberty. Public morals and public opinion, offended by this abuse, found in him their most eloquent advocate. The precepts and examples of the ancients and of the scriptures, contrasted with the prevailing moral and religious dissolution; and the consciousness of an honest patriotism struggling against mercenary obsequiousness to foreign courts, raised in him a spirit which already gave earnest of his future endeavours to reform the whole condition, ecclesiastical and political, of his country; it only remained to be seen whether he could succeed in obtaining the wide field and the commanding position which such an enterprise demanded.

These he obtained at Zürich in the year 1519.

Zürich was, if not the sole, yet the principal, town in the Confederation, which had never allowed itself to be persuaded to accept the French pensions. Conrad Hoffmann, a canon of the cathedral, who enjoyed extraordinary respect, maintained the patriotic cause against foreign service and foreign pensions; he was eloquent, and he did not shrink from uttering severe truths to his audience. It was chiefly through his influence that Zwingli, in spite of much opposition, was elected secular priest at the cathedral.§

Ulrich Zwingli here at once took up the position with regard to these two parties, which from that time he steadily maintained.

His first attacks were directed against all party alliance with foreign powers, even with

* Schuler, Huldreich Zwingli, Gesch. seiner Bildung zum reformator. Notes, p. 7.

† Huldrych Zwingli, the Priest's fabulous Poem of an Ox and certain Beasts, to be understood of the present Course of Things.

‡ Epistola ad Joachimum Vadianum; ex Eremo 13 Jun. 1517, Epp. i. p. 24. Locum mutavimus Gallorum technis. Fuimus pars rerum gestarum: calamitates multas vel tulimus vel ferre didicimus.

§ Bullinger, Reformationsgeschichte, p. 11; "Especially because he heard, how that he preaches violently against pensions and pensioners — against the leagues and wars of the princes."

the pope He is said to have declared that Cardinal von Sitten, who recruited for the pope, did not wear a red hat and mantle without reason, "if it were wrung," said he, "you would see the blood of your nearest kindred drip from its folds" He laughed at the eagerness with which a wolf that only devoured beasts was hunted, while the wolves that destroyed men were suffered to go unmolested.

The effects of the Lutheran movement just then began to be felt in Switzerland No man was better prepared, or more eager, to take part in it than Zwingli He too had had a battle on his own ground with a vender of indulgences, and had succeeded in keeping him at a distance He wrote against the conduct of the court of Rome to Luther, and published an apology for him, in answer to the bull

His preaching, for which he had a singular natural gift, produced a great effect He attacked the prevalent abuses with uncompromising earnestness On one occasion he painted the responsibility of the clergy in such lively colours, that several young men among his hearers instantly abandoned their intention of taking orders "I felt myself," said Thomas Plater, "as it were lifted up by the hair of the head"* Occasionally some individual thought the preacher aimed his remarks at him personally, which Zwingli thought it necessary to guard against "Worthy man," he exclaimed, "take it not to thyself," and then proceeded in his discourse with a zeal which rendered him regardless of the dangers which sometimes even threatened his life

But his efforts were mainly directed to rendering the meaning of Scripture plainer to his hearers With the permission of the chapter, he expounded not only the Perikopes,† but the entire books of the scriptures as he had studied them,‡ for he strove to catch and to communicate the whole current and connexion of the divine thought His doctrine was, that religion consisted in trust in God, love of God, and innocence of life§ He avoided every thing far-fetched or over-learned in his style, and his efforts to render his discourses intelligible to all, were crowned with success In a wide circle of hearers he laid the foundations of that faith which stood fast in the day of the tempest, and afforded him firm support in all his undertakings

In daily life he was of an easy, cheerful disposition. He had learned how to live with men, and how to deal with them, in the republic of a village, in the camp, in the resort of strangers at Einsiedeln He was not free from youthful vices, sometimes of an offensive kind, but his correspondence shows how earnest were his self-reproaches and his endeavours to amend After a time his conduct became irreproachable‖ He laboured to subdue ebullitions of anger, as well as those of other passions, he drove away fantastic humours by music, for he too was a great lover of music, and a master of several instruments —an accomplishment no less common in Toggenburg than in Thuringia¶ He loved a retired domestic life, and his favourite food was that of his country — various preparations of milk, but he never refused an invitation, he frequented the guild meetings of the citizens, the holiday feasts of the peasants, and enlivened every company by his cheerful spirit and pleasant discourse** Laborious as he was, much as he undertook and accomplished, he repulsed no one, he had the art of saying something agreeable and satisfactory to everybody He was well made and robust, charitable and good-humoured, cheerful, accessible, contented, and at the same time full of the greatest and noblest thoughts

If we compare him with Luther, we find that he had no such tremendous tempests to withstand, as those which shook the most secret depths of Luther's soul As he had never devoted himself with equal ardour to the established Church, he had not now to break loose from it with such violent and painful struggles It was not the profound sense of the power of faith and of its connexion with redemption in which Luther's efforts originated, that made Zwingli a reformer, he became so, chiefly because, in the course of his study of Scripture in search of truth he found the Church and the received morality at variance with its spirit Nor was Zwingli trained at a university, or deeply imbued with the prevalent doctrinal opinions To found a high school, firmly attached to all that was worthy of attachment, and dissenting only on certain most important points, was not his vocation He regarded it much more as the business and duty of his life, to bring about the religious and moral reformation of the republic that had adopted him, and to recall the Swiss Confederation to the principles upon which it was originally founded While Luther's main object was a reform of doctrine, which, he thought, would be necessarily followed by that of life and morals, Zwingli aimed directly at the improvement of life, he kept mainly in view the practical significancy of Scripture as a whole, his original views were of a moral and political nature, hence his labours were tinged with a wholly peculiar colour

We must here devote a few words to the question of the priority of his attempts at reform It is not to be denied that, even before the year 1517, he, in common with many others, had evinced dispositions, and

* Autobiographie Platers Misc Tig iii 253

† περικοπαι The passages from the Old and New Testament, selected to be read in churches They were first published in a distinct Lectionarium, by Pope Gregory the Great, in the sixth century, and were adopted by Charlemagne as the basis of the Homiliarium for his whole empire This selection was retained by Luther —TRANS

‡ In the second Zurich disputations he mentions it: he began with Matthew

§ De vera et falsa Religione Veram pietatem, quæ nihil aliud est quam ex amore timoreque Dei servata innocentia Ed Gualth p 202.

‖ To Heinrich Utinger, 4th Dec. 1518 Opp vii Epp i p 55

¶ Bullinger, Reformationsgeschichte, p 31

** Myconius, in Staudlins and Tzschirner's Archiv i ii Ingenio amœnus, ore jocundus

expressed opinions, which tended that way. But the essential point was the struggle with the spiritual power, and the separation from it. This struggle Luther undertook first, and sustained alone: he first obtained freedom of discussion for the new doctrines in a considerable German state; he began the work of liberation. At the time Luther was condemned by Rome, Zwingli was still receiving a pension from Rome. Luther had already stood impeached before the emperor and the empire, ere Zwingli had experienced the least attack. The whole field of his activity was different. While, in the one case, we see the highest and most august powers of the world in agitation, in the other, it is a question of the emancipation of a city from an episcopal power.

But this incident of the great revolution which was now going on, has its interest; this enterprise also demanded intelligence and energy, and it is well worth while to devote some attention to it.

EMANCIPATION OF THE TOWN OF ZURICH FROM THE EPISCOPAL GOVERNMENT OF CONSTANCE.

The city of Zurich, like the other cities of Switzerland, had long maintained a certain independence of the bishopric of Constance, to which it belonged, mainly supported by the collegiate chapter of the cathedral. For some years peculiar circumstances had given a remarkable extension to the exercise of this independence.

The bishop of that time, Hugo of Hohenlandenberg, regarded with great displeasure the traffic in indulgences which was carried on in his diocese by the commissaries of Rome: he had fully consented that the council of Zurich should refuse permission to a vender of indulgences named Samson, who had already come as far as an inn belonging to Zurich on the banks of the Sil, to enter their territory. Zwingli carefully preserved the letter in which he was requested by the ecclesiastical authorities to oppose resistance to men bearing full powers from the Roman Curia.* Meanwhile two political considerations induced the Curia to treat the city with great moderation and respect.

In the year 1520 Zwingli had already secured a considerable number of decided adherents. The town council had actually given the secular priests and preachers in the city, permission to preach according to the divine Scriptures of the Old and New Testament, and to take no notice of any novelties in doctrine or discipline that might have been introduced,† an order which, in fact, involved a defection from the Church of Rome. It could not be said that the affair remained unknown to the Roman court, since two or three papal nuncios and a cardinal were present, but they did not venture on any opposition. Their conduct on this occasion is very instructive, as elucidating the general policy of the Church. They promised Zwingli to raise his pension from fifty to a hundred gulden, on condition that he desisted from preaching against the pope. Zwingli, though in want of this addition to his income, rejected the offer. They then made him the same offer without annexing any condition; but even this Zwingli would not accept.‡ The nuncios, however, were more interested in recruiting the army, with which they hoped to conquer Milan, than in any theological question whatsoever. Although the city was already thoroughly infected with the spirit of defection from the Church, they entered into an alliance with it. "We are not reproached as heretics and apostates," says Zwingli, "but lauded with high titles."§

The ordinary of the diocese favoured the new mode of preaching as a means of resisting the usurpations of Rome; the Roman See tolerated it, in order to attain the object of its political negotiations, and thus the new doctrines were freely promulgated for years, and took fast root in the public mind.

At length, however, serious attention was excited by a violation of the discipline of the Church. In March 1522, the people of Zurich broke the fast, and ate eggs and meat. Upon this the bishop, who found himself menaced with similar acts of insubordination, and saw his dispensations slighted, bestirred himself: he sent a special mission to the council of Zurich, requiring it to maintain the established usages and ceremonies of the Church.

But it remained to be seen whether this was still possible; whether, at this epoch of fervent religious zeal, opinions which had undergone so radical a change, could be brought under subjection to the mere dictum of a spiritual head.

In the conference which followed the communication made to the Grand Council by these envoys, Zwingli maintained that many of the ceremonies of the Church were just those which St. Peter had declared to be intolerable. This assertion received no satisfactory answer, even from the envoys; indeed one of them, Wanner, preacher of the cathedral of Constance, was of the same opinion in his heart.‖ The Grand Council came to a resolution, evasive in form, but very intelligible in fact, that no one should break the fast "without notable cause," and requested the bishop to obtain from the spiritual authorities, or from the learned, an explanation as to the conduct to be observed with regard to the ceremonies, in order not to offend against

* Antwurt Zwingli an Val. Compar. Werke ii. 1. p. 7, further on, the answer to Faber, April 30. 1526.

† "That they all and generally preach in freedom (as is also granted by the papal laws) the holy Gospels and Epistles of the Apostles, conformably with the word of God, and the true divine Scriptures of the Old and New Testament, and that they teach that which they receive and hold from the said Scriptures, and say nothing of other accidental innovations and rules." Answers which a Burgermeister, council and the grand council of the city of Zürich gave to their confederates, Fussli Beiträge, ii. p. 237. See Bullinger, i. p. 20.

‡ Uslegung und Gründe der Schlussreden, p. 359.

§ Zwingli's opinion, in answer to the pope's brief. Werke, Bd. ii. Abth. ii. p. 393.

‖ Ep. Zwinglii ad Fabricium de actis legationis. Opp. i. p. 12.

the precepts of Christ * The bishop answered by impressing again upon the Grand Council the necessity of observing the ordinances and good customs of the holy Church, which he believed to be conformable with the Scriptures In a letter written with greater freedom and animation to the chapter, he indeed admitted that some things might have crept in which were not warranted by the Holy Scriptures, but added that an error shared with the whole of Christendom acquired a right to respect; on no account ought doctrines to be accepted which were condemned by the emperor and the pope, those who would not submit to the bishops, must be entirely separated from them †

There were still some monasteries in the city which were not affected by the first resolution of the Grand Council, a great many persons, high and low, still held to the ancient usages, and consequently this admonition was not wholly without effect The most violent opponents of the monks were recommended to moderate their language in the pulpit or in disputations

But a circumstance purely accidental sufficed, in a short time, to produce a contrary result

About this time a Franciscan monk from Avignon (the same François Lambert whom we had occasion to mention in treating of the synod of Homberg) appeared in Switzerland At an early age he had entered a convent of very strict observance in search of peace and piety, but had found nothing but secret vices and hateful passions ‡ In this state of things, some of Luther's works had fallen into his hands, and he determined to quit his cloister and repair to Luther himself in Wittenberg · This monk, still habited in the garb of his order, and riding upon an ass, now made his appearance in Zurich His Catholic orthodoxy was shaken, but not as yet destroyed He could not bring himself to discontinue the ceremonies of the Church, nor to give up the intercessions of the saints Seated at the high altar of Our Lady's minster, he held discourses to that effect in Latin During one of these, Zwingli called out aloud, "Brother, thou errest!" The orthodox party hoped therefore to find an ally in Lambert, and as they perceived that he was learned and of ready speech, they got up a disputation between him and Zwingli This was held on the 17th of July, in the refectory of the canons But the result was very different from what was expected The Franciscan was a man who loved truth and sincerely sought it He soon perceived the superior weight of his antagonist's arguments, and was at length entirely convinced by the passages of Scripture which Zwingli placed before him He raised his hands, thanked God, and vowed to lay aside all litanies, and to call on his name alone § He left Zurich in the same humble way as he had entered it, and in progress of time we find him in Eisenach, in Wittenberg, at a later period, as we said, in Homberg, and lastly, in Marburg His attempt to give to the German church a constitution different from that established by Luther, is sufficient to perpetuate his memory to all succeeding time

This disputation produced the greatest effect in Zurich It was held on a Thursday On the Monday following (the 21st of July), the council once more called the readers of the Orders, the canons, and the secular priests, into the provostry Zwingli now felt himself strong enough to open the discussion by severely censuring the sermons preached in the convents without any warranty from Scripture The burgermeister renewed the proposal to both parties, to refer their differences to the decision of the dean and chapter But Zwingli declared that he was the preacher, the bishop, of the city he had taken upon himself the cure of souls in it with his vow, he would not suffer that men who had in no respect any true vocation, should preach in the convents against God's word, rather than that, he would mount the pulpit and publicly contradict them Already he had the whole audience on his side, and at length the burgermeister declared in the name of the council, that it was its will, that the pure word of God should be preached in the city, and that alone

Before this conference, preaching according to Scripture was only permitted or recommended to the secular priests, now, it was rendered imperative even on the monks

If we inquire on what authority Zwingli grounded his refusal to conform to the bishop's ordinances, we shall find that it was mainly derived from the idea of the commune ‖ He was of opinion that all that the Scripture says with regard to the Church, was especially applicable to each separate commune (congregation) He seems even to have assumed, that such a body, so long as it did not attempt to introduce any new doctrines or practices, and contented itself with hearing God's word, and deciding all controversies according to that, could not fall into error ¶ He regarded the Grand Council as no less the ecclesiastical than the political representative of the rights of the commune His plan of proceeding was, as he once expressly declared, to continue to discuss each question in his sermons till everybody was convinced, and not till then to bring it before the Grand Council.

* Füssli, Beitrage, ii 15

† His principle was, Communis error facit jus Hæc dogmata non prædicentur, nihil innovetur contra ecclesiæ ritum

‡ Francisci Lamberti rationes propter quas Minoritarum conversationem traditumque rejecit Schelhorn, Commentatio de vita Lamberti Amœnitat literariæ, iii p 312.

§ Bernhard Weiss in Fussli Beitragen, ii 42

‖ *Gemeinde* —We have no word that expresses the double sense, ecclesiastical and civil of this I have therefore been obliged to resort to the French word Commune, which will be generally understood —Trans

¶ Second Disputation Liv W i p 470 "Hence it follows also that this our convocation, which hath met together, not for the injury of certain Christians, but to hear the word of God, cannot err, for it undertaketh not to settle or to unsettle, but will only hear what can be found out from certain portions of the word of God" after which the forms necessary to be established should be determined on, in concert with the ministers of the church The council, says he, holds the supreme power as representative of the commune *

It is manifest that this theory furnished a totally different basis for an infant ecclesiastical society, from that on which the reformers of Germany were building In fact and practice, the difference was not, however, so great, in Germany, the preachers united with the sovereign of the country, in Switzerland, with the civic authorities of the city but the circumstance, that the former were referred to a Recess, while the latter already possessed the sovereignty *de facto,* and now exercised it in spiritual as well as in temporal affairs, forms a very marked distinction in theory, and one very important to the future development of the institution

The bishop issued a new decretal, anathematizing the doctrine, that a Christian was not bound to live according to the rules laid down by the Church, but without the slightest avail, since the very opinion which the commune held to with the greatest tenacity, was that which emancipated it from his authority

The only real difficulty in their way, arose from the obstinancy of certain dissentients in their own body. There were still among them men who denounced Zwingli as a heretic

In order to put an end to this state of things, and on the ground that the explanation which it had demanded had never been given, the council ordained a conference of its secular priests, curates of souls, parish priests, and preachers This was in all respects agreeable to Zwingli's notions He said that God would not ask what the pope and his bishops, or what councils and universities, had decreed, but what was contained in his word The bishop, who does not yet appear to have given up all hope, also sent some delegates, under his vicar-general Faber, not indeed exactly to take part in the disputation, but to be present at it, and to endeavour to reconcile the contending parties † The conference, however, ended completely in Zwingli's favour. What, indeed, could his opponents say, after the principle had once been conceded, that the Scripture, which neither lieth nor deceiveth, was the sole rule of faith? It is matter of surprise that so prudent a man as Faber should venture upon such slippery ground He boasted that he had proved from Scripture the doctrine of the invocation of saints, to a priest infected with the heresy, upon which Zwingli challenged him to adduce the same proof, now, on the spot He failed, as might be expected, thereby affording Zwingli one of his most signal triumphs In short, even zealous adversaries then confessed — what it is impossible to read the report of the proceedings without seeing—that Zwingli obtained a complete victory Hence it followed, that the council expressly authorised him to continue in the course he had adopted, and repeated its admonitions to the clergy, neither to practise nor to teach any thing which they could not prove from the word of God

We must observe well the words, 'practise or teach,' they involve an alteration of the ceremonies as well as of the preaching.

Already the change in the externals of the church was in full progress The clergy married, nuns were at liberty to quit their convents, or to remain in them. "Know, dear Master Ulrich," wrote the steward of the convent of Cappel, to Zwingli, "we are all of one mind with our abbot, — to accept the holy gospel and divine word, and to abide by it till death'§ Although there were still some zealous adherents of the old opinions in the monastery attached to the cathedral, yet the resolution to reform their body was adopted by the canons themselves, and executed in concert with some delegates of the council By far the greater part of the stole fees were abolished, and such arrangements made with regard to tithes and other sources of revenue, that a large and excellent school was established out of the funds But the doubts which agitated the public mind more than any others, were those concerning the veneration of images and the mass, — two questions which were now daily more and more debated. Writings against the canon of the mass already appeared, and acts of violence had been committed upon the sacred images The council deemed it necessary to lay these questions before a special ecclesiastical assembly, which was convoked in October 1523

It was impossible for the independent character of an association detaching itself from the great hierarchical body, and assuming a constitution of its own, to exhibit itself in a more striking light, than at this meeting The Bishop of Constance took good care to send no more delegates The aged Conrad Hofmann, formerly Zwingli's great abettor, in vain repeated that a commune was not qualified to dispute concerning things of this kind ‖ Zwingli's great principle was, that the church consisted not of pope, cardinals, bishops, and their convocations, but of the commune, the Kilchhori (church-hearers) that was the church, like the first church at Jerusalem (Acts, xv)¶ And the present meeting did, in

* Ante omnia multitudinem de quæstione probe docere ita factum est ut quicquid diacosii (the grand council) cum verbi ministris ordinarent, jam dudum in animis fidelium ordinatum esset Denique senatum diacosion adivimus, ut ecclesiæ totius nomine quod usus postularet, fieri juberent Diacosion senatus summa est potestas ecclesiæ vice Subsidium de Eucharistia Opp iii 339

† "Nit zu disputiren sondern allein uffhoren, rath geben und schidlut zu seyn" "not to dispute, but only to listen, to give counsel, and to be peace makers" Faber Warlich Unterrichtung bei Hottinger, i 437

‡ Proceedings of the assembly in the worshipful city of Zurich by Hegenwaldt with extracts from Faber's Warlicher Unterrichtung (true account) in Zwingli's Works, i p 105

§ Jacob Leu, the steward, to Zwingli Epp i 307

‖ "I was ten or thirteen years at Heidelberg, and I went to the house of a learned man, the same was called Dr Joss, a good and godly man, and with him I ate and drank oft there I continually heard that it was not seemly to dispute concerning these matters" Chunrad Hoffmanns Schriftlicher Furtrag wider Zwinglis Reformation. Füssli Beitrage, iii 93

¶ "'Ja Hong und Kussnacht ist eine gewissere Kirche

fact, consist only of the clergy of the town and country of Zurich, with a few strangers (as, in the example above quoted, it was remarked, there were messengers from Antioch), who under the presidency of the burgermeister, Marx Roust, met at the town-house, to take counsel together concerning two of the weightiest questions that could occupy Christendom Master Leu (Leo Judæ), secular priest of St Peter's church, and Zwingli laid before the meeting the propositions, which they were prepared to defend, the one, that it was unlawful to use any image in the worship of God, the other, that the mass was not a sacrifice. they invited every man who objected to these propositions to confute them out of Scripture One after another rose for this purpose, but their arguments were easily answered Those who had the most zealously opposed the new doctrines as heretical, were then called upon severally, by name, to prove their words Some did not appear, others were silent, others declared themselves at length convinced, and merely apologised for having shared the general error At the close of the proceedings, the Abbot of Cappel, whom we have already mentioned, exhorted the men of Zürich now undauntedly to espouse the cause of the Gospel * Hereupon the priests were commanded not to preach against the two articles which had been triumphantly established at the conference Zwingli drew up instructions for them, which were published by authority, and may be regarded as the earliest of all the symbolical books of the evangelical churches

Thus did Zurich sever itself from the bishopric (and hence from the whole system of the Latin hierarchy), and undertook to found a new form of church government on the basis of the commune or congregation

Though the political constitution of the city rendered it impossible to complete the structure in exact conformity with the plan thus laid down, it is undeniable that the inhabitants of the town and country took a voluntary share in all the changes No innovation was attempted to be put in practice till the result was rendered certain by the express approbation of the city communes, the Grand Council did not originate opinions, it only adopted them Already had the clergy of the chapter of Zurich repeated the resolutions of the city, afterwards the several communes (congregations) announced their approbation of the proceedings of the civic body, in separate acts of adhesion The whole population was filled with that positive spirit of Protestantism which has ever since distinguished it, and which has, from time to time, displayed its ancient spontaneity of action in the most remarkable manner

RELATIONS OF THE SWISS REFORMERS TO LUTHER CONTROVERSY CONCERNING THE LORD'S SUPPER

It is clear that there was nothing in these proceedings that can justify us in regarding them as a mere repetition of what had been passing at Wittenberg As the growth and development of the characters of the two reformers, so were also the nature of the civil authority to which they adhered, and of the oppositions they had to combat, widely different Essential divergencies in the direction of their ideas, and in the character of their doctrines, also manifested themselves, in spite of the various analogies between them

The principal difference is, that, whereas Luther wished to retain every thing in the existing ecclesiastical institutions that was not at variance with the express words of Scripture, Zwingli was resolved to get rid of every thing that could not be maintained by a direct appeal to Scripture Luther took up his station on the ground already occupied by the Latin Church his desire was only to purify, to put an end to the contradistinctions between the doctrines of the Church and the Gospel Zwingli, on the other hand, thought it necessary to restore, as far as possible, the primitive and simplest condition of the Christian Church, he aimed at a complete revolution

We know how far Luther was from inculcating the destruction of images, he merely combated the superstitions which had gathered around them Zwingli, on the contrary, regarded the veneration addressed to images as sheer idolatry, and condemned their very existence In the Whitsuntide of 1524, the council of Zurich, in concert with him, declared its determination of removing all images, which it held to be a godly work Fortunately, the disorders which this measure excited in so many other places, were here avoided The three secular priests, with twelve members of the council, one from each guild, repaired to the churches, and caused the order to be executed under their own supervision The crosses disappeared from the high altars, the pictures were taken down from the altars, the frescoes scraped off the walls, and whitewash substituted in their stead —In the country churches the most precious pictures were burnt, 'to the praise and glory of God" Nor did the organs fare better, they too were connected with the abhorred superstition † The reformers

denn alle zusammengerottete Bischofe und Papste' Die Versammlung selbst ist freilich auch keine Kirche, aber sie vindicirt der Gemeinde das Recht der Autonomie. Sie ist der erste Ansatz zur Presbyterialverfassung" "'Yes, Höng and Küssnacht (names of two towns or villages) is a more certain (truer) church than all the bishops and popes banded together' The congregation is, indeed not properly speaking a church but it is an assertion of the independence of the commune It is the foundation stone of the presbyterian form of church government"

* Records of the second disputation (26 27, 28 Wynmonats), Zwinglis Werke, i 539 There exists also a report of it by Johann Salat clerk of the Court at Lucerne It is noticed in Füssli, Beitragen, iii 1

† Bernhard Weiss, p 49 Bullinger Reform Gesch i p 102 Leben Leonis Judæ Misc Tigur iii 33 'Anno 24 stalt man ab die processionen der Monchen und Pfaffen,—ordnet Leut, die uber die Sach (Reliquienkasten) giengend und vergrubind die Gebein oder Heilthum Man laht die Orglen aus den kilchen, das todtenlauten ward abgestellt, das wychen des Saltses Wassers Palmen das verrichten der Krankeen,—hernach that man in der Stadt die Bilder us den Kilchen und uf dem Land wo es das Mehr werden mocht" "Anno 24 the processions of monks and priests

would have nothing but the simple Word. The same end was proposed in all the practices of the church. A new form of baptism was drawn up, in which all the additions "which have no ground in God's word" were omitted.* The next step was, the alteration of the mass. Luther had contented himself with the omission of the words relating to the doctrine of sacrifice, and with the introduction of the sacrament in both kinds. Zwingli established a regular love feast (Easter 1525). The communicants sat in a particular division of the benches between the choir and the transept, the men on the right, the women on the left; the bread was carried about on large wooden platters, and each broke off a bit, after which the wine was carried about in wooden cups.† This was thought to be the nearest approach to the original institution.

We come now to a difference, the ground of which lies deeper, and which related not only to the application, but also to the interpretation, of Scripture, in reference to the most important of all spiritual acts.

It is well known how various were the views taken, even in the earliest times, of this mystery, especially from the ninth to the eleventh century, before the doctrine of transubstantiation became universally predominant. It is therefore no wonder if, now that its authority was shaken, new differences of opinion manifested themselves.

At the former period, they were rather of a speculative nature, at the latter, in conformity with the altered direction of learning, they turned more on interpretation of Scripture.

Luther had no sooner rejected the miracle of transubstantiation, than others began to inquire whether, even independently of this, the words by which the sacrament was instituted were not subject to another interpretation.

Luther himself confesses that he had been assailed by doubts of this kind; but as, in all his outward and inward combats, his victorious weapon had ever been the pure text of Scripture taken in its literal sense, he now humbly surrendered his doubts to the sound of the words, and continued to maintain the real presence, without attempting further to define its mode.

But all had not the same reverent submission to the literal meaning as Luther.

Carlstadt was the first who, in the year 1524, when he was compelled to flee from Saxony, offered a new explanation. This was indeed exegetically untenable and even absurd, and he himself at last gave it up. In the attempt to establish it, however, he put forth some more coherent arguments,‡ which gave a great impulse to the public mind in the direction it had already taken upon this point.

The modest Œcolampadius of Basle, among whose friends similar notions were current, began to be ashamed that he had so long suppressed his doubts and preached doctrines of the truth of which he was not thoroughly convinced; he took courage no longer to conceal his view of the sense of the mysterious institutional words.§

The young Bullinger approached the question from another side. He studied Berengarius's controversy, and came to the conclusion that on this important point—the very point afterwards established by the reformation,—injustice had been done to that early reformer. He thought Berengarius's interpretation might even be found in St. Augustine.‖

The main thing, however, was that Zwingli declared his opinion. In studying the Scripture after his manner, rather as a whole than in detached passages, and not without a continual reference to classical antiquity, he had come to the conviction that the *is* of the institutional words signifies nothing more than "denotes." Already, in a letter dated June 1523, he declares that the true sense of the Eucharist cannot be understood, until the bread and wine in the Lord's Supper are regarded in exactly the same manner as the water in baptism.¶ While attacking the mass, he had already conceived the intention of restoring the Eucharist to itself, as he expressed it.** As Carlstadt now brought forward a very similar interpretation, which he was unable to maintain, Zwingli thought he could no longer remain silent. He published his exposition, first in a printed address to a parish priest in Reutlingen (November 1524), then more at length in his essay, On true and false Religion. Although he was little satisfied with Carlstadt's explanation, he nevertheless availed himself of some of the same arguments which that theologian had employed, *e. g.* that the body of Christ was in heaven, and could not possibly be divided *realiter* among his disciples on earth. He rested his reasoning chiefly on the sixth chapter of the Gospel of St. John, which was thus, as he thought, rendered perfectly clear.

No longer ago than the autumn of 1524, the great division of the Church, into Catholic and Evangelical, had been formally accomplished; and already an opinion was broached which was destined to work a violent schism in the Evangelical Church.

were abolished. People were ordered to go in search of reliquaries and dig up the bones or shrines. The organs were taken out of the churches, the death bell abolished, the consecration of the salt and water and palms, the preparation of the sick; afterwards the pictures were taken out of the churches in the city and in the country, wherever there were the most of them."

* Zwinglis Werke, II. ii. p. 230.

† Preface, Werke, II. ii. p. 234.

‡ Dialogue of the ungodly Misuse of the Sacrament. Walch. xx. 2378. Of the unchristian Misuse of the Lord's Bread and Cup. Ibid. 132.

§ Collection of the various declarations of Œcolampadius in his life, by Hess, p. 102.

‖ Lavater von Leben und Tod Heinrychen Bullingers, 1578, p. 8.

¶ To Hans Wyttenbach, 15th June, 1523. Panem et vinum vere esse puto, ac edi etiam, sed frustra, nisi edens firmiter credat hunc solum esse animæ cibum. Omnia sunt planiora si τὰ σῦκα σῦκα, i. e. ficus ficus appellaverimus panem dixerimus panem, vinum vinum. (Epp. i. 238.)

** Deliberavimus usui esse futurum si missa everteretur, qua eversa speravimus etiam Eucharistiam sibi restitui posse. De vera et falsa Religione, p. 269.

Luther did not hesitate to denounce Zwingli as a wild enthusiast, with whom he had frequently had to *contend*, he disregarded the fact that the removal of images in Zurich had been effected under the sanction of the civil authority, and that the Swiss reformers had found a point at which civil order might securely subsist, only a few steps further removed from traditional usage than that to which he had himself advanced Indeed his notions of the affairs of Switzerland were altogether very vague and imperfect He began the contest with great vehemence

This is not the place to enumerate the polemical writings exchanged, or the arguments employed, on either side The historian may, however, be permitted to make one remark

It appears to me undeniable that the controversy was not to be terminated by a purely exegetic process

That the *is* in the text might have a figurative sense, cannot be denied, nor in fact does Luther attempt to deny it He grants it in expressions such as, Christ is a rock, a vine, &c, "because Christ cannot be a natural rock" He only denies that the word had, or must have, a figurative meaning in the case under discussion *

Hence it clearly appears, that the ground of the controversy lay in their general view of the subject

Zwingli's chief objection to the literal interpretation is, that Christ himself says, "I shall not be with you always," thus implying that he would not be present in the Eucharist, and that, according to this interpretation, he must be omnipresent, whereas a local omnipresence is a contradiction in terms The reply of Luther, who had an instinctive aversion to any departure from the simple, clear and literal meaning of words, is a general one —that he holds fast to the infallible Word, and that to God nothing is impossible But it is abundantly clear that he would never have been satisfied with this defence, had he not felt himself elevated above the objections of his antagonists, by the higher region from which he contemplated the whole subject Being harder pressed, he at length enounced the doctrine of the union of the divine and human natures in Christ, which he regards as far more intimate than that between body and soul. Not even death, he says, had power to loose it, the human nature of Christ was raised above all natural existences, above and beyond all created beings, by its union with the Godhead We have here a case, and by no means the only one, in which Luther, without being even conscious of it himself, reverts to opinions which were current before the development of the hierarchical supremacy, and the organisation of the system to which it gave birth In the ninth century, Johannes Scotus Erigena reconciled the doctrines of the Eucharist and the two natures, if not in exactly the same, yet in a very similar manner †

Luther goes on to teach that the identity of the divine and human nature is showed forth *in the mystery of the sacrament* The body of Christ is the entire Christ, of a divine nature, exalted above all the conditions of the creature, and hence also easily communicable in the bread The objection, that Christ says he would not be present always, he conclusively answers by the remark, that Christ was there speaking of his earthly existence

It is evident why the sort of proof adduced by Zwingli had no longer any cogency for Luther His own hypothesis enabled him to abide by the strict meaning of the words, as he was fond of doing, since they no longer presented any contradiction And this hypothesis, which touches the highest mysteries of religion (though, with a reverent awe of dragging the mysterious into the conflict of the day, he rarely brought it forward), was, therefore, perfectly satisfactory to his mind

Luther indeed here appears to us in the most characteristic light

We have often remarked that he deviated from tradition, only so far as he felt himself absolutely constrained to do so by the words of Christ To go in search of novelties, or to overthrow any thing established that was not utterly irreconcilable with Scripture, were thoughts which his soul knew not He would have maintained the whole structure of the Latin Church, had it not been disfigured by modern additions, foreign to its original design, and contrary to the genuine sense of the Gospel he would have acknowledged the hierarchy itself, if it had only left him freedom of speech, but, as that could not be, he was compelled to take upon himself the work of purification He was so profoundly attached to the traditions of the Church, that it was not without the most violent inward storms that he emancipated himself from accidental and groundless additions But he held with the more unshaken tenacity to the great mystery, in so far as it was in accordance with and supported by, the literal meaning of Scripture ‡ His mind embraced it with all its native depth, he was not only susceptible of the sublimest mysticism, but his whole soul was steeped in it

It is true, Luther fell off from the Church of Rome (or rather he was expelled from it), and wrought it more damage than any other man whatever But he never denied its origin If we take a comprehensive view of the great historical movement of opinion and doctrine throughout the world, we shall see that Luther was the organ through which the Latin Church resumed a freer, less hierarchical form, and one more in harmony with the original tendency of Christianity

We must, however, admit that his views,

* Greater Confession, in Walch's Collection of Luther's Works Part xx p 1138.

† De divisione naturæ Neander Kirchengeschichte, iv 472 The difference mainly consists in this, that Scotus assumes more decidedly the glorification of the human nature by the divine Caro in virtutem transformata nullo loco continetur

‡ E g Carlstadt asked, Where has Christ commanded that the elements should be lifted up and shown to the people? (Walch 2876) Luther answered, Where does Christ forbid it? (p 252)

especially of this subject, were always somewhat individual, — not fitted to produce conviction in all men, any more than the point from which he took those views could be shared by all Nor were the more profound and eminent spirits who took an active part in the general movement of the century, by any means so well inclined towards the Church as Luther And as the evidence adduced by Zwingli failed to convince Luther, so Luther's hypothesis produced no impression upon Zwingli

Zwingli had, as we have said, none of Luther's deep and lively conception of the universal Church, or of an unbroken connexion with the doctrines of past ages We have seen that his mind, formed in the midst of republican institutions, was far more occupied with the idea of the commune, and he was now intent on keeping together the communes of Zurich by a stricter church discipline He tried to get rid of all public criminals, put an end to the right of asylum, and caused loose women and adulterers to be turned out of the city With these views of politics and morals, he united an unprejudiced study of the Scriptures, freed from the whole dogmatic structure that had been raised upon them If I do not mistake, he did, in fact, evince an acute and apt sense for their original meaning and spirit He regarded the Lord's Supper (as the ritual he introduced proves) in the light of a feast of commemoration and affection He held to the words of Paul, that we are one body, because we eat of one bread, for, says he, every one confesses by that act that he belongs to the society which acknowledges Christ to be its Saviour, and in which all Christians are one body, this is community in the blood of Christ He would not admit that he regarded the Eucharist as mere bread "If," said he, "bread and wine, sanctified by the grace of God are distributed, is not the whole body of Christ, as it were, sensibly given to his followers?" It was a peculiar satisfaction to him, that by this view he arrived directly at a practical result For, he asked, how can the knowledge that we belong to one body fail to lead to Christian life and Christian love? The unworthy sinned against the body and blood of Christ He had the joy of seeing that his ritual and the views he had put forth, contributed to put an end to old and obdurate hostilities *

Although Zwingli insists much on what there still was of supernatural in his scheme of the Eucharist, it is clear that this was not the mystery which had hitherto formed the central point of the worship of the Catholic Church We can easily understand the effect produced on the common people, by the attempt to rob them of the sensible presence of Christ Some courage was required to resolve on such an experiment but when this was actually made, the public mind was, as Œcolampadius says, found to be far better disposed for its reception than could have been suspected. This is, however, very explicable People saw that they had gone too far to retract, in their defection from the Church of Rome, and they found a certain gratification of the feeling of independence which that defection had generated, in rendering it as complete as possible

Luther had, from the first moment, been treated with the greatest harshness, Zwingli, on the contrary, with the utmost gentleness even in the year 1523 he received an extremely gracious letter from Adrian VI, in which no allusion was made to his innovations Yet, it is obvious that Zwingli's opposition to the existing forms and institutions of the Church, was far more violent and irreconcilable than that of Luther. Neither ritual nor dogma, in the forms which they had acquired in the course of centuries, any longer made the smallest impression upon him· alterations, in themselves innocuous, but to which abuses had clung, he rejected with the same decision and promptitude as the abuses themselves, he sought to restore the earliest forms in which the principle of Christianity had found an expression —forms, it is true, no less than those he abolished, and not substance, but purer and more congenial

Luther, notwithstanding his zeal against the pope, notwithstanding his aversion to the secular dominion of the hierarchy, was yet, both in doctrine and discipline, as far as it was possible, conservative, and attached to the historical traditions of the Church, his thoughts and feelings were profound, and profoundly impressed with the mysteries of religion. Zwingli was much more unsparing in rejection and in alteration, attentive to the practical business of life, remarkable for sobriety of mind and good sense

Had Luther and his disciples stood alone, the principle of the reformation would probably have rapidly acquired stability; but it would perhaps as rapidly have lost its living, progressing power It is difficult to imagine Zwingli as standing alone, but had views like his arisen without those of Luther, the chain of the historical development of the Church would have been violently broken

Thus it was decreed by divine Providence, if we may presume to say so, that these two systems should make their way together. They co-existed, each in its place, each the offspring of a sort of internal necessity, they belonged to each other, they completed each other

But, from the time of the establishment of the inquisition—of the intolerant domination of a dogmatical system—so rigid an idea of orthodoxy had obtained in the world, that these two sections of the great party of reform, regardless of their common antagonist, attacked each other with furious zeal

We shall frequently have occasion to recur to the various movements excited by this hostility We must now trace the progress of Zwingli on his own ground — Zurich and Switzerland

* Expositio fidei, Works II ii 241

DEFENCE.—PROPAGATION.

Although Zwingli had gone much farther than Luther, he was soon opposed by a still more extreme party: he had to contend with the anabaptists.

He was called upon to form a separate congregation of true believers, since they alone were the subjects of the promises. He replied, that it was impossible to bring heaven upon the earth; Christ had taught that we were to let the tares grow together with the wheat.*

It was then demanded that he should at least invite the whole commune of Zurich to take part in the deliberations, and not content himself with the Grand Council, which consisted only of two hundred members. But Zwingli feared the influence of fanatical demagogues and pretenders to inspiration, on a larger assembly. He maintained that the commune was adequately represented not only politically but ecclesiastically, in the Grand Council. The tacit assent of the commune he held to be a perfectly sufficient sanction of the decrees of the Grand Council. This, it was true, exercised the spiritual power, but under the condition that it did not offend against the rules laid down in the Holy Scriptures in the smallest particular; for that had been promised to the commune by its preachers. Zwingli adhered steadily to the idea of the commune, though he could not perfectly realize it; just as, in modern times, even in countries where the principle of the sovereignty of the people is fully admitted, the body of the people do not, in fact, take an active part in the government.

Zwingli was determined not to suffer the newly established order of things to be disturbed. In order to obtain some advantage from it, the oppositionists demanded the abolition of tithes, which, they said, rested on no divine authority whatever. Zwingli replied, that the tithes had either already passed into the hands of third parties by civil contract, or had been applied to the foundation of churches and schools.† He did not, like Luther, take his stand intrepidly on the principle of the supremacy of the civil power; but he was equally resolved not to allow the political edifice which had just been constructed, to be shaken. He saw that the agitation must stop somewhere, unless every thing was to be called in question. He had reached a certain point, but he would not be drawn on one step further; and he had the general will, on which in a republic every thing depends, on his side.

At this juncture anabaptism also made its appearance in Zurich. The rite of the second baptism is the only symbol of that doctrine which requires perfect uniformity of opinion and genuine Christianity as the basis of the commune (congregation). A community founded on such ideas, however, will always apply to temporal the principle which governs spiritual affairs, and accordingly, we very soon find the anabaptists at variance with the constituted authorities. When summoned before the tribunals, they declared that they were not subject to any earthly power; that God was their only sovereign. They did not perhaps maintain in so many words, that no temporal authority ought to be endured; but they taught that a Christian could not fulfil any temporal office, or draw the sword; so that, according to them, Christianity did not recognise the temporal power. They represented a community of goods as that ideal of our condition on earth after which we ought to strive.‡ As, however, notions of this kind had produced such fearful effects during the revolt of the peasants, and as the Zurich anabaptists (as Zwingli affirmed he positively knew) preached the doctrine, that it was lawful to kill, and necessary to kill priests, the whole force of the existing order of things, in concert with the preachers, rose up in arms to rid the territory of them. Some were banished, others fled; a few of the ringleaders were drowned without mercy.§ The new constitution of the Church was firmly established, without peril or injury to the institutions of the city or the state.

Meanwhile, in another quarter a still more dangerous opposition had arisen out of political motives affecting the whole Confederation.

Zwingli had propagated his political, as well as his religious opinions in Zurich; he had combated the abuses of foreign enlistment and foreign pensions with complete success: the priests were compelled solemnly to forswear all pensions, and in the year 1521, Zurich alone, of all the cantons, refused to accept the French alliance. The disasters which this alliance brought in its train, were used by Zwingli, as means of gaining others over to his system. It is necessary to read "The Divine Warning," which he addressed after the battle of Bicocca, "To the oldest and right honest Confederates at Schwyz," in order to perceive the connexion which subsisted between his religious and his political labours. His persuasion was, that reason and piety were blinded by secret gifts from foreigners, and nothing but discord engendered. He urges his countrymen to lay aside selfish considerations. And if any one asked how this was possible, seeing that selfishness has its root in every human heart, he answered, that care must be taken that the word of God be taught clearly and intelligibly, and without any of the encumbrances of human wisdom. For so would God gain possession of the heart. "But where God is not in the heart of man, there is nothing but the man himself, and he thinks of nothing but what ministers to his in-

* Elenchus contra Catabaptistas. Opp. iii. 362.

† Füssli's Beitrage, i. 235.

‡ Confessions and documents in Fussli's Beitragen, i. 229, 249, 258, ii. 263.

§ In Rodolphi Gualtheri Epistola ad Lectorem prefixed to the second part of the Works, 1544, it is protested that Zwingli did not desire this. "Quod homines væsani, non jam infideles modo, verum etiam seditiosi reipublicæ turbatores, magistratuum hostes, justa senatus sententia damnati sunt, num id Zwinglio fraudi esse poterit?"

terests or his lusts." His political views, and indeed all his ideas, are pervaded by that higher morality, which is at the same time mysticism and religion. In Schwyz, where he had a number of personal friends, his addresses made such an impression, that on the 18th May, 1522, the rural communes declined the French alliance, and admonished others to renounce it, "all those whom it had a right to admonish." It was quite to be expected that Schwyz, where Geroldseck and Zwingli and Leo Juda had so long had influence, would now follow the example of Zurich in religious affairs.

By this course, however, Zwingli necessarily created the most formidable enemies. The leading men in the communes, who received foreign pensions, and the hired captains who led the warlike youth into foreign service, constituted factions which were not disposed to let slip their advantages so easily,—oligarchies which, united, governed the popular assemblies. Zwingli himself discovered that a new nobility was as dangerous as the old one. And in fact these governing parties were powerful enough to induce the Schwyzers to revoke their resolution against foreign service. The influence of Hans Hug, Schultheiss of Lucerne, chiefly contributed to maintain the existing policy in the Wald cantons.* At the diet of 1523 a complaint was formally laid against Zwingli, and it inevitably followed that the hostility to his political opinions was reflected back on his religious exertions. Indeed it is impossible to deny that they were most intimately connected. His views on both subjects were simultaneous in their origin, and had thus far been prosecuted together. In the year 1524, the diet required the Zurichers to desist from their innovations. As they gave an evasive answer, the other cantons threatened that they would no longer sit with them in diet, and would send them back the briefs of confederation. Some dissentient opinions were indeed expressed at the diet, and occasionally prevailed. In the year 1525 a very remarkable resolution was passed, the purpose of which was to limit the spiritual jurisdiction,† after the manner of the German diets. But those who were strongly attached to Rome would hear of no limitation of the ecclesiastical jurisdiction, and, in the main, this more orthodox opinion predominated. The prelates who, shortly before, had been in no little jeopardy, felt the ground once more firm under their feet; they formed the closest alliance with the oligarchs. At this point of our researches, we come upon the remarkable actions of John Faber, the Vicar-general of Constance, who at an earlier period had shared the literary tendencies of his High German contemporaries, and encouraged Zwingli to resist the sale of indulgences. In 1521, however, he returned from Rome totally changed, and now devoted his life to the maintenance of the ancient faith. He laboured by every means to promote the alliance we have mentioned, and to render it effective. The conference at Baden in May, 1526, at which Eck was also present, was the expression of the new understanding between the oligarchs and the spiritual power.‡ With greater confidence, and with greater probability, than ever, the orthodox party maintained that the victory was on their side.

Yet this very conference turned out highly injurious to them.

Zwingli did not attend it, probably alarmed at the executions which had just taken place in the see of Constance, for example, that of Hans Huglin; on the other hand, Bern and Basel sent two representatives of the new doctrines, Berthold Haller and Œcolampadius, who were not only far from conceding the victory to their opponents, but, on their return home, excited a patriotic interest in their cause in the minds of their fellow-citizens.§ Bern and Basel also, on their side, demanded their share in the publication of the acts of the conference, and would not quietly allow them to remain in the hands of the Catholic majority. A misunderstanding had already arisen between those cities and the others, on the question of jurisdictions, and an entire division now seemed inevitable.

But a further political crisis was necessary to bring this to an open breach.

If the new doctrine, however, had made enemies by its connexion with politics, it had also secured friends. In all these cities a powerful democratic party in the Grand Councils, together with the body of the citizens, stood opposed to the oligarchies. As the latter adhered to the spiritual power, so the former inclined to reform. Two parties, opposed in politics and religion, were formed, and long was the victory doubtful. There is no question that the spirit of ecclesiastical reform, established so firmly and so continually gaining strength among the people, mainly contributed in the powerful canton of Bern to give the final ascendancy to the more democratical party. The troubles concerning the conference of Baden had the same result. At the new elections in the year 1527, a considerable number of adherents of reform and adversaries of the oligarchs, entered the Grand Council. The first consequence of this was, that the Grand Council demanded the restitution of all its ancient rights. Twenty years long it had acquiesced in the lesser council

* Zwingli's Complaint, Feb. 19, 1523, to Steiner. Epp. i. p. 275.

† E. g. the clergy shall retain what relates to affairs of marriage, or places of worship and sacraments, or errors of faith; but these too shall first be laid before the secular authorities, which shall refer them, only when they deem it necessary, to the spiritual judges. Articles in Bullinger, i. 203.

‡ Zwingli to Vadian, i. 485. "Istud unum caveo, ne optima plebs Helvetica horum nebulonum, Fabri videlicet et Ecciorum, strophis committatur, id autem Oligarcharum perfidia." 3 Kal. Apr. 1526.

§ As the song by Nicolas Manuel shows: "ain Lid in schilers Hofthon." Grüneisen, p. 409. "Egg zablet mit fussen und henden, fing an schelken und schenden:—er sprach ich blib by dem verstand, den Bubst Cardinal Bischof hand." "Egg strove with hand and foot, and began to scold and to abuse:—he said, I hold to the understanding (opinion) that the pope, cardinals and bishops have."—He appears just the same in Baden as in Leipzig.

being composed of Vennern and Sechzehnern * and it now resumed its inherent right to elect the members of the latter body † After it had thus, agreeably to the constitution, united in itself the entire civic power, it proceeded to the discussion of religious affairs The mandates commanding the people to hold fast to the ancient faith were revoked, a disputation was held, at which Zwingli was present, and which ended entirely in his favour All his plans for Zurich were adopted in Bern In the year 1528, the adherents of the old faith were turned out of both the councils The commune was assembled in the church, man by man,—gentlemen, masters of trades, and workmen, all swore allegiance to the two councils ‡ The next question, as might be expected from the twofold character of the reform, was the system of foreign pensions, which had many advocates in Bern, even among the evangelical party Not without a hot contest, and a second appeal to the opinion of the people in city and country, were the pensions refused (24th August), and notice of the same sent to the King of France §

The existing government of Basel stood its ground a little longer, it flattered itself that it would still be able to maintain the balance between the two confessions Gradually, however, the evangelical communes became aware of their superiority, and at length, at a meeting of the people in January 1529, only eight hundred Catholics were present, to three thousand reformers In the following February, a violent commotion broke out The first thing was to alter the constitution The guilds resumed their ancient independence, and acquired the perpetual right of sending sixty of their members to the Grand Council No one was to sit in the lesser council, who was not nominated by the greater, all the Catholics left the lesser council ‖ Psalms and hymns in the German language were immediately sung in the churches, and on the 1st of April a form of divine service on the pattern of that of Zurich was published, breathing the religious earnestness and austere morality which were among the chief internal causes of this revolution, and containing allusions to the suppression of wanton wars

A code determining their relations was now agreed on by the three cities This was in fact a treaty of alliance for the defence of the new order of things which they had established, and into which they contemplated the admission of all the confederate cantons, "when," as they express it, "they shall be so far instructed in the word of God"

Of this event, indeed, there seemed to be a considerable probability In Glarus, Appenzell, and the Grisons, the reforming party was very active, in Schaffhausen the council incessantly vacillated between the opposite tendencies, ¶ in St Gall the victory was already decided In the year 1528, after a change of the council of that city, the Catholic ceremonies were discontinued, and articles of a radical reformation promulgated ** The same took place in Muhlhausen, where the secretary of the city, Gamshorst, one of the statesmen who had taken an active part in the internal affairs of the Confederation and in its relations to the pope and the emperor, encouraged the movement by his well-founded authority In the years 1528 and 1529, St Gall, Biel, and Muhlhausen (the latter not without some difficulty, and only in consequence of the especial interposition of Bern) were received into the Christian civic alliance ††

These changes, great and important as they were, originated in a single profound thought, embracing political and religious objects Zwingli had resolved to purify at once the church and his country from the most pernicious abuses of both kinds He could not have accomplished the ecclesiastical reform without the political, nor the political without the ecclesiastical Nothing short of the concurrent progress of both would have realized his original conception We shall see hereafter how far he was successful

Germany was chiefly affected by his view of the sacrament of the Lord's Supper. Butzer and Capito, the reformers of Strasburg, had taken part in the conference at Bern, and had long been zealous advocates for Zwingli's system Lindau and Memmingen soon followed Strasburg The same doctrine was preached by Somius in Ulm, Cellarius in Augsburg, Blaurer in Constance, Hermann in Reutlingen, and by many others in the towns of that part of Germany In some indeed, the project of attaching themselves by close and indissoluble ties to the evangelical towns of the Swiss Confederation was talked of And this took place at the very moment when an evangelical church, organized according to Luther's views, arose in so many parts of eastern Germany

The antagonism which thus arose between the opinions and the new-born institutions of eastern and western Germany was undoubtedly a great misfortune The polemical writ-

* Local titles of magistrates The sixteen (Sechzehnern) still exist at Bern, though their functions are reduced to a shadow —TRANS

† "Ad viginti annos 4 Pandareti cum 16 e civibus senatum minorem elegerunt, ea conditione ut per eos delectos civium turma non haberet abjicere nunc ablata est illis potestas et concio universa civium senatum deligit" Letter from B Haller to Vadian in Kirchhofer's Berthold Vadian, p 89

‡ Stettler, ii 6

§ Bullinger, ii 13 Haller calls it pecunia sanguinaria, Hofmeister speaks of execrabile fœdus Gallicum Manuel too was one of those who attacked the pensions Grunei sen, 100 Kirchhofer, 133

‖ See Ochs, Geschichte von Basel, v p 626, f The diœcesium suffragio, cum diœcesiis disponenda in Œcolampadius' Report with which Ochs (v 633) torments himself so much, is doubtless diacosion suffragio, cum diacosiis, by which word Zwingli, and also Œcolampadius (e g in his letter to Hess, p 506), usually denotes the Grand Council

¶ This undecided state of opinion appears clearly in the individual case of Hans Stockar, whose journal was published in 1839

** Arx, Geschichte von St Gallen, ii 529, cursory as to the main point, circumstantial in the collateral and spiteful details

†† Bullinger, Reformationsgeschichte, ii p 46

ings of that period filled all minds with mutual antipathy

But this reflection is by no means the only one which the course of events is calculated to excite The antagonism in question arose not merely from a different apprehension of a dogma, it lay in the very origin of the movement on either side, in the political and ecclesiastical condition from which each party had to emancipate itself Whether, as to dogma, an explanation satisfactory, to both parties might not still be discovered, was as yet uncertain But that reform in Switzerland originated in causes and in sentiments native and peculiar to the country, that it struck root in its own soil, and assumed a form and growth of its own, was unquestionably fortunate for the world at large, since it gave to the general principle of the reformation fresh vigour and stability.

CHAPTER IV

POLITICAL CHARACTER OF THE YEAR 1529

The situation of the world was at that time as follows

The great political relations between East and West, upon which, during the middle ages, every thing had depended, were unsettled The puissant prince in whom the warlike power of the East centred, was once more meditating an attack upon Christendom, from which he was justified in anticipating success as complete as that which had attended his former enterprises it was not likely that the very feeble preparations for resistance which had since then been made by the German powers in Hungary, would have the effect of arresting his course A conflict of the German forces by land and the Roman by sea with those of the Ottoman, seemed imminent

But Christendom itself was torn with divisions

Peace was not yet restored between its two highest potentates The emperor had even entertained the thought of stripping the pope of all his temporal authority, while, on the other hand, the emperor's adversaries had conceived a plan for deposing him, with the aid of the pope These projects were not yet entirely abandoned

Nor was the military superiority of the two great powers which had so long stood confronted in arms, more decided From year to year the fortunes of the house of Austria had been in the ascendant, yet France scorned to acquiesce in the loss of the predominant consideration she had long enjoyed, or to renounce her possessions in Italy

To this conflict of political interests was now added that of religious opinions, at this moment less noisy, but pregnant with far more weighty consequences The authority of the Roman Church, which had ruled the West for so many centuries, now encountered an opposition, to which it appeared likely to succumb. Enemies had frequently arisen, but never before did they manifest a religious sentiment at once so energetic and so firm, never had their efforts been so intimately connected with the general intellectual life, and the progress of civilisation throughout Europe, and, accordingly, never had their opinions been propagated with such rapidity and vigour

It had happened, moreover, that the schemes of reform had taken two perfectly different, and even opposite directions The one system attached itself as closely as possible to the existing doctrine of the church, and to the established forms of the state. The other was, from the first, blended with projects of radical political changes, and assumed as its end the restoration of the primitive state of Christendom And they were directly opposed in their views of the most important dogma

These were not disputes about this or that measure to be taken for the future, or about this or that interest already vested; they were contests concerning the interests and affairs of the deepest importance to mankind at large, the relations of the East and the West, of the empire and the papacy, of the two preponderant powers of Europe to each other a contest on the one side for the permanency of the hierarchical powers, and on the other for the introduction of new ecclesiastical forms, and, even with regard to the latter, a contest between those who advocated the preservation of all that it was possible to preserve, and those who desired radical and sweeping changes

As it is clear, however, that all these antagonisms, however they might affect the world at large, chiefly concerned the German nation, and came into collision on the German soil (for Germany had immediately to fight out the battle with the Ottomans on the continent, to maintain its supremacy in Italy, and to bring the religious quarrels to a decision or to a compromise), the whole course of affairs depended on the attitude which the emperor might assume in the general shock and conflict of these various movements

Hitherto the fluctuating nature of events had forced him upon political measures not always consistent with one another; but now that the time for decision was at hand, it was absolutely necessary to adopt a system, and to carry it through

The wish of the German people was, as we have already remarked, that the emperor would place himself at the head of the resistance to the hierarchy, and, supported by all the energy of the nation, assert the rights of the empire, of whatever kind, and drive back the barbarians beyond the Danube It seems hardly possible that the emperor's inclinations should not have gone with this policy. Had he not, from the moment of his accession, spoken of a reformation of the church, and had he not of late frequently repeated the same word? Was not the most violent and dangerous jealousy of his house to be found in those German princes who had espoused the cause of the hierarchy? It would seem that he must necessarily have regarded an alliance with the popular tendencies (on whose irresistible progress all his letters from Germany dwelt) as a means of increasing his power.

But a man placed in the midst of the conflict of opposing powers and influences of such magnitude, is seldom able to come to a perfectly free, deliberate and unbiassed decision. I do not believe that Charles V. ever so much as asked himself the question, which side he ought to espouse. The German nation was not destined to attain to its further development under the guidance of a common head. Charles V. found himself compelled by his personal situation, and by the previous course of events, to adopt a policy contrary to its wishes.

Recent experience had proved that an attempt to carry on a further contest with the pope would involve him in perplexities of which it was impossible to foresee the end. In the presence of this urgent necessity, therefore, he had resolved not only upon a more conciliatory demeanour, but on an alliance with Rome.

It is remarkable how all his foreign relations conspired to confirm him in this resolution.

We have already observed that the honour of his house utterly forbade him to listen to the doubt, whether the Court of Rome was warranted in granting Henry VIII. the dispensation for his marriage, which that monarch now declared to be null.

In the northern states, the enemies who had driven his brother-in-law Christiern into exile, manifested a strong leaning to the German notions of reform, which indeed had nearly become predominant in Sweden. The emperor could only restore his brother-in-law to the throne, and re-establish the influence of the house of Austria in the north, by a union with the various parties still attached to Catholicism.

Yet further, the alliances which the reformed towns of Switzerland contracted with their co-religionists and neighbours of North Germany, caused the Catholic cantons to seek a support in the house of Austria: they forgot their hereditary enmity to it, and in the early part of the year 1529 concluded a formal treaty with King Ferdinand.

In the quarrel with the Woiwode and his adherents in Hungary also, it was very important to the success of Charles's cause that the church should acknowledge his rights.

And if the emperor cast his eyes over the German empire, he could not fail to see that his authority had most to gain from a union with the spiritual princes. We may remember how anxious Maximilian was to fill the episcopal sees with men devoted to his interests, and to gain over the body of the clergy. This became a far easier task, as soon as the bishops, whose spiritual privileges were menaced by the current ideas of the age, looked for protection to the imperial power. Considering the weight which the hierarchical ingredient in the constitution of the Germanic empire still possessed, it was, indeed, no slight advantage to have it as an ally. I have no documentary evidence to prove that these considerations presented themselves to Charles V., but they are certainly too obvious to have escaped him. We all know that, at a later epoch, the dissolution of the spiritual principalities was the signal for the overthrow of the imperial throne. Something similar might have taken place then, however little it might be contemplated. The imperial authority had not firm root enough to sustain itself among merely temporal powers, even had they not been all hereditary: or if it did sustain itself, it could only be by vast and continued efforts; it was infinitely easier to turn the long-established institutions to account. Zwingli once said truly enough, that the empire and the papacy were so closely interwoven, that it was impossible to make war upon the one without attacking the other.

The result of all these circumstances was, that the emperor's policy was totally different from that which would have been agreeable to the German nation. He meditated a reconciliation with the pope, the exaltation of the imperial power, but solely on the established hierarchical basis; resistance to the Ottomans, but entirely in the usual spirit of Latin Christendom: he had no sympathy with the German ideas of church reform,—on the contrary, they were utterly distasteful to him, and we shall see that he determined to extinguish them.

This is mainly to be ascribed to the fact, that he was not only Emperor of Germany, but King of Spain. He had passed the important years of adolescence, in which a man enters definitively upon the path which he pursues through life, in Spain, and had imbibed the opinions prevalent in that country on some essential points.

Catholicism—which, had it really become a lifeless, unmeaning form, must unquestionably have perished in the storms of this century—had deep and living roots in the Roman part of Europe, and especially in Spain.

In Spain, the State, such as it existed in the middle ages,—the State, in which the attributes of the monarchy and the priesthood were combined,—was still in full vigour and activity.

The conflict with Islam, which had so materially contributed to the development of this form of Church and State, was here still going on; the government was constantly employed in christianizing the country, and no acts of violence tending to that end excited either reprobation or remorse. In the year 1524, Charles got a dispensation from the oath which bound him to tolerate the Moriscos of the crown of Aragon.* The victory of Pavia had inspired him with redoubled fervour; he once

* Pope's Brief of the 12th March, 1524. Llorente, i. 427.

used the remarkable expression, that since God had delivered his enemies into his hands, he was bound to convert God's enemies;* and he immediately set about this work in Valencia, where the Christian population was as yet in a minority; the Christian families being estimated at 22,000, and the Moorish at 26,000. A sort of crusade was set on foot against the latter; and at last the Germans, who had followed the emperor into Spain, were forced to march against the Moors of the Sierra Espadan. Hereupon the mosques were transformed into churches, and tithes were collected for the benefit of the twofold hierarchy. Of all the thousands who were baptized, says Sandoval, there were not six whose inclinations were changed; but woe to him who did not prostrate himself at the sight of the host! The most rigorous inquisition watched over every outward demonstration.

This might indeed be necessary. Even in 1528, a man was discovered among the Moors of Valencia whom they secretly regarded as their king.† His design seems to have been to make a rising on the first absence of the emperor. He was put to death together with his whole tribe.

The colonisation of America was carried on in the same spirit. The great discoverer, on his return to Seville, was seen to take part in a procession, habited in the dress of a Franciscan. Columbus thought himself destined to propagate the Christian faith in the country of the Great Khan, which he believed he had discovered. He continually expressed his hope of being the instrument of procuring to the crown the means of re-conquering the Holy Sepulchre.‡ And we may remark in all his successors, curiously mingled with the desire to be rich, powerful, and glorious, the most ardent zeal for the extension of the religion of Rome.§ For the crown, this was a sort of necessity, since it deduced all its rights from the Roman See; such was the official doctrine which it proclaimed to the Indians. It transferred the entire form and character of the Latin Church, only if possible yet more gorgeous and magnificent, to the new world.

It must not, however, be understood that all men were imbued with these sentiments. It is a remarkable fact, for example, that Cortez did not approve the importation of the complete hierarchy into America; he would have no bishops, only an active lower clergy and zealous monks; and occupied himself in devising means for dispensing with episcopal ordination.‖ But so strong was the attachment to the whole mass of established usages, that even he, the conqueror and lawgiver, could make no effectual resistance to it.

Spain was, indeed, not so secluded from the rest of Europe, that the innovating spirit and tendencies of the current literature had not penetrated there. Antonio de Lebrixa, for example, deserves to be placed in the same class with Erasmus and Reuchlin. He, too, devoted his labours to the sacred writings, and published a work under the title, "A Hundred and Fifty Passages of the Holy Scriptures, translated in an improved manner."¶ But the Dominican Inquisition, which Germany would not endure within its bosom, ruled in Spain with absolute sway. The grand inquisitor, Diego Deza, Bishop of Palencia, robbed the learned author of the greater part of his book, and did not attempt to conceal that his intention in doing so was to restrain him from publishing any thing in future on that subject. Indeed it is asserted that this bishop would, if he could, have extirpated the original language of the sacred books.** Deza's successor, Ximenes, was, as is well known, far from sharing these narrow views; he felt that depth and force of the original which no translation can adequately convey, and ordered the text to be published in his polyglot. But he estimated the received version of the Latin church, the vulgate, far beyond its value. He compared the Greek and Hebrew texts, between which the Latin was printed, to the thieves on the right hand and the left of the Saviour.†† It is an indisputable fact, that he altered the words of the Septuagint, and even the Greek text of the New Testament, in accordance with the vulgate; and adopted a passage of great importance as dogmatic evidence, which is found in none of the manuscripts, merely in deference to that translation.‡‡ In short, the slightest deviation from the established system of the Latin church would not have been tolerated. It is a very remarkable fact, that at the epoch we are treating of, the school philosophy rose into consideration in Spain just as it declined throughout the rest of Europe. In the university of Salamanca, Alfonso of Cor-

* Sandoval, i. 673. who is here generally our authority.

† "Uno que se dize rey encubierto, que es nombre de baxa suerte,—publican, que eran muchos con el que estaban determinados depassando el emperador de matar a la reyna Germana y el duque de Calavria su marido e levantarse por rey esto dicho rey encubierto.—Han fecho morir ata 50 hombres que se dezia ser de su lignage y tienen presos mas de ata ciento." Advertimiento de la Corte del Emperador. Bib. du Roi, Paris. Bethune's Collection, 8531, f. 110.

‡ Humboldt, iii. 260.

§ Prescott, History of Ferdinand and Isabella, iii. 418, quotes a very remarkable passage from Gonzalo di Oviedo: "Who can doubt that powder against the infidels is incense to the Lord?"

‖ Report of Cortez, 15th October, 1524, by Koppe, p. 487.

¶ Quinquagenæ tres locorum sacræ scripturæ non vulgariter enarratorum.

** "Bonus ille præsul in tota quæstione sua nihil magis laborabat, quam ut duarum linguarum, ex quibus religio nostra pendet, neque ullum vestigium relinqueretur, per quod ad dignoscendam in rebus dubiis certitudinem pervenire possemus." (Apologia pro se ipso. Nic. Antonii Bibl. Hisp. Nova, i. p. 135.)

†† Prologus ad lectorem. Medium autem inter has (the Hebrew and Greek texts) Latinam beati Hieronymi translationem velut inter synagogam et orientalem ecclesiam posuimus: duos hinc et inde latrones, medium autem Jesum, h. e. Romanam sive Latinam ecclesiam, collocantes.

‡‡ Semler's Accurate Examination of the bad Execution of the Greek New Testament, printed at Alcala, 1766. They omitted the Doxology in the 6th Chapter of St. Matthew, which, though Chrysostom had adopted that reading, they maintained had, even in his time, been interpolated ex corruptis originalibus (p. 117). The passage in question is, as is well known, St. John i. 5—7. In this they adopted the criticism of St. Thomas. Salmeron too says, videtur plus fidei tribuendum Latinis codicibus quam Græcis.

dova proclaimed the nominalist, and, at the same moment, Francisco of Vittoria, the realist, doctrines, as something new and for the first time to be disseminated in the country, they wished to render it unnecessary for Spaniards to resort to the schools of Paris Francisco of Vittoria had the greatest following, he gave a new development to the moral philosophy of the schools Bellarmine called him the happy father of excellent masters, and, indeed, the most eminent Spanish theologians issued from his school * As another proof of the unaltered state of the public mind in Spain, we may mention, that a great part of the "Romancero general" owed its origin to the sixteenth century. The spirit of the ages of priestly dominion still bore exclusive sway in the polity and literature of the country

The natural consequence of this state of public opinion was, an intense hostility to the aberrations, as they were deemed, of the rest of the world. Not only were the ordinances against Luther's heresy executed with the utmost rigour, but even Erasmus, spite of the favour he enjoyed at court, found no mercy from monkish pedantry Diego Lopez Zuniga, a man familiar with both languages, made it the main object of his life to oppose the innovations of the witty and learned Dutchman † During the Lent of 1527, certain Dominicans formally accused Erasmus—or rather his writings, for luckily he was out of their reach—of heresy to the inquisition A tribunal was appointed; and although its members could not immediately come to any unanimous decision, the inquisition thought itself justified in prohibiting the "Colloquies," the "Praise of Folly," and the "Paraphrase of the New Testament" ‡

In every country there prevails a moral atmosphere, from which there is no escape, and we perceive that it was impossible for the young emperor, surrounded by such influences as these, to acquire energy and independence of mind

The archives at Brussels contain a Spanish criticism of Luther and Œcolampadius, written in the spirit of the church, and presented to the emperor, to fortify him against the influences of the new opinions § In this, the full right of the church to impose the punishment due to a mortal sin is insisted upon, otherwise, it is urged, every man would follow only his own inclination The disputed articles of faith are then defended in all their rigour; marriage, confirmation, consecration, extreme unction, are maintained to be sacraments, instituted by Christ himself In conclusion, it is proved that the proper punishment for heretics is burning

These opinions did not obtain such a complete ascendancy over the emperor's mind as to lead him to an abject submission to the papacy, or to stifle his projects of purifying the church from its abuses, and of undertaking the work of its reformation himself, but it is unquestionable that his residence in Spain contributed to confirm him in views of policy with which the exclusive domination of the Latin church is intimately connected It strengthened his antipathy to the unauthorised innovations of individual teachers or bodies We shall soon witness the effects of these sentiments.

The very first instructions he gave the imperial ambassadors who were sent to the captive pope, contain expressions concerning the necessity of extirpating the erring sect of the Lutherans ‖ In consequence of this the pope, in the treaty of the 26th of November, 1527, promises a council, "whereby the church may once more be set right, and the Lutheran sect be rooted out" In the spring of 1528, the imperial vice-chancellor, provost Waldkirchen, repaired to Germany, with a view to revive the Catholic spirit As he travelled from town to town, and from one prince's court to another, it was universally believed that his intention was to form a league against the evangelical party ¶ The exhortations of the pope to that effect grew more and more earnest and vehement We possess a letter of Sanga's, dated October, 1528, in which he tells the nuncio at the imperial court, to press the emperor in the most urgent manner to devote himself more than heretofore to the affairs of religion already, he said, there were people who went further than Luther, already they denied the sacrament of the Lord's Supper and infant baptism —what would posterity say, when it read that, under the greatest emperor who had governed it for centuries, Germany swarmed with heresies! **

Of the emperor's antipathy to them there could be no doubt The executions which took place in the Netherlands, where he was absolute master, afforded sufficient proof of it Erasmus, who knew him well, was persuaded that he would not think himself emperor, if he did not succeed in suppressing Lutheranism ††

And at this juncture events occurred which rendered it probable that he would acquire the power of doing so

We saw how warlike and menacing was the aspect of things, even so late as the beginning of the year 1529, but the emperor's good fortune frustrated the schemes, and broke the spirit, of his enemies

* Nic Antonii Bibliotheca Hisp N I s v Franciscus.

† He too maintained the superiority of the vulgate "Sciendum est," says he of John i 5—7 "Græcorum codices apertissime esse corruptos, nostros vero veritatem ipsam continere" Nevertheless in this very passage the vulgate is interpolated See Griesbach, App 12

‡ Llorente, i 459 Erasmi Epistolæ 989, 1032. He mentions Pedro di Vittoria especially as his antagonist

§ Siguense los errores de Luther y Colampadio su discipulo con la determinacion de l'iglesia The several articles were discussed in succession e g Art 3, as above, Art. 6 Santo es y justo commendarnos a los santos y adorar sus imagines 7 La iglesia puede licitamente tener patrimonio y poseer bienes temporales 8. Justa pena es por los hereges, que seen quemados

‖ Bucholtz, iii 99

¶ Stetten, p 303 Von der Lith, p 217.

** Lettere di diversi, 56

†† Erasmi Epp p 963 In Hollandia mire fervet carnificina This sounds very differently from the remark of Le Clay, Correspondance de Maximilien et Marguerite, ii p 449, in justification of Margaret

The Venetians and the French still cherished the idea of conquering Milan, in the spring of 1529 they marched again from both sides on that capital, they reckoned on the exhaustion and the discontent of the citizens, and the small number of the troops, and were resolved on an immediate attack

It soon became evident what Milan had lost in losing Genoa By the possession of that city, the emperor gained the advantage of being less exclusively dependent on German auxiliaries than heretofore He was now enabled to send a few thousand men from Spain to Genoa, whence they afterwards pushed on to Milan, which the enemy were not sufficiently masters of the field to prevent They were troops of the very worst appearance,—barefoot, half-naked, squalid, and starved But to the emperor they were invaluable Such as they were, they were most cordially received by his commander-in-chief, Antonio Leiva Leiva had hitherto carried on his defence chiefly by the aid of Germans, in September, 1528, he numbered 5000 of that nation, and only 800 Spaniards,* it may easily be imagined how welcome was this reinforcement of his own countrymen, whose bravery would, he knew, be sharpened by their necessities

The allies immediately perceived that they were not strong enough to make a serious attack on the city They therefore determined to surround it at some distance, and to cut off its supplies St Pol even indulged a hope of making some successful attempt upon Genoa, and quitted Milan with that view

But he thus gave his foes an opportunity of striking a great blow, such as the Spaniards had often struck with success Leiva s troops moved forward in the night, without drums or trumpets, and with shirts over their armour he himself, though suffering from the gout, would not stay behind, fully armed and accoutred, even to the waving plume upon his helmet, he caused himself to be carried on a litter to the field Just as the French were breaking up their camp near Landriano,—at the moment when St Pol was giving orders to pull down a house, the beams of which he wanted to force a piece of artillery out of the mud,† they were surprised by Leiva, who gained a complete victory, and led back St Pol and the chief officers of his army, prisoners to Milan.

This victory rendered the emperor as completely master in Lombardy as he already was in Naples A fresh attack upon his forces would have required new and mighty efforts, which no one felt able or disposed to make

Indeed, such a course was the less to be thought of, since the long-pending negotiations with the pope were brought to a conclusion, exactly at the moment of this decisive affair in the Milanese territory.

The proposals made to the pope were, as we have remarked, of the most advantageous nature, both as regarded German and Italian affairs, the supreme direction of which was to be in his hands the emperor promised to follow his advice in every respect; to restore to him the lands belonging to the church, to conclude a general peace with his mediation, and made many other flattering concessions But we are not to imagine that Clement was influenced by these alone The proximate and determining motive was fear In April, 1529, he complained to Cardinal Triulzio of the eagerness with which he was urged to conclude the treaty by the imperial agents. he declared that he would never accede to it, were he but strong enough to resist, but, he added, he was surrounded on all sides by adherents of the emperor, and might at any moment be exposed to some fresh disaster,—he was still, in fact, no better than a prisoner, he saw no difference, except perhaps, that before, he could not run away, and that now he could certainly do that in fact, he must either escape and abandon the states of the church to the enemy, or make the least disadvantageous terms with them he could He expressed all this with so much energy, that he completely convinced the cardinal. "I know not," says Triulzio, "what the holy father will determine upon. But if he consents to sign the treaty, I see that it will be only because he is forced, and dragged into it by the hair of the head "‡

I will not take upon myself to maintain that this feeling exclusively possessed the pope during the whole of these negotiations,—he well knew that Cardinal Triulzio, to whom he said all this, was a partisan of France —but he was not so thorough a dissembler as to feign it altogether, and it is probable that, though generally suppressed, it was occasionally beyond his control

He was likewise influenced by considerations of his own personal interest His connexion with the emperor afforded him the only prospect of becoming master of his enemies in his native city of Florence

For a time he had entertained the hope of attaining to this most cherished wish of his heart by peaceful means, and with that view he kept up a certain degree of intercourse, not direct indeed, but through friends, with the Gonfaloniere Caponi It seemed not improbable that the Medicean and the republican parties would severally moderate their claims, and come to a peaceable compromise.

But at this very juncture, a contrary movement took place in Florence A violent republican party, which, in spite of the entire change of circumstances, would not give up the persuasion that it could maintain itself as firmly as formerly, accused the Gonfaloniere of these connexions and designs as crimes,

* Letter from Leiva to the emperor Sandoval, ii 19

† The morning of the 27th of June: in sul passar dell' Ambra Barchi, 211 According to Leoni the loss was caused by St Pol disregarding the advice of the Duke of Urbino, to send on the artillery in front and to divide his other troops into two columns, the one of which was to support the other Vita di Francesco Maria, 414

‡ Lettera del Cardinale Triulzio a M Hieronymo, Roma, 9 Apr 1529 Bibliothèque du roi, MS Bethune

and effected his deposition (April, 1529), though he was afterwards acquitted of all real delinquency. From that time all posts were exclusively filled by the most violent enemies of the Medici, the pope was spoken of with hatred and contempt, and a reconciliation with him was out of the question. Clement VII fell into a rage whenever he thought of the affairs of Florence. Among other things, the story of his illegitimate birth was brought up again; he was declared to have been disqualified from ascending the papal throne, and even the title of pope was denied him.* The English ambassador found him one day in a state of great exasperation. Clement said he would rather be chaplain nay, groom, to the emperor, than allow himself to be insulted by his own disobedient subjects.† To the feeling of the impossibility of throwing off the yoke imposed upon him, were united revenge and ambition, which he could satisfy in no other way than by submitting to it.

On the 29th of June, a treaty of peace was concluded at Barcelona, between the emperor and the pope, which was chiefly remarkable for the pope's acquiescence in the emperor's domination in Italy, against which he had so vehemently struggled. He renewed the infeudation for the crown of Naples, and remitted the tribute which had always been paid for it, retaining only the gift of the sumpter horse. He no longer positively insisted on the maintenance of the Sforzas in Milan, but consented that their guilt or innocence should be decided by a regular tribunal, he was satisfied with the emperor's declaration that he would take no steps as to the new investiture of the duchy without the pope's consent. He granted the imperial troops free passage through his territory, from Naples to Tuscany or Lombardy. On the other hand, the emperor promised to restore to the see of Rome possession of the countries wrested from it by Venice and Ferrara (but with express reservation of the rights of the empire), and to reinstate the Medicean family on the ducal throne of Florence.‡ The emperor formed the most intimate alliance with that house. He promised the hand of his natural daughter to the young Alessandro de' Medici, on whom the lordship of Florence was to devolve. For so greatly had things altered, that it was now the emperor's turn to protect the pope against the immediate influence of the Ligue. Now, as in the year 1521, the emperor formed an alliance with a pope of the house of Medici. But how vast was the difference! Leo X might have reasonably entertained a hope of becoming master of Milan and Genoa, and of conquering Ferrara. Clement VII was fain to content himself with receiving back the States of the Church from foreign hands, and reconquering his native city by foreign aid.

To this arrangement of Italian affairs other stipulations were appended, though they were not all included in the treaty.

John Zapolya, who had hitherto enjoyed the favour of the apostolic see, was now abandoned by it, and shortly afterwards visited with the most rigorous ecclesiastical censures.§ In respect of English affairs, Ferdinand's ambassador united his entreaties to those of the imperial envoys. The trial had already begun there, in virtue of the commission already issued, but the pope pledged his word to both brothers that no sentence should be pronounced. They, in return, promised him, in the most solemn manner, their assistance in matters of religion. In the treaty of Barcelona the emperor declares, that he has it at heart to find an antidote to the poisonous infection of the new opinions.‖ If, however, it should be found impossible to bring back the minds of the erring by mild measures, if they should refuse to hear the voice of the shepherd, and remain stiff-necked in their errors, "then," continues this document, "both the emperor and the King of Hungary and Bohemia would set all their forces in motion, and avenge the wrong offered to Christ with their utmost power."

Such was the unexpected turn which events took. The emperor was chiefly indebted for his victory to the sympathy in his cause, produced in the German nation by Lutheran opinions. it was only by means of the power which this gave him that he forced the pope to make peace. Yet in the very treaty which he concluded with the pope, he promised him the extirpation of these very Lutheran opinions.

These events, as the pope had foreseen, rendered it impossible for Francis I to avoid entertaining serious thoughts of peace, however unpalatable they were to him.

In the negotiations of the year 1527, the emperor had no longer demanded the restitution of his hereditary dominions so absolutely as before, he had shown a disposition to accept two millions of scudi as an equivalent. But the whole negotiation had been rendered abortive by the king's refusal to give up Milan and Genoa, or to withdraw his troops out of Italy.¶ It appeared as if the French regarded the re-conquest of Milan as a point of duty and of honour. Chancellor du Prat declared that he should never cease to feel the shame and dishonour that had fallen upon him by the loss of that country to the crown of France, during his administration, could he but recover it for his sovereign, he would be content to die the next hour.**

* Varchi, Storia Fiorentina 208. Jovius, Historiæ, 27, 45.

† Casalis in Herbert, 233.

‡ Tractatus Confœderationis inter Carolum V Imperatorem Romanorum — — et Clementum, VII Romanum Pontificem conclusus. Du Mont, iv. ii 1.

§ Katona, xx i 551. Zapolya's Complaint respecting the Bull, from which he saw, "S. Sanctitatem—me et incolis regni per censuras ecclesiasticas devovisse et a capite nostro Jesu Christo, quod in ea erat, resectos declarasse."

‖ Cum Cæsareæ Majestati cordi sit ut huic pestifero morbo congruum antidotum præparari possit.

¶ Ce qui a été dit en la communication tenue à Palencia, in du Mont, iv i 502.

** Bullay, 13 Juill. 1529, MS. Maitre de Barre tells him that the expressions which had come to the knowledge of Margaret, and also of the emperor, prevented the

Nevertheless, the necessity of acquiescing in this loss had arrived

In the first place, a continuance of the war no longer offered any prospect of success Even the king's partisans in Italy reminded him that it would be impossible to put an army into the field before the emperor appeared in Italy, that Charles's alliance with the pope would make him master in Upper as well as in Lower Italy, Florence would not be able to resist him, Venice was herself in danger from the defection of Mantua, and could think of nothing but her own safety he would have to contend single-handed against the emperor, who had the bravest troops in the world, and the favour of fortune *

The kingdom and the court, it was also urged, could no longer suffer the French princes to remain captives in Spain, whence occasionally unsatisfactory reports of their health arrived

Thus, therefore, while preparations for war were going on, while hopes of the king's arrival in person were held forth to the Italians, and an invasion of Germany was projected, the negotiations for peace, which had never been definitively broken off, were resumed with fresh earnestness

It was long reported in Rome that the pope was to undertake the task of mediation,† and that he was to conduct affairs in person at some place on the frontiers of France and Spain, for example, Perpignan To this he seemed well inclined, even in March, 1529, the galleys that were to transport him were still pointed out In the end, however, all this was given up, and the matter fell into totally different hands

At a considerably earlier period we find a secret emissary of Francis I in Spain, through whom, addressing himself immediately to his betrothed bride, Queen Leonora, he expressed his wishes that all obstacles to their union might be removed as quickly as possible, and placed all his affairs with the emperor in her hands The queen was, as may be imagined, delighted at this message, she declared that she had always relied on the king's good intentions, and had therefore overlooked all that had passed As the envoy refused to treat with the Grand Chancellor on the ground that he was a lover of war,—perhaps because his consideration at court was increased by keeping those eminent men whom war would have rendered necessary, at a distance from it,—Queen Leonora declared that the negotiation was now her business, and that she would bring it to a conclusion alone ‡

I cannot ascertain precisely the date of this mission Suffice it to observe, that it was an attempt to withdraw the negotiations from the usual channel, and the regular mode of proceeding

Duchess Louisa next addressed herself to the emperor's aunt, the Governess of the Netherlands Her motives were doubtless chiefly personal, for while her grandsons were prisoners, she could not endure the thought of the fresh campaign which she saw that her son must almost inevitably undertake. She represented to Margaret that it more especially devolved on them, the two oldest female relatives of the contending princes, to endeavour to effect a reconciliation between them § Margaret, too, was of opinion, that the animosity between the two monarchs had been raised to such a pitch by long-protracted hostilities, by the letters and documents that had been interchanged, and by the challenges that had been sent, that women alone could succeed in bringing about an accommodation ‖ The emperor still thought himself bound in honour to insist on the execution of the treaty of Madrid, he wondered not a little that Margaret, entirely contrary to her former character and habits, listened to the flattering language of the duchess ¶ It was no easy task for her to change his dispositions, and indeed she afterwards took credit for its accomplishment At last, on the 8th of April, she received the fullest authority to negotiate that it was possible to imagine ** Charles V promised, on the word of an emperor, on his honour and under pain of forfeiting his private domains, to ratify any terms which she might conclude It was easier for Francis I to grant full powers Among the reasons why it was expedient that not the king, but his mother, should conduct the negotiations, one of the principal was, that she had not, like him, personally contracted engagements with the Italian powers, Milan, Florence, or Venice.

On the 5th July the two ladies entered Cambray from opposite sides, and took up their abode in two houses connected by a covered way, so that they could see and speak to one another without being observed.

peace They were these "puisque le roi avoit perdu Milan estant luy en administration des affaires, il aimeroit mieux la mort que de faillir a le luy faire recouvrer cela fait il étoit content de mourir une heure après"

* Ottaviano Sforza al vescovo di Lodi Molini, ii 210 Egl Instruzione di Teodoro Triulzio, Guido Rangoni et Joachim a Mess Mauro da Nova, Venezia, 15 Luglio, in Molini, ii 219 "In effecto quest' impresa de tanta extrema importantia si deve extimare, quanta possa essere da l'onore al disonore o per meglio dirlo dal vivere al morire de la prima corona, re et regno di Christianità"

† Hieronymus Niger to Sadolet, v Cal April, 1529 "Quotidie in ore habet (pontifex) divinum consilium suum de profectione ad Cæsarem et de pace publica, quo quidem consilio si integris rebus usus fuisset, non laboraremus" Sadoleti Epp lib. viii p 323

‡ Dechiffrement d'une depesche écrite d'Espagne, Bibl du R MS Bethune, 8543, f 182, without date, place or signature Perhaps of the year 1527, at all events, of the time during which the French princes were in prison "Elle me demanda, si vous vouliez mettre en sa main l'affaire d'entre vous et l'empereur, je luy ai dit que pour cet effet m'aviez depesché vers elle—Elle m'a dit, que la fiance qu'elle avoit toujours eu en votre bonne voulonté envers elle, l'avoit tenue en bonne esperance et lui avoit fait porter patiemment tout ce qui avoit passé Qu'elle vouloit mener cette affaire et que autre ne se meslat qu'elle, et c'estoit son propre fait"

§ Teneur du pouvoir, donné a l'archiduchesse DM iv 2, 15

‖ Her own expressions—Hormayr, Archiv 1810, p 103.

¶ Charles V to the Sieur de Montfort, 16 Mars Pap d'état de Granvelle, i 450. Search ought to be made for Margaret's letter which brought the matter to a conclusion, and which must have been written about this time

** As "Procuratrix généralle et especialle avec plein pouvoir auctorité et mandement especiall pour et en nom de nous pour parler—et finallement traiter et conclure bonne ferme secure paix amitié ligue et confédération."

The negotiations could not be very difficult, since the preliminaries must have been agreed on before they were opened France now actually engaged to pay the two millions demanded, to abandon all her claims and connexions in Italy, and lastly, to renounce her suzerainty over Flanders and Artois On the other hand, Charles V gave up some comparatively unimportant claims, e g to Peronne and Boulogne, and, for the present, relinquished his scheme of conquering Burgundy * The principle which then prevailed throughout Europe—that of severing states, and making them independent of each other—was observable in this treaty of peace Whilst France gave up its foreign enterprises, its internal affairs remained untouched Burgundy and Valois at length, after so many bloody wars, separated Burgundy had not indeed realised all its pretensions, but it had gained immense advantages It had succeeded in circumscribing the house of its rival within the limits of France

But it was not to be imagined that every thing was thus concluded Francis I protested against the treaty of Cambray, as he had done against that of Madrid He persisted in affirming that Asti and Milan were his inalienable inheritance, and that of his children, that Genoa belonged to him, that it was impossible for a treaty wrung from him first by his own captivity, and then by that of his children, to be binding upon him † When the verification of it was laid before the parliament, the procureur-general, Maître François Rogier, solemnly protested against it, on the ground that it had been brought about by the violence done to a feudal lord by his vassal, and was therefore contrary to the fundamental laws of the empire ‡ But these protests were only the utterance of the feeling that France yielded to force,—and very reluctantly, they were an act of reservation for the future, wholly insignificant for the present, and therefore attracting no attention

At first every one rejoiced that peace was actually concluded On all the points but those in which an express alteration had been agreed on—and these were but four—the treaty of Madrid was confirmed, they were now both proclaimed together, and entered in the state register The letter in which Duchess Louisa announces the conclusion of the treaty to her son is very characteristic; the safety of his person, she tells him, resulting from the peace which God had granted them, is dearer to her than her own life,§ the personal danger into which he was about to rush, was the chief motive for her efforts The Netherlanders were very proud that such an act had emanated from their regent, the French delegate was asked at a dinner, whether people had imagined that lady capable of such a work, and whether the French were satisfied with it? The Frenchman replied, "that a part of the merit was due to his king, that on the mere word of the archduchess he had discharged 15,000 landsknechts, with whom he could have struck some decisive blow."‖ The pope was more delighted than anybody, he found no words strong enough to express his sense of the service which Duchess Louisa had rendered to Europe It was a peculiar satisfaction to him that the treaty contained no stipulations in favour of the members of the Ligue, of whom he had to complain In spite of all its provisions, he had no belief in any long continuance of the emperor's ascendancy The protests of the French are quite in accordance with Clement's intimations, that as soon as the king had his sons back again, and not till then, remedies would be found for all the other evils ¶

Nor was this the only cause of the pope's satisfaction In the course of the negotiations, as well as in the treaty itself, the king showed himself no less an enemy of the religious innovations than the emperor. In the full powers granted by Francis, he alleges as one of the grounds of his desire for peace, his earnest wish to suppress the heresies which had arisen in Christendom, 'that the Church might be honoured as the salvation of souls required "** In the 43d article of the treaty of peace, it was said, that the emperor and the king were determined to maintain the holy see in all its dignity and consideration, as beseemed their imperial and royal station and power Among the articles of the treaty of Madrid that were confirmed, was the one in which the king promised the emperor his aid against the heretics, no less than against the Turks So entire a change being thus effected in the relations of the great powers, the most important question now was, What would be the course pursued by the King of England, whose projects of divorce had, by a sort of reaction, so largely contributed to the change?

* The Emperor, however, remarks in his counter report of 1536, that he "ursach und gewalt gehabt hatte, noch grössere und mehrers von ihm (dem Konig) zu begeren und abzunehmen dieweil ich damals zu wasser und zu land sighaft von Gott und mit treffenlicher rustung gefasst und—vil sterker denn er gewesen bin" " had at that time cause and power to demand and to take greater and more things from him (the king), since I was then by God's grace victorious by land and water, and prepared with excellent armaments, and much stronger than he"

† Protestation du Roy François contre les Traités de Madrid et de Cambray The title of the document printed in Du Mont, in Dupuy's collection, 179

‡ Protestation du Procureur-General Du M iv ii 52, nr 39.

§ Lettre de Madame au Roi après le traité de Cambray Bethune, 8471 Copie "La seureté, Monseigneur, en la quelle je cognois votre personne par la paix, que j'estime plus que ma propre vie"

‖ De la Pommeraye au connetable, 17 Sept 1529 Beth 8610.

¶ Lettre de Raince, 12 Août, 1529 "Surtout ne pourroit être plus content qu il est de ce qu'il entend qu on a eu memoire de luy, et semble qu'il ayt quelque advis que aucuns des confederes soient aucunement (in some degree) demeurés en derriere, que luy confirme la satisfaction en quoi il est autant ou plus que nulle autre chose et fait bien compte s'ils vouloient aller le chemin qui sera requis, que delivres et retournés en France Messieurs que à tout se aura bon remède"

** "Pour extirper les heresies qui pullulent en la Chrestienté et que l'eglise soit reveree et honorée ainsi qu'il appartient pour le salut de nos ames" Du M ii iv p 16

Wolsey's hope of carrying through these projects had been founded on political combinations which now no longer existed. He thought himself justified in the largest anticipations from the influence of the French court on the see of Rome, and on the gratitude of the latter towards England.

As to the pope, his real opinion was, that the king would do better to take another wife, without any further agitation of the question, and then to call in the Apostolic See as judge.* This, however, the respect for the letter of the laws, which, even in that age, distinguished England, did not permit. The king wished to have the legitimacy of the possible issue of a second marriage fully established: he chose that the power which had bound, should also loose him from his ties. Wolsey hoped that the successes of the Ligue would lead the pope to consent to this. He repeatedly urged Francis to do as much for the dissolution of the marriage, as the King of England had done for the restitution of the children of France; adding, that he had only to declare to the pope that he thought the cause of the King of England just, and that if Rome refused Henry's petition, he should regard it as an offence done to himself, and should never forget it. Francis well knew the importance to himself of Wolsey's continuance in power; and Wolsey reminded him that he should be ruined if this affair were not brought to a successful issue, after the positive assurances he had given the king.† And, in fact, the pope himself wished that the joint importunities of England and France had been such as would have enabled him to excuse himself to the emperor, on the ground of a sort of moral compulsion.‡ But it does not appear that the French thought it expedient to go so far. They had not yet abandoned the idea of a marriage between the Princess Mary, the presumptive heiress to the throne of England, and one of their princes.§

As Henry would not proceed in the affair without the pope, and as no measures seemed likely to be taken for extorting Clement's consent, he was obliged to resort to diplomatic negotiations, the progress and result of which were, from their very nature, dependent on contingencies.

The English delegates who, in March and April, 1528, remained with the pope, did not deceive themselves. "The difficulties and delays which we encounter in this affair, arise," say they, "mainly from fear; we find every one as well disposed as possible to forward the matter, but people are afraid that any unusual favour granted to the king may lead to a new captivity, provided the emperor retains his power."‖ The ambassadors again made an attempt to combat fear by fear. They one day represented to the pope that he would lose the only prince who was really attached to him; "not only the King of England, but the Defender of the Faith," as Wolsey once expressed himself. Then would the papacy, already nodding to its fall, be completely overthrown, to the joy of all men. The pope was not insensible to this danger; he walked up and down the room in their presence, making violent gesticulations, and it was some time before his excitement was calmed.¶ He did, in fact, make some advances to the English in consequence; naming Cardinal Campeggi (who was on the best footing with Henry VIII., and whose appointment was proposed by the ambassadors) legate to England, and granting him authority to declare the papal dispensation on which Henry VIII.'s marriage was founded, operative or the contrary, and the marriage itself valid or invalid, according to his own judgment. This he did in the beginning of June, 1528, while the affairs of the French before Naples were in the most promising state.** The ambassadors had also promised him to induce the Venetians to restore his cities.††

Shortly after followed the defeat of Lautrec before Naples; we have seen what a complete revolution the papal policy instantly underwent in favour of the emperor, and this now necessarily extended to the English affair, in which Charles took so deep an interest.

On the 2d of September, Campeggi was reminded that, however strongly his Holiness might feel himself bound to the King of England, he must also show all possible consideration for the victorious emperor, and not furnish him with fresh occasion for a rupture, which would not only be an obstacle to peace, but would bring utter ruin on the States of the Church.‡‡

In October, 1528, Campeggi came to England. However strong were the expressions which he used with regard to the emperor, it

* Casalis, 13 Jan. Fiddes, p. 461. "Quia nullus doctor in mundo est, qui de hac re melius decernere possit quam ipse rex; itaque si in hoc se resolverint, ut pontifex credit, statim committat causam (in England), aliam uxorem ducat, litem sequatur, mittat pro legato."

† Bellay à Montmorency, 22 Mai, 1528: "en la quelle (l'affaire du divorce) s'il ne s'employoit tant et si avant, qu'il voudroit faire pour le recouvrement des Messrs. les enfans, il pourroit être seur d'avoir causé à mon d. Sr le legat une totale ruine, pour les grandes asseurances qu'il en a toujours baillé à son dit maistre."

‡ D. Knight. Herbert, 218. The pope thinketh he might by good colour say to the emperor, that he was required by the English ambassadeurs et Mr. de Lautrech to proceed in the business.

§ Bellay mentions this motive in a despatch of the 8th Nov. He, for his own part, scruples to concede the point of the nullity of Catharine's marriage, because of the use that might be made of that concession, "où le mariage de M. d'Orleans tireroit. Aucuns de deça disent, que, quoique on fasse, qui espousera la princesse sera après roi d'Angleterre."

‖ Gardiner and Fox Orviet, the last day of March, in Strype's Ecclesiastical Memorials, vol. v. p. 402, that if there were any thing doon novum et gratiosum agaynst the emperors purpose, it should be materia novæ captivitatis.

¶ The same Monday in Easter week, ibid. 423. The pope also gave the French ambassador hopes "qu'entre cy et demain prendra quelque bonne forme de conclusion, qui pourra satisfaire au roy d'Angleterre." Raince; Le Grand, iii. p. 190.

** Commission Viterbii, VI. Jun. (8th June), printed in Herbert, p. 233.

†† This is evident from Casalis's letter in Burnet's History of the Reformation, Records ii. nr. 17. The pope says to the ambassador, Vos scire volo, promissum mihi fuisse, si legatus hic in Angliam mitteretur, futurum ut mihi civitates a Venetis restituerentur.

‡‡ Sanga to Campeggi. Viterbo, 2d Sept. 1528. History of the Popes, i. 126.

was, very soon evident that he had no intention of offering any serious resistance to him. He admonished both the king and Wolsey to desist from their project. He utterly refused to produce the bull by which Wolsey hoped to prove to the Privy Council the pope's favourable intentions towards the king: probably he burned it.* He affected at every step to have recourse to Rome for instructions. He rejected with the utmost vehemence the prevalent notion that, as a marriage with a brother's widow was forbidden in the Old Testament, this was a case in which the pope had no dispensing power. It only remained, therefore, to prove that the dispensation in question was not based on tenable grounds. Here too, however, insurmountable difficulties presented themselves, as the queen, on whose testimony the whole matter depended, constantly affirmed that the marriage with Prince Arthur had not been consummated. She was a woman of so noble and dignified a character, that she was universally believed. She also availed herself of her legal right of protesting against her two judges, on the ground of partiality.†

During these delays, however, the pope became (especially after the affair of Florence) more and more intimately allied with the emperor, who declared that he regarded the interests of his aunt as his own. In May, 1529, the English envoy expressed his fears that the commission of the two cardinals would be formally recalled.‡

This was probably the motive which led the king to open the proceedings without further delay.

On the 31st of March, 1529, they commenced, but on the 29th, instructions had already been sent to Campeggi from Rome, to protract them as much as possible, and by no means to suffer judgment to be pronounced.§ These orders he punctually obeyed. The affair had not got beyond preliminaries and matters of form, when, on the 28th July, Campeggi adjourned the sittings to the 1st of October. He also claimed the holidays of the Roman rota for himself.

After concluding his treaty of peace with the emperor, Clement was still in time to evoke the suit from England to the tribunals of the curia.

On the 9th of July the pope declared to the English envoys, that he shared the opinion common to all the Roman lawyers, that this evocation could no longer be refused. The ambassadors used every possible means of dissuading him from it, but he replied that he was hemmed round by the power of the emperor, who could not only force him to do justice, but in whose hands he himself was. "I see," said he, "the consequences as clearly as you do, but I am between the hammer and the anvil. If I oblige the king, I draw down the most destructive storm on myself and on the church."‖

On the 18th of July peace was proclaimed in Rome between the pope and the emperor. On the 19th, the pope sent word to Cardinal Wolsey that, to his great regret, he found himself compelled to evoke the cause from England to the curia.

Wolsey had always assured his sovereign that he should be able to carry through the affair to which, as affecting him personally, Henry attached the greatest importance. The king now saw himself cited to appear in person in Rome, and what particularly irritated him, under an express pecuniary penalty.¶ He thought this so offensive to his dignity, that he did not choose to let his subjects know it.

Wolsey had also assured him that France would never desert him. Even in May, 1529, he would not believe this possible; he caught with eagerness at every rumour of a new rupture between that country and the empire, and founded fresh plans upon it. But what he refused to believe came to pass.

Nothing remained for King Henry but to accede to the peace. His participation in the war had of late been so slight, that the peace which he concluded seemed but a supplement to that of France; it has hardly a place in English history. It was enough for the king that France undertook to pay the money which he claimed from the emperor, out of the above-mentioned two millions.**

But no one acquainted with the character of Henry, could for a moment expect that he would desist from his great project, the divorce. The desire of having a legitimate heir and successor by Anne Boleyn, was become his ruling passion. Indeed the affair now assumed a far more important character than heretofore.

Above all, the downfall of Wolsey was become inevitable. Already had his anti-Austrian measures experienced opposition, not only in the Privy Council, but in the nation. Any war with the Netherlands was unpopular in England, the English merchants, discontented at the breach of the peace, had been at one time brought only by a sort of compulsion to resort to the markets as theretofore. The king had been mainly persuaded into this policy by Wolsey's assurances that the alliance would be productive of immediate pecu-

* Pallavicini denies (lib ii c xv) the existence of this bull which Guicciardini affirmed. But it is only necessary to read the above-mentioned report by Casalis on his negotiations with the pope in Dec 1528, in order to dispel all doubt. S. D N injecta in meum brachium manu—dixit—bullam decretalem dedisse, ut tantum regi ostenderetur concremareturque. Burnet, Records, ii 17, p 42. What this bull contained we cannot of course make out, as nobody saw it but the king and Campeggi. I am not disposed to believe Guicciardini's assertion.

† Bellay, 17th Nov, 1528.

‡ Gardiner, 4th May, which was confirmed by divers other letters from our agents. Herbert, p 232.

§ Sanga al Cl Campeggio, 29 Maggio, 1529. Sua Beatitudine ricorda che il procedere sia lento et in modo alcuno non si venghi al giudicio. Lettere de' principi, ii.

‖ Burnet, from the ambassadors' despatches, p 76.

¶ "The K Highness supposeth — that it should not be nedeful any such letters citatorial, conteyning matier prejudicial to his persone and royal estate to be showed to his subjects."—Gardiner to Wolsey, 4 Aug. State Papers, i p 336.

** See Commissio ad tractandum de jocalibus recipiendis. Rymer vi ii 19. "Cum oratoribus," says Francis I "Angliæ regis, pro omnibus obligationibus absque pignore contractis convenimus."

mary advantage to himself The cardinal often represented to the French ambassadors what arts, "what terrible alchemy," as he expressed it, were necessary to enable him to withstand his enemies * But all his resources were now exhausted His foreign policy, which had been calculated on a union between England, France, and Rome, had completely failed Despairing of being able to carry through the projects which he had so zealously encouraged, it is unquestionable that he at length advised the king to desist from them But he thus lost, as might be expected, the king's grace and favour, he irritated a considerable party, which Anne Boleyn had won over, and particularly her father, who had been created Marquis of Rochfort old enemies and new rose up against him, and just then Suffolk, who during his stay in France had shown himself little disposed to favour the cardinal's schemes, returned, and now openly quarrelled with him † Norfolk had never been his friend

Thus fell Wolsey In November, 1529, he was deprived of the Great Seal, in December he was found guilty of having infringed the privileges of the kingdom, by an undue exercise of his power as legate Neither the returning support of the French, nor (to use Norfolk's words) "the counsels of his stargazers," could save him.

A still more important point, however, was, that these affairs became the subject of an angry controversy between the king and the pope The declaration of the former, — that he would marry Anne Boleyn, if the pope allowed it, and if the pope did not allow it, he would still marry her — sounds like a jest,‡ but it was the prelude to an event which changed the history of England Wolsey is reported to have urged the pope to excommunicate the King of England, because, in that case, the people would revolt against him § Whether this be well-founded or not, the bare rumour was sufficient to determine the king to put an end at once to the possibility of such an interference with the internal affairs of his kingdom

To return to the emperor It was doubtless advantageous to him that he was for the present delivered from the hostility of England, and had his hands free in that direction, yet he soon expressed a doubt whether he should not be compelled, by the honour of his house, to draw his sword again in the cause of his aunt, Henry's repudiated wife

His letters show that he by no means calculated on the stability of peace, when, in the summer of 1529, he made serious preparations for going to Italy.

This design he had long seriously entertained He seemed suddenly conscious that the years of youth were past for him, he felt himself a man, and wished to take a personal share in the great concerns which had hitherto been carried on in his name, "to show the world," as one of his confidential friends said, "his true self, his mind and heart, which hitherto had been known to them alone"‖ He was animated by a completely personal and chivalrous ambition. He hoped either immediately to bring about a peace in Italy, or to give such an impulse to the war as would lead to its successful termination, then to receive the imperial crown, and to repair to Germany, whither, as he said, he was called by his anxiety lest the greater part of the country should secede from the church of Rome, or be overrun and conquered by the Turks ¶ In reply to a message from his brother, respecting an impending invasion of the Turks, he sent him word that he would not only assist him, but, if possible, take the field himself

Had not this desire been so strong within him, he would not so easily have entered upon a negotiation, in which he ceded to Portugal the claims of the crown of Castile to the Moluccas, for the sum of 350,000 florins The Spaniards were not very well satisfied at this, but the emperor wanted to be rid of these disputed questions, which had already led to sanguinary quarrels in the East,** and, above all, he was in want of money He was well content that the Portuguese found means to pay him by rapid instalments

He now turned a deaf ear to all opposition He said he could not be satisfied with himself till he had taken this journey

On the 27th of July, 1529, the emperor took ship at Barcelona, and on the 12th of August, landed at Genoa ††

In all the plenitude of a power, not (like that of the emperors of old) composed of German elements alone, but formed of a wonderful combination of the south and the north, Charles now appeared on the Italian frontiers of the ancient empire In his retinue we find all the glorious names of Castilian history; Mendoza, Guzman, Pacheco, Manrique, Zuniga, Toledo, Cueva, Rojas, Ponce de Leon, every great house had sent a representative, and the most brilliant among them all was Alvarez Ossorio, Marquis of Astorga They were joined by Navarrese, Catalans, and Aragonese He also brought fresh troops from

* Bellay, 16th Feb 1528, in Le Grand, Hist du Divorce, iii p 84

† According to a letter of Bellay's of the 20th May, the king was persuaded by the cardinal "qu'il n'a tant avancé le mariage qu il eust fait, s'il eust voulu" Le Grand, p 313

‡ From a letter of the emperor to Ferdinand, 10th Jan 1530

§ See the extracts from a letter from Chapuis to Charles in Hormayr's Archiv 1810, p 131 The Joncquim there alluded to is no other than the Genoese, John Joachim, who is elsewhere so frequently mentioned

‖ Philibert of Orange's Instructions to Balanca, Pap d'état, de Granv i 431 Apres avoir veu le tant grand desir quy (l'empereur) montre, de se trouver en quelque lieu pour donner a cognoistre a tout le monde ce que preca nous aultres ses serviteurs avons cogneu, qu'est d'avoir le cœur tel quil a

¶ Sandoval, ii p 25

** Herrera Historia de las Indias, Dec iv lib v p 117

†† L'empereur au Sieur de Montfort Pap d'état i p 413 When difficulties occurred, he said, "que je n'estois en fasson du monde deliberé de lasser de faire ce voyage, et que je ne me pouvois satisfayre de moi mesme si je ne le faisois"

Malaga to reinforce those in Milan and Naples. The imperial power, personified in the emperor, acquired a romantic and highly Catholic character, from the new elements combined with it. It was only necessary to look at this court, in order confidently to predict its intentions.

Let us next observe how, meanwhile, matters had gone on in Germany.

CHAPTER V.

DIET OF SPIRES, A. D. 1529.

WE have seen how great was the influence of political affairs on the rise and progress of religious reform. Had it not been for the divisions existing between the two highest powers of Europe, the decisive resolutions of the diet of 1526 would never have passed.

Since that time, however, no further proceedings of practical importance had taken place in the empire.

The mission to the emperor, which was then resolved on, was withheld under frivolous pretences. The Saxon party confidently maintained that this was solely the effect of the secret intrigues of the spiritual estates, who seemed to fear that the growing differences between the emperor and the pope might lead the former to decide in a manner disadvantageous to them.

A congress of the princes of the empire held at Esslingen, in December, 1526, had no other object than the defence of the country against the Ottomans; the resolutions which it passed were neither important in themselves, nor productive of the slightest results.

In May, 1527, a diet was convoked at Regensburg; but it was so ill attended that those present did not even consider themselves authorised to deliberate upon matters which had been expressly referred to them; *e. g.* the affair of the deputation to the emperor abovementioned. They passed a resolution "to undertake no business whatever."*

In March, 1528, a new diet was appointed to be held at Regensburg; but the pope's adherents were still not without apprehensions as to the probable decisions of the assembled states; affairs in general were indeed still too uncertain to enable them to form any settled opinions themselves. In the first place, King Ferdinand postponed the opening of the meeting from March till May;† then, an edict of the emperor's appeared, which peremptorily forbade it, without assigning any satisfactory reasons; only, to quote the words of the edict, from "notable grounds and causes."‡ We find from records of the papal court, that "no good conclusion" was anticipated there.§

But the more weighty matters of foreign policy were now decided, and a complete change in the internal affairs of Germany was inevitable.

The emperor's sentiments were learned, from a distance indeed, but quite unequivocally. We have already alluded to the proceedings of his vice-chancellor, Waldkirch. He declared to the people of Augsburg, in the plainest manner, that the emperor was displeased with them because they had introduced changes in religion. In Strasburg he threatened the nobles who sat in the council with loss of life, if they did not oppose the abolition of the mass.‖ The impression he made, and the hopes excited by the renewed connexion with the imperial court, may be inferred from this, among other circumstances;—the chapter of Constance, which shortly before had been compelled, to yield to the force of the new opinions, and to emigrate to Ueberlingen, now chose him, the vice-chancellor, as coadjutor.

The peace concluded by the emperor with the pope was of immense advantage to the bishops, as it not only reconciled, but united, the two supreme powers. The clergy could now once more reckon on strenuous and efficient support.

This was the more welcome at a moment when they all felt the dangers by which they were threatened by the progress of reform in Switzerland. We discover from numerous publications expressive of their opinions, what anxiety Zwingli's departure from the established doctrine concerning the Lord's Supper excited in all quarters; it was feared that the Oberland cities, infected with the new heresy, would separate themselves from the empire.¶

Nor can we deny that the violent courses into which the landgrave had suffered himself to be led by Pack's forgeries, had exercised a very unfavourable influence on the cause of the reformation. They had confirmed the Swabian league in its anti-evangelical system; and it now excluded the Memmingen delegates from its council, because Memmingen had abolished the service of the mass, and embraced Zwingli's opinions.

In his brief of October, 1528, to which we have alluded, the pope had solemnly called upon the emperor to take up the cause of religion at the approaching diet with greater earnestness than heretofore: immediate care must, he said, be taken that at least the evil be not suffered to spread. One effect of this was that, on the last day of November, the convocation of a new diet, to be holden at Spires on the 21st of February, 1529, was issued. The States were apprised that no

* I remark that the extract from this recess in Häberlin (xi. 46) does not precisely correspond with the original (Reichsabschiede, ii. 185).

† Neudecker Actenstücke, i. 26.

‡ Proclamation in the Frankfurt Acts of the 10th April, which, however, reached Germany in time.

§ Sanga a Castiglione, Lettre di diversi autori, p. 56. Prudentemente pensò, poter facilmente essere che ne succedesse qualche non buona determinatione.

‖ Röhrich Gesch. der Reform im Elsass, I. 360.

¶ Es weisst der gmein Man nitt glich, ob er sy Schwytz oder ghör zum Rych. The common people do not rightly know whether they are Swiss, or belong to the empire. (Lied gegen Constanz, bei Vierordt, p. 34.)

notice would be taken of the absent, and that those who were present would proceed to business in the same manner as if the assembly were complete.* The subjects specially announced for deliberation were, the armament against the Turks, the violations of the public peace, and, above all, the religious innovations.

This time the announcement of a diet was serious and sincere, the imperial commissioners made their appearance at the time appointed, the ecclesiastical princes came in greater number than usual, and those who did not come, sent the most zealous of their ministers in their stead.† The Bishop of Constance, for example, was represented by the same Faber, who, as we saw, took an active part in the political and religious troubles of Switzerland. He had seen Erasmus on his way, and expressed himself in such terms, that the latter expected nothing but war and violence.‡ The Catholic principle had also gained new adherents among the secular princes. Duke Henry of Mecklenburg, who had hitherto been reckoned among the evangelical party, now entirely concurred with his son Magnus, Bishop of Schwerin,—one of the most violent opponents of change. The Elector Palatine, who had almost formally joined the reformers, forbade his people to attend the preachings. It was thought that he had been persuaded to take this course by his brother, the Count Palatine Frederic, who had once more conceived hopes of obtaining the hand of an Austrian princess. "The Palatinate," says a letter from Spires, "will have nothing more to do with Saxony."

Under these circumstances, surrounded by opinions favourable to their wishes, the imperial commissioners were enabled to bring forward measures of a decisive nature, in the Proposition§ which they delivered on the 15th of March.

While, in consequence of the pope's consent, they announced a council with greater certainty than before, and at the same time touched upon the old question—how affairs were to be carried on in the interval—they proposed formally to revoke the article of the recess‖ of 1526, in virtue of which all existing innovations were recognised and admitted, on the ground, that it gave occasion to "much ill council and misunderstanding,"¶ and to substitute for it another ordinance of a directly opposite tendency, in favour of the spiritual authorities.

This was the notion entertained by most of the orthodox. In the instructions given by Duke George of Saxony to his ambassador to the diet, we find that he too regarded this article as the cause of all the existing troubles.** He demanded that a uniform standard of faith should be established, and that the representative and government of his imperial majesty should not surrender their power.

The first thing was to appoint a committee to deliberate and report upon the Proposition. In this, as was fully to be expected, the orthodox party were greatly superior. Among the electoral votes, only that of Saxony was on the evangelical side. Of the nine princes' votes, five were ecclesiastical and three of the secular decidedly Catholic, while not only Faber, but Leonard von Eck, the leader of the reaction in Bavaria, was a member of the committee. There could be little doubt of the result. On the 24th of March the committee declared its assent to the proposed article, and only added the following provisions. "Those who had held to the edict of Worms, should continue to do so in the districts which had departed from it, no further innovation should be introduced, and no one should be prevented from saying mass. No ecclesiastical body should be deprived of its authority or revenues, on pain of ban and reban. Lastly, the sects which deny the sacrament of the true body and blood of Christ, should in no wise be tolerated any more than the anabaptists." With these additions the report was laid before the States.

All the measures of the States in favour of the evangelical doctrines had been the consequence of the leaning of the majority towards them. The majority was now reversed. What the former had enacted, the present sought to repeal. In the sittings of the 6th and 7th of April they adopted the report of the commission without the smallest alteration.

Nor were the friends of reform to be deluded by the mere sound of the words, into the idea that the only thing intended was to check the progress of the movement. This was undoubtedly the immediate purpose, but, on a careful examination, it was evident that these ordinances were incompatible with the maintenance of the changes already effected in the several countries, on the strength of former recesses.

One leading motive to the previous recess had been, the necessity of appeasing the internal troubles in the several countries, hence

* The printed copy of the extract names the first, the MS copy, the twenty first. "And if you do not appear within ten days after the day appointed, our envoys and commissaries will notwithstanding, discuss and determine affairs with the States then and there present, in all respects as if you and others who absented yourselves on slight and frivolous grounds had been present. All which we shall attend to and execute with firmness and vigour, in the same manner as if all the States, whether present or absent, had agreed to them."

† "I am afraid," writes Jacob Sturm to Peter Butz in the middle of March, "from what I see of the persons here, there will not be much to be obtained."—"In summa, Christus est denuo in manibus Caiaphae et Pilati." Jung Gesch des Reichstags zu Speier, Beil nr 4.

‡ Erasmi Epistolae, ii 1220.

§ See p 152, Translator's note.

‖ *Abschied.* See Preface, Translator's note.

¶ "Your Imperial Majesty," says the Proposition, "hereby repeals, revokes and annuls the above mentioned article contained in the above mentioned recess, now as then, and then as now, all out of your own imperial absolute power (Machtvollkommenheit)". Muller, Historie von der evangelischen Stande, Protestation und Appellation, p 22.

** "Denn dieweil es ein Jeder sol machen wie er wil und gegen Gott und kais Maj vornimmt zu verantworten, so kann kein Einigkeit seyn."—"For since every man is to do as he will and as he thinks he can answer it to God and his imperial majesty, there can be no unity." Instrument in the Dresden Archives.

it had been left to princes and subjects to come to an understanding with one another on religious questions, as they could. Now, those who had prohibited the Latin mass were compelled to tolerate it, and nothing could be expected but an entire dissolution of all that had been settled.

Further, the very existence of the changes that had been adopted, rested on a tacit denial of the episcopal jurisdictions; the authority of the bishops (that is, their spiritual authority) was now established anew. The right of appointing or removing preachers was, among others, unquestionably restored to them.* How could this be endured for a moment?

The reforms were still going on most prosperously in many cities. Some had delayed to take the final step, because they were still in expectation of some new express concession from the diet of the empire, e. g. the admission of both elements in the sacrament. They were now condemned to abide implicitly, and for ever, by the established forms.

Lastly, Zwingli's followers were absolutely excluded from the peace of the empire.

In short, though the dissidents were not expressly admonished in the recess, to return to the bosom of the church they had abandoned, it was unquestionable that by assenting to it they would bring about the total and speedy ruin of the evangelical church, which was just rising into importance.

It appeared as if the religious reforms which had begun to acquire consistency from the situation of the political affairs of Europe, were now about to be overthrown by the changes which those affairs had undergone. The great community of the empire, which for a while had wavered, now resumed its station on the side of the two great combined powers.

There remained also the most important of all considerations for the evangelical party, viz., whether, supposing they were inclined to venture to resist those powers, they had lawful grounds for doing so.

The question arose, whether, in the present case, a resolution of the majority of the states of the empire was binding upon the minority.

This question was of a general nature. When an institution has been established by lawful means, and has actually attained to full life and vigour, can the supreme power morally assume the right to overthrow and annihilate the new structure? Has not the body which has thus legally and efficiently constituted itself, the right to exist, and to defend its existence?

The imperial power had, on a former occasion, found itself unable to heal the general divisions, and had voluntarily abandoned its functions to the several territorial sovereigns; was it justified, now that it had acquired greater strength, in destroying what was in fact the result of its own act of delegation? This nobody could admit; otherwise institutions of the greatest antiquity might, during some of the vacillations to which power vested in a fluctuating majority is exposed, be brought into question. Nothing would be secure or permanent: for when once institutions had received the sanction of law, how were they to be distinguished in principle from those which had subsisted for ages?

In the present case, too, it was to be observed, that with regard to one of the most important of those ordinances,—that enjoining the toleration of the mass,—nothing was said either in the proposition, the report of the commission, or the transcript.† Landgrave Philip would not admit that the majority of the states had the right to pass decrees so deeply affecting the internal affairs of the territories of the minority, without their assent.

In this declaration, Hessen, electoral Saxony, Luneburg, and Anhalt, together with Markgrave George of Brandenburg, concurred.

The cities viewed the matter under another aspect. Their delegates in the committee remarked, that Faber had worked upon the princes mainly by insisting upon and exaggerating the dangerous consequences of the former concessions.‡ To this they replied, that Germany was indebted for the tranquillity she enjoyed, to that very recess which they were now called upon to revoke. If, in these hasty times, they were to pass resolutions of such gravity, directly opposed to the former, nothing could be expected to result but division, and indescribable perplexities and evils.§ As yet the cities were unanimous, those which had remained Catholic, as well as those which had become Protestant. The reply above mentioned is their common work. Vainly did Count Palatine Frederic represent to the reformers that they were disobedient to the imperial edict, that their innovations led rather to discontent and trouble than to the honour of God, they replied, that what they had done was not an act of hos-

* Furstenberg, Wednesday after Quasimodogeniti (7th April). "Es werden in dem allerlei Wortlin ingeschlichen, die den Stadten, als den man ufsetzig und gefer ist nit treglich noch leidlich seyn, mit Namen dass man niemand an seiner Oberkeyt und Herkommen vergweltigen soll, damit wird den Geistlichen, so solcher Artikel angenommen und verwilligt wird, erfolgen, die Prädicanten zu setzen und zu entsetzen, alle Missbrauch wieder zu erheben und andere wieder anzurichten."—"There were all sorts of little words slipped in, which are not tolerable or endurable to the cities, against which, they (the orthodox majority) are violent and dangerous, and especially that their authority and traditional jurisdiction should be forcibly set aside, in order that the clergy (in case the said article is accepted and granted) may continue to appoint and to displace the preachers, to restore all the old abuses, and to establish new ones." Frankf. Acten.

† Extract from the Protest (Beschwerungsschrift), Muller, p. 33.

‡ Matthias Pfarrer bei Jung, nr. vii. "Der Doctor Faber bildt mit solcher Unworheit und Lugen in die Fursten, —was uss der Ler gefolg hab und noch folgen werd, das do frilich in keines menschen gedanken ich geswige thun file und verbittert die Fursten mit solchen Reden."—"Dr. Faber represents with such falsehood and lies to the princes what has followed and will follow from the doctrine, such as truly never could come into any man's thoughts, much less to act upon, and embitters the princes against us with such discourse."

§ "Der erbern Frei und Reichsstate Gesandten Bedenken." "The scruples of the worshipful the envoys of the free and imperial cities," (8th April,) Jung. nr. 26.

tility or insubordination to the emperor, but a measure intended to maintain peace among their people, and for the relief of consciences, that none could have a greater dread of any kind of disturbance than they King Ferdinand entreated them two or three times to assent to the report laid before them, and added, that the emperor would hold this in most gracious remembrance They replied, that they would obey the emperor in all that could further the maintenance of peace and the honour of God *

Overpowering as the majority was, it did not think it expedient to show an utter disregard of so determined a resistance The cities especially, had strongly objected to the use of the word supremacy, in the article concerning the spiritual power — a word which had been carefully avoided in the recess of 1526 The majority at last thought it better to omit this word, and, as before, only to forbid the subtraction of revenues and lands from the church It added, that no one should protect the lieges and subjects of another state against their lawful lords † But this, too, was strongly objected to by the evangelical minority They feared that, if the words were taken literally, a bishop would think himself entitled to regard the preachers as his subjects and lieges, and that, in conformity with the article of the recess, they must be delivered up to him — an obligation which had been disclaimed long before the introduction of the new doctrines Forty years ago, Frankfurt had refused to comply with such a demand made by Archbishop Berthold Moreover, this was only a single point, and their causes of complaint were numerous

But the majority was inflexible, and it now remained for the evangelical party to consider whether they should allow a resolution which threatened them with destruction, to acquire the validity of law

On the 12th of April, the Saxon envoy, Minkwitz, declared in the full assembly of the empire, that they were resolved not to allow this He insisted chiefly on the religious grounds In affairs of conscience, he said, a majority had no force; but besides, by what right did the diet venture to denounce as unchristian, doctrines which a part of the States held to be Christian, before the council, so often demanded, had been holden? The minority would never consent to this, they would not consent that those who had hitherto conformed to the edict of Worms, should now be forbidden to abide by it, for this would be to pass condemnation on their own doctrines The other reformers were greatly rejoiced at seeing their cause pleaded with such zeal ‡ Minkwitz urged the States of the empire to adhere to their former decree; if this had been perverted to any bad purpose (which, he affirmed, on the evangelical side was not the case), the evil might be remedied by a declaration Under these conditions, he promised that the party to which he belonged would assent to the other resolutions.

But all his arguments were vain

On the 19th of April, King Ferdinand, Waldkirch, and the other commissioners appeared in the assembly of the States, thanked them for their "Christian, faithful and assiduous services," and declared their resolutions accepted, so that there only remained to reduce them into the form of a recess They rejected the proposals and objections of the Elector of Saxony and his adherents, solely on the ground that the resolutions were "adopted according to ancient praiseworthy usage, by the greater part of the electors and princes," so that the rest must also submit to them § The evangelical princes, startled at so direct a refusal, which had the air of a reproof,‖ and, as it was read aloud before all the States, must be entered on the records of the empire, retired for a moment into an adjoining room, in order instantly to agree upon some answer. But the king and the imperial commissioners were not disposed to wait for this In reply to a request of the princes, that they would not refuse a short delay, King Ferdinand said that he had received the positive commands of his imperial majesty, these he had executed, and so the matter must remain the articles were determined on ¶ So saying, he and the commissioners left the house Still more irritated by the contempt for their dignity and their rights which this conduct implied, the evangelical States now determined to execute a project which they had conceived some weeks before, as soon as they saw the turn affairs were taking at the diet They resolved to resort to the only legal means of resistance left them It was evidently impossible to make the assembly recede from its resolutions, to submit to them, would be to renounce their own existence. They reappeared in the same sitting — not indeed before the king and the imperial commissioners, but before the States still assembled, — and caused that protest to be read aloud, from which they took the name their descendants still bear—Protestants

They especially insisted on the fundamental principles of the laws of the empire ** They

* Furstenberg, Monday after Quasimodogeniti (7th April) "Keyserlich Maj begeren halber wiren sie ur bittig, wess sie zu der ere Gottes auch frieden und ruhe dienlich gehelfen mochten, sollt man sie allerunterthanig gehorsam spuren " — "In consequence of his Imperial Majesty's desire, they respectfully promise that wherein soever they can be helpful to the honour of God, and the peace and tranquillity of the realm, you shall find them most dutifully obedient "

† So it was inserted in the Recess, § 10 Unterthanen und Verwandte

‡ Furstenberg He conducted their affairs "with the greatest earnestness, bravely, and for the best "

§ Intended message which his royal highness (Konigl Durchlauchtigkeit) caused to be read aloud In the Instrumentum Appellationis of Muller, p 72

‖ They call it "an almost insolent rebuke "

¶ Narrative in the Appellations Instrument, p 75 and in the letter of the Strasburg envoy, 21st April, Jung nr 44

** A legal argument of a general nature which they adduce is, that "auch in menschen Handlungen und Sachen das mirer wider das minder nicht fürdrücken möcht da die Sachen nit ir vil in ein gemein, sundern jeden sunderlich belangt." — "In human dealings and affairs, the

declared that they could not be obliged, without their consent, to give up the privileges secured to them by the recess lately drawn up at Spires, which had been confirmed by such strong mutual promises, and attested by their common seals, that the attempt of the other States to repeal this by their separate act, was null and void, and had no authority over them; that they should go on to conduct themselves towards their subjects in matters of religion, according to the terms of the former recess, and as they thought they could answer it to God and the emperor If the other States were not to be restrained from framing the present recess with the offensive resolutions, they begged that their protest might at least be incorporated with it

This declaration, the mere form of which is most remarkable, was expressed with all possible external deference and courtesy The States were all spoken of as "our dear lords, cousins, uncles, and friends," they were entitled, with the most careful attention to their several distinctions, "You, well beloved, and you, others"* To the former were addressed "friendly requests," to the latter, "gracious consideration" (*gnadiges Gesinnen*), and while they do not for an instant lose sight of their princely dignity, they beg their opponents not to misunderstand the course which they feel themselves compelled to adopt in return, they promise the former to deserve this by their friendship, and the latter, to requite it by their good will The style of the documents of this century certainly have no claim to be called beautiful or classical, but they are suited to the circumstances, and have a marked character,—like the men of that age and all that they do

The king, to whom this protest was delivered, together with some additions made the following day, did not think it expedient to accept it, nevertheless it made an immense impression That a diet could thus end in open disunion, seemed to promise nothing less than immediate violence On the 20th, Henry of Brunswick and Philip of Baden were commissioned by the majority to endeavour to mediate between the parties

The points on which the mediators agreed with the evangelical party are very remarkable.

They conceded that the article concerning the jurisdiction of the clergy over their subjects, and others connected with them by secular relations, should receive certain limitations

The evangelical party, on the other hand, promised that no further innovation should be attempted before the convocation of a council, and especially that no sect should be tolerated which denied the sacrament of the true body and blood of Christ.

The two parties agreed mutually to tolerate their differences as to the service of the mass, no sovereign was to have any thing to say on this head, out of his own secular dominions †

These terms were actually accepted by the evangelical princes, the cities inclining to Zwingli's views were also inclined to consent to them

It is evident, that, had the only question been, to acquiesce in some check being put to the progress of innovation (in so far as that could be effected by legal means), they would have given way, their position was entirely a defensive one it was only against the influence of the spiritual jurisdiction, recognised anew by the diet, that they determined to make a stand

But the composition of the majority left little hope that these proposals would be accepted They might obtain the assent of a few temporal princes, but the spiritual, to whom the revolution in public affairs appeared to open a brilliant prospect of the restoration of their power, disdained to listen to them Nor were all the temporal princes satisfied with the first resolutions of the committee Duke George of Saxony demanded more precise regulations concerning the deserted convents and the married priests, he wanted that all references to the Holy Scriptures at variance with tradition, should be forbidden ‡ But above all it was impossible to gain over King Ferdinand He was irritated that the evangelical princes had framed and published a protest, without first attempting to negotiate with him, that they had sent it to him with so little ceremony, and had even rejected negotiations which he had empowered Planitz to open He was also greatly displeased with the evangelical cities, especially Strasburg, which, shortly before the diet, had abolished the mass, nor could he be prevailed on to allow Daniel Mieg, the delegate of that city, to take his seat in the Council of Regency He therefore now declined any further attempt at a better understanding, and rejected the proposals of the two mediators He refused to allow the protest to be incorporated in the recess, or even any mention to be made of it

In consequence of this, the evangelical

---

more ought not to oppress the less, since the affair does not belong to many of them in common, but to each in particular" Müller, p 114

* *Eure Liebden und Ihr Andern* It is impossible to find in another language terms which represent the precise distinctions implied in these and the following words The reader will understand that they are among the various graduated forms of respectful address.—Trans

† "Also dass kein Churfurst noch andre Stande ussert-halb ihrer weltlichen Oberkeiten (Gebiete) den andern zu oder von sinem alten oder neuen Furnemen oder Haltung der Messen in eynichem Wege vergweltigen, darzu oder davon dringen sol"—"So that no elector nor other estate, out of his own temporal jurisdiction (territory), should compel another to or from his old or new opinions, or, in any way whatsoever, should urge him to or from the maintenance of the mass" Article of Composition Muller, p 42 Walch xvi 422, where, however, great errors occur (e g, *bessern*, instead of *besten*) Jung nr 45

‡ Letter to his ambassador, 17th April He requires the addition, "dass sich niemands unterstehe, die h Schrift weiter zu deuten oder Disputation einzuführen, denn wie dieselbigen angenominenen Lerer oder der merer Tail unter inen thut anzeigen und beschliessen"—"That nobody should venture to comment on the Holy Scriptures, or to introduce disputations further than the said accepted teachers, or the greater part of them, do actually teach and decide"

princes utterly disregarded Ferdinand's request that they would give no further extension or publicity to the protest

A formal instrument, with all the documents annexed, was drawn up, in which the united princes, Elector John of Saxony, Markgrave George of Brandenburg, Dukes Ernest and Francis of Brunswick-Luneburg, Landgrave Philip of Hessen, and Prince Wolfgang of Anhalt, appealed from the wrongs and offences done to them at the diet, to the emperor, the next general free assembly of holy Christendom, or to a Congress of the German nation

On the following Sunday, April 25th, the necessary legal form was given to this manifesto This took place (for the spot is pointed out with an accuracy worthy of notice) "in the lodging of Chaplain Peter Mutterstadt, near St John's Church at Spires, in St John's lane of the same, in the little room on the ground floor" It was immediately made public in order that every one might know that the princes had in no wise been consenting to the new recess, but were determined to hold fast by the former

This declaration acquired great additional weight from the signatures of a great number of the imperial cities

At first they appeared resolved once more to act together as one man For their old rule was, that, if one of them had a grievance to complain of, all the rest were to adopt it, and on no account to separate their interests or their plan of action We observed, indeed, that the first remonstrance of the cities, though containing matter of a highly anticlerical tendency, was signed by all But the hearts of men were too deeply and intensely moved by the interests of religion for them to attend to old rules The imperial commissioners sent for the delegates of the Catholic cities, commended their steady adherence to the faith, and encouraged them to persevere in it John Faber had a great personal influence over some of the smaller, such as Rottweil and Ravensburg Others, it was affirmed, were rendered more docile by the hope of being rated lighter to the taxation for the empire Be this as it may, in the decisive moment when the Chancellor of Mainz asked which were the cities that felt themselves aggrieved, the recollection of their old principles made them hesitate for a moment, —but it was only for a moment The delegate from Rottweil was the first to declare that there were many among the cities that agreed to the resolutions of the recess To this others assented * A list was drawn up in which those who thought themselves aggrieved wrote their names At first Cologne inscribed itself, not so much because it partook of the new opinions, as because it was engaged in disputes with its clergy, but it afterwards revoked its signature Frankfurt, too, was at first among the number, and here the new opinions had taken firm root: it subsequently withdrew, because it did not choose to break with the emperor But the others remained inflexible In the instrument above mentioned, fourteen were named as joining in the protest Strasburg, Nurnberg, Ulm, Constance, Lindau, Memmingen, Kempten, Nordlingen, Heilbronn, Reutlingen, Isny, St. Gall (which here once more appears among the imperial cities), Wissenburg, and Windsheim This includes, as we perceive, all those attached to Zwingli's opinions In the moment of need the Lutheran princes had not hesitated to unite with them

Sovereigns so considerable, especially in the north of Germany,—cities so populous and wealthy in the south and west,—all united in opinion and in will, formed a body which commanded respect They were determined to defend themselves with their combined strength against every attempt at compulsion on the part of the majority

* Fürstenberg's Report in the Frankf Acts, and the priest Matthis, in those of Strasburg "The separation between the cities began on that very day," exclaims Matthis, "that is what the clergy have been hitherto seeking"

CHAPTER VI.

DISSENSIONS AMONG THE PROTESTANTS

The discussions of the diet of 1529 turned rather on a question of public law than on any points of doctrine

All hope of a general agreement of the empire on matters of religion had long been at an end, the division between the two great parties became more and more marked and hostile This division had indeed been recognised and sanctioned by the supreme authority, whose language and attitude in 1526 might be regarded as neutral Now, however, when the first storm was over,—when the ecclesiastical body, after its own violent dissensions, had re-united for the maintenance of its common interests,—when the emperor had once more established amicable relations with the pope,—the Catholic party succeeded in getting possession of the supreme power; the government of the empire, in the hands of the majority, assumed a thoroughly Catholic complexion and attitude

The evangelical party, while emboldened by the consciousness of a recognised legality, and cherishing the hope of further progress in the same direction, suddenly saw itself not only excluded from all share in the government of the empire (which it had for some years mainly conducted), but threatened in its very existence

Nothing remained but for these princes to organise themselves as a minority, determined to endure no oppression, and to resist every attempt of the kind with all their might.

It must never be forgotten, that the noble and courageous idea of taking up this defensive position,—of entrenching themselves behind the laws of the empire, — an idea from which the whole subsequent development of Protestantism resulted, — was founded on the union of the confessions of Saxony and of Switzerland

On the 21st of April, King Ferdinand refused the offered mediation of Brunswick and Baden, on the 22d, Saxony and Hessen concluded "a particular secret agreement," as it is called in the document itself, with the cities of Nurnberg, Ulm, and Strasburg They were perfectly agreed that they would defend themselves, if they were attacked on account of God's word, whether the attack came from the Swabian league, or from the imperial chamber, or even from the imperial government Delegates who were to meet in June, at Rotach in the Franconian mountains, were to determine in what manner they were to assist each other *

No difference was, as we see, made between Nurnberg, which adhered to Lutheran opinions, and Strasburg, which had espoused those of Zwingli

Immediately after the diet, they proceeded to reconsider the terms of this compact Two drafts of it have come down to us, the one framed by the cities, the other by the princes The former proceeds on the principle that a council should be formed of the delegates of the several states, who, being released from their special duties towards their own particular constituents, should act only with a view to the common interests The member of the alliance against whom the attack might be directed, should always appoint the leader of the combined forces This project contains an ordinance in conformity with the constitution of the empire, viz, that the generalissimo should always be a sovereign prince, to whom should be attached a military council consisting of six members, three from the body of the princes, one from that of the counts, and two from the cities In the draft sent in by the cities, great stress is laid on the point, that no resort should be had to arms on any but religious grounds, "only," to use their words, "if they were attacked on account of their faith, or obstructed in the visitations of the churches, under pretext of a spiritual jurisdiction" In that of the princes, which is in the handwriting of the electoral prince, the right of self-defence is especially insisted on, no mention is made of the emperor, the recent edicts are treated as mere assumptions of arbitrary power on the part of states with which they (of the Protestant party) were in every respect equal in rank and dignity, and which, therefore, it was not only their right, but their duty, to oppose †

Whichever of these projects had been preferred, it is certain that the force which the two allies could have called out would have been considerable The electoral prince reckoned that it would be necessary to raise 10,000 foot and 2,000 horse, he advised that their friends, whether near or at a distance, should be invited to join them The fact, that they would have had Switzerland on their side, was of immense importance, the imperial city of Constance had a year ago allied itself with Zurich and Bern, and St Gall, a Swiss town, had signed the protest But this union would not long have remained so entirely inoffensive, and so devoid of any application to the emperor, as John Frederic intended it to be Landgrave Philip and the council of Zurich, who were most intimately connected, had already serious schemes for the restoration of Duke Ulrich of Wurtenberg In the negotiations on this matter between France and Zurich which were opened by the latter, Zwingli expressly stipulated that the landgrave, whom he characterised as magnanimous, steadfast and wise, should be invited to join them ‡ Venice, too, had been applied to Whilst the emperor maintained his ascendancy in the south of Europe, it appeared as if a party, bound together by religious and political interests, would rise up against him in Switzerland and Germany, and would form the centre of a new European opposition At all events, it might be confidently expected that this union would offer an insuperable resistance to the emperor and the majority of the states of the empire

But how short a time elapsed ere the new party was compelled, by the very nature of its own composition, to abandon all these expectations!

At the time that party was organised, the differences existing between the two confessions had been left wholly out of sight This was indeed possible in Spires, under the pressure of a sudden, unexpected, and increasing danger, in presence of the common enemy, they felt the interests that united them, and the necessity for political combination But as soon as they were dispersed, this impression was effaced, and the old antipathies resumed their power

This was characteristic of the century, the efforts to throw off the yoke of the clergy had been prompted by the theological spirit, and this was too earnest and energetic to allow itself to be controlled by any political considerations

The parties to the new league had at first kept it secret from the theologians in Spires, and when at length it was communicated to them, they were obliged to acquiesce in it

But they were the first in whose minds scruples concerning it arose Melanchthon, a man who, with patient and unwearied labour, worked out in his own mind every difficult problem that came before him, returned home robbed of his accustomed cheerfulness § He fancied that if Zwingli's adherents had been

* Article of the Reflections on the confidential Conversation in the Weid Arch

† Bedenken der Eynung des Evangeliums halber (Reflections on the Union on account of the Gospel) in the W A, und Erstgestellte Notel des Berstendnuss, von den von Nurnberg ubergeben (First note (sketch) of the agreement, submitted by them of Nurnberg) Muller

‡ Hottinger, ii 292, 313

§ Letter from Melanchthon to Camerarius, (17th May) Redii neutiquam afferens domum illam quam solebam hilaritatem" To Spengler and Justus Jonas, 1069-1075 1076

abandoned, the Lutherans would have found the majority more willing to make concessions, he reproached himself with not having insisted upon this, as was his duty He was alarmed at the idea that a subversion of the empire and of religion might be the consequence of this compliance On reaching Wittenberg, he spoke to Luther about it, and we may easily imagine what were his sentiments Melanchthon fell into the most painful state of inward strife "My conscience," says he, in a letter of the 17th May, "is disquieted because of this thing, I am half dead with pondering upon it" On the 11th June "My soul is possessed by such bitter grief, that I neglect all the duties of friendship, and all my studies" On the 14th 'I feel myself in such disquiet, that I had rather die than endure it longer' As if with a desire to remedy the wrong that had been committed, he at length endeavoured, on his own authority to put his friends in Nurnberg on their guard against concluding the projected treaty "For the godless opinions of Zwingli must on no account be defended"

His sovereign master, the elector, he could safely leave to Luther's influence

Luther, as we have said, had not hesitated a moment to condemn the alliance with the followers of Zwingli Instantly and spontaneously, on hearing Melanchthon's statement of the facts, he applied to Elector John even now to set aside the agreement concluded at Spires He represented to him that all such compacts were dangerous, and reminded him how the former one had been misused by the impetuosity of the young landgrave "How then," said he, "shall we dare to connect ourselves with people who strive against God and the holy sacrament? We shall thus go to perdition, body and soul'

It can hardly be affirmed that these theological scruples ought to have been utterly disregarded, or that Luther was to be blamed for entertaining them

We must consider that the whole reformation originated in religious convictions, which admit of no compromise, no condition, no extenuation The spirit of an exclusive orthodoxy, expressed in rigid formulæ, and denying salvation to its antagonists, now ruled the world Hence the violent hostility between two confessions, which in some respects approximated so nearly

A union of their respective followers could only be rendered possible, either by disregarding their differences, or by putting an end to them

In Spires, in the tumult of the diet, under the pressure of the common peril, the former had been deemed possible But how could it be realised while the most violent polemical writings were interchanged between the leaders? Considering the convictions which both parties had embraced with fervour, and held to with the utmost tenacity, such a union would have seemed to prove that the original religious motives had not been entirely free from alloy.

Luther was wholly opposed to it, and there needed only an admonition from him, to deter the elector from any such attempt.

Elector John sent indeed his delegates at the appointed time to Rotach, but with strict charge merely to listen, and report to him, he would then consult with the learned men about him whether the thing could be executed without grieving the conscience. He thought that perhaps similar scruples would occur to the people of Nurnberg *

And in fact the opinions of the Nurnberg theologians were precisely those of the Saxon They too exhorted the council to have nothing to do with the 'Sacramenters"†

Hence the meeting in Rotach ended in nothing beyond general assurances of mutual assistance, and preliminary promises, further deliberations were postponed till a meeting, to be held at Schwabach in the following August This, however, never took place It was already countermanded when the delegates from the Oberland arrived, they had made their long journey in vain ‡

Thus the same influential body—the theologians—who had put a sudden and entire check to the warlike preparations caused by Pack s intrigues, three years before, now offered a no less strenuous and successful resistance to an alliance which appeared the only safeguard from arbitrary power The same influence which in the one case had prevented attack, now proved an equally insuperable obstacle to all measures of defence

It is no wonder that Landgrave Philip, who had embraced the former schemes with all the ardour of his haughty and ambitious temper, was offended and grieved at the present turn of affairs He did every thing in his power to keep his Saxon allies to their former resolution, but in vain §

We are not to imagine from this that Landgrave Philip had emancipated himself from the spirit of his age His disposition to con-

* Instruction auf Herr Hansen Minkwitz Ritter gen Rotach (Instructions sent to Master John Minkwitz, knight, at Rotach) He was to observe whether possibly the Nurnberg delegates might not of their own accord say to him, "that they found it would be difficult for them to come into any compact with those who held Zwingli's opinion concerning the sacrament, inasmuch as they would be burthened on account of the divine word of the faith, as if this article were also founded on the divine word and the faith, which must then be received in silence against their consciences," and then he was to say to them, "that a like difficulty and scruple had also fallen upon us since the last diet at Spires" The recess is dated Tuesday after St Boniface, (8th June)

† Chancellor Bruch said at Schmalkalden, that it all came from the counsels of Nurnberg Strobel Miscellaneen, iv 130

‡ Letter to Nurnberg, 23d August They would privately inform their friends of the affair, although it "is quite burthensome to us the delegates, not only on account of our body s weakness, but of the length of the way, and the alarming gangs wandering about the country" (W A) A meeting at Zerbst also did not take place, it w[illegible] off because the elector "had seen good not to conc[illegible], that which he had conferred about with certain princes and states, concerning a friendly understanding, with whom those of the Magdeburg union will not enter" I find that Erich, Bishop of Paderborn and Osnabruck, who had already joined in the first protest at Spires, was also invited

§ Reasons and counter reasons in the letters of the elector and the landgrave Muller, Gesch der Protest p. 256, 261

cede arose from his being less firmly convinced of the truth of Luther's doctrines than his allies were.

As, however, it was no longer possible to disregard the dissensions between the two sections of reformers, it was doubly necessary to make one effort more to reconcile the contending theologians

Landgrave Philip had already seen the urgency of this in Spires, and had written to Zwingli about it He now sent a definitive invitation to both parties to meet at his castle of Marburg, on the Feast of St Michael (A D 1529)

It is remarkable how differently his two invitations were received Zwingli feared that he should be withheld from going by the Grand Council of his city, if he announced his intentions, he thought they would hardly allow him to take so long a journey through so many doubtful or hostile territories Without communicating his intentions even to his wife, or waiting for the expected safe-conduct from Hessen he therefore set out, with the connivance of a few members of the privy council On the other hand, Melanchthon would rather that his sovereign had forbidden him the journey altogether Luther constantly declared that the conference would lead to nothing When he had reached the Werra, it was impossible to induce him to proceed any further till he had received a safe-conduct in all its forms from the landgrave *

On the other hand, the Swiss were filled with the most sanguine hopes, they knew that the prince at whose court they were to meet their antagonists, was entirely on their side in politics, and nearly so in religion The Wittenberg party were sensible that they would have to contend against Philip's wishes, they were determined however not to give way, but to maintain their ground at all risks

The two parties met therefore in a totally opposite temper of mind, and, according to the usual weakness of human nature, proceeded to act under the influence of the moment

Yet, regarded from a higher point of view, this meeting had a sublime and most important character.

The eminent spirits who, on either side, had led the movement with such power, but between whom misunderstandings had now broken out, met together in order to endeavour to elicit, by personal discussion, some means of putting an end to the quarrels which were so great an obstacle to the progress of the common cause

In this light did Euricius Cordus regard it, when he addresses them all, "the princes of the Word," ' the acute Luther, the gentle Œcolampadius, the magnanimous Zwingli, the honest Melanchthon,'' and the others who were come, — Schnepf, Brenz, Hedio, Osiander, Jonas, Crato, Menius, Myconius, each of whom he designates by some eulogistic epithet, and admonishes them to put an end to the new schism. "The church falls at your feet weeping, and conjures you by the bowels of Christ to take this matter in hand with genuine earnestness, for the salvation of the faithful, and to bring about a decision which the world may confess to have emanated from the Holy Ghost "† It was an ecclesiastical council of the dissidents from Catholicism Had it succeeded, means would have been devised to maintain the unity of the new church

Certain preliminary doubts were first satisfied Zwingli had been accused of errors concerning the divinity of Christ He now professed opinions in entire conformity with the Nicene creed He also declared his complete agreement with the Wittenberg divines, on the doctrine of original sin, on which the whole scheme of redemption rests, on the efficacy of the external word, on baptism, as being not a mere symbol It is certain that Zwingli, in his endeavours to make out the meaning of Scripture for himself, had departed widely from the received opinions of the church on all these points In this respect he, like Luther, reverted to the fundamental basis upon which the Latin church rested ‡ On one point alone, the most important of all—the point which occupied universal attention — on the question of the Eucharist, he was inflexible Here he hoped for victory, and pleaded his cause with great vivacity and earnestness His chief arguments were, the figurative meaning of the word is, in other passages, the explanation given by Christ himself, in the sixth chapter of John (concerning which, he said that "it broke Luther's neck"—an expression the latter rather misunderstood), the consent of several fathers of the church, lastly, the impossibility that a body should be in more than one place at one time But Luther saw written on the page before him, "This is my body" He persisted that these were the words of God, about which there must be no quibbling, and which Satan himself could not get over; he would not now enter upon the more profound explanations with which he had previously combated the argument of locality, without which it is impossible to conceive a body, he would not endure the word "signifies," for that made complete abstraction of the body The difference is this Zwingli regards the presence of Christ as connected with the bread, whereas Luther regards the bread itself as the very presence — the present body,—the visible containing the invisible, as the scabbard contains the sword §

* According to Bullinger, whose account of this conference is, generally, very remarkable, the landgrave himself observed this difference, p 214

† The poem is inserted by Melanchthon in the Paralipomenon to the Chronikon Urspergense, p 495

‡ Loscher, Historia Motuum, p 103, examines how far the present resolutions were contradicted by former expressions of the Oberlanders Even Planck, otherwise a great champion of the Oberlanders, admits that in this matter Loscher is right

§ The following passage in the abstract from the records in Scultetus, p 143, seems to me to contain one of the main points of difference Lutherus affirmat (the subject is, the 6th chapter of John) non ipsam manducationem

He too understood the word *eat* in a spiritual sense, but he would not part with the mystery which is involved in the symbol. He thought that his antagonists had probably never had occasion to prove the value and efficacy of their exposition in the conflicts of the spirit; whereas he was conscious that, by the aid of his, he had fought against Satan and hell, and had found there the consolation which is able to sustain the soul in the most desperate tempests that can assail it.*

With a view to the progressive development of religious ideas, it was not, I think, to be wished that Zwingli should have given up his theory, which, by continually referring to the original and historical character of the institution of the great mystery, was of such immense importance to the whole conception of Christianity, independent of the church as actually constituted. On the points on which he yielded he was not so sure or so steadfast, but this he had thought out in all its bearings; here he was master of his subject; it contained the principle upon which his system was founded, and to this he clung with the utmost tenacity.

Just as little was it to be expected, or even desired, of Luther, that he should assent to Zwingli's exposition. His opinions on the indwelling of the divine element, generally, in the Christian church, are the same as those of the Catholics; only he does not recognise it in the numerous incidents handed down from fantastical or sophistical ages. As these fail to afford him the assurance he requires, he reverts to the original sources, to which the Catholics also refer, and receives nothing but what he finds there. Of the seven sacraments, he retains only the two of which unquestionable mention is made in the New Testament. But to these he adheres in spite of every attempt to wrest them from him, or to detract from their mysterious import.

These are, as we have remarked, two views of the subject taken from different points, but equally inevitable.

It was enough that the two parties began to desist from their mutual outcries of heresy. Luther discovered that his antagonists did not mean so ill as he had imagined, while the Swiss abandoned that coarse conception of Luther's scheme which they had hitherto entertained. Luther thought the violence of the polemical writings would now subside.†

In the first place, all the more important articles of faith on which they agreed, were drawn up and signed by the theologians of both parties; the deviations from the Roman confession are carefully stated in it, as well as those from the anabaptist sects; this was a desirable basis of their common progress, and the Marburg conference will be for ever memorable and important for its establishment. The fifteenth and last of these articles relates to the Lord's Supper. They agree on the nature and mode of the solemn rite, and on its purpose, in so far that both believe that the true body and true blood of Christ are here spiritually eaten; the only point in dispute is, whether this true body is bodily in the bread. Here a freer interpretation of Scripture leads to a different view of the mystery from that adopted by the community of the church. They mutually promised that each party would treat the other with Christian charity.

One point, however, Luther would not concede; viz., he would not extend brotherly love to the dissidents (that is, he would not acknowledge that the two parties formed one brotherhood).‡ He thought the difference of opinion far too fundamental; the mystery, the central point of the Christian's faith and service, far too essential, to admit of such a concession.

We perceive therefore that, as far as the future was concerned, and the recognition that, in spite of their differences, they belonged essentially to the same confession, this conference was productive of important results; but for the political purposes of the moment, which Landgrave Philip had had in his eye, it effected nothing.

Indeed, the very contrary of what he had aimed at came to pass.

From Marburg Luther hastened to Schleiz, where Elector John of Saxony and Markgrave George of Brandenburg were at this moment together, in order to consult with them as to the expediency of the Oberland alliance. Not only did Dr. Luther convince the princes that a perfect unity of faith was necessary to a treaty of mutual defence, but they determined mutually to confess the articles whereon this unity was founded, and to admit no one into their alliance who dissented from any one of them.§ No sooner had the Oberland delegates arrived at Schwabach, where a fresh conference was appointed to be held in October, than such a confession of faith was laid before them for their signature, before any further business was entered upon. These are the so-called Schwabach articles, and are seventeen in number. Little acuteness is necessary to discover that they bear the strongest resemblance to the Marburg agreement. The sequence is the same in the first nine arti-

oralem, sed manducationis modum crassum illum, qualis est carnis suillæ aut bovinæ, rejici. Œcolampadius, arrepta inde occasione, de duplici verborum Christi intelligentia disserit; humili sive carnali, et sublimi sive spirituali: humilem sive carnalem verborum Christi intellectum eum esse quem Lutherus asserat a Christo repudiatum: spiritualem sive sublimem esse illum quem Christus jusserit amplecti. Contra Lutherus fieri non posse nec debere, ut ad spiritualem tantum intellectum verba cœnæ referantur, siquidem remissio peccatorum, vita æterna ac regnum cœlorum carnalibus istis ac humilibus ut appereant rebus per verbum dei annexa sint.

* Luther's Explanation, addressed to Landgrave Philip in de W. iii. p. 510.

† Melanchthon says in the Appendix to the Chron. Ursperg:—Triduo duravit colloquium, et durasset diutius spe uberioris tum concordiæ futuræ, nisi horrendus ille morbus sudatorius — — vocatos dispersisset. This was inserted in Bullinger. It shows at least what an impression had been made on Melanchthon.

‡ Luther to Gerbellius, (4th Oct.): — Denuntiatum est eis, nisi et hoc articulo resipiscant, charitate quidem nostra posse eos uti, sed in fratrum et Christi membrorum numero a nobis censeri non posse.

§ The recess of Schleiz was only oral. We see what its contents were from the instructions to the councillors of the elector, and the Markgrave of Brandenburg at the Schwabach conference. Müller, p. 281, and Walch, xvii. p. 669. First article.

cles,* the forms of expression are for the most part identical also, there are but few alterations, the most important among which is in the tenth article, wherein it is taught, that "the true body and blood of Christ is verily present in the bread and wine," to which is annexed the polemical remark, that the opposite party assert them to be mere bread and wine. The Schwabach articles are a somewhat more elaborate edition of the Marburg agreement, Luther's scheme being exclusively adopted in both.† It was, of course, impossible for the delegates from Ulm and Strasburg to sign this confession. They remarked that it was not in conformity with the doctrines preached among them, that they were not apprised of the alteration, and must bring a declaration of the opinions of their constituents on the subject, to the next meeting.

It was easy to foresee that this declaration would be in the negative, and that, under these circumstances, the alliance must be abandoned.

This division took place just at the moment when the emperor manifested the most hostile disposition towards reform.

The emperor having issued a manifesto from Spain, expressive of his disapprobation of the protest, the states which had joined in it had sent a deputation to Italy, charged to justify their measures to him. Nothing, however, could be more directly hostile to their views than the Spanish Catholicism which the delegates encountered in the emperor's court. The emperor only repeated his former declarations. He refused to receive the protest, and was greatly displeased when the envoys laid it on the table of the secretary who was transacting business with them. The whole court was incensed at the audacity of Michael Kaden, one of the envoys, who put into the hands of the orthodox emperor, the temporal head of Catholic Christendom, a writing of a Protestant tendency, given to him by the landgrave. The delegates were compelled to follow the court for a while as prisoners, and escaped from it only by a sort of flight.

But if any hoped that the adverse and menacing circumstances without, would have the effect of re-uniting the two sections of the Protestants, this hope proved utterly illusory.

At the very meeting at Schmalkalden, before which they laid the report of these circumstances (Dec., 1529), the separation between them was first rendered absolute and complete.

The seventeen articles were once more laid before the Oberlanders (who were here far more numerous than at Schwabach). Ulm and Strasburg, whose example was usually followed by the others, definitively declared that they would not sign them. The Lutherans, in an equally decided manner, declared that, in that case, they could not enter into an alliance with them. Their own earnest entreaties, and the zeal with which the landgrave exerted himself in their behalf,—urging that there was nothing to be expected from the emperor but disfavour and violence,—were equally vain. The other party refused even to communicate to them the report of the delegates, unless they would first declare their assent to the profession of faith.‡

In the course of these transactions, another question, rather of a political nature, had come under discussion.

When Luther warned his master not to enter into a league with the Oberländers, he still cherished the hope that a reconciliation with the emperor was possible. This hope was inspired by the view he took of the character of the reformation. He contemplated only its widest objects and effects—the deliverance of the secular power from the pretensions to supremacy and precedency hitherto asserted by the clergy. He represented what innumerable abuses, universally admitted and complained of, he had removed, while on the other hand, he had combated with chivalrous valour against anabaptists and image breakers, the chief merit which he claimed, however, and most justly, was, that he had revived the idea of civil supremacy and secular majesty, and had procured for it universal acceptance. He had so high an opinion of the emperor, that he was persuaded, if it were represented to him that the doctrines of Christianity were preached in greater purity in the evangelical countries than they had been for a thousand years, he must instantly see the truth. Luther was little less imbued with the idea of the empire than with that of the church. I do not mean its momentary condition or aspect, but its import and essence, and he felt almost an equal pain at having to sever himself from it.

Negotiations were in fact set on foot between the elector and King Ferdinand. Ferdinand was moved to them, as he writes to his brother more than once, by his anxiety lest a movement of the Protestants should ensue before his (the emperor's) arrival, which might have ruinous results, the elector, by his natural reluctance to separate himself

* What the Schwabach Art. viii. appears to contain over and above, is to be found in those of Marburg under the title, De usu sacramenti. See the printed copy of the 17 Articles in Walch, xvi. 778, and given with diplomatic accuracy in Weber's Kritische Gesch der Augsb Con. V i. Ap. 2.

† Riederer found the following words in Veit Diedrich's handwriting on Luther's autograph preface to the 17 Articles, of the year 1530. Præfatio ad xvii. Articulos Marburgi scriptos, and upon them founded his assertion that the 17 Articles themselves were drawn up at Marburg. Had that been the case, Luther would have brought them ready with him to Schleiz. In fact, Luther must have been very much occupied. On the 30th of September the theologians arrived, on the 1st, 2d, and 3d of October they debated, on the 4th the Marburg agreement was signed, and on the 5th he went away. The scheme there concocted does however agree pretty well with the character of the 17 Articles, only they must afterwards have been revised, and rendered more distinct in some places, if what was said in Schmalkalden to the cities is true. "The articles are very well considered, and drawn up with brave counsel of learned and unlearned councillors."

‡ Protocol of the meeting, Sunday after St. Catherine 1529. Strobel, iv. 113.

from the head of the empire,—a reluctance which had been greatly enhanced by Luther's arguments, and which sometimes almost shook the confidence of the landgrave in his intentions Philip once bluntly asked the elector, what he had to look to from him if he were attacked *

But it gradually became evident how little was to be expected from these negotiations It was clear that the Protestants would not, as the electoral prince had assumed in his project of a league, have to deal with the States alone Even in the instructions given by the elector to his envoys to Schwabach it was said, "the great danger will now be in the highest places"†

The further question now presented itself, how far it was generally lawful to resist the authority of the emperor Till this was answered, all union and combination was vain, whatever might be the conformity of opinion in other respects

Saxony remarked with justice that, until they were agreed on this indispensable point, any alliance must be merely apparent, would inspire no confidence, and afford no security

Did not the supreme power reside in the emperor? Were they not bound by the words of Scripture, to which they were constantly appealing, to pay him unqualified obedience?

These questions were examined in Saxony itself with scrupulous earnestness The jurists rested their arguments on the principle of law, that self-defence is permitted, they justified resistance The question was then submitted to the theologians, and, in the absence of Luther and Melanchthon, who were then at Marburg, Bugenhagen, upon whom the decision devolved, brought a theological argument to support those of the jurists He declared that if a power, however unquestionably derived from God, set itself in opposition to God, it could no longer be regarded as the sovereign authority

Luther, on his return, gave a totally different opinion He thought that the maxims of law which countenanced resistance were contradicted by others which forbade it, while the latter were supported by Scripture If resistance to every prince who disobeys God's word were to be permitted, people would at last reject all authority whatever at their own discretion

This opinion was shared by the theologians of Nurnberg Johann Brenz gave in a report to the markgrave to that effect

The conflict was in fact between the doctrines of passive obedience, and of the right of resistance

We know how greatly these doctrines, especially in their connexion with religion, contributed to the development of political theories in Europe, it is worthy of remark that they were first brought into discussion in Germany, and at so early a period

But the time was not yet come for the vast consequences with which they were pregnant to be felt. In another age and country they touched the vital point upon which the development of such theories entirely turns, viz. the relation between sovereign and subject in Germany this was not even agitated, the doubt referred only to the relation of a subordinate to a supreme government, of a prince of the empire to the emperor

In Germany the question turned upon the principles of public law peculiar to the empire, rather than upon those which are common to all states Its real bearing was, whether the supreme power of the empire was of a monarchical or an aristocratical nature.

Luther, who saw in the imperial power the continuation of that of ancient Rome, as represented in Scripture, adhered firmly to the idea of monarchy there exhibited He compared the relation between the elector his master and the emperor, with that between a burgermeister of Torgau and the elector Brenz was of opinion that the princes were as little justified in taking arms against the emperor, as the peasants against the nobles and prelates

These comparisons, however, clearly show how little the essential question was defined. On the other side it was contended, that there was no resemblance between the princes of Germany and the Roman prefects of the Scripture, not to speak of burgermeisters and peasants They were subject to the emperor under certain conditions insuring their freedom and rights, with certain limitations, and according to the privileges originally granted them Moreover, they were themselves sovereigns, and it was their duty as such to defend the Gospel ‡

At the Congress of Nurnberg, the Chancellor of Saxony declared (but under the express proviso that it was only his personal opinion), that he was convinced of the legality of resistance to the emperor He adduced the two arguments we have just mentioned; in the first place, that the power of the princes was no less derived from God than that of the emperor, and secondly, that if the emperor desired to compel them to return to Popery, he was to be regarded in the light of an enemy, and no such compulsion was to be endured

These arguments, however, found little approbation As he was one day going to his chancery, Spengler, the secretary of the city of Nurnberg, whom we have had occasion to mention as a man of great experience in legal affairs, went up to him and accused him of error They fell into a vehement altercation, which, however, they had the discretion to carry on in Latin, that it might not be understood by the bystanders

Brandenburg was of the same mind as Nurnberg Chancellor Vogler affirmed that his master had determined, if the emperor in-

* Rommel Urkundenbuch, No 9

† Instructions for Schwabach Müller, 282

‡ Answer to the scruple put forth, that no resistance may be offered to his imperial majesty Hortleder (ii ii 12) places this at "about 1531" but as it relates to the opposition experienced by the last of the protesting delegations, I incline to think it must be dated at the end of 1529, or the beginning of 1530

vaded his dominions, not to defend himself, but to bear whatever it might please God to lay upon him.

This opinion obtained permanent ascendancy, even in Saxony. Luther declared, that even if the emperor violated his oath, he was still emperor—the sovereign authority, set over them by God: if they were determined no longer to obey, they must dethrone him. But to what could it lead if they took up arms against him? Whoever conquered, must expel him and become emperor in his stead, which could be endured by no one.

The only counsel Luther could give was, that if the emperor had recourse to violence, the princes must not indeed assist him, for that would be to sin against the true faith, but they must not refuse to allow him to enter their territory, and to act there according to his will. He repeated, that if the emperor summoned him and the other reformers, they would be forthcoming; the emperor need have no anxiety on that account. For every man must hold his belief at his own risk and peril.

Thus a few months sufficed to put an end to a league which seemed destined to convulse Europe. It was entirely dissolved. Even the territorial alliance did not seem able to afford protection against the emperor. We perceive that the several sovereigns and states thought themselves again bound to act and to suffer single-handed.

It is very easy to repeat the censure that has so often been thrown upon this decision. It was certainly not the part of political prudence.

But never was a course of action more purely conscientious, more regardless of personal consequences, more grand and magnanimous.

These noble men saw the enemy approach, they heard his threats, they were under no illusion as to his views, they were almost persuaded that he would attempt the worst against them.

They had an opportunity of forming a league against him which would shake Europe, at the head of which they might oppose a formidable resistance to his projects of universal domination, and make an appeal to fortune, but they would not—they disdained the attempt.

Not out of fear or mistrust of their own strength and valour;—these are considerations unknown to souls like theirs. They were withheld by the power of religion alone.

First, because they would not mix up the defence of the faith with interests foreign to it, nor allow themselves to be hurried into things which they could not foresee.

Secondly, they would defend no faith but that which they themselves held; they would have feared to commit a sin if they connected themselves with those who differed from them,—on one point only, it is true, but that one of the highest importance.

Lastly, they doubted their right to resist their sovereign and head, and to trouble the long-established order of the empire.

Thus, in the midst of the jarring interests of the world, they took up a position counselled only by God and their own consciences, and there they calmly awaited the danger. "For God is faithful and true," says Luther, "and will not forsake us." He quotes the words of Isaiah, "Be ye still, and ye shall be holpen."

Unquestionably this is not prudent, but it is great.

CHAPTER VII

THE OTTOMANS BEFORE VIENNA.

THE results of the two diets of 1526 and 1529 were not less diametrically opposed than were their decrees.

The former led the evangelical party, protected and sanctioned by the empire, to lay the great foundations of their future existence; the latter not only withdrew this protection, but at the same time divided their body.

The discord which had arisen since the publication of the regulations of Nurnberg, had now become an open breach.

I think we shall be justified in affirming that the contrast in the consequences of the two diets, with relation to foreign affairs, was not less complete.

At the diet of 1526, the house of Austria having sanctioned the progress of the evangelical party, was requited by that cordial assistance of the German nation, which secured to it the supreme power over Italy and Hungary. It was not to be expected that after this house had taken so entirely different a direction, it would receive the same support from the affections of the nation.

"I have heard," says Daniel Mieg (who had been excluded from the Council of Regency) to the Altammeister of Strasburg, "that his majesty has applied for powder: my advice is, not to grant it, since such an affront has been offered us. It were good that we kept our money and our powder too, we shall want them ourselves."*

The conduct of the house of Austria—its schemes of conquest and aggrandisement—had already excited universal anxiety; people had no desire to lend it any serious assistance. An assessor of the Council of Regency, Hammann von Holzhusen, delegate from Frankfurt—a city so conspicuous for its loyalty to the imperial house—remarks, "that many of the states, whether they be Lutheran or not, do not know what they have to expect from Austria; they are afraid the assistance they afford may in the end be turned to the detriment of the empire and the nation."†

* Saturday before Jubilate, 1529. Jung, Biel. No. 37.

† Spires, Oct. 9. "E. W. werden auch fleissik bedenken und ermessen die schwinnen (geschwinden) lauf und brattig (Practiken) so in etlich Jaren vorhanden gewest.

A little later we find letters circulating in Hungary, in which the impossibility of Ferdinand's defending Hungary is inferred from the religious quarrels in which he was involved with the magnates of Germany.*

Such was the state of the public mind when the most powerful enemy the empire had encountered for centuries, the representative of another world, the rival and the implacable foe of Christendom, appeared on its frontiers.

It was just about this time that one Katib, learned in the law, asserted in Constantinople, that the prophet Jesus was to be preferred before the prophet Mohammed. The divan before whom this innovator was accused, sought in vain to confute him, nor was the mufti, to whom the matter was then referred, more successful; he, however, tried and sentenced him to death. This sentence was entirely agreeable to the opinions of the sultan. Katib refused to recant, and suffered death for the name of Jesus, in the middle of the mosque.

Suleiman's highest ambition was to be regarded as the prophet's vicegerent on earth. He was the first of the Ottoman sultans who raised Mecca into consideration; it was he who built the sacred house of the Kaaba, restored the mosque of Chadidscha, constructed aqueducts, and established colleges. "I whose power is sustained by the grace of the Almighty, by the blessing of the greatest of his prophets, by the protection of the first four of his favoured disciples, I, the shadow of God over both worlds"—such was his manner of describing himself in a letter to the King of France. His pretensions were in harmony with these titles. "Dost thou not know," said his son-in-law, Mustapha (A. D. 1528), to Lasky, "that our lord is next to Allah? That as there is only one sun in the heavens, so also there is only one lord upon earth?"

At a time when peace was yet unconcluded in Europe, when he might expect to find the whole combined opposition to Charles V. in full activity, on the 4th of May, 1529, Suleiman set out with an army which has been reckoned at 250,000 men, to wage a holy war. Before him, the Hospodar of Moldavia invaded Transylvania, and put to rout the followers of Ferdinand. Next John Zapolya descended the Karpathians with the small troop that had collected around him; he had the good fortune to meet with Ferdinand's party in Hungary, before they were joined by the Germans, and to defeat them; he met and joined the sultan on the battle-field of Mohacz. Suleiman asked him what had induced him to come to him, notwithstanding the difference of their faith. "The Padischah," answered John, "is the refuge of the world, and his servants are innumerable, both moslems and unbelievers." Zapolya, repulsed by the pope and by Christendom, fled to the protection of the sultan. This need of others for momentary protection had made the Ottoman empire what it was.

In Hungary, Suleiman experienced little or no resistance. The Austrian government did not dare to call out the light cavalry; it feared, in the unfavourable state of the public mind, that this might lead to disturbances. But it was wholly incapable of defending the country by its own resources. The commander of the fleet, who owed his men 40,000 guld., had the greatest difficulty in getting together 800. Means were not forthcoming even to garrison the fortresses.

Suleiman's wezir laughed at the princes of the West, who were forced to extort money from the wretched peasants before they could make war; he pointed to the seven towers, in which his master had gold and silver lying in vast heaps, while his word was sufficient to place a countless army in the field.

It is little wonder that, under these circumstances, the strong party that adhered to Zapolya was completely triumphant. The magnates—the Hungarian Beys, as they are called in Suleiman's journal—rivalled each other in the alacrity with which they repaired to his camp to kiss his hand. Peter Pereny endeavoured at least to rescue the holy crown for Austria; but he was attacked on the road by the Bishop of Funfkirchen, a kinsman of Zapolya's, who took him prisoner with all the regalia, and carried them to the Ottoman camp.† The extraordinary veneration with which the Hungarians regard their crown is well known. They believe it to have been sent down from heaven, and affirm that, at the sight of it, drawn swords have leaped back into their scabbards. "The loadstone does not more strongly attract the iron," says Rewa, "than the crown does the reverence of the Hungarians, and they hold it to be their duty to escort it whithersoever it may be borne, without heeding cost or danger.‡ The Turkish notion was, that it had been handed down from Nuschirwan the Just; and this palladium, in which the Hungarians beheld a divine symbol of their nationality and their kingdom, was now in Suleiman's camp, and accompanied his army.

In this universal defection, it could hardly

und noch sint, also, das alle Chur und Fursten, geistlich und weltlich, auch ander Pralaten, Herrn, und Stadt, sie seyen lotters (lutherisch) wie man denn die nennen will oder nit, nit wol wissen mogen, wes sie sich versehen sollen, und also das dieselbig Hilf, so gemelt mein gnst. und gn. Herrn Chur und Fursten, auch andre Stende und Stet thun werden, dem heiligen Reich und Teutzer Nation und inen selber zu grossen unuberwindlichen Schaden und nachtail reichen und kommen moge."—"Your worships will also carefully consider and ponder the rapid course and practice [of what, is not said] that for some years have taken place and still exist; also, that all electors and princes, be they Lutheran, as people are pleased to call them, or not, know not what to provide, and also that the same succours which are demanded of my most gracious lords, electors and princes, will be granted by other estates and cities to the great and irreparable prejudice and damage of the holy empire, German nation, and themselves." He proposes a meeting of the cities "in order to have discourse and counsel concerning this and other things, to agree upon an opinion and what is to be done herein, and what answer to be given."

* Katona, xx. i. p. 634. Rex Ferdinandus propter dissensionem suam cum imperio et aliis magnatibus Alemanniæ propter fidem, nullum habere potest populum.

† Zermegh, Historia rerum inter Johannem et Ferdinandum gestarum. Schwandtner, ii. lib. i. § 12.

‡ Rewa, De sacra corona regni Hungariæ, Schwandtner, ii. 456. See Tuberonis Commentarii. Ibid. 113, 114.

be expected that the German garrisons would be able to defend the few strong places they still occupied There were about 700 newly raised landsknechts under Colonel Besserer, in Ofen, who held out against several assaults, but when the city was taken, and the castle of St. Gerhardsberg, which commanded it, was nearly in ruins, they despaired of being able to resist the enemy's fire with their long lances, and held themselves justified in consulting their own safety, they forced their leader to capitulate But they knew not the enemy with whom they had to deal Ibrahim Pacha promised, in the most solemn manner, that they should march out free, they had not reached the gates of Ofen, when they were all cut to pieces *

From this moment the barbarian torrent rolled unresisted towards the German frontier "towards a land," says the Ottoman historian, "which had never yet been trodden by the hoof of a Moslem steed "

The mighty power of the East, erected on kingdoms the civilization of which was either in the state of undeveloped infancy or of semi-barbarised decay, here first came in contact with the very heart of western life, where the unceasing progression of the human mind had taken root, and was in full activity

No sooner had they set foot in Germany, than the Ottomans found they had a different foe before them from any they had yet encountered

They describe it as a country of Giaours (they make no distinctions between infidels) a woody land, difficult to traverse, but they remark that it is peculiarly illumined by the torches of unbelief, inhabited by a warlike people, marching under fierce banners, and defended on all sides by castles, cities, and walled churches, they are struck with the fact that as soon as they had passed the frontier, they found every necessary of daily life in the greatest abundance † They felt the presence of a people thoroughly imbued with civilisation, surrounded with the comforts of a long-settled population, brave and religious

Ibrahim told the Austrian ambassadors the following year, that the warning they had sent the sultan, not to advance further, for that Ferdinand their lord stood ready, sword in hand, to receive him, had served only to inflame Suleiman with fresh ardour to seek him out He had expected to find him in Ofen, where he thought a king of Hungary ought to hold his seat but in this he had been disappointed He had then advanced to the Austrian frontier, where he thought Ferdinand would wait for him, on the contrary, the keys of Bruck were carried out to meet him on his approach Thus he reached Vienna, but there, too, he found neither Ferdinand nor his army, he only learned that the king had fled to Linz or Prague At the sight of Vienna, so beautifully surrounded by vineyards and mountains, and yet lying in the midst of a fertile plain, he said that here he would rest, this was a place worthy of an emperor, he had spread out his skirts (i e he had allowed his light troops to disperse on all sides), to show that the real emperor was come in his might ‡

Such is the description of the event, given by Suleiman himself in a letter to Venice He relates how he had taken Ofen, and made himself master of Hungary, and given it to King John, and how the ancient crown of that kingdom had fallen into his hands "My purpose, however," he says, "was not to seek these things, but to encounter King Ferdinand" § He told the first German prisoners that were brought him, that he would seek out Ferdinand, even if he were in the centre of Germany

On the 20th September, he arrived before Vienna, and pitched his camp there From the lofty tower of St Stephen's church nothing was to be descried for miles, over hill and dale, but tents, and the Danube covered with Turkish sails The place is still pointed out near Sommering, where Suleiman's own tent stood, the internal magnificence of which may be inferred from the golden balls and tassels with which its exterior was decorated He encamped in the same order as he had marched The troops from the Porte immediately surrounded him, behind him lay the Anatolian army under its Beglerbeg, extending as far as Schwechat, before him, the Seraskier Ibrahim, with the European Sipahis, the Rumeliotes and Bosniaks, and the Sandschaks of Mostar and Belgrade For, in a country where the state is nothing else but the army, the distribution of the camp represents that of the empire The Hungarians, who rivalled the other subjects of Suleiman in their zeal "to adorn themselves with the collar of obedience," already found their place in this great assemblage It consisted of western Asia and eastern Europe, in the form they had assumed, and were still assuming, under the influence of conquering Islam, they now made their first attempt on the heart of Christian Europe The light troops ascended the

* The groundlessness of the somewhat dramatic and dressed out lamentations of Ursinus Velius (lib vi)—that the Landsknechts had, on this occasion, forgotten the old German valour—which have found their way into modern histories, appears the moment we recur to some simpler statement, as for example, that of the tutor of the pages (Pagenhofmeister) in Schardius iii 238 —"Arx ad voluptatem magis quam vim instructa erat," etc or that of Sebast Frank (which is, by the by, identical with a pamphlet of that time), p 256 where he says the castle was garrisoned by four companies (Fahnlein), "die nitt so vil man oder einzelich personen vermochten als der Türk tausend, noch hat er eilf gewaltiger sturm davon verloren, dass er meynet es weren eitel Teufel im Schloss" —"Who were not so many men or single persons strong as the Turks were thousands, yet were these repulsed in eleven violent assaults, so that they thought there were nothing but devils in the castle" "Wo die nit gewest," adds Pessel, "wer vielleicht die Stat Wien ubereilet worden"—"Had they not been there, the city of Vienna would perhaps have been taken" "Achthundert frummer deutscher knecht Die hielten sich redlich und recht," says the song of Soltau, p 337

† Ssoloksade in Hammer, Wiens erste türkische Belagerung p 101 See Suleiman's Journal, 22d Sept, Osman Gesch iii 650

‡ Lamberg und Jurischitsch in Gevay, 1530 p 36 In Latin, agreeing in the main, but with some peculiarities, p 40

§ Copia della lettera del Sultan Solimano Belgr 9th Nov Hammer, Belagerung, p 77

Danube in search of the fabulous bridge of the horned Alexander — the boundary of the fantastic world of oriental mythology. The beast of burthen of the Arabian desert was driven up to the walls of a German city, laden with provisions and munitions of war; there were 22,000 camels in the camp. The memory of those who fell before Vienna is still celebrated with oriental pomp. Potschewi says in his history, speaking of Iskenderitschausch Farfara, that "immediately on his arrival here, he drank of the cup of Islamite martyrdom, and forgot the world." For the Turkish army believed itself to be waging a holy war against "the infidels, who were like dust before it." In full view of the grandest castle of the latest German emperors, the doctrine of the sublime Porte was proclaimed, that, as there was only one God in heaven, there must be only one lord on earth, and Suleiman gave it to be understood that he was this lord; he declared that he would not lay his head to rest till he had reduced Christendom to subjection with his sword. It was rumoured that he reckoned on a three years' absence from Constantinople for the execution of this design.

Europe was not so dull of apprehension as not to feel the magnitude of the danger.

It was a crisis like that when the Arabians had got possession of the Mediterranean, conquered Spain, and pressed on towards France; or like that when the Mongolian power, after overwhelming the north-east and south-east of Europe, attacked Christian Germany on the Danube and the Oder. Europe was evidently now stronger: it was conscious that it possessed the power "to drive these devils (so they were called) out of Greece;" but the necessary union seemed impossible.

There is a letter of Francis I., of this period, in which he declares that he would now put in execution the purpose he had always cherished, of devoting all the powers of his kingdom and his person to the war against the Turks; he hoped to move his brother of England to do the same; he thought that he could then bring 60,000 men into the field—a force that certainly was not to be despised. He expresses himself with such warmth that he appears to be really in earnest, but he adds a condition which nullifies the whole. He proposes that the emperor should remit one of the two millions which he was bound by treaty to pay him—a proposition to which nobody could expect the emperor to accede.*

The imperial court, too, where the danger was still more urgent, and where the Ottoman maxim, that every country through which the sultan marched belonged to him, became of terrible practical importance, was employed in devising means for rousing the whole of Christendom to arms. The expedient suggested is very remarkable. Hoogstraten, the leading minister in the Netherlands, once opened himself on the subject to the French ambassador. He said, the true way of resisting the Turks was to bring the pope to consent to a universal scheme of secularisation. A third of the church property, sold to the highest bidders, would suffice to bring an army into the field, capable of driving out the Turks and reconquering Greece.†

It is only necessary to look at these propositions, in order to see their impracticability, to see how impossible it was to carry through an undertaking burthened with conditions so remote and visionary.

If Germany meant to defend itself, it was evident that it must look to its own resources alone.

But even here things wore a very doubtful aspect. It was a question whether there were not people so dissatisfied with the existing order of things, as to wish even for Turkish rule. Luther himself had once said that it was not the duty of a Christian to resist the Turks, whom he ought rather to regard as the scourge of God: this indeed was one of the sentences condemned in the papal bull. And now the results of the diet of Spires were calculated to excite the alarm of all the adherents of a reform in the church, and, as we have seen, to incline them to question whether they ought to afford assistance to Ferdinand—the head of the very majority by which their own just demands had been rejected.

As to Luther, it is true that he used the expression just quoted; but in this passage he speaks only of Christians, as such,—of the religious principle abstracted from all other considerations, such as it is exhibited in some passages of the gospel. His indignation and disgust had been excited by the hypocritical outcry for war against the Turks, for the sake of the Christian religion, and the appeals to the faithful for contributions which were applied to very different purposes.‡ In short, he utterly abjured warlike Christianity; he would not bring religion into so close a connection with the sword. But when it came to be a question of real danger, and of aiding the efforts of the civil power to resist that danger, he declared in the most emphatic manner, that it was a positive duty to oppose the progress of the Turks. For that cause was the empire entrusted to the emperor; he and the princes would otherwise be guilty of the blood of their subjects, which God would require at their hands. He thinks it strange,

* Lettres de Gilles de Pommeraye, MS. Bethune, 8619. En cas que led. empereur, pour m'ayder a souldoyer les gens que je menerois en ma compaignie, me voulust sur lesd. 2 millions d'escus en rabattre ung million, je me faisois fort, etc.

† Que ces deux princes conduisissent le pape jusques a ce point que 1° il se contente de ce qu'il a, 2° qu'il permette qu'a l'eglise des six mille duc. de rente on preigne les deux universellement par toute la Chretiente. les quelles seront vendus au plus offrant, et avec l'argent que les princes fourniront (for they were to do something) sera suffisant pour deloger ce diable de la Grèce, qui seroit grandement accroistre l'eglise d'y adjoindre un tel pays que celui la. Lettre de Pommeraye, 17 Sept.

‡ "Therefore they should desist from urging and goading, as the emperor and princes have been hitherto urged, to the conflict with the Turks, on the plea that, being the head of Christendom, the protector of the church, and defender of the faith, he ought to extirpate the religion of the Turks." Vom Kriege wider die Turken. Published about Easter, 1529. Altenb. iv. 525.

that the assembly at Spires was so much troubled whether people ate meat in Lent, or whether a nun got married, while it let the Turk advance, and conquer cities and countries at his pleasure He calls on the princes no longer to regard the banner of the emperor merely as a piece of silk, but to follow it, as was their duty, to the field With a view to convert those who wished for the government of the Turks, he takes the trouble to set forth all the abominations of the Koran He exhorts the people to march forth boldly in the name of the emperor, "he who dies in the performance of this duty," says he, "will be well pleasing to God"

In treating of this great peril of the German nation, we may be permitted to record the opinion of the man whose voice was at the time more potential than any other The address on the Turkish war exhibits, in all its penetrating acuteness, the spirit whose grand task it was to separate the ecclesiastical and temporal elements

So much at least he effected, that the protesters, though in actual dread of war and violence on the part of the majority, and though they had not assented to the resolutions of the diet, made the same preparations for the defence of the country as the others Even Elector John sent several thousand men into the field under the command of his son *

From every side succours hurried to join the general-in-chief of the empire, Count Palatine Frederic, who meanwhile had come up with King Ferdinand at Linz †

These troops were, however, far from being strong enough to attack the Ottoman camp, especially during the first panic The emperor, who heard in Genoa that Suleiman was not coming thither, did not find himself in a condition to hasten with his Spaniards to the assistance of Vienna, as he had promised

For the present, therefore, all depended on the ability of the garrison of Vienna to resist the barbarians

It is worth our while to pause a moment over the particulars of this siege, which at the time engrossed the attention of the world, and was indeed pregnant with the most important consequences Had Suleiman conquered Vienna, he would have found means to fortify it in such a manner that it would not have been easy to recover it from his grasp From this admirable post, he would have commanded the whole territory of the Middle Danube

Nor are we to imagine that Vienna was a very strong place It was surrounded by a ruinous wall, without any of the defences contrived by the modern art of fortification, without even bastions upon which artillery, commanding the enemy's camp, could have been planted The ditches were without water. The commanders of the army of Lower Austria had at first doubted whether they could defend the "wide-spread, uncultivated spots," for a moment they thought they would rather await the enemy in the open field, so that, in case of need, they could fall back upon the fresh troops which the count palatine and the king were busied in collecting, at last, however, they had come to the conclusion that they must not surrender their ancient capital, and had resolved to burn the suburbs, in order to preserve the city within the walls

But though the fortifications were feeble, Maximilian's passion for gunnery now, so long after his death, stood his capital in good stead. Not only in the citadel, and behind the loopholes which had been pierced in the walls, but on all the towers of the city gates, on the houses, on the walls (which were first unroofed), under the roofs, nay, in the very dormitories of the convents, falconets, culverins, mortars, nightingales, and other kinds of artillery stood ready to receive the enemy's assault

The garrison consisted of five regiments, four German (two of which were raised at the cost of the empire, and two by Ferdinand himself) and one Bohemian The troops of the empire, under Count Palatine Philip, Frederic's lieutenant, occupied the wall from the Red Tower to the Carinthian gate, from hence the king's troops, under Eck von Reischach and Leonhard von Fels, extended to the Scots' gate. They were people of every variety of German race, among them many eminent Austrians, besides Brabanters, Rhinelanders, men of Meissen and of Hamburg, and especially Franconians and Swabians, we find captains from Memmingen, Nurnberg, Ansbach, and Bamberg, a master of the watch from Gelnhausen, the schultheiss (magistrate) of the whole army was from Frundsberg, territory of Mindelheim, and the chief provost from Ingoldstadt The Bohemians occupied the ground from the Scots' gate to the Red Tower A few parties of horsemen were posted about on the open places within the city, under the excellent captains Nicolas von Salm, William von Rogendorf, and Hans Katzianer There might be sixteen or seventeen thousand men in all

Whether these troops would be able to resist an enemy so enormously superior in numbers, was, however, very doubtful

Suleiman sent a message to the garrison, promising that if they would surrender the city to him, he would neither enter it himself, nor allow any of his troops to do so, but would continue his march in search of the king But if they refused, he was well assured that on the third day from the present (Michaelmas day), there would be no dinner eaten in Vienna, on that day, he would not spare the babe in its mother's womb

According to the ballads and tales of the time, the answer of the garrison was, that he might come to dinner when he would, they would dress it for him with culverines and halberts But this is not true Their minds were not sufficiently at ease to send so bold

* Spalatin Vita Johannis Electoris in Mencken, ii 1117

† Hubert Thomas Leodius de vita Friderici p 119, literally transcribed in Melchior Soiter de Vinda Bellum Pannonicum, lib i Schardius, iii p 250

and haughty a reply "The answer," says an authentic report of the general, "stuck in our pen" They made the most earnest preparations for defence, but by no means with the persuasion that they should conquer They saw the extent of the danger, but were determined to brave it *

Suleiman had therefore no other alternative than to take the city by force

First, the Janissaries posted themselves, with their battle-axes and firelocks, behind the walls of the ruined suburbs, they were excellent marksmen, and had with them a company of expert archers, no one could venture to appear on the walls or battlements, for the assailants commanded the whole circuit of the town, and the gables of the nearest houses bristled with arrows

Amidst the dust and noise caused by this discharge of weapons, the Ottomans now prepared a very different attack Whoever was their master,—whether, as it was said, an Armenian, or of what other nation,—it is certain that one of the most formidable of their arts of besieging was the undermining of the walls † The men of the West were astonished when they afterwards beheld these mines, with entrances as narrow as a door, and gradually widening, not like the mines they were accustomed to work for metals, but smooth, regular, spacious caverns, so constructed that the walls must fall inwards The Turks had but little artillery, and this was the art which they now brought to bear upon Vienna But they had here to do with a people well skilled in subterranean works The garrison soon perceived the enemy's designs, vessels of water and drums were placed so as to betray the slightest motion of the earth, romantic stories are still told how people watched and listened in every cellar and underground room, and countermined accordingly It was a sort of subterraneous war On the second of October a half-finished mine of the enemy's was found and destroyed Another was soon after discovered, at the very moment when they were beginning to fill it with powder The miners sometimes came so near that they could hear each other work, the Turks then turned in another direction In order at all events to secure the Carinthian gate, the Germans thought it necessary to surround it with a ditch of sufficient depth, but this, of course, was not possible in all places

On the 9th of October, the Turks succeeded in blowing up a considerable portion of the wall between the Carinthian gate and the citadel, and at the same moment they rushed to the storm amidst the wildest battle-cries

But the besieged were already prepared Eck von Reischach, who had learned at Pavia how to receive an assault, had described to his people the rush and shouts of a storming party, and how it was to be met We are told by a contemporary, that Reischach's instructions gave his young landsknechts "a brave and manly heart," it is certain that they stood admirably They answered the Ottoman war-cry with a tremendous, "Come on!" (*Her!*) Halberts, firelocks, and cannon supported each other with the best results "The balls of the carronades and muskets," says Dschelalsade, "flew like flocks of small birds through the air, it was a banquet at which the genii of Death filled the glasses" The German accounts dwell particularly on the valour displayed by the aged Salm, the commander of the army of Lower Austria, at this moment ‡ The Ottomans sustained such a murderous loss, that they were compelled to retreat The ruined walls were instantly restored as far as possible

But the enemy sought to repair this check by an attack on the other side of the Carinthian gate After many false alarms, he blew up a considerable portion of the wall leading to the Stubenthor, and immediately made another attempt at storming His columns were now more closely formed The Asafs and Janissaries had been reinforced by Sipahis of Albanian origin, from Janina and Awlona, armed with their crooked sabres and small shields, they rushed forward in the van of the other troops over the prostrate walls But here Eck von Reischach, with four small companies of intrepid landsknechts, threw himself in their way He was supported, as at Pavia, by Spanish soldiers, skilled in the use of fire-arms,§ and by field-marshal William von Rogendorf They fought hand to hand, and the long battle-swords which the Germans wielded with both hands, mingled clashing with the Turkish scimeters A Turkish historian describes the fires which flashed from the encounter. Thrice did the Ottomans renew the assault Jovius, who described so many battles, remarks that hardly had this century witnessed a sterner encounter ‖ But all the efforts of the Ottomans were vain, they sustained far heavier losses now than before

This reverse entirely damped their courage

On the 12th October they again overthrew a part of the city wall, but when they saw the Germans and Spaniards with their banners displayed on the other side, they did not venture to advance

Already had the notion gained ground in the Ottoman camp that, in the decrees of the Most High, the conquest of Vienna was not for the present destined to Islam The nights were unusually cold for the season, and the mountains were covered in a morning with

* Journal of the siege Hammer, p 66 Clearly an official report, as the postscript and the whole form show, drawn up on the 19th October

† At a later period Marsigli took great pains to ascertain the proceedings of the Turks on this occasion See Stato militare degli Ottomanni, ii c xi p 37 The corps of the Lagumdschi—miners—received fiefs, not pay and were therefore held in greater honour Hammer, Staatsverfassung der Osm ii 233.

‡ Especially in the Journal in Anton, p 34, concerning Reischach, see p 32, 4th October

§ See especially the first Venetian Report in Hammer, p 13?, he mentions Rogendorf, Frich de Rays et alcuni nobili con 4 bandiere de fanti insieme cum li Spagnoli

‖ Jovius, 28, 69, generally follows private accounts The mention of the Count of Oettingen shows that he speaks of the 11th of October

hoar-frost;* they thought with anxiety on the length and danger of the way back, and remembered that no preparation was made for the three years' absence of which Suleiman had spoken. Added to this, there were rumours of approaching relief. An army of the hereditary subjects of Austria was assembling in Moravia, while armaments were actively making in the circles of the Swabian league.

Schärtlin boasts what admirable soldiers he recruited in Würtenberg. Count Palatine Frederic, who had remained in the neighbourhood of Vienna, assumed a more menacing attitude. The peasants had already begun successfully to resist the bands of skirmishers. Suleiman perceived what would be his position if he were attacked here, in a hostile country, without any fortified places, and in the bad season, by an enemy whose valour he had now learned to appreciate. He determined to make one last attempt on Vienna, and if that failed, immediately to raise the siege and retreat. He chose a day which he regarded as lucky, the 14th of October, — the day on which the sun enters the Scorpion. Exactly at noon he assembled a large part of his army within sight of the walls. Tschausche proclaimed rewards, mines were sprung, breaches opened, and the signal for storming was given. But the soldiers had lost all confidence; they were driven forward almost by force, and then came within range of the guns on the walls, so that whole ranks fell without even seeing the enemy. Towards evening a band was seen to advance from the vineyards, and instantly to retire again.†

Hereupon a general retreat began: the Anatolians now formed the main guard; in the night the sultan himself struck his tent; the Janissaries set fire to their encampments in the suburbs, and hastened to accompany their lord. A few days afterwards Ibrahim followed with the rest of the European troops.

It was the first time that an enterprise of the victorious sultan had so totally failed. He now perceived that he was not, so absolutely as his poets boasted, "the gold in the mine of the world—the soul in the body of the world;"‡ that there were other vigorous and invincible forces besides himself, and beyond his power to subdue.

For the moment, however, he had reason to console himself; he had wrested Hungary from the Germans. John Zapolya received the sacred crown from the hands of the Ottoman authorities; though called king, he was in fact only a lieutenant of the sultan.

It might have been thought that Ferdinand would take advantage of the disorder of this retreat, and of the army collected for the relief of Vienna, to reconquer the kingdom; and in fact the frontier towns, Altenburg, Trentschin, &c. fell into his hands; but the castle of Gran held out, and the troops which came up were far too weak to recover Ofen.§ The cause of this failure is evident enough;—the king had no money. It would have required at least 20,000 gulden to set the troops in motion; he could raise only 1400 gulden (and even that sum in base coin), and a few thousand gulden worth of cloth. The discontent was universal. The Tyrolese, who were urgently entreated to take part in this enterprise, had unanimously refused; the people flatly declared they had no mind to serve any longer.‖ Suleiman, on retiring from before Vienna, had rewarded the Janissaries for their efforts, however unsuccessful, with rich gifts; while the landsknechts, who had so gallantly and so successfully defended the city, were not paid even the storming-money (*Sturmsold*) to which they had a sort of right. The consequence was, a violent mutiny broke out among them. Such being the state of things in the imperial army, their adversaries in Hungary were soon predominant. In the upper districts we find several German captains of note (especially that Nickel Minkwitz, who gave the Elector of Brandenburg so much trouble) in the service of Zapolya; from Kesmark he traversed the country and set fire to Leutschau.¶ Meanwhile the Turks made an irruption over the Bosnian frontier, and Croatia was in danger of falling into their hands; a disaster, the consequences of which extended even to the remoter parts of the country. In Bohemia, Zapolya had so many warm supporters, even among the most considerable men of the kingdom, that when Ferdinand went to Prague, at the end of January, 1530, he came to the conviction that he must get rid of all those who had any share in the government, if he meant to be master of the country.** This disastrous state of things, however, only proves more strongly the immeasurable importance of the defence of Vienna.

The emperor advised his brother to con-

* Pomis uvisque immaturis vescebantur: equi strictis arborum frondibus et vitium pampinis tolerabantur. Ursinus Velius.

† "Sie haben kurz den Fuxen nicht wöllen beissen" (in short they would not bite the fox), says the official report (Hammer, p. 68), which is written with the joyous humour of a victorious soldier. Hans Sachs says in his Historia der türkischen Belagerung der Statt Wien, und handlung beyder tail, auf das kürzest ordenlich begriffen (Thl. i. 208),

"Da sach man naus auf manchem thurn,
Das die Türken getrieben wurn,
Von iren waschen mit gewalt,
Mit saybeln prügeln jung und alt,
Aus iren hütten und gezelten,
Aus den weinbergen und den welden,
Das sie anlaufen stürmen solten,
Das sie sich ärsten und nit wolten."

"Then the people saw from many a tower that the Turks were driven with force from their watches, young and old, with blows of sabres, out of their huts and their tents, out of the vineyards and woods; that they should [were ordered to] rush to the assault, and that they halted and would not."

‡ Baki's Kasside, translated by Hammer, p. 7.

§ Ursinus Velius, lib. viii.

‖ Instructions of the military commissaries in Presburg for Count Nicholas zu Salm the younger, imperial councillor and chamberlain to King Ferdinand: Hormayr, Taschenbuch auf 1840, p. 506.

¶ Sperfogel, and the journal of Pastor Moller of Leutschau, whose own full barns were set on fire, Katona. xx. 1, p. 540, 546. Minkwitz is here called Nicholaus Mynkowitz; he went soon after from Kesmark to Ofen.

** Letter from Ferdinand to Charles, 21st January, 1530, in Gevay, p. 68. Entre tant que ils ont le governement, je ne saroie avoir obeisance ne poroie meintenir la justice.

clude a truce with the sultan, since, at this moment, their combined forces were not sufficient to confront him, and no other prince would afford them assistance

Nay, even in Italy, he had felt the reaction consequent on the triumphs of the Ottoman arms

CHAPTER VIII

CHARLES V. IN ITALY

Notwithstanding the numerous victories obtained by Charles V, notwithstanding their sudden abandonment (contrary to all promise) by Francis I, the Italian states were still in a condition to oppose a formidable resistance to the imperial arms

Venice was in possession of her entire Terra firma, some towns in the States of the Church, and several strong places in the Neapolitan territory, which she successfully defended she kept a noble army in the field, which, if it had won no celebrated victory, had never been beaten, under the conduct of a leader who knew how to satisfy the cautious and jealous senate, and, at the same time, to maintain his own reputation Her naval power too was in a flourishing condition an expedition was preparing in Corfu which was to make a descent on the Neapolitan coast at Brindisi

The Duke of Milan, in spite of long and ruinous wars, still held possession of the greater part of his country, and (besides some less considerable) was master of the strongest places at that time in Italy—Cremona, Lodi and Alessandria

It was hardly to be supposed that the Duke of Ferrara, who had defended a territory fortified by nature and art, against innumerable attacks, would not now be able to repel his enemies.

Florence was governed by a party resolved to maintain their liberties even by a struggle for life and death, Michel Angelo Buonarotti, himself a member of it, fortified the city with a fertility of invention and a skill in the execution, which, a century and a half later, excited the admiration of a Vauban,* a sort of levy *en masse* was organised throughout the territory The Florentines were already in alliance with Perugia, which they hoped to get completely into their hands They were also on tolerably good terms with Siena, which was, like Florence,† oppressed by the pope

The States of the Church and Naples were still in a state of universal disquiet and ferment

How often had Italy offered successful resistance to warlike emperors, who crossed the Alps with far more powerful armies than that at the disposal of Charles, even though they were supported by a party in the country! Even when an emperor had gained a firm footing there, this had only served to unite all parties in Italy in a common effort to drive him back. Neither valour nor talent, neither Frederick I nor Frederick II, had been able to give stability and permanence to their domination

And now came this youthful emperor, whose pale face and feeble voice — whose frame, graceful and healthy, but far from robust, gave him rather the air of a courtier than a warrior—who had never seen a serious battle—and were they to submit to him?

The chief circumstance in his favour was, that he was closely united with the pope, in consequence of the affairs of Florence On his arrival at Venice, the Florentines sent an embassy to him, but of course with limited powers, since they were determined at all events to maintain their actual constitution. The emperor answered, that they must, in the first place, recall the Medici, and restore them to the rank they held before their last expulsion ‡ The young Alessandro, whom he destined to be his son-in-law and ruler of Florence, was already in his train § Moreover, he could not endure a government which had always leaned to the Guelph and French party Until, however, this affair was settled, the emperor was completely sure of the pope, who entertained a passionate hatred of the enemies of his house in Florence.

It might possibly occur to Charles V that he might take arms again, and compel his divided antagonists to accept his conditions This the intimate friends whom he had consulted at his departure from Germany, probably expected, for his presence, they averred, would be equivalent to an army of ten thousand men, the world must be shown that nobody could resist where the emperor appeared in person Some old captains of the Italian wars were also in favour of this course. Charles afterwards regretted that he did not pursue it, and especially that he did not immediately enter the Venetian territory, the issue of the attempt of the Turks on Vienna being what it was, he might then have dictated a peace ‖

This issue, however, it had been impossible to foresee, and the first effect of the advance of the grand sultan was rather to awaken in

* Vasari Vita di Buonarotti (Vite d Pitt X., 110)

† Relatio n v Antonii Suriani de legatione Florentina, 1529 Et però cum questo fondamento de inimicitia con il papa, queste republiche hanno trattato insieme qualche intelligentia

‡ According to Jacopo Pitti, Apologia de capucci, a MS. full of excellent information, the ambassadors had the 'segreta commissione, di non pregiudicare nè alla liberta nè al dominio il che notificato con piu segretezza a Cesare, hebbono per ultima risposta, che se volevano levarsi da dosso la guerra, rimettessero i Medici nello stato che erano avanti si partissero dalla citta onde li oratori se ne partirono subito" See Varchi, ix 234

§ Carlo V a Clemente VII 29 d'Agosto Similmente dico, ch'io sto molto contento della persona del Duca Alessandro Lettere di principi ii, f 185.

‖ Charles to Ferdinand, 10 January, 1530 Me trouvois plus loing de vous que n'eusse fait si dez le commencement je me fusse party au pays des Veniciens, et eusse été plus pres pour mieux vous pouvoir succourir et eulx plus voluntaires pour venir a ung meilleur appointement faillant votre necessité comme elle a fait. Brussels Archives.

the Italian powers a hope that they might find that support in the Turks, which France no longer afforded them. Milan and Venice, therefore, drew closer the bonds of their alliance; they determined on mutual succours, and each promised not to conclude a separate peace. War broke out again in Lombardy; Leiva took Pavia, and a few thousand landsknechts under Count Felix von Werdenberg, invaded the Venetian territory along the Lago di Garda, and plundered the Brescian country.* These slight successes, however, decided nothing, and the two states presented a front fully armed and prepared for self-defence.

Suleiman's retreat altered the face of things: the Italians, abandoned on all sides, lost courage;† but the emperor had in the interval constantly evinced such pacific dispositions, that he could not revert to any warlike schemes, without breaking his word and losing for ever the public confidence.‡

It was not agreeable to him indeed to restore the Milanese, which he would gladly have disposed of otherwise, to Francesco Sforza, nor to leave the towns of the Terra firma, which he claimed as emperor, in the hands of the Venetians; but, all circumstances considered, it was not to be avoided.§

It was most important to him to make peace with the Venetians, who still possessed some strong places and good harbours in the Neapolitan territory. By the acquisition of these, Naples would be tranquillized, it would then be able to conduct its own administration, and to contribute to the general expenses of the empire.

In order to retain possession of the Milanese, he must first wrest from Francesco Sforza the fortresses, which were in an excellent state of defence; this could not be done without a serious war, and would unsettle the treaty of peace concluded with France, and even with the pope.

Pope Clement earnestly wished for peace. His former schemes of restoring the independence of Italy, had been merged in his desire to reduce Florence to obedience. Now it was manifest that a renewal of the war, let it terminate how it might, would open to that city a possibility of resistance, while it would greatly diminish his means of attack, by furnishing other occupation to the imperial army. He thought, therefore, he did enough for Milan and for Italy if he procured them a tolerable peace.‖

Every thing that had happened had served to confirm the emperor in the opinion, that he could not maintain his power in Italy without the friendship of the pope.

Towards the end of the year 1529, they held a conference in Bologna, the object of which was, from the beginning, the complete pacification of Italy; negotiations to that effect having already made some progress under the mediation of the pope. On the 5th of November the emperor arrived, and found Clement awaiting him.

The pope and the emperor, like the two royal ladies in Cambray, inhabited adjoining houses, connected by a door of which each had a key.¶

The emperor took care to prepare himself beforehand for every conversation with the veteran politician. He had a paper in his hand, on which he had noted all the topics to be discussed at that interview.

The first point on which he listened to the pope's advice was, to cite his rebellious vassal, Francesco Sforza, against whom he had proclaimed sentence of forfeiture of his duchy, to appear before him.

Sforza was seriously ill. He was obliged to support himself on a staff when he spoke with the emperor, and the pope would not allow him to kiss his foot. But his cause did not suffer; he showed prudence, ability, and good dispositions; he spoke extremely well, and understood how to conciliate his own interest with entire devotion to his suzerain.** With the great men about the court he employed other means of persuasion. Gradually, the old resentment against him was allowed to subside.

The Venetian ambassador also endeavoured to remove the displeasure which the emperor might have conceived against the republic. He obtained an audience of two hours, and had the satisfaction of finding that the emperor understood the situation of the republic, and admitted the justification he had to offer.

The bases of a treaty were therefore soon agreed upon; the Venetians were to give up whatever they possessed belonging to the states of the church or to Naples, and on that condition, were not to be attacked. Francesco Sforza was to receive the fief of the duchy of Milan.

The only difficulty lay in the demands for money both on Venice and Milan. In order to make sure of payment from the latter, the emperor wished to garrison the citadels of Milan and Como with his troops. On the 12th of December, a courier arrived, bringing the assent of the Venetian senate to the pecuniary

* Leoni, Vita di Francesco Maria 410

† Jacopo Pitti Tutti calarono le bracche per la fuga Turchesca, altrimente l'imperatore haberebbe havuto che fare molto piu che non si pensasse

‡ Pour ceste occasion du Turcq j'avois tant parlé de ceste paix qu'il ne m'eust semble honneste la laisser de faire (Lettre a Ferdinand, 10 Janv)

§ Si j'eusse veu moyen d'en faire autrement, n'en eusse usé ainsi Ib

‖ Recollections in a letter from Rome, doubtless from Sanga to the Bishop of Vasona, papal nuncio at the emperor's court Lettere di principi, ii 181–185.

¶ Romischer keyserlicher Majestat eynreyten gen Bononia, auch wie sich bebstliche Heyligkeit gegen seyne keyserliche Majestat gehalten habe, 1529 His Roman imperial majesty's journey to Bologna, also how his papal holiness demeaned himself towards his imperial majesty, 1529 At the conclusion "Und liegen der Keyser und der Babst also nah bei einander, das nit mer dan ein kleyn wand zwyschen inen ist, und haben ein Thur zusammengehn und jeder ein schlussel darzu"—"And the emperor and the pope lie near each other, so that not more than a little wall is between them, and they have a door through which to meet, and each has a key thereof"

** Confidarsi in lei (S M) ponersi in man sua Contarini Relatione di Bologna, 1530.

terms imposed on the republic, as well as to those regarding Milan *

Hereupon, on the 23d of December, a treaty of peace was concluded, which was at the same time one of alliance The Venetians engaged to pay off the arrears of subsidies which they owed in virtue of the treaty of 1523, by instalments, during the next eight years, and, besides, 100,000 sc in the next year † Francesco Sforza was much more severely dealt with, a sum of 900,000 scudi, to be discharged at fixed periods, was demanded of him, 400,000 of which he was to pay within the next year This was, as we perceive, the emperor's system, he treated Milan and Venice in the same manner as he had treated Portugal and France, he waived claims which he might have asserted, in consideration of money The emperor promised to defend Milan and Venice, and the Venetians, on their part, Naples and Milan, in case of an attack

The Duke of Ferrara was still not included in the peace As he was also at enmity with the pope, he had neglected no means of obtaining access to Charles himself It is said that Andrea Doria wrote to him, that his only way of gaining the favour of the emperor, was to show confidence in him ‡ When, therefore, Charles entered Modena, the duke went out to meet him, carrying the keys of the city, and from that moment it is certain that the emperor showed himself favourably disposed towards him The pope was far less placable It was with the utmost difficulty that he was induced to submit his disputes with Ferrara to a fresh investigation by the emperor himself, in whose hands the duke had consented to place Modena as a deposit

In the Florentine affairs, Clement was perfectly immovable Envoys from that republic presented themselves before him again at Bologna, but they were only met by violent explosions of temper on the part of the pope, and bitter reproaches for all the personal affronts that had been offered to himself, and to the friends by whom he was surrounded in Rome The emperor repeated what he had always said, that he was not come to Italy to injure anybody, but to make peace, but that he had now pledged his word to the pope, and must abide by it § The affair had often been discussed in his privy-council It had been decided that, in the first place, Florence had forfeited her privileges by rebellion, and that the emperor had an indisputable right to punish her, and secondly, that the pope was, independently of this, fully justified in his demands; since the vicar of Christ would certainly commit no injustice ‖ Perugia, Arezzo, and Cortona were already in the hands of the imperialists, the Prince of Orange, though not as fully persuaded of the justice of the pope's claims as his master, obeyed orders, and in the month of February encamped with his army in the neighbourhood of Florence. During the carnival, there were daily skirmishes at the gates

The emperor wished to settle all the affairs of Italy now definitively, that he might be at liberty to go for a few months to Naples, where his presence was very desirable He would then have taken Rome in his way, and, as ancient usage demanded, have received the crown there with all the customary solemnities There were persons about him who told him that he had accomplished nothing, if he had not been crowned in Rome itself Others, however, doubted whether the place was of so much importance, and Charles thought it expedient first to ask his brother, whether the affairs of Germany would allow of his absenting himself for the time required for this journey ¶ Ferdinand replied, the sooner he returned the better, if he went to Naples, his enemies would imagine he would never come back It was therefore decided that the coronation should take place at Bologna, the emperor determined to commemorate his birthday and the anniversary of the battle of Pavia, by this solemn act

Solemnities of this kind have a twofold significancy, they connect the present immediately with the remote past; while, at the same time, they have a character determined by the circumstances of the moment.

The coronation of Charles was distinguished by many peculiarities It did not take place at Rome, as had been the invariable custom, but at Bologna; the church of San Petronio was the substitute for St Peter's, the chapels which were used for the various functions were named after the chapels of St Peter's, and there was a place marked in the church which represented the confessional of St Peter's **

Nor did the emperor appear with the same state as his predecessors He had neglected to summon the electors, a single German prince was present — Philip of the Palatinate, who had arrived by chance the day before the coronation — the same who had just acquired a certain celebrity at the siege of Vienna, but he held no official rank or charge at the ceremony An escort of German knights, such as had heretofore accompanied their emperor to the bridge of the Tiber, was out of the question, instead of them, three thousand Ger-

* Gregorio Casale, 13th Dec Molini, ii p 263

† Tractatus pacis ligæ et perpetuæ confœderationis, Du Mont iv, ii p 53

‡ Galeacius Capella, lib viii p 218

§ Jacopo Pitti Rispose loro Cesare gratamente, dolerli del male pativa la Citta perche egli non era venuto in Italia per nuocere ad alcuno, ma per metterci pace, non poter gia in questo caso mancare al papa — nè credere che voglia il papa cose inconvenienti replicaronli li oratori, che la città desiderava solamente mantenere il suo governo —— Cesare disse, che forse il governo parerebbe loro ragionevole, nondimeno haberebbe bisogno di qualche correctione.

‖ Declaration of the emperor's confessor Varchi, p 338

¶ The immediate purpose of the letter of the 10th of January, so often referred to, which I discovered during my second visit to Brussels, and will insert in the Appendix was this inquiry Ferdinand received it on the 18th, and answered on the 28th from Budweis The answer is printed in Gevay, 1530 App No 1 .

** Consurgens electus venit ad confessionem B Petri ——— et in loco humili et depresso ad instar loci ante ingressum capellæ S. Petri de urbe procubuit. Rainaldus, xx 568.

man landsknechts were drawn out on the piazza, gallant and warlike soldiers, but under the command of a Spaniard, Antonio de Leiva, who had made his entrance into the city at their head, carried on a litter of dark brown velvet Whatever brilliancy surrounded the emperor, had attended him from Spain, or had come to meet him in Italy The procession with which he repaired to the church, to be invested with the imperial crown, on the 24th of February, 1530 (having two days previously received the iron crown with somewhat modified solemnities), was opened by Spanish pages of noble birth, then followed the Spanish lords we have already enumerated, vying with each other in pomp and splendour, after them, the heralds—not German, but principally those of the several Spanish provinces the sceptre was borne by the Marquis of Monferrat, the sword, by the Duke of Urbino, the globe, by Count Palatine Philip, and, lastly, the crown, by the Duke of Savoy The electors learned with wonder that their hereditary charges had been committed to others, without even asking their consent After these undelegated performers of their functions, walked the emperor, between two cardinals, and followed by the members of his privy-council A wooden gallery had been erected to connect the palace with the church of St Petronio, hardly had the emperor passed through it, when it broke down Many regarded this as an omen that he would be the last emperor who would be crowned in Italy —a prediction which the event fulfilled He himself saw in the incident only a fresh proof of his good fortune, which protected him in the moment of danger *

He was now invested with the sandals, and the mantle, ponderous and stiff with jewels, which had been brought from the court of Byzantium He was anointed with the exorcised oil, according to a formula almost exactly the same as that used by Hinkmar of Rheims,† the crown of Charlemagne was placed upon his head; he was adorned with all the insignia of the most ancient and sacred dignity of Chief of Christendom But while receiving its honours, he also accepted its obligations, he took the oath which, in the triumphant days of the hierarchy, the popes had imposed upon the emperors—to defend the pope, the Roman church, and all their possessions, dignities, and rights, and as he was a conscientious man, we cannot doubt that he pronounced this oath with the most earnest sincerity The union of the spiritual and temporal hierarchy required to complete the idea of Latin Christendom, was once more consummated

During the ceremony, the French ambassador, the Bishop of Tarbes, stood between the throne of the emperor and that of the pope, with the Count of Nassau They spoke much of the friendship now existing between their sovereigns, which left nothing to desire, except that it should be permanent But it is only necessary to read the report of the ceremony sent by the bishop to his own court, to see that he, at least, meant the very reverse of what he said He pretends to have perceived that the pope sighed whenever he thought himself unobserved He declares in the same letter that the protracted meeting of the two sovereigns had rather tended to generate aversion than friendship, that the pope had said to him, that he saw he was cheated, but that he must act as if he did not see it In short, he declared it certain that time would bring about proceedings on the pope s part, with which the King of France might be well satisfied ‡

From the correspondence of the emperor with his brother, we also see that he felt by no means secure of the pope

It were a mistake to imagine that it would then have been safe or possible for him to act as if he were sovereign lord of Italy, but he knew how to profit by the moment when his enemies were exhausted and deprived of political support, in order to strengthen that ascendency which he had acquired by arms, and thus to lay the basis of future domination

The pope might vent his anger as he pleased in moments of irritation, but he could no longer emancipate himself from the emperor Florence being reduced to subjection after a brave resistance, the emperor conferred upon the house of Medici a more firmly based legitimate power than it had ever possessed, a family alliance was concluded, which rendered impossible in future any of those violent divisions which had hitherto rent the city

The emperor was also secure of Milan Sforza well knew that Francis I had not wholly renounced his pretensions to Lombardy, as was evident from the eagerness with which some Milanese of rank sought to renew their connexion with France Sforza was therefore compelled to attach himself unconditionally to the emperor, to whom alone he could look for protection Shortly after, he too became allied by marriage with the house of Austria An imperial general continued to command the army in Lombardy

Venice retained a far greater share of independence But here, too, the peace had been brought about by a party in opposition to the doge, and relying on its friendly relations with Austria and Spain for its own support Moreover, the republic, menaced by the Ottomans, was compelled to seek assistance in Europe, which no other power but Spain was in a condition to afford It had gradually come to a conviction that the time for conquest and

* Jovius, 27th Book De duplici coronatione Caroli V Cæsaris ap Bononiam historiola, autore H C Agrippa Schardius, iii 265

† The words of the unction in the ritual, "Ipse—super caput tuum infundat benedictionem eandem usque ad interiora cordis tui penetrare faciat" (Rainaldus, p 569, No 23), strongly remind us of Hinkmar's formula of 877 "Cujus sacratissima unctio super caput ejus defluat atque ad interiora ejus descendat et intima cordis illius penetret." But the earlier form is in all respects more beautiful

‡ Lettre de M de Gramont, Ev de Tarbes à M l'Admiral, Boulogne, 25 Fevrier, in La Grande Histoire du Divorce, tom iii p 386

extension of territory was for ever past for Venice, that she was entering on a new era, the character of which would be determined by her relations with Spain

Nor had the emperor been less anxious to attach to himself the lesser princes and republics

The Markgrave of Mantua was raised to the dignity of duke, Carpi was granted to the Duke of Ferrara, by the emperor, to his brother-in-law, the Duke of Savoy, he gave Asti, which Francis I had surrendered, — to his no small disgust; to the Duke of Urbino—at that time the most renowned warrior of Italy — Charles had offered service, and distinguished him with many personal favours in Bologna

The old Ghibelline spirit revived in Siena and Lucca, and was fostered in every possible way by the emperor Whatever might be said of the restored liberties of Genoa, the real effect of the changes that had taken place there was to render Andrea Doria absolute * The name given to him — Il Figone (the fig-gardener) — from his birth-place, the Riviera, soon gave way to another — the Monarch And this monarch of Genoa was admiral to the emperor

Charles bound the great capitalists to his interests by a different, but not less powerful tie, he borrowed money of them

There is no doubt that all these powers might imagine themselves independent, they might certainly have embraced a different line of policy, and, indeed, they occasionally meditated doing so But either their internal or external affairs afforded motives which bound them to the emperor, and these motives were now partly enhanced by design, partly developed by the nature of things, while Charles's power was so vast and dazzling, that a connexion with him was no less flattering to the ambition, than profitable to the interests, of lesser sovereigns

The world thus once more beheld an emperor in the plenitude of power, but the bases on which this power rested were new, the old imperial office and dignity were gone

Least of all could the German nation boast that the Germanic empire had recovered its ancient character and powers

The electors complained that they were neither summoned to the coronation, nor invited to take a share in the treaties which the emperor had concluded with the Italian powers They entered a formal protest, that if any thing should have been agreed to in these treaties which might now or hereafter prove detrimental to the holy Roman empire, they had in no wise assented or consented to it †

The emperor had already been reminded that the conquered provinces of Italy did not belong to him, but to the empire, and had been required to restore to the empire its finance chambers (Kammern), especially those of Milan and Genoa, upon which the imperial government would appoint a gubernator, and would appropriate the surplus revenues to the maintenance of tranquillity and law Such, however, were not the notions of the emperor, or of his Spanish captains The Duke of Brunswick affirmed that obstacles had been intentionally thrown in his way, during his Italian campaign in the year 1528, by Antonio Leiva, the Spaniard, he said, would endure no German prince in the Milanese And this same Leiva had now received Pavia in fief, and held the supreme command over an army in the field German influence was destroyed.

Under these circumstances the emperor, no longer the perfect representative of the national power, took his way over the Tridentine Alps to Germany (May, 1530) ‡

If we inquire what were his own views as to Germany, we shall discover that none but the most proximate presented themselves with any distinctness to his mind

He had promised his brother, whose fidelity to him through all the complications of his Italian affairs had been unshaken, — who, feeble as were his resources, was ever ready to come to his aid, and who had been his most useful ally,—to confer upon him the dignity of King of the Romans The attempts to transfer this dignity to another house — attempts continually renewed and not without danger—must, he said, be put an end to The fitting moment was now arrived, they must take advantage of this full tide of power and victory

It had likewise become absolutely necessary to take effectual measures against the Turks Recent events had shown the Germans that not Hungary alone, but their own fatherland was at stake, the imminence of the danger would render them more complying This was an indispensable condition to the stability of the house of Austria

Yet he distinctly felt that this state of things would not be permanent

During his stay in Italy, a pacific demeanour —not indeed at variance with his disposition, which rather inclined that way, but contrary to his original intentions — had been imposed upon him by the state of things But the warlike schemes of his youth, though suspended, were not abandoned When he turned his eyes on Germany (as he tells his brother in a letter), he wished to confer with him about many things and especially about their future conduct towards that nation,— whether they should remain at peace, or engage in any warlike expedition, whether they should immediately join in a common effort against the Turks, or wait for some great occasion which might justify their enterprise

Every thing depended on the course of religious affairs, and these had already occupied his deliberate attention

* Basadorna Relatione di Milano, 1533 Esso Doria fa il privato e guberna absolutamente Genoa Del che si doleno Genoesi

† Protest of the 30th July, 1530, in the Coblentz Archives

‡ Bucholtz, iii 92 Note

CHAPTER IX

DIET OF AUGSBURG, 1530

By the treaty of Barcelona the emperor had bound himself to endeavour, in the first place, to bring back the dissidents to the faith, and if that attempt should fail, then to apply all his power ' to avenge the insult offered to Christ '*

I do not doubt that this engagement was entirely in accordance with his intentions

Revolting and arbitrary as the opinion delivered to him by his companion, the papal legate Campeggi, appears to us, it is in fact founded on the same ideas Campeggi begins by suggesting the means by which the Protestants might be reclaimed,—promises, threats, alliances with the states which remained true to Catholicism, in case, however all these should be unavailing, he insists most strongly on the necessity of resorting to force,—to fire and sword, as he expresses it, he declares that their property should be confiscated, and Germany be subjected to the vigilance of an inquisition similar to that established in Spain †

All that has come down to us of the correspondence of the emperor with his brother, breathes the same spirit and the same purposes

Ferdinand had, as we know, entered into negotiations with Elector John of Saxony, but he assures the emperor that he does this only to gain time "You may think," adds he, "that I concede too much, and you may thus be hindered from proceeding to the work of punishment Monseigneur, I will negotiate as long as possible, and will conclude nothing, but, even should I have concluded, there will be many other pretexts for chastising them,—reasons of state, without your needing to mention religion, they have played so many bad tricks besides, that you will find people who will willingly help you in this matter "‡

This, therefore, was the design, to try first whether the Protestants could not be brought back by fair means to the unity of Latin Christendom, which was now restored to peace, and to the imposing aspect of a great system; but in case this did not succeed, the application of force was distinctly contemplated, and the right to apply it carefully reserved

It would not have been prudent, however, to irritate the antipathies of offended self-love by threats Clemency ceases to be clemency, if future severity is seen lurking in the background It was therefore determined at present to turn only the fair side to view

The emperor's convocation of the diet breathed nothing but peace He announced his desire "to allay divisions, to leave all past errors to the judgment of our Saviour, and, further, to give a charitable hearing to every man's opinions, thoughts, and notions, to weigh them carefully, to bring men to Christian truth, and to dispose of every thing that has not been rightly explained on both sides " This proclamation was dated from the palace in which the emperor was living with the pope The pope left the emperor's hands free, and, indeed, he too would have been rejoiced if these lenient measures had been successful

But whatever moderation might appear in the emperor s language, the orthodox princes were sufficiently well informed of the temper of the imperial court, and of its connexion with that of Rome, not to conceive the liveliest hopes on its arrival They hastened to draw up a statement of all their grievances, and to revise all the old judgments and orders in council for the suppression of the Lutheran agitation "It pleases us much,' says the Administrator of Regensburg, in the instructions to his envoys to the diet, "that the innovations against the excellent and long-established usages of the church should be rooted out and abolished "§ The emperor at first held his court at Innsbruck, in order, by the aid of his brother's advice, to secure a favourable result of the proceedings of the diet. Of what nature these were, may be inferred from one fact,—that the Venetian ambassador saw an account from which it appeared that, between the time of its departure from Bologna, to the 12th of July, 1530, the imperial court had expended 270,000 gulden in presents Prosperity and power, in themselves sufficiently imposing and attractive, were now, as for centuries in Germany, aided by all the influence of largesses and favours All who had any thing to expect from the court now flocked thither, and it was almost forgotten that the diet ought long ago to have been opened, every man was intent on getting his own business settled without delay ‖

It soon appeared from one example, how great an influence the emperor's presence would exercise on religious affairs His brother-in-law, the exiled King Christiern of Denmark, who had hitherto adhered to Luther, constantly corresponded with him, and openly declared himself a convert to his doctrines, was induced in Innsbruck to return to the old faith The pope was overjoyed when he heard it "I cannot express," he writes to the emperor, "with what emotion this news has filled me The splendour of your majesty's virtues begins to scare away the night, this example will work upon numberless others "¶ He granted Christiern absolution, and imposed upon him a penance which he was to perform after his restoration to his

* Vim potestatis distringent (Charles and Ferdinand)

† Instructio data Cæsari dal revmo Campeggio "con offerte prima, poi con minaccie ridurli nella via sua, cioè del Dio omnipotente" The opinion is attached to the deliberation at Bologna, with which Eck was acquainted See Luther's Warnung an seine lieben Deutschen (Warning to his dear Germans) Altenb v 534

‡ Letter from Ferdinand to the emperor, Budweis, 28th Jan, in Gevay s original documents of 1530, p 67 See the Excerpt from the Chancellor's letter in Bucholtz, iii 427

§ Forstemann Urkundenbuch zur Geschichte des Reichstags von Augsburg, bd i p 209

‖ Relatio viri nobilis Nic Theupulo doctoris, 1533 ne in esso vi erano spese se non di doni fatti a diversi signori (among whom were Italians)

¶ Roma, 3 Giugno, 1530 Lettere de' Principi, ii 194

kingdom The emperor himself hoped that, as he had succeeded, contrary to his expectations, in purifying Italy from heresy, he should not fail in Germany In Rome every thing was expected from the lucky star which seemed to preside over all his proceedings

Circumstances did indeed appear extremely propitious to his designs

The emperor's convocation had been favourably received by the Protestants The prince whose dispositions and conduct were the most important—the Elector of Saxony—was the first who arrived at Augsburg He went without delay to offer his congratulations to the emperor (who had crossed the Alps just at the same time) on his arrival in the empire, which he had learned "with loyal joy," he would wait the pleasure of his majesty, his own chief and lord, in Augsburg * He had invited his allies to follow him, for the diet of Augsburg seemed to be the national council which had been so long expected, so often and so vainly demanded, and which now afforded a hope of the reconciliation of religious differences †

The negotiations of the elector with King Ferdinand had, as may be presumed from what we have just stated, led to no conclusion, but they were by no means broken off Elector John had also various other affairs to discuss with the imperial court, to arrange which he had sent an ambassador to Innsbruck The question, whether it might not be possible to win him over, presented itself, and an attempt was made to prevail on him to come himself to Innsbruck The emperor sent him word that he might rely on all possible friendship from him, and invited him to come to his court, as many other princes had done "He intended to unite with him in the settlement of affairs, which might be arranged by themselves in person '

But here, too, Charles had a proof of the kind of resistance which he would have to encounter in Germany The elector was offended that the emperor had urged him, through the ambassador of another power, to impose silence on the preachers he had brought with him This demand appeared to him an unauthorised attempt to prejudge the very question to be inquired into, and he was persuaded that the compliance which he refused in Augsburg would be extorted from him in Innsbruck, in case he appeared there He saw, too, that the court was already filled with his personal adversaries Nor did he think it expedient to enter upon the business of the diet at any other place than the one appointed In short, he adhered to his declaration, that he would wait the emperor's coming in Augsburg

The imperial court was generally unprepared for the bearing exhibited by the Protestants assembled in Augsburg, for the approbation the preachers obtained in that city, and the popularity they enjoyed throughout Germany In Italy it had been thought that at the first mutterings of the tempest, the Protestants would disperse, like a flock of doves when the hawk pounces down in the midst of them ‡ Chancellor Gattinara first remarked that the court would find more difficulties than he had himself anticipated § Gattinara, an old antagonist of the papal policy, and without question the most adroit politician the emperor possessed, would perhaps have been the man to modify the views of the court so as to render them attainable; even the Protestants relied upon him But exactly at this moment he died at Innsbruck The state of things excited no such serious misgivings in the others what did not succeed in Innsbruck, they hoped to accomplish, by some means or other, in Augsburg

On the 6th of June, the emperor set out for that city He took Munich in his way, where he was magnificently received Accompanied by the temporal and spiritual princes of Austria and Bavaria—the same who formerly concluded the Regensburg league—he reached the bridge over the Lech, before Augsburg, on the evening of the 15th

The most brilliant assemblage of princes of the empire that had been witnessed for a long time, had already been waiting for some hours to receive him, sovereigns, spiritual and temporal, from Upper and Lower Germany, and a very numerous body of young princes, who had not yet attained to sovereignty As soon as the emperor approached, they alighted from their horses and advanced to meet him The emperor too alighted, and put out his hand to each of them in a courteous and friendly manner The Elector of Mainz greeted him in the name of all these "assembled members of the holy Roman empire " Hereupon they all prepared to make their solemn entry into the imperial city As we have just contemplated the imperial coronation, in which Germany had hardly any share, we must pause a moment over this still essentially German ceremony of the solemn entry ‖

* To Nassau and Waldkirch, 14 May, Förstemann, i 162, 164

† 13th March, ibid p 24 See the opinion in Brück, p 11 In einer Ermanung reymenweiss von Hans Marschalk 1530, wird Gott gebeten offenbar zu machen sein Wort 'damit es komme an ein Ort in diesem Reichstag und Concilio " In "an admonition rhyme wise," by John Marschalk 1530, God is prayed to proclaim his work 'whereby a place may be appointed for this diet and council " Here the hopes of former years re appear The emperor is admonished to embrace the divine word, "damit nicht weyter werd geplent das arm volk der Christenheit, welches lang auf schmaler weyd des Glaubens halb irr gangen ist,"—' that so the poor people be no longer deprived of Christianity who, on account of their scanty nourishment of faith, have long gone half astray "

‡ Leodius, lib vii p 139 See how Erasmus speaks of Sadolet —Duæ res nonnullam præbent spem una est genius Cæsaris mire felix altera quod isti in dogmatibus mire inter se dissentiunt End of 1529, or beginning of 1530 Epp ii 1238

§ Raince, Rome 1 Juin Le s père est adverti, que le chancelier se trouvoit aucunement (in some degree—the sense in which Raince often uses it) deçu de l oppinion facille, en quoy il en avoit été, et qu'il commençoit a confesser qu'il s appercevoit les choses en tout cas y être plus laides qu'ils ne pensoient MS Bethune, 8534.

‖ We have several accounts of this ceremony 1st In the Altenburg collection of Luther's works. 2d. In Cyprian's History of the Augsburg Confession, and two pamphlets called, 3d Kaiserl Maj Einreitung zu Munchen, and, 4th, Kais Maj Einreiten zum Reichstag gen Augs-

Foremost marched two companies of landsknechts, to whom the emperor entrusted the guard of the imperial city, as whose newly-arrived lord he wished to be regarded. They were just recruited, and had not that military air which is required in Germany, but there were many among them who had served in the Italian wars, and some who had become rich there. The most prominent figure was Simon Seitz, an Augsburg citizen, who served the emperor as military secretary, and who now, magnificently clad in gold, and mounted on a brown jennet with embroidered housings, returned to his native town with an air of splendid arrogance.

Next followed the mounted guard of the six electors. The Saxons, according to ancient usage, headed the procession, about a hundred and sixty horsemen, all habited in liver colour, with matchlocks in their hands. They consisted partly of the people about the court, princes and counts having one, two, or four horses, according to their dignity, partly of the councillors and nobles summoned from the country. People remarked the electoral prince, who had negotiated the first alliance with Hessen. Then followed the horsemen of the Palatinate, Brandenburg, Cologne, Mainz, and Treves, all in their proper colours and arms. According to the hierarchy of the empire, the Bavarians had no place here, but before they could be prevented, they had taken their place, and they at least filled it magnificently. They were all in light armour, with red surcoats, they rode by fives, and were distinguishable, even from a distance, by their waving plumes. There might be four hundred and fifty horses in all.

People were struck with the difference, when, after this most warlike pomp, the courts of the emperor and the king made their appearance: foremost, the pages, dressed in red or yellow velvet, then the Spanish, Bohemian and German lords, in garments of silk and velvet, with large gold chains, but almost all unarmed. They were mounted on the most beautiful horses, Turkish, Spanish, and Polish, and the Bohemians did not forget to display their gallant horsemanship.

This escort was followed by the two sovereigns in person.

Their coming was announced by two rows of trumpeters, partly in the king's colours, partly in the emperor's, accompanied by their drums, pursuivants, and heralds.

Here, then, were all the high and mighty lords who ruled almost without control in their wide domains; whose border quarrels were wont to fill Germany with tumult and war: Ernest of Luneburg and Henry of Brunswick, who were still in a state of unappeased strife concerning the Hildesheim quarrel, George of Saxony, and his son-in-law, Philip of Hessen, who had lately come into such rude collision, in consequence of Pack's plot, the Dukes of Bavaria, and their cousins, the counts palatine, whose short reconciliation now began to give way to fresh misunderstandings, near the princes of the house of Brandenburg, the Dukes of Pomerania, who, in despite of them, hoped to receive, at the coming diet, infeudation as immediate lords. All these now acknowledged the presence of one above them all, to whom they paid common homage and deference. The princes were followed by the electors, temporal and spiritual. Side by side rode John of Saxony and Joachim of Brandenburg, between whom there was no slight grudge, sufficiently accounted for by the troubles caused by the flight of the wife of the markgrave. Elector John once more bore the drawn sword before his emperor. Immediately after the electors, came their chosen and now crowned chief, mounted on a white Polish charger, under a magnificent three-coloured baldachin, borne by six councillors of Augsburg. It was remarked that he who formed the centre of this imposing group was the only one who looked a stranger to it; he was dressed from head to foot in the Spanish fashion. He had expressed a wish to have his brother on the one side of him, and on the other, the legate, to whom he wished to pay the highest honour; he even wanted the ecclesiastical electors to yield precedence to him, but on this point they were inflexible. They thought they did Campeggi honour enough when the most learned of their college, Elector Joachim, who spoke Latin with considerable fluency (better at least than any of its spiritual members), offered him their congratulations. King Ferdinand and the legate accordingly rode together, outside the baldachin; they were followed by the German cardinals and bishops, the foreign ambassadors and prelates. Conspicuous among them was the emperor's haughty confessor, the Bishop of Osma.*

The procession of princes and lords was again succeeded by mounted guards, those of the emperor clad in yellow, those of the king in red; with them, vying in gallant equipments, the horsemen of the lords, spiritual and temporal, each troop in its proper colours, all armed either with breast-plate and lance, or with fire-arms.

The militia of Augsburg, which had marched out in the morning to receive the emperor, foot and horse, paid troops and citizens, closed the procession.

This was in accordance with the whole import of the ceremony, viz., that the empire fetched home its emperor. Near St Leonard's church he was met by the clergy of the city, singing "Advenisti desiderabilis;" the princes accompanied him to the cathedral, where "Te Deum" was sung, and the benediction pronounced over him; nor did they leave him till they reached the door of his apartment in the palace.

But even here, at their very first meeting—in the church too—the great and all-dividing question which was to occupy this august assembly, presented itself in all its abruptness.

The Protestants had joined in the religious,

burg. The two former are reprinted in Walch, the two latter in Förstemann. Some particulars I extracted from Fürstenberg's letters.

* Contarini. "di spirito molto alto."

as well as the civil ceremonies; and the emperor was perhaps encouraged by this to take advantage of the first moment of his presence, the first impression made by his arrival, to prevail upon them to make some material concessions.

Allowing the remaining princes to depart, the emperor invited the Elector of Saxony, the Markgrave George of Brandenburg, Duke Francis of Lüneburg, and Landgrave Philip, to attend him in a private room, and there, through the mouth of his brother, requested them to put an end to the preachings. The elder princes, startled and alarmed, said nothing; the impetuous landgrave broke silence, and sought to justify his refusal on the ground that nothing was preached but the pure Word of God, just as St. Augustine had enjoined;—arguments consummately distasteful to the emperor. The blood rushed into his pallid cheeks, and he repeated his demand in a more imperious tone. But he had here to encounter a resistance of a very different nature from that he had experienced from the Italian powers, who contended only for the interests of a disputed possession. "Sire," said the old Markgrave George, now breaking silence, "rather than renounce God's word, I will kneel down on this spot to have my head cut off." The emperor, who wished to utter none but words of mildness, and was naturally benevolent, was himself alarmed at the possibility thus presented to his mind by the lips of another. "Dear prince," replied he to the markgrave, in his broken low German, "not heads off" (nicht Köpfe ab).*

The next difficulty was that the Protestants declined taking part in the procession of Corpus Christi, on the following day. Had the emperor required their attendance as a court service, they would probably have given it, "like Naaman, in the Scripture, to his king," as they said; but he demanded it "in honour of Almighty God." To attend on such a ground appeared to them a violation of conscience. They replied that God had not instituted the sacrament that man should worship it. The procession, which had no longer in any respect its ancient splendour, took place without them.

In regard to the preaching, they did indeed at length yield; but not till the emperor had promised to silence the other party also. He himself appointed certain preachers, but they were only to read the text of Scripture, without any exposition. Nor would it have been possible to bring the Protestants to yield even this point, had they not been reminded that the recess of 1528, to which they had always appealed, and which they would not suffer to be revoked, authorised it. The emperor, at least so long as he was there in person, was always regarded as the legitimate supreme authority of every imperial city.†

It is evident, therefore, that the Protestants did not allow themselves to be driven back one step from their convictions or from their rights. The requests of the emperor when present made no more impression upon them than his demands when absent had done. If the emperor had calculated on compliance, these were no flattering omens of future success.

At length, on the 20th of June, the business of the diet was opened. In the proposition, which was read on that day, the emperor insisted, as was reasonable, most urgently on an adequate armament against the Turks: at the same time he declared his intention of putting an end to the religious dissensions by gentle and fair means,‡ and reiterated the request contained in the convocation, that every one would give him, to that end, his "thoughts, judgment, and opinion," in writing.

As the council of the empire resolved to proceed first to the consideration of religious affairs, the grand struggle immediately commenced.

CONFESSION OF AUGSBURG.

The Protestants hastened immediately to draw up a written statement of their religious opinions, to be laid before the States of the empire.

This statement is the Augsburg Confession, and its origin is as follows:

Immediately after the receipt of the emperor's proclamation, the Saxon reformers had deemed it expedient to set forth in writing, and in a regular form, the belief "in which they had hitherto stood, and in which they persisted."§

Similar preparations had been made in various parts, in anticipation of the national assembly which was to be held in the year 1524; and something of the same kind was, at this moment, taking place on the other side; e. g. in Ingolstadt.‖

The Wittenberg reformers took, as basis of their creed, the Schwabach articles, in which, as we may remember, the points of difference between the Lutheran theologians and those of the Oberland were defined. It is very remarkable that, in framing this confession, the

* There is a very authentic account of this in the letters of the Nürnberg delegate, who that same night caused the landgrave to be waked, and told him what was going forward. 16th June; Bretschneider C. Ref. iii. 106. With slight variations, Heller, in Förstemann.

† Letter from Augsburg. Altenb. v. Walch, 16, 873. (In Walch under Spalatin's name but not complete.) Brenz to Isenmann, 19 Juni, Corp. Ref. ii. 117.

‡ I. Mt hat "aus angeporner Güte und Miltigkeit diesen Weg (der Güte) nach vermöge des Ausschreibens furgenommen, der entlichen Hofnung, der soll bei allen verstendigen ein billiges ansehn haben und menniglich dahin bewegen und leitten, dass alle Sachen wieder zum Besten gekehrt und gewendet werden, damit I. Mt inn irem gnedigen Fürhaben verharren und pleiben." "Your majesty has, from your natural goodness and mildness, chosen this way (of gentleness) according to the tenor of the convocation, with the hope it might obtain just consideration with all reasonable men, and move and lead many in such wise, that all things may be again turned and converted for the best, so that your majesty may persist and remain in your gracious purpose." From Förstemann, i. 308, we see how many variations the copies exhibit. That of Frankfurt has still more: e. g. "aus eingeborner Gunstigkeit, der möglichen Hofnung," u. s. w. But the meaning is the same.

§ It was thus that Chancellor Brück first conceived the thought, as his "Zeddel" shows; Förstemann, i. 39.

‖ 19th Feb. 1530. Extract in Winter, i. 270.

feeling of the differences which separated them from a party so nearly akin, was, to say the least, not less strong than that of the original dissent which had caused the first great movement. The separation now appeared the wider, since Zwingli and his followers had, in the meanwhile, recanted some admissions which they had made in Marburg, and which had found their way from the Marburg convention into the Schwabach articles.

These articles were now revised and drawn up afresh by Melanchthon, in that sound and methodical spirit peculiar to him, and in the undeniable intention of approximating as closely as possible to the Catholic doctrines. The expositions of the doctrine of free will and of justification by faith which he added, were extremely moderated; he defined at greater length what were the heretical errors (errors rejected also by the Church of Rome) condemned by the articles; he sought to establish these articles, not only on the authority of Scripture, but on that of the fathers, and especially of St. Augustine; he did not entirely forbid the honours paid to the memory of the saints, but only endeavoured to define their extent more accurately; he insisted strongly on the dignity of the temporal power, and concluded with the assertion, that these doctrines were not only clearly established in Scripture, but also that they were not in contradiction with the church of Rome, as understood from the writings of the fathers, from whom it was impossible to dissent, and who could hardly be accused of heresy.

And indeed it cannot, I think, be denied that the system of faith here set forth is a product of the vital spirit of the Latin church; that it keeps within the boundaries prescribed by that church, and is, perhaps, of all its offspring, the most remarkable, the most profoundly significant. It bears, as was inevitable, the traces of its origin; that is, the fundamental idea from which Luther had proceeded in the article on justification, gives it somewhat of an individual stamp: this, however, is inherent in all human things. The same fundamental idea had more than once arisen in the bosom of the Latin church, and had produced the most important effects; the only difference was, that Luther had seized upon it with all the energy of religious aspiration, and in his struggle with opposite opinions, as well as in his expositions to the people, had established it as an article of faith of universal application; no human being could say that, so explained and understood, this idea had any thing sectarian in it. Hence the Lutherans steadily opposed the more accidental dogmas which have sprung up in later ages; though not disposed to ascribe to the expressions of a father of the church, absolute and demonstrative authority, the reformers were conscious that they had not departed widely from his conception of Christianity. There is a tacit tradition not expressed in formulæ, but contained in the original nature of the conception, which exercises an immense influence over all the operations of the mind. The reformers distinctly felt that they stood on the old ground which Augustine had marked out. They had endeavoured to break through the minute observances by which the Latin church had allowed itself to be fettered in the preceding centuries, and to cast away those bonds altogether; they had recurred to the Scripture, to the letter of which they adhered. But they did not forget that it was this same Scripture which had been so long and so earnestly studied in the Latin church, and had been regarded as the standard of her faith; nor that much of what that church received was really founded on Scripture. To that they adhered; the rest they disregarded.

I do not venture to assert that the Augsburg Confession dogmatically determines the contents and import of Scripture; it does no more than bring back the system which had grown up in the Latin church to a unison with Scripture, or interpret Scripture in the original spirit of the Latin church. That spirit had, however, wrought too imperceptibly to produce any open manifestation which could have served as a bond of faith. The confession of the German Lutheran church is itself its purest manifestation, and the one the most immediately derived from its source.

It is hardly necessary to add that its authors had no intention of imposing this as a permanent and immutable standard of faith. It is simply the assertion of the fact. "Our churches teach"—"it is taught"—"it is unanimously taught"—"such and such opinions are falsely imputed to us." Such are the expressions Melanchthon uses; his intention is simply to state the belief which already exists.

And in the same spirit he wrote the second part, in which he enumerates and explains the abuses that had been removed.

How wide a field was here opened for virulent polemical attack! What might not have been said concerning the encroachments of the papal power—especially during the sitting of the diet, whose antipathies might thus have been appealed to,—or concerning the degeneracies of a corrupt form of worship!—and, indeed, we find a long register of them among the rough drafts of the work; but it was thought better to omit them. Melanchthon confined himself strictly to a justification of the ecclesiastical organisation to which the reformers had gradually attained. He explained the grounds on which the sacrament in both kinds and the marriage of the clergy had been permitted, vows and private masses rejected, and fasts and confession left to the will and conscience of each individual; he sought to show generally, how new and dangerous were the contrary practices, how at variance even with the old canonical rules. With wise discretion he was silent concerning the divine right of the pope, the character indelibilis, or even the number of the sacraments. His object was not to convert, but simply to defend. It was sufficient that he insisted on the distinction between the spiritual calling of the bishops and their temporal power, while defining the former in accordance with the tenor of Scripture, he wholly abstained from attacking the latter. He maintained that, on this point also, the evangelical party had not deviated from the genuine principles of the Catholic church, and that consequently the emperor might well consent to tolerate the new organisation of the church.*

It may be questioned whether the Protestants would not have done better if, instead of restricting themselves so entirely to defence, they had once more acted on the offensive, and appealed to all the strong reforming sympathies then afloat.

We must, however, acknowledge that from the moment they had decided to refuse to admit the adherents of Zwingli into their community, this was impossible. They found themselves almost eclipsed by the popularity of the doctrines taught by Zwingli; the majority of the inhabitants of Augsburg espoused the latter, and nothing less was talked of than a union of Upper Germany and Switzerland, in order to overthrow the entire hierarchy of the empire. Even one of the most eminent of the reforming princes, Landgrave Philip of Hessen, seemed from his conversation to lean to the side of Zwingli.† A special admonition from Luther was required, to induce him to subscribe the confession.

Nor could the Lutherans entertain the least hope of gaining over the majority of the States of the empire, who had already taken too decided a part with their adversaries.

They wished for nothing but peace and toleration; they thought they had proved that their doctrines had been unjustly condemned, and denounced as heretical. Luther brought himself to entreat his old antagonist, the Archbishop of Mainz, who now seemed more peaceably disposed, to lay this to heart. Melanchthon addressed himself in the name of the princes to the legate Campeggi, and conjured him not to depart from the moderation which he thought he perceived in him, for that every fresh agitation might occasion an immeasurable confusion in the church.‡

In this spirit of conciliation, in the feeling of still unbroken ties, in the wish to give force to that similarity which not only lay at the bottom of both religions, but was obvious in many particulars, was this confession conceived and drawn up.

On the afternoon of the 25th June, 1530, it was read aloud in the assembly of the empire. The princes prayed the emperor to allow this to be done in the larger hall, to which strangers were admitted, — in short, in a public sitting: the emperor, however, chose the smaller, the chapter-room of the bishop's palace, which he inhabited; to this only the members of the assembly of the empire had access. For a similar reason he wished the Latin version of the document to be read, but the princes reminded him that on German ground his majesty would be pleased to permit the use of the German language. Thereupon the young Chancellor of Saxony, Dr. Christian Baier, read the confession in German, with a distinctness of voice and utterance which well accorded with the clearness and firmness of the belief it expressed.§ The number of the spiritual princes present was not great: they thought they should be compelled to listen to many inconvenient reproaches. Those in favour of it rejoiced at having made this progress, and were delighted both with the matter of the confession and the manner in which it was recited. Some took advantage of the opportunity to note down the main points. As soon as it was finished, the two copies were handed to the emperor; the German he gave to the chancellor of the empire, the Latin he kept in his own hands. Both of them were signed by the Elector and the Electoral Prince of Saxony, Markgrave George of Brandenburg, the Dukes Francis and Ernest of Luneburg,

* It is well known that neither of the originals of the Augsburg Confession, signed by the princes, has ever come to light. It was for a long time thought that the German copy had been discovered in Mainz, but Weber in his "Kritische Geschichte der Augsburger Confession" has shown with scrupulous industry, that this, like many others, is a transcript without any authentic value. These transcripts present a number of deviations both from each other and from the first edition, which Melanchthon superintended in the year 1530. Fortunately the deviations, though numerous, are not important. The scribes of that time allowed themselves slight freedoms, especially in the law language, which was so little fixed; but, for the meaning and tenor, these seldom are of any moment. Furstemann's second volume contains a very careful collation of some manuscripts. We meet with the original, from the Mainz Chancery, again at the Conference of Worms, 1540. "Dr Eck," says the Brandenburg Protocol of the 4th Dec., "hat die newe confession und apologia angefochten, des syn seint dem augsburgischen Reichstag etlich bletter gemehret, viel verandert und das har in die wolle, vie er sagt, geschlagen und ein new schmalz darein gethon wer, derhalben er — — das Original Keys. Mt zu Augsburg ubergeben aus der maintzischen canzlei begerete, welches denn unversaget und ihme zu ubergeben bewilliget." — "Dr Eck has attacked the new Confession and Apology, to which since the diet of Augsburg some leaves have been added, much altered, and the hair beaten into the wool (felted), as he says, and a new glaze given to it, wherefore he desired to have the original which had been presented to his imperial majesty at Augsburg, out of the Mainz Chancery, which, accordingly, did not refuse, and permitted the same to be given to him." I do not find, however, that Eck produced the collation he promised.

† Letter from Urbanus Rhegius to Luther, 21st May, 1530. Landgrave Philip adduces "innumera Sacramentariorum argumenta," "sentit cum Zwinglio, ut ipsi mihi est fassus." But it was neither this, nor a letter of Melanchthon that moved Luther to apply to the landgrave. This he did as early as the 20th May. (De W. iv. p. 23.)

‡ Philip Furstenberg reports to the city of Frankfurt, 27th June, that there were formal negotiations concerning this. The elector and his kinsmen prayed "Ih. Mt wolt morgen wieder an dem Ort (im Pallast) erscheinen und den Umbstand (die Umstehenden) ire Berantwortung vernehmen zu lassen gestatten, denn sie weren von iren Widderwertigen nit aleyn bei I. Mt sondern auch bei menniglich verunglimpft, aber endlich ist es bei dem Beschend blieben." — "That your majesty would again appear at the same place (the palace), and be pleased to let those present hear your answer, for they have been reproached not only by your majesty, but by many others, with their untractableness. Nevertheless, the message remained unanswered."

§ Furstenberg. "Hell und klar, dass menniglich, so dabei was, der anders deutsch verstunde, alle Wort eigentlich, was doch in solcher Versammlung selten geschieht, verstehen mocht." — "Distinct and clear, that as many as were there present that understood German, could hear every word, which in such assemblies seldom happens." The Catholics thought the permission to read the Confession aloud, a great and unmerited honour. Even two years afterwards, Eck grumbles at it: "Lutheranismus in arcem dignitatum evectus ita invaluit, ut assertores erroris non vererentur in publicis comitiis Augustæ offerre Cæsari novi dogmatis confessionem." Præfatio in homilias V. contra Turcam. A. iii.

Landgrave Philip, Prince Wolfgang of Anhalt, and the delegates of the cities of Nurnberg and Reutlingen

CONFUTATION —THREATS

The evangelical princes expected that their adversaries would come forward with a similar declaration of faith, and that the emperor would then endeavour to mediate between them This expectation was held out by the Proposition, and, in still more distinct terms, by the convocation in virtue of which they were now assembled

It is highly probable that this was actually the emperor's intention he had indeed wished that the Catholic party had brought forward a distinct charge against the reformers, in which case he would have undertaken the part of an umpire between them At the meeting of the States, Ferdinand had once made a proposal to that effect

But the two brothers were not sufficiently masters of the assembly to accomplish this

The majority which had been formed in Spires, and acquired greater compactness in Augsburg, regarded itself as the legitimate possessor of the authority of the empire Though the Catholic zeal of the two brothers was most agreeable to its wishes, it found many things to object to them Ferdinand had obtained papal concessions of ecclesiastical revenues,—a thing which, though permitted in Spain, was unheard of in Germany This excited universal disgust and resistance among the clergy The majority declined constituting themselves as a party, and acknowledging the emperor as judge between them and the Protestants They declared that they had nothing new to propose, they had simply adhered to the imperial edict, if the emperor was in want of a charge to bring against the reformers, let him resort to that of contravention of his edict Nay, more, as it was the immemorial custom that the emperor should accede to the sentiments of the assembly of the empire, they were of opinion that he should now adopt their cause as his own This was in fact, requesting him to use his imperial power in this affair, with the advice of the electors, princes, and estates of the empire It was a matter of perfect indifference to them, that this was at variance with the express words of the convocation, since they were not the authors of it The emperor was, in fact, compelled to relinquish his idea of a judicial mediation

It has been usually asserted that traces are to be found of personal and independent negotiations between the emperor and the Protestants at this diet The fact however is, that from this moment, the whole business was conducted by the majority of the States Concerning the minutest point—e g, the communication of a document—the emperor was compelled to hold a consultation with them, he acted at last only as they deemed expedient

It is much to be regretted that we have no protocols of the sittings of the Catholic majority, we do not even know whether any were drawn up Neither have any full and accurate reports come to light, and they are hardly to be expected, since the most considerable princes were present, and the delegates from the cities did not take part in the sittings

All that we know is, that there was a division of opinion in the majority itself The one party thought that the emperor ought at once to take up arms, and enforce the execution of his former edict The Archbishop of Salzburg said, "Either we must put an end to them, or they will put an end to us, which of the two suits us best?" An equally violent member of the assembly was heard to remark, jesting, that, the confession was written with black ink "Were we emperor," said he, "we would put red rubrics to it" "Sir," rejoined another, "only take care that the red does not spirt up in your faces" All, as this answer shows, were not equally hostile The Archbishop of Mainz, in particular, pointed out the danger which would arise from an invasion of the Turks, in case of an open breach with the Protestants It was at length determined to advise the emperor above all things to authorise a confutation of the confession meanwhile, an attempt might be made to arrange the differences between the temporal and spiritual estates The emperor acted on this advice He gave himself up to the hope that the settlement of these differences and the confutation of the confession would, united, produce such an effect on the Protestants as to induce them to yield *

The situation of the Protestants was thus changed greatly for the worse

Till now they had expected from the emperor's exalted position a fair appreciation of their conduct, and mediation between them and their adversaries, but they very soon perceived that he did not give, but received the impulse, the old and bitter enemies with whom they had so long striven, constituting a majority, now directed all the measures of the imperial authority.

The confutation was set about with the utmost zeal There was no want of labourers Not only the reforming theologians, but their opponents, had repaired to the diet with their respective princes, Faber from Vienna, who was now become prebendary of Ofen, Eck, from Ingolstadt, Cochlaus, from Dresden, Wimpina, from Frankfurt on the Oder With the prince bishops came their vicars, or learned officiating bishops, there were some eminent monks—Capuchins, Carmelites, and especially Dominicans, Paul Haug, the provincial, John

* The extracts in Bucholtz, iii throw peculiar light on these negotiations A remarkable document belonging to them is to be found entire in Forstemann, vol ii p 9 It is without a date but it must be of the 9th or 10th of July, since the emperor mentions a question he had asked the Protestants on the 9th,—i e, whether they intended to bring forward more articles, to which he had as yet received no answer The answer was given on the 10th, but, perhaps, was not delivered till the day following See the reports in Schmidt, viii 244 Melanchthon to Luther, 8th July C R ii 175

Burkhard, the vicar, and the prior, Conrad Colli, who had written against Luther's marriage * It is not surprising that a man like Erasmus (who was also invited) felt no inclination to have his name associated with such as these The men who were here to conduct the discussion were the representatives of the Aristotelic Dominican system, which so long ruled the schools of Europe, and which he had himself combated With the literary weapons which they had hitherto wielded, they had accomplished little Their whole strength lay in their connexion with power They were now no longer private men, they were to speak and to write in the name of the empire

They were not, it is true, left at absolute liberty People dreaded their violence and their diffuseness, for each of them brought his old animosities and his old refutations of Lutheran opinions, which were not now in dispute † Their first draft was peremptorily returned to them by the assembly of the empire, admonishing them to confine themselves entirely to the article of the confession. A second, shorter, which was next presented, was submitted, article by article, to minute discussion by the assembly It was the third of August before the confutation was prepared and could be read aloud in the fore-mentioned hall of the bishop's palace

It consists, like the confession, of two parts, the one treating of belief, the other of practice

In the former, the contested question already approached the point at which it has since remained stationary It was no longer maintained that the sacrament, the mere performance of the act, the opus operatum, merited grace It was no longer taught that a good work done without grace was of the same nature as one done with grace, that the difference between them was only one of degree Those were the doctrines against which Luther had contended A nearer approach was made to the more profound conception of justification through Christ which has since been almost universally adopted. If the Catholics strove to retain the doctrine of the necessity of good works, it was in a different sense from that heretofore affixed to it ‡

This was, however, the only modification to which they consented

On the other points they remained steadfast to the established system They demanded the admission of the doctrine of transubstantiation, of the seven sacraments, and the invocation of saints, they persisted in the denial of the cup, and the injunction of celibacy; they even made an attempt (which, indeed, was certain to fail) to deduce these doctrines from passages of Scripture, or from the usage of the earliest ages of the church, and in this attempt they stumbled again on the false decretals, they would not give up the sacrifice of the mass, and above all, they firmly adhered to the idea of the Latin, as the universal church They defended the use of the Latin ritual in the mass, on the ground that the officiating priest belonged far more to the whole church, than to the particular congregation by which he happened to be surrounded

In short, if, on the one side, the Protestants were driven by the misinterpretation of doctrines, and by abusive practices, to recur directly to Scripture (understanding it in a sense corresponding with the fundamental notions of the primitive Latin church, but irreconcilable with the ideas and fictions of recent hierarchical times), on the other, their antagonists now consented to relinquish some of the most flagrant excrescences in doctrine, and to take into consideration the removal of the abuses which had already caused so many disputes between spiritual and temporal princes, they still, however, persisted in affirming that the whole hierarchical system was of immediate divine origin We see them in search of a method—for they had as yet found none—by which to prove the conformity of their system with Scripture.

This would not have been of so much importance, had they aimed only at self-defence But that was by no means the case The majority not only declared that they deemed this opinion just and Catholic, conformable with the Gospel, but they also demanded that the Protestant minority should erase the refuted articles from their confession, and return to a unity of faith with the universal orthodox church No attention was paid to their agreement in what was essential, ancient, and original, so long as the slightest difference, though only in accidental and unessential particulars, was discernible Whatever had been altered, whether by the inevitable pressure of circumstances, or in consequence of the legal

* Eck brought, among other things, a book already printed at Ingolstadt under the following title Sub domini Jhesu et Mariæ patrocinio Articulos 404 partim ad disputationes Lipsicam Baden et Bernen attinentes partim vero ex scriptis pacem ecclesiæ perturbantium extractos coram divo Cæsare Carolo V Ro Imp semper Augu ac proceribus Imperii Joan Eckius minimus ecclesiæ minister offert se disputaturum ut in scheda latius explicatur Augustæ Vindelicorum die et hora consensu Cæsaris posterius publicandis He mentions first the 41 articles condemned by the pope, "Assero qui bullæ contradixerint, schismaticos esse ac fidei hostes, quos catholicus habet pro ethnicis et publicanis" He then cites the articles which he had defended at Leipzig and Baden, as well as those which he had opposed to the resolutions of Berne, lastly, "errores novi et veteres jam ventilati," under certain rubrics He collects 404, "ex infinitis eorum erroribus hos paucos subitarie excerpsi" In his hurry, he has also mixed up with them some of Erasmus's maxims The other side threw the Propositiones de vino, venere, et balneo, in his teeth, which we still see circulate among the Catholic societies, and which made him an object of public ridicule

† Cochlæus printed some articles of this confutation in his book, Philippicæ quatuor in apologiam Melanchthonis, Lipsiæ, 1534 At the third article, sheet D, it is said therein, damnent diras blasphemias—Lutheri errorem—suum Pugenhagium—Melanchthonem suum—Antonium Zimerman, hominem insigniter Lutheranum—studiosum Lutheri discipulum Burguerum The passages worthy of condemnation from each are quoted Hence it happened, as Cochlæus said, "quorundam consilium qui judicabant ejusmodi responsionem fore nimis acrem et prolixam"

‡ See, besides the confutation, De principum protestantium confessione Joannis Eccii censura archiepiscopo Moguntino et Georgio D S Augustæ exhibita, in Cœlestin, iii 39 As this work, addressed to certain Catholic princes, contains the essentials of the concessions made by some modern Catholics, it puts an end to the imputation of hypocrisy which has been brought forward against them

enactments of a former diet, was to be re stored to its original state The emperor declared himself entirely of this mind At the end of the confutation, which was published in his name, he admonished the evangelical party immediately to return to their obedience to the Roman and Catholic church If not, he must proceed against them as became a Roman emperor, the protector and steward of the church

The time for mildness was over, the time for severity seemed to have arrived

Already had the pope spoken

At the very commencement of the meeting, the emperor had demanded a short statement of the most important demands of the Protestants, drawn up by Melanchthon, which he communicated to the legate, who forwarded it to Rome As far as we are able to ascertain, the following points were mentioned as indispensable. — Sacrament in both kinds, marriage of priests, omission of the canon in the mass, concession of the secularised church lands; and, lastly, discussion of the other contested questions at a council The document was laid before a consistory of cardinals on the 6th of July What a moment would this have been, if they had but entered on the consideration of it in a conciliatory spirit! But they at once declared these articles at variance with the faith and discipline, no less than with the interests, of the church * they decided to reject the petition, and simply to thank the emperor for his zeal

The assembly of the empire had itself exhorted the emperor to act as became the steward of the church

Urged on either side, bound by his treaties, and exclusively surrounded by persons who either had no idea of the real character and views of the Protestants, or had long been their enemies,—Charles assumed the sternest deportment Not content with his general declarations, he showed his sentiments by his ungracious behaviour to individuals, to the Elector John, especially, he expressed his displeasure that he had separated himself from the emperor, the defender of the faith, introduced innovations, and sought to form confederations "His majesty also had a soul and a conscience, and would do nothing contrary to God's word" If the elector would not return to the faith which had been held by their forefathers for centuries,† his majesty, on his part, would not be disposed to grant him infeudation, nor any of the other favours which he craved.

RESISTANCE

The might and energy of Latin Christendom was once more exhibited to the world in the person of the emperor By his brilliant victories he had secured universal peace, even from the Ottoman power he had nothing to dread during the present, or probably the coming year The papal authority, as well as the collective power of the States of the empire, was on his side On the other hand, the Protestants had no religious or political support in any quarter, nor had they even the internal strength which a firm bond of union would have given them

It might indeed be doubted whether German princes and lords, trained in the chivalrous life of courts, and converted to the new doctrines in mature age, by the arguments and instructions of strangers, — to whom a good understanding with their neighbours, and, in their more important affairs, the favour of the emperor, were indispensable, would have sufficient constancy to maintain their opinions in defiance of his express displeasure, and of the power concentrated in his person

The immediate decision of this question depended on the most eminent and powerful among them, to whom the others looked up, and against whom the emperor chiefly directed his attacks—the Elector John of Saxony

Elector John of Saxony, the last of the four excellent sons of Elector Ernest, — educated with the greatest care, at Grimma, to qualify him for either the spiritual or the temporal dignities of the empire—the progenitor of the Ernestine house, which has now such numerous and flourishing branches‡—did not possess the political genius, nor the acute and penetrating mind of his brother Frederic On the other hand, he was remarkable from his childhood for good nature and frankness, — "without guile and without bile," as Luther said,—yet full of that moral earnestness which gives weight and dignity to simplicity of character He is believed to have lived to his thirty-second year, when he married, in perfect chastity,§ there is at least no trace of the contrary The brilliant and tumultuous knightly festivals in which he sometimes took part at the court of Maximilian afforded him no satisfaction, although he always made a distinguished figure at them, he once said, at a later period of his life, that not one of these days had passed without a sorrow ‖ He was not born for the amusements and dissipations of the world, the disgust which inevitably attends them made too deep an impression on him, and gave him more pain than their frivolous enjoyments gave him pleasure With his brother, who was his co-regent, he never had a difference, never did the one engage a person in his service without the full consent of the other From the first appearance of Luther in the world John embraced his doctrines with the most joyful sympathy, his serious and profoundly religious mind was

* Pallavicini, from a contemporaneous Diario, iii iv 280 Articoli opposti — alla ragion della chiesa A sort of ecclesiastical reason of state

† In the reprint in Muller, p 672, it is said, for twenty or thirty years, which is doubtless an error of the pen

‡ These are the house of Weimar, and that of Gotha, in its three subordinate lines, S Meiningen Hildburghausen, S Altenburg, and S Coburg Gotha.—TRANSL.

§ Spalatin, Von Herzog Hansen zu Sachsen Churfürsten, in Struve's newly published Archives, iii 16, unfortunately much less fertile in information than the same author's Nachricht uber Friedrich d W

‖ An expression of his in Beckmann's Anhaltische Geschichte, ii v p 140

gradually but completely embued with them His greatest enjoyment was, to have the Scriptures, which he now heard for the first time, read aloud to him in an evening, sometimes he fell asleep, — for he was already far advanced in years — but he awoke repeating the last verse that had dwelt upon his memory He occasionally wrote down Luther's sermons, and there is extant a copy of the lesser catechism in his handwriting * Examples are not wanting, both before and since his time, of princes whose powers of action have been paralysed by absorption in religious contemplation, but with him this was not the case, notwithstanding the extreme simplicity of his character, he was not less conspicuous for elevation and force of will When, during the peasants' war, the cause of the princes was in so tottering a state, he did not disguise from himself that a terrible convulsion might ensue, he was prepared for reverses, and was heard to say that he could content himself with a horse or two, and be a man like other men, but this sentiment did not prevent his defending his good right as bravely as any of his brother princes, only he used his victory with greater clemency It would be difficult to point out a moment in the subsequent years of his reign, in which he could have indulged in a merely contemplative piety We know of no prince to whom a larger portion of the merit of the establishment of the Protestant church can justly be ascribed His brother and predecessor had merely not suffered the new doctrines to be crushed, he had taken them under his protection in his own dominions, and, so far as it was possible, in the empire But when John assumed the government, there were rocks on either side, on which the whole cause might have gone to wreck, and which could only have been avoided by a policy founded on those lofty convictions that never for a moment failed or wavered The peasants' war was followed by violent tendencies to a re-action, and urgently as the adoption of these was pressed upon him by his worldly-wise and experienced cousin, John did not allow himself to be mastered by them On the contrary, the course which he took at the ensuing diet contributed to the passing of that recess on which the whole subsequent legal structure of Protestantism was reared It soon, indeed, appeared as if the impetuosity of his Hessian ally would hurry the elector into a series of political perplexities of which nobody could foresee the end, but his calmer and better judgment saved him in time, and he returned to that defensive position which was natural to him, and which he was able to maintain His sole object and endeavour was to give to the new doctrines an utterance and a recognised existence in his dominions He introduced into Germany the first evangelical form of church government, which, in a greater or less degree, served as model for all others He speedily put a stop to the arbitrary acts of his nobles, mild and sweet tempered as he was, he was not to be induced to grant any unjust favour, and he censured his son for listening more than was prudent to those about him In all these respects Luther had the greatest influence over him, Luther knew how to set the secret springs of this pure and noble soul in motion at the fitting time, and to keep this upright conscience constantly awake. Thus, therefore, it was John of Saxony who took the lead in that protest which gave its name and position to the whole party For when justice and religion were on his side, he knew not hesitation, he sometimes quoted the proverb, "Strait forward makes a good runner" ("Gradaus giebt einen guten Renner") He was by nature retiring, peaceful, unpretending, but he was raised to such a pitch of resolution and energy by the greatness of his purposes, that he showed himself fully equal to their accomplishment

Here, in Augsburg, had Elector John to stand the test, whether his intentions were unadulterated gold, or whether they were mixed with any baser matter

He felt the reverence for the emperor natural to a prince of the empire, and at first he had no doubt of being easily able to reconcile that sentiment with his religious convictions But it very soon became obvious that this would be impossible, and in order to avert the danger from the head of their prince, some of his learned men reverted to the old idea, that he should not espouse their cause, but leave it to stand or fall by itself They were prepared to deliver in the confession solely in their own names The elector replied, "I too will confess my Christ" ("Ich will meinen Christus auch mit bekennen")

From that time the emperor evinced more and more alienation from him "We have prayed his imperial majesty," says the elector, in one of his letters,† "to invest us with the electoral dignity according to the feudal forms, this has been refused to us We stand at a great cost here, having just now been obliged to borrow 12,000 gulden, his imperial majesty has, as yet, given us no word of promise We cannot think otherwise than that we have been sorely slandered to his imperial majesty, and that this has befallen us through our own kinsfolk"

We see the state of mind to which he had already been brought, and now followed the confutation and the threatening declaration annexed to it

That he, with his narrow strip of land on the Elbe and his little Thuringia, — without any allies on whom he could rely — could offer resistance to the emperor, who had just achieved so exalted and commanding a station, and was enabled to enforce the ancient ordinances of Latin Christendom, was too wild a thought to be seriously entertained for a moment He was, moreover, paralysed by the doubt, whether he had a right to resist,

* Cyprian, Geschichte der Augsburgischen Confession, p 184

† To Nicolas v Ende, Amtmann in Georgenthal, 28 July

and rather inclined to the opinion that it could in no case be justifiable.

Care was taken to let him know clearly what awaited him. A prince greatly in the confidence of the court, told him one day that, if he would not submit, the emperor would attack him with an armed force, drive him from his country and his people, and execute the extremest rigours of the law on his person.*

The elector doubted not that it might come even to this. He came home greatly moved, and expressed his consternation that he was required either to deny what he had acknowledged to be the truth, or to plunge, with all belonging to him, into irretrievable ruin.

Luther affirms that, had John wavered, not one of his council would have stood firm.

But his simple and straight-forward mind viewed the question laid before him in so clear and direct a light, that his decision was inevitable. "Either deny God or the world," said he,—"who can doubt which is better? God has made me an elector of the empire, a dignity of which I never was worthy, let him do with me further according to his good pleasure."

A dream which he had about this time affords a curious proof of what was passing in his mind. He was seized with that sort of stifling oppression in which the sleeper feels as if he were expiring under a crushing weight. He dreamed that he lay under a mountain, on the summit of which stood his cousin George; towards morning the mountain crumbled away, and his hostile kinsman fell down by his side.

In short, the aged prince neither quailed nor wavered. Great events rarely come to pass without those great moral efforts which are the necessary, though hidden germs of new social and political institutions. Elector John continued to declare that the emperor should find him a loyal and peaceful prince in every respect, but that he would never be able to induce him to regard the eternal truth as not the truth, or the imperishable word of God as not God's word.

The man who had the greatest influence in keeping him steady to this determination was unquestionably Luther, though he was not with him.

Luther's sentence of ban was not yet revoked, and though he had remained secure in spite of it, the elector could not bring him to the diet. He left him at Coburg, on the frontier of his territory.

It was a great advantage to Luther that he was not involved in the turmoil of affairs, and of the incidents of the day, he could take a more comprehensive view of what was passing.

He was struck with surprise that the emperor appeared so intimately connected with the pope, and so secure of the French, and that the States of the empire had again espoused the pope's party. He treated these things with a sort of irony. "Monsieur Par-ma-foi," as he called the King of France, would, he thought, never forget the disgrace of the battle of Pavia. Master In nomine Domini (the pope) would not be much delighted with the devastation of Rome; their amity with the emperor belonged to the chapter, Non credimus.† He could not understand how the princes took it so easily that the pope had crowned the emperor without their presence.‡ He compared their assembly with the conclave of jackdaws before his window, there he witnessed the same journeying to and fro, the clamours and pratings of the whole flock, the monotonous preaching of the sophists. "A right useful folk to consume all that the earth brings forth, and to while away the heavy time with chattering."§ It struck him particularly that the state of things when he first rose into notice, seemed to be entirely forgotten; he reminded his friends that, at that time, the sale of indulgences, and the doctrine, that God might be satisfied by pious works, were universally prevalent; that new services, pilgrimages, relics, and, to crown all, the fable of the garment of Christ, were daily brought forward; that masses were bargained for and sold for a few pence, more or less, and held to be a sacrifice well pleasing to God. He called to remembrance that the most effectual weapons for putting down the peasants' war (at least those of a literary kind), had been used by the Protestants, as a requital for which their enemies were now labouring for their destruction. For he had never for a moment doubted how this matter would end: from the time the emperor had prohibited the preaching, he had ceased to have the slightest hope of reconciliation; he saw that Charles would urge all the subordinate princes to renounce their opinions. Not that he thought the emperor himself disposed to violence; on the contrary, he never speaks of "the noble blood of Emperor Charles" without reverence, but he knows in what hands their good lord is; he beholds in him only the mask behind which their old enemies are concealed; and these, he is persuaded, meditate nothing but force, and trust to their superior numbers. He thinks that the Florentine who now occupies the papal chair, will find some opportunity to cause streams of German blood to flow.

But these prospects did not affright him. "Let them do as they list," said he, "they are not at the end yet."

He could not think of receding one step further. "Day and night," said he, "I live in these things. I search the Scriptures, I reflect, I discuss, I daily feel increasing cer-

* Muller, Geschichte der Protestation, p. 715. One proof how widely diffused were anxieties of this kind, is a report which Zwingli received from Venice in the beginning of the year 1530, in which the emperor's schemes are thus described, "the emperor would bring Duke George of Saxony to Duke John, from whom he would take away his *status* (Stand), so that he be no longer an electing prince, and would take upon him to give it to Duke George." Archiv fur schweiz. Geschichte, i. p. 278.

† To Teutleben, 19th June.

‡ To the Elector of Mainz, 6th July.

§ To his Table Companions, 28th April, and to Spalatin, 9th May. (A translation of this sportive letter may be found in a little volume of Fragments from German Prose Writers.—TRANSL.)

tainty, I will not allow more to be taken from me, let what God wills befall me in consequence." He laughs at the demands of the Catholics for restitution. "Let them first," he exclaims, "restore the blood of Leonhard Kaiser and of so many other innocent men whom they have murdered!"

His intrepidity is solely the result of his persuasion that his cause is the cause of God. "Some are sorrowful," he says, "as if God had forgotten us, but he cannot forget us, he must first forget himself, our cause must be not his cause, our doctrine not his work. Were Christ not with us, where then were he in the world? If we have not God's word, who then has it?" He consoles himself with the words, "Trust to me, I have overcome the world."

"The Lord dwelleth in the mist, he hath his dwelling-place in the darkness. Man seeth not what he is, but he will be the Lord, and we shall see it."

"And if we are not worthy, it will be brought to pass by others. Have our forefathers made us to be what we are? God alone, who will be the Creator after us, as he was before us, causes it to be with us even as it is. For he, the God that ruleth the thoughts, will not die with us. If the enemy put me to death, I shall be better avenged than I could desire: there will be one who will say, Where is thy brother Abel?"

In this temper of mind are all his letters of that time written. Never was a man more intensely penetrated with the immediate presence of the Divine Being. He knew the eternal, all-conquering powers in whose service he was engaged, he knew them, such as they had revealed themselves, and he called upon them by their names. He rested with dauntless courage on the promises which they had given to the human race, in the Psalms or the Gospel.

He spoke with God as with a present Lord and Father. His amanuensis in Coburg once heard him praying to himself:—"I know that thou art our God," exclaimed he, "that thou wilt destroy them that persecute thy people; didst thou not thus, thou wouldst abandon thine own cause, it is not our cause,—we have been compelled to embrace it, thou therefore must defend it." He prayed with the manly courage which feels its right to the protection of the Divine Power to whom it has devoted itself; his prayer plunges into the depths of the Godhead, without losing the sense of its personality; he does not desist till he has the feeling of being heard—the greatest of which the human heart, raised above all delusion, is in its holiest moments susceptible. "I have prayed for thee," he writes to Melanchthon, "I have felt the amen in my heart."

A genuine expression of this frame of mind was the hymn, "Eine feste Burg ist unser Gott" ("Our God is a strong tower"), the composition of which is justly attributed to this period.* It professes to be a paraphrase of the 16th Psalm, but is in fact merely suggested by it; it is completely the product of the moment in which Luther, engaged in a conflict with a world of foes, sought strength in the consciousness that he was defending a divine cause that could never perish. He seems to lay down his arms, but it was in fact the manliest renunciation of a momentary success, with the certainty of that which is eternal. How triumphant and animated is the melody! how simple and steady, how devout and elevated! It is identical with the words; they arose together in those stormy days.

Such was his temper of mind, when he exhorted not only his nearest friends, but the elector and his councils, to be of good courage.

He told his prince to take comfort, that no other crime was imputed to him than the defence of the pure and living word of God. Therein indeed consisted all his honour. In his land he had the best preachers, childhood and youth grew up in the knowledge of the catechism and the word of God, so that it was a joy to see them; this was the paradise over which God had set him as guardian; he did not only protect the word, he maintained and nourished it, and therefore it came to his aid. "Oh!" exclaims he, "the young will be your helpers, who with their innocent tongues call so heartily on Heaven."

"I have lately seen two wonders," writes he to Chancellor Bruck. "The first,—I looked out of the window at the stars of heaven, and the whole beautiful vaulted roof of God, and could nowhere see a pillar upon which the Master had placed his roof, and yet it stands fast. The other,—I saw thick clouds hanging over us, and yet no ground upon which they rested, no vessel in which they were contained, yet they fell not, but greeted us with a gloomy countenance and passed on: for God's thoughts are far above our thoughts, if we are only certain that our cause is his cause, so is our prayer already heard and our help already at hand;—if the emperor granted us peace, as we wish, the emperor would have the honour, but God himself will give us peace, that he alone may have the honour."†

A determined will has always the power of carrying others along with it. How resistless must it then be in one so filled with the Spirit of God! Luther exercised perhaps a greater influence over his followers from a distance, than his continual presence could have given him.

All the other princes vied with Elector John in firmness.

It was on this occasion that Duke Ernest of Luneburg won the name of the Confessor. Instead of receding a single step, he received into his intimacy Urbanus Rhegius, the chief

* Cœlestin affirms this. Olearius, on the other hand, mentions that this hymn is to be found in a collection of 1529. He means, however, only a collection of Lutheran hymns, dated 1529, in the Jen. und Altenb. Ausg. luth. Werke, but which, like many other of his assertions, is founded on error. Nowhere else is there any trace of a collection of 1529, and we may be permitted to doubt of its existence. The one published under that title also contains later hymns.

† 4th Aug., in De Wette, iv.

promoter of the reformation in his duchy, and took him home from Augsburg, as the most precious treasure that he could bring his people.

The emperor and the king had promised Markgrave George of Brandenburg to favour his interests if he would renounce the new doctrine; a consideration of the more weight, since Brandenburg had even then claims on certain possessions in Silesia; but the markgrave rejected every proposal of the kind.* Nor was this all; his powerful and zealously Catholic cousin, Elector Joachim, was not less urgent with him to quit the evangelical party, and bitter altercations took place between them. The markgrave declared his conviction that the doctrine could not be called an error, so long as Christ was really Christ: it taught a man to turn himself to Christ alone: of this he had full experience. Without entering seriously on the discussion of this point, the elector mainly insisted on the emperor's determination to restore every thing to its former state. The markgrave replied, that the emperor might abolish what he chose; that he himself must submit, but that he would not assist in the work. The elector asked whether the markgrave recollected what he had at stake. He replied, "They say I am to be driven out of my country. I must commit the matter into God's hands."†

Wolfgang of Anhalt was by no means a powerful prince, nevertheless he said with the greatest calmness, "Many a time have I taken horse in the cause of my good masters and friends, and my lord Christ deserves that I should venture something for his sake also." "Master Doctor," said he to Eck, "if you are thinking of war, you will find people ready on this side likewise."‡

Such being the disposition of the other reformers, it was not likely that the high-spirited landgrave would be brought to concede any thing. The Hessian chronicler, Lauze, relates that, after the confession had been delivered in, certain men had taken the landgrave to the top of a high mountain, and shown him all the good things of the world; that is, had held out to him hopes of favour in the affairs of Nassau and Würtenberg; but that he had refused them all.§ One day he heard that the emperor intended to reprove him; instantly, accoutred as he was, he hurried to court, and begged the emperor to state the acts by which he had incurred his displeasure. The emperor enumerated some, whereupon the landgrave gave an explanation which Charles accepted as satisfactory. But the grand difficulty was yet to come; the emperor required him to show himself a dutiful subject in the matter of the faith, and added, that otherwise he would take the course which beseemed him as Roman emperor. But threats were still vainer than promises. Philip was, moreover, daily more impatient of an assembly in which, conformably to the hierarchical rules of the empire, he held a position by no means corresponding with his power. He begged the emperor to dismiss him; and as the latter refused, he one evening rode away without leave.‖ He wrote from a distance to the Elector of Saxony, to assure him that he would stake body and goods, land and people, with him and with God's word. "Bid the cities," he writes to his council, "that they be not women, but men; there is no fear,—God is on our side."

And in fact the cities proved themselves not unworthy of the princes. "Our mind is," say the Nürnberg delegates, "not to give way, for by so doing we should put the emperor's favour above that of God; God, we doubt not, will grant us steadfastness." The bürgermeister and council were of the same mind as their delegates.

Others at a distance took part in these events in a similar spirit. "Your grace," write the councillors of Magdeburg to the Elector of Saxony, "stands carrying on a perilous struggle in the affairs of all Christendom, under the banner of our Saviour: we pray to God daily to grant you patience and strength."

Things had thus already assumed a distinct shape in Germany. On the one side was a majority, claiming all the rights and privileges of the empire, united with the emperor, and allied with the powers of ancient Europe; on the other, a minority struggling for its existence, isolated and formless, but full of religious fortitude and constancy. The majority, with the emperor at their head, meditated using force;¶ steps were already taken for raising troops in Italy.** The minority had as yet no plan; they only knew that they were determined not to yield.

But, it might be asked, was not every violent measure full of danger to the majority of the States also? They were not sure of their own subjects; the suggestion of the Elector of Mainz, as to the danger with which both parties were threatened in case of a well-timed invasion by the Turks, made a deep impression. From these considerations the original proposal of the pacific party, incorporated in the resolutions of the diet, was adopted, and an attempt at mediation resolved on.

ATTEMPT OF THE STATES TO MEDIATE.

On the 16th of August a conference was opened, in which two princes, two doctors of canon law, and three theologians of each party

* Letter to the kinsmen of the house of Brandenburg (Stammesvettern), 19th July; Förstemann, ii. 93.

† Cotemporaneous notes commencing these negotiations, passim, 630.

‡ Beckmann's Anhaltische Chronik, II. v. 142.

§ Letter of the Nürnberg envoy, C. R. ii. 167.

‖ 6th August. On the 30th July he had entered into an alliance with Zürich, which had a great influence on his conduct. See Escher und Hottinger, Archiv für schweiz. Gesch. und Landeskunde, i. 426.

¶ Butzer feared a "laniena sanctorum qualis vix Diocletiani tempore fuit." 14 Aug. 1530, Röhrich, ii. p. 136.

** Nicc. Tiepolo Relatione. Essendo in Augusta intesi che si offersero (the two dukes of Bavaria) all' imperatore volendo lui muover guerra a Lutheranis, e seppi che tentorno col duca di Mantova d'haver il modo di condur 1000 cavalli leggieri d'Italia in caso si facesse guerra in Germania.

took part, and which soon appeared to promise great results.

The dogmatical points at issue presented no insuperable difficulties. On the article of original sin, Eck gave way as soon as Melanchthon proved to him that an expression objected to in his definition was in fact merely a popular explanation of an ancient scholastic one. Respecting the article on justification "through faith alone," Wimpina expressly declared that no work was meritorious, if performed without grace,* he required the union of love with faith, and only in so far he objected to the word 'alone." In this sense however, the Protestants had no desire to retain it, they consented to its erasure, their meaning had always been merely that a reconciliation with God must be effected by inward devotion, not by outward acts. On the other hand, Eck declared, that the satisfaction which the Catholic church required to be made by penitence, was nothing else than reformation, an explanation which certainly left nothing further to be objected to the doctrine of the necessity of satisfaction.† Even on the difficult point of the sacrifice of the mass, there was a great approximation. Eck explained the sacrifice as merely a sacramental sign, in remembrance of that which was offered up on the cross.‡ The presence of Christ in the eucharist was not debated. The Protestants were easily persuaded to acknowledge not only a true, but also a real presence. This addition is actually inserted in the Ansbach copy of the confession.

It was certainly not the difference in the fundamental conceptions of the Christian dogma which perpetuated the contest. Luther had done nothing more than revive and re-establish the primitive doctrines of the Latin church, which had been buried under the hierarchical systems of later times, and an ever-increasing load of abuses. Such diversities as those we have just mentioned might be reciprocally tolerated, and indeed different opinions had always co-existed. The real cause of rupture lay in the constitution and practices of the church.

And with respect to these the Protestants gave way as much as possible. They were persuaded that the division was an obstacle to good discipline in church and school, and that the government of the church would be both ill-conducted and costly in the hands of the temporal sovereigns. The Protestant princes and theologians declared themselves ready to restore to the bishops their jurisdiction, right of anathema, and control over benefices, provided only that no attempt was made to abridge the liberty of reading and expounding the Gospel.§ They were even disposed to observe fasts, not as an ordinance of God, but for the sake of good order, and, in regard to confession, to admonish the people to confess all matters whereon they felt a want of advice and consolation, — concessions which, in fact, included a restoration of the externals of the church to an extent no longer to be expected.

Nor is there any ground for the assertion, that the refusal of the Protestants to restore the property of the suppressed convents was the obstacle to a reconciliation. Though the Protestants retorted upon their antagonists the charge of worse acts of spoliation — such as the seizure of the bishopric of Utrecht by the emperor — an event of far greater importance than the suppression of a few convents, seeing that the constitution of the church was founded on bishops, not on monks,—yet the Elector of Saxony at last offered to place all the suppressed convents under sequestration, the sequestrees, honourable men chosen from among the nobility of the land, were to pledge themselves to the emperor to allow nothing to be abstracted from the property, till a council should decide on its application.‖

Such were the advances once more made by the Protestants to the church of Rome, and to the majority in the empire. It is difficult to understand how the latter did not meet them with eagerness.

On one point the committee of the majority made a great concession to the Protestants. It expressed the hope of obtaining, at the ensuing council, the general admission of married priests according to the example of the primitive church.¶ It also opposed no scruple to the sacrament in both kinds.

After so near an approximation, of what importance were a few differences in practice? Was it necessary to sacrifice to them the unity of the empire and the nation, and the blessings of peace?

That such was the lamentable result, may be mainly ascribed to the inability of the Catholic leaders to act as perhaps they would have wished. We know that the affair had been already discussed and decided at the papal court. The papal legate, Campeggi, did not neglect to visit the emperor at the critical moment, in order to inflame his Catholic zeal, and bring him back to the views of the Curia.**

* Eck too says in his opinion, "De principum protestantium confessione Johannis Eccii censura (Cœlestin, iii 36) quod opera de sua natura et in se non essent meritoria, sed solum ex Deo et gratia Dei assistente."

† Spalatin, who performed the duties of a notary at the first sitting, in Forstemann, ii p 228. In like manner is Eck's singular expression to be understood (Cœlestin, p 36). Nos ponimus satisfactionem tertiam partem pœnitentiæ, ipsi vero fatentur sequi debere fructus bonorum operum, ubi iterum lis est verbalis, non realis.

‡ Account in Cœlestin, iii 45. Est ergo missa non revera victima, sed mysterialis et repræsentativa.

§ Unexpected answer, Forstemann, ii 256. Compare with the Reflections, idem p 245, p 75. From the latter it appears, that they tried to derive all hierarchical institutions expressly from human laws, including even the Papacy itself, which on those conditions, might be tolerated. How far Luther assented to this may be seen in Reflections signed by him. Walch, xx 2178.

‖ Sachsische Apologia. Muller, p 861, and the Archiv of Forstemann, p 130.

¶ "That the conjugati should be admitted to priests' estate and ordained, in like manner, as was the usage for some centuries in old times in the first churches." Unschluessige und unvergriffliche christliche Mittel. (Undecided and impracticable Christian Measures — Proposals of the Catholic Committee.) Forstemann, ii p. 250.

** Thom Leodius, Vita Friderici Palatini, vii 151. Ut intellexit, ita rejecit. See Melanchthon to Camerarius Corp Ref ii 590. To this also tended Campeggi's first observations. "I santi padri," says he, "con la santità della vita, osservantia delli precetti divini, con summa

He maintained that all the ordinances of the church were immediately dictated by the Holy Ghost.* He worked on the minds of the States by similar arguments, and at length they required that, until the decision of the council, the Protestants should appoint no more married priests to benefices, they persisted in compulsory confession, they would consent neither to the omission of the canon in the mass, nor the abolition of private masses in Protestant countries, and, lastly, they required that the participation in the Lord's Supper, in one kind should be declared not less valid than in both.

These, however, were concessions which would have as completely destroyed the infant work of Protestant organisation as those demanded in 1529. Half-formed convictions would thus have been shaken to their very foundations. The Protestants were prepared not to condemn the sacrament in one kind, but it was impossible for them to resolve to declare it equally conformable with Scripture as their own form, "since," as they affirmed, "Christ instituted the sacrament in both kinds." Nor could they be expected to reintroduce the private masses, which they had so vehemently denounced as utterly at variance with the idea of the sacrament. This would have been to destroy their own work; notwithstanding their conviction that they had undertaken it on just grounds.

As the negotiations advanced, too, every step revealed a greater difference of fundamental principles than the parties had avowed to themselves. The Catholics regarded the ordinances of ecclesiastical authority as the rule which admitted, at the utmost, of rare exceptions. The Protestants, on the contrary, saw the rule of faith and life in Scripture alone, they would admit the peculiar institutions of the Romish church only conditionally, and in so far as it was wholly unavoidable.* The former derived all the ordinances of the church from divine right, the latter saw in them only human and revocable institutions. But little was gained so long as the Protestants were unanimously inclined to regard the Papacy as an earthly and human institution, and therefore needing limitations, since the religious ideas of the opposite party were entirely founded on the divine right of the Catholic church, and the character of its head as Vicar of Christ.

And even had they come to some sort of understanding, and settled some terms of compromise, it would have been almost impossible to put them in execution. What difficulties, for example, would the re-establishment of bishoprics have created! The character of the new church rested mainly on the independence of the lower clergy, and its immediate connexion with the territorial power. The old antipathy of the cities was already aroused by the suggestion, the Nurnbergers declared they would never again submit to the domination of a bishop.†

Another and a less numerous meeting, consisting of only three members on either side, was convened towards the end of August, after the first negotiations were broken off, but on following their discussions with attention, we find that they never approached the point which the former assembly had reached.

Some isolated attempts at conciliation were afterwards made. Duke Henry of Brunswick had a conference with the son of the Elector John Frederick, in the garden of a citizen of Augsburg. In the church of St Maurice the Chancellor of Baden made certain proposals to the Chancellor of Saxony, who was accompanied by Melanchthon: these were discussed for a time, but could lead to no results.

The Protestant party had conceded as much as possible, consistently with their religious convictions, they had reached the farthest limits of compliance, nay, murmurs were already heard in their own body against the concessions that had been made, it was impossible to induce them to advance a single step farther. During these negotiations, Elector John exhorted the theologians to look only at the cause, and to take no thought for him or his land.

Nor was any farther concession to be extorted from the other side, fettered as it was by the pope.

NEGOTIATIONS OF THE EMPEROR.

It was impossible that the emperor should be inclined to acquiesce in such a termination of the diet or to allow it to disperse thus. He was, on the contrary, deeply impressed with the conviction, that an interminable train of still greater evils and troubles must then ensue.‡

At the very beginning of the deliberations, the Catholic majority had repeated the demand for a council, and Charles, who already contemplated an ecclesiastical assembly from his own peculiar point of view, as emperor, had written about it to the pope. Clement VII laid the demand before a congregation which he had appointed to settle matters of faith. Many declared themselves against it, especially on the two following grounds: first, because persons who had rejected the former councils would not consent to a new one, secondly, because any attack on the part of the Turks would be far more dangerous while the public attention was absorbed by these internal affairs. But the pope was bound by the promises he had made during his captivity in the castle of St Angelo, as well as by expressions he had let fall in conversation at Bologna: he therefore entreated the em-

vigilantia e studio si sono sforzati a partecipare del spirito santo, dal quale senza dubio spinti hanno così santamente ordinate tutte le cose della chiesa."

* Brenz spoke of a preceptum dispensabile in casu necessitatis. The necessity is to him the decree of the Romish Church, which, however, he by no means regards as justified thereby.

† Opinion of Spengler in Hausdorf's Leben Spenglers, p. 65.

‡ An opinion presented to the diet (Brussels Archives) says, "La matière ne peut pas demeurer en ces termes sans en attendre pis et inconvénient irreparable."

peror once more maturely to weigh the thing, but if his majesty, who was on the spot, and whose zeal for the Catholic religion was undoubted, held it to be absolutely necessary, he also would consent, but only under the condition laid down by the emperor and States themselves—that the Protestants must, till then, dutifully return to the rite and the doctrines of the holy mother church. He proposed Rome as the most suitable place for the meeting.*

It was in consequence of this correspondence that, on the 7th of September, the emperor sent a message to the Protestants, in which he announced the council, adding, however "that they must in the interval conform to the faith and practice of the emperor, the states, and the universal Christian church."

Did Charles really believe, after all that had passed, that a command of this nature would be obeyed? Such an expectation would only prove that the temper and modes of thinking of the Protestants were for ever closed and unintelligible to him. They had already heard of the intended proposal, and were prepared. They replied, that to comply with such a demand, would be to run counter to God and their consciences; and that, moreover, they were not legally bound to do so, that the council granted was a consequence of previous decrees of the empire, but that no condition like that now attached to it had ever been so much as discussed. No resolutions which the majority might recently have passed in Spires to this effect could possibly bind those who had solemnly protested against the whole proceedings there. In the oral communication the emperor had described them as a sect, against this they entered an immediate and solemn protest.†

We are in possession of the letter which the emperor hereupon sent to the pope, it proves that he was no less mortified than incensed. "They have answered me," says he, "in the stubbornness of their error, whereupon I am reflecting what to do."

As the necessity of having recourse to force already arose in prospect before him, he thought that, although the mediation of the States had so utterly failed, he might be able to effect something by his personal interference. "In order that all our measures may be more completely justified," he continues, "it seems good to me that I should speak with them myself, both jointly and severally, which I think immediately to proceed in." Not, therefore, without giving notice to the court of Rome, he offered the Protestants his personal endeavours to discover means of restoring unity, previous to the meeting of the council.

He deceived himself greatly, however, if he hoped to accomplish any thing with the Protestants by means of such a missive as he now addressed to them. In this he maintained the nullity of the protest, without going into the grounds on which it rested, and solely because it was reasonable and expedient that so insignificant a number should yield to the majority. he likewise expressed his astonishment that the Catholic deputies had carried their concessions so far. As the Protestants had already expressed their final decision, they could not do otherwise than reject a negotiation founded on such assumptions as these. They entered into no discussion of the religious questions in their answer; they only sought to make the legality of their proceedings clear to the emperor. They replied, that they were determined to take their stand on the recesses of the diets of 1524 and 1526—a position from which no majority could remove them—and asked for nothing save external peace.‡

Inevitable as such an answer was, it deeply offended the emperor. He gave the Protestants to understand that he had received the same "with notable displeasure." He says in one of his letters that he cannot describe what vexation this affair causes him. Clinging tenaciously to the idea of the Latin church, and animated by a chivalrous sort of ambition, he had hoped to triumph over all his enemies. Instead of this he saw himself involved in a dispute, the very grounds of which were unintelligible to him.§

In fact, he now thought that all peaceful means were exhausted, and that he must have recourse to arms. In the letter to the pope, to which we have just alluded, he says, "Force is what would now bring the most fruit," and he was only restrained by the consideration that he was not sufficiently prepared. After the second answer of the Protestants had been sent in, he declared to the majority of the States, that, as he could consent to nothing prejudicial to the faith, and as all conciliatory measures had been of no avail, he was ready to risk his possessions and his person in the cause, and with the aid and counsel of the States, to do whatever might be necessary. He would likewise seek assistance from the pope and other sovereigns.

This thought had been entertained in his privy council from the very commencement of the diet. Should the Protestants remain obstinate, and, as their enemies wished, refuse to submit either to the judgment of the emperor or to the council the legate was to be consulted as to the kind of force to be employed.‖

The emperor appeared disposed to treat the Protestants as he had done the Moors in Spain. Had he been fully prepared with munitions of

* All' imperatore di man propria di Clemente (L di pr ii 197). Pregatala prima che esamini maturamente—dico a V. M. che son contento che quella, in caso giudichi esser così necessario, offerisca e prometta la convocatione del concilio, con conditione però, che appartandosi da' loro errori tornino incontinente al viver Catholicamente.

† Remarks on the Anshach Acts, in Förstemann's Urkundenbuch, ii 303. Sachsische Apologia in Förstemann's Arch 136.

‡ Answer of the Protestants, dated 8th Sept. Forstemann's Urkunden, ii 411.

§ Forstemann's Urkunden, ii. Heller's Report, 422.

‖ Si lesdits Lutheriens - - demeurent obstinez, il faut savoir l'intention du Sieur Legat, comment et par quels moyens on pourra proceder contre eux par righeur.

war, and had he not been bound by the resolutions of the majority, he would probably, spite of his natural mildness, have been led by his consistent adherence to engagements, to proceed immediately in this work.

It is, however, not surprising that the majority of the diet had some hesitation in assenting to such a course. Certain interests had been agitated (as we have already mentioned), about which the States were not fully agreed with the emperor;* they were not disposed to follow him implicitly in a crusade. The old sentiments of members of the empire had not yet so entirely given place to religious hatred. On the contrary, at this moment, the project of electing a king of the Romans (to which we shall shortly recur) excited fresh dissatisfaction among them.

The States submitted a project of a recess, which held out, indeed, a menace of war, but at a distance; the Protestants were to be allowed time for repentance till the next 5th of May, in order to explain themselves on the articles on which it had been found impossible to come to an agreement.

Unfortunately, however, this project was also conceived in terms which wounded the feelings of the Protestants. It was said, that they must compel no one to join their sect;—the word and the thing were equally odious to them: it contained ordinances to which they did not think themselves at liberty to submit; *e. g.* not to allow any thing relating to matters of faith to be printed within the period assigned, and to allow monks to confess and say mass; and lastly, it was expressly asserted that the confession had been confuted with arguments drawn from the Holy Scripture. By accepting and subscribing this recess, they would have signed the condemnation of their own cause. They rejected it without a moment's hesitation. They not only explicitly stated the grounds of their refusal, but seized the opportunity offered them by the assertion that the confession had been confuted, to lay before the emperor an apology for it. On all main points the apology is like the confession; but, if I mistake not, the nature and style of the former recede still more widely from Catholicism.

This brought down upon them another storm. Elector Joachim of Brandenburg announced to them, that if they refused to accept the recess, the emperor and States were determined to venture person and property, land and people, in order to put an end to this matter. The emperor declared that he would consent to no further alterations; if the Protestant party would accept the recess, there it was: if not, he, the emperor, in concert with all the other Estates, must take immediate measures for the extirpation of their sect.

But if former threats had been unavailing, these were not likely to make any impression. The religious spirit which, in the rigour of its conscientiousness, had scorned every alliance not founded on perfect uniformity of belief, now showed itself no less inflexible towards the system from which it had seceded.

Such was the end of every attempt at approximation. The minority were determined to maintain their position in all its integrity, and calmly to await whatever their enemies might undertake against them.

Thus the parties separated.

It were a complete mistake to imagine that the Elector of Saxony had any political schemes of opposition to the emperor. On the contrary, it was a sincere affliction to him to be forced to sever himself thus from his emperor and lord; but he could do no otherwise. The moment had arrived, when, being about to depart, he went to take his leave. "Uncle, uncle," said the emperor, "I did not look for this from you (*Ew. Liebden*)."† The elector made no answer; his eyes filled with tears, but he could find no words; so he left the palace, and, immediately after, the city.‡

A complete separation had taken place among the princes of the empire. In Spires this had extended to the princes alone; now, the emperor was not only present, but implicated.

The rupture which had hitherto been concealed beneath the hope of a reconciliation, was now laid bare to view.

The division had already extended to the cities.

First, Reutlingen, and then, one after another, Kempten, Heilbronn, Windsheim, and Weissenburg in the Nordgau, had joined Nürnberg.

Four other towns, Strasburg, Memmingen, Constance and Lindau, which had hitherto adhered to the Swiss views of the Lord's Supper, had given in their own confession — the so-called Tetrapolitana — to the contents of which, so highly important to the internal history of Protestantism, we shall return hereafter.§ To them, too, the emperor caused a Catholic refutation to be read aloud; of course, without the smallest effect. Strasburg showed

* Königklich wirde zu Hungern sc. Revocation der babstlichen bulle so auf den vierten Tail d' geistlichen gutter erlangt. The revocation of the papal bull is demanded for the fourth part of the ecclesiastical lands, by the king in Hungary, &c. Förstemann's Urk. ii. 843.

† *Your well-belovedness*, would be somewhat corresponding to this title, by which the emperor was wont to address his immediate vassals.—TRANSL.

‡ Erzählung der sächsischen Apologia in Förstemann's Archiv. p. 206. Granvella mentions this trait, as a proof of the loyalty and affection of the elector towards his imperial majesty.

§ Fürstenberg (5th July) relates the following: "Es haben die von Strasburg vergangener Tag uns und etlich mehr von Städten bei sich erfordert, und die Bekanntniss irer Lere und Predig, so sie der Keys. Mt. zu übergeben willens, zuvor anhoren lassen, ob sich jemand villeicht mit inen unterschreiben wolt. Wie wol nun dieselbig fast wol gestellt und, etwas subtiler und zugtiger dan der Fursten gewest, so haben wir doch, diweyl bis anher bei uns des Sacraments halber ihre Opinion nit gepredigt, das underschreyben abgeschlagen; dergleichen haben auch andere gethan, uss ursachen von jeglichen insonderheit furgewant."—"Yesterday they of Strasburg invited us and some others of the cities to come to them, and to hear the confession of their doctrine and preaching, which they intend to deliver in to the emperor; and to see whether perchance any will subscribe it with them. Now, although the same be well drawn up, and somewhat more subtle and discreet than that of the princes was, yet have we, seeing that till now their opinion on the sacrament has not been preached among us, refused to sign; the like have also others done, for reasons by each severally assigned."

as much courage as Nurnberg and other cities Had the intended reconciliation taken place between Catholics and Protestants, the four cities would have fallen into little jeopardy But as things turned out in Augsburg, they had less to fear than at first, and they therefore gave the less ear to any suggestions from the other side

It was only to the other cities that the emperor caused it to be announced, on the 24th of September, that Saxony and his kinsmen and allies had causelessly and wrongfully rejected a recess drawn up, in fact, in their favour,—doubtless mainly because they were required to restore the convents, but that he was resolved to put an end to this thing As the other States had promised to stake life and property on the cause, he hoped to find the same zeal in them The cities requested to be allowed first to consult their authorities, the emperor pressed for an immediate answer

Hereupon those who had remained Catholic, the smaller as well as the larger Rottweil, Ueberlingen, Cologne, Hagenau, even Regensburg, attached themselves without hesitation to the emperor

The others, who had hitherto allowed free circulation to the confession, without setting themselves in open opposition to the emperor and the majority, were now in no small perplexity They considered that, by accepting the recess, they should admit the confession to be confuted, and that they should be compelled to fight against their co-religionists, gradually therefore Frankfurt, Ulm, Schwabisch-Hall—and lastly Augsburg rejected it In Augsburg, as may be imagined, this difficulty was most felt, in consequence of the emperor's presence It was thought necessary to resort to the extraordinary measure of convoking the great council in which members of all the guilds took part But the Protestant spirit had already penetrated the body of the citizens too deeply for them to find it possible to renounce it In the very face of the emperor, Augsburg refused to accept his recess *

There were now fourteen cities, and among them precisely the most affluent and flourishing in the empire—Strasburg, Ulm, Augsburg, Frankfurt, and Nurnberg,—that actively opposed the recess They were a minority, but not so inconsiderable a minority as had at first appeared.

Meanwhile, the emperor had business to transact with the majority, who, as we have said, did not attach themselves with such cordiality to his house as the support they now received from him seemed to demand

The grant of the ecclesiastical lands in Germany and Austria, made by the pope to King Ferdinand, was obstinately rejected. The clergy first declared their resolution not to consent to it, and the whole assembly then made the cause their own In a report with marginal notes, written by Granvilla, it appears that they threatened to withhold all subsidies for the Turkish war if this project was persisted in Such an innovation, they declared, such an assumption on the part of the pope, could be endured neither in the empire, nor in the Austrian hereditary dominions † Granvilla made this known to the king, and Ferdinand was at length compelled to let the bull drop

Not till then were the Turkish succours granted nor even then were they such as the emperor had wished them—permanent, which the states declared would only be possible in case of the co-operation of the whole of Christendom On the other hand, a considerable body of troops raised in haste were immediately granted, twice as many as for the Roman expedition of 1521, viz, 40,000 foot soldiers, and 8,000 horse, for six months only at present, but for longer in case of need.

---

* Kress and Volkamer to Nurnberg in Corp Ref ii 422 The correspondence between the city of Frankfurt and its delegates is specially worthy of note "Sollte es aber mit sich bringen, wie es on Zweyfel thut" wrote Fürstenberg on the 31 of October, "dass wir stillschweygend gehellen, dass die Bekenntniss des Churfürsten und seynes Anhangs mit den heyligen Evangelien und Geschriften grundlich abgeleynet worden, welche Ableynung wir doch nie gesehn noch an Tag kommen ist, das ist unsers Erachtens wider unser Gewissen und Verstand und deshalb zu bewilligen ganz beschwerlich und nit thunlich, und wan es gleich desfalls nit zu widerfechten were, khan E W on Zweyffel wol ermessen, wo es zur Handlung kommen solt, was E W derwegen mit Pulver Buxen Geld und andern zu le hen und darzustrecken zugemut word werden wir wollen geschweygen was das uf im hab zuzusagen und zu halten was weiter beschlossen wird"—"Should it however, come to pass, as it doubtless will, that we tacitly admit that the confession of the elector and his followers is fundamentally confuted from the holy Gospels and Scriptures (which confutation we have, however, not seen and which has not yet been made public,) that were according to our judgment, against our conscience and understanding, and to assent to it were very difficult, and not a thing to be done, and if, in like manner, it were not to be controverted, your worships can without doubt well estimate, if it should come to action, what your worships would be asked to lend and contribute in powder, firelocks, money, and other things we will say nothing about what is to be said to this matter, and will hold to what may be further determined." The eminently discreet council of Frankfurt hereupon resolves on this answer to the emperor (14th Oct)—"Dieweil Kais. Mt ein Concilium zu verschaffen sich allergnedigklichst erpotten, und ein erparer Rath kainswegs sich ye versehen, dass Kais Mt dem ewigen Gottes Wort etwas zuwider werde aufrichten oder handhaben helffen, so wolle ein erbarer Rath in Bedacht hochgedachter Kays Mt als eines allergnedigsten gutigen milten Kaisers selbst erbieten sich desselbigen getroisten, auch furan, als einem christlichen Magistrat wol geziemt, und so viel sie gegen Gott der Seelen und Gewissen halb und der Kays Mt von des Reichs wegen Gehorsam zu leisten schuldig, wie pillig allerunterthanigst gehorsamen"—"Since your imperial majesty has most graciously proposed to procure an ecclesiastical council to be held, and since our honourable council has by no means seen that your imperial majesty would ever help to establish or maintain any thing contrary to the everlasting word of God, our honourable council regarding your imperial majesty as a most gracious, kind and clement emperor, proposes to trust to your imperial majesty as it beseems a Christian magistracy, and in as far as they are bound to tender obedience to God, on account of their souls and consciences, and to your imperial majesty on account of the empire, so far most dutifully to obey, as is just and reasonable" In these obscure folds do they wrap up their refusal In the main, they agree with their ambassador

† Les deputes ont dit clerement, que la dite bastive ayde ne sera en manière nulle consentie, si premierement le roi (Ferdinand) n'abolit entierement la bulle du pape, et ce non seulement en l'empire, mais aussi a l'encontre des subjects de tous les estats qui sont demourans et habitans en pays d'Autriche, car ils donnent a entendre que de la sorte ils ne veulent nullement estre en subjection du pape. (Brussels Archives) Granvilla adds the remark, au roi, que S. M regarde, etc

The succours were not to be in money, but in men, and to be levied according to the division of the circles.

Some other internal affairs were likewise transacted.

One main purpose of the diet, announced in the proclamation, was, to allay the disputes between the spiritual and temporal Estates which had recently made so much noise. At a former period the spiritual States had been vehemently attacked; now, they were the complainants. Formerly, this would have given occasion to the most violent contests; now, as these mutual animosities had given way to a common antipathy, a committee, composed of both, was appointed, and a compromise actually effected, which the emperor consented to proclaim as a constitution of the empire.*

The hundred Gravamina were likewise once more brought forward. The temporal princes, accustomed to persist in their resolutions, presented them anew. As the papal legate was not empowered to enter into negotiations on the matter, the emperor engaged to have them agitated by his ambassador in Rome.†

It appears almost as if the abolition of these grievances had subsequently been regarded as conceded, and as if the constitution just mentioned had obtained a certain authority.‡ But these interests now vanished before the far weightier one of the reformation.

The most important question was, what attitude the emperor and the majority would assume in their relations with the States which had rejected their recess.

From all I have been able to discover, it appears that the emperor was more for an immediate resort to force, while the majority were inclined to defer taking up arms.

After being repeatedly asked, they gave in their opinion, that the emperor should issue a new religious mandate on the basis of the edict of Worms. If Saxony, with his followers, should refuse obedience to it, the emperor should summon them to appear before him, pronounce the due punishment, and proceed to its execution.

The recess is conceived in the same spirit.

The emperor therein proclaims his serious determination to enforce his edict of Worms; he specifies a number of infringements of it, all of which he condemns, whether they be called Lutheran, Zwinglian, or anabaptist; he insists on the maintenance of every point of the disputed usages or doctrines, and establishes anew the jurisdiction of the spiritual princes. The imperial fiscal was immediately to proceed judicially against the recusants, even to the punishment of the ban of the empire, which should be executed according to the ordinances of the public peace.

A main point, and one to which we shall shortly have occasion to return, is that the Imperial Chamber was immediately reconstituted and bound to enforce this recess.

An appeal to arms remained, however, as we see from this document, always in reserve; it was an idea to which the emperor incessantly recurred.

In a letter to the pope of the 4th October, he expressed himself with great vivacity on the subject; he informed him that the negotiations were broken off, and their adversaries more obstinate than ever, but that he was determined to apply all his force to subdue them. He wishes the pope to exhort the other princes of Christendom to espouse this cause.§

We have another letter, dated 25th of October, from Charles to the cardinals, in which he earnestly entreats them to promote the convocation of a council. Meanwhile, he wishes to consult them how he is to act in the interval towards the Lutherans, so as to avoid further danger; and especially how he ought to fulfil the functions of an emperor, which had devolved upon him. "We declare to you," adds he, "that for the termination of this affair we will spare neither kingdoms nor dominions; nay, that we will devote to it body and soul, which we have wholly dedicated to the service of God Almighty."‖

On the 30th October he sent his major domo, Pedro de la Cueva, to Rome, to inform the pope that the Catholic princes were indeed of opinion that the year was too far advanced to undertake any immediate measures against the Lutherans, but to exhort him (the pope) by no means to desist from preparations for such an enterprise. The emperor, on his side, however desirable it might be for him to go to Spain, would postpone every thing, in order immediately to put in execution whatever in the pope's opinion might conduce to the service of God and of his holiness.

In Rome the question had long been decided. Campeggi had told the emperor that, without some strong measure, he would arrive at no result. He had reminded him of Maximilian, who had never been able to obtain obedience till he took up arms, and used them successfully against the house of the Palatinate.¶

* Concordata of the spiritual and temporal grievances, collected in the form of a constitution. Bucholtz, iii. 636.

† In Adrian's Catalogus is quoted (No. 196, p. 93), Consultatio et deliberatio consiliariorum deputatorum super gravaminibus quæ nationi Germanicæ per sedem apostolicam inferuntur, which would belong here.

‡ Spittler, Geschichte der Fundamentalgesetze der deutsch-katholischen Kirche (Werke, viii. 501), affirms that the two documents, the Gravamina, which were regarded as actually settled, and the Concordata, lay on the table of the Imperial Council (Hofrath) for daily use.

§ Raince, 18th Oct. Lui (au Pape) escrivoit le dit empereur estre delibere employer tous ses biens et forces et sa propre personne à leur faire la guerre, priant S. Ste vouloir admonester et requerir tous les princes chretiens vouloir aider et entrer à l'expedition de la dite emprise, et sur cela s. d. Ste fait dimanche congregation de cardinaux. MS. Bethune at Paris.

‖ Il vous plaira, selon votre prudence et bonte, adviser comment on se peut gouverner avec eux—(les Lutheriens) — — tant pour empescher qu'il n'advienne plus detriment a la chose publique, que partiellement pour la satisfaction des charges et offices, esquels par la divine clemence fumes constitues, vous advisans que n'epargnerons ni royaumes ni seigneuries pour la consommation de chose tant necessaire, etc. Bethune, 8539.

¶ Molto più a V. Mta. conviensi in questa impressa santa e christiana a farsi obedire con tutte le vie e modi che si ponno trovare, che fece la felice memoria di Maximiliano suo avo nelle imprese che contra i Palatini si

In short, as the Protestants were not to be brought to conform by mild measures, western Christendom and the German empire, represented by the pope, the emperor, and the assembly of the empire, appeared resolved to put them down either by law or by force

It remained to be seen whether the recusants would have the physical and moral strength necessary to make effectual resistance.

gloriosamente finI dipoi la quale sempre fu poi tenuto e riverito e obedito ——ricordando sempre che è impossibile senza qualche gagliarda exactione et ordine estirpare le heresie

BOOK VI.

ORIGIN AND PROGRESS OF THE SCHMALKALDIC LEAGUE.

1530—1535.

As even in the remote times described by Tacitus, the Germans deemed it the heaviest of all punishments to be forbidden to attend the public assemblies and sacrifices, so, during the middle ages, they accounted it an intolerable misfortune to be excluded from the communion of the church and the peace of the empire These two communities appeared to embrace all the good which man can enjoy on this side the grave and on the other

The evangelical States now found themselves on the point of being excluded from both

From the church, encumbered as it was with abuses which they had hoped to reform, they had, since their efforts were unsuccessful, voluntarily severed themselves They clung with fervent and steadfast attachment to the idea of an improved church On the other hand, the established church strenuously resisted every attempt at change, and repulsed every advance unaccompanied by complete submission

Hence it happened that the imperial authority, on which the evangelical party at first thought they might rely for support, having concluded a close alliance with Rome, now threatened them with exclusion from the public peace, —that is to say, with war and ruin

It seemed evident that the evangelical party, with their slender territorial power, still further enfeebled by internal divisions, if once involved in a serious contest with a large majority of the States, the puissant emperor, and the whole of Latin Christendom united, must be instantly and hopelessly overwhelmed

This it is which constitutes the most striking feature of the diet of Augsburg, that in full view of this danger, they resolved never to abandon the religious position they had taken up, and the importance of which filled their whole souls

When, indeed, this resolution was once taken, it appeared, on a calm survey of their situation, that, in spite of the superiority of their opponents, the cause they so intrepidly defended was by no means desperate.

And, in the first place, the tendency to reform was inherent in the course of events and the progress of public opinion, and had innumerable allies lying without the pale of its acknowledged domain, all the force of the principle of which the protestors were the avowed champions, must, without any effort of theirs, come to their aid.

At the same time the whole of the Germano-Roman nations of the west were attacked by the most formidable enemy they had ever encountered In spite of all differences, in spite of the attempt to exclude them from the great political body of which they were members, the Protestants belonged to this menaced and assailed community , they, indeed, were the representatives of a new stage of that intellectual culture, of which the barbarian enemy meditated the extirpation, Europe neither could nor would dispense with their aid

But, lastly, the external unity of Catholic Christendom was only the product of a moment of good fortune and victory, or of prompt and successful policy It was hardly to be expected that such a peace as this would lead to serious co-operation, or would even be of any long continuance

I do not believe that any of the men then living arrived at a full sense of the real situation of things Landgrave Philip was the first who had a dim perception of it, the others, without much reflection on what was passing around them, took counsel only of their consciences

The important thing both for them and for the general progress of society was, that a centre of resistance should be firmly established, so that they might not be overpowered by the first storm, and might on some future occasion take advantage of favouring circumstances, by which their enemies now so largely profited

CHAPTER I

FOUNDATION OF THE SCHMALKALDIC LEAGUE

The church had of herself no political power, for that, she was wholly dependent on the arm of the empire "The anathema," says the Sachsenspiegel, "injures only the soul, the penalties of the law of the land or of the feudal law are consequent on the king's ban "

Hostile as was the temper of the majority at the diet to the Protestants, this ban, spite of their secession from the church, was not proclaimed against them The majority, which had not even permitted the emperor to act as judge, hesitated to put arms into his hands

While war still appeared imminent, they conceived the design of transferring the combat to another field; "they would not fight, but right" (*nicht fechten sondern rechten*), as they expressed it. Of all the great institutions of the empire which had been so laboriously founded for the conservation of the national unity, the only one that still enjoyed some consideration was the Imperial Chamber (Reichskammergericht), which exercised the judicial functions of the emperor, while its character was eminently representative.* This tribunal they resolved to employ for the purpose they meditated. At the diet of Augsburg, the Imperial Chamber was extended and better organised for the despatch of business. The number of assessors was increased from eighteen to twenty-four; retaining, of course, the right of election of the circles; but besides this, it was thought necessary, in order to get rid of long arrears of business, to appoint eight experienced doctors. Further, the court determined to subject itself to a new visitation. The reader will remember the manner in which it was purified, at the time the old Council of Regency fell.† The same spirit presided over the present reforms. Seven of the procurators and advocates were seriously admonished on account of their religious opinions, and an eighth was obliged to absent himself for a time.‡ And this tribunal, thus strengthened, and purged from all inclination to the new opinions, was now most earnestly exhorted to observe the Augsburg recess, particularly in the article concerning faith; the president of the chamber was to be not only empowered, but bound, to remove any who might infringe it, and must do so under pain of the emperor's displeasure.§

The Imperial Chamber was thus rendered a complete expression of the prevailing sentiments of the majority.

The Protestants were well aware of this. In a project for the maintenance of peace, communicated to them at the conclusion of the diet, it was said, that no one should invade another's dominions unlawfully. They inferred from this that such invasion might take place, in pursuance of a sentence of the Imperial Chamber, the nature of which could not be doubtful.

At the same time, however, a new measure was introduced for the government of the empire.

Of late years the house of Austria had more than once had occasion to fear that, in consequence of the nullity of the Council of Regency, and the absence of the emperor, people might either proceed to elect another chief, or might revive and recognise the rights of the vicars of the empire, of whom the Elector of Saxony was one.

In order to put an end forever to plans of this sort, the emperor abandoned all considerations regarding his possible posterity, and, as we have said, determined to raise his brother to the rank of King of the Romans.

It had been objected to Maximilian on a similar occasion, that he was himself not crowned emperor, and therefore, in fact, only King of the Romans; and this was one of the reasons for Charles's coronation in Bologna.

To this the five Catholic electors raised little objection, presuming that their compliance would be requited with favours. The Palatinate was promised compensation for its losses in the Landshut war, and moreover the sum of 160,000 gulden. A final settlement of the affair of Zossen and the Bohemian fiefs, together with other advantages, was promised to Brandenburg; in his letters he tells with great delight what a gracious emperor and king he has.‖ A number of extraordinary, and indeed almost contradictory favours were to be granted to the Elector of Mainz; *e. g.* to procure him, from the court of Rome, the powers of a legate *a latere* for his dioceses, and at the same time, permission to leave these same dioceses to coadjutors, and keep an accumulation of estates and benefices for his own perpetual use.¶ Trèves had for some years been secured by a sum of money. The longest hesitation was on the part of Cologne, the promises made to whom eleven years ago at the election of Charles V. were not yet fulfilled; but at length, having received sufficient guarantee, he assented. Saxony alone held out.

It was suggested by some, that, as Saxony could in no case be won over without concessions which the emperor was determined not to grant, it would be most expedient to take advantage of his defection from the Church of Rome, at once to exclude him. The pope actually sent a brief, according to which Elector John could be stripped of his right of electing, in virtue of a bull of Leo X., subjecting the defenders of Luther to the pains and penalties of heresy.** Deliberations were actually held upon the matter; but the electors had not yet reached such a point as to consent to so formless a proceeding, which might afterwards be turned against any one of themselves. The evidence we have seems to prove, that the elector palatine most strenuously opposed it,†† and that John of Saxony was in fact invited. The pliant pope had furnished a brief to meet this case also, in which he declared that the participation of Saxony, although, in virtue of the above-mentioned

* *Ständisch.*, See Translator's note, p. 52.

† See p. 193.

‡ Harpprecht, Staatsarchiv. des Kammergerichts, v. 82.

§ Recess of the 19th Nov. 1530, §§ 76, 82, 91. All the persons of the imperial chamber should "bear themselves agreeably to the recess of this diet now and here holden, especially in the article of faith and religion."

‖ Letter of the 18th Aug. 1530. Berlin Archives.

¶ The last, in the letter of grace (Gnadenbrief) of the 6th Sept. in Bucholtz, iii. 662. The first, in the Brussels Archives, 7th Sept. Contendemus obtinere a D. N. Clemente VII. facultates ad instar legati a latere pro electore antedicto in omnibus suis diœcesibus, nempe Moguntina, Magdeburgensi, et Halberstadensi.

** Extract in Bucholtz, ix. 17.

†† Taubenheim to El. John. Förstemann, ii. 821. "Wie ichs vermerke, so szolle Pfalz die vornehmste Ursach sein, damit E. Ch. G. nicht ausgeschlossen werden." According to what I observe, the palatine is the chief cause why your E. G. is not excluded.

bull, he might be regarded as excommunicated, should not prejudice the validity of the election.

The warning thus given, and the threat implied in the new instructions to the Imperial Chamber, were the immediate causes of the Schmalkaldic League.

We have seen how little the evangelical princes had hitherto succeeded in forming any permanent union, and even now they wavered as long as the emperor remained in Augsburg, and there was still a doubt what measures he might take in concert with the majority. A congress already convoked was given up again in consequence of some pacific expressions of the emperor.* But now that the recess had appeared, and was of so decidedly hostile a character, — now, that the above-mentioned citation was at the same time sent to the Saxon court, they could no longer defer their meeting.

In a letter to George of Brandenburg, Elector John gives the following reasons. — First, that in answer to a question concerning the instructions given to the fiscal of the Imperial Chamber, the emperor had replied, that he (the fiscal) should not be prohibited from proceeding against those who would not submit to his recess, it would, therefore, be necessary to deliberate on a unanimous exception against such a proceeding. And likewise, that the summons to the election rendered it necessary that they should converse with each other about it, and immediately agree on some common measures of opposition.†

I know not whether I am wrong in supposing that this turn of affairs was essentially favourable to the Protestants.

The all-important point was, that they should not be excluded from the peace of the empire, on account of their ecclesiastical changes.

Had the old modes of thinking still prevailed, a crusade would have been set on foot against them.

But, inasmuch as the majority resolved to attack them by means of the great representative (*standischen*) tribunal, and on the field of the ancient laws of the empire, inasmuch as the emperor invited them to concur in his brother's election, the legality of their participation in the business of the empire, in spite of their ecclesiastical differences, was recognised.

The whole contest was converted from an ecclesiastical into a general,—from a political question, to one of public law, and on this ground the Protestants had now to unite, and to organise their resistance.

On the 22d of December, 1530, John of Saxony, Ernest of Luneburg, Philip of Hessen, Wolfgang of Anhalt, the Counts Gebhard and Albrecht of Mansfeld, the latter of whom was bearer of the vote of Grubenhagen, and also delegates from George of Brandenburg and from several cities, assembled in Schmalkalden. The heights which surround the town were covered with snow. It was not for their pleasure that they passed the festival of Christmas in this small frontier town, in the midst of a rude mountain district.

They resolved, in the first place, that, as soon as any attempt should be made by the imperial fiscal to enforce the law against any one of them, the whole body should come to his aid.‡ They agreed on certain exceptions which they intended to take in common, and appointed two or three procurators to conduct the business before the Imperial Chamber.

This is the essential part of the league, and it affords the clearest evidence that the religious dispute was transformed into one of law. In this all who had originally subscribed the Augsburg Confession, or had since given in their adhesion to it, joined.

They also agreed that they must try to induce the emperor to mitigate the terms of the recess, or perhaps, protest against it altogether.

Had they proceeded to act immediately, it is probable that a uniform external organization of the new churches would have been effected. Most of them were in favour of the introduction of a general church ordinance,—mainly in order to render open vice amenable to ecclesiastical chastisement.

On the other hand, they could not come to so perfect an understanding concerning the second principal subject of deliberation—the election of the king.

Saxony declared his opinion that they should not allow so great a latitude to the emperor, as that he should be able to carry through an affair of this importance single-handed, otherwise, there would soon be an end of the privileges and franchises of the empire. There was a great difference, he said, between an election after a regular vacancy, and an attempt to place a king of the Romans by the side of a living emperor. In the latter case, a consultation of all the electors, and an unanimous resolution, must precede the summons to the election. But nothing of the kind had been thought of. Even the citation which had been sent to himself (the Elector of Saxony), allowed much too short a time, and was as completely null as all the rest of the proceedings. Lastly, it was impossible to suffer Ferdinand, who had distinguished himself by his enmity to the Gospel, to be imposed upon them. While lieutenant, he had contrived the strangest artifices, and as king, he would have the game in his own hands. To

* It was fixed for the Monday after the feast of St Catharine (28th Nov 1530.)

† This is in fact expressed in the paper which is annexed to the letter from Torgau, of St Andrew's Eve (29th Nov.) The elector invites the markgrave, "ir (S. Gn.) selbst und der sachen zu gut," ("for your grace's own sake, and that of the cause.") (W. A.)

‡ Wo der kais. Fiscal, der Bund zu Schwaben oder Jemand anders I. Chf. und Furstlichen Gnaden oder die gemeldten Stadte, eine oder mehre oder jemand von den Iren in Sachen unsern heil. Glauben oder was demselben anhanget (belangen), auf den ausgegangenen Abschied furnehmen und im Schein des Rechtens oder andere Wege beklagen wurde,—das Ire aller Gn. und Gunsten einander in solche beistendig rathlich und hulflich seyn sollen."—"If the imperial fiscal, the Swabian league, or any others, should undertake, in virtue of the recess just published, and under the appearance of law, or in any other way, to accuse your E. and P. Graces, or the above mentioned cities on account of our holy faith, or what is connected therewith—that all your graces should stand by one another with counsel and help."

elect Ferdinand thus, without any stipulation, would be to put arms into the hands of their enemies. They must stand firm as one man, and refuse obedience with common consent. They could negotiate afterwards. They would then have a good opportunity to oblige the king to order the fiscal to stay proceedings, or entirely to repeal the recess.* They might, according to the expression in the original, "put a bit in his mouth."

These views were very readily listened to, and especially coincided with those of Landgrave Philip. They were approved by a large majority of the States.

Markgrave George and his neighbours of Nürnberg alone would not go so far. The former stood in too various and peculiar relations to Ferdinand, to venture to offend him personally. The great desire of the latter was, to show themselves the more especial subjects of the emperor. At the first request on his part, they had delivered up the coronation regalia which were kept at Nürnberg, and had sent an ambassador for that express purpose to the imperial court.

Another question was intimately connected with the former.

Although the attacks more immediately to be dreaded were of a judicial kind, it was impossible not to see that, in case of need, the emperor meditated employing force. It was remarked that in the recess he had enjoined peace on others, but had not promised to observe it himself.† It is certain that a correspondence concerning the necessity of raising troops, was carried on between Ferdinand and the papal court, in the beginning of the year 1531.‡ People asserted that they had heard Henry of Brunswick say, that he and Esk of Reischach were to take the command of the army.

The first question, therefore, to be decided, was, whether it was lawful to resist the emperor.

The opinion of the theologians, who took their ideas of the imperial authority from the New Testament, was, as we are aware, against resistance.

But in a time of such vast changes, when the secular element was universally emancipating itself from the hierarchy, the notions of public law necessarily became cleared of all theological admixture.

The jurists adduced certain arguments drawn from the civil law, concerning the resistance which might be offered to a judge who should take no notice of a legal appeal; chiefly, however, they called in question, whether the power which the theologians ascribed to the emperor was really his by law.§

The theologians had even advised the princes to allow the emperor to proceed in their dominions according to his pleasure; to allow him, for example, to drive out themselves (the preachers). To this it was objected, that such a proceeding would be utterly unprecedented in any other matter, and that the emperor did, in fact, possess no such power.

New ideas on the general nature of the German constitution gradually made their way. It was observed, that if, on the one hand, the princes did homage to the emperor, he, on the other, took an oath which he was bound to observe: the princes were the hereditary sovereigns of the country; the emperor was elected. A doctrine which was long in obtaining acceptance, and was not recognised as consonant with public law until the conclusion of the peace of Westphalia, was likewise then broached:—the doctrine, namely, that the constitution of the German empire was not of a monarchical, but an aristocratical nature. According to this theory, the relation of the princes to their head was not very different from that of the senators of Rome to the consuls, or those of Venice to their doge, or of a chapter to its bishop. But neither canons nor senators had ever been bound to passive obedience. "The States govern jointly with the emperor, and the emperor is not a monarch."‖

To these arguments the theologians had nothing more to oppose. They could now adhere to their text from Scripture, without being compelled by it to condemn all resistance to the emperor. "We did not know," say they, "that the sovereign power itself was subject to law."¶

The earnestness of their scruples was proved by the difficulty with which they shook them off, and by their subsequent recurrence to them from time to time.

Luther was peculiarly impressed with the fact that, as he had continually remarked, the emperor did not attempt to act independently; but always by the advice of the pope, and of the princes of Germany. He pronounced him to be no "Augmenter of the Empire,"** but a captain and sworn vassal of the pope. And should the Protestants now encourage their old enemies—their neighbours of Bohemia, who would use the authority of the emperor's name—by declaring resistance unlawful? "They hope," says Luther, "that we shall not defend ourselves. But if they mean to show their knighthood against the blood of our people, they shall do so with peril and fear."††

* Article, what is to be treated of the following day at Schmalkalden. (W. A.)

† Letter of the Saxon envoy. Förstemann, ii. 711. The Nürnbergers announced as early as the 21st October, that all was, "dahin gericht, wie man die thatliche Handlung wider die Anhenger des Evangeliums zum tapfersten anfange,"—"so arranged, that forcible measures may be the most vigorously begun against the adherents of the Gospel."

‡ A. de Burgo to Ferdinand, 2d March, 1531. Dixi quod esset providendum de viribus et remediis in re Lutherana, quod solum concilium non futurum esset sufficiens, sed paratæ vires facerent bonum concilium, et quod paratis viribus possint illi (æ?) converti, ubi, etc.

§ Etlicher furtrefflicher Rechtsgelehrten in Wittenberg Sentenz. (Sentence of certain excellent lawyers in Wittenberg.) Hortleder, Book ii. cap. vi.

‖ Juristical decision; Hortleder, P. II. B. ii. C. viii. at the end.

¶ Considerations of the Theologians. Ibid. c. 9.

** Mehrer des Reichs: one of the titles of the Emperor. —Transl.

†† See "Warnung an seine lieben Deutschen."—Altenb. v. 538. "Alles ist ein Getrieb des obersten Schalks in der

On these grounds Saxony now proposed to the assembled States a league for their mutual defence, even against the emperor In all previous coalitions of the kind, he had been excepted; but such a course would now be useless, since their enemies now acted under cover of his name *

These views were by no means shared by Nurnberg, or by Markgrave George Their theologians had remained unconvinced or doubtful. Nurnberg declared that it could not found so important a resolution as this on opinions of so revolting a kind The reader will remember that a similar difference existed the year before, between the divines of the two States †

The others, however, accustomed to follow Saxony, or perhaps even rejoiced that she had at length abandoned her scruples, declared their entire assent

A draft of an agreement was immediately drawn up, in which the emperor's name was indeed, carefully avoided, and the causes of alarm obscurely alluded to, in such expressions as this, "It appears as if there existed an intention of crushing the followers of the pure word of God," but it was more explicit in what related to measures of defence The allies bound themselves to hasten to the aid of any one among them, who might be attacked on account of the word of God It was further declared that this league was directed neither against the emperor, nor against any individual whatsoever, which only meant that it would attack no one, and would rigorously confine itself to self-defence

The league included Saxony, Hessen, Luneburg, Wolfgang of Anhalt, the two Counts of Mansfeld, the cities of Magdeburg and Bremen The other assembled princes and States promised to declare themselves within a short time On the 31st of December they dispersed ‡

These nine days may be reckoned among the most important in the history of the world The threatened and despised minority, under the influence of a religious idea on which depended the future development of the human mind, assumed an energetic and even warlike attitude They determined in like manner, as they had confessed the new doctrine and refused to abandon it, so they would now defend the whole position into which that confession had led them,—by legal means, in the first place, but if necessary, by arms. As to the former, all were agreed, as to the latter, the majority (some still entertained scruples as to their legal right), and thus, at the very origin of the innovation, a compact and determined union was formed for its maintenance, which its antagonists were likely to find it difficult to overcome.

The affair of the election soon proved the force and value of this resistance

During the deliberations in Schmalkalden, John Frederic of Saxony, the heir to the electorate, had gone to Cologne, to oppose the election in his father's name

His opposition had, as may be imagined, no effect in preventing a thing which was already decided Ferdinand was chosen at Cologne (5th January, 1531) by the five other electors, and a few days afterwards was crowned at Aix la Chapelle § By his election capitulations he was expressly bound to maintain the existing forms of religion, and specially in virtue of the recess of Augsburg ‖ This recess, which involved all the interests of the Catholic majority, and was the principal weapon in their hands, had now all the value and force of law From this time the emperor left the administration of the empire chiefly to his brother ¶ He reserved to himself only the privilege of being consulted in some weighty cases, e g the granting of banner fiefs, or of high titles of nobility, or the decision concerning monopolies — the most considerable mercantile interests of those days, or such proclamations of ban, or alliances, as might have the effect of involving the country in regular war ** But how complete and valid soever the election thus appeared to be, the opposition of Saxony did not fail to produce a great effect The public voice was, independently of this, against the act of the elec-

Welt"—"All is a manœuvre of the chiefest rogue in the world" He did not advise recourse to arms, but, as he writes to Spengler, "Ego pro mea parte dixi, ego consulo ut theologus, sed si juristæ possent docere legibus suis id licere, ego permitterem eos suis legibus uti Ipsi viderint"

* "Dieselbig Widerparter die Sachen in die kaiserlich Majestat, als ob sy diselbig gar nicht zu thun hatte, schieven wil"—"The same adverse party will shove the thing on his imperial majesty, as if they themselves had nothing at all to do with it"

† Muller's Annales Norici. One disputed question was whether the imperial authority extended to matters of religion The Landgrave of Hessen, particularly, denied this The Brandenburg opinion, however, maintains it Saxony says, in the above mentioned proposals, "Wo sich gleichwol I Mt Amt in des Glaubens Sachen erstrecken sollt, ware das doch durch die Appellation, so an I Maj un ein Concilium samtlich nach rechtlicher Ordnung erschienen ist, suspendirt"—"But even if your majesty's functions should extend to matters of faith, they must be suspended by the appeal which has been addressed, according to legal order, to your imperial majesty and a council"

‡ Recess of the diet held at Schmalkalden, 1530. Last day of December (W A)

§ Spalatin, Verzeichniss der Handlung in Colln, in Struve's Archiv i 62

‖ The words in the copy at Brussels are, "Das wir in Zeit solcher koniglichen Wurde, Ambts und Regierung die Christenheit und den Stuel zu Rom, bebstliche Heiligkeit, auch die christliche Kirch bei dem alten loblichen und wolhergebrachten Glauben, Religion und Cerimonien vermöge des jungsten zu Augsburg aufgerichten Abschiedes bis zu endlicher Determination khunftigen gemeinen Concils in guten Bevelch, Schutz und Schirm haben sollen"—"That we, as holding such royal dignity, should have in our good ordering, protection and defence, the stewardship and government of Christendom and the See of Rome, the pope's holiness, also the Christian church, with its ancient praiseworthy and well established belief, religion and ceremonies, in virtue of the recess newly drawn up at Augsburg, until the final determination of a future general council"

¶ Extract from the original document, Bucholtz, ix 19 —I am struck by the distinction, 'imperium per Germaniam *superiorem* regat" Was lower Germany excepted, because the Saxon vicar of the empire had not given his assent? or (more probably) because the emperor would suffer no interference of the authorities of the empire with his Netherland government?

** The Brussels Archives contain the Sommaire memoire au roi des Romains d'aucuns points esquels il semble à l'empereur que le dit S roi doit avoir consideration et regard touchant le gouvernement de l'empire, pour lequel l'empereur luy envoye ample pouvoir.

tors Above all, the old rivals of Austria, the Dukes of Bavaria, who had never concealed that they aimed at the crown (alleging that members of their house had been emperors and kings when the ancestors of the Habsburgers were still seated among the counts), had now a lawful ground for refusing to acknowledge the validity of the king's election They cared little for the motives which had prompted Saxony's opposition It is remarkable that, on this point, the ultra Catholics united with the leaders of the Protestants At a second meeting held by the allies at Schmalkalden, shortly before Easter, 1531, Grubenhagen, Hessen and Anhalt declared still more emphatically than before, that they would persist with Saxony in refusing obedience to Ferdinand The cities were not all so resolute, yet they also refrained, for the most part, from giving him the title of King of the Romans

Very shortly after Ferdinand complained to his brother, that he bore the title indeed, but that it commanded no respect or obedience, he had no more weight than any other prince of the empire *

From day to day the league assumed a more important aspect

At the second meeting, the treaty for mutual defence, the duration of which was provisionally fixed for six years, was sealed by Saxony, Hessen, Luneburg and Grubenhagen For the ratification by the cities, a certain process was agreed on, which was afterwards adopted As they had not yet determined on a formal military organisation, and as the movements of their adversaries seemed to make some measures necessary, they resolved, for the present, to take a certain number of horsemen into their pay, till they should see "whither these hasty and strange measures would extend"

At a third meeting at Frankfurt on the Maine, on the 5th June, the principal subject of discussion was, the affairs of the Imperial Chamber The allies were not perfectly agreed to whom they should entrust their procurations, some objections were raised to the persons proposed, but on the main point there was no hesitation, the procurators were to be empowered "to act in all their names, and to help to carry through all things regarding their faith and religion, which the fiscal might bring against any of the allies"† They agreed upon a small tax to pay the procurators Strangely enough, the first permanent contribution which was agreed on in the league, as in the empire, had a jurisdictional destination

Such were the fundamental characteristics, juridical and military, which the league exhibited from its very commencement Not all its members, however, shared both these tendencies Brandenburg and Nürnberg would not consent to armed resistance It was therefore arranged that their delegates should not be admitted to the meetings in which measures of defence were discussed Two reports, or recesses, were drawn up, of which the one was described as the general ("*gemeine*"), the other the particular ("*sunderliche*") The former related to the more extensive, and merely peaceful; the other, to the narrower—that is, the warlike coalition ‡ The adherents of the latter, however, still hoped to induce Brandenburg and Nurnberg to join them Brandenburg was immediately threatened by the Swabian league, and the markgrave was told that had he but signed the treaty for mutual defence, the Swabian league would have left him at peace But every thing was yet in a state of mere preparation

Hitherto we have devoted our attention mainly to the relations of the princes; but those of the cities in upper and lower Germany were not less remarkable Negotiations with the upper German cities, leading to the most fortunate results, and justifying the highest expectations, may be traced through all these meetings of the allies

We should, however, be unable to appreciate them, if we did not first attend to the course which the reformation had in the meanwhile taken in Switzerland.

CHAPTER II

PROGRESS OF THE REFORMATION IN SWITZERLAND

The restored unity of Latin Christendom was, as may be concluded, no less dangerous to the dissidents of Switzerland than to those of Germany

It happened that the Catholic movement was directed first against Germany, because the head of Christendom, the emperor, enjoyed an authority universally acknowledged and respected in that country, but every step of its progress was felt to be of imminent danger to Switzerland

The situation of the latter country was, how-

* Yo no soy mas que un principe de los del ymperio por agora, no siendo obedecido por rey de Romanos (B A)

† "Alle und jede Sachen die Religion Cerimonien und was dem anhangt anlangend, so der ks Fiscal villeicht us befel ks Mt oder uf anhalten sonderer Personen oder Parteien wider die ernannten Stadte eine oder mehr fur gewendt hette oder noch furpringen wurde, in irer aller Namen semptlich und sonderlich zu vertreten und usfuhren zu helfen"—"To act and aid in all and every matter relating to religion, its ceremonies, and what belongs thereto, if the imperial fiscal should, by the command of his imperial majesty, or by the suggestion of other persons or parties against the above mentioned cities, have alleged or should allege one or more of such matters, you are in all their names, collectively and severally, to act as their representatives, and to help to carry the business through" The draft was already prepared at Schmalkalden, but was adopted at Frankfurt

‡ Unterthentger Bericht der Sachen so sich in der Handlung zu Frankfurt Trinitatis 1531, zugetragen und im Abschiede nit verzeichnet sind "Humble report of the affairs transacted at the meeting at Frankfurt, Trinity, 1531, and not entered in the recess" (W A) There exist, as we see, three documents concerning this meeting, the general and the particular recesses, and this report

ever, very different from that of the former. There, as in Germany, the reformation encountered a majority armed with traditional privileges, but in Switzerland this majority was enfeebled by a long series of reverses.

We have seen how Zwingli gained over to his opinions the two most powerful of the eight noblest cantons—Bern and Zurich, of those which had joined the Confederation later, Basel, and of those more remotely connected with it, St Gall, Biel and Muhlhausen. In all these he had introduced a new organisation of the church.

On the other hand, he experienced an obstinate resistance from the remaining cantons of these; five of the older—the four Forest Cantons and Zug, were decidedly hostile. The reader will remember which party had been triumphant there in the year 1522, their refusal to give up the pensions and the right of taking foreign service, and their determination to maintain the ancient faith with all its external observances.

Had the several cantons been completely separate states, they might no doubt, have remained peaceful neighbours. But there were districts where the government was shared by the two opposing parties—the lordships and bailiwicks which were subjects of the whole Confederation: here the adverse powers necessarily came into collision. If we reflect that the Confederation had attained to its strength and compactness chiefly by means of its common conquests—that the real knot of the alliance consisted in these—it will be evident how important must be a difference which came to an open breach on this very ground. Here the majority had always enjoyed paramount consideration; it was now to be seen whether it was in a condition to maintain it.

The five older cantons refused to tolerate the new doctrines in the free bailiwicks. The bailiffs, Joseph am Berg of Schwytz and Jacob Stocker of Zug, inflicted on the dissidents fine, imprisonment, stripes and banishment. The preachers had their tongues slit, and were driven out of the country, or put to death with the sword. Germans who had fled from persecution, and taken refuge in Switzerland, were delivered up to the Austrian government of the Vorlande, which put them to death without trial or delay.* All books of the new doctrine, as well as Testaments and Bibles, were seized. In Baden, the dead belonging to the evangelical party were refused decent burial.

The Zurichers had long seen these things with displeasure; and as soon as they felt themselves strong enough to resist, they determined to endure them no longer. One of the main articles in the treaty between Zurich and Bern is, that the two cantons would not allow the people of the common lordships and bailiwicks (the due proportion of the sovereignty over which belonged to them as members of the Confederation), or the congregations which had determined by the vote of a majority to adhere to the evangelical party, to be prevented from so doing by violence.†

This at once roused all the oppressed evangelical spirit in Thurgau and the valley of the Rhine. The Five Cantons despaired of keeping them down solely by the authority of their bailiffs: on the 30th of November, 1528, they assembled all the magistrates and deputies of the communes of Thurgau in Frauenfeld, and admonished them not to separate themselves in matters of faith from the majority of the cantons to which they owed obedience, but rather to aid the bailiff in punishing the rebellious. This meeting, however, had also been attended by deputies from Zurich and Bern, who had come uninvited, and did not fail to offer exhortations and assurances of a contrary tendency. The country people asked to be allowed time for reflection till the feast of St Nicholas, when they assembled again in Winfelden. At first they showed some hesitation, gradually, however, a majority declared itself determined to adhere to the evangelical confession, and was openly supported by promises of assistance from Zurich and Bern. The former had also been applied to by the people of the Rhine valley, as the principal canton of the Confederation and had replied, that "it would not allow them to be driven from God's word."‡

This was an act of self-government on the part of the people. As the governing body was divided, it depended on their free decision which party to espouse. They chose the cause of reform.

In Thurgau there soon remained but nine nobles who had not joined this party, and even these begged only for delay. In the Rhine valley there was only a single parish in which the majority did not vote for the burning of pictures and images, and the abolition of the mass. Finding that the reforming communes, with the help of Zurich, had been victorious over the Catholic council which adhered to the party of the Five Cantons, the free bailiwicks and the country round soon followed.

However strong the assurances given, that the secular obedience due to the established authorities should not suffer, it is obvious that the basis of power—influence, to which the subject willingly submits—was thus of necessity lost to the Five Cantons.

And already a dispute not less unfavourable to their cause had taken place in another district.

Unterwalden had ventured to offer assistance to the Bernese Oberland, where the measures taken by the city for the introduction of reform—and especially the suppression of the convent of Interlachen—had excited irritation and resistance; and without any declaration of hostilities, to invade the territory of one of its co-confederates with banners flying.

* Proclamation of Zurich, 3d March, 1529. See Bullinger, ii 31.

† Original document of the treaty between the cities. Bullinger, ii 11.

‡ Recess at Frauenfeld and Instructions of the Zurichers for Winfelden. Bullinger, ii 27. Bernh Weiss, p 93.

Bern placed itself on the defensive, reduced its subjects to obedience, and compelled the invaders to retreat, but it is obvious what must be the effects of so open a breach of the ancient alliance Unterwalden found support from the four cantons with which it was more particularly connected, but all the City Cantons were of opinion that Unterwalden must be chastised Solothurn and Freiburg promised to assist Bern, as they were bound to do

In this state of political and religious inferiority, and threatened with vengeance, the Five Cantons conceived the idea of applying to the house of Austria for succour. It was, indeed, a general principle with them not to give up alliances with foreign powers

On the frontiers of Switzerland power was still in the hands of those who had put down the insurrection of the peasants, and suppressed the preaching in those parts —Count Sulz and Count Furstenberg and Marx Sittich of Ems, bailiff of Bregenz The clan of Ems, which had recently been strengthened by an alliance with the Castelan of Musso, sustained the cause of Catholicism in the mountains generally, and the Five Cantons had no difficulty in obtaining a favourable hearing from them Meetings were held at Feldkirch and Waldshut, the arms of Switzerland and Austria were displayed side by side, and it was even asserted that the old antagonists of the peacock's feather (the badge of the house of Austria) were now seen decorated with it A treaty was drawn up, in which King Ferdinand and the Five Cantons mutually engaged to remain constant to the ancient faith, to chastise any who might assail it in their respective territories, and, in case this brought down hostilities upon them, to afford each other assistance. Any conquests made within the Confederation were to belong to the Five Cantons, any without its boundaries, to the king

The chief stipulation of the treaty is, that Ferdinand guarantied to the Five Cantons "all that may be subject to or connected with them" (and consequently the common bailiwicks and Thurgau), while the Five Cantons expressly declared that they would not regard Constance as a member of the Confederation, but would leave it to the king *

The Five Cantons were right in replying to the City Cantons, who reproached them with this treaty, that they also had allied themselves with foreigners, but the circumstances were widely different Constance was closely connected with the Confederation, in consequence of the treaty it had concluded with Zurich It had always been the aim of Austrian policy to prevent this, and Maximilian had once, from that motive, taken a large part of the communes into his service the Five Cantons now abandoned Constance to Austria

It is remarkable that this happened at the very time (the beginning of the year 1529) when the majority of the States of the empire once more embraced the side of the house of Austria All political grudges now disappeared before a community of religious interests

Ferdinand sought to strengthen the Swiss alliance by every means in his power In Innsbruck, where it was concluded, he had also summoned a part of the Tyrolese landholders to the council, all the Vorlande, Wurtenberg included, were to be admitted to it. He hoped, perhaps, by this means, to break forever the power of the Confederation,† but, at all events, to oppose an insuperable barrier to the further progress of the new opinions

But it was a question whether a coalition of this kind could really afford protection to the Five Cantons Its measures, tried by the principles of the Confederation, were thoroughly unjustifiable—the invasion of the Bernese territory, no less than the alliance with Ferdinand They were utterly at variance with the idea and with the existence of the Confederation To the success which, thanks to the goodness of their cause, attended the measures of the City Cantons, was now added all the weight of the interests of the country at large, and of indisputable right

Peace was, at all events, out of the question for the Confederation The deputies of the City Cantons who went into the mountain country, in order to warn their old brother confederates against forming this alliance, found the arms of their cities nailed to the gallows, and themselves treated as heretics and traitors, in spite of their presence and efforts, the most terrific punishments were inflicted on seceders The reformation in central Switzerland had also its martyrs Jacob Keyser, a preacher from the territory of Zurich, who went from time to time to Gaster to conduct the worship of an evangelical church in that place, was arrested in the forest of Eschibach, on the high road, and dragged to Schwytz The office of bailiff of Gaster did not at that time belong to Schwytz, and, even if it had, the trial ought to have been heard before the tribunal of Utznach Nevertheless the commune condemned the unfortunate and guiltless man to the flames, which he endured with great constancy ‡

This roused Zurich to open resistance In June, 1529, when a new bailiff of Unterwalden was to make his entrace into Baden, Zurich openly declared that it would not suffer it, nor indeed have any further community with the Unterwalders from henceforth it would not permit them to exercise the office of bailiff in the domains over which they had a common jurisdiction §

Zurich had long since announced to the Schwytzers its determination to avenge itself,

* Original treaty. Hottinger, ii 475

† Invitation to the Wurtenberg districts, in orig doc, No 141 "That the power of the same confederation is divided by the above mentioned union, while his royal majesty and his subjects who adhere to the ancient Christian faith are strengthened with foreign aid, as well as the above mentioned Five Cantons"

‡ Bullinger, Ref Gesch ii p 148 Eidgenossische schweizerische Martyrer, Misc Tig. ii p 35 (insignificant)

§ They are particularly reproached for this in Eck's "Repulsio"

if any violence was used towards the preacher of its feudatories. Keyser's execution was therefore the signal for war.

On the 5th of June the first company of Zürich troops marched out to protect the free bailiwicks from a bloody re-establishment of the ancient faith; soon afterwards another was sent to Thurgau and the Rhine valley, and a third to invest the Schwytz portion of Gaster, which had put the preacher to death. The enemy having instantly assembled at Bar am Boden, the great banner of the city was unfurled on the 9th of June, under the Banneret Hans Schweizer, who had already borne it in the Milanese wars.

For the first time did two Swiss armies, not, as before, of peasants and their lords, but of adversaries equal in rights and fully prepared for war, stand confronted, in consequence of religious differences. "They are so full of hatred to each other," said King Ferdinand, "that nothing but open violence is to be expected."

The evangelical party had, however, at this moment a decided superiority.

The Zürich army had not its equal. It consisted of the brave men who had embraced the cause of the reformation with all the moral earnestness with which Zwingli preached it. No common women were suffered in the camp; no curses or oaths were to be heard, and even dice were banished; the amusements consisted of athletic exercises, such as leaping, hurling, &c.; quarrels hardly ever occurred, and prayers before and after meals were never omitted. Zwingli himself was with them; he had been relieved from the obligation of going out with the great banner as preacher, but he had voluntarily mounted himself, and taken a halberd on his shoulder.

Zwingli was firmly persuaded of the superiority of his party; and as the accounts from all sides tended to confirm him in this opinion, he conceived the most sanguine hopes. It was at least certain that the Five Cantons had nothing to expect from Ferdinand, who was occupied elsewhere, and found himself reduced to make applications to his states, from which but small results were to be expected. Zwingli now thought himself about to reach the goal upon which he had from the first fixed his eyes. He would listen to no propositions of peace, unless accompanied with the two great concessions, on which he had always insisted, *i. e.* that the whole system of pensions should be forever forsworn, and the preaching of the Gospel permitted throughout all the cantons of Switzerland. He represented to the members of the government, that in this way only was unity in the state to be obtained, as well as in the church. "Stand fast in God," exclaimed he; "they give you good words now, but do not be deceived; yield nothing to their entreaties till the right is established. Then shall we have made a war more advantageous than any that was ever made before; we shall have accomplished things which will redound to the honour of God and of the city, centuries hence."*

Had it depended on Zwingli and on Zürich alone, they would have ventured every thing, and have followed up their advantages to the utmost.

But there is a general and a most just dread of beginning war and of shedding blood. Whilst the Zürichers were preparing to take the field, Ebli, the Ammann of Glarus, appeared among them, and represented how often they had shared weal and woe with those whom they were now about to cast off. His address produced the greater effect, because he was known to be an honest man, who at bottom entertained the same views as those which prevailed at Zürich. He obtained a truce. Zwingli alone, who saw farther into futurity than the others, was not satisfied with a compliance which appeared to him ill-timed. "Good gossip Ammann," said he to Ebli, "thou wilt have to give an account of this matter to God."†

Meanwhile Bern also spoke out. The powerful influence exercised by Zürich was not agreeable to the Bernese, and they now declared that they would lend assistance in case Zürich were attacked, but not otherwise.

The notion of the independence of states, which had become prevalent in Germany, also gained ground in Switzerland. Bern deemed the conditions proposed by Zwingli inadmissible, because it would not be right to interfere so much with the independence of the government of the several cantons.

Thus the obstacles which prevented the great reformer from carrying out his views with the armed hand, originated in the evangelical party itself.

Negotiations were set on foot, which, considering the power the adverse party still possessed, and the opinions that still predominated among the Confederates, could not lead to the decisive results contemplated by Zwingli.‡

The utmost that could be expected was, that the Five Cantons should consent to give up the treaty with Ferdinand; should promise compensation for the expenses of the war, and the punishment of those who had used injurious language; and should formally consent to the rule laid down by the City Cantons, that, in the common domains, the vote of the majority should decide the form of religion in each parish. The prohibition of pensions, and the freedom of the evangelical faith, were also discussed; but they were by no means so decisively agreed to as Zwingli had desired. The abolition of the pensions appeared only in the light of a request of the City Cantons to the Five Cantons; and instead of proclaim-

* Opinion and letter in the Appendix to Hottinger, Geschichte der Eidgenossen, ii. 482.

† Bullinger, ii. 170.

‡ Journal of Hans Stockar of Schafhausen, 199. "Dye von Zürych mianttend, uns hye och jn zu zychen, das nun wyder unser Bunttbryef was und uns nitt zustund."—"Those of Zürich thought that to sign this was contrary to our treaty of confederation, and not within our competence."

ing liberty of preaching, it was only said, that the one party would not punish the religious opinions of the other *

But even thus it appeared that no slight advantage had been obtained

The Five Cantons were compelled to produce on the spot their original treaty with Ferdinand, and although the mediators interposed to prevent it being read aloud, from the fear that it might revive old animosities, Ammann Ebli no sooner saw it than he stuck his dagger through the document and tore it, upon which those who were standing near snatched off the wax of the seal

In consequence of the obvious superiority of the evangelical party, reform advanced much more rapidly after the peace

Bullinger mentions the number of places in which a majority formed itself in favour of the new opinions, in his language, "how the word of God was increased" In the year 1529 Zwingli was already able to hold a synod in Thurgau, and to establish the evangelical church there Large abbeys, like those of Wettingen and Hitzkirch, went over, in the former, not more than two monks refused their consent Abbot George Muller, of Baden, stipulated only that the pictures and images which were removed from the church should not be, as in so many other places, destroyed † Lastly, a resolution was passed by the greater and lesser councils of Schafhausen, that the mass and the images should be abolished Hans Stockar relates, not without suppressed sorrow, how, on the Friday after Michaelmas, 'the great God in the Minster' was taken away ‡ The city joined the union with Bern, Basel and Zurich In Solothurn the reformers demanded and obtained a church, and only a reputed miracle perpetuated the veneration for St Urs The evangelical party, protected by Bern, arose in Neuenburg, the Catholics had already taken up arms, and it seemed as if bloodshed was inevitable, when they resolved to allow the majority to decide § It decided for reform The majority was in many cases small, in Neuenburg, it amounted to only eighteen, in Neuenstadt, to twenty-four The same was the case on the other side, under different influences In Rottweil, in the immediate neighbourhood, the six Catholic guilds committed acts of such violence on the five evangelical, that several hundred citizens were obliged to leave the town ‖

But the most important circumstance for the progress of Zwingli's opinions was, that in one of the eight older cantons, which had hitherto remained neutral, — in Glarus, — where the evangelical majority had been much more free in the declaration of its opinions than in the others, it had obtained a complete ascendancy The reformed doctrine had already so far prevailed, that only two or three churches had retained their sacred images Although their congregations begged for nothing more than a short delay, till the emperor and the empire could take some measures for the remedy of abuses, the country communes determined (April, 1530) that these churches too should be purified, and rendered uniform with the others in the country ¶ There might be some recusants, but, politically speaking, Glarus was now evangelical

The advantage of having gained over this canton, which Zwingli, at the beginning of his career, had been obliged to abandon, was much heightened by the enlarged sphere of legitimate influence over others which was thus acquired

The Abbot of St Gall had used every endeavour to check the progress of the new doctrine in his territory (not the city, which had long espoused it, but the country), in spite of which it had made its way there as rapidly as elsewhere This abbot was a prince of the holy empire, but Glarus, Lucern, Schwytz and Zurich exercised a protectorate over him, and, in consequence, claimed no little influence over the internal administration of his domains At this juncture the abbot died, which rendered the change in opinion of two out of the four protecting cantons very important Contrary to their express desire, the conventual authorities contrived, indeed, to bring about an election, which was confirmed by the emperor and the pope, and approved by Schwytz and Lucern, but which Zurich and Glarus refused to recognise, alleging that they lay under far more sacred obligations to the district where the evangelical movement was now going on, than to the conventual authorities Zurich proceeded on the principle, that it was not the abbot who constituted the religious house, but that all the country people, villages and communes were committed to the guardianship of the protecting cantons In concert with the inhabitants, an order was issued, according to which a captain taken out of the four protecting cantons, and a council consisting of twelve members, were to conduct the government But, that they might not have a commander out of Schwytz or Lucern, hostile to the new doctrines, they made it an express condition that the captain should be of the evangelical party, and that he should not receive homage till he had sworn to allow the vassals of the abbey to continue their attendance on the preaching of God's word ** The newly established freedom extended to Toggenburg, even during Zwingli's youth, that town had begun to purchase its exemption from service to the convent, and this redemption it now completed. Early in the year 1531, Zwingli had the joy

* Landtsfried zu Cappel uffgericht (Peace concluded at Cappel), 25th June, 1529, Bullinger, ii 185

† From N Manuel's Missives in Grüneisen, p. 135

‡ Journal, 201

§ Chambrier, Histoire de Neuchatel, p 296

‖ Stettler, ii 36

¶ Tschudi in Hottinger, p 287, note 30 Bullinger, p 289, "Messaltare und Gotzen wurden abgemeeret etliche Gotzen uf besser Gluck entzuckt und verborgen "—"Mass altars and idols (images) were removed, some idols withdrawn and hidden till better luck"

** Ordnung und Satzung wie hinfuro by den Gottshuslüten Rat und Gericht zhalten —Ordinance and rule how, in future, council and judgment are to be held among the people (subjects or tenants) of the house of God (abbey).

of revisiting his native place—now perfectly free—and of establishing in it a church after his own heart.*

Extensive as was this progress, it did not, however, fulfil the views which he had originally cherished, and on the accomplishment of which all depended. The ruling party in the Five Cantons remained inflexible; even on the field of Gappel the commanders were said to have promised each other, in defiance of the first article of the treaty of peace,† not to allow the spread of the new opinions, and even to put to death any who might attempt to disseminate them. It is at all events certain, that nobody ventured to profess them in their dominions, though many were well inclined to them. The suppression of injurious language was not even attempted. The people of Zürich and Bern were represented as a set of mean, traitorous, heretical pedlars, and their preachers, as stealers of the cup and murderers of souls: the mountaineers said, Zwingli was one of the gods of the Lutherans; the undiscriminating bigotry of their priests made no distinction between the opinions of Zwingli and those of Luther. Though the treaty with Austria was published, fresh negotiations were continually set on foot. Deputies from Lucern and Zug were present at the diet of Augsburg. On their journey thither they were most honourably received by the Catholics, and were lodged in the town near the emperor, by his especial desire; they were observed to give him some written papers. They also experienced support from their old allies, Marx Sittich, Eck of Reischach, and Hans Jacob of Landau; and they discussed vast plans, such as an attack on Strasburg; the destruction of the Confederates who might come to its aid; and a simultaneous invasion of the reformed part of Switzerland, from Savoy, the Rhineland and the Alpine country.‡ These projects found the more easy credence, since the nobility of Savoy was actually preparing for a descent on Geneva; and, at the same time, the castellan of Musso, with his kinsmen and allies of Ems, fell upon the Grisons. The Five Cantons took good care to afford no assistance to the threatened districts; indeed the people of Wallis plainly declared that, for the sake of the faith, this ought not to be done. Zürich and Bern naturally combined all these circumstances; and, indeed, the same was done on the other side;§—for example, King Ferdinand feared that if the City Cantons were masters of the Grisons, they would attack the Five Cantons, and when once they had subdued them, would turn their arms against the hereditary dominions and the empire. It was mainly on this ground that he requested the emperor to afford succour, if necessary, to the Five Cantons.‖

* Bullinger, ii. 271, 344.

† *Land friede.*—Peace of the country, *i. e.* domestic or internal peace. We want a correlative word denoting the termination of what we call *civil war.*—TRANSL.

‡ Christian Friedhald of St. Gall, Augsburg, 16th July, in Escher und Hottingers Schweizerischem Archiv, i. p. 433.

§ From a letter from Bern to Zürich, 16th October, 1530. Hottinger, ii. 326. The game was begun too soon: a Savoyard let out the secret that this was the plan of the clergy. See Landgrave Philip's Instructions in Escher's Archives, ii. p. 304.

‖ Extracts from Ferdinand's letter to Charles in Bucholtz, v. 253.

CHAPTER III.

ATTEMPTS AT A RECONCILIATION OF THE TWO PROTESTANT PARTIES.

AT this juncture we find the Confederation in circumstances very analogous to those of the empire.

In the Swiss diet, as well as in that of the empire, an increasing minority, sustained by public opinion, stood opposed to an orthodox majority.

The chief difference consisted in this:—that the emperor and the empire possessed a spiritual, as well as a temporal authority; while the Swiss diet, which could not appeal for support to the emperor (to whom, as such, it had no legal relation), was wholly without the former. On the other hand, however, the Swiss minority had not, like the German, general decrees of former diets in its favour. The conflict was, in Switzerland, more one of fact; in Germany, of law.

Both majorities looked to the house of Austria as their main prop. It appeared, therefore, the interest of the minorities to use the most earnest endeavours to heal the breach that had so long existed between them.

But the misfortune was, that Zwingli had expressed himself, in the year 1530, in a manner rather calculated to excite resentment and increase division, than to bring about any sort of reconciliation. Whether he was irritated by the unfavourable reports which were spread by the Lutherans concerning the conference of Marburg;—or whether he was influenced by Carlstadt, who had just then come to visit him, and soon after obtained a post in Switzerland, it is impossible to determine:—it is enough to say, that hardly was the Augsburg Confession in his hands, when he sent the emperor, though not at all called upon to do so, a statement of his own belief, in which he not only attacked the Catholic church with greater violence than Melanchthon had done (for example, he utterly rejected the institution of bishops), but also retracted concessions he had already made, such as that on original sin: indeed he almost expressly reproached Luther with sighing to return to the flesh-pots of Egypt, and gave the coarsest interpretation to his words.¶

It was therefore no wonder that the Lu-

¶ Ad Carolum Romanum Imperatorem fidei Huldrychi Zwinglii ratio. Quod Christi corpus per essentiam et realiter, h. e. corpus ipsum naturale, in cœlo aut adsit aut ore dentibusque manduceter, quemadmodum Papistæ et quidam qui ad ollas Egyptiacas respectant perhibent, id vero neque tantum negamus, sed . . . . Mitratum genus atque pedatum (says he, further on) credimus *νόθον*.

therans expressed an increased aversion to the followers of Zwingli

The necessity for peace was, however, so urgent, that at this moment the desire to effect a reconciliation arose in another place

The Oberland States, especially Strasburg, belonged, in fact, to both parties

On the one hand, they shared in the peculiar circumstances of the German cities, and in the desire which prevailed with singular strength among them to render the clergy subject to the civil law, and to put an end to the influence of the great religious bodies on the presentation to benefices,—an influence which had been as great in Strasburg as anywhere In all the measures they had adopted, they had constantly referred to the recesses of the imperial diets In consequence of the recess of 1523, the council of Strasburg had issued an admonition to the preachers, "henceforward to preach undaunted the Holy Scripture, pure and unmixed with men's fables, for a worshipful council would support them in the same"* From the diet of 1526, the Strasburgers further deduced their right to make alterations in the ceremonies of the church, especially, to abolish the mass, and from this they did not suffer themselves to be deterred by the admonitions of King Ferdinand, or the Council of Regency † They were consequently among the first who were impeached before the Imperial Chamber In all these respects, they had now to adopt the same means for their defence as the other German cities

On the other hand, however, the dogmatic opinions of Zwingli were very popular in Strasburg, and gradually became completely predominant, statues and altars were removed, the interior walls of the churches, ornamented with paintings, were washed over with stone colour, the preachers proclaimed that no graven image must be tolerated by the godly, no instrumental music was permitted, even the organs were all silenced ‡ Strasburg had likewise the same political interests as the Swiss cantons, in so far as both were menaced by the Austrian power in Alsatia In January, 1530, it joined the union of the Swiss cities, they promised each other mutual aid and, in particular, Strasburg engaged to furnish the Swiss with gunpowder

Such being the religious and political state and interests of Strasburg, it may be imagined that nowhere was the desire for the reconciliation of the contending parties more earnest

And already had a man appeared who devoted his whole life to bring about this reconciliation, as to matters of doctrine

This man was Martin Butzer After the fall of Sickingen, in whose service he was, he had been driven by persecution from place to place, with a pregnant wife (he was one of the first evangelical preachers who had married), and in the greatest poverty, and had at length sought refuge in Strasburg, where he found not only an asylum, but a field for his highest and most strenuous exertions It is reported of him, that, in his youth, when carrying on scholastic disputations, he had invented a method for severing the essential and necessary from the accessory and accidental § By comparing the subject with each of the two contradictory predications, he discovered a third term which reconciled them. Butzer has the reputation of a pliancy not always to be justified He is generally thought to have yielded too much to circumstances It is undeniable that his attempts at mediation were prompted by the pressing necessity for peace without, no less than by his own reflections, but they were, as far as his convictions were concerned, most sincere. He possessed an acute and subtle apprehension of the ideas of others, and a remarkable talent for developing them,—for what may be called secondary production

At first, Butzer had seen in Luther's interpretation of the Lord's Supper, merely a new attempt to turn Christ into bread, as he calls it (*eine neue Verbrotung Christi*),‖ but on a more profound study, especially of the greater confession of the Lord's Supper, it became clear to him that this was not the case In a treatise he wrote, as early as the year 1528,¶ he remarks, that Luther's real meaning was totally different from that generally imputed to him. In this opinion he was confirmed at the conference of Marburg

But he was not more disposed to accede to the notion generally entertained by the Lutherans that the Oberlanders regarded the Lord's Supper as merely bread and wine. We have observed that, at the diet of Augsburg, the four cities found themselves compelled, as they were not allowed to subscribe the Saxon confession, to deliver in a confession of their own Butzer, who had the principal share in drawing it up, made choice of such expressions as might preclude the possibility of this reproach for the future In the 18th article of the "Confession of the four Free and Imperial Cities, Strasburg, Constance, Memmingen, and Lindau,"—the so-called Tetrapolitana—it is said, "The Lord gives, in the Sacrament, his real body and real blood, really to eat and to drink, for the nutriment of souls to eternal life"** It is evident that the word "real" is designedly repeated, but without

* Rorich, i 173, 453 In the first chapter of the Tetrapolitana, the motive assigned for this change is, that the great diet of 1523 commanded that the sermons be taken out of the Holy Scripture, and the authority cited

† Statement of the deputies of the council of regency Jung, Actenstucke, p 66.

‡ Röhrich Ref. v Strasburg, ii p 8

§ Adami Vitæ Theologorum, 102

‖ Fragment of a letter from Butzer to the brethren in Coire, Rohrich ii 135 The letter to Blaurer (ibid p 275) is likewise very instructive Dum ipsi (Lutherani) veram præsentiam tueri voluerunt. his verbis eam affirmarunt quæ si ad vim exiges, localem statuunt Contra nostri, dum localem voluerunt negare, sic locuti sunt, ut visi sint Christum cœna prorsus excludere

¶ Vergleichung Doctor Luthers und seines Gegentheyls —Dialogus, 1528.—(Comparison of Dr Luther and his adversaries)

** First printed in 1531, with an apology of Butzer, in which Hospinian, a zealous Zwinglian, finds the "vera et orthodoxa sententia de cœna domini" Historia sacramentaria, ii 221

prejudice to the spiritual import of the partaking

For Butzer's scheme of reconciliation rested on the assumption that Luther did not, any more than his antagonists, mean that the body was locally contained in the bread, but only that there existed a sacramental unity of the body and blood of Christ with the bread and the wine, and that, on the other hand, the spiritual nature of the partaking did not exclude the real presence of the body of Christ In so far as Luther ascribed a spiritual essence to the body of Christ, Butzer sided with him He admitted that the body might unquestionably have another than a local presence, the bread and wine did not cease to be symbols, but they were symbols of the present, not of the absent body, of the bodily presence,—that is to say, the *real* presence *

The question now was, whether Butzer would succeed in rendering this explanation acceptable to both parties

He first submitted it to Melanchthon at Augsburg, after which he hastened to Coburg, where he showed Luther those passages of his writings which treated the most plainly of the sacramental spiritual partaking, he reported that he had received from both assurances which led him to hope the best

Luther, however, was not disposed to make the task of mediation a light one To guard against mistake, he proposed two questions which left no room for ambiguity the one, whether the body was really in the symbols, the other, whether it was really received by sinners It is remarkable that the latter and more difficult of these questions had already been raised in the 12th century Otto of Freisingen alludes to it, but he thinks it better to evade it, than to command that it be answered in the affirmative † To Luther this affirmative did not appear to be attended with any such great difficulty, since it must at all events be admitted that God's word was heard by sinners,—that God's sun shone even upon the blind. And in fact, Butzer declared himself in a satisfactory manner on both points He acknowledged that Christ was really present in the sacrament, even in the bread and to the mouth, and that, as all the promises of Christ must be true, he did not doubt that the ungodly, as well as the pious, partook of the body and blood of Christ For himself, he accepted both articles With regard, however, to his "Co-servants of the Word," he remarked, that they were convinced of the first, but were not free from doubt as to the second ‡ Luther had previously consented not to press the second at present, if the first were but agreed on this he now repeated, by the admission that the sacrament was in the symbols, he invested it with its proper quality, the question, what sinners received, he agreed to postpone

This was an epoch in which ecclesiastical, nay, even dogmatical questions, were interwoven in the closest manner with political.

In consequence of the first advances made by Butzer, an invitation had been sent to the delegates of the Oberland cities to take part in the deliberations at Schmalkalden, in Dec, 1530 But after an explanation like that above, they were, without further scruple, formally received into the union at the second meeting.§ John Frederick, who filled the place of his father, made it his first business to speak with the deputies of the four cities, he exhorted them openly to preach the doctrine thus agreed on, and to cause it to be made known to all the world They assured him that, as Butzer did not treat for himself alone, but with the authority of his masters, there could be no doubt on the subject ‖ Strasburg, Lindau, Constance and Memmingen had been joined not only by Biberach Ysni and Reutlingen but even by Ulm This powerful city had protested against the recess of Spires, and, in spite of all the emperor's admonitions, had refused to subscribe the recess of Augsburg, —measures of so decisive a nature as clearly to show how strong the reforming spirit must already be But the opposite party in the city long retained considerable strength, and numerous violent re-actions took place At length the citizens gave the council full powers to restore order In a very short time an evangelical confession appeared, agreeing with the Tetrapolitana on the article of the Lord's Supper The cities above-mentioned all signed the treaty of mutual defence at Schmalkalden

Butzer's efforts having thus been successful with regard to Saxony, he proceeded to inculcate his views in Switzerland

Of the two great Swiss reformers, he gained over one without difficulty The peaceful Œkolampadius thought that Butzer was as diligent a promoter of truth as of charity, and

* Melanchthon de Buceri sententia Corp Ref ii 316 See Literæ Buceri ad Pontanum 4th Aug 1530, in Colestin, ii 302 Letter of Butzer's to Duke Ernest of Luneburg in Hess's "Leben Œkolampads," p 317

† Chronicorum liber, viii. Prologus utrum mali veraciter sacramentis communicent, an exterius tantum ea accipiant

‡ We have not, indeed, Butzer's letter itself, but the expressions of Luther, to whom it was addressed, leave no doubt as to its contents (To Wencelaus Link, in De Wette, iv 327) Likewise to Menius Bucerus effecit tantum, ut concedant omnes, vere adesse et porrigi corpus Domini, etiam corporali præsentia, cæteri tantum fideli animæ ac piæ, Bucerus vero consentit et impiorum manu porrigi et ore sumi In Plank, iii 340, these letters are obviously overlooked

§ Instruction uf den angesetzten Tag gegen Schmalkalden, Torgau 25th March "Uns ist also wieder ein Schreiben von Wittenberg zukommen, so der Butzer an Dr Martin und Phil Mel gethan, daraus die zween, wie uns angezeigt ist worden nit anders zu vernehmen wissen, denn das der hinterstelligen Punkt halber auch vollend verglichen" (W A)—"Another letter from Wittenberg has now come to us, which Butzer had addressed to Dr Martin and Philip Melanchthon from which, as it is shown to us those twain can understand no otherwise than that the article concerning the doubtful point had been fully settled"

‖ Account of the transactions at the diet held at Schmalkalden in the week after Judica "Haben keinen Zweivel, sie (ihre Herrn) werden verschaffen, dass dergleichen gepredigt gelehrt und verkundigt werde, auch solches lautbar zu machen"—"Have no doubt that they (our governors) will take care that the same shall be preached, taught, and proclaimed, so as to make it known"

recommended his interpretation to his colleague, Zwingli *

It was impossible, however, that Zwingli should share his sentiments

In the first place, he had far too frequently and too decidedly accused Luther of a coarse and material view of the subject, lightly to abandon the charge. It was also not to be denied that, although Butzer adhered to the idea of the spiritual partaking, he approached nearer to Luther's exposition of the mystery than Zwingli could possibly approve He was too conscious that his view of the subject was to be traced to a totally different origin He did not directly reject Butzer's formula, but the threefold repetition of the word "*real*" was very offensive to him, he thought that people would understand this in the sense of *natural* He had no objection to Butzer's publication of a letter which he had addressed to the Swiss, on the identity of the two doctrines, but he reserved to himself the right of giving a commentary upon it, expressive of his own peculiar opinion He consented indeed to adopt the formula, that the body of Christ was present in the sacrament, but not without the addition of the words, "only to the believing soul," he utterly refused to assent to the proposition that the body of Christ was presented to the mouth † The whole force of his original conception was aroused within him, and he could not be induced to advance one step further on the path of conciliation

This, however, did not prevent Basel, under the guidance of Œkolampadius, from accepting the mediation There was already a report in Switzerland of a peculiar doctrine taught by Œkolampadius, which was said to have a considerable number of adherents ‡

In short, the rumours of a closer union between the two parties of reformers were general, earnest and uninterrupted In a certain sense this had already taken place, Strasburg, and, since July 1530, Landgrave Philip having joined the union of the Swiss cities, at the same time that they were members of the Schmalkaldic league The following fact appears to me extremely striking —Bullinger's History contains a copy of a treaty of alliance which Zurich laid before Basel and Bern, at a congress held in February 1531, with the remark, that it was already accepted by some Germans On nearer inspection I find that, word by word, from beginning to end, it is merely and precisely the formula of the Schmalkaldic treaty. How remarkable, that Zurich should (at least, as it appears from this) have earnestly proposed to its most intimate allies to join the Schmalkaldic league!

There was no point of time at which the Swiss Confederation was so near to an internal reconstitution, in consequence of the progress of church reform, and likewise to a re-union with Germany, as the one we are now contemplating The two factions into which it was divided were powerfully attracted by the corresponding elements of the German mother country Zwingli said, the matter must be settled in Switzerland, before the emperor would have his hands free in Germany Ferdinand feared a general union of all the Protestants In the unusually energetic resistance which he encountered on all hands, he thought he detected traces of the confidence which such a coalition was calculated to inspire §

But religious differences once more formed an insuperable obstacle to their union

At the meeting at Frankfurt on the Main, in June, 1531, the matter was agitated anew

Bern and Zurich had again declared that they would not accept Butzer's formula, not because it appeared to them unchristian, but because it was obscure, and might easily give occasion to dangerous misconceptions ‖

On the other hand, the Elector of Saxony had instructed his envoys, in case the Confederation should not subscribe a confession in harmony with that of Augsburg, to break off all negotiations with them, and to refuse even to be the bearers of any thing they might desire to send him

This again necessarily had an influence on the internal transactions of the Schmalkaldic league

A project of a military organisation was submitted in Frankfurt, which the Oberländers thought very ably conceived and expedient; but they declined to subscribe it, because it did not include the confederate cantons. They declared that the enemies by whom they were surrounded were too strong; allies so remote would not be able to afford them adequate assistance

Without doubt they wished to wait to see how things would turn out in Switzerland

For it was evident that in that country every thing would be referred to the decision of arms, and that this decision would re-act in various ways on Upper Germany

* Utrinsque (veritatis et caritatis) Bucerus mea sententia observantissimus est Proinde confido non ingratum tibi fore quicquid ille in medium attulit 19th Nov 1530, in Hottinger, ii 320

† Letter in Hess, Œkolampadius, p 341

‡ From the otherwise very empty and uninstructive essay of Faber, de admirabili catholicis data victoria, we see this (cap vi Opp iii 145) In a letter of Landgrave Philip dated the Friday after Palm Sunday, (W A) Œkolampadius is regarded as completely agreeing with that party "Since Œkolampadius and the others are of one mind with us in the matter of the sacrament, and it is to be hoped that the others also will come to us"

§ Es cierto que se haran todos unos y peores que nunca por los fuercas y ventaja que de dia en dia van cobrando los que siguen estas sectas Prina, 27th March, 1531

‖ Correspondence between Bern, Basel, and Zürich in Escher and Hottinger's Archiv ii p 290. Basel insists that Butzer's explanation is "also luter, das sie mit irem (der Gegner) natürlichen lyblichen substanzlichen oder wesentlichen Lyb gar keine Gemeinschaft hat"—"so clear, that it has nothing whatever in common with their (the opposite party's) natural, bodily, substantial, or material body"

CHAPTER IV

CATASTROPHE OF THE REFORMATION IN SWITZERLAND

The attack made by Savoy on Geneva was repulsed in 1530; in the spring of 1531, the Castellan of Musso was also driven out of the Grisons. As, on the one side, the cities had not joined the Schmalkaldic league, so, on the other, the Five Cantons had in fact concluded no alliance with Austria. The two parties in the Confederation stood confronted, each limited to its own resources, but more embittered than ever.

The Five Cantons complained, and indeed not unjustly, that their rights as majority were no longer respected. They refused to assent to ordinances like those which had been issued in St Gall. The first captain who, according to the new regulations, was to assume the command there (he was from Lucern), disdained to take an oath to peasants, and rode away.

On the other hand, the evangelical cities were also with apparent justice, incensed that they had not been supported in matters regarding their interests as members of the Confederation, and affirmed that the bond which united them was thus broken; nor were they disposed longer to endure the "coarse, inhuman" vituperation of which they had been the object. The answers of the Five Cantons were, they said, in themselves an insult.*

Zwingli's intention had been to put an end to the thing at once by force.

The difference which existed between Luther and Zwingli was at least as great on political, as on religious points. Luther's policy, if it deserves the name, was entirely dependent on his religious views, and was limited to immediate defence. Zwingli, on the contrary, pursued, from the very beginning, ends of a positively political nature; a complete change in the form of the Confederation was the central point of all his ideas, and he had laid the most extensive plans for its accomplishment. He is, without doubt, in both respects, the greatest reformer that Switzerland has produced.

It had often been complained of as unfair, that the forest cantons, which contributed so much less in men and money to the wars of the Confederation than the populous city cantons, yet enjoyed an equal share of the advantages of victory and dominion. This was the true cause of the dissensions which followed the Burgundian wars. Zwingli found that this state of things had of late become more intolerable. Zug having joined the four forest cantons, a majority had been formed which decided all the business of the diets, and against which there existed no lawful remedy. Zwingli was of opinion that this advantage, which they so recklessly abused, was highly unjust. The guidance of the Confederation much more properly belonged to the two cities of Zurich and Bern, which had always been its most powerful members, and done the most for its interests. It would be necessary to send back the act of Confederation to the Five Cantons, and make a new one, either entirely excluding them from the common bailiwicks (at least on this side of the Alps), or making a fresh division, or at all events putting an end to their influence as a majority.†

We see that Zwingli wanted to place the constitution on a totally different basis, and to establish its unity on the preponderance of actual force. The same principles would then have prevailed through the whole territory, both in religion and politics.

Plans of this sort can never be executed without an energetic co-operation of forces at the favourable moment. The first question was, whether Master Ulrich Zwingli, powerful and respected as he was, were sufficiently so to unite his own party in an undertaking of this kind.

But even in Zurich Zwingli had still to contend with hostile opinions and obstinate private interests. In the Grand Council, which managed the affairs of the church, there were still, towards the end of the year 1528, men who retained their preference for the old usages. Zwingli demanded from the pulpit the purification of the council from the ungodly, who could not endure the word of God. Accordingly, Zwingli's partisans proceeded to interrogate the members of the guilds, one after another, whether they would repair to the Lord's table like other Christians, and excluded those who refused, from the council.‡ But this did not put an end to all the difficulties. Among the noble families there were many who had reluctantly given up the pensions, and had not broken off all connexion with the leaders of the Five Cantons. If Zwingli could not break this connexion, he was determined at least to render it innocuous. The influence of the noble families in Zurich rested upon this,—that whereas only three members of each of the other guilds sat in the Lesser, and twelve in the Grand Council, the noble guild—called the Constafel—had the privilege of sending six to the former, and eighteen to the latter.§ Zwingli had sufficient influence to break down this inequality. He carried the point of putting the Constafel on the same footing as the other guilds.

* Antwurtten und Meinungen der Radtsbotten der christlichen Stetten.—Answers and opinions of the envoys of the councils of the Christian cities. 24th April, 1531. Bullinger, ii. 362.

† Was Zurich und Bern Not zu betrachten sey in dem funfortigen Handel.—What is to be regarded as the danger of Zurich and Bern in the quarrel with the Five Cantons. Hottinger, ii. 457.

‡ Bernhard Weiss, p. 91, fortunately enters more into detail than Bullinger. The difficulties of the situation are moreover apparent from the following passage from Zwingli's own writings.—An non optimi quique ac innocentissimi, cum senatores tum plebeji, sic me colunt ac tuentur, ut nisi id constantissime facerent, minor esset publica tranquillitas. Responsio ad amici haud vulgaris epistolam. Gualth. ii. 323.

§ See Bluntschli Staats- und Rechtsgeschichte von Zurich, i. 359.—Unfortunately, this book contains no further account of the above mentioned relations.

Nothing less than measures of such severity in Zürich itself, could have brought about that politico-religious unity in the public authority which was necessary to Zwingli's plans. But it was clear that secret, if not open counteraction was inevitable. In a very short time he was made to feel this.

Far greater difficulties were opposed to him by Bern. There, where the attachment to the pensions was much more deeply rooted; where a certain jealousy of Zürich always showed itself; the separation which had hitherto existed between the several cantons found stubborn, if not ardent defenders.

I know not whether Zwingli's plan, which seemed so advantageous to the Bernese, was ever even submitted to them. I find no trace of it in the transactions of their diets.

The demands of the city cantons were confined to the three following: first, that blasphemers should be punished; secondly, that the poor people who had been driven from house and home for conscience' sake, should be received again; lastly, that the religious doctrines of the city cantons should be tolerated in the territories of the other cantons;* —demands which the nature of the case rendered inevitable. For what could be the Confederation in which the one member would not receive the oath of the other? What the community of justice in the bailiwicks, where the one portion of the ruling body persecuted the faith in which the other beheld its salvation? How, above all, could the evangelical members of the Confederation look on, while, at a few miles' distance, their co-religionists were thrown into prison? These demands therefore were merely an assertion of the Christian character of the new state of things; a recognition of this was all that they claimed.

At this time, however, the religious creed was far too intimately connected with the civil power, for concessions, even of this kind, to be obtained, except by compulsion. In the Five Cantons, that power was founded on the exclusive sway of Catholicism. Had the authorities consented to admit the contrary opinion, a hostile party would have formed itself in the population, under their own eyes; and, supported by the tendencies of the age, and encouraged by sympathy from without, might easily have became dangerous to themselves. They therefore at once decidedly rejected these demands.

Upon this Zwingli did not hesitate to advise war, and to urge an immediate attack while the advantage was still in their hands: he so far prevailed that Zürich, where no one now ventured openly to oppose him, declared itself for that course.

In Bern, however, his authority was not so great. That city also regarded coercive measures as inevitable, but did not choose immediately to come to extremities. It succeeded in prevailing on its allies for the moment to resort to no act of open aggression against the Five Cantons, but merely to withhold supplies.

This, however, was little likely to content Zwingli. He clearly saw that delay would ruin every thing. He felt that his adversaries at home were once more bestirring themselves, and complained from the pulpit of the support that Zürich itself afforded to the enemy. At one moment he was seriously determined to resign his post. As he was prevented, though with difficulty, from putting this design in execution, he made another attempt to convince the Bernese of the necessity of adopting another line of conduct. We find him holding a secret meeting, by night, in the house of the preacher at Bremgarten, with certain delegates from Bern, while the councillors of Bremgarten kept watch without. But he seems not to have found much encouragement here. Before day dawned, Bullinger conducted his master to the road, through a gate near the shooting-house. Zwingli was deeply depressed. He wept as he took leave of Bullinger. "God keep thee, Henry," said he, "and only remain thou faithful to the Lord Christ and his church."† In August a comet had appeared; Abbot George Müller of Wettingen one day asked Zwingli in the churchyard of the great minster, what that might signify. "My George," answered Zwingli, "it will cost me and many an honest man dear: the church will be in jeopardy, but you will not be deserted by Christ."‡

Things fell out as Zwingli had foreseen,—indeed, as it was inevitable they should. Bern probably hoped that the common people in the Five Cantons would not be able to hold out against the scarcity, and would rise against their governors; but the very contrary came to pass. The people were exasperated because, under the pretence of zeal for the Christian religion, their adversaries withheld the fruits of the earth, which God caused to grow freely for all.§ The governing class turned this disposition of the public mind to the advantage of their own authority. The Zürichers had put forth a manifesto for their justification, and had sent it to Lucern; the council of Lucern treated all those who had received and communicated it to others as traitors, and

* All the negotiations are to be found in Bullinger's Chronicle, from which nearly all authors, even the earlier ones, have drawn most of their information, and which is now printed. The want of the continuation of Zwingli's correspondence is severely felt.

† Bullinger's Narrative, iii. 49.

‡ I may be permitted here to quote the charming narrative of a contemporary, which has been printed in the Schw. Mus. ii. 535. He tells how, when he was at St. Gall in those days, he one night climbed up the Bernegh with Zwingli's friend Vadianus, Dr. Joachim von Watt, and some others;—how, when they had climbed up to the very top, the doctor seated himself in the midst of them upon the ground in the dew, and explained to them the names of the constellations, the opposite motions of the Zodiac and the rest of the firmament, and the wonders of the Creator, whom he desired soon to behold. Hereupon he cast his eyes upon the country, and spoke of the first settlement by the Romans, of the founding and fortunes of the town, how many times it had been burnt, whence each gate thereof had its name, how the neighbouring forest had been cleared, and who had established the flourishing trade of linen weaving; this thought led him back again to the comet, which none doubted to portend the wrath of God. Theophrastus von Hohenheim, then dwelling at St. Gall, and others, interpreted it to foreshow not only bloodshed and the overthrow of the government, but especially the destruction of learned men.

§ Hallwyl in Kirchhofer's Haller, 107.

sentenced them to the rack. And, indeed, the feeling of continual offence was of itself sufficient to render the temper of the two parties more hostile from day to day. Thus all negotiations were abortive. The Five Cantons persisted in demanding of the cities to open the common stores to them, according to the terms of the Confederation, or to grant them their rightful share. The cities refused to enter into the question of right, as, by the terms of the public peace, the withholding of the stores was expressly appointed as the punishment for continued insults and offences. This punishment they now intended to inflict. The mediators, among whom we find Strasburg deputies, proposed that the punishment of the insults complained of should be left to them. To this the cities consented, but the country cantons were not to be induced to agree to it.

No remedy could be devised, war was inevitable, war, under totally different auspices from what Zwingli had desired.

In September the Five Cantons held a diet at Lucern, in order to consult on the means of carrying on the war. At first, Uri, Schwytz, and Unterwalden, *ob dem Wald*, were against an immediate attack, indeed Uri proposed to wait for the resolutions of the approaching diet of the empire. But Unterwalden, *nied dem Wald*, insisted on the necessity of declaring war without delay, and at length all came round to this opinion, "for they could not perish of hunger, they must fetch means of subsistence, and for this they must risk body and soul."*

The friends of the Five Cantons regarded their decision with some alarm. King Ferdinand feared they would succumb, and that the confusion would then become too violent and general to be repressed.

They were undoubtedly very inferior in numbers, but they were united, their leaders were bound together in the closest manner by community of interest and of danger, and were supported by the popular exasperation. They had likewise the advantage, that while no active steps had as yet been taken in the cities, they could rush down from their mountain fortresses, and make a sudden attack on the most vulnerable points. For some days nothing was heard of them, the passes were vigilantly guarded, and no suspicious person was allowed to go out or in. There were, in the high country, friends of the Zurichers, who had promised to give them intelligence if any thing was in preparation, but they were so strictly watched as to render this impossible. A few days only were necessary to make all ready for an outbreak. Suddenly, on the 9th of October, a company from Lucern crossed the borders, and plundered the free bailiwicks. On the 10th, a boat laden with soldiers was seen crossing the lake of Zug, the sound of horns announced their arrival in Zug, and the pipes of the men of Uri was heard on the border. At the above-mentioned meeting at Lucern, it was immediately determined to combine forces at Zug, the council of war had only to fix the day, and then to set things in order for the attack.†

Had the cities been prepared for this assault, they would easily have repulsed it, Zurich had only to guard the pass over the Albis, and she would have time to make the most efficient preparations for her defence. But the Zurichers were up to this moment continually occupied with the coercive measures they had adopted, they had just been devising means to prevent the approach of troops from Alsatia on either side the Reuss. Whilst busied about means of coercion, they found themselves suddenly attacked. Their confusion was the greater, since the attack coming from different quarters, left them in doubt against what point it was more especially directed.

On the morning of the 11th of October, 1531, the militia of the Five Cantons took the oath, and marched, eight thousand men strong, under their five banners to invade the territory of their chief foe, the Zurichers.

In front of them, near Cappel, a troop of about twelve hundred Zurichers had posted themselves.

The great banner had indeed been unfurled the same morning in the city of Zurich, and the militia belonging to it began to assemble; but all this was done with disorder and precipitation. At the same hour a part of the troops marched towards the free bailiwicks. And now, at the decisive moment, it became evident that all were not of the same mind. A secret counteraction had paralysed every measure.‡ Message after message arrived, that the combined forces of the enemy threatened the troop at Cappel, and would utterly destroy it, if assistance were not immediately sent, so that the militia attached to the banner, weak as it was—there were only seven hundred men—was compelled to take the field without further delay.

The only means of salvation would have been, to surrender Cappel and withdraw the troop.

The proposal was indeed made in their ranks to retire before the superior force. But it appeared to these brave men an act of cowardice to retreat a step, even when their inferiority was so manifest. Rudy Gallmann stamped his foot on the ground when the proposal was made, and exclaimed, "God grant that I may not live to see the day when I shall yield one foot of earth to these people. Let this rather be my grave."

Already had the superior enemy advanced and the firing begun, as the banner reached the summit of the Albis. The company was, as we have said, extremely weak. William Toning, captain of sharp-shooters, looked around, and gave it as his opinion that it

* Bullinger iii 73. The first attack upon Bern emanated rather from Obwalden.

† Kurze Beschreibung der funf katholischen Orte Kriegs wider ihre Eidgenossen der funf zwinglischen Orte (Short description of the war of the Five Catholic Cantons against their confederates of the Five Zwinglian Cantons), which, since Haller's time, has been attributed to Gilg Tschudi, but which appears in MS. under the name of Cysat and others. Balthasar's Helvetia ii p 186.

‡ Examination of Rudolf Lavater. Escher, ii 311.

would be better to halt a while, and to wait for reinforcement from the people, who were now flocking to join them, before they marched further. But Master Ulrich Zwingle, who had also marched out with the banner, and, on this occasion, as preacher, in virtue of the office which he had not been permitted to resign, replied, that it would ill become them to look down idly from the mountain on the brave people fighting below. "I will to them in God's name," added he, "and die with them, or help to save them."—"Wait, Töning, till thou be'st fresh again," said the standard-bearer. "I am as fresh as you," answered Töning, "and will be with you."

The company of the Five Cantons had posted itself on a little height surrounded with wood, called the Schürenberg;* here the banner rushed upon them. It was, indeed, the force of Zürich which now stood confronted with the Five Cantons; but carelessness at first, disunion and want of discipline afterwards, had caused it to consist of little more than two thousand men, whereas the city could easily have put ten thousand men into the field.

This little band was now met by the troops of the Five Cantons, four-fold their numbers, not (to say the least) less warlike, and far better commanded. Little remains to be said of a battle which was decided ere it began. The Zürichers had left the thicket at the foot of the hill unoccupied; through this the enemy rushed, almost unobserved, and began the attack with the utmost confidence in his superiority. The valour of the Zürichers was of no avail; they were routed and overthrown in a moment, and a furious carnage began. Of the two thousand Zürichers, five hundred perished; and what was the most grievous, among them were the most eminent and zealous evangelical leaders, for they had been the first to take up arms. There did Rüdy Gallmann find the grave he pointed to. The standard-bearers, Schweizer and Wilhelm Töning, fell, and the banner itself was saved with great difficulty: the guildmaster Funk, the brave Bernhard Weiss, to whom we are indebted for so many excellent reports;† the director Geroldseck, several preachers, and, in the midst of his flock, Zwingli himself. The enemy, drunk with victory, and already dispersed over the battle-field in search of plunder, found him lying under a tree, still breathing, "with his hands folded and his eyes raised to heaven." Is it too much to conjecture that as he lay there weltering in his blood, a thought which he had lately expressed in gloomy forebodings was present to his soul? The prospects of the Confederation, in the sense in which he understood and desired it, he probably felt he must renounce forever; the prospects of the church and of the religion of the Gospel, he could contemplate with unshaken confidence. Thus was he found dying by two common soldiers, who exhorted him to confess himself to a priest, or as it already seemed too late for that, at least to receive the blessed Virgin and the saints into his heart. He made no answer, and only shook his head; they did not know who he was; they thought him some obscure "stubborn heretic," and gave him a death-stroke. It was not till the next day that it was remarked that Zwingli was one among the many distinguished men who had fallen. All flocked to see him. One of his acquaintances from Zug declared that his countenance in death had the same expression as it used to have when inspired by the ardour of his mind in preaching. No sight could be more welcome to his enemies, the pensioners. They instituted a sort of trial of Zwingli, quartered his body, burned it, and scattered the ashes to the winds.

But the Five Cantons were not yet completely victors and masters in the Confederation. The Zürichers now determined to occupy the pass over the Albis, and under the shelter thus afforded, they collected their strength. They had very shortly an army of twelve thousand men of their own and allied cantons in the field. Meanwhile Bern too had taken the field, and its army, together with those of Basel and Biel, was supposed to amount to about the same number. When these troops united at Bremgarten, the Five Cantons saw clearly that they could do nothing against such masses; they therefore evacuated the ravaged territory, and retreated towards Zug, where they encamped at Bar am Boden.

It now appeared as if an offensive war might be carried on by the cities, as Zwingli had always advised; and they did indeed march in pursuit of their enemy; but circumstances were totally altered.

Since their victory, the Five Cantons had become bolder than they had ever been before; on the other hand, it was remarked that the cities wanted an impulse such as Zwingli would perhaps have given them. Zürich had indeed lost its best citizens: people said, "they had lost the rye out of the wheat."‡ The Bernese had never displayed much ardour for war, and consequently they did not engage in it with the necessary energy. They neglected to fall on the enemy at the favourable moment, when he was changing his position. When at length they resolved to attack the very strong encampment in which he now was, from the Zug mountains on the one side

* In the "Kurze Beschreibung," Schönenberg; but there too it ought rather to be Schürenberg. "Ist ein ziemlich hoher Bühel, daruff vor Zyten ettliche hüser und schüren gestanden sind, daher mans genambt hat, wie es noch heisst, zu oder uff Schüren."—"This is a somewhat high hill, whereon in former times stood several houses and barns, whence it had the name by which it still is known, of the barns (Schüren)." Bulling. iii. 111.

† According to Accolti (in Epistolis Sadoleti, vii. 273), of the 300 senators only seven remained. The truth is that seven members of the Lesser, and nineteen of the Great Council were killed in battle, besides sixty citizens and seven clergymen (quam plurimi sacerdotes)! Bullinger enumerates them all. The rest were men from the country. Accolti, indeed, reckons the Zürichers at 20,000 men.

‡ To those unacquainted with the habits of the German people, this expression requires explanation. They do not willingly eat wheaten bread, which they regard as much less nutritious than that made of rye. A peasant will tell you that it is impossible to work upon wheaten bread, there is no strength (kraft) in it.—Transl.

and the valley on the other, and for that purpose occupied the mountain, they did it with so little skill and prudence, that they gave the enemy, whom they meant to surprise, an opportunity to fall upon the division posted on the mountain, and to cut off a great number of men * Notwithstanding their superior numbers, the cities had no longer courage to make a strenuous attack on their brave and conquering enemy. They only hoped to weary him out by surrounding him with a winter encampment

How totally were the daring schemes which Zwingli had cherished, overthrown! It is clear that the politico-religious principle of which he was the representative and the champion, was, in fact, not so strong in Zurich as he had flattered himself, and that it was still weaker in Bern It was not sufficiently powerful to pervade and to animate the existing elements of society. At the decisive moment, mistaken measures were adopted, the ground of which always was, want of that union and high-minded energy which alone could have insured success

The fears which had been entertained by the Catholic party at the beginning of these disturbances were now changed, by such unexpected successes, into the most sanguine hopes

With undisguised joy and exultation Ferdinand sent his brother an account of the battle of Cappel and the death of the arch-heretic Zwingli "This," says he, "is the first advantage which has been gained of late by the cause of the faith and of the church"

On the arrival of the news of the second successful engagement, he began to lay plans. He exhorted his brother to remember what favour God had shown to the defenders of his cause Were the emperor not so near at hand, he himself, feeble and poor as he was, would hasten to assist in so sacred an enterprise But now he could not refrain from exhorting him, the head of Christendom, to do this, never could he have a fairer occasion for acquiring renown Without Switzerland, the German sects would be easily subdued He advised him to send succours openly or secretly to the Catholic cantons He goes so far as to tell the emperor that this was the true way for him to put an end to religious discords, and to become master of Germany †

Nor was Charles V in any degree indifferent to projects of this kind He answered that the excellence of his brother's advice struck him the more, the more he reflected upon it, that the dignity with which he was invested, solicitude for the orthodox princes, the duty of defending the Christian religion and the common weal, and considerations for the house of Austria, rendered it incumbent upon him to do something

The Five Cantons had been joined in their camp on the Zug mountains by some companies of Italians We discover from a letter that this took place with the knowledge of the emperor, he was of opinion that all future assistance must be given in the name of the pope ‡

Nor did he stop here He immediately sent to ask the King of France to give his support to the Five Cantons, and to declare war against those which had fallen off from the faith

But he found little cordiality in Francis, who had seen with great displeasure the close alliance of the Five Cantons with Austria, and, with a view to maintain a counterpoise, had entered into negotiations with the other cantons shortly before this catastrophe The king pleaded to the emperor's ambassadors all the sums he had had to pay in consequence of the engagements he had entered into at Cambray What he had lately inherited from his mother, he wished to apply to the defence of his kingdom The emperor, he continued with increasing bitterness and irritation, had tied his hands for every enterprise where any thing was to be gained, he was friendly only where nothing was to be got but blows and expenses,—against the Turks and the Swiss §

Negotiations were likewise entered into with the Venetian ambassador in Milan The Bishop of Veroli, papal nuncio, prayed the republic for permission to send two thousand Spaniards through the Bergamese territory into Switzerland The ambassador, Giovanni Basadonna, did not immediately consent to this, he wished to see the full powers of the nuncio, and observed to him that the Spaniards, if allowed to interfere in the intestine wars of the Confederation, might easily render themselves its masters He induced Veroli to drop his request The nuncio repaired in person to Switzerland, where he expressed the hope that it might be possible to induce the seceders to return to their ancient allegiance to the see of Rome ‖

It is evident that, had it depended on the emperor and his brother, the victory of the Five Cantons would have been immediately succeeded by a general attempt to establish Catholicism in Switzerland

Meanwhile, however, the Swiss themselves had begun to consider of the means of putting an end to their dissensions

The army of the cities was by no means in a condition to remain under arms, in the mountains, when the bad season set in As the Five Cantons prepared to attack them

* "Das was ungfar um die swei nach Mitternacht Morgens Zinstag den 24 Octobris" "Maria die Mutter Gottes war dero Nacht ihr Kriegszeichen"—"This was at about two hours after midnight on the morning of Tuesday the 24th October" "Mary, the mother of God, was their watchword on that night" Kurzer Bericht

† 1st Nov Vra Magestad a la qual suplico quiera mirar lo que ynporta y usar de la occasion y opportunidad del tiempo, pues es el mas a proposito que se pudo desear i camino para remediar las quiebras de nuestra fe *y ser Vra Md señor de Alemanna* y hazer una cosa la mas sennalada que in nuestros tempos se ha hecho

‡ Bruxelles, 2d Nov 1531 Archives of Brussels

§ Lettre du roi a Mr d'Auxerre, 21 Nov MS Bethune, 8477 Pour la guerre du Turc ou des Suisses) où il n y a que coups et despenses d argent

‖ Relatio V N Joannis Basadone Come el mi disse, andava cum proposito di rimover Lutherani dalla loro mala opinione con mezzo di alcuni suoi amici e cum danari Archives of Venice

again, Zürich, and afterwards Bern, were obliged to accept the peace dictated to them.

It was exactly the reverse of the last internal peace. The cities were now obliged to give up the alliances they had concluded with foreign powers, and, in one form or another, to pay all the expenses of the war.

They were allowed the exercise of their religion. They had not fallen so low that their enemies could dare to assail this. They had suffered some reverses, and their attack had failed, but they were not subdued.

They were forced, however, to submit to a great diminution of their political and religious influence. The Five Cantons intended to chastise, not only the districts which immediately belonged to them — Rapperschwyl, Toggenburg, Gaster and Wesen, — but also those over which the cities had a joint control with them, such as the free bailiwicks in Aargau, Bremgarten, and Mellingen. In the other common bailiwicks, those who had accepted the new creed were to be not indeed commanded, but permitted, to return to the "ancient and true Christian faith." Expressions of this kind the cities were obliged to endure throughout the treaty.*

No sooner had Bern accepted this peace, than the revival and re-establishment of Catholicism began on all sides.

Immediately after the battle of Cappel, me Catholic minority in Glarus bestirred itself, revoked the succours of the canton already determined on, and warned the subjects of the same not to furnish them; they did every thing in their power to favour the turn things had taken. Very shortly a certain number of churches were restored to them; and from that time they have exercised a far greater influence on the public business of the canton than the evangelical party, which was disheartened and enfeebled by the great losses sustained by their co-religionists. Schwytz, therefore, experienced no resistance when it overran Gaster and Wesen, abolished the old liberties, and restored the altars and images, and the mass. Glarus united with Schwytz, and Uri undertook to reinstate the abbot of St. Gall. His abbey was restored to him, and the city compelled to pay him a large sum as compensation. The people who cultivated the lands of the religious house were once more regarded as its subjects, and the abbot maintained that he was not bound by any stipulations in their favour in the treaty of peace; for that he was a free lord, and the protecting cantons could lay down no rule for his government. These tenants gradually all became Catholic again. Fortunately for Toggenburg, at the very last moment, when it withdrew from the cities, it took better securities for its religious freedom, which, though greatly abridged, was not destroyed. The abbot placed the government of the country in the hands of those who had been driven out of it in the recent troubles.

Rapperschwyl was also reclaimed. At the news of the successes of their co-religionists, the Catholics rose, and being reinforced by succours from Schwytz, were completely victorious. The leaders of the evangelical party were obliged to flee, or were put to death. There lived in the town a very skilful gunsmith, one Michael Wohlgemuth, of Cologne, who had the courage to defend himself after the fashion of old times: he barricaded his house, planted his matchlocks at the windows, and defended himself for some time with equal gallantry and success, till at length he was regularly besieged and taken prisoner. He was put to death with horrible tortures. Of the remainder, some submitted, some were thrown into prison, and some exiled. On the 19th of November, mass was performed again.

In the Aargau, the Five Cantons used the rights of conquest with the utmost rigour. Wherever their banner appeared, the preachers retreated from the death with which they were threatened by the German, and still more by the French Swiss. Bremgarten and Mellingen were forced expressly to engage to restore the ancient rites of the church. The aged Schultheiss Mütschli, who had hitherto governed Bremgarten, lay on his death-bed when the newly appointed Catholic authorities sent to order him to quit Bremgarten. "Tell them that I shall not trouble them long," he replied. He died soon after, and lies buried at Oberwyl.

The treaty of peace did not leave Thurgau and the Rhine valley so much at the mercy of the Five Cantons; they were obliged to content themselves with restoring the convents, which recovered their old privileges.

In Solothurn, on the other hand, the Catholics were completely triumphant. Nearly seventy Protestant families were obliged to leave the city.

This second restoration of Catholicism occurring in our history, was not so bloody as the first, which took place in Upper Germany after the peasants' war; but, like that, it was brought about by the casualties of war; like that, it was violent; and it was far more lasting.

The general relation of the two confessions, at that time established in the Alps, has endured down to the present time.

Even the evangelical cantons felt the influence of the restoration. The Constafel of Zürich regained their lost privileges. The people were obliged to acquiesce, so that Catholicism was not again in activity. The Great Council was forced to make such promises to the country districts as greatly limited its authority.

The war had lasted only six weeks, but it had totally changed the prospects of Switzerland. Bullinger's Chronicle contains at the end a short comparison of what the reformers had projected, and what they had actually accomplished. They had desired the uniform introduction of the evangelical faith; the depression of the oligarchies; the abatement of the majority of the Five Cantons. The result

* The copy of the treaty of peace in Hottinger's Appendix to vol. ii. collated anew with the original.

was, that the new doctrine was extirpated from many places where it had been preached; that the Papacy was reinstated in its authority; that the Five Cantons acquired such an ascendancy as they had never enjoyed before, and that the oligarchies had more power than ever.* "Honour is overthrown, arbitrary power is established," says Bullinger. "The counsels of the Lord are marvellous."

CHAPTER V.

THE REFORMATION IN THE CITIES OF LOWER GERMANY. CONCLUSION OF THE SCHMALKALDIC LEAGUE.

THE spirit of reform had embodied itself in two parties of very different tendencies; the one, bold and comprehensive, both as to religious doctrines and political views; inclined to the absolute rejection of the traditional, and ready for attack: the other, conservative (as far as it was possible) even in matters of doctrine; and, on the field of politics, reluctantly brought to make a resolute defence.

The former of these had failed in its projects; it necessarily followed that the whole strength of the growing reformation now attached itself to the latter. The Schmalkaldic league was the more formidable to its enemies, because its rivals were no longer in a state to compete with it.

The cities of the Oberland had already made as near an approach as possible to the religious principle of the Schmalkaldic league; and, since their Swiss allies were compelled to dissolve the ties between them, they had politically no other support remaining than the strength of the united German States.

Their own danger was increased by the calamities of the Swiss. They knew the lively share which the court of Ferdinand had taken in the affairs of the Confederation, and rumours were afloat of warlike preparations in Alsatia, the Breisgau and the Sundgau.

The Oberlanders now no longer hesitated to engage in a definitive consultation on a plan of warfare. This took place at a meeting at Nordhausen, in November, 1531.

But, before we examine the organisation which the league then assumed, we must endeavour to understand distinctly what progress the cause of reform had in the meantime made in the cities of Lower Germany.

REFORMATION IN THE CITIES OF LOWER GERMANY.

The first city that joined the evangelical princes was, as we have seen, Magdeburg. Here, in a city which had pretensions to hold immediately of the empire, and had seen itself, with great disgust, turned over to the jurisdiction of the archbishop;—here, where Luther had gone to school, and where his personal friends were still in possession of honours and employments, his ideas had easily captivated the whole body of the citizens. One day an old cloth-weaver was sitting under the statue of Otho the Great, singing a Lutheran hymn, and offering copies of it for sale. Just then the Bürgermeister Rubin, who had been at mass, came by, and ordered him to be arrested. This was sufficient to arouse the slumbering fire. The agitation spread from the audience collected about the old man, over the whole city. The citizens, who, ever since the year 1330, had taken an important part in secular affairs, thought that they had a right to a no less participation in spiritual. On the very same day, the 6th of May, 1524, the parish of St. Ulrich proceeded to exercise this right. They met in the churchyard, and determined to choose eight men out of their body, who for the future should manage the affairs of the church with their concurrence, and should choose preachers. Other parishes followed this example, and the council did not deem itself called upon to prevent them. Evangelical preachers were universally appointed by the side of Catholic priests.

But a state of things like this could not last. The priests administered the mass according to the ancient ritual; the attacks of the preachers were mainly directed against the mass. There was no peace till either the priests went over to Protestantism, as M. Scultetus did, or were silenced, or sent away. The parishes of St. John and St. Ulrich having opened a formal negotiation with the dean of Our Lady's Church, and he having refused to grant them such priests as they desired, they solemnly renounced his authority, "in order to take refuge with the sole eternal supreme priest, guardian of souls, bishop and pope, Jesus Christ; with him as their captain, would they do battle like true knights."† On the 17th of July, 1524, the sacrament of the Lord's Supper was administered according to Luther's form, in all the churches of the old town. Hereupon the councillors and hundred men assembled in their armour, and the citizens, according to the four quarters of the city, with matchlocks and halberds; they swore to stand truly and firmly by each other, if trouble should come upon the city on account of the abolition of the mass. They had no doubt that the archbishop, Cardinal Albert, would resort to severe measures against them. They therefore hastened to cut a canal from the Elbe to the city ditches, in order, in case of need, to fill the latter with water; the walls were raised, the palisades strengthened with blocks; the workmen in the town taken into their service for a small remuneration. They were resolved

* Bullinger, iii. 353. The state of things is particularly described in an essay written by Leo Judæ in his own justification. "There are two great parties in Zürich, the one will protect God's word and help to secure all justice to it, the other will plant all dishonesty, and uproot the word of God, re-establish the Papacy, and take foriegn service and pensions again. It appears to the pious that the latter party have always more favour and encouragement than they."

† Cause and Proceedings in the imperial, honourable, and Christian City of Magdeburg, pertaining to a Christian Walk and Conversation. By Wolff Cycloff, Doctor of Medicine, 1524. Printed in Hahn's Collectio Monumentorum, ii. 459.

to defend with life and limb the spiritual independence they had asserted. But the time was not yet come when their resolution was to be put to the proof; for the present, matters did not go to that extremity.*

In Brunswick things took very nearly the same course a few years later. The citizens read Luther's books, and translation of the Bible; above all, his hymns produced the strongest sensation; they were sung in every house, and the streets resounded with them. It had become customary here for the priests who held benefices to leave the business of preaching to young men whom they paid, and who were called Heuerpfaffen (hire-priests). It is not surprising that these men generally espoused the new doctrines, and took part with the citizens. Examples occurred of their giving out from the pulpit, instead of the Latin hymn to the Virgin, one of the new German psalms, in which all the congregation joined with the greatest enthusiasm.

Indeed, the people would no longer listen to sermons of any other tendency. Scholastic demonstrations were tumultuously interrupted, and incorrect quotations from Scripture loudly and eagerly corrected by the congregation. The clergy sent for Dr. Sprengel, one of the most respected of the orthodox preachers of the neighbourhood, and already practised in the handling of controversial points; but he could make no impression. At the conclusion of his sermon a citizen called out, "Priest, thou liest," and set up the Lutheran hymn, "Ach Gott vom Himmel sieh darein!" (O God, look down from heaven!) which the whole congregation sang with triumph.

The priests could at last devise no expedient, except to request the council to rid them of their heretical assistants. But the congregations only attached themselves the more firmly to the latter. The town and suburbs united nominated delegates, at the head of whom was Autor Sander, one of the leaders of the whole movement (he belonged to the literary class of innovators of whom we have formerly made mention); they now, on their side, petitioned the council to remove the priests.

At first, the council inclined to the existing order of things, but it was soon carried along by the popular movement. Reforms were at that time going on in various places, in consequence of the decree of the empire of 1526; among others, in the neighbouring state of Lüneburg; Duke Henry of Brunswick-Wolfenbüttel, who would undoubtedly have opposed it, being occupied in his expedition into Italy. Under these circumstances, the council passed the resolution, on the 13th of March, 1528, that in future only the pure word of God should be preached; that the sacrament of the Lord's Supper should be administered in both kinds, and baptism be performed in the German language. Dr. Bugenhagen came from Wittenberg, in order to give a permanent form, of the kind prescribed by Luther, to the new order of things.† The Duke of Lüneburg promised the city his protection.‡

Things took the same course in most of the towns of this part of Germany. In all of them we see preachers arise, the Lutheran hymns become popular, and the congregations take part in religious questions: the council at first makes a greater or less resistance, but at length gives way. In Goslar fifty men were appointed out of the several parishes, and carried the reforms through; there was a disturbance in Göttingen, because the overseers of the commune were at first hostile; in Eimbeck the council was compelled, by the urgency of the commune, to recal the very preacher whom they had lately dismissed at the request of the canons.

Our readers will remember the violent commotions which broke out in all the cities between the years 1510—1516; even in those of Lower Germany. The question now arose, how far the religious impulse was mingled with this democratic agitation, and whether the predominant tendency would not be political.

We find a great difference among the cities in this respect.

There were some in which council and commune united in good time; and in these the municipal constitutions acquired greater strength than ever during the troubles. For not only did they get rid of the influence of foreign prelates, which had always been oppressive to them; but the administration of church affairs and church property that now devolved upon them, gave them a common interest which united them more closely. In Magdeburg ecclesiastical colleges§ were formed, consisting of members of the former council, and the newly elected superintendants of the communes; this gave additional strength to the democratic element which already somewhat predominated in the constitution of the city. The most remarkable town in this respect is undoubtedly Hamburg. Here, too, the reformers followed the advice of Luther, which Bugenhagen had carried out theoretically in books,‖ and practically by his own plans in Brunswick;—to establish in every parish funds or chests (*Gotteskasten*), in

* Sebastian Langhans, at that time mill-bailiff, left a history of the year 1524, which it is very desirable to have printed. Up to that date, Rathmann's Extracts and Collections (iii. 346—400) are very useful.

† The most minute account of these events is to be found in Rehtmeiers Kirchen historie der Stadt Braunschweig, part iii., the original source of which is a contemporaneous statement by Heinrich Lampe, preacher at St. Michael's church: "What happened in ecclesiastical affairs, shortly before and after the reception of the Holy Gospel here in Brunswick;" Gasmer's Funeral Sermon for Lampe (which is the basis of Lenz's "Braunschweigs Kirchenreformation, 1828") is also chiefly taken from that statement.

‡ Duke Ernest mentions in a letter of the 2d of February, 1531, a former compact with Brunswick, in which they mutually promised, "in matters relating to the divine word and whatever depends thereon, to risk life and property with each other." (W. A.)

§ See Rathmann, IV. ii. 28.

‖ In the Appendix to the treatise, Vom rechten Glauben (Of the true Faith), which Bugenhagen published, both in high and low German, in 1526, and dedicated to the bürgermeister, councillors, and the whole community of the honourable city of Hamburg.

order to meet the wants of the clergyman and the school, and to provide for the poor out of the church property, and chose, as trustees of the same, twelve respectable citizens, some of whom had already filled the office of jurats of the church, and to whom twenty-four members of each parish were now attached The same form was adopted in most other towns, what distinguishes Hamburg is, that it served as the basis of a new political constitution The parish superintendants composed the college of the Forty-eight, and, together with their assistants, that of the Hundred and Forty-four, two colleges which may be regarded as a true representation of the hereditary class of citizens (Burgerschaft) Besides this, a fifth and principal chest was established, in which the whole property [illegible] the church was to be united,* and the a[illegible]istration of it was entrusted to the three [illegible] elders of the parish overseers This t[illegible] place with the full consent of the worsh[illegible] [illegible]e council on Michaelmas-day, 1528 It is [illegible]dent that this college contained the germs of a most important institution for the improvement and prosperity of the city, and we know how completely it has fulfilled its destination After a lapse of three centuries, the day of its establishment has just been commemorated with civic festivities †

In Rostock also the council and the citizens formed the closest union in opposition to the Mecklenburg princes, who in the year 1531 sided for a moment with the Catholic clergy ‡

But things were not everywhere thus peacefully settled In Bremen, where the churches had fallen into the hands of the Lutheran preachers as early as the year 1525, and, in 1527, the two convents of the city had been converted, the one into a school and the other into an hospital, so violent a hatred of the clergy had arisen among the citizens during the incessant quarrels in which they had been involved with the priests attached to the cathedral, that they were not satisfied with having stripped them of all spiritual influence in the city They laid claim to a number of fields, gardens and enclosed lands, which, they said, the cathedral had unjustly wrested from the town, and as the council did not uphold them in these claims they chose a democratic body of a hundred and four members, who not only endeavoured to carry through all these measures, but radically to alter the constitution of the city, they overthrew the whole groundwork, and rejected all the documents and charters upon which it rested, proceeded with the greatest violence, and at length were only put down by force of arms §

The movement in Lubek was still more important

Here the patrician families had formed a close union with the clergy, the chapter, council, gentry and great merchants constituted one party ‖ On the other hand, the desire for religious reforms was here as rife among the citizens as in other places, but it was repressed with unrelenting zeal, families were punished only because the servants had sung a German psalm Luther's commentary on the Scriptures was burned in the market-place

Unfortunately for the ruling classes, they had suffered the finances of the city to fall into disorder, and found themselves compelled to assemble the citizens, and to call upon them for extraordinary supplies

The citizens consented They nominated a committed (A D 1529), which gradually increased to the number of sixty-four, in order to deliberate with the council on this grant, but they immediately seized the opportunity to claim, not only more political power, but religious emancipation They demanded that the committee should have a share in regulating the revenue and expenditure of the town, and that freedom of preaching should be granted them The public voice was very soon raised in their favour The people demanded the restitution of the preachers who had been expelled a few years before, here, too, the officiating priest was interrupted by the psalm, "Ach Gott vom Himmel sieh darein!" Satirical songs were sung against Johann Rode, the rector of Our Lady's Church, charging him with having maintained that Christ had redeemed only our forefathers, and that their posterity must seek salvation from him "They who should feed us, are they who mislead us," (Die uns sollen Weiden, das sind die uns verleiten,) says one of these songs ¶ In one great meeting of citizens, those who wished to remain Catholic were asked to stand aside, when only one complied

Overpowered by such manifestations, and deprived by its financial difficulties of all substantial power, the council was compelled step by step to give way

In December, 1529, it recalled the expelled preachers, in April, 1530, it removed the Catholics from every pulpit in the city, in the June of the same year, it found itself compelled to give notice to the churches and con-

* "Nichtesdeweyniger schollen de veer Kisten in den Carspelkarcken, wo se nu stahn, tho Versamelinge de Almiszen blyven, so doch, dathme allendt wes bether tho darinn gegeven, und hyrnamals tho allen Tyden darinn gegeven werden mag, alles getrouwlik in und by de Hovetkysten presentere und averantwehrde" — "Nevertheless, the four chests in the parish church, where they now stand, shall remain for the collection of the alms, so that all which may heretofore have been given therein, or may hereafter be therein given, through all times, may be truly presented and answered for to the principal [head] chest "—Original form of the Foundation of the Overalten (Over elders), Michaelmas-day, 1528

† Lappenberg, Programme of the third secular commemoration of the municipal constitution of Hamburg, on the 29th of September, 1528, wherein the matter which Burgermeister Bartels and the Præses of the Oberalten (Over elders), Rucker, treated in a popular manner in their speeches, is learnedly and instructively developed

‡ Rudlof N Gesch Mecklenburgs, i 81.

§ Roller, Geschichte von Bremen, ii p 380, u f

‖ The priesthood was become very numerous, especially by the institution of vicars In the middle of the 15th century there were in Lubek and the neighbouring churches 169 vicars They were most of them relations of those who had founded masses for the dead See Grautoff, Schriften, i 266 The disposition of the capital lay in the hands of provisors

¶ The song in Regkmann's Chronicle, p 133.

vents to discontinue their established usages At the very same time that Charles V was attempting to re-establish the ancient faith in Augsburg, it was utterly extirpated in one of the most considerable cities of the North This did not pass unobserved at Augsburg The emperor commanded the Sixty-four in the most earnest manner, by a penal mandate, "to desist from what they were about," and told the council, in case this was not complied with, to apply to some of the neighbouring princes for assistance It may easily be imagined what effect these menaces of a distant power were likely to produce in the fermenting city The agitation redoubled, and increased so violently that the council was under the necessity of requesting the Sixty-four to retain their functions, and even of approving their making a fresh addition of a hundred citizens to their body.* Doctor John Bugenhagen was also invited to Lubek to organise a new church, with a commission chosen from the council and citizens † The convents were converted into schools and hospitals, the nuns of St John's were suffered to remain, on condition of their instructing children, in all parish churches, pastors and chaplains attached to the confession of Augsburg were appointed, under a superintendent, Hermannus Bonnus

It followed, of course, that the Sixty-four, whose origin was of a politico-religious nature, were not satisfied with the concessions made by the church, the council was obliged to promise to account to them for the public expenditure, to make no treaty or engagement without their consent, to allow them a short joint superintendence in military affairs, in short, to share all their most important functions with them ‡ The council accustomed to nearly unlimited sway, reluctantly consented There was, it is true, a public reconciliation between the burgermeisters and the president of the Sixty-four, but solemn acts of this kind have never served to eradicate a rooted aversion a few weeks after, Claus Bromse and Hermann Plonnies, the two burgermeisters, found the impotency to which they were reduced, and the mistrust of which they were the objects, so intolerable, that they quitted the city This was at Easter, 1531 No sooner was the departure of the burgermeisters known among the citizens, than a storm of anger arose The people imputed to them, and to the whole council, an understanding with the neighbouring princes, and expected that the city would be attacked. First, the Sixty-four, then the Hundred, and lastly, all the members of the commune were called together, the gates were closed, the members of the council were arrested, either in their own houses or in the town-house; till at length the council, subdued, shackled, tormented, and deprived of its chiefs, determined to give up the great seal of the city to the Sixty-four. The commune did not go so far as to depose them, never would the Lutheran preachers have approved that But, as they sought out a document to prove that the council might consist of a greater number of members than actually held seats in it, and immediately proceeded to appoint the number deficient,—as they nominated two burgermeisters instead of those who had left the town, they did in fact entirely transform the council, and impart to the victorious opinions a preponderant influence over all its decisions. The preachers consented to this with great reluctance, for their idea of the exalted nature and dignity of the civil authority extended to the city councillors, and at every change they earnestly warned the people from the pulpit not to transgress against authority §

Duke Ernest of Luneburg was extremely rejoiced, on his return from Augsburg, to see around him how little people cared for the favour or disfavour of the emperor; on the contrary, how much more prosperous was the evangelical cause in these cities now than heretofore ‖ The emperor had just admonished the city of Luneburg in a private letter, to remain constant to the old faith, the only result of which was, that the city prayed the duke to leave Urbanus Rhegius, the reformer, whom he had brought home with him from Augsburg, for a time with them, for the purpose of organising their church,¶ which he gradually accomplished

So powerfully did the spirit of the reformation diffuse itself through Lower Germany Already it had taken possession of a portion of the principalities, it was triumphant in the Wendish cities, it had penetrated into Westphalia, as we shall see hereafter; it seemed about to pervade the whole character and condition of North Germany

But it was easy to foresee that, before this could come to pass, it would have to encounter many a storm

Very violent political tendencies mingled themselves with the attempt to reform the church, and it was a question how far the former could be guided in the channel of

* In the answer of the citizens, in Regkmann, 139, it is said that this was proposed by the council, "um vieler Ungestumheit willen, Müh' und Verdriess zuvorzukommen,"—' in order to prevent much disorder, trouble, and annoyance "

† Notices in Grautoff, ii 159 The influence which is ascribed in that work to a more moderate party in the council stands, however, in need of further proof

‡ The articles of the commune made, agreed on, and confirmed on the 13th of October, 1530 Becker, Lub Gesch iii. 27, says, not all the demands of the commune were granted, and he then adduces only those expressly mentioned in the journal in Kirchring and Muller, p 166 Is it possible that the title of the articles can be so wrong?

§ In the Chronicle of Hermannus Bonnus it is said that there is no better means of maintaining a stable government than to leave the choice of the council in the hands of the authorities

‖ Ernest to Elector John, Zelle, Monday, 17th of October "Befinde, das wynzig Gottlob in diesen umliegenden Stadten kais Maj Gnaden oder Ungnaden gescheuet, denn sye itzunder heftiger, als vor nie, in allen Stadten predigen und das Wort Gottes furdern "—" I find that, thank God, his imperial majesty's favour or disfavour is very little cared for in the cities hereabout, for they now preach in all cities more vehemently than ever before, and promote the word of God" (W A)

¶ Letter above "hauen heud der Rath und die Gemeyne mir semptlich geschrieben "—" The council and the commonalty have all written to me to day"

established institutions, or how far they would assume a revolutionary character

With these were also connected changes of religious opinion, which did not always remain within the pale of the Lutheran system, and the future direction of which it was impossible to foresee

We shall examine more closely these changes, which are extremely important there came a time when the popular mind, violently excited, rushed into wild and pathless regions

At present, however, these symptoms had not betrayed themselves

At present, the only remarkable fact was, the support which Protestantism, in its peaceful progress, experienced from its new extension, at the very moment when it was most violently menaced by the emperor This support was peculiarly advantageous to the Schmalkaldic league, to which we must now turn our attention

CONCLUSION OF THE SCHMALKALDIC LEAGUE

The Magdeburgers were included in the earlier Protestant associations In the year 1531, being urged by their archbishop to conform to the recess of Augsburg, they looked to the Elector of Saxony as their sole refuge, and implored him "to protect them in their adherence to the eternal word of God " They delayed not an instant to join the league *

Bremen, uninvited, asked the Duke of Luneburg for the first draft of the convention, and declared itself ready to send a representative to the meeting, and to contribute its share of aid †

With Lubek, on the other hand, the duke had to open negotiations This was at a time when the council still retained some power, and, as its sympathies were quite in an opposite direction, it naturally hesitated. But the Hundred and Sixty-four were easily won over On their motion, a delegate of the city appeared at the second congress at Schmalkalden, in March, 1531 He desired first to be informed, what support the princes could afford the city against the ejected King of Denmark, if the emperor should attempt to restore him, and pleaded the necessity of not exacting too much assistance from the citizens But even this reservation was dropped, when the great change which we have described took place in Lubek. Although the delegate received very unsatisfactory answers to his questions, Lubek immediately after acceded to the treaty We find these three cities mentioned in the first sealed formula of the league

At the following meeting in June, they were joined by Gottingen and Brunswick. Brunswick thought that it belonged sufficiently to the league, through its connexion with the Duke of Luneburg,‡ but the allies were of opinion that they should have stronger grounds for sending assistance to the city in case of need, if it was a direct party to the convention An envoy from the margrave at last removed all its scruples

Shortly after, Goslar and Eimbeck followed

So rapidly did the compact of the princes extend over both parts of Germany It now included seven cities of Upper, and seven of Lower Germany

It was impossible longer to delay giving a constitution to such a union We know how urgently this was demanded by events in Switzerland, and the Oberlanders were now fully prepared for it §

A preliminary discussion was held in November, 1531, at Nordhausen, and a definitive one at Frankfurt-am-Main in December

The first question was as to the supreme command of the league

It was an arrangement prompted as much by the nature of things as by habit and tradition, that they should nominate a single head of the league, who should also command them in war Saxony wished that one of the two Welfs, either the Luneburger or the Grubenhagener, should be chosen There was a general wish to avoid the landgrave, who was accounted too rash and too intimately connected with the Swiss

But this was not practicable The landgrave was far too powerful and warlike to suffer himself to be excluded from the command of the league and, since the defeat of the Swiss, nothing more was to be feared from his leaning to their side

But as the Elector of Saxony also did not choose to be thrown into the shade by the landgrave, it was agreed at the meeting at Nordhausen to elect two commanders, and that these two princes should be the men Each of them was to bring up one half of the troops and they were alternately to conduct the affairs of the whole body, if the war was to be carried on in Saxony and Westphalia, the elector to have the command, if in Hessen and Germany, the landgrave

But it is not to be imagined that full powers were given to these two chiefs to act at their good pleasure the question was discussed with equal earnestness, how the deliberations were to be held, and the votes divided, and what relation these should bear to the contributions

The first proposal on the side of the princes

* Magdeburg, Saturday after Estomihi, 1531 "It happened that our most gracious lord cardinal's steward appeared on Ash-Wednesday before us, the whole council sitting, and delivered a missive from our above mentioned gracious lord and thereupon set forth that he had a printed copy, which he would also deliver to us, and as he had before signified to our burgermeister and council, that, in the said printed copy, the recess held at Augsburg, and the order that they should hold to the old usages, were inserted, we would not receive it "

† Letter of Duke Ernest, Tuesday after St Clement

‡ Letter of the city to Ernest of Luneburg 22d March, 1531 "Since we have settled with your princely grace concerning our natural relation as subjects, and have included therein our separate treaties with regard to the Christian matters undertaken in God's name "

§ Melanchthon to Camerarius, 30th December "Scis ejus periculi partem ad nos pertinere " A letter from Ulm (Saturday after St Simon and St Jude) announces that the greatest joy prevailed at Ferdinand s court, in the Sundgau, Breisgau, and Alsatia, the people had been warned to hold themselves ready for war, in the lands of the Abbot of Kempten they had been ordered when attacked to take up arms instantly and assemble

was to create five votes; two for Saxony and Hessen, two for the cities, and the remaining one for the other princes and counts conjointly. The ordinary contingents, reckoned at two thousand horse, and ten thousand foot, were taxed at seventy thousand gulden a month; of which the princes were to pay thirty thousand, and the cities forty.

The objection to this plan is obvious at the first glance. The greater half of the votes, and the lesser of the contributions, were allotted to the princes. The cities did not neglect to propose a different scheme, in which perfect equality was observed. Each party was to contribute thirty-five thousand gulden, and each to have four votes.

How was it to be, however, if these votes were equally divided on any question? an inconvenience carefully avoided in all deliberative bodies. The cities proposed to give a casting vote to the electoral prince of Saxony, who would otherwise have no voice. But to this the landgrave would by no means consent. He replied, that he wished his friend and brother all the prosperity in the world; he should be glad to see John Frederic Roman king and emperor; but that, in this affair, they must maintain perfect equality, according to the original agreement.

They therefore reverted to a project very similar to the first. Nine votes were created, of which four were divided between Saxony and Hessen, and four among the four cities; the ninth was to be held in common by the remaining princes and lords. The only advantage the cities gained was, that the contributions were more equally divided. Of these four votes, the Oberland towns had two, and the Lower Saxon the other two; and they took an equal share of the contributions upon themselves. Of the two Lower Saxon votes, Magdeburg and Bremen had the one, Lübek and the remaining towns the other.

In this manner were the affairs of the league arranged, as soon as it was concluded. The constitution is merely the expression of the fact, and of the relations of the parties; of the former, inasmuch as those on whose coalition all depended were now its recognised chiefs; of the latter, inasmuch as the legal influence on its resolutions was determined by the relative force and the contributions of the members.

After all that has been laid before the reader, it is unnecessary to observe, that the principle of reform, at once conservative and defensive, such as Luther conceived it, was here most perfectly and eminently represented; but if I am not mistaken, it may be added, that this league, by thus combining the two great provinces of Upper and Lower Germany, which had hitherto always been separated, was of the highest value to the unity of development of the German mind. There was now another centre besides the diets; there was a unity not imposed by the command of the sovereign power, but arising spontaneously from the force of circumstances, and combining a political and military, with an intellectual character. Luther was the great author, who, intelligible to both parties, found access to both, and pre-eminently contributed to the foundation of a uniform national culture. It was a union which extended to the uttermost boundaries of Germany on either side. Not only the neighbouring Magdeburg and central Strasburg, but bürgermeisters and town councillors from Riga sought aid and protection from the Elector of Saxony, on whom, under God, all their hopes were fixed. They came in the name of the evangelical party in Dorpat and Reval, praying to be defended against the attempts of their archbishop, who threatened them with the execution of the recess of Augsburg.*

The league had likewise a great political import. All who had any thing to fear from Austria, or any thing to complain of in her past conduct, rallied round it;—the Duke of Guelders and Juliers, from whom Ravenstein had been taken; the King of Denmark, who was in daily dread of a fresh attack from Christiern II., aided by Austria; and lastly, an election opposition headed by Bavaria. In February, 1531, we find the Bavarian councillor, Weichselfelder, in Torgau;† in August, Leonhard Eck visited Landgrave Philip at Giessen; in October, a congress of all the States hostile to Ferdinand was held at Saalfeld. Here they mutually promised "by their true words as electors, princes and counts,‡ on their honour, truth and faith, not to consent to the election, and, above all, to the administration, of Ferdinand; and in case they were attacked for the same, to support each other." Some months afterwards the form of these mutual succours was agreed on.§

It is curious to see in what light these things appeared at a distance; how, for example, Henry VIII. expressed himself concerning them in a conversation with the Danish ambassador, Peter Schwaben. The emperor, Henry thought, ought to have yielded at Augsburg, on the few points on which they could not agree,—but Campeggi probably hindered him. "The emperor is foolish," said he; "he understands nothing of Latin. They should have taken me and the King of France as umpires; we would have summoned the most learned men in all Europe, and would soon have decided the affair." He then proceeded to speak of the election. "Why do not the princes," said he, "choose another king?—the Duke of Bavaria, for example, who would be quite a fit man. They must not allow the emperor to deceive them as he has deceived the pope." "Sir," added he, as if alarmed at his own frankness, "nobody must know that I have said this. I am an ally of the em-

* Letter of the Council, Wednesday before Palm Sunday, and also that of the Syndic Lehnmüller, the Wednesday after the 29th March, and 5th April, 1531. (W. A.)

† The Bavarian councillors were expected at the second congress at Schmalkalden, as a letter from Philip to Dr. Leonh. Eck (undated, but without doubt of the 31st January) shows.

‡ Neudeckers Urkunden, p. 60. The counts of Mansfeld are those alluded to.

§ May, 1532. Original document in Stumpf, No. v. p. 20.

peror. In fact," continued he after a pause, "it would be a disgrace to the emperor if he were forced to leave Germany without putting an end to these troubles. I see the time is come when either the emperor must make himself renowned, or the Elector of Saxony."

Thus, then, things were come to such a pass, that a sagacious neighbouring sovereign could compare the elector's chances of renown and universal consideration with those of the emperor.

We must not, however, take this for more than it is worth; we are well aware that the king flattered his own secret hostility to the emperor with thoughts of this kind.

But so much is clear notwithstanding;—that the federative position which the aged elector acquired now, at the close of his life, was a very high and significant one.

If the aggressive tendencies of the reformation in Switzerland had been crushed in the attempt to break down the influences opposed to it, a similar calamity was not to be feared for the league, whose attitude was purely defensive. Even if the emperor had taken advantage of the Swiss reverses and begun a great war, he would not have found it so easy, as perhaps Ferdinand thought, to suppress Protestantism, and to make himself absolute master of Germany.

Moreover, circumstances had occurred which rendered this utterly impossible.

CHAPTER VI.

OTTOMAN INVASION. FIRST PEACE OF RELIGION.

1531, 1532.

DESTINY (if we may be allowed to use the word) had for a time left the emperor at liberty to put an end to these religious troubles in one way or another. For two years he had been at peace.

But this period presents a singular spectacle. We behold those who threaten war and destruction separate, and each betake himself to his own affairs; while, on the contrary, those who are threatened adhere with unshaken pertinacity to their designs, and succeed in founding an effective politico-religious coalition. The check which reform had sustained in Switzerland was advantageous to its consolidation in Germany.

It always happens, and especially under circumstances like those of Germany, that the obvious necessity for common defence is a far better bond of union than the most elaborate plan of attack.

The emperor did not neglect to urge the electors to more vigorous measures. Immediately after Ferdinand's election, they formed a league for the defence of it against all attacks whatsoever. In the spring of 1531, the emperor proposed to connect with this a more extensive coalition, for the purpose of preventing all attempts of the seceders injurious to the true faith.* To this, however, the electors did not accede; they thought that sufficient security was afforded by the rules and recesses of the empire. We know that there were other points on which the States of the empire did not perfectly agree with the emperor; the diplomatic correspondence of the time shows that demonstrations and professions of friendship were traversed in every direction by under-currents of secret animosity.

Moreover, every attempt to reduce the Protestants was rendered impossible by the danger which incessantly hung over Europe from the East.

At length its most formidable foe once more arose in his might. His recent attack on Vienna had rather irritated than intimidated him.

We have now to contemplate, not only the warlike preparations of the Ottomans, but their effect on Germany. If even the dread of war was favourable to the Protestants, we may expect to find that its actual outbreak was much more so.

OTTOMAN INVASION.

In the year 1530, both Ferdinand and the emperor entertained the idea of terminating the affair of Hungary by a treaty with the sublime Porte. As John Zapolya boasted that he paid no tribute, the court of Vienna hoped that the sultan might be gained over by the offer of a sum of money; and even flattered itself that it might be possible to recover the whole of Hungary, such as King Wladislaus had possessed it. In this spirit were the proposals conceived which Ferdinand sent to Constantinople, in May, 1530.†

In fact, he hoped nothing more from the war with the woiwode. A fresh attempt on Ofen had failed. The Hungarians of both parties were evidently weary of internal discord; they had even a project of proceeding to elect a third king, whom all might acknowledge. Ferdinand therefore consented to a truce with Zapolya. His hopes were turned towards Constantinople—hopes which were destined to be entirely crushed.

It was well known in Constantinople, that a general enterprise against the Turks was incessantly talked of in Germany, Italy and Spain; that the pope and the empire had

* Original document in the Berlin Archives under the title: "Keyser Carls Bedenken, wie die Election eines römischen Königes zu Cölln geschehen und auf König Ferdinand gericht, wider den Churfürsten von Sachsen und Andre so dieselbe gestritten, moge gehandhabt werden."—"Emperor Charles's Reflections how the Election of a King of the Romans, which took place at Cologne, and fell upon King Ferdinand, is to be maintained against the Elector of Saxony and others, who have contested it." There is in Brussels an extract from the elector's answer in the French language, in which the emperor's offer is described in the words: Offrant derechef avec le roy son frere d'accomplir et fournir à une notable et durable entreprise.

† Instructions to Lamberg and Jurischitz; Gevay, Urkunden und Actenstücke, Heft i.

granted money for it, and that the emperor hoped to render his name glorious by such a campaign. But it was also known that the money, though granted, was either not forthcoming, or could not be applied to its destination, that Christendom, spite of all treaties of peace, was full of open or secret divisions, and the threat of uniting its forces against the Ottomans was treated with derision. "The King of Spain," it was said, "has encircled his brow with the diadem of the empire, but what then? is he better obeyed? He is emperor, who extends his dominion with the sword." When the envoys appeared with the proposals above mentioned, the grand vezir Ibrahim changed colour, and dissuaded them from even submitting such to the sultan,* for Hungary belonged not to the Janusch Kral (as he called the king-waiwode), but to the sultan, who therefore took no tribute from that country, but, on the contrary, gave succours to his servant and lieutenant who governed it. The sultan had twice conquered Hungary with the sword, with his own sweat and blood, and that of his warriors, and it belonged to him of right. Indeed, even Vienna, and all that Ferdinand possessed in Germany, belonged to him, since he had invaded those countries in person, and had hunted there. Charles V threatened to attack the Turks, he should not need to go far, they were making ready to advance to meet him. "I am the sultan," said the letter which Suleiman gave to the ambassador, "the great emperor, the highest and most excellent, I have reduced the Greek crown to subjection, the White and the Black Sea,—with God's help and my own labours, after the fashion of my father and grandfather, with my own person and my sword, have I conquered for myself the kingdom and the King of Hungary." He replied to the Austrian proposition with the demand—made far more in earnest—that Ferdinand would surrender all the fortresses which he still possessed in a part of Hungary.†

Suleiman lived only in the thought of making Constantinople once more the capital of the world, he called Charles V merely King of Spain, he claimed the exclusive title of emperor (which the East called Caliph of Rum), and was determined to restore it to its full significancy.

We see from a letter of Ferdinand's of the 17th March, 1531, what a powerful impression the insolent answer brought by his ambassadors made upon him. He represents to his brother how contrary it is to all reason and honour to suffer a kingdom like Hungary, so great and noble and fertile, and so many innocent souls, all created in the image of the living God, to fall into the hands of the Turkish tyrant. It was also to be considered that this would lay open all Europe to him. The sultan would take possession on the one side of Bohemia and Moravia, on the other, of Inner Austria and Istria; from Signa he would not have far to go to the march of Ancona and Naples.‡

In a succeeding letter, he conjures the emperor not to defer the preparations for resistance, because the advance of the Ottomans was still doubtful, "For the danger is great," says he, "the time short, and my force insignificant or null."§

When it was seen that the sultan's projects were serious, that he really contemplated, either immediately, or after a short delay, marching on the German frontier, this prospect naturally dictated the policy of the two brothers.

It was a moment like that in the beginning of the tenth century, when the Hungarians first possessed themselves of their settlement, and pushed on from thence westward, plundering and laying waste by the way. The West had indeed made enormous progress, and had far better means of defence than it then possessed, but the enemy was also incomparably more powerful and more dangerous.

On considering how he was to be encountered, it became obvious that the greatest obstacle to an efficient defence was the divided state of Germany. "The succours of the empire," said Ferdinand in his first letter, "will come up very slowly. You must hold it for certain, that Luther's adherents, even if they are convinced of the necessity for their aid, and inclined to grant it, will yet withhold it, because they fear that if the Turks are conquered, and the peace with France, England and Italy continues, our arms will be turned against them; they think that the victorious soldiery will not be satisfied with the blood they have shed, but will seek out more to slake their thirst."

We have already seen how great an influence Ferdinand's counsels had on Charles V. They were, indeed, always well-timed and judicious, and bear the stamp of resolution and promptitude. Ferdinand now had no hesitation in advising his brother to come to a peaceful arrangement with the Protestants, in so far as that was possible, without prejudice to the essential points of the Catholic faith. He said that their zeal must be allowed to consume itself, for the more water was thrown on it, the fiercer it burned. They must be conciliated at a diet. They would willingly grant aid against the Turks, as soon as they saw themselves secure in all that related to "their vain superstitions."‖

As early as February, 1531, an attempt was made by the emperor, as was always the case

* Report of the envoys and the letters of Suleiman and Ibrahim. Gevay, Urkunden und Actenstücke, Heft i.

† From Suleiman's letter, Gevay, Urkunden und Actenstücke, Heft i. p. 91. Pity that this is rather an extract, as well as No. vii., than a translation.

‡ Gevay, i. 99. The same opinion appears again in the second part, but somewhat altered.

§ 27th March. Vra Magestad si es razon ni cordura, de estar assi desapercebidos y desunidos, alla defensa necesaria debaxo desta sombra de operation dudosa, cerca de lo qual suplico a V. Md. quiera mirar y tener proveydo lo que convenga porque el peligro es muy grande y el tiempo breve, y mi pusanza muy poca o ninguna. (Br. A.)

‖ Assentandose esto avria mas disposition y menos ympedimento para resistir al Turco assi en los principes como en las otras personas, a lo qual ayudaran de mejor gana, estando assecurados dello que toca a sus vanas creencias. (Prima 27 Marzo.)

in Germany, as soon as any division assumed the appearance of danger, through the intervention of the Palatinate and Mainz, to bring about a reconciliation; but as the Protestants demanded, as a preliminary to all negotiations, that the proceedings of the Imperial Chamber should at least be stayed for a time, nothing came of it. The emperor declared that it would be difficult for him to undo any thing that had been determined by the Estates of the empire.*

But Ferdinand now urgently pressed for this concession. On the 27th April, he sent the emperor an opinion of the council of war on the plan of defence against the Turks. Meanwhile, in order to avert the danger arising from the coalitions and practices of the Lutherans, he advised his brother no longer to resist their demands.

The emperor therefore, in convoking a diet at Regensburg, directed his fiscal "to suspend the proceedings, which he had been authorised by the recess of Augsburg to set on foot in religious matters, till the approaching diet."† This rendered negotiation at least possible, and afforded a prospect of uniting the strength of the empire to meet any pressing emergency.

This prospect was, however, as yet very remote.

King Ferdinand, the author of these conciliatory measures, would sometimes have preferred to come to an agreement with the Turks, even under the most unfavourable conditions. In the days in which the events in Switzerland had awakened all his zeal and ambition against the innovators, he determined to make immense concessions with regard to Hungary. In the instructions of the 5th November, 1531, he desired his ambassadors, whom he sent to Constantinople, to begin by refusing to cede any part of his Hungarian dominions; but, in case the sultan should absolutely decline to treat on these terms, they were then to listen to his demands. They were to try at least to keep possession of the castles nearest to the German frontier, or to negotiate their surrender for the sum the woiwode had formerly offered. But if this also could not be obtained, if the sultan should be inflexible, and insist on a free surrender of all the castles to the woiwode, they should have full powers to consent even to that; only with the reservation, that both these castles and the whole kingdom of Hungary should revert to Ferdinand at the death of the woiwode. So great were the concessions Ferdinand was prepared to make.‡ For so remote a contingency as the death of his rival, he was willing to surrender all that yet belonged to him in Hungary. So high was the price he set upon peace with Turkey. He wished his brother and the pope to be included in the truce. If his brother broke it, it should be the same as if he broke it himself. And indeed Charles V. exhorted him to leave nothing untried, in order to conclude a treaty with the Turks.

But these offers were already vain. Before an ambassador had reached the Turkish frontier, news arrived of the vast warlike preparations of the sultan by land and by sea. On the 26th April, 1532, Suleiman set out on the campaign that was to decide the struggle with his mightiest foe, the Emperor Charles, in whose person, as far as it was possible, the power of the West was represented.§

A Venetian chronicle has left us a description of this expedition, which reminds us of the pomp of the earliest eastern monarchs.|| The march was opened by one hundred and twenty pieces of artillery; then came eight thousand Janissaries, overjoyed at being led against the Germans, and followed by troops of camels loaded with an enormous quantity of baggage. After them came the Sipahis of the Porte, two thousand horse; to whom was entrusted the holy standard, the Eagle of the Prophet, gorgeously adorned with gems and pearls, which had already waved at the conquest of Rhodes. To this were attached the young boys who were exhibited as the tribute from subject Christians, and were educated at the Porte; dressed in cloth of gold, with long locks like women, red hats with white plumes on their heads, and lances of exquisite Damascus workmanship in their hands. Behind them was borne the sultan's crown, which had shortly before been brought to Constantinople by a Sanuto from St. Canziano at Venice, at the cost of 120,000 ducats. Then followed the immediate retinue of the sultan,—a thousand men of gigantic stature, and of the greatest personal beauty that it was possible to find; some leading hounds in a leash, others holding hawks on their fist, all armed with bows and arrows. In the midst of them rode Suleiman, in a garment of crimson velvet embroidered with gold, a snow-white turban decorated with precious stones, dagger and sabre at his side, and mounted on a chestnut horse. He was followed by the four wesirs, the most remarkable of whom was Ibrahim, who bore the title of chief counsellor of the sultan, vicegerent of the whole empire of the same, and of all his slaves and barons; after them came the remaining lords of the court, with their attendants. The whole wore an appearance of discipline and obedience, and moved on-

* Instructions how we two, Ludwig, Count Stolberg, and Wolf von Affenstein, knight, are to treat with his imperial majesty: Tuesday after Estomihi (23d February). Likewise: Summary note of what we have negotiated with his imperial majesty. (W. A.)

† "For excellent and sincere reasons we commend thee earnestly, that thou wilt completely stay such proceedings on account of religion, as thou hast in hand, in virtue of our recess of Augsburg, between now and the next coming diet." Copy of a letter of the Elector of Mainz, 25th July.

‡ Instructio de iis quæ—Leonardus Comes de Nogarolis et Josephus a Lamberg — apud ser^{mum} Turcarum imperatorem nomine nostro agere debent, Gevay. ii. (1531.) Sicubi vero de hac quoque conditione fuerit desperatum, videlicet quod Turcus gratuito et sine pecunia castra illa omnia Waywodæ reddi voluerit, tum demum sic fortuna volente fiat per eosdem oratores nostros de iis omnibus promissio.

§ Avviso venuto di Ragusi di un nuovo esercito messo da Solimano per ritornar una secunda volta alla città di Vienna l'anno nuovo 1532, in der Chronica Ven., which Guazzo uses, but with great freedom.

|| Marchiando con gran solazzo verso Vienna.

wards without the slightest tumult or disorder

Such was the pomp and majesty with which the Sublime Porte rose up and advanced to take possession of the empire of the world From all sides the armed bands of its subjects hastened to join its standard The army which crossed the frontier of Hungary in June was reckoned at two hundred and fifty thousand men

Such was the camp in which Ferdinand's ambassadors at length arrived But what negotiations were likely to have power to stem this torrent?

I do not find that the envoys adhered very strictly to their instructions They proceeded, however, so far as to promise both the sultan and the wesir a yearly tribute for that part of Hungary which was still in Ferdinand's hands On the wesir this made some impression, but the sultan utterly rejected it "For who would assure him," he said, "that while he was at peace with Ferdinand, his brother, the King of Spain, would not attack him? But he would seek out that monarch, who, for three years past, had boasted of achieving great things If the King of Spain has the courage," added he, "let him await me in the field With God's grace, I shall come up with him, and then let God's will decide between us"

The ambassadors were asked how long it took to reach Regensburg, they answered that, by the shortest way, a man must ride for a month This long march the Ottomans seemed resolved to undertake

And in Regensburg the States of the empire were just assembled to hold the long-deferred diet, on the 17th April, the proceedings had been opened

The emperor wished for an augmentation of the succours already granted him in Augsburg An opinion of the council of war had been given in, according to which ninety thousand men, of whom twenty thousand were to be light horse, were required * The emperor wished to have sixty thousand from the empire, promising, in that case, to furnish thirty thousand at his own expense But it was quite contrary to all the precedents of the empire to increase a former grant None of the delegates or envoys of the States were prepared for it, and the subsidies already voted—forty thousand foot and eight thousand horse—were larger than any ever granted before On the 28th of May, the emperor declared himself satisfied, and only urged that the troops might be assembled as rapidly and in as effective a state as possible The place of meeting was not, as at first intended, Regensburg, but Vienna,—nearer to the enemy The whole body of troops were to meet there on the 15th of August For the first time, the military constitution of the empire was in real and active operation

Even while the diet was sitting, meetings of the circles were convoked, commanders appointed, and their pay provided, and the whole armament gradually put in a train

But the thing on which the execution of all these decrees depended was, the result of the negotiations with the Protestants

What would be the consequence of their rejection was soon seen, when the emperor prepared to bring his own army into the field He was particularly in want of fire-arms and of powder, and he was obliged to apply to the cities of Strasburg Augsburg, Ulm, Nurnberg, Constance and Frankfurt, to come to his aid with theirs They were all Protestants †

Even the Catholic States observed to the emperor that, before making war abroad, they must be secure of peace at home ‡

It may even be asserted that the religious dissensions of the Germans were not among the feeblest of the motives that prompted Suleiman's undertaking Whenever the ambassadors in the Turkish camp said that the emperor enjoyed the dutiful attachment of his subjects, they were asked, whether he had made peace with Martin Luther The ambassadors replied, that indeed disputes sometimes arose in Christendom, but that they did not interfere with the general welfare, the peace in question would soon be concluded §

This was now to be seen Let us turn our attention to the negotiations, momentous as is the crisis at which we are now arrived, these are interesting and important on other and more lasting grounds

NEGOTIATIONS WITH THE PROTESTANTS

When, in the summer of 1531, the negotiations were opened, the Catholics thought to resume them at the point where they had been broken off at Augsburg

But it was immediately evident how widely circumstances were altered The Protestants no longer made, they received, petitions They declared that it no longer seemed to them advisable to attempt to bring about a unity of religion, they, for their parts, were determined to adhere to their protest and confession, and would render a further account of them before a Christian council

They had a corresponding answer ready for every other proposal.

They were requested no longer to deprive the clergy of "their own" They replied, that

* They demanded 32,000 foot with long spears, 10,000 with short arms, P000 good marksmen 500 arquebuses, and a few thousand men to serve the artillery This was reckoned at 118 pieces, falcons, falconets, culverines, nightingales carronades, mortars, &c —Opinion of the Council of War The Berlin archives contain the letters of Barfuss, concerning the first proceedings of the diet, in which we see that the opening of it took place on the 17th April

† Furstenberg to Frankfurt, 7th June

‡ Denken Chf FF und Stande, wo der eusserlich krieg statlichen sol volnbracht werden, dass zuvor die hohe Notdurft erfordern wolle, anheym den Frieden zu halten, damit ein yder wiss, wie er neben dem andern sitz,——dass auch in allen andern Artikeln vermog E K M Ausschreybens daneben furgeschritten, gehandelt,—einer mit dem andern beschlossen werde —The electors, princes, and states think, that if foreign war is to be carried on grandly, the first thing necessary will be, to keep the peace at home, so that every man may know how he sits next to his neighbour,—that also in all other articles in virtue of Y I M 's summons, affairs should be proceeded with, negotiated, and one with another concluded.

§ Report of the ambassadors, p. 31

if the bishops were allowed to retain their jurisdiction (for that was what was chiefly meant by "their own"), it would be putting a sword into their hands, wherewith at any time to extirpate the true doctrine.

Farther, the emperor renewed the request that the exercise of the ancient ritual, especially the communion in one kind, should be permitted. Bruck, the Chancellor of Saxony, replied that, in that case, the communion in both kinds must be permitted throughout the empire; peace could not be established so long as the liberty with regard to the two most important sacraments was not perfectly equal throughout the nation.

Lastly, the election was mentioned. Turk, the Chancellor of Mainz, expressed his opinion that the opposition of the Protestant party was raised only with a view to promote their religious interests. Dr Bruck replied, that he could assure him that his party had no fear whatever for their religion; it had penetrated too deeply into the hearts of the people: every one now knew how to discern right from wrong. The serious intention of the Protestants was, that the king should either allow the thing to come to a legal settlement, or content himself with ruling over those who had elected him.*

Such are the most important points of these negotiations, which fill huge bundles of documents in various archives.† The elector palatine kept up a constant correspondence with the landgrave, the Elector of Mainz with the Elector of Saxony, and both of them with each other, and with the other members of the Schmalkaldic league. Occasionally, imperial plenipotentiaries came to Weimar; the Elector of Mainz took the opportunity, during his journey between Halle and Aschaffenburg, to speak with one or other of the most influential functionaries of Saxony; lastly, the two chancellors met in Bitterfeld, and drew up new proposals, which they sent to Brussels. The emperor turned pale when this affair, to which he had such a repugnance, was brought before him again; but he did not refuse to hear it, asked his brother's advice, and moderated or confirmed his propositions accordingly.

So long as there remained the faintest possibility of an accommodation with the Turks, we need not wonder that no progress was made in these affairs. In Schweinfurt, where the conferences were held in the beginning of the year 1532, not the smallest advance was made; the mediators deemed it best to let the business of the election entirely drop; and in Nurnberg, whither the negotiations were transferred, in order to be nearer the emperor, the mediators at first only renewed the old proposals, and even added some limitations.‡

It was not till positive intelligence was received that the sultan's progress could not be arrested, and that he was advancing in greater force than ever, that the two parties began earnestly to endeavour to accommodate their differences.

Not that they had the smallest idea of coming to a perfect agreement. The Protestants aspired to nothing more than to see the position they had taken up at least provisionally recognised by the emperor. They demanded the proclamation of a general peace, and the suspension of the proceedings of the Imperial Chamber, by which they felt themselves aggrieved.

But even these proved extremely difficult to obtain.

The mediators had again used the expression, "No one shall dispossess another of his own." No wonder if this provoked the opposition of the Protestants. There was again no mention of any peace, except that between the several States, whereas the Protestants demanded that the peace "between his imperial majesty and themselves should be also proclaimed to all the States of the German nation."

Another obstacle to an arrangement was, the description of the council. The Protestants had demanded "a council in which questions should be terminated according to the pure word of God." This description was pronounced to be insidious, and not Catholic. But as "a general free council, such as was determined on at the diet of Nurnberg," were the words substituted, the Protestants had ample reason to be content, since they had always insisted on an adherence to the resolutions of that diet.

But the difficulty arising from the proceedings of the Chamber was much greater.

* Dr Bruck's Report of what he negotiated with Dr Turk in Bitterfeld, Wednesday in the Christmas holidays (27th December, 1531). There was a second meeting, on Thursday after the Purification B V M (5th February), concerning which there is a similar report in the Weim Arch.

† In Weimar, Cassel, Magdeburg, Vienna. (See Bucholtz, Bd ix. Erhard, Ueberlieferungen, Bd. i.)

‡ Endliche Mittel und Furschlag worauf Kais Mt uf d' Schweinfurtischen Handlung empfangenen Bericht — zu handeln befohlen. — Final means and proposals whereupon his imperial majesty, on the receipt of the negotiations at Schweinfurt, has commanded us to treat. Monday after Boniface (10th June). It is an error in most editions of Luther's Works (e g, Walch, xvii p 2202), that the proposals were given in at Schweinfurt. The Protestants sent their answer on the 12th June. In Art I they missed the words, "who adopt in future into their doctrine the confession and apologia they have already made which they acknowledge themselves bound by Christian duty to accept." Art 2 concerning the council, they allege that the words, "that it shall determine according to the pure word of God alone," are wanting. So it goes on, and it is evident that they did not in the least give way. On the 18th July, on the contrary, they prayed, "that as to outward things, not belonging to God's word and to conscience, a general, permanent, internal peace may be treated of, and that the same may be concluded." This turn of things was expressly confirmed by a letter from John Frederic to the count of Nuenar, Sunday after St James (30 July, 1532), wherein he complains that he has been detained eight weeks at Nurnberg, and then reports the negotiations. "His imperial majesty's mind is kept in such a state by the two electors, that nothing advantageous could be transacted; and we on our parts remarked so many difficulties therein, that we could not treat on those articles with the approbation of God or with a good conscience. Hence we have at last entirely rejected the articles, which ought to have been conducive to unity, since such were the terms offered, and have discussed how a general peace should be brought about in the empire." (Weim Arch.)

The idea of attacking the Protestants by process of law, was far more that of the majority than of the emperor. The tribunal itself was, as we have seen, an institution representing the States. We remember how much trouble it cost to set limits to the influence of the imperial court over it. In the proceedings of that tribunal against the Protestants, resolved on at Augsburg, and already in full progress, the Catholic party beheld its most powerful weapon. And in these they obstinately persisted, notwithstanding all their occasional declarations of the necessity of a peace. In the draft of a recess which they laid before the emperor on the 10th July, an article declares that, in matters of religion, the recess of Augsburg must be adhered to generally, and especially by the Imperial Chamber.* The papal legate also refused to give his assent to an inhibition of the imperial fiscal in affairs of faith.

Such were the perplexities in which the emperor was involved. In order to resist the Turks, the tranquillity of the empire was absolutely necessary. But the sole condition which could assure peace to the Protestants, the Catholics refused him the power to grant.†

At length the imperial court came to this compromise — in the public proclamation, to announce only the peace, but to give the Protestants a private assurance of the suspension of the legal proceedings. This, too, was not so complete as the Protestants wished. They had demanded a declaration that the emperor would, neither through his fiscal, nor through his chamber, nor in any other court of justice, and also, neither officially nor at the instigation of any other person or persons, allow proceedings to be taken against Saxony or his kinsmen and allies. The emperor was not to be induced to agree to so many express clauses. He only promised, that he would stay all law proceedings instituted "by his majesty's fiscal and others,"‡ in matters of the faith against the Elector of Saxony and his associates, until the convocation of the council. This promise did not absolutely offend the majority, and yet might be interpreted in the sense of the Protestants, and as satisfying their principal demand.

On the other hand, that party had determined on a great concession, which is indeed implied in those words. Their original meaning had been that the assurance given them should also avail for all those who might join their confession in future; they had even demanded freedom of preaching and of the Lord's Supper according to their ritual, for the subjects of foreign dominions. But this, again, it was impossible to obtain from the emperor. The principal motive which he used to overcome the objections of the legate, was, that he put a check to Protestantism by means of this treaty.§ The second demand was, in fact, the same which the city cantons of Switzerland had made, — the same which had led to war in that country, and to such disastrous consequences. Luther himself said that it could not be complied with by their opponents, could it be hoped, for example, that Duke George would freely admit the evangelical doctrine into Leipsig? Impossible, — they, on their side, would not permit neighbouring princes to interfere in the internal affairs of their country. Luther was, as we have seen, a faithful ally of the territorial power of the princes. His conception of the empire likewise prevented his approving such a demand. He said it was as if they, the Protestants, wanted to take advantage of the emperor, that is to say, to usurp an influence over the conduct of public affairs, in consequence of the necessity for defence. He was rather comforted that "the emperor, the supreme authority ordained of God, should so graciously offer to make peace, and give such clement and liberal commands for that end." "I esteem it no otherwise," says he, "than that God held out his hand to us." That the progress of the evangelical faith was thus impeded, disquieted him little, he said, "everybody must believe at his own peril," that is, must be sufficiently strong in his belief to encounter whatever dangers it might subject him to.‖ Elector John was entirely of the same opinion, it was in harmony with the purely defensive attitude he had assumed from the first, his ruling sentiment was, the necessity for a perfect justification of all he did by his own conscience. He did not suffer himself to be carried away by the brilliant extension of the league, at the head of which he stood, to swerve from the principles on which it was originally founded. He, too, thought, like Luther, that they ought not to give up the present good, the greatest on earth — peace, — for the sake of a contingent addition to their numbers. And accordingly he did not allow any limiting clause to be inserted in the treaty, — he bound himself by no promise for the future, — except that those States alone should be admitted into it, who belonged to the league, including Markgrave George and Nurnberg, all the princes and States, in short with whom we are already familiar, and who had been joined by Nordhausen and Hamburg. The Landgrave of Hessen, who entertained the contrary opinion, was at first not contented, but he afterwards acquiesced.¶

* Letter from Planitz to Taubenheim, 11th July.

† Declaration of the emperor, sent by Planitz to Saxony, Thursday after St John the Baptist (27th June). "And since the above mentioned States have seen good to abandon all further means and negotiations for peace, and adhere to the recess of Augsburg, his majesty requests with peculiar earnestness of the above mentioned States, that they will consider what may be the consequences to the cause of the faith."

‡ He could be brought to nothing beyond the addition of the words, "and others." In the original draft his majesty's fiscal only was mentioned. The negotiations remained wavering till the day of the final resolution, the Tuesday after S. Mary Magdalene.

§ Granvella urged the "inconvenient irremediable, sans quelque traite pour (?) infecter le reste de la chrétienté, comme l'expérience l'a evidemment demontré."—Bucholtz, ix p 32.

‖ Reflections of Luther and Justus Jonas. De Wette, iv 339. In his somewhat later reflections he reminds his prince, in his relations with his neighbours, of the principle, quod tibi non vis fieri, alteri ne feceris.

¶ Opinion of his theologians, Neudecker Urkk 199.

It may be regarded as a peculiar favour of Providence, that the aged Elector of Saxony lived to witness these days of peace. We have seen above how much of the merit of founding the evangelical church was due to this simple-hearted man. He now enjoyed great consideration in the empire. Even a member of the imperial court (Count Nuenar) describes him as "the one father of the German land in things human and divine."* But his mind was too much imbued with the sentiments of a prince of the empire, to be satisfied so long as he was at variance with the emperor. It formed part of the fulfilment of his destiny, to have regained the friendship of his chief; to have lived to see the legality of the position he had taken up with regard to the supreme power, acknowledged, after it had been so strenuously denied; and thus to have made a most important step towards the permanence of the religious establishment of which he was the founder. In August, both the public declarations and the private assurances of the emperor appeared. Shortly afterwards, when the elector had been once more taking the pleasure of the chase, with his two daughters and the fugitive Electress of Brandenburg, and had come back in a very cheerful mood, he was struck with sudden death by apoplexy. "He who can trust on God," says Luther, in the epitaph he wrote for his master and friend, "abides in security and peace."

Meanwhile, however, the emperor, pressed by necessity, determined to make concessions to the Protestants, which had neither been suggested nor approved by the majority; a line of conduct which altered his whole position. The experiment which he had made in Augsburg — to govern with the majority — he now relinquished; while the majority, seeing that they did not find in him the support they expected, raised such an opposition to him at the diet of Regensburg as he had never before experienced. The States made reproachful representations concerning his entire system of government; — the delays of business; the appointment of foreigners, even to places in the chancery; the arrears of his share of the salaries of the Imperial Chamber; his arbitrary conduct towards Würtenberg, Maastricht (which he was accordingly compelled to separate from Brabant and reinstate in its ancient liberties), and Utrecht.† Not only did he not dare to publish the assurances above mentioned in favour of the Protestants, but he was compelled, in direct contradiction with them, to confirm the decrees which had been passed at the recent visitation of the Imperial Chamber, wherein the execution of the recess of Augsburg was enjoined afresh. Nay, the majority even held out a sort of distant menace of the possibility of a coalition of the two religious parties against him. On reading in the recess of the empire, that the States vehemently pressed for a council, we are not at first particularly struck with the fact; but if we weigh these words with greater attention, and mark their origin, we shall see its vast importance. In the summer of 1531, Bavaria and Hessen had jointly determined upon this point: at a meeting between Landgrave Philip and Dr. Leonhard von Eck, at Giessen, it had been determined that, if the pope deferred the council longer, they would urge the emperor to summon one of his own authority; if the emperor also, from one cause or another, neglected to convoke it, an assembly of the States should be called to discuss the means of restoring the unity of religion and of putting a stop to crime.‡ It is obvious that the opposition to the emperor was one means of uniting two leaders of the hostile parties in this determination; still the fact is very extraordinary. It was, indeed, not with the emperor's good will that he promised, in the recess of Regensburg, that if the general council was not convoked by the pope within six months, and was not actually held within a year, he would summon an assembly of the empire, to deliberate on the evils that afflicted the German nation generally, and on the means of removing them. He distinctly felt that this resolution was forced upon him, and might become dangerous. And, indeed, he avoided summoning another diet for eight years, from the fear that it should constitute itself a national assembly, and pass decrees on religious affairs entirely at variance with his own.§

Such was now the aspect of things in Germany. Not only did the two religious parties stand confronted in a hostile attitude, but new divisions had broken out in their own ranks. The Catholic majority was discontented with the emperor; while the Landgrave of Hessen exchanged sarcastic, nay, insulting letters with the electoral prince, John Frederic of Saxony, who now filled the place of his father.‖ Hessen and Bavaria, on the other hand, had formed a closer political connexion; but this could lead to no result, since the contrast between the two religious tendencies was nowhere so strongly exhibited as in the persons of these two

* William von Nuenar to John Frederic, 11th June (W. A.), "Dann wir haben leyder keynen mynschen, den wir für ein vater des duytschen vaterlandes in gotlichen und menschlichen Sachen achten mogen, denn allein U. F. G. Herr Vater und U. F. G., wir wollen widder mit gotlicher Hülfe um U. F. G. stan." &c. — "For unhappily we have no man whom we can reverence and respect as a father of the German fatherland in divine and human things, save only Y. P. Grace's father, and Y. P. G.: we will again, with the divine help, stand around Y. P. Grace," &c.

† Letter from Fürstenberg, 8th July. The emperor replied to a reproach of this kind, that the suggestion was wholly "untimely and inconsiderate, and, as it appeared to H. M., not made with the knowledge of all the States; all in biting and sharp words." Fürstenberg finds the reproaches very just; but he was not pleased at them, because they were likely to irritate the emperor, who had left his wife and child in order to attend to the business of the empire.

‡ Correspondence in the Weim. Arch.; extracts therefrom, and article of the agreement of Giessen in the Appendix.

§ Declaration of the emperor to the pope, in the year 1539. Rainaldus, xxi. 104. Rem esse periculi plenam, alia indicere comitia, perpensa maxime sanctione ordinum imperii, — ut Pp. Clemens de convocando concilio rogaretur, quo non convocato Cæsar illud convocaret, — ac si huic muneri is deesset, ut concilium nationale cogerent.

‖ There is a whole roll of these letters copied in the W. A.

princes The emperor and Saxony had framed an accommodation, but it was easy to foresee what difficulties would attend its execution

The emperor no longer appeared, as at Augsburg, in the full vigour to be expected from his time of life He was ill the whole summer, a hurt in the leg, which he got by a fall while hunting the wolf, took so dangerous a turn, that his physicians thought his thigh must be amputated, and one night the sacraments were administered to him The injury was afterwards renewed by the part he imprudently took in a procession, and perhaps by excesses of another kind, during the diet, he repaired to the baths of Abach in the hope of a cure, and was sometimes inaccessible even to his brother When the States went to announce to him that the succours for the Turkish war were granted they found him in his bedroom, sitting on a wooden bench without cushions, in the plainest dress, with a green bough in his hand, with which he was brushing away the flies, "in his vest," says the Frankfurt ambassador, "with so lowly an air, that the meanest servant could not bear himself so humbly."*

CAMPAIGN AGAINST THE TURKS

And this feeble and sickly emperor, — this empire torn by such deep-rooted dissensions,— were now to sustain the attack of the mighty chief of the Ottomans, at the head of his countless bands How different was his appearance! When Ferdinand's ambassadors had audience of him, not far from Belgrade, they were first conducted far and wide through the camp, both of the foot and horse soldiers, splendidly accoutred, then through the ranks of the Janissaries, who met them with a somewhat insolent air, until they were received near the emperor's tent with trumpets and clarions, and at length were permitted to enter and to behold the lord of all these armies in his splendour, sitting on a golden throne, near him was a splendid crown, and before him, on the pillars of the throne, two magnificent sabres in scabbards inlaid with mother-of-pearl, and a richly ornamented bow and quiver The ambassadors valued the jewels they saw at 1,200,000 ducats On the 20th July, the Turkish army crossed the Drave over twelve bridges of boats in the neighbourhood of Essek Suleiman marched through Hungary, as if it had been his own undisputed territory The castles which he passed sent out their keys to meet him He punished the magnates who had deserted Zapolya, his approach struck terror into the others, and many of those who had remained true to Ferdinand, and now saw themselves abandoned, fell off from the house of Austria

Germany now began to make serious preparations for defence

The first who appeared in the field, even before the negotiations had come to an end, were the Nurnbergers They were bound to furnish only one company, but "for the honour of the empire and the weal of Christendom" they had equipped two; altogether eight hundred men, among whom two hundred were armed with matchlocks and fifty with arquebuses Meanwhile, they, with some of their neighbours, recruited a hundred reiters in Brunswick (among whom we find a Kamp, a Bursberg, and a Munchhausen), who were hospitably received on their arrival in the city, furnished with beer, wine and oats, and on the 21st of August, took their way against the enemy under Sebastian von Jessen and Martin Pfinzing Besides this, Nurnberg gave the emperor fifteen pieces of heavy artillery, 175 hundred-weight of powder, 1000 lances for the infantry, 200 coats of armour for the heralds, and a large stock of flour † Such were the munificent contributions of a single city, and all the others vied with Nurnberg The imperial deputy, who carried to Ulm the requisition to prepare for war, had not returned to his quarters, when he heard the sound of the drum, calling the people to arms Augsburg instantly declared itself ready to send all its artillery to Vienna It appears from a letter of the Frankfurt envoy, that the firmness with which the emperor had resisted the majority, had produced a great impression on the cities ‡ For a moment, the Protestants raised the question, whether it would not be expedient to keep together, and to fight under a captain of their own, but this suggestion was speedily dismissed, it would have involved a fresh division, and they chose rather to serve according to the order of the circles Meetings were held in all the circles at which a captain was nominated, to whom each State in the circle delivered a list of the men it intended to furnish It was his business to see that the complement was actually under arms, whom it admonished to be obedient to their appointed leader He had also the right to fill all offices with the most capable men of the circle The persons from whom he was to receive his pay were determined, and were in return to enjoy certain privileges § In the circle of Lower Saxony, doubtless on account of the daily increasing religious dissensions, it was found impossible to come to a unanimous choice of a captain, the emperor, therefore, in virtue of the right which in this case devolved upon him, nominated the young Markgrave Joachim of Brandenburg At the beginning of August, the whole empire was in a state of warlike preparation "Daily," says Cardinal Campeggi, in a letter of the 8th, "do we see the finest companies of horse and

* Furstenberg, Tuesday after Whitsuntide, and in other letters Ferdinand to Maria, 3d April, 1532 Gevay, p 74

† Mullner's Annals "all this was destined to the fortification and provisioning of the city of Vienna"

‡ "Es erwindet fürwahr nicht an Ks Mt und wird I Mt gnedig Gemüt und Herz auch von den Stadten dermassen gespürt, dass sie I Mt mehr als ihre gebuhrliche Hulfe senden"—"There will truly be nothing wanting to your I M, and your I Majesty's gracious mind and heart are so understood by the cities that they send more than their proper contingent"

§ Proceedings of the meeting of the circle of the Upper Rhine, at which Philip von Daun was appointed Frankfurt Records

foot pass through Regensburg, they go forth in high spirits, and doubt not of victory" The emperor, too, was full of courage He remarked, that he could only be the gainer in this war, whether he were the victor or the vanquished Were he conquered, he would leave behind him an illustrious name, and secure his entrance into paradise, if he were victorious, he would not only gain favour in the sight of God, but perhaps extend the empire to its ancient limits, live glorious on earth, and bequeath a great name to posterity * He appeared to wish nothing more earnestly than to meet his adversary face to face

Meanwhile a most glorious, not to say marvellous, feat of arms had already been achieved in Hungary

We are acquainted with the name of Nicholas Jurischitz, one of the two ambassadors of King Ferdinand to the sultan, in 1530, 1531 At that time, when the envoys found all negotiations fruitless, they said they saw that Hungary was destined to be the grave both of Turks and Christians Jurischitz now seemed resolved to prove the truth of this prediction He was just about to leave the city and castle of Gunz (where he filled the office of captain) to a lieutenant, and to join his sovereign with a small band of ten heavy and twenty light horsemen, when the approach of the Turks filled the town with crowds of fugitives He determined to remain, to afford these unhappy people at least a momentary defence, and to arrest the progress of the great army for a few days He never entertained a hope of making any successful resistance to such an enemy "I had made up my mind," says he, "to certain death" The Turks appeared in full force and began the siege in the customary manner, planted their cannon on the nearest heights, dug mines and tried to enter by the breaches Jurischitz had no other soldiers than his thirty reiters, the rest were all inhabitants of the town, or fugitive peasants, they might amount to about seven hundred in all Yet they drove back the Turkish storming parties eleven times, and made that dauntless resistance which nothing but the determination rather to die than surrender, could have inspired At length, however—as was inevitable—all was vain The Turks had thrown up two great heaps of rubbish to the height of the wall, on one of these they planted their largest guns, which now commanded the walls and under cover of their fire a broad way could be made from the other to the wall The assault thus prepared was made on the 28th of August by Janissaries and horsemen, and it was impossible, as may easily be imagined, to make any resistance to such a superiority both of numbers and position The besieged were soon driven into their last entrenchment, where they still maintained the fight, though with failing strength, already the Turkish banner floated from eight different points on the walls Jurischitz expected nothing but death "I rejoice," said he, "that God's grace hath appointed me so honourable an end" But he was reserved for a wondrous deliverance The defenceless fugitives—women, children and aged men—now beheld themselves given over to the fury of their terrible and barbarous foe At the moment when he was rushing upon them they uttered a cry, in which the imploring appeal to Heaven was blended with the shriek of despair, that piercing cry which nature forces unconsciously from the living creature when threatened with inevitable destruction If this can be called a prayer, never was prayer more instantly heard The conquering Ottomans recoiled with alarm from the terrific sound The resistance they had encountered had long appeared to them almost miraculous, and they now thought they saw fresh troops issue from every house, they imagined they beheld in the air a knight in full harness, brandishing his sword at them with menacing gestures. They retreated "The Almighty God," exclaimed Jurischitz, "has visibly saved us" †

We might liken this to the Delphic god who opposed the irruption of the Gauls into Greece, to the apparition which called aloud to Drusus, in the centre of Germany, "Thus far, and no farther," or to other of those sudden turns of fortune which, at the moment of their occurrence, have impressed the minds of men with a sense of the presence of a higher Power (under whatever form they conceived it),—but we will not venture into these regions, it is enough for us to say that dauntless valour and complete self-devotion were crowned with their usual success

Suleiman resolved to leave his brave enemy, who could not have held out one hour longer, under a guard, and to march onward

In the interval, however, the emperor had had time to collect his forces He himself had raised 12,000 landsknechts, who had mustered in the neighbourhood of Augsburg Spanish grandees had come to win honour under the eye of their emperor, in the war against the infidels The Duke of Ferrara had sent a hundred huomini d' armi Other Italians arrived, under the conduct of the young Ippolito de' Medici, nephew of Pope Clement VII King Ferdinand's hereditary domains had done their best, and no means were neglected to raise money, he had even applied to several Netherland nobles, and to devout rich women, urging that no one could better employ his wealth than in the defence of Christendom ‡ But the militia of the empire formed the main strength of his army The great muster took place in the Tulner field, near Vienna The numbers cannot be precisely ascertained, the most credible accounts vary from 76,000 to 86,000 men On one point, however, they are all agreed,—that it was the finest army

* Niccolo Tiepolo, Relatione di 1533 Il che diceva sempre, che si vedeva non solamente pronto a questa impresa, ma quasi arder di desiderio che li venisse occasione di sorta che potesse honestamente esponere la persona sua a tal fortuna

† Letter from Jurischitz in Gobel's Beitragen, p 303—Also what Jovius heard from his own lips, lib xxx. p 105 Sepulveda, x 17—23

‡ Letter from Ferdinand to Maria Gevay, ii 23.

that had been seen in Christendom for centuries It combined the qualities which had won the great victories in Italy; German strength and discipline, Italian activity, and the dogged craftiness of the Spaniards But the German ingredient was by far the largest

Suleiman had advanced in the expectation that the divisions which reigned in Christendom, and especially in Germany, would tie the emperor's hands and render a vigorous and effective resistance impossible When he saw before him so numerous and well-appointed an army, he had not the courage (which he had so often vaunted) to seek them in the field.

Despatching his Akindschi, 15,000 in number, towards Austria, he himself marched into Styria and appeared before Grätz * The Akindschi were light troops, commanded by a chief, the crest of whose helmet was a vulture—the symbol of swiftness and rapacity They were, however, driven by one band of Germans into the hands of another, and almost annihilated, Grätz defended itself, and, in the mean time, tidings arrived that Doria had obtained signal successes over Zai-beg in the Ionian seas Suleiman recognised the ascendancy of the star of his rival, and determined to withdraw from so perilous a struggle by a rapid retreat †

The emperor had, as we have observed, wished to give battle to the enemy for a decisive victory might have restored Hungary to his brother But he was satisfied with this less brilliant result "God's grace has granted us the glory and the happiness," he writes to the pope, "to have put the common enemy of Christendom to flight, and to have averted the mischief which he designed to inflict on us"‡ He was fully sensible that this was not a mere momentary advantage It was a gain forever, that the fear of the warlike array of the Germans —the impression of their superior force, had rendered the sultan averse to engage in the struggle, and had determined him to retreat

Doria, too, had gained brilliant advantages for the emperor He had driven the Ottoman squadron out of the Ionian seas, pursued them beyond Cerigo, and taken Coron, Patras and the Dardanelles in rapid succession Large cannon with Arabic inscriptions were brought to Genoa, and placed in the Doria chapel on the Molo §

The satisfaction of King Ferdinand was far less complete than that of his brother He had really hoped to recover Hungary—Belgrade not excepted, in the full tide of victory But the troops thought they had done enough in having repulsed the enemy from the frontiers of Germany The captains produced their instructions, in which no mention was made of the conquest of Hungary The commander-in-chief, Count Palatine Frederic, refused to advance. The main cause of this was, that Ferdinand had lost the favour of the nation by the zeal he had evinced for the Papacy, the people would make no conquests for him They wished rather to see him weaker than stronger, as soon became evident.

* True description of the second expedition into Austria From an old Nürnberg printed paper of 1539, in Göbel's Beiträgen, p 309 The writing is taken from the correspondence of the Count Palatine

† Schartlins Lebensbeschreibung, p 35 Hammer, iii p 118.

‡ Sandoval, ii.

§ Jovius, lib xxxi. Historia del Guazzo, p 124

CHAPTER VII.

INFLUENCE OF FRANCE RESTORATION OF WURTENBERG.

1533, 1534.

It had appeared as if Latin Christendom, united under the emperor and the pope, were about to fall with all its weight upon the seceders from its body, and to annihilate them

Instead of this, however, it happened that one of its chiefs was compelled, in order to ward off the attack of the powerful foes who more immediately threatened himself and his house, to come to terms with the Protestants, and to grant them temporary immunity The positive concession was not the only thing they gained; it was a no less important advantage to them to be thus associated in the great national enterprise, and to contribute their full share to the defence of their common fatherland

But meanwhile the intestine discords which we have noticed had broken out afresh among those from whom the Protestants had the most to fear

King Francis was unquestionably bound by treaties to assist the house of Austria against the Turks, but his pride forbade him to do this in the manner the emperor desired. Francis offered to attack the Turks in Egypt; but the imperialists suspected that his real purpose was, to arm under this pretext, and then to fall on Genoa and Naples, and they utterly refused his offer ‖

We have observed with what vehemence he rejected the proposal for a combined war against Switzerland

In the matter of the council, too, his answer was evasive He was much more anxious for the favour of the pope, who sought to avoid, than for the friendship of the emperor, who wished to convoke it ¶

For he never for a moment thought of regarding the concessions which he had been forced to make in Cambray (especially the renunciation of all claim to Genoa and Milan), as definitive He regarded these possessions as his own property, of which he had no right

‖ Letter from A de Burgo to Ferdinand. Rome, 2d March, 1531 Bucholtz, ix 90

¶ Gregorio Casali au Grand Maistre, 5 Maggio, 1531, Le Grand Histoire du Divorce, iii 542 Questa corte fin adesso è stata in gran timore del concilio, hora sono alquanto assicurati sì per le ultime lettere dell' imperatore, che sono state meno furiose delle altre, sì anche per quello si spera in voi altri

to rob his children, and he felt his honour wounded as often as he thought he had lost them

An alliance with the pope seemed to him the only means for their recovery

From day to day new differences broke out between the pope and the emperor

The emperor's earnest importunity for a council was very distressing to the court of Rome It had been represented to him, that while he demanded money from the pope, he deprived him of the means of raising it, since not a man was to be found who would advance a loan on ecclesiastical revenues, the reduction of which was expected from the council Besides this, Clement VII felt himself offended that so little respect was shown to his recommendations, that, in the granting of vacant benefices, less attention was paid to the interest of his nephew, Ippolito, than he had anticipated, that Cardinal Colonna, a sworn enemy of the court of Rome, was left at full liberty to do as he pleased in Naples But what chiefly inflamed the old resentment was, the emperor's decision in the affair of Ferrara The emperor had promised the pope, that if he saw the right was not on the side of his holiness, he would pronounce no decision at all Nevertheless, he now decided in favour of Ferrara "This," says a confidant of the pope, "has wounded his holiness's heart"—"Would to God," exclaims the chargé d'affaires of King Ferdinand, "that the emperor had not pronounced that sentence!" He thought he observed that the imperial party at court and in the sacred college had been weakened by it *

The King of France, on the other hand, had proposed to the pope the most honourable alliance that had ever been conferred on a papal house He offered the hand of his son, Henry of Orleans, whose prospect of the throne of France was by no means remote (and who, in fact, subsequently occupied it), to the pope's niece, Catharine de Medici.

The value attached to this connexion by the pope may be inferred from the treaty which he concluded on the 9th of June, 1531

The king's demands were by no means humble, above all, the creation of a principality for the young couple, consisting of Pisa and Leghorn, Reggio, Modena, Rubiera, Parma, and Piacenza, with these, Urbino, which had for a time belonged to Catharine's father —nay, even Milan and Genoa, were to be united The pope was to promise his aid to reconquer these districts †

The pope entered earnestly into the negotiations In the presence of the French ambassadors, Cardinal Grammont and the Duke of Albany, he declared himself ready, as soon as the marriage should be concluded, to cede Pisa, Leghorn, Modena, Reggio, and Rubiera, to the young couple, and whenever he and the king should deem it practicable and expedient, Parma and Piacenza, for which, however, the king was to grant compensation to the church, to be determined by commissioners appointed by both parties He expressed himself very willing to contribute his share to the reconquest of Urbino Concerning Genoa and Milan, he gave no decisive answer But he declared that he found the secret articles, in which this demand was contained, generally reasonable and just, and desired their execution as soon as a good opportunity should present itself ‡

It is evident how close was the common interest thus established between the king and the pope, in the entire reconstitution of Italy, and how totally this interest was at variance with that of the emperor

It followed, of course, that the pope kept his engagements with France as secret as possible

In August, 1531, he once ventured to say to the Austrian minister plenipotentiary, that he held it to be absolutely necessary to do something for the satisfaction of the King of France, he saw that the emperor would never give up Genoa and Milan, but would it not be possible to hold out hopes to that effect, without really fulfilling them?§ But the impression which even such a suggestion was calculated to make, was very unfavourable At least the pope said to the French ambassador, in allusion to it, that he saw himself under the necessity of concealing his good intentions towards France, and of begging for delay, but that the French needed not for one moment to doubt of his dispositions He several times admitted in confidence, that the emperor had pushed his advantages too far in the last treaty, and that it were to be wished that he would restore to the king his rightful property In March, 1532, the ambassador was convinced that it was the pope's sincere desire that the king should rule in Milan and the emperor in Naples, then he would believe that, placed between them, he might enjoy some power ‖

At the period we are come to, we no longer expect schemes like those which all this weighing of advantages, this leaning to France, which he sought to conceal, at length led the pope to contrive

In May, 1532, he sent a proposal to King Ferdinand, to abandon what he possessed of Hungary to the woiwode, and to indemnify himself for the loss in Italy, and especially in the Venetian territory He had utterly forgotten the lessons which others had learned from the war of the Ligue of Cambray The woiwode, whom he (though in the secret tribunal of conscience) had relieved from the censures which he had once pronounced against

* A de Burgo, 8th June, 1531, p 99

† Articles secrets of the marriage treaty, signed, like that, on the 24th April Among other demands was, "Ayde et secours audit futur epoux pour luy ayder à recouvrer l'etat et duché de Milan et la seigneurie de Gennes, qui luy appartiennent."

‡ Nre St père ayant vu les articles secrets les a trouvés et trouve très raisonnables —MS Bethune 8541, f 36 —I found the article and declaration in the King's Library at Paris

§ Burgo, 11th August, 101

‖ Despesches de l'eveque d'Auxerre, ambassadeur pour le roi Francois I près le Pape Clement, 11 Sept, 28 Oct, 4 Janv, 20 Mars. Bibl Royale MS Dupuis, nr 260.

him, in favour of the brothers of Austria, was now to ally himself with them against Venice The King of France was to do the same, and, as a recompense, was to have a part of the Milanese and a part of Piedmont Francesco Sforza was to be created Duke of Cremona, and to be propitiated by a territory formed out of the Milanese and Venetian domains — in short, a scheme exactly in the spirit of the restless policy of his immediate predecessor The desire to see the King of France once more powerful in Italy, had clothed itself in the most singular forms in his mind *

Negotiations were actually set on foot for the furtherance of this project, nor did it appear utterly out of the question to Ferdinand's plenipotentiary, nor probably to Ferdinand himself, but in the meantime the Ottoman invasion approached and demanded exclusive attention, and, while he was so occupied, circumstances altered

The emperor instantly reappeared in Italy It may be true, as has been affirmed, that want of money led him to dismiss his great army, and to leave his brother with an insufficient force another motive, however, doubtless was, that it was become extremely urgent for him to hold personal communication with the pope On the 5th December, he repaired to a fresh conference with him at Bologna.

The affair of the council necessarily claimed precedence of all others The emperor did not deceive himself as to the pope's desire to evade it † But he probably hoped that his presence, and fresh representations of the state of things in Germany (especially the danger of a national assembly), would extort some concession from the pope. The conferences began without delay the pope created a congregation for them, consisting of Cardinals Farnese, Cesis, and Campeggi, and Aleander, Archbishop of Brindisi, who held consistories on the matter The question was, whether a council should be definitively convoked, or whether an attempt should first be made to allay the pending quarrels between the Christian princes For these quarrels were always alleged by the pope as the excuse for his procrastination In the first consistory the cardinals declared for immediate convocation, on the ground that the attempt to effect the reconciliation alluded to was too remote and uncertain But the pope deferred receiving the decision till the next sitting, and in this, on the 20th December, it fell out in accordance with his wishes The majority declared, that until the reconciliation was effected, the council could not be held, nor any common measures be adopted against the Turks or the Lutherans ‡ The displeasure of the emperor may easily be imagined An attempt was made to save appearances, declarations were published that the council should, at all events, be held, and deputies were sent to Germany to make a show of preparing for it, but all this was, if I may use the expression, mere fencing These missions had no other serious purpose than that of persuading the Germans to abandon the thought of the national council This was the only point on which the emperor and the pope understood each other §

The maintenance of peace in Italy next came under discussion The emperor thought he had to expect an attack of Francis I on Genoa, and his scheme was, to prevent this by a coalition of all the Italian States for their mutual defence But in this, too, he experienced but feeble support from the pope In the presence of the emperor, Clement spoke indeed in favour of such a coalition, but in secret he gave the Venetian ambassador to understand, that in what he had said there, he had merely expressed the opinion of the emperor, not his own, and that he might cautiously intimate this to the republic ‖ The Venetians declared that their relation to the Ottoman prevented them joining this coalition, which was formed solely to favour Andrea Doria Another obstacle arose from the misunderstanding between the pope and Ferrara With the utmost difficulty, Clement was brought to promise the duke security for eighteen months ¶ At length the treaty was concluded, and the contributions which each was to furnish in the event of a war, determined But the negotiations themselves suffice to show how little cohesive force the league possessed They were, indeed, rather advantageous to Francis, inasmuch as they afforded him a fair occasion for complaining of the hostility which the emperor betrayed in these precautions

If the emperor had hoped to loosen the ties between the pope and the king by a compact of this kind, he had fallen into a gross delusion Against so honourable a family alliance as that proposed, no objections or representations were likely to have any effect.

In the following autumn the pope set out in person to conduct his niece to France. At Marseilles he had a meeting with King Francis, which was of incomparably more importance than his recent interview with the emperor

Unfortunately, from the nature of the case

---

* Andreas de Burgo to the Cl of Trent, 23d May, 1532, very circumstantial, see letters of 20th August, and 11th September

† He wrote this to his brother as early as the 29th July, 1531 Plus va l on avant, plus l on apperco t que le pape n'y (for the council) a voulenté et que le roy de France luy ne veult depiaire, pensant par ce moyen le tenir guigné (Brussels Arch)

‡ This information is not given by Pallavicini, but it is authentic nevertheless I took it from a despatch of the French ambassador, the Bishop of Auxerre, dated 24th December, 1532 " Sire, au premier consistoire, une partie des Cardinaux opina, qu'il falloit pourvoir de faire ung concille tant pour obvier aux Lutheriens que au Turc, disant que la chose seroit trop longue de vouloir a cette heure appoincter les princes chretiens, fut par notre st père la chose remis a correcture jusqu'au pronchain consistoire, qui fut vendredi dernier, auquel fut conclu par sa S^{te} et a la pluralité des voix que sans accorder lesd princes chretiens ne se pouvoit faire ny concille ny pourvoir au Turc ny auxd Lutheriens "

§ Extract from the Instructions to the nuncio, Ugo Rangoni Pallavicini, lib iii c xiii (V i p 327)

‖ " Que ce qu'il avoit dict present l'empereur, il l avoit dict comme opinion de l'empereur, mais non pas comme la sienne, et qu'il le fist entendre saigement à la S^{rie} " L'eveque d'Auxerre, 1 Janv 1533

¶ Compare Guicciardini (at that time vice-legate at Bologna, who was called to the conferences), lib. xx. p 109

(the negotiations being all conducted orally), we have no authentic documents concerning them The emperor received warning from Rome that it was not possible but that the pope and the king had some designs against him ;* and the testimony both of the Florentine confidants of the pope, and of so acute and excellent an observer as the Venetian ambassador, unanimously goes to prove that this was the case

Not only were French cardinals nominated at Marseilles, a much more important fact was, that the pope consented, at the king's request, to recal his nuncio in Switzerland, the Bishop of Veroli, who was thought to be well affected to the emperor †

Other circumstances soon show what had been concerted between the two sovereigns

The Duke of Orleans, husband of the pope's niece, laid claim to Urbino as the inheritance of his wife, and the papal nuncio in Germany did not conceal that the pope meant to support his claim ‡ He was, he said, certainly forbidden by treaty to attempt any changes, but it was impossible to call that a change, which was merely a restitution Urbino was a fief of the church, and it could not be believed that the emperor would espouse the cause of any papal vassal against the church ‡

This matter, however, assumed a much greater importance when the king renewed his claims to Milan more energetically than ever He demanded that Sforza should be provided for by a pension, and Milan instantly ceded to him §

If we bear in mind that these were the stipulations of the marriage treaty, it will appear extremely probable that the real subject of the conference at Marseilles was, the mode of carrying them into execution And, indeed, it could not be otherwise than most welcome to the pope to see his niece a powerful Italian princess

His near connexion with France freed him from any immediate fear of the emperor We shall see how he tied the hands of that monarch, and indeed tried to change the whole direction of his policy, by complying with his wishes in the English affair

The question only remains, how he meant to bring him to give way in Italian affairs,—whether by open force, or by indirect means ||

The Venetian ambassador affirms, that the pope declined the former, but gave his assent to the latter.

The political opposition to the house of Austria (which had succeeded in imposing its will on Catholic Europe by force of arms) had been a little allayed, but it now revived, and resumed its former projects The scheme of the king and the pope was, to make use of foreign hostilities to further their own ends

The Venetian ambassador mentions that a movement on the part of the Ottomans had even been talked of in Marseilles, but he will not positively affirm it ¶ on the other hand, he asserts without the smallest doubt, that a general recourse to arms in Germany was under deliberation Guicciardini too maintains, that the king communicated to the pope his design of setting the German princes in motion against the emperor **

I find nothing that can invalidate the credibility of these assertions, or can, on any reasonable grounds, be set against them

For the connexions which the king at that time maintained with the German princes were solely of a political character

He especially abetted the opposition to the election of King Ferdinand When, in May, 1532, the opposing princes formed a closer union, and even agreed on a regular military constitution, Francis I bound himself, in the event of war, to pay 100,000 gulden to the Dukes of Bavaria The boldest and most extensive plans were occasionally put forth, for example, the one talked of, in February, 1533—an invasion of Charles's territories by the French, simultaneously with an attack on those of Ferdinand by Zapolya †† The German empire was incessantly traversed by agents of the king, the most of whom were Gervaise Wain, a native of Memmingen, and Guillaume du Bellay, in order to keep the opposition alive, and to knit closer all the threads that bound it together

But the affairs of Wurtenberg soon became even more important than those of the election

---

The efforts to restore the Duke of Wurtenberg to the throne may be dated from the very day of his expulsion Innumerable negotiations and conferences had been set on foot for that purpose ,‡‡ but all had been frus-

---

* Letter in Sandoval, xx § 20 Que no se descuyasse, porque no era possible se no que el papa y el rey avian tratado algun negocio contra el The emperor himself mentions these things, "Que l'on y voudroit practiquer au prejudice des choses traitées entre ledit Sr Roy et nous" Papiers d etat de Granvelle, ii p 73

† Sanchez, in Bucholtz, ix 122.

‡ Letter from the archbishop of Lunden to Granvelle, 15th February, 1534 The nuncio had said 'Scire se ob id bellum futurum in Italia et pontificem auxilia daturum duci Aurelianensi contra quoscunque pro recuperatione dicti ducatus

§ Extracts in Raumer, Briefe aus Paris, i 262

|| The emperor himself afterwards saw the affair in that light After the breaking out of the landgrave's war, he charged his ambassador to declare to the king. Que ces moiens qu'il semble être pour nous vouloir contraindre sont bien loin, etc Papiers d'état de Granvelle, ii 109

¶ It is certain, nevertheless The pope himself who wished to call the attention of the emperor to the subject, gave him the news L'empereur au comte de Reux, 19 août, 1535 Pap d'et du Cl de Granvelle, ii 341 que le roy de France luy avoit respondu en parlant de la desfension et provision a l encontre dudit Turcq que non seulement iceluy roy de France n'empescheroit sa venue contre la dite chrestienté, mais la procureroit

** Relatione di Francia di M Marino Giustiniani, 1535 Giudico che l intelligentia coi Turchi fusse medesimamente deliberata in Marsiglia con Clemente Pontifice, comme fu ancora quella di Germania Guicciardini, xx 111, havendogli (al papa) communicato il re di Francia molti di suoi consigli, e specialmente il disegno che haveva di conciliare contro Cesare alcuni di principi di Germania, massimamente il landgravio d Hassia See Sandoval, lib xx § 20 Hereupon they parted, completely satisfied with each other

†† Stumpf, Baierns politische Geschichte, i 94

‡‡ E.g the negotiations between Landgrave Philip and

trated by the decided hostility of the Swabian league, and at the diet of Augsburg, Ferdinand received from his brother the investiture of Wurtenberg in the most solemn manner

In the year 1532, however, an event occurred which gave a fresh cogency to the claims of the sovereign house

After the expulsion of Duke Ulrich, his son Christopher, then only five years of age, was also carried out of Wurtenberg It was reported that, at the last house in which he slept in his own country, the boy played with a lamb, and when he went away earnestly entreated the host to take care of it, promising that when he came back he would reward him for his trouble It was long, however, before this childish dream was fulfilled The boy grew up in Insbruck and Neustadt, under Ferdinand's guardianship He was not very well taken care of, less perhaps from evil intention than from the general disorderly state of the affairs of the court, he himself tells us that his condition excited pity, sometimes he suffered absolute want, and once he was even in danger of being carried off by the Turks But early suffering is a better school for princes than the idleness and the flattery of a court, fortune was, in the main, his true friend She gave him, as a teacher, the learned and excellent Michael Tifernus, who attached himself to his charge with entire devotion The history of this man is extremely characteristic of his times When a child, he was carried off by the Turks whence, nobody knew, but at length they dropped him on the road. The poor little foundling was taken to Duino (Tybein) near Trieste, from which town he took his name there he was brought up by charitable people, and afterwards sent to a college at Vienna, where his education was completed He carefully watched over the safety of his docile and intelligent pupil By degrees the lad was introduced at court, for there was no intention of breeding him in a manner unseemly for a prince, and in 1530, he was with the emperor in Augsburg Here he inevitably learned his true position in the world, for he became a centre of attraction to people who incessantly reminded him of his claims to sovereign power. How then could he see with indifference the banners of Wurtenberg and Teck in Ferdinand's hand, at the ceremony of the investiture? The feeling of his right grew with his growth, and strengthened with his strength, but he was obliged to repress and conceal it In this excited state of mind, he received notice that he was to accompany the emperor, with whom he had willingly gone to the Netherlands, through Italy and Spain It is very probable that he felt no inclination for this expedition, especially when he remembered that, immediately after the expulsion of his father, there was an idea of sending him to Spain. Christopher was, moreover, determined not to abandon "his rights in Germany" He said plainly that he would have nothing to do with the journey to Spain. Accordingly, when the imperial court crossed the Alps to Italy, after the Turkish war in 1532, he contrived to escape with his tutor They wandered away from the rest of the retinue unobserved, and took the road to Salzburg Guided by peasants familiar with the mountain passes, they were at a great distance before they were missed and followed If all the circumstances related in the 16th century were true, their flight was accompanied with various perils, one of their horses fell ill, and in order to avoid being betrayed by its body, they determined to drown it in a lake, and while the young prince fled on the remaining horse from his pursuers, Tifernus lay hidden in the long rushes on its margin * In short, they disappeared from the court, and it was generally believed that they had fallen victims to bands of soldiers or peasants in the mountains † But they had reached a secure asylum, probably under the protection of the Dukes of Bavaria, whence the complaints of Christopher, and his demands for the restitution of his inheritance, were suddenly proclaimed aloud to the world ‡

The re-appearance of a prince of the house of Wurtenberg, with legitimate claims unimpaired by time, of the ancient race and name, and possessed of the affections of his born subjects, was of itself a very important event At that moment it was rendered doubly so by the circumstance, that the Dukes of Bavaria, to whom Christopher's father had been peculiarly odious, and whose coalition with the Swabian league had been the main instrument of his expulsion, now gave their support to his son

The Swabian league was indeed already on the eve of dissolution One motive for this was, the long-existing one,—that the princes could not accustom themselves to submit to the council of the league, in which prelates and cities enjoyed equal rights and equal influence with themselves, and an adroit member sometimes guided the decision of the assembly at his pleasure § In 1532, Hessen, Treves and the Palatinate formed a separate coalition, in which they promised each other not to agree to the renewal of the league ‖

Duke Henry of Brunswick, in the year 1530, which have since been minutely discussed in the controversial writings.

* The ground work of this story is in Gabelkofer, extracted by Sattler and Pfister (Duke Christopher) Pfister says (p 80) that Charles had begun to pay attention to Christopher in Vienna, and took him with him to a meeting he had with Hadrian VI in Bologna This is not true Heyd, too (Duke Ulrich, ii 332,) seems to me to go too far, when he concludes from an expression of Christopher's, "that he had inquired into his affairs ever since the diet of Augsburg," that the young prince was not there

† Letter from Christopher to his mother, 18th October Heyd, ii 339

‡ The first letter of the 17th November Sattler, ii 229

§ Landgrave Philip says, in a subsequent letter (25th December, 1545) "Befinden, wie es im schwäbischen Bund zugangen, dass Dr Eck, so oft er gewollt, des Mehrer hat machen können, es sey gleich den andern Standen gelegen oder ungelegen gewesen welches auch verursacht das der schwabische Pund daruber zerrissen worden"—"I find how it has gone on in the Swabian league, that Dr Eck, as often as he pleased, was able to play the leader, whether the other States liked it or not, which has also caused the rupture of the Swabian league"

‖ Friday after St Bernard The agreement is in the Archives of Trèves at Coblenz.

The cities, too, were dissatisfied, especially at the rigorous Catholic proceedings of the league tribunal. Ulm, Augsburg and Nurnberg united for their common protection But the highest discontents were caused by the affairs of Wurtenberg In the year 1530, Wurtenberg shared all the privileges of Austria, and was even left out of the matricula of the Imperial Chamber It seemed that it was to enjoy an exemption from all the burdens of the empire And meanwhile the expenses of the war, which the league had incurred in the conquests of 1519, were not yet paid * The emperor and the king clearly saw how important it was for the possession of the country, to be able to call out the well-appointed veteran troops of the league, their plenipotentiary, the Bishop of Augsburg, took all possible pains, in the year 1533, to hold it together † But already the result appeared very dubious under the existing circumstances, no one would undertake the defence of Wurtenberg for Ferdinand Bavaria declared that he regarded the cause of Duke Christopher as his own

In December, 1533, a meeting of the league was held at Augsburg, for the definitive adjustment of the affair

The poor, despoiled, and almost forgotten young prince now appeared with a brilliant band of supporters, councillors from electoral Saxony, Brunswick, Luneburg, Hessen, Munster, Juliers, Mecklenburg, and Prussia Ferdinand's commissioners found themselves constrained to treat with him, and to offer as compensation Cilli, Gorz, or Nellenburg The young duke, however, would no longer listen to these proposals He declared that the agreement upon which they were founded had never been fulfilled, and hence was at an end ‡ He conducted himself with prudence and circumspection, taking care never to advert to the causes of his father's expulsion He only steadily maintained, that unheard-of injustice had been done to his house, and to himself particularly, seeing that not one of the stipulations made and agreed to had been observed He solemnly declared, however, that, in spite of this, he should never think of revenging on the leagued States the injuries they had inflicted on his house This assurance was repeated in his father's name by the Hessian envoys The impression made by these circumstances rendered it impossible for the commissioners to advance a single step When the meeting dispersed, it was obvious to every one that the great league on which the power of Austria in Upper Germany mainly rested, was near its dissolution §

A French envoy was present at this assembly We are so fortunate as to possess the pathetic discourse which he pronounced in favour of Duke Christopher,‖ but the simple fact that so powerful a neighbouring monarch espoused the cause of the young prince, produced a greater effect than all his eloquence

This happened at the same time that the king and the pope were together in Marseilles As soon as the pope left that city, the king, secure of a good understanding with Rome, hastened to take advantage of favouring circumstances for a decisive movement

In January, 1534, he contracted a still closer alliance with the German princes as to the affair of the election He engaged, in case it should lead to a war, to take upon himself a third part of the costs For the present, he paid the 100,000 crowns of the sum he had promised, which were deposited with the Dukes of Bavaria

He felt that his objects would be more immediately furthered by supporting the claims of Wurtenberg, upon which affair he immediately entered

Landgrave Philip, personally attached to Duke Ulrich of Wurtenberg, and hostile on various grounds to the house of Austria, had long determined to undertake the restoration of the exiled house at the first favourable opportunity This had been one principal aim of his whole policy during many years Circumstances now favoured his designs He wanted nothing but money, in order to strike the blow as quickly as possible, and without any obstructing engagements with other German princes

The alliance between King Francis and Landgrave Philip was mainly negotiated by Count William of Furstenberg, one of those partisan leaders who attached themselves first to one side and then to another After serving the house of Austria in the year 1528, he had now thrown himself into the party of France

From Marseilles, the king proceeded to the eastern frontier of his kingdom, under the conduct of Count Furstenberg ¶ Landgrave Philip also came from Cassel, and passed through Zweibrucken, on the 18th we find him at St. Nicholas on the Meurthe

A meeting between him and the king immediately took place in Barleduc All the pending questions were here discussed, the council and the election, the interests of Hessen and Nassau, and those of the Netherlands and Gueldres The king professed himself on every point a friend of German independence, and, in general, of the Protestant princes,**

* Ferdinand to Charles 27th April V Md sabe la dicha liga no quire mas servir en esto hasta ser pagados dello que por ello les fue promctido y esto al presente por su parte tengolo por imposible

† The instructions and statement are in the Brussels Archives See Appendix

‡ See Complete Refutation of the Treaties; last day of July, 1533 Hortleder, i iii vii

§ Extract from Gabelkofer in Pfister, Duke Christopher I, 102—116, expressly remarked by Baut (Heyd, ii 424)

‖ "The prince would be an exile, in foreign lands men would point at him and say, that is he who once—who now—who without any fault of his"——he did not finish the sentence, because he read, as he said, in the eyes of the assembly, that they felt his meaning Discours de M de Langey, in the Appendix to the Memoires of Bellay Coll univ tom xviii p 336 He was moreover, commissioned (p 271), 'd'essayer tous moyens possibles à faire que cette ligue de Suabe ne se renovast, mais que de tous points elle se dissolust"

¶ Letter from Philip to Furstenberg Munch, Fürstenberg, ii p 37

** Letter of the landgrave to the elector, Rommel, iii p 51, which is remarkable, as well for what he says, as

the main question, however,—that on which all depended,—was the design upon Wurtenberg The landgrave, who had no want of troops or munitions of war, demanded, in the first place, money to put them in motion The king, expressly bound by the treaty of Cambray not to take part with the enemies of the emperor, among whom was the Duke of Wurtenberg, scrupled thus formally to agree to send subsidies for his assistance, in open violation of that treaty They hit upon the expedient of disguising the payment of the sum of 125,000 crown dollars, which Francis engaged to supply, under a contract for the sale of Mompelgard, the duke reserving to himself the right of re-emption In a subjoined agreement, the king declared that he gave the duke 75.000 dollars as a present On the 27th of January, the treaty was concluded,* the landgrave set out on his return without delay, and on the 8th of February was again in Cassel He now lost not a moment in making his preparations He hesitated, as may be supposed, to confide his secret to paper, but so numerous were the messages with which he despatched his confidential councillors, that sometimes he had not one of them left at home, to the Elector of Treves and the elector palatine he went in person † He also took part in the compact concerning the election, but when he sent the ratification of it to the king, he added that he should not wait for the Dukes of Bavaria, he was already preparing to go to work by himself ‡ The king was delighted at the prospects which were thus opened to him On Easter Monday, 1534, he said to an agent of the woiwode, who was with him, that the Swabian league was dissolved, that he had sent money to Germany, and had many friends there, and allies already in arms, that he, Zapolya, would soon be able to dictate a peace §

One danger the landgrave had to avert before he openly took arms The electors who had chosen Ferdinand, would perhaps fear that a successful campaign against him might, in the end, prove ruinous to themselves It appeared very possible that they would be induced by this consideration to take up the king's cause, and indeed a diet of electors was already fixed to be held at Gelnhausen Unquestionably the chief motive of Philip's journey was to tranquillise the electors of Treves and the Palatinate So far, he said, from thinking of a war on account of the election, the basis for a final accommodation of that matter would now be laid Bavaria promised that, if Wurtenburg was restored to the hereditary house, it would make no further opposition to the election, hereupon Brandenburg, Cologne and the Palatinate, promised not to obstruct the landgrave in his undertaking Treves even consented to contribute succours ‖

King Ferdinand suddenly found himself in a state of complete isolation

The emperor was at a distance, the King of France hostile, the pope (as afterwards more clearly appeared) extremely doubtful The old hostility which had formed the bond of the Swabian league had expired, Duke Ulrich solemnly confirmed the assurances of the landgrave, that the cities had nothing to fear from him Neither the engagements entered into by the electors at the king's election, nor their religious differences, now operated in his favour The clergy were as much his enemies as the laity ¶

For no German prince could see with approbation an ancient German sovereign house thus despoiled of its inheritance

The Wittenberg theologians and his own subjects warned the landgrave that he would bring Hessen into danger, he replied, half jestingly, "I will not ruin you this time" He took a wider view of the state of things than they did, and felt himself sure of his cause

He had to contend only with Ferdinand,—nay, only with Ferdinand's Wurtenburg forces, and for these he felt himself fully a match

Whilst he himself was mainly occupied in collecting a magnificent body of cavalry—the arm in which, in the 16th century, Lower Germany surpassed the rest of Europe—Count William of Furstenberg, with the aid of Strasburg, assembled twenty-four companies of foot on the Upper Rhine and in Alsatia, where the best landsknechts remained all the winter, waiting to be called into the field They were from Pomerania and Mecklenburg, Brunswick and Eichsfeld, the Westphalian bishoprics, and the archbishopric of Cologne, while the heart of them was formed by Philip's own Hessian vassals, without question the militia most frequently called out in all Germany at that time, and now not very willing to answer the call The two bodies met at Pfungstadt, in the Odenwald On Tuesday, the 5th May, the news arrived that the enemy had also collected a fine army in Stuttgart, and would doubtless appear in the open field All were in the highest spirits, and eager for the fight On Wednesday the 6th, just after midnight, they broke up their quarters The landgrave, on horseback, with his lance in his hand, reviewed the troops In their van were the wagons with munitions and stores, driven by six thousand peasants, all men capable of bearing arms Next came a company of light horse, and then the artillery, followed by the great squadron of heavy-armed reiters, under the chief standard, borne by the hereditary

for what he does not say According to this, the king only offered to negotiate between Ulrich and Ferdinand

* Notices hereupon in Rommel, ii p 298, it were much to be wished that the treaty itself were printed

† Tellement que luy meme en personne a ete contrainct d'aller devers l archeveque de Treves et le comte palatin Lettre du chancelier du landgrave à Langey MS Bethune, 8816, f 55

‡ Sommes déja près de conduire le tout en effet Cassel, 9 Mars MS Bethune, 8493

§ From the interrogations of Casali and Corsini, who were arrested and examined in Hungary, 1535 In the Brussels Archives

‖ Letter of Philip, in Stumpf, Appendix, No 14 See another of his letters to Dr Eck, mentioned by Stumpf in the text, p 153

¶ Wolfgang Brandner had already represented the matter very justly to the king, in July, 1533 Bucholtz, ix. 76.

grand marshal of Hessen, after them the foot soldiers, both those brought up by the landgrave, and the Oberlanders, to whom Duke George of Wurtenberg sent a very considerable reinforcement There were about 20,000 foot and 4000 horse, an army which, though far from being the largest that had been seen even in those days, was yet, for a single prince of the empire, and one not even belonging to the first class, numerous beyond all expectation, excellently equipped, and perfectly provided with all things necessary for war Care had been taken to enlist as many officers as possible of the evangelical faith, which was that of the majority of the common men It was the first army of a politico-religious opposition to the house of Austria, on the part of Germany and of Europe, that had appeared in the field

On the other side, the Austrian government in Wurtenberg had been arming Convents of monks and nuns, cathedral and rural chapters had raised contributions, and the cities had paid a war-tax * The old commanders of the Italian campaigns, Curt of Bemmelberg, Caspar Frundsberg, Marx of Eberstein, and Thamis,† surnamed Hemstede, had collected bands of landsknechts we meet again the well-known names of the adversaries of Hessen in Sickingen's wars,—Hilch von Lorch, Sickingen's sons, and Dietrich Spat The king himself did not appear; his place was filled by Philip of the Palatinate, lieutenant of Wurtenburg,—the same, who had distinguished himself at the defence of Vienna Although the troops were not equal to those of the landgrave in number (they might amount to about 10,000 men, including a considerable number of Bohemians), they had courage enough to wait for him on his way, in the open field at Laufen on the Neckar They did not even take the trouble to obstruct his passage over the river

The first engagement took place on the 12th of May The king's troops sustained the assault tolerably well Not only, however, was the count palatine, their leader, wounded, but the landgrave's superiority became so manifest, that they saw they had no chance of making any successful resistance In the night, Dietrich Spat set out to bring up more cavalry Early in the morning of the following day, the army itself sought to take up a more secure position

But it was not likely that the fiery landgrave would suffer them to accomplish this. In an instant, he was in motion He would listen to no objections, he saw well what an advantage it would be for him, with his superior cavalry and his good artillery, to fall upon the enemy when dislodged from his position It was by such a movement, that the bands of armed peasants had formerly been routed The Austrian army had, indeed, experienced landsknechts and brave officers but the want of horses brought them into the same perilous situation as that which had proved fatal to the peasants By a charge of cavalry on their flank, Landgrave Philip detained the enemy in a vineyard till his artillery could come up He then hastened back to bring up the infantry for a decisive attack But before they could come up, the cavalry and artillery had already combined their efforts with such effect, that the enemy fell into complete disorder, and retreated across the Bidembach The few reiters that remained escaped to the Asperg, the foot soldiers were dispersed, and many perished in the Neckar ‡ The landgrave himself was astonished that leaders of such reputation had made so little resistance.

A field of battle is, in general, the place on which the collective forces of two opposite states of moral culture come into collision, and try their respective strength Landgrave Philip had the most fortunate combination of European circumstances, the secret or declared good wishes of all Germany, and a host of religious sympathies, on his side Ferdinand had only himself to trust to, he defended a dubious right and unpopular ideas, and he had proved the weaker in the land he possessed

But this battle is also deserving of all attention on account of its consequences It decided the fate of one of the most important German principalities The country fell at once into the power of the conquerors Duke Ulrich re-appeared after his long absence, the citizens, after ratifying the treaty of Tubingen, did homage to him for his capital city of Stuttgart, in a meadow on the road to Canstadt, the other towns and villages followed their example Nor did the castles hold out for Ferdinand Either their commanders were in their hearts inclined to the returning princes of the land, or they feared for their estates, which had already fallen into the hands of the conquerors, or they yielded to force Even the Asperg surrendered on the 8th of June

Thus was Wurtenberg once more in the hands of a Wurtenberg sovereign Duke Ulrich's enemies had given him, in derision, the nickname of broom-maker, the other side now retorted the jest, and said that he was come to sweep all the spiders' webs from out the land The people were delighted to see once more the hunting-horn,§ after which they

* Spanish report in the Appendix

† This is doubtless the Von Thonis in the song in Heyd, Battle of Laufen, p 88

‡ Neue Zeitung von des Landgrafen zu Hessen Kriegshandlung, bei Hortleder, I vol iii c. 12 is neither graphic nor correct, especially as to time Philip's letter to his councillors (Rommel, ii 319) gives the best account The other reports, however, are still more useless than the Neue Zeitung Jovius makes out that the count palatine was wounded on the day of battle, probably merely for the sake of effect (lib xxxii p 123) Nicolaus Asclepius Barbatus insists upon the circumstance that the landgrave attacked, "ea manu quæ hostium numero vix responderet" It is clear that he could not attack with all his troops at once, but he had a most decided advantage in point of numbers Tethinger gives a kind of general description of "equitum fremitus, armorum crepitus strepitusque," of no value whatever Von Heyd's careful monograph, Die Schlacht von Laufen, Stuttgart, 1831, contains a fragment of another letter by Philip, coinciding with the first, and a very good passage from Gabelkofer (Beil iii v), which confirm the statement made above,—besides some new landsknecht songs, very interesting and valuable

§ A badge of the house of Würtenberg.—TRANSL

had so long yearned; and proclaimed in their songs the happiness of the country that had recovered its native prince. Politically, it was of great moment that a prince, who might be regarded as the most complete representative of the opposition to Austria, was now called to play a part in the centre of Upper Germany. His well-known sentiments left no doubt from the first, as to what his conduct would be in religious affairs.

The behaviour of Pope Clement VII. on this occasion was very remarkable. The ambassador of King Ferdinand implored his assistance in this imminent danger, which, he said, might also become extremely formidable to the Church and to Italy. The pope brought the matter before the next consistory; he repeated the ambassador's words, and even heightened his expressions; but as to the assistance to be rendered to the king, he did not so much as make a suggestion. Hereupon a letter arrived from Ferdinand himself to the pope, and the affair was again brought before the consistory. But the pope chose this moment to revive the emperor's demands with regard to a council, which were so intensely odious to the Curia; the consequence was, that, though the subsidies already granted to the emperor and the king were paid, the proposal for further aid was sent back for the consideration of a congregation. The pope said, the king lay ill of a disease which no slight tinctures or syrups could cure,—nothing less than a violent medicine. Accordingly, the congregation decided that, as it could not grant the king a large subsidy, it was better to grant him none. To the great vexation of the ambassador, the news had arrived, that the landgrave on his entry into Würtenberg had attempted no hostile measure against the churches; whereupon the pope declared that the war was a private one, in which he would not interfere; if the enemy should attack the Church, it would then be time enough for him to think of subsidies. The ambassador remarked, with all the vivacity consistent with his respect for the pope, how important the affair was; how dear it might cost the Holy See, nay, the city of Rome and all Italy. But the pope too was excited and almost angry; he asked, where then was the emperor? and why he had not provided against these disasters? he (the pope) had long ago called his attention to the conduct that was to be expected from the landgrave.* In short, the pope was not to be moved to take any part in the affair—not the slightest. He would wait till he heard of the ruin of the Church before he would do any thing to prevent it; at present, he regarded the matter merely from a political point of view. The German princes—as, for example, Duke George of Saxony—reproached the pope with being in an understanding with the king, to keep Germany in a state of confusion, in order not to be forced to convoke a council.†

Such a state of things seemed to open the most brilliant prospects to the King of France.

On the 18th of June, the victors had reached Taugendorf, on the Austrian frontier. "My friends," said Francis, "have conquered Würtenberg,—only onwards! more!" Meanwhile Barbarossa too had appeared at sea, plundered the Neapolitan coast far and wide, and then fallen upon Tunis, which he captured. He assumed a most threatening attitude towards Spain, as we shall have occasion to show hereafter. Francis I. thought that the emperor, oppressed by the various dangers which menaced his house, would yield to his demands. He demanded Genoa, Montferrat, and a part of Milan, immediately.‡ The schemes with regard to Urbino began to be agitated.

In Germany a flame seemed to be kindled which would not easily be quenched.

As soon as the emperor received the news of his brother's defeat, he despatched a messenger with a considerable sum of money, with which to bring an army into the field to chastise the landgrave.§ Nothing could better have suited the views of his enemies.

But in Germany, people were not inclined to allow things to go to such lengths, either on the one side or the other.

The aggressors did not feel themselves strong enough to carry on a protracted war, and least of all would they fight for a foreign interest.

If Francis I. had intended to turn the animosities of the Germans to his own account, they, on their part, had designed to use the French for the attainment of their own ends: that was all.

* Bericht des königl. Gesandten Sanchez an Ferdinand, 13 Juni, 1534. (July is probably an error of the copyist.) Bucholtz, ix. 247. All that surprises me is, that Bucholtz fancies himself to have disproved the assumption I have here made, that the pope was informed beforehand of the landgrave's intention to take up arms. He has underlined all the civil speeches which the pope made to the nuncio, in order to keep him quiet; as if any weight was to be attached to such things, and the historian were not to judge from actions. But Sanchez was by no means so devout a believer in the pope as our Bucholtz. He acquaints his master with the course which things are taking, "ut melius M^e V^ra istorum mentes et cogitationes intelligat, quibus technis parent isti rem longius differre." He suspects: "suborta mihi fuit suspectio, S^tem S. non satis efficaci fervore procedere;" he is indignant at the excuses that are made: "dolore et indignatione assensus replicui, cum tamen reverentia debita;" and ends by convincing himself that nothing will be done: "opinor papam daturum nobis bona verba." If I may venture to offer another conjecture with respect to this affair, I would suggest that King Francis I. had really promised the pope that the landgrave's enterprise should have no consequences which might affect the church; a condition always made by the kings of France, when they supported the Protestants during the Thirty Years' War.

That such a promise could not have been kept, especially in times of such vehement zeal, is obvious.

† L'empereur au comte de Nassau, 29th Août: Papiers d'état du C^l Granvelle, ii. 171: Se sont indignez les electeurs, princes et autres . . . à l'occasion de la responce faite par le duc Georges de Saxen au nunce de pape là où il le touche (le roi) grandement avec le dit st. père de non chercher autre chose que d'entretenir la dite Germanye en trouble et s'entendre avec le dit st. père pour empescher le concille.

‡ This appears from the instructions of the emperor to the count of Nassau, 12th August, 1534, from which Von Raumer has given extracts in his Briefe aus Paris, i. 262. Since then printed in the Pap. d'état du C^l Granvelle, ii. 15.

§ We have a minute report on this subject by the Bishop of Lunden, who went from one Rhenish court to another, in order to negotiate the matter; 1st August, 1534. Br. Archives.

It was certainly agreed in the treaty concerning the affairs of the election, that neither party should conclude a peace without the other; but, as Philip of Hessen observed, the war in question had not then broken out.* He had taken care to prevent this before he took up arms. The Dukes of Bavaria had remained quiet; the French deposit lay unemployed in their coffers.

The whole question was, whether King Ferdinand could resolve to give up Wurtenberg.

He, too, was placed in a very doubtful position. Should he, in order to recover what he had lost, imperil all that he possessed by a better and more unquestionable right? He was told that if he was not ready for battle in a few days, all would be lost. His councillors, Rogendorf, Hofmann, and the Bishop of Trent, joined in the opinion that he had better determine to give up Wurtenberg.

A meeting of German princes was already opened at Annaberg, on this and other business.

In order to take part personally in the proceedings, King Ferdinand repaired to Cadan, a little place in the neighbourhood, between Annaberg and Saatz.

He did not, indeed, consent to renounce Wurtenberg, absolutely and forever, for, he said, he had been most solemnly invested with the fief in the presence of the assembled diet —his brother had grasped the banner with his own hand; he could not, and would not, suffer himself to be despoiled of his right. But he consented that Duke Ulrich should take possession of Wurtenberg as a sub-fief of Austria, though with seat and voice in the empire.† With this, Landgrave Philip, and at length Duke Ulrich himself, was satisfied.

In return, the Elector of Saxony now declared himself ready to acknowledge Ferdinand as King of the Romans. He did not confess that he had been in the wrong, on the contrary, he demanded that a clause should be annexed to the Golden Bull, laying down such directions for future cases, as might amount to a sanction of his conduct in the present case.‡ But this reservation did not prevent him from going to Cadan on the 27th of June, nor from paying to his former adversary all the honour due to a King of the Romans. His adherents, too, to whom this opposition alone had given a legitimate ground for refusing allegiance to Ferdinand, could now no longer withhold it. By degrees all acquiesced.

The ambassador of Charles had just commenced his negotiations on the Rhine against the landgrave, when this intelligence arrived and caused him to suspend them.

Whilst King Francis was daily hoping to hear of further hostilities in Germany, peace was already concluded. From this quarter, at least, he could expect nothing more, calculated to forward his Italian schemes.

On the contrary, it was evident that the landgrave's enterprise, though its success was to be entirely attributed to a concurrence of European circumstances, would nevertheless produce no effect on political relations in general: its results were bounded by the frontiers of Germany, and there they were by no means exclusively political, as had been anticipated, but were also of the greatest importance to religion. Some other stipulations were made at Cadan, which eventually contributed greatly to the permanence and stability of Protestantism. But they belong to another cycle of events, which we shall contemplate hereafter.

CHAPTER VIII.

PROGRESS OF THE REFORMATION DURING THE YEARS 1532—1534.

It is evident that an event like the peace of Nurnberg must inevitably contribute, in a very high degree, to confirm and develope the principle of the reformation, in those countries where it had been established in consequence of the recess of 1526.

The Protestants had not suffered the episcopal jurisdictions to be re-imposed upon them; they thought themselves guarantied, by the emperor's promise, from further proceedings on the part of the Imperial Chamber, and at the same time from the immediate hostilities of the majority of the States of the empire.

Hereupon, the Saxon diet, assembled at Weimar towards the end of 1532, no longer hesitated to ordain the resumption of the visitation of the churches, which had naturally been interrupted at a time when every thing was in suspense.§

The mass, which in some places had been adhered to, was now entirely prohibited: the few convents that still existed were ordered to adopt the evangelical doctrine, and were forbidden to receive novices. A universal sequestration of conventual lands was organised, with the co-operation of the States. Their design was to apply the proceeds to some of the most pressing wants of the country, espe-

* "Alldiweil man der wale sachen halben nicht krieget." "All this while there is no war on account of the election business." Philip's instructions to his envoys to the king, Rommel, iii. 65.

† Letter of George von Carlowitz, in Sattler, iii. Urk. p. 104.

‡ "Das künftiglich, wann bei leben ains Röm. Kaisers oder konigs ain Rom. König soll erwelt, alle Churfursten zuvor samen beschaiden werden, davon zu reden, ob ur sachen genugsam vorhanden und dem Reich furderlich sey ainen Rom. König—zu erwehlen, und wann sie sich da verainigt das alsdann und nicht eher der Churfurst zur koniglichen wahl erfordert werde."—"That in future, when in the lifetime of a Roman emperor or king, a king of the Romans is to be elected, all electors should be convoked beforehand to consult about it, whether there be causes sufficient, and whether it be profitable to the empire to elect a Roman king, and when they are there assembled, that then, and not before, each elector should be called upon to elect a king." Matuzisch sachs-sches Bedenken, ibid. 101.

§ Extracts from the Reports of Visitations, Seckendorf, iii. § 25. Add. iii. The instruction is dated 19th December, 1532.

cially to pay off the public debt, for which they had likewise just granted a tax. But as they expressed themselves very humbly on this subject, and even held out a prospect of re-payment, if necessary,* the elector insisted with the greater earnestness on the necessity of keeping in view the original purpose of the endowments. The first care was for the parish churches. The idea had originally been, that the parish churches might be provided for out of the small foundations, confraternities, endowments for masses for souls, and, where these were insufficient, new rates, levied upon the communes. But this proved wholly impracticable. The communes — burghers and peasants, as well as nobles — were vainly reminded how much their masses and indulgences had heretofore cost them, they answered, that times were altered. It was therefore necessary to apply to the parishes a large portion of the conventual property, which, at first, while many monks were still to be maintained, and an expensive administration to be kept on foot out of it, yielded no very large revenue.† It is scarcely credible in what a state they were found. But at length the end was accomplished. "With great care, trouble, and labour," says Myconius, himself one of the Visitators, "we brought it to pass that every parish should have its teacher, and its allotted income, every town its schools, and all that belongs to a church."‡ The visitation now extended to the domains of the princes of Reuss and Schwarzburg. The clergy there showed less refractoriness than ignorance and immorality, it was impossible to retain them, however willing they were to remain, they were almost all replaced by disciples of the Wittenberg school. This metropolis of Protestantism was now rather better provided for.§ The old order of things was utterly overthrown, and Wittenberg stood at the head of the new church. From her had emanated the doctrines which had already begun to be rendered imperative on the preachers,‖ and ordination was conferred by the spiritual members of her university.

This system was also adopted almost unchanged in Hessen, where the original sketch of a constitution of the church, founded on the idea of the commune, as conceived by Zwingli, had long been abandoned. Visitations were held, the parishes were put upon a better footing, as the landgrave boasted, than they had ever been, superintendents were appointed, and divine service was conducted after the manner of Wittenberg. The chief difference was, that the church in Hessen was far richer than in electoral Thuringia and Saxony, which rendered it practicable to make some large endowments. In the year 1532, the convents of Wetter and Kaufungen, with revenues which had been estimated as equal to a small count's fee, were consecrated to the portioning of noble young ladies in marriage. In the year 1533, the houses of Haina and Merxhausen, and, shortly after, those of Hofheim and Gronau, were converted into national hospitals. Ten monasteries in the upper and lower principalities were gradually incorporated into the university of Marburg, and a part of the revenue of five others devoted to the same purpose. A theological seminary was established, supported by contributions from the sovereign, and all the (Burgerschaften) town corporations of the country.¶

In Luneburg, the jurisdictions of Bremen, Verden, Magdeburg and Hildesheim had already been separated. They were now entirely abolished and the supreme superintendency over all these districts was confided to Urbanus Rhegius. He deemed it his duty to remain in this laborious and not very secure post, although he was invited to return to the Oberland, of which he was a native. His sovereign, Duke Ernest, was his zealous supporter. We frequently see him, accompanied by his chancellor and one of the preachers, visiting the monasteries in person, and recommending the cause of reform, and, indeed, most of the monks, as well as the prioresses, with their nuns, went over to the evangelical faith. Sometimes the priors or canons had a common interest with the duke, for example, in Bardewik, which the Archbishop of Bremen wanted to incorporate with Verden. Gradually the Saxon forms predominated here as in Hessen. An annual church visitation was held.**

In Franconian Brandenburg, too, the monasteries were successfully put under the civil administration. There were still monks in many places, but some of them had taken wives—even here and there an abbot.†† But no fresh elections of abbots or abbesses were

* "Zu einer Furstreckung und Mithulfe, jedoch der gestalt dass solchs der Notturft und Gelegenheit nach wieder erganzt worde." "For a loan and aid, but in such wise that the same be restored according to need and occasion." Transactions of the diet at Jena. Erhardi 1533.

† As an example we will cite the parish of Umpferstedt. The decree of the visitors was as follows. "Als wir — — befunden das die pfarhe zu Umpferstedt und Wigendorf zur unterhaltung eines pfarhers vast zu wenig hett, so haben wir verordent, nachdem das Dorf Umpferstedt dem Closter Oberweymar an alle myttel und eygenthumlich zugethan seyn soll das einem iden pfarrer zu Umpferstedt von gedachtes Closters zu Oberweymar Guteln zugelegt und gegeben werden soll eines yeden Jahres ein Acker Holz samt dem Closterholz zu Drostet, ein Acker oder anderthalb ungefährlich Wisewachs zu Neuendorf und ein halb weimarisch malter korns von Adam Rosten zu Weimar, von beiden Dorfern die Decimation."—"Seeing that we — — have found that the parish of Umpferstedt and Wigendorf hath two little for the support of a priest, we do hereby order and direct that, seeing the village of Umpferstedt is claimed as pertaining and subject to the convent of Oberweymar every priest at Umpferstedt shall duly receive from the property of the said convent of Oberweymar each year one acre of wood, over and above the convent wood at Drostet, an acre or an acre and a half, more or less of forage from Neuendorf, and half a Weimar measure of grain from Adam Rosten at Weimar, besides tithes from both villages."

‡ Lommatzsch, Narratio de Myconio, p. 55.

§ Its whole revenue amounted to 2811 g. 11 grs., to this 1900 g. more were added. Hitherto Luther's salary had been 200 g., it was now increased to 300 g.

‖ Knapp, Narratio de Iusto Iona, p. 17.

¶ Extracts from the Reports. Rommel, i. p. 191, and note.

** Schreiben des Urbanus Rhegius an die Augspurger, 14 Juli, 1535, bei Walch, xvii. 2507. See Schlegel, ii. 51, 95, 211.

†† Report by Cornelius Ettenius, p. 498.

allowed: in some cases we find administratrixes, as, for example, Dorothea of Hirschhard, in the chapter for noble maidens at Birkenfeld. An order of chancery was drawn up, according to which, the surplus of the revenues of the monasteries was to be thrown into a common fund, and reserved for any cases of need occurring to the state generally. All the proceeds of other foundations and benefices that might become vacant, were to be applied to the maintenance of parish churches and schools. In the year 1533, an ecclesiastical ordinance was drawn up, in concert with Nürnberg, for the governance of churches and convents.*

All, as we perceive, was yet in its infancy, and nearly formless; a regular and stable ecclesiastical constitution was as yet out of the question. Thus much only is evident,—that the secular authorities generally obtained great advantages over the spiritual.

A portion of the ecclesiastical revenues fell into the hands, either of the sovereign, or of the nobility, or of the community at large. In all the reformed countries a clergy, indebted for its position and importance to the zeal and efforts of the civil power, was substituted for one whose rights were exclusively derived from episcopal ordination.

We find a proof how little the laity were inclined to submit to any domination on the part of the new clergy, in the ecclesiastical ordinance of Nürnberg and Brandenburg, just alluded to.

The clergy of those districts wished for the re-introduction of the power of excommunication, for which those of Nürnberg formally petitioned; those of Brandenburg were at least not opposed to it, and indeed in their report they adduced arguments in favour of that institution. But they could not prevail. The laity would not submit to this despotism, and, in the publication of the ordinance, the paragraph treating of it was expunged.†

Wittenberg itself was opposed to it. Luther said,‡ that public sentence of excommunication ought to be preceded by previous inquiry, and followed by a universal avoidance of the excommunicated: now the former could not easily be conducted; the latter would cause great confusion, especially in large towns. He clearly saw that it was not the province of religion to maintain public order by any coercive measures whatsoever, which properly belong to the state alone. The church of Wittenberg contented itself with refusing the sacrament of the Lord's Supper to notorious sinners, without attempting to interfere with the civil relations of society. The preachers condemned vice in the pulpit, and admonished the authorities not to tolerate it.

Nor did the spiritual power achieve any greater conquests elsewhere. In the year 1533, a provincial synod was established in Strasburg, which included various secular elements, together with the spiritual; a commission of the council (which, indeed, had precedence), the wardens of the city churches, the doctors and teachers of the liberal arts. In the articles which it adopted, the office of preventing blasphemy and open scandal was specially committed to the civil authorities;§ whereas the council never would consent to the introduction of church discipline, properly so called. In affairs of faith, they said, nothing was to be effected by commands; as they could not possibly be enforced, the publication of them could only be attended with loss of consideration. The blameless life and conversation of the clergy (each of whom was to be seriously admonished in private), the good example of the higher classes, and exhortations to the lower by the masters of the guilds, appeared to them the only practicable means to the attainment of the object.‖

The church was regarded as an institution for the propagation of religion—not so much outward as inward. Every thing approaching to papacy was avoided. To free themselves from the coercive power of the spiritual body—the exercise of which was most oppressive, while its relaxation was most destructive to morality—was the chief aim of the whole movement. And if the people would no longer endure the influence and the spiritual tyranny of the prelates, neither were they disposed to confer analogous powers on the inferior clergy who had abandoned the hierarchical system. The demand for a more rigid church discipline was immediately met by the conviction, that the Christian principle ought to act upon the will, by penetrating the heart; not to subdue the former by force, nor to alienate the latter by coercion.

While, however, the reformers were busied with these arrangements and considerations, and thought themselves perfectly secured by the concessions of Nürnberg, it proved that this was not entirely the case: the higher clergy of the Catholic church were far too powerfully represented in the constitution of the empire, and too expressly supported by the laws of the empire, so easily to abandon their cause.

The emperor, indeed, issued an injunction to the Imperial Chamber from Mantua (6th November, 1532), to stop all hostile proceedings concerning religious matters till his further commands.¶

A great number of prosecutions of that kind were already begun. Accusations were laid, by the higher clergy against Strasburg, Constance, Reutlingen, Magdeburg, Bremen and

* Lang, ii. 42.

† Considerations of the Clergy of the Margravate concerning Church Discipline. Strobel, Miscellaneen, ii. p. 148. Even so recently as in 1741, the worthy Hausmann did not venture to tell what he knew of this matter. Hausmann in Spengler, pp. 55, 297.

‡ Bedenken bei, D. W. iv. p. 389.

§ The sixteen articles of the synod of 1533. Röhrich, ii. 263, and especially Art. 15.

‖ Declaration of the council of 1534, id. p. 41.

¶ Harpprecht, v. 295. Saxon delegates were sent thither to carry on the business. Schreiben von Planitz, Mantua, 7th Dec. They received through Held this answer: "Und so weit die Forderungen am Kammergericht und zu Rothweil belangen thut, wüszte sich I. Mt. wohl zu erinnern des Vertrags," &c.—" So far as the demands made on the Imperial Chamber and at Rothwill are concerned, his imp. majesty was mindful of the treaty," &c.

Nurnberg, as well as against some sovereign princes, among whom were Ernest of Luneburg and George of Brandenburg. Most of the confiscated property was reclaimed, and occasionally the interest due to a chapter, or an endowment in a town was withheld, or an attempt was made to remove married priests, or to place zealous Catholic priests in a Protestant city, against the will of its inhabitants.

The Protestants thought they were permanently protected by the emperor's injunction. The Imperial Chamber, however, was not of that opinion.

The Chamber was bound to the observance of the recess of Augsburg, it well knew that the majority had committed the war against Protestantism to its hands, and no man, or body of men, will ever willingly surrender functions which confer power. On the other side, could it venture to disobey an injunction of the emperor, from whom its authority was derived, and in whose name its judgments were pronounced?

In this dilemma, the Imperial Chamber devised the expedient of declaring that the pending trials were not affairs of religion, but breaches of the public peace, and acts of spoliation, and that the offence charged was, transgressions of the recess of the empire.

The first case in which this distinction was taken, was in the course of the proceedings concerning the claim of the city of Strasburg to the revenues and jewels of the chapter of Arbogast. The city advocate, Dr Herter, said, that was indeed the suit against Strasburg, an affair in which all Protestants were civilly interested, but that it also concerned religion, and therefore could not be proceeded in, conformably with the emperor's recent proclamation. The bishop's advocate replied, that his gracious master had nothing to do with the Protestant body, that the business regarded things wholly distinct from religion. The Protestants said, that a peace of the kind understood by the Chamber could be of no value to them, nor would his imperial majesty have troubled himself to ordain such a one, the truce included persons, property, and co-dependencies. Nevertheless, they could obtain nothing further from the court, than a resolution to ask the emperor for an explanation of his words.

The emperor was still in Bologna, as it were the guest of the pope, and in daily communication with his holiness, when this question was laid before him. He dared not offer a fresh offence to the pope, already vacillating, nor dared he offend the majority of the States. And yet he could not revoke his truce. He gave an answer as dark as the response of an oracle. "The words of our injunction," says he, "extend only to affairs of religion, what, however, affairs of religion are, does not admit of any better explanation than that which the affairs themselves afford."* Probably Held, an old assessor of the Imperial Chamber, who had accompanied the emperor to Bologna, was the inventor of this interpretation. Obscure as it is, it leaves no doubt of its tendency. The government wished to confirm the Chamber in the course it had taken.

A commission which visited the tribunal in May, 1533, also admonished the members of it afresh to maintain the recess of Augsburg, especially in regard to religion.†

Fortified by this double admonition, the Imperial Chamber now knew no moderation. The plaints were received and reproduced, the objection raised by the defendants, that the Chamber was not the proper tribunal for religious matters, made no impression, the accusers charged them with an offence against the imperial authority, the inevitable consequence of which was sentence of ban.

Had the Protestants submitted to this, their union would have been totally useless.

They first addressed themselves (according to a resolution of their meeting at Schmalkalden, in July, 1533) to the elector palatine and the Elector of Mainz, who had negotiated the peace and who now took part, by their councillors, in the recess of visitation. The electors declared that they could not take this matter upon themselves. Hereupon the Protestants appealed to the court itself. As a proof that the pending trials turned upon affairs of religion, they cited the traditional maxim of the church of Rome,—that every thing relating to a benefice is to be considered a spiritual matter. Their sole purpose, they said, in concluding the peace, was to guard themselves from the complaints and accusations of the clergy,—that in consequence of the change of doctrine they were robbed of their usufructs. But besides this, they had been expressly promised that the proceedings at Strasburg should be stopped. They pressed for a distinct explanation, whether the Imperial Chamber would stay the proceedings in compliance with the emperor's commands, or not. The direct answers of the Chamber were obscure and evasive, the indirect—its actions—were perfectly clear. In November, 1533, the guildmasters and council of Strasburg were declared guilty. The city advocate again objected, that it was no longer an affair concerning Strasburg alone, but all Protestants, upon which the bishop's advocate asked the judge of the Imperial Chamber, Count von Beichlingen, whether his grace would allow his sentence, given doubtless after mature reflection, to be impeached in so unfair a manner. Judge and court, after a short delay, declared, that if within fourteen days nobody should come to terms on behalf of the city of Strasburg, judgment would be executed on the demand of the bishop's advocate.

At the same time difficulties were vexatiously thrown in the way of the Protestant procurator, Helfmann, because he persisted in taking the oath to God alone, and not to the saints also.

* 26th Jan 1533. Harpprecht, v 300

† "Dem Abschied von Augsburg, sonderlich der christlichen Religion und Glaubens halber, nachzukommen und stracks zu geleben."—"To follow the decree of Augsburg, especially touching the Christian religion, and to live strictly according to it."

The Protestants saw that the concessions they had obtained in the treaty of Nurnberg were, under these circumstances, of no avail to them. Meanwhile they were far from abandoning their claims: on the 30th July, 1534, they proceeded to a formal recusation of the acts of the Imperial Chamber.

The Council of Regency was abolished, the emperor at a distance, King Ferdinand not yet secure of the allegiance of his subjects, and the administrative powers which the emperor had committed to him, very imperfectly recognised. To all these elements of disorder was now added, that the authority of the tribunal which was the sole remaining representative of the unity of the empire, was repugned by a large portion of the States.

It is obvious how much these troubles tended to heighten the discontent which the rapid success of Landgrave Philip in his Wurtenberg campaign had already seriously aggravated.

They were accordingly among the most important subjects of discussion at Annaberg and Cadan.

One main inducement for the Elector of Saxony to give way as to the election was, that King Ferdinand, from whom hitherto nothing could be expected but a hostile influence on the Chamber, now bound himself, ' seeing that a misunderstanding had arisen concerning the peace of Nurnberg," to bring about an abandonment of the proceedings commenced against those included in that treaty. These words must be well weighed. The admission that a misunderstanding had arisen, the promise of a complete stop to proceedings, were clearly intended to silence, as far as it lay in the king's power, the cavils of the Imperial Chamber. So the Protestants understood it.* We do not know the injunction which the king hereupon issued to the Imperial Chamber, but it is the fact, that we find no complaint of any further proceedings of that tribunal.

The benefit of the truce extended, of course, only to those who were included by name in the peace of Nürnberg. But another point was determined at Cadan which tended materially to the spread of Protestantism.

King Ferdinand had at first not only wished to bind the Duke of Würtenberg by the terms of the peace, to receive his country as a fief held of him, but also, to attempt no alteration in religious matters, and an article was actually proposed, stipulating that the duke should leave everybody as he had found him in the matter of religion.† But if Ferdinand obstinately persisted, as we have seen, in the former demand, the elector was equally inflexible in rejecting the latter. It was impossible, he said, that he could ever consent that the word of God should not be preached according to his own confession and that of his deceased father, he could not obstruct the free course of the Gospel, he would not, even were the duke willing, rather would he withdraw his opposition to the election, the article in question must absolutely be erased.‡ Upon this the duke received the joyful intelligence that he was to remain unshackled as to religion, and have power to take measures for Christian order in concert with his subjects.§ The only restrictions imposed on him were in regard to those who, being possessed of certain regalia, were not properly to be considered his subjects.

These, then, are the decisions which render the peace of Cadan so important to the cause of Protestantism. It is clear that no such result was contemplated in the attempt on Wurtenberg, that the Protestant theologians hoped nothing, the pope feared nothing, from it. But, concluded by one of the chiefs of the evangelical party, in favour of a prince who during his banishment had imbibed similar sentiments, and ratified under conditions like those we have described, this peace could not fail to bring about a total alteration of the religious state of Wurtenberg.

The form which the reformation here assumed was also to a certain extent prescribed by the course of events.

Had the duke's restoration been brought about sooner by one of those political combinations which Zwingli contemplated, it is probable that his views of church government would also have gained an ascendancy in the duchy.

But now, the war having been conducted by Hessen, and the peace brought about by Saxony, after the defeat of the Swiss and the approximation of the Oberlanders to the Saxon confession, that result was not to be expected. On the contrary, the duke adopted the form of expression in use since that approximation, he announced that he would tolerate no one who preached any other doctrine than that of the true body and blood of Christ in the Lord's Supper. An article of the peace of Cadan was expressly directed against the Sacramenters.‖

At the same time he invited Ambrosius Blaurer, one of the most eminent Oberland

---

* Saxon memorial to the congress at Vienna 1535. The pretext of the Imperial Chamber, that it did not listen to any religious affairs, was, according to this, obviated by the treaty. "Indem das sich K Mt verpflichtet hat, obwol uf berurten nurnbergischen Frieden etwas Missverstand, —welcher Missverstand eben des Kammergerichts Gegenfürwendung gewest —furgefallen, soll er doch aufgehoben seyn" — "Inasmuch as his imperial majesty has bound himself, although a certain misunderstanding has occurred concerning the above mentioned treaty of Nürnberg" (which misunderstanding was neither more nor less than this pretext of the Imperial Chamber,) "that it should be removed."

† That is, without doubt, the meaning of the somewhat obscure words, "Das Herzog Ulrich einen jedern in dem Fürstenthumb Wirtenberg der Religionsachen halber in dem Wesen wie sie bis uf sein Einnehmen (gewesen), verfolgen, und zugestellt werden" — 'That Duke Ulrich should allow all men in the duchy of Wirtemberg to continue and be established in the state in which they were, as to religious matters, up to the time of his restoration."

‡ We know these negotiations from a letter of the Elector of Saxony to the king. Sattler, iii p 129. On the margin, by the side of this article, is written "Sol aussen pleiben"—"Must be left out."

§ Through Hans von Dolzk, Letter from Ulrich, ibid 124.

‖ Letter to Blaurer 22d December, 1534. The addition "Wie Euch denn selber alles wohl wissen ist,"—"As all is known to yourself," shows that Ulrich, from the first, held the same language.

theologians and an intimate friend of Butzer's, together with the Marburg professor Erard Schnepf, a decided follower of Luther, to organise the church of Wurtenberg They began by agreeing on a formula satisfactory to both Their agreement is a symptom of the gradual consolidation of the unity of the German evangelical church *

Thereupon Blaurer undertook the reformation of the country above and Schnepf that of the country below, the Staig † The priests were no longer convoked according to the rural chapters, as heretofore, but according to the secular division of the country into bailiwicks, and after the main points of the evangelical doctrine had been expounded to them, were asked to state what the government had to expect from them Spite of all the exertions of the Austrian government for the maintenance of the religious edicts, there were still a considerable number even of the priests who joined the evangelical party at the first invitation. In the bailiwick of Tubingen there were seven, the remaining twelve asked for time to consider ‡ Under these circumstances the ritual was altered without difficulty In many places the mass was voluntarily abandoned, in others, it was discontinued according to order Schnepf instituted a form of the Lord's Supper with which the Oberlanders were satisfied

The monasteries were next taken in hand Duke Ulrich made no secret of "his intention of applying their property to the payment of the public debt, and the relief of the people from intolerable burdens" As he had been so long out of the country, and had taken upon him Ferdinand's debts to the Swabian league, it is not to be wondered at that he found himself in pecuniary difficulties, for which this was the only remedy §

He did not suffer himself to be restrained by the limitations laid down in the peace of Cadan The Austrian government had led the way, it had asserted the rights of the state over endowments of doubtful sovereignty, and could not make much objection if its successor did the same

The whole country was thus in a short time transformed Duke Ulrich had the merit of devoting particular attention to the university. We find many distinguished names among the teachers, the system of stipends adopted in Hessen was introduced with increased effect into Wurtenberg Tubingen gradually became one of the most distinguished nurseries of Protestant learning

Wurtenberg was a conquest of Protestantism based on the old hereditary rights of German princes, a conquest of double value, inasmuch as it was achieved in precisely that region where the Swabian league had hitherto obstructed the progress of the evangelical faith ‖ Throughout the Oberland this now acquired fresh activity, in Alsatia, where the influence of Strasburg had not been impaired, in the neighbouring dynastic domains, Markgrave Bernhard of Baden, Count Philip IV of Hanau, Louis of Falkenstein, William of Furstenberg (the joint leader in the Wurtenberg war), gradually reformed the church in their territories, as did also numerous imperial cities. Scarcely could the news of the battle of Laufen be known, when Michael Kress, the parish priest of Weissenburg in the Wasgau, discontinued the mass (June, 1534), the council concurred with him, and warned the discontented servants of the chapter to quit the town without delay The greatest impression, however, was made by the conversion of Augsburg The reformed doctrine had long been gaining ground there, but the old opinions had still powerful supporters, among whom were the Fuggers, and had any thing been attempted against the bishop and chapter, the law or the Swabian league would have hastened to their assistance It is obvious, however, that a state of things in which the minds of men were daily embittered by conflicting or hostile preaching, was not tenable in a community that pretended to some political weight in the empire, these points of difference now constituted the most important part of public affairs The evangelical party, which had long been the majority, now took courage, under the political influences of those times, to assert their rights ¶ A disputation was proposed to the clergy As they either entirely refused to enter into it, or would do so only under conditions which the city could not accede to, the greater and lesser council, with the burgermeister Wolf Rehlinger at their head, passed a resolution, that no more papistical preaching should be allowed, no mass tolerated, except in the church immediately belonging to the bishop This happened on the 22d July Hereupon most of the chapels were closed, a part of the clergy left the city,

* They both confessed, Corpus et sanguinem Christi vere i e substantialiter et essentialiter, non autem quantitative aut qualitative vel localiter, præsentia esse et exhiberi in cœna, a formula, the scholastic fashion of which scandalised many of the evangelical party

† In Schnurrer's Erlauterungen der W K und Ref Gesch it is stated as a fact, (p 127,) that many whom Schnepf sent away as doubtful, went a few miles further and were accepted by Blaurer Schnurrer refers for this to Fussli's Epistolæ Reformatorum p 99 There is a letter of Haller to Bullinger in which the former relates what he had heard from Thomas Blaurer in August, 1534, —consequently at the very beginning of the difference between the two parties, quam male conveniat Wirtembergensibus ministris (as the Schnepfians are full of sneers at enthusiasts), et dum quibusdam de Schnepfio periculum sit cum ad ministerium apti sint, quum prima prope sit interrogatio de eucharistæ causa, si Lutheranus fuerit, quantumvis alioquin doctus, admittatur, sin minus, rejiciatur et ab Ambrosio recipiatur It is clear that Thomas Blaurer speaks of it only as a danger,—a possibility Jac Sturm was of the same opinion "Schnepf schuhe die unsern, werde die in Anstellung der Kirche meiden"—"Schnepf is shy of our people, and will avoid them in his appointments to the church" But it remains to be proved whether circumstances really turned out as Schnurrer sets forth

‡ Bericht Ambrosii Blaurers was er mit den Pfaffen Tubinger Umts ausgerichtet (Report of Ambrose Blaurer what he effected with the priests of the Tubinger bailiwick) Sattler, iii App No 16

§ Schnurrer Erlauterungen, p 149, No. 1

‖ Cassarus, in Mencken i p 1798 this took place "Non sine totius Sueviæ pfafforum monachorumque consternatione"

¶ Cassarus, passim Stetten, 335. Zapf, Leben Stadions, p 82.

while another rallied the more closely round the bishop and the chapter.

Analogous motives regarding the internal affairs of the city led, about the same time, to the formal conversion of Frankfurt, though without so marked an influence of political causes.*

We need not adduce any more facts to show that the new religion, though certainly favoured by the course of political affairs, possessed great independent force and activity; it had prepared the very events which contributed to its emancipation.

It was sometimes sufficiently strong to maintain itself in complete contradiction to what the political situation of the country seemed to require; as, for example, in Anhalt.

For what could be more perilous for the majority of the Anhalt princes (in whose name one of them — Prince John — had subscribed the recess of Augsburg), than to retract in direct opposition to those powerful neighbours whose favour was absolutely essential to them,—Duke George of Saxony, the Elector Joachim of Brandenburg, and the Archbishop Albert? One of the brothers, Prince George, was an ecclesiastic, and already prebendary of Magdeburg and Merseburg cathedrals; his prospects seemed bound up with the existence of the Catholic church. Yet it was he who contributed the most to the change. He declared that, near as he lived to the birth-place of Lutheranism, he had been deceived as to its true character; it had been represented to him in the most unfavourable light possible; he had been told that good works were forbidden by it, good ordinances subverted, and license given for all unchristian practices. But he had convinced himself of the contrary. He had found that the Holy Scriptures were taught conformably with the ancient Romish church.† He gradually became so zealous, and so persuasive in his exhortations to his brothers, that a Dominican friar having indulged in violent language against the use of the sacrament in both kinds, on Holy Thursday of the year 1532, in the pulpit at Dessau, they displaced him, and appointed in his stead Nicholas Hausmann, a friend of Luther. Duke George of Saxony instantly threatened them with the emperor's displeasure; he predicted the utter failure of their attempts, and the ruin of Prince George's prospects in the church; but he made no impression upon them, either by representations of this kind, or by his doctrinal arguments.‡ They went on fearlessly. The circumstance, that a member of the reigning house also held a high office in the diocese, was of great importance. As archdeacon and prebendary of the church of Magdeburg, Prince George deemed himself entitled to exercise a regular spiritual authority in his dominions. In virtue of this combined spiritual and temporal power, he convoked the clergy of the Anhalt country on the 16th March, 1534, and admonished them in future to administer the Lord's Supper in both kinds.§ The archbishop cardinal was dissatisfied, as may be imagined, but Prince George insisted that the spiritual jurisdiction belonged in the first place to him, as archdeacon, while the archiepiscopal superintendence remained with the cardinal. Spite of all opposition, he gradually filled the benefices south of the Elbe with disciples of Luther. But when the reform was about to begin in the country on the other side, within the jurisdiction of the Bishop of Brandenburg, matters were altered. At first, Prince George requested the bishop to ordain whatever priests he might send him. But as the latter naturally refused to admit married priests into the Catholic church, Prince George no longer hesitated to send his candidates to Wittenberg, where Luther examined them, and, if he found them attached to pure and sound doctrine, gave them a certificate, and ordained them.

It was fortunate that things anywhere took so peaceful a course.

In other parts, as, for example, in Pomerania, there were the most violent intestine struggles. Indeed, there had always been peculiar exasperation between parties in that country. In some of the towns there had been iconoclastic riots, and with what hatred the adherents of popery requited them, may be seen in the satirical songs which are extant. The nobility and clergy of the whole country were leagued against the towns. The two princes, George and Barnim, quarrelled. Even in 1531, the Protestants had feared that George would take an active share in the war which threatened them. But Barnim — the same who had taken part in the Leipzig disputation — sent word to the league, that what his brother built up, he would pull down,¶ that he had wished for a division of the provinces and a separate government, in order that he might be able to support the religious reforms. At this moment, however, Duke George died, and his son Philip, young, eager for instruction, and rather at variance with his Catholic step-mother, was more easy to gain over. It is probable that Barnim and Philip, at an interview at Cammin, in August, 1534, agreed to undertake in their dominions what had already been effected in so many others. At a diet at Treptow, in the following December, they laid before the meeting a project of a reformation, which was, in fact, founded on a proposition of the towns, and,

* Kirchner, Geschichte von Frankfurt, ii. 84. I shall revert to both these cities.

† Letter from George to the emperor, in Fürst Georgs Schriften und Predigten (Prince George's Writings and Sermons), p. 368.

‡ Letter of Prince Joachim to George, Furst Georgs Schriften und Predigten, p. 384. Luther rejoices at this commencement, "Etiamsi id factum non sit sine gravi periculo, magnis principibus contrarium suadentibus, imo super etiam minantibus." Letter to the three brothers John, Joachim, and George, in Lindner's Mittheilungen aus der Anhaltischen Geschichte (Communications from the History of Anhalt), part ii., which contains some letters wanting in De Wette.

§ Instructions to the envoys of John and Joachim of Anhalt to the archbishop. (Dessau Archives.)

¶ Proceedings at Schmalkalden, Judica, 1531. He declined joining the Schmalkaldic league "because the domains were still undivided between him and his brothers."

with some trifling alterations, joyfully accepted by them. The excellent Pomeranian, Doctor Bugenhagen, was invited to undertake a visitation of the churches in the manner of Wittenberg. But the nobles and clergy raised a most violent opposition. The Bishop of Cammin, who had been entreated to direct the changes, utterly refused; the Abbot of Altencamp produced a mandate of the Imperial Chamber, forbidding the dukes to make any innovation. The knights were made to believe that a league was in agitation between the princes and the towns, which could only turn out to their injury; and therefore refused to take the smallest share in the reforms.*

This was, indeed, the state of a great part of Lower Germany. Duke Henry of Mecklenburg, who, in 1534, took the sacrament in both kinds, was opposed by his brother Albert, together with the greater part of the country. The resistance which the change still experienced in Holstein, appears in a letter of Landgrave Philip to Duke Christian, as to the means of gaining over the nobility. Almost everywhere we find the chapters and the equestrian order (Ritterschaften) in array against the reforming tendencies of the cities. In Westphalia, especially, the most violent contest had broken out.

The course and progress of things in the cities of Westphalia were the same as in those of Saxony. Lutheran hymns were sung by boys in the streets, by men and women in the houses, first in an evening, and then by day; and Lutheran preachers arose. Here and there a convent voluntarily broke up, as at Hervord, while the priories of monks and nuns which remained adopted the reformation.† The priest of Lemgo, who had been a steady adherent of John Eck, was at length convinced by the writings of his antagonists, and travelled to Brunswick in order to inspect the nature and mode of the change; he returned an evangelical preacher, and introduced reform into the town. The old bürgermeister Flörken, who had been a great admirer of the hierarchical system, and held it to be the only legitimate form of Christianity, was obliged to yield to the innovators, who confuted the scholastic doctrines out of the Epistle to the Romans.‡

There were, however, but two or three places in which the movement was so peacefully carried forward; elsewhere, it gave occasion to scenes of violence and blood, especially in Soest and Paderborn.

In the former city, the bürgermeister and councillors had been compelled, against their will, to sanction the Lutheran preaching, and to adopt the Confession of Augsburg, and an evangelical form of church government.§ But since they remained in office, it was impossible to avoid continual irritation between them and the leaders of the evangelical party in the commune. There was a tanner, named Schlachtorp, who was peculiarly odious to them; and thinking to re-establish their tottering authority, at least in civil matters, they seized on the pretext of an excess of which he and two or three others, heated with wine, had been guilty, to arrest him, bring him to judgment, and condemn him and his companions to death. Nobody was prepared for such a sentence—for their only crime in fact was some insulting and irritating language—Schlachtorp least of all, for otherwise he could easily have made his escape. No representation as to the trifling nature of the offence, no intercession, was of any avail; the day of execution was fixed. In order to protect them in this act, the council entrusted the most loyal of the citizens, who were still in part Catholic, with arms. We must accompany the victim to the scaffold. When he reached it, he turned to the multitude of his fellow-citizens of his own opinions, who were assembled in great numbers, though unarmed, and after protesting that he died for the cause of religion alone, he began to sing the hymn,—"Mit Fried und Freud fahr ich dahin." (With peace and joy I go hence.) The whole multitude joined in. They were convinced that the unfortunate man was a victim to arbitrary power; but the council wielded the sword of justice, and they did not think themselves justified in interposing. The executioner asked which of the condemned would die first. Schlachtorp craved that honour, sat down upon the chair, suffered his shirt to be pulled off, and presented his neck to the stroke. As fortune would have it, the executioner did not take good aim, and the stroke, instead of falling on his neck, fell on his back; so that Schlachtorp and the chair in which he was seated were overturned, and, though fearfully wounded, he was still living. The other executioner came forward, raised him up, and placed his neck in a position to receive a second stroke. But meantime Schlachtorp had recovered his consciousness; he thought he had given justice her due, and was absolved from all further obligations; though his hands were bound, by a rapid turn he snatched the sword, already again uplifted, from the executioner's hand, and grasped it with a strength redoubled by the mortal peril, till he had torn the cords from his hands with his teeth; when he brandished the weapon, crimsoned with his own blood, around him with such force, that neither of the executioners dared to approach him. All this was the work of a moment. But in that moment the sympathy of the people, which had been repressed with such difficulty, burst forth. The magistrates ordered the executioners to desist; the crowd carried Schlach-

* Letter of Abbot Johann Huls (8th June), and the Pomeranian Order of Knights (25th October, 1535), in Medem, Gesch. der Einführung der ev. Lehre in Pommern, 197, 231.

† "Wolte," says Luther, "dass die Klöster alle so ernstlich Gottes Wort wolten beten und halten."—"Would that the convents all would so earnestly pray (*i.e.*, read with devotion), and keep God's word."

‡ The other bürgermeister who then resigned was Andreas Kleinsorg, grandfather of Gerhard von Kleinsorgen, who wrote a history of the Westphalian church, of a Catholic tendency.

§ The Catholic clergy were commanded "ut honeste viverent—abolita superstitione tantum." Most of them quitted the city.

torp, holding the captured sword in his hand, in triumph to his house, where, on the following day, he died from loss of blood and violent agitation. Never was there such a funeral seen as his. Men and women, old and young, evangelical and Catholic, accompanied the body, all pressing to see the sword of justice which was laid on the coffin. This incident raised the ferment of all spirits and the exasperation against the council to such a pitch, that the latter thought itself every moment menaced with violence and tumult, and at length deemed it best to leave the town (July, 1533). A new council was then appointed, and the evangelical organisation completed.

The events which occurred at Paderborn also lead us to the foot of the scaffold, though not to witness so terrible a catastrophe. Here, too, the common people had, by violence and intimidation, obtained liberty of preaching, and had already delivered over several churches to Protestant preachers, no negotiation of the Landdroste,* no orders of the diet, had availed to reclaim them. Such was the state of things when the newly elected administrator of the chapter, Hermann of Cologne, rode into the town at the head of the leading men of the land and an armed retinue, to receive their homage. Hermann was by nature no zealot (we shall meet him hereafter on a totally different path), but the representations of the canons and the council, joined to some resentment at the disregard shown to his authority, at length moved him to a violent step. He once more, and, as he said, in order to take a gracious leave, invited the citizens to the garden of the monastery of Abdinkhoven, on their arrival, they were surrounded with armed soldiers; the leaders of the evangelical party were seized and thrown into prison. They were accused of a design to deliver up the city to the Landgrave of Hessen, put to the torture, and sentenced to death in presence of the assembled people, and in sight of the scaffold, already strewn with the sand that was to drink their blood. But things were not allowed to pass here as in Soest. The first executioner declared that they were innocent men, and that he would rather die himself, than put them to death. An aged man was heard to call out of the crowd, into which he had crawled, leaning on his staff, that he was as guilty as the condemned, and that he demanded to be executed with them; at the same moment, the women and young maidens of the town rushed out of an adjoining house with disordered garments and dishevelled hair, and implored, weeping, mercy for the prisoners.† The tears came into the eyes of Elector Hermann (one of the house of Wied), who, as we have said, loved not deeds of violence; and as he saw that his temporal lords were also moved, he granted the condemned men their lives. But their doctrines were effectually put down. Those inclined to them were kept under strict supervision, and fined at the pleasure of the authorities. A recess was drawn up, by which the new doctrines were forbidden under the severest penalties.‡

Such were the conflicting powers in Westphalia: on the one side, spiritual princes, cathedral chapters, knightly orders and city authorities, closely bound together, on the other, bodies of citizens vehemently excited, and inflamed by zealous preachers, the one class not less wilful and violent than the other. The former scrupled not to employ their jurisdictional and magisterial powers with the extremest severity to suppress the new opinions, the other, obedient so long as the strict letter of the law was concerned, were ripe for revolt at any moment when that appeared to be in the least degree violated. The spiritual government, which held together the higher classes by the bonds of a common interest, was attacked by the lower, who rejected its authority, with all the violence of incipient rebellion.

Nowhere, however, did these conflicting elements come into fiercer collision, than in the centre of spiritual organisation, in that place where the word used to denote the convent founded on the banks of the Aa, at the time of the first introduction of Christianity, had superseded the ancient name of the place and the district, and had become the name of the town and the country—in Munster.

Bernhard Rottman, a Lutheran preacher, who had already been driven away, fixed himself again at the church of St Maurice in the suburbs, and became so popular, that at length the bishop, urged by the clergy of the city, sent him a safe-conduct, and desired him to go. The consequence of this, however, was, that his followers in the city itself received him, they first built him a wooden pulpit in a churchyard, but soon after—rather by the threat, than the actual application of force—opened to him the church of St Lambert.§ A committee of the citizens was next appointed to defend the new doctrines against the clergy and the council. Other Lutheran preachers appeared, and a disputation was held, the object of which was, to show the abuses of the established mode of worship. As they found no able defender, the sentiments of the people gained influence over the council (which, consistent with the ancient constitution of the country, was open to popular influences), and at length obtained a majority. They then proceeded without delay to a final arrangement. At a solemn meeting at the Schauhaus, all the parish churches were delivered up to the newly come preachers, by the council, aldermen (oldemänner) and guildmasters. The clergy, together with the mi-

* A sort of magistrate, high bailiff.—TRANSL.

† Hamelmann Hist renov evangelii, 1328, here, my chief authority.

‡ "We will that now and henceforth no strange man or woman, serving man or maid, who come out of such towns or villages as are attached to the new doctrine, or are accused of the same, be received as servants in our city of Paderborn," 1532, 15th October. Kleinsorgea, p. 361.

§ So the oldest and simplest report relates. "Dorpius Wahrhaftige Historie, wie das Evangelium zu Münster angegangen." "True history how the gospel was assailed at Munster."

nority of the council, quitted the city. The religious revolution was, as so often happened in those times, connected with civil changes.

But those who had been expelled were less inclined in Munster than elsewhere to despair of their cause: they found natural allies in the knights (Ritterschaft) and the chapter. Here, too, advantage was taken of the accession of a new bishop, Francis von Waldeck, to excite the whole country against the city. All communication with it was cut off, its rents and the interest of its moneys were withheld, and the citizens themselves taken prisoners wherever they were caught. The condition attached to the removal of these oppressive measures was, the restoration of the old religion.

The evangelical party, however, who thought themselves in the right, were not disposed to yield. If force were appealed to, they felt themselves strong enough to resist, and the best opportunity soon offered for striking a blow which must decide the contest.

The bishop had just ridden with the States to receive homage at Telgte, a mile from Munster. The injunction to the citizens, to conform again to the ancient faith, was issued from this place, on the Christmas-day of 1532. They instantly resolved what course to pursue. During the following night they marched upon Telgte, nine hundred strong, partly brave citizens, partly tried soldiers, armed with matchlocks and two or three small cannon, laid on four-wheeled wagons. Fortune favoured them so far that the bishop's mounted posts did not fall in with them. They arrived at Telgte in the gray of the morning, broke in the gates, took possession of the streets, and found their way into the houses where their enemies were quietly sleeping. They took them nearly all prisoners, the princes, councillors, the highest members of the cathedral chapter, and of the equestrian order, together with their own councillors who had quitted the town, the prince himself, by good luck, was gone, they suffered the deputies of the small towns to depart, but they carried all the rest—all their opponents—back to Munster on carts.* At about eleven o'clock the train, announced by the joyous beat of the drum, re-entered the city in triumph.

The people thus for the present attained their end. The bishop could not make a regular attack upon them, for even had he had the means, he would have been restrained by fear of the vengeance the citizens might take on the prisoners in their hands. The anxious families of these prisoners now endeavoured to put an end to the hostilities they themselves had excited.† By the mediation of Hessen, a peace was at length concluded in February, 1533, according to the terms of which, liberty to follow the Confession of Augsburg, both as to ceremonies and preaching, was guarantied to the city for its six parish churches, while, on the other hand, the citizens were to permit the exiles to return, and allow the ancient ritual to subsist for the bishop, chapter and monastery. The landgrave as mediator, the bishop and chapter, the delegates of the order of knights (among whom were a Raesfeld, two Drostes, and a Buren), and the councillors of the cities, signed the treaty of peace. All seemed now set at rest. The bishop appeared in the city, and received the homage, an evangelical church ordinance was published, in which a provision was made for the poor, and negotiations were opened for joining the Schmalkaldic league.

Had these things remained, says Kersenbroik, the clergy of Munster would have fallen under a yoke never again to be thrown off. We may add, that had these things remained, Protestantism would now be the prevalent religion of town and country in Westphalia. The neighbouring communes, Warendorf, Beckum, Aalen, Coesfeld, already imitated the example of Munster. The bishop himself, who was not more fixed in his opinions than Hermann of Cologne, would at length have been borne with the stream, and Munster would have decided the fate of Westphalia.

But a signal example was to be given to the world, of the dangers inevitably attending a change in long-established things.

The principle of the reformation was once more in living progress, it was spreading victoriously through all Germany; but for that very reason, its effect on the actions, the wants and the passions of men admitted neither of restraint nor calculation. It is true that the Protestants had at length acquired a regularly constituted organ, whose legality and compatibility with the condition and welfare of the empire had obtained recognition, though at first an unwilling and partial one, but even to this the innovators could not entirely adhere. The members of the Schmalkaldic league, in whose favour the peace had been made, were specified by name, and these did not yet venture to unite with others. The new opinions were compelled to make their way by their own strength, and it naturally followed that they struck into paths deviating from the constituted evangelical church.

At an earlier period of the reformation, the movement in the towns of Lower Saxony was with difficulty arrested at the results of its first successes, or appeased by the mere freedom of divine worship according to the new ritual. In Magdeburg, community of goods had been preached under some lingering influences of

* Instructions and Report of Thanne von Hardt, Marshal of Munster, in the Cleves Records, Dusseldorf Archives. Negotiations and attack as already related. "Alsdann etlich unser gewaltigen Heren von Munster, desgleichen rede, verordente, eins Domcapitels und der Ritterschap, ok somige ander des Adels, ok somige von den Steden gefenglich genummen."—"Then certain of our powerful lords of Munster, the council of the same, the delegates from the chapter of the cathedral and the order of knights, and some of the nobles and some of the citizens were taken prisoners."

† Letter of Bishop Francis (after confirmation), 17th Jan. 1533, "sind wir durch etzliche Grafen auch ein trefflichen Adel und Verwandte, sunderlich den von Buern und Mengersheim umb Erlösung derselben die also in unserm Dienst niedergelacht, sehr heftig angesucht."—"We are very vehemently solicited by certain counts, also excellent nobles and kinsmen, especially by them of Buern and Mengersheim, for the liberation of those who have thus succumbed in our service."

the peasants' war, and it required as determined a will as that of Amsdorf, who was chosen superintendent of the church of Magdeburg, to assert and maintain the pacific intentions of Luther In Brunswick, an inclination to Zwingli's views showed itself soon after the creation of the Lutheran church-establishment, even among the preachers who had assisted in constructing it, they rejected the organ and singing in parts, and especially certain hymns sung during the communion, expressive of the Lutheran view of that institution, but the council of the city, and especially the syndic Levin of Emden, declared themselves against every innovation, and would not suffer any thing at variance with the received ordinances of the church to be devised, doubtless they feared that it would not be easy to set limits to a new movement We observe similar appearances in Goslar They arose in part from the Zwinglians who had been driven out of Brunswick, but here, too, Amsdorf watched over the integrity of the Wittenberg ordinances, and their opponents were driven away

Movements of a kindred nature, but far more violent, now took place in Munster The preachers who had arisen during the conflict (of whom the most zealous, Rottmann, now held the office of superintendent) not only betrayed a leaning to the Zwinglian view of the Lord's Supper, but what (considering the manner in which opinions were at that time implicated) was much more important, — a wide departure even from Zwingli in relation to the other sacrament Rottmann rejected infant baptism All the lovers of peace in Munster, all who were satisfied with what they had obtained, were alarmed, the council, democratically as it was constituted, opposed him, a disputation was held, the result of which was, a formal declaration against Rottmann The university of Marburg too gave in an opinion against him, and certain Hessian theologians came to support the council in its resistance to the innovators With all this, however, the new council, which had still to contend with the tendencies of the Catholic party, was not strong enough to have recourse to energetic measures Rottmann and his followers remained in the town, and their secret influence was the greater, the more it was openly controlled They were not inclined to submit to a secular authority, owing its existence to a religious movement which had been headed by themselves

In this state of things they fell upon the thought of publicly introducing in Munster an element of the general moral and intellectual confusion to which they had already been somewhat inclined — Anabaptism. This has frequently crossed our path in the course of our history, and we have seen how, expelled and persecuted by every legitimate authority, it yet always exercised a resistless power over the minds of men

The importance of its admission into Munster was by no means confined to that city It was an event of universal significancy

The principle of reform, now embodied in a regular system, again saw tendencies rise around it, by which it was, in its turn, threatened with destruction

If, on the one side, it had established itself on impregnable foundations against the assaults of the ancient church, it was destined to encounter, from the opposite quarter, dangers which at some moments seemed to threaten its very existence

The arena for the free struggles of the intellect was now thrown open, it was soon to appear that conquests on that field are neither easy to win, nor to maintain.

CHAPTER IX

ANABAPTISTS IN MUNSTER CURSORY AND GENERAL VIEW OF ANABAPTISM

AT a moment when the great ecclesiastical institutions which for centuries had held all consciences enthralled by ordinances more or less arbitrary, was shaken, partially overthrown and robbed of its influence, it was not probable that the minds of men could be brought again to concur in one positive set of opinions

The wonder is less that this could not be completely effected, than that it was actually accomplished to so great an extent

At the moment before us, however, antagonist principles were about once more to come into violent collision

We saw the resistance that Zwingli, as well as Luther, had to encounter from a third party, which rejected infant baptism We observed at the same time, that this rejection formed by no means the exclusive point of dissent, but was merely the badge of a party which differed on innumerable other points, and exhibited infinite shades and varieties

It were well worth while to explore this eccentric state of opinion, to collect the strange writings in which it found utterance, and to trace out their inward connexion

So far as I can gain a general view of the matter, it appears to me that there were, in regard to doctrine, two distinct lines of opinion, diverging from the same point

The dogma of justification occupied the attention of the Anabaptists, as well as of their cotemporaries, and gradually led them to the discussion of the questions of the two natures in Christ, and the powers and qualities of the soul They all adhered to the belief of the freedom of the will (and in that respect were opposed to Luther), but they differed in the conclusions they drew from it

The one party thought the question a very simple one They held that man could unquestionably earn salvation by virtuous conduct and by his own efforts, that Christ was rather our teacher and father than our redeemer. This opinion was particularly expounded by Hans Denk, a very distinguished young man; — learned, conscientious and modest, at least he acknowledged, what scarcely any other of his associates would grant, that it was possible he might err The basis of his doctrine is, that God is love, which, he said, flesh and blood could never have understood, had it not been embodied in certain human beings, who might be called divine men, or the children of God But in one of them, love was supremely exemplified,—in Jesus of Nazareth He had never stumbled in the path marked out by God, He had never lost his unity with God, He was a saviour of his people, for he was the forerunner of all those who should be saved This was the meaning of the words, that all should be saved by Christ *

Intimately connected with Hans Denk was Ludwig Hatzer, they translated a part of the prophets into German together Hatzer, however, was not only licentious in his life, but pushed his doctrines to their extremest consequences He was the first man of that time who denied the divinity of Christ We are not able to say how he arrived at this opinion, nor by what arguments he maintained it, the book he wrote upon it was never printed, and Ambrosius Blaurer burned the last manuscript copy

Hans Kautz, of Bockenheim, near Worms, put forth similar doctrines He maintained that Jesus Christ of Nazareth was our Saviour, inasmuch as he left footsteps, by treading in which we might attain to salvation, whoever taught more than this, converted him into an idol †

It is difficult to believe how widely these opinions were diffused We find them in Salzburg, without being able to trace how they got there They were professed by a community of poor people who rejected all divine worship, lived together in solitary places, and established confraternities by voluntary contributions, they called themselves Gardener-brethren (*Gartnerbruder*) They believed that the desire to do good was inherent in man, and that if he fulfilled the law, it was enough, for that God drew us to himself by that necessity of acting justly, which He had imposed on us that Christ was by no means the fulfiller of the law but a teacher of Christian life,‡—doctrines of no very profound, but of a perfectly innocuous character Nevertheless, they drew down upon these poor people the most terrific punishment Some of them being discovered at a meeting in the house of a parish priest, had, without hesitation, given the names of the absent members of their society Hereupon, they were all delivered up to justice Those of weaker faith, who allowed themselves to be persuaded to recant, were first beheaded and then burnt. Those who refused to recant, were consigned alive to the flames "They lived long," says a cotemporaneous account, "and called aloud upon God, so that it was most piteous to hear" In other places they were brought together into the house where they had frequently held their meetings and preached to one another, fastened in, and the house set fire to "They cried out most lamentably together, and at length gave up the ghost God help them and us all!"

There was a beautiful girl of sixteen, who could by no means be induced to recant,—for indeed the soul is at that age stronger and more capable of the highest flights of devotedness to a great moral sentiment, than at a more advanced period of life,—it is certain that she was guilty of the things whereof she was accused, but in all other respects she had the consciousness and the expression of the purest innocence. Everybody supplicated for her life The executioner took her in his arms, carried her to a place near where horses were watered, and held her under the water till she was drowned, he then drew out the lifeless body and committed it to the flames §

The other party, of whom mention was made, was led to totally different conclusions on the same questions of redemption and justification They assumed a fundamental separation between flesh and spirit. Instead of holding that man is able of his own strength to do that which is right, and is saved by righteousness, and that this is the doctrine preached by Christ, they maintained, that the flesh alone sinned, and that the spirit was not affected by its acts, since it did not participate in the fall that the whole man was rendered as free by the restoration, as before the fall, or even more so Inasmuch as they ascribed this restoration to Christ, they taught that his humanity was of a peculiar nature, that he took nothing of his mother at his birth, but in him the pure word was made flesh, for the flesh of Adam was accursed These views were also very widely disseminated, there are Anabaptist hymns in which they are distinctly expressed ‖ It is not improbable that

* Passages from his Buch von der Liebe (Book of Love). Arnold, i 1305 He was not consistent in his opinions Œkolampadius (Epp Zw et Œc p 169), maintains that he retracted shortly before his death "Etiamsi nec illa purgatissima erant" See Vadian to Zwick, in Fussli, Beitrage, v 397

† Röhrich Gesch der Ref in Elsass i 338 Zwingli refers to him in the Elenchus contra Catabaptistas, in which he says, Apud Vangiones Denckii et Hetzeri cum Cutiis nescio quibus nihil obscure plenam perlitationem per Christum negant, quod nihil aliud est quam novum testamentum conculcare "

‡ Newe Zeyttung von den widdenteufern und yhrer Sect, 1528 — New Journal of the Anabaptists and their Sect, 1528 Appended are 13 articles, "welche sie sur warhaftig halten," "which they hold for true," *e g*, "Es sey ein inniges ziehen des Vaters damit er uns zu yhm ziehe, das sey wenn man lere recht thun von aussen "—"Sie mogen Guts thun von yhnen selbst wie sie erschaffen "—"That there is an inward attraction of the Father, whereby he may draw us to himself that is, if we teach men to do rightly from without (i e in outward acts) "They may do good of themselves, as they are created to do"

§ Newe Zeyttung In Zauner's Salzburger Chronik, v. 119, there are some further notices concerning these priests, &c, although the anecdote above was unknown to him

‖ The song, for example, which is inserted in the history and traditions of Munster, (Munsterischen Geschichte und Sagen,) p. 291 The prisoner is there asked whether Christ be of the flesh and blood of the Virgin Mary

"Das hab ich nie gelesen, hab ich vor ihnen bekannt,
Wie soll der von Erde wesen den Gott uns hat gesandt "

Caspar Schwenkfeld, who also rejected the church, as then constituted, and infant baptism, and denied that the body of Christ was created, contributed greatly to their development.* Melchior Hoffmann, who busied himself so much with these points, was certainly instigated by him. Hoffmann declared himself at first for unconditional election by grace; but he afterwards maintained that every man might be made partaker of grace; those only were lost without hope of mercy, who, having been once enlightened, fell off again from the truth. He proposed to unite all in whom any sign of grace manifested itself, into one congregation by second baptism.†

Many and still greater diversities showed themselves among the Anabaptists in respect of conduct and practice.

Some regarded infant baptism as useless, others as an abomination; some demanded the strictest community of goods, others went no further than the duty of mutual help. Some segregated themselves as much as possible, and held it to be unchristian to celebrate the Sabbath; others declared it culpable to follow after singularities. Sebastian Frank, who knew them well, and was even thought to belong to them, gives a long list of divergencies which he had observed among them.‡

It was impossible that they should not come into collision with the civil power in various ways.

This was obviously the case with those who refused to perform military service, or to take an oath. They esteemed it a crime to take away life under any circumstances whatsoever, and regarded an oath as sinful and forbidden. This could not possibly be allowed in the cities, the defence of which was still entirely confided to the citizens themselves; nor in those, like Strasburg, where the whole allegiance was connected with the oath of citizenship (Bürgereid), which was taken on the yearly swearing day (Schwörtag).

As we advance, we find others who thought themselves called upon to reform the institution of marriage, on the plea that none was valid, save such as was concluded in the spirit. One of this class of reformers was the tanner, Claus Frei, who had deserted his wife, and rambled about the world with another woman, whom he called "his only true spiritual wedded sister."§

All, however, agreed in declaring the church government, formed by the combined authority of the magistrate and the priest, insupportable; and maintained that if everybody were allowed to preach, there would be no such thing as schism. They declared that the institutions framed by the evangelical leaders were nothing else than a new kind of papacy.

They were persuaded, too, that these could not last long. One of the most essential points of their creed is, the apocalyptic expectation of a speedy and total revolution and a complete victory, which Münzer and Storch had fostered. Following their example, the later leaders had also indulged in the most magnificent visions, each on his own behalf, and had contrived to procure belief in them, at least among his immediate friends and followers.

Hubmayr likened Nicolspurg, where one of the house of Lichtenstein hospitably entertained him, to Emmaus; "for it began to be night, and the last days were at hand."

Melchior Hoffmann, a travelling tanner, already mentioned, whom we meet with in Alsatia, in Stockholm, in Livonia, in Kiel and in East Friesland, — one while intimately connected with powerful princes, and another, pining in prison,—at length returned to Strasburg. This city, he declared, was destined to be the seat of the New Jerusalem, whence, according to the Apocalypse (c. xiv.), a hundred and forty-four thousand virgin apostles were to issue forth, to gather all the elect of God into the fold.

By degrees, the idea of introducing such a state of things by force was agitated.

Hans Hut imagined he could prove out of Moses and the Prophets, that the Anabaptists were destined, as children of God, like the Israelites of old, to root out the ungodly, to which God himself could call them.‖

In the Würtenberg territory, a man named Zuberhans, who was taken prisoner in the year 1528, confessed that he and other true believers had determined to begin the work on the following Easter; seven hundred of them were to meet at Reutlingen, and to proceed immediately to overthrow the government of Würtenberg, to put the priests to death, and to effect a complete revolution.¶

Melchior Hoffman did not threaten to use the sword himself, but he was persuaded that recourse must be had to it. He had been for a time in personal communication with Frederic I., King of Denmark, and he declared him to be one of the two sovereigns by whom, when the times should be come (for they had not yet arrived), all the first-born of Egypt should be slain, till the true gospel should possess the earth, and the marriage of the Lamb be accomplished. But all his disciples had not his moderation. Some of them were of opinion that the times were actually come, and that they were themselves destined to wield the sword. Thus these opinions very quickly rose from the more strange than dangerous peculiarities of the Quietists (*Stillen im Lande*), to the furious violence of fanatical world-reformers.

"That have I never read, as I confess'd before you,
How should He have been of earth, whom God hath sent to us."

* Bullinger, writing to Vadian, says of Schwenkfeld, "Hoffmanni dogma de carne Christi cœlitus delata primus invenit, etsi jam dissimulat." Butzer accuses him of the whole of the Anabaptist doctrines. Epp. Ref. p. 112.

† Extract from his Exposition of the 12th Chapter of Daniel, in Krohn's Geschichte der Wiedertäufer (only concerning Melch. Hoffmann), p. 90.

‡ Die dritt Chronika Von den Päpsten und geistlichen Händeln. (The third Chronicle of the Popes and religious quarrels), p. 165.

§ Röhrich, ii. 93, 101.

‖ Sebast. Frank, p. 169.

¶ Sattler, Herzöge, ii. p. 174.

Every part of Germany was traversed by wandering apostles of these various sects, no one knew whence they came, or whither they were going Their first salutation was, The peace of the Lord be with you! and with this they connected the doctrine of a fraternal community of all things They then went on to discourse of the corruption of the world, which God was about to chastise, and remarked that the power He had given to the Turks might be regarded as a beginning of that chastisement They next turned to the expectation, then very widely diffused, of an impending mystical transformation of all things Rumours had come from the East of the birth of Antichrist, which had already taken place at Babylon amidst signs and wonders, some even said he was grown up and worshipped as a god * In the West, the successes of the emperor, Charles V, had excited the most extravagant hopes He was to conquer Jerusalem, and to issue a commandment to put to death every man on earth who did not adore the cross, he would then be crowned by an angel of God, and die in the arms of Christ † In some places people seriously expected the end of the world, the day and hour of which was fixed To dreams of this sort, the Anabaptists attached their prophecies They declared that the messengers of God who were to seal the elect of God with the sign of the covenant, were already abroad in the world When the time was come, those who were sealed were to be gathered together from the four ends of the earth, and then would Christ their king come among them, and deliver the sword into their hand The ungodly were to be utterly swept away, but to the elect a new life was appointed, without laws, or authorities, or marriage, in the enjoyment of overflowing abundance ‡

It is evident that the Anabaptists proceeded upon principles which leaned on the one side to mysticism, and on the other to rationalism, but they always concurred in the feeling of the necessity for the strictest union, and in the arrogance of an elect people, these, combined, led to views, at once transcendent and sensual, of the mission of a Messiah There was no novelty in what they promulgated These were, in fact, only the same promises which the Talmud held out to true believers among the Jews —that, at the end of days, all the peoples of the earth should be destroyed, or should become the servants of the elect, who should live in glory, and feast on Behemoth and Leviathan But such was the universal fermentation in the minds of men, that they produced a certain effect. They addressed themselves not, as before, to peasants, but to artisans The dark and dingy workshop, where continuous toil still leaves the spirit free for a certain degree of meditation was suddenly illumined by these notions of a near and blessed futurity,—a dream too intoxicating not to find believers

The German governments of both confessions delayed not to put in force against them all the severity which they were bound by the constitutions of the empire to employ

The Protestants were for a while perplexed: the constitutions of the empire had been declared, at the meetings at Schmalkalden, too severe,§ and they at length came to the resolution not to punish men for their belief, but only for the crime of promulgating insurrectionary doctrines There is a little book extant, printed at Wittenberg, in which this distinction is more fully expanded, the Berlin copy of it contains notes in the margin, written by an Anabaptist, in which he persists in affirming that the Anabaptists have nothing to do with the insurrectionary disorders ‖ But the very difficulty was, to separate tendencies so intimately blended In Saxony, the government adhered steadily to the principle of examining the doctrines taught by each man, and dealing with him accordingly ¶ Landgrave Philip, on the other hand, always leaned to milder measures, he contented himself with keeping Anabaptists, who openly professed revolutionary opinions, in prison The Oberland governments, supported by his example, declared they would not stain their hands with the blood of these poor people, and in Strasburg, children were permitted to attain the age of seven, before their parents were compelled to have them baptized **

In the Catholic countries, on the contrary, where heresy was even more severely punished than revolt, executions took place in mass The Gardener-brethren were treated with the same rigour as at Munich, "some were deprived of their limbs, others beheaded, others cast into the Isar, and others burned alive at the stake" Similar punishments were inflicted at Passau, where thirty perished in dungeons †† There are circumstantial accounts of the deaths of George Wagner at Munich, Hatzer at Constance, and Hubmayr at Vienna, who all perished in the flames How terrible is the cry uttered by Jacob Hutter, when the Anabaptists, who had sought refuge under the protection of the nobles of Moravia, were driven forth again! "We are

* A letter published in the year 1532 by the Rhodisern, in Corrodi's Geschichte des Chiliasmus, iii p 20 His mother's name was Rachuma (the Merciful) On the night in which he was born (5th March), the sun shone, and disappeared the following day It rained pearls, which typified the people that had bound themselves by oath to follow him

† Antonius Pontus, Hariadenus Barbarossa, in Matthæi Analecta veteris ævi, i p 1, mentions it, "ut vulgatissimum ita antiquissimum verbum divinum"

‡ Der Wiedertaufer lere und geheimniss aus h Schrift widerleght durch Justum Menium (The Doctrine and Mystery of the Anabaptists confuted out of the Holy Scripture, by Justus Menius) In Luther's Works, Wittenberg edition, ii. 262

§ "Zu geschwinde"—"too hasty" Recess of the Meeting at Frankfurt Trinity, 1531

‖ Das weltliche Oberkeit den Weidertauffern mit leiblicher Strafe zu wehren schuldig sey, Etlicher Bedenken zu Witenberg, 1536 The secular authorities are bound to put down the Anabaptists by corporal punishment Some Reflections at Wittenberg, 1536 In the notes the Maulchristen (Mouth Christians) are particularly attacked, the evangelical doctrine is not censured

¶ Melanchthon, in Luther's Letters, by Lindner, p 21.

** Sattler, iii 44 Röhrich

†† Winter, Geschichte der baierschen Wiedertaufer, p 35.

in the desert, on a wild heath, under the bare heavens!" Yet even there toleration was denied them.*

But with all these persecutions the governments did not attain their end, — least of all, indeed, where they were the most inhuman, as in the Netherlands. Here, the Lutheran opinions had, from the first, found very general acceptance; violently as they were repressed, we find a confession, dated in the year 1531, that if coercion were withdrawn, all the people would receive them. It was this forcible repression of the principles of the reformation which prepared the soil for the doctrines of the Anabaptists. Jan Matthys, a baker at Leyden and a disciple of Hoffmann, combined with the fanatical and mystical views of religion of his master, the notion that the restoration of all things was at hand and must be brought about by the sword. He declared himself to be the Enoch who was to announce the things to come, formally established himself as a prophet, and sent twelve apostles to the six neighbouring provinces, who made numerous proselytes, and sealed them with the mark of the covenant of the Anabaptists. We may trace the progress of Jan Bockelsohn from Leyden to Briel, Rotterdam, Amsterdam, Enkhuysen and Alkmar, baptizing wherever he went, and establishing small associations of ten, twelve, and fifteen true believers, who, in their turn, propagated his doctrines. In Holland, generally, we find a very powerful Anabaptist party, which started up suddenly in all directions, and sought to conquer a field for the further development of its forces.

It happened that affairs were now in such a state in Munster, that people were well inclined to receive them. The apostles of Jan Matthys, who made their appearance there, gained access not only to the artisans, but also to those very preachers who had been nourished with the marrow of the evangelical doctrine.

RISE OF THE ANABAPTISTS IN MUNSTER.

This was not the first example of such leanings; Capito of Strasburg betrayed them for a time, though in him they yielded to maturer reflection.

The motives, however, which led Bernhard Rottmann to give himself up to them without reserve, were, if we may believe a report originating with Melanchthon, of a very personal nature.

There lived in Munster a certain Syndic Wiggers, from Leipzig, a worthy and honourable man, but married to a woman of very equivocal conduct. Her husband's house and garden were daily thronged with her passionate admirers, among whom was Bernhard Rottmann, an attachment of the most violent nature was soon formed between them, and at the death of her husband, which occurred soon after, it was commonly reported that she had poisoned him.† Rottmann immediately married her. There is no need to substantiate all the rumours that were circulated, in order to explain the coldness and aversion with which every man of decency and honour regarded Rottmann. The consequence of this was, that he strove to re-establish his reputation by excessive severity of manners. He began to discourse on the corruption of the world, and the necessity for works of charity, and expressed himself dissatisfied with the state of things brought about by the Lutheran reformation. In dogma, too, he continually receded further from the reformers, whether from the influence of the secret emissaries of the Anabaptists, or from the suggestions of his own mind, we are not able to discover. After having altered the ceremony of the Lord's Supper,‡ he began, as we have said, to impugn the lawfulness of infant baptism. As soon as the number of the Anabaptists became considerable, he openly joined them. Rottmann and his colleagues had just fallen into violent disputes with the council. They had at first been compelled to give way and to quit the town. What better allies could they have found than the new prophets, whose predictions and doctrines exercised so great and wide an influence? The Lutheran system ascribed great power to the civil government — even to the magistracy of a city, — for the recognition of the independence of the secular element in the state was of its very essence. On the other hand, Anabaptism was decidedly hostile to it; its own aspirations after an exclusive despotism were incompatible with any other authority. Nothing could be more welcome to the preachers of Munster, in the struggle they were carrying on. One of them assigns as the motive for the cordiality with which they had received the prophets, that he might predict ("vorwittigen" is his expression) that God the Lord would purge the whole country of Munster, and drive the ungodly out of it.§

The important coincidence was, that the growing Anabaptism of Holland happened to find its way into Munster at a point of time when the politico-religious movement had, as yet, no definite aim, and a half-suppressed

* Missive from Jacob Hutter to the Governor of Moravia. Annales Anabaptistici, p. 75.

† Locorum communium collectanea a Johanne Manlio excerpta, p. 483. Habebat conjugem mirabilem quæ cœpit insanire autore Rotmanno, quapropter et virum veneno interemit. In Kersenbroik this is not stated with such certainty. On the other hand, a still severer version of the same story is to be found in the Postilla Melanchthoniana. Extracted in Stobel Von der Verdiensten Melanchthons um die heil. Schrift, (Of the services rendered by Melanchthon to the Holy Scriptures,) 1773, p. 89.

‡ Dorpius, Wahrhafftige Historie wie das Evangelium zu Munster angefangen. (True history how the gospel began (to be preached) in Munster.) Sheet C. "Brach semel in ein grosse breite schüssel gos wein darauff, und nachdem er die Wort des Herrn vom nachtmal dazu gesprochen hatt, hies er die so des Sacraments begerten zugreiffen und essen. davon ist er Stuten Bernhard genannt worden, denn semel heisst auf ire sprach stuten." — "He broke white bread into a large wide dish, poured wine thereon, and after he had spoken the words of the Lord at the Last Supper, he told those who desired the sacrament to take and eat; hence he was called Stuten Bernhard, for white bread is called Stuten in their tongue."

§ Confession of the Anabaptist preacher Dionysius von Diest, surnamed Vynne, in Nieserts Munsterischer Urkundensammlung, i. p. 48.

party was rousing itself for fresh struggles with the existing order of things The leaders of this party seized upon it, partly from conviction, partly as means to their own ends, and it was thus adopted by a numerous community, amidst whom it could expand all its forces

At the end of the year 1533, Munster was filled with Anabaptists On the festival of the Three Kings, in 1534, the prophet Jan Matthys appeared with his fanatical apostle, Jan Bockelson of Leyden A considerable burgher of the city, Bernhard Knippeidolling, who, being formally expelled from Munster, had connected himself with the Anabaptists in Stockholm, received them into his house The two Dutchmen, with their remarkable dress, their enthusiastic deportment, their daring, and yet, to the people of those parts, attractive manners, made a great impression in Munster Religious opinion was still in a state of violent oscillation, and on the watch for novelty It was to be expected that women, and especially nuns, would be easily carried away by doctrines which proclaimed the coming of a life of holy sensuality Seven nuns of the convent of St Ægidius were baptized at once, and their example was soon followed by those of Overrat The citizens' wives next went by stealth to the meetings of the Baptists, and brought their jewels as the first fruits of their devotion Their husbands began by being indignant, and ended by being converted After the preachers of the city had themselves received baptism, they administered it Rottmann taught these new doctrines with all the talent and all the zeal which he had before devoted to the cause of the reformation It was the same voice which had seduced men from the church of Rome,—the voice which no one could withstand People said he carried a philtre about him, by which he bound all whom he baptized forever to himself

He was soon strong enough to be able to set the council, which had thought to control him, at defiance Women reproached the burgemeister for favouring a Hessian preacher, who could not even speak the language of Munster, nuns spoke with scorn in the open market of the Hessian god whom men ate, girls of sixteen cried aloud, Woe to sinners! the journeymen blacksmiths forced the council to liberate one of their comrades who had been imprisoned for preaching

Nevertheless, the Anabaptists were not yet masters

On the 8th of February a tumult occurred, in which, excited by a real or an imaginary danger, they took possession of the market-place, while, on the other hand, the council and the anti-Anabaptists invested the walls and gates It was soon evident that the latter had a great superiority both in numbers and strength, being joined by auxiliaries from the neighbouring peasants and the bishop They dragged cannon to all the entrances to the market, and many thought that the matter must now be decided, the market-place secured, and the Anabaptists, of whom so many were strangers, be expelled. The houses of those who had not been rebaptized were already marked by garlands of straw, as a protection in the approaching pillage On the other hand, enthusiasm and fear, courage and danger, produced in the Anabaptists an exaltation of mind in which they beheld the most extraordinary visions,—a man with a golden crown, a sword in one hand and a scourge in the other, or a human form with gouts of blood dropping from his clenched fists Or they fancied they saw the city full of lurid fire, and the man on the white horse of the Apocalypse, riding on the flames and brandishing a sword * It became a question whether wild fanatics like these should be attacked with artillery, and the Hessian preacher Fabricius, who had been the object of so much contumely, exerted all his influence to prevent it, he admonished those who were prepared for the fight, to spare the blood of brethren. Some members of the council, too, were moved with pity, if not with secret sympathy. They also reflected that they should certainly meet with resistance, and that perhaps, in the universal confusion, the bishop would make himself master of the city In short, instead of proceeding to the attack, they began to negotiate. Plenipotentiaries were named, and hostages mutually given, at length it was settled that every one should enjoy freedom of conscience, but should keep the peace, and obey the civil authorities in all temporal things † The Anabaptists regarded their deliverance (and with justice) as a victory In one of their writings on the restitution it is said, "the faces of the Christians (for this name they arrogated exclusively to themselves) became beautiful in colour" Children of seven years old prophesied in the market-place, "We do not believe," adds the writer, "that a greater joy was ever known on earth"

And in truth from this hour, they daily advanced to a decided superiority in power

They had now, for the first time, acquired a legally recognised existence Men of congenial sentiments flocked to Munster from all sides, husbands without their wives, wives without their husbands, sometimes whole families together Rottmann had promised to every man who would repair thither, tenfold compensation for all that he abandoned

So sudden was the revolution, that on the 21st February, when the election of a new council took place, the Anabaptists had the majority The electors were no longer appointed according to the flesh, but according to the spirit, they were all inspired artisans

* Restitutie des rechten und warrachtigen verstandes forniger articule eine in Munster gedruckte Schrift, aus der Arnold (Kirchen- und Ketzer historie) die Beslyytre den hat abdrucken lassen —"Restitution of the right and true understanding of foregoing articles a writing printed in Munster, of which Arnold (Kirchen und Ketzerhistorie) has reprinted the concluding discourse" See the Confession of Jacob Hafschmidt, in Niesert, p 155

† Dorpius, D iii. "Das ein jeder solt frei sein bei seinem Glauben zu bleiben, solten alle widder heim, ein jeder in sein haus ziehen, frieden haben und halten"—"That every one be free to abide by his faith, and all shall go home again, every man to his own house, and have and hold peace"

Nor were these men at all disposed to spare their adversaries, or to tolerate their existence near themselves. On the 27th February a great meeting of armed Anabaptists was held at the town-house. It began with prayers, which lasted for some time; the prophet seemed to be sunk into a deep slumber; suddenly, however, he started up and declared that such of the unbelievers as would not be converted must instantly be driven out; such was the will of God. He made no secret of his designs. "Away with the children of Esau!" exclaimed he, "the inheritance belongeth to the children of Jacob." Rapacity was combined with enthusiasm. Hereupon the streets resounded with the fearful cry of "Out with the ungodly!" It was on a stormy day, in the middle of winter. The snow, which still lay very deep, began to melt; a violent wind drove the rain and sleet through the air. The houses were broken open, and all who would not abjure their baptism were driven from their homes and hearths. An eye-witness has painted the wretched spectacle of mothers, who could rescue nothing else from their houses, with their half-naked babes in their arms; little children wading barefoot through the snow; old men, who left the city leaning on a staff, stripped of the last penny of the miserable remnant of the earnings of a long and toilsome life.*

The Anabaptists were thus not only the masters of the city, but its sole occupants. What their adversaries had scrupled to do to them, they inflicted with fanatical eagerness. They divided the city among themselves; and communities from different parts of the country took possession of the religious houses. The movable property of the exiles was collected together, and seven deacons were appointed by Matthys to distribute it gradually to the faithful, according to their several necessities.

The Anabaptists would have immediately proceeded to extend their dominion beyond the city, had not the bishop, now supported by the neighbouring princes, encamped around it with a splendid army.

Cleves and Cologne had at first hesitated whether they should merely keep off the infection from their own territory, or render assistance to the bishop. But the consideration, that the Landgrave of Hessen might send him succours, and that, in case these were victorious, a change might be attempted in the see under his influence, induced both these western neighbours to follow his example.† They found that the bishop was ill armed and ill advised; they saw what danger might ensue if the Anabaptists succeeded in gaining over the smaller towns subject to the see, and they therefore determined to send succours, first of artillery and infantry, and then of cavalry; always, however, under the condition that the see should compensate them for their outlay. The bishop now strained every nerve; fresh taxes were levied, and all the jewels from the churches were devoted to the expenses of the war; the bishop's vassals took the field at their own cost. In April and May, 1534, the city was beleaguered on all sides. If, as it was very well provided with the requisites for war, the allied troops could not flatter themselves that they should immediately reduce it, they at all events attained no inconsiderable advantage by confining the disorders within the walls of Münster.

The matter of immediate interest is, to watch the internal and spontaneous development of this singular phenomenon. We shall see a religious element (such as, under one form or another, had appeared in the ecclesiastical movements of preceding ages) at work within a narrow sphere, but in complete freedom, and producing the most remarkable results.

CHARACTER AND PROGRESS OF ANABAPTISM IN MÜNSTER.

It might be presumed that, from the time the Anabaptists were masters of Münster, hardened by success in the narrowness of mind common to sectarians, they would not only tolerate nothing that was likely to oppose them, but even nothing that was not completely identified with themselves. Accordingly, all the pictures and statues in the cathedral and the market-place were destroyed. The almost entire disappearance of the monuments of the Westphalian school of art, which, if in existence, would assert their place by the side of those of Cologne, is to be ascribed to the wanton barbarism with which they were destroyed at this period. Rudolph von Langen had brought back from Italy a noble collection of old engravings and manuscripts, illustrative of the great recent revolution in literature; these were solemnly burnt in the market-place.‡ The reformers even held it a duty to destroy all musical instruments. Nothing was to remain but the Bible, and even that subject to the interpretation of their prophets.

Every thing was to be in common among those who had undergone the second baptism. The rule which had been laid down as to the property of the exiles, was very soon applied to the possessions of the faithful. They were ordered, under pain of death, to deliver up their gold and silver, their jewels and effects, to the chancery, for the common consumption. In short, a sort of St. Simonism was established. While the idea of property was abolished, each man was to continue to exercise his craft. Regulations are extant, in which journeymen shoemakers and tailors are specially men-

* Kersenbroik. Historia Anabaptistica MS.; for it is necessary always to compare the German translation of this work, of 1771, with the original. Mencken's reprint contains scarcely a third of the original, and just the most important things are left out.

† Protocol of a sitting of the council at Berg (Düsseld. A.) "Nachdem zu besorgen, das Hessen mit underlouffen, und vielleicht eine verenderung der stifte gescheen mochte." — "Afterwards it is to be feared that Hessen might interfere, and perhaps an alteration of the see take place."

‡ Kersenbroik. In campum dominicum cum incredibilis librorum multitudo perlata esset, qui etiam ultra viginti millibus dorenorum valebant,—incomparabilem urbis thesaurum flamma subita absumit.

tioned; the latter being enjoined to take heed that no new garment or fashion be introduced. There are also rules for the smiths and locksmiths; in short, every trade was treated as a public charge or office. The most honourable of all these was, as may be imagined, the defence of the country. Even boys were trained to this, and acquired an extraordinary dexterity in shooting with the bow, which was not yet entirely superseded by firearms. Those to whom a special office was committed, were exempted from the service of the watch. The whole community formed one military-religious family. Meat and drink were provided at the common cost; the two sexes, "brethren and sisters," sat apart from each other at meals; they ate in silence, while one read aloud a chapter of the Bible.*

It is obvious that a community so singularly constituted could not consist with the forms of municipal administration, in which the bürgermeister and city councillors possessed power and pre-eminence. The prophet, Jan Matthys, who devised the new institutions, very soon seized on the supreme authority, which contemporary writers describe as truly royal—absolute.† Matthys, however, did not survive the Easter of 1534. At a tumult in which he was foremost—for his fanaticism was not of the cowardly sort—he was killed.

We have already mentioned that he had been accompanied to Münster by Jan Bockelson, surnamed of Leyden, the son of a magistrate (Schulz) of the Hague, and a Westphalian serf woman who had been bought from her husband.‡ In his wanderings as journeyman tailor, he had been as far as Lisbon on the south and Lübek on the north, and had at length settled in Leyden, near the gate leading to the Hague. He soon grew discontented with his business, and opened a sort of inn, where he and his wife sold beer and wine. It was his great ambition to make a figure in the poetical association which Leyden, like most of the cities of the Netherlands, at that time possessed, called the Kammer van Rhetoryke. The flow of his verses (Refereyne) was the easiest, his scholars were the most distinguished; he wrote dramas, in which he played a part; and it is very likely that he here became imbued with the spirit of hostility to the church which was common to the schools of rhetoric of that day. In this state of mind, Anabaptism fell in his way, and took complete possession of him. He speedily acquired a tolerable knowledge of the Holy Scriptures; though, as is usual with such autodidactic artisans, he utterly confounded national and religious elements, and applied whatever seized upon his ardent imagination, with all its accidental circumstances and relations, to the actual world. He possessed an agreeable exterior, natural eloquence, fire and youth;§ even before Matthys' death he played a certain part, and after that event (which he said he had predicted) he took his place. And in boldness at least, he was nowise inferior to his predecessor. The opinion was already afloat, that, even in civil affairs, it was our duty to disregard all human laws and ordinances, and to hold merely to the word of God. The public attention was turned upon the new prophet. After he had remained silent some days, "because God had closed his mouth," he at length declared, that there must be twelve elders in the new Israel, as in the ancient, and immediately proceeded to name them. Rottmann, on his side, assured the congregation that such was the will of God, and presented the newly appointed elders to it. The preacher and the prophet now dispensed with all the civic forms of election, and nominated the magistrates. The people universally acquiesced, and accepted them. Six of them were to sit to administer justice every morning and afternoon; the prophet, Jan Bockelson, was to proclaim their sentences to the whole people of Israel, and Knipperdolling to execute them with the sword.

It is evident that this was a new step in the progress of visionary religion, or rather of fanatical prophecy. A table of laws was announced, composed exclusively of passages from Scripture, especially the books of Moses.

The extravagant abuse to which such an application of Scripture naturally leads, soon became evident in other ways.

Jan Matthys had already abandoned his wife, who was advanced in years, and had married a young girl called Divara; he had persuaded her that this was the will of Heaven, and had brought her to Münster. Jan Bockelson coveted not only the post, but the wife, of his predecessor; but as he was already married, he put forth the doctrine, that it was allowable for a man now, as well as under the old covenant, to have several wives. At first, the natural good sense of mankind revolted against such a proposition. We may remember that propositions of this kind had been long before submitted to Luther, who had rejected them on the ground that marriage was a civil ordinance, and therefore must be obeyed. In Münster, arguments of this nature were utterly despised; people insisted on living merely in accordance with the

* Kersenbroik, fol. 213. Ordinatio politici regiminis a 12 senioribus recens introducta. § 9. Ut in cibis administrandis legitimus servetur ordo, præfecti ejus rei, officii sui memores, ejusdem generis fercula uti hactenus fieri consuevit singulis diebus fratribus sororibusque in disjunctis et disparatis mensis modeste et cum verecundia sedentibus apponent. It appears, indeed, as if this related more particularly to those engaged in the defence.

† Hortensius, p. 301. Joannes Matthias hanc autoritatem sibi pararat, ut unus jam inde supra leges esset, unus scisceret, juberetque quæ viderentur, antiquas et abrogaret leges, aliasque pro libidine conderet.

‡ Confession of Jan Bockelson. "His father was called Bockel, and was a Schulte (magistrate) in Sevenhagen." It should be Grevenhagen, in which place Kersenbroik was prætor. Bockelson's mother was a serf woman of Schedelich, from Zolke, in the Münster territory.

§ "Doch find'ich von jenem in Truck ausgangen, dass er von Angesicht, Person, Gestalt, Vernunft ein redsprech, rahtweiss anschlegig, an Behendigkeit unerschrockenem stolzen Gemüt von künen Taten und Anschlegen ein edel wohlgeschickt und wunderbarlich Mann sey gewesen."—"But I have found from that printed book, that he was in countenance, person, stature and intellect, an eloquent, sagacious, cunning man; of prompt, dauntless, and haughty spirit; of bold deeds and designs; a noble, capable, and extraordinary man." Sebastian Frank, die andere Chronik, 266.

Holy Scriptures. Rottmann preached the new doctrine for several days in the churchyard of the cathedral.* Things were not, however, come to such a pass, that so crying an insult to good morals and to all honest usage and tradition could escape opposition, even under existing circumstances. All that remained of the old-established citizens, all who were not utterly given over to the new opinions, rallied around a smith of the name of Mollenhök. The watchword of "the gospel" was heard once more; there was a talk of recalling the exiles, and restoring the old constitution of the city, and some of the prophets and preachers were actually imprisoned. But they were now become too strong for opposition; there were too many enthusiastic strangers in the town; and the common people were intoxicated by the doctrine of equality. Mollenhök's party were soon compelled to take refuge in the town-house; and cannon being posted in front of it (partly drawn by women), they waved their hats out of the windows, in token of surrender. They ought to have known that this would not save their lives. Never were prisoners more pitilessly treated than these, by men who were but yesterday their "brethren in the spirit." Many were bound to trees and shot. "He who fires the first shot," exclaimed Jan Bockelson, "does God a service." The others were beheaded.†

It was consistent with that fanatical narrowness which acknowledges nothing but its own creed, to punish every deviation from it with death and destruction. Terror is the necessary and invariable offspring of a system of belief which rejects every other. At the proclamation of the table of laws above mentioned, extermination from among God's people was denounced against every man who should disobey them. Above all, wo to him who should call in question the divine commission of the lawgiver! Even Matthys had caused the punishment of death to be inflicted on one Master Truteling, a smith, a man of good repute, who had addressed some disrespectful words to him. We stated that Knipperdolling undertook the office of executioner. He had the power of putting to death any man whom he detected in disobedience to the new laws, on the spot, and without trial; for the wicked, it was said, must be rooted out of the earth. Preceded by four heralds, with a drawn sword in his hand, he traversed the streets, carrying terror wherever he went.

But since every thing, however wild and eccentric, must still follow the laws of its peculiar nature, nor can stop in its career till it has displayed its original instincts in the clearest light, this monstrous phenomenon, having vanquished all external opposition, now entered on the last stage of its internal development.

The spiritual power, in conflict with the temporal, had called prophecy to its aid; and had first opposed, then defied, and finally overthrown, the civil authority; it had then driven out or exterminated all its opponents, and had established a sort of government, over which it exercised absolute sway. But it had not yet reached its culminating point. Theocracy, being founded on the claim to a peculiar preference and favour of the Divine Being, has a natural tendency to assume a monarchical form. The chief prophet could not content himself with merely proclaiming the will of the elders to the people of Israel, although they were in fact appointed by him; he conceived the project of becoming the king of that people.

Another prophet, who had arisen by his side, one Dusentschuer, formerly a goldsmith, spared him the trouble of announcing his intentions. Dusentschuer declared that God had revealed to him that John of Leyden should be king. The preachers, who always advocated the most extravagant ideas, immediately supported him; indeed, John himself afterwards avowed that, without their assistance, he could neither have introduced polygamy, nor established monarchy. He accordingly granted them a share of his power. After the people had given their assent to his new dignity (every man subscribing his name), he declared that he could not tarry alone in the sanctuary; the congregation must join him in praying to God for good servants of his house. After all the people had prayed, Rottmann appeared, and read from a paper the names of those who were pointed out by the divine approbation for the highest dignities. One of the highest was himself. He was the president or speaker (worthalter), — like the presiding bürgermeisters of the free cities; Knipperdolling, who had frequent fits of prophetic ecstacy, was statthalter, or lieutenant; while the king's privy council was composed of preachers and the most eminent of the fanatics. In short, the principle of spiritual fanaticism now attained to absolute sway in this monarchi-theocratic government.

The mystical views which lay at the bottom of the whole Anabaptist movement now assumed a more distinct form. The hopes which had hitherto seemed dim and remote, appeared more attainable, more possible to be realised.

The Anabaptists deduced from Scripture that in the beginning God had created all things good by the word; but they had not remained good, and God's ordinance now required their restoration by the word. But all things had their course in triads—in three periods. One was to be succeeded by another, so that the past should be eclipsed by the present; till at length a third should appear—that, namely, to which there should be no alteration or end.

The first age of the world ended with the

* In a contemporaneous notice in Spalatin's Annales Reformationis, p. 302, it is stated that Rottmann also took four wives.

† Ne ex crebris bombardarum tonitruis hostes oppidanos inter se dissidere suspicentur neque tantam pulveris jacturam faciant, decretum est reliquos sexaginta sex gladio ferire, quæ pœnæ executio Knipperdollingo committitur, qui singulis diebus aliquot pro arbitrio suo productos et tandem ad unum omnes capite plectit, nisi quod propheta interim animi et exercitii causa in nonnullos animadverterit. (Kersenbroik.)

deluge. It had now reached its second epoch. God had resorted to various means of turning men to himself; he had sent them Abraham and the prophets, had showed them signs and wonders, had given his written word, lastly, had sent his only Son: but all in vain — men would not tolerate righteousness near them, much less let it rule over them; therefore must the wrath of God go forth, even as in the days of Noah, and be poured out upon the heads of the wicked, in order to bring about the third age, and the perfecting of the whole world. This moment was now arrived.*

Rottmann, in his treatise on temporal and earthly power, viewed the matter from another side, but the tendency of his opinions was the same.

He says, that it was God's will that all men should be subject to him alone, should behave as brethren, and should live quietly and joyfully under him. But in consequence of the fall, the divine government had ceased, and an earthly power become necessary. This, however, was in its very nature bad, and was constantly becoming worse. Four monarchies had been ordained by God from the beginning. The first had been likened by Daniel to a beast: but the fourth, or last, was a monster which had not its equal upon earth for bloodthirsty tyranny. But the time of this, too, was come; its cracking betrayed the nearness of its fall; all its wealth and treasure would become the spoil of the true brethren.†

He exhorted them to seize the present moment, that it might not be with the Christians as formerly with the Jews, who did not perceive the time of their visitation.

The objection, that the kingdom of Christ was not of this world, they put aside in their own peculiar manner.‡ They made a distinction between a spiritual kingdom, which belonged to the age of suffering, and a corporeal kingdom of glory and splendour, which Christ was to enjoy with his true disciples for a thousand years.§ They were persuaded that the kingdom of Munster would endure until the commencement of that millennium, and ought therefore to foreshow it, and be an image of it. They regarded the siege which they had to sustain as necessary: for the sacrifice must be offered up in the desert; the woman must suffer their strife; the court of the temple must be filled with dead. God, however, would not only avert the arm of force, but would also put his sword into the hand of his people without delay, that they might destroy all that did evil from the face of the earth. "Thrust in thy sickle and reap, for the time is come."‖

This was also the mystical reason for their appointing a king over them; for the prophecies referred especially to a king who was to be the lord of all the earth. Dusentschuer called Jan Bockelson king of the whole world.

This young visionary artisan was entirely persuaded that the whole future destiny of the world rested on him. He called himself John, the rightful king in the new temple. In his edicts he says, that in him the kingdom announced by Christ was incontestably come, that he sat upon the throne of David.¶ He wore round his neck a chain of gold, to which hung the symbol of his dominion,—a golden globe transfixed with two swords, the one of gold, the other of silver, above the handles of which was a cross. His attendants wore the same badge on their green sleeves; for green was his colour. Like all upstarts, he loved magnificence. Thrice a week he appeared with his crown and golden chain in the market-place, seated himself on his throne, and administered justice, Knipperdolling standing one step lower, with the sword. When he rode through the town, two boys walked beside him, the one carrying the Old Testament, the other a naked sword: all who met him fell on their knees.** There were some who expressed

* Von der Verborgenheit des Rykes Christi ende von den Dagen des Herrn (Of the hidden Mystery of the Kingdom of Christ, the end of the Days of the Lord) cap. v. Arnold, Kirchen und Ketzer geschichte, i. 994. Pity that the last seven chapters were left out, merely for the sake of sparing a few leaves.

† Rottman, Von tydliker und irdischer Gewalt (On temporal and earthly Power), MS. in Munster. Extracts from it in Jochmius Geschichte der Wiedertaufer, p. 128. It is remarkable what a striking resemblance these notions have with those proclaimed by Robespierre after he thought he had put down atheism. Compare his speech at the fête de l'Etre Supreme, 8th June, 1794. "L'auteur de la nature avait lie les mortels par une chaine immense d'amour et de felicite; perissent les tyrans qui ont osé la briser! Francais republicains, c'est a vous de purifier la terre qu'ils ont souillée, et d'y appeller la justice qu'ils en ont bannie." Buchez et Roux, Histoire Parlementaire, xxxiii. p. 179. The difference lies only in the religious ideas: the intention — to establish a primitive state of universal happiness — is exactly the same.

‡ A specimen of their exegesis is to be seen in the Confession of a Deist, formerly a Priest. "Christus spreckt, myn rike ist nicht van duser werlt, heft dusen Verstand: Christus rick ist ein rick der Gerechticheit und der Wairheit: dat rike avers duser werlt ist ein rike der bosheit und ungerechticheit."—"Christ says, 'My kingdom is not of this world,' the meaning of which is, that Christ's kingdom is a kingdom of justice and truth, but the kingdom of this world is a kingdom of wickedness and injustice."

§ See the conference of John of Leyden with Corvinus.

‖ Rev. xiv. This is the reference in the original. But the words quoted are, "Schenket ihr doppelt ein, denn die Zeit ist vorhanden." (Pour ye in double, for the time is at hand.) Such differences in the two versions are, however, of very frequent occurrence.—Transl.

¶ One of his laws, given in Latin by Kersenbroik, and with slight differences by Herrsbach, is to be found in German, in the Archives at Dusseldorf. It begins very characteristically: "Kundlich und openbar sy allen Liefhebberen und Testendern der Warheit, und gotlicher Gerechticheit, sowol den Unvorstendigen, als in der Verborgenheit Gottes Verstandigen. So und in welmaten de Christen und ere Testendere sick under dem Panier der Gerechticheit als ware Israeliten in dem nyen Tempel in jegenwerdicheit des Richs vorlanges verseen, durch den munth der Propheten belovet, vermitz (vermittelst) Christum und seiner Aposteln in Kraft des Geistes angefangen und geopenbaret, und nu an Johann den Gerechten in dem Stule Davids geloffliche und unwedersprechlichen vorhanden, schicken wandern und haben sollen."—"Be it known and proclaimed to all lovers and followers of the truth and godly righteousness, as well those who understand not, as they who understand the mystery of God. Inasmuch as the Christians and their adherents have sent forth under the banner of righteousness, as true Israelites in the new temple, in the present existence of the kingdom long foreseen, promised by the mouth of the prophets, begun and revealed by means of Christ and his apostles in the power of the spirit, and now come in (the person of) John the Rightful, the promised and incontestable occupant of the throne of David."

** Ant. Corvinus de miserabili Monasteriensium Anabaptistarum obsidione ad G. Spalatinum, ap. Schardium, ii. 315. Aulam præfecturis ac officiis ita instituerat, ut si natus rex fuisset, prudentius non potuerit: erat enim in excogitandis iis quæ regalem pompam decebant, mirus artifex.

disgust at his pomp, and at the number of his wives, to which he was continually adding "Out upon you!" exclaimed he, "but I will rule over you, and over the whole world, in spite of you!" Even Knipperdolling could not help mixing buffoonery with his terrible functions He once caused himself to be suspended over the heads of the crowded multitude in the market-place, that he might breathe the spirit into them all He danced indecent dances before the king, and seated himself on his throne! These men were like madmen, a secret and irresistible consciousness of the untruth of all their wild visions forced itself upon them Knipperdolling, indeed, had once a serious quarrel with the king, but it was soon made up, Knipperdolling did penance, and all things returned to the track of credulous obedience In October, 1534, the whole city celebrated the Lord's Supper in the following manner —Tables were set for all the adult women (who were far more numerous than the men), and for those of the men who did not hold watch on the walls,—four thousand two hundred persons, John of Leyden and his wife Divara appeared with all their courtiers, and served at the tables, it was a regular meal After this they took wheaten cakes, ate of them first, and gave of them to the others—the king the bread, the queen the wine, saying, "Brother (or sister), take and eat, as the grains of wheat are baked together, and the grapes are pressed together, so are we also one" Then they sang the psalm, "Allein Gott in der Hoh' sey Ehr" (To God alone in the highest be honour) * So far, this ceremony might appear religious and innocent But mark the sequel The king thought he perceived at the feast "one who had not on a wedding-garment" He fancied that this man was Judas, ordered him to be led out, went out himself, and cut off his head, he believed he had felt himself commanded by God to do this, and returned cheerful and delighted to the feast †

Of all the phenomena which attended this monstrous delusion, the mixture of piety, sensuality, and blood-thirstiness is the most revolting, however reluctantly, we must pursue our observation of it somewhat farther

There was a woman in Munster who boasted that no man could control her, this boast had irritated the desire of John of Leyden to have her among his wives, she lived with him for some time, but growing tired of him, she gave him back the presents she had received from him and left him The Anabaptist king regarded this as the greatest of all crimes, led her to the market-place, beheaded her himself, and kicked away the corpse with his foot. Hereupon all his other wives joined in singing, "To God alone in the highest be honour"

Every thing being overthrown and transformed, and universal equality established, nothing remained, save the self-love and self-will of the visionary fanatic to whom all paid willing homage In him spiritual pride and sensual desire, frenzied enthusiasm and natural coarseness, formed a strange, we might say a grotesque mixture, which is very remarkable, viewed as a psychological product Freedom was, of course, out of the question, among men who had given themselves up to courses of so horrible and disgusting a character How frightful is the contrast between the innocence of the little sect of the Gardener-brethren of Salzburg and their delirious depravity!

Yet it riveted the affections of men, they fought for it with the intensest animosity

A woman of Sneek, in Friesland, named Hille Feike, who had travelled to Munster to seek, as she said, the salvation of her soul from God's word, felt herself incited by the story of Judith, which she had heard read at table, to follow her example She actually set out, on a similar errand, dressed in all the bravery she could collect, with jewels furnished her from the treasury, and provided with a sum of money But the unusual splendour of her dress excited suspicion She was taken before the bishop whom she had intended to kill, and being questioned, she confessed her design, and was put to death ‡

On the 30th of August, 1534, the bishop made an attempt to storm the city, but he found it excellently prepared to receive him. A small body of picked men stood in the market-place, ready to hasten, under the king's orders, to those points which were most threatened Others were posted in the alleys of trees behind the walls The main force awaited the enemy on the walls, between the men stood women and boys the latter armed with bows and arrows, the former with large cauldrons, in which, as they said, they were cooking the enemy's breakfast At five in the morning the great Hessian cannonade, called the Devil, gave the signal in the camp, the landsknechts moved upon six different points at once, and succeeded in passing over the ditches and stockades, they placed their ladders, and already more than one standard-bearer had planted his colours on the walls But the besieged had allowed them to come on thus far unmolested, in order to overwhelm them with more certain destruction The fire of musketry now poured down among the crowded ranks The women threw down wreaths of burning pitch on the necks of those who were climbing, or they poured the seething lime which they had mixed in their cauldrons over them,§ the storm was totally re-

* Neuste Zeitung von den Wiedertauffern zu Münster, 1535

† Dorpius, "and he was so pleased with this murder, that he continually laughed"

‡ Bekanntnisse Hyllen Feyken aen pyn am Freydag nach Nativitas Joh Baptistæ —Pynlig Bekanntnisse Hyllen Feyken am Saterdag na J B Niesert, i 40, 44

§ Here is another specimen of Kersenbroik's descriptive powers Piceas coronas adhibita face incendunt, atque ita fragrantes furculis quibusdam ferreis in ascendentium colla injiciunt, qui horrendis flammis ipsa arma penetrantibus miseris modis excruciati sorsum deorsumque cursitant majorique motu flammas exsuscitant et frustra chirotecis e crassioribus femorum pellibus ad hoc comparatis ardentia serta eximere tentant, ita enim fragranti pice et resina contrahuntur ut manus inde retrahere nequeant tandem quidam eorum proni concidunt, seseque in terro algenti præ intolerabili cruciatu ita volvunt ut herbæ cir-

pulsed without need of any assistance from those posted in the interior of the city; the inhabitants had displayed military talents and courage which robbed the landsknechts of all spirit for a renewal of the onslaught.

The prince bishop was obliged to content himself with surrounding the city with blockhouses, for which he had to levy a new tax.

The spirits of the Anabaptists were naturally raised by so brilliant a victory.

In October, after the communion described above, some of the faithful were charged to go into the neighbouring cities, and to relate the signs and wonders that had been done amongst them. In the very hour in which they received these orders, they set out to execute them. They all fell, as was to be expected, into the hands of the bishop's people, and expiated their design with their death.

This, however, by no means induced John of Leyden to renounce his vast projects.

We may remember that a universal fermentation had seized on the lower classes, especially the artisans, in the German towns; and that the Anabaptist spirit took root more particularly among these classes. At this moment we meet with the same appearances in almost every part of Germany. In Prussia, the Anabaptists enjoyed the protection of one of the most powerful men in the country, Frederic von Heideck, who was in high favour with Duke Albert; and they even gained over a portion of the nobility.* Great as was the number of fugitives from Moravia, we still find them there by thousands. In 1534, the Saxon visitators found the valley of the Werra filled with them, and in Erfurt they avowed that they had sent forth three hundred prophets to convert the world.† In the year 1534, we trace single emissaries in Anhalt, and in Franconian Brandenburg, where people had to produce their baptismal register before they could be admitted to the second baptism. In Würtenburg, the duke's hereditary marshal, a Thumb von Neuburg, kinsman of Schwenkfeld, gave them asylum for a time in his lands in the Remsthal.‡ In Ulm, there were threatenings of new opinions bordering on Anabaptism, like those of Sebastian Frank or Schwenkfeld; while in Augsburg an Anabaptist king actually arose. In Switzerland they were always to be found in the Protestant cantons; and as their denunciations were chiefly directed against the bad life of pretended Christians, the zealous Haller sought to turn their appearance to account, for the purpose of establishing a better church discipline.§ In Strasburg, many pertinaciously adhered to the belief that Hoffmann would come forth from his prison in glory and splendour; they also added an Enoch to this their Elias. Dreams and prophecies of this kind were rife along the whole course of the Rhine; in Cologne and Treves, troops of light cavalry traversed the country, to prevent or disperse assemblages of Anabaptists.‖ But their stronghold was the Netherlands. In Amsterdam, where, a short time before, an emissary from Münster had made numerous proselytes, they more than once ventured to show themselves openly. When Count Hoogstraten, the privy councillor of the regent, came thither in October, and endeavoured to introduce some more rigorous measures both against Lutherans and Anabaptists, a nocturnal tumult arose, which very nearly led to the most formidable consequences.¶ From that time there were incessant rumours of the design of the Anabaptists to take possession of the city. Leyden was kept in a constant terror of fires and tumults.** In the beginning of the year 1535, a meeting of nearly a thousand Anabaptists took place in the Gröningerland, which the stadtholder was obliged to disperse by an armed force.†† In East Friesland, a prophet expressed the hope that the whole of Upper and Lower Germany would rise, as soon as the king should go forth with his mighty banner. Even those who did not share in their opinions, thought that if John of Leyden could only win a few successful battles, he would find followers enough to convulse the world, as the Longobards or Franks had done of old.‡‡ We have seen that John of Leyden laid claim to the whole world as his property. He once gravely appointed twelve dukes, amongst whom he formally partitioned the world, and in the first place Germany. He treated the neighbouring princes of the empire as his equals. In a letter to Landgrave Philip of Hessen, he calls him "dear Phil" (lieber Lips), as the landgrave's most intimate brothers in arms were wont to do.§§ He begged him to take up the Bible, and especially to study the lesser prophets; there he would find, as he says, "Whether we have usurped the power and title of king, or whether this matter is ordained of God to some other end."

But before things were ripe for a general and combined effort on their part, the empire was roused to take energetic measures to stem the rising torrent.

PREPARATIONS FOR AN ATTACK ON MÜNSTER. REDUCTION OF THE CITY.

The mode in which this took place, may

cumquaque flammas emarcescerent: hinc magno clamore animam evomunt: alii vero conceptas flammas restinctori in fossas proruunt et pondere armorum depressi subsidunt.

* Baczko, iv. 219.

† Seckendorf, Hist. Luth. iii. § 25, p. 71.

‡ Lang, ii. 33. Sattler, iii. p. 104.

§ Haller and Frecht in Ottius, p. 69, 81.

‖ Protocol of the Council of March, 1534.

¶ Lambertus Hortensius Tumultuum Anabaptistarum, liber unus, Schardius Scriptt. rer. Germ. ii. p. 306. These Netherland reports are the most important thing in Hortensius.

** Brandt, Histoire de la Reformation, i. p. 50.

†† Letter of the Stadtholder of Friesland to the Bishop of Münster. Lewarden, 25th January. (Düss. A.)

‡‡ Sebastian Frank, Andre Chronik, p. 267.

§§ 14th Jan. 1535. Printed in the little book: Acta Handlungen Legation und Schriften, so durch Landgraf Philippsen in der Münsterschen Sache geschehen.—Documents of the Proceedings, Legation, and Correspondence of Landgrave Philip, concerning the Affairs of Münster. 1536, sheet ii.

serve as a perfect specimen of the conduct of affairs in the empire generally.

It would have been natural to expect that this triumph of opinions, so severely prohibited by all successive recesses of the empire, in a considerable city, and the new vigour thus given to them in many other places, would have caused the whole empire to arise in its strength to crush a danger threatening to every condition of men.

Yet the affair was left almost entirely to the Bishop of Münster, and his political friends.

We have seen how their jealousy of Hessen, and their own danger, had induced Cologne and Cleves to come to the bishop's assistance.

Each of them sent, in the first place, some artillery; though only on the security of the chapter, and under condition that any damage done to the guns should be repaired.

The councils of Cologne and Cleves then had a meeting to deliberate on what was further to be done.

They met on the 26th of March, 1534, at Orsoy, and determined to send the bishop succours of men, but not of money; each prince to send two companies of landsknechts at his own cost. On the 7th of May, at a second meeting at Neuss, they added, that each should also have two hundred fully mounted horsemen before Münster, in readiness for the storming of the city. The Duke of Cleves had already commanded his subjects to take no foreign service, nor to permit any one belonging to them to do so, till this matter was terminated.

Meanwhile, the bishop required other aid than that of troops. As the resources of his country were not sufficient, he incessantly pressed for a "brave sum of money" on loan. At first, there was an idea of raising him a thousand gulden on security; but as this turned out to be either impracticable or insufficient, it was resolved, at a fresh meeting between the council of Münster and those of Cologne and Cleves, at Neuss, on the 20th of June, that each party should contribute twenty thousand gulden — sixty thousand in all — in order to provide every thing necessary for the assault;* the bishop, however, engaging to repay the two other powers, after the conquest of Münster. We have seen, however, the bad success of that enterprise. When the councils met in camp in the beginning of September, they hoped to find the city reduced; they found nothing but the consequences of defeat, and universal discouragement. The erection of the block-houses took place in consequence of the common resolution of the three sovereigns. They agreed again to raise fifty thousand gulden for that purpose.

But it was sufficiently evident that Münster would never be reduced in this way. They determined, as had been proposed from the first, to apply to the nearest circles, and to engage their co-operation.

Cologne belonged to the circle of the electorate of the Rhine; Cleves was head of that of Westphalia and the Lower Rhine. The circles had begun, for the first time, to take an important part in affairs during the last Turkish war; and the princes were now authorized by the recesses of the empire, to require their co-operation in this matter.

It was first discussed in Mainz, at a meeting of the circle of the electorate of the Rhine. Cologne and Cleves reckoned their outlay, and demanded compensation; and, more especially, that the other states of the circle should immediately share it. But the only result of this was, that, in spite of all their resistance, the meeting ordered them to keep up the block-houses; agreeing, however, to deliberate further on the matter at a general assembly.†

On the 27th of October, the states of the circle of the Lower Rhine and Westphalia met in a convent at Cologne. As a general meeting was in prospect, they declined voting any permanent succours. But in order to be prepared at any moment to send such as might be demanded in haste, they agreed to raise the same sum of money as a month's tax for the last Turkish war would have amounted to.

Meanwhile, the more distant circles, like those of Hessen and Saxony, were invited to join in the deliberations. Saxon councillors met those of Cologne and Cleves at Essen, in the beginning of November; the Hessian, shortly after, those of the Palatinate, Mainz, Treves and Würzburg, at Oberwesel. Their deliberations acquired great earnestness and energy, from their fear lest the bishop should apply for aid to the house of Burgundy, which might seize this opportunity to get possession of Münster; for Mary had already asked for succours for that city, from her states in the Netherlands. Rather than this should happen, Saxony bound itself to take an equal share of the expenses of the blockade. Here, too, ambitious schemes were at work; but mutual jealousy compelled every one to keep within legitimate bounds.

The meeting of the three circles — the two above named and that of the Upper Rhine — determined on at Mainz, took place in December, at Coblenz. They expressed their readiness to bear the expenses of the continued blockade. Three thousand men were to be kept before Münster, and to that end fifteen thousand gulden were to be raised monthly. Count Whirich von Dhaun was appointed commander; four councillors of war, from Cologne, Treves, Cleves and Hessen, were to accom-

* "That each prince, Cologne, Cleves, and Münster, should contribute and pay 4000 soldiers, for the support of the knechts who now lie before Münster, and 1000 miners for a month (which gives a sum of 12,000 knechts and 2000 sappers and miners); and also, shall altogether furnish 10,000 Emden gulden, for the purchase of powder; which, reckoning each knecht's and miner's pay at four Emden gulden, together with the actual 10,000 E. g., amount in all to 70,000 E. g., which are equal to 60,000 gold gulden; so that each elector and prince has undertaken to contribute 20,000 gulden."

† Extract from the recess of Mainz, in the Düss. Arch. "The electoral councillors consider of the most useful and profitable way, how other princes and states of the empire, besides their own electoral circle, the circle of the Upper Rhine, and that of the Lower Rhine, and Westphalia, may be induced to take part in this business."

pany him, and the troops were to take the oath to the states of the circles *

It is evident, however, that even this was rather a measure of defence against any attack on the part of the besieged, than one at all calculated to effect the subjugation of the city For this the circles did not think themselves powerful enough, they determined to call the entire empire to their aid

The course of this affair, as we have already remarked, strikingly illustrates the character of the German commonwealth The measures necessary to reduce to obedience a city in open rebellion, did not originate with the supreme head of the empire, but the sovereign to whom that city belonged, and his nearest neighbours, were left for a long time to struggle with it unassisted, till the growth of the danger gradually widened the circle of allies, and at length drew the whole body of the empire though not without partial opposition, into the contest

One of the first acts that Ferdinand had to perform after his recognition as King of the Romans, was, to convoke a general assembly at Worms on the fourth of April, in conformity with the petition of the three circles

The States were not, it is true, unanimous, the Elector of Brandenburg, for example, maintained that the three circles were able alone to make an end of the Anabaptists, and refused to take any part in the measures for that object But by far the greater number of the States sent delegates A resolution was passed to levy one month and a quarter of the last general tax for the empire, on all the States The amount which this might be expected to produce was not great enough to enable the allied princes to bring any considerable accession of force into the field The only advantage was, that they were now sure of being able to continue the blockade till they could obtain a decisive result The appointment of the commander-in-chief, which had taken place at Coblenz, was confirmed by the imperial authorities, only with the addition of two councillors to the other four after the conquest of the city, the emperor and the States were to decide on the course to be pursued with it

It were superfluous to enter into any minute recital of the deeds of this little army It is sufficient to say that it succeeded in cutting off all communication with the city, and in reducing it by hunger

The chief hope of the besieged was, that they should receive help and supplies from the country where their doctrines were the most widely diffused, and whence they themselves had mostly sprung Zealous Anabaptists from the Netherlands had come to see the state of things in Munster, and had gone back and announced the approaching triumphal procession of the king, whom they also acknowledged, and whom they were to accompany through the world The cry of, Death to all priests and nobles! was revived, with the addition, that the only lawful sovereign in the world was the King of Münster † About Easter, 1535, they were all in motion. The West Frieslanders took Oldenkloster, not far from Sneek, the Groningers marched upon the monastery of Warfum, while the Hollanders, many thousand strong, crossed over to Overyssel, thinking to meet others of the faithful at the hill convent in the Hasselt country

It seems as if they had intended to make these convents, whence Christianity had once radiated, centres from which to spread Anabaptism over the land, and then to go to meet their appointed king But the organised and armed force of the provinces was stronger than these irregular bands The Groningers and Hollanders were dispersed on their way without difficulty ‡ Oldenkloster, which the Anabaptists had possession of, made some resistance, and was not retaken without loss. They afterwards made an attempt to conquer Amsterdam for the King of Zion, and actually got possession of the town-house one night,—though, indeed, for that one only § They did not choose to observe the conditions under which their co-religionists had succeeded in obtaining power in Munster, and ascribed that success to a miraculous interposition of God, which they expected to be extended to themselves, and, of course, expected in vain

The prophet had incessantly encouraged the people of Munster with the hope of the assistance of his countrymen, whom, he said, neither sword nor any other deadly peril, neither fire nor water, would prevent from making their way to see their king · but as these prophecies were not fulfilled, some murmurs arose among them ‖ By degrees the famine became insupportable, Those of weaker faith began to doubt of the whole matter, and quitted the city They were at first repulsed by the camp. women with their children were seen sitting in the ditches by the stockade, through which some compassionate landsknechts handed them food, but it was found impossible to drive back whole

* The recess of Coblenz is only to be found in Kersenbroik I sought it in vain in Coblenz and in Dusseldorf

† "Slan doot alle Monniken und Papen und alle Overicheit de in der werlt sint, went allenne unse Konink is de rechte Overicheit "—" Slay all monks and priests, and all sovereigns in the world, since our king alone is the true sovereign " Beninga Historie van Oostfriesland, bei Matthäus Analecta vet ævi, iv p 660, where some characteristic details are to be found

‡ Extraict de ce que Maistre Everard Nicolai conseiller au grand conseil ordonné a Malines escript a son frere Mr Nicolas Nicolai Les Anabaptistes par instigation et messaiges se sont esmeus et rassemblés en nombre de plusieurs mille sur la coste de la mer d'Hollande pour de la neviger au pays d Overyssel où ils devaient à certain jour prefix tenir communication de leurs affaires dedans un monastere qui s'appelle Bergklooster auprès de la ville de Hasselt, &c Nicolai was gone there expressly to convert them According to him, there were twenty wagons and three thousand people He found, however, only five men and thirteen women, whom he soon convinced of their error

§ Hortensius Tumult Anabaptistarum, bei Schardius ii 310

‖ Nie Tydongen en den Erzb tho Cullen (New tidings to the Archbishop of Cologne) Niesert, p 198. According to a letter of the commander of the 7th of May, a soldier who had escaped said, there was great distress, the common people murmured, the king with his retinue only sought to prevent an insurrection

troops into the city. They presented a spectacle which recalled to their learned contemporaries the horrors of Saguntum and Numantia. Skeletons covered with a shrivelled skin, with a neck scarcely able to support the weight of the head, meagre lips, and hollow, transparent cheeks;—all of them filled with horror at the famine they had shared and witnessed, and hardly able to stand. But many were still determined "not to flee back to Egypt," as the king expressed it. They rejected the summons sent them in the beginning of June, by the commander-in-chief, with the indignation of men assured that they have truth on their side. Not that they concealed from themselves that they should perhaps be trampled under the hoofs of the last monster described by Daniel; but they clung to the hope that he would soon be crushed by the corner-stone, and the kingdom be given to the saints of the Most High. They are said to have intended, when all was lost, to set fire to the city, and rush out upon the enemy's guns.

And perhaps it would have come to this, had there not been found a traitor willing to help the besiegers (who had not yet forgotten the disastrous assault of last year) to cross the ditches and walls. If they had only the inner walls and the musketry to contend with, the result could not be doubtful. Those who remained in the city could not be in much better plight than those who had quitted it; the king only and those belonging to his court,—his councillors, friends, the new dukes and governors, and such privileged persons, had sustenance for a short time.* When the bishop disclosed his plan to the landsknechts, and promised them that the commander, with the nobles and captains, should lead the way, they expressed themselves willing; for they were tired of their straw-beds in the block-houses. The scene before us is a deplorable one;—on the one side wild, violent men, hurried away by their dreams into excess and crime, now famished and desperate, yet still drunk with enthusiasm; and on the other, bands of landsknechts kept together with difficulty; sluggish and listless in their movements, and only roused to make a decisive attack when there could remain no doubt of the result. Here was no field for glorious exploits. At the appointed hour, on St. John's eve, 1535, a few hundred landsknechts crossed the ditches where they were the narrowest, and mounted their ladders where the walls where the lowest. They knew the Anabaptists' watch-word, deceived the sentinels, and then threw them over the walls: thus they took a bastion, made their way to the cathedral close, and, without waiting long for their comrades, shouted their war-cry and beat their drums. The Anabaptists sprang from their beds and rushed together to defend themselves. The result was for a moment doubtful; but only until the main body of the besiegers pressed in through a gate opened from within. The Anabaptists then fought with fury, and did great mischief to the assailants with their musketry; they killed a hundred and fifty nobles and officers, who were in the foremost ranks of the enemy: but it was the struggle of desperation. As the king was attempting to retreat to the strongest bastion, he was taken prisoner. Rottmann, resolved to escape the ignominy that awaited him as captive, rushed into the thickest of the fight, and found his death there. A few hundred of them still defended themselves behind a heap of carriages near St. Michael's chapel, with such bravery, that their assailants determined to allow them to capitulate. It appears that the terms granted were not observed. They were told they should be allowed to go home, and that when the bishop came he would determine what further should be done. It is true, indeed, that he would hardly have spared their lives. But the landsknechts, exasperated by the loss of their comrades, were not to be prevailed on to wait for his coming; they rushed after the people retreating into their houses, and it was almost impossible to stay the slaughter; and this, when stayed, was only succeeded by more formal executions.†

For, as things now stood, it is not to be wondered at that the entire extirpation of Anabaptism was contemplated. Even the women were driven out of the city, and every one who afforded them shelter was threatened to be treated as an Anabaptist. No one knew what became of them. Gradually, those who had been driven out of the city before, and who formed about a third of the former popula-

* Corvinus ad Spalatinum: Vidi ipse multos ibi libros, quorum detracta coria victum miseris suppeditarunt—immo scio pueros quoque comesos ibi esse, id quod ab iis auditum mihi est, qui in reliquias quasdam capta urbe ejus rei testes inciderunt.

† Here, as well as in the account of the conquest of the city, I follow a pamphlet called "Warhafftiger bericht der wunderbarlichen Handlung der Dueffer zu Münster in Westvalen, wie sich alle sachen nach eroberung der stat und in der Eroberung zugetragen; die noch vor der Execution des Jan von Leiden geschrieben worden, sie hat sein Bildniss in Holz."—"True account of the wonderful affair of the Baptists in Münster in Westphalia, how all things after the conquest of the city and during the conquest happened; which was written even before the execution of John of Leyden; it has his effigy in wood (engraving)." Kersenbroik, however, relates otherwise: Donantur vita et positis armis urbe protinus, præeuntibus quibusdam militiæ ducibus, exire jubentur. Cum vero liberum exeundi commeatum impetrassent, multi eorum ad ædes suorum necessariorum forte aliquid inde allaturi sese subducunt atque iter ab aliis ad exeundum paratis sponte sua divelluntur, ubi cum longiorem moram fecissent, jam tuto egressos eodem certe commeatu confisi sine ducibus subsequi contendunt, qui a militibus intercepti mactantur. I leave every one free to judge,—but this appears to me like a dressing up and apology. The old account above says:—"Ward auf beiden partheien so vil gehandlet das ein yetlicher solt wider heim in sein haus ziehen, bis auf die Zukunft des bischofs des gnädigen herrn, dann solt weiter in den sachen gehandlet werden. Darauff ward jenen glauben zugesagt, und zoch ein yetlicher wieder heim in sein haus. Als aber die landsknecht grossen merklichen schaden empfangen—fielen sie mit grimmigen zorn in die heuser und wo sie der einen funden, rissen sies mit den köpfen aus den heusern auf die strassen, howens zu stucken, stechns all zu tod. Kurz demnach ward umbgeschlagen daz man kein mer todtschlagen solt," &c.—"It was agreed by both parties that every one should go to his own home again till the coming of the Lord Bishop's Grace, and then the matter should be further handled. Thereupon this was trusted to, and every man went to his own home again. But as the landsknechts had suffered great and notable damage, they fell with furious rage on the houses, and where they found any one they dragged him by the head out of the house into the street, hewed him to pieces, or stabbed him dead. Shortly afterwards they slew all round, till there were no more to slay," &c.

tion, returned; but as even they were not held entirely guiltless, they were obliged to pay a small acknowledgment to the bishop for the recovery of their estates. No one suspected of Anabaptism could be re-admitted into the city, without giving security to the amount of four hundred gulden. Cleves and Cologne endeavoured to mitigate the severity of the re-action, and especially expressed their disapprobation of the plan of building a fortress in the city.* We shall see, at a subsequent period of our history, what were the plans of these two sovereigns, in regard to religion; plans, which they required the bishop to promise beforehand to adopt. A deputation of the empire also demanded the restoration of the city to its ancient rights and privileges. But of this there was not the slightest hope. The bishop, chapter and equestrian order, or nobles (*Ritterschaft*), were, indeed, only preserved from utter destruction by the help of their neighbours; and the army which had won the victory for them had been assembled in virtue of a decree of the empire; but the administration of the empire was very far from having energy enough to take the affair into its own hands. On the contrary, the chapter and nobles seized this opportunity entirely to annihilate the independence of the city, which had long been odious to them. In spite of the intervention of the two powers above mentioned, it was decided to build a fortress in Münster, and even at the cost of the city itself; the half of its revenues were to be applied to that purpose: the commander of this citadel was to be taken from among the nobility of the country, nominated only with the consent of the chapter and body of nobles, to whom he was to swear allegiance, and whose commands he was to obey, even if the sovereign were present.† The town council, too, was for the future to be nominated with the consent of the chapter and the nobles. The city, which had nearly emancipated itself from the yoke of the nobles and clergy, was thus once more entirely subjected to it, as a consequence of the insurrection. The chapter and the nobles got possession of far more power than the prince; as Bishop Francis, who had to encounter their violent opposition, afterwards experienced. The restoration of Catholicism, in all its rigour, followed of course in the train of these events.

Meanwhile, the captive king and his councillors, Knipperdolling and Krechting, were already brought to trial. The king was at first full of defiance, treated the bishop with insolent familiarity, jested with those who reproached him with his polygamy, and protested that he would never have surrendered the town, even if all his people had died of hunger. In the first conversation which several Hessian theologians had with him, he manifested the greatest obstinacy. But he very soon requested another conference, in which he said that none of them in Münster had any certain knowledge of the millenium, the clear perception of which had been revealed to him in prison; he now confessed that the resistance he had offered to the authorities was unlawful, polygamy rash and untimely, and he even acknowledged the obligation of infant baptism.‡ He promised, if he were pardoned, together with Melchior Hoffmann and his wives, to try to bring all Anabaptists to silence and submission. In this disposition he remained, even after he must have known that it could avail him nothing. He confessed to the bishop's chaplain that if he were to suffer ten deaths, he had deserved them all. Knipperdolling and Krechting, on the other hand, were perfectly obdurate: they appeared far less versed in theological questions than John of Leyden, and their convictions being founded on less knowledge, were more stubborn; they persisted in declaring that they had only followed the admonitions of God. They were all condemned to be put to death with red-hot pincers in the market-place of Münster.§

Protestants and Catholics witnessed the execution, which was the result of their combined efforts; but what was already their temper towards each other! One of the Hessian divines above mentioned, describes, in a letter to the court chaplain of Saxony, the delight of the mass-priests at the execution. Some, however, he adds, appeared to want, to complete their satisfaction, that the Lutherans should be disposed of in the same manner. The Lutherans did not disguise from themselves, that, for the present, there remained no hope for the progress of their doctrines in Münster.‖

The effect of this catastrophe on the Anabaptists was, that the anarchical principles they had professed, although they still found champions, were gradually abandoned; and the milder form of their opinions remained the prevailing one. This change, it is clear, could be of little immediate avail to them; they were not the less obnoxious to severe and bloody persecution.

This later and mitigated period gave birth to the spiritual songs which have been, from time to time, republished from their hymn-books. They contain such sentiments and

* Proceedings at the meeting at Nuyss, 1535, 15 July. They objected that for this the consent of emperor and empire were necessary; it was contrary to the privileges of the city, and it would be better to raze the walls, and fill up the ditches.

† Kersenbroik gives the Articuli de propugnaculo, which are not quite correct in the German re-translation; e. g. § 4. Neque hic sine capituli et nobilitatis consensu inauctorabitur, neque exauctorabitur; the translation of which is, "he should neither be appointed nor dismissed without the approbation of the chapter."

‡ Gesprech oder disputation Antonii Corvini und Johannis Kymei mit Johann von Leiden. Printed contemporaneously at Wittenberg. In sheet G there is a confession of John of Leyden, "mit miner eighene hand ondertekent," "undersigned with my own hand."

§ Des Münsterischen Königreichs an und abgang, Bluthandel und End; the rise and fall of the kingdom of Münster; trial and execution; Samstag nach Sebastiani, Anno 1536. The frontispiece represents the tower of St. Lambert's church, with the iron baskets in which the bodies were exposed, that of the king rather higher than the two others. The pamphlet is merely a history of the execution.

‖ Corvinus ad Spalatinum, l. 1. 318. Tanto Anabaptistis iniquior sum, quanto certius comperi illorum malitia factum esse ut vix mutire nunc audeant qui antea veritati erant addictissimi.

expressions as the following:—They are beset on every side by crafty and malignant serpents; the great dragon hath arisen, and rideth in his wrath through Germany; but they are resolved not to suffer themselves to be frightened by fire, or water, or sword; they know that God can save his true children, and that He will, in every case, take care of the soul, even though the flesh should bleed. "The tyrants of the Burgundian court" are arrayed against them; they imprison men and women, and make inquisition into their faith. These, however, display a single and steadfast mind; they will not deny Him who is the eternal good, and they seal their belief in him with their blood.* Therefore they are thrown into prison.' *They are happy, for they see themselves* surrounded by the heavenly hosts and martyrs; they behold God in the sun of grace, and know that no man can banish them from their fatherland, which is with God. They call to mind analogous events; such as the miracles in the old martyrologies (treating them after their manner).† Lastly, they prepare to lay themselves as victims on the altar, and to be led to the place of execution; the clear fountain of the divine word consoles them with the hope of being made like unto the angels.‡

In Germany, the utmost they could obtain for their opinions, under their mildest forms, was some degree of toleration.

But at the moment of their total overthrow in Münster, many had fled in despair to England. Here, amid the storms of the seventeenth century, their whole system of opinions assumed a most remarkable form. For example, a great deal of what is peculiar in the mode of life of the Quakers is a mere reproduction of what Justus Menius imputes to the Anabaptists.

But the colonies of North America now lay open to them. Those things for which there was no room in a constituted society, where such experiments could produce nothing but disorder and destruction, were practicable in a world where every thing had to be created. In Providence and Pennsylvania the moral and religious ideas of the Anabaptists were first developed and reduced to practice.

CHAPTER X.

BÜRGERMEISTER WULLENWEBER OF LÜBEK.

THE disturbances created by the Anabaptists were not the sole interruption to the regular progress of the reformation in Germany. The source whence these had sprung gave birth to other movements, which, although they took very different directions, threatened to become equally formidable.

A spirit of anarchy and insubordination had prevailed in the towns ever since the beginning of the sixteenth century; and now that the commonalty took so active a part in carrying out the reformation, the religious movement could not fail to be tinctured with this democratic spirit.

Nevertheless, respect for established political institutions was a leading principle of the German reformation. In by far the greater number of towns, the lawful authorities kept their place; indeed, there were only two of the larger ones in which the old councils were *completely overthrown*, Münster and Lübek.

To these two cities, therefore, all restless and innovating tendencies impetuously rushed.

At Münster, where the clergy had always been paramount, attempts were made, as our readers have seen, to establish a kind of socialist theocracy.

A strong moral or intellectual impulse, if allowed its free course, will always set at work the most peculiar powers and instincts of the organization upon which it acts; now Lübek, the centre of the Hanse towns, had interests of a mercantile and warlike nature; and precisely these were the most powerfully acted upon by the prevailing democratico-religious spirit. The incidents which occurred there were not less remarkable than those in Münster, but of a totally different character.

But in order to understand them, we must first cast our eyes round the theatre on which they were acted.

The first consideration that will strike us is, that the power of the old Hansa rested on two main points; first, the union of all the maritime towns of Germany, from Narwa to Bruges; and, secondly, the ascendancy which the more central of them—the so-called Wendish cities—had acquired over the Scandinavian kingdoms.

In that age Scandinavia was still of the greatest importance to the commerce of Germany. Calculations were published at the time, of the possible products of the mountains of the great peninsula, the plains of the Vorlande, and the surrounding sea; the copper and iron of Sweden; the furs of the northern, and the masts of the southern parts of Norway; the produce of the cattle-breeding and the agriculture of Denmark; above all, the profits arising from the herring fishery, which supplied the whole of northern Germany as far as Swabia and Franconia; and lastly, the advantages of the command of the sound.§

As governments were now continually springing up, anxious to improve the natural resources of their country for their own profit, the northern kings had long been trying to oppose a check to the excessive influence of the cities.

This would not have been of great moment,

* See the Lied des gefangenen Wiedertäufers (Song of the imprisoned Anabaptist), Die zwei Jungfrauen von Beckum, (The two Virgins of Beckum,) "O lieber vater und herzog mild," ("O beloved Father and clement Duke,") in the Münsterischen Geschichten und Sagen, p. 277, f.

† See Pura, in the Wunderhorn, i. 146, and Algerius, in the same, p. 353.

‡ Abschied vom Leben (Farewell to Life), Münst. Gesch. u. Sag. p. 284.

§ Summarium von allem was die drei Reiche Denemark, Schweden und Norwegen an whare und anderm vermügen; im Archiv zu Brussel. Summary of all that the three kingdoms, Denmark, Sweden, and Norway, possess in wares and other property. In the Archives at Brussels.

had not the union between the latter been dissolved. In the private war which broke out in 1427, between the Wendish cities and Erich, the sovereign of the united kingdoms of Scandinavia, the Netherlands severed themselves from the former, obtained peculiar privileges, and followed their own separate interests. Lubek was, indeed, in the fifteenth century, strong enough to prevent their acquiring an ascendancy, but it was not able completely to counteract their influence in the East.

When Christiern II, the last of the kings who wore the united Scandinavian crowns, married the sister of Charles V, he was not only intent on securing powerful political allies, but also on gaining a firm support for his commercial schemes in the Netherlands.

We accordingly find that he was assisted in his attempt on Sweden by the Netherlands—especially by the dowry of the Burgundian princess, and immediately afterwards, in defiance of all treaties, began to violate the privileges of the Hansa. Hanseatic merchants were detained at Schonen, ships coming from Riga carried off, and new and exorbitant duties imposed. The king's wish was, to emancipate himself completely from Lubek, and to raise Copenhagen to be the great emporium of the trade of the North. The Hanse towns were fully persuaded that the king, contrary to all he had signed and sealed and sworn, aimed at nothing less than the ruin of the maritime towns.

The gallant resistance made by Lübek is well known. It was she who sent to Sweden Gustavus Vasa, the enemy and rival before whom Christiern's star paled, and supported him with all her might. When Stockholm surrendered to him, the keys of that city were presented to the two town-councillors who accompanied the Lubek fleet, by them they were then delivered to the new king, who had just granted them a most liberal and advantageous charter.*

Nor was the share which Lubek took in the change of affairs in Denmark much less important. When Frederic of Holstein accepted the crown offered him by the aristocracy of that country, and repaired to Copenhagen, a Lubek army accompanied him by land and a Lubek fleet was ready to support him by sea.

Severin Norby, who still for a while kept Christiern's flag afloat in the Baltic, at length succumbed mainly to the exertions of the navy of Lubek, which burnt his ships on the coast of Schonen.

From that time, Christiern incessantly menaced the country from which he had been driven, with an invasion. He formed an alliance with England, raised troops in Germany with the aid of his kinsmen and friends, sent ships to sea against the Hanseats from Zealand and Brabant, and, as he still had communication with the interior of the country, and an imperial party still existed in the towns, he was always feared. Lubek enjoyed the franchises it had obtained, without molestation, mainly because the two kings could not do without her assistance against their menacing foe.

Their alliance was drawn closer when Christiern, notwithstanding the Protestant zeal he had formerly manifested, returned to Catholicism, and now, supported by efficient aid from the emperor, seriously prepared to make an effort to recover his throne. It is, however, clear that there was not always the best understanding betwen the brothers-in-law. While Christiern was arming in Friesland, an imperial envoy endeavoured to bring about a reconciliation between him, King Frederic of Denmark, and the Hanse towns. King Frederic declared that he would submit to an arbitration if Christiern consented to do the same, and, above all, to suspend hostilities; a proposal which the envoy hastened to lay before Christiern in Friesland. That monarch, however, answered him with violent complaints, that after being so long an exile from his country, he was not yet to be permitted to return to it, nor to be restored to his rightful throne.† Instead of disbanding his troops, he marched without delay into Holland. That which he could not obtain by fair means, he extorted by force—ships and money. He knew that the court of Vienna approved of his undertaking (if not at the present moment, yet on the whole), and wished for the same results. The emperor had often enough declared that he regarded Christiern's cause as his own. Netherland merchants afforded the king voluntary assistance, the houses of Frei of Campen, Schultis of Enkhuysen, Bur of Amsterdam, and Rath of Alkmar, were mentioned as those to whom he was chiefly indebted for the funds necessary to his designs; and he, in return, granted them the most advantageous charters. On the 15th October, 1531, they set sail from Medenblik.

The Lubekers now addressed themselves to the Schmalkaldic league. They declared that nothing less was intended than the destruction of Protestantism, and that there was an express understanding with all the bishops to that effect. King Frederic offered to join the Schmalkaldic league with his hereditary domains, if at least the most considerable members of it, Saxony, Hessen and Luneburg, would conclude a similar treaty with him in respect of his elective kingdom.‡ For, he said, that, however strong his attachment to

* Regkmann lubliche Chronik, otherwise a mere repetition of Bonnus, has an article peculiarly confirming this statement.

† Literæ Banneri ad Cæsarem, de gestis apud Vandalicas civitates, s. a. Brussels Archives.

‡ The acceptation generally given must be so modified. "Your grace will be pleased to know," says King Frederic in a letter to Landgrave Philip dated St John's Day, 1531, "that we are earnestly well inclined to enter upon a union and alliance of our kingdom, and also our hereditary domains, concerning secular affairs, commerce and transactions, with you and our beloved uncle, the Elector of Saxony, together with the Duke of Luneberg." If this alliance should be concluded, "we are consequently not disinclined, but, on the contrary, fully minded, then to contract a union, understanding and alliance, on behalf of our hereditary dominions alone, with all electors, princes, counts and estates attached to the evangelical party." The landgrave hoped that Hamburg, Rostock, Wismar and Stade would also join.

the evangelical cause, he would be prevented from expressing it by the power of his bishops, every one of whom had a great following of nobles

Thus, as a counterpoise to the influence which Catholicism had exercised on the one side, an attempt was made to implicate the scarcely formed anti-catholic league in these political affairs But it did not succeed Elector John would not hear of this twofold character of a member of the league, nor indeed was it necessary No sooner had King Frederic given the Lubekers sufficient security for the trade with Holland,* than four Lubek men-of-war put to sea, before the Danes had made any preparations Christiern had indeed landed in the mean time in Norway, and had, without difficulty, gained possession of the whole of that country, with the exception of a few fortified towns, but the Lubek cruisers burnt his ships on the coasts, provisioned Aggerhus, and formed a central point for the greater force which assembled in May, 1532, relieved Aggerhus, and compelled Christiern to negotiate, to capitulate, and finally to surrender himself into the hands of his enemies As far as I have been able to discover, it was the delegate from Lubek who counselled the perpetual detention of Christiern.

As the Dutch were parties to this defeat, they instantly began to feel the consequences of it. In the summer of the year 1532, above four hundred merchant vessels were lying useless in the ports of Holland, there were ten thousand boatmen out of employment, and wheat rose to double its usual price † While Christiern was in Norway, King Frederic had allowed himself to be prevailed on to sign an ignominious treaty, but in virtue even of that he now claimed compensation, which he rated extremely high, and which the Netherlands refused to pay The king dismissed the ambassadors of the stadtholderess with an unfriendly message, upon which the Lubekers took the confiscated church treasures out of the sacristies, and fitted out a squadron with them, which, in the year 1533, lay in the Sound

Upon this, the great towns of Holland fitted out a fleet to chastise that of Lubek—"the rebel and foe to his majesty"

They insisted on the high dignity with which their sovereign was invested, as if that gave a greater colour of right to their proceedings!

It seemed as if matters must come to a decision by arms, now and for ever, between the two divisions of the ancient Hansa, especially since the democratic faction in Lubek, the rise of which during the religious troubles we have noticed, was now at the helm, and engaged in these affairs with the most ardent zeal

In the early and primitive days of Lubek, when, as in Venice, a share in the administration of public affairs was regarded as a burden, a statute was framed, according to which, a man who had sat two years in the council, was at liberty to quit on the third ‡ People had, however, long been accustomed to regard this burden as an honour, and were jealous of sharing it with anybody Nevertheless, the rising faction interpreted the statute to mean that no one should be allowed to sit more than two years in the council, consequently, that a third part of the college must be renewed every year The most active supporter of this construction was George Wullenweber, one of the directors of the Hundred and Sixty-four, he probably thought it the best means of getting possession of the supreme power, with an appearance of legality, and it was entirely approved of by the excited citizens In February, 1533, the council was renewed, and Wullenweber was one of the first elected to it, scarcely had he sat a fortnight, when (8th March) he was chosen burgermeister This completed the overthrow of the constitution of Lubek Wullenweber now united the power of a popular leader with that of a lawful magistrate He seemed determined immediately to prosecute the war with Holland with the utmost vigour, ordering even the great chandeliers of St Mary's church to be taken down, and cast into guns

But before he proceeded farther, changes took place which gave his activity a totally different direction

It was natural that the northern governments, delivered from the enemy they had so long feared, should not cling so closely to the cities which had hitherto afforded them protection They were now once more free to feel the oppression which these protectors exercised over them,—the obstruction which they offered to their own commercial activity In the victory of Lubek over Holland, they could not possibly see any direct advantage to themselves, for there, too, a democratic faction, against which they had a natural antipathy, had gained the upper hand Had they not reason to fear that it might excite similar agitations among their own subjects?

While things were in this state, King Frederic died at Gottorp, in April, 1533, and a number of pretenders to the Danish crown arose Frederic's sons, of whom the one, Christian, was inclined to Protestantism, the other, John, was trained in the Catholic faith, had both numerous adherents, the latter, especially among the higher clergy It is affirmed that a distant relation, Joachim of Brandenburg, also put in claims to the succession, and ventured to entertain hopes Others thought of

* Bonnus and Regkmann — — — "with the assurance that they would again assist the city of Lubek against the Hollanders, and not allow them afterwards to sail through the Sound with so many ships"

† Wagenaar, Niederlandische Geschichte, ii 423

‡ "Des dridden Jaers sol he frye sin des Rads men he mögne id dann mit Bedde von eme hebben, dat he socke den Rad"—"The third year he should be free from the council, unless he be requested to offer himself as a member again"—Becker, ii p 54 I do not know on what grounds Barthold rests his interpretation of the statute, in his article on Wullenweber, in Raumer's Taschenbuch, for 1835, p 37 It is as follows—No man shall sit for more than two years in the council unless the citizens propose an extension of the term, for some special reasons

the Elector of Saxony The memory of Christiern was not yet wholly effaced, but the house of Austria hastened to set up a new pretender in his place, Count Palatine Frederic, to whom the emperor gave the daughter of Christiern in marriage

In this general uncertainty, Lubek thought it might also have a voice, and that it perceived in what direction its interests lay Wullenweber went to Copenhagen, and addressed himself first to the council of state on the subject of the Dutch war, but he found no encouragement He then turned to the nearest Protestant pretender, Duke Christian, and offered him his assistance to obtain the crown Christian had, however, sufficient prudence and reserve to decline this Wullenweber saw that he should gain nothing by a war with Holland, if, meantime, he lost Denmark He conceived the idea of taking advantage of the confusion of the moment, and establishing in that country the dominion of his city (and consequently his own), on a firmer and more extensive basis than ever He thought that he might reckon on the sympathy of a party in the country, and at the same time on the support of one of the great powers of Europe

A part of the Lubek fleet which had put to sea against the Dutch, had touched on the English coast, when its commander, Marcus Meier, had ventured to land without a passport, and had been arrested and lodged in the Tower of London This happened just at the time in which Henry VIII (as we shall have occasion to relate more at length) had entirely broken with the see of Rome, and had determined to emancipate his kingdom from the power of the pope, he was, therefore, looking round on every side for allies to assist him in his defence We have a resolution of his privy-council, in pursuance of which an embassy was to be sent to the Hanse Towns (among other places), in order to form an alliance with them * Considering also the growing coolness with the emperor, it could not be a matter of indifference to the English whether the throne of Denmark was filled by a prince in the interest of the house of Burgundy, or in that of its opponents It is, therefore, no wonder that the king, instead of punishing the commander of a fleet which had taken the sea against the Netherlanders, invited him to his presence, and negotiated with him. From the documents extant, it appears that Marcus Meier promised, in the name of his party and his city, that no prince should mount the Danish throne, whom Henry VIII did not approve Henry, on the other hand, showed himself ready to support Lubek in its undertaking, and hoped to gain over the King of France to the same cause

Meier returned to Lubek, full of this most unexpected result of his expedition

This man had formerly been a blacksmith at Hamburg, but had left his trade to enter the army. He served first in that body of adventurers which Christiern II collected in Friesland, and conducted into Holland and then to Norway Here he was taken prisoner, but he immediately seized the opportunity to take service with Lubek This unquiet community was just the element for him, he attached himself to the rising chiefs of the popular party, and as early as the year 1532, the command of the troops destined for the Turkish war was entrusted to him, and he marched to the frontier and back again, through the whole German empire, at their head He next, ready for either kind of warfare, went to sea, and he returned from England, decorated with a gold chain and the honour of knighthood He now began to play a great part in Lubek, keeping a vast retinue of servants and horses, and going, after the somewhat barbaric fashion of that age, dressed with the utmost possible splendour,† he was young, handsome, and brave, and, of course, found favour in the eyes of the principal citizens' wives By a marriage, contracted shortly after his return, with the rich widow of the lately deceased burgermeister, Lunte, he gained a footing among the patrician families, and, at his wedding, the captain of the city, surrounded by a mounted band, escorted him from the Holstein Gate

Marcus Meier had, from the first, been on intimate terms with Wullenweber, their intimacy now became closer than ever. At the sittings of the Hansa they appeared at the head of a numerous retinue, in glittering armour, and preceded by trumpets The good fortune that had hitherto attended them, gave them confidence in the future

Their first efforts were directed towards ruling in Lubek itself

There were still in the council some of the former members, and these, as may be imagined, did not concur in all the propositions of the innovators At Easter, 1534, they were turned out of office without ceremony, notwithstanding the utter repugnance of such a proceeding to the principles laid down by Luther The superintendent, Bonnus, would no longer look on, while the authorities were attacked, dismissed, and banished,‡ he, therefore, sent in his resignation

Their main object now was to have their hands free in politics and war, and they therefore determined, though after some hesitation, to conclude a truce with the Dutch for four years, even on the condition of granting the free passage through the Sound, demanded by Holland

They could now direct all their thoughts and plans towards the North, where things assumed the most favourable aspect for them.

In the Danish cities, nay, even in the capital of Sweden, as well as on the south of the Baltic, there were civic bodies impatient of the yoke of an oppressive aristocracy

* Propositions for the King's Council in Strype's Memorials Ecclesiastical, i 238 State Papers, i 411.

† Sastrow, i 115

‡ Letter of Hermannus Bonnus to the extraordinary Council, 4th May 1534. Starke, Lubekische Kirchenhistorie, i, Beilage, iii v.

In Denmark the citizens had discovered, after the lapse of some time, that the expulsion of Christiern II. had been of no benefit to them. All the immunities from burdens which that king had granted them, had been gradually revoked. They were especially indignant that the nobility, not content with the enormous privileges it enjoyed, endeavoured to get the profits of commerce into its hands.* The two bürgermeisters, Jorg Mynter of Malmöe, and Ambrosius Bogbinder of Copenhagen, both Germans, entirely shared Wullenweber's democratic sentiments. Protected by Frederic, Jorg Mynter had introduced the reformation into Malmöe, and would not allow it to be put down, as the national council seemed to intend. They promised the Lübekers that, as soon as their men-of-war should appear off the Danish coasts, they would abandon the council, and fight openly on their side. It appears as if it had been concerted that both cities should join the league of the Hansa; but on this point the authorities are not unanimous.

Very similar views were entertained by Andres Handson, master of the mint at Stockholm; with whom all the German citizens, and a part of the Swedish, seem to have been in an understanding. King Gustavus affirmed that their designs aimed directly at his life, and that powder was laid under his seat in the church, with the intention of blowing him up in the sight of the assembled congregation.

If we remember that, in all the Hanse towns, nay, in all nether Germany, the popular inclinations had manifested themselves in a similar manner, and though repressed for the moment, were by no means entirely extinguished;—if we combine with this the popularity acquired in the West by Anabaptism (which was only a religious cloak for the democratic principle), we shall perceive how mighty was the agitation which shook the North German world. It was a ferment like that preceding the revolt of the peasants, which had not then penetrated Lower Germany, but had been arrested and quelled on its frontiers. Now, however,—after a lapse of ten years,—Lower Germany was in a state of agitation not less violent. At the time of the peasants' war, some few towns partook of it; now, they were its leaders and champions. Lübek, which Bonnus calls the capital of all the Saxon tongues, led the way. What was to be expected if bold demagogues were already masters there, and had at their disposal the means for the execution of their plans?

But the cities now, like the peasants before them, could not do without a commander of noble birth. They engaged the services of Christopher of Oldenburg, who, though a canon of Cologne cathedral, was a brave warrior and a zealous Protestant. As a child, his mind had been richly stored with history; and when, at a riper age, he had repaired to the court of Philip of Hessen, it was thoroughly imbued with that mingled spirit of war and religion which then reigned there; he had afterwards assisted in putting down the peasants, and in delivering Vienna; he was not without elevation of mind, and had all the parts and qualities of a gallant soldier.

It was, however, impossible that a member of the house of Oldenburg should adopt the quarrels of a few bürgermeisters without solid grounds; or, at the least, without a plausible pretext.

The Lübekers determined to allege that they were about to liberate and reinstate on his throne the captive king Christiern, whom nobody had more bitterly hated, or more successfully sought to injure, than they. Yet there was a certain tincture of truth in this. The object they had immediately in view, was not their mercantile interests (which Christiern had thwarted), but the democratic, or rather anti-aristocratic, which he had always espoused.† But they took ample precautions as to the former. Count Christopher promised that, if he conquered, he would cede Gothland, Helsingborg, and Helsingör to the Lübekers, whose ascendancy in the Baltic would thus have been secured forever. Nay, he gave them the assurance that he would deliver King Christiern into their hands, as soon as he had rescued him from prison.‡ What a power over the three Scandinavian kingdoms would they have acquired by the possession of the person of their legitimate monarch!

For they were resolved not to suffer Gustavus Vasa to remain in Sweden; they had even thought of setting up the young Svante Sture as a temporary rival and competitor.

In May, 1534, Count Christopher entered Lübek. The present intention of the inhabitants was to seize upon the property of the cathedral, which they meant to confiscate at the death of the bishop. Christopher took Eutin without difficulty. His attack on some castles in Holstein, such as Trittow, which he conquered, and Segeberg, was merely in order to give occupation to Duke Christian, and in the mean time, undisturbed by him, to attain his ends in Denmark.§

Disregarding the means of defence which Duke Christian instantly raised, and the advantages which he obtained, Count Christopher, eager to complete the great work, put to sea at Travemünde, on the 19th June, 1534, with twenty-one ships of war.

Never did an invading army find a country

* Address from the Commons of Copenhagen to Queen Mary, May, 1535, (Brussels Arch.,) specifies the reasons for their irritation, "Darum das dieses Richs Raidt und der Adel, über das sie unsern rechten König—entsetst, lusher mit manigfaltiger unredlicher Beswerung nicht weniger uns denn alle andere Stette und gemeinen Mann im ganzen reich fon unsern, christlichen Freiheiten und Gerechtigkeiten gezwungen, die Kaufmannschap hinweggenommen," &c.—"Because that the council of this kingdom, and the nobility, besides that they have deposed our rightful king, have hitherto, with manifold, dishonest, and intolerable conspiracies, forcibly suppressed our Christian liberties and rights, taken away our privileges as merchants," &c. The last complaint is also reported in the Rerum Danicarum Chronologia, in Ludewig Reliquæ MSS. ii. p. 70, auf. Nobilitatis osores gravissimi ob negotiationes quas exercebant ditiores.

† See Havitfield, G. ii. Pontanus ap. Westphalen, 1144.

‡ Declarations of Wullenweber in his Interrogatorium; authenticated by Gebhardi, ii. 135.

§ Wullenweber declared that these schemes related only to Denmark.

better disposed for its reception. The burgermeister Mynter put out to meet the fleet, with the news that he had raised a revolt in Malmoe, and had got possession of the citadel, which he had destroyed. Hereupon Christopher cast anchor some miles in front of Copenhagen. As soon as he showed himself, the insurrection, for which every thing was ready and which, like those in Germany, was directed against the nobles and the clergy, broke out in Seeland. In Roschild the multitude plundered the bishop's palace and delivered up the city. They fell upon the castles of the nobles and rased them to the ground. The majority of the nobles, solely to save their lives, consented to renew their former oath to Christiern II., and in an unusual form. On the 15th of July, Copenhagen went over, Laaland, Langeland, and Falster followed the example of Seeland without delay. Nothing was wanting but the arrival of the count in Malmoe, to carry all Schonen with him. In Funen it seemed for a moment as if the revolt of the peasants, which had just arisen, would be put down by the council of state and the nobility; but some small succours from the count sufficed to insure victory to the peasants, and recognition to the exiled king. There remained only Jutland. A pirate, named Clemint, who had joined Count Christopher in Malmoe, fell upon Aalborg, and collecting the Jutish peasants around him, soon drove the nobles and their heavy cavalry out of the field.

While these tidings were coming in, the syndic of Lubek, Doctor Oldendorp, one of the most active members of the reforming party — a man "of unquiet spirit," to use the words of old Kantzow — travelled through the Swedish cities, to invite their participation in this undertaking. He was personally a representative of the democratic interests, and he now unfolded the most flattering prospects that it was possible to conceive; it may easily be imagined how he was received by the people. A few of the old councillors opposed him, but in vain. The Stralsunders threw their burgermeister, Claus Smiterlow, into prison, carried the cannon on board the ships of war, and elected a new council. The expenses of the war were to be paid by forced contributions from the richer sort, without any assistance from the people. The old burgermeisters of Rostock were compelled by force to give their assent to the preparations for war. All the towns of the surrounding countries were roused to attempt great things. Reval and Riga sent contributions. Nothing was heard of but Lubek. "Had the cities succeeded as they hoped," says Kantzow, "not a prince or a nobleman would have been left."*

Meanwhile, the people of Lubek did not neglect to cultivate their friendship with England. On the 30th May, they sent three councillors to that country, to express to the king their sentiments as to his quarrel with the pope to offer him their alliance against the see of Rome, and at the same time to request his support and assistance in their own affairs.†

We have before us the copy of a treaty of the 2d August, 1534, according to which they also left the king the free disposal of the crown of Denmark, in case he desired either to take possession of it himself, or to recommend another candidate,‡ while he, on his side, confirmed all their ancient privileges, gave them a sum of money, and promised them further support.

One symptom of the impression which these events made in Europe, may be found in a letter of the Archbishop of Lund, in which he begs the emperor to reflect on the consequences of an alliance between the Hanse towns and England, how easily Holland might then be invaded, and an insurrection raised there, and conjures him to take some means to prevent it. He added, that if the emperor thought himself bound by his treaties with the house of Oldenburg, he might declare war in the name of Frederic of the Palatinate and the youthful Dorothea. There was living in Lubek one Hopfensteiner, formerly in the service of the Archbishop of Bremen, who incessantly entertained the imperial ministers with reports of the great regard still paid to the emperor's interests in the Hanse towns, and represented an enterprise of this kind as very easy. The Archbishop of Lund offered, in case of need, to carry on the war in his own name.§

But before the imperial court, or the government of the Netherlands, could resolve on a measure of so decisive a kind, the Lubekers had met with a resistance in the North, which daily assumed a more formidable character.

Duke Christian of Holstein was a man of tranquil, North-German temper: a nature not lightly moved, but when once urged by necessity, capable of acting with admirable perseverance and discretion. He had already shown of what he was capable, by the manner in which he had introduced the reformation into the duchies. His mind and character were profoundly penetrated with the religious and moral spirit of the German reformation. He sang the Lutheran hymns with as much

* Kantzows Chronik von Pommern, in the accurate edition of Böhmer, p. 211.

† Oratores missi de villa de Lubicke, in Rhymer's Fœdera, vi. ii. 214. Further information on these affairs may be expected from the continuation of the State Papers. It is remarkable that the king wished also to form an alliance with the Hamburghers, "for the redressing and amending of the injuries doon to his majestie by the Bishop of Rome." Articles were to be laid before them for their acceptance, e. g., "Against Goddes prohibitions the dispensation of the Bishop of Rome or of an other man is utterlie nought and of no value," the same which were after laid before the Lubekers, and also some others specially relating to the bishop's government. they were to send twelve ships to the king's assistance, and raise 10,000 men at his cost—3000 horse and 7000 foot. Printed in the Report of the Rec. Commission, App. C.

‡ If he would do neither, for he was as yet undecided, they engaged to repay his loan. "Alle und itlik Geld, so S. K. M. der Stadt thom besten vorstrecket." — "All and every money which H. R. M. had advanced for the benefit of the city." Words of the treaty, which Dr. Schmidt had the kindness to procure me from the Bremen Archives.

§ Literæ Archiepiscopi ad Cæsarem et Dm de Granvella, in the third volume of the Imperial Documents at Brussels. The letter of the 1st of August, 1534, which I intend to give in the Appendix, is particularly worthy of note.

fervour as any worthy artisan of an imperial city. Perjury he visited with new and increased penalties. To read the Bible, to listen to passages from history, to converse at table with some learned divine or wise statesman, to follow the discoveries in astronomy—such were his pleasures. His political and military acts were, as we see, based on deep and solid grounds, and prompted by elevated motives and tendencies.*

To this prince the leaders of the popular party in Lubek had, as we have stated, offered the crown of Denmark; he had declined it, because he would not owe it to force, and they had, in consequence, directed their first hostilities against him, being at length irritated, and earnestly supported by his subjects and his neighbours (and among them the Landgrave of Hessen), he at length took the field with a considerable force, in the intention of chastising the Lubekers for their attacks.† In September, 1534, he appeared before the city, and, in order to cut off the communication with the sea, proceeded without delay to block up the Trave. Marcus Meier protested that he should not succeed in this. But Meier's arrangements only proved his complete unfitness for serious warfare. The Holsteiners first took possession of the bank of the Trave as far as Tremsmuhle; they then took up a strong position on the opposite bank, on the Burgfeld, and connected their posts by a bridge which effectually closed the river. All attempts of the Lubekers, both by land and water, to get possession of this bridge, were fruitless; they were repeatedly beaten before the eyes of their wives and children, and were forced to yield other important points. The city which was laying plans to get the whole North under its influence, saw itself cut off from all communication with the sea at its very gates.

The first and most urgent of all necessities for Lubek was, to rid itself of so imminent a foe. Already misunderstandings broke out in the city; the citizens were discontented, the Hundred and Sixty-four resigned, and even in the council the men in power encountered resistance. They were compelled to enter upon negotiations with Holstein, which they were no longer in a condition to conduct according to their wishes. We have no accurate information either concerning the preceding movements in the town, or these negotiations; but it is evident that the latter embraced the affairs of Denmark as well as those of Holstein, and that a considerable approximation was made between the parties. Christian seemed inclined to make some concessions, and Wullenweber declared that he would have consented to the terms of peace, had not Dr. Oldendorp prevented him. Thus it happened that they agreed on nothing but the affairs of Holstein; Lubek ceded all that she had taken from Holstein. But a stranger peace was never concluded. Whilst the contracting parties agreed about Holstein, each reserved to itself the right to continue the war with all its might concerning the affairs of Denmark.‡

But these also were decided by the personal qualities of Duke Christian.

Such were the straits in which the states of Denmark found themselves, in consequence of attacks from without and revolt within, that they had, at length, although not without strenuous resistance on the part of the clergy, determined to elect the duke to the throne.

By this measure, all the fears of the Protestants of that kingdom, which had been very lively, were dissipated. In their manifesto, the Lubekers had spoken of the introduction of pure religion as the chief object of their undertaking. This was now of course without a meaning, and all the sympathy that they could look for on this score, had vanished.

Now, moreover, the interests of Denmark were defended by an able and courageous champion. As he would perhaps have yielded too much in the camp before Lubek, so he would afterwards, perhaps, have consented to extend anew the privileges of the Lubekers;§ but they would be contented with nothing less than the disposal of the kingdom and the crown. There was now no other resource, therefore than the sword. Without loss of time, Christian turned with his victorious troops from Lubek to Jutland. Even in December, 1534, he succeeded in retaking Aalborg, and pacifying the whole province. His two brothers-in-law, the King of Sweden and the Duke of Prussia, took up arms for him, the former by sea and land, and the latter by sea only. His other brother-in-law, the Duke of Pomerania, sent him subsidies which arrived just at the critical moment. Two or three Hessian companies, which he had had with him at Lubek, marched with him to the North. Throughout a great part of Norway, he was already acknowledged king.

On the other side, the Lubekers once more collected all their forces.

They succeeded in gaining over to their cause a neighbouring prince, Duke Albert of Mecklenburg.

Duke Albert, who had adhered with great fidelity to the party of the deposed and imprisoned Christiern, subsequently declared that he had received no pay from Lubek; his only motive was, "that it seemed to him good and praiseworthy to set free an anointed king, who, contrary to bond and seal, had been thrown into prison."‖ It was said that the crown of

* Eragius, Historia Christiani, III p 395. Hemming, Oratio funebris ad calcem historiæ Craginæ.

† Chytræus, Hist Sax. p 408.

‡ Regkmann's Chronicle (p 176) agrees with the Interrogatorium of Wullenweber, if accurately compared. Only Regkmann gives some conjectures, e g that Wullenweber's enemies would not permit that Lubek should be aggrandized by him.

§ According to a letter of Hopfensteiner, 20th of January, 1535, the king promised, first, that the captive king Christiern should be well taken care of, secondly, satisfaction given to Count Christopher; thirdly, restitution of what Lübek had expended on the kingdom of Denmark, "in his father's time," fourthly, much more liberty and justice than they have hitherto had; and also certain towns as pledges;—"but they would not consent."

‖ Albert's Declaration, Monday after Reminiscere, 1537. (Brussels Archives.)

Denmark, or even that of Sweden, had been promised to him as a recompense for his services. It does not appear that any such direct and positive engagement was entered into; according to Wullenweber's declaration, the promise made to him was, that Lubek would protect him in the possession of whatever he might obtain from King Christiern.* It is possible, however, that more distinct views were held out to him; according to Hopfensteiner,† the plan of the Lubekers was, that, if King Christiern was liberated, Duke Albert should continue to govern Denmark as regent, while the king should be maintained suitably to his rank in Lubek; they enjoying all the advantages they had ever claimed,—Helsingor and Helsingborg, with the tolls, Gothland, and perhaps even Calmar and the Swedish mines. On the 9th April, Duke Albert embarked at Warnemunde. He seemed to have made preparations for a permanent residence in Denmark, taking with him his wife, who was with child, his court, and even his huntsmen and hounds, in order that he might enjoy the pleasures of the chase, after the German fashion, in the thick forests of Denmark. It was of great advantage to the Lubekers, that a distinguished prince of the empire, sovereign of no inconsiderable territory, had espoused their cause. It inspired the Danish towns likewise with courage and confidence. Hitherto they had borne the whole weight of the contest alone; but Albert brought some independent power to their aid, and was rather to be regarded as an auxiliary than a salaried commander. Wullenweber, who accompanied the duke, at length succeeded in bringing about an understanding between him and Count Christopher, who had, at first, shown considerable dissatisfaction. Shortly after, a Lubek squadron brought further reinforcements, under the Counts of Hoya and Tecklenburg.

Meanwhile, Marcus Meier, who had been sent to Schonen, had bestirred himself there with great success. He executed one of his usual daring and dexterous manœuvres. Being taken prisoner, he turned his ill luck to such good account, that he got possession of the very castle in which he was imprisoned—Warburg, in Holland.

The two parties were, as we perceive, very equally matched; perhaps that of Lubek and the cities was somewhat superior in numbers.

The question was no longer, as perhaps at an earlier period, whether the ecclesiastical reform would extend to Denmark; its destiny was completely secured by the accession of a Protestant king. The question rather was, whether the ecclesiastical reform would combine with a political revolution; whether the democratical principle, which, emanating from Lubek, had spread itself over the whole North, would be triumphant there, or not,—the same question which, from the moment of its first agitation at Wittenberg, in Carlstadt's time, had kept Upper (and more recently Lower) Germany in that state of ferment which had just been so terribly quelled in Munster.

The whole force of the democratic principle was now united at this remote point of the North. Had it conquered, it would have caused a fresh and mighty reaction in Germany.

On the 11th June, 1535, on the spot where of yore Odin was worshipped with sanguinary rites — where legends of the greatness of the house of Oldenburg, mutilated by its own divisions, have their seat—on the island of Funen, not far from Assens, near the Oxneberg, this awful question was decided. On both sides were Germans and Danes. The royal party were led by Hans Rantzau, who had won his knighthood at Jerusalem, and had traversed the whole of Europe, and who combined, in a still higher degree than his master, zeal for Protestantism, and love of arts and science,‡ with address in the council and valour in the field; the troops of the cities were commanded by the Count of Hoya. Rantzau conquered,—like Landgrave Philip at Laufen—like the princes in the peasants' war—by the superiority of his cavalry and artillery. It was in his favour that the enemy did not wait for him, but made the first onset, and fell into disorder. The best men of the cities' army fell, and it sustained a total defeat.§

At the same time, the fleets met at Bornholm. The king's fleet included Swedish and Prussian, that of Lubek, Rostock, and Stralsund ships. It was now to be decided whether the princes or the cities were henceforth to be masters of the seas. The battle had already begun, when they were parted by a storm; but the royal fleet was evidently superior; the Danish admiral, Skram, who commanded it, captured a great number of Lubek trading vessels on the coasts.

Christian III. was thus victorious by land and by sea. Funen had been forced immediately to submit, and did homage to him at Odensee. With the help of the fleet, which arrived at that moment, he crossed over to Seeland, where he was received with great joy by the nobles. The inhabitants of Schoningen did him homage, as soon as he appeared. Warburg was soon retaken, and used as a pledge between Denmark and Sweden. In the beginning of August, 1535, the conquests made by the cities were once more reduced to Malmoe and Copenhagen.

Notwithstanding this, the possession of these two points would still have rendered a resumption of their former plans possible, had not the discontents which had arisen at the first reverses, ripened meanwhile into a complete revolution.

And lastly, that interposition on the part of the authorities of the empire in the internal

* Interrogatorium.

† Hopfensteiner, 26th November, 1534, at which time the negotiation was already begun. The prospect of gaining Mecklenburg contributed the most to bring about the rejection of Christian's proposals. Wullenweber declares that he neither prevented the peace, nor engaged Duke Albert on his side, but that this was done by others: this account is perfectly consistent.

‡ Chytræus: oculus nobilitatis eruditæ in his terris fulgentissimus. See Christiani, N. Gesch. von Schleswig und Holstein, i. 479, ii. 54.

§ Cragius, Historia Christiani III. p. 95.

affairs of Lübek, which the imperial envoys had two years before demanded, was now energetically put in practice. The city was admonished, by a mandate of the Imperial Chamber, to reinstate the expelled bürgermeisters, and all the members of the town-council. In itself, this mandate would have had little effect; but it expressed a demand which was now imperiously heard in almost all the other cities of Lower Germany, and was, therefore, supported by public opinion. Above all, the Lübekers felt that they were beaten; their world-embracing plans had encountered an invincible, nay, a triumphant resistance; the energy of the democratic spirit was broken by their failure.

On the 15th August, 1535, the council convoked the commons, and laid before them the mandate of the Imperial Chamber. The moment in which Wullenweber was on a journey of business in Mecklenburg was not taken without design. The commons first convinced themselves that the mandate contained nothing about the re-establishment of the ancient ecclesiastical forms; and, being satisfied on that point, declared themselves ready to obey it, and to put a stop to all innovations in temporal things. At the next sitting of the council, George von Hövelen, who had been made bürgermeister against his will, rose up and took his old place among the councillors. The councillors appointed by the commons perceived that, under these circumstances, they could not maintain their posts, and quitting their chairs, they resigned their dignity. We may imagine the astonishment of Wullenweber, when he returned and found so complete a change effected in his absence. He had long ceased to possess the popularity which had raised him to power, and no effort to regain it had been of any avail. He, too, was compelled to resign. Recalled by his fellow-citizens, escorted into the town by a hundred and fifty old friends, and the ambassadors from Cologne and Bremen, — for the Hansa happened to be sitting, — Nicholas Brömse re-entered Lübek.* A recess was drawn up, in virtue of which the evangelical doctrines were retained; while, on the other hand, the council was reinstated in its former rights. The Lutheran principle, which demanded only a reconstitution of spiritual things, and allowed the temporal, wherever it was possible, to subsist, was here, too, triumphant.

It was obviously no longer to be expected that the Danish war could be carried on with vigour. Gert Korbmacher, the miner, who joined another expedition to the Sound, expresses his disgust at the little earnestness that was shown in it.

The war, however, went on, though feebly enough, and sometimes new and extensive plans were connected with it.

From the trial of Wullenweber, it appears indisputable that he had intended to resume his schemes and enterprises. There were at that time a few bands of landsknechts, under the command of a colonel named Uebelacker, recruited in the name of the Count Oldenburg in the Hadeln country. Wullenweber set out to join them. On his trial, he declared that his intention was to lead these troops across the Elbe at Boitzenburg, and before the walls of Lübek, without delay; his partisans would have opened the Mohlenthor to him, he would have overthrown the council, and have established a completely democratical government, together with Anabaptism. But even in his examination, these plans appear in the light of half-matured projects; and before his death, Wullenweber utterly denied them,† and especially retracted all personal accusations of participation which had been extorted from him. It is difficult to reject a confession, the most material points of which were made without the fearful agency of the rack; but it is utterly impossible to ground any belief on a declaration which the accused retracted at the moment of his death. The existence of these plans, therefore, must for ever remain problematical. If they ever existed, they could have had no other result than that which we have already witnessed. Wullenweber fell—as he had been forewarned—into the hands of his bitterest enemy, the Archbishop of Bremen, who, as in his quality of spiritual lord he could not stain his hands with blood, gave him up, to his brother, Duke Henry of Brunswick. Here he was subjected to the examination above mentioned,‡ accused by both Denmark and Lübek, and because he would not deny all that he was accused of, condemned to die according to the old forms of the German law. The justice of the land pronounced that "he might not have done unpunished, that which he had done." He was beheaded, and then quartered.

Wullenweber is a perfect representative of the rash and perverse spirit which was rife, during that period, among the inhabitants of the German cities. He had begun, like so many demagogues in other towns; the talent of leading a mobile population at his pleasure, and the natural force of the political and religious interests, elevated him to a station whence he could dare to intrude, self-supported, among the great powers of the world. He knew no moderation; failures did not teach him caution; he evoked once more the ancient spirit of the Hansa, prevailed on Ger-

* Becker, Geschichte von Lübek, aus Reimar Kock und Lambert von Dalen, ii. 91—95.

† In Article 31, he says, "They have never entirely concluded the affair of the Anabaptists; but one thing brought on another."

‡ In Regkmann's Chronicle there is a report of his last accusation and execution, with some of his letters written from his prison. Strangely enough, the defence has thus been published without the accusation. This, which is contained in the trial, I intend to print in the Appendix. The trial, which I found in the Weimar Archives among the Wolfenbüttel papers, has been of great use and value to me. Wullenweber confessed but few of the charges, and those the most doubtful ones, under the torture. On the other hand, there is much of another kind without any immediate relation to the criminal accusation, and rather of an historical nature, which is occasionally strikingly confirmed by passages of the Chroniclers not generally considered authentic, or by forgotten documents. Of course I have admitted nothing that Wullenweber denied again before his death.

man princes to engage in his wars, and contracted alliances with foreign potentates Motives of all sorts—democratic, religious, mercantile and political—were confusedly blended in his mind, he entertained the project of making the reformed Lubek the centre and head of the democracy of the North, and himself the director of this newly organised world But he thus deserted the sphere of the ideas which had given force and success to the German reformation, the powers which he attacked were, at length, too strong for him, the reverses which democracy suffered on every hand, reacted on his native city. the ground was thus cut from under his feet, and he fell into the hands of his enemies. Having failed to conquer the North, the only alternative that remained to him, was to die on the scaffold

It is altogether a remarkable generation which we here find engaged in conflict Bold demagogues who have raised themselves to power, and stubborn patricians who never for an instant gave up their cause, princes and lords who make war for war's sake, and others who steadily contemplate an object, which they pursue with persevering resolution all robust, violent, aspiring natures, all connecting some public interest with their own private advantage Among them, and second to none in capacity, the aged king, to whom the greater part of all that was contended for, legally belonged, whose name sometimes resounded in the fight as a war-cry, but who expiated the sins of his youth by an endless captivity Victory declared herself on the side of the strongest She could neither be won by those who had not yet thoroughly secured their own cause, nor by those who had adopted projects to which they were in fact strangers Victory remained with the duke, raised to the royal throne, who fought with ardour and energy for himself, and who was connected with the existing and the past by his policy, and with the progressive and the future, by his religion All the intrigues of foreign potentates were abortive In the year 1536, Christian III (we shall see hereafter under what combinations) took possession of his capital, and remained master of the field

Independent, however, of all personal considerations, it may be affirmed that the enterprise of Lubek was no longer compatible with the spirit and circumstances of the times Those great communities which, in the middle ages, pervaded and bounded together all states, and the organisation of which is one of the most striking peculiarities of that period of history, were now on the eve of complete decomposition. In presence of an all-embracing sacerdotal order, and of an equestrian order which bound the whole nobility of the West in a sort of corporation or guild, civic bodies might also aspire to extend their commercial monopoly over kingdoms far and near But, with their cotemporary institutions, they too were doomed to fall The principle which pervades modern history, tends to the mutual independence of the several peoples and kingdoms, on every political ground That Lubek should emancipate herself from the hierarchy, yet think to maintain a commercial supremacy (and not by the natural superiority of industry, capital, or skill, but by the force of compulsory treaties and edicts), involved a historical contradiction

But it must not be supposed that the influence of Germany over the North was thus destroyed. On the contrary, it was now established on a more liberal, but a firmer basis than ever It was no longer the influence of force, but of intelligence Who does not know what efforts were made in earlier ages to carry Christianity into the North from Germany? yet an accurate investigation will convince us that England was far more instrumental to its conversion That alliance of a specially religious nature which Anscharius and his successors failed to bring about between Germany and the northern kingdoms, was now effected, though in another manner, by the reformation The destruction of the influence of Lubek did not prejudice Protestantism, scarcely had Christian III taken Copenhagen, when he proceeded to introduce its doctrine and rites as they prevailed in Germany, under the direction of the same Wittenberg theologian, who had reformed so many parts of Lower Germany—Doctor Bugenhagen. This system of faith struck root there, with the same rapidity and depth with which it had established itself in Germany, and formed the basis of the intimate union of the whole moral life of the North with that of Germany From that time, the same current of thought, the same development of ideas, has distinguished the German and the Scandinavian portions of the great Teutonic family In the North, too, the church severed herself from the restless domain of politics, her whole activity was confined to the intellectual regions

We have observed the same result in all the events of the latter years of our history

Zwingli, who contemplated not only a purification of faith and doctrine, but a radical change in the Swiss confederation, and especially the progress of democratic ideas, had fallen, his political projects had failed, in the last days—perhaps the last moments—of his life, he could seek consolation only in the prospects of the church The Anabaptist movement, which aimed at so complete a change of all the conditions of society, was suppressed, and, in Germany, annihilated. Even the general agitation of the middle classes of the trading cities, which had been connected with the schemes of Lubek, proved fruitless, and necessarily subsided. It seemed as if the religious principle which had arisen in its own peculiar strength, could endure no such intimate connexion with politics

The chief anxiety of the reformers was, to protect their faith from all interpretations which could lead its followers into these devious and dangerous paths

To this anxiety may be attributed the introduction of symbolical books among the Protestants. In order to secure themselves from the propagation of Anabaptist opinions, the Wittenberg teachers once more solemnly adopted the resolutions of the early assemblies of their church, in which the doctrines of the Trinity, and the two natures in Christ, were originally established; as had already been expressed in the Confession of Augsburg. They held it necessary to render conformity to these doctrines indispensable both to theological advancement in the universities, and to appointments in the church.*

Not that they meant by any means to hold up their Confession as an eternal and immutable rule or form of faith. In the negotiations carried on with England in the year 1535, the case was expressly pronounced possible, that some things in the Apology and Confession might, on further examination of God's word, be found susceptible of correction and improvement.† Nor, keeping in view the relations with Switzerland, can it be denied that the doctrine itself was in a state of living progress and construction. The connexion formed by Saxony with the Oberländers, which, spite of a great approximation, did not amount to a complete adhesion on the part of the latter, involved an influence of their dogmatic views on those of Saxony; we shall shortly see how earnest were the efforts made to bring about a complete amalgamation.

The example of Saxony was soon followed by the cities of Lower Germany. In April, 1535, the preachers of Bremen, Hamburg, Lübek, Rostock, Stralsund and Lüneburg entered into a convention, in which they determined, that, in future, no one should be permitted to preach who did not solemnly subscribe to the sound doctrines contained in the Confession and Apology. This appeared to them the only means of keeping down Anabaptists and other heretics, who would otherwise throw every thing in church and state into confusion.‡

And, we may ask, was not this in conformity with the principle in which the whole Protestant movement had originated?

The intention of its authors was not to prescribe new laws to the world; they had no desire to shake the foundations of political and social life, as actually constituted; their only object was, to emancipate themselves from a hierarchy which, exclusive and worldly as it had become, still laid claim to absolute and divine authority.

In this undertaking vast progress had now been made; but it was far from being thoroughly accomplished. Mighty powers, constrained by their nature and interests to resist all attempts at separation, were still arrayed against it. We shall still have to tell of the stern conflicts and the various fortunes of this high intellectual warfare.

* Statuta collegii facultatis theologicæ in Förstemann, Liber Decanorum, p. 152. Volumus puram evangelii doctrinam, consentaneam confessioni quam Augustæ—exhibuimus, — pie proponi; — severissime etiam prohibemus spargi hæreses damnatas in synodis Nicæna, Constantinopolitana, Ephesina et Chalcedonensi, nam harum synodorum decretis de explicatione doctrinæ, de Deo Patre, Filio, et spiritu Sancto, et de duabus naturis in Christo nato ex virgine Maria assentimur, eaque judicamus in scriptis apostolicis certo tradita esse.

† Petitio illustrissimorum principum data lagatis serm[ae] regiæ dignitatis, 25th December, 1535. The king was to promise to conform to the Confession and Apology: nisi forte quædam — ex verbo Dei merito corrigenda aut mutanda videbuntur.

‡ Bericht von etlicher grossen Gemeinen Prediger Unterredung. Report of the conference between certain great preachers. In Schröder's Evangelischem Meklenburg, i. 301, "qui velut obliti humani nominis omnia sursum ac deorsum miscent tam id republica quam in causa Christianæ religionis — — ne dissimulatione malum irrepat atque magistratus auctoritas labefactetur."

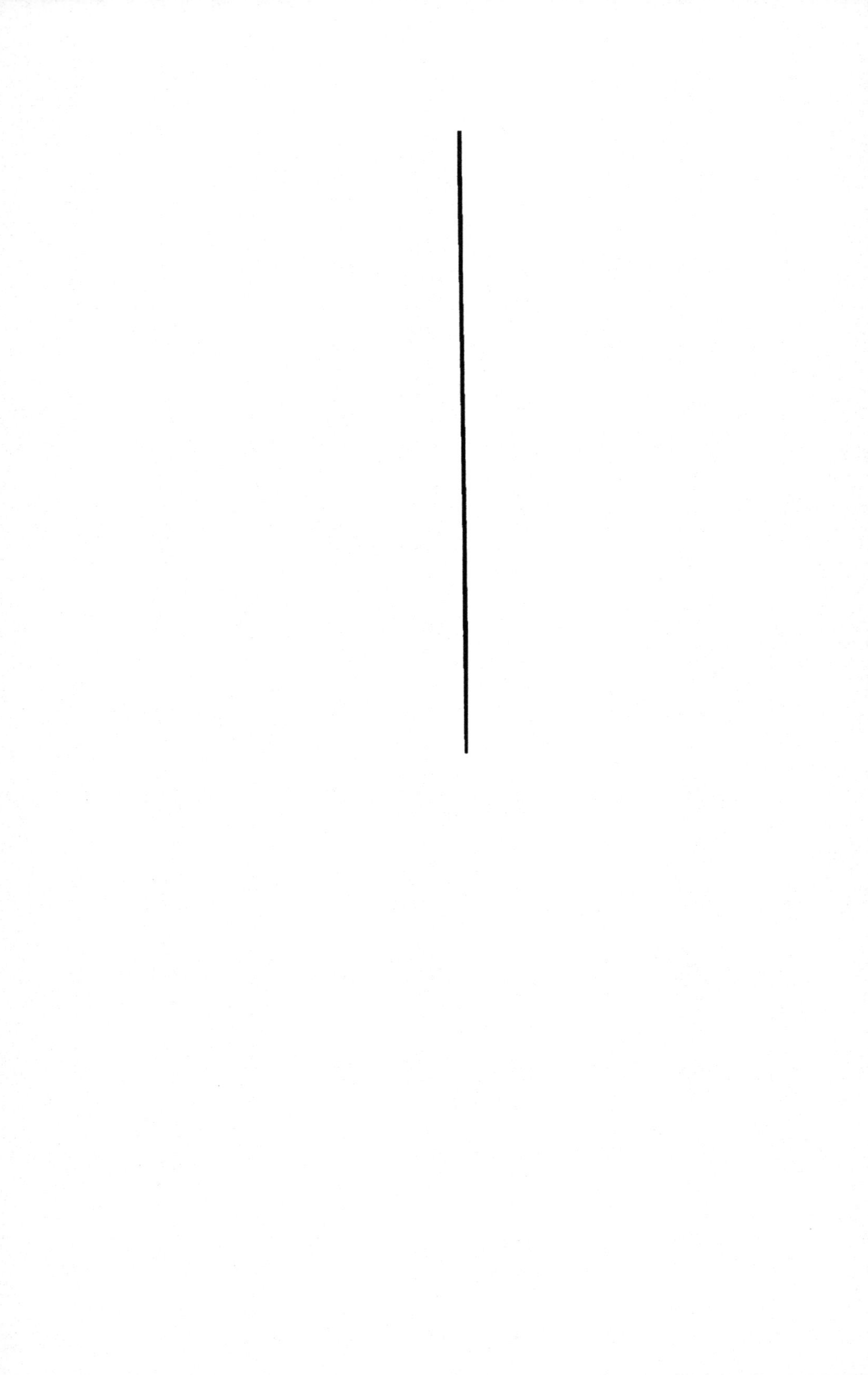

CPSIA information can be obtained
at www.ICGtesting.com
Printed in the USA
BVOW06*1449130917
494798BV00010B/327/P